The P.C. Support Handbook

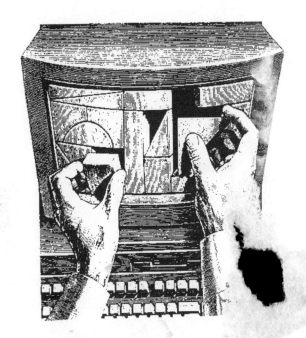

The

Configuration
and
Systems
Guide

09.

Europa

12th

2008

Dumbreck
Publishing

The P.C. Support Handbook
© 2008 by Dumbreck Publishing
ISBN 978-0-9541711-3-1

Introduction

The fact that you hold in your hands a copy of the 12th edition of this book, is testament to the ever evolving nature of computing. Over a decade ago, when the first edition of this book was being written, technologies were in use that are today almost considered museum pieces.

While an understanding of legacy technologies is important to the computer technician, we must focus on the sort of equipment that is in use in the widest number of locations, and also provide our readers with an idea of the technologies that are likely to dominate in the near future.

After all, those who work with computers will find themselves specifiying the latest equipment for new purchases, while maintaining a range of older computer systems and peripherals.

So, we have to try and keep a broad range of coverage in every edition of the book.

From legacy devices that are still relatively commonplace, through current technologies like PCI-E and 64-bit processors right up to the latest wireless or high-speed serial technologies.

Anyone involved in or learning about repair, maintenance and general support of PCs should have a broad base of knowledge from which to draw. We hope this book should give you that sort of knowledge.

David Dick

Acknowledgements

We would like to acknowledge and thank the following people for their contributions:

Philip J Irving, Senior Lecturer at the University of Sunderland, for material on multi-user systems.

Chic Thomson, for miscellaneous written material.

Hilary Austin, for the original cover artwork on which this edition's cover is based.

W H Anderson, for the artwork on the inside front page.

Christopher Columbus, for making possible the invention of the coffee perculator.

And our readers, for keeping this publication going all these years.

Contents

Computer Basics

Today, computers are used in a wide variety of applications. Almost all aspects of life, work and play are influenced by their use. Sometimes, the computer chip is even embedded inside a piece of equipment such as a video recorder or a washing machine. In these cases, the chip is dedicated to a particular function and the user is only given a small degree of control over its operations.

In industry and commerce, the computer comes in all shapes and sizes, from the hand portable carried round by the busy executive to the giant mainframe that crunches its way through millions of tax bills. The larger machines handle complex operations such as automatic banking, weather forecasting, traffic control, scientific modelling, Computer Aided Manufacturing, etc.

This book is concerned with the *'microcomputer'*. This is the machine that sits on the office desktop. Despite its relatively small size, it is becoming more powerful every year. It can store larger and larger programs and can run ever faster. Above all, it is programmable - it is not tied to a single program or activity.

Typical uses of microcomputers are:

> Budgeting, Payroll Processing, Word Processing, Databases, Stock Control, Project Management, Desk Top Publishing, Graphic Design, Multimedia, Electronic Music, Communication between offices and within the office, World-wide electronic mail, Internet access, etc.

Advantages of computers

- They can carry out repetitive and large volume tasks without fatigue.
- They are much less error prone than humans, providing an output of consistently better quality.
- They are much quicker than humans. Masses of information are always readily available.
- They are more reliable than humans, allowing for better planning and control of output.
- They can work 24 hours a day, in the dark, with minimum heating and little supervision.
- They are immune from human conditions - such as sick leave, maternity leave, strikes, etc.
- They occupy less space than humans; they don't need seats, desks, canteens, toilets, etc.
- Over a period of time, they are cheaper than humans, due to savings in wages, power and accommodation and savings through improved output and quality.

Disadvantages of computers

However, all is not on the plus side.

- Computers can be expensive to install and maintain.
- Trained personnel are required to use the computer applications.
- Trained personnel are required to maintain the machines, the programs and the company data.
- There are problems of compatibility between computers. Programs from a Macintosh system will not run on a PC; PC programs will not run on a Macintosh without special add-ons. There is no *'standard'* computer, although those based around the IBM PC model account for most business and commercial use - providing a common system for exchanging data.
- There are problems of *'concurrency'*. If data (e.g. a price list) is duplicated on several machines and changes are made, which computer holds the most up-to-date version?
- Storing masses of data on computers, particularly when computers are connected together, presents a real security problem. By law, companies have to prevent unauthorised access to their data; this may come from employees or from outsiders *'hacking'* in to the system using modems.
- Any failures in the system threaten the users' activities. Where all a company's activities and data are stored on a single computer, any breakdown in that computer leaves the company unable to function.

Above all, computers are stupid! There is great truth in the phrase - "*Garbage In Garbage Out*". If you enter wrong information into the computer, you get incorrect results! If you place correct information in the computer, but the program is wrong - you still get incorrect results! The computer is merely a machine with no intelligence other than that programmed into it. For example, if the programmer forgets to tell a computer that no employee in the company is likely to be over 80 years old, it will happily accept an employee's age as one million. Consequently, the company's statistics are completely flawed, showing an average employee age of several thousand!

At the end of the day, computers are tools for use by humans and cannot fully replace human common sense and experience.

What is a computer?

There have been *'computers'* for a long proportion of society's history. The abacus and mechanical devices have long been used as an aid to calculation. Today's definition of computers really describes the electronic computing device. A computer is essentially an information processor that is able to perform substantial computation with little or no intervention by human operators.

To function, a computer requires both hardware and software elements. The physical machinery involved in the computer system is called *'hardware'* and consists of components such as the processor unit, monitor, keyboard, disk drives and printer. If it can be touched, it must be hardware. The more efficient the hardware, the quicker the programs will run. Software programs are bought or created for the computer. These carry out specific tasks such as word-processing or accountancy. The better designed the software, the more facilities are offered to the user.

In the microcomputer market, the IBM PC is by far the most common machine, without around 90% of the world share. The *'PC'* stands for *'personal computer'* and the machine first appeared in early 1980's. All subsequent PC machines have been built round this basic architecture. Of course, most machines in everyday use are not manufactured by IBM. They may be Compaq models or Packard Bell, etc. These are termed *'clones'* since they follow the basic architecture of the IBM model. In practice, they perform like an IBM PC in almost all respects (within the limits of copyright).

Microcomputer components

The main components that comprise the typical PC are:

- The main system unit
- Input devices
- Output devices
- Storage devices

The typical process for using a computer is:

1. Load a program into the computer's memory (e.g. a word-processing package). The program is initially held on some storage device such as a floppy disk, CD, or the computer's internal hard disk. A copy of this program is transferred into the memory of the computer; the disk still stores the original copy. The program is then run from the version stored in memory.

2. Input any data (e.g. type in a report).

3. Process the data (e.g. spell check the report).

4. Output the data to screen or printer (e.g. print the report).

5. Save the data (on to a floppy disk or the internal hard disk).

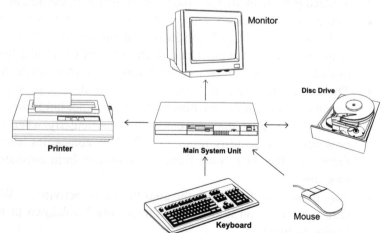

A brief description of the units is:

Main System Unit: This case houses the CPU (Central Processing Unit, also called the Micro Processor Unit or MPU) chip which carries out all the computer's programming tasks and a range of support chips to communicate with the other hardware devices.

Keyboard: The keyboard allows the user to type in input to the computer (e.g. commands to do things, words for a report, choices from menus, etc.).

Monitor: A screen that allows the facts, pictures, etc. generated by the computer to be viewed.

Disk Drive: Stores the programs and information that the user needs.

Mouse: A pointing device that makes some operations, such as using Windows or drawing packages, easier to use than with the keyboard.

Printer: Produces a permanent copy of the program's output (e.g. a letter or a graph) on to a sheet of paper.

Main System Unit

The main system box comes in a variety of shapes from tiny hand-held plastic cases for portable use to large metal tower cases for network servers and power workstations. Inside each case, there is a main electronic board, called the *'motherboard'* that houses the CPU, memory, etc.

Motherboard

This comprises a printed circuit board, about the size of an A4 sheet of paper in the case of standard desktop computers. It has all the computer's processing chips mounted on it, either being soldered directly to the board or being plugged into sockets on the board. All the power, data and addressing information is carried between components on the copper tracks etched on to the printed circuit board. Each motherboard is designed to handle a particular computing processor, since modern processor chips have more sophisticated needs than older processors. Thus, manufacturers supplied motherboards specially made for use with 386 chips and these are of different design from motherboards intended for use with Pentium chips. Even within the Pentium range of CPUs, a range of different motherboard designs and connections are used.

CPU (Central Processing Unit)

The main chip in any computer system is the Central Processing Unit. The speed and design of this chip largely determine the overall speed of the computer. Early PCs used a chip known as the 8088 and this was followed by the 8086, 80286, 80386SX, 80386DX, 80486SX, 80486DX, the Pentium Pro, the Pentium MMX, the Pentium II and III, Xeon and Pentium 4 chips. The 8086 machines ran at a speed of 4.77MHz while the current Pentium processors run faster by a factor of almost 1000 times.

Apart from their raw speed improvements, modern chips have other in-built advantages over earlier models. For example, modern computers handle data at a faster rate due to their data bus being 64 bits wide; older models only had a 32 or 16-bit bus and the earliest XT machines had only an 8-bit bus. While the older systems are no longer for sale, machines of all types and speeds are currently in use in commerce, industry and in the home.

The CPU is the heart of the computer system and is a silicon microchip. Its function is to interpret and execute the required instructions (see chapter on Computer Architecture).

Memory

To work, the computer has to temporarily store the program and data in an area where it can be used by the computer's processor. This area is known as the computer's *'memory'* or sometimes as *'primary storage'*. Memory consists of computer chips that are capable of storing information.

That information may be:

- The program that keeps the computer running (e.g. Windows).
- The instructions of the program that the user wants to run (e.g. a database or a drawing program).
- The data that is used or created (e.g. letters from word-processing or records from a database).

When the user wishes to run a program (e.g. a game), a <u>copy</u> of the program is loaded from the user's disk and placed in the computer memory. The program is then run from the computer memory.

This makes it possible for the machine to be a word processor, graphics designer, Internet browser, games machine and many other functions. The machine, in fact, will run whatever program is currently in memory. If another program is loaded, that becomes the new function of the machine. This is what makes the computer so versatile - it is not tied to any one activity.

The memory chips consist of a large number of cells, each cell having a fixed capacity for storing data and each has a unique location or address. This type of memory is known as RAM (Random Access Memory) and its contents are *'volatile'*. This means that the program and the data held in the memory is lost when the machine is switched off. This is not a problem for the program as it is only a copy - the original program is still stored on disk.   However, any data created (e.g. a letter or drawing) is only sitting in the memory and will be lost, unless it is saved to disk before the computer is switched off.

Another type of memory is known as ROM (Read Only Memory) and this is non-volatile (i.e. the program code exists even when the machine has been switched off).   The ROM BIOS (Basic Input Output System) chip is used to store chunks of the system's own programs (e.g. to check for the user typing at the keyboard, or to handle disk activities).   When the computer is powered up and running, some of the system programs are run directly from ROM.   Most system programs are loaded into the computer memory from the hard disk when the machine is first switched on.

The operating system takes up a certain amount of the computer's available memory, so not all of the memory is actually available to the user.   Sophisticated software packages such as Microsoft Excel and Microsoft Word take up large amounts of RAM and the user may create large worksheets and documents using these packages that can use up the rest of the available memory.

This means that the more memory in a machine the more efficient the computer runs.   Each year, machines are supplied with more memory and users can usually add extra memory to an existing computer.

For more information, see the chapter on memory.

Measurement of capacity

Capacity describes the amount of data a storage device, such as a CD-ROM, a hard disk, or a memory chip can hold at any one time and is measured in bytes. One byte represents one character. A character can be a letter or a number, or any of the many special characters found on the keyboard including a space.   There are many other characters used in the internal workings of the microcomputer that are never seen in print. For example, the *'beep'* for the computer's internal loudspeaker is stored as a single character.   Of course, devices also store pictures, video clips, etc. and their size is also measured in multiples of bytes.

In computing, where operations are often considered in units of 2, the Kilo or K actually means 1,024 characters with similar definitions for the larger numbers.

Kilo is 2 raised to the power of 10, or 2 x 2 x 2 x 2 x 2 x 2 x 2 x 2 x 2 x 2.

Tera is 2 multiplied by itself 40 times, or exactly 1,099,511,627,776.

KB (Kilobyte)	1,024 characters
MB (Megabyte)	1,048,576 characters
GB (Gigabyte)	1,073,741,824 characters
TB (Terabyte)	1,099,511,627,776 characters

A rough measure of storage requirements is:

> 1 byte can store 1 character
> 1 KB can store a few paragraphs of text
> 1 MB can store the text of a reasonably sized book
> 4MB can store a typical MP3 audio clip
> 4GB can store a typical DVD movie

Input devices
Input devices are used to enter or input data into the CPU. The main input device on computers is the keyboard. There is a wide range of other input devices including the mouse, optical scanners, pressure pads and other sensors, graphic tablets, touch screens, communication devices and audio and video capture cards.

Output devices
Output devices convert data from the computer into forms that humans can understand or use. There are two main output devices on the microcomputer system, the monitor screen and the printer. Other output devices include graph plotters, modems, audio boards with speakers, and robot arms.

Backing store
This is also known as external memory or secondary storage and is used for the long-term storage of data. The bulk of information (programs and data) used by computer applications are stored on backing store and must be transferred to main memory before it can be processed by the CPU. Backing store devices include magnetic disks (removable floppy disks and built-in hard disks), CD-ROMs and magnetic tape.

The power of the machine
The power of the machine is usually indicated by the speed of the processor; the faster the speed of the chip, the more instructions it can process in any given time.
The following measurements of time are used:

Millisecond	=	1/1,000th of a second
Microsecond	=	1/1,000,000th of a second
Nanosecond	=	1/1,000,000,000th of a second

These measurements are essentially used to describe the time taken for the computer processor to perform one cycle, in which time it may perform a basic operation or part of a more complex operation.
For a while, an alternative measurement known as MIPS (Millions of Instructions Per Second) or GigaFLOPS (billions of Floating Point Operations Per Second) was used. This was an estimate of the number of instructions or operations able to be processed by a computer. Recently however the raw speed rating is most often quoted, which can be slightly misleading.

Different models of computer are designed to run at different speeds. Of course, the faster the machine, the greater the purchase price. One measure of speed of a machine is the number of cycles per second at which it can operate (measured in MHz - MegaHertz - millions of cycles per second). The first and slowest PC was just under 5MHz. The fastest speed is always being improved upon and is currently around 4000MHz, with ever faster systems appearing all the time.

The choice of machine depends very much upon its expected use. If the machine was used entirely for word processing, a lower speed machine is perfectly satisfactory. Since the slowest part of the process is the typist's thinking and typing time, there is little to be gained by very fast processing in between long pauses at the keyboard.   On the other hand, where there is going to be a great deal of machine processing, such as graphics calculations and other number crunching, a faster machine becomes essential.

For even faster processing, the machine can be fitted with an extra chip - called a 'co-processor'. Older CPUs had an optional 'maths co-processor' which took on most of the mathematical calculations, leaving the main processor free for other tasks. Since the tasks are being shared, the whole program runs much more quickly. This facility is already built into the Pentium chips and many modern motherboards provide a socket for an extra Pentium CPU chip to boost the computer's performance.

Of course, the raw speed of the CPU is not the only factor in determining the machine's overall speed. Other factors, such as the speed of the disk and video card, the amount of RAM available, whether the machine has an efficient caching system, etc., also determine the machine's performance.

Monitors

Most programs send the output from their calculations to a screen (apart from those such as payroll programs that send most of their output to the printer, with only a summary going to the screen). The screen is contained in a unit called the *'monitor'* - sometimes also called the VDU (*'visual display unit'*).

Monitor types

The earliest monitors were monochrome, displaying data using only black and white (i.e. white text on a dark background or vice versa, or perhaps using a green or amber screen)

All monitors are now colour models and applications are written to provide text and graphics in colour. Sometimes this is used to enhance the use or appeal of the product. On other occasions, such as graphic

design, PCB design, etc., the use of colour is essential.

Screen output can vary from user messages and prompts, to displaying complex graphs, pie charts and video.

For many years, the main monitor construction was the CRT (cathode ray tube) type, which is very similar to the type used in televisions. Recently, there has been a marked increase in the use of LCD (liquid crystal display) screens. These have the benefit of being seen under most lighting conditions. They are also much lighter than CRT models and take up less desk space since they use narrow panels.

Screen resolution

The PC supports different degrees of screen resolution. The higher the screen resolution, the better the quality of the picture, allowing graphics to be displayed. The resolution of a screen is measured in *'pixels'* (picture elements). Each pixel is an independent dot appearing on the screen. The resolution of a screen is given by the number of pixels in the horizontal and in the vertical plane.

The most common screen resolutions are:

VGA	640 x 480
SVGA	800 x 600 up to 1600 x 1200

Other standards, such as the Hercules, CGA and EGA resolutions are long extinct and are rarely seen.

The higher resolution models produce a sharper, more detailed picture. The highest resolution becomes a necessity where desktop publishing, CAD or other graphic applications are to be run. Microsoft Windows and Windows applications are greatly improved with higher resolution monitors. A 1024 x 768 screen will reproduce a greater number of Windows icons on the screen at any one time than a 800 x 600 screen. Monitors with higher resolution require more demanding construction and these are more expensive to buy.

All monitors have on/off switches and controls for screen brightness and contrast; some models have other, more sophisticated controls. All monitors have two connecting cables; one to connect power to the monitor and one that connects to the system unit's video output socket.

Keyboard

This is the main input device to the computer that is used to enter data directly into the machine, for processing. The keyboard has a single cable attached to it and the plug at the end of this cable is attached to the keyboard socket on the computer main system unit. This cable takes the power from the unit to the keyboard and returns information on any keys pressed back to the motherboard.

The computer keyboard consists of a normal typewriter layout with some additional keys, a group of function keys, a numeric pad on the right, and a group of direction keys also on the right side.

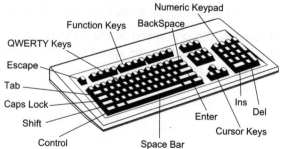

When you press a key that is engraved with an alphabetic character you will see a lower case letter on the screen. Pressing a key with two engravings will display the character in the lower half of the key top. To get capital letters and the characters on the top half of the key top you must hold down one of the SHIFT keys while you press the other key. If most of your keying requires the use of capital letters, you can press the CAPS LOCK key, which remains ON until you press it again, and this produces the upper case with alphabetic keys only.

The CTRL and ALT keys allow the same key to carry out several functions. For example, pressing the "L" key, the CTRL and "L" keys together and pressing the ALT and "L" keys together may provide three different results.

The keyboard also provides keys that allow movement across the screen or the insertion or deletion of screen text. The use of all the keyboard's keys is explained in the chapter on Computer Peripherals.

Disks

A computer needs somewhere to store its programs and data when they are not in the machine's memory. The most common storage medium is the disk system. Programs are loaded from disk to run in the computer memory, as previously mentioned. Additionally, when the program has created its data, it can store it on the disk for later use.

There are two main types of disk storage medium - the hard disk and the floppy disk.

How disks work

The physical characteristics of all magnetic disks are similar. Thin, non-magnetic plates are coated on both sides with magnetic recording material. A special set of heads is used to both record data on to the disk and to read data from the disk. The method is identical to that used for recording videotapes or audio cassettes. The only real differences are that the medium is a disk instead of a long strip; and the information being transferred is digital data, instead of audio or video information. So, the disk is a direct access device, which means that the reading/writing heads can move directly to the track and sector where the desired information is stored (unlike tape, which is a serial device, where you have to search from one end of the tape to find the information).

Hard disks

A hard disk is supplied with all microcomputers and is mounted inside the machine casing. These disks hold an incredible amount of information, anything from old, long defunct 10 Megabyte models to current 1 Tbyte and even larger models. It is known as a 'hard disk' because it is made from a solid sheet of aluminium. It is then coated with ferric oxide and a number of such disks are stacked on top of each other and placed in an airtight casing. Each disk surface has its own read/write head and they are linked so that they will all move in unison. The disks spin at a constant speed. The slowest models ran at 3600 rpm (12 times faster than a floppy disk) and current models range up to 15,000rpm. Apart from their large capacities, hard disks have a much better access time than a floppy disk. A hard disk's mechanism allows it to read in data, write a file and find files much faster than a floppy disk.

The disks are mounted on a vertical shaft and are slightly separated from each other to provide space for the movement of read/write heads. The shaft revolves, spinning the disks. Data is stored as magnetised spots in concentric circles called 'tracks' on each surface of the disks. Each disk contains several hundred tracks for the storage of data.

It is possible for the read/write heads of disks to come into contact with debris on the disk surface, such as dust or smoke particles. This might cause the head to "crash" into the surface of the disk, damage the disk, and corrupt the data. Special devices have been developed to get over this problem. One such device is the Winchester disk drive. Winchester disks are sealed units containing the disks and the read/write unit. These types of disks are the hard disks used on the microcomputer and are fast and reliable. Hard disks are usually fixed within the microcomputer cabinet and are therefore not very portable. Hard disks are faster to access information and have much higher storage capacity than floppy disks.

Floppy disks

These are flat disks of polyester film with and iron-oxide magnetic coating. The disk is covered with a protective jacket, and reading/writing to the disk is performed through the head access slot. Floppy disks have a capacity of 360KB to almost 3MB, although the most widely used type stores 1.44MB. Floppy disks are very portable and can be used by different microcomputers (provided they are of a similar type).

The construction of hard disks and floppy disks is covered in detail in the chapter on 'Disks and Drives'.

Floppy sizes

Floppy disks used to be produced in a 5.25" size but now all floppy disks are 3.5".

Each of these disks is capable of being formatted to different capacities, dependent on their quality (i.e. whether they are double/high/quad density). At its basic format, the old 5.25" disk stored up to 360 Kilobytes. The later 5.25" disk drives handled quad density disks, each disk having a capacity of 1.2 Megabytes. The current 3.5" disk has a basic format of 720 Kilobytes, with the more common high-density version holding 1.4 Megabytes. A 2.88 Megabytes version made a brief appearance but did not last long on the market.

Disk recording terms

Sector	Division of magnetic surface of disk into separate but continuous pie-shaped information zones by either magnetic or physical coding of disk.
Soft Sector	Sectors defined magnetically by software.
Hard Sector	Sectors defined physically by punching holes around inner/outer disk diameter. Now outdated.
Initialisation/Formatting	Magnetically coded pattern recorded on disk to identify each track and sector.
Double-Sided	Disk made for use on drives with two recording heads.
Single-Density	The standard density for floppy disks. No longer used.
Double-Density	Recording twice the amount on disk compared with single-density. This is 360k for 5.25" disks and 720k for 3.5" disks. Now outdated.
High/Quadruple-Density	Method of recording four times the amount on disk as possible with single- density. This is 1.2MB for 5.25" disks and 1.4MB for 3.5" disks.

Care of disks

- Never touch the recording surface of a floppy disk because a small amount of grease will be deposited, to which dust will stick.
- Never bend a floppy disk.
- Insert a floppy disk into a disk drive carefully to avoid bending or crushing the disk.
- Keep disks away from excesses of temperature.
- Keep the disks away from any form of magnetic field. That includes telephones, printer motors, speakers, power transformers, etc.
- Write on a disk label <u>before</u> applying it to the floppy disk; as writing on the disc itself can potentially damage it, especially for the larger 5.25" disks.

Printers

The printer is used to produce a paper copy (often called a *'hard copy')* of the letters, reports, graphs, etc. produced by the program. They have two connector cables; one for the mains supply and one to take the data from the computer to the printer. The manufacturers produce two different types of connection for printers and these are known as serial and parallel systems. These names describe how the data arrives at the printer from the computer. Serial printers (including USB connections) accept data one bit at a time from the computer. Parallel printers have more wires and receive 8 bits, i.e. one byte, at a time. Most printers have only a serial or a parallel connection, while a few have sockets for both types. There are different printers for different jobs. All have different qualities as described next.

Dot Matrix

On a dot matrix printer, characters are formed by striking an inked ribbon with a rectangular array of needles. The dots of ink are transferred to the paper, producing a pattern that can comprise letters, numbers, or even graphics. These types of printers are relatively cheap and fairly fast, printing from 50 to 400 characters per second. The quality of print from a dot matrix printer is much improved if the number of dots that make up a particular character is increased.

The earliest machines used a vertical row of seven print needles that printed 5 times for each character. Each character was thus formed from a 7 x 5 array of dots. The latest machines use 18 x 24 arrays of pins or 24 x 24 or 48 x 24 arrays.

These printers are commonly in use where quality is less important than cheap and quick copies and are mostly employed for mass print runs, such as bills, statements, reminders, or pay cheques.

Ink Jet Printers

An inkjet printer is a *'non impact'* printer, preferring instead to spray dots of ink on to the paper. The ink is stored in a small plastic case about the size of a matchbox and this case also comprises the printing

head. A small printed circuit board on the ink cartridge takes the signals from the computer right up to tiny holes in the ink reservoir. The ink is attracted through the holes and carries on to strike the paper. This produces an output that approaches the quality of the laser printer, at a fraction of the cost. It typically produces a resolution of about 600 dots per inch and is very quiet in operation. Colour inkjet models use four ink heads and mix their outputs to achieve an even greater range of colours. The inks used are the primary print colours (cyan, magenta and yellow) and black. These are known as CMYK printers.

Laser Printers

A laser printer works on a similar principle to the normal photocopier; in fact, a laser is like the second half of a photocopier. With a photocopier, the image from an inserted master is scanned and turned into a stream of digital information. This digital information is then used to modulate a laser beam on to a drum. The electrostatic charge thus built up attracts the toner powder, which is eventually transferred to the paper. With a laser printer, the stream of digital information is

supplied directly by the computer, via the printer cable. So, the laser printer is like a cut down version of a photocopier.

The resolution of a laser printer is measured in the number of dots in an inch and is normally 600 dpi, with modern versions now at 1200 dpi or higher. They are thus capable of both high quality text and graphics. A typical laser is capable of printing either 8 pages per minute or 12 pages per minute. These speed figures describe the number of pages that the printer can produce once the image is ready to print. In fact, the normal laser printer makes up a copy of the picture in its own internal memory, prior to starting the printing process. This time has to be added to the time for printing. So, for a single copy, the printing speed is fairly slow; if many copies are required, the image is still only built up once and the overall speed becomes closer to the printing speed.

The size of the printer's memory has an influence on the final quality of print that can be handled. If the printer has only a small internal memory, say 256k or 512k, then it will not be able to store a complete A4 page of graphics. To reduce retail prices, many manufacturers produce models with small internal memories. Of course, most printers can have their memory size upgraded by adding extra memory boards, although this is fairly expensive.

Due to their mechanics, laser printers are very quiet in operation. There is no impact noise, as the paper is not struck; there is only the sound of the motor and its roller mechanisms.

Print quality

Laser printers produce true letter quality print. Dot matrix printers can produce almost letter quality or NLQ (near letter quality) by increasing the number of dots in the character or by passing over the same line twice. Dot matrix printers can produce faster output in draft mode. This produces a readable document fairly quickly. The printers can be switched from one level of quality to another by a hardware switch on the printer or by sending a signal through the software to the printer. Inkjet printers produce a quality which somewhat less than a laser but much better than a dot matrix.

All impact printers use ribbons - either ink-impregnated fabric or one-off ribbons. With fabric ribbons, the quality can be poor at the beginning of the use of the ribbon due to overinking, while the quality also suffers at the end of the ribbon's life due to lack of ink. Laser printers and inkjet printers, on the other hand, maintain a constant quality of output, with the quality suddenly dropping off as the toner or ink reservoir runs low.

Proportional printing

The standard print size on most machines is 10 characters to an inch. It is possible to change this using either a hardware switch on the printer or by sending special codes to the printer. The number of characters printed to an inch can be increased (making the print smaller) to 12, 17 and 20 cpi. It is also possible to print expanded characters and to produce characters with proportional spacing. With proportional spacing, a character only occupies as much width of the paper as it actually needs. So, the letter *'m'* uses more space than the letter

> This is an example of proportional spacing
> This is an example of standard width printing

'i'.   As a result, proportional spacing results in more professional output, similar to typeset documents as seen in books.

However, one problem with proportional spacing is lining up data into columns as seen in this example.   Since each digit occupies a different page width (e.g. an eight is wider than a one), figures do not line up in neat columns.   In this respect, a fixed-width character set produces more readable results.

> 9866 99.55 88
> 2311 18.11 28
>
> 9866 99.55 88
> 2311 18.11 28

The selection of pitch sizes can be achieved by setting the buttons on the printer front panel, for plain text applications.   Windows applications set the pitch using software, through the selection of Windows fonts (see chapter on *'Windows Configuration'*).

Printer fonts

Dot-matrix printers and all laser printers allow the user to choose the shape or style of the type to be output.   The term *'typeface'* describes the shape of the letters and characters.   So, a plain unadorned character would be one typeface, while a fancy Gothic script would be another typeface.   If a typeface has feet and twirls, it is said to be a *'serif'* typeface.   If it is a plain typeface, it is described as a *'sans serif'* style.   Each typeface comes in a variety of sizes, measured in *'points'*; there are 72 points to one inch.   So, a 36-point character is a half-inch character.   The collection of all the sizes of a particular typeface is called the *'fonts'*.   A half-inch character would be

> This is a serif typeface
> **And this is sans serif**

available in the 36-point font of a particular typestyle.   In addition to the character's outline and size, the user can usually have control over whether the character is printed in normal, bold, italic and underlined.

Printer buffers

Computers send data to the printer at a much faster rate than the printer can print it out; this is because the printer is a slow mechanical device. This would leave the user sitting waiting until the printer had finished the print job before he/she could carry on using the machine. To increase efficiency, all printers have a block of memory built in, called the *'print buffer'*. This is able to read a chunk of data from the computer and, if the block of memory is large enough, the entire file can be transferred to the printer in one operation. This would immediately free the computer for other processing. To keep the retail price down, most printers have a nominal buffer size and additions to this are regarded as extras. However, Windows can be configured to use some of the computer's memory as an additional printer buffer.

Printer paper

Printers can use different types of paper. A common type of paper is continuous stationery. This is held in place and moved by tractors gripping the sprocket holes at the side of the paper. There are two basic sizes; 13 x 11 inches, which will allow a maximum of 132 standard characters per line and 66 lines on every page and 8 x 11 inches, which gives 80 character lines. This may be plain paper or specially printed paper providing office stationary or commercial facilities such as accounts. This may be single or multi-part stationary (i.e. more than one sheet with carbon backing so that several copies of the data are printed on the different copies of the sheet).   Self-adhesive labels are also commonly used on continuous rolls, so that mailing labels are quickly produced.

Many printers also allow the use of single sheets of paper using a friction mechanism as on a typewriter, to hold and move the paper. Cut sheet feeders may also be supplied to guide the paper in the printer. Again, the paper may be plain or pre-printed. Some printers also allow acetate sheets to be inserted so that OHP slides (overhead projector) may be created. These use special acetate sheets that will not melt in the normal heat in a laser printer.

Pointing devices

Windows applications make very good use of a mouse or other pointing device for choosing menu options, drawing activities, etc. Although the activities can be carried out using the keyboard cursor keys, it is much more cumbersome than using a mouse or other pointer.

Mouse

By far the most common pointing device is the mouse, although other devices such as trackerballs, touch screens, pens and joysticks are available. The mouse has won support through its accuracy and ease of use. The most common is the type that houses a large heavy rubber ball, which protrudes from its base.
When the mouse is moved over a surface (preferably a *'mouse mat'* - a mat with the correct friction to optimise the ball's movement), the ball rotates inside its case. The ball movement rotates two rollers, one for vertical and one for horizontal movements. Moving the ball diagonally will rotate both rollers. The mouse converts hand movement into a stream of electrical pulses that is passed via the serial port to the computer. The quicker the mouse is moved, the faster the pulse stream; the further the mouse is moved, the longer is the pulse stream. The incoming signals are used by the program to produce pointer movements on the monitor screen.

The mouse has two, sometimes three, buttons on its casing to allow the user to click on a particular choice or lift/drop the pen while drawing. Some mouse drivers allow the buttons' functions to be transposed, so the mouse can be used more easily with left-handed operators.

Some models have a central wheel that allows the user to scroll up and down screen contents and some use infra-red or wireless connections to avoid the limitations that a mouse cable can sometimes produce.

Finally, some drivers, such as in Windows, allow an option to leave a trail as the cursor moves, so that the cursor position can be easier identified, which is useful on portable computer screens.

Other hardware items

Modem

A modem (*'modulator/demodulator'*) allows a computer to communicate with another computer at great distances over the ordinary telephone network, or over specially hired lines. It translates (modulates) the data that is held in the computer as electronic pulses into audible tones that are capable of being sent down telephone cables. The modem at the receiving end translates (demodulates) the tones back into electronic pulses for use by the receiving computer. For more details, see the chapter on data communications.

CD-ROM

This computer CD player works in a similar way to an ordinary CD player, except that the data that is read is computer digital data instead of audio data. The disks used with such players can store around 650Mbytes of data, which is equivalent to about 500 high-density floppy disks. The disks are removable and not easily damaged. The only drawback is that the basic system only reads data from disk to computer. Read/write systems are available but are more expensive. DVD disks work in a similar way but store much more data (typically 4.7GB). For more information, see the chapter on disks and drives.

Scanner

A scanner is a device that analyses a printed piece of work (e.g. a picture, drawing or even text) and converts the image into a file that can be further processed. A scanned file of a picture or drawing might be incorporated into desktop publishing and a scanned piece of text from a book, etc. may be converted back into ASCII text using a software package called OCR (optical character recognition).

Add-On Cards

When an extra device such as a modem is to be added to a system, the user can choose to fit external equipment that attaches to the computer's port connections or fit an internal board. Some other devices such as sound-producing cards are most commonly available as internal boards. These boards contain all the electronics and hardware to carry out their particular function and are plugged into spare unused slots on the
motherboard. These slots are known as the computer's *'expansion slots'*. The add-on board is fitted and the software to make it function is then installed. Many devices that once were only available as add-on cards, such as sound cards and video capture cards, are now available for connection through the computer's USB ports.

Assembling the system

When a computer is first purchased, it arrives in several boxes. The monitor is in one box, while the system unit, keyboard, mouse, manuals and disks are usually packed separately. The monitor has its own power cable and video cable permanently connected to it in most cases, while the system unit comes as an independent component with separate cables.

The steps to assembling the system are:

- Choose a suitable location for the computer. Avoid situations of excessive heat, cold, damp, dust or vibration. Also avoid locations close to magnetic disturbance such as lift motors, power transformers, etc. A good location would be one with a flat, stable surface and good air circulation.
- Carefully unpack the components from the boxes. The contents of the boxes should then be checked against the system checklist, to see that all components have been delivered.
- Read the assembly instructions carefully to ensure that you understand the necessary steps and that any special precautions are understood.
- Gather any tools that you may require. Normally, the only tool is a Philips screwdriver to secure connections to the system unit. Some connections use thumbscrews to make a secure connection and do not require a screwdriver - read the manual.
- Carefully connect the components together, in the order directed by the computer manual. Do not force any connections; if a plug will not easily connect to a socket, it may mean that a connector pin has become bent. It might also mean that the wrong socket is being chosen, or the plug is being inserted upside down!

A typical order of assembly is:

- Place the system unit on the surface to be used.
- Place the monitor on top of the system unit.
- Attach the video cable from the monitor to the video out socket of the system unit. Ensure that the plug and the socket are of compatible types. The old, obsolete CGA and EGA monitor cables had a 9-pin plug on the end of its connector cable, while a modern VGA or SVGA monitor has a 15-pin plug.  The two are not interchangeable. Note that the edges of the plugs are shaped so that they only connect one way round. On some connectors, the plug is secured to the system unit with metal screws and a screwdriver is required to tighten the screws. With other connectors, the plug has plastic thumbscrews that are tightened by hand.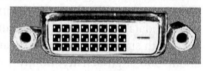

  Many TFT monitors now use a DVI (digital visual interface) connection. This provides higher quality results and should be used where the monitor and the graphics card both have a DVI interface (the monitor and the card might also provide a normal 15-pin interface). The DVI interface has a 24-pin socket as shown in the illustration.
- Connect the mains lead to the system unit. The lead has a normal 3-pin plug on one end and a connector similar to those used in electric kettles on the other end. Do not plug the socket into the mains at this time; simply plug the other end of the cable into the computer's mains inlet socket.
- Connect the monitor to the mains supply. Some monitor mains cables have normal 3-pin plugs and these plug directly into a mains supply. Other monitor power cables have a plug that matches a socket at the rear of the system unit. These are useful, since switching on the system unit also supplies power to the monitor. So, if the monitor power switch is left on, both units can be powered up from the computer's on/off switch.
- Connect the keyboard to the system unit. These are usually 5 or 6-pin plugs and are produced in two sizes. The larger size plug was used with older computers. It has 5 pins and has a matching socket on the system unit, as shown in the illustration. With the smaller size keyboard plug, there is also a matching socket. and the plug can only be connected one way since the socket has a key to guide the plug. This smaller socket size is the same type as used for a dedicated mouse socket. Care should be taken to plug the keyboard into the correct socket. Where the two sockets are of the same size, the system unit should either clearly label them as 'KBD' and 'Mouse', or colour code the sockets and

plugs. Generally, the keyboard socket is coloured purples and the mouse socket is coloured green. Recently, keyboards have become available that attach to the PC via a USB socket, and some even use infrared or radio based wireless technologies (explained in more detail in the '*LANs*' chapter).

- Connect the mouse to the system unit. The mouse may be of the PS/2 type mentioned above and care should be taken to ensure that the plug is inserted into the correct socket. Some mouse plugs connect to the system unit's serial port connector. The serial socket usually has nine pins and is marked as '*Serial*', '*COM1*', or '*RS232*'. Sometimes the socket is already used (e.g. for a modem) and the mouse connects to the second serial socket. In older PCs, the second socket may have 25 pins and the mouse connects via a 9-pin to 25-pin adapter. Like the keyboard, there are both USB and wireless mice available.

- Connect the printer to the system unit. A common cable is the '*parallel*' or '*Centronics*' type, which has a 25-pin cable. The cable at the system unit side terminates in a 25-pin plug that connects to the socket marked '*Parallel*' or '*LPT1*'. The other end of the cable connects to the socket on the printer, as shown in the illustration.

A few printers have a serial connector and connect to the socket marked as '*COM1*', '*Serial*' or '*RS232*'. Some computers have two serial sockets (e.g. to connect a mouse and a printer at the same time. In these cases, the computer is set up to recognise one of the serial outlets as a printer port and the other as a mouse port. The manual should be checked to determine the use for each port. Most printers now have a USB cable that connects to one of the computer's USB sockets. The printer illustrated on the previous page has both a Centronics port and a USB port.

- Connect the printer to the mains supply and ensure that it is supplied with paper and is on-line.
- Check that the monitor is at an angle that affords easy and comfortable viewing and adjust this if necessary; the monitor rests on a plinth that allows the monitor angle to be altered.
- Connect the loudspeakers to the '*line out*' socket on the sound card (the socket is marked with the engraving shown on the left and may be coloured green). If the card has two line out sockets, the first is used for the main speakers while the second is used for rear speakers. If greater volume is required, cables can connect the card's line out to another system such as a domestic audio system.
- If the computer is to be used to record audio, a microphone can be connected to the 'microphone' socket (engraved with the diagram shown on the right and may be coloured red). Additionally, the output of an audio device such as a cassette deck or audio CD player can be connected to the sound card's 'line in' socket (the engraving shown in the middle and may be coloured blue). Windows has a utility that allows the volume levels of each device to be individually set (see the chapter on Windows Configuration).

Getting up and running

The steps involved are:
- Connect the printer to the mains supply, switch on the printer and run a self-test. The method for doing this will vary from printer to printer and the printer manual should be consulted. With a dot-matrix printer, this usually involves holding a key depressed (such as the LF key) while the unit is switched on; when the key is released, the printer prints out a sample of its output. With a laser printer, this normally involves taking the printer off-line and carrying out a key sequence (e.g. pressing the Shift and Test buttons) or running a test through software once the computer is running.
- Plug in the monitor and system unit mains connectors to the mains supply and switch on the mains at the wall sockets.
- Switch on the monitor and check that the mains indicator light illuminates.
- Switch on the system unit. The computer ON/OFF switch is located on the main body of the computer. It can be a button on the front, or a switch at the side or the rear. Before

switching on, ensure that the floppy disk drive is empty. There will often be an additional switch to power the monitor, usually on the front of the monitor casing.

After being switched on, the microcomputer will take about 30 seconds to establish its operating system before it can be used. The computer checks itself to see that its main board, its memory and other key components are working. If the machine passes the self-test and the keyboard and monitor are correctly connected, the monitor screen will display the Operating System interface, which usually means the Windows Desktop.

This first level of operation is the point at which you can choose *'Shut Down'* from the *'Start'* button (on a Windows-based system), or safely switch the microcomputer system off (on a DOS-based system). It is most important always to return to this level if you have been using another piece of software.

Failure to do so can result in either or all of the following circumstances –

- Loss of data through incomplete file update.
- Loss of automatic backup copy of a file.
- Partial update and consequential corruption of any file that is open at the time.

If the system does not work properly, the computer's manual on basic troubleshooting should be consulted.

Setting up a laptop computer

Laptop, also called 'portable' systems, use the same technology as full-fledged desktop systems, with some important differences:

- Although a laptop system can use an external monitor, it has a flat panel screen built in, so that it can be carried around more easily. If an external monitor is to be connected, it is done in the same way as to a desktop machine, but a function key sequence is used to change the output from the integral flat screen to the external monitor. Consult the manual to find the proper function key sequence to do this for any given system, as it differs from one supplier, and sometimes one system, to the next.

- Similarly, an external mouse, and sometimes even an external keyboard, can be used. These generally attach to a normal PS/2 connector at the back of the laptop. These, however, don't normally require a function key switch to be pressed before they can be used.

- Laptops often make use of infrared connections, for example to communicate with desktops, cameras, etc.   Ensure that the laptop is positioned such that the infrared sensor points at the device to be used.

- Laptop systems are supplied with power from one of two sources: an external AC/DC converter (unlike the straight AC 'kettle' lead used in desktops) or an internal DC battery. A component inside the laptop known as the *'DC Controller'* detects which source to use, and modulates the power to the various parts of the system. Thus, if the battery light on a laptop is flashing, it can be plugged into an AC socket via the adapter, to maintain power, without needing to reboot.

- Upgrade cards for laptop computers come in the shape of PCMCIA cards (also called *'PC cards'*) that can be inserted or removed while the system is running, unlike the internally fixed cards found inside a desktop computer. Such cards include modems, network interfaces, and so on. See the Computer Architecture chapter for more details on these cards. Any cards that are needed should be inserted, and connected to any external lines or devices as necessary. For example a PCMCIA modem will come with a small lead that attaches to a standard phone cable.

- When extra functionality is required, the laptop can be attached to a *'docking station'*. The docking station allows quick connection to various external devices, usually including a keyboard, mouse, monitor, network connection, and full-size desktop-style expansion cards. An alternative is to use a *'port replicator'*, which is similar to a docking station, the main difference being the lack of expansion slots. Its main function therefore, is to allow all ports to be connected quickly and simultaneously, hence the name. In either case, attaching the laptop to the station is usually a simple case of clicking it into place at a slight angle then laying it flat.

Using the computer

The machine should be used in a way that protects both the operator and the machine.   These issues are covered in the chapters on *'P.C. Support'* and *'Display Technology'*.

Software & Data

Computer Software

Software is the program that is bought, or created, for the computer. Without software, a computer is just a black box of electronic equipment that is incapable of any useful function. Software tells the computer exactly what to do and when to do it. Such programs are written in a form of code that only that particular type of computer understands. This machine specific code is called *'machine code'* and code written for a Macintosh or a Unix system will not run on a PC, for example. The code used by the computer is written using one of the many programming languages. The computer requires step-by-step instructions to reach a solution to a given problem. This series of instructions is known as a program.

The difference between programs and data

- Data is facts or information available for, or the result of, processing. The source of data is usually via the keyboard where an operator types information such as names and addresses, payroll information, measurements, etc.
- Programs are the instructions for processing data. Programs are created by a systems analyst and a programmer. They specify and write a set of instructions that the computer understands and which is able to process the data supplied. Programs can be simple or complex, and can be written by a single programmer or be created by a whole team working for a "*software house*".

Software falls into two main categories - Application software and Systems software.

Application Software

This consists of general-purpose programs and those developed for computer users to solve specific tasks. Typical applications are Word, Excel, Access, PhotoShop and MS Project.

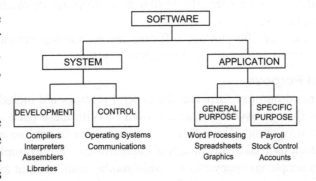

Systems Software

This consists of programs that enable users to make efficient use of the machine. They co-ordinate and maximise the use of the computer's circuitry. Examples of systems software are MSDOS, Windows, Unix and communication utilities.

Application and System software act as interfaces between computer users and computer hardware. If this software did not exist, very few computers would be in use. As application and system software become more sophisticated, computers become easier to use.

System Software

System software can be divided into two categories - Control and Development Software.

Development

This software is concerned with the <u>creation</u> of other software; it comprises sets of software tools to allow programs to be written and tested. Knowledge of the appropriate programming language is assumed. JavaScript, for example, is a commonly used language for writing web page programs, while 'C' is commonly used for creating real-time programs.

The writer can choose from the following tools:

- Editors (to enter and modify the program lines)
- Assemblers (to write in machine-specific language)
- Compilers (to turn the writer's program into a form to be saved and run by the machine)
- Interpreters (to convert the written program and run it, one line at a time without being previously compiled)
- Libraries (to store commonly used bits of program, so that the writer can include them in his/her program without having to re-write them from scratch)
- Diagnostic (or '*debugging*') utilities to detect *'bugs'* - errors in the logic of the program.

Development software also includes Computer Aided Software Engineering (CASE) tools. These are not programming languages as such, and are not used on their own to develop software, but are used as aids to normal software development methods.

Control

This software appears on all computers in one form or another. The most common control software is the computer's *'Operating System'*. This is the software that controls the machine's disk, screen, keyboard and printing activities, etc. The most commonly used system is Microsoft Windows. This is described in detail in the chapter on *'Windows Configuration'*. Other commonly used system software is Linux and various Network Operating Systems (NOS).

Application Software

These are the software applications that are used by organisations to input, store and process data. This software can be further sub-divided into Specific-purpose and General-purpose categories.

Specific Purpose

These packages are written to carry out a prescribed set of tasks and the user has very little control over the process.

The advantages of using specific purpose software are:

- Little training, since the program produces a series of simple tasks that is easy to carry out.
- Comprehensive error checking. All likely errors that can be made by users are predicted in advance and the program is written to prevent the user from entering erroneous information (e.g. an age of -17 or entering numbers for a person's name).

The big disadvantage is that programs that are specific to a company's needs are not available off the shelf and have to be specially written as a *'bespoke application'* by a software house, which is a very expensive option.

Examples of specific purpose software are accounting systems, payroll systems, expert systems, stock control systems and transaction processing systems.

General Purpose

With general-purpose software, the general routines are included in the package but the user has a great deal of influence over how they are used. With these packages, the user controls the software and not the other way round. These facilities are available to anyone who uses the package. The difference lies in how each user takes advantage of the facilities. For example, one user's output from a word processor may be a simple company memo, while another user's output may be a best selling novel or a love poem The differences between specific-purpose software and general-purpose software are even more striking when looking at graphics and Desk Top Publishing packages, where the flair, imagination and artistic abilities of the user are more significant than the packages' abilities.

Examples of general-purpose software are word processors, graphics packages, CAD and DTP packages Some commonly used software packages are examined next.

Databases

A database is a collection of data that is stored on computer files. Many of today's applications are based on databases – customer management systems, stock control systems, payroll systems, ordering systems, and so on.

A database file stores a collection of individual records. Each record is a store of details (e.g. customer details in a mailing list or product details in an on-line catalogue). Typical database activities are:

- Adding a new record (e.g. a new customer into a mailing list)
- Reading records (e.g. by a telephone sales operator)
- Altering a record (e.g. changing the price of an item)
- Deleting a record (e.g. removing a deceased customer from a list)
- Creating reports (e.g. totalling sales for each customer).

For large organisations, databases are specially designed and written to the customer's specification. For smaller organisations, databases are constructed by tailoring the facilities of existing commercial packages (e.g. Access, dBase, FileMaker, etc.). In both cases, careful consideration has to be given to who can access different types of information (e.g. only the personnel section may have access to personal staff records).

Accounting

Since all organisations survive and prosper on the basis of their financial stability, most departmental software feeds data into the financial system. Sales systems, booking systems, payroll systems, stock control systems, and so on, all link to ensure that the necessary monitoring and control of the organisation's finances remain sound.

At the heart of any organisation is its financial accounting system. This keeps track of all financial transactions and is constantly being added to as new sales and purchases are made.

The basis of the accounting system is a set of ledgers. In times past, these were books into which entries were hand-written. Today, the system is computer-based and this provides improved working through computerised calculations, automatic posting of entries, rapid production of balance sheets, profit and loss statements, cash flow reports and comparisons with previous months/quarters/years.

An accounting system uses the following ledgers:

Sales ledger

This records all the goods and services supplied by the organisation and stores all payments or debts to the organisation. A typical entry might contain:

- The date of the transaction.
- The customer details (e.g. an account number).
- The financial details. This may be:
  - The invoice number (the document sent to the customer outlining the goods and their costs, requesting payment within a specified period) and amount.
  - The credit note number (when a customer returns goods) and the amount credited back to the customer against a previously issued invoice.
  - Details of monies received in payment (or part payment) of a previously issued invoice.

In this way, the financial dealings with each customer is recorded. Adding a new invoice into the system increases the customer's debts, while each credit note or receipt of payment reduces the debt.

In a relational database system, entering a customer's account number pulls details from a separate customer file, such as invoice address, delivery address, credit limit, special instructions, etc.

This ledger is used to query individual account details – to settle disputes, print out customer statements, etc. It can also provide reports that cover the entire ledger, such as bad debts (those customers who have not settled within the agreed payment period), customers who have not made any purchases in the recent month/quarter, customers who have spent more than a certain amount in the last year, etc.

Purchasing ledger

This records all the goods and services purchased by the organisation. The details of the entries are similar to those in the sales ledger. The difference is that the entries record all the debts incurred and payments made by the organisation. The invoice numbers and the credit note numbers will be those issued by the various suppliers. The ledger is used to query accounts with individual suppliers, or list all unpaid debts.

Nominal ledger

Details are entered into the sales and purchasing ledger on a daily basis and record details of each transaction. A summary of these transactions is recorded in another ledger called the nominal ledger (or general ledger). This ledger is used for the production of the organisation's final accounts, producing both a Profit & Loss Account and a Balance Sheet as explained below:

Balance Sheet	This tracks how much a company is worth and comprises the fixed assets (e.g. property), plus the current assets (e.g. unpaid invoices, cash, stock) minus the current liabilities (e.g. unpaid bills, unpaid taxes, etc.).
Profit & Loss Account	This indicates how much money a company has earned, or lost, over a specified period. It comprises the sales minus direct costs (e.g. labour, materials) minus indirect costs (e.g. advertising) minus overheads (e.g. premises, janitorial services, legal services, and depreciation).

The nominal ledger also provides the source for creating transaction reports that can be used for management information, customer analysis and error checking.

Payroll

This is a good example of specific-purpose software. The user is prompted to enter details such as employee number, number of hours worked, number of night hours, etc.   The database will have previously stored details of the employee's grade and salary scale. The program then calculates the deductions such as tax and National Insurance and determines the final net wage of the employee. The program then prints the employee's payslip. The role of the user is restricted to feeding the machine with the appropriate answers. A menu may allow different reports to be generated but there is no opportunity to deviate from the pre-programmed activities.

Expert systems

Another example of specific-purpose software is an expert system. The knowledge of practising experts is built into a software package in a way that allows the knowledge to be accessed by those using the software. Experts systems are used in medical, scientific and many commercial areas. They are also used for repairing equipment (see an example on computer faultfinding on the author's web site). Users answer questions or input data and are guided to accurate conclusions. Of course, like all systems using data, the accuracy of the output is only as good as the quality of the data stored in the system.

Stock control

Every organisation keeps track of its stock. This may vary from office stationary to aerospace engines. A company that manufactures or trades goods has the responsibility of maintaining sufficient stock to satisfy customer demand. A number of problems have to be tackled:
- Having too little stock, resulting in failure to deliver or delays in delivery.
- Having too much stock, tying up valuable resources and causing cash flow problems.
- Having stock that expires before sale (e.g. stocks of last year's calendars or perished goods).

These problems are minimised by a combination of market forecasting (to avoid stocking excessive or unfashionable goods) and an efficient stock control system.

The heart of a stock control system is a database of all goods that are stocked.

The stock information in the file can be accessed by sales desk operators or directly by customers (e.g. in some stores and on many web sites).

Typical entries in a stock control record are:

Stock code	The unique code used to identify individual products.
Description	The description of the product as displayed on the screen.
Stock unit	The amount by which the product is sold (e.g. singly, by the dozen, etc.)
Stock level	The amount of that product currently held in stock.
Re-order level	The figure to which the stock will drop before replacements are ordered.
Re-order quantity	The amount that will be ordered when replacement stocks are ordered.

Other probable entries will include the details of the supplier of the product, the cost price, the selling price, any VAT qualifications, and any special instructions (e.g. obtaining import licences).

Some data will be open to general access (e.g. letting customers and sales staff read the current stock levels) while alteration of entries will be restricted to those who despatch goods (reducing reduce stock levels) or receive incoming goods (increasing stock levels).

Word-processing

This software has fixed facilities to enter text, modify it, move it around, format it (e.g. make it bold or underlined) check it for correct spelling or grammar, etc.   These facilities of word processors have been extended from simple text processing to handling other contents such as tables, charts and graphs.

Its usefulness to organisations has been enhanced by its ability to use templates for standard letters and invoices. They are also capable of importing data from other packages (e.g. an image from a graphics package or a graph from a spreadsheet).

It is universally used for writing reports and general correspondence. However, it has evolved into a powerful tool for creating web sites, compiling mailshots and mailing lists, and producing presentations.

DTP

This software is used for the creation of material intended for printing. It creates a master copy of a leaflet, brochure or book from which the printing is carried out. It has the facilities of a word processor with improved support for text flow, text leading and kerning, indexing, colour management, outputting to PostScript and PDF formats, etc.

Spreadsheets

This software provides the tools for entering text, numeric values and formulae into a matrix of cells, to create a computational model for delivering specific calculations. These facilities are constructed so that inexperienced operators can use the final package. So, one company might tailor a spreadsheet to provide a budget program while another company might produce a sales forecasting program as a management model for making strategic decisions. Spreadsheets are used for storing and processing existing data. They are also used to predict the effects of various factors on a company's profitability or competitive edge, by entering different data into a projection of the company's operations. This is known as 'what if' (e.g. what would happen if VAT was increased to 20%, what would happen if sales rose by 3%, etc.).

The data is held in the spreadsheet's rows and columns and the contents can be sorted (e.g. into alphabetic or numeric order), searched (e.g. to find a particular value) and filtered (e.g. to find out which rows have products with a zero VAT rating). The results can be displayed as a set of figures. They can also be displayed pictorially, using 2-D or 3-D charts.

Note:

Spreadsheet and database packages cannot be used straight out of the box. They have to be configured to meet the specific needs of the organisation. Fortunately, the person tailoring the package need only know the package's functions, tools and script language. This means that a commercial system can be developed within the company, saving the huge costs involved in ordering a custom designed product from a software house.

Licensing Agreements

Software can be obtained in a variety of different ways and in a variety of different pricing structures.

The main channels are:

Commercial

This is the most common method of acquiring software. Thousands of products are available with the most common programs being produced by large software houses and corporations such as Microsoft and Macromedia. These are copyrighted programs with strictly enforced licences.

The various options are:

Single licence

Often referred to as an End User Licence Agreement (EULA), a single copy is supplied with installation disks or CDs and user manuals. The software can only be installed on a single machine. Each extra machine is added by purchasing another complete package.

Site licence

A small number of physical copies of the software and manuals are supplied in this case, to reduce costs. The organisation is licensed to install the software either on a set number of computers (e.g. a 20-user licence), or in some cases on any system located within a single physical location. Typically, user-based site licenses can normally be expanded as needed by buying additional licenses. Site licenses are used where individual licenses for each computer would be too expensive.

Enterprise licence

Similar to a site licence, an enterprise licence allows the software to be used on any systems owned in any location by a particular organisation. It is generally based on the number of users, and each enterprise licence will be different as a result.

Licence by use

This allows the software to be installed on a large number of computers, but the licence only allows a fixed number of users to be operating the software at any one time. A 20-user licence on these terms would allow the software to reside on 100 machines as long as there was never more than 20 operators using the package at any one time. Increasing the users on this system is identical to the site licence arrangements. This is sometimes called '*per-person*' licensing.

Licence by station

This allows a fixed number of machines to have the software installed. If it's a single-user licence, the software must reside on a single machine; if it's a 10-user licence, then only ten machines can have the software installed. This is sometimes called '*per-seat*' licensing.

Network multi-licence

If an organisation has a local area network, an individual software package for all the computers will reside as a single copy on the file server. Many single-user packages will refuse to work over a network and special network versions have to be bought. In addition, network versions contain facilities to allow many users to read and update the same data without getting in each other's way. If a 20-user network version of a package is bought, then only 20 operators can use the package at any one time. There can be 30, 40 or 100 machines on the network and the package will be available at any one of the computers. When a 21st operator attempts to access the package, the software will not be able to be accessed by that user. Purchasing upgrade disks extends the system. If, for example, a 4-user upgrade were purchased for an existing 20-user system, then the disk would be run to change the maximum allowable from 20 to 24.

Licences may allow the user to make a back-up copy of the installation disks and most allow the user to install the program on a machine or to sell the program provided no copies are kept. Licences usually prohibit the renting/leasing of the program and prohibit additions/alterations to the software. Licences often also attempt to limit the manufacturer's liability for any problems caused by use of the software.

Application Service Providers

Application Service Providers (ASP's) introduced a relatively new form of licensing. With the increasing speed of Internet access, and growing power of server equipment, it became feasible to attach a server to the Internet (or a private network) that would perform application tasks for client systems. For example, a user could be able to log on to the Internet from his office machine, his home machine, or a laptop with a dialup line, and access the word processing, database, spreadsheet and/or other applications on the server for which he or she is licensed.

This method makes upgrading of software hassle-free for end users, and can help prevent 'over-licensing' – a phenomenon which occurs where an organisation ends up with licensed software which it has paid for but no longer needs.

At one time widely touted as being likely to become the dominant licensing strategy, the ASP model has failed in most markets to achieve this goal. This is largely due to the need for connectivity, and the associated costs.

Product Activation

A system that is not yet implemented, but which has been discussed now for years, is the theory of Product Activation, whereby systems are supplied with a huge range of software on the hard disk, all of which are rendered inactive. When the user purchases a software license, he simply receives an activation code that allows him or her to use the software. This system is likely to be in development for some time yet, due partly to technical concerns but more largely to the need to enforce licensing legalities.

NOTE: Windows implements Product Activation differently. See the Operating Systems chapter.

Public domain

Often abbreviated to '*PD*'. These programs are not copyrighted by their authors and can be distributed and used free of charge. Users are allowed to alter any program code. This type of software is normally restricted to small programs and utilities. These programs are largely obtained by downloading them from the Internet and from bulletin boards.

Freeware

This is similar to public domain except that the alteration of program code is not permitted. The author retains the copyright over the program and its code. The user is allowed to use and copy the program. It is also sometimes described as '*Bannerware*'. A common variation is '*Open Source*' software, which encourages users to add their own code and promotes a software sharing community.

Shareware

These are copyrighted and usually full-working versions of programs. The author retains all rights over the program and can alter it or withdraw it from public use if desired. Unlike the normal commercial sector, these are freely distributed on a *'try before you buy'* basis. This normally involves allowing the free use of the software for a limited period (typically 30 days) so that a user can evaluate the usefulness of the product for the specified purpose. If the product is satisfactory, the user has to register the program by sending the author the prescribed fee. This fee acts as a licence to use the software and may also provide a printed manual, free updates and telephone or mail support. If the product is not found to be satisfactory, the user should stop using it. These programs are obtained from the Internet, from bulletin boards, CDs supplied with magazines or from shareware distributors. The user is not allowed to alter the program code.

The quality of shareware programs varies tremendously, from the insultingly bad to entirely professional products. Some products are *'clones'* of well-known spreadsheet and word-processing packages. Such packages provide broadly similar facilities at a fraction of the normal commercial price. In other cases, the shareware version is a cut-down equivalent to a well-known product, offering fewer facilities. However, since most users only use a small proportion of a package's facilities, this need not represent a real loss of program functionality for the user. If cost is a factor and compatibility with existing packages is not an issue, then shareware products can be a cost-effective purchase.
In America, the Association of Shareware Professionals provides a standard of writing, support and protection. In the UK, the equivalent body is the Association of Shareware Professionals (UK) Ltd, Treble Clef House, 64 Welford Road, Wigston Magna, Leicester, LE8 1SL.

Shovelware

This is not an actual licensing category but is included for completeness. The term has come to describe the habit of supplying large amounts of shareware/PD software on the one CD disk, particularly common as give-aways with computer magazines. It also covers the cramming of many illegal copies of major application packages on to one CD-ROM for sale as a pirate copy.

Copyright

Software, once written, can be copyrighted and protected by the UK Copyright, Designs and Patents Act of 1988. The Act was subsequently slightly amended by an EC Directive (which takes precedence) in 1992 and is now referred to as the Copyright (Computer Programs) Regulations. The Act defines a computer program as a *'literary work'* and the copyright applies to the program for the life of the author, plus fifty years. In the case of an employee, the copyright is owned by the employer. The Criminal Justice Act makes the Trading Standards Office responsible for copyright law enforcement and breaches of copyright are considered to be criminal offences.

Software Piracy

The copying of software to avoid paying the licence is widespread and is estimated to cost hundreds of millions of pounds in the UK alone; world losses are estimated to be several billion dollars. Huge amounts of money are invested in developing software and potential income is lost through piracy. As a result, the development costs are recouped through increased retail prices to the legal purchasers. When a user opens a sealed pack of new software, he/she is deemed to have accepted the conditions printed on the envelope. These lay down whether the software is a single user/single computer licence, the restrictions on its use, etc. It is illegal to:

- Copy copyrighted software without permission from the copyright owner.
- Copy the software's manuals and program notes, without permission from the copyright owner.
- Distribute copyrighted software without permission from the copyright owner.
- Distribute the software's manuals and program notes, without permission from the copyright owner.

Police have search warrant powers to enter premises where there is a suspected breach of the Copyright Act involving computer software and a number of highly publicised fines have been imposed on well-known public and private organisations. Maximum penalties are 6 months/£5000 in the Magistrates

Court and 2 years/unlimited fines in the Crown Court. Six-month jail sentences have already been given in a number of cases of selling counterfeit software. Successful prosecutions have also been brought against the importation of pirate software, under the Trademarks Act, with sentences up to 4½ years. There is now some evidence that employers are taking the issue of piracy seriously and many now have policies to prevent unlawful copying of programs or bringing unlicensed software into the workplace. In some cases, culprits face disciplinary measures up to the level of dismissal.

Anti-Piracy Agencies

One of the major groups is the Federation Against Software Theft which was formed in 1984 to combat computer piracy and is supported by the subscriptions of its around 900 members (mostly corporate users or from the computer industry). It works closely with local police forces and council Trading Standards departments. Its purpose is twofold:

- To educate and advise computer users against software piracy.
- To support software developers and law enforcement agencies in preventing and detecting computer piracy and to aid the prosecution of offenders.

A group of computer auditors can descend, without warning and at any time, upon a suspected company and serve an 'Anton Piller' court order allowing a search for illegally copied software. An Anton Piller order is a court order that requires a company to allow the inspection team to search the premises and produce a permanent record of all software installed on the premises. The inspection team is usually compiled from computer experts and lawyers and their records may be used in evidence in any legal action against an offending company. The consequences of such an action are severe and include:

- The individual responsible for the installation of the software may lose his/her reputation or even his/her job. Even if that person is not personally responsible, he/she will still be held liable and will pay the price for poor control of staff.
- The offending organisation may have to delete all illegal software and purchase new packages.
- The offending organisation may have to pay for its use of the illegal software.
- The offending organisation will have to pay for all the inspection and legal costs.
- The offending organisation will suffer extremely bad publicity.

To date, FAST has not lost a single court case. They can be contacted at

York House
18 York Road
Maidenhead
SL6 1SF (Tel 01628 622 121, www.fast.org.uk).

FAST has concentrated largely on large corporations but has began to focus on the SoHo (small office/home office) market. This will mainly be an educational drive, with the legal drive directed against those who produce and market illegal copies.

There are a number of other active agencies.

The ELSPA, the European Leisure Software Publishers Association, has its own crime unit. They pay particular attention to pirate games CDs and can be contacted at 0870-5133405.

The BSA, Business Software Alliance operates internationally, specialising in combating piracy of business applications. Its members include Microsoft and Novell.

In the UK it works closely with FAST and can be contacted at 0207-340-6080; its Software Crimeline is 0800-510510.

'Intercept' is a group including major software companies such as IBM and Microsoft. It has laid some stress on the detection and elimination of computer pornography.

Although not an enforcing agency, the British Computer Society has a number of specialist working groups in this area - the Law Specialist Group, the Technology of Software Protection Group, the Computer Security Specialist Group and the Data Protection Group.

The BCS is at First Floor, Block D, North Star House, North Star Avenue, Swindon, S21 1FA, Tel 01793-417417 (www.bcs.org.uk).

Microsoft provides software to large corporations under its 'Select' scheme and it now intends to invoke a clause in that contract that allows for spot-check audits of software.

Software Audits

In an organisation with many PCs, keeping track of the contents of each machine's hard disk is difficult. A systematic approach has to be adopted to catalogue all the software in use on the machines in an easy form that can be compared with the software licences held by the company. A manual search through all the files on each hard disk and the collation of the results would be very time consuming. Automated systems are available in the form of *'software auditing'* programs such as Lan Auditor, Asset Explorer, and ABC Lan Licenser.

Since most PCs are now connected to local networks, most auditing packages are designed to collect information over the network cabling. There is no need to visit individual PCs and the work can be carried out centrally. Of course, auditing programs are available for organisations that do not network their computers. In such cases, visits have to be paid to each machine.

Steps in an audit

- Gather together the entire organisation's licences. In the best organisations, there will already be a responsible person (e.g. MIS manager or Finance Manager) who has these documents catalogued. In most organisations, they are scattered and will have to be tracked down using invoices, manuals, installation disks, local knowledge, etc. This task can be carried out while the other audit tasks are being performed.
- Inform the users about the procedures. This is particularly true for a first audit, as its aim will include educating users on the problems of illegal software, threats from virused games and the organisation's discipline policy on these matters.
- Gather the information. In a non-networked situation, each computer is visited and the auditing procedure is:
    1. Insert the audit floppy disk into the computer and run its program. (after a virus check)
    2. Supply the program with details of the machine being tested (e.g. machine serial number, room number, or other identifying code).
    3. Wait while the program searches the machine's hard disk cataloguing all the known programs in its list. This list includes all the most common applications and can be added to by the user. The program saves the machine's program details to a file on the floppy disk.

In a networked system, the information can be gathered from each remote computer and stored directly to the auditor's hard disk.

- Compile the results. The auditing software can provide a variety of views - i.e. details for each machine as well as totals for particular application packages. It produces a report that combines all the facts from each machine and lists how many copies of each program were found in the company's machines. This is the list that can be compared to the company's licence provision and unlicensed use detected. The reports can be sent to the screen or the printer.
- Decide on action. All experience shows that a mass of unlicensed software will be uncovered. All software not required by the organisation (e.g. games) can rapidly be removed. However, the reports may also highlight any shortages of licences to cover the use of some packages. Waiting for the next financial budget allocation is not a legal option. Either the software has to be immediately removed or extra licences immediately purchased.

Software Installation

Each application has its own differing step-by step routine to install software. In most cases, the installation routine is straightforward. The package contains a CD or a set of disks and an installation guide. The guide may be part of the package's manual or may be a separate booklet. In Windows, software supplied on CD should autostart on inserting the disk, thus beginning the installation procedure automatically. If not, locate the CD drive in Explorer and look for an installation program, probably called *'install.exe'* or *'setup.exe'*. Floppy disk software is now rare except for device drivers, but if more than one floppy is supplied; the first disk normally contains the setup program.

Before installation:
- Make sure that all relevant materials are to hand. This includes not only the installation media, but also the license details (in particular any serial number that may be required).
- Check the system's specifications (such as amount of RAM or processor speed) compared to the minimum stated for running the product, to ensure that the software can be used normally.
- The media should be checked for viruses so that the systems on which it is being installed do not become infected. Ideally a backup of the system should be made in case anything goes wrong during the installation.

During installation:
- Some configuration may take place during the installation process. Configuration is explained below.
- Record any installation problems, for fault tracking purposes. Installation problems can include corrupted or missing source files, compatibility problems with existing software (particularly if DLLs are overwritten by the install procedure), or a simple failure to install, usually with some form of error message.

After installation:
- The software must be configured after installation. During application set up it may require information to allow it to perform its function properly. For example Microsoft Office products will ask for a user name, so that the author of any file can be identified. Some applications need more detailed information, such as which folder to store created files in. The setup information required varies for each package, and the manual should be consulted.
- After the software is installed and configured, the software should be tested. Due to the wide range of software available there is no single correct way of doing this, and of course the level of testing carried out will vary depending on the importance of the system. For example, a secretary's word processor can be deemed satisfactory if it opens, saves and prints; while a research lab system would require very thorough testing to a rigorous plan developed in advance. It would be futile to try to check every function of the software, so the major relevant functions must suffice. This testing may also have to be carried out at a later stage, in response to faults that develop, (e.g. if important files are accidentally deleted, moved, or corrupted) so proper records of the test should be kept.
- Almost all packages include registration. This should be carried out, since legitimate packages registered with the producers of the software benefit both the supplier and the software user. The user normally receives added benefits such as additional technical support. Registration can usually be done by post, or on-line by email or web-based registration.

Further alterations

When the installation program finishes, the new piece of software is stored on the hard disk and is available for use. In nearly all cases the application will set up a program item and a suitable icon to make access to the program easier; these may include an icon on the Start Menu, the Desktop, and/or the Quickstart bar.

In all applications, the settings can be changed later, if for example the user wishes to use the program in a different manner or if the machine is transferred to another department. With Windows, there are a number of additional settings that can be made outwith the installation process, such as altering the keyboard repeat rate timing, changing the sensitivity of the mouse or altering the system's memory usage. These issues are covered in other chapters.

In addition, some software may have additional components that can be installed or removed as needed. For example Microsoft Word can have any of a range of text input and output filters installed. Sometimes this is done through the Add/Remove Programs section of the Control Panel, but just as often it is done via a menu option in the program itself, and in some cases by more obscure means such as manually editing configuration text files.

Maintaining legality

Before installing software, the support technician should confirm that the software is licensed for installation on the particular machine. A well-run organisation will require documentation on the installation. The technician should fill in a report that states the date of the installation, the person who carried out the installation, the name of the package and other relevant details.

Software Uninstallation

Every piece of software eventually becomes obsolete. When it does, it is usually replaced by more up to date software, and this in turn requires either the replacement of the entire computer system, complete reinstallation of all software, or more likely, the uninstallation of the old software to make room for the new.

Uninstallation is rarely carried out precisely, since many factors change during the use of a package.

DLL or other files may be copied or moved, and therefore cannot be deleted. Registry entries may be left over, as may empty or nearly empty folders on the hard disk. All of this means that a fresh operating system install is preferable where it is practical, on any major software uninstall. However, time constraints may make this impractical, and the options left are uninstallation, or installing the new software on top of the old. The latter option potentially leaves even more problems, as overlapping DLL functions or conflicting settings can cause havoc. Uninstallation is therefore a good idea in many cases.

This is normally carried out either by a specially provided *'Uninstall'* icon, or by selecting *'Add/Remove Programs'* from the 'Control Panel' menu found in the Windows *'Settings'* option. Again, it is a good idea to backup the system before uninstalling software, where reasonably possible, in case faults develop as a result. The system should be tested once again after uninstallation. If faults occur once the new software is installed and proper tests are not carried out at this stage, it will be impossible to tell whether the uninstallation or the new installation have caused those faults.

Normally the uninstallation process is almost entirely automated. The user should <u>never</u> try to 'remove' a package simply by deleting the folder the program is contained in – this will leave links, DLLs, registry entries and so on lurking around the system. Some packages provide useful information on any folders, files, registry entries or program files that could not be removed during the uninstall procedure, and these should be removed manually where practical to do so. Registration details should be kept even after the software is uninstalled, since even though the software may appear to be gone there can still be traces of the package on the system, and the registration details will prove that the package was there quite legally.

Information in organisations

Organisations are formed for a variety of reasons: e.g. to make profits, to serve the public, or as social gatherings. An organisation often produces better results than the efforts of individuals and in many cases, such as building cars or bridges, the results can only be produced efficiently with a collective effort.

A group of individuals may loosely co-operate in some activities such as sport, clubbing, charity work, etc. As soon as those individuals co-operate in a more structured way (e.g. forming a football team) they have developed into an organisation. Their group could not exist without being organised (for setting up matches, organising transport, electing a captain, applying for grants, etc.).

Individuals in the organisation gather information (e.g. the secretary consults train timetables while the treasurer maintains the club bank account). In commercial organisations, there is a legal responsibility to maintain financial and other records.

With a few exceptions, organisations can be classified into three general categories:

- Public service – those which provide facilities or aid to the general public. For example schools, libraries, hospitals, emergency services, social security, etc. are all run by local government or national government departments.
- Industrial – these are organisations involved in the mass production of goods. Although some industrial organisations also sell their own goods to the public, the majority sell through a commercial agent.
- Commercial – there are organisations that exist purely to sell goods supplied by others, or to provide services at a charge.

Organisations vary widely in their size. For example, a company specialising in repairing thatched cottage roofs may employ only a few highly skilled workers. The company might only work within a relatively small geographical area. On the other hand, a huge retail chain will have hundreds (or thousands) of stores throughout the world and will benefit from its massive purchasing power and brand name. Its workforce may be largely unskilled or semi-skilled. Organisations also vary greatly in their purpose. Some provide goods while others provide services. There are even differing interests within the same market area. For example, a state hospital's prime objective is to return a good record on health performance while a private hospital is primarily judged on its return for shareholders.

Organisations vary widely in size, purpose, and structure – from a local swimming club, to a district council, to national government to international bodies such as NATO and the United Nations. Nevertheless, they share some common features. They all need information and communications to function, and they all have some form of management structure and (at least in theory) they are all accountable to their members (e.g. shareholders, voters, club members).

Organisational structures

Organisations adopt different strategies in organising their management. Each has an impact on the ratio of managerial staff to the size of the workforce, the levels of decision-making and responsibility and the overall efficiency of the organisation.

Hierarchical model

The most widely known and used management structure is the *'hierarchical model'*. In this model, there are various layers of management above those who actually do the core work. Those further up the management 'tree' manage those below. For example the workforce in a plant might report to a foreman, who in turn reports to the plant manager, who then reports to the local area manager, who eventually reports to the General Manager of the company. This model has the advantage of laying out clear levels of  responsibility and relieves those in higher positions of dealing with the intricacies of the organisation's functions. Each member of the organisation communicates 'upwards' to this/her manager, and the manager in turn communicates 'down' the tree in order to issue instructions. Foremen and middle managers have levels both above and below them. They both receive and issue instructions. One problem with this structure is the scope for delays and misinterpretations in communications between levels.

Flatter model

A model that is gaining in popularity is the flat management model. Although not truly flat, there is a less pronounced hierarchy, promoting 'sideways' communic-ation between workers who are considered effectively equal. For example, 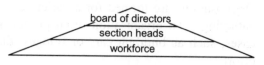 a software development house may have project leaders and managers, but the majority of the work will be carried out by programmers, placing less emphasis on hierarchical structures. A flatter hierarchy is intended to promote teamwork and remove unnecessary layers of management. One problem with this structure is the tendency to offload the tasks that were once carried out by middle management onto the workforce – in addition to their current workload.

Division of organisations

Large organisations split the structure into more manageable divisions. A supermarket chain, for example, might split its structure on geographic lines, with a London division, a Welsh division, etc. Regional managers would have responsibility for implementing the company's plans for their regions.

In addition, organisations may create distinct divisions as a means of separating out key activities. Thus, a company may be structured on geographical lines, with either a hierarchical or flat structure for each separate district or region. It often has a departmental structure, with managers and sub-managers for each department in the company.

It may also support functional sections, such as order processing or stock control. In a small to medium organisation, several functions may be organised within a department. In a larger organisation, each department may concentrate on a single function, such as marketing or sales.

In all cases, there will be sideways communication and even diagonal communication. This may be structured (i.e. staff in sales have to talk to staff in shipping) or may be informal (i.e. the *'grapevine'* that passes news and gossip but also stimulates ideas and suggestions).

Computer Data

Although a variety of organisations exist, they all work with data and information in some form, and they must all be able to communicate data and information, both internally and externally. The development of computers is driven by the need to collect, manipulate, communicate, and analyse data of all forms.

Information and data

There is a distinction to be made between 'data' and 'information'. Data is purely an accumulation of facts and figures, while information is data that has been processed in such a way as to highlight trends, summarise collections of data, and present other useful material.

For example, a transaction at a supermarket checkout will record the date and time of purchase, along with the items sold, and payment method. These facts on their own are not useful to the organisation, except at the time of purchase or in case of a refund being requested. But when many similar items of data are collected together they can be manipulated to produce figures for overall income, profits, best selling items, busiest times of the day, and so on. When combined with other data, even more information can be produced, for example combining sales figures with expenses will allow the organisation's total profit to be calculated. Thus, processed information can be used in a variety of applications, including strategic planning and operational control (see MIS departments, later in this chapter).

In most cases, data in both its raw and processed state is valuable. Raw data, for example, can be used to send out mailing lists - while processing the same data can produce information on the total numbers in any one town, etc. Indeed, data and information have become commodities for trading. Lists of affluent purchasers (e.g. those recorded as buying expensive cars, art, conservatories, etc) are sold on to companies for mailshot purposes. Of course, the information is only as good as the data that was used to compile it.

Data sources

Almost all medium to large businesses are split into various internal departments. For example, there is likely to be staff and equipment dedicated to sales, purchasing, marketing and so on. The division between departments is often well defined in company documents, which specify the responsibilities of each. Additionally, they may be separated geographically. For example a restaurant chain may have a head office in a particular city, which contains the marketing and personnel departments for the entire organisation. In addition to internal departments, the organisation must communicate information with several external bodies. Customers require information on products and services, prices, where to find the products, points of contact and so on. The suppliers need to be told which items are being purchased, where to deliver the items, and how payment will be made. Government agencies will also be concerned with the organisation's activities, ensuring they comply with laws and regulations, and so on.

Some of the more common sources of data are:

Internal data sources
- Departments (Accounting, Sales, Purchases, Development, Maintenance, Operational control, Personnel or 'Human Resources', Product Design, Training)
- Individuals (timesheets, suggestions box, interviews, unofficial *'grapevine'*)

External data sources
- Other organisations (orders, invoices, returns, government agencies e.g. Inland Revenue, Customs & Excise, Health and Safety Executive).
- Individuals (letters from the public).
- Information providers (market research organisations).
- Service providers (on-line databases).
- Product providers (manuals, technical specifications).
- Reference publications (Government pamphlets, tax tables).
- Public records (legal case histories, balance of payments figures, Hansard).
- Technical resources (see the PC Configuration chapter)

Departmental Functions

Each department in an organisation has its own function, its own software and its own data.

In some cases, the data may be exclusive to that department for legal reasons (e.g. personnel records are subject to privacy laws) or commercial reasons (e.g. the design department's research work is sensitive). In most cases, the data is shared within the organisation. Consider the example of a company's stock control file. It is shared by the Sales, Despatch and Purchasing departments. The Sales department can't sell goods that are not in stock, the Despatch department has to update stock records when goods are shipped out, and the Purchasing dept has to order goods when stocks are running low. Of course, although they are sharing the same set of data, each department probably has a different software application to examine and/or alter that data.

The table shows the general classifications of department, their organisational information and the processing software they use:

Sales		
Responsible for handling customer enquiries and processing customer orders.		
Internal	**Sources of Data/Information**	**External**
Price lists, stock level details, sales targets, special offer details, product specifications.		Customer orders (mailed, telephoned, faxed, on-line ordering)
The department requires sales order processing software that calculates the order costs, confirms the order, notifies the despatch department to send out the order and notifies the finance department of invoice details. It may use booking software (e.g. to sell cinema/theatre/concert seats, airline seats, holidays, etc.) It may also use an EFTPOS or BACS system to receive payments.		

Personnel		
Responsible for human resources management (i.e. recruitment/training/welfare/discipline)		
Internal	**Sources of Data/Information**	**External**
Personnel records (promotion, discipline, health, etc). Training programmes.		Letters of complaints/praise from the public. Employment legislation, Trade Union laws.
The department requires personnel handling software that records personal data records on staff members, including grade, wage level, qualifications, health records, pension records, criminal records, discipline records, staff appraisal records, staff interview records, etc.		

Purchasing		
Responsible for knowing when to order, how much to order, negotiating prices and confirming safe receipt of goods.		
Internal	**Sources of Data/Information**	**External**
Stock control procedures, re-order levels, order amounts, budget restrictions, purchase order documents.		Catalogues, specifications, purchase contracts
The department requires stock control software (to monitor existing stocks against required stocks) and purchase ordering software (to initiate orders for the appropriate stock amounts). In a smaller organisation, this would be part of the Finance Dept.		

Design

Only required where a company produces its own products. The department may work to a specific brief (e.g. develop a solar-powered pump) and may also carry out its own research and development work (e.g. developing new drugs or materials).

Internal	Sources of Data/Information	External
Historical records on previous work. Test results, past and present. Materials specifications.		Laws governing any restrictions (e.g. on embryo research, drug classifications, weapons research, etc.). Databases on research papers, symposiums, etc. Patents for existing products

The department requires the software appropriate to the type of design it is engaged in. Examples include CAD (Computer Aided Design), scientific modelling and emulation tools, and statistical analysis tools.

Marketing

Responsible for predicting and creating market demand for products and services.

Internal	Sources of Data/Information	External
Sales figures, Company Research & Development results.		Market Research, Government initiatives (e.g. on training, grants and subsidies.)

The department requires software to analyse sales trend figures for regions, districts, departments and individual sales items.

Finance

Responsible for the financial affairs of the organisation, both internally (e.g. paying wages) and externally (e.g. receiving payments and issuing payments to customers).

Internal	Sources of Data/Information	External
Company accounts, VAT payments, Payroll details		Sales orders, Remittance advice, Purchase Invoices, Returned goods, VAT receipts.

The department requires accounts software to process and record all invoices and remittances, along with all other company incomings and outgoings, to produce annual accounts statements. It also requires payroll software to process employee wages, including overtime, sick pay, maternity pay, student loans, etc, to produce wage statement of gross and net pay, deductions such as tax and national insurance. It may also use BACS software to eliminate handling cheques.

In a large organisation, the payroll function would form a separate department.

Operations

Responsible for the day-to-day running of the organisation.

Internal	Sources of Data/Information	External
Production figures, management decisions, internal memos.		Delivery schedules, Health & Safety Work legislation

Departments may need software for process control (e.g. operating robots or machinery) and operation monitoring and recording. An operations manager may also be charged with ensuring the smooth operation of the data flow procedures.

Some documents, such as those on policy on health and safety, individual privacy, privileged company information and data protection, cover all departments of an organisation.

Other information categories can be developed, such as:

Scientific   (e.g. scientific formulae, periodic tables, properties of materials, test results).

Engineering (e.g. quality controls, tolerances, templates, computer numeric control systems).

Social   (e.g. national census, voters rolls, music charts, club membership lists).

Another categorisation of information is into *'primary'* and *'secondary'* sources. Primary sources are those recorded at the time of the event, while secondary sources are set down after the event.

Primary sources are frequently more accurate and should be used wherever possible.

Examples of primary information are product specifications, original film footage, authenticated statistics, health and attendance records, and historical records.

Examples of secondary information are product reviews, film reconstructions, politicians' reports, employee appraisements and history books.

Information flow

Whether the communication is between peers, or from manager to subordinate, the means of communication can take several forms. Verbal communications are fast, but prone to misinterpretation and cannot be retrieved later for reference. Paper media can be archived, but often takes up a lot of space, and can be difficult to manage. However, some people are more comfortable with having a hard copy of information, and in fact some information may only be accepted if it is in writing.

Electronic information has its disadvantages, such as extra training requirements, higher initial cost, and the need for support of information systems. Nevertheless, in most cases the advantages are greater – the speed of delivery of communications, the ability to quickly analyse data, and efficiency of storing data, amongst other benefits.

It is often useful to generate an '*information flow diagram*', detailing the internal departments and external groups, as well as the information that typically flows between them. This is useful when implementing or maintaining IT systems in the organisation, as it indicates which personnel need to be able to pass information on to whom.

A typical information flow diagram (not to be confused with a Data Flow Diagram, which is used in software development) might look like the one shown, which details the information inflows and outflows of the sales department in a typical business.

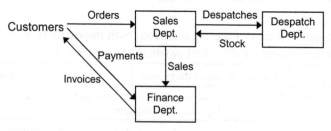

The diagram outlines the type of information that is passed between departments and outside bodies (e.g. customers, suppliers, Inland Revenue). It could also define the format of each item. For example, internal flows may be through updating databases, sending e-mails, or pre-defined reports, while external flows may be through Internet orders, printed paper (e.g. invoices, statements, etc).

Supporting information flow

Information technology can be useful in facilitating the efficient communication between internal departments and between the organisation and the outside world. Fax machines, teleprinters, pagers, and portable phones are all useful, but the main application of Information Technology in business communication is based around computers.

Example benefits are:

Email	The huge boom in commercial e-mail demonstrates is usefulness in sending text and attached data (such as budget spreadsheets, graphics of layout plans, etc.) across the globe almost instantaneously. Mobile phones allow text messaging and WAP-enabled models allow Internet access.
Instant messaging	The ability to create private 'chat rooms' on the internet allows multiple members of staff from around the world to engage in a typed discussion in real time (see the chapter on using the internet).
Video conferencing	The connection of cameras, microphones and loudspeakers to computers, along with the accompanying Internet interfaces, allows users to communicate on a face-to-face basis, potentially improving relations and trust between the participants.
Tele conferencing	The ability of users to have an Internet telephone conversation while sharing access and control of a software application, such as a spreadsheet or accounts package. Usually, an area of the screen (referred to as a '*whiteboard*') allows the users to scribble ideas for discussion.
EDI	Electronic Data Interchange is a system used to exchange data in a standard format. This makes electronic transactions easier since the buyer and seller can have different computer systems and still transfer documents.

Web pages	A large base of government and other public body information is available, along with the ability to e-mail queries to individual departments. Many commercial sites provide online catalogues and other information.
Intranets	Creating an internal web site that can only be accessed by staff attached to the company local area network (see the chapter on LANs). This allows the web site to contain sensitive data (e.g. profit margins) that is not for public consumption, for reference by staff only. It can also provide the equivalent of a staff notice board, with news, vacancies, etc. being posted on the site.
Extranets	This is essentially an intranet with limited outside access to approved individuals (see the chapter on LANs). This could allow sub-contractors, customers or suppliers to see a specified range of internal company information.
EFTPOS	Electronic Funds Transfer at Point Of Sale. A payment model where the money is taken from the customer's bank account when a purchase is made by debit card. The card is swiped in the retailer's premises.
BACS	The Banks Automatic Credit System links the banks and finance houses, allowing money to be transferred between accounts without the need for issuing and cashing cheques. This EFT (Electronic Funds Transfer) system is used between companies to buy and sell goods and services. It is also used to pay wages and pensions.

Data Production

Examples of differing producers of data and information are:

Type of Activity	Type of Data	Type of Information
Weather Centre	Temperatures; barometric readings; wind speeds	Trends in the weather; average sunshine/rainfall for a particular month.
Finance Dept	Invoices paid; income receipts	Balance over a period; main spending areas.
Opinion Polling	Purchasing preferences; voting intentions; public attitudes	Degree of success of an advertising campaign; voting and public opinion snapshots and trends.
College/University	Student details, examination results	Student numbers; proportions by sex, race, etc; total successes in each performance band.

The list could be greatly extended as almost all organisations maintain records for a wide range of purposes. In each case above, information is the result of processing the data in some way. The information is further condensed as it goes further up the organisation's structure. The foreman may require basic daily information for operational reasons, while middle management will want the same information covering a longer term but with less specific detail. Top management will take an even longer view and require even further condensing of the information.

Usage of information

The main uses of the stored information are recording, monitoring and planning:

Historical recording	Used to store for later use (e.g. tax returns, VAT receipts/payments, targeted mailshots, etc).
Monitoring	Used to determine comparisons and trends (e.g. stock control, climatic changes, stock market trends, etc).
Planning	Used to determine future action (e.g. build more schools/roads/houses, extend factories, etc).

The MIS Department supplies information appropriate to the level of management in the organisation as shown below:

Management Level	Responsibilities	Information Required
Top Management	Long-term strategic decisions (e.g. market trends, new products, expansion/ contraction.	Market research, comparisons with competitors.(i.e. both internal and external information)
Middle Management	Tactical decisions on a month-by-month basis.	Future orders, company targets (i.e. company wide information)
Junior Management	Daily operational decisions.	Daily production/staffing/stock figures (i.e. departmental information)

Strategic, tactical and operational information can be produced using a variety of software packages. A database or spreadsheet may suffice in some cases, but it is often more efficient to use specific purpose software such as personnel management systems (operational), accounting packages (tactical) or data analysis packages (strategic).

Decision Support Systems (DSS) are specially tailored applications to provide detailed insights into specific areas that may not appear in normal MIS reports. DSS systems are essentially fact-based (e.g. finding out which customers placed the largest orders last month) and can be enterprise-wide or desktop-based. They usually employ spreadsheets, relational databases, statistical analysis packages or financial modelling software.

MIS Departments

Large organisations will have their own *'Management Information System'* - a department equipped to gather data and produce useful information for management at all levels. The department's aim is to improve the quality of management decisions by:

- Speeding up the time taken for a significant event to be notified to management.
- Providing all information necessary for the support of planning, control and operational functions.

All the clerical operations of staff are set up and processed through the MIS department.

Data Handling

Where large amounts of data are stored in a single computer, a number of potential problems have to be addressed and preventative/corrective measures implemented.

These include:

Loss of data	Preventing loss due to system breakdown or data corruption (see Computer Security Chapter). Also covers the failure to produce the data on time for effective use.
Integrity	Ensuring that data is:
	<u>Complete</u> (all required facts and figures are entered).
	<u>Accurate</u> (all entries are correct - perhaps using double entry of data and/or entry validation procedures such as range checking, format checking and the use of check digits).
	<u>Consistent</u> (e.g. a price list on one computer stores the same values and descriptions as a price list on another computer).
Usefulness	Ensuring that the data held is:
	<u>Relevant</u> (the data stored matches the organisation's needs).
	<u>Suitable</u> (the data is stored in a way that allows easy processing)
	<u>Timeless</u> (historical data is unaltered by subsequent data input)
Legality	Storing data in a legal manner (see the Data Protection Act).
Security	Preventing unauthorised access to data (see the Computer Misuse Act).

An organisation's Management Information Systems (MIS) Department has overall responsibility for the above issues and would institute protective measures in consultation with the P.C. support technicians. The MIS department has the responsibility of ensuring that users are confident about the data that they use – from the point of collection, through processing, to the final presentation and use of the information.

Data processing systems

Organisations use a variety of methods to process their data.

Batch systems

Larger organisations often use *'batch processing'* where a collection of jobs is saved and run in one large batch (usually overnight). The data is usually sorted into order (e.g. alphabetically) before being processed. This system is useful where there is no demand for rapid results from the organisation's activity, since the processed output may appear long after the source data is available. Example uses are payroll (where the output is only required on a weekly or monthly basis) and census statistics.

Real-time systems

Modern banking involves cash points and Point-Of-Sales outlets where a high-street transaction alters the user's bank balance as soon as transaction is completed. This is an example of a real-time system, where the input is immediately accepted and processed very quickly so that further action can be taken using the results of the processing. Real-time processing is essential for transaction processing, as the result of the transaction often affects other transactions. For example, a withdrawal at a cash machine must be updated instantly, to prevent the customer making a further withdrawal that exceeds the amount left in the balance. Similarly, an airline seat cannot be sold twice, so the seat must be withdrawn from sale the instant that it is purchased. Real-time systems use a computer processor to control or monitor activity that is happening in real time. Other examples are robotics, alarm systems, music sequencers and speech recognition.

On-line systems

On-line systems use a computer to access a larger system, such as remote banking, or access to central company databases. It is often used in conjunction with real-time activities.

Time-sharing systems

This method is used by large mainframe and Unix systems, where the processing power of the central computer can be accessed by users on desktop system (see the chapter on Local Area Networks).

Centralised/distributed systems

Organisations employ different approaches to storing and processing their data, depending upon their needs. At one time, all processing of data took place in the organisation's central computer. As the cost of desktop computers has fallen, there has been a marked trend towards users processing data on their local systems.

For large, widespread organisations, there are additional decisions regarding how their masses of data should be stored. If all the data is held in a giant single database in one location (i.e. a centralised database), it is easily controlled and updated. Since there is only one copy of the database, all remote sites access the same set of data. Security can easily be placed on areas of the database (e.g. areas protected under the Data Protection Act or for reasons of commercial secrecy). On the other hand, all the remote sites have to access the same master site and this can produce substantial delays in retrieving data. It is also vulnerable to failure, with a problem at the master site resulting in all locations losing access to data.

An alternative is to distribute the database, with either the entire database being replicated on all other locations, or parts of the database being stored at each location. This prevents the slow performance associated with centralised databases, since each location may have its own exact copy of the master database (or at least a part of it). It also allows processing to continue, even when the master database is off line for any reason. However, there are problems associated with distributed databases. If each location has its own copy of the entire database, there is a danger of each location altering parts of its copy. This means that no two copies of the database are identical (a problem known as 'concurrency'). This can be solved by altering every other copy of the database at the same time as altering the local copy, in turn generating much more data traffic between locations.

The choice of approach depends on factors such as how often data is altered, who has ownership and access rights to particular sections of data, the speed of the links between sites, whether data processing is to take place locally or centrally, etc.

The Data Processing Cycle

The acquisition and use of data consists of several different stages, all of which must be implemented intelligently in order to provide useful information. As with all 'cycles', this is a circular process, meaning that it can be continued as many times as is desired or even indefinitely. This is done either to constantly monitor the organisation's operation, or to provide further and deeper analysis. The stages of the cycle are:

Preparation

Before data can be acquired, the system must be prepared. In a broad sense this might mean the installation of the data processing system as a whole, but it can also mean laying the groundwork for the following stages by deciding on the type of data to be gathered, methods to use and so on. This stage should determine who is responsible for data collection, when it will be carried out, and how it should be collected. For example should the general populace be surveyed in the street, should customers be phoned for details, are logs to be manually entered into computer, and so on. If data is to be collected on paper or directly into computer, then appropriate forms should be created for recording the raw data. This document must be carefully designed to ensure that the correct types of details are entered, when the input stage takes place.

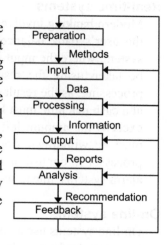

Input

The actual entering of information. This usually consists of both the collection and input of data into the processing system and may involve some or all of these steps:

- The keyboard entry of data that already exists in paper form (e.g. timesheets).
- Downloading data from a remote source (e.g. local branches of an organisation).
- Copying data sub-sets from existing computer files (e.g. from an Internet order form).
- Using machine readers (e.g. like those used to read Lotto forms), to extract data from standard input sheets.
- Reading data from forms using OCR (Optical Character Recognition) systems.
- Reading bar codes (e.g. for stock control)

The main concern at this stage is '*Quality Assurance*' - ensuring the data entered is accurate. Controls should be in place to ensure that no nonsensical data is accidentally entered (see 'Data Controls').

Processing

This is the stage in the cycle that turns raw data into information that can be worked with. Once the data has been entered, it can be processed in any way the organisation deems useful. For example, the same till receipts could be processed in such a way as to gather information on the times of day items were purchased, to gather information on items sold, or so on.

Output

At this stage, it is information rather than data that is being dealt with. The output of the information does not always mean printing the information out, because many pages of information can be as difficult to work with as many pages of raw data. Instead the information may be used to generate reports. For example the output of information on till receipts could involve generating a report which details the fifty best selling products, or the busiest sixty-minute period of each day of the week.

Analysis

Before any action is taken based on the information gained, it must be analysed. This involves going through the information and finding any trends that are apparent. For example, it might be found that lunchtime is the busiest time during weekdays, indicating that it might be a good idea to take on part-time staff to help cover the busy periods. Although it is possible to look for specific information such as this, an alternative approach known as '*data mining*' involves methodically looking at large sets of data in the hopes of uncovering some useful nugget of information. For example it might be found that two products are often bought at the same time by the same customer, indicating the possible effectiveness of a special promotion whereby one product is half price when bought alongside the other.

Feedback

The final stage of the data processing cycle is the feedback stage. This stage essentially concentrates on the actual results of the cycle as compared to what was expected. Depending on the results, the organisation may decide that the methods used in the cycle should be changed, and therefore the cycle should begin again at the preparation stage. Similarly, it may be decided to input new data, to process it in a different fashion, to provide different reports, or even to analyse it in a different way. The feedback stage therefore provides a view of how the cycle progressed, allowing the analyst to decide whether to carry out another cycle, with or without any changes to the process used.

Data Controls

When processing data, it is not enough to simply enter figures. The information must be accurate, valid, and concurrent for it to be of use. If the data is of a personal nature, then the Data Protection Act requires the information be kept up to date.

This means that the data must be entered and maintained in a controlled fashion.

Likely measures to control data accuracy include:

Input controls

These controls aim to prevent inaccurate data entering the processing stage.

- Minimisation. The amount of keyboard entry can be reduced by using machine-readable forms, bar codes, punched cards, etc. This greatly reduces the scope for incorrect entries.
- Simplification. For example, instead of the data field for a customer code being 10 digits (easy to enter incorrectly), it could be four letters and six numbers.
- Confirmation. The data entered at the keyboard should be displayed on the screen in a form that the operator can easily read and that allows alteration of the data.
- Verification. This requires two operators to key in the same data. The two sets of data are compared and any discrepancy is notified, so that the data sets can be examined.
- Validation. When entering new data at the keyboard, the system should be set up so that only values that make sense are accepted. For example, when entering a person's age, a negative number, or an extremely high number should be invalid. The data should be verified before being stored on the system, and any unacceptable data should be rejected and notified to the data entry clerk.

These controls are a mixture of procedural controls, software controls and operator training. Management can instigate measures such as minimisation, simplification, etc. but the data entry staff must be able to spot some errors before they are entered as valid data. Such errors might include forms that are incomplete, vague (e.g. is a digit a 0 or a 6) or incorrect (e.g. a travel expenses form from an employee who is on sick leave).

Processing controls

These controls aim to detect errors during the processing of data.

- File controls. These detect invalid file operations, such as adding the same customer twice to a database or attempting to add transactions to a closed file.
- Validation. The processing software should detect errors that may have slipped in as valid input (e.g. a claim for Business Class travel from an employee who is only authorised for Economy Class, an overtime claim that puts an employee over the maximum allowable working hours, etc.). It may also carry out the range-checking activities mentioned in Input Controls.
- Reconciliation. For example, if an input form contains a list of prices and a price total, the software should check that the manually calculated total agrees with the computer-calculated total.

Security controls

These aim to prevent corruption or loss of data through accidents (fire, flood, etc.) or deliberate action (e.g. theft, sabotage, viruses, hacking). These issues are covered in the chapter on 'Computer Security'.

System Life Cycle

Similar to the data processing cycle explained elsewhere, the System Life Cycle is a technique used to select, install, and maintain IT systems in an organisation. The software that is available off the shelf rarely meets the specific needs of an organisation. A small company may adapt to the software but a larger organisation will develop its own software so that the software mirrors the way that the company works. This, in turn, means that the system hardware must be purchased and configured to support the operational needs of the software.

Although the stages in this development cycle may vary depending on the particular organisation, there are a few common factors.

- **Proposal definition:** This is the first stage of the system life cycle. As the name suggests, this stage investigates exactly what is required of the system. The aim should be to create a comprehensive document detailing the necessary systems for proper implementation of Information Technology in the organisation. It includes an explanation of why the system is required, what benefits can be expected, timescales for implementation, likely organisational changes, budget considerations, etc.

- **Feasibility Study:** Once the proposal is developed, it is critically examined before any further time and money is spent. The project has to justify itself in terms of technical feasibility (can the system work, will it require extra hardware, what will be the impact of organisational changes, what training needs are involved, can it be implemented in the desired time) and economic feasibility (what costs are incurred in implementing the system, can the benefits of the new system be quantified, is there an overall gain from the new system).

- **Information Requirements Analysis:** When the system is approved, the next stage is to define what data and information will be created and processed through the system. This should include the functional requirements of the system and be as specific as possible. It should include the data that will appear on every internal form and report and the content for every database query. It should lead to the development of the overall logic of the company database (known as the *conceptual schema*).

- **Design:** The next stage is to draw up a detailed design document. This will include the conceptual design (e.g. the system's inputs and outputs, the form and screen layouts, operating and training considerations, etc.) and physical design (e.g. database design, hardware specifications, data communications, backup and security considerations, etc.). Allocating the proper resources to designing a system will greatly reduce the maintenance required once the system is installed, as many potential problems will be highlighted and dealt with before the system is even in place.

- **Implementation:** The actual implementation of the system should, perhaps surprisingly to some, be the simplest and fastest part of the systems implementation process. For many organisations, there may be a need for data conversion – converting the data currently held by the system into the new format expected by the new system. Of course, the finished system has to be thoroughly tested before being brought into operation.

- **Conversion:** Whether new software is being rolled out, or new computers or networks are being installed, the aim should be to minimise confusion to the users and effect a smooth crossover into the new system. This requires adequate staff training and is often carried out by a period of 'parallel running', where the old system and the new system are operated together for a period of time. While this involves extra manpower (to keep two systems going), it ensures that the new system works before the old system is disbanded. This prevents any major disasters or data loss.

- **Maintenance:** The cost of any IT system is not purely reflected in its development and installation costs. There is a running cost of maintaining the system. While this includes upkeep of any physical components, it also implies fixing errors in software, maintaining accurate data where required, and even redevelopment of parts of the system that might prove inadequate.

Like other cycles (such as the Data Processing Cycle or the Software Development Life Cycle), the System Life Cycle should not be a one-off process. Instead, there should be continual redevelopment, with feedback coming from any one stage in the process and being used to return to an earlier stage. For example if during the Implementation stage it turns out that certain equipment is significantly more expensive than previously thought, it might be necessary to return to the Feasibility Study to reconsider. However, in any such case care should be taken to avoid *'feature creep'*, a phenomenon whereby apparently 'helpful' capabilities are added to a system that are not part of the requirements analysis, and indeed are not needed in the system. Such additions are normally of little practical use and cause unnecessary delays in the project.

CASE Tools

The design and development of large data handling and system projects are complex and error-prone activities. Computers are often used to both clarify and speed up the process. The software used is called CASE (Computer Aided Software Engineering). Its uses the power of the computer to simplify the information gathering and the computational effort and presents graphic representations of processes. The tools cover a range of activities such as structured analysis, software development, change management and project management. A wider definitions of CASE tools covers activities such as compilers, code generators, configuration management, collaboration tools, reverse engineering, etc

Database Design

CASE tools can play a major role in developing large database systems. They aid the systems analysis stage by identifying the user's data requirements (what data they will create/amend/use) and processing requirements (what they expect in terms of reports, summaries, transaction processing).

The software then produces the main elements for the database design. This includes a *'Data Dictionary'* (details of all the separate items of data to stored in the system), and *'Data Flow Diagrams'* (charts showing how data is accessed/moved within an organisation).

The software can also provide facilities for designing the database user interface. It may also generate much of the program code for the final database program.

Project Management

The planning for a project should begin at the earliest stage, with the detailed tasks being progressively identified. Many managers wish to concentrate on project implementation, seen as *'getting the job done'*. More enlightened, and usually more successful, managers realise that skimping on the design or testing stage affects the quality of the final product. A carefully planned design ensures that the project is successfully started and adequate testing ensures that it is successfully completed.

Large projects benefit from the use of project management software, to ensure that the most efficient use is made of resources and to achieve a working product in the shortest possible time. If a company is planning the creation of a training video, it has to consider that a video crew might require a long advance booking, a well-known personality for the presenter/voice-over may only be in the country over a short time period, etc. and the activities have to be planned to prevent hold-ups.

The illustration below shows a very basic Gantt chart produced by Microsoft Project software. It is illustrative only. It is not indeed to be used as a model. A real working chart would have many more activities and more linkage between activities. Nevertheless, it shows how the software can be used to plan tasks, monitor tasks for slippage, alter tasks and produce reports for management information.

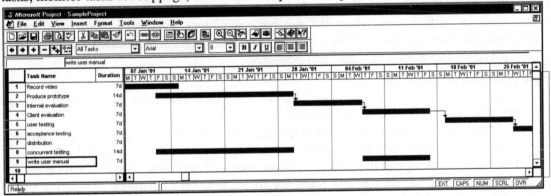

An alternative approach is a Pert Chart. It contains the same information as the Gantt but displays the information in a different way.

E-Commerce

Another consideration is how an organisation's e-commerce operations fit into the business information system. At its simplest, an e-commerce operation may only consist of a web site that provides product information, with orders being placed in the conventional way. However, e-commerce provides the most benefit when it is integrated into the company's existing IT structure. An online, transaction based system requires additional resources both hardware (web servers, modems, extra communication lines) and software (web creation software, security software and software to interface the web site customers with the company systems).

The key issues are:

Product definition	The existing product database may only store items by their product code and price. Customers browsing the web site will need product descriptions and perhaps a photograph of the product. Customers also value searching facilities, to locate products in the database.
Stock levels	Customers should have access to the stock levels for each item, to confirm availability before placing an order.
Order/payment systems	On-line order forms and credit card handling facilities have to be added to the system.
Order confirmations	The system should automatically send the customer an e-mail confirming the order details, prices and delivery times.
Order tracking	The customer should be able to visit the web site at any time and check on the progress in despatching an order.
Integration with existing distribution system	Online orders should be automatically entered into the company's distribution system.
Selling overseas	The internet opens up the possibility of sales throughout the world, with the added complications of differing taxes on goods, export restrictions and shipping charges.
Newsletters	The customer database can be e-mailed regular company newsletters or special offers.
Availability	The site is available 24 hours per day, 7 days a week. The web site, and the company IT network, has to have sufficient capacity to cope with potential demand.
Security	Linking the company databases to the outside world increases the risks of hacking and strict security measures (e.g. firewalls) must be implemented.

After the initial setup costs, there are financial advantages to e-commerce that arise from extra trade, reduced staffing costs, savings on printing costly catalogues and regular pricing updates, automated mailshots, etc.

Data Protection Act

The single biggest use of computers is for the creation of databases to store masses of data. This data includes personal information on individuals as employees, clients, patients, etc. The data also includes sensitive financial information on contracts, deadlines, specifications, etc. Since 1984, holders of such data - 'Data Controllers' - are governed by the Data Protection Act and are legally obliged to register. EU Data Protection Directive (95/46/EC) further tightened UK legislation in this area and became the 1998 Data Protection Act.   Despite its name, the Data Protection Act is more concerned with protecting people and protecting them from the effects of wrong information.

The central points of the Act are:
- Data should not be available to unauthorised viewers.
- Subjects of the data should have the right to view their own data.

There are, however, a few areas where the Act has exemptions, such as national security and the prevention and detection of crime.   Other exemptions include personal, household and recreational use of data and data used for calculating wages and pensions.

The eight principles of the Act are:

1. Data must be processed fairly and legally. The data must not be obtained through subterfuge or impersonation, for example.
2. Data shall only be held for specified purposes. Data users have to tell the Data Protection Commissioner (previously known as 'Registrar') what uses the data is intended for.
3. Data shall not be beyond that required for the specified purposes. A file of customers, for example, should not contain any reference to the religion or political persuasion of the customers.
4. Data shall be kept accurate and up-to-date.   Where circumstances change (e.g. medical records), the data must be kept in a current condition.
5. Data shall not be kept longer than is necessary.   If data is held on patients for, say, a controlled experiment, the data on individuals should not be kept after the trial is completed; the generalised data, cropped of subject names, may be kept for reference.
6. Personal data must be processed in accordance with the rights of individuals ('Data Subjects').
7. Data shall be protected against unauthorised access.
8. Personal data must not be transferred to non-EU countries unless they have a similar system of data protection.

Rightful access

Wherever personal details are recorded, there is scope for error. These errors could be typing mistakes or the confusion of records (how many John Smiths live in Britain?). These mistakes have, in the past, resulted in patients being given medical treatment meant for others, for example. Individuals could also find themselves being refused employment, promotion, benefits, credit or other rights, as a result of incorrect data. It is vital that the subjects whose data is being stored have access to their own records to check their accuracy. This could include taking away a copy of the data. Where the information is inaccurate (e.g. wrong age), the user should be able to have it altered. Where the information is incorrect (e.g. wrong person), the user should be able to have the data erased from the file. The Data Protection Commissioner will arbitrate in any disputes between subjects and organisations holding data on them. The subject may also apply to the courts for correction or deletion of incorrect data.

Unauthorised access

It is also important that only those authorised to view the data have access to personal records. Many bodies keep very personal data on individuals, covering areas such as health details, marital details, financial details and promotion and discipline details. It is the responsibility of the body to ensure that there are adequate measures to prevent unauthorised access. A normal procedure would be to ask a subject to complete a request form to view their data. This might incur a search fee of, say, £10. When the form is submitted, the subject is obliged to provide some proof of identity. In this way, only the actual subject will be able to see his/her own data.

Compensation

Data subjects can receive compensation where incorrect data has caused them harm. Examples of this might be from the loss of data, the use of incorrect data, or the unauthorised disclosure of data. The results might be physical damage (the wrong medicine), financial damage (passed over for promotion) or psychological damage (ridiculed by workmates about an exotic disease, unorthodox religious or political persuasion).

The Data Protection Act requires that users of personal data (i.e. Data Controllers) be registered with the Data Protection Commissioner.

Copies of the notification pack can be obtained from the Office of the Data Protection Commissioner at

    Wycliffe House,
    Water Lane,
    Wilmslow,
    Cheshire, SK9 5AX
    Tel: 01625-545745
    or visit www.ico.gov.uk for enquiries.

Users must instigate procedures whereby the subject can request and gain access to his/her data.

Operating Systems

With the earliest computers, users had to have a great knowledge of each item of hardware. When DOS (Disk Operating System) appeared, computers became available to ordinary users. The user could carry out a range of activities by giving relatively simple commands, in the knowledge that the operating system would translate the simple user command into the set of hardware tasks needed to carry it out.

The operating system could be considered as the foreman of an organisation. When the manager (i.e. the user) gave an order for work to be carried out, the foreman took on the job of ensuring that the actual physical task was carried out. The manager need not know where the resources are kept and what activities are involved - that is the job of the foreman. All operating systems have 2 main objectives:

1.   To use the resources of the computer efficiently.
2.   To conceal the difficulties of dealing directly with the hardware of the computer.

The Operating System (OS) is the lowest level of software on a computer, and applications or utilities such as word processors or anti-virus programs run 'on top' of the operating system. The OS automatically loads when the computer boots up, and must finish loading before any applications or utilities can be loaded and run. As a result, the type of operating system must take into account the way, or ways, in which that system is used.

There are several general classifications of computer systems. This describes how they are used, but does not necessarily imply the use of any particular operating system.

Personal Computers

A Personal Computer, or PC, is one that is primarily designed for use by one individual. Typical use in an office environment include word processing, spreadsheets, databases, presentations, email, and so on, all of which are intended for the individual in whose office the machine is located. Home use includes gaming, Internet surfing, electronic music, etc. PC operating systems must be flexible, as individual users requirements are prone to change within an organisation.

Batch Processing Systems

This is a general description of how processes are routinely handled on the system. As the name suggests, a batch system carries out processes in a batch, finishing one process before it moves on to the next one. The processes are usually referred to as 'jobs', and a batch of them is usually run overnight, to carry out repetitive processing on large amounts of data. For example, banks still use batch systems to process some types of daily transactions. Few operating systems are designed solely for use as Batch Processing systems. Batch systems are usually optimised to perform one task only.

Real-time Systems

More or less the opposite of a batch system, a real-time system, as the name suggests, has to control or monitor external activity in real time. A real-time system tries to guarantee an appropriate reaction to every data input, within a specified timescale. This maximum response time is known as the '*latency period*', and the time given depends on the function being performed.

Most real-time systems are either built into microchip hardware, or are application programs rather than operating systems. Typical examples include robotic systems, alarms, and speech recognition systems. A real-time system must be equipped with the correct level of hardware to be able to provide the correct response time.

Time-sharing Systems

Some computer systems are designed on a time-sharing basis, which means that the processing power of the main computer is shared between a number of '*terminals*'. This type of system is described in more detail in the '*Multi-User Systems*' section, later in this chapter.

Parallel Systems

In some cases, computer systems are designed to split problems up into different parts, which are to be processed independently. Since many tasks are related, this can be difficult to do, but can result in the jobs being processed significantly faster. In such a system, the various processes are said to be running 'in parallel' with each other. Parallel systems are generally either Multi-Processing systems or Distributed Systems (see later).

PC Operating Systems

Although there is a wide variety of Operating Systems, the vast majority of IBM-compatible PCs use a version of Microsoft Windows, with the remainder using mainly Linux, which is a version of Unix. Windows, however, originated as an add-on to an older, now obsolete operating system called DOS, and still incorporates and builds on many DOS concepts.

Microsoft DOS and the Windows Command Prompt

For many years, the only major operating systems for PCs was Microsoft's MSDOS (Microsoft Disk Operating System). Today, DOS itself is extremely unlikely to be found in use, and many new users have never seen or used it, since they have been brought up using the Windows family of operating systems. However, a very similar Command Line Interface (CLI) based in many ways on DOS is still available even in the most modern versions of Windows, called the Command Prompt.

Why learn to use Command Prompt?

There are almost no DOS-based machines in commercial use any more. However, machines which are Windows based still use many of the original DOS concepts such as file extensions, sub-directories and paths, and the Command Prompt box is still useful for certain administrative tasks. Finally, when things go wrong and you can't get back into Windows, you revert to the command prompt to restore the system.

Using the Command Prompt interface

When the computer loads the command line interface, the essential portion of the Command Prompt is loaded into the computer memory. The prompt will then be displayed to the user. This normally shows the drive that the system is currently logged on to (i.e. currently looking at), as below:

```
C:\ >
```

The above prompt tells the user that the current logged drive is the 'C' drive, the machine's internal hard disk. This should be accompanied by a flashing line, known as the 'cursor' and indicates that the machine is waiting for an instruction.

To save memory space, only the essential and most-commonly used commands are loaded into the Command Prompt when it runs. These commands are called 'resident' commands. All the other programs remain on the disk until called by the user. If the user needs to use any of these commands (called 'transient' or 'external' commands), then the Command Prompt loads them into the computer's memory. If all the possible utilities were loaded into the computer on switch on, the Command Prompt would take much longer to load, and would take up much more memory.

Using basic Command Prompt commands

The simplest commands comprise a single word instruction, which can be entered in either upper or lower case. The Command Prompt will not being to process a command line, though, until the 'Enter' key is pressed to enter the command. For example, to see what version of operating system is installed on the machine, the command would simply be VER, followed by pressing the Enter key.

Other drives can be accessed by entering their drive letter followed by a colon and the Enter key. For example if a floppy is available, the prompt can switch to the floppy drive by simply entering A:

Other simple commands are:

CLS	Clear the screen and reset the command prompt to the top left corner of the screen.
VOL	Display the name ('or LABEL') given to the current drive.

For more complex commands, the command is followed by various options, called 'parameters'. For example, to delete a file from a disk, there is no point in simply telling the computer to DELETE - the computer has to be told what file to delete. Here, the parameter would be the name of the file. So, to erase a file called REPORT, the command would be

```
DEL REPORT
```

Parameters can be a single item or can be more than one item - sometimes separated by spaces, or commas, etc. Many built-in commands perform functions that can be performed in Windows Explorer, for example:

LABEL ACCOUNTS	Changes the volume label of the current drive to 'ACCOUNTS'
MD REPORTS	Makes (creates) a new Directory (folder) called 'REPORTS'
RD REPORTS	Removes the 'REPORTS' directory, as long as it is empty.
DELTREE REPORTS	Removes the 'REPORTS' directory, and all its contents.
FORMAT A:	Begin formatting the disk in drive A:
COPY REPORT1.TXT REPORT1.BAK	Makes a copy of file 'REPORT1.TXT' and calls it 'REPORT1.BAK'
REN REPORT1.TXT JANREP.TXT	Renames file 'REPORT1.TXT' to 'JANREP.TXT'
MOVE REPORT1.BAK BACKUPS	Moves the file 'REPORT1.BAK' into the folder 'BACKUPS'

Starting and stopping programs in the Command Prompt

External programs, i.e. any application that is not loaded as part of the Command Prompt itself, can be run by entering the name of the program at the command prompt. If the program is in the current directory, or if it is in one of the directories in the PATH (see later), then it will begin execution, and will continue until it completes its job, or is stopped by the user. In the Command Prompt, programs can be stopped in several ways. A full-fledged Command Line application can be closed down by using the appropriate menu commands, and basic command-line programs can often be terminated by pressing Control-Break at the keyboard.

Getting help in the Command Prompt

From DOS 5 onwards, on-line help has been available to the user. DOS 6 onwards has particularly useful help pages complete with examples of usage. Simply typing 'HELP' will produce a list of topics. Typing a command followed by /? will produce assistance. Typing HELP followed by the command will produce explanations, syntax data and examples.

Using a printer with the Command Prompt

All printers can create an exact replica of any text that appears on the screen.
This can be done in a number of ways:

- The "Print Screen" or PrtScr can be used to print the current contents of the screen, and pressing Ctrl and PtrScr together will 'echo' on-screen output to the printer. However, in a Command Prompt running under Windows this may require the print properties of the Command Prompt to be edited, and depending on the version of Windows those print properties may not even be available.

- Redirecting output to the printer. This method sends output that was heading towards the screen to the printer instead; no output is displayed on the screen. This is achieved by placing > PRN at the end of a command. So, giving the command VER > PRN would send the OS version number to the printer instead of the screen. This redirection can be used with many Command Prompt commands.

- Using the PRINT command, for example: PRINT INFO.TXT.

Filenames and Extensions

To aid future recognition of files, there are certain conventions followed by DOS and still used as the basis for Windows filenames. Firstly, all file names may have three parts:

Filename

The File Name consists of alphanumeric characters and some punctuation characters, with a minimum of 1 character. The maximum size of the filename in DOS is eight characters.

REPORT.DOC

File Name   Dot   File Extension

However, Windows introduced Long FileNames (LFNs), which can be accessed in the Command Prompt interface by putting the filename in quotes, for example   PRINT "My Documents.TXT".

The filename part is compulsory and the file system will not accept a file without a name. The file name used should express the contents of the file. A file given the name of 'HH' or 'Z1' may have significance when it was first saved - but will probably not convey much six months later.   More meaningful names such as 'BUDGET03' or 'APR_MEMO' should be used.   The Excel spreadsheet program, for example, is called 'EXCEL.EXE', while the Command Prompt help program is called 'HELP.COM'.

File Extensions

DOS allowed a file to have up to a three-letter extension; since Windows 95 longer extensions have been allowed. So files called 'MEMO', 'MEMO.03' and 'MEMO.TXT' are all valid filenames. The extension can be chosen to describe the format of the file's contents.   The use of file extensions is optional but is recommended.

Files can have widely differing types of contents, but can be separated into two main classes:

- The **programs** themselves; i.e. applications such as word-processors, spreadsheets and accounting packages.   Most large commercial packages are comprised, not of a single file, but of a collection of linked files.

- The **data** used by applications; i.e. database records, spreadsheet worksheets and graphics files. These are stored in special formats used by the particular package. Data files used in one package cannot be used in another package without converting the file format first. It is therefore important to know the format in which data is stored.

Dot

When a file extension is used, a dot must be used to separate the filename and extension.

Pre-defined file extensions

Where the user has a choice, files can be given any file extension that helps convey the file's internal format. However, a number of file extensions are commonly used and these have to be avoided. Examples of these extensions are:

Program file extensions

There are a number of extensions that are reserved for executable programs. The most important of these are the COM, EXE and BAT extensions, since any file with one of these extensions is regarded by the operating system as being a program file. This means that the program can be run by simply typing the program name, without the dot or extension, and pressing the Enter key. For example:

> HELP.COM is a command file that is run by typing HELP then Enter.
> MSD.EXE is an executable file that is run by typing MSD then Enter.
> MYPROG.BAT is a batch file that is run by typing MYPROG then Enter.

COM and EXE files are composed of instructions, usually many thousands of instructions, in the special 'machine code' recognisable by the computer's CPU but unreadable by humans. BAT files are also program files but are in plain English format; they are less versatile than machine code programs but are much easier to write. DOS also added a number of other file extensions, such as SYS, CPI and BIN, for its own internal use.

Note that simply giving a file a COM, EXE or BAT extension does not convert that file into a program file. If a file called REPORT.DOC contained a company report in plain English, changing the file name to REPORT.EXE would have no effect on the file's internal contents. If the user tried to run the file by typing REPORT followed by Enter, the only result would be an error message. Each of the three program extensions has a different meaning, since the system has to handle each type differently.

Windows extensions

Microsoft Windows also claims a number of extensions to itself. These are in addition to the program file extensions that it also uses. Typical Windows extensions are BMP (Bit Mapped Pictures) used for creating background wallpaper effects, INI (information files) used for storing details of Windows configurations and Windows application details, and GRP (Group) used to store details of what utilities are included in the same Windows group. Other Windows extensions include DRV, TMP, PIF, FOT and TTF.

Application extensions

Individual applications claim extensions for their own use. This makes the use of a program easier, since the housekeeping is then carried out by the program itself. If the user wishes to open up a file called REPORT, there may be various files with that same file name but different extensions. There may be REPORT.DOC, REPORT.XLC, REPORT.DBF and so on. The word-processing application created the text file with the extension .DOC. The user only had to choose the file name as REPORT, the application automatically added the .DOC extension. Similarly, the Excel spreadsheet program added the .XLS extension to the worksheet saved by the user as REPORT. The database package also automatically added the .DBF extension to the file of records that the user saved simply as REPORT. Now, when the user is in a particular application and requests to open the REPORT file, the application will know which file to open by the extension on the end. The spreadsheet package will ignore the other files named REPORT and only work with the file called REPORT.XLS. The same is true of the word-processing and database packages. The technicalities of this are hidden from the user, who need never even know that the files have been given any extensions.

There is a wide range of application extensions and some are even used by more than one application. This can confuse matters unless files of the same type are kept in their own particular compartments (see later).

Example extensions are:

ANNUAL.XLS	A worksheet created in Excel
CLIENTS.MDB	A database file created in Access
SCREEN.HLP	A help file (common with many applications)
ADVERT.SWF	A graphics./animation file created in Macromedia Flash
SALES.DOC	A word-processed file created in Word.

Language extensions

Many programming languages (called high-level languages) create programs by the user initially writing the instructions in an English-like format using a form of word-processor.   This text is then converted into the machine code instructions required by the computer.   This conversion can be a permanent process and the machine code instruction can be saved as a separate, independent EXE file (a process known as 'compiling') or the instructions can be simply converted and acted upon immediately, with no second file being created (a process known as 'interpreting').   In both cases, the original text is preserved, in case the writer wishes to add to or modify the instructions.   The extensions given to the text files depend upon the programming language in which they run. Typical examples are:

GAME.BAS	The text of a Basic program. Can be compiled or interpreted.
UTIL.PAS	The text of a Pascal program to be compiled.
PAYROLL.CS	The text of a C# program to be compiled.

Other extensions

A number of other extensions are commonly in use and are regarded as a standard between packages. In other words, every package recognises the file as being of the same format. Examples are:

READ.ME	A text file usually included on the program disk, containing last-minute information about the release.
MEMO.TXT	A file containing plain English text.
MARGARET.GIF	A graphics file in Graphics Interchange Format, used regularly on the Internet.
STREETS.LST	A list containing related items, such as names or addresses.
NAMES.SRT	A file containing a list of items in a sorted order (e.g. names in ascending order or debts in descending order).

Obtaining a list of files in the current directory

The command to show a list of files in the current drive and directory, the command DIR is used. It displays a list of files, giving their names and extensions, file sizes and the dates and times that they were created or last modified. For example, typing DIR while in the C:\ folder might show:

```
16/06/2008   12:32    <DIR>           Program Files
17/06/2008   13:05    <DIR>           WINDOWS
04/08/2004   13:00           250,032  ntldr
16/06/2008   17:11     2,145,386,496  pagefile.sys
```

It is possible to display the contents of a drive or directory that is not the current directory. For example, if the prompt is currently on the hard disk, then typing DIR A: will display the contents of the floppy disk, without changing the fact that the prompt is at the hard disk.

If a folder has so many files that a DIR listing scrolls right off the screen, the DIR /P option will force it to pause after each screenful, or the DIR /W option will show a wide-format, abbreviated list. Additionally, the /A parameter can be added to show only certain entries in the list; for example /AH will show hidden files, /AD will show only directories, and /A-D will show everything except directories.

Directories / Folders

A hard disk can contain many thousands of files.   This could make finding and operating on any given file very difficult, as each file would be mixed in with the thousands of others.   It is essential, therefore, that files are stored in a logical way, so that they are easy to retrieve and manipulate.   DOS introduced an electronic disk filing system that is derived from the concept of an office manual filing system, where every file is kept in a filing cabinet under a different name or heading.   Files could be stored by the office department or function.

Consider, for example, searching for the discipline record of John Smith, the repair worker. The office may have six filing cabinets but only the one labelled 'Personnel' will need to be searched, thus removing five-sixths of the data from the search.   The Personnel filing cabinet will have three drawers and only the one labelled 'Discipline' need be opened - the others are labelled as 'Promotion' and 'Sick Records' and are thus ignored in the search. When the drawer is opened, three wallets are found, labelled as 'Clerical', 'Production' and 'Maintenance'. Only the Maintenance wallet need be opened, again narrowing down the search.   Finally, an alphabetical search is made of the files in the Maintenance wallet, until the file of John Smith is found. The above process provides a very speedy access to any individual file - assuming that files have been stored in a logical order in the first place.

Users of computer systems need to have the same ease of access to their computer data files as they have with their manual paper system.   This is the role of the filing system.   The file system provides an electronic equivalent to the manual system. It holds its files in different compartments (called *'directories'* or *'folders'*) on the disk, just as the manual system holds files in different physical compartments. If a database is in use, a directory can be created to hold the database files; if a word-processor is being used, then a directory can be created to store all word-processed files, and so on.

The creation of compartments (directories) containing other compartments (sub-directories) results in a structure called the *'tree'*.

The diagram opposite only represents a small fraction of an actual structure; a real hard disk may have many hundreds of directories, each containing many different files.

Although the structure is called a tree, the top level is known as the ROOT directory because all other directories grow out from it.

Spreading from the root directory are branches (directories and sub-directories) and leaves (the data files and program files).   Each branch of the tree (i.e. each directory) may contain leaves (i.e. files) or other branches (i.e. sub-directories).

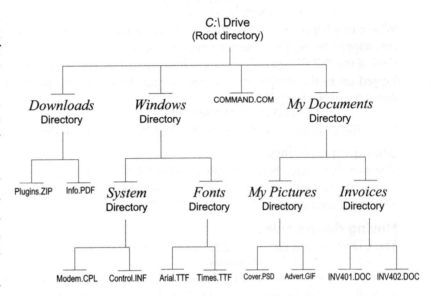

In the example, the root directory contains one file and three sub-directories called "Downloads", "Windows" and "My Documents".   The directory names can describe the application contained within it (e.g. "Windows") or can describe the function or organisational structure of the company (e.g. "Invoices").

Some guidelines for directory construction are:
- The number of directories and their structure should mirror the needs of the organisation.
- Each directory and sub-directory should be named to clearly label its contents.
- Only the relevant files for a directory should be stored in that directory.
- Do regular housekeeping to ensure that directories are kept up-to-date.   Ensure that only relevant files are being stored in each directory; move files to other directories where appropriate; remove files that are no longer used to prevent the disk becoming clogged up with old unwanted files.

Paths

To get to any file, a path is taken from the root directory, through any other directories and sub-directories until the file is reached. So, each file can be fully described in terms of its name and where it is stored.

The full file description is comprised of three parts:
- What disk it is on.
- What directory it is in.
- What the file is called.

Here are a few examples of files included in the above example diagram:

C:\COMMAND.COM
"C:\Downloads\INFO.PDF"
C:\WINDOWS\SYSTEM\CONTROL.INF
"C:\My Documents\My Pictures\Advert.GIF"
"C:\My Documents\Invoices\INV4001.DOC"

If the same files resided on a floppy disk, filenames might be

```
A:\COMMAND.COM
"A:\Downloads\INFO.PDF"
etc.
```

Where a file or a folder includes a space in its name (e.g *"My Pictures"*) the path is enclosed by quotes. Since each file can be described in terms of its path as well as its name, files with the same name and extension can now exist on the same disk - as long as they are stored in separate directories. For example, two files called REPORT.DOC could exist on the same disk in different parts of the directory structure as shown:

```
C:\CLIENTS\UK\REPORT.DOC
C:\CLIENTS\EU\REPORT.DOC
```

Where this happens, the two files can have exactly the same contents or can be completely different files that happen to use the same filename and extension.

Giving the full file specification is a little laborious but can be very useful. For example, the user can be logged on to the floppy drive as the current drive and still print out a file that is sitting down in a sub-directory of the hard disk e.g.

```
PRINT C:\EU\REPORT.DOC
```

When the printing is over, the user is still sitting looking at the floppy drive, as before.

Changing directory

The user can switch between making a hard disk or the floppy disk the one to be currently looked at. The user will also wish to control which sub-directory is the current one for any operations on that drive. This is accomplished with the CD or CHDIR command.

Moving downwards..

The CD command can be used to move the user down into a lower level of the directory structure, eg:

```
CD "My Documents"
```

would move the user out of the current directory into the "My Documents" directory. If a DIR command were given, only the contents of the "My Documents" directory would be displayed.

```
CD INVOICES
```

would then move the user from the current directory, the "My Documents" directory, into the INVOICES sub-directory. If a DIR command were given, only the contents of the INVOICES sub-directory would now be displayed.

If the user wished to go directly to the INVOICES sub-directory, this can be achieved with the command

```
CD "My Documents\INVOICES"
```

These examples move the user from the current directory into a lower directory. There are times when the user is neither in the root directory or the "My Documents" directory.

In these cases, the user can give the full path in the command and move straight to the specified directory from anywhere in the structure. Thus:

```
CD "C:\My Documents\INVOICES"
```

makes the INVOICES directory the current directory of the 'C' drive, no matter where the user's current drive is at the time of giving the command.

If the CD command is used without any parameter it will display the drive and directory that the user is currently in.

Note:

Use of this command does <u>not</u> switch the use from one drive to another. For example, a user may be on the A: drive and issue the command 'CD C:\WINDOWS'. The user would remain in the A: drive but when the command 'C:' was given, the user would be in the WINDOWS directory.

Moving back up the structure..

If the user is in any sub-directory, there is a command to move the user back up the structure.

```
CD..
```

moves the user back up one level of the structure. So, if the user was in the "My Pictures" sub-directory, the CD.. command would move the user into the "My Documents" directory. No matter how far down the structure the user happens to be, repeated use of the CD.. command will eventually return the user to the root directory. There are occasions when the user is down several layers of the structure and wishes to immediately return to the root directory, without a whole series of CD.. commands. The Command Prompt allows an immediate return to the root directory with the command CD\

Deleting files

Many files eventually become outdated (e.g. old correspondence, drafts of letters, budget figures, etc.). Others may be archived to tape or similar media. If any such files are no longer needed on the hard disk, they can be removed, allowing the space to be given to future files.

To delete a file, the DEL or ERASE command is used as follows:

> DEL REPORT.DOC

This will delete the file, if the file is in the current directory.

The path can be included in the command as:

> DEL "C:\My Documents\INVOICES\ENG.DOC"

This command has a /P switch which prompts the user to confirm that the deletion should be carried out - e.g. DEL *.*/P

Wildcards

Consider having to copy 50 files with the .PAS extension from one directory to another, or having to delete 30 files with the extension .BAK from a directory, or wishing to display a list of all files in a directory with the extension .DOC. Fifty separate COPY commands or thirty different DEL commands can be given but this is tedious and error-prone since some files might be overlooked. What is required is a method of handling files in groups - moving a group of files, or deleting them. Similarly, it is useful to have a DIR command that only displays a desired subset (say all .DOC files) from a directory.

The Command Prompt provides this facility by using 'wildcards'. A wildcard is a character used as part of a normal command's parameters. Wildcards use the question mark (?) and asterisk (*) characters.

The * Wildcard

The * wildcard is used to replace a group of characters. In the Command Prompt, it can replace zero or more characters.

Examples

> DIR *.PAS

will display only those files in the current directory that have the .PAS extension.

> DIR BUDGET.*

will display all files with the name BUDGET, regardless of the extension.

> DIR G*.*

will display all files that start with the letter 'G', regardless of the extension.

> DEL A:*.PAS

will delete all files from the floppy disk with the .PAS extension.

> COPY C:\WINWORD\FILES*.DOC A:\ARCHIVE*.BAK

will copy all the .DOC files from the WINWORD\FILES directory of the hard disk in to the ARCHIVE directory of the floppy disk, with each file having its extension changed to .BAK.

Note:

There is a potential danger to be avoided when using the * wildcard.

Consider the command

> COPY C:\BUDGET.* A:*.BAK

This command will copy all files with the name BUDGET in the hard disk's root directory into the floppy disk's root directory and give them the extension .BAK. If the C drive's root directory contained files called BUDGET.XLS, BUDGET.XLC, BUDGET.DOC and BUDGET.DBF, then they will all be copied on to the floppy disk as BUDGET.BAK. Since only one file can have the name BUDGET.BAK the first three files are lost and only BUDGET.DBF is stored on the floppy disk; all other files will have been overwritten by the next file copy.

The ? Wildcard

The ? character is used in a command to replace any single character in a filename. Unlike the * character, the ? character does not represent a group of characters. If a number of characters are to be wildcarded, then there will have to be multiple occurrences of the ? character. The length and structure of files have to be known to use this option.

For example:

DIR MEM???03.DAT

will find the files MEMJAN03.DAT, MEMFEB03.DAT, MEMAPR03.DAT, etc.   Any memos written in 2001 or 2002 are ignored by this command.   The * wildcard option could not be used here, as DIR MEM*02.DAT would display all files beginning with MEM and using the DAT extension - the 02 part of the command would be ignored, since the * wildcard takes precedence and replaces the last letters of the filename.

Note:

The user should always use the chosen wildcard with the DIR command before using it with the actual command desired. For example, DEL *.DOC will delete all of a user's .DOC files - but will also delete everyone else's .DOC files !   A quick check with DIR *.DOC would soon reveal the inclusion of any unwanted files.

File Attributes

Every file on a disk has a set of *'attributes'*.   These are flags that indicate the current status of the file (e.g. whether it is a system file or not). These are normally hidden from users but if the command

ATTRIB *.*

is given, the status of all the files in the current directory is displayed.   Each filename is accompanied by up to four possible letters - A, R, S and H.

These attributes can also be set by the user, with the ATTRIB command and the options are:

Read

One of the attributes flags stores whether a file is able to be both read and written to (known as READ/WRITE) or can only be read (known as READ ONLY).   If a file is read-only it can still be accessed by users and can appear in directory listings, can have its data extracted and used for calculations, can have its text printed out, etc.   However, it cannot be deleted and cannot have its contents altered.   Any attempt to delete a read-only file will be disallowed and an error message will result.   Similarly, any attempt to alter the contents of a file, such as a word-processed file, would be disallowed.

This means that files can be set to prevent accidental erasure, with the command ATTRIB +R *.*   The 'R' indicates the read-only flag and the '+' indicates that the read-only is being set on.   In the example, all the files in the current directory would be set to read-only. To remove the read-only flag , the plus sign is replaced by a minus sign and the command becomes ATTRIB -R *.*   The command can also be used with individual files (e.g. ATTRIB +R REPORT.DOC) or with selective wildcards (e.g. ATTRIB +R *.EXE).

Archive

A file's archive bit can also be set by the user and is mostly used in conjunction with the BACKUP command, to control which files are selectively backed up.   The BACKUP command can make a backup copy of all files or can be set to only make a copy of files that have not been previously backed up. The way that the BACKUP command knows whether a file has been previously backed up is via the archive flag. When a file is created or modified, its archive bit is set to on (indicating that it should be backed up).   When a file is backed up, its archive bit is automatically set to off (indicating that it has been backed up). A future backup process will only select the files with archive bits set on and will ignore files with archive bits set off. The user can alter the files' archive flags with commands such as ATTRIB +A *.BAK and ATTRIB -A *.BAK

Hidden / System

These flags hide the file from the normal view of the user and therefore it does not appear in directory listings, cannot be copied and cannot be deleted.   The user should not normally adjust these flags. The commands DIR/AS/S and DIR/AH/S will list all files that are set as system and hidden files.

Data Organisation

This section considers the best method of storing data on the hard disk of a single computer. A hard disk on a newly supplied computer is often empty apart from the Windows, Program Files and My Documents directories and a few system files. The way that the rest of the disk is organised can affect the efficiency of the disk's later use.   The data on the disk should be organised in such a way that it is:

- EASILY IDENTIFIED
- EASILY DELETED
- EASILY BACKED UP
- EASILY PROTECTED

Previous to Windows, most application programs were stored in a directory off the root, and the data files were stored in a sub-directory of that directory. This meant that if a project required work in more than one package, the data files would be scattered around various directories. This poses problems for security and backup purposes.

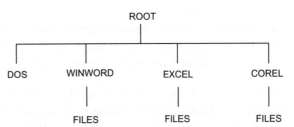

Windows provides a '*Program Files*' folder to store the application programs, and a '*My Documents*' folder to store files, although some packages can be set to default to another drive or folder. It is surprisingly common for users to simply put all their data files in '*My Documents*'.   This would throw all the files into a single folder, thereby mixing together all the data files for different projects.

This is convenient in the sense that all the possible data files for Word are found in the same folder. However, over time, the data will relate to many different projects and it is very easy to lose track of which files belong to which project.   Consequently, there is confusion over which files to backup, copy, or delete at the end of a project. This results in many old unused files cluttering the hard disk.

A common solution is to create different sub-directories for each project. For example, the data files for the first project are in C:\My Documents\Project 1, while the documents for Project 2 are in C:\My Documents\Project 2, and so on. If each project contained many files of different types, it could be split up again. So, for example, the word-processed documents for Project 1 are in C:\My Documents\Project 1\Correspondence, while the Excel budget calculations are in C:\My Documents\Project 1\Budget.

Since the program files are already stored on the installation disks, there should be no need to involve the '*Program Files*' section of the disk structure in any backup strategy. The only exception is for an application that is heavily customised and the backup may be necessary to store the customisation details.

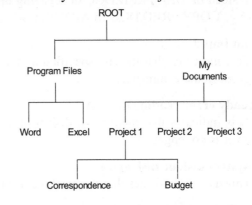

A variation on the above approach is to partition the existing hard disk into two or more distinct areas (see the chapter on Disks and Drives). After partitioning, the original 'C' drive will appear as separate 'C', 'D', etc. drives. The operating system and application programs could be stored on the 'C' drive, while the other partition(s) stores data.

For those computers with more than a single hard disk, there is no need for partitioning, since 'C', 'D', etc drives will already exist.

Command Prompt Error Messages

A number of errors are possible when typing in Command Prompt commands:
- The user may make a typing error (e.g. 'DIT' instead of 'DIR')
- The user may give an incomplete command (e.g. 'DEL' without naming the file to delete)
- The user may make a logical error (e.g. 'COPY FRED FRED' is trying to copy a file onto itself)

- The user may make an incorrect hardware compatibility choice (e.g. 'FORMAT A:' when a drive is 1.4MB capacity and the disk is only 720k capacity).
- The user may have specified a non-existent file (e.g. 'DEL FRED.DOC' when the file is no longer on the disk).
- The user may omit to specify a file's path (e.g. 'COPY FRED.DOC A:' when the file FRED.DOC exists but is not in the current directory).
- The user may have left a data disk in the A: drive when the machine was switched on (so that the computer is unable to load the operating system from either the hard disk or the floppy disk).
- The user may not have set up the hardware to make the command possible (e.g. issuing a PRINT command when there is no printer attached to the computer; or issuing a 'COPY *.* A:' command when there is no disk in the A: drive)

The Command Prompt is not particularly user-friendly when a mistake is made. Part of the job of the COMMAND.COM file is the analysis of commands (called *'parsing'*).   While all the above errors are detected, the amount of help given is very limited. The Command Prompt does not respond to errors with helpful advice; it produces cryptic messages that the user has to interpret.

The most common Command Prompt error messages are:

Bad command or file name
> This message indicates that a command has been given that is not part of COMMAND.COM or is not an external COM, EXE or BAT file in the current directory.   This error message is often due to a mistyping of the command and the entered command should be re-checked.   If the command is found not to be a spelling error, it is likely that the program is not in the current directory or in a directory specified in the PATH statement; the command should be altered to specify the path where the program file resides.

Invalid parameter
> This indicates that either too much or too little information has been specified as parameters after the command.   Forgetting to leave spaces between parts of the command (e.g. 'DELFRED.DOC 'instead of' DEL FRED.DOC or breaking up an otherwise legitimate parameter with extra spaces (e.g. 'COPY FRED.DOC M ARY 'instead of' COPY FRED.DOC MARY often causes this error').

File not found
> This indicates that the file specified as a parameter is either mistyped or is not in the directory given in the command.

Not ready error reading drive A
> This indicates that there is no disk in the floppy drive or, in the case of 5.25" drives, the disk lever is not engaged.

Non-system disk or disk error
> This usually indicates that the machine has been started up with a non-boot disk in the A: drive.

Abort, Retry, Ignore, Fail ?
> This indicates that a *'critical error'* has occurred. This may indicate a hardware malfunction such as the network going down or there being no disk in the drive. Often it indicates that part of the disk is unreadable.   With hard disks, the surface integrity should be checked with a utility; with floppy disks it's often best to recover as many files as possible and replace the disk. Choosing Abort ignores the disk operation and control is passed back to the program or application.   Choosing Retry instructs the system to attempt the disk operation for another time. Choosing Ignore ignores that particular cluster read; this may move the program on to a subsequent read operation, resulting in a loss of data. Choosing Fail will inform the program or application that the disk operation failed.

Access Denied
> This indicates that the disk is write-protected or that files have their attributes set to read-only.

Microsoft Windows

Without doubt the most successful operating system is Microsoft's *Windows* series. This OS has its humble beginnings in several versions of Windows that were nothing more than DOS environments. Even the first version of Windows, however, was as a *'GUI'* - a graphical user interface - and it used a range of icons (miniature pictures) to represent computing functions, so simplifying activities. For example, if the user was word processing and clicked the printer icon, the document would be sent to the printer. In this way, it is hoped to reduce the time users spend trying to <u>understand</u> the machine and more time spent actually <u>using</u> the machine.

Each version of Windows provides enhancements on the previous version, such as speed improvements and new facilities, but they all use the same basic GUI principles.

After Windows version 3.11, the operating system was entirely revamped, and for a period there were two distinct classes of Windows operating system. One is the user-oriented Windows 95, Windows 98, Windows 98 Second Edition (or Windows SE), and Windows Millenium Edition (Windows ME), all of which are often collectively called Windows 9x. The other is the network-oriented Windows NT versions, and Windows 2000, which is based upon NT. Windows XP sees the merging of the two paths once again to provide a single operating system for both home and office use, albeit through two slightly different versions of the same OS. Windows XP still uses much of the underlying functionality of Windows NT, rather than Windows 9x, but includes a new interface and other additions.

Windows has many features, such as:

- Supports multi-tasking. If desired, one application can be seen on the screen while the other application is working away in the background. Alternatively, both applications can be on the screen at the same time, each application occupying a different portion, or window, of the screen.
- Allows easy copying of data between programs.
- Full on-line help system. This includes a full hypertext system where the user can type in a search entry, find out about that item and be given options to view items of a similar category. This hypertext system is similar in concept to very basic HTML (see the Web Sites chapter).
- Provides a set of common features and techniques for all Windows applications. This means that every application written for use under Windows will use the same techniques (e.g. the same way to load and save files, the same way to import a picture, etc.). This results in users being able to adapt to a new Windows application quickly, since skills learned in a previous package are re-used. With DOS-based applications, each package would do the same job in a different way; one package would expect a particular function key, another would require a particular key combination using Alt and Ctrl keys, while yet another would expect the operation to be achieved through menu options.

The Windows environment allows for extensive configuration to meet the needs of the user (e.g. screen colours, use of memory, background wallpaper, choice of printers, sensitivity of the mouse, etc.); this is covered in the chapter on Windows configuration. Windows can be keyboard-operated but it is really designed for mouse operation and is certainly much easier and quicker to use with a mouse.

A comparison of DOS and Windows

In today's market, the Windows operating system is dominant, where once Microsoft DOS was the leader. There are several fundamental differences between DOS and Windows, some of which brought important benefits for most business users. The chart below details the most important differences between the two operating systems.

	DOS	Windows
User Interface	Command-based: The user must learn the command set in order to perform activities.	Icon-based: users can access programs by selecting one of several icons available.
Filing System	8.3 filenames: DOS is restricted in the size of the names that can be given to files, as explained earlier, as well as being unable to use several 'reserved' characters in the filename.	Long filenames: names of up to 255 characters in length can be given to files, and may include some (though not all) of the characters previously reserved.

I/O system	Limited driver support: Many peripherals, such as printers, needed a separate driver for most major applications.	Driver standardisation: All drivers are installed in the Device Manager, enabling any application to make use of any peripheral without needing additional drivers.
Memory manager	Basic memory management: DOS itself includes only very basic memory management, and requires several drivers to make effective use of extended memory.	Virtual memory manager: Windows automatically uses all memory available, and uses virtual memory (see later) without needing a driver to do so.
Process Scheduler	Single-tasking: With a few limited exceptions, DOS can run only one program at a time.	Multi-tasking: Many programs can run simultaneously, which can improve versatility.

All of these factors contributed to make Windows easier to learn and use than DOS. Windows itself borrows many concepts from earlier operating systems such as the system used on Mac computers.

Using the mouse

The Windows interface and all applications that work within Windows use the mouse in the same way. The main mouse activities are listed below.

Point   The mouse is moved so that the screen pointer is positioned over the desired item - e.g. an icon or object.

Click   Click the left mouse button while the pointer is positioned over the desired item. This is most commonly used to select an object.

Double Click   Click the left mouse button twice while the pointer is positioned over the desired icon or object. This is most commonly used to execute an activity - e.g. open an icon or run a program.

Drag   Move the mouse while holding down the left mouse button.

Shift Click   Hold down the *'Shift'* key while clicking on the desired item.

Shift Drag   Hold down the *'Shift'* key while dragging the mouse.

Wheel   Many mice today have a 'mouse wheel' in the centre, that can be used to scroll through data by rotating it up or down.

Closing vs Minimising

When the user is finished using an application, that application can be closed by clicking on the *'File'* menu option. This produces a pull-down menu and clicking on the *'Exit'* option closes the program. The top right-hand corner of applications for Windows 95 and later operating systems has a set of buttons as shown in the diagram. Clicking the *'Close'* button will also close and exit the application. On the other hand, the user can click on the minimise button that appears on the leftmost button of that set. The application is reduced to an entry on the Task Bar at the bottom of the screen. This is known as *'minimising'* and the application remains active, frozen at the point at which it was minimised. If the application is later clicked on the Task Bar, it is restored to full-screen, ready to proceed at the same stage it is was at when it was minimised. The diagram shows Microsoft Word and the Lexmark Printer Utility both being held in a minimised state.

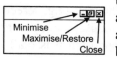

Using the Clipboard

A big advantage of using Windows is that information in one document can be copied or transferred into another document. This could involve the copying or

transferring of data from within the same application - e.g. copying or transferring a paragraph of text from one Word document to another Word Document. It could also involve the copying of data from one application to a different application - e.g. copying a picture from a Word document into PhotoShop for editing. The stages are:

- Move to the application that contains the desired information.
- Highlight the information to be copied/transferred.

- Use the *'Copy'* or *'Cut'* option to fetch the information from the source application. If the information is <u>cut</u>, it is removed from the source document; if it is <u>copied</u>, a replica of the information is used.
  In both cases, the information is placed in a temporary store, known as the *'Clipboard'*.
- Move to the application that is the destination for the data.
- Move the cursor to the spot in the destination document where the information is to be placed.
- Use the *'Paste'* option to place the information into the document at the cursor position.

The contents of the Clipboard can be pasted as many times as required - into different parts of the same document or into different documents. While the machine remains in Windows and no further information cuts are carried out, the Clipboard will store the information. This is automatic, unless leaving an application results in a particularly large piece of information being left in the Clipboard. In that event, the user is asked to confirm that the information should be left in the Clipboard.

Copying Windows to the Clipboard

It is also possible to copy the entire Windows screen, or any individual window on the screen, to the Clipboard.   The two options are:

- Pressing the *'Print Screen'* key while in Windows results in the entire monitor screen area being saved to the Clipboard.
- Pressing *'Alt'* and *'PrtScrn'* results in the active window area being saved to the Clipboard.

The screen is copied to the clipboard as a bitmap image, which can then be pasted into graphics packages, Microsoft Word, or any of a range of other applications.

Windows 95

Windows 3.1 was not a full operating system, as it required DOS to be installed. Windows 95, however, has its own drivers for memory management, CD handling, etc.   This makes it an operating system and graphical user interface in one package.   Although a version of DOS is installed along with Windows 95, most users never need to go beyond the Windows interface.

Since Windows 95 wants 4MB of memory for its own use, even more RAM is required to provide memory for use by the applications. Using a local bus or a PCI bus system will result in improved graphics handling.

Windows 98

The basic 32-bit architecture of Windows 98 is largely identical to that of Windows 95. Many of Microsoft's additions to Windows 95 such as Internet Explorer, the OSR2 (Operating System Release 2) update pack, new drivers, etc are now included in Windows 98. In that respect, existing users of Windows 95 who have already added these features will not find Windows 98 to be greatly altered.

	Minimum	Realistic Minimum
CPU	386DX	486/Pentium
Memory	4MB	8MB, preferably 16MB.
Video card	VGA	SVGA
Bus	ISA	PCI or Local Bus
Mouse	Normal	Mouse with right-hand button

Windows ME

In 2001 Microsoft introduced the Windows Millennium Edition, or Win ME for short. This is intended to be a personal Operating System and so lacks all of the groupware features of Windows 2000. It also uses the Windows 95 kernel instead of the NT kernel.   The interface is very similar to

	Minimum	Realistic Minimum
CPU	486DX	Pentium
Memory	16MB	32MB or more.
Video card	VGA	SVGA
Bus	ISA	PCI
Mouse	Normal	Mouse with right-hand button

Windows 98, with only a few cosmetic changes. Although it still has a DOS command prompt available, it is more difficult to find, and only operates in protected mode, meaning that very old real mode DOS programs will not work.   It is essentially an upgrade of Windows 98, with the added features listed below.

Windows NT

The original version of Windows NT was version 3.1.It used the same Windows 3.1 interface, but had a powerful 32-bit 'back end'. Versions 3.5 and 3.51 were essentially upgrades to NT 3.1, but none of them could match Novell's operating systems at the time in terms of sales. Windows NT version 4.0, released in 1996, used the popular Windows 9x interface as well as incorporating many technical advances, and as a result it was much more successful.

Windows NT is based around the concept of a network '*domain*' (as opposed to the '*workgroups*' formed by Windows 9x systems) that uses a Primary Domain Controller (PDC) and a Backup Domain Controller (BDC). For proper operation the user rights must be '*synchronised*', and the logon scripts and system policies must be '*replicated*', from the PDC to the BDC. Although it is recommended for servers to use Windows NT Server and client systems to use Windows NT Workstation, the clients can just as easily be Windows 9x systems.

Although there is a Workstation version of Windows NT available, the Windows NT system is really aimed at servers, and not Personal Computers. As a result it is covered in this book mainly to serve as an introduction to the technologies that are used in Windows 2000 and Windows XP.

Windows 2000

Windows 2000, known during beta testing as Windows NT 5.0, was released in February 2000, and retained the 9x style interface. It is, however, designed for use as a corporate desktop platform, and a lot of effort has been put into making it easy to install and administrate. It shares much

	Minimum	Realistic Minimum
CPU	200MHz Pentium	300MHz Pentium
Memory	32MB	64MB
Hard disk	600MB	1GB
Video Card	VGA	SVGA
Bus	ISA	PCI
Mouse	Normal	Wheelmouse

in common with its predecessor, Windows NT 4.0, but includes several improvements and is generally more user-friendly so that it can be easily used in PCs as well as servers.

Windows XP

This operating system was introduced in late 2001, and 'XP' is apparently short for 'experience'. It sports an improved interface with a greater degree of customisation, and improved user management and security. Although

	Minimum	Realistic Minimum
CPU	233MHz Pentium	300MHz Pentium
Memory	64MB	128MB
Hard disk	1.5GB	3GB
Video Card	SVGA 800x600	SVGA
Bus	PCI	PCI
Mouse	Normal	Wheelmouse

looking quite a bit different from previous Windows versions, XP's interface still bears many similarities to its forebears. Underneath, however, the NT kernel powers Windows XP, so many of the control panel options operate quite differently.

Windows 2003 Server

This system is essentially the Windows 2000 Server OS with various enhancements. For example, the IIS server is disabled by default, to increase security.

	Minimum	Realistic Minimum
CPU	133MHz Pentium	550MHz Pentium
Memory	128MB	256MB
Hard disk	1.5GB	3GB
Video Card	VGA	SVGA
Bus	PCI	PCI
Mouse	Normal	Wheelmouse

Windows Vista

Windows Vista is the latest in the Microsoft Windows line of operating systems. It is available in several versions, including: Home Basic, Home Premium, Business, Enterprise, and Ultimate editions. Each of these has varying capabilities and accessories – for example, the media control capabilities of Windows XP Media Centre edition are built in to the home premium edition of Vista. A 'starter' version is also available, with a bare minimum of features, and not even sporting the full version of the new 'Aero' interface introduced with most versions.

The system requirements are hard to pin down, because there are so many versions, and even in each version the operating system will adapt its interface for that hardware. However, the absolute minimum (called 'Vista Capable') and recommended minimum (called 'Premium Ready') specifications are as shown in the table.

Component	Vista Capable	Premium Ready
Processor	800MHz	1GHz
Hard Disk	10GB	40GB
Optical Disk	DVD-ROM	DVD-ROM
Memory	512MB	1GB
Video	DirectX 9 compatible	128MB graphics card

Facilities of Windows

Each version of Windows builds on the last, adding, replacing or changing new functions, tools, and interfaces. The following lists the facilities introduced by Windows, roughly in order of the version or date at which they were added:

- The *'Documents'* option from the *'Start'* menu stores and display a list of the last 15 files used on the computer, allowing simple recall of commonly used files. Single click on any of the file names and the file is opened inside its appropriate application. So, if a file called 'REPORT.DOC' is clicked, the system loads Microsoft Word and then opens the REPORT.DOC file within it.

- Provision of pop-up help windows. If the user allows the mouse pointer to linger over a command button, a pop-up window displays the function of that button.

- Allows the user to allocate long filenames of up to 255 characters. It should be understood that Windows 3.1 and DOS programs still use the old eight-dot-three naming system. So, any files created under Windows 95 that are saved under DOS or Windows 3.1 will have their files names truncated. A Word file called *'Consumer Report on Beef'* would probably be re-saved as *'CONSUM~1.DOC'*.

- Increasingly efficient video capabilities. With many versions of Windows, video playback became smoother, higher quality, and/or with better compression.

- Support for plug-and-play - the system recognises p-n-p components and automatically assigns resources. Newly installed p-n-p compatible cards are automatically recognised by Windows.

- Creation of a *'Recycle Bin'*. Files that the user deletes appear to be deleted but are in fact stored in their complete form and can be accessed at any time via the Recycle Bin. The user can recover a file from the Bin or can permanently empty the Bin's contents.

- Extensive *'Help'* facilities, accessed through the Start Menu. These change in each version of Windows, usually to provide better user-friendliness and more comprehensive information.

- Diagnostic facilities through the provision of a *'Hardware Wizard'*.

- Easy handling of applications through an *'Add/Remove Programs'* facility.

- Internet Explorer built in. New versions often coincide with new versions of Windows.

- Inclusion of Outlook Express, with e-mail and newsgroup facilities.

- Support for multiple monitors. Up to eight video cards can be connected to the machine, each handling its own monitor. This means that a much larger desktop size can be set, with each monitor displaying a different area of the desktop - or a different application.

- Support for USB and FireWire, and improved Plug and Play.

- Diagnostic tools have become increasingly powerful, although there is still not a comprehensive diagnostic or troubleshooting facility supplied with any version of Windows.

- The drivers supplied change with each version of Windows – early versions simply kept adding more drivers, but in recent versions they have stopped supporting some older hardware.

- FAT32 allows single disk partitions greater than 2GB and stores data in smaller clusters, minimising wasted disk space.

- Better use of AGP graphics cards and MMX processors.

- The rewriting of many existing Windows components results in increased stability from one version to the next.

- The *'System Restore'* utility. Over time, with programs alterations, components will have been added, deleted and modified. From Windows ME onward, these changes are noted and saved. This allows a user to return the system to the state it was in at any previous point, before an alteration was made.
- A *'System File Protection'* utility guards against any overwriting or deletion of important system files that may occur during the installation of other software.
- A *'Hibernation'* utility allows the machine to be closed down, with the current active programs and files being noted. When the machine is switched on later, the computer automatically opens these original programs and files.
- A *'Windows Image Acquisition'* utility builds the downloading images from digital cameras into Windows, rather than requiring the separate utility supplied with the camera.
- The *'Movie Maker'* application provides video capture facilities for those with video capture cards. It automatically creates separate clips for each scene in the video. It also provides basic video editing facilities such as cropping, amalgamating clips, and adding fades and voiceovers.
- Updated versions of the *'Media Player'* included the playing of CDs and the playing of streamed audio and video. It also includes a 'CD ripper' that converts a track from an audio CD into a compressed WMA file (the Windows alternative to MP3).

- Support for multiple processor motherboards, and a wide range of hardware.
- Ability to user both the NTFS and FAT filing systems. (See the Disks and Drives chapter)
- Eventually with Windows NT a pure 32-bit environment developed, and a *'microkernel'* design. These together provide vastly improved reliability. Even if an application crashes, it normally does not affect other applications, as often happened in Windows 9x systems.
- Introduction of a 'Hardware Abstraction Layer' (HAL), that serves as an interface between the kernel and the hardware devices. The HAL deals with low-level communication with devices, presenting a more abstract interface that allows the kernel to use more general instructions.
- Network management features built in, including user rights, logon scripts, user profiles, system and group policies, WINS and DNS management, and so on. Use of the policies and profiles allows customisation of the environment to suit the hardware of each machine, and/or the requirements of each user or group of users.
- System Difference (SYSDIFF) utility, allowing network administrators to track the changes made to the system by a particular program's installation, and automatically apply those changes to other machines, making system setup easier.
- Security features built in, such as the requirement to log on.
- Intelligent Mirroring across networks allows a user to sit down at any machine on the network and be presented with their 'own' desktop, menus, and even documents.

- Several cosmetic improvements, such as menus *'fading into view'*, hiding less used menu items, and notification for printed jobs.
- Active Directory (AD) services, which can incorporate DNS services, thus eliminating the need for DNS replication between the PDC and BDC.
- Improved Group Policies that allow each individual user to have a personalised desktop, customised and personalised menus and toolbars.
- Support for the FAT32 or NTFS5 filing system. (see the Disks and Drives chapter).
- Use of Organisational Units (OU's) within domains. This allows domain administrators to delegate administration of certain aspects of user management within any given OU.
- Uses the Microsoft Management Console (MMC) that was previously only available with an NT option pack. This is explained in more detail in the *'Faultfinding'* chapter.
- Enhanced Accessibility for people with disabilities. See an explanation of *'Narrator'* in the *'Windows Configuration'* chapter.
- Web pages can be stored on the hard disk to make them available offline. This technology was introduced in later editions of Win98, and is now mainstream.

- Built in support for multiple languages, switchable in the task bar.
- Easier upgrades, as long as the machine to be upgraded satisfies the compatibility lists.
- More wizard-based administration, including a wizard to connect to a network.
- Unicode has been used throughout Windows since Windows 2000, and the new European currency symbol is fully supported.
- Support for multiple processor motherboards, DVD, infrared and FireWire have been added.
- A new file system enhancement called *'Encrypted File System'*, can be used to secure data, in the event of the hard disk or the whole machine being stolen.

- Windows XP introduced the *'Luna'* interface. This still consisted of a startbar, taskbar and system tray along the edge of the screen; and a desktop containing icons. However, although the appearance of every part of the interface had been changed, and many names were also changed, the methods used to access the interface remained largely the same.
- Integrated support for CDR writing. The user can save files to CDR from Explorer rather than having to use a third-party program. See the chapter on Computer Security for details.
- A *'device driver rollback'* function, that can restore the previous state of a machine, before incorrect, corrupted or badly configured drivers are installed.
- *'ClearType'* technology, to make fonts easier to read on laptop systems.
- Network connection Firewall software built in, to improve security.
- Remote Desktop, Media Player 8 and more wizards such as the digital camera wizard.
- Encouragement for *'digital signing'* of device drivers to ensure compatibility.
- Windows XP introduced controversial *'product activation'* measures that allow Microsoft to collect user information in order to install the operating system.

- An integrated web server and streaming media server.
- Support for 64-bit processors, and Symmetric Multi-Processing (SMP).
- Improved network clustering, including Network Load Balancing (NLB), to provide redundant fail-safe servers.

Windows Vista facilities

The following is a synopsis of updates and capabilities that changed in the most recent version of Windows, ie. Windows Vista.

Cosmetic changes
- New Interface style, named 'Aero'.
- New, "streamlined" start menu.
- Windows may be semi-transparent.
- Windows fade when they become unresponsive.

Security
- "Protected mode" - Internet Explorer now runs in a "sandbox" in an attempt to prevent web sites using Explorer to damage a system.
- Vista gives the user the ability to delete ActiveX controls.
- User Account Control (UAC) – this part of the system will ask before running new executables, and run programs in User Mode unless otherwise authorised. These authorisations come in the form of 'elevations' to improve the access granted to any piece of software. This is to address the problem of so many applications running with full administrator access.
- The UAC also allows for a range of privilege levels. 'Standard users' can now view the calendar, install fonts and perform other mundane tasks that were often blocked in more secure implementations of XP networks.
- 'Secure Desktop' is used for sensitive functions such as entering passwords, the UAC, and so on. Secure Desktop greys out the background and only allows interaction with the foreground window.

- 'BitLocker Drive Encryption' can provide encrypted security for an entire hard disk.
- 'Kernel Patch protection' makes rootkits (malicious software that make use of low level operating system functions) more difficult to use.
- Security Centre, which allowed access to the Firewall, Automatic Updates and Virus Protection settings in XP, now also includes Spyware Protection (aka Windows Defender) and General Security for system-related security settings such as UAP.
- Unsigned drivers are no longer permitted, for security reasons.
- 'ReadyBoost' facility can make use of an attached USB drive as cache memory.
- Parental controls built in.

User Interface

- Improvements to Internet Explorer – including tabbed windows, RSS feed capability built in, page previews, and (many would say not before time) print scaling.
- Voice input in multiple languages.
- Language management allows the logon screen to use multiple languages.
- More information can be displayed during common processes such as copying, moving files, etc.
- When copying, the user has the ability to choose a new filename instead of overwrite an existing file with the same name.
- Ability to set different sound volume levels for different applications.
- The Alt-Tab menu, previously called 'fast switching', is now called 'Windows Flip', and includes a 3d version.
- 'Live Icons' in explorer and 'Live thumbnails' in taskbar and Windows Flip allow the user to see what an entity contains before opening.
- 'Sideshow' capability, which uses a secondary display as a control panel for the primary output, for example as a media player controller.
- Windows Sidebar, an enhanced desktop menu and application system, provides quick access to various facilities, and has the ability to add new 'gadgets' written in Java.

Using Windows

Since Windows versions from '95 onwards share a great deal of common user interface, the following descriptions cover all systems.
Differences are highlighted within the text.

Using the Mouse
The Windows interface and all Windows applications use the mouse in the same way. From version 95 onwards, the Windows operating systems makes extensive use of the right mouse button.

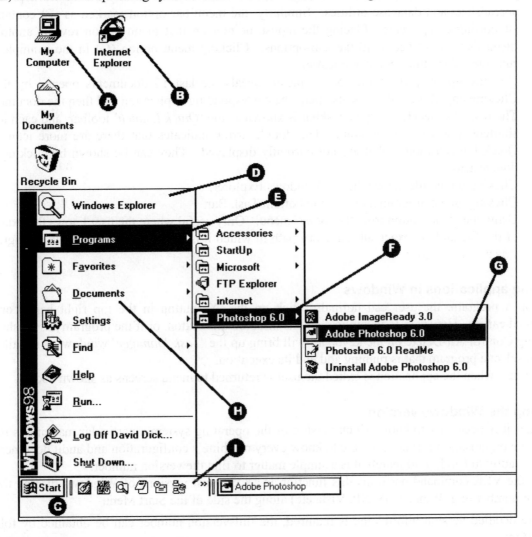

Launching applications in Windows
The above illustration shows the '*Desktop*' and '*Start Menu*' of Windows 98, later versions of Windows still use these concepts although the appearance of the Start Menu continues to change, as shown later in this chapter. The 'classic' appearance shown above is still available, though, as an alternative option, even in Windows XP and Vista.

Together, the Desktop and Start Menu provide various methods of accessing and running applications:

1.   The icon marked   **(A)** opens the '*Explorer*' program, which displays files and folders on the computer's disks. Accessing Explorer by the '*My Computer*' icon also provides quick access to the computer's printers, networking facilities and the Control Panel.
2.   Icon **(B)** shows an icon for a user's application that has been placed directly on to the Windows desktop. This is a '*shortcut*' to the application and the program can be run simply by clicking on

the icon. In this way, the user's most commonly used programs can be displayed as soon as Windows is loaded.

3. The button **(C)** is labelled *'Start'* and clicking this button displays the menu shown on the left of the screen.   The menu option **(D)** displays an application that has been placed on the start menu as an alternative means of accessing often used programs.   Clicking on its menu bar loads and runs the program.

4. One of the *'Start'* menu options is titled *'Programs'* and moving the mouse pointer over the button, marked as **(E),** displays a menu showing all the programs available on the computer. Clicking one of the menu options, such as item marked *'FTP Explorer'* in the example, loads and runs that particular program.

5. In some cases, an entry in the Programs menu is not a single program but a collection of similar programs. For example, the *'Microsoft'* option contains the Office suite of word processing, spreadsheet and database utilities. Similarly, the menu bar option marked as **(F)** contains four supporting components. Placing the mouse pointer on that menu option reveals another sub-menu that allows access to the sub-options. Clicking menu option **(G)** in the example shown runs the Adobe PhotoShop application.

6. Clicking option **(H)** on the *'Start'* menu reveals the last 15 documents opened by the user. Clicking any of these documents opens the corresponding application and then the document.

7. The row of icons **(I)** along the taskbar is known as the *'Quick Launch'* toolbar, and each icon is a shortcut to a different program. The double arrow indicates that there are more icons on the Quick Launch toolbar that are not currently displayed. They can be shown by clicking on the double arrow.

8. Clicking on the file name when in Windows Explorer.

9. Clicking on the program name on the bottom Task Bar.

10. Using the *'Run'* option from the *'Start'* menu. Only useful where the user knows the exact name of the file and the exact sub-directory path in which it is stored, or wishes to run a program that was recently used.

Closing applications in Windows

To stop a program, the user can normally click on the 'X' button in the top right hand corner, as explained earlier. However, if an application has disabled this button, or if the program has crashed, then pressing Control-Alt-Delete on the keyboard will bring up the *'Task Manager'* window which allows the user to select a program that is running and end its execution.

In all cases, when the application is exited the user is returned to menu screens as shown above.

Finding the Windows version

At times it is necessary to know which version of the operating system a particular machine is running. In a large organisation it is not possible to know every machine's configuration and audit documents may not be readily to hand. Fortunately it is a simple matter to find the version number.

While the VER command performs this function in DOS, most versions of Windows display the main version number (e.g. Window 98, XP, Vista etc) along the side of the Start Menu.

If more detailed version information is required, the full version number can be obtained by following these steps:

*   Click *'Start'*.
*   Click *'Control Panel'* – you may need to click *'Settings'* first in order to find it.
*   Choose *'System'* from the options displayed in the *'Control Panel'* menu.
*   If you are running Vista, the basic computer details should appear immediately. On other versions of Windows, you may need to click the *'General'* tab.

The full version number is more explicit, for example "Microsoft Windows ME, version 4.90.3000"

'Start' Menu Options

Apart from running applications and accessing documents and other file types, the *'Start'* menu offers a number of useful facilities. The most notable options are listed in the table below.

Favorites	Provides quick access to commonly used files, folders and webs sites. (Windows 98/2000 only).

Search	Called the *'Find'* menu prior to Windows ME, this contains one or more options:
	   For Files or Folders - Searches the computer's disk drives (and network drives if on a network) for specific files or folders. Searches can be for specific names, specific contents, specific dates or specific sizes.
	   Specific file types - XP and Vista can search for Documents, Pictures, Music etc.
	   Computers - If a local area network is installed, this will search for a specific computer by its network name.
	   People - Searches for people listed in the Address Book.
	   On The Internet - Opens Internet Explorer's *'Search'* facility.
	   E-mail - Searches Windows Mail messages for the word specified.
	In Windows Vista, the Search facility is simplified and indexed for faster results, but no longer includes a link to search for computers, people or on the Internet.

Connect To	In Vista, this allows the system to connect to any available network. In XP, the 'Connect To' option may instead be a link to the Network Connections folder.
Computer & Network	These two options (which are named 'My Computer' and 'My Network Places' in XP) are simply links to the folders of the same name in Explorer.

Settings	The *'Settings'* option only appears on classic style Start menus, and contains three or more sub-options depending on the version and setup. These include: Control Panel, Network Connections, Printers, and Taskbar & Start Menu.
	   Control Panel - As explained below.
	   Printer - As explained below.
	   Taskbar - Sets the options for the Taskbar and the Start Menu.
	   Folder Options - In Windows 98, accesses the same dialog as the *'View/Folder Options'* selection from Explorer. Not accessed through the start menu in other Windows versions.
	   Active Desktop - Includes options to customise or update the Windows 98 active desktop. In XP this is accessed through the Display option of the Control Panel; in Vista the Active Desktop has been removed.
	   Windows Update - If installed, runs the Windows Update through Microsoft Explorer. In XP/Vista, this is done through the Add/Remove programs option in Control Panel.
	   Dial-Up Networking - In Windows ME, the Settings menu contains a link to the Dial-Up Networking window. In Windows 2000, this is called the *'Network and Dial-Up Connections'* option, and has more functions including network connection management.
	   Network Connections - In Windows XP and Vista, if using the classic interface, there is a link to the Network Connections section of the Control Panel.

Control Panel	Provides functions for setting various system details, such as adding new hardware, adding and removing software, and configuring network settings.
Default Programs	In Vista, this is a link to the Default Programs section of the Control Panel, where the user can set which program is used for various types of files and data.
Printers	Called *'Printers and Faxes'* before Vista, this provides options to add new printers, to set printer ports and to set the configuration of printers.

Help and Support	Provides comprehensive help in three ways, which vary depending on the system:
	   Home - Newer versions of Help have a home page with links to get users started.
	   Contents - Help is organised in a systematic way providing information in a hierarchical fashion with the user delving deeper if he/she wants more information on a subject. In Vista the Contents page is accessed by pressing the 'Browse Help' button on the top bar.
	   Index - The user can scroll through a long list of help topics or can search by entering a word or phrase. The Index is not available in Vista Help.
	   Search - This will look through all the help files available to find occurrences of the word you type into the search box. (Called *'Find'* in some versions)

Run	A pull-down menu lists the programs that were recently loaded via the *'Run'* facility. One of these can be selected or the user can click the *'Browse'* option to search for a specific program to be run. The Run option may instead be listed under *'Accessories'* on a PC that is using the Aero interface.
Shut Down / Turn off	Shut Down options vary by system, but typically include 'Turn Off', 'Restart', and low-power modes such as 'Stand By' / 'Sleep' and the more energy-efficient but slower 'Hibernate'.
Log Off	On systems where logins are available or required, this option will return the user to the login screen, possibly closing down applications in doing so. There may also be 'Switch User' or 'Lock workstation' options.

The Windows XP Start Menu

In Windows XP, the '*Start*' menu looks fairly different from that of other versions, although almost all options are the same.

'*My Documents*' is a link to the My Documents folder, which before XP was accessed through Explorer or the Desktop.

'*My Recent Documents*' is the new name for the Documents folder, which stores links to recently used files.

'*My Pictures*' and '*My Music*' are links to the folders of the same names, and the '*My Computer*' icon in XP is on the Start Menu instead of being on the desktop.

'*My Network Places*' is essentially the new name for Network Neighborhood, although it uses Windows NT/2000 functionality. The Control Panel and Printers settings are accessible directly from the Start Menu.

XP also places shortcuts to the most recently used programs onto the Start menu, and the user can access the programs from there. The illustration shows six recently used programs, including Notepad and the On-Screen Keyboard.

Note however that the XP Start Menu can easily have its appearance changed to the 'classic' style used by previous versions of Windows.

The Windows Vista Start Menu

The Vista start menu builds on and expands the Luna interface from Windows XP. The word 'Start' has been removed, and the Shutdown and Lock Computer buttons are also represented by icons without their names. Many links are renamed slightly and put in a different order, and a 'start search' box is placed at the bottom of the left hand pane. As the user types, this facility will search for items within the Start Menu that match the words typed, to allow the user to more quickly locate the link they are looking for.

The major change in this version is the 'All Programs' option. In Vista, this will not expand into a new area of the screen as you select folders, as it did in XP. Instead, it will replace the most frequently used icons in the left hand pane with a basic Explorer-like interface that will allow the user to locate and run the program they are looking for.

The 'Run' capability is now stored in the Accessories folder by default, and the additional shut down / log out options are accessed via the small arrow next to the padlock ("Lock this computer") icon.

Other Accessories

One of the options in the '*Programs*' menu is a collection of utilities under the heading '*Accessories*'. These are supplied as standard with Windows 95 onwards and include:

Available with Windows 95	
Multimedia Utilities	Media Player, CD Player, Sound Recorder and Volume Control.
System Tools	System Monitor, and Disk utilities - Backup, Disk Defragmenter, DriveSpace (not with Windows 2000) and ScanDisk.

Calculator	A calculator providing scientific functions and conversion between different number bases.
Clipboard Viewer	Facilities to view, save and delete the contents of the Clipboard.
Dial-Up Networking	Uses a modem to connect a computer to a network, or to another computer with a modem.
HyperTerminal	An improved version of Terminal, transferring files between two computers over the telephone network. Requires the computers to be connected to modems.
Phone Dialer	A utility allowing users with modems to place telephone calls from the keyboard or from a stored pick list.
Direct Cable Connection	A utility to allow two computers to share their resources. One computer can access the files and printers of the other computer.
Paint	A more basic version of Paintbrush, with facilities to create and edit bitmap pictures. Provides line drawing, box drawing, text overlay, fills, etc.
Imaging	A simple tool to add lines, boxes and text to an existing image. Also provides facilities to scan images and documents, when a scanner is fitted to the computer.
Notepad	A simple word-processing program for small files, less than 64k.
WordPad	An improved version of the old Windows 3.1 Write word processing program

Introduced with Windows 98

DVD Player	Used to play DVD disks where the computer has a DVD drive.
Disk Cleanup	Detects temporary file, Internet cache files, etc that are using up valuable disk space.
System Info	A very powerful utility for testing the computer's system files, Registry, etc.
Maintenance Wizard	A utility to automate checks for disk errors, etc, at times set by the user (e.g. overnight).

Introduced with Windows 2000

Fax	Used to send, receive and organise faxes.
Accessibility Options	Improved usability and readability for the visually or physically impaired.
Synchronise	Used to keep the contents of a desktop machine synchronised with laptops, PDA's etc.

Introduced with Windows XP

CD-R writing	Although not found in the Accessories folder, this is a new XP capability (see the chapter on Computer Security for details on its use).
Settings transfer wizard	A wizard that allows users to transfer their program settings or data files from one computer to another.
Utility Manager	A small program that allows the user to quickly start up Accessibility programs.
Program Compatibility Wizard	A wizard that Helps users to properly set up programs that were not designed for Windows XP.

Introduced with Windows Vista

Windows Sidebar	A collection of small tools that can appear along the side of the screen, such as a clock, 'sticky' labels, live news feed, and so on.
Snipping Tool	This small application allows the user to capture sections of the screen into a graphic image.
Problem Reports and Solutions	This is intended to help the user troubleshoot problems, download important upgrades, and generally solve problems with the computer.

The actual applications appearing on the list depends on how the user's machine is configured.   This depends on the version of software installed and the number of items installed onto the hard disk from the installation CD.

Explorer

Windows Explorer allows access to disk operations at file and directory (folder) level. Explorer has one or more screen panels. The left panel is the '*Explorer bar*' or '*Navigation Pane*', which normally shows the '*folder tree*'. The folder tree displays a graphic representation of the structure of the currently chosen disk drive, using an icon for each folder or other object.   It also allows access to the Control Panel, Printers folder and other special folders. The main panel is the '*folder window*' and it displays icons and names representing the files, folders and other objects within a selected folder. In the folder tree window, the currently chosen folder is highlighted.

To select a new folder to view, the user clicks the mouse pointer on the folder name or its folder icon. A plus sign or a small horizontal arrow on a folder indicates that it contains sub-folders that are not being currently displayed.

The terms '*expanding*' and '*collapsing*' are used to describe the display or non-display of folders.

In the example shown, the '*mmbook*' folder has been expanded and all the sub-folders at the next level are revealed.   In turn, the '*pics*' folder has been expanded and all sub-folders within '*pics*' are listed.   The '*graphics*' sub-folder has been selected and its contents are viewable in the right hand panel.

The display options for Explorer vary depending on the Windows version in use, but can include:

Classic Mode

The illustrations show both the 'original' interface as introduced in Windows 95, and the current version of the same mode as it appears in Windows Vista.

The Windows XP version looks broadly similar to the original mode, but the pane on the left (called the 'Explorer Bar') can show Folders, a Search interface, Favorites, or History.   In Windows Vista, the left hand bar is called the '*Navigation Pane*' and can show Folders and Favorite Links.   However, the Search option in Vista is located in the top left corner, and Vista makes more extensive use of indexing and keywords so that searches are much faster.

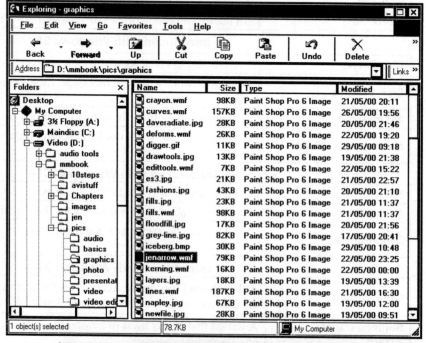

The Vista version of the 'classic' interface also replaces the Status Bar with a more detailed '*Details Pane*', and also offers a '*Preview Pane*' which defaults to the right hand side of the window, as shown.

Show Preview and filters

In Vista, this mode is basically the same as Classic mode, but it hides the menu bar (File, Edit etc). The user can still access this menu bar by pressing the 'ALT' key on the keyboard.

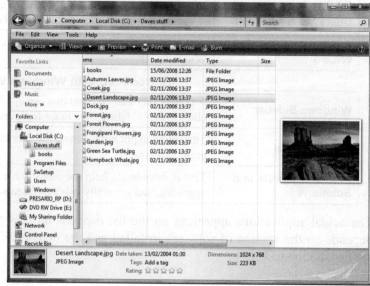

View as a Web Page.

Prior to Windows XP, the option existed to show folders in explorer as if the user was viewing them on a typical web page

This is shown in the illustration opposite. The right-hand panel displays the folder's files and highlighting a file provides file details (type, size, date created/modified). If the file is a graphic file, it is displayed (as with the globe example shown).

The View as Web Page mode was replaced with the 'Show Common Tasks in Folders' option in XP.

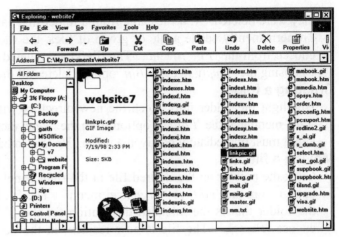

Show Common Tasks in Folders

Explorer for Windows XP can display the Folders window at the left-hand side, as with previous versions. However, if the panel is not shown, and it is in this mode, it will instead show several boxes that provide information and allow user feedback.

The contents of the boxes are context-specific, which means they vary depending on which object(s) are selected. However, they generally include one or more 'task' boxes which contain shortcuts to common operations in this context; an 'other places' box that allows quick navigation to other drives and locations; and a 'details' box that displays information on the current object or objects.

Explorer for XP also introduced an option to view the current folder's files as thumbnails, if they are graphic files, or as a 'filmstrip' which is essentially a slide show.

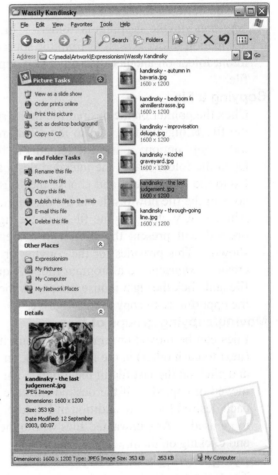

The main Explorer activities can be carried out using the mouse and/or keyboard and these are:

Expanding a folder

Double click the mouse pointer on the desired folder or single-click on the arrow or plus icon to its left; if using the keyboard, highlight the desired sub-folder with the cursor keys then press the right arrow key.

Collapsing a folder

Double click the mouse pointer on the desired folder; if using the keyboard, highlight the desired sub-folder with the cursor keys then press the left key.

Deleting a file

Highlight the desired file in the right panel by clicking the mouse pointer on it; press the Delete key; when prompted, confirm the file's transfer to the Recycle Bin.

Deleting a folder

Highlight the desired folder icon and press the delete key; when prompted, confirm the transfer of the folder and all its files and sub-folders to the Recycle Bin. 'Deleting' files and folders, in fact, only sends them to the Recycle Bin area where they can either be recovered or permanently deleted.

Undeleting

Since files and folders that are *'deleted'* are actually sent to a folder called the *'Recycle Bin'*, they are available for recovery. Double-clicking the Recycle Bin icon on the desktop opens a window that displays all the items available for recovering. The desired files can be selected and the *'Restore'* option, which may be either on the *'File'* menu or the toolbar, restores them to the folder from where they were deleted. If a file came from a folder that has since been deleted, the folder is also restored. To permanently delete a file or group of files, the file(s) should be selected and the *'Delete'* option chosen from the *'File'* menu.   The file(s) are deleted and the disk space is recovered for future use. Choosing the *'Empty Recycle Bin'* option deletes all the files currently in the Bin.

Creating a folder

Highlight the folder into which the new directory will be added; choose the *'New'* option from the *'File'* menu and the *'Folder'* option from the *'New'* menu.   An unnamed sub-directory will be created and it must immediately be given a name. Vista also has a 'New folder' option under 'Organize'.

Moving a file

Click the pointer on the desired file in the right panel so that the file is highlighted. Chose the *'Cut'* option from the *'Edit'* or *'Organize'* menu.   The file is now removed from the source folder. Open the folder that is the intended destination for the file.   Go to the *'Edit'* or *'Organize'* menu and choose *'Paste'*.   The file is now resident in the destination folder.   Another technique involves dragging a file from the right panel to a folder in the left panel.   This works for data files that are moved between folders in the same drive. For program files, it will not move the file but will place a *'shortcut'* in the destination folder.   In this way, the program can be loaded and run from the destination folder as well as from the source folder where the program file remains. Dragging any file into a folder on another disk drive will copy that file into that folder, whether it is a program or data file.

Copying a file

Click the pointer on the desired file in the right panel so that the file is highlighted. Go to the *'Edit'* menu and choose the *'Copy'* option.   The file remains in the source folder. Open the folder that is the intended destination for the file. Go to the *'Edit'* menu and choose the *'Paste'* option.   The copy of the file now resides in the destination folder.

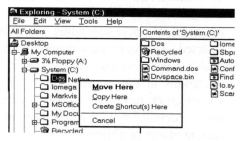

Alternatively, dragging the file with the right mouse button pressed will present the user with a menu of choices as shown.   This provides for the copying or moving of a file into the destination folder.   It can also create a *'shortcut'* to a program file.   A quick way to copy a file to a floppy disk is to highlight the file and click the right mouse button. A menu opens and clicking the *'Send To'* option offers the user the opportunity to copy to the A: drive.

Moving/copying groups of files

Files can be moved or copied as a group in a single operation.   If the group of files are contiguous (next to each other) in the file list, click on the first file in the desired group, hold down the 'Shift' key and click on the last file in the group.   This will highlight the entire group of files, which can then be moved or copied.   If the desired files are not contiguous, hold down the Ctrl key while clicking on each desired file.   An addition in Explorer is the ability to click and drag a rectangle around the files to be used.   Any unwanted files within the rectangle can be deselected by holding down the Ctrl key and clicking on them.

Copying/moving a directory

The technique is identical to moving/copying files except the folder is highlighted instead of a file.

Renaming a file or folder

Highlight the desired file or folder in the right panel. Choose the *'Rename'* option from the *'File'* or 'Organize' menu. When prompted, type in new file name. The file remains in its current directory but is renamed. Alternatively, click the pointer on the desired file in the right panel, wait a moment (so that it is not perceived as a double-click) then click again, to be able to rename the object.

Printing a file

Highlight the desired file in the right panel. Choose the *'Print'* option from the *'File'* menu or main toolbar. The *'Print'* option will only appear if the file is capable of being printed.

Setting file/folder attributes

Right-click on the file whose attributes are to be changed, and select *'Properties'*. The bottom part of the dialog will show two to four tick-boxes, one for each file attribute that can be changed. Only early versions of Windows allowed changing of the System attribute, and the Archive attribute is usually found by clicking the 'Advanced' button.

Formatting a drive

Ensure that the media to be formatted (eg floppy, memory stick etc) is properly installed, connected and/or inserted.

Select the floppy disk drive in the left panel and click the right mouse button. This produces a menu from which the *'Format'* option can be selected. A *'Format'* dialog box is opened as shown. The 'capacity' drop-down allows the user to choose between different disk sizes if available. The user can choose to give the disk a name by typing an entry in the 'volume label' box. The different formatting options include:

Type	Purpose
Quick Format	Can only be used with disks that were previously formatted. Saves time by not checking for errors on the disk surface.
Full	Checks for surface errors and marks them as bad sectors. This is the default if 'Quick Format' is not chosen.
Create an MSDOS startup disk	This will create a disk that is capable of being used to start up the computer, for example in order to fix faults.

When the options are chosen, clicking the *'Start'* button begins the formatting.

File system options typically include NTFS and FAT32, while the allocation unit size allows the user to set the size, in bytes, or each sector on the disk. (see the Disks & Drives chapter)

Copying a disk

This utility makes an exact replica of one disk on to another disk; any previous contents on the destination disk are lost. Insert the floppy disk to be copied in the drive. Select the floppy disk drive in the left panel and click the right mouse button. This will produce a menu from which the *'Copy Disk'* option can be selected. A *'Copy Disk'* dialog box is opened. If the machine has a single floppy drive, that drive letter will be highlighted in both windows. Where a machine has several floppy drives, they will appear in both windows and the user can choose the source and destination drives for the copy.

Clicking the *'Start'* button initiates the copying process. Where two different drives are involved, the user only has to wait until the process is completed. Where the user nominates the same drive as both the source and destination drives, the program prompts for the switching of the disks when required.

Controlling printing

In Windows, files sent to the printer are first stored as a *'print job'* in a *'print queue'* until the printer is ready to deal with them. This also permits more than one job to be kept in the queue at any time, allowing the user to get on with other tasks while the system is printing. However, it may be necessary to pause or even cancel a document that is in the print queue.

Double-clicking on the *'Printers'* option in the Control Panel will bring up the printers folder in Explorer, listing the installed printers. Double-clicking on the relevant printer will then open the printer queue. From here, the user can single-click to select a print job, and then pause or cancel it from the *'Document'* menu.

Taskbar

When working in Windows, a number of applications will often be running at the same time. Some of these may have been automatically loaded at the startup of Windows (see the chapter on Windows Configuration) or they may have been loaded during the Windows session. Each time an application is loaded, it is added as a button to the Taskbar and when the application is closed the button is removed from the Taskbar. The Taskbar usually sits along the bottom of the screen and the buttons show every application that is currently open. Switching between applications only requires the appropriate button on the Taskbar to be clicked.

Windows provides additional access, since pressing the Windows key or the CTRL and ESC keys brings up the *'Start'* menu, superimposed over the current application window.

Leaving Windows

Through the various versions of Windows there have been a variety of different methods used to close down the Windows system. In all cases the option to leave Windows is located on the Start Menu. It was initially named '*Shut Down*', but was renamed '*Turn Off Computer*' for Windows XP before returning to being called '*Shut Down*' for Vista.

Option	Function
Shut down	Saves data or changes to applications before closing down.
Restart	Closes down then restarts so that any new settings may take effect.
Sleep / Standby	Go into a low-power mode for short periods of inactivity.
Hibernate	Save the system state to disk and go into a very low-power mode for long periods of inactivity.

In Windows Vista, the shutdown option uses the standard on/off symbol, while the other options are accessed via an arrow to the right.

In other versions of Windows, the Turn Off or Shut Down option displays a small menu of options in the centre of the screen, from which the user can select the type of shut down they wish.

Using Microsoft Networking

Windows includes integrated support for networking. At least three pieces of driver software are required in Windows to use networking capabilities. These are the network card driver, the protocol driver, and the network client. See the LANS chapter for more details on these components.

Once these drivers are properly installed, and the physical cabling is in place, Windows will be able to access the network. The interface, resources and functions that will be available to the user depend on the type of network that is installed, but normally include shared resources such as network printers and file server drives.

Microsoft supplies its own networking client with all versions of Windows from 3.11 onwards. This normally runs through the TCP/IP protocol, and allows the user to logon to Windows '*domains*' (run by servers) or '*workgroups*' (peer networks). If additional drivers are installed, peer-to-peer file and printer sharing is possible through Microsoft Networking.

Note that file and printer sharing installation is not required to be able to access the files and printers of other systems – the software is only required when wishing to share the facilities on the current system to others on the network.

Networking in Windows Vista / XP

In Windows Vista and XP, every user is required to log in to the computer (although this may happen automatically and the user may be unaware of it). These login details will typically be used when logging into any Windows network.

In these versions of Windows, connecting to a Windows workgroup can be as simple as entering the name of the workgroup or domain in the 'System' dialog box of the Control Panel.

Networking in other Windows versions

In older versions of Windows, log in is not required for a standalone system; installing network drivers however will force users to log in, using a login box like the one shown here.

For those systems that access the network through an NT domain or Novell Netware server, there will be an additional text box where the domain name should be entered. Do not confuse Windows domain names with Internet domain names! Ask the network administrator if you are unsure which domain to use.

To log in, enter your username and password (the password will be hidden as you type). If this is the first time that username has been used on the system, it will ask the user to confirm the password so that it can store these details in a PWL (PassWord List) file on the local hard disk. Note however that unless you are logging into a server, this is merely the Windows password. If this is the case then hitting the '*Cancel*' button or the '*Esc*' key

will bypass the login stage. Additionally, unless logging into a server, or unless using Windows NT/2000/XP, Windows will only attempt to validate the password from its own local list of PWL files. This means any unused username will become a valid login from Windows' point of view. Although the PWL files are stored in an encrypted form, there are programs available that can decrypt these files so network managers should be aware of this as a potential security hole.

The easiest way round this is to enter the correct password for the network, and then the '*Set Windows Password*' dialog appears, change both fields to a blank password. This will fool Windows into thinking that the user does not have a password, thus making the issue of PWL viewing irrelevant. This method also avoids problems caused when the network password is changed and the local Windows password remains the same.

Other login methods can be more complex. For example, standard NT and 2000 login boxes contain further options such as dial-up logins, language selection or workstation only logins. Additional client software such as Novell clients may have further capabilities or options.

Accessing shared files

If a user is logged in with access to a Microsoft Network, any shared resources become available to that user. Folders and drives can be accessed through Explorer in the normal way, through selecting '*Network*' (or '*My Network Places*' or '*Network Neighborhood*') and navigating through workgroups, machine names and resource names.

However, this can be a cumbersome and sometimes confusing method, especially if there are a large number of machines on the network. An alternative is to '*map*' a network drive. This provides a local route to a remote resource for easy access. For example, if a local machine has an A:, C: and D: drive, it could map the (currently unused) E: drive to the network folder \\OFFICE\INVOICES. In this case 'OFFICE' is the name of a machine and 'INVOICES' is the name of a folder or drive on that machine which has been shared. Once the mapping is successful, the user can access that folder or drive as if it were a local drive with the letter E: designated to it.

This mapping can be achieved in one of two ways.

If the user knows the UNC (Universal Naming Convention) address of the resource, then it can be mapped by choosing *Tools / Map Network Drive* and entering the UNC path to the resource.

If the path is not known, the user can navigate through Network Neighborhood to find the resource he

wishes to map, then right-click on it and select '*Map Network Drive*'. The latter method will fill in the appropriate path automatically, as shown in the example.

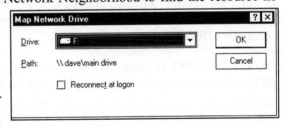

The '*Reconnect at logon*' checkbox will tell Windows to attempt to reinstate the mapping every time it logs on. If it fails it will offer the user to stop mapping this drive at logon.

Accessing shared printers

For printers, there is an equivalent to drive mapping, known as '*Connecting*' or '*Capturing*'. This can be done by right-clicking on a remote, networked printer, and selecting 'Connect' or 'Capture'.

The Printer Capture process has a similar effect to mapping a drive: all data sent to the selected local LPT port is redirected to the network printer. For example LPT1 could be redirected to \\OFFICE\LASER. As with the mapping operation it is possible to tell Windows to reconnect the printer at the next logon.

NOTE: In Windows XP and Vista, the 'connect' dialog does not show an LPT port. It will simply capture the first available LPT port; if you need to change which LPT port the printer is using, go to the Printers folder, right-click on the printer, choose 'Properties', and click on 'Ports'.

Printer drivers

Sending data straight to a remote printer raises the issue of ensuring that the proper device drivers are in use. If a remote PC shares its printer, then that printer must have appropriate drivers installed on its hard disk. The local user can therefore install the printer driver from the remote machine. This is done by right-clicking on the printer and choosing '*Install*'. This will run through the same installation procedure as if it were a local printer. This install procedure will set up a port redirection just as if the Printer Capture process had been performed. Therefore, the user need only capture a port when printing to another identical model of printer in, for example, another department or floor.

Running DOS programs in Windows

Despite its improvements over DOS, technicians often have to revert to using a DOS boot disk or the Command Prompt to fix faults. Furthermore, the command prompt is sometimes used for low-level control of networking and related functions in Windows systems, particularly servers.

The majority of command line programs that are still in use are small utility programs. These are capable of running in a window. This is usually accomplished by double clicking on a command line executable file – but bear in mind that depending on the setup of the system, if the program completes its task quickly it might just 'flash' up on the screen for a moment before disappearing, and any screen output may be lost.

To avoid this, the user can start a 'Command Prompt' window, sometimes called a 'DOS box' even though it isn't technically an instance of DOS but a DOS-like command-line interface. This can be done by locating the 'Command Prompt' option in the Start Menu or by typing 'COMMAND' in the 'Run' dialog from the Start Menu. When the Command Prompt loads, the user can navigate to the location of the utility and run it, and the output will remain on screen as the command prompt is still running until the user types 'EXIT'.

However, some legacy DOS applications require *"real mode"* operation. This can only be supplied in Windows 95 and 98, and only by leaving Windows entirely. The Shut Down window in these versions of Windows provide a *'re-start in DOS mode'* option, which closes Windows down and provides a DOS prompt. Before the prompt appears, though, the system will execute the batch file DOSSTART.BAT, found in the Windows directory, in much the same way as the AUTOEXEC.BAT file is used in *'ordinary'* DOS.

DOSSTART.BAT is generally used to load real-mode drivers, such as the MSCDEX CD-ROM driver, DOS mouse drivers and so on. Typing *'exit'* will leave DOS, and load Windows back up again.

Windows NT based systems, including Windows 2000, XP and Vista, do not use 'plain' DOS, but have their own DOS-based command prompt, known as CMD rather than COMMAND.

CMD provides many useful additions to prior versions of the command prompt. There are numerous network-related command prompt utilities, for such things as scheduling network tasks or spooling print jobs. CMD also has a file and path auto-complete feature accessed by pressing Tab, as well as various other features such as *'true pipes'*, where piped programs run simultaneously, allowing larger amounts of data to be piped since there is no need for temporary files.

Components of an Operating System

Since the computer has a variety of resources, the operating system is often viewed as consisting of several layers, even if the OS is stored in a single file on the disk. The various layers of the operating system can be seen in the diagram.

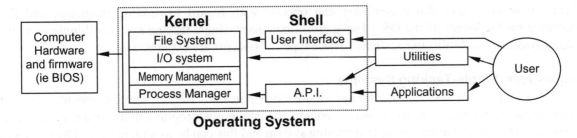

Operating System

As can be seen from the diagram, the user never deals directly with the computer hardware, or even any low-level parts of the operating system. If the user was forced to deal with low-level details of system operation, as the first computer users were, it would be impossible to use efficiently.

The following table briefly outlines the main functions of the various part of an OS:

Process Manager	Processes hardware and software interrupts. Deals with processor errors such as divide by zero. Schedules tasks to share processor time (in a multi-tasking system). Co-ordinates communication between tasks (in a multi-tasking system).
Memory Management	Allocates memory, and co-ordinates access to memory Ensures that processes stay within their memory boundaries (in multi-tasking systems) Most OS'es provide virtual memory if required.
Input/Output system	Communicates with peripherals and hardware components. Co-ordinates IO response systems including Interrupts and DMA.
File system	Organises and accesses files and folders on storage media such as hard disks. Maintains user file space quotas (on multi-user systems). Control file or record locking procedures (see LANs chapter).
Application Program Interface	Provides system services for applications. Supplies an interface between the application and the OS.
User Interface	Allows the user access to programs. e.g., the Start Menu in Windows. Allows the user to view or change system settings. e.g., the Control Panel. Provides these functions through a consistent interface.

The Kernel

This part of the system is so named because it is the 'central' part of the OS. Any interaction with the computer's hardware is via a *system call* to the kernel, which requests a function to be carried out by one of the kernel's layers. Many of these system calls take the form of interrupts, which are intercepted by the Process Manager, but the actual code that interacts with the device is usually part of the IO system.

The Process Manager

The process manager deals with *interrupts* (See the Computer Architecture chapter), and low-level errors such as division by zero. Its main purpose, however, is in 'multi-tasking' systems, where it also enforces whatever method of multitasking is being employed – see below for details.

The kernel also provides mechanisms for tasks to communicate with each other. If two programs try to access the same resources (such as a file or peripheral device) it can cause problems. For example two programs could both try to save data to the same file.

If not managed by the kernel, this could result in the file receiving the data from two programs simultaneously and containing garbled information.

This is solved by using 'semaphores'. The idea behind this system is that a variable is used, like a flag, to indicate whether a device is already in use or not. Only the process that 'picks up' the semaphore is allowed to use the device. Semaphores are explained in detail later.

There are several ways that a computer can operate with regard to running programs, and this is dependent on the kernel of the OS. These are: Single-user, single-tasking systems; Single-user, multi-tasking systems; and Multi-user systems. These types of systems are explained below.

Single-User, Single-Tasking Systems

This is the simplest of systems and the most common one in use. Here, a single computer is used by a single operator at a time (i.e. 'single-user'), only ever running one program at any one time (i.e. 'single-tasking'). This only requires a simple operating system and this can be as simple as MSDOS. A single-user machine is only connected to its own range of input and output devices. If there are two machines in an office and they both need fax facilities, they both require to have fax boards fitted. If both machines require lots of disk space, they both require to have large hard disks fitted. If both users require a particular package, it has to be installed on both machines. If they both use the same data, copies of the data have to be placed on the disks of both machines. The only shared resource might be a printer with an extra switch box that allows the printer to be connected to a number of machines, with only one being actually switched through to the printer at any one time. This system was predominant in the days of DOS and very old software may still expect to have full, undivided access to resources. Single-user, single-tasking systems are still used for such activities as EPOS (Electronic Point-Of-Sale) or data entry stations, where the user is not expected to want to use other software.

In the home, most games also operate in effectively single-tasking mode. Specialist uses of single-tasking machines include electronic music (using a 'MIDI' interface to connect the computer to an electronic instrument) and video capture (converting images from camcorders or video players into graphics images or sequences that can be stored on disk).

Multi-Tasking Systems

This system allows a single user to run more than one program at the same time. So, a user can open a database package and a word-processing package at the same time. While the word-processor is being used to type a report, the database can be compiling all the facts from the database. Both programs are functioning at the same time. The word-processor is the one seen by the user and this is described as being in the 'foreground', while the database search is said to be operating in the 'background'. Running Windows applications is a good example of a single-user machine being used for multi-tasking. The user can open up both the Excel spreadsheet and the Word word-processor and data from Excel can be copied over directly into a document being written in Word. Both packages can be seen on the screen at the same time, with each occupying a different area, or 'window' of the screen. Other examples of multi-tasking systems are Windows 2000, XP and UNIX.

In many multi-tasking systems, a single programs can be loaded more than once. A 'process' (or 'task') is therefore a single occurrence of a program loaded into memory. Not all processes that are running are necessarily user programs. For example, a typical Windows PC might be running Explorer and Microsoft Word, but could have also loaded several tasks on boot-up, such as a virus-checker. Additionally, there are a large number of processes that operate without the user ever needing to know about them – such as the mouse driver, disk caching and so on.

Process Management

When the processor changes from executing one task to another it is said to have 'changed context'. This entails saving various details about the process, so that it can be resumed later. Therefore, when a user starts a new process, it creates a data structure called a Process Control Block (PCB).

A typical PCB includes:
- the location of all memory allocated to the process, details of any files that are being worked on, and any events it may be waiting on. This information is held in a '*process control block*' for each process, and all of these are grouped together into a '*process table*' so that the kernel can properly maintain the processes.
- An ID number (called the Process ID or PID in UNIX), by which the Operating System and other processes can reference it.
- The ID number of the process that created this process, known as its '*parent*'. In UNIX this is called the Parent PID, or PPID.
- Processor state information, including registers and stacks – see the Architecture chapter.
- Process Control Information, such as files being worked on, memory allocated to the process, and any events it may be waiting for, interprocess communications, process privileges, etc.

Multi-tasking techniques
There are several ways to achieve multi-tasking:
- Using multiple processors. This is known as '*multi-processing*'.
- Using a single processor that uses techniques that allow it to run multiple tasks.
- Distributing the processes between a number of independent but linked computers. (called '*distributed processing*' or '*distributed systems*')

Even when using a multi-processing system, it is unlikely that each processor will have just a single task. Therefore, apart from distributed systems, which are discussed later, multi-tasking must find some method of running, or appearing to run, multiple tasks at the same time on any given processor. There are two ways of doing this, known as '*pre-emptive*' and '*non pre-emptive*' multi-tasking systems.

Non Pre-emptive multi-tasking
A basic type of multi-tasking system is called '*co-operative multi-tasking*', where each task voluntarily gives up processor time to the other tasks. This is a form of multi-tasking that does not involve pre-empting tasks from execution. Normally, a process will stop using the processor when it is awaiting input or output to or from a device. However, this system requires that every program is written properly, because a program that fails to give up the processor while awaiting input will stall the system. Also, processor-hungry task could very easily hog processor time. Windows 3.1 used a co-operative system, and was well-known for tasks not giving up the processor, thus effectively preventing multi-tasking from working efficiently. Because of this problem, the majority of multi-tasking systems, especially on PCs, are pre-emptive.

Pre-emptive multi-tasking
The most widely used solution is '*time-slicing*'. Time-slicing involves swapping programs in and out of

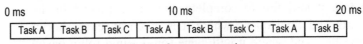

execution many times a second, so that every program gets a 'slice' of processor time.
The illustration shows how just 20 milliseconds could be split between three tasks. Since the processor time is divided into such small periods of time, it appears to the user that all processes are in constant execution. This example is allocating equal amounts of time to each task, which is sometimes called '*round robin*' scheduling.

A time-slicing system is called '*pre-emptive multitasking*' because processes are involuntarily stopped from running to allow processor time to be allocated to another task. The Process Manager layer of the OS must decide on how much processor time to allocate any given task, and 'pre-empt' it from execution when another task is to be given time.

In a pre-emptive system, each process may be in one of three states:
- Running. This process is currently executing.
- Ready. The process is in a queue, waiting to use the processor.
- Suspended. The process is waiting for an event, such as input from a keyboard.

Obviously, a program will make many 'state transitions' in the course of execution. When a program begins executing, it will be in the 'running' state. If it is pre-empted, it will finish the machine code instruction it is carrying out (the processor cannot be interrupted in mid-instruction) and then cease running. The task is capable of running, but will be prevented from doing so by the kernel. It has therefore become 'ready'. It joins a queue of processes waiting for their time slot, and will soon return to the 'running' state.

However, if a 'running' process has to wait for an external event, it cannot continue execution, even though it has been allocated time. It moves to the 'suspended' state, and the next process in the queue is immediately given processor time by the kernel. When the external event that the process is waiting for does occur, the suspended process does not immediately go back into execution; instead it joins the queue and becomes 'ready'.

These state transitions are illustrated in the diagram.

Although initially the round robin system seems a fair way of allocating time to processes, on closer examination jobs fall into two categories:

- Those that are CPU intensive
- Those that are not CPU intensive

CPU intensive jobs are those that require large amounts of time on the CPU (such as large mathematical problems). The non-CPU intensive jobs will rarely fill their time slice on the processor, as they will almost always become blocked awaiting input/output. Thus with round robin, the CPU intensive jobs effectively have more time per cycle on the CPU which is unfair on the other applications. Also, it wastes resources because actually switching between jobs (context switching) takes time and it may slow down I/O bound jobs. Often, it is the I/O bound jobs that are required to execute more quickly.

Multilevel feedback queues

UNIX operates a method of scheduling known as multi-level feedback queues in an attempt to resolve the contentions of round robin scheduling. With this type of scheduling, a new process enters the queuing system at the top level and is given an appropriately long timeslice for that level, in an attempt to make it complete in one timeslice. The top level is known as Level 1, and operates in a FIFO (First-In, First-Out) system. Should the process fail to complete in one timeslice, then after leaving the CPU it is placed in the second level queue where it is given a shorter timeslice (again, equal to all other processes in this queue). Should it still fail to complete upon timing out, then it is placed in the third queue where it is given an even shorter timeslice (equal to all the other processes in that queue). Finally, should it still fail to complete, then it is placed in the fourth and final queue where it is given an even shorter timeslice, and where it will cycle (on a round robin basis) until completed.

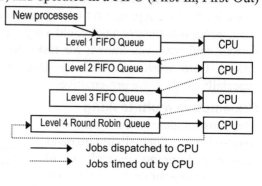

Thus the CPU intensive jobs very quickly find their way into the fourth queue taking up less resources than the less CPU intensive jobs.

The above assumes only one processor is available as part of the computer system. In general, UNIX machines tend to have multiple processors but only one undertakes the *"main"* processing; the others handle communication, etc.

In order to increase the processing power available, UNIX machines are often *"clustered"* around a shared or networked filing system (NFS). This means that a user wishing to use the system could log into a machine of their choice and access files created on another machine. If the user was accessing a database held on the other machine, then it is possible for the machine hosting the database to perform some processing before passing on the requested information. This is a form of *'distributed processing'*. Distributed systems are explained later in this chapter.

User Mode and Kernel mode

Some operating systems (including Windows NT, and some versions of Linux) support the concept of *'user mode'* and *'kernel mode'*. This idea is that processes in kernel mode have more privileged access to computer resources without the usual restrictions. Since this can be dangerous, most applications run in user mode for the majority of the time, and are subject to the normal restrictions on memory access and so on (as explained later). Device drivers, interrupt handlers, and the operating system itself are examples of software that would normally run in kernel mode, since these software routines may be required to act on behalf of any other process.

Multi-User Systems

Each year, more and more PCs are being connected together by special cables and software, to produce *'networked'* systems. Such systems range from a few PCs wired together using Windows software, through to many hundreds of computers linked together with highly complex LAN (local area network) software such as NetWare, NT or Unix systems.   This provides many advantages such as:

- Sharing software resources. All the application programs can be held on a main computer, known as the *'file server'* with only a single copy used for each program. When a computer wishes to run a program, a copy is sent from the server to the computer. Since there is only one central copy of all programs, additions and upgrades are much easier to perform.
- Sharing data resources.   With copies of data being held in separate machines, the information held in each computer soon varies from that held in the other copies.   If the data is held centrally, there is no need to have multiple copies in all individual machines. This means that the one central copy is the most current copy available for all users.
- Sharing hardware resources.   If the printers, plotters, modems, etc. are attached to an appropriately configured server or peer station, they are available to all computers connected to the system. This means that even the most expensive piece of equipment can be made available to all computers in the organisation and results in substantial savings over duplicated equipment.
- Communications - since all the machines are interconnected, they are able to send messages to each other via *'E-Mail'* (electronic mail) software.
- Added security.

A multi-user system is a network of computers (or *'terminals'*) that are all connected to a large central computer, known as the *'server'*. Some servers only provide shared data and peripherals – this is a multi-user system, but a fully multi-user operating system also shares processor time between its various terminals. This can even allow the terminals to be 'dumb', which means they have no processor power of their own. Unix is the most widely used Multi-User Operating System (MUOS).

Note that a MUOS that provides processing in this way must by definition be multi-tasking, because each user will presumably have at least one task running. Therefore, every multi-user system uses some form of time-sharing, usually time-slicing.

Distributed Systems

A distributed system is any network of computers, which may even be completely independent of one another, but which co-operate by sharing processing time. A system that is not using all of its processing time (for example, an idle PC or one which spends most of its time waiting for the user to type in data) can carry out a process for another machine on the network.

An example of a Distributed System is the Remote Procedure Call (RPC) protocol that is used on a wide variety of systems from Windows to Unix. This allows a process on one computer to call up a subroutine that is running on a remote machine. This has many uses, such as remote administration, and communications.

Problems with multi-user systems

Complex operating systems with several processes running concurrently can save on the amount of resources required by sharing. Thus several users can share one printer, for example. As there are fewer devices than there is demand, there can be contention between 2 or more processes for a device or devices. If not carefully controlled, in such positions deadlock becomes a serious threat to system integrity. The illustration shows two tasks, which each take control of a resource. If these resources can only be accessed by one task at a time, then the resources have been 'consumed', and no other task may use the resource.

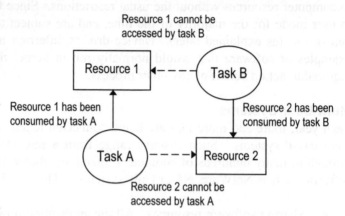

Two or more processes are said to be 'deadlocked' (or in a 'deadly embrace') if each waits on a resource held and not released by the other, as shown in the example. Starvation then occurs as processes wait on future execution sequence before they can proceed. Given time, more and more processes join the queue waiting for these devices and end in starvation. Effectively, the system grinds to a halt.

Systems cannot be allowed to deadlock and the solution involves forcing processes to release a resource they are holding before requesting another resource. Access to the resources must also be controlled if they are not to conflict. The following solutions to deadlock problems have been devised:

Semaphores

Semaphores are a manual method of controlling access to a piece of code requiring a shared resource. For instance if a user wishes to print, they should check that the printer is available before attempting to use it. If it is not, then they should wait until it is.

Semaphores operate in a very similar way to that which early trains used to obtain access to a single (bi-directional) piece of track:

There is only one track key, and only the train driver with the key is allowed onto the track. If the key is in station A, a driver from station A may use the track but drivers at station B can not. When driver A reaches station B, the key is dropped off there. Now, a driver at station B may use the track, because they have access to the key, but drivers at station A may not access the track, because they no longer have the key. This method ensures that only one train driver may use the track, thus regulating the flow of traffic on the track, as well as ensuring that crashes do not occur (assuming all the drivers follow the rules!).

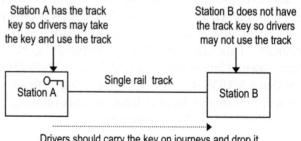

Systems programmers operate a similar principle by declaring a semaphore. The semaphore is initially set to 1 (available). When a process requires a resource; it executes a wait (on a named semaphore). If the value of the semaphore is 1, then 1 is deducted and it is allowed to proceed. If another process requires access to the same resource, as the semaphore is zero it will have to wait. When the first piece of code finishes with the shared resource, the programmer codes it so that it will SIGNAL the appropriate semaphore (adding 1 to its value). A waiting process will then wake up (subtract 1 from the semaphore) and then proceed.

Just as it is possible for the train driver to forget to replace the key and bring the railway to a halt, it is possible for the systems programmer to forget to SIGNAL the semaphore (or even put the SIGNAL command in the wrong place). In order to work, semaphores must be implemented very well. Thus just as automation has replaced keys on railway tracks, so semaphores in code have been superseded.

Monitors

Monitors were introduced as a solution to the semaphore problem. Basically, the system programmer places the code accessing the resource between the two relevant monitor statements. Working in an almost identical manner, it is the responsibility of the operating system to control access to monitored code.

Memory Management

This part of the operating system deals with volatile memory storage, much like the File System deals with non-volatile disk storage. The duties of this system include tracking memory usage, allocating and de-allocating memory when requested, and protecting certain areas of memory from unauthorised access. For example, the area of memory in which the kernel is stored can be read from, but any attempt to overwrite it should be disallowed by the memory management system.

Requests for storage of data are sometimes treated differently from requests to store programs in memory, as programs may require faster memory to operate efficiently. Sometimes this requires swapping the locations of processes in memory, so that a process of greater priority can execute more quickly. However, this is not used in modern PCs as PC main memory is normally of uniform speed.

The Memory Management System often has to 'clean up' memory by removing 'orphaned' memory. This is memory that has been allocated to a program that is no longer running, and has not been properly de-allocated. This might be as a result of the program crashing, for example.

Virtual Memory

If the system does not have enough physical memory space to store data or programs, it can create a disk file that acts as if it were memory storage space. Obviously, disk access is much slower than real memory, but slow memory is better than not enough memory. Increasing physical memory space will reduce virtual memory use, and improve performance. Having less physical memory space results in more virtual memory use, reducing performance arising from the increased time overheads caused by the extra swapping involved..

Virtual memory's contents are managed by this layer of the OS, although the file itself will be accessed through the File System. Virtual memory works by splitting the computer's memory into chunks known as 'pages', which are usually of 16k in size on Windows PCs, or 4k in size on UNIX systems. By doing this, pages can be swapped between 'page frames' in memory and the 'swap file' on the disk.

Obviously, care must be taken to load the next pages of the program when they are needed otherwise the program will be prevented from running. Preferably, the pages need to be loaded in advance of being required otherwise unnecessary delay will be caused. Failure to load a required page in advance is termed a 'page fault'.

When a particular page is required, it can be fetched from disk and used to replace another page that is already in memory, using a number of possible 'page replacement policies'. The continual swapping of pages between memory and disk allows the computer to run a much larger program than would otherwise be supported.

The two most commonly used page replacement policies are 'least-recently used' and 'least recently loaded'. The first method replaces the page that has not been used in the longest time, in the assumption that it is less likely to be needed. The latter method replaces pages that were loaded into memory the longest time ago.

When swapping out a page, the operating system must know (via a flag) whether the page is "dirty" (a page that has been modified) or "clean" (a page that has not been modified). If the page is clean then there is no need to save it back to the storage media and so write time (and associated disk access time) can be saved. By operating in such a fashion, the system can execute a program whose entire size is larger than computer's memory or combined jobs whose size is larger than the computer's memory. The operating system is using the computer's disk storage to create "virtual memory" limited only to the size of hard disk storage (which may be several GB). Whilst this is a useful facility, it must not be relied upon. Disc storage is many times slower than memory, which causes significant delay.

Memory paging can also be useful in multi-tasking – see later in this chapter for details.

Thrashing

Although virtual memory sounds like a dream come true it must be remembered that disk access is many thousands of times slower than the CPU. This means that pages retrieved from disk take much longer - hence the Operating System tries to minimise the number of faults. Users must try not to push Virtual Memory systems beyond their limits. If too many programs or too much data is loaded in comparison to the computers real memory then there is a risk of the system *"thrashing"*.

Thrashing is the term given to the situation where the computer spends more time loading and saving pages to and from disk than it does doing useful work. When systems start to thrash it is immediately noticeable - it is not uncommon for a machine's response time to fall from 5 seconds to 5 minutes when it starts to thrash. The solution is usually simple and inexpensive - more real memory!

Computer systems also use virtual memory to save details of processes in execution and may swap out processes that have suspended (blocked) waiting for disk I/O, etc. For this reason the systems need a swap file which is usually limited to 1.5 to 2 times the size of the computer's actual memory.

Memory Segmentation

DOS PCs use a memory *segmentation* system, in order to access memory. Early Intel PCs had a smaller address bus, which meant that they could only access 64k of RAM. The workaround that Intel developed was to provide a memory *segment*, and a memory *offset*, instead of one address. This is illustrated in the diagram opposite.

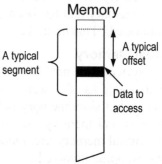

The segment referred to a 64k chunk of memory that could be located at any memory location that was a multiple of 16. The offset was the location within that 64k segment that the program wished to access. This method is still supported, for reasons of backwards compatibility, even though it has been the source of many headaches for programmers.

It is also possible to use segments instead of pages as the basis for virtual memory.

Memory Allocation in multi-tasking systems

If multiple programs or multiple sets of data are resident in memory at any one time there cannot be a guarantee of where those programs will load. The programs could load in low memory one day and high the next. For instance, if Fred loads his program first then it may be in low memory but, if Jo loads hers first, Fred's will then load into higher memory. Thus programs on a multi-user multi-tasking operating system like UNIX cannot dictate where they will load. For this reason they must not use specific memory addresses but instead must be relocatable (i.e. operate where the operating system dictates they will load).

To achieve this, relocation registers are used. Such registers require programs to operate on a base and offset principle. With this principle, the program is allocated a "base address" and all addresses in this program must be offsets to that address. Consider a simple program of which line 1 effectively says *'Jump to line 10'*. In a base offset situation the compiler would change this to *'Jump 10 lines'*. Thus if the base register was allocated as 40 the program would jump to line 50 and would therefore still work.

It is interesting to note that DOS does not employ such a method fully, and that is why there is the 640K memory problem with DOS.

Associated Problems

Whilst such a technique allows several programs to be resident in memory and to run successfully, there are further complications. The major complication is the division of the computer's memory – how much space should be allocated for each program?

In the first attempts at sharing memory (static partitioning) designers needed to determine how much space should be allocated for each program. If the limit were set too small, then the larger applications would not fit. If it were set too high, then memory would be wasted and other applications would be unable to fit in. Thus allocating fixed space was very quickly considered unacceptable.

It was determined that Operating Systems needed to vary the size of the memory allocation (variable partition memory) allocating just enough space for the programs to operate in. Again, the Operating

System is responsible for the control of this. As programs terminate, the Operating System must reclaim this space.

Although a vast improvement over static partitioning, this is far from perfect. Firstly, consider size. If the first program to load is large, then there may be insufficient room to load another. Indeed, there may be insufficient room to load the data to work with the program!

Such situations were particularly common when new versions of programs were installed - it is very unlikely that a revised application is smaller than its predecessor and more memory (if available) may need to be installed.

Further, consider the case where several programs and data are co-residing in memory. When one of the smaller programs terminates, it will leave two *"holes"* in memory (one from the data and one from the program). Together, these may amount to enough memory to run a further application but because they are two separate chunks rather than a whole (contiguous) chunk, a further application cannot run. This leads to uncontrolled memory fragmentation.

It is very difficult to devise algorithms that will deal with uncontrolled memory fragmentation and so a better way had to be found.

Memory Paging

To address these problems, the concept of paging was born. In a paged system (such as UNIX) a process is split into a number of chunks known as pages (typically 4K in length).

Memory is divided up into page frames of the same size. The process of program loading then consists of loading page into page frames, until the entire program is loaded.

As processes vacate the system, frames will become empty. By allowing parts of another process to be loaded into these vacated frames, maximum use is made of memory. Relocation of the job is affected by paging because it is possible for programs to be *"split up"* and loaded in a non-linear fashion. In such cases, memory becomes fragmented, as shown in the illustration, but because this is controlled by the Operating System, it is acceptable.

Process A Page 1
Process A Page 2
Process A Page 3
Process B Page 1
Process B Page 2
Process A Page 4
Process B Page 3

Paging presents further benefits:

- It allows the computer to run a program that is larger than its memory
- It allows the combined size of all programs to be larger than main memory
- Programs can begin execution immediately without waiting until fully loaded into memory

Paging can be used to split memory into units that can be swapped in and out to achieve virtual memory, as described previously. When used in this way it is sometimes called '*virtual paging*'.

An alternative system, which uses variable sized 'segments' instead of fixed-size pages, is known as '*virtual segmentation*', which should not be confused with memory segmentation under DOS.

Memory Protection

It is essential that each process does not interfere with another process or its data. However it is desirable (e.g. oracle indexes) that process code and data can be shared. Thus the operating system must undertake to manage the machine's memory and allow only authorised processes to address their parts of memory. It does this by monitoring memory address calls made by the processes and intercepts these if they are not valid for that process. Usually it will report to the process that it has an "invalid address reference". For this reason, UNIX is less susceptible to virus attacks than DOS, which operates no such control. Note that in DOS this error message could mean that there is no more memory however, in UNIX there could be the memory but it isn't allowed to be used.

Memory Management on Multi-User Systems

Managing memory is more complicated in a multi-tasking or multi-user system. Often several users wish to execute the same program. Consider a class that is studying ORACLE on a UNIX system. If there are 25 in the group and ORACLE took up just 2MB, it would require 50MB RAM just to load - a huge waste of resources. Resources can be conserved by loading only one copy of the program, and allowing 50 users access to it. Programs that can be used in such a way need to be compiled as *"re-entrant"*. This means that each user can run a different part of the same program by taking a *"thread"* through the program.

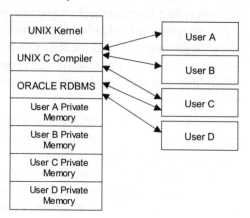

The diagram shows a section of computer memory. Users A, B & C are all using the same copy of the compiler. Users C & D are both using the same copy of ORACLE.

Input / Output System

The IO System is concerned with the precise details of any communication with various hardware peripherals and system components. For example, if a Windows user clicks to copy or delete a file, he or she is actually telling the User Interface to create a system call asking the IO system to access the hard disk. The file system is also involved in this example, telling the IO system where to find the file to delete. Similarly, an application that wishes to create files on the disk will normally create the system call by using a routine in the API.

The IO system is programmed with details of accessible control registers found on controllers such as the UART chip, which are used to control the operation of the device, while the data bus is normally used to transfer data from the processor to these chips. Input and Output occurs in two forms:

- Programmed IO
- Direct Memory Access.

Programmed IO is simply IO that is directed by the processor, while DMA is an improved method.

Device Drivers

Every input and output device requires a small piece of software to organise communications with the device. The IO system is normally capable of communicating with several devices. Others, however, require a 'device driver' (or 'device handler') that is programmed with the details of how to communicate with the device.

Device drivers are sometimes considered to be part of this layer of the OS, even though they are often supplied separately. This is because the device driver performs the same IO functions with one specific device. In fact, the IO system could be thought of as simply a set of basic device drivers, including perhaps the keyboard, display adapter, serial and parallel ports, and motherboard chips.

A *monolithic* OS, such as Unix, has all hardware device drivers built in to the OS file on the disk. On the other hand, a *modular* system such as Windows, is able to add or remove drivers as required.

Resource Sharing

The type of resource shared determines the sharing mechanism. For instance, a processor can be shared by moving processes on to it in a controlled fashion (see the Process Manager, earlier in this chapter). However, a printer must be given over to a process until the specified print job is complete – otherwise two processes would print over each other's job and garble the output. Similarly, two requests to save data to disk must be treated one after another, and not at the same time, or the results will almost certainly be disastrous.

Unix systems use programs known as 'daemons', which organise requests for data transfer to and from the device from multiple users. This places requests in a device queue until the current request is dealt with. 'Spooling' (Simultaneous Peripheral Output On-Line) is the name for a system that stores peripheral output in a queue while awaiting processing. However, for historical reasons, the name 'spooler' is usually reserved for print spoolers. Spoolers are for output only, and generally indicate large-volume data transfer, while device handlers in general are more often used for such devices as hard disks and CD-ROMs.

Direct Memory Access (DMA)

Some devices require data to be transferred between the CPU and the device at the fastest possible speed. These are usually devices handling bulk data such as network cards, scanners, sound adapters and hard disks. Slower devices such as floppy drives and serial/parallel ports do not have as demanding a speed transfer requirement. The slow devices use the CPU to organise the transfer of data between memory and the devices. All the data has to pass through the CPU and this ties up a lot of processing time, slowing down the computer's throughput.

To handle the faster devices, the PC uses a special technique known as 'Direct Memory Access'. An extra chip handles the transfers to and from memory, leaving the CPU to get on with other tasks. This results in a more efficient system and increased throughput.

The IO system's role in this is to negotiate details such as the locations in memory to access, whether data is to be read or written, and which DMA line to use.

File System

All programs and data are held on a storage device until they are ready to be used. The most common storage device is the magnetic disk, although CD/DVD disks or memory 'flash cards' are also in use. A file is collection of related data. The data may be instructions to the computer (program files) or database, spreadsheet or similar information (data files). Hard disks are likely to be storing thousands of such files at any one time, so a hierarchical structure is employed, where files are stored in 'directories' (or 'folders') and sub-directories, so that related files can be kept in one folder for ease of reference. This is analogous to a physical filing system, where files such as employee records might be kept in a folder labelled 'employees'.

Each file has a unique name; no two files are allowed to have exactly the same name in the same disk directory. This unique name is used by the computer to later find and load the file from anywhere on the disk. If a file is saved with the same name as an existing file of that name, the new file's contents replace the existing file contents. Filenames are covered earlier in this chapter.

The File System (FS) is required to keep track of the location and size of files and folders, as well as the attributes of all files. File attributes vary depending on the operating system, but usually include whether the file is read-only or read/write, amongst other things. File attributes in PC based systems are explained later in this chapter.

The FS also keeps track of all files that are 'opened'. An open file is one that is being viewed, edited, or otherwise processed. The FS keeps a list of 'file handles' that details the file name, location, and mode of opening for every file that is opened. File opening modes are used by programmers, and they include read-only (where a file is opened only to be viewed), and read/write (where a file can be changed). Do not confuse file opening modes with file attributes – a read/write file may be opened in read-only mode, though the reverse is not the case.

The FS opens and closes files at the request of programs as they run. It also reads and writes to the files, and 'seeks' through the file when data is requested from a non-sequential location in the file. It is also the FS that carries out the formatting of disks, both hard and floppy.

The disk caching system (explained in the memory and disk chapters) is generally considered to be part of the File System layer. A related type of facility, known as a RAM disk, may be part of the FS but is often a separate utility. This system sets aside some system memory to be used as if it were hard disk space. Since RAM is much faster than hard disk space this provides a temporary, volatile, but extremely fast storage area for files.

The File System of a Multi-User Operating System has the additional responsibility of ensuring the proper security restrictions are followed. In general, only system administrators will be allowed to access all files on all drives, while most users will probably only be allowed to run certain program files, and save to their own 'home' directory on one disk drive.

There are many different types of file systems, but the ones most used on PCs are FAT and NTFS – see the chapter on 'Disks and Drives' for details.

The Shell

Just as the Kernel consists of the inner workings of the operating system, the 'shell' is the surrounding layers that provide an interface to applications or directly to the user.

Applications Program Interface

Not all OS's have a component known as an API, but all provide some method of facilitating programming on the computer. For example, DOS software interrupts are available to simplify DOS programming. Windows does have an actual API, which is a set of named routines that provide a wide variety of system functions.

User Interfaces

This is not always considered to be part of the OS proper, as it can normally be replaced entirely with a new interface. The UI is also known as the *'shell'* and they can be broadly classified into two types – *Graphical User Interfaces* or GUIs (such as Windows or Mac systems) and *Command Line Interfaces* or CLIs (such as DOS or UNIX).

The User Interface has several tasks, the most important of which are to allow the user to start and stop programs, to provide a consistent interface, and to allow the system to be configured.

Command-Line Interface

A CLI uses a program called a *'command interpreter'*, which accepts commands typed at the keyboard, and interprets them into instructions for the operating system to carry out. In DOS, the command interpreter is COMMAND.COM, while in UNIX the command interpreter could be the Korn shell or the C Shell, for example.

CLI's often have a cryptic command set that must be typed exactly at the keyboard, making them more difficult for beginners to learn. On the other hand, CLI's can be quicker and more powerful for experienced users.

Graphical User Interface

Unlike CLI's, GUI's have a much more user-friendly *'point-and-click'* interface, that uses a 'WIMP' design. This stands for Windows, Icons, Menus and Pointers, and describes the four main ways in which the user interacts with a GUI.

Instead of having to learn a set of CLI commands, a GUI user only needs to know which window, icon, or menu to use. There is no chance of a typing error, and the user can often just browse through the menus until he or she comes across the option they wish to use, instead of having to look in a complex manual for the system.

Numbering Systems

Computers work with all kinds of information – numbers, text, pictures, sounds, programs and so on. All of this has to be stored somehow. Early computers used punched card. Modern PC's use hard disks, floppy disks, digital tapes, CD-ROMs and DVDs. But they all have something in common: each particle of data can be stored in one of two different states. For example:

- Each location in punched card can be either punched or unpunched.
- Each magnetic particle on the surface of a hard disk or floppy disk can be magnetised, or demagnetised.
- Each location in a CD-ROM can be either flat, or raised.
- Each memory cell can either contain an electrical charge, or no electrical charge.
- An electrical signal can be either positive, or negative.

A system that can be in one of two states at any one time is called a '*binary*' (base two) system. Because there are no states in-between, the examples are also *digital* systems. This is different from, for example, a volume control, which is *analogue* because the dial's precise location is never exactly a whole (or '*integer*') number. A typical volume control may also be labelled from one to ten, making it a '*decimal*' (occasionally called '*denary*') system.

Decimal and Binary

Because computers work only with binary systems, computer designers have to represent every piece of data in a binary form so that computer can use it. Text, sound, graphics, even decimal numbers have to be converted into binary form or the computer cannot use the data.

Mathematicians know the decimal system we use every day as '*base ten*', because each digit can be one of ten different symbols, from zero to nine. That means that every digit in decimal is worth ten times as much as the previous digit. For example, using the familiar school method of giving each digit a value, the number six thousand, seven hundred and fifty-three is represented as follows:

....	10000	1000	100	10	1	1/10	1/100	....
		6	7	5	3			

In other words, six thousands, seven hundreds, five tens, and three ones. To give it a more precise mathematical notation, the example would look as follows:

....	10^4	10^3	10^2	10^1	10^0	10^{-1}	10^{-2}	....
		6	7	5	3			

This indicates that the first digit, the number 6, is in fact 'worth' 6 times 10^3. That means the leftmost (called the '*most significant*') digit is in this case worth six times ten to the power three, in other words 6 x 10 x 10 x 10, or six thousand. The other digits are worth 7 times 10^2, 5 times 10^1, and 3 times 10^0.

Note that the 'ones' column is thought of as ten to the power zero. This is because any number raised to the power zero is always equal to 1.

The example shows that each digit's value is equal to the previous digit's value, multiplied by the base. In this case, the base is ten, so each digit is worth ten times the last digit. However, the same concept can be used with any base numbering system. The base, or '*radix*' R is used as follows:

....	R^4	R^3	R^2	R^1	R^0	R^{-1}	R^{-2}	....

Binary is known as '*base two*', because each digit can only be one of two values, represented either by a zero symbol or a one symbol. This is useful to computers because binary numbers can easily be represented by any of the binary systems that every computer employs. For example, a memory location can represent a 'zero' by the absence of electricity, or a 'one' by the presence of electricity.

Since binary is base two, the column values could be represented as follows:

....	2^4	2^3	2^2	2^1	2^0	2^{-1}	2^{-2}	....

Although mathematically correct, it is often easier to think of the columns like this:

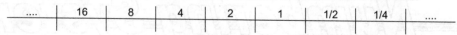

For example, the binary number 10100_2 (the '$_2$' indicates base two) could be seen as:

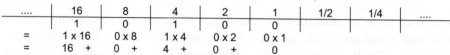

	16	8	4	2	1
	1	0	1	0	0
=	1 x 16	0 x 8	1 x 4	0 x 2	0 x 1
=	16 +	0 +	4 +	0 +	0

In other words, the binary number 10100 represents one times 16, no 8's, one times 4, no 2's and no 1's, for a total of 20 in decimal. In this way, a binary number is converted into the decimal number it represents.

In physical terms, then, the number 20_{10} (20 in base 10) could be transmitted from one part of the computer to another using several data lines, each of which carries either a high or low voltage to represent a one or a zero. A data line containing eight wires, named D0 to D7, could transmit the number 10100_2 as shown in the diagram.

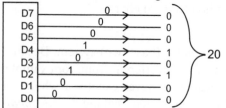

This system carries eight <u>binary digits</u> (called '*bits*' for short), and is therefore capable of transmitting numbers from zero (0000 0000) to 255_{10} (1111 1111), a total of 256 different possible numbers.

Binary digits have to be grouped together in this way, in order to store any useful information. Common groupings are as follows:

- <u>NIBBLE</u>: Although not often used, a nibble is the name for a group of just four binary digits, capable of storing numbers from zero to 15.

- <u>BYTE</u>: A group of eight bits, as in the example, is called a byte. This is short for '*by eight*', and is the basic unit of computer information. The lowest order bit, i.e. the one which has the least value, is called the '*Least Significant Bit*' (LSB) while the highest order bit is known as the '*Most Significant Bit*' (MSB).

- <u>WORD</u>: This term does not refer to a fixed amount of bits, despite popular misconception. The 'word size' of a computer is the number of binary digits that are transmitted along its data bus in one clock cycle. Therefore, a processor with a 16-bit bus uses 16-bit words, while a 32-bit processor uses 32-bit words. However, for historical reasons, many programmers and authors assume a word to be 16 bits. Therefore, a group of 32 bits is often called a 'double word', and 64 bits is called a 'quad word'.

- <u>KILOBYTE</u>: Modern computers deal with enormous quantities of data storage, and expressing sizes in bytes becomes difficult. A kilobyte (kB) is the number of bytes that can be given individual memory addresses using a ten binary digit address. A kilobyte is therefore 2^{10} bytes, or exactly 1024 bytes. However, for simplicity, kilobytes are usually simply thought of as '*thousands of bytes*'.

- <u>KILOBIT</u>: Many communications systems transfer just one binary digit at a time, and therefore measuring in bytes introduces unnecessary complications. Therefore, a kilobit (kb) refers to 1024 bits, rather than bytes. For example, a typical modem transfers data at 56kbps, or 56 kilobits per second. A kilobyte is equal to eight kilobits.

- <u>MEGABYTE</u>: For larger amounts of data, a group of 2^{20} bytes is referred to as a Megabyte. (MB) Although commonly thought of as a million bytes, it is actually 1024 kB, or 1,048,576 bytes. Some systems measure in megabits (Mb) rather than megabytes (MB).

- <u>GIGABYTE</u>: This is a group of 2^{30} bytes, or approximately a billion bytes. More exactly, it is 1024 MB, or 1,073,741,824 bytes. It is abbreviated to 'GB'. Some systems measure in Gigabits (Gb) instead of Gigabytes (GB).

These groupings are used to measure both hard disk capacity, and memory capacity, but <u>not</u> processor speed. Speed is measured in Mega*Hertz* (MHz) and Giga*Hertz* (GHz), which are not measured in base two. Therefore, a speed of exactly 2GHz really is exactly 2 billion Hertz.

Note:

There is no real standard for abbreviations of bytes and bits, so a lot of books and magazines use terms like kb and KB interchangeably. To avoid confusion, this book uses an upper-case '*B*' to represent bytes, and a lower-case '*b*' to represent bits. For example, a modem usually works at 56kbps, while a motherboard data bus might run at up to 3.2 GB/s.

The table shows some groupings of binary digits that are used in computers:

Some important data sizes		
Number of binary digits	**Range of Numbers or addresses**	**Example bus sizes and capabilities**
1	2	Can store either a one or a zero.
2	4	
3	8	
4 (Nibble)	16	Values range from zero to 15.
5	32	
6	64	
7	128	
8 (Byte)	256	The XT Data Bus – values range from zero to 255.
9	512	
10	1,024	If an address bus were this size, it could access 1 Kbyte.
11	2,048	
12	4,096	
13	8,192	
14	16,384	
15	32,768	
16 (Word)	65,536	The AT Data Bus – values range from zero to 65535. Also DOS segment address size – can access 64Kbytes
20	1,048,576	The XT Address Bus – can access 1Mbyte
24	16,777,216	The AT Address Bus – can access 16Mbytes
32 (Double word)	4,294,967,296	The 386/486 Address Bus – can access 4 Gbytes Also 386/486 Data bus – values range from zero to c. 4 billion.
36	68,719,476,736	Address Bus of Pentium II onwards – can access 64 Gbytes
64 (Quad word)	18,446,744,073,709,600,000	The Pentium Data Bus – values from zero to around 18 billion billion, but the whole bus does not normally represent a single integer.

Storing decimal numbers as binary

The earlier example showed how binary numbers are stored, and how a binary number could be translated into the decimal number it represents. However, to get the binary numbers into the computer in the first place, they have to be converted in the other direction – from decimal to binary.

This is done by repeatedly dividing by the base (which is 2 in this case, since binary is base two) until the quotient is reduced to zero. The remainders from each division are recorded and constitute the binary equivalent of the decimal number.

For example, the decimal number 13_{10} (the '$_{10}$' indicates base ten) is converted into binary as follows:

2	13	Divide the number by 2.
2	6 remainder 1	The answer ('quotient') is 6, with remainder 1. Divide by 2 again.
2	3 remainder 0	The answer ('quotient') is 3, with remainder 0. Divide by 2 again.
2	1 remainder 1	The answer ('quotient') is 1, with remainder 1. Divide by 2 again.
	0 remainder 1	The answer ('quotient') is 0, with remainder 1. Stop dividing.

This indicates that the number 13 in decimal consist of 1 x 1, plus 0 x 2, plus 1 x 4, plus 1 x 8. This makes the binary equivalent 1101. This is composed of the remainders of the divisions, but note that the numbers are read from the bottom up.

Hex Numbering

All data is stored and moved around in binary format - no matter how the program or the user might wish to regard it or organise it. However, binary numbers can comprise very long strings of 0's and 1's when it is representing a large number. For example, the binary number 0101100110011100111001 is, in fact, the decimal number 1,468,217. The binary version is hard to visualise; users find it hard to look at two binary numbers and know which is the largest. As a result, binary numbers are difficult to handle and are prone to human errors.

When dealing with very large numbers, it is often convenient to express the number in base 16, instead of base 10 or base 2. This is known as hexadecimal (often shortened to 'hex') and it is simple to convert from binary to hexadecimal. Also, the data on an 8-bit bus can be represented by just two alphanumeric characters instead of eight binary digits.

Binary	Decimal	Hex
0000	0	00
0001	1	01
0010	2	02
0011	3	03
0100	4	04
0101	5	05
0110	6	06
0111	7	07
1000	8	08
1001	9	09
1010	10	0A
1011	11	0B
1100	12	0C
1101	13	0D
1110	14	0E
1111	15	0F

The hex system requires symbols to represent from 0 through to 15. Since 10 to 15 are outwith normal single decimal digits, the letters A to F are used to represent 10 to 15.

The table shows the relationship between binary, decimal and hex.

Hex Conversions

These are similar to conversions between decimal and binary, except that the base used is 16 instead of two. Here are some examples:

Converting hex number 2B3 to a decimal number:

....	65536	4096	256	16	1	1/16	1/256	....
	0	0	2	B	3			

$$= \quad 0 \times 65536 \quad 0 \times 4096 \quad 2 \times 256 \quad 11 \times 16 \quad 3 \times 1$$
$$= \quad 0 \quad + \quad 0 \quad + \quad 512 \quad + \quad 176 \quad + \quad 3$$
$$= \quad 691$$

So $2B3_{16} = 691_{10}$.

Converting 349 to a hex number:

16	349		Divide the number by 16.
16	21	remainder D	The quotient is 21, remainder D (13). Divide by 16 again.
16	1	remainder 5	The quotient is 1, remainder 5. Divide by 16 again.
	0	remainder 1	The quotient is 1, with remainder 0. Stop dividing.

So, 349 is 15D in hex.

Large numbers can be represented quite compactly in hex. For example, the 640k memory boundary in the computer is A0000.

Hex is the preferred way of describing memory addresses and port locations.

Note:

Since not every occasion will see a hex number using the A to F characters, there can be confusion. For example, the number at the top of a 4k block of memory is 1000 in hex. This is not the same as the decimal number of one thousand. To prevent confusion, hex numbers are often followed by the letter 'h'. Thus, the number 4096 would be 1000h when given in hex. Similarly, 'd' and 'b' can be used to denote decimal and binary numbers.

Representing text in binary

Not all data stored in memory or carried on the computer buses will represent numbers. Often it will represent alphabetic characters and punctuation symbols. When the data is in alphabetic form, the ASCII (American Standard Code for Information Interchange) numbering scheme is employed. Each of the range of alphabetic characters, numeric digits, punctuation symbols, etc. is given a unique number. For example, the letter D is represented by 68, the number 7 is represented by 55, the comma by the number 44 and so on. Upper case letters have a different code from lower case letters and the full set of printable characters uses numbers from 32 to 127. The set of numbers between 0 and 31 is non-printable. They are mainly used to control printers (the number 12, for example, provides a Form Feed control character for a printer). A single byte provides 256 different numbers (0 to 255) but, since no ASCII character number is greater than 127, the codes are contained in a 7-bit sequence.

IBM created an extended character set to take advantage of the codes from 128 to 255. Printers using the IBM character set can print out various box drawing and other symbols.

The range of ASCII printable codes is:

Decimal	0	1	2	3	4	5	6	7	8	9
30			space	!	"	#	$	%	&	'
40	(	)	*	+	,	-	.	/	0	1
50	2	3	4	5	6	7	8	9	:	;
60	<	=	>	?	@	A	B	C	D	E
70	F	G	H	I	J	K	L	M	N	O
80	P	Q	R	S	T	U	V	W	X	Y
90	Z	[	\	]	^	_	`	a	b	c
100	d	e	f	g	h	i	j	k	l	m
110	n	o	p	q	r	s	t	u	v	w
120	x	y	z	{			}	~	DEL		

Printer control characters include:

12	(0C in hex)	Form Feed
13	(0D in hex)	Carriage Return
10	(0A in hex)	Line Feed

An example showing different ways of representing a string of characters is given below:

ASCII	H	e	l	l	o		!
Decimal	72	101	108	108	111	32	33
Hex	48	65	6C	6C	6F	20	21
Binary	01001000	01100101	01101100	01101100	01101111	00100000	00100001

Appropriate Data Representation

The binary value stored in a particular memory location could represent any one of several types of data. It may be an ASCII code, an integer number, a real number, or a program instruction, to name only the most common data types.

Consider the following examples:

"67"	is stored internally as 36h 37h	It is storing two ASCII characters
67	is stored internally as 43h	It is storing an integer number
"C"	is stored internally as 43h	It is storing a single ASCII character
6.7	is stored as 40h D6h 66h 66h	It is storing a floating point number

If the computer is asked to use the contents of a particular location, for example to display its contents to the screen, it has to know whether it is meant to display the number it finds there, or the ASCII character represented by the number. This is settled by the context in which the print request is made. If the printer is asked to print a string of characters, it will convert the number into its ASCII equivalent before printing it; if the printer is asked to print out the numbers that it finds, the number is printed out without any text conversion.

If an operation is performed on data that is inappropriately represented, it normally causes errors or even crashes. For example, a program that asks for a number from the keyboard will receive that number in ASCII format. If that number is to be part of a mathematical calculation, using it as an ASCII code will give the wrong result. It must be stored as a binary number, which means it will have to be converted from ASCII into an integer before storing in memory.

Other errors can result from the handling of negative numbers (e.g. –17) or numbers that have a fractional part (e.g. 1.25). If the system does not understand negative or fractional numbers they will be stored as positive (e.g. 17) or whole numbers (e.g. 1) causing errors in calculations.

Other Numbering Schemes

Less common numbering schemes are in use and these include:

EBCDIC

The Extended Binary Coded Decimal Interchange Code (EBCDIC) is an 8-bit code that was introduced by IBM and ICL for their mainframe computers.   It is of little interest to PC users except where data has to be converted between EBCDIC-based machines and ASCII-based PCs.

BAUDOT

This is a five-bit code that was popular for telegraphy, telex and computer-controlled radio communications systems (popular with radio amateurs).   Since it a five-bit system it can only support 32 different combinations.

By using two codes (called *'Letters shift'* and *'Figures shift'*) the system shifts between using the numeric codes to represent alphabetic characters and using the same numbers to represent numbers and punctuation symbols.

BCD

Where the data is only in numeric format, each individual number can be converted into its binary equivalent and handled separately.   Since each individual number will only be between 0 and 9, only four bits are required to store each number.

So, the decimal number 5931 would produce a BCD equivalent of:

5	9	3	1
0101	1001	0011	0001

whereas the normal binary equivalent would be 1011100101011.   This only occupies 13 bits compared to the BCD equivalent.   Since each BCD number has its own collection of four bits it is often used to drive LED meters in instrumentation, monitoring and control computer systems.

OCTAL

Octal numbering works with a base of 8 and therefore uses a 3-bit system.   It is little used today and is only mentioned for completeness.   Conversion between decimal and Octal is similar to that already described for decimal/hex conversion, substituting 8 for 16 in the calculations.

Computer Arithmetic

The computer constantly carries out arithmetic and comparison operations.   These operations may be requested by the user in an application package (eg spreadsheet calculations) or may be used by the computer system (eg for graphics and video).

Binary addition

In denary, adding two numbers might result in a carry over between columns.   In the example, adding 7 and 8 produced 15.   This is another way of saying one lot of ten and 5 units.   This was represented by carrying a one from the units column into the next column.

Tens	Units
	7
	8
1	5

Similarly, adding 1 and 1 in binary produces no lots of 1 and one lot of 2.   Again, there was a carry from the units column into the next column.   In binary addition, the calculation on any column has to take into account the possibility of a bit being carried over from a calculation on the previous column.

2^1	2^0
	1
	1
1	0

The general rule for binary addition is:

$$0 + 0 = 0$$
$$0 + 1 = 1$$
$$1 + 0 = 1$$
$$1 + 1 = 0 \text{ carry } 1$$

Consider adding 6 and 7 together. Six has a binary pattern of 0110, while seven has a pattern of 0111.

	2^3	2^2	2^1	2^0
6=	0	1	1	0
7=	0	1	1	1
result	1	1	0	1

Addition takes place from the lowest value upwards; this means from the right-most column through to the left-most column.

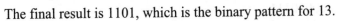

The example of 6+7 would be processed thus:
- Adding the bits in this column (ie 0+1) produces a 1 without a carry.
- Adding the bits in this column (ie 1+1) produces a 0 with a carry into the next column.
- Adding the bits in this column, plus the carry (ie 1+1+1), produces a result of 1 plus a carry into the next column.
- Adding the bits in this column, plus the carry (ie 0+0+1), produces a result of 1 with no carry.

The final result is 1101, which is the binary pattern for 13.

It is common for arithmetic to take place on full bytes of data.
For example, adding 109 and 54 produces:

$$\begin{array}{r} 01101101 \\ \underline{00110110} \\ 10100011 \end{array}$$

However, adding 130 and 140 produces:

$$\begin{array}{r} 10000010 \\ \underline{10001100} \\ 100001110 \end{array}$$

This calculation has produced an answer that cannot be stored in a single byte. The number of bits needed to store the result (i.e. 9 bits) has overflowed the size of the storage area (i.e. 8 bits). This final carry has to be detected and acted upon otherwise the carry is ignored and the computer thinks that 130+140=14!

Binary subtraction

The general rule for binary subtraction is:

$$0 - 0 = 0$$
$$1 - 0 = 1$$
$$1 - 1 = 0$$
$$0 - 1 = 1 \text{ borrow } 1$$

Consider subtracting 3 from 5:

	fours	twos	units
5=	1	0	1
3=	0	1	1
	0	1	0

In the right-most column, taking 1 unit from 1 unit results in 0 units. In the 'twos' column, there is nothing in the top row to subtract the lower 1 from. So, the 1 is borrowed from the column on its left. However, since each column increments by a factor of 2, borrowing from its left is, in fact, borrowing four - or two lots of 2. Subtracting one lot of two from two lots of two leaves one lot of two, which is placed in the middle column of the result.

Negative numbers

The examples on the previous page used simple examples. The example additions only used positive numbers; the subtraction example avoided negative numbers and subtracted the smaller number from the larger number to avoid a negative result. In practice, the computer has to store and calculate negative values.

In addition, it may be desirable to use negative numbers for other purposes. The computer need not have separate addition and subtraction operations. The calculation of 7-3 can be represented as 7+(-3). Both calculations are identical. The second representation allows the computer to avoid a subtraction; it simply adds together two values - one a positive number and the other a negative number. A subtraction problem has been converted into an addition problem.

A byte has eight bits and can store a range of contents varying from all zeros (ie 0) through to all ones (ie 255), storing 256 possible different values.   However, this does not allow for negative numbers to be stored.   If the most significant bit of the byte was ignored, then the byte would store from 0 to 127 (ie seven ones).   The eighth bit can then be used to store an indicator of whether the number was positive or negative.

A zero value in the eighth bit (Most Significant Bit) indicates a positive number, while an eighth bit containing a value of one indicates a negative number.

MSB   LSB

| 0 | 1 | 0 | 0 | 0 | 1 | 1 | 1 |

In the first example, the MSB is 0, so the number is positive.   So, the value in the first example is 71.

MSB   LSB

| 1 | 0 | 0 | 1 | 0 | 0 | 1 | 1 |

The MSB in the second example is 1, indicating a negative number.   This could be used to represent the negative number –19.   However, this has a serious drawback – normal binary additions using this method can produce the wrong result.

For example, the calculation of 7-3 can be represented as:

$$\begin{array}{ll} +7 & 00000111 \\ +(-3) & \underline{10000011} \\ \text{result} & 10001010 \quad = -10 \end{array}$$

This has produced the wrong answer and so other methods are used for storing and manipulating negative numbers.   The most common of these is known as 'two's complement'.

Two's complement

With two's complement, sometimes written as 2's complement, positive numbers are represented in their normal binary conversion.

Negative values are converted using the following rules:

Decimal to 2's Complement Conversion Rules	Worked Example for value of -3
Drop the negative sign	3
Convert to binary	00000011
Invert all bits (convert all 1's to 0's and all 0's to 1's). This stage is known as converting to One's Complement.	11111100
Add 1 to the result	11111101

So, -3 is represented by 11111101.

The earlier calculation of 7-3 is now represented by:

$$\begin{array}{ll} +7 & 00000111 \\ +(-3) & \underline{11111101} \\ \text{result} & \underline{1}00000100= +4 \end{array}$$

The carry resulting from the addition is ignored, producing the correct answer of +4.

Any carry resulting from these calculations is always discarded.

If the MSB (eighth bit) is zero, the number is positive and is converted back to decimal in the normal way.

In some cases, the result of a calculation produces a negative value.

Consider the calculation 4-8.

$$\begin{array}{lll} +4 & 00000100 & \text{2 converted to binary} \\ -8 & \underline{11111000} & \text{this is 8 in 2's complement} \\ \text{result} & 11111100 & \text{result has MSB set to 1} \end{array}$$

The resulting value cannot be immediately converted to a decimal number.

If the MSB is set to 1, then the following rules apply:

2's Complement to Decimal Conversion Rules	Worked Example for value of 11111100
Invert all bits (convert all 1's to 0's and all 0's to 1's).	00000011
Add 1 to the result	00000100
Convert to decimal	4
Place a minus sign in front of the number	-4

Representing fractions in binary

All of the numbers discussed so far, whether positive or negative, have been 'integer' numbers, also called 'whole' numbers. If the user wishes to store a fraction such as 3.14, which is more correctly known as a 'real' number, then additional detail is needed. There are two methods of representing real numbers in binary. These are known as 'fixed-point' and 'floating point'. Note that, just as in decimal, it is not always possible to store a fractional number with 100% accuracy. The fraction 1/3, for example, cannot be completely accurately represented by a single number, either in decimal or in binary.

Fixed-Point numbers

In this method, the 'radix point' (the full stop symbol that separates the whole number part from the fractional part) is assumed to be in a fixed position. For example, a 16-bit fixed-point number might place the point in the middle, allocating the top 8 bits to the whole part, and the lower 8 bits to the fractional part. In this system, the number 3.14 would be represented as follows:

....	2	1	1/2	1/4	1/8	1/16	1/32	1/64	....
	1	1	0	0	1	0	0	1	
=	1×2	1×1	$0 \times 1/2$	$0 \times 1/4$	$1 \times 1/8$	$0 \times 1/16$	$0 \times 1/32$	$1 \times 1/64$	
=	2 +	1 +	0 +	0 +	0.125 +	0 +	0 +	0.015625	
=	3.140625								

Note that this is not the exact number we wish to represent. In some cases, using more binary digits will provide enough precision to accurately represent the number. In other cases, there will always be some degree of inaccuracy, however small.

The main problem with this system, however, is that it has a fairly limited range of numbers that can be represented. With the example 16-bit fixed-point number system above, only numbers from zero up to almost 256 can be represented. If a similar, 32-bit system was used, it would still only represent numbers from zero up to almost 65536.

Floating Point numbers

Rather than simply continuing to add new digits onto a fixed point system, a different system can be devised where the radix point 'floats' around, allowing a greater range of numbers to be represented.

Numbers are sometimes referred to in 'scientific notation'. This means the number is described in terms of a 'mantissa', a 'base' and an 'exponent'.

For example, the number 1,234,567 could be written as :

$$1.234567 \times 10^6$$

In this case, the mantissa is the first number, the base is ten, and the exponent is equal to six. This is equivalent to saying: 1.234567 x 1,000,000. Note that by increasing or decreasing the exponent, it can be ensured that the mantissa is always lower than 10, but no lower than 1. (unless of course we are storing the number zero!) This is called 'normalising' the number.

A similar system is employed in computers. Although the implementation may vary, a common standard for floating point numbers is the IEEE 754 standard, which describes two levels of precision, both of which can store either positive or negative numbers. They allocate the following digits:

	Sign	Exponent	Fraction
Single precision (32 bits)	bit 31	bits 30 to 23	bits 22 to 0
Double precision (64 bits)	bit 63	bits 62 to 52	bits 51 to 0

Note that since we are working with binary numbers, the base is assumed to be 2. Also, similar to the decimal representation, the mantissa will always be normalised so that it is below 2, but no less than 1. This means that the digit before the radix point can be assumed to be a 1, except in the case of representing the actual number zero. If we do wish to represent the number zero, then all of the fraction and exponent bits must be set to zero.

However, in order to represent numbers between decimal zero and decimal one, we need to be able to use negative exponents. For example, the number 0.5 could be represented as 1×2^{-1}. In order to do this, the exponent subtracts a 'bias' from the stored exponent. In order to maximise the range, this bias is half of the maximum number that can be represented with the exponent bits. In other words, the bias in single precision numbers is 127, while the bias in a double precision number is 1023.

The sign of the number overall is stored in the sign bit, which is a 1 for negative, or a zero for positive.

So, for example, the number -20.25 is stored in single precision as:

Sign	Exponent	Fraction
1	10000010	01001000000000000000000
Negative	131 decimal	0.265625 decimal

Thus, this number represents a negative number, with the exponent of $131 - 127$ (the bias) = 4, and a mantissa of $0.265625 + 1 = 1.265625$. The scientific representation is therefore -1.265625×2^4, which is equal to -20.25.

Hex addition

Hex numbering requires a multiplier of 16 between columns, compared to multipliers of 2 and 10 for binary and decimal respectively. The carry over methods involved in the earlier examples of decimal and binary addition also apply to hex addition, except that the carry between columns involves a base of 16. The least significant column stores single units with the column's contents allowed to range from zero (ie 0 lots of 1) to F (ie 15 lots of 1). The next column stores how many 16s help comprise the number stored; it can range from 0 lots of 16 to 15 lots of 16. Each subsequent column's contents increase by a factor of 16.

In the table below, the columns represent 1s, 16s, 256s and 4096s - reading from right to left.

The example shows 75 and 211 being added together. 75 converted to hex is 4B while 227 converts to E3. The addition of the first column combines B (ie 11) and 3. This produces an answer of 14, which is E in hex. The second column adds 4 and D (ie 13). This produces an answer of 17. Since the column only stores factors of 16, there is a carry over into the next column and a remainder of 1 placed in second column.

	16^3	16^2	16^1	16^0
75=	0	0	4	B
211=	0	0	D	3
result	0	1	1	E

The final result is 11Eh, which is 286 in decimal.

Hex subtraction

Hex notation is the most common way to describe memory locations and address location in computers. For example, the program necessary to drive a SCSI hard disk may be described as sitting in memory between C8000h and D0000h.

To find out how much memory this occupies, the two hex figures should be subtracted; the difference in hex can then be converted to decimal if required.

16^4	16^3	16^2	16^1	16^0
D	0	0	0	0
C	8	0	0	0
0	8	0	0	0

The subtraction would be processed thus:

- The right-most column produces a 0 since 0-0 = 0.
- The second column also produces a 0 (i.e. 0-0 = 0).
- The third column also subtracts 0 from 0 producing 0.
- The fourth column subtracts 8 from 0, forcing 1 to be borrowed from last column. Borrowing one lot of 16^4 effectively means borrowing 16 lots of 16^3. 8 from 16 leaves 8 in the third column.
- Since there was a borrow from the last column, the value of D is reduced to C. Subtracting C from C leaves 0 in the last column.

This means that the memory requirements were 08000h.

This converts to hex as

0	x	1	=	0	
0	x	16	=	0	
0	x	256	=	0	
8	x	4096	=	32768	
		Total	=	32768	

The program occupies 32768 bytes of address space - i.e. 32k.

Logic operations

Users constantly use logic operations when carrying out day-to-day activities:

- To make a word bold in Word requires both that the word is highlighted **AND** the Bold option is clicked on the Toolbar.
- DOS **OR** Windows can be used to copy files.

In the first example, <u>both</u> conditions had to be met before the result was met.

This can be shown with the use of a '*truth table*'.   A Truth Table is a table that shows the results of all possible sets of input conditions.

For the first example, it would be:

Condition A	Condition B	Result (or output)
Word not highlighted	Bold option not clicked	Word not Bold
Word not highlighted	Bold option clicked	Word not Bold
Word highlighted	Bold option not clicked	Word not Bold
Word highlighted	Bold option clicked	Word made Bold

In the second example, <u>either</u> condition being met produced a positive result.

The truth table for the second example is:

Condition A	Condition B	Result (or output)
DOS not used	Windows not used	File not copied
DOS not used	Windows used	File copied
DOS used	Windows not used	File copied

With computer circuitry, the state of particular electrical bus lines or the states of particular bits of data are used to determine the result of an action.   The logic circuits are often called '*gates*'.   The most common types are the AND gate, the OR gate, the NOT gate, and the XOR gate.

AND

A typical way to demonstrate an electronic AND logic is the use of a battery, a lamp and two switches.   The switches are wired in series with each other. This means that both have to be switched to light the lamp.

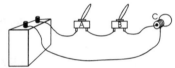

Its truth table is shown below, with the left table describing it fully in words while the right table shows a shortened form:

Condition A	Condition B	Result (or output)
Switch A Off	Switch B Off	Lamp not lit
Switch A Off	Switch B On	Lamp not lit
Switch A On	Switch B Off	Lamp not lit
Switch A On	Switch B On	Lamp lit

Switch A	Switch B	Lamp C
OFF	OFF	OFF
OFF	ON	OFF
ON	OFF	OFF
ON	ON	ON

If a zero is taken as a condition being OFF (or a condition being false) while a one represents a condition being ON (or a condition being true) then the most common method of showing a truth table is as shown.

A	B	C
0	0	0
0	1	0
1	0	0
1	1	1

The right-most column describes the expected outputs while the other columns described the variety of possible input conditions.   Of course, there may be more than two inputs and this would result in extra input columns.

OR

In this example, the switches are wired in parallel and switching on either of the switches will light the lamp.

This is known as an OR configuration and its truth table is as shown.

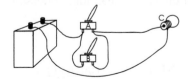

A	B	C
0	0	0
0	1	1
1	0	1
1	1	1

NOT

In this case, the lamp is permanently wired to the battery and will normally remain lit.   If the switch is thrown it will place a short circuit across the battery/lamp and the lamp will be extinguished.

Throwing the switch reverses the normal condition (ie the lamp changes from lit to unlit) and this logic is known as a NOT.   It has a simple truth table.

A	B
0	1
1	0

XOR

This is the term for an Exclusive OR, also sometimes known as EOR.   The truth table shows that when there are no input conditions, there is no output; this is identical to a normal OR.   The table also shows that where either of the inputs is on, the output is set to on.   This is also identical to a normal OR.   However, if both the inputs are set, the output remains off.

A	B	C
0	0	0
0	1	1
1	0	1
1	1	0

Logic combinations

Another way to show a logic gate is as a box with one or more inputs and a single output.   All computers use logic gates (as do VCRs, washing machines and all kinds of other electrical appliances).   The computer's CPU, disk controller, etc. have logic gates built into their chips' circuitry.

The different types of gate (AND, OR, etc.) are used in various combinations to carry out the required tasks.

Consider the following requirement for a VCR:

The motor will spin when the cassette is inserted and when the "Record" or "Play" button is pressed

This examines three conditions in the following way:

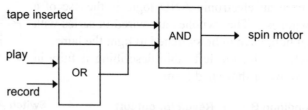

tape inserted AND (*record pressed* OR *play pressed*)

The diagram shows how logic chips could make such a test and the truth table shows the results of various conditions.   The truth table uses YES and NO as table values.   This is an alternative to using 0

Tape inserted in VCR	Play button pressed	Record button pressed	Spin motor
N	N	N	N
N	N	Y	N
N	Y	Y	N
Y	N	N	N
Y	N	Y	Y
Y	Y	N	Y

and 1 or OFF and ON.

Bitwise Logic

Truth tables use '*Boolean*' variables – this means each input and output state can be either TRUE or FALSE.   Clearly, this can quite easily be represented by a binary digit, and thus a Boolean logic operator (such as AND or XOR) can be used on a binary value.

For example:

```
         01010011              01010011               01010011              01010011
AND      10010111       OR     10010111      XOR      10010111      NOT     01101000
         00010011              11010111               11000100
```

These examples perform logic operations on more than one binary digit at a time, which has a variety of uses in programs and computing. To process these logic operations, the processor must contain arrays of logic gates, each individual gate working on one binary digit of each group of digits that are to be processed. The most common example of bitwise logic is in using 'masks'.

Bit masks

Any alphabetic text may require to be converted to upper case. A lower case letter 'a' is ASCII value 97, which is 01100001 in binary, while upper case 'A' is ASCII 65 or 01000001. In fact, the difference between the lower and upper case version of any letter is 32 and this is binary 0010000. Subtracting 32 from the binary pattern would convert from lower to upper case. Since all lower case letters have bit 6 set to 1, a 'mask' can be used as an AND filter to let all of the binary pattern, apart from the 6th bit (value 32), appear in the output.

```
example input    01100001
AND with 223     11011111
example output   01000001
```

Logic operations are 'bit-wise' operations; the condition of any output bit is purely the result of the logic operation on the corresponding input bits, independent of the result of any other bit operation. So, for example, bit 3 in the output byte was determined solely by the contents of the third bit in the two inputs - with no carry being used.

Conversely, alphabetic text may require to be converted to lower case; this is the reverse of the previous example. Since no uppercase alphabet letters have the 6th bit set, 32 has to be added to the input to provide a lower case output. This is achieved by ORing the input with 32 - a binary mask of 00100000.

```
example input    01000001
OR with 32       00100000
example output   01100001
```

Using the XOR bitwise operator

The XOR operator, for example, can be used for transmission error checking.
Consider the example of transmitting an upper case D. Upper case D is ASCII 68 or 01000100 as a byte in binary. If that pattern is transmitted from one computer to another computer at a distant location, the receiving end can re-transmit what it received.
This will be returned (ECHOed) to the sender and the patterns can be compared. using XOR.

	1st example	2nd example
Pattern sent	01000100	01000100
Pattern returned	01000100	01100100
Result of XORing	00000000	00100000

In the first example, the pattern returned was identical to the pattern sent and XORing results in a byte full of zeros.

In the second example, the data was corrupted during transmission and XORing produces a value, which is not all zeros. Therefore, testing for a byte value of zero reports on a successful or an unsuccessful transmission of that character.

The XOR operator can also be used to zero a number. If any number is XORed with itself, it will produce an output of zero (eg 129 XOR 129 = 0). This can be used to switch graphics off and on. It is also a handy way to clear the contents of a CPU register.

Computer Architecture

The Basic System

A computer consists of various elements - CPU, memory, and a range of Input/Output connections to devices such as disks, keyboard, monitor and mouse.   Most of a computer's operations are concerned with the movement of data between these elements (e.g. reading a program from disk into memory, reading spreadsheet data, recalculating results and storing them back to memory).   Some of these data transfers are purely internal to the computer (as in the case of spreadsheet updating).   Other data transfers are to outside peripherals via cards plugged into expansion slots on the computer motherboard or motherboard sockets (as in the case of printing a spreadsheet).

The diagram shows a simplified view of a computer system.   The Address Bus and Data Bus link all the memory and input/output devices to the CPU and the main components are:

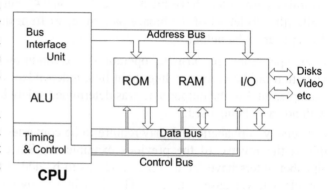

Address Bus

Each memory location has a unique address number. The CPU has to be able to read or write data to any of these addresses. The CPU accesses a memory location by putting the desired address number, in binary format, on to the Address Bus. Devices such as the parallel and serial ports are also part of this addressing system.

Data Bus

When the appropriate memory location is accessed, the CPU can either fetch data from it or write data into it; such data is transferred along the Data Bus.

Notes:

- Some of the memory is in the form of 'ROM' (Read Only Memory). This is a chip with program coding permanently burned into it.   Its contents are not lost if the machine power is switched off. Some, or all, of the system/video/disk BIOS is stored in ROM form.
- Information never flows into the CPU from the Address Bus.   The Address Bus is only used to allow the CPU to access various peripheral chips.
- Since ROM cannot be written to, data only flows on to the Data Bus from the ROM chip - and never in the opposite direction.
- Since RAM can either be read or written, there is a need to allow data to flow between memory and the CPU in either direction (only one direction at a time!)
- The I/O expansion bus also has to be capable of both receiving and transmitting data on the Data Bus (e.g. a modem has to transfer data in both directions).

Control Bus

This bus transports several control signals. Many CPUs have two major control lines, one that is brought to a low voltage level to indicate that a read is taking place and one that is brought to a low voltage level to indicate a write taking place. Naturally, only one of these lines can be brought low at any one time.   The PC range of processors, the xxx86 range, treats memory and I/O devices differently and therefore has separate control lines for each.

The PC's main control lines are:

MEMR	goes low to indicate a read of memory
MEMW	goes low to indicate a write to memory
IOR	goes low to indicate a read of an I/O device
IOW	goes low to indicate a write to an I/O device

The Address Bus and the Data Bus are simply the electrical paths between the CPU and the other chips. They exist as the copper tracks of the computer's printed circuit board and the chip sockets are soldered to these tracks. To allow other peripheral cards to attach to the buses, the buses connect to special sockets called *'expansion slots'*. The cards plug in to these slots and pick up the bus connections, as well as power, from the edge connections.

CPU

In the diagram, the CPU has been expanded into three parts:
- **The ALU** - Carries out all the calculations and decision-making tasks.
- **The Bus Interface Unit** - Takes the data to and from the CPU (held inside its internal *'registers'* - i.e. small memory stores) along the external Data Bus to read/write memory and devices. The Data Bus is a two-way bus, as it must carry information in both directions. The Bus Interface Unit also places the required location addresses on to the Address Bus, in order that the required devices can be accessed for reading or writing.
- **The Control Unit** - Decodes all program instructions and dictates all the CPU's control and timing mechanisms.

Note: All of the aforementioned components are found in every microprocessor, not just PC-based computers. See later in this chapter for a brief history of processors.

How the computer works

The CPU is the intelligence of the machine but it still needs a pre-written program to create, use and modify the user's data. If the computer needs to compare two numbers, or add two numbers, this is carried out <u>inside</u> the CPU and the numbers have to be fetched into the CPU from the computer's memory chips. Similarly, any program instructions have to be fetched into the CPU so that they can be acted upon. This means that CPUs work with

- programs that are stored in memory
- data that is stored in memory

The memory store can be the computer's main RAM memory or it can be the system ROM (e.g. the BIOS chip). It cannot run programs straight from the disk - it loads the program from the disk into the machine's RAM memory and then runs the program from the memory. Similarly, all data - whether incoming or outgoing - will have to reside in memory at some stage. So, programs and data from disk, tape or CD and data from keyboard, mouse, networks, sensors, etc. are all placed in memory for the CPU to access.

The program, no matter its origin, will end up as a series of instructions stored in the low-level language that the CPU understands. This is the CPU's *'instruction set'* and is different for different CPU variations. Since the CPU can only process numbers, all programs and data are reduced to sequences of numbers. The most complex Windows application is simply stored as a long set of numbers; the most beautiful graphic is similarly reduced to a stored set of numbers. The way that these numbers are interpreted by the CPU gives the program or data its meaning.

Data Handling

The normal process of a computer is a sequence of getting instructions from the program, interpreting them and acting upon them - mostly resulting in the manipulation of data. Therefore, the CPU is constantly reading instructions from the program in memory. It does this by fetching a copy of the instruction from the memory, along the data bus, into the CPU for interpretation. If this instruction requires an alteration of the user's data, this altered data will need to be transmitted from the CPU on to the data bus and used to overwrite the old data held in memory.

Of course, it is essential that the programs and data are held separately and are not allowed to overwrite each other. To achieve this, the programs and data are stored in different portions of the machine's RAM memory. If the CPU knows where each is stored, it can get at each for reading data from, or writing data to, these specific areas. Every individual memory location has its own unique location number, known as its *'memory address'*. The CPU can only read from, or write to, a particular address by asking specifically for that address - that is the purpose of the address bus. Only one address number can be on the address bus at any one time and only the memory location with the same address number will respond to that address data. So, if the number 7700 is placed on the address bus by the CPU, only location 7700 will be accessed.

Controlling the Flow

There is one final complication. Once a location is accessed, it needs to know whether it is supposed to dump a copy of its contents on to the data bus or whether it is meant to alter its contents to that currently on the data bus. That is the purpose of the Control Bus. When an address is accessed, the lines on the control bus will state whether the location is to be read or written. These control signals are organised by the CPU and are either *'read'* or *'write'* instructions dependent on the task required.

Examples of typical operations may be:

- reading a new instruction from the program (i.e. the copy stored in memory).
- reading the contents of the ROM (remember that ROM can't be written to).
- writing to a data memory location (e.g. updating a cell in a spreadsheet).
- writing to a device memory location (e.g. sending a character to the printer).
- reading from a device memory location (e.g. reading a joystick or mouse position).

The process of getting each instruction from memory, interpreting the command and carrying it out is known as the *'fetch-decode-execute cycle'*. The following pages give a simplified version of this process but it should be noted that all computers use variations based on the system outlined. The precise details vary with the specific architecture of each CPU and the modern techniques used to speed up the process.

Inside the CPU

The diagram shows a simplified layout of a CPU architecture as used in the early basic XT PC. Many improvements are built upon this general framework.

The components are grouped under two headings:

Bus Interface Unit

This comprises the Instruction Queue, Control Unit and Address Segment Registers. These components move data in and out of the CPU and translate program instructions into CPU tasks.

The BIU also uses the Cont-rol Bus to control many of the computer's other components such as memory and peripheral devices.

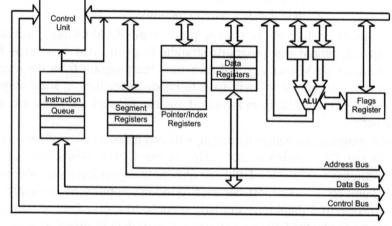

Execution Unit

This comprises the Data Registers, the Pointer Registers, the Flags Register and the Arithmetic Logic Unit. These components carry out the arithmetic and logic calculations and determine program flow using the pointer registers.

Fetching instructions

The BIU is capable of fetching a number of program instructions in a single procedure. The Instruction Queue shown stores up to six instructions at any one time. The instructions are individually taken off the top of the queue and sent to the Control Unit where they are decoded. Since these instructions are already inside the CPU, they are more quickly available than fetching from memory via the Data Bus. This pre-fetching is a simple form of *'pipelining'* and is carried out while the Execution Unit is busy executing internal instructions (e.g. arithmetical calculations). In this way, fetching and execution can be overlapped in time.

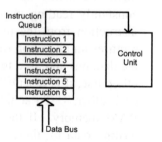

Decoding instructions

A single machine code instruction will, in practice, require a number of operations to be carried out. For example, the instruction *'CMP DL, AL'* requires that the contents of two registers be compared. This translates into smaller sub-programs to fetch the contents of register DL and place it in the ALU, fetch the contents of register AL and place it in the ALU, initiate the ALU comparison and set the flags register to reflect the results of the comparison. The Control Unit is responsible for decoding all instructions into sub-programs and transmitting the control signals in the correct sequence, with the required timings.

Storing data

The CPU has a number of internal short-term memory stores; these are used for storing values that are currently required. The number of registers used and their size varies with different CPUs.

The simple model has four data registers and these are:

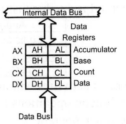

Description	Title	Use
AX	Accumulator	General Purpose. Also used to store values prior to, and resulting from, arithmetic operations.
BX	Base	General Purpose. Also used for forming base-displacement addresses.
CX	Count	General Purpose. Often used for counting.
DX	Data	General Purpose. Also used for accessing machine and system interfaces.

The above registers are 16 bits long and all 16 bits can be read or written to in one operation. However, to allow more flexibility, each register can be treated as two separate 8-bit registers. Thus, the AX register is 16-bit, while the lower byte is addressed as AL and the upper byte is addressed as AH.

Other Registers

Another set of registers is designed specifically to locate data held in memory - they *'point'* to the required locations. These registers are:

Description	Title	Use
SP	Stack Pointer	A stack is an area of memory allocated to store data. The stack works in a LIFO manner - Last In First Out. Items are placed in the stack and peeled off later in reverse order. The Stack Pointer is used by the CPU to implement the stack but is not often manipulated by the programmer.
BP	Base Pointer	This is used to access data that has been pushed on to the stack.
SI	Source Index	They can be used to form indexed addresses or to point to strings.
DI	Destination Index	
IP	Instruction Pointer	Other CPUs refer to this as the Program Counter. The register stores the address that holds the next instruction to be fetched. As the program runs, the IP will continually update to reflect the flow of the program code.

A further set of registers, known as Address Segment Registers, combine to store the addresses used for data transfers. No register in the example system is more than 16 bits wide. This stores a memory address range of 2^{16}, providing only 65,536 unique address locations.

Since even the oldest PC had 1MB of addressable locations, a 16-bit register is insufficient to store all required locations. This led to the *'segment + offset'* principle of memory addressing. One register is used to store the upper part of the memory address (the segment) while another register is used to store the lower part of the address (the offset). The combined registers form the required address.

A typical address might be DC00:0015. The first four hex characters store the segment address and the last four characters store the offset from that segment address. The *'effective address'* is calculated by multiplying the segment address by 16 and adding on the offset. Therefore, the effective address of DC00:0015 is DC015h.

The Address Segment Registers are:

Description	Title	Use
CS	Code Segment	Used with IP to form the address of the next instruction to be fetched
DS	Data Segment	Used with SI to form the address of a particular item in memory.
SS	Stack Segment	Used with SP for stack accesses.
ES	Extra Segment	Similar to DS. Used for additional data accesses.

Note The segment address is commonly used (e.g. within the BIOS, DOS commands such as EMM386, memory maps, etc) with the offset assumed to be 0000h.
For example, the 640k memory boundary may be quoted as A000h. More correctly, this should be A000:0000.

There are two types of machine code programs. One has the extension .COM (e.g. FORMAT.COM) and the other uses a .EXE extension (e.g. ATTRIB.EXE).   With COM files, the entire program including all its data and resources fits within a single 64k segment.   When run, DOS decides which segment to use and only a single 16-bit register is required to address the entire program code.   With EXE files, which are usually of large size, the program occupies several segments and the segment+offset method using two registers is required.

The ALU

The diagram shows the Arithmetic Logic Unit as a V-shaped object being fed by two *'operands'*.   An operand is a value that is about to be used for arithmetical or logic operations.

Arithmetic	+ - * /
Logic operations	AND OR NOT XOR
Operand comparisons	Is one operand greater, smaller or equal to another operand
Operand values	Is an operand's value positive, negative or equal to zero

Typical activities within an ALU are:

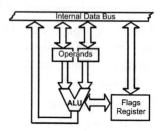

Arithmetic operations typically fetch one operand from the Accumulator and the other operand via a register.   After the arithmetic operation, the result exits the ALU and is placed into the Accumulator. These data movements take place via the CPU's internal busses.

The CPU also has a Flags Register (known in some other CPUs as the Status Register).   This is a 16-bit register where individual bits are set (i.e. 1) or cleared (i.e. 0) to notify specific results from the ALU's operation.

Flags Register

The Least Significant Bit, Bit 0, is set to indicate that an arithmetic operation resulted in a carry. Bit 6 is set when a previous instruction (e.g. Compare or Subtract) produced a zero result.   Bit 11 is set when an overflow occurred (i.e. the result is too large for the register to store it).   The program can test these flags and take appropriate action (if Bit 6 is set then jump to another piece of code; if not carry on).

The program to execute

The diagram shows an extract from a program, displaying two instructions from a larger program.

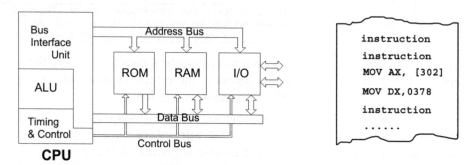

The first instruction is to read the contents of location 302 into register AX. This could be reading the value from an external sensor via an add-on data acquisition card. The next instruction places the value of 0378 into register DX.   This could be setting the system up to write to the parallel printer ports, as 0378 is the normal location of the LPT1 port.

The instructions and their values in hexadecimal are:

MOV AX,[302]	A1 02 03
MOV DX, 0378	BA 78 03

Each of these instructions would be stored in different memory locations and would be in a pure hexadecimal numeric format as shown in the example below:

Location in RAM	Location Contents	Meaning of Contents
1017	??	Part of previous instruction
1018	A1	MOV into register AX the contents of the following address
1019	02	Part of address 302
1020	03	Rest of address 302
1021	BA	MOV into DX the following number
1022	78	Part of 0378
1023	03	Rest of 0378
1024	??	Part of next instruction

The addresses shown for storing the instructions are illustrative only. Each instruction happens to occupy three bytes of memory and addresses are entered in reverse order - 0378 is stored as 78 followed by 03.

The Fetch-Decode-Execute Cycle

The steps in running the example instructions would be:

FIRST INSTRUCTION

1. The CPU's Control Unit places the value of 1018, from the Instruction Pointer, on to the Address Bus. This is the location that stores the beginning of the instruction to be fetched. Only the RAM byte at location 1018 responds to this action.

2. The Control Unit brings the MEMR control line low. This signal tells the memory chip that the contents of the location 1018 should be placed on the Data Bus. The memory chip dumps the current contents of location 1018 - i.e. the value A1 in this example - on to the Data Bus.

3. The CPU reads the value A1 off the Data Bus and restores the MEMR line to high.

4. The CPU reads locations 1019 and 1020 in the same way. It knows that the instruction consists of three parts by decoding the first value read in. The Control Unit knows that the value A1 translates to moving a value into the AX register from a port address. It also knows that the port address is two bytes long. Therefore it knows that it has to fetch two more bytes of data to make up the entire instruction.

5. The next two reads are used to determine the address for the port read. The CPU now knows that it requires to read the contents of port location 302.

6. The CPU stores the value 1021 into the Instruction Pointer - this is the location to fetch the next instruction when it has finished carrying out the current instruction.

7. The value A1 is converted by the Control Unit into a sequence of control signals, both within and outside the CPU itself, paced by the system clock.

8. The CPU places the value of 302 on to the Address Bus. This is the location that stores the beginning of the instruction to be fetched. Only the data acquisition card will respond to this activity.

9. The CPU brings the IOR control line low, telling the card that the contents of the location 302 should be placed on the Data Bus. The card chip dumps the current contents of the location on to the Data Bus.

10. The CPU reads the value off the Data Bus and restores the IOR line to high.

11. The value read from the Data Bus is placed in the AX register. The instruction has been carried out.

SECOND INSTRUCTION

12. The CPU places the value 1021 from the Instruction Pointer on to the Address Bus. 1021 is the location storing the beginning of the next instruction to be fetched. Only the RAM location 1021 will respond.

13. The Control Unit brings the MEMR control line low. This tells the memory chip that the contents of the location 1021 should be placed on the Data Bus. The memory chip dumps the contents of location 1021 - i.e. the value BA - on to the Data Bus.

14. The CPU reads the BA value off the Data Bus and restores the MEMR line to high.

15. The CPU then proceeds to read locations 1022 and 1023 in the same way. It knows that the instruction consists of three parts by decoding the first value read in. The CPU knows that the value BA translates to moving a fixed value into the DX register. It also knows that this value is two bytes long. Therefore it knows that it has to fetch two more bytes of data to make up the entire instruction.

16. The CPU stores the value 1024 into the Instruction Pointer - this is the location to fetch the next instruction when it has finished carrying out the current instruction.

17. These next two reads are used to determine the value to be placed in register DX. The CPU now knows that it requires to place the number 0378 into the DX register.

18. The DX register has 0378 placed in it. The second instruction is completed.

The CPU would then fetch the third instruction by reading the contents of location 1024. The flow chart shows the sequence of events in processing an instruction.

It should be noted, however, that programs do not continually run in an unbroken sequence.   At certain points in the program, depending upon the result of some test, the CPU may fetch an instruction from another part of the program. Since the instruction does not reside at the address stored in the Instruction Pointer, it has to alter the IP to store the exact address where the new instruction is stored.   The process is known as 'branching'.

```
         ┌─────────┐
         │  Start  │
         └────┬────┘
              │
              ▼
        ┌──────────────┐
        │  Fetch the   │
        │ Instruction  │
        │ and Decode it│
        └──────┬───────┘
               │
               ▼
 ┌────────────┐   ┌──────────────┐
 │Fetch the next│  │ Increment the│
 │ byte of the │  │ Instruction  │
 │ instruction │  │   Pointer    │
 └────────────┘   └──────┬───────┘
        ▲                │
        │   No     ▼
        └────◇ Have all
             │ bytes been
             │  fetched?
                 │ Yes
                 ▼
        ┌──────────────┐
        │ Execute the  │
        │ Instruction  │
        └──────────────┘
```

Interrupts and Polling

The computer runs a program by the repeated use of the fetch-execute-decode cycle, systematically working through the program instructions.   Once a program has started there has to be provision for the user to control the flow of the program (e.g. by key presses or mouse clicks).   The CPU also has to handle external error conditions (e.g. writing to an unformatted floppy disk or a memory parity error).   If the CPU had to continually test whether the keyboard or mouse had been used, etc, a great deal of machine time would be wasted through this 'polling' of devices.   A more efficient method is to allow the CPU to proceed as normal and only interrupt the program when an event is triggered.

The program sequence can be interrupted at any point by outside events, such as:

- Those generated by the computer's own hardware (such as a user pressing a key or the computer's built-in clock being incremented).
- Those generated inside the CPU in response to an unexpected condition (e.g. a divide-by-zero error).
- Those generated by add-on cards connected via the expansion slots on the motherboard such as the mouse port, serial port devices, network interface cards, etc.
- Those deliberately embedded inside the software program so that it can gain access to external routines in the ROM (e.g. BIOS routines) or the RAM (e.g. user-created routines).   These are called 'software interrupts' and examples are sending a character to a parallel printer (one of interrupt 17h routines) or one of the many DOS services provided by interrupt 21h (such as reading and writing to disks, reading the built-in clock, etc.).   Examples of interrupt 21h calls include display characters to the screen, or getting input from the keyboard.

256 different routines are available and each routine has its own interrupt number from interrupt 0 up to interrupt 255.

The first 16 are allocated to hardware interrupts, which means that they are designed to detect activity from hardware elements. The first eight interrupts are allocated for system activities such as detecting mathematical overflow errors or the user pressing the PrtScr key.   The next eight interrupt numbers are mainly for the use of peripheral add-on cards (for the interfacing of modems, mice, etc.).   These are called IRQ0 through to IRQ7.   (IRQ stands for Interrupt ReQuest)

A further eight interrupt lines are available from IRQ8 through to IRQ15.   These are allocated to interrupt 70 onwards as shown in the table. These IRQs are serviced by an extra controller chip.

Num	Description
00	Divide Error
01	Single Step / Debugging
02	Non-Maskable Interrupt / Parity Error
03	Breakpoint / Debugging
04	Overflow
05	Print Screen
06	Reserved
07	Reserved
08	IRQ0 - Timer
09	IRQ1 - Keyboard
0A	IRQ2 - Cascade to second PIC
0B	IRQ3 - COM2
0C	IRQ4 - COM1
0D	IRQ5 - LPT2
0E	IRQ6 - Floppy Controller
0F	IRQ7 - LPT1

70	IRQ8 - Real-Time Clock
71	IRQ9 - Re-directed IRQ2
72	IRQ10 - Reserved
73	IRQ11 - Reserved
74	IRQ12 - PS/2 Mouse
75	IRQ13 - Maths Processor
76	IRQ14 - Hard Disc
77	IRQ15 - Reserved

There is room for confusion because the IRQ numbers that users see and set within utilities do not equate to the interrupt numbers within the system.   A look at the chart will show that IRQ0 is interrupt 08, IRQ1 is interrupt 09 and so on.

Note that the interrupt numbers are given in hexadecimal notation (i.e. in base 16). Examples of the first few interrupts and their uses are shown in the table.

When an interrupt occurs, the normal program is suspended and the chosen *'interrupt service routine'* is run instead. When the interrupt routine is completed, control is passed back to the main program, which carries on from the point where it was interrupted.

MI & NMI

There are two types of interrupt that are external to the CPU:

- Those that prevent the computer program from proceeding any further. Examples of these problems are falling supply voltage in the computer or a memory parity failure. These are so serious that they cannot be disabled via software - i.e. they are interrupts that are unable to be masked. These are known as NMI (Non Maskable Interrupts) and are not normally altered by the user or technician.

- Those that denote non-fatal errors or are deliberate acts within a program (e.g. BIOS calls). These interrupts are commonly used by application packages as it makes sense to use the existing routines provided within the BIOS chip. These are known as MI (Maskable Interrupts) and allow operations that require strict timing - such as disk activities - to carry on unhindered. In these cases, the interrupt request is only carried out when the CPU is ready to handle it.

Since there are two levels of interrupt, there is a separate electrical line for each on the motherboard.

Prioritisation of Interrupts

It is likely that more than one interrupt will occur at any time and the CPU has to be told which ones are the most important to service. The table shows the priorities for various interrupt conditions. Note that the first column shows system interrupt numbers and not IRQs. If the CPU is servicing a low priority interrupt and a higher priority interrupt is triggered, the CPU suspends the lower interrupt routine and only returns to it when the higher priority interrupt has been successfully completed. This practice of interrupts interrupting other interrupts is called the *'nesting of interrupts'*.

Interrupt Type	Priority	Example	Source
Int 0	1	Dividing a number by 0	Inside the CPU
Int 4	1	Overflow - Calculation result is too large to store	Inside the CPU
Software	1	Interrupts calls within program code	Inside the CPU
Int 2	2	NMI - Memory parity error	External to CPU
Hardware	3	MI - Keyboard, I/O, etc	External to CPU
Int 1	4	Single stepping during debugging	Inside the CPU

The hardware interrupts from the slave PIC are serviced first, followed by those generated in the master PIC. IRQs 8, 13 and 14 are pre-allocated to the clock, coprocessor/FPU and disk controller respectively. In addition IRQ 9 is used to cascade to the master PIC. Similarly, IRQs 0,1,2 and 6 in the master PIC are pre-allocated. The remaining IRQs are either available (i.e. not yet allocated to any device) or are alterable (e.g. a sound card can use IRQ5 nominally allocated to LPT2).

The IRQs are serviced in the following order: 0, 1, 2, 8, 9, 10, 11, 12, 13, 14, 15, 3, 4, 5, 6, 7

Hardware Interrupt Handling

Program interrupts are handled by dedicated chips called the *'interrupt controllers'* or *'Programmable Interrupt Controllers'* (PICs). These connect to the various hardware lines that require servicing. These can be seen in the expansion slot connector diagrams later in this chapter. One PIC handles the lower eight interrupts while another (Slave PIC) chip handles a further eight interrupts and channels them through the first PIC.

The routines for handling all these interrupts are stored in the computer's memory. This is likely to be within the machine's BIOS chip although a routine could also be stored as a TSR somewhere in the main memory area. When an interrupt occurs, the CPU has to know where the routine for that particular interrupt is stored. This achieved by holding the addresses of all the interrupt routines in the first 1k of the conventional memory - from address 0000h to 0400h. This is known as the *'interrupt vector table'* and each interrupt number has a corresponding 4-byte address that points to where the interrupt handling routine can be found. The diagram shows the relationship between the various components and activities.

Example

Here are the steps that result from the user pressing a key on the keyboard.

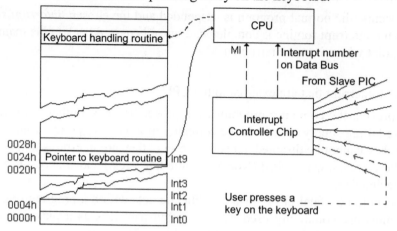

- The user presses the key.
- This activates the hardware line from the keyboard to the Programmable Interrupt Controller (PIC).
- The PIC activates the MI line to the CPU.
- The CPU takes a note of where it is in the main program so that it can return to that point again later.
- The PIC places the interrupt number (9 in this case) on the Data Bus.
- The CPU uses this number to fetch the address of the keyboard handling routine. Since each interrupt vector is 4 bytes long, the wanted vector is stored at an address given by multiplying the interrupt number by four. So, in this example, the vector is stored at 9x4 = address 36 (which is 24h in hexadecimal).
- The CPU fetches the vector from the interrupt vector table - in this case the four bytes stored from address 24h onwards.
- The CPU runs the routine that is located at this address.
- When the routine is completed, control is passed back to the main program. The CPU remembers where it stopped processing the main program and returns to that point for further processing.

The above sequence will be identical for any add-on cards that are using the IRQ lines.

The NMI (Non Maskable Interrupt) Line is not handled through the PIC and has its own logic chips and its own direct line to the CPU.

Software Interrupt Handling

Interrupt calls that are made within a piece of software are handled in a slightly simpler fashion than that shown above. The CPU is informed of the interrupt number by the software call, the normal operation of the program is suspended and the interrupt number is multiplied by four as in step 6 above. It then carries out steps 7 to 9 as already explained.

Plug-and-Play PCI Interrupts

The older ISA system worked, but because the number of IRQs available was almost always limited to 16, upgrading systems was often a hit-and-miss affair and involved a lot of manual configuration. The PCI system can use Plug-and-Play technology, with several benefits including the ability to share an IRQ between devices.

Plug and Play needs three key elements:
- The PC must support it (this is provided in all new computers).
- The adapter cards must support it (almost all new cards and devices have this feature).
- The operating system must support it (Windows 95 onwards do; NT, OS/2 and DOS don't).

PCI systems have a PnP-specific BIOS, which extends the normal BIOS POST operations to include device configuration. This auto-configuring of cards makes alterations and additions to hardware a simpler process. With all other buses, the addition or swapping of cards involves ensuring that there is no clash of memory addresses, IRQs and DMA channels between the existing and the new devices (see the chapter on *'Hardware Installation'*). These problems are intended to be eliminated with PCI since the BIOS will maintain a list of all memory addresses, IRQs and DMAs in use and provide non-conflicting allocations for new cards. Each of the new PCI plug-and-play cards has its own *'configuration space'* - usually a set of memory registers that are solely devoted to storing configuration information. The Plug and Play BIOS chip interrogates these registers to determine the card manufacturer and type and the range of options it can handle. The cards are all capable of working with a range of different memory addresses, IRQs, etc. The BIOS determines the best settings for the cards and sends data to be stored in each card's configuration space detailing what the specific settings for the card are.

With Windows 3.1, the basic plug and play services were supplemented by providing *'BIOS extensions'* (software to link the BIOS facilities and the extra facilities). Windows, from version 95 onwards, has the additional services designed into the operating system.

Plug and play is fully implemented when users have the required combination of PnP BIOS, PCI motherboard, PnP operating system or BIOS extensions and all add-on cards being of the PnP variety. Additionally, some software still ignores best practice and bypasses some BIOS routines. True full PnP depends upon all the required features being present - partial benefits can be gained from a lesser specification although this will still involve some manual installation. PnP still functions when the computer has some older (non PnP) cards installed, as the PnP BIOS assigns the PnP cards' configurations around those of the existing non-PnP cards.

IRQ sharing

The PCI chipset has its own interrupt handling circuitry and does not use the two PICs previously explained. The conversion from PCI handling to the conventional handling and prioritisation is carried out by circuitry following an agreed standard known as *'Serialised IRQ Support'*. The Plug and Play BIOS will build up a *'PCI IRQ routing table'* that keeps track of IRQs assigned to PnP devices in specified physical slots. Each PnP device can use up to four interrupts, known as INTA to INTD for each particular device. The routing table combines this information into *'link values'* that distinguish between devices that share an IRQ. Sometimes, problems with the information in the Routing Table mean that sometimes simply moving a PnP card into another physical slot can resolve some hardware conflicts. It is theoretically possible to run a PnP system without IRQs as used on ISA systems; PnP IRQs are used mainly to remain compatible with legacy hardware. However, an IRQ-free system would require truly *'legacy-free'* hardware with no ISA slots, and also no motherboard ISA devices such as PS/2 mouse and keyboard connectors, serial and parallel ports and so on.

IRQ Steering in Windows

Windows 95 OSR2 and later operating systems support a system called PCI Bus IRQ Steering. This allows the operating system to assign IRQs to devices, overriding the assignments made by the BIOS, although in most cases this is not necessary. If problems arise, the BIOS can be set up to 'set aside' IRQs for older, non-PnP ISA devices to prevent conflicts. PCI Steering systems can change IRQs dynamically, for example if a PCMCIA card is attached to a laptop it can be detected and assigned an IRQ. IRQ Steering is the software interface that allows the Windows operating system to control a computer that shares IRQs between devices. The illustration shows the IRQs allocated on a typical machine, along with the IRQ Steering on the shared IRQs.

However, PCI Steering is not without its drawbacks. When changing IRQs it can cause the system to hang on occasion, and some devices may conflict with others when PCI Steering forces them to share an IRQ. If this is the case, Windows PCI Steering can be disabled through the Control Panel, and the BIOS usually has a setting called *'PnP Aware OS'* which can be set to *'No'*.

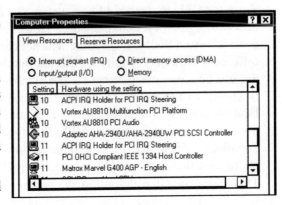

Note: Practical consideration of IRQ usage is covered in the chapter on *'Hardware Installation'*.

Processor Speed

The speed of any microprocessor is often judged purely by the internal clock speed – in other words, the time taken for each processor cycle. However, this is not the be-all and end-all of CPU performance. The following factors also affect the overall speed of the processor:

- Bus size. The width of the data bus determines how much data can be transferred between the CPU and main memory in any given cycle. Obviously, a larger bus size means more potential throughput. The amount of data transferred is known as a '*word*', and thus this measurement is also called '*word length*'.
- Cycles per instruction. Each machine code instruction takes a number of clock cycles to execute. There are many factors in this, such as the time taken to decode instructions, the number and usage of internal registers, and so on. Generally, though, RISC instructions tend to be executed faster than CISC instructions.
- Instruction coding. The type of machine code instructions available also has an effect on performance. SIMD (Single Instruction, Multiple Data) instructions also provide improved performance by eliminating the need to repeat the same instruction on multiple items of data.

Speeding up the process

It is assumed so far that each new instruction is fetched from the memory <u>after</u> the previous instruction has been fully executed. If this were so, the only way to increase the computer's efficiency would be to increase the rate at which the CPU was clocked through the fetch-decode-execute cycle. Already, clock speeds have been raised from the original 4.77MHz to around 3GHz. However, the laws of physics and the cost of manufacture restrict the ability to continually raise machine clock speeds. Very fast CPUs, for, example, would require very fast address buses and data buses, since these support chips would have to be able to keep up with the demands of the CPU. This would result in a very expensive motherboard. In practice, other methods are used to speed up the CPU's efficiency. These include:

- increasing the data bus width so that a larger data word is handled with each read or write, thus saving on the time required to execute several smaller reads or writes.
- pre-fetching techniques, to read several instructions at a time, saving subsequent reads.
- pipelining techniques, to decode one instruction while carrying out another, saving time.
- using two ALUs, or two or more CPUs, so that several instructions can be processed simultaneously.
- using a maths co-processor, or FPU, to carry out the number crunching while the main CPU carries out other tasks. These are add-on chips to older CPUs, while today's chips have the FPU built in.
- clock multiplying - making the operations inside the CPU chip run faster while maintaining the existing speeds for the main buses and motherboard devices.
- introducing efficient memory caching systems, either built in to the CPU chip and/or as external secondary cache.
- Using multiple processor cores, or even multiple processors.

Measuring performance

Comparison of performance between different computers requires some standard for measurement. Different systems are in use but they all seek to measure the *'throughput'* of the computer - how much work it can get through in a given time, usually one second.

CPU standards

Since the CPU is stepped by the system clock at speeds ranging from 4MHz to over 2GHz, this could be a starting point for comparison. However, many instructions require more than one clock cycle to complete, so a 900MHz machine will not carry out 900 million instructions per second. In addition, different CPUs may require a different number of clock cycles to carry out the same kind of activity. So, one common measurement is the number of instructions that can be carried out in a second. This is known as the 'MIPS' rating (<u>M</u>illions of <u>I</u>nstructions <u>P</u>er <u>S</u>econd). Another standard notes that floating point operations (handling real numbers) are the most demanding of a computer's processing time and therefore measures 'MFLOPS' (<u>M</u>illions of <u>F</u>loating Point <u>O</u>perations <u>P</u>er <u>S</u>econd) or even Gigaflops. However, these standards do not take into account the word size of the CPU. An instruction that handles a 32-bit number will operate faster than one that only handles 8-bit numbers. This has evolved a definition of *'memory bandwidth'* that looks at the millions of memory bits accessed per second. This standard is dependent on clock speed, the average clock cycles for instructions and the memory word length; it is therefore a more accurate reflection of machine performance. Intel introduced the iCOMP index for comparing 32-bit systems.

Machine standards

The above measurements, though important, do not accurately measure the whole machine's performance. A slow disk system, slow memory chips or a poor graphics card can easily mar a fast CPU performance. For this reason, utilities are available to produce a factor that takes into account all components of the system. Scores are produced for each component (e.g. CPU, maths co-processor, memory, video, and disk) and an overall performance score. Examples of these utilities are PC Bench, PC Tools and Norton Utilities. The figures still have to be interpreted by the user. For example, a machine mostly used for graphics would require the best video and CPU performance while a machine mostly used for databases would benefit greatly from a good disk sub-system; a multimedia workstation would require all components to be top performers.

Application standards

From the user's point of view what matters is the speed in carrying out real-world applications. The time taken to perform normal application tasks is a more useful yardstick of a computer's performance than simple CPU speed or machine speed measurements. AMD use an *'XP'* system (not to be confused with Windows XP) whereby their processor's performance is rated according to the equivalent level of Pentium clock speed. For example, the AMD 3800XP chip theoretically presents the same level of performance as a 3.8GHz Pentium, even though the AMD 3800XP chip has a physically slower clock speed. In older machines, a similar system known as the '*P-rating*' system was used. For machines with Windows-based applications, performance-measuring utilities include WinBench and WinStone.

Von Neumann Model

Computers were, and still largely remain, based around the model developed by Von Neumann in the 1940's. The main points are:

- The same memory is used for storing both input and output.
- The memory holds a 'stored program' of instructions.
- The Program Counter maintains the program flow by pointing to the next instruction.
- The CPU can adopt one of a finite range of states.
- The action taken by the CPU depends upon its current state and current input.
- The instructions are fetched and executed one at a time.

Treating each stage of the fetch-decode-execute cycle as separate sequential activities produces system bottlenecks and other approaches have been developed to increase throughput.

Pre-Fetching & Pipelining

As mentioned, the CPU has its own internal registers that are, in effect, fast access memory stores. These are fast because they are already internal to the CPU and don't suffer the slow fetch times associated with the addressing of external memory chips. Unfortunately, these registers are also used for holding intermediate data for calculations and comparisons. The solution lies in providing other internal stores within the CPU, capable of providing fast access to instructions and/or data. This is called the *'pre-fetch buffer'* and Intel's 8086 began with a buffer area capable of storing six pre-fetched instruction bytes. When the wanted instruction was read from memory, the CPU fetched the next instruction(s) at the same time. The system was designed so that the buffer would be refilled every time it dropped to below five bytes and the CPU was not already accessing memory.

The 80386 attempted a form of *'pipelining'* to speed up operations within the CPU. This system realised that while instruction 1 is being executed, instruction 2 and probably instruction 3 are already stored in the CPU. It is able to apply the decode phase to instruction 2 while concurrently carrying out the execute phase for instruction 1. This was a sound theory but was never fully exploited in the 386 chip.

The 486 took the pre-fetch a stage further, with its *'burst mode'* approach. The first initial access of a memory address is still relatively slow but reading the subsequent adjacent memory addresses is much faster. This, coupled to a block of 8k of static cache RAM built into the CPU, resulted in much improved processing times. The sequence in a 486 was defined as instruction fetch, instruction decode, address generation (described by Intel as *'Decode 2'*), execution and write-back (writing its results back to an internal register). This system allowed instruction 1 to be at the write-back stage, while instruction 2 was at the execute stage and instruction 3 was at the decode stage. Modern Pentium chips break the pipelining into multiple operations. This speeds up performance and is known as super-pipelining.

Superscalar Architecture

The Pentium moves the process even further with a *'superscalar architecture'*, which means that it has two separate ALUs.   Each of these pipelines is capable of processing an instruction and the resultant system is capable of processing two instructions simultaneously. Since not all instructions have to be carried out in a serial fashion, this will speed up some sections of code. This capability would not be used where an instruction must follow another in time (e.g. the second instruction is dependent upon the output of the first instruction). The Pentium has two internal 8k caches, one for storing instructions and the other for storing data. Pre-fetch buffers supply the two ALU pipelines, known as the U-Pipe and the V-Pipe.   A new *'Branch Prediction'* unit examines the instruction cache, predicts the most likely flow of instructions and feeds the pipelines accordingly. This technology, in processing multiple instructions, moves away from the original Von Neumann principle on which computers were designed.

Parallel Processing

Both pipelining and superscalar systems are elementary forms of parallel processing, in that more than one processing task is taking place at any one time. Full parallel processing is available with the use of two or more separate CPU chips. These communicate with each other to share tasks most effectively. This is the basis of the *'transputers'* that are being developed at the supercomputer end of the market. However, PCs are already available employing two or four Pentium chips.   These are currently aimed at the network server market, so that server tasks and database engine tasks can be carried out simultaneously. Standalone dual Pentium systems offer around an 80% increase in performance.

Hyperthreading

Recent processors have introduced 'Hyperthreading' technology.   The first processors with this capability were the 3.06GHz Pentium 4's, but it has already been added to lower specification processors. Hyperthreading is only available when supported by the processor, the motherboard, and the operating system.   At present, the only operating system which fully supports Hyperthreading is Windows XP, although some Linux versions support it to some degree. Hyperthreading allows a single physical processor to operate as if it were multiple 'virtual' processors. In theory, this provides most of the benefits of a multi-processor system, using only one processor. This has a significant effect on improving speed for processor-intensive tasks such as graphical design, with some reports stating around a 25% speed increase, but is of considerably less importance in a typical office desktop system.

System Clock

The computer's system clock provides the pulses that are used for all timing in the CPU, on buses, etc. The clock is a piece of circuitry that provides a train of pulses at very precise intervals. It uses a slice of quartz that oscillates at a fixed rate when a voltage is applied to it. The tiny changes in current are picked up by the clock circuitry and are used to supply a fixed pulse rate to the computer. The final working frequency of the clock circuitry is usually determined by the setting of jumpers on the motherboard.

Clock-Multiplying

Introduced with Intel's 486 processor, all CPUs are clocked to run faster than the main computer bus speeds. This is termed *'clock multiplying'*. By having extra memory, known as *'cache memory'*, built in to the chip, the CPU can read ahead and pre-fetch both data and program instructions. This way, the amount of traffic between the chip and the bus is reduced by around 50%.   As a consequence, the <u>internal</u> speed of the CPU can be doubled or tripled without straining the CPU/bus interface. For example, the overall system could run at 25MHz while the CPU ran at 50MHz.

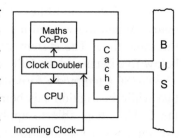

The first Intel chips to benefit from clock multiplying were the 486 range. A clock-doubled 486 chip was known as a *'DX2'*. So, a 486DX2/66 was a 486 machine with a 33MHz clock being doubled inside the CPU to 66MHz.   Intel's *'clock tripled'* CPUs were designed to treble the internal running of the CPU compared to the normal clock rate of the system.   This was the *'DX4'* range and they took a 25MHz machine and ran the CPU at 75MHz.   The 100MHz model of the chip could either treble a 33MHz system or double a 50MHz system to produce the 100MHz internal clock rate.

Pentium Settings

The technique continues in the Pentium range and its clones. The *'clock'* frequency (i.e. number of pulses per second) is divided down and used to supply the timing pulses on the PCI bus. The same clock frequency is also multiplied by a chosen factor and clocks the internal operation of the CPU. Links on jumper blocks are set to determine the clock's working frequency; other jumpers set the multiplication factor.

Although a wide variety of clock speeds and CPU multipliers were produced, the vast majority on sale today are at 200MHz to 333MHz (although see 'quad pumping' below), with a clock multiplier of between x7 and x28.

The example shows a 100MHz clock being divided down by a factor of three (i.e. for every three pulses incoming pulses the divider sends out a single pulse) to provide the 33MHz rate used by the PCI bus. The same 100MHz signal is multiplied up by a factor 5 (i.e. for every one incoming pulse the multiplier sends out five clock pulses).

Typical Clock Multipliers				
CPU	Basic Clock Frequency			
Multiplier	100MHz	200MHz	266MHz	333MHz
X7		1400MHz	1866MHz	2333MHz
X8		1600MHz	2133MHz	2667MHz
X8.5				2833MHz
X9		1800MHz	2400MHz	3000MHz
X9.5		1900MHz	2533MHz	3166MHz
X10		2000MHz	2667MHz	
X10.5		2100MHz		
X11		2200MHz	2933MHz	
X11.5		2300MHz		
X12		2400MHz		
X12.5		2500MHz		
X13	1300MHz	2600MHz	3466MHz	
X14	1400MHz	2800MHz	3733MHz	
X15	1500MHz	3000MHz		
X16	1600MHz	3200MHz		
X17	1700MHz	3400MHz		
X18	1800MHz	3600MHz		
X19	1900MHz	3800MHz		
X20	2000MHz			
X21	2100MHz			
X22	2200MHz			
X23	2300MHz			
X24	2400MHz			

A Pentium with a 233MHz clock speed and a multiplier of 10 produces a CPU speed of 2.33GHz. Similarly, an Athlon at 133Mhz with a multiplier of 13 produces 1.73GHz CPU speed.

Operations via the separate memory bus are processed at the basic clock rate. Early Pentium and Pentium Pro systems used a 60MHz bus, but this was later replaced with a 66MHz bus. The Pentium II uses either a 66MHz or 100MHz bus, while the Pentium III bus was from 100 to 166MHz. Pentium 4 buses ran from 100MHz up to 266MHz, while Core 2 use a bus from 166 to 333MHz.

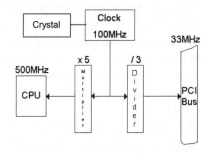

Some CPUs have fixed multipliers (see *'Overclocking'* in the *'Hardware Installation'* chapter).

Quad Pumping

Many intel buses use multiple channels, in a technique they call *'quad pumping'*, which raises the effective bus speeds by a factor of four. Since it is not an actual bus speed, this speed is instead referred to in terms of its data transfer capacity, and as such measured in 'MegaTransfers per Second' (MT/s). For example a 266MHz system could be quad pumped to 1066MT/s.

Maths Co-processors

Early PCs allowed the addition of an extra chip to improve the computer's number crunching operations. The 8086 chip had the 8087 companion chip, the 80286 had the 80287, the 80386 had the 80387 and the 486SX had the 80487. The 486DX and the Pentium range of chips have their own maths co-processors built in to the CPU, often referred to as the Floating Point Unit (FPU).

The demand for maths co-processor chips resulted from the design of the 80xxx series of CPU chips. The computer's main CPU is best at handling integer calculations; its speed drops dramatically when confronted with floating point (i.e. fractions) calculations. The companion chip for the 80xxx series - known as a *'maths co-processor'* - runs in parallel (hence the term *'co-processing'*) with the main CPU.

Mathematical tasks normally undertaken by the CPU are delegated to the co-processor. The maths co-processor chip, unlike the main CPU, is not designed for a general-purpose role; it is tailored to carrying out its functions in the most efficient way possible. The co-processor built in to the 486DX chip, for example, has relatively large 80-bit registers, to manipulate very large numbers with great accuracy.

This provides great potential advantages:
- The co-processor is much quicker at mathematical calculations.
- The main CPU is freed to carry out other tasks.

However, there are a number of other considerations:
- This great improvement only occurs for a <u>proportion</u> of the machine time, since the computer only spends a proportion of its time on mathematical calculations.
- Some applications benefit much more from the maths co-processor than others. For example, there is no advantage for word processing, as the number crunching element is almost non-existent. Besides, by far the slowest link in the chain is the user. The machine spends most of its time waiting for the typist. There is also little benefit for database operation, as most database activity requires file accesses, which are very slow compared to any processing activity. The collation of figures for reports would involve some calculations including real numbers expressing currency. Even here, many reports tend to maintain integer counts and totals. However, dramatic performance increases can normally be expected with computer-aided design packages. These rely heavily on the calculation of curves, etc. and are all equipped to use a maths co-processor to best advantage. Similarly, graphics, Desk Top Publishing and other graphic-oriented applications also rely on substantial amounts of number crunching to calculate arcs, vector co-ordinates, etc.

CPU Cache Memory

Standard memory speeds have not progressed at the same rate as processor speeds. As a result, the CPU can process data faster than the data can be fetched from memory or placed in memory. The Pentium III front side bus operates at no more than 133MHz while the CPU can run at up to 1.3GHz. The Pentium 4 system has an effective memory transfer rate of up to 1066MHz, while the CPU can run in excess of 3GHz. Consider that a 3.06GHz CPU cycles every 0.3ns while the fastest access time for main memory is around 0.9ns. This means that the CPU has to stand idle while data is transferred in from memory. This waiting is enforced by *'wait states'*, which prolong the CPU's access cycle time. While this matches the performance of the CPU to that of the computer memory, it slows down the effective CPU operating speed.

The simple solution to this bottleneck is to use much faster RAM as main memory. However, CPU speed is growing faster than RAM speed, so this is not a cost-effective solution. It would also be extremely wasteful to have expensive RAM sitting doing little, while most of the computer activity centres round only a small portion of the memory at any one time.

A favoured solution is to use a small block of very fast RAM between the CPU and the main memory. This is known as *'cache memory'*. Any data held in the cache memory can be transferred to the CPU at greater speeds, due to its faster access time, normally equal to the internal clock speed of the CPU. This means that the CPU can access memory without the need for wait states. The result of using cache memory is to dispense with wasted CPU time and to increase computer efficiency. Since the block of fast SRAM is likely to be substantially smaller than the computer's main memory, the cache memory can only hold a portion of the data that is resident in main memory. The aim is to ensure that only the data most likely to be required is stored in cache memory. This relies on two established facts, collectively known as the *'principle of locality'*.

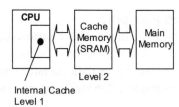

- The running of application programs involves jumping and looping through different parts of the long list of program instructions. Despite this, most program activities are sequential - an instruction follows from a previous program instruction, with occasional jumps to other program areas. When arrived at the new program area, the machine then progresses sequentially through the new area. Often, the same few instructions are repeated over and over again as part of some iterative process.
- The data for programs is often grouped together in sequential fashion. For example, a payroll program will process employee 75 after employee 74, and so on. Also, data recently read is likely to be the data to be written. The same payroll program, for example, will read an employee's wage record, calculate new figures and write the new results over the old record data.

If the data is often accessed sequentially, then a group of data is transferred from main memory into cache memory. This one-off transfer will take place at the slowest speed - i.e. that of the main memory, wait states and all. Any subsequent requests for data are transferred to the CPU at the higher cache memory speed. Concentrating the program's main data into the fast memory ensures that the performance is optimised. When another area of data is requested - one not already stored in cache - the data is transferred from main memory into cache memory, along with the contiguous data in main memory. The fetch of the first piece of data, in this case, is actually slower than normal, since an entire block of data was transferred at a wait-state speed. However, since subsequent fetches from that memory block are faster, the <u>overall</u> effect is to speed up processing.

Therein lie the limitations of cache memory:

- If the cache contains data transferred due to a previous CPU request, there is no guarantee that the next CPU request will be for data from the same block. In that circumstance, there is no *'cache hit'*, i.e. the requested data is not to be found in cache memory. The requested data, as part of a new block of data, is transferred from main memory to cache. This means that the time taken to transfer the previous block was largely wasted and the efficiency of the computer has been reduced.
- The benefits of caching vary with the type of application in use. A program that uses a lot of data transfers benefits from a large cache memory. On the other hand, a program that is processor intensive (any number-crunching application) requires less data transfers and does not benefit to the same extent.

Despite these limitations, cache memory greatly improves the computer's overall processing times.

Cache Organisation

Just as any cache memory is better than no cache memory, the way that the cache memory is organised and read/written has a bearing on its performance. The material so far has outlined how data is fetched from main memory to cache, to CPU. Of course, any data that is <u>written</u> to cache memory also has to be reflected in changes to main memory. A number of different methods of reading and writing exist and they affect the performance of the cache. Predictably, the faster the method, the more costly the product. Users have no control over the method of reading and writing cache, other than at the purchasing stage.

Read Methods
LOOK THROUGH
   The CPU requests data from the cache. If it is not in the cache, the CPU requests the data from the main memory. This would involve a second read request, which would slow the process.

LOOK ASIDE
   The CPU interrogates the cache memory and the main memory at the same time. If the data is in the cache memory, it is transferred at the faster rate; otherwise, it is fetched more slowly via main memory.

Write Methods
WRITE THROUGH
   The CPU updates the cache and the data in the cache is used to update the contents of main memory. An improvement on this method is to store all writes to main memory in a queue within the cache and copy from the queue to main memory. This requires an area of cache memory to be set aside to store the data queue but it has the advantage of allowing the cache to write data to the main memory at a quiet time on the data bus - and without tying up the CPU. This method is used with some 386 CPUs and all 486 CPUs.

WRITE BACK
   This is similar to the improved *'write through'* method, except that the main memory is only updated if there is a difference in the contents of the cache and the corresponding section of main memory. This is the method used with all CPUs in the Pentium range.

Cache Architecture
The data transfers are carried out by dedicated *'cache controllers'*. When the CPU requests access to the data at a particular address, the cache controller checks whether that address appears in the cache memory. If the address is already in the cache memory - a *'hit'* - then the address contents can be used by the CPU without recourse to the main memory. If the address is not found in cache memory - a *'cache miss'* - the cache controller has to access the main memory (and update the cache memory).

The hit rate of the cache is determined by:
- The cache size. A large cache stores more address information and increases the likelihood of the required data being in cache. This can be improved by adding increased memory to the cache and is a good way to improve a machine fitted with slow main memory chips of, say, 70ns or 100ns access time.
- The bus size between main memory and cache. A wide bus transfers data between main memory and cache memory at a faster rate, for those occasions when a cache miss is encountered.
- The way the cache is organised. The common methods are 'direct mapped' and 'associative cache'. These control the link between main and cache memory and cannot be altered.

With large caches, a lot of time can be spent searching the cache. If the wanted data is not present, then the extra time has been wasted. However, if multitasking is required, then a large cache size speeds up processing. Off-the-shelf computers are supplied with a variety of cache options. Older computers had from zero to 256k of cache. Modern computers have 512k up to 2MB of cache.

Primary/Secondary Cache

Pentium chips already have a small area of cache memory built in to the CPU chip. This is known as *'Primary Caching'* or *'Level 1 Caching'*. This is often considered inadequate and can be supplemented with the addition of extra *'Secondary' or 'Level 2'* caching, which may be external but is internal on modern chips. The Pentium II has two 16k L1 caches but reverts to an external cache that runs at half the speed of the CPU. The Celeron Pentium II has 128KB of cache while the Xeon has a 512KB, 1MB or a 2MB L2 cache, both types running at full CPU speed. The Pentium 4 uses 20KB of L1 cache and 256KB of L2 cache.

The table shows some common memory speeds:

	486DX	Pentium	Pentium Pro	Pentium II	Xeon	Pentium III	Pentium 4
System	33MHz	66MHz	66MHz	100MHz	100MHz	100MHz	400MHz
CPU	100MHz	233MHz	200MHz	450MHz	400MHz	550MHz	2GHz
L1	10ns	4ns	5ns	2-3ns	2ns	2ns	0.5ns
L2	30ns	15ns	5ns	4-6ns	2ns	4ns	0.5ns
Main Memory	60ns	60ns	60ns	10ns	10ns	10ns	1.2ns

Direct Memory Access

The concept of DMA is explained in the Operating Systems chapter. However, the OS is not the only part of the computer that deals with DMA transfers. The motherboard, chipset, and CPU must all be designed with DMA capabilities, to allow the computer to be able to take advantage of this technology. All modern PCs are equipped with DMA capabilities, usually in the form of bus mastering.

Bus Mastering

In a basic, non-bus mastered system, the data bus is under the control of the main processor. The CPU is the *'master'* of the bus. Some types of data bus, however, allow the chipset to become the *'bus master'*, and direct all of the memory data transfers. This is not really supported by the ISA bus (both on design and speed grounds). The MCA, EISA and PCI buses are designed to handle multiple bus mastering, where a system of interleaved bus transfer cycles means that a high speed bus can service several slower speed devices (e.g. network interface cards). The bus mastering system on a common PCI bus therefore provides DMA capability, along with other benefits such as IRQ Steering.

Benefits of DMA

At its best, DMA can carry out data transfers between memory and other devices on the data bus, while the CPU works on processing instructions in its cache. However, the benefits can vary widely. The performance of a DMA system depend on many factors, such as:
- The amount of data the DMA system is asked to transfer. Small transfers might occur with little interruption to processing time. However, long transfers might empty the CPU cache, resulting in the DMA transfer having to be interrupted so that more instructions can be passed to the CPU.
- The bandwidth of the data bus, and the processing speed of the CPU. If the bus transfers more data within a given time, there is an improved chance of any given DMA transfer completing before causing any disruption to the processor. However, the faster the CPU runs, the more it will have to use the data bus and therefore the less effective the DMA system becomes.
- The CPU utilisation. A program that is processor-intensive might require very little access to the data bus, making background DMA transfers highly effective. However, a program that relies heavily on processing data that is coming from an external source, such as compressing incoming video signals, will benefit little from DMA.

Actual figures for speed improvements caused by DMA are difficult to measure. However, the graph shows in general terms the sort of performance improvement the system can bring. The system is

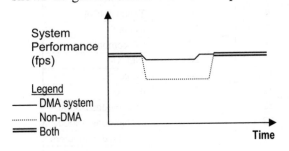

measuring screen updates in frames per second. Note that even the DMA system does suffer some loss of performance during a transfer – this is due to the CPU's reduced access to the data bus. However, the loss of performance is not as great as with a non-DMA system, as the latter will force the CPU to multi-task between screen updates and CPU-controlled I/O. Because of this, the non-DMA system also takes longer to complete the data transfer, and return to its normal level of performance.

Processor Development

The very first computers were composed of high-energy vacuum tubes. These '*first generation*' computers were enormous, power-hungry machines the size of a large room. The '*second generation*' appeared when the transistor was developed, and were smaller, more efficient and more reliable. However, they were still very cumbersome, being composed of numerous Printed Circuit Boards (PCBs) that each had a limited purpose.

The '*third generation*' were based on Integrated Circuits (ICs), which are etched silicon chips containing large numbers of transistors. Nevertheless, every computer needed many of these chips to perform their functions. The last giant leap in computing came in 1971 with Intel's development of the 4004 chip, widely acknowledged as the world's first microprocessor.

The 4004 was designed for use in a printing calculator, but proved so versatile that Intel bought back the rights to the design, and began work on improving it. Several chips followed during the mid-70s, such as the 8-bit 8008 and 8080 chips, but these achieved only limited success. In the meantime, numerous other 8-bit chips cropped up, with widely varying popularity. The two most successful of these were themselves 8-bit chips based in part on the Intel range, and included the Zilog Z80 and MOS 6502. The Zilog Z80 was used with the CP/M operating system, which was later to become the basis for the DOS operating system. The 6502 was an inexpensive chip, and so was chosen for the Apple II computer.

However, it was not until Intel released the 8088 chip that personal computers started to become widespread. The 8088 was in fact a cut-price version of the 16-bit 8086 chip that used only an 8-bit external data bus. This enabled cheaper add-on cards, which prompted IBM to use the chip in their then new XT computers.

Intel's main rivals have been Motorola. Although they had limited success with the 6800 chip, it was the successor 68000 series of chips that were to be Intel's main competition for some time, as it was chosen to be the processor for the Apple Mac computer.

More recently, however, RISC (Reduced Instruction Set Computing) chips have become popular, based on the idea of a smaller set of machine code instructions, that execute faster. Acorn, who developed a number of home computers in previous decades, is widely credited with developing the first commercial RISC chip intended for personal computers. This was the ARM1 (Acorn RISC machine, later renamed the Advanced RISC machine), although few of this chip were made. Instead, the ARM2 was the first widely manufactured ARM chip, basically a slightly improved ARM1. ARM chips are generally very well designed, providing good performance despite their slow clock rating, and having considerably lower power requirements than Intel processors. For this reason, many ARM chips have seen wide use as embedded processors within a range of consumer electronics, from palmtop computers to car electronics. ARM chips have also influenced a number of subsequent RISC designs, including that of the PowerPC 601 chip.

The table overleaf shows some of the characteristics of the most influential chips prior to the 286.

	Year	Transistors	Clock speed	Data bus	Address bus	Used in
Intel 4004	1971	2300	740kHz	4	10	Calculator
Zilog Z80	1976	8500	2.5MHz	8	16	Tandy TRS-80
MOS 6502	1976	9000	2MHz	8	16	Apple II
Intel 8086	1979	29,000	4.7MHz	16	20	PC compatibles
Intel 8088	1979	29,000	4.7MHz	8	20	IBM XT
Motorola 68000	1979	68,000	8MHz	32/16	24	Apple
Intel 286	1982	134,000	8-12MHz	16	24	IBM AT
ARM2	1985	25,000	8MHz	32	26	Archimedes A3000
ARM3	1989	300,000	24-33MHz	32	26	Archimedes A5000
ARM250	1992	100,000	12-16MHz	32	26	Handheld computers
ARM600	1991	360,000	20-33MHz	32	32	Handheld computers

Multi-processor systems and multi-core CPUs

The ever-increasing clock speeds of CPUs has slowed down, due to the limitations of current technology. To get faster computers, the processing power of a PC is now enhanced by using more than one CPU.

This is achieved by having a motherboard with two CPUs on board, or by having a single chip which has two or more CPUs built into it.

Multi-processor systems are still generally relegated to server systems, with multi-core processors providing a more cost-effective solution for desktop systems.

Effectively, a multi-core processor is two or more processors on a single chip, possibly with each core having its own cache. Both AMD and Intel produce multi-core processors, and the technology is already commonplace in high end computers.

There are some important differences between the two technologies. Dual-core processors must share the front-side bus connection, while a dual-processor system does not have that bottleneck, for example. On the plus side, licensing of software is often on a per-processor basis, so it may be cheaper from a software point of view to run on a multi-core system than a multi-processor one.

Furthermore, Windows XP and Vista are able to support up to two processors on a system, however many cores those processors might have.

From an application point of view, the user should be aware that not all applications are capable of using multiple processors or cores. In particular, large number crunching applications that you may expect to benefit from this may find themselves utilising only 50% of the processor time; the second processor or core lying idle. To fully utilise both processors, the system needs to be running both a suitable operating system *and* suitable software.

The range of Intel CPUs

From the beginning of the PC range of computers, the main CPU has been from the Intel range, supplemented by other manufacturers with *'clones'* or improved versions of each chip in the series.
The series consists of the following chips:

8086

These are no longer manufactured or sold. Since it only had a 20-bit address bus, it was only capable of addressing 1MB of unique addresses. This meant that it was unable to support extended memory and was completely incapable of running Windows and most modern DOS applications. Its speed was much slower than its successors - e.g. the Pentium can be hundreds of times faster than the XT, when measured in MIPS.

286

Like the 8086, they are no longer sold, and are rarely found in current commercial use. They are slow, running at speeds from 10MHz to 20 MHz. With a 24-bit address bus, the AT was able to address up to 16 million different address locations. To complement this, the AT had two operating modes - *'real mode'*, where it used only 8086 code and acted like a fast XT and *'protected mode'*, where it was able to access beyond the 1MB address limit and employed its added features. It also ran at about 4 times the MIPS rate of the XT. Since *'real mode'* is the natural mode for normal DOS operations, the *'protected mode'* was intended for multi-tasking operations, Windows, OS/2, etc. Unfortunately, the chip was not really powerful enough for these tasks.

386

Also out of production, these chips ran at speeds from 16MHz to 40 MHz and could carry out the effective multi-tasking operations (i.e. run two programs at the same time) that eluded the 286. It was also the minimum processor for running Windows, with a machine with at least 4MB of RAM. It introduced substantial improvements in both memory management and an enlarged instruction set. The chip was available in two varieties - the 386SX and the 386DX. The SX version had a 32-bit internal data path but had only a 16-bit path between the CPU and the computer's memory. So, the SX model could only transfer data in 16 bit chunks at a time. The DX model had a 32-bit data bus between the CPU and the memory chips, allowing larger data transfers and therefore faster throughput. The ability to use external cache memory, usually about 64k, also improved performance. The 386SL model was a low power consumption model used in portables.

486

This chip, now obsolete, ran at speeds from 20MHz to 100MHz. Little change was made to the 386 instruction set, with the emphasis being placed on performance enhancements. This chip was also available in SX and DX varieties, with the DX having a built-in maths co-processor. Motherboards using the 486SX chip provided a spare maths co-processor socket to upgrade to a DX. Apart from the raw CPU clock speed, the 486 was faster than previous chips because it carried out the most common instructions in a single clock cycle (compared to two or three clock cycles for the 386 chip). This was a move towards the RISC philosophy (see later). The 486 chip also had a built-in 8k block of cache memory. This, coupled to a new 'burst mode', meant that data was transferred at a far higher rate than the 386 system. Burst mode allowed memory transfers from consecutive memory locations to be achieved at the rate of one per clock cycle. The clock-tripled 100MHz DX4 ran faster than the first Pentiums - i.e. the 60MHz and 66MHz models. Since the DX4 range used only a 3.3 volts supply, compared to the normal 5 volts, they consumed less power and created less heat, making them good choices for portables.

Pentium

It was significantly faster than a 486 and was effectively two CPUs in the one chip with a 256-bit internal bus and a 64-bit external data bus. On most occasions, this allowed two instructions to be executed in parallel, greatly speeding up throughput. The chip also had the main mathematical operations (i.e. add, divide and multiply) hard-wired into the chip; its maths co-processor was up to 10 times faster than the 486DX maths co-processor. All Pentium models are 'superscalar'; the basic Pentium chip had two integer processing pipelines. It also had a 'branch prediction' facility that 90% of the time correctly predicted the flow of the program and fetched the instruction from a buffer area. The Pentium also had a 16k internal cache. It used CISC technology with some RISC elements. 60MHz and 66MHz chips required a 5 volt supply while models from 75MHz upwards use a 3.3 volt supply for both core operations and input/output operations.

Pentium Pro

This chip used six different pipelines and 40 general-purpose registers. All the pipelines operated simultaneously, offering greatly improved processing capability. To fully utilise this architecture, the Pro read the incoming program instructions into an 8k instruction cache. The instructions were then turned into fixed-length RISC-like 'micro-operations' by three parallel decoders and sent to one of the free pipelines. In this way parts of the original instructions were being processed independently rather than sequentially. The CPU had an 'out-of-order' approach so that instructions that couldn't be immediately executed (e.g. waiting for data) were not placed in a pipeline where they would prevent other micro-operations from being processed. In this way, bottlenecks were minimised. The results of the micro-operations were then assembled in the correct order for use by the external software application.

For even greater speeds, the Pentium Pro had all the necessary logic on board to allow four CPUs to be connected to the same motherboard for parallel running. This is known as 'symmetric multiprocessing'.

The chip used 16k of level 1 cache in a 'unified' mode. The Pentium used two banks of cache - one for instructions and one for data. If the instruction cache was full the CPU could stall, even if there was spare capacity in the data cache.   The Pentium Pro regarded its two 8k caches as a single block of 16k available dynamically for either data or instructions, balancing any changes in load and minimising CPU stalling.

There was also 256k or 512k of second level cache built into the chip.   With many CPUs, the cache was a plug-in unit or was soldered to the motherboard.   With the Pentium Pro, the cache was internal to the chip and directly connected to the CPU itself.   This meant that the cache operated at the full CPU speed while some other external caches operated at only half that speed. This made the Pro's caching much more efficient. The Pro's design is optimised for 32-bit working and actually runs 16-bit code slower than a Pentium. For maximum results, it needs to run 32-bit program code with a 32-bit operating system (eg Windows 98/NT).

Pentium MMX

This is a version of the Pentium with 57 additional instructions in the CPU instruction set.   These are multimedia and communications extensions to the CPU giving them the title 'MMX' - multimedia extensions.   The new instructions use a technique known as SIMD - Single Instruction, Multiple Data. One instruction can work on up to 8 bytes of data simultaneously. This provides very fast repetitive processing of data - ideal for video decompression, sound synthesis, multimedia, 3D rendering and other graphics-intensive activities.   MMX aware programs - i.e. those using the new MMX instructions produce speed improvement in these areas.   It also runs existing programs faster because of its 32k internal cache (16k for code and 16k for data).

The Pentium MMX contains a more efficient branch prediction unit.   The instruction pipeline also works one level deeper - it can carry out more work in advance than a normal Pentium. MMX chips have 8 enhanced internal registers that are 64 bits wide, comprising virtual registers using the normal registers along with the Floating Point registers).   It uses 2.8v for core operations and 3.3v for input/output operations. This reduces power consumption and reduces heat, but means that an MMX chip cannot be used to upgrade a motherboard that does not have a dual voltage supply on Socket 7 CPU holder.   Intel has introduced an 'Overdrive' MMX chip that only runs on 3.3v and is intended for upgrading with older, Socket 5, motherboards.   In either case, the motherboard's BIOS chip needs to be MMX compatible.

Pentium II

Previously known as the 'Klamath', it is an improved Pentium Pro with MMX additions.   Its initial release was a 233MHz CPU with a 100MHz processor/cache interface and a 66MHz system bus.   The built in second level cache is taken out of CPU and is mounted, along with CPU on a plug-in card.   This card plugs into a special connection slot known as 'Slot One', which means that the Pentium II needs a completely re-designed motherboard.   It uses a 2.9v supply to reduce heat dissipation.   The external second level cache only runs at half the CPU speed, which means that the performance is diminished. However, the 32-bit performance, coupled with MMX capabilities, placed Pentium II machines in the lower multimedia and graphics workstations market. The newer Slot 1 Deschutes chip uses the same slot as the standard Pentium II but starts at 300MHz speeds.   In conjunction with the newer BX chipset, it will also run at system bus speeds of 100MHz (compared to 66MHz).   A version aimed at the budget PC market, known as the Celeron, has a 66MHz bus only, as well as reduced cache size.

Pentium II Xeon

The Xeon is intended for high performance workstations and network servers.   It requires yet another new motherboard with a ' Slot 2' connection. It is based on a Pentium II with a lower supply voltage and initial speeds around 400MHz to 450MHz.   It requires a higher specification motherboard with faster memory and a newer chipset (the 450NX). The Level 2 cache runs at the same speed as the clock and is available in 512KB, 1MB and 2MB sizes.

Pentium III

This chip is the current entry-level standard for computers (the minimum standard that is still in production), although rapidly being replaced by the Pentium 4. The Pentium III uses the Slot 1 connection for early models, and Socket 370 for later models. It has a bus speed of 100MHz or 133MHz. The internal second level cache is 512k but still runs at only half the CPU clock speed.

The Pentium III introduces KNI, Katmai New Instructions, comprising 70 new machine code instructions aimed at 3D graphics, MPEG2 video encoding/decoding, AC3 audio and image processing. These work on the same principle as the MMX (Single Instruction Multiple Data) moving large amounts of data with a single instruction. The MMX chip's registers were used for both normal storage and MMX operations. The CPU was forced to halt normal register operations to switch into MMX register operations - and vice versa. The switching time overhead reduced overall throughput. The PIII has a new separate set of 128 registers for SIMD operations, thereby speeding up both SIMD and normal register activities.
The Pentium III Xeon is essentially the Pentium II Xeon with the added KNI instructions.

Pentium 4

The Pentium 4 was introduced with a 100MHz Front Side Bus, with an internal multiplier of x13 to x22. This gives a processor speed of 1.3GHz to 2.2GHz. However, it was at first only available with the Intel 850 chipset, which required RAMBUS memory and used a quad pumped bus. Later Pentium 4's became available with other chipsets, having a bus speed of 133MHz or 166MHz, and capable of using DDR memory. The instruction set includes Streaming SIMD Extensions 2 (SSE2) to improve Internet performance as part of Intel's *NetBurst* architecture. The Pentium 4's other main features include *'Hyper Pipelining'* based on larger instruction pipelines and deeper prediction techniques, a *'Rapid Execution engine'* that consists of two clock-doubled Arithmetic and Logic Units, and more recently the *'Hyperthreading'* technology explained earlier in this chapter. Later versions of Pentium 4 have support 'x86-64', also known as 'Intel 64', which is Intel's 64-bit architecture, and the Pentium D line are dual-core versions of the Pentium 4.

Core 2

The successor to the Pentium 4 is Intel Core 2. It actually has much in common with the Pentium 4, but multi-core and 64-bit architecture support is present on all Core 2 processors, and it also includes such technologies as SSE3, SpeedStep (for dynamic control of processor speed), and TEX (Trusted Execution Technology – which provides hardware-level private key support). It comes in several forms – Core 2 Duo (Two cores), Core 2 Quad (4 cores) and Core 2 Extreme (2 or 4 cores, with their clock multiplier unlocked).

Although the processors are named 'Core 2', there are very few processors available from the original 'Intel Core 1' line. The "Core Architecture" was developed from mobile processors which provided better energy efficiency and lower heat, although it had to ditch the NetBurst architecture in the process. Apart from a few mobile models, it quickly proceeded to the Core 2 technology which is widely used in both desktops and laptops.

Alternatives to Intel
Athlon, Athlon XP, and Athlon 64

The main challenge to the Intel line of CPUs comes from AMD with its Athlon-related processors including Duron, Sempron, Opteron and Phenom. The Athlon (K7) chip uses its own proprietary slot connector (Slot A), with a specially designed motherboard and an AMD750 or VIA KX-133 chipset. It supports both 100MHz and 133MHz bus speeds, double pumped so that transfer rates reach 200MT/s or 233MT/s and is capable of using DDR memory.

The Athlon is also available, along with the Duron, in a Socket A format. Matching motherboards are available with a range of supporting chipsets such as the SiS 730, the VIA KT-133, the KT-266 the KT-333 and the AMD 750. The Athlon MP processor is designed for dual processor systems and aimed at the video editing, graphics rendering and server markets. It uses a 760 MP chipset that supports a 133/266MHz front side bus, ATA100, AGP4x and PC2100 DDR RAM.

At the time AMD adopted the 'XP' speed system, they released new models of the Athlon, and these were known as the Athlon XP line of processors. They had bus speeds of 133MHz, 166MHz, and 200MHz, again double pumped.

When Intel started *quad*-pumping, though, the double-pumped AMD chips fell behind in speed, so AMD developed the "Athlon 64" line of 64-bit processors, which proved successful in contrast to Intel's largely unsuccessful Itanium 64-bit products at the time. It supported such technologies as SSE3, MMX, and included single-core and dual-core (called '*X2*') processors. More importantly, though, it utilised the brand-new Hypertransport Front Side Bus system, with speeds from 800MHz to 2000MHz. Although CPU speeds ranged from 1800MHz to 2600MHz, the 'XP rating' of these chips was between 2800-6400.

Other AMD CPUs

In order to compete with the newest low-cost Intel CPUs such as the Celeron D, AMD responded with an upgrade to their previous low-cost Athlon XP chips. These were named '*Sempron*', and are very similar to the XP they replaced, except for an increased bus speed of up to 166MHz to 400MHz.

Sempron chips come in two forms: one for Socket A mainboards, and one for Socket 754 mainboards, and as with the Athlon they are advertised not by their actual clock speed, but by '*benchmark measurements*' that essentially compare the Athlon chip with it's Intel equivalent. Thus, the 1.67GHz Sempron is named 2400+, while the 1.8GHz version is named 3100+.

'Turion' is a range of AMD CPUs designed for laptops and other mobile devices, while 'Opteron' is a range of 64-bit server CPUs that can run either 32-bit or 64-bit code natively, unlike other 64-bit processors at the time of its release.

Most recently, the 'Phenom' range was released, featuring triple-core and quad-core designs which were all on one chip, contrasted to Intel's quad-core CPUs which are actually multiple chips on one module. Phenom also contains a built-in memory controller, and some models have their multiplier unlocked.

Cell

In 2002, Sony, Toshiba and IBM (STI) applied for a patent for the '*Cell*' processor which was still in early development. This processor was initially intended simply as the processor for the upcoming PlayStation 3 games console, but many industry analysts suspect that the Cell architecture is powerful enough to challenge current PC industry norms.

The Cell architecture is centred round the concept of distributed processing. Each computer or other device may contain one or more '*hardware cells*', each capable of performing processing. The software program is also split, into '*software cells*' that are also containers for the data to be processed. The program can therefore be split up and handed to individual hardware cells for processing.

This distributed nature means that hardware Cells, in addition to performing processing, are also given the task of distributing software Cells to other hardware Cells as and when required. This maximises the processing power available across all the Cell-based products in the network.

The element of the hardware Cell that might be considered the 'CPU' is named the Processing Element ('PE') in Cell architecture terminology, and consists of 1 controlling 'processing unit' (PU) and 8 sub-units or 'attached processing units' (APU) that do the main processing.

Each APU is basically an independent processing core, and each hardware Cell contains eight of them. Furthermore, a system is expected to contain multiple hardware Cells so, for example, a PS3 is expected to contain a total of 32 APUs. As you might imagine, software for a Cell system is more complicated than for an ordinary PC, but the potential speed improvement is likely to be very high.

Summary of Intel P.C. Processors

	8086/88 the 'XT'	80286 the 'AT'	80386	80486	Pentium
Introduced	1978	1982	1985	1989	1993
Number of Pins	40	68	132	168	273
Transistors	29,000	120,000	275,000	1.2m	3.1m
Data Bus Size	8088 8 bit 8086 16 bit	16 bit	32 bit	32 bit	64 bit
Address Bus Size	20 bit	24 bit	SX 24 bit DX 32 bit	32 bit	32 bit
Addressable Memory	1MB	16MB	SX 16MB DX 4GB	4GB	4GB
Clock Speed (MHz)	4.77 / 8	10/20	SX 16/33 DX 33/40	SX 20/25 DX 33/50 DX2 50/66 DX4 100	60 to 233
Performance (in MIPS)	0.75	2.66	11.4	54	112

	Pentium Pro	Pentium II	Xeon	Pentium III	Pentium 4	Core 2
Introduced	1995	1997	1998	1999	2001	2006
Number of Pins	387	Slot 1	Slot 2	Slot 1 / Socket 370	423, later 478	478 or 775
Transistors	5.5m	7.5m	7.5m	9.5m	42m	291m
Data Bus Size	64 bit	64 bit	64 bit	64 bit	64 bit	64 bit
Address Bus Size	36 bit	36 bit	36 bit	36 bit	36 bit	36 bit
Addressable Memory	64GB	64GB	64GB	64GB	64GB	64GB
Clock Speed (MHz)	150/266	166/600	400/450	450/ 1GHz	1.3GHz-3.06GHz	2.2GHz – 3.3GHz
Performance (in MIPS)	300	900	n/a	2012	2661 to 5340	~60,000

Effects of address and data bus sizes

As can be seen from these tables, the increasing data bus and address bus sizes have had a considerable effect on the power of the system. As data bus sizes have increased, the bus has become capable of transferring more data bytes in one bus clock cycle. For example, a Pentium system can transfer eight bytes in one cycle, while a 486 can only transfer 4 bytes at once. This means more program instructions and/or data is supplied to the CPU in one bus clock cycle. Since the CPU's clock cycle is typically several times faster than the bus's clock cycle, keeping it supplied with data is crucial to processor efficiency.

As for the address bus, this has a direct impact on the amount of memory that the machine can address, and therefore access. For example, a Pentium 4 with its 36 bit address bus is capable of accessing up to 64GB of RAM, while a basic Pentium can only access 4GB of RAM. This is useful, even if the machine is not currently fitted with this amount of memory, in order to allow for future upgrades.

If cost were not a factor, then manufacturers and consumers could simply opt for higher and higher bus sizes, and all performance requirements could be met. However, cost is usually a major concern. With PC motherboards, the demand for high speed processing means it is unusual for manufacturers to drop behind in data bus sizes for long. Where a board's performance exceeds user requirements, the extra expense in its purchase is only justified if there is also a need to provide for future requirements.

Comparison of PC Bus Architectures

The following pages examine the performance characteristics of the range of personal microcomputers that have been manufactured, sold and used over the last two decades. All the machines discussed will be around for years to come. Production of XT, AT, 386, 486 and some Pentium ranges has ceased but there are still some of these machines in use in certain sectors. In any case, the support technician has to be able work with the whole range of machines, from the oldest DOS-based machine to the newest Pentium or Athlon.

As microcomputers have developed, there has been a race between the improving performance of the CPU, the memory, the peripherals - and the buses that connect them.

When considering various buses, the following questions should be asked:

- How much memory can be accessed?
- How fast can it be accessed?
- Is access to different components at different speeds required?
- How much does it cost?
- How flexible is the machine - (e.g. will cards or CPU modules from one machine still work in the new machine)?

When examining various systems, there is no abstract 'correct answer'. The system for a user is only correct or incorrect for that user's needs. A user requiring a high-bandwidth multi-user file server would find an old 486 PC absolutely useless; a high-performance machine would be a necessity for such applications.

On the other hand, a high-performance (and therefore very expensive) machine is wasted if it is only used for simple word processing since the speed of the system is only relevant for small periods. By far the greatest time sees the machine idling while the user thinks of the next word to type.

The XT

The earliest PCs were the XT range, dating from the early 1980's and designed and manufactured by IBM. Many other companies produced 'clones' - machines based on the architecture of the IBM XT, with only small differences to avoiding infringing IBM patents. These are often also known, more kindly, as 'PC compatibles'.

Data Bus

The XT Data Bus was 8 bits wide (a single byte) and could therefore transfer a number between 0 and 255 at a time.

Address Bus

The Address Bus was 20 bits wide and so could access up to 1MB of memory (2 raised to the power 20 gives over a million unique address locations).

Clock Speed

Every computer has an oscillator that gives regular timed kicks to the CPU. These pulses are used to move the CPU through the individual activities that comprise each machine code instruction. Each machine code instruction can require one, two, three or four different clock pulses to ensure its completion. The XT was based on the 8088 processor and had a normal clock speed of 4.77MHz (i.e. 4.77 million clock pulses per sec.)

Data Rate

The 8088 chip took four clock pulses to complete a transfer of data on the data bus. So, the data transfer rate is

bus width*clock speed/(8*clock pulses per transfer)

The wider the bus width, the more data can be transferred at a time; the greater the clock speed, the faster the transfer activities can be completed. On the other hand, some chips take more clock pulses to complete a transfer than others.

In the case of the XT, the data transfer rate is

8*4.77m/(8*4) = 1.2 million bytes per sec = 1.14MB/s

Expansion Slot Layout

The diagram shows the connector layout of the expansion slot. The slot connections carry not only the address and data lines, but also a range of power and control lines.

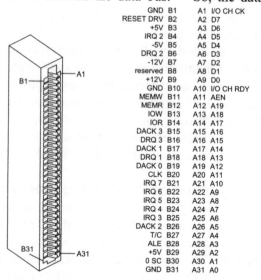

GND	B1	A1	I/O CH CK
RESET DRV	B2	A2	D7
+5V	B3	A3	D6
IRQ 2	B4	A4	D5
-5V	B5	A5	D4
DRQ 2	B6	A6	D3
-12V	B7	A7	D2
reserved	B8	A8	D1
+12V	B9	A9	D0
GND	B10	A10	I/O CH RDY
MEMW	B11	A11	AEN
MEMR	B12	A12	A19
IOW	B13	A13	A18
IOR	B14	A14	A17
DACK 3	B15	A15	A16
DRQ 3	B16	A16	A15
DACK 1	B17	A17	A14
DRQ 1	B18	A18	A13
DACK 0	B19	A19	A12
CLK	B20	A20	A11
IRQ 7	B21	A21	A10
IRQ 6	B22	A22	A9
IRQ 5	B23	A23	A8
IRQ 4	B24	A24	A7
IRQ 3	B25	A25	A6
DACK 2	B26	A26	A5
T/C	B27	A27	A4
ALE	B28	A28	A3
+5V	B29	A29	A2
0 SC	B30	A30	A1
GND	B31	A31	A0

The AT

The successor to the XT was the AT PC, which used the 80286 chip with its improved capabilities.

Data Bus

The width of the data bus was increased to 16 bits; this ensured greater throughput, as it could handle numbers from 0 to 64k at a time.

Address Bus

This was increased to 24-bit width, allowing addressing of up to 16MB of memory. It was now possible to consider add-on memory (see section on extended memory). With the XT models, there was no point in adding extra memory chips above the 1MB range, since the 8088 chip and the 20-bit address bus was unable to access the additional memory addresses.

Clock Speed

The standard clock speed was increased to 8MHz, although faster machines (10MHz or 12MHz) were also produced. The 80286 was also able to transfer data in only two clock pulses, compared to the four required by the 8088.

Data Rate

The data transfer rate was dramatically improved, due to the effect of greater data bus width and the improved chip design. The data transfer rate for an 8MHz system is

$$16*8m/(8*2) = 7.629MB/s$$

However, there was a problem using the memory chips that were available at that time. Their access time (the time required to read/write data to memory locations) was slower than the new improved chip and bus transfer rates.

Since the system can only run at the speed of its slowest element, the effective clock speed was reduced to that which memory could handle. This introduction of *'wait states'* was a reflection of the state of the art of chip development. The CPU would waste some clock cycles, waiting for the memory to access. With improved chips, the access time is faster and adverts talk of *'zero wait state'* systems. In practice, most AT ISA buses run at around 5MB/s.

It was important that all cards then in use with XTs would also be able to work in AT machines. Therefore, the bus layout would have to compatible - and still provide the extra data and address bus connections. This was achieved by keeping the original XT expansion bus and adding an extension section to the bus for the extra connections. In that way, XT cards would fit in the expansion slot, while AT cards would also use the slot extension.

This system is termed the *'ISA'* system (Industry Standard Architecture) and the 16-bit implementation remained the main system until the introduction of PCI.

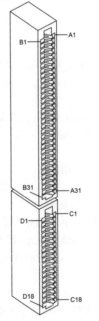

GND	B1	A1	I/O CH CK
RESET DRV	B2	A2	D7
+5V	B3	A3	D6
IRQ 2	B4	A4	D5
-5V	B5	A5	D4
DRQ 2	B6	A6	D3
-12V	B7	A7	D2
reserved	B8	A8	D1
+12V	B9	A9	D0
GND	B10	A10	I/O CH RDY
MEMW	B11	A11	AEN
MEMR	B12	A12	A19
IOW	B13	A13	A18
IOR	B14	A14	A17
DACK 3	B15	A15	A16
DRQ 3	B16	A16	A15
DACK 1	B17	A17	A14
DRQ 1	B18	A18	A13
DACK 0	B19	A19	A12
CLK	B20	A20	A11
IRQ 7	B21	A21	A10
IRQ 6	B22	A22	A9
IRQ 5	B23	A23	A8
IRQ 4	B24	A24	A7
IRQ 3	B25	A25	A6
DACK 2	B26	A26	A5
T/C	B27	A27	A4
ALE	B28	A28	A3
+5V	B29	A29	A2
0 SC	B30	A30	A1
GND	B31	A31	A0
MEM CS 16	D1	C1	SBHE
I/O CS 16	D2	C2	A23
IRQ 10	D3	C3	A22
IRQ 11	D4	C4	A21
IRQ 12	D5	C5	A20
IRQ 13	D6	C6	A19
IRQ 14	D7	C7	A18
DACK 0	D8	C8	A17
DRQ 0	D9	C9	MEMR
DACK 5	D10	C10	MEMW
DRQ 5	D11	C11	D8
DACK 6	D12	C12	D9
DRQ 6	D13	C13	D10
DACK 7	D14	C14	D11
DRQ 7	D15	C15	D12
+5V	D16	C16	D13
MASTER	D17	C17	D14
GND	D18	C18	D15

The 386/486

The range of micros based on the 80386/486 chip brought even better potential performance:

- DATA BUS - 32 bits wide (handling numbers from 0 to 4GB).
- ADDRESS BUS - 32 bits wide (able to address up to 4GB of memory).
- CLOCK SPEED - 20MHz up to 66MHz.
- POTENTIAL DATA RATE = 32*66m/(8*2) = 132MB/s.
  (i.e. 32-bit bus, 66MHz clock, 2 clock pulses per transfer).

These demands were way beyond the capability of the normal ISA bus and alternative methods had to be found, if computers were to use this progress.

To date, there have been four main responses:
1. The MCA bus.
2. The EISA bus.
3. A separate memory bus.
4. Local bus systems - VESA, PCI and AGP (see the chapter on *'Display Technology'*).

MCA

The IBM response was the introduction of the *MCA* (Micro Channel Architecture) bus with their new PS/2 range of machines in 1987. In fact, IBM introduced both 16-bit (for their 286 machines) and 32-bit versions of the bus. The design broke with tradition, both in construction and method of operation.
The XT, ISA and EISA systems all use *'synchronous'* buses. In these systems, the data transfer rate of the bus is tied to the clock speed of the machine's processor. The MCA is *'asynchronous'* and runs as fast as it can in any particular situation.

Advantages:
- The standard speed for these boards was 20MB/s, which can be specially increased to much greater speeds.
- The MCA add-on boards are physically much smaller than all other types of board.
- MCA buses cause less electromagnetic radiation.

Disadvantages:
- Using a 16-bit board brings the machine performance back down nearer to the old ISA boards.
- IBM had strict licensing policies for MCA.
- The technology was largely ignored in the PC market and even IBM eventually dropped it from its range of PCs.

EISA

The licensing demands and conditions of IBM produced a mixed response from other manufacturers. Some, like Olivetti and Research Machines, produced MCA machines under licence. Others, led by Compaq, produced their own improvement to the ISA bus. This is known as *EISA* (Extended Industry Standard Architecture).

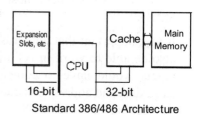

Standard 386/486 Architecture

Data Bus - 32 bits wide (0-4 Billion)

Address Bus - 32 bits wide (0-4GB)
The bus widths are identical to those of MCA. The big advantage of EISA systems is their *'backward compatibility'*. Any card designed for the ISA system can be used in an EISA bus. This involved a little ingenuity, since the EISA bus has enlarged data and address buses compared to the ISA bus.

Bus Layout
The EISA expansion bus, at first glance, looks identical to an ISA bus. It is the same length and appears to have the same number of connectors on each side of the connector block.

The trick in the design of the EISA bus is that it has two levels of connectors. The upper level is identical to the ISA bus, allowing normal ISA cards to be plugged in and used. It also has a second set of contacts that are set deeper into the expansion connection. These provide the extra address and data connections for EISA cards.

Plastic keys stop the ISA cards from penetrating to the bottom level of contacts. EISA cards have notches that match the keys. This allows the card to be pushed deeper into the connector and the card's extra connectors make contact with the lower level of bus connections.

Data Rate

The EISA bus is synchronous and has to run at the slow speed of 8MHz, to allow it to use any slow speed ISA cards.

So, the actual maximum data transfer rate achieved is:

$$32 * 8m / (8*2) = 15.2 MB/s$$

An additional special data rate mode allows data to be transferred in a single clock cycle and this increases the data transfer rate to a maximum of 32MB/s. Overall then, the bus has to run at the speed of its slowest card. An EISA bus with an ISA card installed will only run at ISA speeds.

MCA systems, because of the IBM reputation, enjoyed success in sales at the high performance end. EISA systems were common in network file servers but manufacturers produced few other add-on cards. PCI has replaced them both in PCs and in network servers, while AGP is now used for graphics cards.

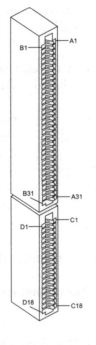

Left	B signal	B pin	A pin	A signal	Right
GND	GND	B1	A1	I/O CH CK	CMD
+5V	RESET DRV	B2	A2	D7	START
+5V	+5V	B3	A3	D8	EXRDY
X	IRQ 2	B4	A4	D5	EX32
X	-5V	B5	A5	D4	GND
polarising	DRQ 2	B6	A6	D3	polarising
X	-12V	B7	A7	D2	EX16
X	reserved	B8	A8	D1	SLBURST
+12V	+12V	B9	A9	D0	MSBURST
M-10	GND	B10	A10	I/O CH RDY	W-R
LOCK	MEMW	B11	A11	AEN	GND
reserved	MEMR	B12	A12	A19	reserved
GND	IOW	B13	A13	A18	reserved
reserved	IOR	B14	A14	A17	reserved
BE 3	DACK 3	B15	A15	A16	GND
polarising	DRQ 3	B16	A16	A15	polarising
BE 2	DACK 1	B17	A17	A14	BE 1
BE 0	DRQ 1	B18	A18	A13	LA 31
GND	REFRESH	B19	A19	A12	GND
+5V	CLK	B20	A20	A11	LA30
LA29	IRQ 7	B21	A21	A10	LA28
GND	IRQ 6	B22	A22	A9	LA27
LA26	IRQ 5	B23	A23	A8	LA25
LA24	IRQ 4	B24	A24	A7	GND
polarising	IRQ 3	B25	A25	A6	polarising
LA16	DACK 2	B26	A26	A5	LA15
LA14	T/C	B27	A27	A4	LA13
+5V	ALE	B28	A28	A3	LA12
+5V	+5V	B29	A29	A2	LA11
GND	OSC	B30	A30	A1	GND
LA10	GND	B31	A31	A0	LA9
LA8	MEM CS 16	D1	C1	SBHE	LA7
LA6	I/O CS 16	D2	C2	A23	GND
LA5	IRQ 10	D3	C3	A22	LA4
+5V	IRQ 11	D4	C4	A21	LA3
LA2	IRQ 12	D5	C5	A20	GND
polarising	IRQ 15	D6	C6	A19	polarising
D16	IRQ 14	D7	C7	A18	D17
D18	DACK 0	D8	C8	A17	D19
GND	DRQ 0	D9	C9	MEMR	D20
D21	DACK 5	D10	C10	MEMW	D22
D23	DRQ 5	D11	C11	D8	GND
D24	DACK 6	D12	C12	D9	D25
GND	DRQ 6	D13	C13	D10	D26
D27	DACK 7	D14	C14	D11	D28
polarising	DRQ 7	D15	C15	D12	polarising
D29	+5V	D16	C16	D13	GND
+5V	MASTER	D17	C17	D14	D30
+5V	GND	D18	C18	D15	D31
MACKn		D19	C19		MRE on

Separate Memory Bus

To maximise the computer's efficiency, data must be transferred between the processor and memory (and vice versa) as quickly as possible. When a slow speed card is used in the computer, this should not be allowed to slow down these CPU/memory transfers. The solution from the 386 models onwards is to provide a separate high-speed bus linking the processor and memory.

All the communication between CPU and memory is carried over this bus. The normal ISA bus remains to handle disk, video, expansion slots, etc.

Advantages:

- The memory chips runs as fast as the CPU allows, while slower speed cards are catered for on the separate slower bus. The system runs at its maximum speed.
- Now that the memory has its own separate bus, a block of even faster memory (cache memory) can be introduced between the main memory and the CPU. The cache memory is used to handle pages of memory data at a time (see notes on memory).

Local Bus systems

Technological change left the original PC bus design lacking in terms of bus width and bus speed.

Bus width

The width of the data bus is a major factor in determining how much data can be transferred over a given period. This data could be memory reads/writes, disk read/writes or graphic card read/writes, along with data associated with a range of peripherals such as printers, modems, scanners, etc. The original IBM XT model had a data bus that was just 8 bits wide. The bus was common to the CPU, memory, etc. and the expansion slots that were used to plug in add-ons. This was increased to 16 bits for the AT model and 32 bits for the 386 and 486 machines. The bus architecture was then changed to that shown in the diagram above. Although the bus between CPU and memory was widened, the data bus to the expansion slots was kept at 16-bit. This was to allow add-on cards designed for the older architectures, both 8-bit and 16-bit, to still be used on the newer machines. So graphics cards, although capable of greater throughput, were restricted to slower 16-bit data transfers. The problem also extended to disk controllers, which were similarly slowed down.

Bus speed

The XT data bus was common to local chips and to extension boards and was clocked by the same CPU clock chip. So all chips and peripherals were clocked to run at 4.7MHz. Modern architecture may split the local and extension chips into separate buses, but the ISA expansion bus, if present, is still separately clocked at a slower speed to allow old add-ons to be used. Therefore, a computer with a much faster front side bus could still have an ISA slot (i.e. expansion bus) running at between 8MHz and 12MHz. For best performance, PCI cards should be used where possible, with the exception of the graphics card which is best suited to an AGP port.

The Local Bus solution

All current computers use *'local bus'* architectures, where the expansion bus is clocked more slowly than the CPU, for the benefit of slower add-on boards. However, a *'local bus'* connects the memory, video

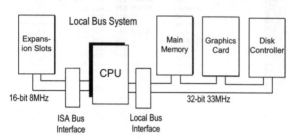

and disk controllers to the CPU on a full 32-bit or 64-bit bus. This bus is clocked at a much higher rate - up to that of the CPU - for maximum data transfer. Consequently, all cards that run on the local bus outperform their equivalent ISA card versions. Video perform-ance, in particular, is spectacularly better but the benefits are also available to disk controllers and other local bus cards. The local bus boards still run ordinary application software and require no special operating system arrangements. Currently, the technology appears both in add-on cards and implemented on the motherboard.

There are two major variations in local bus technology - the older VESA Local Bus and the current Intel PCI bus.

VESA Bus

The first local bus standard was the *'VL Bus'* from VESA (Video Electronic Standards Association). It was used in a wide range of cards. The bus was tied to the speed of the machine's CPU, as the processor had to manage the timing of every card on the bus. The VESA standard provided for clock rates up to 66MHz, although plug-in cards were only used on systems up to 40MHz, as the physical characteristics of the electrical connectors and timing problems affect performance beyond 40MHz. With 33MHz systems, there was a three-device limit. Practically, the VL-Bus system was optimised for 386/486 32-bit architecture at 33MHz working. The VESA local bus system did not progress beyond the 486, with the PCI system taking over at Pentium level.

PCI Bus

Current systems use the Intel PCI (*'Peripheral Component Inter-connect'*) Bus. Initially designed as a 32-bit connection system for motherboard components, it developed into a full expansion bus system. The diagram shows a typical PCI motherboard config-uration for Athlon, Pentium, Pentium II and a few rare early Pentium III chipsets, although the details vary slightly with different CPUs and different memory systems.

All Pentium 4 and nearly all Pentium III systems use a hub-based architecture as shown later.

The PCI bus exists as a local fast bus, separate from the slower ISA bus. In the example shown, a bridge controller (the *'South Bridge'*) allows the use of older ISA cards on a normal ISA bus. However, it decouples the CPU clock and data path from the bus and interfaces to them through another chip in the PCI chipset (the *'North Bridge'*). The PCI bus is therefore independent of the machine's CPU. It works equally well with the 486, and the Pentium/Pentium II, and is used with the DEC Alpha workstation and the PowerPC. All that is required is that each CPU has its own CPU-PCI chipset. The chipset comprises two chips. The North Bridge handles the CPU, memory, cache and the PCI bus, while the South Bridge handles USB, IDE drives and the ISA bus. Current

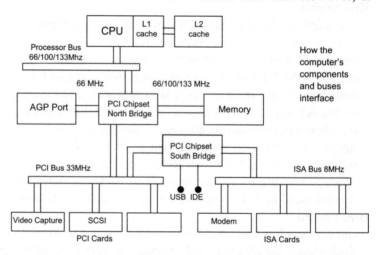

Athlon chipsets retain an amended North Bridge/ South Bridge arrangement which, among other things, drops support for the ISA bus.

The system bus was initially designed for a maximum operating speed of 66MHz although this has not been fully implemented. Current PCI buses run mainly at 33MHz, even though most motherboards run at 100MHz or 133MHz. The PCI bus is synchronised to the system bus but is reduced to a proportion of its speed. Early systems used a 66MHz front side bus, while current Pentium systems use 100MHz or 133MHz. Athlon-based motherboards currently support up to 200MHz. A new standard (PCI-X) is being proposed for fast networking systems, using a 64-bit bus running at 133MHz. Also, the PCI Special Interest Group (PCI SIG) is working on what

Comparison of Bus Systems		
Bus Type	Clock Speed	Max Data Rate
XT	4.77MHz	1.14MB/s
ISA	8MHz	7.629MB/s
MCA	10MHz	20MB/s
PC Card	8MHz	20MB/s
EISA	8MHz	33MB/s
CardBus	33MHz	133MB/s
VESA	50MHz	133MB/s
PCI	33MHz	133MB/s
AGP	66MHz	266MB/s
AGP 2x	66MHz	533MB/s
AGP 4x	66MHz	1066MB/s
AGP 8X	66MHz	2132MB/s

it calls *'Future IO'*, while Intel is developing its own *'Third Generation IO'* standard, also known as *'PCI Express'*.

The PCI Bus conforms to the *'Energy Star'* requirements by running at 3.3 volts, although a 5 volt PCI card is detected and still supplied with 5 volts.

Some older computer motherboards had a mix of expansion connectors - e.g. EISA with VESA, ISA with VESA, PCI with VESA, PCI with ISA and some even had ISA, VESA and PCI. For maximum performance, only PCI cards should be used where possible. The exception to this rule is for graphics cards, where AGP should be used if available.

THE PCI SLOT

The PCI standard allows up to 6 PCI connectors for use in personal computing equipment. It comes in several forms. The 5V PCI standard is designed for use in desktop systems, the 3.3 V PCI standard is to be used in portable computers, and the Universal PCI system is for motherboards that are likely to be used in either type of system. Each type is available in 32-bit and 64-bit configurations. The universal PCI connector is essentially a mix of the 5V and 3.3V versions: the voltage on the I/O pins is 5V where there is a 5V bus, and is 3.3V where there is a 3.3V bus. For this reason, the Universal PCI slot is tabulated here. For 32-bit PCI connectors, only pins A1/B1 to A62/B62 are used. 64-bit cards use pins A63/B63 through to A94/B94. 64-bit PCI cards are very rare and so the details of this part of the interface have been omitted.

INTEL PCI CHIPSETS

The PCI chipset has a crucial role in connecting the CPU and memory with the rest of the computer's resources. It provides the interfaces for the bus, disks, keyboard, memory, I/O ports along with handling interrupts, DMA and timer functions.

All PCI chipsets support the *'Plug-and-Play'* system that is designed to make configuration of device settings an automatic process. See the section on interrupts, earlier in this chapter for more details.

REAR OF PC			
PIN	SIGNAL	PIN	SIGNAL
B1	-12v	A1	Test Reset
B2	Test Clock	A2	+12 V
B3	Ground	A3	Test Mode Select
B4	Test Data Output	A4	Test Data Input
B5	+5V	A5	+5V
B6	+5V	A6	Interrupt A
B7	Interrupt B	A7	Interrupt C
B8	Interrupt D	A8	+5 V
B9	PRSNT1#	A9	Reserved
B10	Reserved	A10	+ V i/o
B11	PRSNT2#	A11	Reserved
B12	Keyway	A12	Keyway
B13	Keyway	A13	Keyway
B14	Reserved	A14	Reserved
B15	Ground	A15	Reset
B16	Clock	A16	+V i/o
B17	Ground	A17	Grant
B18	Request	A18	Ground
B19	+V i/o	A19	Reserved
B20	Address 31	A20	Address 30
B21	Address 29	A21	+3.3V
B22	Ground	A22	Address 28
B23	Address 27	A23	Address 26
B24	Address 25	A24	Ground
B25	+3.3 V	A25	Address 24
B26	C/BE 3	A26	Int device select
B27	Address 23	A27	+3.3V
B28	Ground	A28	Address 22
B29	Address 21	A29	Address 20
B30	Address 19	A30	Ground
B31	+3.3V	A31	Address 18
B32	Address17	A32	Address 16
B33	C/BE 2	A33	+3.3 V
B34	Ground	A34	Cycle Frame
B35	Initiator Ready	A35	Ground
B36	+3.3V	A36	Target Ready
B37	Device Select	A37	Ground
B38	Ground	A38	Stop
B39	Lock	A39	+3.3 V
B40	Parity Error	A40	Snoop Done
B41	+3.3 V	A41	Snoop Back-off
B42	System Error	A42	Ground
B43	+3.3 V	A43	PAR
B44	C/BE 1	A44	Address 15
B45	Address 14	A45	+3.3 V
B46	Ground	A46	Address 13
B47	Address 12	A47	Address 11
B48	Address 10	A48	Ground
B49	Ground	A49	Address 9
B50	KeyWay	A50	KeyWay
B51	KeyWay	A51	KeyWay
B52	Address 8	A52	C /BE 0
B53	Address 7	A53	+3.3 V
B54	+3.3 V	A54	Address 6
B55	Address 5	A55	Address 4
B56	Address 3	A56	Ground
B57	Ground	A57	Address 2
B58	Address 1	A58	Address 0
B59	+5 i/o	A59	+V i/o
B60	Acknowledge 64bit	A60	Request 64bit
B61	+5V	A61	+5 V
B62	+ 5V access Key	A62	+ 5V Access Key

The first Intel PCI chipset was the FX chipset, which supported EDO RAM, pipeline burst cache and bus-mastered EIDE. It could cope with 128MB of RAM but could only cache the first 64MB. Further

Intel chipsets include the HX, VX, TX, LX, EX, BX, GX, ZX and NX. These added a variety of new capabilities, such as supporting larger RAM sizes and types, and supporting USB, UDMA, FireWire and so on.

The majority of the 'X' series of chipsets are no longer on sale except with laptop computers, but there are certainly plenty of computers still in use containing these chipsets.

Hypertransport

This recent technology was developed by AMD. It is a pair of uni-directional bus lines, in other words one set of connections is used to send data, and another set used to receive. It is not intended purely for PC motherboards, and as a result there are a number of different bus sizes, from 2 bit to 32 bit. This technology is likely to be used to connect the northbridge part of the chipset to the southbridge, since the Front Side Bus that connects the memory, northbridge and CPU is already very fast.

Infiniband and PCI-X

With PCI beginning to show its age, competing technologies began developing as prospective replacements. The Compaq-led *'Future IO'* and the Intel-led *'Next Generation IO'* eventually converged, to create the Infiniband design that may soon take over from PCI. Just as parallel ports gave way to serial USB and FireWire connections, the Infiniband system will be a serial replacement for the parallel based PCI system. It will use IPv6 networking technology, allowing for a vast number of devices to be added, and is said to have a bandwidth of up to 2.5GB/s, while standard PCI has a top bandwidth of 532MB/s. It is no longer a bus system, though, since it uses a switched point-to-point system instead.

PCI-X is another technology designed as a replacement for PCI. This system increases the bus speed from 66MHz to 133MHz. The advantage that PCI-X has over Infiniband, however, is that PCI cards will still work in a PCI-X system.

PCI Express

Not to be confused with PCI-C, PCI Express or PCI-E is not backward compatible, as it is serial rather than parallel in design. PCI-X is a 64-bit interface that could handle up to 1,066Mbytes/sec. However, since it requires a separate controller for every slot, it is an expensive and bulky option. Consequently, most development has centred on PCI Express, also referred to as PCIe and previously known as 3GIO, whose main features are:

- It uses a serial interface, unlike the parallel interface of PCI and PCI-X.
- Each 4-wire connection, called a *'lane'*, has its own dedicated bandwidth that is unaffected by the traffic on any other lane (unlike PCI and PCI-X whose channels share the bandwidth).
- Each lane can pass 250Mbytes/sec in each direction, since each lane has both a send and a receive pair of wires.
- Lanes can run in parallel to increase bandwidth (e.g. sixteen lanes – known as PCI Express x16 – can handle 4Gbytes/sec.).
- A single lane, an *'x1'*, is a slot of only about 1", with x16 slots being about the size of an existing AGP slot.
- It provides more power (up to 76 Watts) to video cards, to support future even faster and more demanding cards
- It also supports hot-plugging.

PCI and PCI-X devices share a common bus and have to vie with each other for attention. With PCIe however, each device is connected directly to a common switch via its lane(s). This allows devices to pass data on a peer-to-peer basis, lowering the strain on the chipset.

The table shows a comparison of various bus systems.

Bus	Max Bandwidth
ISA	8 Mbytes/sec
PCI	133 Mbytes/sec
PCI-X	1066 Mbytes/sec
PCI-X 2.0	4,266 Mbytes/sec
AGP 1x	266 Mbytes/sec
AGP 8x	2,133 Mbytes/sec
PCI-E Single-Lane	250 Mbytes/sec
PCI-E 4-lane	1,000 Mbytes/sec
PCI-E 8-lane	2,000 Mbytes/sec
PCI-E 16-lane	4,000 Mbytes/sec

In the table, the PCIe figures are for a single direction. If the lane is carrying data in both directions, these figures would be doubled.

There is no effective upgrade path to PCI Express, as a new motherboard, graphics card, and DDR2 memory are required. Transitionally, some motherboards provided both PCI and PCIe slots, allowing older devices still to be used. Existing AGP cards are not compatible with the new 164-pin x16 slot. A motherboard may however provide one x16 slot (i.e. 16 lanes) for a graphics card, along with a number of single lanes for various peripherals.

The main benefits of PCIe are experienced in disk controllers, Gigabit LAN cards and other applications that are bandwidth-intensive (e.g. processing huge video files).

ExpressCard

The PCI Express system not only replaces the old PCI bus and AGP 8x; it is expected to replace PCMCIA card standards with a new interface called 'ExpressCard'. This is a co-operative effort between the PCMCIA group and the PCI-SIG group.

Essentially, it extends the PCI Express bus to an external socket on a mobile (or desktop) computer, providing a much faster external interface.

It needs new ExpressCard peripherals, as existing PC Cards do not fit in an ExpressCard slot.

The ExpressCard standard specifies a single slot supporting both the USB 2.0 and PCI Express interfaces, with cards of both types both being hot-pluggable.

The smaller of the card formats, ExpressCard/34, is designed for most of the common applications. It is about half the size of a PC Card, measuring 23mm x 75mm x 5mm.

The wider variation, the ExpressCard/54, is also 5mm thick but is wider to allow it to house tiny hard drives, smartcard readers, CompactFlash cards, etc. The standard also allows for card to extend outside the case of the computer, to house even larger future applications. It also offers the ability to extend the bus outside the computer by up to 5 metres.

The 8xx series Intel chipsets

The 810 series, or Whitney, chipsets were introduced in mid-1999 and were a significant departure for Intel and for mainboard design. No motherboards designed for the 810 chipset and beyond have any ISA bus slots. As explained earlier, previous motherboard architectures used a series of three busses, each running at a different speed. These were typically 8MHz for the ISA bus, 33MHz for the PCI bus, and 66/100/133MHz for the system bus (also called the 'CPU bus' or 'host bus'). The three busses were interconnected by two so-called bridge chips, the North Bridge connecting the CPU to the PCI bus, and the South Bridge connecting the PCI to the ISA (see the discussion of the PCI bus in the previous section).

In the 810 chipset, there are still three busses and two bridges but there is no support for ISA expansion. The slowest bus is the PCI bus. The bridge chip called the I/O Controller Hub (IOCH or ICH) connects

from the PCI bus to the new 66MHz Accelerated Hub Architecture (AHA) bus. This hub has built in support for keyboard, mouse, floppy, printer, serial and USB devices as well as audio CODECs.

The bridge chip between the 66MHz AHA bus and the system bus is called the Graphics Memory Controller Hub (GMCH or GCH). This chip has an integrated AGP controller and Hardware Motion Compensation support to improve software reproduction of DVDs.

The same chip supports analogue video out for conventional monitors and digital video out for flat panel displays. It has system management functions which allow the mainboard to be monitored over the network, ACPI compliant switching of power etc. These chipsets will form the basis of a range of machines with

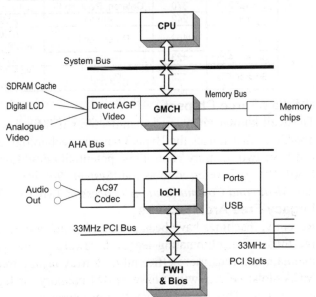

integrated sound and video, and eventually separate video cards may become a limited market for specialist applications. The 810 chipset is capable of handling Pentium III chips but is mainly targeted at the budget Celeron-based products.

The 820 Chipset, designed for higher performance Pentium III machines, supports RDRAM memory and AGP4x video systems. It also supports a faster 133 MHz system bus, if 133MHz memory is also used.

The 840 Chipset is designed for high memory bandwidth applications, and multi-processor Xeon-based systems, as used in servers or very powerful workstations. It can provide up to a theoretical maximum of 3.2GB/s of memory bandwidth with either RDRAM or SDRAM memory.

The 845 chipset is essentially an 840 chipset that is capable of accessing DDR memory instead of RDRAM. The 845E and 845G chipsets also contain built-in graphics and USB2.0 support, while the 845G is also capable of an effective system bus speed of 533MHz. The 845PE is optimised for hyperthreading, and supports PC2700 memory.

The 850 Chipset is used exclusively with Pentium 4 processors, and is based on Intel's new '*NetBurst*' architecture aimed at improving Internet facilities. It only uses RDRAM memory, but utilises dual channels to retrieve data from two memory modules at a time. Since RDRAM chips transfer 16 bits (2 bytes) of data in each clock cycle, using two channels means 32 bits (4 bytes) are transferred, and with Rambus at either 800MHz or 1066MHz this adds up to 3.2GB/s or 4.2GB/s of data transferred. The system bus between the GCH and the CPU in an 850-based system runs at only 400MHz or 533MHz, but with a bus width of 64 bits (8 bytes), so this matches the speed of the Rambus memory, allowing the full speed of the Rambus to be utilised.

However, Intel has more recently decided to switch to DDR memory. Its 865 and 875 chipsets support DDR333 and DDR400 memory modules, as well as Serial ATA and Hyperthreading technology. The 875P model also implements the CSA (Communications Streaming Architecture) link that provides a high speed (266MB/s) connection from a Gigabit Ethernet controller directly to the North Bus, freeing up bandwidth on the PCI bus for other devices.

The range of sockets and slots used for housing CPUs over the years is shown in the table.

Socket Number	Number of Pins	Type of CPU	Common chipsets	Common clock speeds	Common multipliers
Socket 1	169	486	-	16MHz – 33MHz	1x to 3x
Socket 2	169/238	486	420TX	25MHz – 50MHz	1x to 3x
Socket 3	169/237	486	420EX, 420TX	25MHz –50MHz	1x to 3x
Socket 4	235	Pentium	430LX	60MHz – 66MHz	-
Socket 5	273	Pentium, K6	430FX, 430NX	50MHz – 66MHz	1.5x to 2x
Socket 6	320	486 DX4	-	25MHz – 40MHz	2x to 3x
Socket 7	321	Pentium, K5	430FX, 530TX	40MHz – 133MHz	1.5x to 6x
Socket 8	387	Pentium Pro	440FX, 440GX	60MHz – 75MHz	2x to 8x
Slot 1	242	Pentium II	440BX, 440FX, 810, 820, 840	60MHz – 133MHz	3x to 11.5x
Slot 2	330	Pentium II Xeon	440GX, 840	100MHz- 133MHz	4x to 7x
Socket 370	370	Celeron, Pentium III	810, 815, 820	66MHz – 111MHz	4.5x to 14x
Slot A	242	Athlon	AMD750	100MHz – 133MHz	5x to 10x
Socket A	462	Duron, Athlon	AMD750, KT266, nForce	100MHz – 133MHz	6x to 15x
Socket 423	423	Pentium 4	845, 850	100MHz	13x to 20x
Socket 478	478	Pentium 4	845, 850, 865, 875	100MHz – 133MHz (quad pumped)	15x to 26x

NVidia nForce Chipset

The well-known video card manufacturer nVidia has produced its own motherboard chipset. This is notable in that it uses the HyperTransport technology explained earlier in this chapter, and also in that it can have two memory controllers, potentially doubling the memory data rate. In the nForce chipset the North Bridge is referred to as the '*System Platform Processor*' (SPP) and the South Bridge is known as the '*Media and Communications Processor*' (MCP). This chipset uses Socket A and AMD processors.

Legacy-Free Architectures

Recently, machines have been produced which are advertised as '*legacy-free*'. This concept is based on the theory that eliminating legacy hardware should produce a more elegant solution that is easier to maintain and runs more efficiently. A truly legacy free motherboard will have no ISA, EISA, VESA or MCA slots; neither will it have SIMM memory, or legacy connectors such as serial, parallel, and PS/2 connectors. This means legacy-free machines must make extensive use of USB devices, for keyboards, mice, and other external attachments (with FireWire coming along later). Current legacy-free machines tend to have little room for internal upgrades, with only a few half-height PCI slots. In fact, some have no PCI slots at all, integrating the sound and video into the motherboard.

A compromise is what is known as '*legacy light*' machines. These take out some but not all legacy components. For example, new Pentium III and 4 motherboards have no ISA slots, removing the need for a South Bridge in the chipset, yet many such motherboards still support PS/2 keyboards and mice.

External Interfaces

The preceding pages have covered the <u>internal</u> architecture and the available internal add-ons. Every PC also has a number of <u>external</u> connections (known as '*ports'*), to allow the machine to communicate with the outside world. A range of input and output devices (sometimes a device is both an input and output device) can be connected to these ports.

- Input devices include - keyboard, graphics tablet, scanner, modem, sensors, camcorder.
- Output devices include - printer, monitor, plotter, modem, actuators, robots.

Peripheral interfaces have a number of common characteristics:

- Data conversion - translating data from the form held inside the computer into the form required by the device (e.g. from computer binary to ACSII for the printer).
- Buffering - the temporary storage of data between the CPU and the peripheral (e.g. holding data until the modem is ready to transmit it).
- Control Signals - the transmission of control information to a device (e.g. moving disk drive heads).
- Status Signals - the reception of information on device readiness (e.g. testing if a printer is on line or out of paper).

Most interfaces are two-way devices. A printer port, for example, has to send control information and data to a printer but it also reads status information back from the printer. Of course, the printable data only goes in one direction (PC to printer). With other devices, the data may flow in both directions; this is the case with a modem that must both transmit and receive data.

Interface methods

All connections to the computer and its adapter cards use one of these interface methods:

Parallel

Data is sent with all the byte's bits being transmitted simultaneously over a set of wires. Used by most printers, disk drives, etc.

Serial

The data is transmitted one bit at a time over a single connector wire. The RS232 serial port is slower than parallel transmission but serial transmission is much cheaper (particularly over long distances). Keyboards, monochrome monitors, some printers, the mouse, and LAN cabling use this method. There are a number of other interface standards that use serial methods, such as USB and FireWire.

Analogue

Analogue signals have an infinite number of different states, as would be expected from real-world audio or video sources. They require special adapters to interface to the computer and examples are modems, microphones and video sources such as cameras and VCRs.

Buffering

Buffers are memory blocks used to temporarily store data until it is required, preventing slow speed devices from slowing down the CPU. Buffer memory areas are to be found inside printers, modems, video and network interface cards. The computer itself also creates and uses buffer areas, usually in higher memory areas of the main system memory. They are used for disk reads and writes and for keyboard buffering.

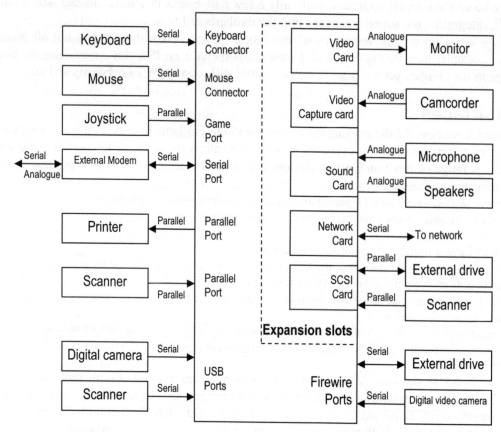

External Ports

To facilitate the connection of external devices, PCs have a number of external ports at the rear of the machine.   Normally, a PC has at least a parallel port and a serial port, although some machines may have more. All machines have a keyboard interface and an outlet for attaching a monitor.

Some motherboards also have joystick ports and USB sockets.

The Parallel Port

Also known as the *'Centronics'*, *'LPT'* or *'Printer'* port. With the introduction of improved parallel ports, the original connection is also now known as the SPP (*'Standard Parallel Port'*).

By convention, the whole cable is described as a Centronics cable. In fact, the plug that fits the printer socket is a 36-pin Amphenol plug to fit the printer's Centronics socket. The plug at the computer is a normal 25-pin male D-type connector.

Parallel port devices

A whole range of storage and other devices exist for connection to the computer's parallel port.   These include 3.5" floppy drives, 5.25" floppy drives, fixed hard disks, removable cartridge drives, optical R/W drives, CD-ROM drives and tape streamers (fast-running tape decks using 1/4" cartridges or DAT tapes, for data backup and restore purposes).   Peripherals other than storage devices include scanners, video cameras, sound cards and LAN adapters.   The advantages of parallel port peripherals are:

- Ease of connection.   There is no need to open machines to fit or configure cards.
- Portability. The peripheral is a free-standing device that connects to any computer.
- Can be used to extend laptops and notebooks, which lack internal space for expansion.
- Allows a machine with the IDE card limit of two hard disks to attach a third, external, drive.
- Sharing resources. A printer, for example, is not tied to a particular computer; it is neither fitted into a machine nor requires a special adapter card.   This allows the peripheral to be easily moved to another location where it can currently be most usefully employed.
- Sharing Data. Devices such as the ZIP drive allow 100MB, 250MB or 750MB of data to stored on a removable disk that can then be inserted into any other ZIP drive for reading.
- Easy recovery from machine failure.   In the event that a machine breaks down, its data is held on a mass-storage device that can be quickly transferred to another working machine.   A portable 20GB hard disks or a 24GB DAT streamer would handle most of an organisation's data comfortably.

To ensure that the computer's only parallel port is not lost to the device, parallel port peripherals normally provide an additional parallel port.

Parallel transmission

In parallel transmission, the data port has eight separate wires connecting the computer to the external device. There is a separate pin in the socket for each data wire, plus other pins for the control information. Five volts on a wire represents logic 1, while zero volts represents logic 0. In this way, an entire byte of data can be transmitted at a time. With a printer, the value of each bit is carried on a separate wire in the parallel cable and is read by the printer's electronic circuits.

There are problems in sending parallel transmissions over long distances. Due to the different 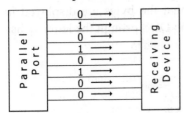 characteristics of each wire, the time taken for the data to pass down each wire is different. So, over a long distance, the individual bits that comprise a particular byte may not all arrive at the destination at the same time - even although they were transmitted simultaneously. This effect is known as 'skew' and is the reason that parallel transmission, although faster than serial, is restricted to short cables up to two metres in length. Parallel transmission is used for most printer cables (although it is possible to buy serial interface printers).

EPP

The IEEE 1284 standard was introduced in 1992. This has become known as the Enhanced Parallel Port (EPP). Like the normal bi-directional ports, the EPPs are capable of either sending or receiving data on the data pins. The main advantage of the EPPs is that they do not require the CPU for flow control as the chips on the cards carry out these tasks. The EPP performance is a major advance, with typical data transfer rates of 800KB per second (a 2MB/s maximum).

Enhanced Parallel Ports are also 'backward compatible' with older, non-EPP devices. This means that a computer with an EPP has the following characteristics:

- Any device that is EPP compatible will attach to an Enhanced Port and will detect that the port is of the EPP type. Subsequent data transfers will be at the maximum rate allowed by the port. This allows the newer printers and network adapters to operate at their best potential.
- Any device that is not EPP compatible will still attach to an Enhanced Port but the port will operate in standard mode.

If an EPP compatible device is attached to a standard Parallel Port, the device will work in standard mode.

For the user, this should be an automatic process as the device software is able to test the port type and configure itself accordingly. The EPP was designed for use with hard drives, CD-ROMs, LAN cards, etc.

ECP

The Enhanced Capability Port was promoted by Microsoft and Hewlett Packard and is designed for interfacing to the modern range of printers and scanners. While it is capable of operating in other modes, the ECP mode provides added features such as DMA operation and RLE (Run Length Encoding) compression of data. Compression ratios of up to about 64:1 are supported, making it an ideal interface for the transferring of scanned bitmaps.

Windows 95 onwards has built-in support for ECP ports and the IRQ and DMA can be set up in the 'Device Manager' menu. Naturally, the printer must also be ECP capable.

The parallel port interface

IBM defined the first parallel port as LPT1 and the second and third, if fitted, as LPT2 and LPT3. The system can differentiate between these ports and any other devices because the hardware for LPT1, LPT2 and LPT3 (and the serial ports similarly) only responds to certain defined port address ranges.

The three possible ranges for parallel ports are:

Port	Data to Printer (output)	Printer Status (input)	Printer Control (output)
Option 1	3BC	3BD	3BE
Option 2	378	379	37A
Option 3	278	279	27A

When the computer is booted up, one of the address ranges above is allocated to LPT1, LPT2 and LPT3 as the defaults. The system is checked for parallel ports, any devices found are allocated to the ports and the information is stored as part of a device list stored in main memory. Plug and Play systems will dynamically allocate the port addresses. The addresses in use on any particular computer can be found using the MSDOS MSD utility or the *'System/Ports'* option in Device Manager found in Windows Control Panel. If this is not available on the machine, the DEBUG utility can be used. When DEBUG runs, the DOS prompt is replaced by DEBUG's minus sign prompt. When the command

d0040:0008

is entered, a set of hex numbers will appear on the screen. A typical line might be

78 03 BC 03 00 00 00 00

The first two bytes indicate that LPT1 is in use at address 0378 (note that the bytes are displayed in reverse order) and that LPT2 is in use at address 03BC. To get back to the DOS prompt the letter 'q' has to be entered at the minus prompt.

Parallel Cable Connections

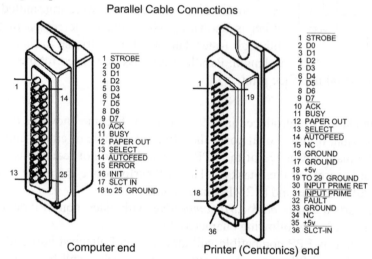

Computer end   Printer (Centronics) end

The parallel port's pin connections

This table shows how the pins are used to control a printer when in Standard Parallel Port Mode.

Pins	Direction	Active signal	Functions in SPP mode
2 to 9	Out	-----	**D0 to D7:** Used to take the data byte out to the printer.
10	In	1=normal 0=acknowledge receipt of data	**ACK:** (Acknowledge) Used by printer to tell computer it has received and printed the transmitted data and is ready for more.
11	In	0=printer busy 1=printer not busy	**BUSY:** Used by printer to tell the computer that it is busy printing and that it cannot currently accept any more data.
12	In	0=printer has paper 1=out of paper	**PE:** (Paper Empty) Used by printer to tell computer it is out of paper
13	In	0=printer offline 1=printer online	**SELECT:** Used to indicate to the computer whether the printer is online or offline.
14	Out	Active low	**AUTOFEED:** Produces a printer carriage return and line feed after each line is printed - when this line is held low.
15	In	1=no error 0=printer error	**ERROR:** Printer indicates an unspecified operational error
16	Out	Active low	**INIT:** Computer initialises (i.e. resets) the printer when pulsed low and then returned to high.
17	Out	Active low	**SELECTIN:** Allows printer to be brought on or off line by computer. When brought low by the computer, your printer lowers the SELECT pin in response.
18 to 25	-	-	Ground

Notes:

- A high logic level is regarded as being +5 volts, while a low logic level is regarded as being zero volts.
- The second column (marked as *"Direction")* indicates whether the signal is going out of that parallel port pin, or coming in from a printer.
- The third column (marked as *'Active Signal'*) indicates what voltage change to expect on a pin when the signal is made active. For example, pin 11, the printer's BUSY indicator, is an

active high input. This means that the pin is normally held at zero volts and is taken up to +5 volts when the printer is busy. Pin 15, on the other hand, is an active low input (i.e. it is normally held at +5 volts and this is reduced to zero volts if an error occurs in the printer).

- Some pins are held in one state for a long time while others change state regularly. For example, the Paper Empty, ERROR and SELECT pins remain in the one state during an entire printing task, while other pins such as STROBE and ACK flip between states regularly.
- Usually, a high voltage on a pin corresponds to a logic 1 stored in a register bit. There are three pins that are exceptions to this rule. The BUSY, AUTOFEED and SELECTIN pins are known as *"Hardware Inverted"*. This means that a high voltage on these pins corresponds to a logic 0 in the register bits, while a zero voltage on the pins corresponds to a logic 1 in the register bits.
- The SELECTIN signal takes the printer off line. This was often used with daisywheel and golf ball head printers where the document to be printed would have special printer codes embedded in the text. When the text altered (e.g. to an Italics font) the printer would be automatically taken off line to allow the operator to change print heads.
- An input pin on the parallel port can have its state altered by connecting it to either +5 volts or to ground, indicating a 1 or a 0. However, directly altering the voltage on the pins risks damaging the port's electronics and may not result in a clean enough signal. The wiring should include a line-driving buffer, such as a 74LS244 or 4050 chip to protect the computer. Only attempt this if you are competent with electronic circuits.

The port's electronics

The motherboard's parallel port socket is wired through three data registers. These are small memory storage areas that store information that will pass between the port and the printer.

The three registers are:

Register Name	Register Purpose	Pins used
The Data Register	Used to send characters <u>OUT</u> to the printer.	Wired through eight pins (pin 2 to pin 9)
The Printer Control Register	Used to send control information <u>OUT</u> to the printer.	Wired through four active pins (pins 1, 14, 16, 17)
The Printer Status Register	Used to store printer information coming <u>IN</u> from the printer	Wired through five active pins (pins 10, 11, 12, 13, 15)

The diagram shows the relationship between the parallel port pins and the register contents.

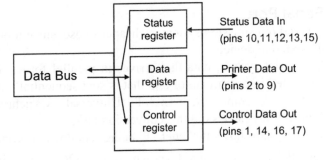

Printing via the parallel port

Whereas the serial port has its own chip to carry out data transmission, the Standard Parallel Port requires these tasks to be carried out by the computer's CPU. The computer can feed data to the printer much faster than the mechanical printing process can deal with it, and so a system of flow control (known as *'handshaking'*) must be used.

The process varies slightly but a general description is as follows:

- Using the CPU, move a byte of data along the Data Bus into the parallel port's Data Register. All eight bits in the register are then placed on pins 2 to 9 of the parallel port.
- Check to see if the printer is busy, by examining the state of the BUSY line. If the printer is busy, it will not accept any data, thus any data that is written will be lost.
- When the printer is free, pulse the STROBE line (pin 1) low for approximately 5 microseconds to 1 millisecond before restoring to a high level. This should energise the

printer end and result in the printer reading the data off the data lines and switching its own BUSY line high.

- Check the BUSY line (pin 11). When the printer is ready to receive the next data byte, it will switch its BUSY line low again.
- When the BUSY line goes low, repeat the process.

In other systems, the printer informs the PC that the data is received by bringing the ACKNOWLEDGE line (pin 10) low for about 5 milliseconds.

If the printer runs out of paper, the printer's electronics automatically alter the value on pin 12 on its Centronics socket from low to high. This changed value is carried back to the parallel port by the printer cable.   The changed value arrives at pin 12 of the port and alters the value in the Status Register. The computer reads the Status Register and knows that the printer is out of paper.

Many modern printers, particularly lasers, ignore all control signals apart from the STROBE signal.

The Parallel Port as an Input/Output Port

Standard Mode

The Standard Mode, also known as the *'Centronics'* or *'Compatibility'* Mode, is purely an output system and does not expect any input other than status information (e.g. out-of-paper or paper-jam information). No user data enters the computer using this mode.

Nibble Mode

The Standard Centronics interface has four lines that are used to signal problems to the computer (such as shortage of paper). If the control software is written to examine these lines, then the parallel port offers the possibility of being a two-way device.   Since the data being read into the parallel port is only four bits wide, only half a byte, i.e. a *'nibble'*, can be transferred at a time. This is described as *'four bit mode'*.   Incoming data is therefore substantially slower than outgoing data and is typically 80Kb per second. All parallel ports can operate in this mode, since every port has these four input lines.

Byte Mode

Four-bit working is inadequate for fast data transfer and a full bi-directional parallel port was first introduced as early as 1987, with the IBM PS/2 range of computers. Here, the eight data lines are capable of both reading and writing data, allowing the port to be an input as well as an output device. This significantly speeds up data transfers to a maximum of 300Kb per second. However, the system is still hampered by the CPU having to carry out all the port's handshaking and flow control activities.

Serial Port

A serial transmission system is cheaper to use, since it only requires a single channel between the PC and the external device.

In a serial system, data that arrives in parallel format from the bus is converted into a stream of bits that is sent sequentially along the single cable.   A chip called UART (Universal Asynchronous Receiver Transmitter) carries out this conversion task.

The diagram shows the letter 'T' being sent down a serial cable.

Serial Port   01010100→   Receiving Device

The PC uses a standard known as RS232C and is implemented as COM1 and, if fitted, COM2, COM3 and COM4.

An updated version known as RS-232D meets CCITT V.24, V2.28 and ISO IS2110 standards.

Another version, the RS 422 / RS485, is used extensively to control equipment. This allows multi-drop connections from a controller, via a two-wire bus to up to 32 devices at a range of up to 1200m/4000ft.

Common devices to be found on a serial port are printers, plotters, modems, remotely controlled instruments and machinery. Although the example above shows data being transmitted out of the port to a device, it should be stressed that the RS232 port is essentially a bi-directional port. This means that data can also be passed in to the port from an external device.

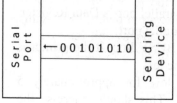

Serial Port   ←00101010   Sending Device

The diagram on the left shows the letter 'T' being received into a serial port.

A good example of an input device is a serial mouse. Other examples are bar code readers, electronic tills and remote monitoring equipment. In the case of a modem, the port will transfer data both <u>in</u> and <u>out</u> of the PC.

The serial port is often used for instrument control. The computer sends out commands on the RS232 port to the instrument's serial interface. The commands may set up the instrument for certain purposes and initiate the resultant readings, which are transmitted back to the computer on the same serial cable. This can be used over short distances for activities such as manufacturing test beds and the digital control of electronic or radio equipment. When used via modems or dedicated telephone lines, longer distances are achieved. This allows for the remote control of apparatus and remote data logging.

Like the parallel ports, the serial ports are detected at power up and their addresses stored in memory. The normal address for COM1 is 3F8h and the normal address for COM2 is 2F8h.

As with the parallel ports, the serial port addresses in use on any particular computer can be found by using the MSDOS MSD utility or the Windows *'Ports'* option from the *'Device Manager'* menu, available from the *'System'* option of *'Control Panel'* option of the *'Settings'* menu. In XP, *'Device Manager'* is accessed through the *'Hardware'* tab of *'System'*.

Alternatively, the DEBUG utility can be used to interrogate the table with the command:
d0040:0000
The RS232 port and serial communications are covered in detail in the chapter on *'Data Communications'*.

PC Cards (PCMCIA) & CardBus

Announced in 1990, the PCMCIA standard (<u>P</u>ersonal <u>C</u>omputer <u>M</u>emory <u>C</u>ard <u>I</u>nternational <u>A</u>ssociation) appeared as a standard interface for portable computer users. All major hardware and software suppliers support the standard. The standard aims to allow the easy connection of a range of add-ons. PCMCIA products are now referred to as *'PC Cards'*.

The PCMCIA connection is the portable's equivalent of the expansion slots on a desktop machine. An add-on card is about the size of a credit card and the original intention was to allow the easy connection of additional memory chips

Memory Cards

The cards have a 68-pin plug at one end and connect to sockets inside palmtop/notebook computers and digital cameras. Once inserted, they act like a normal bank of memory configured as a RamDisc. This means that it looks within Windows like an extra disk drive and can be read/written like a hard disk.

It can be purchased as a complete unit and it is also sold as an adapter to take standard flash memory cards such as SmartMedia, CompactFlash, and Small ATA cards. They are either Type I or type II devices and they operate on the 3.3v or 5v power taken from the computer.

They either use SRAM which needs a small lithium backup battery to retain stored data once the card is extracted from the computer or they use Flash RAM which does not need battery backup.

When a card is withdrawn, it retains the data stored in its chips until it is required again.

This provides portability, as the card can be pulled out of one machine and inserted in another machine, just like a floppy disk.

The cards mostly use static RAM as the storage medium with the more expensive Flash RAM providing larger capacities. Memory cards are available with capacities ranging from 32MB to 1024MB.

Since these cards have no moving parts, they are immune from shocks and vibration. They also operate down to 0° C and as high as 55° C. This makes them a good option for rugged environments.

PCMCIA Interface

PCMCIA is now used mainly as a hardware I/O standard, allowing the connection of a whole range of devices already associated with desktop PCs. These include disk drives, CD-ROMs, sound cards, digital cameras, video capture cards, data acquisition cards, modems, faxes, and LAN interface cards. These connect through the PCMCIA interface and ignore any ISA, MCA or EISA bus that might be on the machine. The system dynamically assigns I/O addresses and IRQs to the cards during the boot-up or when cards are inserted.

Advantages

- Speed. Flash RAM has a claimed access time that is 10,000 times faster than a hard disk.
- Software could packaged in this credit-card format.
- Easy change of cards, while the computer is still running - known as *'hot plugging'* or *'hot swapping'*. The new card should be automatically detected and recognised by the interface, based on the information stored and supplied by the card. The functions of some of the pins on the interface are re-mapped according to the device detected. By default, the card is assumed to be a memory card. Since the process is automatic, there is no need to re-boot the computer each time a card is changed.

Disadvantage

- The range of add-ons remains much more expensive then their desktop counterparts.

Physical Versions

- Type 1 of the standard covers the use of the card as a memory storage device. This defines the physical thickness of the card as 3.3mm and size 54mm by 85mm.
- Type 2 announced in 1992, expanded the PCMCIA standard use to cover the connection between card and machine as the basis for designing a range of I/O (input/output) add-on cards for LAN adapters, SCSI controllers, modems, sound cards, video capture cards, etc. This card is 5mm thick and has a size of 48mm by 75mm. This is the type most commonly fitted to portable computers and digital cameras. While the larger type 3 was intended for disk drives, manufacturers have miniaturised their drives so that they fit in a type 2 socket. Examples are the 2GB and 5GB drives from Toshiba and Kingston.
- Extended versions of Version 1 and Version 2 standards are available. These have the same width and thickness as the normal version but allow for extra long cards to be used. This allows even more complex circuitry to be mounted on the cards but means that the cards will protrude from the computer's casing by up to 135mm.
- Type 3 is 10.5mm thick to allow for the inclusion of larger peripherals and small hard disk drives such as the 520MB Kingston drive, the 270MB SyQuest drive and the Hitachi MP-EG1A 260MB digital camcorder's drive.
- Type 4 is 16mm thick to allow for the inclusion of larger capacity hard disk drives. IBM, Western Digital, Hewlett Packard, Maxtor and Connor have produced hard disks to this format, with disks sizes as small as 1.3" and 1.8".
- Type 5 is 18mm thick and was announced by Toshiba for its wireless network cards.

All types plug into the same 68-pin interface socket, arranged as two rows of 34 pins.

Standards

- PCMCIA 1.0 stated the minimum specification for early cards.
- PCMCIA 2.1 specified the interfaces used with the 16-bit cards.
- PCMCIA 3.0 is the new CardBus system and supports 32-bit working, DMA and 3.3volt working (older cards require 5 volts while newer portables work on 3.3volts). It has a 32-bit address bus and a 32-bit data bus. It supports bus mastering and runs at 33MHz, providing a throughput of 132MBps. Windows, from version 95 Release 2 onwards, has built-in CardBus card and socket services.

There is still work to be done to finalise file formats so that a card from one machine can be read by another machine. The hardware writing and reading is agreed but the format of the data interchange is still to be agreed. The device driver software has been given the title of *'enablers'*.

The low-level *'Socket Services'*, those that read the card data and link to the higher level *'Card Services'*, should ideally be implemented in BIOS. Unsurprisingly, Award and Phoenix (manufacturers of BIOS chips) lead the field in Socket Services. These services configure the card for the machine that is using it. Some cards use their own proprietary enablers, ignoring the Card and Socket Services. In general, software support is lagging the development of this new hardware.

Universal Serial Bus

The Universal Serial Bus (USB) was developed by Intel and it promises to be the new general-purpose PC port. It is expected to replace serial ports, parallel ports and internal interface cards as the means of connecting slow to medium speed external devices such as keyboards, mice, modems, scanners, etc.

Pin	Purpose	Colour
1	+5 v	Red
2	D-	White
3	D+	Green
4	Ground	Black

Unlike the large 9/25 pin serial connections and the 25/36 pin parallel connections, the USB requires only four wires in a light flex cable. There is one wire for the common ground, two to identify data in each direction and a 5v power supply wire. A fifth wire might be connected at the motherboard end, wired to a protective shield around the USB cable. The illustration shows a USB chassis socket.

It has many distinct advantages:

- The bus is relatively fast with a maximum date transfer rate of 12Mbps and a lower rate of 1.5Mbps for slow devices such as keyboards and mice.
- USB is Plug and Play compliant. So, devices can be 'hot swapped' - i.e. fitted and removed without rebooting or reconfiguring the machine. The configuration problems previously associated with adding and altering equipment is eliminated. If a new device is fitted while the computer is switched on, it is automatically configured.
- Since one entire USB system requires a single IRQ, problems of running out of machine IRQs will disappear.
- The bus provides its own power supply to any low-power devices that connect to it. There is no longer any need for each external device to have its own power unit. This should make peripherals cheaper and eliminates the tangle of power connections at the rear of machines. However, adding multiple devices may place a strain on the computer's own power supply.
- Devices were once designed to only work their own manufacturer's interface cards (e.g. scanners, some mice). USB devices do not have this restriction. This should make the new USB models of the devices cheaper and easier to connect.

USB allows a single port to connect many devices together is in daisy chain. Up to 127 devices can connect to a single USB port if hubs are used to expand the system. A hub is a star-like connector that connects a group of devices to a single connection point.

The diagram shows a PC with two USB ports. Port 2 connects directly to a hub and this has three outlets connected to USB devices. Typical USB hubs support four, five or seven port outlets.

Port 1 connects to two devices that are daisy chained to the port. One of these devices also acts as a hub and has two further devices connected to it.

A number of monitors are available with multiple USB ports mounted on the base. So, a PC port may connect to a monitor with the speakers, headphones and microphones connecting directly to the monitor. Or a keyboard could be designed as a hub, with a mouse, joystick and light pen attaching to a connection at the rear of the keyboard.

Many USB devices are now available such as digital cameras, mice, joysticks, monitors and keyboards. A digital camera with a USB cable can connect to the computer's USB port and will work without any additional software. The camera is automatically detected and the camera's memory is seen as an additional drive on the system. This allows the captured images to be copied from the camera to the computer's hard disk.

USB is supported by all modern PCI chipsets (i.e. HX, VX, TX, LX, BX, 800 series) but is only supported in Windows from version 95 Release 2 onwards. USB facilities are unavailable to all Windows 3.1 users and many Windows 95.

USB2

The current standard for Universal Serial Bus is USB 1.1. This specifies the data rate of up to 12Mb/s, with low speed signalling at 1.5Mb/s, on the same interface as mentioned earlier. The consortium developing USB includes companies such as Intel, Microsoft, Hewlett Packard, Lucent and Philips. It released a new standard (USB 2) at the start of the year 2000. USB 2 is entirely compatible with the existing cables and plugs, but runs at up to 480MHz. This frequency was chosen after calculations showed that it was as high as could be achieved on the existing cabling. Windows XP supports USB2, with the use of additional Microsoft drivers (available from the Microsoft website). USB2 co-exists with the IEEE 1394 FireWire (see below).

Generally, USB 2 will connect computer peripherals like Ethernet interfaces, printers, and so on, while FireWire connects Audio/Visual and multimedia applications like digital camcorders, digital TV equipment etc. Few USB2 peripherals are available so far, but USB2 hubs and devices are easily integrated with older USB1.1 equipment.

USB2 hubs and devices are easily integrated with older USB1.1 equipment. A *'transaction translator'* allows high-speed and low-speed devices to be used simultaneously without any affect on each other's speed. The USB 2.0 controller works out how to connect and route signals between 1.1 and 2.0 peripherals.

The ability to easily attach and use multiple USB devices simultaneously is a big benefit of USB 2.0. So, for example, a PC can have a scanner, an ADSL modem, a webcam, several USB hard disks, a removable memory key and several printers (e.g. laser and inkjet), a keyboard and a mouse all working at the same time. However, this raises a few problems:

Bandwidth

A port's available USB bandwidth is *shared* between devices. If several peripherals all want high-speed data transfers, they have to share the available bandwidth. A solution may be the fitting of an additional USB card in one of the computer's PCI slot. Since the bandwidth is restricted on any individual port, adding additional ports increases the total USB bandwidth that is available.

Power

Each port can only provide 2.5W of power (500mA at 5Volts) and this has to be shared by all devices that do not provide their own external power supply. While low-power devices such as keyboards and mice consume less than 100mA each, high-power devices such as digital cameras and bus-powered hubs, require over 100mA each. Windows displays a warning message if it detects an attempt to draw too much power from a port. Since the 2.5W limit applies to a single USB port, devices can be attached via a second or third USB port (if the PC provides them). Alternatively, a *powered* hub can be fitted, so that the hub can provide the extra power to its attached devices. FireWire, the rival to USB 2.0, provides up to 15W of power.

Processor time

Just as power is shared between devices, the computer's CPU has to share its processing time between the applications (e.g. video-conferencing, printing, loading and saving files, etc.). Although many devices can be *connected* simultaneously, the software for each may be slowed down if too many applications are *run* simultaneously. USB carries out most data transfers itself, compared to full bus-mastering systems). As a result, heavy data peripherals (e.g. scanners, optical drives, broadband downloads, etc.) can overload the CPU, producing bottlenecks.

This is a particular problem with older machines that have slower CPUs.

Compatibility Rules

USB 2.0 is both backwards and forwards compatible with USB 1.1. This means:
- Fully compliant USB 1.1 cables will work at USB2 speeds; cheaper-quality cables may need to be replaced.
- peripherals, including a 1.1 hub, will work on 2.0 ports, but at 1.1 speeds.
- 2.0 peripherals will work on 1.1 ports, but at 1.1 speeds.
- 2.0 peripherals connected to a 2.0 port via a 1.1 hub run at 1.1 speeds.
- Connecting a 1.1 peripheral in a 2.0 port will not affect the speed of any 2.0 devices connected to other 2.0 ports.

Each set of USB ports only uses one IRQ, regardless of the number of peripherals attached to them

Connectivity Rules

There are two different types of USB plug connector.

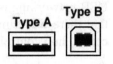

Type A is the flat rectangular plug that is inserted into the USB socket on the computer. Type B is the squarer plug that connects to peripheral devices. This has a smaller version known as the mini-B (see later). Occasionally, a device will use its own lead with a Type A for the PC end and its own proprietary plug at the peripheral end.

Hubs and socket extensions have a Type A plug at the PC end and one or more Type A sockets for peripherals to plug into.

USB only guarantees trouble-free operation with a cable length of 5m between the PC and the peripherals.

USB to parallel or to serial adapters.

Some users have expensive existing peripherals that they do not wish to upgrade (e.g. colour printers, modems, monitoring equipment, etc.).

USB-to-parallel and USB-to-serial adapters can be used and they often comprise a cable with the translation electronics enclosed in the plug. From a user's point of view, the cable allows a parallel or serial peripheral to be connected to a USB socket. These adapters work as long as the software works with 'logical' ports (eg. COM1 or LPT1) and doesn't demand the actual physical hardware address of the device. Additionally, most USB-to-parallel adapters are not bi-directional, while many parallel devices provide bi-directional services to their software.

Extending USB Connectivity

Hubs

A hub is an external box you connect to a PC's USB A socket and it, in turn, provides additional USB A sockets. This can be used to allow the connection of extra peripherals and page 149 of the book shows multiple peripherals being connected through several hubs.

Powered hubs, also known as active hubs, can also be used to extend the distance between a peripheral and the PC beyond the 5m limit. A 5m cable is used to connect the PC to a hub and a further 5m cable is used to connect the hub to the peripheral. If required, extra hubs can be placed in this daisy-chain to further extend the distance between the peripheral and the PC. There is a five-hub limit to any daisy-chain, so a peripheral can be up to 30m away from the PC.

The hubs acts as bi-directional repeaters, boosting the signals and passing them between devices. They also ensure that high-speed data is not sent over any low-speed links.

Upgrading to USB 2.0

If a PC has no USB ports, or has only 1.1 ports, USB 2.0 can be added without having to replace the motherboard. Most computer stores sell a USB PCI card that plugs into an unused PCI slot in the existing motherboard. This usually brings out four USB sockets to the rear of the computer.

USB Networking

The FireWire interface was designed as a peer-to-peer system. So, for example, connecting a FireWire cable between two PCs allows them to communicate with the minimum of setting up.

USB, however, was designed as a host-to-peripheral system so a direct cable connection cannot be used between the USB sockets of two PCs. Apart from the fact that this would short the two power supplies, USB is not designed to carry out normal peer-to-peer communication.

This is overcome by using a USB bridge, also known as a USB to USB adapter.

USB OTG

USB networking is concerned with making two PCs talk to each other. USB manufacturers then realised that there was a market for a system that let two *peripherals* talk to each other, without the need for a central hub controller. This facility was already available using FireWire.

Consequently, the USB On-The-Go (USB OTG) specification was developed as an addition to the USB 2.0 specification.

While USB 2.0 uses a host/peripheral method, with the host being the PC's hub controller. OTG extends this to introduce peripherals that act *as 'dual role devices'* (DRDs). This means that these peripherals built with this capability can play the role of either a host or a peripheral when required, still using the same OTG connector. So, for example an OTG-enabled digital camera would act as a peripheral when connected to a PC – but would act as a host when connected to a compatible printer. In the first example, it functions in a way that is 100% compliant with USB 2.0. In the second example, it would be able to print pictures without the need for a PC being connected. In the same way, a camera or camcorder could save its media straight to an external USB disk drive, without needing a PC.

Apart from cameras and camcorders, OTG has obvious applications for PDAs and mobile phones.

The USB OTG Working Group gives the following examples of use:

Mobile phone to mobile phone -	exchanging contact information
Mobile phone to digital camera -	emailing photographs
Mobile phone to MP3 player -	downloading music files
Mobile phone to external drive/PDA -	downloading files
Digital camera to digital camera -	exchanging photographs
Scanner to printer -	photocopy documents
Scanner to external drive/PDA -	save scanned documents
PDA to PDA -	exchange files
PDA to printer -	print documents

Many of these functions were carried out with dedicated interfaces. For examples, different makes of PDA used their own proprietary cradles to connect to PCs. Each PDA also use its own proprietary brand of external keyboard. USB OTG means that cradles will no longer be required and any OTG-enabled keyboard will work with any OTG-compatible PDA. Of course, each OTG device still needs to provide its own driver to interface with the OTG system.

USB OTG is faster and cheaper to implement than Bluetooth, a current popular interface methods for peripherals.

OTG-enabled peripherals use miniature USB plugs and sockets, called the mini-A and mini-B. These use five wires instead of the usual four.

Wireless USB

Wireless USB provides the features of USB 2.0 without the need for any cables and hubs. It is much faster than the wireless systems currently used for a keyboard or a mouse, providing 480Mpbs at up to 3m range and a still very respectable 110Mbps at up to 10m.

Its intended uses include connecting PCs to home entertainment systems, disk drives, printers, scanners, digital cameras and flash memory sticks.

FireWire

Another high-performance serial bus is IEEE-1394, commonly known as *'Firewire'*. This was developed from the Apple computer range and is also known as the *'Multimedia Connection'* since it allows camcorders, scanners, disk drives, DVD players, CD-ROMs and printers to share a common connecting bus. The common interface means that it is also suitable for the home networking of PCs.

Like the USB system, it supports up to 63 devices. However, FireWire does not require the use of hubs as each device has a common connection to all other devices - including the PC. The standard connecting cables are 6-wire; two for the power and four used to connect to consumer audio and video products (TV sets, VCRs, amplifiers, etc). The four bus wires are configured as two twisted pairs, crossed between ends to provide transmit and receive pairs. FireWire devices have several sockets and a 1394 cable plugs into the sockets of the devices to be connected. There are no cable length restrictions (as with LANS) and no need to set device ID numbers (as with SCSI). The only restriction is that the devices must not be cabled in a way that wires the system as a loop.

Sony uses a four-wire variant (known as *'i-link'*) for its products, using the IEEE-1394.1 standard.

Despite its simplicity, FireWire is an extremely fast interface that can move data at 100Mbps, 200Mbps or 400Mbps. Even the slowest speed is capable of simultaneously delivering two full-motion video channels running at the high video rate of 30fps, accompanied by CD quality stereo sound. It multiplexes data such as compressed video and digitised audio along with device control commands on the common bus.

Many DVC (Digital Video Cassette) systems use FireWire on their camcorders. Other major players such as JVC, Hitachi and Philips will also have FireWire systems on their D-VHS (Digital VHS) recorders. Since DVC requires 3.5Mb per sec (i.e. 28Mbps), it cannot be handled by USB (12Mbps limit) but is well within FireWire's capabilities. On the other hand, a 90-minute video could require almost 19GB of hard disk space. This places this aspect of FireWire at the professional end of the video market.

FireWire devices, like USB devices, are hot swappable.

FireWire is fully supported from Windows 98 onwards and as an upgrade to Windows 95.

FireWire 2

Version 2.0 of FireWire has now appeared. Known as IEEE 1394b, it can potentially run up to 1.6Gbps, four times faster than basic FireWire and is easily the fastest external bus that is currently available. It also claims to travel greater distances without degradation, and carries greater power on its cable than the first implementation (allowing more devices to be powered directly by the computer). A 3.2Gbps version for use with optical fibre cables is being developed; this is aimed particularly at multimedia and video distribution

Relative Uses

Both FireWire and USB are competing with Ultra SCSI and Fibre Channel for the high-speed bus market. The likely uses of USB and FireWire are complementary rather than competing.

- USB remains the option for input devices (mouse/keyboard/joystick), audio (sound/music/ telephone), printers, scanners, storage devices (floppy, tape) and slow speed communications (modems, ISDN)
- FireWire offers a higher performance for top-end devices such as DVD drives, DVC cameras, D-VHS recorders and wide-band networking. Some CD-ROM drives and fast hard disk systems also use FireWire interfaces.

Wireless interfaces

There are a range of wireless data communications standards. Most of these are used mainly in LAN and WAN networks, so they are described in full in the *'Local Area Networks'* chapter.

However, two technologies that are becoming more common in non-networked computers are IrDA (and infrared standard) and Bluetooth (a radio standard). These technologies have found more traditional computer uses – for example, a wireless mouse and keyboard that run on IrDA protocols.

Comparison of serial interface performances		
Interface	**Cabling**	**Max Data Rate**
Serial (RS232)	Twisted Pair	115kbps
Infrared (IrDA)	Optical Beam	4Mbps
USB 1	4-wire Cable	12Mbps
USB2	4 wire Cable	480Mbps
FireWire (IEEE 1394)	6 wire Cable	400Mbps
FireWire (IEEE 1394b)	6 wire Cable	1.6Gbps
Bluetooth 1.1	Wireless	720kbps
Bluetooth 1.2 (under development)	Wireless	2 to 3 Mbps
Bluetooth 2.0 (under development)	Wireless	Up to 12Mbps

Wireless technologies, and Bluetooth in particular, are often referred to as 'Personal Area Networks', as the computer is considered to be the 'master' and the devices to be 'slaves' in a tiny network known as a '*piconet*'.

Infra-Red protocols and connectors

CIR – Consumer IR
CIR is a medium-range IR port for control of consumer goods such as hi-fis, VCRs and so on. It is a relatively simple 4-pin connector, compared to IrDA's 6-pin connector to the Infra-red receiver. Similar consumer-based remote control protocols include NEC, RC-5 and RC-0.

ASK-IR
ASK-IR has a basic data rate of 9.6kbps, though speeds of up to 38.4kbps are possible.

SIR
The first IrDA standard was SIR (Serial Infra-Red). It was capable of a data rate of just 9600bps to 115.2kbps, and is now superseded by the FIR protocol that is used in version 1.2 of IrDA for most applications. However, it has a higher distance than FIR, and so is still used by devices that require a long range, but a higher data rate than CIR offers.

MIR
Introduced in IrDA 1.1, MIR (Medium speed Infra-Red) offers a higher data rate of 1.152Mbps. It offers a middle ground between SIR and FIR, both in terms of speed and range.

FIR
Stands for Fast Infrared transmit mode (IrDA 1.1 Standard), which is the capability to transmit data up to 4 Mbits/sec. SIR stands for Serial Infrared transmit mode (IrDA 1.0 Standard), which is the capability to transmit data at 115.2 Kbits/sec.

VFIR
As you might expect, VFIR stands for Very Fast Infra-Red, and is likely to be adopted in the next version of the IrDA standard. It is expected to reach a data rate of 16Mbps.

Display Technology

For many years the term *'Computer Video'* was used to describe the techniques used to transfer computer images to the monitor, and the piece of equipment that generated the image is indeed still often called the *'video adapter'*. The images displayed could be mainly static (as in the case of databases or word processing) or could be animated (as in the case of games, graphic simulations, etc). These days, 'computer video' describes the specific technique of showing real-life video footage for multimedia presentations. This chapter examines the technology of monitors and computer graphics cards and discusses the technical and operational factors to be considered when choosing - and using - such devices.

The visual output of the early mainframe computers was only plain text and numbers. Usually this output was directed to a line printer. Even when screens became more common, they were mostly used to *'monitor'* the computing process. The introduction of the personal computers brought the first moves towards a more attractive presentation. IBM machines introduced its *'IBM character set'* for screen and printer and this provided some line and box graphics. There was no need for sophisticated screens and early monitors were crude, low-definition devices.

Two main developments have led to greatly improved monitor design:

- Programs have become increasingly more graphics based (Computer Aided Design, Desktop Publishing, Windows, multimedia, etc.). These programs required monitors that could display ever more detailed output.
- Users were spending much longer periods in front of the monitor, as the computer developed into more of a personal tool. This raised questions of eyestrain, fatigue and other harmful effects that had to be addressed.

Monitors, and their hardware and software drivers, are becoming increasingly complex devices. There is a wide choice of specifications, techniques, performances and prices. There is no overall *'correct'* choice; there is only an appropriate choice for a particular use. For example, it would be a waste of a company's resources to buy a £2,000 large screen, high performance monitor and graphics accelerator card for a PC that is used only for occasional word processing. On the other hand, the same expensive monitor and card might be absolute necessities for detailed work in a design office.

Monitor Construction

Monochrome Monitors

The construction of computer monitors is identical to that of television screens. The monitor is based around a CRT (cathode ray tube) that contains the main elements shown in the diagram, plus control and amplifier circuitry. The electron gun, or *'cathode'*, produces an electron cloud that is then drawn as an accelerated stream towards the front screen of the CRT, which is held at a very high voltage. When the electrons strike the coating on the inside of the tube they cause a temporary phosphorescence of that area of the tube surface. This causes a bright spot to appear in the middle of the monitor screen.

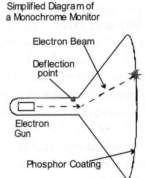

Simplified Diagram of a Monochrome Monitor

Electron Beam

Deflection point

Electron Gun

Phosphor Coating

To produce a picture from this system, the two other requirements are:

- The whole of the screen should be covered by the beam.
- The beam should be modulated, to provide a grey scale.

Scanning

The CRT monitor is a serial device. Each individual area of the screen has to be illuminated to different degrees to provide a picture. It is not practical to have a separate gun for each spot on the screen. The one gun has to handle the whole screen surface. The process of ensuring that the electron beam systematically

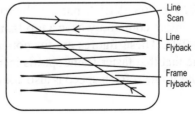

Line Scan

Line Flyback

Frame Flyback

covers each part of the monitor screen is known as *'scanning'*.

The screen scanning process executes in the same way that a book page is read - from left to right and from top to bottom, one line at a time. The finished picture is, in effect, composed of a set of parallel lines, called a *'raster'*.

To achieve this, electronic circuitry is introduced to deflect the electron beam in both the horizontal and vertical directions. The movement from left to right, and the accompanying rapid *'line flyback'* from right to left is carried out by the *'line scan'* circuitry. The slower movement down the screen and the final rapid *'frame flyback'* is carried out by the *'frame scan'* circuitry. These scans are synchronised by line and frame scan oscillators.

Commencing from the top left corner of the screen, the beam is moved rightwards at a constant, pre-determined speed. When it reaches the rightmost edge, the electron stream is switched off, while the deflection circuits 'fly back' the position to the left edge of the screen, ready for the next line of scan. The period when the stream is switched off is known as the *'line blanking'* period. This process is repeated hundreds of times, until the entire screen is covered. The exact amount of lines depends on the resolution of the screen standard in use - anywhere between 480 lines and 1600 lines or over. When the last line is traced on the screen, the electron stream is again switched off - the *'frame blanking'* period, while the beam is returned to the top left corner of the screen.

Modulation

In a TV receiver, the intensity of the beam can be varied continuously across the scan of the line, limited only by the quality of the controlling electronics. For computer monitors, each line is considered to have a certain amount of elements along its length. Each element can then be illuminated or not, to produce the picture intelligence. Each of the picture elements is known as a *'pixel'*. The number of picture lines and the number of pixels across each line are a measure of the *'resolution'* of the screen picture. A SVGA screen, for example, has a resolution of 800 x 600 - i.e. is has a matrix of 800 pixels across by 600 pixels down.

If a monitor were to have a modulating input signal that was TTL (transistor-transistor logic) the input voltage would switch between +5 volts and 0 volts. The electron stream would either be completely on or completely off. Such a monitor would not be able to provide shades of grey. If the flow of electrons can be stepped in discrete stages, then a grey scale can be implemented. The input here would be an analogue signal, which is capable of providing degrees of modulation of the electron beam. In an ideal world, the modulating signal would vary in infinitely small steps, to display a huge amount of picture detail. While the monitor can cope with fairly small changes, a large amount of memory is required to store such variations making high-resolution graphics cards more expensive.

Frame refresh speeds

The screen produced by the above process has only a short life, as the glow from the phosphoresced areas rapidly dies away. The whole process has to be repeated regularly enough so that the persistence of vision of the human eye perceives the screen as a continuous display, with no detectable flicker. Where the picture has a dark background, any flicker is less noticeable. Where there is a white background, the constant cycle of lighting a pixel, letting the pixel illumination dull, followed by again fully illuminating the pixel causes the most pronounced flicker. This can be particularly noticeable with Windows, since most backgrounds are light-coloured. Initially, 40 frames per second was considered adequate and a refresh rate of 50Hz (cycles per second) was used. This was discovered to be too slow, as it still produced enough flicker to cause eyestrain and headaches. 40Hz is the rate at which most people can detect flicker. Many people are capable of detecting and being bothered by flicker at up to 70Hz. At 72Hz, flicker ceases to be a factor.

Over the years, the frame refresh speeds - i.e. the vertical scanning frequency - has gradually increased. At the end of 1997, VESA recommended 85Hz as the refresh rate for 14" monitors. VESA has set 70Hz as the lowest acceptable rate for SVGA graphics adapters, with 72Hz as the acceptable standard. With 1024 x 768, VESA has set the rate at 70Hz, although larger screen sizes often use 76Hz. Modern monitors commonly have a top frame refresh speed exceeding 100Hz and some models have a top rate of 160Hz. These figures are for non-interlaced systems. The pace of improvement has been tempered by the fact that faster frame speeds increase the system bandwidth and thereby cost more to manufacture.

The frame refresh speed is also commonly known as the *'vertical scan range'*.

Line refresh speeds

The frame refresh speeds and screen resolutions have a direct bearing on the required speed from the line scan circuitry. Consider the frame refresh time being kept constant and the resolution being increased. The system has to produce more horizontal lines in the same time, so the line scan time has to be shortened, to get each line drawn faster. This results in a higher line scan frequency. Similarly, if the resolution remains constant but the frame refresh is speeded up, there will still be more lines drawn in the same time - the line frequency has to be increased. A VGA monitor has a line frequency of 31.5KHz. This means that 31,500 screen lines have to be traced out every second. Consider a SVGA screen (i.e. 800 x 600) with an 80Hz refresh rate. 48,000 screen lines would be required to be produced each second (i.e. 600 lines scanned 80 times per second). Monitors have a lower line refresh rate of around 30KHz and maximum refresh rates depend upon the quality of the product. Typical upper rates are around 100KHz for older models and up to 160KHz for top quality models.

The line refresh speed is also commonly known as the *'horizontal scan range'*.

Bandwidth

When a monitor is driven at a high resolution with high frame refresh speeds, much data has to be placed on the screen in a very short time. The ability of a system to achieve high throughput is measured by its *'bandwidth'*. The bandwidth is measured in MegaHertz (millions of cycles per second) and describes how quickly the electronic circuitry can change from the system voltage state to a zero voltage state; this in turn determines how many pixels can be handled per second. A high resolution screen will have more dots along each screen line. This will demand a greater throughput and hence a higher bandwidth. Similarly, a high frame refresh rates involves writing to the screen more often, which also increases the data moved in any one time period - i.e. the bandwidth is increased.

Running in VGA (640x480) mode only requires a bandwidth of 21.5MHz at the commonly used refresh rate of 70Hz. This bandwidth is determined by multiplying the horizontal resolution, vertical resolution and the frame refresh rate (i.e. 640 x 480 x 70 = 21,504,000)

Higher resolution SVGA modes might require a bandwidth of up to 270MHz (i.e. 2048 x 1536 x 85). The higher the system bandwidth, the more demanding is the monitor circuitry. This partly explains why a high-performance monitor is more expensive than poorer models.

Simply lowering the frame refresh rate would lower bandwidth and reduce monitor costs. This is an unacceptable solution, since it produces severe flicker problems. As a result, monitor resolutions and refresh rates have not improved at the same speed as many other computer components.

Interlacing

To provide high-resolution screens at lower cost, a system of *'interlacing'* is contrived. The picture is built up in two halves. Firstly, all the odd lines are built up. This is immediately followed by filling in all the even lines. If the frame speed is unchanged, then the whole picture takes twice as long to build up as a non-interlaced model. This reduces the required bandwidth and hence cost. The problems of a jerky
picture at low refresh speeds are reduced, since each frame refresh manages to update the whole screen, albeit only every other line. This used to be an acceptable compromise, although non-interlaced monitors are the best performers and are now universally sold. Non-interlaced models are also sometimes referred to as *'sequential'* systems. They draw every line, both odd and even, in a straight sequence until the whole screen is painted before returning to the top of the screen.

Synchronisation

The internal circuitry of the monitor contains oscillators to produce the necessary line and field scans. The start of these line and field scans must coincide with that required by the computer's graphics output. The cable between the computer and monitor carries the modulation information. It also carries line and frame synchronising pulses from the computer. These pulses are used to keep the oscillators in the monitor running at the correct timing. Without these synchronising pulses, the screen would soon suffer from *'line tear'* and *'frame roll'* as the slight timing differences between the two units became aggregated. The sync signals are usually two different TTL lines varying from 0v and 5v, one each for the line and frame pulses.

Dual Sync / Multi-Sync

Some older monitors only operated on a single line frequency. When attached to a computer graphics card, it adjusted its running speed to synchronise to that of the video output. This was a minor automatic adjustment and extended only to very limited frequency boundaries. Producing this single standard model required less complex circuitry and is cheaper.

'Dual Sync' monitors sensed the frequency of the incoming signal and locked to it if it is one of its two pre-set line frequencies - normally 31.5Khz and 35.5KHz.

Modern monitors are capable of automatically locking to a range of different line and frame scan frequencies within the bandwidth it is designed for. They are said to be 'multi-sync', 'multi-scanning' or 'autosync'.

If the upper limit of this scanning range is high enough, an element of future proofing is introduced, since the monitor will be able to handle any future specification upgrades (new standards will involve higher refresh rates). The fact that a monitor's circuitry can synchronise to a range of different refresh speeds, does not necessarily imply that it will perform equally well at all the standards it can cover. Indeed, models that are designed for high-resolution SVGA modes often perform less well when trying to handle lower standards.

Typical scan frequencies for the range of screen resolutions are given in the table.

	Line Scan (max)	Frame Scan (typical)
VGA	31.5KHz	60Hz, 70 Hz
640 x 480 VESA	37.5KHz	75Hz
SVGA 800 x 600 VESA standard	35.5KHz	56Hz
	37.8KHz	60Hz
	48KHz	72 Hz
	46.8KHz	75Hz
	53.7KHz	85Hz
1024 x 768 VESA standard	48.3KHz	60Hz
	56.5KHz	70Hz
	60KHz	75Hz
	68.7KHz	85Hz
1280x1024 VESA	80KHz	75Hz
	91.2KHz	85Hz

An autosynched monitor is ready, if the facility is provided, to auto-size the screen image so that the new picture occupies the entire screen area.

Aspect Ratio

This is the ratio of the screen's width to the screen's height. Monitor CRTs, like conventional TV screens, are built with a ratio of 4:3. To maintain a uniform screen display, the screen must be driven at the same rate - i.e. there should be 4 pixels across the screen for each three pixels down the screen. If this is achieved, then all the pixels on the screen will be square and graphics drawing is simplified. Most VGA and higher modes are in the 4:3 ratio, thus avoiding the need to stretch pixels to fit a 4:3 screen. Stretching would result in non-square pixels; for example drawing a box whose dimensions were 20 pixels by 20 pixels would not produce a box, but a rectangle. Similarly, a circle would produce an ellipse. These problems could be overcome - at the expense of further complexity (i.e. more calculations, more time).

Only outdated standards suffer from this problem. The SVGA standard, for example, is 800 x 600, which is exactly a 4:3 ratio.

Whilst only a few manufacturers currently produce video monitors to native widescreen video standards, such as 16:9 and 2.23:1, these standards are becoming more popular in games and DVD presentations. They are generally accommodated by "letterboxing" the displayed image on a standard 4:3 screen. A band above and below the image is unlit. The computer's graphic card has to support widescreen mode.

Colour Monitors

It was commonly held that a colour monitor was always better than a monochrome model. This was not true. Indeed, in some cases a monochrome monitor produced sharper results than a colour version. The techniques required to manufacture colour screens required a much more accurate alignment than was necessary with monochrome screens. A colour monitor displaying a monochrome screen may not have been as clear as the same display on a monochrome monitor. Certainly, a poorly adjusted colour monitor was much more difficult to use than a poorly adjusted monochrome monitor. Improvements in CRT construction, and the advent of TFT screens, have overcome many of these earlier problems.

There are many good reasons why users wish, or need, to use colour monitors:

- Art and graphic packages really require colour if they are to be used to the maximum effect. Professional packages allow for *'colour separations'*.   The various coloured components of the picture create their own separate printouts on a printer. The masters are taken to a commercial printer, where a separate print run is made for each colour. Each run overlays on the same sheet, to reproduce the original artwork.
- Multimedia and video almost always require colour for maximum realism and impact.
- Computer Aided Design packages make use of colour to represent different elements of the design. A street plan, for example, might show water routes in a different colour from electricity supply routes. Also, when technologists design a printed circuit board, each layer of connecting tracks is a different colour, with the silk screen layer being a different colour again. These jobs could be accomplished with a monochrome screen, but the viewing would be much more difficult, therefore less productive.
- Application programs are written to make use of colour to highlight menus, chosen options, etc.   A red message on a blue background is perfectly clear on a colour screen. When viewed on a monochrome screen, it is seen as one shade of dark grey on another shade of dark grey.   Colour screens make the reading of such menus easier, with less eyestrain.
- Sales and business presentations are greatly enhanced by colour.

Colour Principles

The human eye processes various light sources that are either:

- reflected from the printed page (known as *'subtractive mixing'*).
- directly targeted at the eye (known as *'additive mixing'*).

Subtractive Mixing

Natural daylight reflecting off a non light-absorbent paper (i.e. white) allows the full light spectrum to be reflected. These reflected wavelengths are mixed inside the eye and interpreted as white.   Adding ink or paint pigment to the paper surface results in the area affected selectively absorbing some of the wavelengths from the white light source. The viewer sees the resultant colour <u>reflection</u> from the mix. Since the introduction of the pigment have taken away some of the wavelengths, the process is termed *'subtractive mixing'*.

Primary Colour Mix	Result
Magenta + Yellow	Red
Cyan + Yellow	Green
Cyan + Magenta	Blue
Cyan + Magenta + Yellow	Black

The primary pigments are Cyan, Magenta and Yellow and the result of mixing them in equal quantities is shown in the table.   Other colours and hues are obtained by mixing the primary colours with unequal quantities.

In practice, it is easier to introduce a black ink (i.e. one that absorbs all light wavelengths) than to achieve the absolutely equal amounts of Cyan, Magenta and Yellow required for the same effect. Subtractive mixing uses the *'CMY colour model'* and CMYK printers use this principle and add a black ink for more consistent blacks and to achieve faster print speeds.

Additive Mixing

The colour monitor exploits the fact that the three primary colours, as detected by the eye, are red, green and blue (Hence the name RGB).   In this case the light is not reflected but is directly transmitted from the CRT screen to the eye. Any other colour of light can be obtained from mixing the three primary colours of light in the appropriate ratios.

For example, mixing red and green light produces yellow light, while mixing red, green and blue in the same proportions produces white light. Since the monitor CRT uses three different light <u>sources</u> to produce the colours, the process is termed *'additive mixing'*. If no light sources are added to the mix, no wavelengths reach the eye and the screen is perceived as being black.

CRT Construction

The monochrome monitor screen was only concerned with *'luminance'* - i.e. how bright a particular pixel on the screen should be. Screen brightness might vary from being off (i.e. black) through to fully on (i.e. white) and shades of grey (i.e. guns partly on).

The colour monitor is concerned with luminance - but it is also concerned with the <u>colour</u> of each pixel - known as the *'chrominance'* information. The colour output from the PC is sent out as three separate signals - one each for the red, green and blue components.

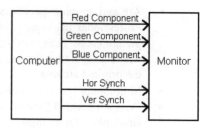

Other outputs carry the vertical and horizontal synchronisation signals. These video outputs are produced by the graphics card of the computer. A specially constructed monitor is required to produce the colour display.

The Shadow Mask Tube

The diagram shows a commonly used model of colour tube, which is called the *'shadow mask tube'*. The tube was originally invented by the Radio Corporation of America and first demonstrated as early as 1950. Although originally produced for colour TV tubes, the same technology is used in most current CRT monitors. More modern, improved, and more expensive alternatives exist in the *'Trinitron'* tube (see later).

The Shadow Mask tube is really three tubes in one and has three electron guns, one each for the red, green and blue components of the screen. Each of these guns produces an electron beam that can be either switched off and on (as in the RGB monitors) or have its intensity varied (as in analogue monitors).

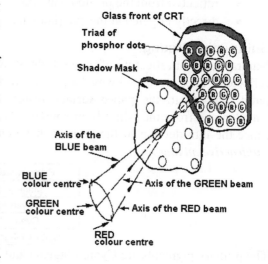

The inside of the tube is coated with many thousands of tiny dots of red, green and blue phosphor. These dots are arranged in triangles comprising a dot of each colour. It is this cluster of dots, referred to as *'triads'* or *'dot trios'*, which provides the luminance and chrominance for a single pixel.

When a colour phosphor is hit by an electron beam it emits a beam of coloured light and the mixing of the various beams of colour takes place in the viewers' eyes to produce the final perceived colour for each triad.

It is the job of each gun to emit, modulate, focus and accelerate its own electron beam towards its own set of phosphor dots. However, as a single beam scans, it would illuminate dots that were part of another colour set. To prevent this, a metal sheet is placed inside the tube, between the guns and the screen, about 1cm from the screen. This screen is perforated with tiny holes and these are aligned so that only the 'red' beam will ever be able to illuminate the red phosphors, the 'green' beam will only ever illuminate the green phosphors and the blue phosphors are only ever illuminated by the electron beam from the 'blue' gun. There is a single hole in the mask for each triangle of dots. The rest of the screen is *'shadowed'* off from the beam by the mask - hence the name *'shadow mask tube'*.

Since the holes only occupy a minority of the area of the mask, the mask absorbs the vast majority of the emitted electrons. As a result, colour tubes need much greater beam currents and a higher final anode voltage than a monochrome tube.

SIGNAL			COLOUR
R	G	B	
0	0	0	Black
0	0	1	Blue
0	1	0	Green
0	1	1	Cyan
1	0	0	Red
1	0	1	Magenta
1	1	0	Yellow
1	1	1	White
COLOURS AVAILABLE WITH RGB			

To obtain a pure white screen, all the guns are driven at the same amplitude. If any of the guns suffers partial or total failure, the picture will have a *'colour cast'*. A total failure of the red gun, for example, would result in a cyan cast (the complementary colour of green and blue). A partial failure of the blue gun produces a yellowish tinge to the display. Changing characteristics of components might lead to colour casts and these are usually eliminated by altering variable controls on the printed circuit board. Some monitors may provide external controls, to allow the drive of each gun to be altered.

Colour Purity

Colour purity confirms that a pure red (or green or blue) video drive produces a screen that is uniformly red (or green or blue) all over the screen area. Achieving and maintaining the alignment of each beam with its corresponding set of mask holes and phosphor dots is a tricky business. This work is carried out by trained staff, who have to open up the monitor case to carry out the adjustments.

The first adjustment is CENTRE PURITY, which ensures that the beams pass through the colour centres. If centre purity is incorrectly adjusted, then a pure red picture would begin by producing red at the left side of the screen. It would then drift away to other colours. Another adjustment is EDGE PURITY, which tackles the more common problem of obtaining purity in the corners of the monitor screen. Here a red picture would produce pure red at the screen centre, with loss of purity at the extremities. These tests are carried out by using a test screen of solid red, followed by the same tests for the other guns. In practice, loss of colour purity is not normally sufficiently severe to produce other than 'hot spots' - area where the solid colour suffers a change in tone.

Note: This effect can also be caused by shadow mask magnetisation (see next section). The purity should only be adjusted if de-gaussing proves ineffective.

Convergence

Any picture on a colour monitor is a mixture of three separate pictures. Even a monochrome display on a colour monitor is only a mixture of the red, green and blue pictures, in equal quantities. It is essential that the three pictures be correctly aligned with each other. This involves ensuring that any one graphics pixel is achieved by illuminating the phosphors in the same triad. Failures to align are normally at their worst away from the screen centre. For example a screen filled with a white grid might display properly at the centre while the vertical lines at the edges may be yellow (red + green) with a blue edge (known as

Misaligned Blue picture

Red and Green pictures aligned

'colour fringing'). Such misconvergence can vary by 0.5mm to 1.5mm across the screen and is a major cause of eyestrain.

Static Convergence is concerned with aligning the undeflected beams (i.e. converging the triad in the centre of the screen). Dynamic Convergence is concerned with the total area covered by the beam travel.

Note that a tube may have perfect colour purity and still be badly misconverged. Convergence tends to alter with age. At least one model has external controls for convergence - all the others have internal variables for use by trained technicians. Misconvergence is not a problem with Trinitron tubes or monochrome tubes, which only have a single gun.

It is not generally the job of the support technician to fix these problems; the technician only has to detect them and report them for repair.

Degaussing

The electron beams are easily deflected by magnetic fields. The shadow mask is metal and therefore able to be magnetised. If this happens, the unwanted magnetic fields will distort the beam - causing problems with purity. Likely sources of unwanted magnetic fields are loudspeakers and power supplies. In monitors, as in TV sets, a coil surrounds the tube. When the monitor is first switched on, the coil is automatically energised. A high alternating field is produced by the coil, which is gradually reduced over a period of seconds. This removes any residual magnetic field that may have been present on the shadow mask.

In adverse conditions, such as using computers on production lines, near heavy machinery, etc., the excessive local magnetic fields may render the automatic degaussing apparatus only partially effective. In these circumstances, the technician can manually degauss the screen using a degaussing coil or wand. These are plugged in to the mains supply and gradually moved in a circular motion over the face of the shadow mask tube for about a minute. Still maintaining this movement, the coil or wand should be slowly moved away from the face of the screen. At about 6 - 10 feet distance, the degaussing device can be switched off. Do not switch off the device close to the screen; otherwise the device acts as a gaussing device, instead of a degaussing device! All new monitors provide degaussing at switch-on as standard. An extra refinement is to have a degaussing button that will carry out the function at any time during the running of the system.

Trinitron Construction

The Sony Corporation of Japan developed the Trinitron CRT in 1968. Although the tube's construction

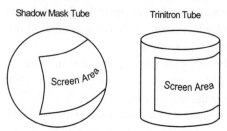

follows similar principles to the shadow mask tube, its approach produces a significantly different performance. The screen area (the part seen by the user) of a shadow mask tube resembles part of the surface of a sphere. The screen is curved in both the vertical and horizontal directions. This system provides for easy focusing of the electron beams on to the phosphor inner coating. The screen area of a Trinitron tube looks like part of the rounded surface of a cylinder.

The vertical direction is flat although the horizontal direction remains curved in most models. A few monitors, such as the Sony Multiscan F500, are flat in both planes.

The Trinitron tube has the following advantages over the shadow mask variety:

- Distortion of displayed lines is minimised.
- The screen corners are sharper.
- It suffers less glare from lighting.

Another major departure is in the distribution of the tube's phosphor coating. The Trinitron tube moves away from the triad cluster of coloured phosphors. Instead, the phosphors are arranged in vertical strips in alternating colours. These strips stretch continuously from the top to the bottom of the screen. A set of three colours is called a *'triplet'* instead of a triad.   Their construction sometimes covers a greater width than a triad, resulting in a poorer horizontal resolution than a shadow mask tube. To overcome this, Hitachi introduced an *'Enhanced Dot Pitch'* tube that is more densely coated in the horizontal direction, resulting in more horizontal triplets.

Because the screen is composed of stripes of colour, instead of independent clusters, the quality of the

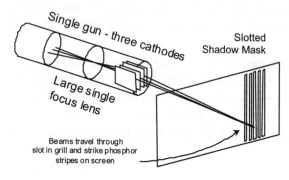

final picture is regarded as being superior - although some have not found it to their tastes. The shadow mask is replaced with an aperture grille that has a vertical slot for each vertical phosphor triad. The aperture grille contains less metal than a shadow mask. However, because the Trinitron tube has larger areas of phosphor to excite, it has to pass more current. This causes the grille to heat up, and distort in extreme cases. For this reason, Trinitron tubes that are run at high brightness levels sometimes exhibit convergence errors due to heat distortion in the aperture grille. This

disappears when the tube is run at a lower brightness.

The third important difference is in the construction of the guns. Instead of having three separate colour guns, as in the shadow mask, the Trinitron employs a single gun with three cathodes - it produces three beams.   The three beams have a common focus plane, which results in a sharper image and better focusing over the entire screen area. The use of a single focusing lens allows a larger gun dimension than the individual guns of the shadow mask tube. This results in higher beam density. This, together with fewer losses in the mask, results in a much brighter picture. Trinitron quality is measured in *'slot pitch'* or *'grill pitch'* instead of dot pitch. A 0.26mm slot pitch is about 0.28mm or 0.29mm dot pitch. The aperture grille is held in place by two fine supporting wires that run across the screen. This results in two fine horizontal lines appearing on the screen when a plain light pattern is displayed, but this generally does not present problems to users.   The Trinitron tube is used in a range of Sony, Taxan, Philips and Eizo monitors.

Energy Saving

Many manufacturers now take positive steps to reduce the power consumption of the computer, the monitor, or both, during periods of inactivity.

Typical power consumptions of CRT monitors are around 70W for a 15" model, 80W to 100W for a 17" model, 100W to 130W for a 19" model and 120W to 180W for a 21" model. This compares to around 35W for a 15" LCD monitor and around 40W for a 17" LCD monitor.

Power-saving efforts on CRT monitors centre round:

The Energy Star Programme - this is the voluntary code of practice agreed between the American Environmental Protection Agency and manufacturers. The code stipulates that units should be capable of entering a *'low power'* state of 30W maximum.

The DPMS System - this is the power-saving method recommended by VESA and can be used to meet the Energy Star standard. It is known as the *'Display Power Management Signalling'* system and depends upon the monitor and the graphics card both being DPMS compatible. Spare lines on the monitor connecting lead are used to carry the control signals from the PC to the monitor. The graphics card signals to the monitor how to control its energy-consuming components - i.e. the HOR and VER drive circuitry, the very high CRT voltages and the current to the tube's cathode. Differing power savings can be made, dependent upon the time required to bring the monitor back to full operation. The *'Suspend'* operation lowers power consumption to about 10-20% of its normal level and allows for a fairly fast recovery time. The *'Active Off'* operation lowers power consumption to about 5% but has a slower recovery time.

TCO-92 - this is a more stringent standard from Sweden that requires a 30W maximum on standby and 8W maximum on power down.

Meanwhile, Hitachi has produced its own power saving system that is not VESA compatible. It uses a serial port connection between the monitor and the computer. The provided software allows the serial connection to power down the monitor when it is not in use and controls the normal monitor settings.

Note

Although the main unit consumes less power than the monitor, steps can be taken to save energy by closing down the disk drive power or reducing the disk speed and by running the CPU at a reduced speed. Most computers are now available with the energy-saving techniques implemented either in software or in the BIOS. The facilities range from a single power-down facility to independent power-down times for CPU slow-down, hard disk power-down, monitor power-down and system power-down; intervals can be from one or two minutes up to one or two hours. Major manufacturers such as AMI and Phoenix incorporate these features in their new BIOS chips. In 1994, VESA introduced a standard for implementing power management via the BIOS (known as VBE/PM, the VESA BIOS Extension for Power Management). Many monitors now switch themselves off if no incoming signal is detected.

Resolution

The quality of a screen picture, in terms of its detail, can be defined by its *'resolution'*. The screen resolution is measured by the number of pixels across the screen, by the number of pixels that can be displayed in the vertical direction. The number of colours for each resolution in the table shows the most common figures. The colours available for higher resolutions are really limited by production costs, rather than technical considerations.

Even these high resolutions are unable to fully meet modern needs. Advertisers used to talk a lot about WYSIWYG (What You See Is What You Get). This means that the screen displays the image in the exact size and detail as would be expected in the final printed output. The higher resolutions of modern printers place an increasing demand on WYSIWYG DTP and graphics systems.

Consider that an A4 sheet is approximately 97 square inches - say 80 square inches printable area after taking borders into consideration. A typical laser printer or inkjet printer has an output at 600 dpi (dots per inch), or 360,000 dots per square inch. So, to display a full A4

Mode	Resolution
Base VGA	640 x 480
SVGA	800 x 600
8514/A	1024 x 768
XGA	1024 x 768
EVGA/SVGA	1024 x 768
WXGA	1280 x 768
SXGA	1280 x 1024
SXGAW	1600 x 1024
UXGA	1600 x 1200
WUXGA	1920 x 1200
QXGA	2048 x 1536
QSXGA	2560 x 2048
QUXGA	3200 x 2400
QUXGA-W	3840 x 2400

sheet on screen - at printer resolution - would require 80 x 360,000, or a full 28,800,000 dots. Clearly, even the highest screen resolution is incapable of fully displaying detailed DTP and CAD work. With current printers having 1200dpi or higher capability, the problem is greatly worsened.

These limitations are minimised by the *'zoom'* facility offered by many packages; this allows a close up view of a small area of the printed output. While zooming allows the fine detail to be inspected, it is no longer at the correct physical size. Many would argue that this is not a problem since users could not visually resolve 360,000 individual dots on a one inch square in any case.

Dot Pitch

In a shadow mask tube, the holes in the mask are set at pre-defined intervals across its surface. The triads of colour phosphors are laid on the inner screen at a matching pitch. The distance between the centre of one triad to the centre of the next nearest triad is known as the *'dot pitch'*. The dot pitch, therefore, is a measure of the finest quality possible in the picture from that particular monitor. The dot pitch is measured in fractions of a millimetre. The lower the dot pitch value, the more closely spaced are the individual illuminated spots - hence the better picture detail. Since adjacent triangles are offset, the dot pitch value is usually a diagonal measurement.

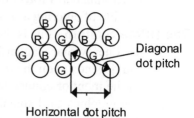

Users, however, view their monitors in terms of the screen resolution mentioned earlier. The dot pitch requires to be converted into the maximum horizontal resolution that the particular monitor can support. The value of the horizontal *'dots per inch'* is a more useful measure when deciding the quality of a monitor.

The horizontal dot pitch normally works out at a factor of around .866 times the manufacturers quoted diagonal dot pitch.

The table shows the <u>maximum</u> number of dots that can appear across different screen sizes.

Advertised screen size			14"	15"	17"	19"	21"
Theoretical width of screen			11.2"	12"	13.6"	15.2"	16.8"
Diagonal dot pitch	Horizontal pitch	Dots per inch	Maximum theoretical number of horizontal dots				
0.22mm	0.19mm	133	1492	1599	1812	2025	2238
0.25mm	0.22mm	117	1313	1407	1595	1782	1970
0.26mm	0.23mm	112	1263	1353	1533	1714	1894
0.28mm	0.24mm	104	1172	1256	1424	1591	1759
0.31mm	0.26mm	97	1094	1172	1329	1485	1641

The exact figures will vary by manufacturer and those in the table are working approximations. Manufacturers tend to err on the side of over-estimating the active image area of their screens. An inspection of a range of 17" monitors reveals that the actual screen diagonal size varies from 16.34" down to as little as 15.25". If the actual viewable area is less than the calculated area, then it follows that the actual number of viewable pixels is also likewise reduced. This means that the above table significantly overestimates the specification of the monitors. The real world performance is less than that shown. In the case of the 15.25" view from a 17" monitor, it means that the number of viewable pixels is less than 90% of the figure shown in the table. As a result of pressure, monitor manufacturers now often quote both the monitor size (e.g. 17") and the viewable screen size (e.g. 15.9").

As can be seen, there is a direct relationship between dot pitch, screen size and the maximum screen resolution. A .28mm dot pitch monitor has around 1424 dots per line on a 17" screen but has only around 1172 dots per line on a 14" screen. The 17" monitor in this case is capable of handling 1280 x 1024 mode with ease. The 14", on the other hand, has fewer dots on the screen than the number of individual pixels required by the 1280 x 1024 picture. The result is a marked loss of detail and the blurring of small characters. Since even the table shows idealised figures, the 14" monitor is best run at no more than 800 x 600.

Although the smallest dot pitch is more desirable, they are more costly to manufacture. .21mm and even .2mm dot pitch monitors are available but are expensive. Typical dot pitch sizes for colour SVGA monitors are 0.25m and 0.27mm. Some manufacturers claim that a .28mm 14" monitor is a 1024 x 768 model and this is only true if an inferior picture is acceptable, since each individual pixel cannot possibly be separately displayed. For large-screen monitors, the dot pitch can be greater without any loss of detail. Alternatively, the dot pitch can be reduced; in this case, more detail can be crammed on the screen (e.g. more columns of a worksheet).

Even where a screen's construction quality allows for the reproduction of high resolution, the higher resolution modes may not be able to be used. A 14" monitor, for example, would display tiny icons and extra small text if it were driven at high resolutions.   The table shows the most likely resolutions to be used with a particular screen size.

Resolution	Best Monitor Size
640 x 480	14"
800 x 600	15"
1024 x 768	17"
1280 x 1024	19"
1600 x1200	21"

Video Standards

VESA

The Video Electronics Standards Association was formed out of a group of independent vendors of graphics controllers, who were unprepared to allow IBM to continue to set the standards. Members include Intel, Orchid, Taxan, Tseng Labs and Video 7. The slowness of IBM in developing beyond VGA and its eventual production of an IBM-bound product in XGA, led VESA to produce their own advanced 800 x 600 standard in 1989; this became known as the Super VGA Standard (see below). VESA involves over 200 companies internationally.

Common Graphics Modes

Below is a brief description of the most popular graphics modes currently to be found in use.

Old Modes

The earlier ranges, such as MDA, Hercules, CGA and EGA, are no longer manufactured and these graphics mode are only seen in very old cards.

They are listed in the following table for reference and completeness.

MDA Mono Display Adapter.	This was the original screen for the earliest personal computers, as defined by IBM in 1981. It only supported a monochrome text mode of 80 x 25 characters.
HERCULES	This is the earliest high resolution graphics standard. It introduced a graphics mode and could display 720 x 350 pixels, in monochrome only.
CGA Colour Graphics Adapter	The original IBM standard for colour monitors. Although introducing colour, the CGA standard had a poorer resolution than the Hercules model. Its maximum resolution was 640 x 200 pixels in 2-colour mode and 320 x 200 in 4-colour.
EGA Enhanced Graphics Adapter	Introduced by IBM in 1984 and was a great improvement on the CGA standard. It was able to display 16 colours from a palette of 64, at the much improved resolution of 640 x 350. Like the MDA, Hercules and CGA systems, the EGA is no longer available.
MCGA Multicolour Graphics Adapter.	This is basically a cut-down version of the VGA system. To save memory on the video card, it had no 640 x 480 16-colour mode. Since memory is now relatively cheap, MCGA is ignored in favour of VGA. The 256 colour low-res mode of many VGA cards was often referred to as MCGA mode.
EVGA Enhanced VGA.	Introduced by VESA in 1991. A non-interlaced, 70 Hz refresh rate 8514/A standard that is only common in large-size screens.
XGA Extended Graphics Array	Originally an interlaced standard from IBM that is more versatile than the 8514/A. The 8514/A and the XGA systems failed to replace VGA as IBM hoped. Originally, XGA was only compatible with the IBM MCA bus. The 1024 x 768 mode is interlaced but the VESA standard is non-interlaced. The card supports 256 colours at SVGA and 1024 x 768 - and 65,536 colours at VGA.

VGA

Video Graphics Array.   Introduced by IBM in 1987 and remains a popular mode. It introduced the first screen with square pixels, i.e. a 4:3 aspect ratio. It was also the first standard to dispense with TTL levels of screen drive and introduce varying levels of colour intensity. It handles a palette of 256 colours at 320 x 200, and 16 colours with a resolution up to 640 x 480. It also supported refresh rates of 60Hz or 70 Hz. The 16-colour version quickly became the industry standard. Although long overtaken by superior resolutions, it is still useful for troubleshooting, as it is the basic Windows resolution in Safe Mode.

SVGA

Super VGA. The original VESA specification was for a 16-colour 800x600 screen. This produced over 50% more dots than VGA, for the same screen area. This allowed for example, spreadsheets to display more worksheets columns on the screen, by displaying 132 characters instead of the usual 80 characters. It was also very useful for Windows and its applications, since the user could see more icons on the screen at any one time as well as having improved resolution. This was the most common standard supplied with new models. Later VESA standards allowed for greater resolutions and colour depth. It covers refresh rates of 56Hz, 60Hz or 72 Hz. Some high-res modes that are not true VESA modes are still referred to as SVGA – see below.

High resolution graphic modes

Although not a VESA standard or the name of a video adapter, the terms SXGA (Super XGA) and UXGA (Ultra XGA) have become commonplace to describe the 1280x1024 and 1600x1200 resolution modes, respectively. Note that UXGA has an aspect ratio of 5:4 instead of 4:3 like most other modes; using UXGA mode on a 4:3 screen will result in a very slightly squashed image. Conversely, using any of the 4:3 graphics modes on a 5:4 ratio screen (which is unusual even for portable computers) will result in a slightly stretched image.

QXGA refers to 'Quad XGA', and as the name suggests this mode is four times the size of XGA, at 2048x1536. Similarly, QSXGA is Quad SXGA mode, and QUXGA is Quad UXGA. In addition, there are now a range of wide screen modes available, including WXGA (Wide XGA), SXGAW (SXGA Wide), WUXGA (Wide UXGA), and QUXGA-W (QUXGA Wide). These offer resolutions of 1280x768, 1600x1024, 1920x1200, and 3840x2400. Other, less common modes are also in use. Typically, a widescreen format is around 20% wider than a normal display mode, bringing it to an aspect ratio of 5:3, 25:16 or 8:5. None of these are exactly the same as a standard widescreen television at an aspect ratio of 16:9, so there will still be empty edges of the screen if this type of display is used.

CVT

Specifications above the VGA standard have always suffered from a confusing mixture of names. Some manufacturers gave the name 'SVGA' to any product that was a better resolution or colour depth than standard VGA, for example, whether the screen mode was VESA-compliant or not. Also, the term XGA originally meant the specific video card of the same name by IBM, while it is now commonly used to describe one of the XGA card's resolution modes.

In an attempt to create a common approach, Vesa has introduced the *'Co-ordinated Video Timing'* (CVT).

This specifies any screen using a *'yMz'* code. The *'y'* indicates the number of megapixels that the screen displays (in the same way that a digital camera's resolution is specified). The *'z'* indicates the aspect ratio of the screen (e.g. a value of *'3'* indicates a normal 4:3 aspect ratio while a value of *'9'* indicates a 16:9 widescreen format). We know from earlier in this chapter that the total number of screen pixels is the result of multiplying the vertical resolution by the horizontal resolution (e.g. a 640x480 screen needs 640x480 pixels =30720 pixels = 0.3072 megapixels). Equally, we can calculate the horizontal and vertical resolutions if we know the total megapixels and the screen aspect ratio.

For example, a .307M3 screen has a 4:3 aspect ratio and the formulae for screen calculations are:

Horizontal resolution = 1000 x square root of aspect ratio x number of megapixels
= 1000 x square root of (4/3 x 0.307020) = 640

Vertical resolution = 1000 x square root of number of megapixels divided by the aspect ratio
= 1000 x square root of (0.307020 / 4 x 3) = 480

Examples of screens defined by this code are:

CVT code	Megapixels	Resolution	Aspect Ratio	Typical use
.409M9	.408960	852 x 480	16 : 9	Widescreen plasma
.786M3	.786432	1024 x 768	4 : 3	TFT or CRT screen
1.31M4	1.31072	1280 x 1024	5 : 4	

Screen Sizes

Higher resolution monitors allow more information to be simultaneously displayed on the screen - more of a worksheet, more of a database record, an entire A4 page of DTP.

Advantages
- Less time is spent on scrolling a window on the output.
- More data visible on screen at the same time means fewer errors.

Disadvantages
- Putting more information on the same size of screen means that text, icons and graphics are all smaller than before - and therefore more difficult to read. A 14" model of SVGA monitor, for example, is only useful to those with gifted eyesight.
- To maintain the required readability requires a bigger, and therefore more expensive, monitor. The user is forced to move from a 15" model to a more expensive 19" or 21" model.
- Bigger screens have problems maintaining an even resolution over the entire screen area. Some extreme areas become slightly fuzzy, due to convergence problems. An even quality can be maintained using *'dynamic beam focusing'*, but this involves extra, costly, construction complexities.

The average monitor is between 15" and 19". Larger 20" to 24" models are becoming widespread for DTP and CAD use. For specialist work, multimedia and other presentations, monitors are available up to 60", at staggering prices.

Notes
- When a manufacturer's specification refers to the screen size, it is describing the measurement between any two diagonal corners.
- This measurement usually does not describe the <u>actual</u> screen area. It is common for the phosphor coating to only extend over a proportion of the front screen, resulting in a permanent, unlit border round the screen.

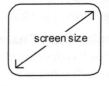

- The unused area of the screen does not result in any loss of resolution; it just means that the graphics detail is compressed into a smaller area than the screen dimension suggests.
- Although a small size monitor is capable of displaying a high-resolution screen, it is often not a practical situation, since the size of the text can be too small to be readable. This is being countered by the introduction of *'anti-aliasing'*, a technique in the video card that adds artificial shading to lines and letters, to give an appearance of added sharpness.

Screen Drives

RGB

This is the most straight forward of the colour drive methods and is the method used for the now obsolete CGA and EGA standards.   For CGA, four connections are used to convey the picture information from the computer to the monitor (other connections are used for the signal ground and the horizontal and vertical synchronisation signals). The RGB system operated by switching the red, green and blue guns off and on from zero volts to around one volt. Any gun, at any time, is either fully switched on or fully switched off. The fourth connection allows any of the eight colours to be displayed in one of two intensities (i.e. - red appears pinkish, etc.). EGA systems provided two wires for each gun - one for on/off and one for intensity. This resulted in 64 possible colours. These drives were described as *'TTL'* types (<u>T</u>ransistor to <u>T</u>ransistor <u>L</u>ogic).

Analogue

For accurate design work, a monitor with sharp images in a range of colours is perfectly adequate. However, for artwork, a greater degree of diversity of colours is required.   After all, a 'real' picture has many shades and hues. With RGB drive, any gun, at any time, was either fully on or fully off. This is unable to meet more sophisticated needs. Ideally, each of the guns should be able to have its intensity varied from fully off to fully on - and <u>every</u> intensity in between. The permutations provided would provide the rich variety encountered in normal life. It is argued that, for art and graphic work, a greater <u>variety</u> of colours on screen has a greater impact on the viewer than increased screen <u>resolution</u>.

If a video card runs the three colour drives at 64 different intensity levels, the possible colours produced are 64 to the power 3, which is 64x64x64 = 262,144 colours. When the drives are 256 different levels, the result is 256x256x256= 16,777,216 different colours.

Note: The construction of some monitors may not allow the display of much more than about 256,000 different colours. The computer system - its memory, its graphics hardware and its software drivers - can now handle over 16 million colours. The drive variations to provide the 16 million colours will still be sent to the monitor but, mainly due to the characteristics of the phosphors, the full range of colours may not be reproduced.

TV-Out

Many display adapters now combine a conventional 15-PIN D-SUB video connector (or a modern DVI connector) with a 'TV-Out' facility. This uses one of several types of connectors to send video output to an ordinary or digital television, allowing these models to use some TVs as monitors, which can be useful. However, they suffer from poorer quality, as the extra signal processing circuitry introduces more noise and more signal distortion. The two connectors that may be available on a TV-Out capable video card are those of Composite or S-Video. Both could be more accurately described as 'AV-out' rather than TV-out.

With the composite method, the output from the PC is a single signal that combines the three colour components and the synchronisation signals. The monitor has to separate these signals, before applying them to the monitor circuitry. The S-Video connector is a four-wire cable that transmits separate signals for chrominance (colouration) and luminance (brightness). This offers a slightly better quality of signal than the composite method.

Note however that not every television has composite or S-Video connectors. Many have only SCART connectors, for which a special converter adapter will be required.

Display Data Channel

VESA has developed a system, known as DDC, whereby the graphics card and monitor can communicate with each other using one of the unused pins on the video connector cable. This is of special significance when used with the Plug and Play facilities of Windows 95 and later. The monitor holds information on its specification and this 128-bit information block is continually transmitted to the graphics card. The data block is called the 'Extended Display Identification' - EDID. The graphics card can then adjust to the best drive for that monitor. For example, graphics cards will always automatically use the maximum refresh rates supported by the monitor for a particular resolution. It will also automatically use the best screen mode available. These changes take place without any activity on the part of the user although the user is still free to choose the setup if desired.

The current standard has two levels - DDC1 and DDC2. DDC1 describes the basic operation and DDC2 is further split into B and AB categories. The B specification supports a larger range of video modes DDC1 while the AB specification supports a new bus, termed the ACCESS.BUS to control the monitor/graphic card communication. The ACCESS.BUS is a serial system that hopes to rival USB. Almost all new monitors are both DDC1 and DDC2 compliant.

Health & Safety

EC directive 90/270/EEC was passed in May 1990. It took effect from 1st January 1993, with all new and modified workstations coming under its terms. All workstations, both existing stations and new sales, were covered by 1st January 1996. The directive ensures that workers using VDUs are:

- given full information on the use of office equipment
- provided with monitors to required standards on ergonomics and emissions.

In the UK, the Health and Safety at Work Act, through the Health and Safety (Display Screen Equipment) Regulations, embodies the EC directive and the British Health and Safety Executive will provide guidelines on the directive. The directive sets out minimum requirements in a range of areas such as VDU, keyboard, desk, chair, lighting, noise, heat and humidity, along with employer obligations to train employees, reduce employee VDU time, protect employees' eyesight and enact worker consultation and participation. The standards of the directive are contained in its annexe and this is largely based on the ISO standard 9241 *"Ergonomic requirements for office work with visual display terminals"*. Of course, the HSE and employers' organisations such as the CBI have differences with the trade unions on the interpretation of individual items of the directive. The aim should be the creation of a safe, functional and productive working environment for the benefit of all.

The legislation ensures that employers will provide VDU operators with a free eyesight test when requested by an operator. If necessary, the employer will also provide *"corrective appliances"* (spectacles). The definition of a VDU operator is one who uses a VDU for between 3 and 5 hours per day. The HSE provide a pamphlet entitled *"Display Screen Equipment Work"* that explains definitions for different types of VDU user. Legislation also covers the hardware design. As a result of EC action, from 1st Jan 1997, monitors, like other goods, will carry the *'CE'* mark - an EC safety mark. This covers limits of EMI (electromagnetic interference) and EMS (electromagnetic susceptibility).

Radiation

The harmful effect of electromagnetic radiation from monitors has been an issue that is controversial and still not satisfactorily resolved. Some reports, mainly from Sweden, Finland and Denmark, suggest that monitor radiation can induce leukaemia and brain cancer. Others, including the UK Health and Safety Executive, dispute the reports and there are claims that the reports are under-researched and discredited. Still others accept that there is a cancer danger from monitor radiation - but small in comparison to cancer dangers from smoking and diet. Computer monitors produce high magnetic fields. These are essential to the running of the monitor, as high currents are required for the beam deflection circuitry. They are no different from the magnetic fields that are emanated from all 50Hz mains electrical equipment and wiring. It is the effects of sustained exposure that causes concern. After all, a user would not normally sit in front of an electric kettle for 8 hours a day but a computer user could easily spend 8 hours a day less than two feet from a monitor. In this respect, it is similar to the claims of harmful effects of living under high-voltage power lines.

Radiation from monitors occurs mostly from the rear, although an appreciable amount also occurs from the front. The fields diminish sharply with distance.

For increased safety, the following steps can be taken:
- Use an LCD screen, or other non-CRT display, if this is acceptable.
- Use a monochrome monitor, if possible. These have lower radiation levels.
- Purchase a low radiation monitor (usually tagged as 'LR'). Note that if a monitor has a special screen coating to reduce radiation, this coating also reduces the screen brightness.
- Position the monitor about 30" from the user.
- Ensure that no other workers are seated less than 4' from the rear of the monitor.

The EC Directive 90/270 talks of radiation levels being reduced to *'negligible levels'*. Radiation is categorised as both ELF (Extremely Low Frequency - i.e. 5Hz to 2KHz) and VLF (Very Low Frequency - i.e. 2KHz to 400KHz). The Swedish MPR-II standard (also called MPR 1990) has become an international standard, because it specifies actual radiation levels.

However, the Health and Safety (Display Screen Equipment) Regulations exempt the UK from the requirements of MPR-II. Nevertheless, almost all monitors on the market are at least MPR-II standard. The Swedish regulatory body NTUEK, in contrast to the UK, works on the assumption of a link between radiation and cancer and has mandatory minimum radiation levels.

Another standard that is sometimes quoted (e.g. from Hitachi) is the TUV standard from Germany. This standard covers both radiation levels and refresh rates. It is a combination of the MPR standard and ISO 9241, which covers image quality.

The Swedish TCO 1992 standard lays down rules on electromagnetic radiation levels, heat emission, automatic low power switching and electrical safety. To carry a TCO '92 label, the monitor must have a more stringent set of radiation levels than MPR-II as shown in the table. It must also meet other conditions such as having an automatic power-down function, a declaration of its energy overhead, and compliance with European fire and electrical safety requirements

Frequency Band	Electric Field (in volts per metre)		Magnetic Field (in nano Teslas)	
	MPR-II	TCO	MPR-II	TCO
ELF	25	10	250	200
VLF	2.5	1	25	25

(EN 60950). The man-ufacturer must also have concluded a certification agreement with TCO. TCO '95 has the same radiation and power saving requirements as TCO '92 but includes extra issues such as improved screen ergonomics (e.g. screen linearity, luminance uniformity) and banning the use of CFCs and heavy metals in the monitor manufacturing process. TCO '99 outlines even stricter screen ergonomics (even luminance, contrast levels, flicker), halving the standby power consumption of all devices except the base unit, and restrictions on painting and metallicising plastic components.

Physical Layout

The layout of keyboard, monitor and documents in relation to the user's vision and easy physical reach is of great importance. Prolonged periods of body inactivity, particularly in bad seating, can itself result in backache and neckache. Add uncomfortable seats and badly laid out desks and the situation is worsened. Bad desk layouts not only contribute to back problems - they are also a source of eye problems, as users strain to read monitors and documents in adverse conditions.

In a normal day, the human eye experiences a variety of muscle movements. The eye normally moves rapidly from one object to another, with the vertical, horizontal and focusing changes that are entailed. In contrast, prolonged viewing of a VDU involves prolonged muscle tension, to maintain concentration on a relatively small flickering viewing area. VDU users complain of a range of symptoms from redness, watering and ache through to focusing difficulties, loss of clarity and double vision.

A range of measures to improve user conditions includes:

- Size of desk. An inadequate desk surface usually results in an unmanageable clutter, loss of productivity and user stress. Consider placing the CPU unit under the desk, or using mini-tower CPU units. Most desks are about 70cm high, which satisfies the average user.
- Seating position. The seat should be comfortable and be of the swivel type, preferably on castors. The seat height and backrest should be adjustable. Certain users may require footrests to maintain adequate posture.
- Size and type of monitor screen. The screen size should be adequate for the job being carried out. Detailed CAD or DTP work on a small screen is a sure way to cause eyestrain and lost working days.
- Position of monitor. The monitor should be moved to suit the user and not the other way round. EU regulations require that monitors have positional adjustment (e.g. a tilt and swivel base or adjustable monitor arm). The VDU user should be able to rotate the display from side to side as well as tilt the screen up and down. Many users prefer to stand the monitor directly on the desk surface, rather than on top of the computer case. Some desks have glass top so that the VDU can be situated under the glass. This frees the desk space but may introduce extra reflections from office lighting. A preferred position would involve the user being stationed about 30" from the monitor and looking down on it from a small angle. Flickering first affects the edges of a user's vision. If a user sits close to a monitor, the effects of flicker are more pronounced.
- Position of monitor controls. These should be front-mounted for ease of access. Thumbwheel controls provide greater precision setting than tiny knobs.
- Protection of monitor controls. Ideally, the controls should be covered by a flap, to prevent accidental changes to settings.
- Regular breaks - necks suffer most when forced to maintain a fixed position for long periods; eyes suffer from maintaining a fixed focal distance. Those employees on permanent screen operations - data entry workers, database operators, program coders, etc. - should have scheduled breaks in their working day.
- Use of document holders - these can be adjusted for the most comfortable reading position. This avoids the continual refocusing involved when reading documents that are left on the desk.

Screen Glare

The aim is to minimise the amount of office light that reflects from the screen surface of the monitor. Screen glare makes reading the screen data extremely difficult and is very tiring to user eyes. The aim is to have as little contrast as possible between the screen and its surroundings. Preventative measures include both lighting and environment changes and choice of monitors.

- Avoid fluorescent lighting completely. The room lighting should be diffused. Both the Lighting Industry Federation and the Chartered Institute of Building Service Engineers provide booklets that cover the problems of poor lighting and the lighting required for areas where VDUs are in use.
- Don't place a monitor in front of windows or other bright light sources. If there is no alternative to having a monitor face a window, use blinds or curtains.
- The room walls and furnishings should have matt surfaces with neutral colouring.
- Use monitors with FST tubes, as they suffer less glare than conventional tubes.

- Use monitors with fast refresh rates as this minimises flicker effects. Some monitor tubes use long-persistence phosphors to minimise flicker, but they also tend to blur movement.
- Use monitors whose screens have anti-glare silica coatings. The screen can also be etched to refract the light. A smooth panel can be bonded to the surface of the screen. This lets light out, but minimises glare by breaking up light that strikes the screen.
  By preventing light entering the tube, the picture contrast is improved - as in Trinitron tubes.
- Fit a non-glare filter in front of the monitor screen. These are mostly made from glass, although some are plastic. But beware, the Association of Optometrists believe that filters reduce glare - at the expense of making the screen more difficult to read. Keep the screen clean with an anti-static cleaning compound.
- Use VDU spectacles when working at screens; these are specially tinted and can include prescription lenses.
- Where the application allows user-defined screen colours, choose screen colours carefully. There is evidence that dark lettering on a light background aids readability. It is more protective to the eyes when handling text, as there is no need for the user to constantly adapt to differing contrasts. On the other hand, dark backgrounds suffer less from the effects of flicker.

Stress

Employees who spend long periods on VDU suffer greater levels of stress than other employees. The source of such stress appears to be the high levels of productivity expected of data-entry workers, poor working environment and the low esteem associated with jobs that have been computerised. This is covered by the EC directive, which states

"the employer must plan work activities in such a way that daily work on a display screen is periodically interrupted by breaks or changes of activity, reducing the workload at the display screen".

This is based on the old adage that *'a change is as good as a rest'*. A balanced load of VDU work and other work will improve working conditions and will probably lead to more productivity in the long run.

The Health and Safety Regulations requires that employers carry out risk assessment. This involves assessing the risk to their employees' health and safety, employing competent safety officers, devising appropriate safety measures, and training staff in these safety measures.

Adjustments/Controls

Many of the reported monitor problems of users are easy to resolve. Often, a monitor is simply badly adjusted, or has gone out of adjustment over time. A few simple tweaks may be all that is required to restore normal working. Most monitors provide the basic control over its operations in the form of an On-Screen Display (OSD), with older monitors using adjustable knobs or thumbwheels; a few controls require a screwdriver adjustment.

Most quality monitors allow a fair degree of additional trimming of monitor performance, as follows:

Brightness

This varies the density of the electron beam(s) and hence the amount of screen illumination. In monitors with poor power regulation, an increase in brightness might lead to a shrinking of the picture size. This may appear with manual alterations to the brightness control - or may occur when the screen content switches from a mainly black content to a mainly white content. The monitor power supply cannot cope with the increased current demands and the voltage to the screen scanning circuitry drops. The reduced voltage means that the scan drive is reduced and the picture occupies a smaller proportion of the screen area. At the extremes, this cannot be cured by user adjustment and the monitor has to be sent for repair or be replaced.

Contrast

This control increases the amplitude of the drive to the gun(s), increasing the ratio between different levels of screen brightness. Too much contrast drives the light grey details into displaying as white, thereby losing detail. Too little contrast makes all colours tend to grey, producing a wishy-washy screen.

Hor/Ver Position

These controls adjust the starting points, and hence the stopping points of both the horizontal scan and vertical scan. The effect of these adjustments is to move the picture vertically or horizontally along the screen and this is used to centre the picture.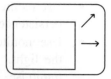

Hor/Ver Size

The position controls determine the commencing point of the scans. The size controls vary the <u>amplitude</u> of the beam swing in the horizontal and vertical planes and this determines the actual size of the illuminated portion of the screen. Some monitor models can be adjusted so that the scans fill the entire screen area, eliminating the black border. This increases the effective viewing area and aids readability. However, with shadow mask tubes particularly, this may result in the loss of pixels at the corners (this is particularly a Windows problem, where icons like the minimise/maximise icon sit in the extreme top right-hand corner of the screen).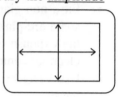

Pre-Set Controls

Monitors come with the following different approaches to their controls:

- Entirely manual - the user has to make adjustments each time the monitor is used for a different mode. This is thankfully now uncommon.
- Auto-sensing. This works entirely automatically and is the most common approach.
- User choice from either a set of in-built stored settings or from a set of user-entered settings that were digitally set and stored. If none of these options are taken, the system works in auto-sensing mode.

Where digital controls are used, there are usually 8 or 9 settings, although there can be up to 30 predefined modes and user-defined settings. Now, the monitor circuitry automatically sizes and places images as it switches between resolutions. A block of built-in memory is used to store size and positional information for different analogue and digital sources.

Less Common Controls

VER/HOR Convergence Controls

Some monitors, such as the Iiyama Vision Master, allow the user to adjust the convergence of the three colour elements of the picture. In most monitors these are internal controls, as best results are obtained using test equipment. A signal that comprises three colour grids is injected into the monitor, so that the alignment of the colours is achieved more easily. Without a test generator, the adjustment is a more hit-and-miss affair.

Pincushion Control

Like the control above, this control is also concerned about the picture's shape, as opposed to its size or position. It is difficult to maintain linearity at the extremes of the picture area and the result is *'pincushion distortion'* as shown in an exaggerated form in the diagram. The Compaq V70 monitor, for example, allows the user some control over the screen's beam linearity.

Trapezoidal Distortion

With trapezoidal distortion, the edges of the screen remain straight but the scan length at the top of the screen is progressively lengthened with each successive line scanned. This produces a trapezoidal shape as shown in the diagram. Again, the shape has been exaggerated for clarity.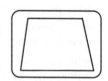

Rotation

This control, if available, is used to rotate the picture. Normally this only ranges a few degrees in either direction, to allow the user to make sure the picture is straight.

Hor/Ver Lock

Also called horizontal and vertical phase. Controls are often marked as HSYNC and VSYNC. These controls vary the locking between the incoming synchronisation signals from the computer video circuits and the monitor's internal oscillators. This adjustment corrects *'roll'* and other problems caused by the two being out of sync.

Other Controls

Many monitors provide additional controls to those listed above. These may include Parallelogram controls (to adjust any vertical 'skew'), moiré controls (to reduce display artefacts), colour purity, and individual RGB controls. The latter controls are used to match on-screen colours to printer colours, and are relatively unusual. They can be found on the Mitsubishi Diamond Pro and Philips Brilliance monitors.

> **CAUTION**
> Internal pre-sets exist for brightness, convergence, etc. Leave these well alone. These adjustments are intended for trained service staff. And, don't forget that there can be as much as 25Kvolts on the final anode of the cathode ray tube!

Flat Display Panels

In the past couple of years, CRT replacements in the form of flat LCD/TFT panels have started to appear. Other technologies include Gas Plasma displays and IBM's HPA. The technology used in these displays has been perfected in laptop computers over the years and is based on individual pixels being addressed in an array. Such displays may either use a standard video card or may be based on a specialist proprietary digital card (see DVI, below). The differences between flat panel displays and CRTs are:

- As explained earlier, the actual viewing surface of a CRT is less than its quoted screen size. With Flat displays, the entire viewing area is visible and exactly corresponds to the quoted screen size.
- CRT displays have to be constantly refreshed to avoid flicker effects, as explained earlier. Pixels on a flat panel display do not fade between refreshes, such that a frame rate of around 60Hz produces a flicker-free picture. Increasing the frame rate above about 60Hz produces no perceived improvement, while increasing the systems' bandwidth requirements.
- Because flat panels are built from a fixed matrix, they have a native resolution. Driving the display at a different resolution involves scaling (interpolation) of the incoming signal to either shrink it or expand before using it to drive the display. Scaling up may cause pixellation making the image chunky and difficult to read. Alternatively, a signal of smaller resolution can be displayed as a small image in the centre of the screen. Scaling down may result in the loss of some important detail. CRT displays always use the entire screen area for display and cannot scale down.
- Some flat panels need a proprietary adapter card that is not compatible with other displays (CRT or Flat Panel). Some use DVI interfaces, which are expensive and complex. Others are compatible with standard analogue SVGA outputs but require expensive internal electronics to digitise the signal.
- Viewing angles are smaller, and output brightness is usually less than the equivalent CRT display.
- Because of the low manufacturing yield and scarcity, flat panels tend to be expensive.
- There are only a few manufacturing plants for large LCD "blanks" and the etched glass screens. Because of this, commercially available LCD screens over 19" are extremely expensive.

Flat panel displays took some time to catch on, but have now all but replaced CRT displays in new sales. Nonetheless there are still plenty of CRTs in use in legacy systems. It can be expected that as flat panel technology continues to mature, they will become even cheaper and more common. In the meantime, they are most useful in certain areas where space, privacy or subliminal flicker are issues. The forthcoming '*Mira*' smart display technology from Microsoft is essentially a portable flat screen that can use wireless communications to connect to a nearby PC, although its usefulness may be limited by the fact it cannot be used for entertainment such as DVDs and games.

Note: In flat panel devices, there are no dots. Therefore the measurement of the distance between one pixel and the next is called the '*pixel pitch*' when referring to flat screens.

DVI Interfaces

Flat panel displays are digital devices, while VGA is an analogue cable. Driving a flat panel display via a VGA cable results in unnecessary loss of detail during the conversion process, and the solution is a new digital cable – DVI. Although DVI interfaces have been around for some time, it is only relatively recently that a standard has been agreed upon. Despite the name, DVI comes in three flavours: DVI-d (digital only), DVI-a (analogue only) and DVI-i (integrated digital and analogue). The connector has three rows of pins for digital only and shared digital/analogue connections, and five pins for analogue only connections. The ATI Radeon cards, for example, provide DVI output connectors.

DVI is also useful with CRT monitors that have DVI inputs, as it means the digital signal can be converted to analogue by the monitor rather than the display card, enabling the monitor to fine-tune the conversion process to suit the characteristics of the particular monitor.

The principle of operation of each of the major types of flat panel displays is explained below:

Liquid Crystal Displays

The Liquid Crystal Display is the most popular alternative to cathode ray tube monitors and is widely used in portable and notebook PCs. It employs the following principles:

Light is only a very high frequency radiated wave. In fact, light is *'unpolarised'* - it is composed of waves in angles of every plane. In an LCD display, the source of this light is usually a fluorescent source behind the screen - such models being described as having a *'backlit'* display. This light is passed through a polarising filter. Only the waves in a single plane will pass through this filter. This single plane is known as the *'plane of polarisation'*. This polarised light is then presented with another polarising filter. If the second filter has the same plane of polarisation as the first filter, then the light is able to

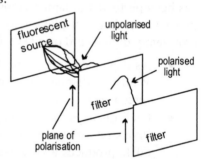

pass through and be viewed by the user. If the plane of polarisation is opposed to that of the first filter, then no light wave is able to pass through. It follows, then, that if the second filter can alter its plane of polarisation, it will control the flow of light waves to the user. If the diagram was considered as a single pixel and was repeated thousands of times over, as a matrix, then it would constitute a VDU screen.

In practice, it is not possible to continually alter the plane of polarisation of the second filters. Instead, a cell is composed of a piece of *'nematic'* liquid crystal between the filters. The planes of polarisation of the two filters differ by 90 degrees. Now, the light from the fluorescent source still passes through the first filter in a single plane only. This time, the effect of passing through the liquid crystal is to twist the wave 90 degrees, along the crystal's plane. When the wave reaches the second filter, it is at the correct angle to pass through since they are both aligned. So, the normal state is to pass light. That is why most LCDs have a lit screen as default.

The second diagram shows the effect of applying an electric field to the cell. The molecules of the liquid crystal will line up, its plane will become straight and there is no 90-degree twist to the light wave as it passes through. The light's plane is now different from the second filter and no light will pass through the filter. So, if each pixel area has its electric field switched on or off, pixels are lit or unlit - i.e. a functioning VDU has been created.

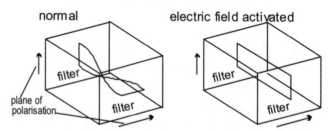

LCD Construction

In practice, the display is not constructed pixel by pixel. Instead, the screen is manufactured as a single entity, with a layer of liquid crystal sandwiched between layers of glass. This, in turn, is sandwiched between polarising sheets. A grid of wires is used to access any particular area of the screen surface. A voltage is applied to the appropriate vertical and horizontal co-ordinates, to activate that particular pixel. This is called *'direct multiplexing'* and although relatively easy to manufacture, it is difficult to control drive to the cells.

The main problems are:
- The voltage on the control wires cannot be too high; otherwise there is a likelihood of turning on cells adjacent to the wanted cell.
- The small allowable voltage swings do not provide enough control to achieve satisfactory grey scales and good contrast.
- The scanning arrangements are inadequate.   The data on every pixel in a line can be stored and applied to the vertical wires at the same time.   However, It is only possible to address a single row at any one time.   So, for example, a VGA screen of 480 lines would result in each line only having its pixels set every 1/480th of the time.   The greater the vertical resolution the less time is available for holding a particular cell in the 'dark' state.   During the rest of the time, the cell is reverting to its 'light' state, with a consequent deterioration of picture contrast.

TFT Displays

To solve these problems, an *'active matrix'* is employed. This uses TFT (thin film transistors) in a matrix, with a single transistor located at the junction of each vertical and horizontal control wire.   The voltage at each cell can now be increased, since smaller level signals can be placed on the control wires that are amplified by the transistor.   Since this higher voltage now only occurs right at the cell, there is little chance of activating adjacent cells. The result is a sharper picture. Additionally, the higher voltage swings result in faster cell changes and therefore greater contrast. Finally, the higher voltage range available allows much greater control over grey scales. TFT LCDs also improve on scanning difficulties. The short time available for each cell remains unavoidable. However, the construction of the TFT screen results in a capacitance effect on each cell.   This maintains the desired charge while the cell is not being addressed and maintains the desired 'dark' state longer, improving screen contrast.

TFT displays are not without their problems however. Individual transistors can fail, causing pixels to become 'stuck' permanently in a certain colour. These are called *'dead pixels'*, and part of the ISO standard 13406-2, which deals with flat panel display quality, defines three classes of pixel reliability. Class 1 standard displays, which are only now beginning to appear, are guaranteed to have no pixel faults, while class 2 and class 3 flat panels have a set maximum number of faults.

Colour LCDs

LCDs are also available in colour versions.   These are expensive, since they have even greater production quality control problems than monochrome versions.
They are available in both passive-matrix and active-matrix versions.

Advantages Of LCDs
- No electron beams, thereby eliminating problems with linearity, misconvergence, pincushion distortion, and sizing/positioning.
- Low power consumption and low voltages.
- Light weight, making them ideal for inclusion in portable computers.
- No radiation or flicker problems, unlike CRTs.
- Flat displays, therefore easy to hang on a wall or locate in work area.

Disadvantages
- Restricted viewing angle.
- Poor contrast.   Supertwist displays give more contrast but introduce a certain tinge. This is correctable with special film coatings and extra construction complexity. It is called *'triple supertwist'*. It is more expensive to manufacture and is used in the best LCD displays.
- Slow speed.   When the liquid crystal structure has been pulled into a straight configuration, under the influence of the electric field, it takes a relatively long time to restore to its former state. This explains why LCD screens often 'smear' when scrolling or attempting other fast screen updating.
- Costly to manufacture, due to difficulties of quality control.

Passive Matrix

The cheaper of the versions, this screen is effectively a sandwich of three LCD screens, each screen emitting red, green or blue. All modern systems increase efficiency by using *'dual scan'* displays. These split the screen in two vertically and each half is simultaneously scanned and lit. So, a single screen is painted in half the time - i.e. the refresh rate is doubled and flicker is halved.

Active Matrix

Each colour triad comprises the necessary red, green and blue LCD elements and each is activated by its own switching transistor. In this way, the TFT mechanisms described above take place on light waves of pre-determined colour. Since each element is individually switched, the *'ghosting'* associated with older screens is eliminated. In addition, TFT elements are less sensitive to heat and brighter backlights can be used. Unfortunately, these screens are expensive to produce, since even a VGA monitor would require almost a million transistors to be assembled on the one screen. A single non-working transistor means that a pixel has lost one of its colour elements. Too many defects mean that the screen has to be scrapped. About a third of all units produced are unable to meet this very demanding quality control.

Plasma Displays

Gas plasma displays are produced by filling the space between two glass plates with neon /xenon gas and then exciting it with a suitable voltage, usually greater than 80V. The exciting electrode is etched onto the glass. The original gas plasma displays were orange and black and had high power consumption. Recently however various companies have resurrected the technology, extended it to full colour and are using it for display panels, High Definition Television (HDTV) displays and desktop monitors. Among the prime movers of this technology in Europe are Philips BV whose FlatTV is plasma based.

Large plasma displays are becoming more common for such locations as airports, hospitals, trains stations, and even domestic television. Many are capable of handling both computer and audio/video input.

OLED Displays

The most recent display technology to be developed is Kodak's OLED (Organic Light Emitting Diode) technology. This consists of an 'electroluminescent' material coating on a plastic film. The material glows when electric current passes through, producing both colour and light, therefore eliminating the need for an additional light source. OLEDs are currently in development, and can potentially bring about low power consumption, extremely thin flat screens. They are already in use in cameras, and mobile phones using OLEDs are currently in development, with computer displays in the pipeline if the brightness level is acceptable on a large display.

Rear Projection Displays

Another recent innovation is the technique of using a small projector at the back of the display unit. The most notable form of RPD is the Digital Micro-Mirror Device, which works by passing light through a roughly one-inch square chip carrying thousands of tiny mirrors. Each mirror is mounted on an electrode, which allows it to be tilted 10 degrees to either side, thus either reflecting light toward the screen or away from it. These electrodes can switch so quickly that they can effectively present many shades of grey simply by switching quickly back and forward between blocking and reflecting light. This greyscale light is then passed through a spinning colour wheel

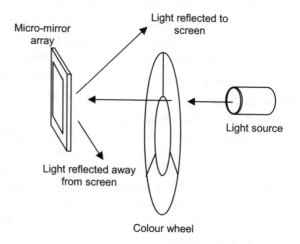

which is co-ordinated with the electrodes, in order to produce a full colour image. RPDs can be roughly as large and thin as a plasma screen, and are of similar price, though this may change in the future. However, RPDs have none of the heat problems associated with plasma screens.

Graphics Cards

The rapid development of computer applications such as video, animations, walkthroughs and photorealistic graphics has stretched both the demands on the computer monitor and graphics card technology. Graphics cards have undergone significant improvements from the early versions that were designed for text and some crude chunky graphics.

The electronics to drive the monitor is mounted on a separate graphics card that slots into the expansion bus on the computer's motherboard. The monitor cable plugs into a socket on the video card.

Graphic Card Performance

There are a number of factors to be considered when purchasing a graphics card. Such a purchase might be as part of an entire system. It is also possible to buy a matching graphics card and monitor, to upgrade the graphics facilities of an existing system. The main considerations are:

- RAM size/Resolution/Colour Depth
- RAM type
- Internal bus size
- Chip Set used
- Extra facilities (e.g. video handling, 3D, TV)

- Bandwidth
- External bus type
- Refresh rates
- RAMDAC used

Graphics RAM Size

Screen Memory

The number of colours that a monitor can produce is theoretically endless. Tiny voltage changes to any of the monitor's guns will alter that colour and hence the mix perceived by the viewer. The limitation is in the ability of the computer graphics card to store all the possible colour permutations (in the form of a large range of voltage levels) for each screen pixel. All graphics standards use a *'memory mapped'* method of handling screen output. An area of computer memory is reserved for holding the individual pixels that comprise the screen picture. This screen memory is <u>additional</u> to the computer's 640k user area. In all but the lowest resolutions, extra memory for storing the screen's composition is located on the graphics controller card. The data in this memory area is used to regularly update the picture.

The computer's CPU (or graphics chipset) has the task of constantly updating the screen memory area. The electronics on the graphics card reads this information and uses it to control the drive to the monitor. For a simple, monochrome system the storage may only require a single bit per pixel. If the bit is 0, the pixel is left unlit; if the bit is 1 then the pixel is illuminated. In colour systems, extra pixels are required, to store the colour and hue of the pixel.

In text modes, the bit pattern for each displayable character (i.e. the alphanumeric set, punctuation and the IBM extended character set) is pre-stored and is copied into the screen memory area. It is a much more complex task in graphics mode. To place a straight line on the screen, the CPU must calculate the position of every pixel in that line and write this information to the appropriate screen memory locations. For an arc, there is the added time required to calculate the curve's co-ordinates. The main memory of the PC was not designed for the current high-resolution screens. The amount of memory put aside to hold the screen information is totally inadequate by today's standards. Out of the 1MB memory area, a maximum of 128KB is laid aside for graphics memory. This would directly address a 640 x 200 screen of 256 colours. To go beyond this specification, the machine has the additional graphics information stored in <u>extra</u> memory with special software routines to access this extra hardware. Consequently, graphics cards have their own memory chips to store graphics information.

The RAM size required is determined by the maximum screen resolution and the maximum colour depth (i.e. how many colours to be displayed).

The formula to calculate the amount of memory required for a particular screen standard is:

HORIZONTAL RESOLUTION x VERTICAL RESOLUTION x COLOUR BITS / 8

The number of bits for each pixel depends on the number of colours that the pixel has to display.

For monochrome, only one bit per pixel is required (pixel is either lit or unlit).

For 4 colours, 2 bits per pixel are required, providing 2 to the power of 2 combinations. For 16 colours, 4 bits are required, providing 2 to the power 4 combinations.

For 256 colours, 8 bits are required (i.e. 2 to the power 8 combinations).

A 16-bit system can provide 65,536 different colours for each pixel (called *'high colour'*), while a 24-bit system provides 16.7million colours (often termed *'true colour'*).

Some cards offer 30-bit depth producing 1,073,741,824 colours! Other cards use 32-bits to handle true colour with added effects.

The equation given produces a memory requirement specified in bytes. Dividing the result by 1024 gives a requirement measured in Kilobytes (KB). There are 1024 bytes to a kilobyte. Dividing by a further 1024 produces a measurement in MB (MegaBytes).

Examples

A 16-colour VGA screen would require

640 x 480 x 4 / 8 = 150 Kbytes

A 16-colour SVGA screen would require

800 x 600 x 4/8 = 234Kbytes (i.e. at least a 256k card)

A 256-colour VGA sized screen would require

640 x 480 x 8 / 8 = 300 Kbytes (i.e. at least a 512k card)

A 256- colour SVGA screen would require

800 x 600 x 8/ 8 = 469 Kbytes (i.e. at least a 512k card)

A 256-colour 1024 x 768 screen would require

1024 x 768 x 8 / 8 = 768 KB (i.e. a full 1MB card)

Bits per pixel	Colour Depth
4	16
8	256
16	65,536
24	16.7m

A 24-bit, true colour 1024 x 768 screen with 16.7 million colours would require

1024 x 768 x 24 / 8 = 2.25MB (i.e. a 4MB card)

Finally, a top of the range system with true colour at 1600 x 1200 would require

1600 x 1200 x 24 / 8 = 5.49MB (i.e. an 8MB card)

SVGA cards used to be supplied in 256KB and 512KB versions; they now come from 8MB to 256MB.

Notes

- If a board's design allows for future expansion, then extra memory can be fitted to the card to allow it to cope with greater resolutions. Many cards allow up to 8MB of memory to be fitted while some cards allow up to 40MB to be fitted.

- Where the fitted RAM size is vastly greater than is currently required for a particular mode, the memory can be divided into *'pages'* - each page containing the data for a full graphics screen. This allows rapid switching between screens, since the second screen can have its pixel pattern built up in memory, while the first screen is being displayed. This is the basis of on-screen animation. An additional use for extra memory is for storing 3D texture maps and other special effects data.

- Most cards can display a number of colours from a larger possible palette (e.g. 16 colours from 64 or 256 from 32,767).   A piece of software may wish to use more colours than the card is capable of displaying at any one time. The 'extra' colours are displayed by *'dithering'* using the existing colours, producing a rather coarse hatching effect. This allows cards with poorer specifications to still run the application.   This may be acceptable in some applications but photo-realistic graphics, video clips and multimedia applications would demand a wider displayable colour range.

Bandwidth

The term *'bandwidth'* describes both memory and graphics needs and there are important differences. The general description of monitor bandwidth was given earlier.   With colour monitors, the graphics data is sent in parallel to three separate guns and the amount of colours being used is not relevant to the bandwidth calculation.   The restriction on any one channel's capabilities is measured by the resolution required and the refresh rate.

The formula to calculate the required graphics bandwidth is:

HORIZONTAL RESOLUTION x VERTICAL RESOLUTION x REFRESH RATE / 8

So, a 640 x 480 display with a 70Hz refresh rate requires to cope with

640 X 480 X 70 / 8 = 2.56MB /sec, i.e. over 20 million different pixel values per sec

while a 1600 x 1200 display with a 75Hz refresh rate requires to handle

1600 X 1200 x 75 / 8 = 17.17MB /sec, i.e. over 135 million different pixel values per sec

Memory bandwidth is much greater than graphics bandwidth for the same screen because it has to store and transfer the colour details for each pixel.

So, a 640 x 480 display, with a refresh rate of 70Hz and 256 colours requires to transfer

640 X 480 X 70 X 8 / 8 = 20.2MB /sec, i.e. over 160 million different pixel values per sec

while a 1600 x 1200 display with a 75Hz refresh rate and 16m colours requires to transfer

1600 X 1200 x 75 X 24 / 8 = 412MB /sec, i.e. over 432 million different pixel values per sec

Where a card is intended for multimedia and video use, the bandwidth capability of both the monitor and the graphics card become crucial factors.

RAM Type

Video cards use RAM to store pixel information. Just like the RAM used on the motherboard, the video RAM may be of various different types. Previously, a wide range of memory types has been used in video cards. VRAM (Video RAM) is a type of memory developed specifically for video cards, which is a dual port system. This allows data to be sent from the CPU to be stored in video memory via one port, while the video memory is being used to update the screen through the other port. WRAM (Windows RAM) was another video memory technology that was basically a modified Dual-Port RAM system designed to speed up common Windows functions. Video cards have also used EDO RAM, SGRAM and other types.

However, in modern video cards, there are two types of memory in use. The first, and cheapest, is SDRAM (Synchronous Dynamic RAM). SDRAM is a type of memory that operates at a certain frequency, synchronised to the clock of the component it is attached to. Video cards often have their own subprocessor onboard, meaning that video SDRAM may be at an entirely different speed to SDRAM found on a motherboard.

The second, and more expensive form of RAM is DDR (Double Data Rate). This is still an SDRAM technology, but provides improved speed by allowing data to be transferred twice within a single clock cycle (once on the rising edge of the clock signal, and once on the falling edge). This theoretically doubles its throughput, though in practice the speed gain is not quite so high.

The Memory chapter explains these technologies in more detail.

External Bus Type

A very wide range of graphics cards is available, using every type of data bus system. Since the fastest data buses have the greatest throughput, the graphics card should be matched to the fastest bus. So, a computer might be able to accommodate a graphics card on either its ISA expansion slot or its PCI expansion slot. Although an older ISA or PCI graphics card will work in the system, a PCI-E or AGP card would provide better performance. Similarly, a VESA card should be used in an older VESA local bus machine, although an ISA can be used. PCI cards and VL cards are not interchangeable, and modern motherboards support the faster PCI-E or AGP rather than VL or PCI.

Bus size is important as well as speed – a 32-bit card can transfer twice as much as a 16-bit card, all other things being equal. The 8-bit and 16-bit ISA ports are virtually obsolete and are never used for graphics in any recent systems. Graphics cards for PCI Pentium boards use a full external 64-bit data bus, but even these are no longer used in new systems. AGP cards use their own high-speed 32-bit bus, as well as using techniques similar to DDR memory transfer to achieve x2, x4 or x8 speed.

Internal Bus Size

The bus size in a graphics card's specification refers to its internal architecture, the path between the card's RAM and the card's graphics processor. The most critical element in graphics performance is not data flow into the graphics board; it is how the board organises and manages the frame buffer held in memory inside the graphics board. Having a 64-bit internal bus greatly speeds up throughput, enhancing the card's performance. The card's memory is organised into interleaved banks, allowing one bank to be written to while the other is being read. This increases throughput without the expense of VRAM.

However, with increasing resolution, even 64-bit buses can act as a bottleneck and 128-bit versions are now common. In fact, there are now even 256-bit cards available, such as the GeForce256 Annihilator. Note that the internal bus size being doubled does not affect the bus connecting the card with the motherboard, and will not result in the card being twice as fast overall. In fact, in some circumstances the difference will be negligible.

Refresh Rates

Greater resolution and greater colour depth (i.e. bits per pixel) both mean that the card has to move more data for a single frame. This means that cards commonly have lower refresh rates at higher resolutions and at greater colour depths. For example, even a high performance card like the GeForce FX 5200 card has a wide variation in refresh rates. It handles 240Hz at resolutions up to 1024x768, 170Hz at 1280x1024 but is only 60Hz at 2048x1536. An older S3-based ISA card from 1992 fares much worse with respective rates of 70Hz for VGA, 60Hz for SVGA and 1024x768 and an unacceptable 45Hz interlaced format at 1280x1024.

Chip Set Used

To reduce costs, all SVGA graphics cards are based round a limited range of different VLSI chips, sometimes referred to as the *'graphics engine'*. These chips are dedicated to the one task and different manufacturers produce a range of chips with different performances. Although there are a range of graphics chip manufacturers, the driving force of 3D graphics for computer games has led to cut-throat competition for high-quality 3D video cards. As a result such cards come and go each year, replaced by newer and better models.

All these chips, and others, provide varying performances. It is best to compare the working speeds of the chipsets as used on various cards. This may use *'Wintach'* readings, measuring how cards cope with actual applications packages or general card tests may be used, measuring the bit manipulation features. Example chip/card features are:

Chip	Graphics Card	Interface	Memory Type	RAMDAC(s)
ATI Radeon HD2900GT	ATI FireGL V7600	PCI-E x16	800MHz GDDR4	600MHz
nVidia GeForce 9800 GX2	XFX 9800 GX2	PCI-E x16	2000MHz GDDR3	600MHz
NVIDIA Quadro NVS 285	PNY Quadro NVS 285	PCI-E x16	DDR2	350MHz
Matrox Parhelia-LX	Matrox Millenium P650	AGP 8x	DDR	400MHz

Display Acceleration

As soon as the PC progressed beyond the CGA standard, the standard machine BIOS (Basic Input/Output System) was inadequate and required extension. The added graphics functionality is provided by an extra EPROM (Erasable Programmable Read Only Memory) chip on the graphics card. The efficiency of this BIOS extension affects the screen writing speed. Some SVGA cards copy the extension software into an area of RAM to speed up screen handling. This technique is known as *'ROM shadowing'*.

Another way of improving the speed of a display system is to use an '*accelerator card*'.

Accelerator cards

Early graphics cards left the computer's CPU to do all the screen handling. This is the simplest and cheapest method but it is also the slowest. This is most noticeable in real-time rendering of 3D images, for computer games and CAD applications, where frame rates can drop to as low as 10fps or less if the CPU is sharing its time between graphics processing and other tasks. For some intensive uses such as video playback or editing, even 2D performance can become strained.

The problems worsen if the system is upgraded. Moving up to a resolution of 1600x1200, for example, or implementing more detailed 3D models, means the CPU has to handle an even bigger amount of screen data - with no extra computing power to process it.

The solution is to use a graphics card with its own processing capabilities. The first of these '*graphics accelerators*' were concentrated on improving 2D performance, and were capable of drawing such 2D objects as text, lines, rectangles, ellipses and area colour fills, with minimal involvement from the main CPU. Many also included '*'bitblitting'* (bit-to-block transfers - i.e. memory flooding), a common technique in software that required fast 2D performance such as the computer games of the time. The 8514/A and XGA display adapters were the first to use graphics acceleration techniques of this sort, but even the most modern video card still contains some 2D acceleration.

More recently, however, it has become almost universal for graphics cards to contain a powerful onboard Graphics Processing Unit (GPU), which can handle the intensive graphics computations 3D scenes require, leaving the processor to deal with other matters.

Like main processors, graphics processors can also be overclocked, and this shares the same benefits and risks as main processor overclocking, except that they mainly apply to 3D operations such as computer games.

As with any other peripheral device, an accelerator card requires installation of its own software drivers. In Windows, these include the graphics adapter driver, and a graphical language driver such as DirectX or OpenGL for 3D applications.

Card Performance

There can be significant variations in the efficiency of each card's method of handling graphics functions. For example, one particular card may need less information passed to it, in order to carry out a particular graphics function, compared to another card. Some cards will carry out a smaller range of graphics functions, the remaining functions being left for the computer's main CPU to process.

There is no doubt that graphics accelerator cards substantially improve a system's performance. However, manufacturers' claims should be put in perspective: the claims only consider the graphics functions being tested in isolation. When considered as <u>part</u> of the overall activities of an application program or computer game, the performance is nowhere near so spectacular.

Also, note that the particular capabilities provided by a card should match the needs of the user in order to make best use of what can be an expensive part of the system. For example, a top of the range 3D accelerator may cost as much as £400, which could be money well spent on a design system, or a high-end gaming system. However, a user that does a lot of video editing or DTP would likely be better off with a card that concentrates on 2D performance, provides higher resolution, or offers such extra facilities as multiple monitors or colour calibration.

3D Cards

Games and animations such as walkthroughs and flybys show a quick succession of frames with each frame showing the viewer a different viewpoint on the scene. As the viewpoint is moved, so the shading, shadowing and fine detail will alter. Each scene comprises a range of objects (buildings, people, etc) and each object is made up from many individual graphics polygons, usually triangles. Each triangle has its own colour and surface detail (e.g. grains of sand, bricks, leaves). The scene will have one or more supposed sources of illumination; this could be the sun, streetlights, etc. As the viewpoint is moved the light source will illuminate the triangles differently. To produce a 3D effect, the user is shown perspective (i.e. distant objects are made smaller than close objects) and defocussing (i.e. distant object are not as clear as close objects; they are usually dimmed or 'fogged').

The commonly implemented features in 3D cards are:

Facility	Explanation
Z-Buffering	Since x and y describe the horizontal and vertical co-ordinates, 'z' refers to depth. A Z-buffer stores the depth information of objects (e.g. the dog is behind the tree). This allows *'hidden surface removal'* - i.e. time is saved by not drawing parts of an object that are obscured by foreground objects.
Flat shading	The polygons are filled with a uniform colour, which is not as effective but is very quick. Flat shading can be implemented to improve frame rates.
Gouraud shading	Obscures the boundaries between polygons by drawing realistic colour gradients; produces smoother and more natural shapes.
Phong shading	Achieves better results than Gouraud shading but is more demanding of processing power.
Texture mapping	Filling polygons with the same graphics bitmap (e.g. woodgrain or feathers).
Bump mapping	Similar to texture mapping, this technique uses a *'map'* of raised or depressed areas that is applied to a surface to produce an irregular 3D shape.
Anti-aliasing	Curved and diagonal edges produce a 'staircase' effect known as *'jaggies'*. If the colours of the boundary's surrounding edges are blended, the effect is minimised.
Perspective correction	If an object is receding into the distance, the bit maps used to texture should also gradually diminish. So, a brick wall bitmap would draw smaller and smaller bricks as the wall shrunk towards the horizon.
Mip mapping	Similar to the above, except that new patterns are rendered for distant polygons.
Bilinear/trilinear filtering	Large areas when rendered can appear like a patchwork quilt, with blocks of slightly differing colouring. Filtering determines a pixel's colour on the colour of the surrounding pixels thereby producing a more uniform transition.
Alpha blending	Controls an object's translucency, thereby providing water or glass effects. It is also used to mask out areas of the screen.
Logarithmic fogging	More distant objects are fogged to grey.

The routines to constantly calculate all of these objects and display them on the screen (typically at 20 pictures per second) require a great deal of computational power.   This is called *'rendering'* and it strains even the most powerful PC.   To overcome this problem, many of these computational routines are embedded in graphics card's chipset and called by special software drivers.   Initially these drivers, known as APIs (Application Programming Interface), were written by graphics card manufacturers for their own range of cards.   The routines for a Matrox card would not work with a VideoLogic card, and so on.   As a consequence, games supplied with one card would not work with another graphics card, as the games were specially written to use the card manufacturer's APIs. Games bundled with the Diamond Stealth 3D 200, for example, are specially written for the card's VIRGE chipset.

There was a need for standard interfaces and this has been met by Silicon Graphic's OpenGL and Microsoft's Direct 3D. OpenGL is not designed for the games market but for high-end graphical workstations. With the rise of comparatively cheap PC 3D cards this market is shrinking. Windows 95 Release 2 and later Windows operating systems provide DirectX facilities, which includes Direct3D. Card manufacturers only have to write drivers to interface their cards to the Direct3D API's functions.

Microsoft's DirectX

Microsoft has produced a number of APIs under the title DirectX.   These are:

Direct 3D	Provides a standard interface for 3D object display and rendering.
Direct Draw	Reduces CPU time by allowing software direct access to alter video memory.
Direct Sound	Reduces CPU time by allowing software direct access to sound hardware. Also provides synchronisation of video and sound data.
Direct Play	Aids running applications over networks or communications lines.
Direct Input	Speeds up mouse and joystick responses.

RAMDAC Used

The graphics information is stored in memory in digital format and has to be converted into analogue values to drive the gun(s) of the monitor. A chip, known as a RAMDAC (RAM digital/analogue converter) carries out the conversion function.   The frame buffer data for each pixel is read in the order that it will be sent to the monitor for display. This data is passed to the RAMDAC for conversion. With 24-bit colour, the numbers stored in memory exactly relate to the intensity of the red, green and blue elements of each pixel.   This makes the digital to analogue conversion simple.

However, this is not the method with lower colour depths. It is common that a card can only handle a subset of its full range of colours at any one time.   For example, a card capable of 65,536 different colours may only be using 256 colours in a particular mode.   This subset of colours is known as the *'palette'* and is stored in a look-up table in memory.   During normal activities, the screen's pixel colour information is stored as a sequence of logical colour numbers. The colour number for each pixel is read from memory, translated into the values for each gun and these values are given to the RAMDAC to produce the actual colour that will appear on the monitor.   Each Windows application package stores information about the palette it uses. When the application is run, Windows sets the RAMDAC to use that palette.   When several applications are open at the same time, each application may have different sets of colour numbers in their required palettes. This can result in unexpected colour changes, as the range of colours supported by the card is less than the range of colours requested by the applications. RAMDAC performance is measured both in colour depth (e.g. 24-bit) and conversion speed (up to 400MHz).

Card Connections

The output from the graphics card appears on a socket at the rear of the computer case.

The diagram shows the types of connector used with PCs.

The older CGA connector and EGA connector are identical and each has two rows of pins while the VGA/ SVGA/ XGA connector has three rows of pins. The chart shows the purpose of each pin.

The DVI-D connector provides a digital output, while the DVI-I connector provides both a digital and an analogue output.

Pin	EGA	VGA/SVGA/XGA
1	Ground	Red
2	Red Intensity	Green
3	Red	Blue
4	Green	Not Used
5	Blue	Not Used
6	Green Intensity	Red Return
7	Blue Intensity	Green Return
8	Horizontal Synch	Blue Return
9	Vertical Synch	No Pin (used as key)
10		Ground
11		Not Used
12		Not Used
13		Horizontal Synch
14		Vertical Synch
15		Not Used

Many cards also offer other connections to extension devices. The range of connections includes:

Video Input	The ability to display input from live video sources such as VCRs and camcorders, as provided in the Media Vision 1024 card. An extra daughterboard may have to be fitted for this.
TV Aerial Input	A number of graphics cards, such as the ATI Wonder Pro, now have a built-in TV tuner, allowing both viewing of television programmes on the monitor and the capture of television programmes to hard disk.
TV Output	Some graphics cards are capable not only of TV input but output as well. The user may decide whether to output the display to TV or monitor, or possibly both.
RGB output	Used for connecting to high-quality monitors and other video devices that use RGB connectors.

AGP

The Accelerated Graphics Port was developed in response to the huge memory and consequent data transfer overheads required for 3D graphics. A large number of texture maps have to be stored in memory. This allows rapid access to the texture data for the rapid rendering of 3D objects.   Fetching directly from disk would be far too slow to maintain the frame refresh rates.

However, 3D rendering produces two main problems:

- The memory requirements of these maps can exceed the actual amount of memory in the graphics card.
- Huge amounts of data need to be transferred to produce rendered screens at up to 30 frames per second.

The solution is twofold - use some of the computer's existing memory and access it at far faster data rates.   This requires a new motherboard with a new bus system - the Accelerated Graphics Port.

The Accelerated Graphics Port is only available on Pentium systems and these motherboards have their own AGP card slots and use the 440LX chipset onwards. The graphics card no longer sits on the 33Mhz PCI bus. As the diagram shows, the card is plugged directly into the separate AGP 66MHz bus that connects, via the chipset, to the CPU and memory. With modern CPUs, AGP functions are built in.

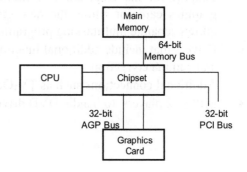

All AGP modes use a 32-bit parallel connection to the

graphics card. The computer's memory is shared between the application program's usage and the graphics card usage. For even faster performance, AGP cards can be purchased with substantial extra memory chips on the card.

The basic mode of working uses the 66MHz system clock to provide a maximum throughput of 264MBps. This is known as *"AGP 1x"*.

Although twice as fast as the PCI bus, the data rate of the AGP bus may be either greater or lesser than the data rate between the chipset and the main memory, or between the chipset and the CPU itself, depending on the speed of the Front Side Bus and/or the speed of the memory bus.

The initial AGP 1.0 specification was enhanced to strobe the graphics chips at multiples of the clock frequency, hence the terms AGP 2x, AGP4x and AGP 8x.

The '*AGP4x*' mode was introduced as part of the AGP 2.0 specification, while the '*AGP8x*' mode was introduced with the AGP 3.0 specification.

The maximum performance of each mode is shown in the table.

	AGP 1x	AGP 2x	AGP 4x	AGP 8x
Clock speed multiplier	1	2	4	8
Effective clock speed	66MHz	133MHz	266MHz	533MHz
Video throughput	264Mbps	528Mbps	1056Mbps	2.1Gbps

An addition to AGP 2.0 is the '*AGP Pro*' specification, which is essentially the same as AGP 2.0, but provides more power to the video adapter via additional pins on the AGP slot. AGP Pro is a fairly specialised technology, used almost exclusively by top-end design workstations.

Normal 2D graphics do not require this extra performance and normal applications will not particularly benefit from AGP techniques. Since support for AGP did not appear until a new DirectDraw in Windows 98, the shared memory usage ability of AGP cards were inactive until then. In the short-term, AGP provides a faster data transfer rate. In the long term, AGP 8x is the last of the parallel transfers modes between motherboard and graphics card. Future implementations will use " PCI Express" which is a high-speed serial interface.

Other Facilities

The preceding pages outline some of the more important features of graphics cards.

However, many more factors may prove important for a particular user or for a particular activity.

These might include:

- Support for DPMS power saving. The ability of the graphics card to control the power usage of the monitor at times when there is no user activity.
- Virtual Screen or virtual desktop. A user may wish to display a great deal of detail on the screen (e.g. many Windows groups or many Windows applications open at the same time). This would normally require a large screen monitor otherwise each window would be too small for comfortable viewing. An alternative is to use a normal monitor screen size and only view a part of the full screen at any one time. Moving the mouse to an edge of the screen scrolls the display in that direction. Thus a 640x480 screen can act as a window on a larger 1280x1024 display held in screen memory.
- Zoom. The virtual desktop provides a scrolling window on a larger screen. The zoom facility allows the user to magnify any portion of the screen, usually to allow detailed editing of graphics or DTP. There is no scrolling in this case. The Number 9 GXE64 Pro card, for example, magnifies the screen up to 5 times normal size.
- Support for the connection of multiple monitors - either through installing multiple graphics cards or fitting the new graphics cards that have twin video outputs. This allows separate multitasking programs to be run on separate monitors.
- Drivers that include additional functionality, such as colour calibration, monitor controls, and gamma correction.
- Additional connections such as TV-Out, TV-In, or DVI sockets.
- MPEG-2 players, to handle DVD drives.

Video Handling

Many graphics cards support a range of full motion video options, including MPEG, QuickTime, Video for Windows and Intel Indeo formats. Video playback is often achieved by fitting an extra board or using additional video handling software.

Video for Windows (AVI) is the most common PC video format although MPEG systems are becoming very popular. MPEG initially required special hardware to decode the compressed files, although with the advance of CPU power software methods have overtaken more expensive dedicated hardware decoders in many instances. The popularity of DVD players has led to a resurgence of dedicated hardware decoder cards, as these also provide *'theatre quality'* audio output.

The SLI 3D Graphics Interface

The chapter on Display Technology shows how a screenful of information is built up in the graphics card's memory, before being sent to the monitor. In particular, page 178 discusses the bandwidth requirements. It shows that higher resolution screens and faster screen refresh rates place greater strain on the graphics card.   The AGP bus and the current graphics cards needed a replacement technology, if future graphics demand were to be met.

A previous approach, called SLI (scan line interleaving) used two graphics cards, with one card rendering all the odd screen lines while the other card rendered all the even screen lines. The two sets of lines were then interleaved before being sent to the monitor.

The latest system, introduced by Nvidia in June 2004, is also called SLI but this stands for *"Scalable Link Interface"*.   It also uses two 3D graphics cards carrying out parallel processing. In Split Frame Mode, one card renders the top section of the screen image, while the other card renders the lower section of the screen image.

The Nvidia
SLI Connector

The top of each card has a slot connector and the two cards are linked together by a U-shaped bridge connector which fits across the two slot connectors. This allows the cards to communicate and have the GPUs (Graphic Processing Units) share the load.

The SLI load-balancing technique is to ensure the cards share the rendering load equally.   This means that the load is not always split 50/50 between cards. A scene may contain lots of detail in one section of the screen and have little detail in the other section (e.g. the top section may be mostly static plain blue sky). In these cases, the screen *data* is not shared 50/50 between cards, it is the *rendering* load that is shared equally.   This means constantly distributing both the geometry and pixel shading tasks between the two GPUs, including inter and intra-frame algorithms.

This method also ensures that both cards take the same time to render their share of the screen. The proportions rendered by each card are hence *'scalable'* and are always changing.

The rendered data from the slave GPU is sent over the SLI interface to the master GPU, where the two screen sections are composited before being sent to the monitor.

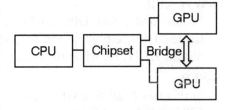

Motherboard

SLI is designed for the PCI Express interface.   AGP is not suitable, as it only supports a single graphics device. Also, SLI provides greater bandwidth, isochronous data transport (guaranteeing audio and video synchronisation delivered on time) and the ability to run four monitors at once (two from each graphics card).

The motherboard has to provide an SLI chipset and two x16 PCIe slots for installing the graphics cards.

Graphics Cards

The two SLI graphics cards need to be finely balanced and closely synchronised, to achieve proper dynamic load balancing. This means that the two cards have to be *exactly* matched. They have to be from the same manufacturer and have the same model number.   It is not even sufficient to have two cards that use the same GPU.   They must have the same GPU speed, use the same number of PCIe pipelines, etc.

Initially, this means that SLI systems are targeted at the high-end market

Power

Using two top-end cards means that the power requirements for the PC are greatly increased, with a typical demand of 75W per PCIe slot, plus that from any additional auxiliary power connectors. The 6800 series cards draw their additional power from separate 6-pin +12v connectors fed directly from the power supply or from special motherboard connectors. SLI configurations can demand power supplies with rating up to 550W.

With the extra power comes extra heating, as the cards will emit great amounts of heat. This demands that an SLI system be cased in a system with superior airflow.

Performance

In theory, doubling the graphics rendering power should provide twice the graphics performance, with the most benefit being seen with high resolution, high image quality content. Of course, other factors come into play. With the improved graphics performance and improved PCIe bus, the CPU becomes the potential bottleneck. The CPU now has to handle the increased data provided by two GPUs pumping out greatly increased frame rates and this requires a fast CPU.

The performance improvement also depends upon the application being run. All existing software, including those using DirectX and OpenGL, should run on an SLI graphics system without modification. That is not to say that they will all run equally fast. The SLI drivers decide on the best mode to use to run an application.

In most cases, this would be SFR (Split Fame Rate) mode, as described above. However, certain games and applications might be run in AFR (Alternating Frame Rate) Mode, which is similar to the earlier scan line interleaving technique.

In the worst cases, it could run in Compatibility Mode, which runs on only one graphics card and provides no improvement over traditional single-card systems. In most cases, and certainly as new applications are introduced, SLI performance should approach the doubling of performance compared to a single graphics card.

Quad SLI

For even greater graphics processing (2560x1600), four GPUs can be fitted to a motherboard that supports quad SLI.

Quad SLI uses two graphics cards, each card having two GPUs on board. SLI bridges connect the first GPU with the third GPU, then the second GPU to the fourth. The system boasts of having six Teraflops of computing power, allowing graphics processing at 48 Gigapixels per second. Its maximum resolution is 2560x1600.

It can operate in one of several modes.

4-Way AFR

In this mode, each GPU renders every fourth frame. So, for example the first GPU would handle frames 1,5,9, etc while the second GPU handles frames 2,6, 10,etc.The Third GPU would handle frames 3,7,11, etc while the fourth GPU handled frames,4,8,12, etc.

4-SFR

In this mode, all four GPUs are used to render each frame. As with dual SLI, the workload to each GPUs is balanced for maximum performance.

AFR of SFR

In this mode, the first set of GPUs render the odd frames (e.g. frames 1,3,5, etc.) while the second set of GPUs render the even frames (e.g. frames 2,4,6, etc.).

Crossfire

An alternative to SLI is the 'Crossfire' system from ATI. It also uses two graphics cards but connects them via an external cable, rather than SLI's internal bridge connector.

It provides SFR and APR, along with some other sharing techniques.

It has the advantage that it can work with graphics cards that are not matched, although the system then operates at the speed of the slowest card.

HDMI

Connecting consumer Audio/Video equipment together can involve a variety of different interfaces – VGA, DVI, SCART (for Europe), composite, component, S-Video, etc.

This has led to a drive towards improving and standardising on a new interface.

This has been driven by two sources:

- Manufacturers such as Sony, Panasonic, Hitachi, Toshiba and Philips - who wanted a standard interface that was based on digital connections rather than analogue connections.
- Movie producers such as Warner Bros, Disney, Fox, Universal and satellite and cable operators – who wanted an interface that eliminated piracy of movie content.

These interests created a working group that released the HDMI 1.0 specification in December 2002, followed by the HDMI 1.1 specification in May 2004.

What it is

HDMI stands for *'High Definition Multimedia Interface'*. It aims to be the standard for the digital transport of uncompressed video and audio information from a device (e.g. set-top box, DVD player, etc.) to a display (e.g. digital television, LCD monitor, Plasma screen, etc.).

It is essentially the DVI interface (see the book) with added features. Like DVI, it transfers uncompressed RGB video in real-time.

However, it also provides:

- Support for high resolutions, up to 1080i (1080 lines, each line being 1920 pixels – i.e. 1920x1080). This delivers standard PC formats up to high definition television and improves images on large-screens and home cinema systems.
- Support for standard stereo up to 8-channel digital audio surround-sound, uncompressed at 24-bit. This delivers both compressed audio formats such as Dolby Digital, through to uncompressed streams, with sampling rates of from 32kHz to 192kHz.
- Support for CEC (*'Consumer Electronics Control'*), providing features that manufacturers may opt to incorporate in their devices. CEC allows for facilities such as timer programming, one-touch record, tuner control and deck control. HDMI allows communication between its attached devices and control through a hand-held remote.
- Support for plug-and-play.
- Support for future expansion. HDTV (High Definition Television), for example, uses less than half of the 5 Gbps bandwidth that HDMI provides.

Quality Benefits

The above list shows that HDMI is *'bigger'*, but the manufacturers also claim that it is *'better'*. Under HDMI, the audio and video quality should improve for two reasons:

- The signals are uncompressed and therefore don't suffer the quality losses associated with compressing and uncompressing signals.
- The signals remain digital throughout and therefore avoid the quality losses associated with analogue interfaces (e.g. the digital signal from a DVD player being output as analogue and then converted back to digital within the display). It also minimises unwanted noise.

Nevertheless, this new system only minimises rather than eliminates unwanted effects. This is for three reasons:

- Not all signals are transferred in digital format for their entire journey. For example, HDTV is transmitted as a compressed MPEG stream before being decoded and output as uncompressed video.
- Even digital-to-digital conversions can, and often do, degrade picture quality. Digital conversions take place between the decoder and the production of the HDMI signal (known as TMDS – Transition-Minimised Differential Signalling).
- Many video resolutions have to be *'scaled'* to match their display's native resolution. Where the image size is greater than the screen resolution, pixels have to be removed from the image. More likely, smaller images have pixels added to make them fill a large screen resolution, the values of the extra pixels being 'estimated'. Since these processes interfere with the original image, they affect the quality of the displayed image. Signals originated from a digital source are affected in the same way as an analogue source.

So, if a source of AV begins life as digital, is transmitted digitally, transferred digitally within the consumer system – and the final display is an exact match of the resolution of the original source – the optimum quality is achieved within DPMI.

That said, DPMI quality provides significantly improvements by removing some of the factors that degrade AV quality.

How it works

HDMI operates entirely digitally. There is no analogue processing and there are no analogue connections between devices and displays.

HDMI is based on DVI. They both use the same encoding scheme and produce identical video quality results.

Their video signals are fully compatible. As a result, HDMI digital televisions can display video from DVI devices, including PC DVI graphics cards. DVI-equipped displays can present video from HDMI devices, although without the audio and the CEC features.

Unlike DVI, the HDMI interface cable carries both audio, video and control information. Even better, there is only a single cable between the device and the display. This cable replaces all previous AV cables (e.g. Composite, Component, S-Video, stereo audio cables, etc.). In addition, HDMI uses High Bandwidth Digital Content Protection (HDCP).

Connections

By using a single cable to connect the HDMI device to a display, the set of existing cables is replaced and this produces the following benefits:

- Simpler (no working out what plug fits into each socket).
- Foolproof (the plug only inserts in one direction).
- Neater (no mess of wires). The consumer version of the plug is almost half the width of a DVI plug. It connects in a similar fashion to a USB plug, without the screw pins used by DVI plugs.
- Cheaper (single cable is cheaper than multiple cables).

The HDMI standard provides for two types of plug:

- Type 'A', with 19 pins, provides a single TMDS link with a video sampling rate up to 165MHz and is designed for consumer products such as TV and DVD.
- Type 'B', with 29 pins, provides a dual link with a video sampling rate up to 330MHz and is designed for resolutions exceeding 1080i (e.g. PCs and future high resolution displays).

While a DVI cable has a 5m limit on its useable length, HDMI cables work satisfactorily up to 15m. Since both systems have no error correction, lost information becomes a greater problem with increased distance (unless expensive fibre optic cables are used).

Copy protection

The MPAA (Motion Picture Association of America) is eager that HDMI become the standard interface. This is because the HDMI specification includes HDCP (High-bandwidth Digital Content Protection). This protection scheme aims to prevent unauthorised copying of HDMI material.

As the diagram shows, video content can be encrypted before being added to the TMDS link. At the display

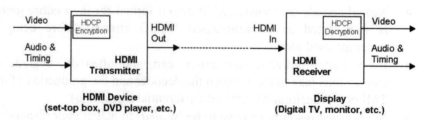

end, any encrypted video content is decrypted before being sent to the display. The use of HDCP is optional but will certainly be used by the large commercial media giants to protect their video content.

The system requires that both the device and the display have HDCP support. So, for example, if the display is not DHCP compatible, it may display a low resolution image or even no image.

Playing HDTV DVDs on a HDTV player into a HDTV-compatible TV will operate correctly. The problem arises when displaying HD material on a DVI-connected monitor using a PC with Vista installed. In this case, the graphics card and the monitor must both be HDCP-compliant. For almost all users, this requires both to be replaced as they have only recently appeared for sale.

The encryption works by encoding an encryption key into the HDMI signal. This encryption is supplied, under licence from *'Digital Content Protection LLC'* (a subsidiary of Intel), when an HDMI-enabled item is purchased. If the display device also has a licensed decrypter key, the video content is decoded and displayed.

DHCP also checks the receiving device every few seconds. As long as the receiving device has an authentic key, the encrypted content is transmitted. If not, the transmitting device may refuse to send out any content.

Digital Content Protection LLC will operate renewable keys. So, if the company believes that a set of keys has been compromised, it can place those keys on a revocation list and provide new keys to the licensed user.

Computer Memory

Memory Usage

The memory inside a computer stores a variety of information.

- A computer loads a program into its main memory, from where it can be run. A computer program is a list of instructions for the CPU, each instruction being stored as a numeric code.
- Computer programs exist to manipulate data. The data may be loaded from disk or CD, entered from the keyboard, downloaded via a modem - and a range of other input devices. The data may be in the form of database records, wages data, etc. Whatever its format, the data is always held in the form of numeric values.
- The computer stores some of its own system programs (such as the components of Windows) and its own system information (such as the nationality of the keyboard in use, screen display information, etc.).

All of these must share the same pool of memory held inside the computer. In addition, the machine stores much of the code it requires to handle its hardware in programs that are permanently blown on to chips. If the computer is to avoid getting into utter confusion, it must allocate these activities to separate areas, each with its own distinct boundaries within the machine's addressable memory.

Memory Access

The machine has to separate one program instruction from the next. This is achieved by storing the machine instructions in different memory locations. This means having each consecutive instruction stored in each consecutive memory address. It is important to differentiate between an address and its contents. The address is a unique location in memory. The contents of this address may be part of an application program or system program, or may be data.

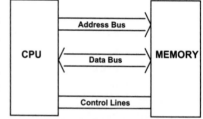

The CPU will fetch an instruction from the memory by placing the instruction's memory address on the Address Bus and a Read signal on one of the Control Lines. The memory chip places the address's contents on to the Data Bus and this is picked up by the CPU. The CPU then carries out the instruction. If the instruction involves writing a piece of data to memory, the appropriate location is placed on the Address Bus, the value to be written is placed on the Data Bus and a Write signal is placed on one of the Control Lines. Once the instruction is completed, the CPU can fetch the next instruction, often stored in the next consecutive program memory address. The simplified diagram uses a single bus for both data and program instructions. This is very common and is called the *'Von Neumann'* architecture.

Memory Organisation

As discussed earlier, the computer's memory, both RAM and ROM, is regarded as a contiguous list of locations, and each location is identified by its unique memory address. In the most recent RAMBUS chips, the memory locations are indeed arranged in a contiguous manner along the memory bus. In all other types of RAM, however, the memory is organised as a matrix of storage cells, as in the diagram. For simplicity, the diagram only shows 16 rows and 16 columns, providing 256 addressable locations or cells. Any cell in the matrix can be accessed by specifying its row and column co-ordinates. The memory chip circuitry has to translate any memory address into the corresponding co-ordinates.

In the example, the CPU requests access to address 227 (i.e. 11100011 in binary. This binary pattern is placed on the address bus.

The four least significant bits (0011) are used by the column decoder to determine the column co-ordinate, known as the Column Address Select (CAS) line. In the example the CAS value is 3. The four most significant bits (1110) are used by the row decoder to determine the row co-ordinate, known as the Row Address Select (RAS) line - in this case 14. The row and column address lines then access only the single unique cell that corresponds to the address supplied. Note that the convention is to number address bus lines and data bus lines commencing with line 0. So, a 16-bit address bus would number its lines from A0 to A15 and an 8-bit data bus would number from D0 to D7. As can be seen, any cell in the

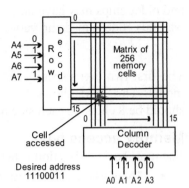

matrix can be individually accessed. Hence the description as a random access device. Also, accessing each cell will incur the same circuit switching time overhead. This is the chip's *'access time'*.

To simplify the diagram, only the address lines are shown. There will also be data lines to transfer data in and out of the cells to the CPU. A data transfer will either be a read operation (the cell's contents are copied on to the data bus) or a write operation (the contents of the data bus are copied into the cells). To instruct the chip on which operation is required, it is fed read/write information on its control lines. If the CPU requires data from memory, it issues a read instruction along with the address to be read. To write data to memory, the CPU places the data on the data bus and issues a write instruction along with the address location.

The diagram shows only a matrix of 256 bits. A practical chip would involve the same architecture, only on a larger scale. The diagram describes a 256 x 1 bit chip, since only one bit at a time can ever be accessed. To read or write a byte, eight of these chips would require to be accessed in parallel. Example commercial DRAMs are 256k x 1 devices, 64k x 4 devices (four 64k devices parallel configured in the same chip) or 1M x 8 devices (a full byte-wide set of 1MB matrix capacity)

Note The cells accessed may contain a program instruction or program data. The circuitry can't distinguish between instructions and data and the programmer has to ensure that the correct addresses are being accessed.

UMA

Unified Memory Architecture is a memory organisation standard set by VESA. Motherboards supporting UMA allow the CPU and video system to share the same pool of main memory. There is no need for video cards to be fitted with 4MB, 8MB or more of their own separate memory, making these cards significantly cheaper. Additionally, chunks of the memory on the current standard video cards are unused when the card is used in low resolution or low colour depths. This may be occurring while there is a real shortage of main memory for user applications and data. With UMA boards, lowering the resolution or colour depth reduces the amount needed by video and the remainder is released for use by programs. Unfortunately, such systems are slower by up to 10% due to the extra processing required to manage the memory and because of the loss of memory from the normal pool available for Windows, applications, etc. UMA provides cheaper but slower computer systems.

AGP

The Accelerated Graphics Port, described in more detail in the *Display Technologies* chapter, is a more modern standard that allows the video card to utilise main memory. Unlike UMA it uses its own high-speed bus to access the RAM, instead of the slower PCI bus. In addition, main memory used by AGP cards is <u>in addition</u> to memory on the video card, not replacing it. Both of these facts make the AGP system much faster than a UMA system. In AGP enabled systems, the BIOS will contain a setting to determine how much RAM the AGP card may use. This is known as the *'Video Memory Aperture'* and is measured in megabytes. High end graphics cards normally use their own high-speed memory rather than sharing system RAM, so shared AGP memory is usually only used by cheaper or older graphics cards.

Memory Types

A range of memory products exists, with differing characteristics. These characteristics are explained in more detail later in this chapter, but the main differences are:

- Capacity. The amount of memory a module contains is measured in Megabytes (MB).
- Access type. Some chips may have their contents altered, while others cannot.
- Speed. Faster chips are of course generally more expensive.
- Connector type. A memory module may only be used in a system that supports that particular type of module.

It is sometimes difficult to tell apart chips of one type from another. The most obvious difference is the connector type, but chips of the same connector type can be confused. While manufacturers are increasingly including labels on the chips that explain the chip size, speed and so on, some still do not, and older chips may have no easily understood markings. Many chips carry only a numeric code, and the way this code is made up varies from one manufacturer to the other. For example:

48LC16M8A

The first two digits specify the product range, with the letters 'LC' indicating that it is a Low Current model. The '16M' shows that each chip is of 16 Megabytes capacity, while the '8A2' indicates that there should be 8 chips on each side of the module, and chips on both sides.

Memory access type
The most basic distinction is between two types of memory:

- Those whose contents can only be read, during the running of a program. Some memory's contents may be permanent, while other memory chips may be removed from the computer and re-programmed. These are referred to as Read-Only Memory chips (ROM), but also include PROM, EPROM and EEPROM chips.
- Those whose contents can be read and also written to. This type of memory is called RAM (Random Access Memory), and examples include DRAM, SRAM and DDR.

Read-Only memory types
The basic *'Read Only Memory'* chips are *'non-volatile'*; their contents will not be lost if the power is removed. These chips are used in a wide range of electronic control circuits, from industrial machine tools to domestic washing machines. They are also the ideal choice for computer control.

ROM BIOS
A computer's most basic control programs must be non-volatile. The computer's essential functions are controlled by system software and there is a potential Catch-22 situation, in that

"the computer needs a program to be loaded, so that the computer can load a program"

By placing part of the operating system software (called the '*system BIOS*') into a ROM chip, the basic machine control programs are available to be run as soon as the computer is switched on. The programs in the ROM provide the machine's basic input and output functions, to allow application programs to be loaded and run. Unfortunately, if the system is to be updated, the BIOS chip has to be replaced with a new chip that contains the new program routines. This requires opening the computer case and is a job for experienced support staff or technicians. As a result ROM BIOS chips have been replaced by EEPROM, or *'Flash ROM'* which allow BIOS updates to be carried out in software.

ROM chips are *'mask programmed'* devices; the layers of the integrated circuit are manufactured using specifically designed masks. These produce chips that are only capable of performing the required pre-determined programs. Due to the cost of manufacturing ROMs, they are only used in large quantity runs. This, in turn, means that they are only made when the manufacturer is certain that the programs they contain are debugged. These chips are also fitted in video, network and disk controller cards.

PROM
This stands for *'Programmable Read Only Memory'*. With ROM, the internal program is dedicated at the production stage; the physical construction of the chip reflects the program that it stores. A cheaper method for small and medium scale use is a ROM-type chip that can be programmed, after the construction stage. Such chips are mass-produced by a chip manufacturer, who has no idea of the use to which they will be put. Once a computer manufacturer purchases the chip, the company's programs can be embedded in it. This is achieved by *'blowing'* fusible links inside the chip, to form the binary codes representing the program's machine code instructions. Every intact link represents a binary 1, with a blown link representing a binary 0. Like the ROM, the PROM chip is also non-volatile.

EPROM
The initials stand for *'Erasable Programmable Read Only Memory'* and it was introduced as a development tool. The problem with ROM and a programmed PROM was that, once produced, they were unalterable. This is perfectly fine for a computer manufacturer - once the program contents are fully debugged. The EPROM is used to test the program. Like PROM, its links are blown to the needs

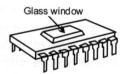
Glass window

of the test program. The EPROM can then be used on the test computer. If the program is satisfactory, it can be used to create mass ROM or PROM versions. If the program needs alteration, the EPROM is subjected to ultra-violet light for a few minutes. This 'heals' the ruptured links, allowing the chip to be blown to the next test program. The blowing and wiping clean process can be repeated many times over, before the chip fabric starts to degenerate. An EPROM chip is easily identified as it has a glass window on top of the chip to allow entry of the ultra-violet light. Due to its more expensive construction, it is only a viable alternative to ROM and EPROM for small-scale use. Example EPROM chips would be the 2764-20 (64k - i.e. 8k x 8 bits) and the 27512-20 (512k - i.e. 64k x 8 bits). The equipment required to program and erase EPROMs can be cheap enough for individual or hobbyist use. For continual development use, the EPROM is often replaced with a *'ROM emulator'*. This is a piece of equipment that plugs into the ROM socket and acts like an EPROM. It contains RAM to avoid the program-erase cycles. Since it is self-powered, it appears to the main computer as a piece of ROM.

EEPROM

A variation on the EPROM is the **EEPROM** - the *'Electrically Erasable and Programmable Read Only Memory'*. Like EPROM, it has holds its contents when the power is removed. However, its contents can be overwritten without resorting to prior cleaning with ultra-violet light. This type of chip is used in many *'flash'* memory devices. The SmartMedia range of cards used in digital cameras and MP3 players, for example, are EEPROM based. EEPROM tends to have high access times in comparison to ROM and RAM, but is still fast compared to disk storage. For example a typical access speed for SmartMedia is around 25 milliseconds.

Main Memory

The variations on ROM memory outlined earlier are primarily concerned with the computer's basic control functions, with application programs being loaded from disk into main memory. However, this is not always the case. Many palmtop computers use ROM to store application programs, to overcome the storage problems associated with such small machines. Due to their tiny physical dimensions, there is no space for a hard disk to store application software. So, the machine stores a word processor, spreadsheet, personal organiser, etc. in ROM. In most computers, however, the application software is loaded into, and run from, main memory. In addition, there is a need for an area to store program data and video data. These memory areas use RAM, which stands for *'Random Access Memory'*. Unlike ROM technology, RAM chips are volatile which means that the data stored in the chips only remains there as long as the chips are powered. When the machine is switched off, the chips lose their contents. That is why users are always reminded to save all their data before switching off their machines. In fact, to ensure complete data integrity, the application should be exited before switching off. This ensures that any data held in the computer's memory buffers are flushed away to disk. A database, for example, will not save each record as it is entered; it will save a number of records into a buffer area and then save the groups of records. Although they appear to the user as having been saved, they are still vulnerable to loss, if the power is switched off. The term *'random access'* is used to distinguish it from serial access devices. With serial access devices, such as tapes, the data is read in with one item following the other. The last item takes longer to fetch than the first item. Random access means that any cell address in the entire memory area can be accessed with a uniform time overhead.

Note: Confusingly, ROM chips are also random access devices. The difference between ROM and RAM variants is not in their access methods, but in their volatility (or lack of it) and speed.

Random-Access Memory

This type of memory is further split into two basic forms: Dynamic Ram (DRAM) and Static RAM (SRAM). Both types use arrays of transistor switches to store the binary data. The main difference lies in how the transistors are switched and it is this that affects the chips' characteristics.

Note : Both types use different circuitry and are therefore <u>not</u> interchangeable.
Static RAM cannot be plugged into sockets intended for Dynamic RAM and vice versa.

DRAM

Dynamic Ram, or DRAM, is commonly used for the computer's main memory. An incoming data signal with logic level *'on'* (i.e. logic 1) to a cell is used to charge a capacitor, which holds the transistor in its switched state. The charge in this capacitor quickly leaks away and the transistor would lose its information. To prevent this, the capacitor has to be constantly *'refreshed'*. The contents of the capacitor have to be read on a regular basis. If it contains a value, the capacitor is fully re-charged to maintain its 'on' state.   When an incoming logic level wishes to store an 'off' state (i.e. logic level 0), the capacitor is discharged.

With a main memory of 640k, and 8 cells to every byte, this involves reading and writing to 5,242,880 different cells. If the machine has a 128MB memory, then over a billion cells have to be refreshed regularly. For this reason, DRAM - despite technological improvements - is a relatively slow memory system. 120ns or 150ns would be considered as slow access times for modern DRAM, while 70ns or 80ns would be average and 60ns would be considered fast.   Example DRAM chips are:

> 4164-12   with 64k x1 bit organisation and a speed of 120nS
>
> 44256-70 with 256k x 1 bit organisation and 70nS access time
>
> 41256-60 with 256k x 1 bit organisation and 60nS access time

IBM produce a 256MB DRAM and Hitachi produce a 2GB DRAM. On a practical note, modern DRAM uses a simple 5V or 3.3V supply. Earlier DRAM needed both 5V and –5V. The move to single sided DRAM means that a modern motherboard can work with only +5 and +12V supplies, although the RS232 ports will be compromised.

SRAM

Static RAM, or SRAM, does not use the capacitive method. Each cell represents a single bit and the value is held by a more complex set of transistors that are configured as a bistable (commonly called a 'flip-flop').   The output of this flip-flop can be 'set' or 'reset', to store either a binary 0 or a binary 1.   In this chip, the cell's state will maintain itself, until it is either altered by a new value, or has its power removed. There is no need to constantly refresh the cells' contents. The result is that the static RAM chip is significantly faster than dynamic RAM. An access time of 10ns or more would be considered slow, while 5ns would be average and 2ns would be considered fast.

Static RAMs have one major drawback. They require a more complex structure, with a greater component count for each cell.   As a result, the fastest static RAM is larger and much more expensive than dynamic RAM.   For this reason, it is not used for the main memory chips of the computer. They are, instead, used for fast cache memory (see later section).   Most SRAM chips are of the DIL (dual in line) or SIL (single in-line) type and are of the SIMM (single in-line memory module) or SIP (single in-line package) variety.

NVRAM

Non-Volatile RAM, as its name suggests, is memory storage that does not lose its contents when the computer (or any other device that uses memory) is switched off. The two main types of NVRAM technology in use are battery-powered SRAM, such as that used in CMOS data storage; and EEPROM chips, such as those used in Flash memory cards. Other NVRAM technologies are in development for commercial use, such as FRAM – Ferromagnetic RAM, which uses magnetic cores to store data.

NVRAM technologies are used in Flash BIOS chips, and as storage for digital cameras, MP3 players and so on. Examples include Sony's Memory Stick, SmartMedia, and CompactFlash.

Memory speed

In older chips, the speed of the chip was termed its 'Access time' (occasionally called its 'period') and was measured in nano-seconds (i.e. 10 to the power minus 9), with smaller values meaning faster chips. More recent chip types are described in terms of their 'clock frequency' which is measured in MegaHertz, with a larger frequency representing a faster chip.

However, equally important as the data transfer speed, is the amount of data transferred in each cycle. The memory bus size determines how many bytes are transferred in one go, and the total amount of data a chip is capable of transferring each second is termed the module's 'data throughput'. It is measured in Gigabytes per second (GB/s), and can be calculated by multiplying the number of bytes transferred in each cycle by the number of cycles per second.

There are a number of ways that have been developed to improve on access times.   These include:

Fast Page Mode Access

The normal basic access method splits the incoming address value into a Row Address and a Column Address. Where access to the memory is random (i.e. an incoming address is completely different from the previous address accessed) the process already described has to be undertaken. However, there are many times when the access is sequential (i.e. the data to be fetched consists of a block of contiguous addresses). Examples of sequential access would be fetching graphics data or a block of text. With sequential access there is no need to recalculate the Row Address for each cell and a block of data can be accessed by changing the Column Address values alone. The data fetched is known as a *'page'* and is accessed at a faster rate than conventional methods.

Interleaving

This also speeds up sequential accesses and is achieved by splitting the memory up into two or four separate banks. All digital circuits move between high and low states and, after being switched, need a specific time to recover before being switched again. This slows down memory access rates. With interleaved systems, sequential data is stored over the various memory banks. This means that one bank can be accessed while the previous bank is in recovery time. This reduces waiting time and increases sequential data access rates. It also allows banks to perform read/write operations at the same time.

Synchronous Operation

Normal DRAM works asynchronously - the CPU and the memory chips have to use an elaborate set of signals to control data operations. The time to generate these signals and the time for the signals to be recognised impose time delays upon the data transaction. Synchronous operation ties the CPU and the memory in step with the same clock. This eliminates the need for much of the handshaking signals and the generation by the CPU of a wanted address location results in the transfer of a copy of the location's contents without the need of any further CPU to memory communication. Commonly used with Pentium cache RAM (486s used asynchronous cache), it is now appearing for use with main memory.

Fast Access Memory Types

Ranges of memory chips take advantage of the above techniques, and others, to improve memory performance. These memory types currently are:

EDO RAM

This stands for *'Extended Data Out'* memory and is used both for main memory and in video cards as a replacement for VRAM (see below). It is an extended version of page-mode working. With normal page-access memory, the data is removed from the chip's output buffer when the Column Address line is de-activated. With EDO, the data stays available while the chip is getting set up for the next access. Access delays are reduced in this way and a complete memory transaction can take place in a single clock cycle instead of the normal two clock cycles. This will not double the chip's overall speed, since it only improves sequential access times. Overall, typical speed improvements of 5% to 10% are expected. Can't be used in 386s, 486s or older Pentiums. Available as 72-pin SIMMs or 168-pin DIMM versions (at 3.3v or 5v).

BEDO

Burst Mode EDO memory was essentially EDO with the addition of burst mode operation plus some tweaks to the memory access cycle. Only supported by the FX chipset.

VRAM

This is a variation on DRAM chips, where normal data write operations and constant sequential reads occur at the same time. This is especially useful for video memory and is explained in the chapter on *'Display Technology'*.

SDRAM

Synchronous DRAM uses synchronous working as outlined earlier. For even faster working, it also uses both interleaving and burst mode techniques. This ensures speeds up to 100MHz, in burst mode, compared to EDO's 50MHz maximum speed and BEDO's 66MHz maximum. Because of its reliance on its clock speed, SDRAM performance is measured in MHz, such as PC133 memory, which is 133MHz.

WRAM

Windows RAM was developed by Samsung especially for use in video cards. It is dual-ported like VRAM but supports a block write mode for faster data rates.

MDRAM

Multibank RAM applies the interleaving technique for main memory to second level cache memory to provide a cheaper and faster alternative to SRAM. The chip splits its memory capacity into small blocks of 256k and allows operations to two different banks in a single clock cycle.

SGRAM

The *'Synchronous Graphics Ram'* is based on SDRAM, but can operate in burst mode for both write and read operations (SDRAM can only read in burst mode). Although faster than early SDRAM, it is largely unused now. They have 10ns, 12ns and 15ns access times.

RDRAM

Dispenses with the page mode type of interface in favour of a very fast serial interface operating at 800Mbps to 1200Mbps. This *'Rambus'* interface is a fast local bus between CPUs, graphics controllers and block-oriented memory. Initially adopted for some Nintendo machines, this system was preferred by Intel, but has recently been abandoned in favour of DDR.

DDR SDRAM

Originally developed for video cards, DDR (Double Data Rate) is a type of SDRAM that has recently become cost-effective enough for main memory. In the best situations, it can transmit data on both the rising and falling edges of the clock pulse. In real situations this is rarely achieved, but overall DDR is still faster than SDR (Single Data Rate) memory. The diagram shows that the internal bus must be twice the size of the external bus in order for DDR to operate.

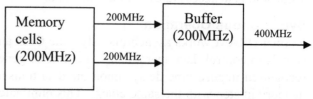

DDR2

The second version of DDR is of a lower voltage (1.8V as opposed to the 2.5V of DDR), and includes a few new technologies in its design such as electrical termination to prevent signal noise, and a longer pre-fetch buffer. However, the headline change to DDR2 was the increase in the bus clock speed. DDR ranged from 100MHz to 166MHz, which was 'doubled' to 200MT/s-333MT/s. DDR2 begins with a memory speed of between 100MHZ and 266MHz, but it uses two the bus speed is 200MHz to 533MHz. This, in turn, is 'doubled' to 400-1066MT/s. Essentially, then, DDR2 is double the speed of DDR. The diagram shows that the internal bus must be four times the size of the external bus in order to use DDR2.

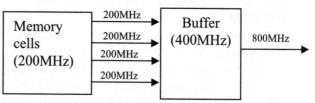

Description	Bus speed	Transfers per second	Throughput
PC3200	200MHz	400MT/s	3200MBps
PC4200	266MHz	533MT/s	4264MBps
PC5400	333MHz	667MT/s	5336MBps
PC2-6400	400MHz	800MT/s	6.4Gbps
PC2-8500	533MHz	1066MT/s	8.5Gbps

As can be seen from the table, DDR2 types continue to be named after the data throughput, measured in millions of bytes per second.

DDR3

Continuing in the footsteps of DDR2, which has a bus speed double that of its internal speed, DDR3 has a bus speed *four times* that of its internal memory speed. So, even though the clock is still 100-200MHz, the bus speed is 400-800MHz, and the transfers per second is 800-1600MT/s.

Description	Bus speed	Transfers per second	Throughput
DDR3-800 (PC3-6400)	400MHz	800MT/s	6400MBps
DDR3-1066 (PC3-8500)	533MHz	1066MT/s	8528MBps
DDR3-1333 (PC3-10667)	667MHz	1333MT/s	10667MBps
DDR3-1600 (PC13-12800)	800MHz	1600MT/s	12.8Gbps

GDDR

The memory on graphics cards should be faster than that used as motherboard main memory, due to the increased speed demand placed upon it. To meet this need GDDR (Graphics DDR) was developed. It is capable of operating at faster speeds and at lower voltages. Faster speeds increase chip temperatures but operating at lower voltages compensates accordingly. Like DDR, GDDR2 memory operates at 2.5v. GDDR3 memory, however, operates down to 1.8v as with DDR2. GDDR4 currently has a maximum effective rate of 4Gbps and GDDR5 can theoretically reach speeds of 4.5GB/s.

Physical Address Extension
For systems with lots of physical memory (NOT virtual memory), the PAE addressing system allows the memory above 4GB to be accessed, up to a maximum of 64GB. It is available on all Intel processors since the Pentium Pro, and many modern AMD processors as well. PAE makes use of an API named Address Windowing Extensions (AWE) to allow software to access the additional memory.

Chip Connection Types
RAM and ROM chips are available in a variety of different physical constructions. Note that most RAM memory is not supplied as single chips, but in '*memory modules*' that consist of several chips.

DIP chips
Dual in-line packages; sometimes also known as DILs. These are the traditional outline for industry logic chips and other integrated circuits and were used on early PCs. They are rectangular blocks with connecting pins down two opposite sides. The pins can be soldered directly on to the computer motherboard, or plugged into board-mounted receptacles, called '*I.C. sockets*'.

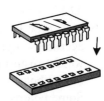

SIP modules
The SIP (Single In-line Pin package) is found in older models. It is very similar in its construction to the SIMM board, except that its connections are to a row of pins instead of a row of printed circuit pads. These pins are then plugged into a special socket on the motherboard or soldered into place.

SIMM modules
The '*Single In-line Memory Module*' is the standard for most machines and consists of a set of memory chips mounted on a small printed circuit board. There are most commonly eight or nine chips on the board, dependent on whether parity checking is in use. The board has an edge connector similar, although smaller, to that used on add-on cards. The memory board plugs

into a special set of slots on the motherboard. Since the board is clipped into place, it provides a more secure connection than earlier DIP chips. The constant heating and cooling of memory chips made them regularly expand and contract until they sometimes popped out of their holders - an effect known as '*chip creep*'. This is avoided with SIMMs making their use more reliable. SIMMs are available in two basic types - 30-pin and 72-pin; this refers to the numbers of pads on the edge connector.

30-Pin SIMM
These are mainly used with now obsolete PCs such as 286's to 486's. Each SIMM board has an 8-bit data width, with an extra ninth bit if parity is used. SIMM boards are used in sets of four, to connect to a 32-bit data bus. Chips used on SIMM boards advertised as '*1 x 8*' indicates that it is of 1MB capacity - i.e. 1 mega-bit times 8. When used in sets of eight, each chip stores a single bit of each data byte. The more common '*1 x 9*' board uses nine chips, with the extra bit included for parity checking. Newer '*composite*' SIMMs use improved chips that replace three conventional memory chips. Thus, a 3-chip board and a 9-chip board both provide the same amount of memory but with different chips on the board. These boards, despite having the same capacity, are not usually interchangeable.

72-Pin SIMM
These are used with some 386DX's, some 486's and older Pentiums. They are supplied with 8 or 9 chips on the board. They have a 32-bit data width and will have four extra bits if parity is being used. The extra

30-pin	72-pin	Parity	Access Time
x8	x32	No	70ns
x9	x36	Yes	70ns
-	EDO	No	60ns

pins to the board carry the address lines and control lines from the motherboard. It can be thought of as four separate 8-bit chips used to construct a 32-bit wide data path. So, a chip advertised as '*1 x 32*' indicates that it is of 4MB capacity - i.e. 1 mega-bit times 32, divided by 8. Similarly, a '*1 x 36*' is a 4MB chip including parity checking. An '*8 x 32*' is a 32MB SIMM while an '*8 x36*' is a 32MB SIMM with parity. 72 pin SIMMs are available in 1MB, 2MB, 4MB, 8MB, 16MB, 32MB and 64MB varieties.

SIMM Banks

Motherboards provide slots for inserting SIMMs and these groups of slots are known as *'SIMM banks'*. The motherboard manual should be consulted, as different configurations are possible. For example:

386/486

The average 386/486 motherboard has eight 30-pin SIMM slots and the slots can be configured to take either 256k, 1MB or 4MB modules. Most motherboards split the eight slots into two banks of four slots. The four slots in the bank must be populated and the four SIMM boards fitted must be of the same type. It is not possible, for example, to have two 4MB modules and two 1MB modules in the bank. There would have to be four 4MB modules or four 1MB modules. This is because a 32-bit data bus width needs to connect to 32 bits of RAM. Since each 30-pin SIMM provides 8 bits, four boards allow the full 32 bits of data to be accessed at the same time. If data was accessed a byte at a time, it would require four separate memory accesses to build up a 32-bit data word, resulting in much slower transfer rates. Some other models, including Pentium motherboards, have only two banks of 2 slots.

Some boards also demand that the configuration of the second bank be identical to that used in the first bank. So, if the first bank contained four 2MB modules, the second bank would also have to contain four 2MB modules. Some motherboards provide jumpers so that the second bank can have a different configuration from the first bank. This allows the first bank to have, for example, four 2MB modules while the second bank has four 1MB modules - giving a total of 12MB. It is also important that each SIMM board uses chips with the same access times. If SIMMs have different access speeds, the computer will either operate at the speed of the slowest board or the system may crash if the BIOS has not been configured for the slowest speed.

Since the 486 has a 32-bit data width, it can be fitted with a single 72-pin SIMM.

Pentiums

The Pentium has a 64-bit data bus and requires two 32-bit SIMMs be fitted at a time. The two SIMMs must be of the same capacity - i.e. using two 16MB SIMMs provides 32MB of main memory. Although all Pentiums support 72-pin SIMMs, there are variations in the type of memory supported by particular motherboards. Try to avoid mixing parity and non-parity SIMMs. Fitting parity SIMMs to non-parity motherboards will probably crash the system; fitting non-parity SIMMs to a parity system will probably disable the parity checking of existing parity SIMMs. Try to avoid mixing memory speeds as adding a slower SIMM usually brings the whole bank down to its access speeds.   It is usually possible to mix pairs of SIMMs- e.g. one pair of 16MB and a pair of 4MB.   VX and HX chipsets allow each bank to have different memory types (e.g. FPM in one bank and EDO in another bank) and run each bank at its best speed.   FX chipsets allow the mixing of EDO and FPM in the same bank, with all SIMMs being treated as FPM. Some early Pentiums used 30-pin SIMMs.

FPM and EDO SIMMs are identical in appearance.   To find out what is currently installed on a computer either check the motherboard manual, use a SIMM tester (this may involve visiting a repair shop) or watch the messages on booting up the computer. Many BIOS chips will produce a message such as *"BANK 0 : EDO"* if EDO is installed.

DIMM modules

Standard now in most computers is the *'Dual In-line Memory Module'*. It is a 168-pin module that has electrical contacts on both side of the board. It has a greater reliability than SIMMs and is available as a 64-bit non-parity or as a 72-bit parity device. This 64-bit data width directly matches the Pentium's data bus width, allowing a single DIMM to be fitted.   Since the system requires fewer memory slots, the motherboard can have a more compact layout. The extra 8 bits on a 72-bit module are used for storing error detection data, such as parity or ECC (see later).

DIMM boards are most commonly fitted with

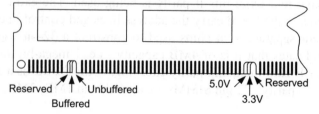

SDRAM chips. Using DIMMs does not in itself lead to any speed improvement, as it is only a connection type.

It is the use of SDRAM on DIMMs with interleaving that makes these particular DIMMs faster. DIMMs appear in both rare 5v and common 3.3v versions. They also appear in both the common unbuffered version, or with additional chips that buffer the memory from the data bus. Older DIMMs were available with built-in buffering chips but became out of favour on newer modules as the buffering chips slowed down data access.

Since 3.3v modules must not be used in a 5v system, the modules have different notch spacings. This prevents damage caused by inserting the wrong memory module type. Similarly, the notch spacings prevent buffered and unbuffered modules from being incorrectly inserted.

Older motherboards had both SIMM and DIMM slots but were often incapable of using both at the same time. In these cases, the manual should be consulted, as some or all of the SIMMs may have to be removed to allow the DIMM to function. Modern motherboards come with DIMM slots or RIMM slots only.

As the speed of DRAM and in particular SDRAM increased the manufacturers stopped referring to the speed of memory parts in nanoseconds (nS). A series of standard memory speeds was proposed by Intel and adopted by the industry for SDRAM. Standard DIMMs are therefore available in PC66, PC100 and PC133 varieties, according to the bus speed.

With the adoption of Rambus & RIMMS, and the introduction of DDR memory as system memory, conventional SDRAM did not progress beyond the PC133 specification. Although there are still systems containing conventional SDRAM in use, currently produced systems use RDRAM or DDR DIMMS.

DDR DIMM modules
Double Data Rate DIMMs are now used in many motherboards. They use DDR SDRAM chips as described earlier. However, this necessitates the use of a DDR capable chipset and motherboard, so it is important to distinguish DDR DIMMs from other types. As a result the DDR DIMM has only one notch, making it physically incompatible with standard DIMM slots, and uses 184 pins.

The names given to DDR chips, as shown in the table on the next page, do not refer to the clock speed as with other 'PC' class memory specifications. Instead they refer to the total bandwidth in millions of bytes transferred per second. Thus, a DDR DIMM using an effective bus speed of 200MHz is listed as PC1600 instead of PC200. This was done in order to make DDR DIMMs more attractive in comparison to RIMM memory such as PC800. Note however that this is not measured in Megabytes per second but in millions of bytes per second. With a bus size of 8 bytes and an effective bus speed of 200MHz, the system can transfer up to 1600 million bytes per second, but this has to be divided by 1024 to get Kbps, and by 1024 again to get Mbps. Similarly, a 266MHz system drives a PC2100, a 333MHz system drives a PC2700,a 400MHz system drives a PC3200, and a 533MHz system drives a PC4200 DDR DIMM.

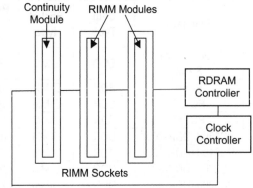

DDR is not generally as fast as RAMBUS memory, but it is considerably cheaper, and has become quite popular as a result.

RIMM modules
The *'Rambus'* memory technology is also called RIMM, which according to the Rambus Corporation does not stand for 'Rambus In-line Memory Module' but is simply a name to distinguish the technology. It is very similar to a DIMM connection. It is also a 184-pin module that has electrical contacts on both side of the board. It is specifically designed for RDRAM, and DIMMs and RIMMs are not interchangeable - a RIMM will not fit in a DIMM slot and vice versa.

RIMMs use RAMBUS technology. This is an extremely fast but essentially serial technology, as opposed to the more usual parallel arrangement. This is because it was originally developed to suit the setup of Nintendo games machines. The typical RIMM system provides four RIMM sockets. Each socket must contain either a RIMM module or a so-called RIMM continuity (or C-RIMM) module. This continuity module is just a short circuit to allow serial memory signals to pass through. New motherboards that have RIMM sockets fitted come with RIMM continuity modules as part of the supplied hardware kit.

Due to the bus structure of a RIMM module, the system has to ensure a consistent memory speed. This is achieved by delaying the response from electrically closer chips to allow further chips to 'catch up'. Thus, a RIMM system will respond slower the more memory that is installed. RIMMs also transfer data in 16-bit chunks instead of 64 bits like DIMMs. However, even with all this in mind, RIMM is generally faster than DIMM. This is in large part due to the high speed of the bus. The types of RIMM that are used in PCs (as opposed to consoles) can reach 1200MHz, and RIMMs used with Pentium 4 motherboards utilise dual channels to double throughput again. In fact, newer RIMM modules are essentially a dual pair of chips on one module, giving double the throughput from the start.

However, with such high speeds, the RIMM chips heat up quite quickly, so they come with metal heat spreaders over the chips. RIMMS therefore look quite different to the previous memory technologies, although they are still using multiple chips inside.

SO-DIMMs and SO-RIMMs

In Notebooks, DIMMs and RIMMs take up too much valuable space. For this reason many notebooks use Small Outline (SO) DIMM and RIMM sockets, which are functionally the same, but smaller in size.

Typical Chip Capacity

Memory chips come in a range of capacities and the table shows the most common varieties:

Chip type	Typical lower capacity	Typical higher capacity
30-pin SIMM	8 x 64K chips (512KB)	8 x 256K chips (2MB)
72-pin SIMM	8 x 256K chips (2MB)	8 x 4MB chips (32MB)
168-pin DIMM	8 x 2M chips (16MB)	8 x 16M chips (128MB)
184-pin RIMM	8x 4M chips (32MB)	8 x 32M chips (256MB)

Typical Chip Speeds

The table shows the expected performance from the range of memory types:

Standard	Chip Type	Socket type	Physical bus speed	Effective bus speed	Bus size	Max. Data throughput	Equivalent period
Typical 72-pin SIMM	EDO	SIMM	33MHz	33MHz	32 bits (4 bytes)	63MBps	60ns
PC66	SDR	DIMM	66MHz	66MHz	64 bits (8 bytes)	503MBps	15ns
PC100	SDR	DIMM	100MHz	100MHz	64 bits (8 bytes)	763MBps	10ns
PC133	SDR	DIMM	133MHz	133MHz	64 bits (8 bytes)	1014MBps	7.5ns
PC1600 (DDR-200)	DDR	DIMM	100 MHz	200MHz	64 bits (8 bytes)	1525MBps	5ns
PC2100 (DDR-266)	DDR	DIMM	133 MHz	266MHz	64 bits (8 bytes)	2029MBps	3.7ns
PC2700 (DDR-333)	DDR	DIMM	166 MHz	333MHz	64 bits (8 bytes)	2541MBps	3ns
PC3200 (DDR-400)	DDR	DIMM	200MHz	400MHz	64 bits (8 bytes)	3200MBps	2.5ns
PC4200 (DDR-533)	DDR	DIMM	266MHz	533MHz	64 bits (8 bytes)	4264MBps	1.8ns
PC800	RDRAM	RIMM	800MHz	800MHz	16 bits (2 bytes)	1525MBps	1.2ns
RIMM 3200	RDRAM	RIMM	800MHz	800MHz	32 bits (4 bytes)	3050MBps	1.2ns
RIMM 4200	RDRAM	RIMM	1066MHz	1066MHz	32 bits (4 bytes)	4264MBps	0.9ns
RIMM 4800	RDRAM	RIMM	1200MHz	1200MHz	32 bits (4 bytes)	4800MBps	0.8ns

Comparative memory chip sizes

The diagrams below show the outline and size of the common range of memory modules. These diagrams are full-scale, allowing a chip to be laid on the page to determine its type.

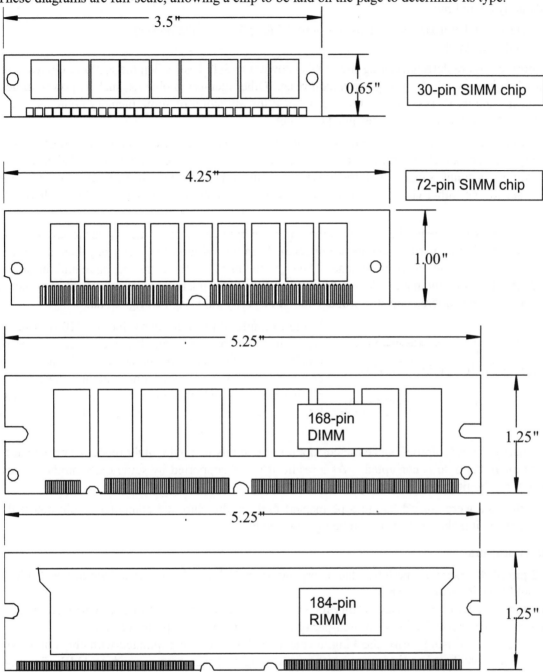

Data Integrity

The movement of data in and out of memory is carried out by the 'memory controller'. This circuitry can be configured to check the integrity of the data being held in memory. Lower-end models tend to have no integrity checking, mid-range systems tended to have parity checking, while top-end systems such as network servers have ECC (see later).

With the production of ever more reliable memory chips, parity has tended to be dropped, leaving ECC provided on systems requiring the ultimate in reliability (known as 'mission critical' systems).

Parity

Many machines have built-in parity bit writing and parity checking. This technique attempts to ensure that the data stored in any particular memory location is identical to the original data written and has not been accidentally altered by:

- electrical disturbances (such as transients - i.e. spikes - on the power)
- faulty RAM chips

Faulty memory chips are detected during the POST (Power On Self Test) when the ROM BIOS tests out the system when it is switched on or given a hard reset. Other memory problems, such as power surges, can occur during the user's session and these can cause the alteration of some memory contents. It is these problems that parity checking is designed to detect.

Users see memory as being a byte in width. The eight bits of the byte are used to store the program data. In fact, parity memory attaches a ninth bit to each data byte. This is the *'parity bit'*. When data is written to memory, a count is made of all the binary 'one' bits in the data byte. If the total is odd, then the parity bit is set to one, otherwise it is set to zero. This is an automatic process by the motherboard circuitry.

When the data comes to be read, the same calculation on the byte's contents is made prior to sending it to the CPU. If the calculated parity contents are different from the value in the parity bit, then an error is known to have occurred and an error message is given to the user. If the expected value and the stored value are identical, it is likely that the data is unchanged (this is not guaranteed, since a number of bits in the byte could have been altered and still produce the same parity value as the original data).

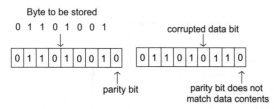

In the example illustration, the value 01101001 is being stored in a memory location. It has an even number of binary 1's, so the parity bit is set to 0. If the data is corrupted as shown in the second diagram, there would be five binary 1's, which should result in a 1 in the parity bit. Since the parity bit contains a 0, the error is detected.

A single bit parity is not foolproof, since the corruption of two bits in a byte might render a correct parity check even though the byte is corrupted. As a result, it is not supported by some older motherboards; parity SIMMS can be fitted but the parity bit will be ignored.

Note that if the data were altered due to a permanent fault on the chip, the computer would detect the faulty address when it makes its self-test on being powered up.

Practical Examples

With 72-pin SIMM memory modules, data is organised on 32-bit width and each byte of the 32-bit word would have its own parity bit.

A DIMM module with parity uses 64 bits for data storage and a further 8 bits for parity storage. Modules have been quoted as *'x64'* for non-parity versions and *'x72'* for parity versions.

As a consequence of using parity checking, memory modules may be populated with chips in groups of nine. For example, nine 1M x 1 chips would use eight of the chips to produce 1MB of storage (1M x 8 bits) while the ninth chip is used to store the parity for each byte.

A non-parity system can be fitted with parity RAM; the parity bits are simply not used. However, a parity system has to be fitted with parity RAM or it will not work.

Fake Parity

A simple check was used to determine whether a SIMM was parity or non-parity. A two or eight chip SIMM was non-parity while three or nine chip SIMMs were parity types.

However, a few SIMMs have been used on parity motherboards that utilise *'fake parity'* or *'logic parity'*. This reduces the price of the SIMM by not providing the extra memory to store the parity bits. Writes to the SIMM discard the parity calculations since it cannot store them. During memory reads, the SIMM generates the correct parity bit expected by the motherboard. The motherboard is fooled into thinking that parity checking has been carried out and no memory errors have been found.

ECC

Parity circuits are designed to detect memory errors; they are unable to correct them. The Error Correction Code (ECC) system, also known as *'Error Checking and Control'*, detects and corrects single bit errors. A five-bit error checking code is used to provide reliable detection of corruption. Since there is great detail in the checking code, the information can be used to restore the data byte to its original value. Any corrections are made without the user even knowing that a problem had occurred; it will not produce error messages.

ECC systems will also detect multiple bit errors. Unlike parity systems, ECC will detect multiple bit errors where two bits appear to self-cancel (i.e. one bit changes from 0 to 1 while another bit changes from 1 to 0). It does this by using a Cyclic Redundancy Check, (or CRC) which is a special type of mathematical polynomial, implemented in binary.

The same CRC system is used to ensure data integrity on Hard Disks, CD-ROMs, Networks and serial communications systems.

Practical Examples

Two SIMMs that are x36 (i.e. 36 width bus) or a single x72 DIMM module provides a total bus width of 72 bits. Of these, 64 bits are used for data transfer and 8 bits are used for ECC information.

However, x36 and x72 chips are also commonly used for parity systems. In these cases, the way the integrity locations are used depends upon whether the memory controller works on a parity or an ECC system.

CMOS

CMOS (Complementary Metal Oxide Semiconductor) is a low power consumption memory chip. In PCs, it consists of a small block of additional memory that is used to store information about the computer (e.g. type of drives in use, amount of memory in the machine, etc.).

It is not part of the computer's memory map and is associated with the computer's real-time clock chip. The real-time clock is always supplied with power as it has its own rechargeable battery. This means that the contents of the CMOS will remain, even when the power is switched off. The CMOS ensures that the details of the machine's configuration are always available when the machine is first booted up. It is also the reason that the PC knows the time and date when it is first started.

The contents of the CMOS memory can be altered via the BIOS setup procedure offered during bootup. Depending upon the BIOS type, pressing the Delete key or the f1 key during bootup will take the user into the BIOS setup routine.

Memory Summary

A summary of the main memory definitions is given below:

Type	Summary
DRAM (Dynamic Random Access Memory	Once was the only type used for main memory. It is used for the User Area, System Area and both Extended and Expanded Memory.
SRAM (Static RAM)	Fast access memory normally used for caching inside the CPU (see below).
NVRAM	Non-volatile RAM. A term used to describe any method of retaining memory contents without a power supply, such as EEPROM or battery-powered chips.
EDO	Extended Data Out. A newer, faster alternative to DRAM chips. EDO SIMMs have access times of 50ns, 60ns or 70ns.
BEDO	Burst Mode EDO memory. Sends a group of data bytes to the CPU without involving the CPU in much of the process. Faster than ordinary EDO memory.
SDRAM	Synchronous DRAM. Keeps the CPU and memory timed in step, thereby minimising the control signals between them and greatly increasing data transfer rates compared to both DRAM and EDO.
SGRAM	An even faster version of SDRAM that can operate in burst mode for both write and read operations (SDRAM can only read in burst mode).

VRAM (Video RAM)	A dual-port memory technology used in some older video cards to speed up screen updates.
WRAM	Windows RAM. Developed by Samsung for video cards. It is dual-ported like VRAM but supports a block write mode for faster data rates.
Multibank DRAM (MDRAM)	20ns access time memory. A cheaper alternative to SRAM for caching and a faster alternative to DRAM for video cards.
Rambus (RDRAM)	A serial access memory technology able to transfer data at 600 to 800MHz. Synchronised to the bus clock and provides data on both edges of the signal.
DDR (Double Data Rate)	A type of SDRAM that is able to transmit data on both the rising and falling edges of the clock cycle, theoretically doubling data throughput.
PC Modules	A PC Module is a modern memory module that is designed to cope with a specific bus speed and throughput rate, as indicated by the PC number, such as 'PC133'.
Cache RAM (Level 1)	Memory built in to a CPU and sitting between the CPU and external memory to speed up data access. In modern processors the cache RAM runs at the speed of the processor core, and is used to cache machine code micro-operations.
Cache RAM (Level 2)	Initially found on the motherboard, modern PCs have L2 cache on the CPU, also clocked to the processor core, and used to buffer data from memory.
CMOS RAM	Small block of additional memory is used to store information about the computer (e.g. type of drives in use, amount of memory in the machine, etc.).
ROM BIOS	The ROM chip fitted in every PC. When the machine is switched on, it tests the system and boots the OS.
BIOS Extensions	The ROM chips that are fitted to add-on cards to control their operations (e.g. video cards or disk controller cards).

The PC Memory Map

The IBM XT PC appeared in 1981 with an 8088 processor and only 16k of main memory (with a recommended figure of 64k). These chips had a 20-bit address bus and could only address 1MB of memory. This now seems a ludicrous limitation, in the days of 1GB applications.   In 1978, though, when the 8086 was brought out, memory chips were extremely expensive and personal computers would have been lucky to have 100 kilobytes of memory. 1MB was only found on large mainframe computers. The ability of the 8086/ 8088 chips to address a full megabyte of memory was regarded as a luxury that was unlikely ever to be used.

This may have been a reasonable assumption at the time but holds up poorly in the light of the drop in memory prices, the development of more powerful processors and the creation of huge software applications.   Overcoming these design shortcomings is dealt with elsewhere.

The diagram that displays the allocation of memory to different parts of the computer system is known

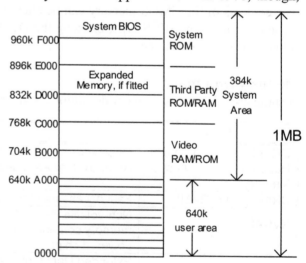

as a 'memory map' and is explained below in terms of a basic configuration, without any memory management.   The entire machine memory is divided, for historical reasons, into segments of 64k.   The segments are not shown to scale on the diagram, to aid clarity.

The map shows both decimal numbering and its hexadecimal notation equivalents, since the latter is commonly shown on computer system manuals.

Note

Many memory maps use 4 hex characters to describe map addresses. For example, the 640k boundary is often shown as A000h. The full effective address of 640k is, more correctly, A0000h or A000:0000.

User Area

Occasionally called *'Low-DOS'*, the lower 10 segments make up the 640k user area. In a Command Prompt instance or a Boot Disk, this is where the operating system and the user applications reside. The bulk of this area is provided for application programs, but some is devoted to system programs and variables. In a Windows system, the concept of a user area is abandoned, with all memory being managed by the operating system and assigned to programs as if it were one continuous section of memory.

System Area

The remaining six segments, a total of 384k, are variously called the *'system area'*, the *'upper memory area'* or *'high DOS'* area. This is occupied by the ROM BIOS, various device drivers such as video adapters and disk controllers, and video memory. These are not all shown on the memory map, since individual configurations can vary greatly. The map, as an example, shows the location of expanded memory. In fact, the great majority of PCs do not have these expanded memory expansion cards fitted. The exact map locations for scanners, modems, data acquisition equipment, etc. would vary, since their actual addresses might well have to be altered to prevent clashes of addresses. This would be performed by the plug and play system, but in older machines it might be accomplished manually by setting the values of DIP switches mounted on the cards.

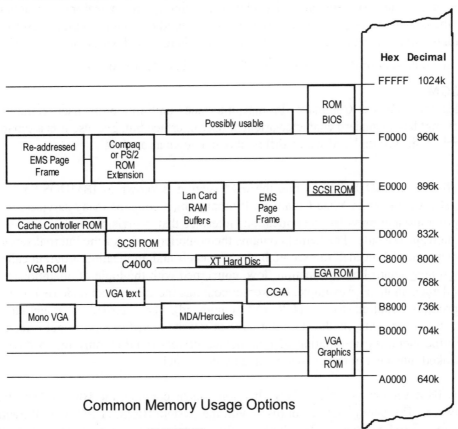

Common Memory Usage Options

The diagram also shows that two 64k sections of memory are set aside for the computer's video needs. The exact amount of video memory that is used depends on the screen standard in use (refer to the chapter on Display Technology for more details on video modes). As can be seen from the diagram, only the most basic of video modes can fit within the RAM allocated, such as the long defunct MDA, Hercules, CGA and EGA modes, as well as the rarely used Mono VGA mode and the VGA text mode used in Command Prompt sessions. The higher resolution modes of EGA and some modes of VGA adapters manage to fit into the High Memory Area by appropriating varying areas of RAM between

A0000 and C8000. Full VGA and super VGA modes cannot fit into main memory, even commencing at A0000, and have to use extra memory on graphics boards.

Much of the upper memory space is unused because the designers overestimated the amount of space that would be required by future add-ons and extra system ROMs; the idea that programs would be available as plug-in ROMs never developed.

This space can be used for other purposes, as described in the section on memory management. The diagram shows the most common memory areas and their uses.

Notes

- Any memory block is exclusive to one use. For example, if the address range D0000h to E0000h is being used for expanded memory, any LAN card or disk controller card would have to be set for operation in another - unused - part of the memory map.
- The ROM BIOS is always located from F0000h to FFFFFh. This is because the PC always looks for an instruction at FFFFFh when the machine is switched on. This instruction starts the bootup process.

Command Prompt and the Memory Map

The Command Prompt is fundamentally a program loader and file handler and consists of three elements:

- A command processor
- A system kernel
- A hardware-specific BIOS

The separation of the system into parts allows the maximum flexibility when it comes to developing the system and producing improved versions. The first two software components are written to be independent of the physical requirements of the hardware. They are concerned with the functions and interface to the user. The last component has the responsibility of controlling the actual hardware components of the computer system. Since only the BIOS is hardware-dependent, the user interface and system kernel do not have to be revised to accommodate new hardware devices that might be developed.

The basic Command Prompt or Boot Disk requires three files in order to boot up:

COMMAND.COM

This provides the standard Command Prompt interface, and interprets user commands. The Command Prompt has a standard character-oriented user interface but, because it is a separate module, it can be supplemented or replaced with a different one, known as a 'shell'.

MSDOS.SYS

The Microsoft title is MSDOS.SYS, while the IBM version is known as IBMDOS.SYS. This is the DOS kernel, still used even in Vista Command Prompt, which contains many services. It is called by application programs and provides an applications interface that is invisible to the user. It is called by the general interrupt 21h call. The kernel contains the compiled code for the internal services, such as file management and I/O, needed to execute both commands and application program calls. Note that this is the high level control of information flow, concerned with the logic of operations and not their hardware implementation. For example, the kernel contains the file system code (e.g. the sequence of steps and prompts required for a FORMAT command). The kernel is essentially hardware-independent. So, a hardware vendor does not have to rewrite MSDOS.SYS to get it to run on a new machine. Furthermore, the installation of new device drivers requires only that a device driver be written and linked into a list of drivers maintained by the kernel.

IO.SYS

Known in its IBM version as IBMIO.SYS, this component contains the BIOS (Basic Input Output System) software. This should not be confused with the System BIOS, or ROM BIOS, which is burnt onto a chip to control bootup. The IO.SYS file contains hardware-specific code, including a collection of built-in drivers for screen, keyboard, hard and floppy disk, clock and serial and parallel ports. Some, or sometimes all, of the BIOS may be stored in ROM. The BIOS code deals with devices on a low level. For example, it moves the disk's read/write head or writes characters to the video display. It also contains initialisation code that is temporarily brought in to interpret the lines of the CONFIG.SYS file at machine start-up. Because the hardware details are hidden from the rest of the operating system, additions at BIOS level make it possible to add support for new devices without having to make extensive changes to services in the kernel.

Note
All these components have to be present for the Command Prompt or a System Boot Disk to function. They are not needed to load the Windows XP or Vista GUI. Normally the files are hidden.

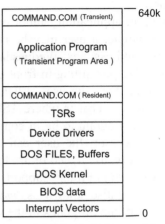

COMMAND.COM (Transient)	640k
Application Program (Transient Program Area)	
COMMAND.COM (Resident)	
TSRs	
Device Drivers	
DOS FILES, Buffers	
DOS Kernel	
BIOS data	
Interrupt Vectors	0

User Allocation
The user allocation is shown in the unscaled memory map.   The bottom 256 bytes are always reserved for the machine's interrupt vector table. This is a set of pointers that contains the addresses of particular sets of code to be run, if particular interrupts are triggered.   These pointers are held in RAM, so that an expert programmer can alter them to change program functions. For example, a programmer can prevent the PrtScr key from carrying out a screen dump, instead pointing to code that plays a tune! This area should not be touched by the inexperienced. The DOS kernel is the heart of the operating system and has to be permanently present in main memory. The actual amount of space that it occupies depends on the DOS version and whether memory management techniques have been applied.   DOS can leave as little as 537k for user use (DOS v4.01) and as much as 617k (DOS 5 with memory management).

Notice that COMMAND.COM is loaded as two separate portions. The lower section is known as the 'resident' portion and it handles program termination (i.e. pressing Ctrl-Break) or user program errors resulting in program termination. This section provides all the standard DOS error messages. The upper section is known as the 'transient' portion and provides the user's interface to the Command Prompt.   It provides for EXE and COM files to be run and also contains the batch processor (to interpret and execute batch file commands). This portion also processes the 'internal' commands (DIR, COPY, etc.).

The memory needs of the buffers, device drivers and TSRs have to be added to the overheads of the Command Prompt itself. They occupy a significant proportion of the so-called 'user area'.   The user allocation of 640k can quickly diminish to 500k, or even less.

When the demands on the system are extreme, there can easily be conflicting demands for machine configuration. The setup for one application might slow down another's operations. In some cases, it may prevent another application from loading.   At worst, it may allow a program to load, then prevent the work from being saved back to disk. Such difficulties are usually overcome by the re-allocation of programs within the machine memory - a technique called 'memory management'.

Device Drivers
A device driver is simply a piece of software that is used to provide the correct interface to a particular piece of computer equipment. The equipment might be some external device, such as a printer, plotter or mouse; it might be an internal device, such as a graphics card. It might also be a different way of treating conventional equipment such as a RAM disk or screen writing. The Command Prompt, after all, has its own default software for driving the screen, printer, etc.
Consider how a printer and a plotter handle data. The output to a printer is transmitted one character at a time, as a series of ASCII characters. The received ASCII value is used by the printer to select the appropriate sequence of dots, in dot matrix, laser or inkjet printers, or appropriate rotation on a daisy wheel printer.   Regardless of the printer type, there is a standard output from the computer's printer port. Plotters, on the other hand, work in an entirely different way. The final print is a result of a series of lines drawn by pen activities.   These activities consist of pen up, pen down and pen horizontal movements.   Such movements are not the standard output from a printer port. The plotter device driver is the software that translates the data into the corresponding sequence of pen movements. Similar conversion software is required for mice and graphics cards. The software is particular to the piece of equipment in use and therefore the driver would be supplied along with the equipment.
The Command Prompt supplies a few of its own device drivers. These are optionally installed by the user and are therefore taking up memory space if the user has a requirement for them. The most used of these are the MSCDEX and MOUSE drivers, which allow the Command Prompt to utilise CD and DVD drives, and a mouse or other pointing device, respectively.

TSRs

Often, an application cannot provide all the functions that a user might wish. For example, a user may be running a word-processor and wish to enter the client's address, next Wednesday's date or a net price after adding mark-up and taxes. Despite sitting in front of a very expensive database and calculator (i.e. the computer), the user still has to resort to the filofax, calendar or pocket calculator.   That is where TSR programs aid productivity. They allow more than one program to be in computer memory at one time. Without leaving the word-processor, the user can temporarily call up an on-screen calculator or other utility, use it, and return to the word-processing program.

The Command Prompt supports the use of TSRs (*'Terminate and Stay Resident'* programs), also known as *'memory-resident'* programs.   These differ from command line programs in the way that they use memory and the way that they are called. A command line program is invoked by executing the appropriate COM or EXE file. This results in the program taking the amount of memory it requires.   When the program is exited, the memory is released. A TSR program is also installed by executing a COM or EXE file. This loads the program into the lowest available memory above the device drivers. In some cases, the program is immediately run and is eventually exited by the user. In other cases, it loads itself into memory and immediately returns to the command prompt. To the unwary, it may appear that nothing happened. In either case, when the program terminates, it does not release the memory space it occupied. Instead, the program remains in memory and can be called up to be run. A normal command line program, or even another TSR program, can now also be loaded into memory and loads commencing from the upper address of the first TSR. As the diagram shows, TSRs can be stacked up in memory. Some may be single utility programs, while others may contain a suite of facilities.

All TSR programs sit inactive in their memory areas, while the main program runs.

At any time, TSRs can be called by the user pressing *'hot key'* combinations; perhaps holding down the ALT key and a particular letter key, or pressing both Shift keys simultaneously.   Even while the main application is running, the Command Prompt is checking in the background for keyboard operations. As soon as it detects the TSRs hot key combination, control is passed to the TSR program, with the main application being temporarily suspended. Most often the TSR program 'pops up', i.e. the screen of the application is seen as a background with a foreground window displaying the TSR program. The main application is still sitting in main memory and is frozen at the point of TSR invocation. When the user exits the TSR, the main application re-occupies the whole screen and carries on from where it was suspended. The TSR program remains in its own memory area awaiting a future invocation.

Disadvantages

If one or more TSR programs are installed, they may not leave enough space in the memory to allow a large application to be loaded. Some TSRs have an *'uninstall'* parameter; used memory space is recovered by executing it a second time with this parameter. In most cases, however, the only way to reclaim the memory space is to reboot the machine. This initialises the system with a new low marker, indicating the starting point for the loading of applications.

TSRs are often included in the AUTOEXEC batch file, so that they are automatically installed in memory at switch on. This is a convenient way to configure a machine to have regularly-used TSRs in place. Of course, in these cases, rebooting the machine will not reclaim the space, since the AUTOEXEC file will always install the TSR.   The line invoking the TSR will have to be removed from the batch program script and only installed by the user from the prompt, when required.

TSRs that are always used should be included in the AUTOEXEC.BAT file, while others should be manually invoked. TSRs are available for a wide range of uses, such as spell checkers, thesauruses, calculators, keyboard enhancers, communications programs and small databases and text editors.   The most famous of these is the Sidekick program, which has a wide range of facilities and is flexible in its installation options. For example, if memory space is tight, a limited version can be installed which omits the notepad, calendar and dialler.   Other files can be run to install other variations. It should be noted that a few TSRs load in at the top of available memory.

The most common TSRs are SHARE.EXE, KEYB.COM and a range of different virus checkers.

Note

Although more than one program is in memory, it is not *'multi-tasking'*. Multi-tasking systems run several programs 'simultaneously'. Usually the CPU time is, in fact, shared between each process, each having a *'time slice'* in a rota. The time slots allocated to each program are small, so the CPU quickly moves from application to application. To the user, each program seems to be running continuously. With TSRs on the other hand, several programs reside in memory, but only one program ever runs at a time. If a TSR is invoked, the CPU time is devoted entirely to that process. When the TSR is exited, the CPU time is devoted solely to the application program.

Overlays

Even at best, the useable area of base memory in a Command Prompt is around 620k. Even modern machines with 4GB of RAM are limited by the DOS 640k barrier if they run a Command Prompt. How then, does a machine manage to run a large Command Prompt program? If an application is 10MB, 20MB or 50MB in size, it cannot possibly fit into the user memory area. One solution rests in only loading and running a <u>part</u> of the program at any one time. Accordingly, the program is divided up by the programmer into sections of code that are able to fit into memory; these are called *'overlays'*.

These overlays are not independent programs; they are not EXE files that can be executed from the Command Prompt. Instead, they must be loaded into memory by the core program, which will be an executable file. They may sometimes be identified by the file extension .OVL or similar. Since the overlays cannot be run independently, the application always maintains a core program in memory. This keeps track of all data and decides what overlays should be brought in at any particular time.

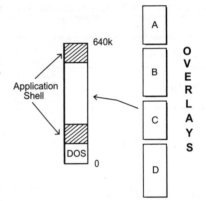

For example, a word processor would not keep its thesaurus or spell-checker in memory at all times, since they are not frequently required. If the user requests a spell-check, then the core program would fetch the spell-checking overlay from disk and place it in the main memory. When spell checking is finished, another overlay can be fetched from disk and its contents can overwrite the spell-checking overlay. This is not the ideal way to run an application, since time is taken in swapping overlays from disk. Alternative methods of handling large programs exist, either accessing the memory more efficiently or accessing memory above the 1MB limit.

Paging

Overlays suffer from two main problems:
- They require the <u>programmer</u> to split the program into manageable chunks.
- They can be inefficient. A 200k overlay may be loaded just to access one of its 2k long routines.

As a result, overlays have been largely replaced by the use of *'virtual memory'* which uses *'paging'*. Paging techniques are used on Windows systems, which could have several gigabytes of actual memory, because the user is able to run several large programs at once, thus the system often still does not have enough RAM to fully load them all.

Paging solves the first problem by having its own *'paging unit'* inside the processor's memory management unit. This divides the program into chunks and handles the loading and unloading of these chunks to and from memory. These chunks, known as *'pages'* are normally at least 4k in length and this minimises the wasted time involved in handling excessive chunks of program.

Paging also provides a *'virtual memory'* system, where the program can be larger than the physical size of the computer's memory. A modern PC typically has a maximum physical address range of 64GB. Thus, many millions of 4k pages are supported. Since computers have only around 512MB to 4GB of memory installed, any extra pages required for a program can be stored to disk. When a particular page is required, it can be fetched from disk and used to replace another page that is already in memory, using a number of possible *'page replacement policies'*. The continual swapping of pages between memory and disk allows the computer to run a much larger program than would otherwise be supported.

ROM Shadowing

The code inside the system BIOS ROM consists of a set of utilities. The internal POST program checks out the computer hardware on bootup. Thereafter, a set of utilities can be called upon by the Operating System or by applications. Examples are program code to read a character from the keyboard or write a character to the screen. Similarly, the ROM chip built in to a video card has code to handle the card's screen handling activities. The routines contained in the ROM chips are accessed on a very regular basis but the time required to access code from a ROM is several times longer than accessing data from RAM. If the BIOS code and video code were held and accessed in RAM then their operations would be greatly speeded up and the machine performance would be significantly improved.

Facilities exist to copy the system BIOS and the video ROM code from the ROM chips into normal RAM - a process known as 'ROM Shadowing'. Shadowing is normally enabled or disabled via the BIOS setup. The BIOS setup normally allows for either only enabling the System BIOS or only enabling the video BIOS code, or enabling both. The chosen ROM code is copied into unused areas in the system area (i.e. 640k to 1MB).

DOS Memory Usage

The main memory of a PC is used for a variety of purposes. The following chart shows the main allocations of RAM; see the memory management section for more details.

Type	Summary
Environment	Part of main memory that is set aside for storing information about the current prompt, search paths and user-defined variables.
User Area	Also known as Base Memory and Conventional Memory. All DOS programs and parts of Windows applications run in this area. Extends from address 0 to 640k.
UMA (Upper Memory Area)	Also known as the System Area and the High DOS area. Extends from 640k to 1MB and is used by the ROM BIOS chip and the ROM chips that are fitted on expansion cards. The parts not used by ROMs are available to provide the window into Expanded Memory, with unused areas being called Upper Memory Blocks (see below).
UMBs (Upper Memory Blocks)	Unused areas of the UMA. Can be used to store device drivers and TSRs if the machine has been memory managed.
EMS (Expanded Memory)	The original way to create extra memory beyond the 1MB limit. A block of memory (often chips on a separate card) can have a part of its contents viewed at any one time through a 'window' in the UMA. No longer used, but emulated for very old programs.
HMA (High Memory Area)	The first 64k block of memory above the 1MB boundary. Used to store part of DOS when the system is memory managed.
XMS (Extended Memory)	The area of memory above 1MB. Used by Windows and by a wide range of utilities such as disk caches, ram drives, print spooling, etc.

Breaking the 1MB barrier

As mentioned previously, the early PCs could only address 1MB of main memory due to their 20-bit address bus. Apart from memory addressability, IBM made a design decision that has affected PC development ever since. It decided that the top of the map should be given over to system use. There was no problem with the XT range. Their processors could address 1MB and their boards allowed for the fitting of up to 1MB of ROM/RAM. The restrictions became clear when the processor range was upgraded. The 80286 chip had a 24-bit address bus, capable of accessing 16 million different memory locations; the Pentium chips have 64-bit address buses, capable of accessing 64GB of memory. Memory chips are now comparatively cheap and extra memory can easily be fitted to the motherboard.

This extra memory could have been accessed with relative ease - if only IBM had decided that the system area would be located at the bottom of the memory map. As it stands, there cannot be a contiguous block of memory, since the 384k system block breaks up the user memory area. This causes difficulties for programmers and hardware manufacturers alike.

IBM must privately regret the impediment they have inflicted on their own product range. There is no technical difficulty in producing a PC product with a different memory map. The system area could be placed at the bottom of the memory map, allowing limitless future expansion above it. The problem is not one of technology; it is one of compatibility. No existing software or add-ons would work with this new machine and this has been the deciding factor in maintaining the present architecture - warts and all. All subsequent PC hardware and software developments struggle to get the best from this bad situation.

Note: Later chapters explain the operation of a computer system running DOS-based applications and games. All newer games and all Windows 95 and later applications use a memory management system that automatically handles <u>extended</u> memory, while hiding its operations from the user.

XMS and EMS

In the modern PC computing world, operating systems such as Windows and Linux have memory management systems built in, and are able to overcome the 1MB barrier on their own. DOS, however, has no such luxury. In order for a DOS program to access memory beyond the 1MB limit, special techniques must be employed. The two technologies that were successful in this regard were the e**X**tended **M**emory **S**ystem (XMS) and **E**xpanded **M**emory **S**ystem (EMS).

XMS

This technology, developed by Microsoft, adds memory to the memory map above the 1MB line. As a result, extended memory is available only on 286 or later machines, which are capable of addressing above 1MB.

EMS

The EMS technology works by swapping data in and out of a section of conventional memory. Due to this design, the EMS system can only access a small area of expanded memory at a time.

Since it works with conventional memory, it can be used on machines earlier than the 286. On the other hand, it is slower, more awkward to use and more expensive than extended memory. This is due to the way the expanded memory is organised and accessed.

Disks & Drives

Disk Basics

The computer's disk systems are designed for the long-term storage of programs and user data. When the power is removed from a machine, the contents are lost from memory, so the disks (sometimes called 'backing store') are used for their preservation. The disk systems used to store data range from large hard disk packs used in large mainframe computers, to tiny 1.5" and smaller hard disks in portable notebook computers. In addition, almost all PCs allow data to be stored on removable disks called 'floppies'. This allows data to be moved around by carrying disks from machine to machine, or sending a disk through the mail. Hard disks, on the other hand, are permanently built-in to the machine and are not normally accessible by the user. Some new systems employ removable hard disks, to exploit the high capacity of hard disks while retaining the mobility of floppy disks but these are still relatively uncommon.

Despite the wide differences in size and storage capacity, all magnetic disks work on the same basic principles. Even the newer optical disks, while using substantially different technology, adopt the same general approach. Disk drives are 'direct access' devices, which means that the reading and writing of data can occur at any part of the disk. Tape storage, on the other hand, is a 'serial access' device - the system has to search in a series from one end of the tape until the wanted data is found.

Tracks

Data is written to a disk magnetically in a similar way to recording on audio tape or videotape. In this case, however, the media used is not a long continuous cassette of tape but the same type of surface material in the shape of a disk. The disk is rotated to allow access to all parts of its surface. So, data is written in circles round this disk. Regardless of the type of disk, the data is organised on the disk in concentric circles known as 'tracks'. The tracks number from the outside of the disk to the inside, with the outermost track being called track 0. The number of tracks on a disk varies from 40 or 80 on floppy disks to about 1000 on some hard disks. The 'density' of a disk is the number of tracks that the disk can handle e.g. for 3.5" disks, Double Density means that it can support 80 tracks per side.

The density of a disk is often quoted in TPI - tracks per inch. A typical 3.5" floppy is a 96tpi disk, meaning that each track is 1/96th of an inch wide. So, an 80-track disk format would use up slightly less than one inch of the available disk diameter. A 48tpi disk is usually used for 40 track disks.

Writing/Reading Data

A disk is coated on both sides with a magnetisable material, to allow it to store a magnetic pattern that will represent the computer's data. Iron-oxide coatings were universally used in older drives, with improved cobalt-oxide coatings appearing in newer models. The coating is magnetised under the influence of a coil of wire called the read/write head (the same coil that writes data is also used to read back data when required). The disk is mounted on a vertical shaft that spins it at 300 rpm in the case of floppy drives and from 4000 rpm to 15,000rpm for hard disk drives. The read/write head can be moved to any track on the disk by an electric actuator and it floats just above the surface of the disk. This movement is organised by electronic circuitry known as the 'disk controller'.

So, by moving the head to the desired track and waiting until the desired portion of the track rotates under the head, any part of the disk can be accessed for reading or writing. Writing involves energising the coil to create a magnetic field, which in turn creates an altering magnetic pattern on the disk surface. At a later date, when the magnetised area of the disk is passed under the head, the magnetic fields on the disk induce a current in the read coil. These pulses of current are cleaned up and used to convert back to the binary data that was originally recorded.

The dimensions of the read/write head areas are dependent on the number of tracks that are used on that disk. If a 5.25" floppy disk drive only has to cope with 40 tracks, its head is twice as wide as another 5.25" drive that has to cope with 80 tracks on the same disk radius. On a large capacity hard disk with many hundreds of tracks, the head dimensions are even more finely engineered. The heads commence their numbering from head 0.

Sectors

A floppy disk holds from 4.5k to over 18k of data on a single track, with a hard disk storing 30k to 50k. To make the most economical use of tracks, they are divided into compartments known as *'sectors'*. Sectors number from 1 upwards and each sector normally holds 512 bytes, i.e. 1/2k, of user data. Therefore, a 9-sector track on a 5.25" DD floppy stores 4.5k of data, while a 36-sector track on a hard disk stores 18k of data. The number of sides and the maximum number of tracks are determined by the hardware of the disk drive and are outwith the control of the user. However, the size and number of sectors are set under software control (hence the description *'soft-sectored'*)

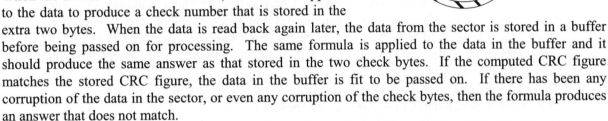

In fact, at the end of each sector there are two bytes that are additional to the 512 of the sector. These do not contain user applications and data; they are used to ensure the integrity of the data in the sector. These are known as *'Cyclic Redundancy Check'* bytes.

When the data is written to the sector, a formula is applied to the data to produce a check number that is stored in the extra two bytes. When the data is read back again later, the data from the sector is stored in a buffer before being passed on for processing. The same formula is applied to the data in the buffer and it should produce the same answer as that stored in the two check bytes. If the computed CRC figure matches the stored CRC figure, the data in the buffer is fit to be passed on. If there has been any corruption of the data in the sector, or even any corruption of the check bytes, then the formula produces an answer that does not match.

When the machine's built-in test routines in the BIOS find this error, they send an error code to the application program that is using the disk reading code. For example, if the Operating System is using the BIOS code to read a sector, a corrupted sector will produce an error message. The CRC bytes occupy disk space but do not appear in the figures for usable disk space (e.g. a 1.4MB disk is the user's figure after taking into account CRC bytes).

Clusters

In practice, sectors are mostly grouped in a unit called a *'cluster'*. The cluster is the smallest area of disk that can be used to store an independent item of data. So, if a particular disk used 4 sectors to a cluster, a batch file of only a few hundred bytes would still consume 2k of disk space. If a program or a piece of data requires more than one cluster's worth of space, it can be stored in subsequent unused clusters. The number of sectors to a cluster is determined by the Filing System (FS) used on the disk.

Formatting

All disks, floppy or hard, have to be formatted - a process sometimes also called *'initialisation'*. This lays down data on the disk that is never seen by users; it is solely used to distinguish between one track and another and between one sector and another. The read/write head is moved to the desired track and sector before reading or writing data in that sector. So, every block of data can be uniquely addressed by the read/write head used, the track used and the sector used to store it. Before any read or write operation is started, the system ensures that it has really arrived at the correct track and sector. A mechanical or electronic glitch may position the head over the wrong sector, resulting in either reading the wrong data or overwriting data. To overcome this, the data sections laid down on a disk are preceded by a Sector ID that contains the track number, the sector number and the sector size. If the information in the sector ID matches the desired location, the read or write operation proceeds normally. In the event of an incorrect head movement, the sector ID will not match the wanted location and the head is returned to track zero for another attempt. The Sector ID requires 57 bytes, so a sector size is really 571 bytes (57 for the Sector ID, 512 for the user data and 2 for the CRC).

Preparing a hard disk with sector IDs is known as *'low level formatting'*. A complimentary *'high level formatting'* process consists of preparing the disk for use by the operating system. A low level format, normally performed by the hard disk manufacturer, is carried out by the disk controller card and results in a disk that has its sectors identified and organised according to the required interleave. A high level format uses some of these sectors to set up the structures needed to store details of the files and their whereabouts. For Windows systems, this includes the boot sector area, the File System and the root directory, all of which are dealt with later. Modern hard disks rarely allow a low-level format, and when they do they require a special utility. A high level format is carried out by a software program such as Explorer or the FORMAT command. With floppy disks, this command carries out both low and high level formatting.

See the chapter on *'Operating Systems'* for instructions on formatting via Windows.

Floppy vs Hard Disks

Floppy disks comprise a single disk with two sides, while a hard disk will comprise several disks, with more sides and therefore greater storage capacity. This, coupled to the more precise engineering of hard disks, means that hard disk capacities far outpace those of floppies. The largest commonly used floppy disk stores 1.44MB of data while the smallest hard disks currently produced store 80GB of data, with larger models storing up to 1TB of data. Fetching data from a hard disk is much faster than from a floppy disk. This is due to factors such as:

- The increased speed of rotation of a hard disk (this is 50 or more times faster than a floppy disk).
- With the exception of power saving modes, a hard disk is spinning continuously while the computer is switched on. By comparison a floppy drive motor is only energised when data is to be read or written.   This means that a hard disk is always ready at the correct speed of rotation while a floppy drive has to get up to the correct operating speed before any disk activity can take place.
- The data is packed more tightly on a hard disk, so more data is read off from the reading of a single track compared to a floppy disk's track.

As programs become more sophisticated, they become ever larger, with some packages needing hundreds of megabytes of disk space. The extra capacity and vastly better speed make hard disks the obvious choice for storing application programs. Where large data files are in use, such as databases and graphical/DTP activities, there is also a speed advantage to storing the data on a hard disk. Floppies have the advantage of being cheap and portable and are a popular choice for storing backup copies of data. Software used to be supplied on a set of floppy disks, but is mostly now supplied on CD-ROMs.

The floppy drive is normally known as the A: drive.   If a second floppy is fitted in a machine, it is known as the B: drive, while the first hard disk is called the C: drive. Most machines have a single hard disk, although others can be added as Drive D, Drive E, etc. Some hard disk systems only allow two hard disks per machine, while others allow four or more hard disks.

Floppy Disks

Floppy disks for PCs come in two sizes - the old, obsolete 5.25" and the current 3.5" size. This refers to the diameter of the disks inside the protective casing. Both disks are made from mylar plastic coated with ferric oxide. A normal PC can have one or two floppy drives, each being of either 3.5" or 5.25" type. A modern floppy disk drive has two heads (one for each surface). The earliest floppy disks were single-sided (i.e. only one read/write head on one side of the disk) but these are almost all gone from use, leaving all floppy drives as double-sided models. The table shows the characteristics of various floppy disk types.

	Tracks/ side	Sectors/ track	Formatted Capacity	Unformatted Capacity	Sectors per cluster
5.25" Double Density	40	9	360k	500K	2
5.25" Quad Density	80	15	1.2M	1.6M	1
3.5" Double Density	80	9	720k	1.0M	2
3.5" High Density	80	18	1.4M	2.0M	1
3.5" Extra Density	80	36	2.8M	4.0M	2

5.25" Disks

The disk sits in a vinyl wallet, or *'jacket'*, to protect the magnetised surface from exposure to dust or grease.   The disk spins at 300 rpm inside the jacket, so the jacket lining is coated with a soft, non-woven material that is very lightly lubricated to minimise friction. The write-protect notch allows or prevents writing to the disk. A tab can be placed over the notch to disable any writing to the disk. In this way, important data can be written to the disk and then protected against accidental erasure or modification. When the tab is removed, the disk can again be written to.

The wallet has a slot in both sides, to expose the surface so that the read/write heads can reach the magnetised coating on the disk. The read/write head is brought close to the disk surface by the action of closing the disk drive lever after the disk is inserted.   When not in use, the disk should be kept inside its cardboard sleeve, to protect the exposed area.

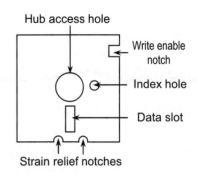

The lower density product - i.e. Double Density - uses 40 tracks and 9 sectors per track.   This means that there are 360 sectors on each side, giving a total of 720 sectors on the entire disk.   Since each sector is 512 bytes, the disk can store 360k of data.   The higher density version - described as Quad Density - increases the number of tracks to 80 and the number of sectors in each track to 15, giving a storage capacity of 80 x 15 x 2 sides x 512 bytes = 1.2MB. A double density disk has a coercivity of 300 Oersteds while a quad density disk has a coercivity of 600 Oersteds (see later).

3.5" Disks

The inner disk of this type of floppy is constructed similarly to the larger floppy, except that it has smaller dimensions and a higher quality coating. It can store more data than the 5.25" despite its smaller proportions.   The 3.5" is more robust since it is housed inside a rigid plastic case. The read/write slot is protected by a metal or Teflon slider that covers the slot when the disk is outside the drive. When the disk is placed in the drive, the drive mechanics push the slider back so that the read/write head can gain access to the magnetic surface. 3.5" disks have a write-protect hole that can be covered or uncovered by sliding a plastic cover over it. When the hole is covered, the disk can be written to. This is the opposite of the 5.25" disk that can only be written to when its write-protect notch is <u>uncovered</u>.

Double Density disks have 80 tracks with 9 sectors per track. This gives a capacity of 80 x 9 x 2 sides x 512 bytes = 720kB.   High Density disks have 80 tracks and 18 sectors in every track. They have double the capacity of double density disks - giving a capacity of 1.44MB. Some dealers offer '2MB disks'. These are just high-density disks, being quoted with their unformatted capacities.   When the formatting data is placed on the disk, the disk is left with a usable capacity of 1.44MB. The coercivity of a 720kB disk is 600 Oersteds and a 1.4MB disk's coercivity is 700 Oersteds.

When data is written to a disk, the level is taken as being 100%.   When that same data is read from the disk, its level is lower than the original figure. This reduction is known as the 'clipping level'. A known-brand disk normally returns a clipping level of around 50%, while bulk disks are around 40%. Disk drives, however, are able to adequately cope with clipping levels down to about 20%.

A high-density disk has a permanent extra hole punched in its body; this hole is not designed to be covered and uncovered like the write protect hole. The hole's presence or absence indicates whether the disk is a double density or high density version. The drive decides to use high or low head currents by checking for the presence or absence of this hole.

Protecting floppy disks

The disk media is easily affected by the environment and users should be encouraged to practise good housekeeping. As the diagram shows, the gap between the head and the oxide coating is tiny compared to commonly found elements in the real world.   A smoke particle is around 250 microns, a fingerprint is around 300 microns, a dust particle is around 400 microns, while a human hair is a gigantic 0.03 ins.

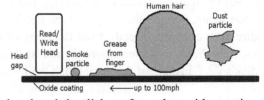

If a particle of smoke or dust was to be trapped between the head and the disk surface, the oxide coating would be torn from the disk and the surface would almost certainly be permanently damaged. The data contained in that sector, cluster, or even entire track would be lost forever. In extreme cases, the drive's head itself could also be damaged. This problem is greatly minimised with hard disks, as the mechanism is contained within a sealed unit.   But, with floppy disks, the danger is much greater. That explains why users are recommended not to smoke in the presence of computers. Of course, smoking does not automatically mean that damage will occur.   Luckily, smoke and dust particles often bounce off the surface and are not trapped in the head gap.

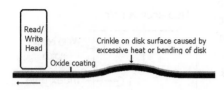

Read/Write Head

Oxide coating

Crinkle on disk surface caused by excessive heat or bending of disk

However, there is an added danger with 5.25" disks. The disk surface is open to outside corruption through the head access slot. If a user holds a 5.25" disk such that a fingerprint or palm print is placed on the disk surface, a layer of grease is deposited on the oxide coating. If this happens, a smoke or dust particle can become embedded in the grease. Now, the particle won't bounce off and is more likely to be dragged into the head gap.

Other problems can be caused by leaving the disk exposed to excessive heat. This may warp the disk surface as shown in the diagram. If a 5.25" disk is forced into a drive, or bent in any other way, the disk is similarly warped or crinkled. This raised portion will hit the read/write head as it rotates and part of the disk surface will be scraped off, with resultant damage to the disk and the loss of data.

Apart from protecting the disks themselves, there is a need to take care of the disk drive mechanisms. From time to time, computers have to be transported from one place to another. The sudden jolts to the machine could cause the read/write heads to bounce around and crash against each other. A cardboard or plastic insert can be placed in the drive and the drive door closed. This layer of card prevents the heads from bouncing around and allows the drive to be moved around in safety. With hard disks, this is not possible as they are housed in sealed cases. Hard disk heads must be moved to a part of the disk surface where no data is stored. Here, they can safely rest on the disk surface without scraping the oxide coating. This is called *'parking'* and is covered later.

Do's & Dont's of disk handling
- Avoid keeping computers in dusty surroundings; enforce smoking bans in computer areas.
- Avoid placing or storing disks in excessive temperatures.
- Don't touch the exposed surface of a 5.25" disk; keep unused disks in their protective envelopes.
- Avoid magnetic fields - don't place disks on top of printers, loudspeakers, telephones, etc.
- Floppy disks should never be folded or bent in any way.
- Always insert floppy disks carefully into drives.

Detecting disk changing
A floppy disk drive needs to detect that a disk has been removed from a drive and a new disk has been inserted. This may take the form of a microswitch inside the drive that is depressed when the disk is inserted. The switch changes state when a disk is removed and changes state again when a new disk, or even the same disk, is inserted. The status of this *'media change line'*, line 34, is used by various applications and utility programs. If a drive is not fitted with this mechanism, or the mechanism becomes faulty, the machine will not know that a disk has been changed. This can lead to unexpected results. For example, a user looks at the directory contents on a disk and then swaps the disk and looks at the directory again. Instead of displaying the new disk's contents, the files of the original disk are displayed once again. Since the system does not know that the disk has been changed, it is displaying the old directory contents directly from the copy of the FAT and directory stored in memory rather than reading the new directory information. Worse still, any new writes would be based on the memory version of the disk's FAT instead of the actual disk FAT - with data being written to the wrong part of the disk.

Hard Disks

Hard disk systems are composed of:

- A sealed drive unit.
- Disk controller electronics, either on a controller card or built in to the drive.
- Connecting cables between the drive and the computer motherboard.

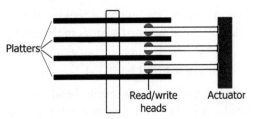

While the floppy is a single plastic disk, hard disk units consist of two or more disks in the one sealed unit. The extra disks boost the drive's storage capacity and each of these disks is known as a *'platter'*. The term applies to both sides of that particular disk. So, if a drive had three platters, it would contain 6 sides. Like floppies, areas of the hard disk's coating are magnetised and demagnetised to store the data. The disk is aluminium and coated with ferric oxide or cobalt oxide. In some newer models, the disk is made of glass.

The original XT hard disk was composed of two platters and had a capacity of 10MB. Modern drives can have many platters, but the number of platters is not necessarily an indication of disk capacity. An old disk drive with many platters could still have less capacity than a modern drive with fewer platters.

The older models of hard disk drives were 5.25" and newer models are 3.5" (or even 2.5") in diameter. There is no relationship between the size of the disk and its capacity. The 3.5" models are generally faster and quieter than the 5.25" version. A full-height drive is about 3.25" high, while a half-height drive is about 1.63" high. Virtually all 3.5" drives are half-height models.

Cylinders

Many specifications and publications refer to the term *'cylinders'* when describing a disk's construction. Mostly, the term is used freely as the equivalent of *'tracks'*. With hard disks there are a number of different platters and the heads are mechanically linked and are therefore placed over a <u>set</u> of tracks at any one time. The collection of tracks covered is known as the drive's *'cylinder'*.

In a hard disk, each platter has an identical set of cylinder numbers and these number from zero upwards. So, cylinder 2 would be the third track on side 0, the third track on side 1, the third track on side 2 and so on. Since a floppy disk has only two sides, the term is never used. The inner tracks are smaller than the outer tracks, so the data is stored more densely in the sectors of these tracks.   The density of the innermost track determines the drive's maximum capacity.

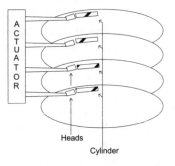

When a disk is constructed, it is provided with one or more extra inner tracks. These are used to provide a landing zone for the read/write heads. When machines are powered down, (very old machines may require a *'park'* command) the read/write heads are moved to sit in the landing zone so that they will not be able to scratch the surface of any sectors used for storing data. A drive rated as 771 tracks might only format the disk to 770 tracks, using track 771 as the landing zone. Some systems also use spare inner tracks to compensate for bad tracks. This can result in different utilities displaying different results; some are counting the tracks for data while others are counting the total tracks.

With IDE and SCSI systems, the electronics can be used to hide the *real* surface structure from the machine. As far as the machine is concerned, the drive has say 953 tracks, with each track containing 36 sectors. This will indeed be the *'logical'* view given to the machine by the drive. In fact, the drive may well have a completely different physical layout.   Since the disk's outer tracks cover a much greater surface than the inner tracks, the outer tracks can be used to store up to three times more sectors per track than the inner tracks.   This is known as *'zone bit recording'* and provides greater storage with improved reliability. The exact internal layout need not be known by the machine or by the user, since the electronics on the drive make the drive appear to have the normal regular track and sector layout.

Heads

Each side requires its own read/write head and these number from zero upwards. All the heads are mounted on the same actuator arm, so that they all move in unison as a single unit. When one head is on the sixth track in from the edge, then all the other heads are also on the sixth track of their disk sides. This achieves efficiency and economy of head motion. All the sectors in the same cylinder number (of all platters) are used, before moving the head inward to the next cylinder number.

The maximum read without moving the head to another track is calculated by multiplying the number of sides by the number of sectors in the track; this is then multiplied by the sector size, usually 512 bytes.

So, for the old XT machine, 4 x 17 x 0.5 = 34k could be read.
For a 12GB hard disk,   16 x 63 x 0.5 = 504k could be read.

Each platter has a read/write head for each side. Where a drive is reported to have an odd number of heads, it is due to the extra head and side being used for storing positional information instead of data. The smaller the dimensions and tolerances, the more likely that the drive could go out of alignment.

To prevent this and the effects of temperature changes (see later), one disk side is sometimes given over to *'servo tracks'* that ensures that the head assembly maintains its tracking. As long as the head on the servo track's side is kept in alignment, then the other heads must maintain alignment, since they are mechanically linked.

Elevator Seeking

Modern hard disk electronics use a technique known as *'elevator seeking'*. The requests for disk reads are stored in a queue so that reads located in the same disk area are read while the head is at that location. The reads are not in the same sequence as originally requested and the electronics sorts out the data to compensate. This technique reduces the amount of head movement thereby speeding up disk access.

Calculating disk capacities

Like floppy disks, the capacity of a hard disk is found by multiplying the total number of sides by the number of tracks by the number of sectors per track by the number of bytes per sector.

For example, the hard disk issued with the IBM XT machine had 2 platters, 17 sectors and 305 tracks. Since each sector was 512 bytes, it had a capacity of 4 x 17 x 305 x 512 = 10MBytes. The IBM AT machine had the same specification, except that it had 615 cylinders. So, its capacity was 4 x 17 x 615 x 512 = 20Mbytes. Modern disks of course are capable of much larger capacities. However, there are a number of other factors that have to be taken into account when attempting to calculate the usable surface of a hard disk.

A worked example

Consider the case of a disk advertised as a *"200GB"* disk.
This may be based on the following formula

```
      sides       tracks        sectors
      6  x 1,033,656  x   63    = 390,721,968 sectors at 512 bytes = 200,049,647,616 bytes.
```

However, this is not a 200GB disk. The final figure has to be divided by 1024 to arrive at the total expressed in KB (since there are 1024 bytes in a kilobyte). Dividing the result by a further 1024 gives the answer in MB and dividing by a final 1024 produces an actual disk size of 186.31GB. This is a full 13.7GB less than the manufacturer's advertised size.

However, this is not the end of the story. The disk space that is actually available to the user to store programs and data is smaller still. The hard disk is consuming the following overheads:

The Partition, DBR, FAT and Directory are covered later. A further 46.61MB of disk area is used for file management (i.e. 48,877,056/1024/1024). This leaves a user area of 186.31GB - 46.61MB = 186.25GB. The so-called 200GB hard disk, in fact, provides a user area of just over 186GB.

	Sectors	Bytes
Partition	36	18432
DBR and reserved sectors	3	1536
FATs	95392	48840704
Directory	32	16384
Totals	95463	48877056

To compound matters, some manufacturers and suppliers used to quote the <u>unformatted</u> size of a hard disk. The sector numbering which is written during formatting consumes a considerable amount of the disk surface and the *'formatted capacity'* is a more accurate reflection of the true usable size of the disk. The total capacity of a disk is generally around a quarter more than the final formatted disk capacity.

Comparison of sector coding

The BIOS always identifies a particular sector by a three-dimensional co-ordinate - the cylinder number/side number/sector number. On the other hand, many programs refer to sectors by their ascending sequential number - in the above example going from 1 to 23,547,888.

The conversion of logical sector numbering and the actual physical layout of sectors/tracks/heads is carried out by the machine's BIOS.

Increasing disk capacity

The capacity of disk surfaces is continually rising as improving technology allows the packing of ever more data on to each square inch of disk surface. This increased packing density, also known *as 'areal density'* relies upon:

- Improved surface coatings
- Improved head technology

Disk coating

To achieve higher data density, the number of tracks is increased and the length of a sector is shortened. This means that the area free to be magnetised to store a single bit is diminished in both directions, both in length and in breadth. If no steps were taken, the magnetised effects on the disk surface would influence each other and upset the data storage. To prevent this, the disk has a surface coating that is difficult to magnetise. This reduces the interference between the adjacent magnetised areas.

The degree of resistance to magnetisation is known as *'coercivity'* and is measured in units called *'Oersteds'*. It measures the amount of magnetic force that is required to change magnetic particles from sitting in a North-South orientation to a South-North orientation. A low coercivity disk will have its magnetic particles in the disk coating more readily affected than those of a high coercivity coating. A 3.5" floppy disk has a coercivity of 700 Oersteds, while modern drives have ratings of around 2,000 Oersteds. Research is continuing to produce surfaces with higher ratings, allowing more data to be stored on the disk surface.

Disk heads

The write head uses a magnetic field to alter the flux pattern of the disk coating. The magnetic field from the head spreads out like an umbrella, increasing in width as it approaches the disk surface. The first diagram shows how a head with a large gap requires a large surface to store a single piece of data.

In the second diagram, the head is flying much lower, the gap is smaller and the area covered by the magnetic pattern is much reduced. Reduced head gaps result in greater areal density. The original flying height of read/write heads was over 12 microns and now range from 1 to 6 microns.

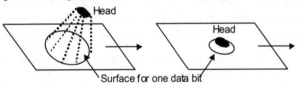

The current tiny high capacity drives are achieved by having the heads fly at less than one micron above the disk surface. With the head being closer to the surface, the head's magnetising effect is also increased.

This technique is currently maximised through *'Proximity Recording'* where the head flies at only 0.8 microns from the disk surface.

Another technique is to make the head of narrower width so that the tracks are closer together and more tracks can be placed on the disk surface. This allows for increased capacities (i.e. more data on the same disk size) or smaller diameter disks (i.e. the same data on a smaller size). Increased packing density also means that manufacturers can make disks cheaper by having less platters and heads.

Magnetoresistive heads

As the area allowed for each bit is reduced, the signal picked up by the normal inductive read head is weaker, reducing the reliability of the data read. Techniques to improve the signal pickup include:

Technique	Effect	Limitations
Move head closer to disk surface	Increased flux at head increases signal	Head gaps already very small
Place more turns on head coil	More sensitive head increases signal	Increases losses at fast speeds
Move data past head faster	Greater rate change of flux increases signal	Head speeds already very fast

One of the improvements in head technology is the Magnetoresistive (MR) head. MR heads have the following features:

- Separate read and write heads.
- The write head remains an inductive head but with much less windings on the coil. The extra windings were required for adequate data reads but resulted in writing too wide a track. Fewer windings means the head produces a narrower magnetic pattern and more tracks can be placed on the surface and more bits can be placed on each track.
- The reduced inductance of the write head also means that it can write at faster speeds.
- The read head is made from an alloy whose resistance changes in the presence of a magnetic flux.   It is velocity independent - i.e. it is the presence of the flux and not the rate of change of flux that produces the read signal; increasing or decreasing the disk speed has no effect on the signal.
- The read head is tiny and can detect a much reduced data area.   Areal density can therefore be increased.
- The read track is smaller than the write track so even slight head misalignment will not produce noise (the read head remains within the written track and does not read data from adjacent tracks).

PRML

Traditional drives translate the incoming signal from the head into digital data using *'peak detection'* - reading a peak value as a binary 1 and lower values as a binary zero.   This is an increasingly difficult task for the electronics when the incoming analogue stream is very fast and contains noise.   PRML (Partial Response Maximum Likelihood) converts the incoming signal into a digital waveform and runs it through a series of filters.   A group of bits is compared at a time, producing a more reliable data translation. The increased reliability allows for a more efficient coding method when writing data. This results in greater capacity from the same disk area.

Maximum Disk Handling

Available disk drives sizes grew at a rate that overtook the computer's handling capacity.   Early DOS versions, prior to v3.31, had sixteen bits embedded in the disk boot sector to store the total number of sectors allowed per logical drive.   Since the maximum different binary combinations from a 16-bit address is 65,536 and each sector is 0.5k, the maximum disk partition size on early PCs was 32MB.

This restriction has long since been lifted, when a four byte area was put aside in the boot sector area. This is a 32-bit number and can theoretically store a partition size up to 2 Terabytes. However, at first the BIOS for PC compatibles had a design that limited it to handling a maximum of 1024 tracks on any one hard disk, 63 sectors per track and a maximum of 255 read/write heads. The IDE interface, on the other hand, can handle a maximum of 65,536 tracks, 255 sectors per track and 16 heads. A disk system can only work at its lowest common denominator; there is no point in the BIOS supporting 255 heads, for example, if the IDE electronics can only handle a maximum of 16 heads.

This meant that an old IDE disk system could only operate with a maximum disk size of 16 heads covering 1024 tracks with each track holding a maximum of 63 sectors. With the normal sector size of 512 bytes, the maximum disk size supported is:

	BIOS	IDE	Actual best
Sectors/track	63	255	63
Number of heads	255	16	16
Number of cylinders	1024	65536	1024
Maximum capacity	7.8GB	127.5GB	504MB

$$16 \times 1024 \times 63 \times 512 = 504MB$$

This restriction could be overcome by bypassing the drive mechanism program code in the BIOS.   The normal calls to the BIOS disk routines (i.e. interrupt 13h) are intercepted and sent to a conversion routine which translates between the normal physical CHS (cylinder/head/sector) values and logical CHS values which can have a greater range than those contained in the BIOS. Ultimately, the logical values, when multiplied together, cannot exceed the product of the BIOS values.

ATA drives address the problem by using LBA (logical block addressing) on the disk controller card along with an LBA-aware BIOS chip. For very old machines whose BIOS code did not support LBA working, a software patch was installed which extends Int 13h working. Every sector on the drive is numbered in sequence from zero upwards.   The extended BIOS takes the CHS information that is passed to it (via the DOS Int 13h call used for disk reads/writes) and translates it into a 28-bit address specifying the disk sector.   Although the extended 13h functions use 32 bit for addresses, the ATA drives only use 28 bit addresses, limiting the maximum working to 127.5GB ($2^{28}*512/1024/1024/1024$).

Nevertheless, the maximum partition size remained at 2GB for some time. This limit was imposed by the design of the FAT16 filing system used by DOS, Windows 3.1 and the first release of Windows 95. The second release of Windows 95, OSR2, and Windows 98 use FAT32 - a 32-bit file system. This took full advantage of LBA working to handle disks up to 127.5GB as a single partition. The SCSI interface, due to its disregard for physical disk geometry, has no limitations on the number of heads it can support; SCSI drives have always used a form of LBA working.

Windows NT has its own filing system (NTFS), which was adopted by Windows XP and Vista. This does not use the BIOS for its disk handling and can therefore handle beyond the size limit imposed by older system BIOSes, addressing up to 2 Terabytes of storage space.

File System	Maximum Disk Size
FAT16 on Win9x	2GB
FAT16 on Win NT/XP/Vista	4GB
FAT32 on Win98	127GB
FAT32 on Win ME or later	2TB
NTFS	2TB

Head Actuators

The set of read/write heads in a hard disk assembly is moved in unison, under the influence of a single actuator mechanism.   The head mechanisms come in two varieties:

Stepper Motors

Stepper motors rotate by a small pre-determined amount when the motor coil is energised. Each step moves the read/write heads in or out exactly one track.   This is a cheap system but is slow and is no longer used. Stepper motor systems are also more prone to temperature changes than voice coil types. The physical dimensions of the disk expand and contract with temperature changes.   Since the stepper motor always moves the heads by the same amount with each step, they might not position the head exactly between the track boundaries.   That explains why users are recommended to switch on their computers for some time before using them, if they have been lying in a cold office overnight. If the heads and tracks are not in exact alignment, then data reads might be inaccurate, as the read head may be reading partly from a neighbouring track.   Even worse problems may result if the user tries to save data under these conditions. The data may be written partly on the wanted track and partly overwrite data on a neighbouring track.   Stepper systems also require a *'park'* utility to move the head away from the active disk surface when the machine is being transported. When the power is removed from a stepper motor drive, the read/write heads settle on the disk surface at the last track stepped to.

Voice Coils

A voice coil actuator is the more modern method and is given its name from the coil that moves the cone of a hi-fi loudspeaker. Like the loudspeaker coil, the head coil is within the influence of a permanent magnet. When the current through the coil is increased, the coil moves. Since the coil is connected to the head and actuator arm, the arm moves and therefore the heads are moved. This movement is against the action of a spring. When the current is removed, the spring pulls the heads to an area of the disk surface that does not store data; this is achieved without the user having to run a *'park'* utility - in effect, these disks *'auto-park'*. Voice coil systems are faster and more reliable.

The disk in a voice coil drive will shrink and expand with temperature changes, just like any other hard disk. The voice coil mechanism, however, is designed to overcome this particular problem. Instead of moving the heads by an exact amount, regardless of the prevailing disk temperature, the heads are moved to exactly the correct part of the track. In effect, the heads may move by a slightly different amount for differing temperatures.

The heads find out the exact stopping positions for each track by sensing positional information laid down on a special track laid aside for the purpose.   As the disk expands, the positional information will also move outwards and the heads will come to rest at the new altered position. This extra track is called the *'servo track'*.

Disk Reliability

Manufacturers usually quote their disks' reliability figures in terms of *'Mean Time Between Failure'* or *'MTBF'*. With older drives MTBFs were of between 20,000 hours and 50,000 hours - i.e. between about 800 days and 2,000 days of continuous use. Modern drives are quoted as having MTBFs of between 300,000 and 500,000 hours. Allowing for manufacturer's optimism this still results in drives that would never become faulty during their useful lives. In this context, 'useful life' would be the functional, rather than mechanical or electrical, life of the drive. Drive technology is moving ahead at a rate that encourages organisations to upgrade their drive systems prior to them becoming faulty beyond repair.

Protecting Hard Disks

Hard disks require most of the safety precautions already mentioned concerning floppy disks to be observed. The need to keep the disk unit away from strong magnetic fields, avoiding smoke and dust, etc. apply as much to hard disks as floppy disks. On the one hand, the hard disk is in a sealed unit and therefore has a better chance of surviving a hostile climate. On the other hand, the repercussions of disk failure are much more serious. If a floppy disk is damaged, it can be thrown in the waste bin at little financial loss. If a hard disk is damaged, it is a very costly item to replace. In addition, a damaged floppy disk should have its backup copy immediately to hand and so productivity is not affected. With a hard disk failure, a new disk has to be ordered up, fitted and have all the backup files restored before the machine is ready for use.

Apart from the above environmental problems, hard disks are particularly vulnerable to knocks and jolts. Unlike the floppy drive, the user is unable to mechanically stabilise the head assembly. If the case of the machine should be jolted while the machine is powered up, the head may make contact with the surface of the disk and scrape off some of the coating from the tracks. If this happens, the data in these sectors is lost and considerable permanent damage can be caused to the disk surface. This is termed a *'head crash'* and it renders sectors unusable. If the head crash happens when the head is positioned over the system areas (see notes on the Master Boot Record and DOS Boot Record) then the entire disk can be rendered unusable. This is because the system files cannot be relocated to any other sector - they must be found in specified tracks and sectors of the disk.

To minimise possible damage, modern drives have auto-park mechanics; that means that the read/write head is positioned out of the way of the data tracks when it is not involved in read or write operations. If this mechanism were not in place, as with very much older drives, then switching off the machine would result in the head dropping onto the disk surface. This would result in damage when the hard disk is powered up and spins with the head lying on the surface. These older drives required the user to run software utilities that placed the head out the way of data tracks before switching off the computer.

Disk reliability technology

Recently, Quantum has introduced new protection technologies, named DPS (Data Protection System) and SPS (Shock Protection System). DPS is a system that can distinguish a disk hardware fault from a fault elsewhere in the computer as a whole; while SPS is designed to buffer data to be written in the event of the drive suffering from a physical shock. Both systems improve the reliability of the disk.

A more widely available system is SMART (Self Monitoring Analysis and Reporting Technology), which works in conjunction with a SMART-enabled BIOS. See the Faultfinding chapter for details.

Disk Speed

The speed of a disk drive is based on:

- The time to get to the required data (known as the *'access time'*)
- The time taken to read that data from the disk (known as the *'data transfer rate'*)

Access Time

The time taken to reach the required data is based on two factors:

1. The time that the head takes to get to the wanted track (seek time) measured in milliseconds. Each track-to-track jump time may be different, since some head movements will wish to move across a larger amount of the disk than other movements. Due to the way that files are written, most track-to-track movements are not very distant. So, the average access time is calculated on the basis of 1/3rd of the tracks, instead of the expected half of the tracks. A poor seek time would be 12ms and a fast seek time would be 4ms. Drives with seek times lower than around 25ms are using voice coil actuators rather than stepper motor actuators.

2. The time taken to get to the wanted sector (latency period). This is the time spent waiting for the wanted sector to rotate to the position directly under the read/write head. On average, this is half a disk revolution. At 3600 rpm, this would be 8.33ms, at 4500 rpm this would be 6.67ms, at 10,000 rpm it would be 3ms, and at 15,000rpm it would be 2ms.

The original PC's 10MB hard disk had an access time of 80ms and the AT was quoted at 40ms. Modern drives range from about 12ms to under 4ms.

Data Transfer Rate

The rate at which a small amount of data (e.g. a single sector) is transferred is determined by the above factors and is a physical restriction that cannot be adjusted by the user. When a number of sectors require to be read, the most common case, the way that the disk is low-level formatted plays a large part in achieving the maximum data transfer rate. Low level formatting separates each sector with 'sector IDs' that determine the sector boundaries. The maximum data transfer rate is reached when the head reads from a contiguous set of sectors, without having to move the head to another track. In such a case, the rate would be determined by the sector size, the number of sectors per track and the speed at which the data passes under the read head.

With a floppy drive, the disk rotates at 300 rpm and so the 18 sectors on a 1.44 MB floppy would be read in 0.2 secs. The transfer rate would be:

$$0.5k \times 18 / 0.2 = 45k \text{ bytes/second or } 360Kbits/sec$$

Now, even a slow hard disk spins much faster, at 3600 rpm, giving a track reading time of only 0.01666 secs. So, for a hard disk with 36 sectors the data transfer rate would be:

$$0.5k \times 36 / 0.01666 = 1.08MB/second \text{ or } 8.6Mbits/sec$$

With models rotating at 10,000 rpm the track reading time is 5.99ms and the data transfer rate would be:

$$0.5k \times 36 / 0.00599 = 3.01MB/second \text{ or } 24Mbits/sec$$

So, reading a 1MB file from a large hard disk can take third of a second, around sixty times faster than reading from a floppy disk. Of course, the access time for both drives has to be included and this slightly reduces the dramatic gap in performance between the two drive types. Most controllers also have to decode various timing pulses before sending the data to the computer. Dependent on the type of card used, this produces various levels of delay and affects the overall data transfer rate. The above figures are maximums, in that they assume that all the data is read in one contiguous read, with no additional track-to-track movements.

Another major factor in determining data transfer rate is the efficiency of the electronics in the disk controller card. A very fast disk requires that the controller be able to transfer the data to the motherboard at the same rate. This is covered later.

Interfaces

The 'controller' is the electronic circuitry used to control the operations of the drive mechanism and the head read/write activities. In modern machines, this circuitry is built on to the machine's motherboard but older systems implemented this on a separate expansion card.

In early systems, manufacturers produced their own interface arrangements and this meant that users had to always use the manufacturer's specific card and drive components. Nowadays, one group of manufacturers, including for example Western Digital, produces controllers while other manufacturers, like Seagate and Maxtor, produce the hard drives. Consequently, a number of standard interfaces have been arrived at, to allow the devices to communicate. While the interface card is mainly for controlling the hard disk, most boards also have built-in electronics to control floppy disks.

The mechanics of drives mostly work in the same way but there are differences in the way that the drive communicates with the motherboard.

The most common interfaces are described below.

ST506 and ST412

These drive interfaces have been obsolete for decades now. The ST506 had a maximum disk capacity of 140MB and it read raw data from the disk drive in a serial fashion, stripped the timing and other information, and then passed the actual data on to the computer.

ESDI

A consortium of manufacturers who required better performance than the ST506/ST412 standard produced the Enhanced Small Device Interface, which is also now completely outdated. ESDI is also a serial method but introduces several improvements including putting the electronics on the drive itself to improve speed. It could typically achieve a transfer rate of 1.25MB/sec.

IDE

The system, introduced by Compaq in 1987, stands for Integrated Drive Electronics, sometimes described as Intelligent Drive Electronics, or even Imbedded Drive Electronics. This system is really an ST506/ ST412 setup that puts the entire controller circuitry on to the drive itself, to eliminate any losses between drive and controller. With this improved reliability, IDE drives have increased the number of sectors per track, allowing even greater data density on the drive. Most have 34 or more sectors per track and a 63 sector per track drive is not uncommon. They take into account that the data from the disk is now in faster parallel format, to produce fast performances. Theoretical data transfer rates of up to 5MB/sec are possible although around 4MB/sec is more typical.

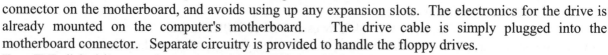

The fact that the IDE system is designed to appear to the machine as an ST506 system means that the original AT BIOS chip can always accommodate an IDE; there is no need to change the BIOS chip to get it to communicate with the drive system.

IDE drives connect to the computer via an integrated IDE connector on the motherboard, and avoids using up any expansion slots. The electronics for the drive is already mounted on the computer's motherboard. The drive cable is simply plugged into the motherboard connector. Separate circuitry is provided to handle the floppy drives.

Two IDE disk drives can be connected to an IDE motherboard socket and most motherboards provide two such sockets, allowing a maximum of four IDE devices. These may be a mixture of disk drives, ZIP drives or CD-ROM drives. The motherboard sockets are usually marked as "*Primary*" and "*Secondary*" or as "*IDE1*" and "*IDE2*".

An IDE cable has three plugs - one at either end of the cable and one along the length of the cable. One fits into the motherboard and the other two plug into the disk drives (or other IDE devices).

UDMA66/100/133 drives need a special low crosstalk cable, which if not supplied with the motherboard can be bought for a few pounds. This is an '80-wire' cable, but still uses only 40 pins. Each pin has two wires, which are twisted around each other to reduce crosstalk, thus allowing higher data rates.

An older system, now no longer used, had a *'pass-through'* board that plugged into a spare expansion slot. There were no electronic processing components on this board and it was used solely as a means of making connection to the motherboard (hence the term *'passing through')*. The board contained only bus buffering chips and some address decoding chips and it had a 40-wire ribbon cable that connected to the IDE drive. 16 of these wires are used as a parallel bus for faster data transfer.

IDE was a popular choice of drive due to its general reliability and its relative cheapness (caused by the reduced circuit complexity as a result of the data interpretation work being done on the drive). However, it does have the one drawback. If problems are encountered, the drive cannot be low-level formatted. IDE drives are low-level formatted at the factory and only give the appearance of an ST506 system to the machine. So, if the problems cannot be resolved at a higher level, the design of the IDE drive prohibits using the usual software to carry out low level operations such as low-level formatting and interleave setting.

IDE systems use logical addressing which leaves the job of translating logical sector numbers into actual head, track and sector information to the electronics on the drive. This is an advantage since it simplifies operations, with the drive taking over some housekeeping. For instance, if the drive detects that a track is deteriorating, it can transfer the data to a spare track and mark the original track as bad - all without the knowledge of the main machine. As far as the OS is concerned, the data is still in the original track - the task of translating what the OS thinks is the wanted sector into the actual new location is the job of the drive circuitry. That is why the normal utilities that work an absolute sector level have problems with IDE drives. However, file utilities such as defragmenters operate at a higher level and can therefore still work with IDE drives.

IDE drive controllers are unable to co-exist on the same machine with ST506 controllers or ESDI controllers. If a machine is to be given a second drive as an IDE drive, the original drive must also be an IDE type. Most IDE drives are compact 3.5" models.

Setting IDE drives

Where more than one disk drive is connected to a computer system, the computer has to be able to recognize them individually, know which one is the boot drive, etc. This is achieved by adjusting settings on each drive, so that they are recognised as being unique.

On older drives, these adjustments were provided on the printed circuit board of the drive. On modern drives, they are at the rear of the case on a *"jumper block"*. The block has two rows of pins and various pins can be bridged with small metal connectors with plastic covers.

Motherboards support two IDE connectors (channel 0 and channel 1). Each channel can support a *'chain'* of two IDE devices (known as device 0 and device 1).

Device 0 is the *'master'* device and device 1 is the *'slave'* device of each chain. The master device on channel 0 is usually used as the boot drive (see notes). Channel 0 is also known as the *'Primary'* channel, with Channel 1 being known as the *'Secondary'* channel.

This means that if a computer has four drives fitted they would be known as:

- The primary master
- The primary slave
- The secondary master
- The secondary slave

Modern systems mount the controller's electronics directly in the drive itself, rather than from a controller card. Where there are two drives on the one cable, only one controller is in operation. This is known as the *'master'* drive. The second drive uses the master's controller for its control instructions. This is known as the *'slave'* drive. This ensures that only one controller is ever active on a single channel.

Disk drives are usually supplied already configured as master drives and may need to be altered if they are to be used as slave drives.

Notes

- The BIOS can be set to select the boot device. So, even if a drive is jumpered to be the boot device, the BIOS can be set to boot from a floppy drive or from a CD-ROM drive.
- The actual jumper settings vary from manufacturer to manufacturer. The installation notes that come with the drive should be consulted.

Drives and the BIOS

The early XT machines expected the user to set switches on the controller card to inform the system of the drive number in use with the card. The XT controller card had its own BIOS chip and it stored a table of the most popular types of drive. Each number in the table corresponded to a set of disk parameters. This was satisfactory at the time, since only a limited range of disk types and sizes were available. From the AT onwards, the motherboard BIOS made provision for disk handling and it originally contained a disk table of types 0 to 14.

The machine's BIOS uses an area of CMOS (Complimentary Metal-Oxide Silicone - a type of low-power RAM) that is permanently powered by the machine's internal automatically recharged batteries. This same battery keeps the internal clock operating. The CMOS stores the details of the number of disk drives in use, their type and size. The hard disk details include the number of cylinders, number of sectors per cylinder, number of heads and write pre-compensation tracks. The user runs a setup program and chooses the appropriate description; the type number is used to set up the parameters in the CMOS memory.

Below are extracts from an AMI BIOS:

Drive Number	No of Cylinders	No of Heads	Start of WPC	Landing Zone	Sectors/ track	Disk Capacity
1	306	4	128	305	17	10M
2	615	4	300	615	17	20M
3	615	6	300	615	17	30M
4	940	8	512	940	17	62M
...	...	...	...	...	...	...
45	968	10	65535	968	34	161M
46	751	8	0	751	17	50M

Since the original table originated with the XT, the list is far from exhaustive or up-to-date. The original table grew to some 47 entries, some of which still describe small disk sizes that are no longer in use. To further complicate matters, some manufacturers' tables list their own versions of what characteristics match what table number.

Entries 0 to 14 are identical to the entries in the original AT set. However, a number of entries thereafter have been altered to allow the inclusion of higher-capacity drives than previously specified. This, of course, means that the modified numbers in the table only correspond to that manufacturer's BIOS and will not be available in other BIOS tables. Indeed, the table may well not be the same in future issues of the same manufacturer's BIOS.

Unfortunately, since disk technology is racing ahead, there are many disk types that are not covered by the existing tables held inside most BIOS chips, regardless of manufacturer. A way had to be found to future proof the BIOS, otherwise the chip would have to be updated whenever new drive types became available.

Entry 47

Fortunately, BIOS manufacturer (e.g. IBM, AMI, some Phoenix, etc.) deliberately left the details for table entry 47 left undefined. This allowed a custom configuration to be entered by the user as entry 47. In this way, a BIOS will not age too quickly.

If option 47 is chosen as the drive type, the user is then prompted to enter the following information:

Entry	Meaning
Cylinders	The number of cylinders
Heads	The total number of read/write heads
Write Precompensation - WPC	The starting cylinder for write precompensation to take effect
Landing Zone - LZ	The cylinder to be used as the landing zone for parking the read/write heads
Sectors per track - ST	The number of sectors per track
Size in MBs	The capacity of the disk expressed in Megabytes

The entries listed are the ones to be commonly displayed by a utility. In fact, there are two other entries held in the table. These are:

- Size in millions of bytes - this holds the disk's capacity in millions of bytes, as opposed to Megabytes.
- Control Byte - the individual bits in this byte are used hold information such as whether the disk has more than eight heads, is a servo drive, etc.

Since the values in the table do not cover new drives, the values that are placed in the CMOS can be any set of values which result in the same, or less, sectors than the actual drive used. As long as the formula

total tracks x number of sectors per track x number of heads

produces a value that is equal or less than the sectors value given in the drive specification, the IDE electronics can handle the logical to physical translations. If the total value of sectors exceeds the actual physical sectors, incorrect clusters are overwritten and data is lost.

EIDE

The rapid development of the other parts of the computer system has left the disk subsystem as the bottleneck for many activities.

Although IDE was very popular, it had a number of disadvantages:

- Its peak data transfer rate, at 4.1MB/sec, was inadequate. The low transfer rate was not a limitation with ordinary 16-bit ISA busses, since they were only capable of working up to a maximum rate of around 3MB/sec. The PCI and VL busses could handle much faster rates, but the IDE controller card was designed to fit into the ISA expansion slots of these machines. Such machines were therefore incapable of handling even the IDE's peak rate and an improved disk interface would be wasted on ISA based computers. A disk interface capable of plugging into the PCI or VL expansion bus could utilise the faster potential on these buses - hence the development of EIDE.
- It is only designed to interface hard disks. Other devices are not easily connected to the interface, although some CD-ROMs now provide IDE connections.
- It can only handle two drives per controller. Many machines do not support more than a single controller, limiting the computer to a maximum of 1GB spread over two drives. At best, a computer will support two controllers, allowing 2GB of disk capacity.

1995 saw the more widespread use of an improved interface known as EIDE or E-IDE (Enhanced IDE) capable of handling four devices. The devices are mostly disk drives but the interface easily handles CD-ROMs and ZIP drives. It is also cheaper than the other alternative fast interface - the SCSI interface.

The EIDE interface offers significant improvement in speed over the standard IDE interface, with a range of possible rates as laid in ANSI specifications. An EIDE disk drive remains compatible with the normal IDE system. Such a drive can be connected to an IDE controller and will work happily, although its transfer rate will slow down to that of the normal IDE performance. It is this compatibility that gives the Enhanced IDE its name.

This originated the current range of improved non-SCSI drive systems that remain backward compatible with older computers. So, for example, a UDMA/66 drive produces a full data transfer rate of 66.6MBps when connected to a motherboard and BIOS that are both ATA/66 compatible. However, its 40-pin plug still connects to an older motherboard IDE connection (the extra 40 wires in the cable are shields for the 40 pins) - although, of course, it runs at the reduced data transfer rate.

ATA INTERFACE

ATA (AT Attachment) is the general standard for connecting disk drives and it currently has four flavours:

- ATA-1 describes the original normal IDE working.
- ATA-2 is the foundation of a range of EIDE interfaces. It also incorporates ATAPI (ATA Packet Interface), which describes the ability of the interface to work with other devices beyond disk drives. If a scanner or CD-ROM is described as having an ATAPI standard, it means that it connects to the IDE controller.
- ATA-3 is the upgraded specification that introduced PIO Mode 4 and Multiple Word DMA 2. It also brought in power management - particularly useful for portable computers.
- ATA-4 is the specification that encompasses the newer Ultra DMA drives, also known as Ultra-ATA, Ultra DMA/33, Ultra DMA/66 and Ultra DMA/100.

ATA devices cover a wide range of transfer times, using different data transfer methods.

There are three data transfer methods:

PIO	The Programmed Input/Output method has the computer's CPU in control. The CPU itself reads the data from the disk interface and writes it to memory (or vice versa for disk writes). Used by the original 80286 PC disk controller and also modern IDE controllers. PIO has six different working modes: <table><tr><td>PIO Mode</td><td>Speed</td><td>Standard</td></tr><tr><td>0</td><td>3.3MBps</td><td>ATA</td></tr><tr><td>1</td><td>5.2MBps</td><td>ATA</td></tr><tr><td>2</td><td>8.3MBps</td><td>ATA</td></tr><tr><td>3</td><td>11.1MBps</td><td>ATA-2</td></tr><tr><td>4</td><td>16.7MBps</td><td>ATA-3</td></tr><tr><td>5</td><td>22MBps</td><td>Not yet implemented</td></tr></table>

DMA	With the Direct Memory Access method, the circuitry on the disk controller card relieves the CPU of much of its memory read/write activities. The CPU tells the DMA controller which disk to access and what memory area to read/write and the DMA controller handles all the data transfers. This is termed *'Bus Mastering'* since the CPU controls all data transfers during this period. During this time, the CPU is freed to carry out other tasks. These tasks cannot involve memory access but can be computer calculations. There are six variants of DMA transfers: <table><tr><td>DMA Mode</td><td>Speed</td><td>Standard</td></tr><tr><td>Single Word 0</td><td>1.04MBps</td><td>ATA</td></tr><tr><td>Single Word 1</td><td>2.08MBps</td><td>ATA</td></tr><tr><td>Single Word 2</td><td>4.17MBps</td><td>ATA</td></tr><tr><td>Multiple Word 0</td><td>4.7MBps</td><td>ATA</td></tr><tr><td>Multiple Word 1</td><td>13.3MBps</td><td>ATA-2</td></tr><tr><td>Multiple Word 2</td><td>16.7MBps</td><td>ATA-3</td></tr></table>

ULTRA- DMA	Ultra DMA uses techniques such as improved timing and data pipelining to double the maximum data transfer rate achieved by the standard DMA method. It also introduces CRC testing to ensure the integrity of data moving on the bus. This is in addition to the CRC checks discussed earlier, relating to integrity checking when writing to the disk surface. Ultra-DMA drives will connect to existing IDE motherboards but will not provide the higher transfer rates. Motherboards using LX and TX chipsets onwards support Ultra-DMA drives. There are several variants of Ultra-DMA transfers:

DMA Mode	Speed	Standard
0	16MBps	ATA-4
1	24MBps	ATA-4
2 (UDMA/33)	33MBps	ATA-4
4 (UDMA/66)	66MBps	ATA-4
5 (UDMA/100)	100MBps	ATA-4

SCSI

The SCSI interface standard is the Small Computer Systems Interface (pronounced *'scuzzy'*). This is an old interface, adopted as an ANSI standard in 1986, which has made a serious impact on the general storage market. The SCSI drive has the controller circuitry built-in and, like the EIDE, it uses logical addressing methods. The drive is connected via a 50-wire or 68-wire cable to an adapter card that connects to one of the computer's expansion slots. Since the controller circuitry is on the drive, the card is described as a *'host adapter'* rather than a controller card. Its only real job is to allow SCSI devices to connect to the computer bus. Since it is a simple device, it is able to connect up to seven or sixteen different devices. The connecting cable can have a number of connector plugs along its length, to connect to a number of internally fitted SCSI devices. External devices, such as DAT drives and external CD-ROMs or even hard disks, can connect to the bus via a D-shell connector on the SCSI adapter card.

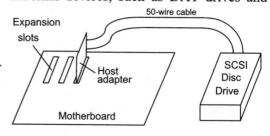

When several devices are connected, the system is described as being *'daisy chained'*. The total length of the chain must not exceed 19 feet (reducing to 9 feet for Wide SCSI and only 5 feet for SCSI-3), to minimise transmission errors. Each end of the chain must also be fitted with terminating resistors. These terminate the cable and prevent signals being reflected back down the cable as noise. The terminators may consist of resistors built in to the device and activated by DIP switches, or they may be separate terminating plugs or *'blocks'*. Each external device has two connectors - one for connecting to the existing chain and one for either extending the chain or terminating the chain.

The intelligence built in to the host adapter is designed to relieve the machine's CPU from the tasks of organising the control of the various devices attached to it. The machine CPU can transfer these responsibilities to the circuitry of the host adapter card so that it can carry out other activities.

The IDE drive receives instructions that are both disk-specific and low-level. The SCSI controller, on the other hand, communicates at a higher level and is data-specific, leaving the physical considerations entirely to the device's on-board circuitry. The generalised nature of this interface means that it is able to connect more than just disk drives to the motherboard. A range of devices, such as CD-ROMs, tape drives, scanners, etc. can be connected to the SCSI interface with ease. Each device must be given a different ID number. With SCSI-1 and SCSI-2, these range from 0 to 7 and the host adapter usually defaults to ID 7. Wide SCSI-2 and SCSI-3 support up to 16 devices. The ID number is set in each device with the DIP switches or jumpers on the cards. Adaptec, a major SCSI adapter manufacturer, pioneered the ASPI (Advanced SCSI Programming Interface). This is a single driver that lets the OS communicate with the adapter card and another driver for each device on the chain.

Since each device on the chain may be able to communicate at a different data rate, the adapter card has to alter its data rate to match each device it is working to any particular time. The card can work at the faster rates for faster devices and will slow down to the rates of the slower devices. To achieve this, the card has to set its standard for communicating with each device.

SCSI Versions

A range of different SCSI standards has evolved with the following data transfer rates from the device to the adapter card. These use different data bus widths and different electronic controls.

Type	Data Rate	Data Path	Comments
SCSI-1/ SCSI-2	5MB/sec	8-bit	50-pin connector. Asynchronous
SCSI-2 Fast	10MB/sec	8-bit	50-pin connector. Synchronous
SCSI-2 Fast Wide	20MB/sec	16-bit	68-pin connector
SCSI-3 Ultra	20MB/sec	8-bit	50-pin connector. Also called Fast 20.
SCSI-3 Ultra-Wide	40MB/sec	16-bit	68-pin connector
Ultra-2	40MB/sec	8-bit	Also called Fast 40, or LVD.
Ultra-2 Wide	80MB/sec	16-bit	68-pin connector
Ultra 80	80MB/sec	8-bit	Also called Fast 80
Ultra160 (or U160)	160MB/sec	8-bit	An implementation of Ultra-3
Ultra320	320MB/sec	16-bit	Also called SCSI-4

Bus widths are either 8-bit or 16-bit. This is the bus between the controller and the drive; the controller may well have a 32-bit interface via the PCI connector.

Fast SCSI doubles the transfer rate by using more stringent electronic parameters that allow timings to be altered and overheads reduced. Ultra SCSI's electronics run at double the normal clock frequency and this produces transfer rates that are double that of Fast SCSI.

Since the data transfer rate between the adapter and an ISA based computer works out at around 2Mb/sec; a SCSI adapter that connects to PCI bus produces far better results.

Note that some material refers to Ultra-2 SCSI as LVD ('*Low Voltage Differential*'). Ultra-2 SCSI was the first type of SCSI to use LVD technology, but Wide Ultra-2, Ultra-3 and Ultra320 also use LVD technology. LVD uses lower voltages, allowing greater integration and therefore slightly reducing the cost of an LVD drive.

SCSI systems do not use the machine's BIOS, having placed a device driver in the CONFIG.SYS file to install the necessary control software. This means that a SCSI drive can cohabit with an IDE system in the same machine without any conflicts. In addition, since devices of different transfer rates can work with the same adapter, upgrading to a faster SCSI hard disk will involve no changes to the SCSI adapter. Some CD-ROMs, scanners and Postscript printers have SCSI-2 interfaces.

Notes:

- The best EIDE performances compete with the middle/top SCSI performance but SCSI systems also have an edge on performance in multitasking environments. The CPU can send an instruction to a SCSI device and carry on with other tasks until the device responds. With EIDE, the CPU has to wait until the device responds before carrying out other tasks thereby slowing down throughput, particularly in situations of multiple I/O requests.
- The performance of the interfaces has outstripped the speed of most current drives. Drives typically have a sustained data rate of 5 to 40 MB/s. Even the most modern and fastest drives (such as the 15,000 rpm Cheetah) can only provide a sustained transfer rate of up to 69MB/sec.
- An ultra-wide controller card, such as the Adaptec 2940UW, has both 68-pin connectors (for ultra-wide devices) and 50-pin connectors (for SCSI-2 devices).

SCA Connectors

The Single Connector Attachment system is not limited to SCSI devices, but SCA usage so far has been almost entirely in SCSI systems. SCA is essentially a method of connecting data and power lines to the attached devices through a single interface. The current specification of SCA is an 80-pin connector.

Serial ATA

The most recent development in storage device interfaces is the Serial ATA interface. Just as the parallel port gave way to the USB serial bus, the parallel 40-pin IDE ribbon cable eventually gave way to this 4-wire serial cable. This is accompanied by a new form of power cable, with ground pins longer than the other pins to facilitate 'hot-swapping'. (the capability to remove and replace drives while the machine is running)

As its name suggests, it moves data between the drive electronics and the mainboard in a serial manner. This contrasts with the older parallel system that is still currently in use on most computers, which is now renamed PATA (Parallel ATA).

Advantages

Serial ATA offers distinct advantages over the parallel interface:

Easier setup

Each drive is allocated its own cable and its own dedicated bandwidth, unlike SATA which connected up to two drives per cable and shared the bandwidth. This eliminates the fiddly master/slave jumper settings and their problems. Unlike PATA drives, SATA units are hot-swappable. This means that drives may be connected and disconnected while the system power is on.

Faster transfers

PATA transfer rates were 100MBps, with bursts reaching 133MBps. The first implementation of SATA, by contrast, was 1.5Gbps. However, unlike PATA, the serial method used by SATA allows it to be further increased. Thus the next implementation, Serial ATA II increases the data transfer rate to 3Gbps. Future implementation will be at 6Gbps. These speeds are the *maximum* transfer across the drive to motherboard link – they are not necessarily the rate that is achievable in practice. Since these data rates are currently well in excess of the drive's ability to read/write data to the disk surface, the fastest speeds are only achievable when reading from the drive's internal cache.

Increased reliability

At a physical level, SATA systems are more reliable since their connections are simplified and are more robust. They use wafer connectors instead of pins (i.e. the edges rub together instead of a 'pin and hole' approach'). This eliminates the dangers of bent pins when inserting plugs. Also, the reduced number of contacts on the connections means there are fewer potential failure points.

At a signal level, SATA systems are also more reliable. While PATA drives apply CRC checks (see description in main book) to all data carried across the cables, SATA also carries out CRC checks on the commands being that are passed. This results in a claimed detection rate of 99.998% of all possible errors (commands and data).

Reliability is also improved through SATA operating voltages only requiring 250mV. This compares with 5V required by PATA, a level that is hard to obtain when chip core voltages are now below 5v and falling still further.

Improved cabling

Standard PATA cables are short and wide. These cables have a 45cm (18") limit to their length and their 40-wire or 80-wire cables mean that they are wide and bulky. This results in restrictions to the smooth airflow inside the computer case, with potential overheating and component failure. It also means that access within the case is restricted.

SATA cables can be up to 1 metre (around 40") in length. Since SATA cables only need 7 wires, they are much slimmer than PATA cables. These longer, slimmer cables allow cables to be routed round the case, tucked away and causing no airflow restrictions. This results in a neater internal layout and improved system cooling. They also offer advantages in systems with physical restrictions, such as small form factor systems and consumer electronics boxes.

Connections

Like PATA, SATA systems use two connectors, one for connecting power and one for transferring data. However, the two systems' connections are not compatible.

Compared to PATA's 40 or 80 wire data cable, SATA uses just seven wires. It has two data channels, one for sending data and a separate channel for receiving data. The table below shows the connections as viewed from the controller. The data connections are reversed at the device end, with the controller's *'Transmit'* pins connecting to the device's *'Receive'* pins and vice versa.

Pin	Signal	Purpose
1	GND	Ground
2	A+	Transmit +
3	A-	Transmit -
4	GND	Ground
5	B-	Receive -
6	B+	Receive +
7	GND	Ground

The power cable looks like a longer version of the data cable and has 15 connections. These provide three different voltages, these being 3.3V, 5V and 12V. Each voltage has three connectors, providing positive, negative and ground connections for each voltage. Added to these nine connections are six further connections that provide SATA's hot-swappable features.

The connectors are designed so that they cannot be inserted the wrong way round.

Upgrading

SATA works without any alteration to a user's operating system. So, for example, Windows works equally efficiently with PATA or SATA.

Eventually, new computers will provide both SATA-enabled motherboards and SATA disk drives. For these users, SATA is already installed.

For users wishing to fully upgrade to the SATA standard, the requirements are:

- SATA-enabled motherboard
- SATA drive
- SATA cables
- SATA-enabled power supply

Alternatively, to save costs, users can simply fit a SATA controller card into an existing motherboard and fit an adapter between an existing power supply and the new SATA drive. Users who purchase a SATA-based computer can still use their old PATA disk drives by fitting a PATA to SATA adapter between the disk drive and the disk controller.

Comparison table

	Parallel ATA	Serial ATA
Max data transfer rate	133MB/sec	1.2Gbps to 6Gbps
Hot swappable	No	Yes
Power cable	4 pin	15 pin
Data cable	40 pin	7 pin
Max cable length	18"	1m (approx 40")
Connection type	Pin	Wafer
Signal voltage	5V	250 mV

eSATA

Connecting external drives to a PC is popular but the external interfaces (USB2 and Firewire) transfer data more slowly than the disk drive can provide.

eSATA (External SATA) was developed as a more efficient serial external interface and is currently claimed to be up to six times faster than existing external drive interfaces.

It can connect with a cable that is up to 2m long and plugs into an eSATA socket. For older PCs that are without an eSATA connection, an eSATA controller PCI card can be installed on the PC.

Solid State Drives

Developments are containing to replace hard disks with flash memory although, as yet, only a 32GB version is commercially available.

Solid state drives, when fully developed, offer:

Faster access times

Immunity from damage from physical jolts and bumps

Lower current requirements, resulting in longer battery life in portables and less heat.

miCARD

The MultimediaCard Association has agreed a specification for a memory card that plugs directly into a USB port, without the need for a memory card reader.

Called the miCARD, it is essentially a MMC memory card with an attached USB interface. The card can be removed from a digital camera or mobile phone and inserted into a standard USB port on a PC. At 21mm x 12mm x 1.5mm, it is smaller than the current MMC card. It provides a transfer rate of up to 480Mbs on a USB2 port.

This is similar to the existing product for SD card produced by SanDisk. Their SD card has a flip-up cover that reveals a board with contacts for insertion into a USB socket. Lexar's version is known as a USB FlashCard.

FireWire Disks

The relatively new FireWire standard (see the Architecture chapter for more details) can be used to connect external hard drives and other storage devices. In theory this means the drives could use the full data transfer speed of the FireWire interface. However, it should be noted that in most cases the hard disks used are simply normal IDE drives with interfaces that allow it to be used through a FireWire bus. Although this gives the advantage of an external, mobile disk, it does not use the full speed capability of the architecture.

Write Precompensation

IDE and SCSI systems use the disk surface to the maximum advantage. They write more data on the more spacious outer tracks and less data on the more compressed inner tracks. To the outside world, however, they present a logical view that represents the disk as having an identical number of sectors in every track. For other systems, this facility is lacking and this can cause problems of reading and writing data evenly over the disk surface. The sectors that are on the inner tracks on a disk (the higher numbered tracks) are smaller in size than the tracks on the outer surface of the disk. Yet, the track has to hold the same amount of data, for say 36 sectors, whether it is on the inner or outer edges of the disk. It follows then, that the data is more compressed on the inner tracks than on the outer tracks. The computer data is written on to the disk surface as a stream of magnetised sections, with each section having its own north and south poles like any other magnet.

A small unmagnetised area separates magnetised sections from the each other. Problems arise when the inner tracks locate these 'magnets' closer together, with smaller spaces between them. Their proximity results in the magnetised areas affecting each other, with similar poles repelling and opposite poles attracting. The slight alteration of the magnetic pattern may be sufficient to prevent the data being read back correctly. To correct this, the writing process can treat the inner tracks differently from the outer tracks, by taking into account the likely distortions when placing the data on the surface. The writing process is compensating in advance for the problem, so that the final written information will be where it ought. It is this 'compensating in advance' that gives the process the name 'precompensation'. When the data is later read, the inner and outer tracks are read and processed in the same way. Since precompensation is concerned with writing data to the correct place on the disk surface, it only affects the writing process and is not used for reading data.

The parameters for each drive include a write precompensation number. This is the number of the first track at which to apply precompensation when writing data. If a 953 cylinder disk has a precompensation value of 150, then write precompensation starts at track 150 onwards. If the value for the same drive is 953, then no precompensation is applied to that particular disk (this might also be stored as -1).

The reduced physical size of disk area for the storage of each data bit can cause another problem. The electric current used to produce the data writing to the outer tracks could result in each data write occupying too large a disk surface area in the inner tracks. The separating non-magnetised areas disappear and the data elements begin to overlap into each other. To prevent this, the current supplied to the write head is reduced on the inner tracks, creating a smaller write area on the disk surface.

Disk Cache

The speed of a computer's throughput is not solely determined by the raw speed of the CPU. Many applications are disk based and large database applications are especially disk-intensive in their operations. So, a large proportion of the time is spent in disk activities rather than processing activities. Windows also makes heavy use of disk operations, particularly if machine memory is small and swap files are in operation. Additionally, Windows uses many DLL (Dynamic Link Library) files. These sub-programs are usable by various applications and function like overlay files. However, this technique also increases the number of disk accesses required to run applications.

There has been continual progress in CPU development from the days of the 8088 processor. Disk development, although making rapid progress of late, has remained the main bottleneck in the system as it is still largely limited by the mechanical nature of its operations.

Cache controller cards have been developed as a highly successful method of improving disk access times. They work on the same principle as memory cache systems explained previously. Memory cache acts as a high-speed buffer between the fast CPU and slower memory. With disk caching, memory chips are used as a high-speed buffer between the fast CPU and very much slower disk devices. It is also argued that the reduced need for disk accesses results in reduced disk wear, prolonging the disk's life
In fact, DOS buffers are an elementary form of caching. Each buffer stores 512 bytes of data - the same size as a disk sector. With buffers set at 20, 10k of memory is set aside for disk caching. With today's giant applications, this is totally inadequate and most modern disk drives use *'track buffering'* instead of sector buffering. This means that an entire track (or more likely several entire tracks) is read at a time into a memory buffer that is located on the drive's own electronics circuit board.

True disk caching can be implemented in two ways:

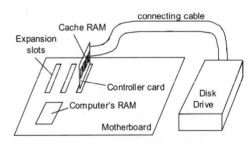

1. Using memory chips that are not part of the PC's normal memory map. In older systems, they were located on a separate disk controller card. The controller card was used to replace the normal IDE or SCSI controller and was plugged into an ordinary ISA expansion bus on the motherboard, as shown in the first diagram.
   This has now been replaced by the system shown in the second diagram. The cache memory chips are now located inside the disk drive case.
   Modern drives have from 512k up to 16MB of this built-in cache memory. In both cases, they provide extra memory that is dedicated to interfacing slow disk access with fast CPU access.

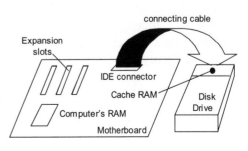

2. Using a chunk of the computer's memory, under the control of the Operating System, such as by using the System Cache option in the System Properties section of the Control Panel.

Both caching systems work in the same way.   The CPU demands data at a much faster rate than the disk mechanism can fetch it.   The cache memory in the disk drive - or in the computer memory - stores copies of the data that was previously read or written. It also reads ahead - it reads in data from sectors beyond that requested. If the machine wishes to read a file, there is a fair chance that the data is already stored in the cache memory. If so, then it can be transferred at a much faster rate than would be the case with reading directly from disk. If the data is found in cache, then it is described as a 'hit'; if it has to be fetched from disk, then it is a 'miss'.   To improve the 'hit rate', the controller predicts the next data to be read (see notes on the principle of locality) and pre-loads this data into cache memory.   This is particularly effective with database records and other data that is organised on a sequential basis.

Caching algorithms can deliver around 90% of data requests from the high-speed cache, avoiding interrogating the hard disk.   On the other hand, when there is a cache 'miss', the system actually operates more slowly than a non-cached system.   There is wasted time, while the cache is fruitlessly searched, before the data is fetched from the disk.

Of course, if a very large quantity of data is to be handled, a small controller cache, or a small cache, will have only a limited effect on efficiency.   The larger the cache memory size, the more likely that the data will be found without recourse to disk access.   If the user is working with huge database records, or large graphics files or DTP files, then each read required could be larger than the actual cache size and large disk reads would be required on every occasion.   This will slow down throughput and give a poor hit rate.

> **Note**: This effect should be borne in mind when measuring cache efficiency. It is possible that the same machine might be perfectly efficient at handling other processing chores.

When fresh data is read in, there are occasions when the cache is already full of older data.   The controller decides what data should be overwritten by the new data.   This is either based on algorithms called the 'Least Frequently Used' or the 'Least Recently Used' methods. As the names imply, either the least popular (the data least requested) or the oldest data is chosen to be overwritten. The LRU (Least Recently Used) algorithm is most commonly used, as it is the fastest.   This is the method used by Windows to decide which DLLs should be sent to the swap file when its memory resources become tight. Implementing cache in hardware offers the benefit of greater throughput, since little processor time need be dedicated to cache activity; the controller's built-in CPU decides when data should be read from or written to disk.

Write Caching

Some caching only operates for disk reads. If required, the benefits of caching can be applied to disk writes. With write-behind caching, data to be written to disk is not written immediately, but is held in the cache memory until the machine's CPU is free. In this way, the machine's throughput is not slowed down by forcing the CPU to deviate from other work to carry out the disk writes.

While write-behind caching improves machine performance, it also leaves data vulnerable. While these systems have a time limit (say four seconds) of holding write data in the cache, this still leaves scope for problems. If there is a power failure, for example, data that is being held temporarily in the controller memory will be lost. Similarly, any command that reboots the machine might cause this to happen while data was still in the cache.   In these circumstances, the data should be flushed to disk prior to rebooting - or the write-behind facility itself should be disabled.   Disk controllers can have the system set between either write-through or write-behind.

Windows Caching

Windows 95 replaced the old DOS SMARTDRV cache system with a system called VCACHE, which is more 'intelligent' also caches CD-ROMs. Windows XP and Vista have write-caching enabled as part of the System Cache, but this can be disabled through the disk's Properties dialog, in the 'policies' tab. Alternatively, to assign a larger amount of memory as cache, this can be done from the System Properties in Control Panel, by clicking the 'Advanced' tab, going to Performance Settings, then the 'Advanced' tab again, and finally the 'System Cache' option.

FAT Disk Organisation

When a hard disk is formatted using any form of FAT filing system, it creates four areas of the disk (like a floppy), and there is an additional area for the Master Boot Record (not required for floppies).

The actual order on a disk is as follows:

- Master Boot record
- Boot Record
- FAT (File Allocation Table), including a backup copy of the FAT
- Directory
- Data Area

Each of these areas occupies differing amounts of disk space, dependent upon the disk's overall capacity. Each is described next, with the order changed to ease the explanation.

Data Area

This is by far the largest area of the disk and it contains all the data files and directories (a sub-directory acting in a similar fashion to a data file).

The formatting process sub-divides the data area into many equal sized portions known as *'sectors'*. A sector is the smallest area of the disk that can be independently identified. Sector sizes can be 128, 256, 512, 1024 or 2048 bytes but has standardised on a sector size of 512 bytes. Sector size is under software control, hence the description of *'soft-sectored'* disks. Older systems actually punched holes in the disk to define sector boundaries and were described as *'hard sectored'*. These holes were punched in the inner track of the disk and a photoelectric cell detected a light beam as it shone through each passing hole. The number of light pulses detected, when compared to an index hole, determined which sector was being read. This meant that the size and shape of the disk could not be changed but it had the advantage of using the entire surface of each track. Soft sectored systems are more flexible but require to use some of the track area for the synchronising information previously supplied by the punched holes.

The ability to control the layout of data on a disk was exploited in some early copy protection schemes. To prevent unlawful copying of disks, manufacturers resorted to non-standard formats such as including a sector that was larger than the rest, or having eight sectors on a particular track instead of nine. Since DOS did not know of their changed layout, the disk could not be read by normal COPY, XCOPY or DISKCOPY commands and the disk could not be duplicated. The disk could still be run, as the program coding would know of the non-standard sections and treated them accordingly.

Note that some utilities report on sectors as *'sector 17551'* while others may refer to *'cylinder 2, head 3, sector 4'*. This is because the Operating System does not wish to know the exact location of a sector in terms of heads and tracks; it prefers to number sectors in continuous ascending order - sector 0,1,2,3,4....15001, 15002, 15003 and so on.

Disk layouts in PCs can be viewed as having two formats:

1. The physical format that is used by the ROM BIOS. This sees the actual layout in terms of the number of heads, the number tracks, the number of sectors per track and the sector size. These are termed the *'absolute sectors'* and an absolute sector is identified by its cylinder/head/sector.

2. The logical format as used by DEBUG and various other disk utilities. This sees the sectors as continually incrementing from sector one, commencing on the first head and the first track and moving inwards. These are termed the disk's *'relative sectors'* and consist of single numbers. These absolute sectors can be mapped into the actual physical absolute sectors.

Cylinder 0/head 0/ sector 1 contains the hard disk's master partition information and is therefore not included in the sector numbering scheme. Cylinder 0, head 1, sector 1 is the equivalent of sector 0. This sector contains the Boot Record and is normally also ignored in the numbering scheme. The remaining sectors on the disk are then included in the sector numbering.

Example

> In a typical 36-sector disk with 4 heads, side 0 track 5, sector 3 is an absolute sector.
> To get to that position, four full tracks of 36 sectors must have been scanned by all four heads.
> So, 4x36x4 = 556 sectors. The head, having returned to head 0 is moved to sector 3.
> This means that the relative sector is 556 + 3 = 559.
> Therefore, the absolute sector given by side 0, track 5, sector 3 maps to relative sector number 559.
> Note that this will only be the case with disks with four sides.
> If the disk had six sides, the relative sector would be (6x36x4)+3 = 867.

Clusters

With hard disks, like floppies, space for data is allocated on the basis of `clusters'. A cluster is the smallest group of sectors that can be utilised as a single unit. A cluster is the smallest disk space that will be allocated to a file, no matter how small the file may be. There can only be one file in any one cluster, although one large file can span many clusters. A cluster is composed of one or more sectors.

The cluster size varies with the disk and its formatting. The actual number of sectors in a cluster depends on the type of disk. A table of typical examples is shown on the following table:

Filing system	Disk Size	Sectors/cluster	Cluster Size
FAT12	720kB 3.5" floppy	2	1,024
	1.44MB 3.5" floppy	1	512
FAT16	< 16M	8	4,096
	< 64M	2	1,024
	< 128M	4	2,048
	< 256M	8	4,096
	< 512M	16	8,192
	< 1GB	32	16,384
	< 2GB	64	32,768
FAT32	< 8GB	8	4,096
	< 16GB	16	8,192
	<32GB	32	16,384
	>=32GB	64	32,768
NTFS	Any size	1	512

There is a compromise between maximising read speeds and getting the maximum use of disk space. Large cluster sizes lead to faster access times and faster transfer times but it does waste disk space for smaller files. However, since many larger applications use large files both for programs and data, it makes sense to use larger cluster sizes in the larger capacity disks. Floppy disks always have very slow access times due to their design. Since speed is not the major factor for floppies, they can concentrate on storage efficiency. The 1.44MB disk, for example, only has a single sector as a cluster.

The clustering of sectors only occurs in the disk's data area - the directories and FATs are organised on an individual sector basis.

The larger the cluster size, the greater potential loss of disk space due to lost capacity in underused clusters. For example, a small batch file of 30 bytes consumes 512 bytes on a 3.5" HD disk - and as much as 32k on a large hard disk. Since a file is never likely to use exact multiples of the cluster size, it follows that there is quite a bit of wasted space on a disk. The DIR command only shows the amount of data stored in a file and does not give the actual amount of disk surface allocated to store the file.

Consider the illustration, which is for a hard disk with 32k clusters. The first two columns display the file names and extensions. The third column shows the file sizes as displayed when a DIR command is issued at the Command Prompt.

```
              Displayed   Space
                size      taken
AUTOEXEC BAT      482     32768
BACK     TXT      962     32768
BACKCHK  DAT       28     32768
COMMAND  COM    47845     65536
CONFIG   SYS      224     32768
FILELIST DOC     4880     32768
GETCHAR  COM       32     32768
HISCORES 3D       275     32768
MENU     BAT      572     32768
PCXLIST            57     32768
POWERPNT INI      414     32768
VGA_BIOS EXE    77133     98304
WORD     BAT       25     32768
               -------   -------
Totals         132,929   524,288
               -------   -------
```

According to the DIR report, the 13 files appear to consume 132,929 bytes of hard disk space and they appear to have an average file size of 10.2k.

In fact, they consume 524,288 bytes - a difference of over 291,000 bytes and the average file size is actually 40.3k.

The best case is the COMMAND.COM file, which produces very little waste. The file has been allocated 47,845 bytes and actually consumed 65,536 bytes, with 17,691 bytes being wasted. The worst case is the WORD.BAT file, which only uses 25 bytes of the 32,768 byte cluster.

Master Boot Record

The Master Boot Record comprises a single sector - sector 1 (i.e. side 0/track 0/sector 1).

The sector contains a partition table and other information.   A partition is a portion of the hard disk that appears, and can be treated as, a separate disk drive. Not only do partitions act like separate hard disks, they are allocated disk drives letters such as 'D', 'E', etc.

A partition is a set of contiguous tracks and a partition has to start on the first sector of a track and end on the last sector of a track.

A disk can have more than one partition and this may be adopted for a number of reasons:

- Through necessity if older OS versions are in use (see the earlier section on 'Maximum Disk Handling').
- For operational convenience (e.g. placing all applications in one partition and data in another partition).
- To allow completely different operating systems to reside in different partitions of the disk. Examples of this are:
    - Windows on one partition and UNIX on another partition.
    - Windows 2000 on one partition and Windows 95 on another partition.

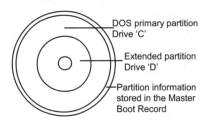

The actual disk surface would be configured to logically appear as several separate hard disks - disk drive 'C' would be supplemented by drive 'D', drive 'E' or even drive 'F', etc.

The Disk Management program (or *'FDISK'* in systems before Windows NT/XP) is the utility that creates disk partitions. After partitioning, each partition can be formatted to the layout for the particular operating system.

The partition table stores the location and length of each of the disk partitions.   There must always be a partition table, even if the disk contains only a single partition.   The number of partitions on a disk and the size of partitions can be later altered with the Disk Manager but, since this process destroys the data in partitions, a full backup would be undertaken before altering disk partitions.

Most OS's support up to 24 partitions (i.e. 'C' through to 'Z') but the partition table in the MBR can only store four entries.   To overcome this, disk partitioning tools allow the disk surface to be divided into one or more *'primary'* partitions and a single *'extended'* partition.   This uses four or fewer of the partition table's entries but the extended partition can then be further divided into many *'logical'* partitions, each with their own drive letter.   Typically the primary partition will be 'C', while extended partitions may be 'D' (unless it it already taken by another device such as a CD-ROM), 'E', 'F' etc . The logical drives do not appear in the MBR partition table, but they have their own boot record, file system and root directory.   As such, it functions as an independent disk drive and can be treated as such when it comes to formatting and ordinary disk read, write and copy activities.

Each partition will contain:

- A boot record, as explained below.
- File system information – such as a Master File Table (MFT) for an NTFS drive, or a File Allocation Table in a FAT16 or FAT32 drive.
- A directory structure for the files in that partition.
- The data area for that partition.

If a disk has more than one partition, then the above is repeated for each partition, although there will still only be one Master Boot Record with the disk's partition table. Where there is more than a single partition, the partition table stores a marker for the active partition. When the machine is booted up, the MBR contains a startup program that passes control to the boot program in the active partition.

Where a disk has more than one partition, the Boot Record is repeated at the start of each partition.

The diagram opposite illustrates the layout of a disk that is partitioned into three logical drives, two of which are on an extended partition.

The format of the Master Boot Record can be viewed with certain disk editing tools such as Norton's Utilities.

Boot Sector

The first sector of any FAT partition area is the Boot Sector, occasionally called the DOS Boot Record, or *'DBR'* – a legacy from older systems. This sector contains disk information and the code that is used along with IO.SYS and MSDOS.SYS to both cold boot and warm boot the machine. It contains a short machine-code program to load the operating system from disk to memory – assuming the disk is formatted and contains an operating system. The boot record is always created, even if the area is not formatted as a system disk. The boot

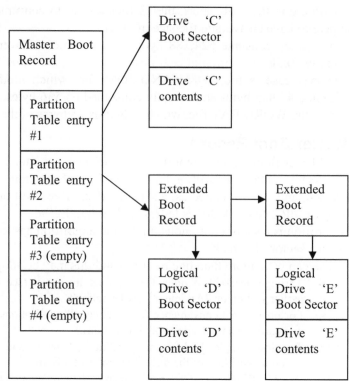

record also stores details of its own formatting - e.g. bytes/sector, sectors/track, etc. For a floppy, there is no master boot record, so the boot sector will be in sector 1 of track 0, side 0. If this sector were viewed with Norton Utilities, the first few lines of the screen dump would look like this for a 720k disk:

```
Side 0, Cylinder 0, Sector 1
EB3C904D 53444F53 352E3000 02010100 02E00040 0BF00900 ó<ÉMSDOS5.0.  etc
12000200 00000000
```

There is a three-byte offset followed by:
- Eight bytes containing the system ID
  (in this case the hex characters 49 42 4D 20 20 35 2E 30 representing the text 'IBM 5.0').
- Two bytes containing the number of bytes per sector (in this case 00 02; since Intel stores numbers in reverse order, this is 0200, which is 512).
- One byte containing the number of sectors per cluster (in this case 02).
- Two bytes containing the number of reserved sectors at the beginning
  (this is 01 00, or 1, for current-sized floppy disks).
- One byte containing the number of copies of the FAT (in this case 02).
- Two bytes containing the maximum number of root directory entries supported
  (in this case 70 00 , or 0070h which is 112).
- Two bytes containing the total number of sectors on the disk
  (in this case A0 05, or 05A0h, which is 1440).
- One byte containing the format ID
  (in this case F9 for 720k or 1.2M . A 360k floppy is ID FD,
  A 1.44MB disk is ID F0 while hard disks are ID type F8).
- Two bytes containing the number of sectors per FAT (in this case 03 00, or 3).
- Two bytes containing the number of sectors in each track (in this case 09 00, or 9).
- Two bytes containing the number of read/write heads (in this case 02 00, or 2).
- Two bytes containing the number of special reserved sectors (in this case 00 00, or zero).

Note:
The numbers are displayed in hexadecimal, or *'hex'*, a numeric system using the base of 16 rather than the decimal base 10. Numbers in any column start at 0 and rise to a value of 15. Since numbers above 9 cannot be shown as a single character, they are replaced by letters of the alphabet.

The number 10 is represented by the letter A, the number 11 by the letter B and so on up to 15 being represented by the letter F. The right-most column in a hexadecimal number is to the base 1, while the next column is to the base 16, the next to the base 256 and so on, incrementing by a factor of 16 in each column. To distinguish hexadecimal numbers from decimal numbers, the suffix 'h' is usually added to the number.

So 11h and 11 are different, 11h being 17d. In the example display above, the total number of sectors on the disk was 05A0. Starting from the right-most column the number can be calculated thus: 0 lots of 1 + ten lots of 16 + 5 lots of 256 = 0 + 160 + 1280 = 1440.

The comparative figures shown by Norton for a 1.4MB disk are:

Side 0, Cylinder 0, Sector 1
EB3C9049 424D2020 352E3000 02020100 027000A0 05F90300 ó<ÉIBM 5.0. etc
09000200 00000000

These are similar results to the 720k disk, with the exception of:

- the number of root directory entries allowed which is 00E0 or 15x16 = 240.
- the total sectors on the disk which is 0B40 or 11x256 + 4x16 = 2816+64 = 2880.

The comparative figures shown by Norton for a 210MB hard disk are:

Side 1, Cylinder 0, Sector 1
EB3C904D 53444F53 352E3000 02080100 02000200 00F8C900 ó<ÉMSDOS5.0. etc
24000C00 24000000

The main points to note are:
- There are 8 sectors per cluster.
- There are 0200h = 512 entries allowed in the root directory.
- There are 00C9h = 201 sectors storing the data for each FAT.
- There are 0024h = 36 sectors in every track.
- There are 00C0h = 12 read/write heads on the drive.

File Organisation

The FAT filing system handles file saves and file reads using a combination of the disk DIRECTORY and the disk FILE ALLOCATION TABLE (known as the 'FAT'). The disk Directory stores the list of the files on the disk along with file information such as creation date, etc. (the columns that are viewed when a DIR command is given). The FAT is a table with an entry for each cluster and is used to map the storage of files. Buffers are used to cache copies of the FAT and directory.

Directory

The File Directory is a table of all the files on the disk. A hard disk can accommodate 512 directories in the root directory and a 1.4MB floppy can store 224 entries. The DBR stores the number of directory entries that are allowed for a particular disk. Each directory entry is 32 bytes in length and stores information such as the file name, extension, size, attributes and time and date of creation, as shown in the table.

Purpose	Number of bytes
File Name	8
File Extension	3
File Attributes	1
Unused	10
Date Created/Last Updated	2
Time Created/Last Updated	2
First Cluster	2
File Size	4

The **filename** is allocated 8 bytes and the characters must be in upper case. The filename must contain at least one character and if the name is less than eight characters, then the entry is padded with space characters (i.e. ASCII character 32). If the first letter in the entry is a dot (2Eh) then the entry is for a sub-directory. If the second byte is also a dot, then the entry contains information on the parent directory of the current directory - the cluster number held in the entry points to the parent directory that calls it.

The **extension** is three bytes long and can consist of no characters at all. Again, any unused bytes are padded with spaces.

The **attributes** byte consists of eight individual bits, each containing separate information about the file. Each bit has the following meaning, if the bit is set to 1:

Bit 0 : the file is read-only (it cannot be modified or deleted).

Bit 1 : the file is hidden (it cannot be seen by DIR commands).

Bit 2 : the file is a system file (same as hidden).

Bit 3 : the entry is a volume label (it is the disk's volume label and must be in the root directory. The name and extension data can be combined, allowing a volume label of up to 11 characters.

Bit 4 : the entry is a sub-directory (it points to the sub-directory chain in the FAT - see later. The entry has no data in the file size field).

Bit 5 : the file will be used in an archiving program, such as BACKUP.

Bits 6 and 7 are unused.

So if a file has an attributes value of 23h or 35d, it means that bits 0,1 and 5 are set - so the file is a hidden, read-only file with the archive flag set.

The **time** data is stored in two bytes that record the time that the file was created or was last changed. The system uses a 24-hour clock. The value is valid to the nearest 2 seconds and is calculated thus:

Time value = hours x 2048 + mins x 32 + secs/2

So, a time of 22:31:12 would result in a value of 22 x 2048 + 31 x 32 + 12/2.

This results in a value of 46,054, which is B3E6h, and would be read in a utility as E6 B3.

The **date** is also stored in two bytes and stores the date that the file was created or was last altered. The value is calculated thus:

Date value = (current year - 1980) x 512 + current month x 32 + current day

So, the 15th October 1993 would be stored thus:

(1993 - 1980) x 512 + 10 x 32 + 15 = 6991 = 1B4Fh or 4F 1B on a sector editor.

The **first cluster** data points to the beginning of the file's allocation chain, as explained later.

The **file size** data is four bytes long and contains the size of the file.

All entries in a newly formatted disk have the first byte in the name set to 00. When a DEL, COPY, DIR, etc. command is given, the file system stops looking for files when it reaches a 00 first byte - knowing that there are no further files on the disk.

A directory entry for a file also includes the first cluster number on the disk that stores the file - this points to starting point in the FAT so that the rest of the file can be traced should the file require more than a single cluster.

Undeletion

When a file is erased in a FAT system, the first byte of the filename is set to E5h - all the other Directory information is left undisturbed. This ensures that the file is ignored in any file activities such as DIR and COPY, as files commencing with the E5h character are by-passed. The contents of the file are not deleted since this would involve needless extra time-consuming disk activity. If a new file to be written needs the space occupied by a deleted file, it can overwrite it at any time. Since the 'deleted' file's data is left intact, it can be easily recovered. If there has been no further file saves that have overwritten the deleted file's directory or FAT areas, a deleted file can be recovered. An 'unerase' utility, such as the MSDOS UNERASE command or certain disk tool utilities, can be used to search for filenames that begin with the E5h character. The rest of the filename is then presented to the user, who can type in the file's commencing letter. This letter is written back to the directory entry so that it replaces the E5h value. The file will again be recognised by DOS commands and is recovered.

Windows provides a 'recycle bin', so that files that are supposedly 'deleted' are actually moved to the bin for actual deletion at a later date. This is a more user-friendly way to restore deleted files, but once the file is actually deleted the UNDELETE program will not work due to Windows' use of long filenames. Other file recovery programs exist, however.

File Allocation Table

Commonly called the 'FAT', the table immediately follows the boot record. The disk space required to store the FAT depends on the size of the disk (e.g. a 1.4MB floppy needs 18 sectors to store its FAT, a 20MB AT disk needs 82 sectors and a 201MB disk requires 402 sectors).

Examples of the different disk sector layouts are:

Disk Type	System	Boot sector	FAT sectors	Directory sectors	Data sectors	Total sectors
720k	FAT12	1	6	7	1426	1440
1.4M	FAT12	1	18	14	2847	2880
201M	FAT16	1	402	32	411225	411660
500M	FAT16	1	489	32	1 million	1 million
20G	FAT32	1	39063	32	40 million	40 million
100G	FAT32	1	48829	32	200 million	200 million

The partition table is not included in the hard disk calculations. Since floppy disks only support a maximum of 4096 clusters, the FAT size is set at 12 bits, since 12 raised to the power of 2 is 4096. 12-bit tables are an inheritance from the days when disks were extremely small and all disk space was precious. With larger disks, 16-bit FATs are used, to allow up to 65,636 entries. FAT32 can theoretically store billions of FAT entries, but this is allowing for future increases in disk size and current disks do not use its full capabilities. The table contained in the FAT stores an entry for every cluster on the disk.

The value held in the FAT indicates whether that cluster is:

- Already in use (i.e. is storing user data).
- Free for use (i.e. can be used for storing a new file, or part of a new file).
- Marked as Unusable (i.e. there is a faulty sector in that cluster).

The possible values in the FAT are:

Purpose	Contents
In Use (part of a chain)	Another cluster number
In Use (end of a chain - EOF)	FFF8-FFFF
Free/Available	0000
Reserved	FFF0-FFF6
Bad Cluster (marked by FORMAT)	FFF7

With floppy disks, the value for unusable is FF0-FF7, while EOF values are in the range FF8-FFF. Like the directory area, the FAT values are set to 00 when the disk is first formatted. The first entry in the FAT is always the disk ID. This is F9 for a 720k or 1.2M floppy, FD for a 360k floppy, F0 for a 1.44MB floppy and F8 for a hard disk).

Reading a file

If a file is short, under 4k, it will only occupy a single cluster. In such a case, the cluster number stored in the directory entry points to the sole cluster of the program. However, most files are longer than 4k and would therefore occupy several, or many, clusters. The collection of clusters for that file is known as a 'chain' or 'allocation chain'. The start of the chain is the commencing cluster stored in the directory entry. In the example, this is cluster 77.

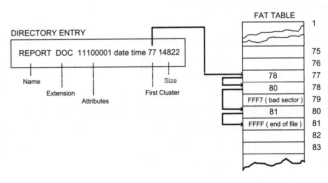

If entry 77 is examined in the FAT table, it will indicate whether any further clusters are required to be read for that file. For a small file of a single cluster, entry 77 would store the end of file marker - a value between FFF8 and FFFF. No further clusters are read.

For larger files, as in the example, entry 77 stores the location of the next cluster that comprises the file's chain (cluster 78).

Cluster 78, in turn stores the location of the third cluster in the file's chain. Notice that this is cluster 80, since cluster 79 was not written to due to it being a bad cluster. Cluster 80 then points to the fourth cluster of the chain. In fact, this is the <u>last</u> cluster of the chain, as indicated by end of file marker stored there.

The system continues to read data until the end of the chain is reached, or the data read equals the size of the file as stored in the directory.

Creating a file

When a <u>new</u> file is written to disk, its details are placed in the Directory, in the first unused entry. This may be a previously unused entry, or it may be overwriting an erased entry. The first FAT entry that is marked as free is used to store the first cluster of the file and two bytes of the directory entry are used to store this initial cluster location. If the file is small enough to fit in the single cluster, the FAT entry is set to FFFF, to indicate end-of-file. For larger files, the next free cluster is found, further user data is stored there and the contents of the initial cluster number in the FAT table are updated to point to this second cluster. This will continue until the entire file is stored - at which point the FAT entry for the last cluster to store that file's data is given the end-of-file value FFFF.

When the disk is formatted (or re-tested later with a utility), faulty sectors are isolated by placing the value FFF7 in the corresponding FAT entry. The file system will not allow any software to write to these clusters, when allocating new files.

Notes:

- Since the FAT is a central part of the entire disk operation, a second copy is also stored on the disk. Both copies are updated for each file write. The primary FAT is the working version used for reads; the secondary copy is used as a backup in the event of FAT corruption problems. When writing to a file, both FAT copies are updated; when reading files, only the main FAT is used.
- The CHKDSK command does not make good any difference in the two FATs, although add-ons, such as Norton Utilities can detect and repair any FAT damage.
- Scandisk (or CHKDSK in previous versions) only reports on the FAT entries that are already marking clusters as bad; it does not detect any newly faulty clusters, unless a 'disk surface scan' is chosen. This is not available in CHKDSK so a third-party product must be used with older systems.
- To save storage space, 12-bit FATs only occupy the FAT space that they actually require. For floppy disks, early small hard disks under 16MB and small partitions - in fact, any situation where there are fewer than 4096 clusters - the 12-bit code is used and occupies 1½ bytes. So, FAT entries are bunched into pairs with a pair occupying three bytes of the FAT. This improves storage at the expense of a more complex algorithm to extract the chain values from the FAT. This means that a user cannot directly examine a floppy disk's file chain by directly reading the values in the FAT. Fortunately, many utilities allow the FAT to be viewed directly with the conversion being carried out by the utility. With FAT-16 hard disks, the task is more direct, since the FAT entries are 16-bit. This means that each entry in the chain occupies a distinctive pair of bytes in the FAT and tracing of the chain is simplified.

Handling Sub-Directories

The above example was a simple case where all files resided in the root directory of the hard disk. In fact, most files will reside within sub-directories of the disk, to various layers of depth. This means that the sub-directories and their files must fit within the structure outlined above.

This is achieved by making a sub-directory an entry within the main root directory, similar to making an entry for a normal file. It will have a directory entry similar to a file directory entry. In this case, however, the *'Directory'* attribute is set to indicate that it is not a file. In this instance, the *'First Cluster'* stored in the directory entry points to a cluster similar to the layout in the diagram. The cluster holds information on the files in its directory in the same way they are stored in the root directory. The cluster stores all the normal date, time and size information.

It also stores the starting clusters of these files which can then have their chains traced in the usual manner, as previously described.

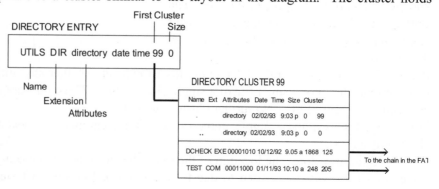

The first two entries in the directory cluster are the single dot and double dot that appear whenever a DIR command is issued in a sub-directory.

These are compulsory entries. The dot entry refers to the sub-directory itself and the double dot entry points to the parent sub-directory (i.e. the directory that called it).

At the first level down from the root, all sub-directories have a double dot entry with a cluster number of zero, to indicate that it was called from the root directory. If the cluster number is not zero, then the sub-directory is more than one level down from the root directory and it stores the cluster number of the sub-directory that is its parent.

A large hard disk with a 4096 byte cluster can hold a maximum of 128 entries, since each directory entry is 32 bytes long. The 128 entries may be a mixture of files and other sub-directories. When using smaller disks, or when requiring to store more than 128 files, a second or further directory clusters would be required to store all the additional entries. Where more than a single cluster is devoted to a sub directory, the FAT table is used to point to the next cluster in the sub-directory chain. With a single-cluster sub-directory, the FAT entry will store the end of file marker.

Note:

Since the files and directories in the root directory are created in purely chronological order, many hundreds of files will already be present in the root directory prior to some important directories being created. These directory entries appear well down the list of root directory entries. Should the sub-directory wish to be accessed, the whole directory must be sequentially searched until the sub-directory entry is found. This can slow down file accesses and it would improve matters if directories could appear further up the directory table. Fortunately, Norton has a utility called DS.EXE, which can re-write the directory so that sub-directories appear at the top of the table, prior to single files. The directories and files can be sorted into alphabet order or, if desired, the order of individual directories can be decided to allow the most-frequently accessed directories to appear at the top of the directory table.

FAT Problems

The FAT and directory are the parts of the disk that are continually read and written. Every time a file is created or modified, the directory and FAT entries are updated. Since these areas are the most used on the disk, they are most at risk of corruption through hardware, software or power problems.

These problems are rarely hardware faults. They are usually software glitches that have made rogue writes to the FAT, or users switching off the power before a program has completed its disk housekeeping, or users switching off the power to escape from a problem they don't understand. Most such faults can be detected and fixed using a disk checking program – see the 'PC Support' chapter for details.

Fragmentation

Often, a file is stored as one contiguous block of disk space.

However, files can end up occupying several non-contiguous areas of the disk when:

- An existing file is added to. Unless it is the last file in the FAT table (very unlikely), the extra data will have to be placed in the first free clusters.
- A new file is allocated the space of a smaller erased file. Again, the extra data is forced to overflow into a non-contiguous area of the hard disk.

The resultant diffusion of files across the disk can be viewed using the `disk map' facilities of Windows 'Disk Defragmenter', or a third party defragmentation utility. The continual movement of the head from one area of the disk to another slows data retrieval, by up to 25%.

Fragmentation can be overcome by backing up and restoring the disk, although this is a bit drastic. A better option is to use utilities such as 'Disk Defragmenter', , or a third party defragmentation utility. These re-order the allocations to achieve contiguous space for files. The result of defragmenting is to have each file occupying consecutive disk clusters. Defragmentation is covered in the 'PC Support' chapter.

Allocation Errors

The file's size is held in the directory entry. From this can be calculated the number of clusters that it ought to require to be stored. If a file's size indicates that it requires 4 clusters and CHKDSK detects a chain of 3 or 5 clusters it produces an *'allocation'* error message.

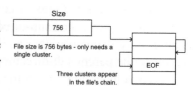

Invalid Cluster

Every chain in the FAT table ought to terminate in an end of file marker. If CHKDSK discovers that a chain terminates in a value of zero or a bad file marker, it will produce a *'file has invalid cluster'* message. CHKDSK will tidy up the situation by truncating the file. If the situation remains undetected, then the cluster will be used in a future file allocation. So two file chains will point to the same cluster (see the later section on cross-linked clusters).

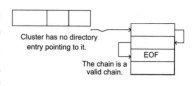

Lost Clusters

If the user aborts an application in the middle of a disk write operation, the application should complete the file activity before closing down. If the application is poorly written, or if there is a power glitch or the user has simply turned off the machine prematurely, the file activity may be halted before completion. Since the last act of a file write activity is the updating of the file's directory entry, the chain can end up written to disk without being pointed to by a directory entry. Other causes of *'lost clusters'* messages are applications that only partially delete their temporary files and programs that write directly to the directory and FAT areas.

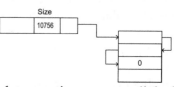

Every time a file is deleted, the Operating System should mark all the clusters in the chain as being free, thereby putting them back into the general pool for future file allocations. Anything that prevents these clusters being marked as free results in them being ignored in the allocation of future files - even although they are not being used to any good purpose.

Disk checking utilities, such as the 'Check Disk' tool that comes with Windows XP, drive might occasionally report 'lost allocation units' or 'lost clusters' when scanning a FAT, and provide the user an option to *"Convert lost chains to files"*. If the user decides not to, then the clusters in the chain are marked as free in the FAT table, to return them for further use. If the user opts to convert them, then the program attaches a directory entry to the chain. Since the original file name is not known, it will have a name like FILE0000.CHK, with any subsequent recovered files being titled FILE0001.CHK, FILE0002.CHK, etc.

The recovered files can be examined to see if the contents are usable. Often, the recovered file is a valueless temporary file or the file may be in machine code and therefore unreadable without a disassembler utility. However, text files may be examined and the file may be brought back into use and renamed if desired.

Cross-Linked Clusters

If the chains of two different files point to the same cluster, a *'cross-linked clusters'* message results. This is usually the result of clashes of software or disk hardware problems. Most operating systems do not have a utility to repair this situation. However, utilities, such as Norton's Disk Doctor, can carry out an intelligent repair. If there is no utility to hand, the only other method is to save the affected files with new names, delete the original affected files and then rename the files back to their original names. This is not usually fully successful and a file may end up with too much data or data loss.

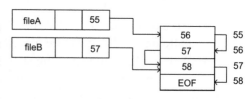

An examination of the recovered file's contents is possible if they happen to be text files; it takes a lot more skill to unscramble files containing machine code instructions. If at all possible, EXE, COM and overlay files that have been cross-linked should be replaced with the original files from the installation disks.

Directory Corruption

If the directory area becomes corrupted, the chains that comprise the files are still intact in the FAT area, but the directory entries no longer point to the start of the chains as they once did. If the user edits the directory with a disk editor such that the first cluster field contains 00, then the CHKDSK/F command will recover the file into a new file called FILE000.CHK and can then be renamed. In this way, the file is recovered without the need to carry out any intensive search of FAT chains.

Of course, if many files were corrupted, the above process would produce many files that would have to be interrogated, identified and renamed.   This might be an essential, if boring, task where a data file has no backup copy.

In the case of application files, it is much quicker to simply re-install the application.

WINDOWS 95/98/ME

Windows 95, 98 and ME reorganise the old file structure to provide the following benefits:

- Supports large partitions (Not in Windows 95 Release 1).
- Minimises disk wastage by using small cluster sizes (Not in Windows 95 Release 1).
- Supports long filenames.

FAT32

With Windows 95 Release 2 (OSR2) onwards, the filing system FAT32 was introduced, as distinct from the 16-bit FAT16 that hard disks use with DOS, Windows 3.1 and Windows 95 Release 1.

The earlier chart showed the makeup of a 32-byte directory entry.   Two bytes were allocated to point to the starting cluster of a chain.   16 bits can only store up to 65,536 different numbers making that the maximum number of clusters for a disk of even the biggest size. This means that an 8GB disk would have

to use clusters of 128k (i.e. 8GB/65536) and a 32GB disk would require a cluster size of 512k. This means that a small batch file of 100 bytes would occupy a 0.5M of disk space!

Max Disk Size	Sectors /cluster	Cluster Size
< 8G	8	4096
< 16G	16	8192
< 32GB	32	16384
> 32GB	64	32768

FAT32 future proofs the computer by using two of the ten 'reserved' bytes in the Directory to provide a four-byte address for clusters.   A 32-bit location can store four thousand million different numbers; this allows the maximum size of a disk to be 4G x 512 bytes - i.e. 2 Terabytes.   It also means that the size of a cluster could be theoretically reduced to a single sector.

To minimise the size of the disk's two FAT areas, a compromise minimum cluster size of 4k is the minimum used.   FAT16 and FAT32 are incompatible, so if a FAT32 computer were booted with a floppy using FAT16, the FAT32 disk would not be readable.   Fortunately, FAT16 layouts can be converted to FAT32.

The Drive Converter supplied with Windows 98 and ME, which is accessed through the System Tools folder of the Start Menu, can convert FAT16 partitions into FAT32 partitions, but is unable to reverse this process.

Long Filenames

One of the benefits in Windows 95 and later, is having file names up to 255 characters in length, accept spaces and full stops, allow upper and lower case - and still remain backwards compatible with DOS and Windows 3.1.   When upgrading Windows, there is no need to re-format the disks as the long filenames can be integrated into the existing Directory and FAT structures.   The older files continue to use the storage methods described earlier, while newer versions of Windows files use extensions to the existing system to provide both 8.3 and long file name versions of files that it stores.

The 32 byte Directory entry described earlier remains in use under Windows.   This only provides for eleven characters for the file name.   This cannot be increased without making the file structure incompatible with DOS and Windows 3.1.

The solution lies in the attribute byte, shown in the diagram.   The purpose of each bit in the byte is explained earlier. There is no occasion when the first four bits are all set at the same time (i.e. the directory entry cannot be both a volume label and a system file).

REPORT.XLS

| REPORT | XLS | ? | Time | Date | Cluster | File Size |

Microsoft takes advantage for long filenames by setting the first four bits (i.e. the byte stores the value 15 or 0Fh). DOS and older Windows applications do not test for this and therefore only see the traditional 8.3 file format. Windows applications and utilities check for the attribute byte being set to 0Fh and detect that a long file name is present. It then uses a chain of LFN (long filename) directory entries, each entry storing another part of the name; this works as an altered version of sub-directories as explained earlier.

Expenditure 98.XLS

| EXPEND~1 | XLS | 0F | Time | Date | Cluster | File Size |

Since DOS and older Windows applications require the traditional file naming, the long name is truncated to six letters, a tilde sign and a number as shown in the example. Traditional 8:3 filenames are unaffected. Where a file's first six characters are identical to another file, the number at the end of the file name is incremented.

Long File Name	Truncated File Name
REPORT.DOC	REPORT.DOC
Minutes of October	MINUTE~1
Minutes of November	MINUTE~2

Many of the older utilities were designed to run at a low level and do not understand the mechanisms being used by newer Windows versions. Consequently, they cannot be used and newer versions of disk utilities have to be purchased. Microsoft's Disk Defragmenter and ScanDisk utilities, as supplied with Windows 95/98, understand the new structure and are safe to use.

A problem technicians might experience with FAT32 drives is that older System Disks and alternative operating systems may not recognise FAT32 partitions. It is very easy to forget that a machine has a FAT32 partition and then wonder why the partition cannot be seen when the PC has been booted from a System Disk for diagnostic purposes.

NTFS

This is the native File System for Windows NT and is also used in Windows 2000/XP, which is NT based. NTFS is in turn based on the HPFS filing system used in IBM's OS/2 operating system, which is no longer produced. It is from HPFS that NTFS gets most of its capabilities. For example, both systems support filenames up to a maximum of 256 bytes, but NTFS partitions can be up to a maximum of 16 EB or ExaBytes, (i.e. 2^{64} bytes or 17,179,869,184 Gigabytes). It is estimated that all of the words ever spoken by every human being throughout all of history would occupy 5EB of storage. Furthermore, where the performance of FAT and its derivatives degrades as the partition size gets bigger, NTFS's performance is the same on a huge disk as it is on a tiny one. NTFS has also increased security and networking support, and a set of security permissions much more like UNIX's, as befits a system designed for deployment on servers. Other operating systems, including DOS, Windows 3.1, 95 and 98 cannot read NTFS partitions, so a machine with an NTFS partition that is booted from a floppy will look like it has no hard disk. Windows 2000, however, supports both NTFS and FAT 32, NTFS being the recommended file system. It is not possible to make an NTFS floppy disk.

The internals of an NTFS partition are very different from those of a FAT partition. The NTFS partition is listed in the Master Boot Record and Partition Table, as outlined above, and it does have a Volume Boot Record (VBR) just like its FAT cousins. However, the VBR's format is radically different and is principally just a pointer to the first record in the partition's structure (the MFT). The NTFS partition is built around a unit called a *'Master File Table'* or MFT. Where FAT contains a set of pointers or cluster references, an MFT holds much more information about the files and directories that are its concern. Indeed, for smaller files or directories the MFT can even contain the data!

The first record in the partition's MFT is called the *'descriptor'*, and it contains details of the MFT itself. The second is an identical copy of the Descriptor, which (like in FAT) means that faults can be remedied. The third record in the MFT is a log file record. It is an NTFS file that contains a log of file system transactions. This can be used to restore the file in case of mishap. The rest of the MFT contains records for all the files and directories on the partition. NTFS files and directories are *'Objects'* that have both user-defined and system-defined *'attributes'*. The contents of the file are a user-defined attribute. Whereas FAT has directories that contain information like size, date, and RASH attributes these travel inside the MFT record along with the other attributes and the data itself. Directories in NTFS are just sets of pointers to MFT records, nothing more, because all the attributes can be read from the MFT record along with the data.   If the data is less than 1500 bytes, it is stored completely in the MFT record. If it exceeds 1500 bytes, the MFT record holds a list of pointers to other clusters that are called *'extents'*. Any record in the MFT, including the descriptors and the log file, can use extents to store extra attributes.   Where attributes are stored as part of the MFT record they are referred to as resident attributes, where they are stored on an extent they are called non-resident attributes.

When a data file contains information from another file then that data will be added in an *'extent'* which is entered in the original files MFT record and referred to as a *'stream'*. This can be used to make data move transparently. Thus, a word processor document that contains a spreadsheet will do so in another stream that exists on an extent of the word processor files MFT record.   To give a concrete example, a file can be saved as c:\myfile.txt. By then opening c:\myfile.txt:secret, another stream has been opened to put data in. This is stored and carried between NTFS partitions transparently. No indication will exist that the secret part of the file exists.

Initialising a Disk

Disk drives fitted in new computers are supplied pre-formatted.   If not, the disk has to be initialised before use. In addition, there are occasions when the best solution to surface problems is to be clean the disk back to scratch.   This involves:
- Low level formatting
- Partitioning
- High level formatting

Any files on the hard disk are destroyed by the formatting/partitioning process and must be backed up before the process is started.   However, if Partition Magic or similar programs are used, then non-destructive partitioning can be carried out and partition sizes can be re-allocated without loss of existing disk contents.   Without these utilities, an archive would need to be created to temporarily store the files, which would be restored later onto the formatted disk.

Low Level Formatting

Low Level Formatting routines create the gaps between the disk's tracks and sector and write the sector IDs. All new IDE and SCSI disks are supplied pre-formatted and only require a low-level format under exceptional circumstances.   The manufacturers recommend against this practice.   The routines for low-level formatting are usually tucked away and are accessed in one of three ways:
- Via a hard disk drive utility supplied with the drive or *'Disk Manager'* by Ontrack.
  Used in IDE and EIDE systems.
- Via a BIOS routine called from the setup menu offered during bootup. Used with SCSI drives.
- Via a BIOS routine called via DEBUG.   Used in some old systems.
  Run DEBUG and at the minus sign prompt enter G=C800:5 or G=CC00:5 or the address given in the disk controller manual.   This displays a menu allowing the low level formatting of the disk.

Partitioning

Creating partitions is achieved using software tools such as the Disk Management tool in the Administrative Tools found in the Control Panel, or during OS installation.   The illustration shows the Disk Management tool.

Note that only one partition can be *'active'* at any one time and some Operating Systems expect to be installed on the primary partition.

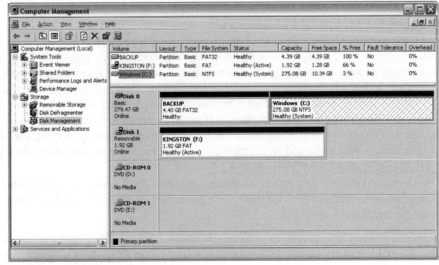

Partitioning Steps

The steps involved in partitioning a drive are:

- Delete any previous disk partitions, by right-clicking on the partition you wish to remove and selecting '*Delete Partition*'. Note of course that you cannot delete the partition on which the current Operating System is installed.
- Create a new partition, by right-clicking on the 'Unallocated' space on the appropriate drive and selecting '*New Partition*'. The 'New Partition Wizard' will pop up. Click '*Next*'.
- Select whether to make the new partition a Primary or Extended, and click '*Next*'.
- If you wish to create a Primary partition, the next few pages will ask you to select how much of the available space you wish to allocate; which drive letter to assign to the new partition; and whether to format it immediately.
- On the other hand, if you wish to create an Extended partition, you will only be asked how much space to allocate to it.
- Click '*Finish*'.

To create a new logical drive within an extended partition:

- Right-click on the extended partition and select '*New Logical Drive*'. The wizard will appear again. Click '*Next*'.
- '*Logical Drive*' should be selected. Click '*Next*'.
- Select how much space to allocate to this logical drive; which drive letter to assign; and whether to format it immediately. Click '*Finish*'.

High Level Formatting

Once a partition is created, the drive(s) on that partition must be formatted before they can be used. The Disk Management tool allows you to format as part of the partitioning process, or it can be done at a later date. Note: Formatting a floppy disk performs both a low-level and high-level format.

Protecting Files

Computers are susceptible to temperature extremes, power cuts or fluctuations and magnetic fields. This can lead to a sudden machine breakdown and the collapse of the program it is running. Worse still, it can lead to the loss or corruption of important data. In most organisations, the data held in the machine is more important than the machine itself. Replacing a faulty hard disk is simple and relatively inexpensive. However, if large amounts of data are lost, then countless person-hours are required to replace this data. In many cases, the data can be reconstituted from paperwork (e.g. customer forms, order forms, etc.). In other cases, the data has no paperwork equivalent (e.g. telephone orders or data that was automatically gathered in real time from remote stations) and this can be lost forever.

Despite all efforts to achieve reliability, these losses remain a distinct possibility. The only defence is to ensure that important data is copied away at regular intervals, thus creating backup copies. In the event of machine failure and data loss, the user can reconstitute the data using the backup version. See the Computer Security chapter for more details.

Compression Utilities

There are two main reasons for compressing files:

TO STORE DATA MORE EFFICIENTLY

> With the ever-increasing size of application packages, particularly Windows products, there is an inescapable rule of computing that says, *"no matter how big your hard disk is, it's not big enough"*. The 8GB disk that was meant to solve all storage problems rapidly fills up and the previous 1GB system looks decidedly small. The room full of 40MB machines is relegated to running older applications with the hope of a future upgrade. To relieve storage problems, software houses proposed an alternative approach. Instead of making bigger disks, the files could be made smaller! If certain applications or data are used infrequently, they can be stored in a sub-directory in compressed form. When they require to be used, the files can be decompressed. Files storing video, audio and large graphics would be too large to store unless they were compressed.

TO TRANSMIT DATA MORE QUICKLY

> The increased use of data communications, including the Internet, has demanded ever-improving methods of compression to reduce download times. If a file is half its original size, it will only take half the time to transmit over the telephone network.

Compression does not create new files. It takes existing files and packages them in a more compact form. The files cannot be used without first being restored to their original form. They are only stored or transmitted in a compressed format; they have to be used in their original format. Some utilities require the user to carry out the decompression before using the file. Other utilities make the process invisible to the user who is completely unaware that compression and decompression are taking place.

Compression can work at one of two levels:
- On an individual file, or group of files, basis, such as PKZIP or LHA.
- On an entire disk basis, such as with Stacker, SuperStor or Windows DriveSpace.

File Compression

ARC and ZOO were early compression utilities and are still in use. PKZIP is currently the most-commonly-used file compressor program. These are all shareware programs. Other shareware utilities include LHA (which uses .LZH files), SLIM, PAK and ARJ. Some use a *'lossy'* algorithm; it sacrifices some tiny details for increased space savings. This is acceptable for graphics or sound files, whereas other data files and program files require being stored with absolute accuracy. Absolutely accurate reproduction requires *'loss-free'* algorithms. Most files, whether programs or data files, contain a large amount of repetitious and redundant information. If the storage of this information is re-organised, vast savings can be made, dependent on the file's format. Some graphics file formats, for example, are already stored in a compressed form and these will produce poorer results than plain ASCII files.

The table shows some typical compression results:

File used	Original size	Compressed Size	Program used	Percentage saved
CONTROL.HLP (in Windows)	121,672	87,028	PKZIP	29%
MONEY.CS (in Visual Studio)	46,225	11,081	PKZIP	77%
NEWMACRO.DOC (in Word)	110,383	43,007	PKZIP	62%
NETWORK.BMP (digitised image)	1,146,880	49,152	Converted to JPEG in Paint Shop Pro	96%
SONG.WAV (digitised music)	34,178k	3,100k	MP3 encoder	91%

These results are achieved by attacking the file's areas of repetitious data. Consider, for example, a graphics file that has large areas of blue background. Instead of storing every blue pixel separately, the area could be stored as *'5000 pixels of blue'*. This is called *'Run Length Encoding'*, or RLE. When decompressed again, the coded information restores 5000 separate elements of pixel data.

If a file is compressed with a particular utility, it has to be uncompressed by the same utility, since different utilities use different algorithms to achieve compression / decompression.

There are only three or four compression algorithms and utilities use variations on these. The PKZIP and ARC utilities use the LZW (Lempel-Ziv-Welch) algorithm, while others uses a form of Huffman coding to produce JPEG files.

The LZW method requires that a table be created, which places different strings from the file in different elements of the table. So, element 400, for example, would represent a particular string in the file being compressed. The code 400 can now replace every other occurrence of the string in the entire file. The string could be an English word within document files, or a run of pixels in graphics files. As the file is compressed, the table is filled up and is used as reference to replace strings with shorter codes in the compressed version. When de-compressing, each occurrence of the code in the compressed file results in the actual string being retrieved from the lookup table and being restored in the decompressed version. In this way, the original file is reconstructed with no losses. The V42bis standard for modem data compression uses BTLZ, a British Telecom variety of the Lempel-Ziv algorithm.

Facilities
- To simplify the storage and manipulation of compressed files, most utilities can compile a set of files into one single compressed file.
- To automate file decompression, some utilities create a self-expanding file. The file, or files, is compressed into a single file which then has the decompression utility embedded into the file. This creates a single .EXE file which, when called, runs the decompression code and reconstructs the individual files. It should be noted, however, that the sub-directory would still hold the .EXE file in addition to the decompressed file(s). This can occupy substantial extra disk space if not deleted.
- The compression of a group of files into a single file also simplifies downloading. It is often used in application packages' distribution disks, with the ARC or CAB format (as used by Microsoft).

Disk Compression

Rather than tackling compression at a file level, some techniques address the disk as a whole. They concern themselves with *'disk compression'* rather than *'file compression'*. These utilities are often known as *'disk doublers'*, since they can make the hard disk store up to twice as much data as before. To achieve this, the files on the disk are compressed and decompressed *'on the fly'*. This means that files are compressed before being saved to disk and decompressed when read from disk. This happens in real time, hence the expression *'on the fly'*. With file compressors, the individual files remained as normal files and could be copied in their compressed state. With disk compressors, this is not possible due to the way that the files are stored.

In the past, separate compression software was needed in order to compress an entire drive. Windows 95 introduced '*DriveSpace*', but it was not compatible with FAT32. Modern Windows versions have compression built in to the device manager; simply right-click on the drive, select 'Properties' and the option will be available to compress the drive.

An example of a disk compression method is as follows. The disk is effectively sectioned into two. The smaller section is the normal section on which the machine will boot up; it contains some system files including configuration files and the CONFIG.SYS and AUTOEXEC.BAT files. A huge hidden file within the partition is used as the store for the compressed files. This much larger section is called the CVF (compressed volume file) by the compression utitity, and is named as DRVSPACE.000. To keep the process invisible to the user, the utility then swaps round the 'C' drive and the 'D' drive. This means that when the machine is booted up, the system is configured from the normal partition (i.e. the <u>actual</u> 'C' drive) and then the compressed section is presented to the user as the logical 'C' drive. The normal section can still be accessed as the 'D' drive.

There is no need to format or partition the disk to achieve this; the task of creating these sections is carried out by the utility's installation program. The installation creates, in effect, an extra drive within a drive complete with its own file system.

With disk compressors, calls to the disk routines are trapped by the extra software layer sitting between the Operating System and the disk controller and the data is compressed before being written, or decompressed after being read. Buffers are used to hold the data while it is being processed. As far as DOS is concerned, it is dealing with a perfectly ordinary disk drive; the driver presents the compressed section as an extra logical disk drive, e.g. drive 'D'.

Since the utility is hardware-independent, it can be used with a range of storage devices.
It will work with floppy disks, ZIP disks, optical drives and even RAM drives. The drive types used can be IDE, EIDE, SCSI, or others.

If an existing disk is to be compressed, the installation will also involve an initial compression of all files already on the disk. If an old machine is fitted with a 500MB or 800MB hard disk, the cost of installing a disk compressor is not economic, given the rapid fall in hard disk prices.

Large capacity removable disks

There is a phenomenal growth in mass-storage devices such as CD-ROM and floptical disks. These are now widely available in the commercial and home market and the forecast is for continuing future growth. The read-only versions are used to hold application packages, databases, educational encyclopaedias, clip art collections and PC support information. Increasingly, programs are being freely distributed in a demonstration format so that users can test the package's abilities. The entire program is already on the CD and a user can call the distributor to purchase the package by credit card. The user is then given a password code to allow them to access the entire package. All the above programs or data are written permanently at the manufacturing stage and cannot be altered by the user.

The WORM drive (write-once read many) is also used for archiving company audit material; the data is written to disk and cannot be altered thereafter. This is usually in CD-R format and provides a secure method of mass storing information than was previously committed to microfiche. There are also two types of device that can be user modified. The new generation of rewriteable CD-ROMs and MO disks (large capacity floppy disks) use magneto-optical systems that allow the data on the disks to be modified.

CD-ROM

The simplified diagram shows the basic layout of a side view of a section of a CD-ROM disk.   The plastic disk has an embossed surface consisting of areas of normal thickness ('lands' or 'hills') and sunken areas ('pits').   The disks are stamped out from a master disk. After the high initial costs of creating the master disk, individual CDs can be stamped out very cheaply as can be seen by the number of computer magazines that include free CDs of shareware and program demonstrations.   The changes of height along the track represent the data on the disk, although the coding method is more complex than the simple storage of the data's 1's and 0's. The top surface of the disk is coated with a layer of reflective aluminium (the shaded area of the diagram) and this is covered with a protective plastic layer; the total disk thickness is 1.2mm.   Pressed CD-ROMs are known as 'silver disks' due to the colour of the aluminium used.

The disk is read from its underside by firing a laser beam at the revolving surface.   The beam reflects from the aluminium coating and is diverted to a photo sensor by a prism.   The normal depth areas - the 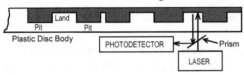 'lands' - reflect back most of the laser beam while the 'pitted' areas scatter the beam as shown in the diagram.   So, the photo sensor will detect different reflected strengths from the two different surface areas.   The laser beam passes through focusing lenses so that the beam is a tiny spot at the point of contact with the disk surface.

The spot is only 1 micron in size - one millionth of a metre. This means that much more data can be packed on to the disk surface compared to standard magnetising methods. This explains the ability to pack up to 650MB of data on to a single disk. Since the head does not require being close to the disk surface, it does not suffer the risk of head crashes associated with normal floppy and hard disks.

The disk contains only a single track, organised as single spiral similar to a long-playing record, except that the disk is read from the centre outwards.   The laser, prism, lenses and photodetector are all enclosed in a single unit that is moved between the inner and outer parts of the spiral. It is the equivalent of the ordinary read/write head of a hard disk. Reaching a wanted sector requires the head to be moved to the approximate location on the spiral track.   The head then follows the track until it reaches a sector header; this header information is then used to locate the wanted sector.

Although CDs use a number of error detection and correction techniques, they should still be handled with care. Grease from a fingerprint diffuses the laser beam while surface scratches deflect the beam.

Disk Organisation

The disk is 120mm in diameter with a 15mm hole is punched in the centre. A 6mm area of the surface, next to the hole, is used by the drive mechanism to clamp the disk while rotating. The next 4mm area is used to store information regarding the disk's contents; this is known as the VTOC (volume table of contents). The data area width is 33mm and comprises a single track spiralling outward about 20,000 times and totalling around 3 miles in length. The outer area of 3mm is used for handling the disk.

```
centre hole
table of contents
handling area
data area
clamping area
```

Most CDs have a 2352 bytes sector size of which 2k or over is used for data and the remaining bytes for error-detection and synchronisation information.

Hard disks specify a particular disk area in terms of track and sector.
CD-ROMs, showing their origins as audio disks, specify areas in terms of minutes, seconds, and sectors within each second.

Thus, a 74 minute CD has a capacity of
74 x 60(secs) x 75(sectors) x 2k = 650MB of user data area.

A single-speed drive reads 75 of these sectors per second, giving a transfer rate of 150kB/s.   A double-speed drive reads 150 sectors/sec while a 52x drive reads 2400 sectors/sec, giving transfer rates of 300kB/s and 7800kB/s respectively.   The original single speed model spins at 300rpm and other models are multiples of this - i.e. a quad speed rotates at 1200 rpm and a 52x rotates at 15,600rpm.

There are several methods of organising and accessing data on the disk:

CLV - Constant Linear Velocity.

This was the most common method and is that used with audio CDs and many computer CD disks. All disk sectors are of identical length. The outer spirals on the surface are longer than inner spirals and can store more sectors per spiral than those closer to the centre. The disk is consequently spun slower when reading outer tracks compared to inner tracks. A 4x drive may spin at over 2100 rpm on inner tracks and only 800rpm on outer tracks. This system achieves the same amount of data read per second, no matter where on the disk the data is stored. A good quality motor is required to cope with the constantly changing rotational speed.

CAV - Constant Angular Velocity - also known as Full CAV.

It is currently used in hard and floppy drives. The disk motor rotates at a constant speed making it easy to manufacture. The outer spirals store fewer sectors per inch than inner spirals, resulting in each spiral storing the same number of sectors. Consequently, CAV drives transfer the same amount of information for every revolution, regardless of the head position.

CAV technology is increasingly adopted by CD drive manufacturers for reading disks. The writing of CD disks still uses CLV techniques, storing more data on outer spirals.

Since the CAV motor spins at a constant speed, more data per second is read from outer spirals than inner spirals. This explains why a CAV CD drive may be described as being a *'20/40x'* model. The innermost spiral reads at 20x speed while the outermost spiral reads at 40x speed. The top data transfer rate only occurs at the outermost spirals. CDs are written from the inner spiral outwards and many CDs do not fill all the available disk capacity. As a result, the average performance of a CAV CD drive is nowhere near the maximum rating.

CAV drives have faster access times than CLV models since they do not suffer delays while the motor speed changes between inner and outer spirals. Pioneer, for example, claim that their 10x has a 65ms access time in CAV mode compared to around 150ms for CLV models.

PCAV - Partial Constant Angular Velocity.

Many CD drives are now a CLV/CAV hybrid, using CLV (i.e. changing speeds) on the outer tracks and CAV (i.e. constant speeds) on the inner tracks.

CD-ROM Performance

The performance of CD-ROM is determined by the following factors:

- The access time of the drive.

  These times vary from 65ms to 100ms for newer models and 350ms to 900ms for older models. Compared to hard disk speeds, these are very slow times. That is because there is one single continuous spiral track. The read head cannot first go to the exact track and wait for the wanted sector to come round. It has to make an approximation to the correct distance in, then wait for the first sector header to tell the system where the head is positioned. It then makes a second seek to get to the correct position. This slows down the sector access times.

- The data transfer rate of the drive.

  The most common rates are:

Data Rate	Description	Data Rate	Description
150kBs	single-speed	1500kBs	10x
300kBs	double-speed or 2x	2400kBs	16x
450kBs	triple-speed or 3x	4800kBs	32x
600kBs	quad speed or 4x	7200kBs	48x
1200kBs	8x	7800kBs	52x

  These figures do not give a complete picture since a quad speed drive will not provide double the throughput of a double speed, and so on.

  This is for a number of reasons:

  - The higher transfer rates only apply to long sequential reads. If the head has to make a number of random access seeks, the faster transfers are offset by the substantial individual access times. The result is an average figure somewhat less than the performance suggested by the 8x, 10x, 24x, ratings.
  - With CLV models, there is an additional time delay while the motor changes speed when moving between inner and outer tracks.
  - For the same reasons above, the sustained data rate shows up better with bigger files.
  - AVI video files are often created to run at double speed and drives with faster rates have to work at the slower rate to be compatible with the data being presented.

- The detection and elimination of read errors. Errors occur due to slight imperfections in the boundaries of cells or from fingerprints or scratches obscuring the data read. For small data losses, the error detection system also has an error correction system that alters the read data to the original information. This is an improvement on normal disks and provides a more secure storage medium.
- The size of the drive's buffers. The current drives cache sizes vary from 16k to 1024k, mostly available in 128k or 256k. The cache size can have a significant influence on the smooth flow of multimedia content. Memory used for disk caching can be used to gain a reasonably useful improvement in CD-ROM performance.

Practical notes

- CD drives are available as internal and external models.
- With some models, the disk is placed in a plastic caddy for extra protection from scratching or dust. This case is then placed into the CD drive for use. A slider on the underneath of the caddy is then moved aside, in the same manner as that of a 3.5" disk, to reveal the recorded surface. Other models simply require the disk to be placed in a tray like audio CD players or placed in a top loader.
- Four different interfaces can be used to connect the CD to the computer. Some older models use a connection from a SoundBlaster Card or other sound card; these have the required circuitry to control the CD-ROM. Other older systems connected to a special proprietary interface card. Most modern systems connect to the IDE or the faster EIDE (known as *'ATAPI'- Attach Packet Interface*) interface. Faster still is the SCSI interface. This is also a cheap option if a SCSI card is already in use for the hard disk. External models use USB or SCSI connections to the computer.
- For DOS Startup Disks, the hardware requires two drivers - the hardware-specific driver supplied with the particular CD (although a generic CD driver is typically used) and MSCDEX.EXE, the Microsoft CD-ROM Extensions for DOS. The first driver is installed via CONFIG.SYS and the other is installed via AUTOEXEC.BAT. The MSCDEX utility is a TSR that reads the standard ISO 9660 CD disks (i.e. it makes CD files look like normal files); it also provides audio support. The equivalent in Windows 95 onwards is the 32-bit CDFS driver.
- Front panel features include the volume control, headphone socket, activity light and disk eject button.
- Dust protection is improved through double door mechanisms, unit seals and automatic lens cleaning systems.

CD Standards

Many of the standards are named after the colour of cover used to report on the new standard. So, the standard for audio on CD became known as the Red Book standard because it had a red cover.

Standard	Purpose
Red Book	Audio CDs
Yellow Book	Computer data (e.g. application installation CDs)
Green Book	CD-Interactive applications, games and, entertainment
White Book	Video CDs
Blue Book	Music CDs with text
Orange Book & Purple Book	Recordable CDs
Photo CD	Kodak's multi-session picture storage

ISO 9660

Often known as *'High Sierra'*, since it was first discussed in the High Sierra Hotel in Nevada in 1985. By 1987, a superset of High Sierra, known as ISO 9600, was agreed as the common standard for computer CD-ROMs.

All drives conform to this standard for handling files and directories, with different drivers to allow the standard to work with PCs, Macintosh computer and Unix systems. The PCs version is implemented with the MSCDEX or CDFS driver software.

Red Book

Established in 1980, it is also known as CD-DA (Digital Audio). The *'Red Book'* standard was the first of the series and defined the specification for the audio CD currently in use. It specified that the audio would be stored in digital format and be subject to error detection and correction. Each sector stores 1/75th of a second of digitised audio and occupies 2352 bytes. Data is stored as uncompressed Pulse Code Modulated (PCM) samples, in stereom with 16-bit audio depth, and with a sampling rate of 44.1KHz and a theoretical maximum of 74 minutes of audio per disk. It can handle 99 audio tracks and its TOC stores the starting point of each track (measured in minutes, seconds and sectors).

At 44.1KHz (i.e. 44,100 samples per second), and two channels (stereo) of two bytes each (16 bit audio) that means 176,400 bytes of data per second of audio.

The standard also specifies that audio data is to be stored in sectors each containing 1/75th of a second of digitised audio. Therefore, each sector (also sometimes called a *'large frame'*) contains 1/75th of 176,400 bytes, or 2532 bytes. This is further split into 98 frames of 24 bytes each. Since each sector stores 1/75th of a second, a full 74-minute CD stores 783,216,000 bytes of audio, or nearly 747MB. Finally, the Red Book standard allows for 99 audio tracks per CD, with the disc's TOC (Table Of Contents) containing the starting point of each track.

Since Red Book is an audio standard, measurements are normally expressed in terms of minutes, seconds and sectors. Nearly all common CD standards are built upon the Red Book as a basis, and it is therefore not uncommon for other standards to refer to minutes or seconds of storage space rather than kilobytes or megabytes.

The Red Book audio specification includes a number of error detection and correction techniques. One form of error detection is called *Cross-Interleaved Reed-Solomon Code* (CIRC), and is often able to fix several bad frames in any sector. A method of error correction involves the insertion of sound values interpolated between surrounding values or repeated from the previous value. A single error corrected this way will not be noticed because individual frames contain less than a thousandth of a second of sound each.

In addition to the normal audio data in a Red Book CD, there are additional bits that normally remain hidden to the user, and which are only available in Red Book CDs. Most of these contain the error detection and correction data mentioned above, but there are also 8 bits per frame that can sometimes be accessed for use. These are called *'subchannels'* and are assigned letters from P through W.

- The 'P' subchannel is used to indicate the beginning of each track.
- The 'Q' subchannel is where the Table Of Contents is stored during the Lead-in, and gives time information during the music tracks. In addition to being available only to Red Book CDs, the 'P' and 'Q' subchannels are only available to the CD producer when the disc is created in Disc-At-Once mode.
- The 'R through W' subchannel (The remaining 6 subchannels are combined because they are used for the same data) can store additional information such as graphics or MIDI information. These discs are sometimes referred to as CD+G (Graphics) and CD+MIDI discs, but are uncommon.

Philips and Sony introduced the "Scarlet Book" format in 1999 as a range of alternatives to the standard Red Book format. Red Book stores audio data in uncompressed format while Scarlet Book uses lossless compression to reduce the file size and therefore allow six channel sound. The format envisages single layer and multi-layer disks.

Yellow Book

The *'Yellow Book'* standard of 1985 defined the computer data CD specification that is now commonly described simply as CD-ROM. This standard is really a storage medium with improved error correction and has three modes:

Mode 1 uses a maximum disk capacity of 650MB to store computer data. It uses the same 2352 byte sector size as Red Book but uses 2k of each sector for data with the remaining bytes being used for synchronisation and error correction codes.

The usable capacity is calculated thus:

sector size x sectors per second x seconds per minute x disk capacity in minutes

The answer is divided by 1024 (to get answer in KB) and then divided once more by 1024 (to get the answer in MB)

In this case the answer is 2352 x 75 x 60 x 74 /1024 / 1024 = 741.85MB

Mode 2 was the original attempt at CD-I and provided for compression of audio and graphic information. It offered a 742MB maximum capacity since it dropped the error correction bytes, allowing each sector to store 2336 bytes of data. Since the disk was spinning at the same speed, its data transfer rate was also greater - 170kB/s instead of the normal 150kB/s. Mode 2, however, was unable to access computer data and audio/visual data at the same time, since they were stored on different tracks of the disk (only one mode is allowed per track). This limited its usefulness and Mode 2 was never developed.

Mode 3 was termed Mixed Mode as it allowed computer data tracks and audio tracks to be placed on the same disk. Usually, the first track contains the computer data with the remaining tracks containing audio data. The audio tracks could be played through a domestic audio CD player in which case the player would be stepped over the data track. A CD-ROM drive would recognise the computer data tracks and would be able to play the audio through its audio output. However, it could not do both at the same time.

Some references to Mixed Mode refer to a drive that can handle both Mode 1 and Mode 2.

CD XA

It is possible for audio and graphic information to be stored in different CD tracks. When each of these data items is used separately there is no problem but multimedia demands that both audio and graphic information be presented in a synchronised manner and this is not easily achieved. The Extended Architecture (XA) specification allows both audio and graphic data to be stored in the same track in an interleaved fashion, thus allowing greatly improved synchronisation. This extends the Yellow Book Mode 2 by having a Form 1 for computer data (2k of data/sector with error detection) and a Form 2 for audio and video data (2324 bytes of data/sector with no error detection). Since Form 1 and Form 2 work under the same XA Mode, they can both be placed on the same track. XA also saved space in the storage of audio by using a method called ADPCM (Adaptive Delta Pulse Code Modulation). This stores the difference between sound samples rather than the values themselves and results in smaller values being produced and saved.

Green Book

This is also an extension of the Mode 2 of the Yellow Book, designed for playing CD-I interactive applications. It stores files compressed to the MPEG format and interleaves the picture and sound elements. All CD-I tracks are in Mode 2 XA format. Unlike White Book, it does not provide the standard ISO 9660 access and requires a special CD-I player, a PC upgrade such as ReelMagic, or a special device driver, since a normal CD-ROM drive cannot handle the format. Dedicated CD-I players are available with their own CPU and video memory and these connect to a monitor or TV.

CD-Bridge

As the name implies, this standard allows a drive to handle CDs that were both XA and CD-I compatible. This special bridge CD disk is really a CD-I disk with extra XA information added to it. The Photo CD disk explained below is an example of a bridge disk. The disk has more than one disk label and this allows the same disk to be played in a CD-I player or an XA CD drive.

White Book

Used for Video CD - i.e. the storing of full-motion MPEG-1 video. The output cannot be taken directly to any ordinary video card. It has to feed a decompression card to restore MPEG files to their original size. MPEG-1 compression results in a CD with up to 74 minutes of VHS-quality video and stereo sound track. Videos that are longer than 74 minutes have to be split up over two disks. MPEG-1 handling now appears on many video cards, with software or hardware decompression. Video CD uses XA's Mode2/Form2 working and requires a Mode 2/Form 2 compatible player.

Blue Book

Also known as CD Plus or CD Extra, this is designed to provide multiple sessions on a disk. The first session contains audio tracks and the second session contains computer data. The main TOC (table of contents) contains information on audio tracks and points to a further TOC storing data tracks. If the disk is used in a normal hi-fi CD audio player, it will not attempt to play the data tracks as it will not recognise the second TOC. A blue book drive will recognise and use both TOCs.

The most likely use for Blue Book systems appears to be in the music industry where a CD can be played both in a standard audio CD player and in a computer CD drive. In the latter, photographs and text about the performers can then augment the music. This, along with White Book covers most manufacturers' approaches to multimedia CDs.

Orange Book

Also known as CD-R (CD-Recordable), this describes the writing of CD disks.
The three parts to the standard are:
I. The use of Magneto Optical drives, which allows data to be written to disk, then erased or overwritten.
II. The use of the 'Write Once' format, where the data is written in a single session or multiple sessions but cannot be altered after it is written.
III. The Rewritable format (CD-RW), which allows the disk to be re-written up to 1000 times. This requires a Multi-Read CD drive or a DVD drive to read disks written by a CD-RW writer.

CD Writers can produce disks in CD-ROM, CD-DA, Mixed Mode, XA and CD-I format and a quad-speed drive will record an entire disk in about 18mins.

Purple Book

Developed by Philips and Sony as a double density CD (DDCD) format. The disks use a narrower track pitch and shorter pit lengths, so that they can store 1.3GB per disk. They also offer a faster scanning velocity and an improved error correction system – but they cannot be played on existing CD-ROM or DVD-ROM drives.

Kodak Photo CD

CDs are capable of storing large graphics files and the Kodak Photo CD system allows photographs taken with an ordinary camera to be placed on CD disks. When the film is taken to the developer, the images can be reproduced in both standard photographic print format and in CD format. Such photographs can be viewed in the same way as any other graphics file stored on a CD. A standard CD can store 100 photographs and the full 100 may be built up over a period of time with additional photographs being added at later dates. This is not a problem as Kodak can add any new photographs to the CD. However, an older CD is not capable of reading any added data since each new additional group has its own unique storage key and this cannot be accessed by the old technology. If this extra facility is required, a *'Multi-session'* model must be purchased, as this is capable of reading any subsequent additions. Almost all models currently on the market are now multi-session. CD-I players or CD drives that support XA Mode 2/Form 1 are capable of reading these files.

Recordable CD

For large quantity production of CDs, a master copy is laser cut into a glass master copy and this is used to stamp out the lands and pits on the reflective layers of each blank CD. The master copy costs around £500 to produce but subsequent stamped CDs are relatively cheap (which is why they are given away with computer magazines and audio magazines).

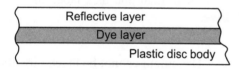

For small quantities, this is an expensive option. CD-R (CD-Recordable) systems utilise a CD writer that uses disks of a different construction from the standard pressed disks. Recordable CD blanks have a layer of dye that can be spot heated by a laser beam to fuse the dye with the plastic substrate and create pits.

The blank disks, known as *'gold disks'*, are supplied with a *'pre-groove'* moulded on its surface. The groove provides tracking information for the drive's head servo and provides a cheap way to ensure quality tracking. The individual blank disk is more expensive than a pressed disk but there is no expensive master to create.

CD-R disks should be able to be read on any normal CD drive. CD Writers are also capable of reading normal CDs. The dramatic fall in the price of CD writers has led to their widespread use as a backup device. Current models record at up to a maximum of twenty-four speed.

Future Technology

A range of techniques is being developed to improve both the capacity and speed of CD-ROMs.

Creating multiple levels of disk.

> IBM is developing a sandwich of ten CD-R disks. By changing the beam's point of focus, different disks in the sandwich are used.

Spread laser technology.

> CD-ROMs using a spread focus laser beam that reads the track across a broad area, typically seven to nine parallel sets of pits, and then uses a digital signal processor to extract the data. Early production versions quote data rates that are a true 72x.

Universal Disc Format

Universal Disc Format, or UDF, is a format designed to allow easier and more efficient recording of CD-ROMs. It was developed by the Optical Storage Technology Association (OSTA), which is a group of hardware and software vendors, and its current version is 1.50. UDF supports a technology called *'incremental packet writing'*, (see *'CD Recording technologies'* below) which means that data can be written to CD-Rs in packets without having to create a disc image. Using UDF, a CD-R can be formatted, at which point any system equipped with a CD-R drive and UDF compliant CD writing software can send packets to record on the disc. Drivers using UDF can allow a CD-R disc to appear as a drive letter, which can be read from and written to in a similar fashion to hard disks or floppies.

UDF, however, is not compatible with ISO 9660. In order for other systems to read a UDF disc, there are two options. The reading system can have a UDF driver installed – note that any system which is capable of writing UDF discs can also read them. Alternatively, a UDF disc can be *'finalised'* by writing an ISO 9660 readable volume, which consumes approximately 20MB of CD space. Even when the disc is finalised, a CD-R drive can still write to the disc. However, further changes will require to be finalised once again, consuming another 20MB, if they are to be ISO 9660 compatible.

Storage concerns

Depending on the recording software, the system may already take into account all recording overheads and simply present the user with a simplified drag-and-drop interface. However, if not, then the user must be aware of several factors affecting storage capacity of CDs.

As stated earlier, CD-ROMs do not use their full capacity for storing user data. A large portion of CD storage space is used in low-level error detection and correction, as well as data modulation. However, these cannot be removed under any circumstances and so they are of no concern to CD producers.

After these, the CD is left with 74 minutes of audio, or nearly 747MB of data as explained under the *'Red Book'* explanation. Red Book is the only standard that can use all 747MB of storage space for user data. All other standards use at least some of that space for synchronisation and additional error correction codes.

CDs are normally manufactured with a maximum of 74 minutes capacity, giving a total of 333,000 sectors. Some manufacturers are capable of producing CDs of up to 81 minutes length by compressing the spiral greater than normally. However, these are not standard CDs and do not follow the Red Book format. As such they are not guaranteed to work on all CD players, and are best avoided where possible. On the other hand, shorter CDs can be played in any standard CD player – 60 minute CDs are not uncommon, and there is a special *'mini'* CD just over 3 inches wide. These smaller disks can still be played in almost all CD players, because data is recorded from the inner spiral outwards.

From a standard CD with up to 333 thousand sectors, the following <u>theoretical maximum</u> storage capacities can be calculated:

Red Book	333,000 sectors x 2352 bytes = 783,216,000 bytes (approx 747MB)
Yellow Book Mode 1	333,000 sectors x 2048 bytes = 681,984,000 bytes (approx 650MB)
Yellow Book Mode 2	333,000 sectors x 2336 bytes = 777,888,000 bytes (approx 742MB)
XA or CD-I Form 1	333,000 sectors x 2048 bytes = 681,984,000 bytes (approx 650MB)
XA or CD-I Form 2	333,000 sectors x 2324 bytes = 773,892,000 bytes (approx 738MB)

Unfortunately, storage on a CD is not just a simple matter of just writing sectors away to disk. CD has its roots in audio, and so each disk is split up into *'tracks'*. In an audio disk, each track normally does represent one musical piece, and the Volume Table Of Contents lists up to 99 track locations. If a basic computer CD-ROM is produced, without additional music or video tracks, then the entire CD-ROM will comprise a single data track, either in Yellow Book Mode 1 or CD XA Form 1.

Things get more complicated, however, when other types of disks are produced. Generally, all data within a track must be of the same mode. However, a CD-XA or CD-I track will allow each sector to be either Form 1 or Form 2, so that data of both types can be interleaved to improve synchronisation. That means that, for example, a CD-XA video and data track could have 25 sectors of computer data and 25 sectors of video data, then back to computer data and so on. The storage capacity can only be calculated then by understanding just how many sectors will be Form 1 and how many will be Form 2.

Then there is the case of multiple tracks. Red Book CDs containing nothing but audio, and written in a single session, are the only type that can have tracks back to back. Every other type of CD must have a gap between each track. That gap is 2 seconds before audio tracks, and 3 seconds before every other type of track. Three seconds is 225 sectors, or 450KB in Yellow Book Mode 1, which is no longer available for recording data.

Finally, there is the consideration of multiple sessions. CDs written in a single session have an area called a *'lead-in'* before the tracks, and a *'lead-out'* area after the tracks in that session. If the CD is recorded in more than one session then each individual session must have its own lead-in and lead-out.

Each lead-in area occupies 4500 sectors, while the lead-out area occupies 6750 sectors for the first session and 2250 for each subsequent session. These overheads can seriously eat into the storage capacity of a CD, so for any distributable CD it may be wise to have as few sessions as possible.

For example, an often-used CD format is to have a single Red Book session of audio, followed by a second session of CD-ROM data. This format allows most computers to access the data, while normal audio units will only recognise the audio session. The audio in the Red Book session can be written back to back, and if it takes up say 45 minutes, then that corresponds to 202,500 sectors. Add to this the 4500 sector lead-in and the 6750 sector lead-out. The Red Book session would therefore consume 213,750 sectors, leaving 119,250 sectors for the second session. With the lead-in of 4500 sectors and lead-out of 2250 sectors, the data session has a maximum useable data area of 112,500 sectors, or approximately 219MB.

For computer data, the storage considerations do not end there, unfortunately. While audio or video data can be stored 'as-is', computer data requires a logical format in order to access the data. This might be an ISO 9660 format, Joliet, or some similar standard. In all cases, the logical standard requires some data on folders, filenames, and so on. ISO 9660 also stores a path table, and a root folder record. Furthermore, each folder will require disk space, and there is additional wastage when storage of a file leaves the last sector less than fully utilised. It is impossible to give hard and fast figures on the amount of space this will consume, but CD images should always be created with these additional overheads very much in mind, in order to avoid last minute trimming of files.

CDs written using packets in UDF have the added burden of a table that has to keep track of all packets and the files they belong to. This means a UDF packet written CD-R is reduced to around 600MB of space. CD-RWs written using UDF also use *'sparing'* techniques to prevent over-using areas of the disk, which further reduces available space to about 500MB.

DVD

The current CDs have the following capacity limitations:
- Most hard disks are now much larger than the 650MB storage of a CD. So, backing up drives involves writing to several CDs per drive.
- A full-length movie stores on two CDs and requires the disk to be changed during viewing.

The response is the high-capacity *'Digital Versatile Disk'*. It is mainly viewed as a mechanism for distributing films and the first DVD disks are of this type. It also provides an ideal medium for a wide variety of applications ranging from training material to encyclopaedias. Their large storage capacity makes the writeable versions a good choice of backup medium.

The disk retains the conventional CD diameter of 120mm but can be double sided and can have two separate layers capable of storing data. The largest capacity types have a sandwich of two layers (i.e. four storage surfaces). With double-sided versions, the disk is flipped over to use the other side.

Single layer disks, both single and double sided, are manufactured in a very similar way to current CD-ROMs. The second layer comprises a resin layer with partially transmissive qualities. The reflections from both layers vary only slightly in intensity requiring a particularly sensitive detection system.

Product	Capacity	No of layers	No of sides	Mode	Comments
DVD5	4.7GB	1	1	Playback	
DVD9	8.5GB	2	1	Playback	
DVD10	9.4GB	1	2	Playback	
DVD18	17GB	2	2	Playback	
Version 1.0 DVD-R	3.95GB or 7.9GB	2	1 or 2	Record-once	Mostly DVD-ROM compatible
Version 2.0 DVD-R	4.7GB or 9.4GB	2	1 or 2	Record-once	
Type 1 DVD-RAM	2.6GB or 5.4GB	2	1 or 2	Record-many	Cartridge based, not DVD-ROM compatible
Type 2 DVD-RAM	4.7GB or 9.4GB	2	1 or 2	Record-many	
DVD-RW	4.7GB or 9.4GB	2	1 or 2	Record-many	Single-sided currently available
DVD+RW	4.7GB or 9.4GB	2	1 or 2	Record-many	Single-sided currently available
Blu-ray Disc	23GB to 27GB	1	1	Record-once	
AOD ("Advanced Optical Disk")	15GB to 36GB	1	1	Playback & Record-many	In development (see later)

The range of products is shown in the table. A 4.7GB disk stores the equivalent of around 133 minutes of video and three audio streams. DVD5 disks are the types that are currently used for mass DVD distribution.

The DVD specifications are known as *'books'* and are shown in the table.

Book Name	Contents
	DVD Specifications for Read-Only Disc
DVD-ROM	Part 1: Physical specifications Ver. 1.03 Part 2: File system specifications Ver. 1.03
DVD-Video	Part 3: Video specifications Ver. 1.13
DVD-Audio	Part 4: Audio specifications Ver. 1.2
	DVD Specifications for Recordable Disc
DVD-R (3.9G)	Part 1: Physical specifications Ver. 1.0 Part 2: File system specifications Ver. 1.0
DVD-R for General	Part 1: Physical specifications Ver. 2.0 Part 2: File system specifications Ver. 2.0
DVD-R for Authoring	Part 1: Physical specifications Ver. 2.0 Part 2: File system specifications Ver. 2.0
	DVD Specifications for Rewritable Disc
DVD-RAM (2.6G)	Part 1: Physical specifications Ver. 1.0 Part 2: File system specifications Ver. 1.0
DVD-RAM (4.7G)	Part 1: Physical specifications Ver. 2.0 Part 2: File system specifications Ver. 2.0
	DVD Specifications for Re-recordable Disc
DVD-RW	Part 1: Physical specifications Ver. 1.1 Part 2: File system specifications Ver. 1.01
	DVD Specifications for DVD-RAM/DVD-RW/DVD-R for General Discs
DVD Video Recording	Part 3: Video recording Ver. 1.1
DVD Stream	Part 5: Stream recording Ver. 1.0

Aimed at the production of quality video disks, they support both the original MPEG-1 (i.e. 352x 240 at 30 fields per second) and the current MPEG-2 (i.e. up to 720x480 at 60 fields per second) video standards. DVD disks interleave the video and audio streams.

Video Standards
The DVD standard supports a range of screen aspect ratios, from 1.33:1 (the 4/3 standard of normal TVs and monitors) to 2.25:1 (wide screen movies).
Most movies are produced at 1.85:1 and domestic wide-screen TV's display at 1.78:1 (usually advertised as 16:9 sets). When movies are played in DVD players, users can control how they are displayed, including *'squeezing'* the image (everyone looks tall and thin) and *'letterbox viewing'* (all the movie is displayed but the upper and lower portions of the screen are black).
Each DVD movie disk has a *'country lock'* - a code specific to a region of the world. DVD disks will only run in players that have the same zone code. Region 1 is USA while Europe is Region 2. This attempts to prevent US disks being played on European DVD drives.

Audio Standards
DVD supports three *'theatre quality'* sound formats - Dolby AC-3 surround sound, MPEG-1 audio and MPEG-2 audio. Europe favours MPEG-2 surround sound, while the USA, Japan and the rest of the world use Dolby AC-3. MPEG-1 is described as *'2.0'* (i.e. two channel stereo) while AC-3 is *'5.1'* and MPEG-2 is either *'5.1'* or *'7.1'*. The number after the dot indicates whether the sound includes support for a low-frequency effects sub-woofer. The numbers before the dot indicate how many main sound channels are supported. So a 5:1 has a centre sound channel, a channel at all four corners of the sound room, and a sub-woofer. MPEG-1 samples at 44.1 kbps while MPEG-2 and AC-3 sample at 48 kbps (see chapter on multimedia for an explanation).

How DVD stores 4.7GB on a single side

A CD's basic capacity is 747MB, although 650MB is left for the user after error correction overheads are deducted.   DVD uses a combination of more precise engineering, higher laser frequency, and improved modulation and error correction techniques, to dramatically improve the capacity of a single disk side.

	Standard CD layout	DVD layout	Improvement Factor	New Capacity
Smaller pit length	0.972 microns	0.4 microns	2.4300	1.82 GB
Narrower track pitch	1.6 microns	0.74 microns	2.1622	3.93 GB
More surface used for storing data	86 sq cms	87.6 sq cms	1.0186	4.00 GB
Better error correction	25% of data area	13% of data area	1.1062	4.42 GB
More efficient channel bit modulation	08:14+3	08:16	1.0625	4.70 GB

DVD Data Rates

The table above shows how DVD manages to store much more information on the same surface area than a CD.   However, this has other implications, primarily on the data transfer rate of a DVD drive in comparison to a CD-ROM drive. The reduced pit length means that a DVD drive spinning at the same speed as a CD drive will read 2.43 times as much data. However, the base (single speed) velocity of a DVD is almost four times the base (single speed) velocity of a CD-ROM drive.

These two factors together mean that a single speed DVD transfers data at the same rate as an 8x CD-ROM drive, and a 6x DVD has a data rate similar to a 48x CD-ROM drive.

Advantages of DVD Drives

- Choice of up to eight language tracks.
- Choice of up to 32 tracks for subtitles and menus.
- Newer DVD drives can read all formats (i.e. all DVD modes and CD-ROM, CD-R and CD-RW disks).

Disadvantages

- Requires an MPEG-2 decoder and a sound card that can handle the disk's audio formats. These cards are available separately as upgrade kits or are available bundled with DVD drives.   Software implementations are available (e.g. CompCore's SoftDVD) although their performance is poorer since they use CPU resources rather than dedicated hardware.
- Older DVD drives cannot read CD-R and CD-RW disks.
- Normal CD drives cannot read DVD disks.

Recordable DVD

Like CD-ROM, there is more than one option when considering production of DVDs. Pressing of DVDs is similarly expensive unless large numbers are pressed, and so there are DVD-R and DVD-RAM drives available to create single disks or small runs.

DVD-R

Book D of the DVD specification is DVD recordable, more commonly called DVD-R.   This is a write-once system that creates a DVD that many household and computer DVD players can read. However, it is not re-writeable, limiting its usefulness as a backup medium.

Like CD-R, DVD-R uses a laser beam to permanently transform a dye recording layer.

The DVD-R format supports incremental writing (see earlier explanation) although the DVD can only be read in a DVD recording drive until the disk is finalised. A finalised disk can then be read in a DVD player.

In fact, there are two kinds of DVD writers and two types of DVD-R media:

DVD-R for General (DVD-R(G))	This is the format designed for consumer products. As such, it is unable to make bit-for-bit copies of DVDs. It is produced in a 4.7GB format.
DVD-R for Authoring (DVD-R(A))	This format is designed for professional use and is available in 3.95GB or 4.7GB sizes.

The DVD-R(G) is the type that is generally advertised and sold through computer shops, magazines, etc. and is simply referred to as DVD-R.

A DVD-R(G) writer cannot write to a DVD-R(A) disk and vice versa. The production of two systems is regarded as an attempt to prevent unauthorised duplication of commercial DVD disks. The DVD-R(A) system is much more expensive than a comparable DVD-R(G) system. Disks created by either type of writer can be read by most players. Players make no distinction between the two types of media.

DVD-R is technically able to write to both sides of a dual sided DVD, though dual-sided media is rare. Alternatively, a "DVD+R9" drive is one that is able to write to dual-layered discs, giving 8.5GB of space. However, there are as yet no dual-layered, dual-sided media available to store the maximum 17GB that the DVD technology can accommodate.

DVD-RAM

Book E specifies DVD-RAM principles. It uses magneto-optical rewriteable technology and is available in the older type cartridge-based and the new type which allows the disk to be removed from the cartridge after writing. DVD-RAM is based on the original agreed specifications of the DVD Forum, the major manufacturers.

DVD-RAM can use one of two media types. The DVD-RAM specification version 1.0 allows only 2.6GB per side, while the newer version 2.0 specification allows 4.7GB per side, equal to a mass-produced DVD 5. This makes it useful for creating DVD masters. Some drives are able to read and write to both types of DVD-RAM.

DVD-RAM disks, once removed from their cartridge, can only be played on a few models of standard DVD player but mostly have to be used on other DVD-RAM drives. Double-sided DVD-RAM disks have to be turned over manually to access both sides.

Despite the format's poor compatibility with other drives, it has great advantages as a backup medium. Due to its use of magneto-optical technology it provides:

- Longer shelf life, around 30 years compared to 10 years for DVD-RW and DVD+RW.
- Vastly more rewrites. The disk can be re-written to more than 100,000 times.

The main producers of this type of writer are Pioneer, Hitachi and Toshiba.

DVD-RW

The Forum also produced a rewriteable standard, known as DVD-RW.

DVD-RW is a read/write system that operates on a Phase Change system similar to CD-RW disks. The disk surface is of an alloy material that can change back and forth from a crystalline to a non-crystalline (amorphous) structure.

Its development was delayed many times, and the initial aim of a 2.6GB DVD-RW was changed to the currently available 4.7GB version.

The main producers of this type of writer are Pioneer, Yamaha, Panasonic, Mitsui and Ricoh.

The disk can be read by most domestic DVD players and computer DVD drives, and can be re-written to around 10,000 times.

DVD+RW

Sony and Philips broke with the Forum specifications and introduced own format called 'DVD+RW'.

It was developed by Sony and Panasonic outside of the DVD Forum as a rival to DVD-RW. Initially both companies believed 2.6GB was too little, and aimed at 3GB rewriteable disks, but this too has been increased to 4.7GB per side. It also suffered from many delays in production, but the companies involved have more of a stake in previous CD technologies and as a result DVD+RW is likely to be more backwards compatible than DVD-RW. It uses a similar technique to DVD-RW in as much as it writes by creating crystalline/amorphous areas on the disk surface.

The main producers of this type of writer are Philips, Sony, Ricoh and Hewlett Packard.

The disk can be read by most domestic DVD players and by most computer DVD drives, and can be re-written to up to 10,000 times.

There are many other DVD 'standards' in use or in development, such as the 8cm mini-DVDs used in new digital camcorders or the 15GB single-sided disks under development. Even after years of DVDs being on sale, there is still a confusing mass of options, even though DVD-R has finally emerged as the most widely used 'standard'. Sony has decided to produce DVD-RW systems for consumer products and DVD+RW for computer systems, while other manufacturers are concentrating on manufacturing writers that can handle multiple formats.

The table shows some of the main features of each type of format.

	DVD-R	DVD+R9	DVD-RW	DVD+RW	DVD-RAM
Types available	Single sided Double sided	Single sided Double sided Dual layered	Single sided Double sided	Single sided Double sided Dual layered	Single sided Double sided
No of rewrites	Once only	Once only	1,000	100,000	1,000
Data transfer rate (typical)	Up to 16x (177.28Mb/s)	2.4x (26.59Mb/s)	2x (22.16Mb/s)	2.4x (26.59Mb/s)	1.4x (15.52Mb/s) 4x (44.32Mb/s)
Play on domestic DVD player	Yes	Few	Nearly all	Some	Nearly all
Play on computer DVD-ROM drive	Yes	Few	Nearly all	Some	Nearly all

Compatibilities

The range of formats, writers and players leads to problems of compatibility – i.e. a disk from one system not working on another system.

Some very old DVD-ROM drives cannot even read CD-R disks and only read pressed CDs. All newer drives can usually read all formats except DVD-RAM.

However, the system used for re-writeables make them incompatible with each other. For example, DVD+RW can't be read by DVD-RW systems and vice versa.

The table shows the compatibly between systems (i.e. whether a disk recorded in one type of drive will be readable in another type of drive).

	DVD-R	DVD-RW	DVD+RW	DVD-RAM
Pressed DVD-ROM	Yes	Yes	Yes	Yes
DVD-R	Yes	Yes	Yes	Yes
DVD+R9	Few	Few	Few	Few
DVD-RW	Yes	Yes	Mostly	Mostly
DVD+RW	Mostly	Mostly	Yes	Mostly
DVD-RAM	No	No	No	Yes

Of course, standard CD drives cannot read DVD disks of any type.

DVD recording drives generally write in their native format, although dual-format drives are available that will write to both DVD+R/+RW and DVD-R/-RW formats.

There are many other DVD 'standards' in use or in development, such as the 8cm mini-DVDs used in new digital camcorders or the 15GB single-sided discs under development. Even after years of DVDs being on sale, the number of options available can still lead to confusion at times.

Dual Layer DVDs

Dual layer disks (i.e. the DVD9 format) consist of a sandwich of two disks of polycarbonate, each with its own reflective coating and dye recording layer.

Each layer has its own read/write laser system. The top layer functions like a normal DVD disk. However, the top layer is semi-transparent allowing the second laser to access the dye layer underneath. The result is a disk with a capacity of 8.5GB, just short of being twice 4.7GB.

These disks need a dual-layer reader/writer, as the existing DVD readers/writers can't handle the new format. Of course, dual-layer readers/writers can access existing single-layer DVDs.

Like single-layer DVDs, dual-layer disks area available in both DVD+R/+RW and DVD-R/-RW formats With double-sided disks, the disk has to be taken out of the reader/writer and turned over to access the other side. With dual-layer disks, both sides are accessed without turning over the disk.

Current DVD developments

Although dual-layer DVDs provide a welcome improvement in storage capacity, there is a demand for even greater capacity. This is particularly driven by the emergence of High Definition video, which has a much higher definition than current video systems and consequently occupies much more storage – up to 12.GB per hour of HD video.

High-definition video camcorders and recorded HDTV material (movies, concerts, etc.) is currently the big marketing area.

Developers wanted to keep the disk size the same as current DVDs (i.e. 12cm) so the extra capacity had to be met by storing more pieces of data on the same disc surface area. This has been achieved by using blue lasers instead of the current red lasers.   Blue lasers operate at a higher frequency (i.e. a shorter wavelength) than red lasers – only 405nm compared to 650nm for a red laser and the 780nm used in CDs. Since the beam focusses on a smaller surface area of the disk, it is able to cut pits that are smaller than with red lasers.   Since the pits are smaller, more of them can be placed on the disk surface. This means packing more data capacity per spiral and allows the spiralling tracks to be positioned more closely together. As a result, the disks have a much-increased optical storage capacity.

There are currently two competing formats using blue laser technology – the HD-DVD and the BluRay formats.   Since they both use different laser heads and closer tolerance mechanisms than current DVD systems, both new systems require the use to install a replacement reader/writer.   Both systems have strong support from major players in the computing and entertainment industry.

HD-DVD

HD-DVD is supported by Intel, NEC, Toshiba, Sanyo, Time Warner and Universal Studios.   It is also supported by Microsoft's Vista through its Windows Media Video 9 compression system).

It uses the same 0.6mm protective surface layer as current DVDs, making the new players easily backwards compatible. It appears in 15GB single layer and 30GB dual layer capacities, with a 45GB triple layer being developed. HD-DVD is now losing out to Blu-ray in the race for acceptance and is gradually being withdrawn.

Blu-ray

Its major backers include LG, Hitachi, Samsung, Philips, Apple, Walt Disney Pictures, Twentieth Century Fox, MGM, Dell and Hewlett Packard. It is also supported by Sony, through its film division and its PlayStations from version 3 onwards.

The Blu-ray disk has a protective surface layer that is reduced to just 0.1mm, compared to 0.6mm for current DVDs. This reduces the effects of beam distortion and allows the beam to focus closer to the disc surface. As a result, the spot is five times smaller, so capacity is five times larger.   Blu-ray disks are in 25GB single layer and 50GB dual layer formats.   An eight layer version is being developed, with a promised 200GB capacity.

Blu-ray disks have a higher storage capacity than HD-DVD disks but are currently more expensive to produce.   Blu-ray players are also backward compatible with current DVDs.

Note
> The demands of High Definition TV and video, with 720 lines or 1080 lines of resolution, require not only greater storage but also higher data rates.   High-resolution moving images mean shifting and processing more data for each frame of video.   In response, Sony's DSP (digital signal processor) can handle data rates of 36Mbits/sec, compared to a standard DVD's rate of around 4Mbits/sec. A 2X version of the format doubles the data transfer rate from 36Mbits/sec per second to 72Mbits/sec.

Although both formats were initially targeted at the consumer electronics market, they both quickly found their way into the general computer storage market, with some drives being capable of reading/writing to both HD-DVD and Blu-ray discs.

Magneto-Optical Drives

Magneto-optical (MO) drives use metal granule coatings on the disk surface. Unlike normal hard disks where the surface area is evenly coated, the MO disk has a raised bump for every data bit on the entire disk.   Each data bit occupies an area of just 1 micron in diameter. This surface is then covered by a plastic or glass-based protective coat. The 5.25" types are double-sided disks with two independent sides glued together. The 3.5" type is single sided. The completed disks of both types are enclosed in cartridges similar to the construction used for 3.5" floppies, although larger and about 11mm in thickness. Each disk side has tracks with discrete physical cells capable of storing data.

Each data cell is written to in at least two stages - erase the old data and write the new data, sometimes accompanied by a third stage to verify the write operation.   Mostly, these are carried out during separate revolutions of the disk resulting in writing to a disk being substantially slower than reading from a disk. Phase change systems (see later) allow the write operation to be carried out in a single pass.

The coating used has a very high coercivity, which means that it is normally very difficult to change its magnetic polarity.   However, the coating is also susceptible to heat.

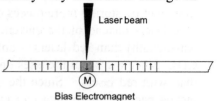

To alter the contents of a cell, a laser beam is directed at it, on a high-power setting.   This raises the temperature of the cell to just under 200° C.   This greatly reduces the coercivity for a brief period and during this period a magnet is used to set the cell to the desired polarity.   When the cell cools again, the magnetic polarity is effectively locked into the disk.   Only the cells that need to have their contents altered require to be subjected to this process.

A new system called *'LIMDOW'* (Light Intensity Modulation/Direct Overwrite) carries out the operations in a single pass, greatly speeding up disk writing.   The LIMDOW system modulates the light intensity instead of the magnetic field, to write to the surface.

To read the disk, the laser beam reverts to a low-power setting and is reflected off the disk.   The magnet is not used in the read process.   This method does not rely on the <u>amount</u> of reflection as used in the CD-ROM.   Instead, it analyses the <u>polarity</u> of the reflected beam, since the beam is slightly polarised according to whether it is reflected from a '0' or a '1' cell - a phenomenon known as *'The Kerr Effect'.*

The most commonly used disks employ CAV (Constant Angular Velocity), which places data on the tracks using a fixed speed motor.   This results in data on the outer track being less densely packed than data on the inner tracks.   It is a simple but wasteful system.   Other systems use ZCAV (Zoned Constant Angular Velocity), which keeps the motor speed constant within any one track but has a faster speed on outer tracks than inner tracks.

Magneto-optical disks are robust, with life expectancies up to 30 years.   Manufacturers claim that the disks have write/rewrite cycles of between 10 million and 1000 million.   All these drive systems use SCSI interfaces.

Current MO drives are available in a range of capacities.
- 230MB systems (e.g. Olympus PowerMO 230)
- 640MB systems (e.g. the Fujitsu DynaMO 640)
- 1.3GB systems (e.g. some HP drives)
- 2.6GB systems (e.g. the Plasmon DW260)
- 5.2GB systems (e.g. the Sony RMO-S551)

Drives offer only slow access times of between 12ms and 90ms, with most being around 25ms.   They perform like slow hard disks.   The One Technology One Pro MO has the fastest current seek times of 12ms but this is still slower than modern hard disks.   Rotational speeds vary from 1800rpm to 3600rpm and data transfer rates vary from 522kBs to 10MB/sec.

The hardware is expensive to buy initially but the disks are relatively cheap so it is an economic proposition for large storage needs.   The more data that is stored the cheaper it becomes in terms of pence per MB.   Some rewriteable optical systems can be configured to also act as a WORM drive, where data security is important.

> **Note**   An MO drive uses a motorised ejection of the disk under software control.   Although there is an eject button, it is not operational with the power switched off.   The drive should not be moved when a disk is in the drive.   The head is held in a locked position when there is no disk in the drive, but the head is free to move when a disk is inserted.   Moving the drive without the head being locked might cause damage.

Phase-Change Disks

Some systems, such as the Plasmon PD2000 and the Matsushita PD, do not use magnetism to alter the state of the disk surface.   These are called *'phase change'* systems and use a disk whose coating can adopt one of two conditions - amorphous or crystalline.

The drive mechanism's laser beam can produce two levels of heat at the disk surface.   Heating the coating to just below melting point produces a crystalline structure during the rapid cooling down period. Heating to just above melting point destroys the crystalline structure producing the amorphous state at that point on the surface.   Unlike conventional MO systems, phase change drives can write the surface in a single pass and this reduces the time for write operations. During read operations, the different surface structures reflect different amount of light from the scanning laser beam and these differences are detected and interpreted in the same way as normal CD drive systems.

Floptical Disks

These are based on ordinary floppy disk technology with the disk surface being magnetised to store the data.   The disk is also stored in a normal 3.5" plastic case. The difference lies in the addition of special optical servo tracks to the disk surface to ensure very accurate alignment.   These extra tracks appear between magnetic tracks and are used to ensure that the read/write head positions itself exactly in the middle of the desired track.   An infrared LED light source reflects off the servo tracks and is picked up by a photodetector. The information indicates the exact position of the read/write head.   This increased accuracy allows more tracks to be place on a 3.5" disk size and this results in higher capacity disks. Since the tracks are very narrow, a special narrow head is used to read and write the data.

With drives that are backward compatible - i.e. can also read standard 720k and 1.4M floppies - the drive mechanism also has a second wider head to read these wider tracks.

The most popular floptical drive is the 120MB Panasonic LS-120.

Removable Cartridges

Large capacity disks using conventional magnetised surfaces are available, each with their own particular drive mechanism. This means that disks cannot be exchanged between different cartridge drives. The Iomega 'Zip' drives have a capacity of 100MB or 750MB, while their 'Jaz' model has capacities of 1GB and 2GB.   The Zip drive has a seek time of 29ms and the Jaz seek time is 12ms. The Zip has an inferior performance compared to IDE or SCSI hard disks, while the Jaz is almost comparable. Interface types used are the SCSI, IDE or proprietary cards, with the parallel port being used for external models.

IBM Microdrive Disks

IBM has historically always been at the forefront of increasing storage densities for magnetic drives. As well as making huge volumes available on conventional drive sizes, this increased density also manifests itself by making reasonable volumes available on tiny disks. Their recently announced Microdrive Product is a standard magnetic hard-disk which is sufficiently smaller than a PCMCIA card that it can be mounted on a PCMCIA card. The device then becomes a drop-in replacement for proprietary Compact Flash memory, which is used in digital cameras, MP3 players and PDAs and has a typical volume of 8MB. The IBM Compact Flash Microdrive has capacities of 170MB or 340MB, and 1GB devices are promised. This allows huge increases in the storage capacity, and therefore usefulness of the devices that support Compact Flash storage.

Future DVD Technology

Current DVD disks have too low a capacity for storing high-definition video and HDTV material (movies, concerts, etc.) is seen as the next big marketing area.

Increased optical storage capacity is possible with the use of blue violet lasers. These have a higher frequency (i.e. a shorter wavelength) than red lasers and the beam can therefore focus on a smaller area of the disc surface. As a result, smaller pits can be cut on the disk surface. This means packing more data capacity per spiral.

There are currently two competing formats using this technique. Both use the normal 120mm disk size associated with CD and DVD Disks.

Blu-Ray

This format is being developed by a nine member group including Sony, JVC, Sharp, Pioneer and Panasonic. Its specification includes three disk capacities – at 23.3GB, 25GB, and 27GB. Each version is a single-layer disk, although double-layer disks (with double the capacity) are also specified. Panasonic already has a working 50GB rewriteable prototype. A 2X version of format is being developed to double the data transfer rate from 36mbps per second to 72mbps.

AOD (Advanced Optical Disc)

The AOD format is being developed by Toshiba and NEC, as a rival to Blu-Ray. They look to the DVD Forum to ratify AOD as a replacement for current DVD usage. Although still in the design stage, the intention is to store 20GB on a single layer recordable disk, 15GB on a single layer pre-recorded disk (with the potential of doubling both these capacities).

Although both formats are initially targeted at the consumer electronics market, they will both eventually find their way into the general computer storage market.

Computer Peripherals

A computer peripheral is a piece of equipment that adds extra power or functionality to the central basic system. Since every computer has to have a motherboard, CPU, and memory, these cannot be classified as peripherals, whereas a scanner or a digital camera is clearly not an essential. There is a grey area in between. For example, a computer can control a robot without the need for a monitor but the monitor is essential for desktop use. In any case, the book cover monitors, graphics cards, sound cards, disk drives, modems, etc. in other chapters.

This chapter looks at:

- The keyboard
- The scanner
- The uninterruptible power supply
- The mouse
- The bar-code reader
- The joystick
- Printers

Getting data into the computer

Very few computer programs run without any input from the people using the system. Games expect input from joysticks, databases expect input from the keyboard, drawing packages expect input from the mouse, and so on. This chapter looks at some of the devices used to put information into a computer.

The Keyboard

The keyboard is a piece of hardware that lets users enter alphabetic, numeric, cursor, function key and other information into your computer.

The keyboard's main features are:

- The computer keyboard consists of a normal typewriter layout with some additional keys incorporated, and a group of function keys (situated on the left with older models and along the top with newer models), a numeric pad on the right, and an optional group of direction keys also on the right side.

- The keys for numeric zero (0) and alphabetic (O), and numeric one (1) and alphabetic 'l', the 12th letter of the alphabet, cannot be interchanged.

- Most keys have an automatic repeat function, which means that if you hold a key down for more than a pre-determined time (say half a second), the key starts to repeat itself. So, you can enter a whole line of the same character with a single press of a key.

- The normal setting for your keyboard means that when you press a key that is engraved with an alphabetic character you will see a lower case letter on the screen, and a key with two engravings will show the character in the lower half of the key top. To get capital letters and the characters on the top half of the key top you must hold down one of the SHIFT keys while you press the other key. If most of your keying requires the use of capital letters, you can press the CAPS LOCK key, which remains ON until you press it again, and this produces the upper case with alphabetic keys only.

- There are many operations that need to be carried out on a microcomputer that could need a wide range of keys or commands to carry them out. You cannot be given a giant keyboard layout, as this would cause great confusion as well as occupying the entire computer desk area. Manufacturers of modern microcomputers have evolved a standard key-sequence procedure to enable these operations to be achieved while still using a standard-sized keyboard. This involves the use of the CTRL and/or the ALT keys in conjunction with one of the normal keys in the same way as the SHIFT key would be used to give capital letters. This operation is usually indicated in documents as CTRL-B, CTRL-G, etc (or ^G where ^ indicates the use of the control key)

- The keyboard contains an 'Enter' key which is the key with the bent arrow on the right of the centre section of the keyboard. In DOS and in some applications, this key MUST be pressed after a line of text or a command to tell the computer to process that line. It is sometimes also called the RETURN key.

- The keyboard has a single cable attached to it and the plug at the end of this cable is attached to the keyboard socket on the computer main system unit. This cable takes the power from the unit to your keyboard and returns information on any keys pressed back to the motherboard.

- Modern keyboards may have extra keys for special functions such as Windows or Internet operations.

- Some keyboards even include a fingerprint scanner or bar code reader, to prevent unauthorised access to the computer. Only the operator whose fingerprint is recognised is allowed access.

The Control Keys

This set of keys does not produce any printable characters; they are used to control the editing and display activities and are as follows:

Enter ⌨ This key has two functions. One is to move the cursor from one line to the next, as would be expected with a typewriter carriage return key. The second function is to enter a program command. In DOS, the Enter key terminates an entry sequence and lets the machine know that the letters typed in so far constitute a command to be carried out.

Backspace ⌨ This key moves the cursor to the left by one position each time it is pressed. As it travels backwards, it erases any character it passes over.

Shift ⌨ While held down, this activates upper case letters and the top half value of various keys.

Caps Lock This changes the alphabetic keys on the keyboard between shifted (Capital) and unshifted (Lower-case) mode.

Control ⌨ This key accesses the alternate functions of other keys. Hold the Control key down and press the key with the desired function.

Del ⌨ This key removes characters from text at the cursor position, without moving back one character like the backspace key.

Tab ⌨ The Tab key functions similarly to a typewriter tab key. DOS has preset positions on the horizontal line, so that when the Tab key is pressed it moves to these preset positions. The Tab key may also be used in a number of applications such as Microsoft Word.

Ins This key activates an insert mode in which characters can be entered at the cursor position. Characters already on the line are moved to the right to make room for characters entered. If this key is not active, typing a character at the keyboard will result in that key overwriting the character at the current position of the cursor.

Ctrl/Break Control and Break pressed together causes most running DOS programs to halt.

PrtScr When in DOS mode, this key causes the information displayed on the screen to be sent to the printer. Control and PrtScr together will cause the printer to echo everything displayed on the screen.

The **Pause** and **Scroll Lock** keys are rarely used, although some software applications program them for their own particular use.

The QWERTY Group

These are the keys found on a standard typewriter and are used to enter commands or type text. The user can type correspondence, give DOS commands, choose from menus, etc. by pressing these keys.

The Numeric Keypad

The numeric keys along the top of the keyboard are repeated and grouped together at the right-hand side of the keyboard, known as the 'keypad'. The proximity of the numeric keys is an aid to speedy input for users who are involved in a lot of numeric data entry work. For those not involved in such work, the keypad also doubles up as a cursor movement set of keys.

The Num lock key is used to activate and deactivate the number keys on the right-hand keypad. When Num Lock is engaged, key presses in the keypad group are interpreted as the entering of numbers; when Num Lock is not engaged, the same key presses are interpreted as Page Up, Page Down, and other cursor movement key operations. The application package may report that the Num Lock is engaged or the keyboard may have a Num Lock light that lights when in this mode.

Function Keys ⌨

These are marked F1 .. F12 (or up to F10 on some keyboards). They are programmed to perform different functions within different software applications. In DOS they allow the user to retrieve and edit single commands

Cursor Keys

This key moves the cursor up one line each time it is pressed, in certain programs.

This key moves the cursor down one line each time it is pressed, in certain programs.

The cursor-right key moves the cursor one character to the right each time it is pressed. It does not delete any character it passes.

The cursor-left key moves the cursor one character to the left each time it is pressed. It does not delete any character it passes.

End   The End key, inactive in normal DOS activities, is program dependent and moves the cursor to The last character in the current line or screen.

Home   The Home Key, inactive in DOS, is software dependent and moves the cursor to the home position - usually the top left corner of the screen.

PgDn   The Page Down key moves the screen contents up in predetermined increments.

PgUp   The Page Up key moves the screen contents down in predetermined increments.

Windows keys

Most keyboards have extra keys, allowing some Windows activities to be run by a single key press.

This key brings up the Windows Start menu.

This key brings up the Windows Context menu, whose options depend on the activity at the time. Other options include Sleep, Wake, Power, e-mail, and www buttons.

Keyboards are available in a wide range of designs. Most people use the standard layout, but keyboards are available that split in two, have non-standard key layouts or have improved ergonomic designs. They are also available in cordless and waterproof versions.

How keyboards work

When a key on the keyboard is pressed, it makes certain connections to a chip inside the keyboard. This chip knows what key has been pressed and sends a code, along the keyboard cable, to the computer. There is another chip inside the computer for handling the keyboard's input. When it receives the code from the keyboard, it converts it into data that can be used by the computer. This process is explained in more detail in the following pages.

Detecting a key press

A keyboard is a case that contains a set of switches. There are over a hundred different keys on a keyboard and the system has to cope with any of these being pressed. It must even cope with more than one key being pressed at a time (e.g. pressing the shift key and the letter "q" to get an upper-case "Q").

Since the keyboard has over 100 different keys, it is not practical to have a separate wire for each switch back to the computer. Instead, it does this by arranging all the keys on the keyboard into a set of rows and columns.

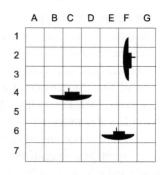

Children play the game of *"Battleships"* where two opponents lay out their ships on a grid. In turn, one player shouted out a row and column and the other player checked if one of his/her ships sat on that location. So, for example, if one player shouted out "B3", the other player would look along to column B and then look down to the third row.

Every box on the grid had a unique location that was identified by its row and column. In the example, there are seven rows and 7 columns, providing 49 different locations.

The keys on the keyboard are organized in a similar way, this time using a grid of wires as shown in the diagram. Each dot on the diagram represents a switch that connects the horizontal and vertical wires at that location.

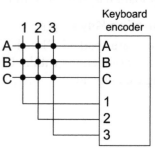

The grid of wires is connected to a special chip called the *"encoder"*.

In this example, there are three columns by three rows, giving nine different places where they join.

If a switch is wired across each place where the wires cross, there are locations for nine different keys. Although there are nine different keys, it only needs six connections to the keyboard's encoder chip. If the grid was made up from six rows and six columns, 36 different keys could be connected and only 12 connections would need to be wired to the encoder.   Now, if the grid was made up of 10 wires by 10 wires, 100 different keys could be connected with only 20 connections to the encoder.

The keyboard encoder is built so that making a connection between its pin A and pin 1 produces a unique code. Connecting pin A and pin 2 produces a different code, and so on   Since there are nine different permutations in the example, the encoder produces nine different codes.

Now, all that has to be done is to wire a keyboard switch across each junction and make sure that the engraving on the key's top is linked with the unique code that is produced. In other words, if you hit the key marked "G" on the keyboard, the encoder should produce a code that will eventually be understood as being the letter "G".

How the keyboard talks to the computer
The diagram shows how the keyboard connects to the computer.
There is a chip at each end of the keyboard cable:
- one in the keyboard, called the *"keyboard encoder"*.
- one in the computer, called the *"keyboard controller"*.

The sequence of events is:

The Keyboard Encoder

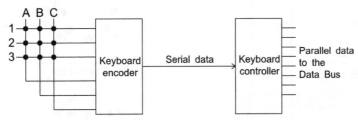

- A key on the keyboard is pressed.
- The key connects two points in the matrix.
- The connection is detected across two pins in the keyboard controller.
- The encoder *"debounces"* the signal (see later).
- The encoder produces a unique *"scan code"* (see later) that corresponds to the changes on its matrix pins.
- The encoder transmits this scan code to the computer, using a serial transmission of data along the keyboard cable (see the wiring of the keyboard cable later in the book).

Keyboard Controller
- The controller receives the data stream from the keyboard.
- The controller generates an interrupt, IRQ1, to let the computer know that it has received data.
- A BIOS routine translates the scan code into an ASCII character for placing on the Data Bus.

Keyboard Controller

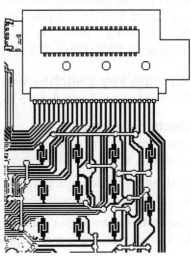

How keyboards are constructed
The diagram shows a typical layout of the main key switch circuits inside a keyboard. For simplicity, the diagram only shows the upper right-hand side of the keyboard - the area where the numeric keypad is to be found.   It shows part of the main board and the matrix of tracks can clearly be seen.

The tracks and contacts may be on a solid board, but they are more likely to sit on a plastic sheet. All the tracks from the main board are plugged in to a small printed circuit board that contains the keyboard encoder and a few other components.

To the left of the controller there is a socket for plugging in the keyboard cable.

The board also has three LED lights, to show whether the Num Lock, Caps Lock and/or Scroll Lock are active.

 This illustration shows a magnified section of the board layout. It shows the plates that make up both ends of a switch and tracks from these plates run back to keyboard controller.
If the two plates were shorted together (more on this later), this change is detected by the controller's circuitry.

There are various types of switches that can be used to bridge these plates and these are covered later.

The keyboard connections

The keyboard connects to your computer via a cable that plugs into a socket at the rear of the computer case.   The older keyboards had a 5-pin DIN plug that was about 1/2" in diameter.   They were called *"AT"* plugs. Modern keyboards use a 6-pin mini DIN plug that is about 3/8" in diameter and these are called *"PS/2"* plugs.

Since many mouse sockets also use PS/2 plugs, there is room for confusion, especially if the two sockets on the computer are not labelled as *"mouse"* and *"keyboard"*.

These diagrams show the types of connectors used on keyboards and say what each pin is used for.

Description	Pins	AT Connector
Keyboard Clock	1	
Keyboard Data	2	
	3	
Ground	4	
Power Supply	5	

Description	Pins	PS/2 Connector
Keyboard Data	1	
	2	
Ground	3	
Power Supply	4	
Keyboard Clock	5	
	6	

Note that not all pins on the plugs are used. Pin 3 is unused on the AT plug and the PS/2 plug does not use pins 2 or 6. The controller's chips are powered through the *"Power Supply"* and *"Ground"* pins.

The *"Keyboard Clock"* pin is used to ensure that the keyboard encoder and the keyboard controller are properly synchronized. The output from the keyboard appears on the *"Keyboard Data"* pin and is at *"TTL"* level, which means that it is either at 5v level or zero volts level.

Wireless keyboards

A range of keyboards are available that have no wire between the keyboard and the computer. Instead, the keyboard communicates using infrared or radio frequencies, including Bluetooth. A receiver module is plugged into the computer to receive the keyboard data and this module is powered from the power pins on the PS/2 port. The receiving module for a Bluetooth keyboard will connect through one of the computer's USB ports. The keyboard transmitter uses batteries that are fitted inside the keyboard.

How the key switches work

Different types of switch have been used in keyboards. The most common types are explained below.

Mechanical keys

The simplest form of keyswitch is the mechanical switch, as it acts in the same way as the doorbell switch in any house.

Pushing the switch makes a contact between two plates and releasing the switch breaks the circuit.

The first diagram shows a key cap (the part you see and press) connected to a small block of foam. A piece of conductive material is attached to

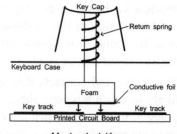

Mechanical Keys

the bottom of the block. When you press the key, the foil shorts across the key plates on the main board. As soon as you let go of the key, the return spring pushes the key back up and the contact is broken.

Another type of mechanical switch is the rubber dome type.

A piece of rubber is moulded into a dome shape and the dome is pliable. Inside the dome is attached a small block of carbon, which is also a conductive material.

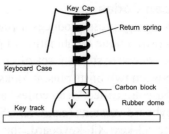
Rubber Dome Keys

Pressing the key on to the dome compresses the dome and the carbon block shorts across the plates in the matrix. When the pressure is lifted, the dome returns to its previous shape.

Membrane switches

The membrane switch also relies on the electrical contact between two plates going to the controller. In this case, however, there are two separate sheets, each with their own tracks and plates.

In between these sheets is a thin layer of insulated material that has holes punched in it at the places where the plates are positioned. As a result, there is a small gap between the two plates.

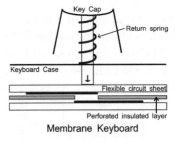
Membrane Keyboard

When you push a key, the rod attached to the key pushes the top plate down into the gap, so that it makes contact with the bottom plate.

Releasing the key allows the top sheet to flex back to its normal position and the contact is broken.

Capacitive keys

This keys works in a different way from the rest.

The other keys relied on making two plates touch each other.

In this case, the two plates never actually touch.

When you press a key, the top plate is brought closer to the fixed lower plate.

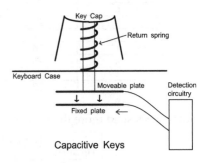
Capacitive Keys

This changes the capacitance between the plates (like tuning a radio) and the change is detected by a special electronic circuit.

Key bounce

With digital circuits, the electronics can switch a voltage from fully on to fully off, or vice versa, in a very short time indeed. So short, in fact, that it seems to be instantaneous.

Things are a little different, however, with mechanical switches. Imagine dropping a ball on to the floor. It eventually goes from a high position to the floor level, but only after bouncing off the floor a few times. The mechanical switches act in this same way. This *"bounce"* only takes place for a very short time. But since computers operate extremely fast, this is detected as the key being clicked several times. So, if you hit the 't' key once, it might appear on the screen as "ttttt".

In other cases, pressing a key and releasing it very rapidly can set up a bouncing action producing the same result. To overcome this, the keyboard controller contains *"debounce"* circuitry.

Once the initial change in voltage is detected, the circuit prevents any further changes from being detected for a short time. This is enough to prevent any bounces from creating false triggering of the controller.

Repeating characters

Each key produces a change when pressed and another change when the key is released. If the keyboard processor detects a 'make' change and does not detect a 'break' change within a certain time, it sends out the key code repeatedly until the key is lifted. The pace at which it sends out the repeat character is called the *"typematic rate"* and this rate can be set within the BIOS, using DOS or Windows. You can also change how long the key will be depressed before the character starts repeating.

Scan Codes

Every key press produces a change on a pair of pins on the encoder. Each key produces that change on its own unique combination of pins.

The encoder stores a set of codes, one for each pin combination.   When the encoder detects a change between two of its pins, it looks up the code that matches it and sends the code to the computer.

These are called "scan codes" and the set of scan codes vary, depending upon the keyboard in use and the keyboard versions (e.g. UK, US, etc).

The 83-key XT keyboard, the 84-key AT keyboard, the 102-key enhanced keyboard, and the 104-key *"Windows keyboard"* all have differences in scan code output.

The encoder has a small area set aside as a buffer. This means that it can store a list of keypresses for later transmission to the computer.   This is necessary because sometimes keys are pressed in combination.

You will already be familiar with the fact that pressing the Shift key and any letter key produces the capitalised version of that letter.   Using Shift, Alt and Ctrl keys in conjunction with another (e.g. Ctrl-A or Alt-P) produces a set of scan codes.

Here some examples of the scan codes sent from the keyboard to the computer:

Key	Scan Code	Key	Scan Code	Key	Scan Code
a	1E	<	33	Spacebar	39
b	30	>	34	Tab	0F
c	2E	=	0D	Enter	1C
d	20	-	0C	Backspace	0E
e	12	/	35	Caps Lock	3A
f	21	#	2B	Num Lock	45
g	22	0	0B	Scroll Lock	46
h	23	1	02	Left Shift	2A
i	17	2	03	Right Shift	36
j	24	3	04	F1	3B
k	25	4	05	F2	3C
l	26	5	06	F3	3D
m	32	6	07	F4	3E
n	31	7	08	F5	3F

Some keys send more than one scan code. These include:

Cursor keys		Windows keys	
Up Arrow	E0 48	Left Windows	E0 5B
Down Arrow	E0 50	Right Windows	E0 5C
Left Arrow	E0 4B	Application	E0 5D
Right Arrow	E0 4D		

If you hit one of these keys, the encoder sends the two scan codes, one after the other.

In fact, hitting the Print Screen button sends four codes - E0, 2A, E0, 37.

The encoder's buffer stores the four codes while they are being transmitted to your computer.

You may have noticed that some applications place different meanings to what appears to be the same key.   For example, hitting the Shift key on the left of the keyboard produces a different result from hitting the Shift key on the right of the keyboard.   That is because the scan codes for each key are different (2A and 36 respectively).   Most applications, such as Word, use either key to produce a shift from lower to upper case.

Keyboard lockout

The "Data Communications" chapter looks at handshaking as a way to regulate the flow of data. This technique is also used with keyboards.   Apart from synchronising the keyboard data to the computer, the clock line is used for handshaking. When the computer pulls the clock line low, the keyboard is placed in a state of *"lockout"* - it is prevented from sending data to the computer. Instead, the characters are stored in the encoder's buffer until the computer is ready to accept them.

The Mouse

While keyboards are the best way to enter textual information, such as names, address, prices, etc - it is very poor at providing positional information. Although it has keys for up, down, left and right, this is not sufficiently accurate for modern applications such as drawing packages, design software, etc.

In particular, Windows is designed so that menu choices are easily selected with the use of a mouse.

The mouse has become very widespread and very popular because of its accuracy and ease of use.

For these reasons, most computers are supplied with both a keyboard and a mouse.

The main components of a mouse are

- The main case that you move around.
- Buttons (usually two but can be up to five) for clicking selections.
- A cable that connects to the computer (although some are now cordless).
- Hardware and software at the computer end, to handle the mouse and its data.

Some types also have a small wheel mounted between the keys and this can be rolled with your finger to scroll through the screen content. Alternatively, it can be pressed in and then it acts like a third button. This type is called an *"Intellimouse"* and it provides quicker and more flexible use of applications that can use it. There are two main types of computer mouse:

- The mechanical mouse
- The optical mouse

In both types, the mouse casing houses a large heavy rubber ball that protrudes from its base. When you move your mouse over a surface, the ball rotates inside its case and this results in a stream of electrical pulses being passed to the computer. The quicker the mouse is moved, the faster the pulse stream; the further the mouse is moved, the longer is the pulse stream. The incoming signals are used by the program to produce pointer movements on the monitor screen.

The mechanical mouse

The ball sits inside the case, with only enough protruding from the bottom of the case to allow it to make contact with a mouse mat or other flat surface.

The mouse can be moved in any direction and this means that the ball can be rotated in any direction.

As the diagram shows, the ball rotates two rollers as it moves.

If the ball is moved exactly in a vertical direction, only the bottom roller is rotated, as there is no significant friction on the side roller. Similarly, moving the mouse purely in the horizontal plane means that only the side roller is rotated. If the mouse is moved diagonally, both rollers will be rotated.

Each roller is connected to a rotating sensor system. With a mechanical mouse, the roller rotates a small insulated disc on which there are etched copper tracks.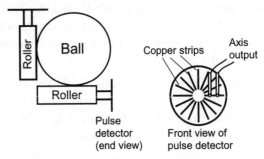

Springs rest on the disc and as the disc rotates, the copper tracks will regularly short across these springs. Each time the springs are shorted, it is detected as a new pulse by the mouse circuitry.

There is one detector for the vertical direction (known as the Y-axis) and one for detecting horizontal movement (known as the X-axis).

This type of mouse is not in common use but is sometimes used in very cheap models.

The opto-mechanical mouse

The mechanical mouse was in widespread use but was not very efficient and had a short life. The most common mouse today is the opto-mechanical type.

It still uses the same roller system as the mechanical mouse but uses a different pulse detection system. The rubber ball still rotates the rollers and each roller still has a disc attached to it. However, this time the disc is plastic and it has slots cut round it as shown in the diagram. A light source, usually from a LED, sits on one side of the disc. As you move the mouse, the disc rotates and the light shines through the slots when a slot lines up with the light source.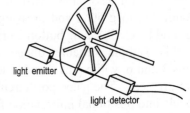

When this happens, a light detector, sitting on the other side of the disc, picks up this light and converts it into an electrical pulse. The more you move your mouse, the more the disc is spun and more pulses are generated.

The optical mouse

The biggest problem with the average mouse is that it suffers from the wear and tear of being constantly used - and is open at the bottom, allowing all sorts of dirt to enter the mechanism.   To overcome this, a purely optical mouse was developed. It does not use a rubber ball to detect mouse movement. In fact, it has no internal moving parts at all.

Instead, the underside of the mouse is sealed but is transparent. This allows the mouse to shine a light down on to the surface that it is sitting on.   This light is reflected back into a light sensor. As the mouse is moved, the changes detected on the surface are converted into electrical pulses.

Early models required that a special mouse mat be used with an optical mouse. Modern versions, such as the Microsoft Intellimouse Explorer, work on any surface. You can even roll the mouse up you arm or over your clothes and it will work.   This model scans the surface 1,500 times per second and provides greater accuracy than a conventional mouse.

The Trackerball

This is also sometimes known as a *"trackball"* system.   It is really only a mouse turned over on to its back. It works in exactly the same way as the mechanical or opto-mechanical mouse already described. However, in this case the mouse is not moved across your desk or mouse mat. Instead, you use your hand to rotate the ball. This means that the trackerball needs a lot less desk space.

The Joystick

The joystick is the common device used for getting positional information into a computer while playing games.   It is also used for flight simulators and virtual reality systems. Sometimes, the joystick is disguised as steering wheels and pedals or *'joypads'*.   While the layout is different, these devices still work on the joystick principle.

The normal joystick connects to the computer through a game port. This can be a dedicated add-on card or the connection may be provided on a sound card or a multi-function card.

The connection is a 15-pin sub-D socket. This connector can handle four press switches (activated by pressing buttons) and four resistive inputs whose values are altered by moving the joystick lever's position.   This allows two joysticks to be connected to a single socket, with each joystick having two buttons and a lever.

The joystick lever is mechanically linked to two variable resistors that are mounted inside the stick. Moving the joystick in the vertical direction alters the voltage output of one of these resistors, while moving the joystick in the horizontal direction alters the voltage output of the other resistor.   Moving the joystick diagonally alters the output of both resistors.

The diagram shows the wiring of a single basic joystick.   Pin 1 takes a five-volt supply to the two variable resistors and the output of these resistors is sent to pins 3 and 6. The voltage level on pin 3 at any one time represents the horizontal position of the joystick (i.e. the x-axis) while the voltage on pin 6 represents the vertical position of the stick (i.e. the y-axis).

The diagram also shows two press buttons.   Pins 4 and 5 are connected to ground and pressing button 1 brings pin 2 down to ground level. Pressing button 2 brings pin 7 down to ground level. In this example, variable voltages are detected by the game port on pins 3 and 6, while pins 2 and 7 detect voltage drops when buttons are pressed.   The game port circuitry converts the altering voltage levels into positional information for the computer program.

To connect a second joystick to the port, the ground level on pin 12 can be taken to a further two buttons that connect to pins 10 and 14.   A five-volt supply from pin 9 can connect to two variable resistors and the varying x-axis output is taken to pin 11 and the y-axis output to pin 13.

The port address for the joystick is from 200h to 20Fh, normally 201h. The basic joystick is simple and does not require an IRQ or DMA allocation. There is no interrupt activity and so the program has to specifically ask the game card for a reading of joystick settings.

The byte at address 201h uses its 8 bits in the way shown:

Bit 7	Bit 6	Bit 5	Bit 4	Bit 3	Bit 2	Bit 1	Bit 0
Button 4	Button 3	Button 2	Button 1	y-axis stick 2	x-axis stick 2	y-axis stick 1	x-axis stick 1

The status of any push button can be determined at any time by reading the value of the corresponding bit. A value of 1 indicates that the button is not being pressed. The value changes to 0 when the button is held down. The value of any variable resistor is read by sending an OUT command to the port. This starts a timer. When the value of the bit of the particular resistor being read flips from 0 to 1, the timer value is read. The value in the timer is proportional to the stick position.

Apart from the game port, joysticks may also connect to the keyboard. These more elaborate versions have multiple buttons that can be programmed to carry out normal keyboard commands.

Joysticks are now commonly available with USB connectors. A wide range of additional features are now available, including force feedback (to simulate the feeling of a gun recoiling or of going over bumps, striking objects, etc.), programmable buttons, throttle wheels and so on. The concept of variable resistors and push buttons is also used in the manufacture of steering wheels, car pedals and other separate game-playing devices.

Bar-code reader

Everyone has seen a bar-code reader in action. Every time you visit a supermarket or DIY store, the checkout operator runs a reader across the items and the electronic till registers the item name and price. This is known as EPOS (Electronic Point Of Sale) and bar codes can also be found on goods in bookstores and music stores. It is also widely used on mailing labels, luggage handling, ID cards and many other applications. In some cases, the goods are passed over a glass plate. In other cases, the operator moves a reader gun or wand across the label or simply points the gun at the label. Bar code readers can be connected to cash registers, automated handling equipment, and also to ordinary PCs. The information the scanner reads is then used to look up a database to find a description of the item. The information may be general (e.g. a thousand items with the same code) or may be unique (e.g. a code specific to a single item or person).

The simplest bar code label is printed as a set of parallel vertical stripes. The stripes have various widths and varied spacing. The combinations of stripe widths and gaps are used to represent numeric digits. This is similar to the way that Morse Code uses different durations of audio tone to represent characters.

The wand reader

The diagram shows the way that the simplest wand reader works.
A light is shone on the label.   If the light shines on a black stripe, the light is absorbed and nothing is detected by the sensor.
However, if the light beam is shone on a white area, the beam is reflected from the label and is detected by a light sensor.
As the label is moved under the light beam, the sensor picks up a series of reflections and converts them into a stream of digital data for use by the computer or other connected equipment.

The CCD reader

The wand reader method reads off the data from the label in a serial fashion, with one digit after another being read. Another method is to read the entire label's contents at the one time. The entire label is illuminated and the reflections from the bar code stripes are focused on to a set of sensors, called a CCD (this device is described in the section on scanners). This system is commonly used and is the type where the operator does not have to swipe the reader across the label. The operator simply points at the label and the data is read off. Although the data is read off in a single operation, the data itself is made up from several numeric characters. So, the electronics inside the reader convert the incoming data into a set of digits for transmitting to the computer in a serial fashion.

Bar Code Standards

There are hundreds of different bar code formats that have been developed but only a few are regularly used. The most common sets of bar code standards are EAN and UPC.

The EAN (European Article Numbering) system is the standard for Europe and, through the EAN International, for the rest of the world except North America.

The UPC (Universal Product Coding) system is used in the USA and Canada.

EAN-8 and EAN-13 are the codes regularly used in retail labelling. As the names suggest, they store 8 or 13 numeric digits.

The example shows an EAN-13 label.   The last digit (the right-most digit) is not part of the item code. It is a check digit used to prevent read errors. Start and stop codes, known as *'guard patterns'*, are added to the label (see the slightly longer bars in the example).   Each person who uses a handheld wand reader will pass the wand over the label at a different speed. The additional patterns placed at each end is used to calculate the speed of the wand movement, so that an accurate interpretation can be made of the rest of the scan. See www.ean-int.org for more details.

Other numeric-only codes include Codabar and Interleaved 2 of 5. Bar codes that support alphanumeric characters include Code 39 and Code 128 (set A and setB).

PDF417 and Maxicode are two-dimensional (i.e. multi-layered) bar codes as shown in the example of a PDF417 label. This allows them to store much more information (e.g. the PD can store 1100 bytes of data).   This allows information such as size, price, description, etc. to be read directly from the label, instead of being looked up on a database.

Printing bar codes

This. is carried out using a specially written labelling program – or using a normal word processor such as Microsoft Word. Bar code fonts are available as freeware and shareware on the Internet.   Once the font is installed, the text for the label is entered as normal numeric or alphanumeric characters (depending on the bar code type). The entered characters are then highlighted and the bar code font style is chosen from the word processor's font list. This converts the text to its corresponding set of bars for printing out as a label.

Scanners

Many computers are now sold along with a bundle of extras such as speakers, modems and scanners. The scanner allows you to take a sheet of paper and copy its contents into a file on your computer. The paper may have printed text on it, or it may contain a diagram, a chart or a photograph.

Scanners are used for a variety of purposes, common examples being:

- Converting simple line drawings (e.g. line art, logos, hand-written signatures, diagrams, charts) into graphics files.
- Converting photographic images (e.g. photographs, driving licence, bus pass) into high-resolution, multi-coloured graphics files.
- Using OCR (optical character recognition) software to convert scanned printed pages into text files.

Scanners are available for a variety of purposes:

- Flatbed – This looks like a small photocopier and is the most common type. It usually scans an area slightly larger than an A4 sheet of paper although larger A3 models are also available. Many flatbed scanners are not limited to scanning objects with flat surfaces, and can provide a useable image from most objects placed on the glass bed.   This allows pages from books and magazines to be scanned, as well as 3-D objects such as a human hand, coins, and so on.   Anything that is scanned on a photocopier at the office party is capable of being scanned on a flatbed scanner.
- Sheetfed – This allows a set of documents to be fed to the scanner page at a time (usually for OCR or document archiving). This can be a scanner that is specially built for this kind of work, or a sheet feeder device can often be added to an existing flatbed scanner.
- Drum – used for high end reprographics.
- Pen – This type is very small and portable. The scanner pen is hand operated and the device is rolled across the image to be scanned.   It is useful for reading text from a page but larger areas have to be read in many passes and then stitched together.
- Film – This type scans in negatives or slides from conventional cameras. It may be a scanner specially built for the job – or it may be an adapter that is added to a flatbed scanner.

Models are also available in a variety of resolutions and colour depths. Early models were solely monochrome, whereas current scanners range from 600dpi through to 4800dpi models, at up to 48-bit colour depth.

How a scanner works

Consider the operation of a photocopier. It has two separate phases.

- The first phase captures the image from the document that is placed on the glass.
- The second phase writes a copy of the image on to a sheet of paper.

These operations can be also be carried out by two computer peripherals - a scanner and a printer. The scanner can capture the image and the printer can print a copy of that image. Indeed, software is available to use them together to act as a photocopier. So, a scanner is really just the first half of a photocopy machine. The most common type of scanner is the flatbed model and the description for this type follows, although the general principles apply to all scanner types.

The photograph (or other object) is placed face down on the scanner glass bed and the capture software is started. This can be a piece of software specially written for the job, or can be any graphics package that has a capture facility built into it.

A bright cold cathode light and a scanning head are mounted on a frame that is able to travel down inside your scanner chassis. It is slowly moved down the document by a stepper motor.   The light is shone up on the surface to be scanned and the reflected light from one narrow strip of the document is focussed on to a scanning head. The scanning head contains a single row of light sensors using a CCD.

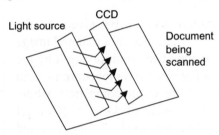

The CCD (charge-coupled device) is a small solid-state chip that contains a set of light sensors. Each sensor is a tiny photodiode that produces a value of electrical charge that varies according to the amount of light that hits it.

When you press the scan button, a microchip reads the amount of charge in each cell.   The values from each row are read off and make up the serial image output stream. The scanner's electronics move the image data out of the CCD and convert them from varying light intensity levels into digital values that can be saved as a file to disk.

Since there are a fixed number of sensors in the row, the maximum quality of the picture is decided by the number of sensors.   The quality is measured by the number of *"pixels"* that appear in the final picture. A pixel is a *"picture element"* which is smallest dot that will appear on the scanned image. The quality of the scanner's image is quoted in either *"dpi"* which is dots per inch or *'"ppi"* which is pixels per inch.

The number of pixel sensors has a bearing on the final quality of the scanned image, with greater resolution being achieved by CCDs with a greater number of pixels.

The scanner captures a document's detail one line at a time.   Since most flatbed scanners handle an A4 sheet, the width of the scanned area is a minimum of 8.27", with most models having an 8.5" scanning width. If a scanner supports a maximum scanning resolution of 600dpi, the CCD in the scanning head will contain 8.5 x 600 = 5,100 sensors.   Even a top-quality 2,400dpi optical resolution requires just over 20,000 sensors.

Either way, the scanner gathers the image data as a series of pixel data and this is sent to the computer via the cable interface.

The quality of the final image depends on the quality of the scanner components - and on the resolution of the scanning mechanism. Since many measurements are metric, conversions have to be done into inches to calculate file sizes (see later).

Optical resolution

As explained above, the construction of the CCD determines the maximum scanning resolution. This is called the *'optical resolution'* and is usually 600dpi, 1200dpi or 2400dpi in the horizontal plane. The stepper motor moves the head in amounts set by the user. If you choose 600dpi for the vertical resolution, the head is moved 1/600th of an inch for each vertical scan. If the scanning head is moved down the bed in movements that are equal to the CCD sensor spacing, the final resolution is equal in both planes (e.g. 600dpi x 600dpi or 1200dpi x 1200dpi).

If the head assembly is moved in smaller steps, the vertical resolution becomes greater than the horizontal resolution (e.g. 600dpi x 1200dpi, 600dpi x 2400dpi or 1200dpi x 2400dpi).

Interpolated resolution

Most manufacturers also quote a figure for their scanner's *'interpolated resolution'*. This is a much higher figure, up to 9600dpi, to make the specification appear more impressive. Since the scanner cannot actually detect any more data than its number of CCD sensors, the *'extra'* data for the higher resolution is interpolated (i.e. estimated). If, for example, a scanner has an optical resolution of 600dpi and an interpolated scan of 1200dpi is chosen, there is twice as much data to be stored in the file for each line than is being physically scanned. The scanner software looks at the actual readings on adjacent CCD sensors and works out the likely values of colour and contrast that would appear in between. No extra original information has been extracted from the photograph, but the file size is four times larger. In addition, since the process averages out the values at edges, the final scanned image is slightly softened.

File sizes

When choosing a model, consideration has to be given to the capabilities of the rest of the computer. The size of a scanned image is calculated by taking the area to be scanned and multiplying it by the number of dots per inch. This gives a file size for a monochrome scan (i.e. each screen dot is either completely black or completely white, with a single bit storing the value of each scanned dot). A 256-level grey scale image is achieved by sampling the level of light reflected from each dot and storing it as one of 256 levels. In this way, a single byte stores the dot's value. A 24-bit colour scan is three times the size of a 256 grey-scale scan. A technique, known as *'oversampling'*, uses 36-bit up to 48-bit colour.

File sizes for various scanning resolutions (from an A4 sheet at 24-bit colour)	
Scanning resolution	Uncompressed file size
300dpi	25MB
600dpi	100MB
1200dpi	398MB
2400dpi	1.56GB
4800dpi	6.22GB
9600dpi	24.89GB

An A4 sheet of paper is the size of a standard sheet of typewriter paper. The dimensions are 210mm x 297mm, or 8.27" x 11.69", when converted to inches. If the entire page were to be scanned in colour, the file size for a range of different scanning resolutions is given in the table.

Take the example of scanning at 600dpi. The page is 8.27" wide, so this requires 8.27 x 600 = 4962 dots of horizontal resolution. The page is 11.69" long, requiring 11.69 x 600 = 7014 dots of vertical resolution. The number of dots to represent the entire A4 sheet is then 4962 x 7014 = 34,803,468 dots. This represents the size for a monochrome image, each dot being either black or white.

To store a colour image, each dot is represented by varying amounts of red, green and blue. A byte is required to store each of these colour values. So, the file size is multiplied by three to get the final size in bytes. In the example, a staggering 100MB of storage space is required for an A4 image at a respectable 600dpi.

Since a photograph in a magazine can expect to be printed at a minimum of 4800dpi, a scanned A4 image would not even fit on an entire DVD disk - unless it was compressed.

This single file requires huge storage space and provides huge memory problems in trying to load and manipulate the image in paint and photo-retouch packages. Careful thought has to be given to the use of scanners before choosing the specification.

Interfacing scanners

Early models of scanner used dedicated interface cards or connected via the parallel or SCSI ports.

Most current models connect via the USB port, while some connect via a FireWire port.

All current scanners are designed to interface with a TWAIN driver. Since a TWAIN driver is the one used in all current software packages, such as PhotoShop or OCR packages, it means that any software package is able to work with any make or model of scanner.

Printers

In choosing the printer for a computer system, there are a number of factors that should have an effect on the selection process. For example:

- The quality required. If the printer is for occasional home use (e.g. to print letters to friends etc) or internal business use (for example internal memos or code printouts) then in most cases a low-quality printer will be sufficient. There is no point buying a high-end laser printer if all that will be printed is the occasional leave request form, for example.
- The volume of output. Computers in the home tend to be lightly used, while some office machines can be in almost constant use. The usage requirements affect which type and model of printer to buy. It is a waste of money to buy a high-end super-fast laser printer if it will only be used on odd occasions, while buying a cheaper printer for high volumes of printing is false economy because the printer will wear out much faster, and printing may be slower.
- Cost considerations. There is more to be considered here than simply the initial outlay of purchasing and installing the system. The idea of '*Total Cost of Ownership*' (TCO) suggests that other factors should be taken into consideration, such as: consumable costs (ink, paper); maintenance costs (for replacement parts as well as the engineer's time); warranties; etc.
- Maintenance requirements. What type of warranty does the printer have, for example?   Whenever a printer breaks down in a workplace, there can be a significant reduction in productivity. Also compare the *Mean Time Between Failures* (MTBF) of printers if prolonged downtime will cause serious problems. The higher the mean (average) time between failures, the more reliable the printer is.
- Special requirements. If, say, the user wishes to be able to print on envelopes, opacities or so on, then it should be ensured that the desired printer has that capability. Other factors that may be demanded include duplex printing, colour output, large page sizes such as A3, etc.

The table below shows the general performance of various types of printer categories:

	Dot Matrix	Inkjet	Laser
Quality	Moderate	Good	Excellent
Printing speed	Slow to moderate	Moderate	Moderate to Fast
Printer cost	Low	Moderate	High
Consumable cost	Low	Moderate	High
Reliability	Good	Good	Good

Of course, individual printers may vary, and statistics on printer speed (expressed in ppm - pages per minute) reliability (expressed in MTBF - mean time between failures) and similar factors can be found in printer manuals or by checking recent computer magazines.

Once the desired printer has been selected, its purchase should be handled in a similar way to a PC purchase. Check that it comes with the kind of warranty wanted. If the organisation has its own in-house support then a cheaper warranty covering parts may be sufficient, while many small businesses without such support might well require back-to-base or even on-site maintenance warranties.

How printers work

Your printer is used to produce a paper copy (often called a '*hard copy'*) of the letters, reports, graphs, etc. produced by your programs. Although there are different types and models of printer, every printer contains at least the following components:

- Power cable connector
- Print head
- Interface circuitry
- Data cable connector
- Printer carriage
- Power supply

These components are explained in more detail below. Depending on the type and model of printer, additional components could be used in the printer.

Power and data connectors

The printer needs two things before it can begin printing. It needs to know what to print, and it needs to have electricity to allow the components to operate. The page information is sent to the printer from the computer via the data cable, while the power is supplied from the mains via a power cable.

The power cable for a printer is a standard *"kettle"* lead. This is the same type that connects to the PC and the monitor. These leads are interchangeable, even though printer power leads tend to have a distinctive 'L'-shape, and so the power connector on the printer is the same as the power connector on a PC.

The data connector, on the other hand, can be of several types, such as:

- 25-pin D-type parallel connector on the PC end of the cable, with a Centronics connector at the printer end. This is the most widely used connector on parallel printers (i.e. Printers that receive data via the computer's parallel port).
- 9-pin D-type Serial connector. This connector is used for serial printers. (i.e. Printers that receive data via the computer's serial port) although this is not a common type.
- Universal Serial Bus. The more recent USB system is an option on many printers, although older PCs might not have USB ports to take advantage of this connection type. Some printers provide both parallel and USB connections.
- Network connector. If the printer is to be used on a computer network, it may have one or more types of network connector to allow it to plug straight in to the network. If this is used, then it should not be connected to any PC through any other of the connectors it may have. However, on stand-alone systems, this connector is not used.
- IrDA connector. Some printers have built-in infrared capability, and there are adapters that can turn a parallel printer into an infrared printer. This allows laptops with IrDA capability to print without having to go through the process of physically connecting to the printer.

Serial vs. Parallel

There are two different types of connection for printers, known as serial and parallel systems. These names describe how the data arrives at the printer from the computer. A serial printer accepts data in a series of single data bits from the computer; a parallel printer has more wires and so it can receive 8 bits (i.e. one byte) at a time. Most printers have only a serial or a parallel connection, while a few have sockets for both types. Now the USB (Universal Serial Bus) interface is a common method of attaching printers. The USB is similar in basic operation to a serial port, though the connectors are very different and the USB is capable of having more than one device attached to a single port.

Standard vs. bi-directional

The standard parallel port on a PC is designed for data output only. This is due to the fact that the main parallel device, the printer, is only used for output. However, as time went by and technology progressed, printer manufacturers realised that some form of feedback from the printer would be helpful. For example, the user may not realise when the printer runs out of paper. Modern printers often detect such problems and report them immediately to the PC.

The user would then be made aware of the problem and be able to rectify it before trying to print anything. In order for the printer to communicate these problems to the controlling PC, the parallel port on the computer system has to be able to accept data input as well as send data output.

There are two broadly similar methods to allow this input and output to happen on the same cable. They are known respectively as the Enhanced Communications Port, (ECP) and the Enhanced Parallel Port. (EPP) Both of these ports are identical physically to the standard parallel port, only the method of operation of the port is different (see the chapter on Computer Architecture for more details).

In most cases, a printer that is designed to take advantage of ECP or EPP communications with a computer will still operate on a standard parallel port, but without the feedback information.

Power supply

Although the printer has a mains power connector, the motors and electronics use a much lower voltage than the mains voltage. Like the PC, it has to reduce the voltage supplied to components within the printer. The power supply of a printer is not interchangeable in the way that PC power supplies are interchangeable. If the printer power supply is damaged, the only options are repair or replacement with an identical model of power supply. And as with all power supplies, repair is a safe option only for experienced electrical engineers.

Print head

In many ways, the most important part of the printer is the print head. This component is the one that actually does the work of getting the image placed onto the paper. The way in which it does this varies depending on the type of printer, but the vast majority of printers in use today use a print head that forms an image by creating a pattern of dots on the page.

For example, if the user wished to print out an order form, and the first letter on the document was the letter 'K', then that letter could be represented by the pattern of dots shown in the illustration. Although it is clear that the letter is indeed the letter 'K', it is not particularly good quality. However, if that pattern of dots was much smaller, say perhaps the size of one of the letters in this paragraph, then the 'dottiness' of the pattern would be considerably less noticeable. In fact, the more dots we can cram into a square inch, the more difficult it is to notice the dots at all – simply use more dots to make up each letter or picture on the page!

This is where the measurement known as '*dots per inch*' (dpi) comes from. The higher the number of dots that a print head can squeeze into an inch square determines just how high quality the output will be. 300dpi (300 dots per inch vertically by 300 dots per inch horizontally) is a reasonable basic resolution for any printer, but high quality laser printers can achieve up to 2,400 x 600dpi or sometimes even higher for professional purposes.

High resolution printers that use this method are occasionally referred to as '*near letter quality*' (NLQ) printers. This is to distinguish them from printers that use a set of pre-determined letters etched onto plates, which give '*letter quality*' (LQ). However, these two terms are outmoded since the arrival of extremely high quality laser printers that produce output that is indistinguishable from true letter quality printers while still being able to print graphics and varying fonts.

Printer carriage

An inkjet print (or dot matrix) head does not span the entire page. In most cases, it does not even span the width of the page. The print head normally only covers a tiny fraction of an inch squared in area. This is not enough to cover the entire page, and so the print head has to be moved across the width of the page to print one row of the image. This movement is the job of the printer carriage mechanism. It is simply a mechanical device for moving the print head back and forward across the width of the page.

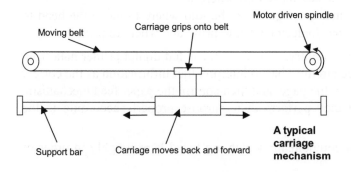

A typical carriage mechanism

This allows the print head to create an entire row of dots across the page in one movement. However, a single row is far short of an entire page.

The solution is to print row after row, while pulling the paper slightly further through the printer so that each row is printed below the last. This job is performed by the paper transport mechanism (see later).

For ease of understanding the print head is not shown in this diagram – it would attach to the carriage as it moves horizontally.

Paper transport mechanisms

Also known as the *"paper feed mechanism"*, there are two methods of moving paper through the printer. These are:

Friction feed

This is the type of feed used in ordinary typewriters.

The paper is held between the main roller and a number of small rollers. As the rollers rotate, the paper is pulled through. This has the advantage that ordinary paper can be fed into the printer; the printer can handle ordinary A4 sheets of paper or pre-printed stationary. It can also handle continuous stationery or fanfold paper but this can cause problems. Since the paper is not of consistent thickness and the rollers do not maintain a constant friction, continuous paper gradually is pulled through unevenly. This effect is known as '*skew*' and becomes a greater and greater problem with the length of the paper being pulled through. With single sheets, the effect of skew should be so slight as to be unnoticeable. Most photocopiers and many fax machines use friction feed systems.

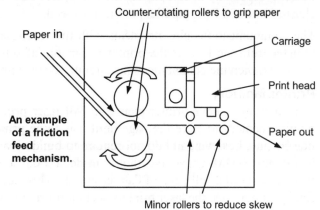

An example of a friction feed mechanism.

Tractor feed

This mechanism uses belt-driven pins on each side of the paper.

These pins engage in holes that are punched down both edges of the paper. This ensures that the paper is pulled through evenly.

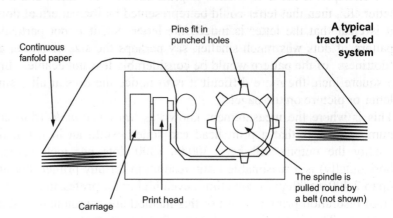

A typical tractor feed system

Pins fit in punched holes

Continuous fanfold paper

The spindle is pulled round by a belt (not shown)

Print head

Carriage

The disadvantage is that it requires the purchase of specially made paper with holes along either side. Fortunately, fanfold paper is in easy supply.

Most fanfold paper comes with tiny perforations, so that the holed edges can be removed. This type of fanfold also has horizontal perforations at intervals so that the final result looks like a normal sheet of A4 paper.

Feed holes

Perforations

Interface circuitry

The print head and the printer carriage mechanism are both concerned with physical operations, like moving the print head around and getting it to put ink on the page. However, something has to control the print head and the printer carriage so that this ink is placed in the correct location. In the previous example, where the letter 'K' is being printed, the print head does not know that it is the letter 'K' being printed. It is simply told where to place dots of ink on the page. Likewise, the printer carriage has to be told where to move the head to before it starts printing that letter 'K'. Something has to decide what to print, and where to print it.

Both of these jobs are performed by the interface circuitry. The circuitry is fed digital printer data from the PC via the data cable connector. The interface circuitry has to interpret that information as the correct sequences of dots placed in the correct locations on the page, and then control the paper feed mechanism, the printer carriage and the print head so that they perform their purpose properly according to the desired output.

The Interface Circuitry itself consists of several components, which are listed here roughly in order of use, from PC to final printout:

- Communications circuitry
- Raster Image Processor
- Printer Memory
- Printer Buffers
- Control Circuitry

These components are explained in more detail over the following pages.

Communications Circuitry

As with a PC, the printer requires some control over the flow of data. Printers are generally quite slow devices, especially in comparison with a typical PC. Very few printers indeed can cope with data being churned out of a PC's parallel port at full speed.

The communications circuitry deals with the reception of printer data, and the synchronisation of data transfer from the PC. If the printer is capable of sending information to the PC (such as out of paper warnings) then the communications circuitry deals with the transmission of this data to the PC.

Printer Memory

Not all printers have printer memory. All laser printers, because they print an entire page at a time, require memory to store the page until it is to be printed. Dot Matrix, Inkjet and similar printers print line by line, however, and do not require to build up an entire page image. The printer memory (which is usually SIMM chips like those inside a PC) store data, usually generated by the Raster Image Processor, until a full page of data is stored. This can then be used by the control circuitry to create the final printout. See the laser printers section for more information on printer memory.

Printer Buffers

As mentioned above, printer memory is not required in a line printer such as an inkjet. However, all printers do have a small area of RAM called a buffer.

Computers are always much faster than printers, and if a computer had to wait every time a single character was printed this would result in significant delays. The printer buffer helps alleviate this problem, by allowing the communications circuitry to fill up the buffer before having to delay the PC from further communications. The control circuitry can then begin printing information from the buffer rather than directly from the PC. This makes the whole printing process slightly more efficient, sometimes even allowing a small print job to be processed in a single transfer. Like printer memory, many printers allow additional buffer upgrades.

Control Circuitry

The print head (or heads, in a colour printer) need to be told which dots to print and when, and in some printers even how much ink to use. The printer carriage and paper feed, on the other hand, need to be controlled to ensure that the print head is facing the correct part of the page at the correct time. This is the job of the control circuitry.

The control circuitry is given data on the desired page or line data, from printer memory or buffers. This information is then converted into the correct sequence of electrical signals to control the print head and the printer carriage mechanism appropriately.

Raster Image Processor

The part of the circuitry that generates the sequence of dots to be printed is called the Raster Image Processor. (RIP) In order to interpret information from the PC, the interface circuitry is programmed by the manufacturer to accept information in a certain format, and control the printer carriage and print head in order to print out pages accordingly.

There are many printer data formats, but the most common include:

*   Plain (ASCII) text
*   Epson escape codes
*   Binary image data
*   Postscript format

These are explained in more detail below.

ASCII text

The American Standard Code for Information Interchange (ASCII) is a data format that is used to represent information consisting purely of text and punctuation marks. It is not possible to print graphics using ASCII.

ASCII is an internationally recognised set of numeric codes that represent upper case letters, lower case letters, numbers, and various punctuation marks and other symbols. For example, ASCII code 67 represents the upper case letter 'C', while ASCII code 32 represents a space. (for example a space between words in a sentence)

Although all printers support standard ASCII codes, the ASCII system is not used purely for printing. Far from it – ASCII codes are used to represent text within the computers themselves, as well as when transmitting text over a modem, storing text on disk, and so on. In fact almost every computer system that deals with plain text uses ASCII.

When a printer receives an ASCII code to print, it has to convert that 8-bit number into a pattern of dots that it uses to output the character represented by the ASCII code. For example, if the ASCII code 75 is to be printed (the upper-case letter 'K'), then the pattern of dots might be as shown earlier. Every other printable ASCII code has a separate pattern of dots, and they all depend on the resolution of the printer and the font styles that printer is able to output.

ASCII control codes

Those ASCII codes from zero to 31 do not represent actual characters, but instead are reserved for '*control codes*' that have special uses.

The most important of these are:

10   This is the ASCII code for Line Feed (LF). This code tells the printer to feed the paper up one line. This code is interpreted by the circuitry as a request for the paper feed mechanism to advance the paper one line. It is normally used alongside the ASCII code 13, described below.

12   The ASCII code for a Form Feed (FF). This code will tell the printer to feed the paper an entire page on. How this works depends on the type of printer. For example a dot matrix printer might move the paper on enough to line up the print head with the start of the next page, while a laser printer might not even print anything until a full page of data or a Form Feed is received. Some printers have a 'FF' or 'TOF' (Top Of Form) button to perform the same function.

13   Carriage Return (CR). This code tells the printer circuitry to move the print carriage back to the start of the line to begin printing another series of data. However it does not necessarily mean that the paper should be moved on to the next line of the page. Because of this, the Carriage Return and Line Feed codes are used together in most cases when a new line of output is desired, and are often referred to together as 'CR/LF'. A CR/LF combination will move the print head back to the start of the line and move the paper on to the next line. Together, this makes the printer ready to print the next line of data.

Most software packages and printer drivers, when communicating data to the printer, send both the CR and LF codes. However, some assume that the printer will supply a line feed when a CR code is sent, and so they do not send an accompanying LF code.

To deal with this, most printers have a setting that determines whether the printer automatically inserts line feeds with each carriage return. Sometimes this setting is a switch marked 'CR/LF' or 'ALF' (Automatic Line Feed) while on many laser printers it is an option accessed through a menu.

Setting the automatic line feed option incorrectly can lead to constant reprinting over the same line (if the printer never receives a line feed code and does not automatically generate one), or printing double spaced lines instead of single spaced lines. (if the printer receives a line feed code but also generates another one itself when it receives the carriage return code).

Extended ASCII codes

Standard ASCII is a seven-bit code, in other words it uses seven binary digits to store or represent each ASCII code. Seven binary digits allow a range of 128 possible codes, ranging from zero to 127. This is enough to represent 32 special control codes (such as CR and LF); 52 alphabetic characters (26 each of upper and lower case); 10 numeric characters (zero to nine); and 34 punctuation marks or symbols. (such as the '?' character or the '£' symbol)

However, a standard data byte is 8 bits long, giving a range of 256 codes, from zero to 255. This can represent an additional 128 codes that are not used in standard ASCII.

Rather than let that extra capacity go to waste, most printer manufacturers look to extend the ASCII code set. The first to do this was Epson, who used the upper 128 codes to represent characters that were to be printed in italics. IBM, on the other hand, used the upper 128 codes to represent foreign characters (such as letters with accents, or foreign currency symbols), and also to represent basic line graphics. (for drawing boxes around text, and so on)

These two systems became widely used in plain text printing, and so many printers support both modes. The printers achieve this support by allowing the user to decide whether to use the Epson extended ASCII character set or the IBM extended ASCII character set. How this is set depends on the printer; it may be through DIP switches inside the printer case, or chosen through a menu on the printer interface.

Epson escape codes

Although the Epson extended ASCII set allowed for italic characters, it did not have enough codes to represent other modes of printing, such as bold or underlined. Epson developed a solution to this that still used only an 8-bit byte for each code.

The ASCII code 27 is one of the special ASCII control codes (see above). It represents the 'Escape' character. The escape key is the one on the top left of your keyboard, and it is used to interact with programs. As far as storing or printing text is concerned though, the escape key, and hence the escape code, has no use. Epson realised that this code could be put to use, and developed a system they called 'ESC/P'. In this system, standard ASCII text was sent to the printer as normal. When the 'Escape' code is received by the printer, this informed the printer that the next byte of data was not an ASCII code but an *'escape code'*.

These escape codes could be used to send many kinds of information to the printer. For example the P.C. could tell the printer to start (or stop!) printing in bold, underlined, strikethrough or double-strike typeface. It could change font size or style, change between draft and full quality print, and so on.

For example, the ASCII code 71 represents the letter 'G', while the ASCII code 27 (escape) followed by the escape code 71 tells the printer to begin printing in double-strike mode.

Binary image data

Standard ASCII text is excellent for representing pure text, but it has no graphics capability at all. Even IBM's extended ASCII character set only provides a very basic set of line drawing characters.

In order to output graphics or customised fonts that are not recognised by the printer, the page must be printed as a graphic image. Every page printed by a modern PC printer is composed of dots, usually so small and closely packed together that they are not recognisable as dots to the naked eye.

With ASCII text, the printer simply converts an ASCII code into a particular pattern of dots, and then prints that pattern. With an image file, the pattern of dots is already known. For user-defined fonts, or pages that mix text and graphics, the whole page must be converted into a large image before transmitting to the printer.

This image is not in ASCII text or any other human-readable format. The pattern of black and white dots is transmitted as pure binary information. Unfortunately, the format of the binary information varies between some manufacturers and even sometimes between different models of printer.

For example, a user could print an A4 page with margins set so that the output is 7 inches in width. A 300dpi printer would expect 7x300=2100 binary data bits (263 bytes) to represent each horizontal line, while a 1200dpi printer would expect 7x1200=8400 data bits (1050 bytes) per horizontal line.

Furthermore, there are some printer settings that may be user-adjustable. For example, a modern laser printer will offer the capability to print at different resolutions for different pages. The software will need to inform the printer when it wishes to change resolution. Other printer-specific settings might include setting the page type (e.g. A4 or American Letter size etc.), the tray to use (manual feed, upper paper tray, lower paper tray etc.) and so on.

Printers with special capabilities, such as colour output or duplex (two sides of the paper) printing, will have even more to take into consideration when sending binary data from the PC to the printer.

All of these differences mean that binary output must be customised for the type of printer that is in use; otherwise the output will almost certainly be totally unrecognisable.

Before Windows became widely used, software packages had to be written so that they were capable of sending data in various binary formats to accommodate several printer types. However, the Windows operating system allows a *'printer driver'* to be installed, that is capable of translating the user's document into the correct series of binary digits for that particular printer. In fact, Windows allows several printer drivers to be installed, so that if you have multiple printers attached or available through a network, the user may select any one printer for a particular document.

Printer Emulation

Some printer types are more widely used than others. Among dot-matrix printers, the Epson FX80 was at one time by far the most widely used. The HP DeskJet series are the most common inkjet printers, and the Hewlett Packard LaserJet series are the most common laser printers.

As mentioned earlier, before Windows became common, software had to be written such that they could prepare binary data for various printer types. Any new printer would then in theory require a new add-on to the software. Many manufacturers however realised that they could *'emulate'* the operation of one of these popular printers.

Many laser printers, for example, are able to emulate the operation of a HP LaserJet III. If the software sent binary data that a LaserJet III could recognise, then a printer set to emulate a LaserJet III could understand the data and print as desired.

Setting the emulation of a printer may be achieved by DIP switches inside a dot matrix printer, or by a setting on the control panel of a laser printer, for example.

In Windows, emulation is only required if the printer driver is not readily available – perhaps if the printer is obsolete and no longer supported by the manufacturer.

Postscript

While the user is creating a page in an application such as Microsoft Word, it is not stored as a binary image. The text is stored as ASCII, with images stored as bitmaps or vectors, and control codes throughout to indicate typefaces, font sizes and so on. To print this page as an image to the printer, it is converted to a series of lines of data bits representing black and white dots, as explained earlier

PostScript is a method that allows pages to be regarded as objects instead of binary collections of dots. This can improve print quality as it allows the printer to select certain settings rather than relying on the software which may not know the best way to print on any given printer.

Instead of converting the entire page into a single giant binary file, the page data is transmitted as a text file in a language called '*PostScript*'. This text file contains information that allows the printer to recreate the page. For example, it contains text formatting information, data on objects in object-oriented images, and information that allows the printer to interpret a bitmap image embedded in the PostScript file.

There are other printer languages, such as Hewlett Packard's HPGL, the Printer Control Language (PCL) and so on, which are sometimes grouped together under the heading of Page Description Languages (PDL). They all perform similar functions, but PostScript is the most widely recognised printer language, and is used in high-quality DTP productions. It is not necessary for ordinary home or business use.

Printer types

There are different printers for different jobs. All have different qualities as described next.

Impact printers

This involves an inked ribbon being struck against the paper, impressing ink from the ribbon onto the paper to produce the shape desired. Because of the constant striking of the ribbon, impact printers usually generate a lot of noise when they are in use. There are a variety of forms of impact printer, of which the Dot Matrix is the only type that is still in use to any real degree.

Dot Matrix

Dot matrix printers operate by using a number of pins on the print head, usually arranged in a rectangular pattern. The printer selects which of these pins it wishes to strike the ribbon to create the final pattern on the paper. This pattern could resemble a letter, a number, or part of a graphic image.

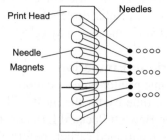

Dot matrix printers are the oldest printers still in use. They are among the cheapest available, and can be reasonably fast, some printing up to 400 characters every second.

The quality of output from a dot matrix printer depends mainly on the number of pins on the print head. Early dot matrix printers involved a vertical row of seven pins that impacted five times along the page to create a matrix of 7x5 dots that each character consisted of.

More modern dot matrix printers have a rectangular array of 18x24 up to 48x24 pins on the print head.

Some dot matrix printers increase the quality of output by having two modes – *draft* and *quality*. Draft mode allows the printer to print each line in a single pass, while quality mode means that each line consists of two passes. This two-pass mode is of course slower by a factor of two, but both the resolution and the heaviness of print can be increased when printing in two passes.

The quality of dot matrix printing is also affected by the quality of the ribbon. Often, a new ribbon contains more ink than might be anticipated, resulting in smeared or smudged printouts for a short while. However, as the ribbon nears the end of its useful life it contains less and less ink, which has the opposite effect – resulting in printouts that may not be dark enough.

Dot matrix printers are used for bulk printing, where cost of printing is more important than print quality, for example printouts of inventories, or long sections of program code. Most dot matrix printers can take fanfold paper including specialised stationary, making them better suited to printing off long runs of items such as mailshots, reminder notices or pay slips.

Colour dot matrix printers

Dot matrix printers are able to print in colour, by using a ribbon that has four rows, each with a different ink colour. The ribbon is moved up and down to print each different colour. As a result, each line has to be printed in four different passes to allow all of the colours to be used.

This is obviously much slower, and colour dot matrix printers are no longer widely used.

Other Impact printers

A matrix of dots is not the only way to push ink from a ribbon onto paper. Daisy wheel, thimble, barrel, and chain printers all operate in a similar manner to typewriters. Each character has a typeface permanently located on a daisy wheel, thimble, barrel or chain. The raised character shape is caused to impact against the ribbon, creating a replica of the shape on the paper; similar to the way a rubber stamp leaves ink only where it has raised areas. The use of whole character shapes instead of a number of dots means that every printout has true '*letter quality*', but at the expense of being unable to cope with varying fonts, italics and so on without replacing the impact device, which would involve a significant delay. Also, they are completely unable to deal with graphics at all.

Non-impact printers

Impact printers have a number of disadvantages - they are noisy, relatively slow, and produce limited quality. There are a number of techniques that allow printing without using impact mechanisms, from cheap bubble-jets for home use through to professional wax transfer or dye sublimation printers. Due mainly to cost and speed considerations, the two most widely used non-impact printer types are inkjet and laser printers.

Ink Jet Printers

Ink jet printers avoid using impact to transfer ink, by instead spraying dots of ink onto the paper surface. A small plastic case contains the ink, which is drawn from the reservoir through a pattern of tiny holes on the print head. How said ink reaches the page depends on the technology used - there are a number of inkjet printing methods. The original method was *continuous stream* printing, but the two methods most widely used today are *thermal* (or '*bubble jet*') and *piezoelectric* (or *mechanical*) inkjet printing methods.

Continuous stream inkjets

The first inkjet printers to be developed used conductive ink, in other words ink that could be given an electrical charge. The charged ink was then sprayed in a continuous stream of tiny droplets. Since each droplet was charged, an electromagnetic field could be used to deflect the droplets onto the page, similar to the way a compass needle is moved by the Earth's magnetic field. However, the ink had to be sprayed in a continuous stream, so unused ink had to be deflected away from the page into a container. This could be extremely wasteful.

The continuous stream method was fairly fast at the time it was introduced, being able to print over a hundred characters per second, but is very slow by today's standards.

Another problem with continuous stream inkjets is that it is susceptible to magnetic interference. The charged stream of ink is analogous to the charged stream of electrons in a television set. Just like a television set, if you put a strong magnetic device nearby (like a paperclip holder or a magnetic screwdriver) it will interfere with the final result.

Thermal inkjets

A thermal inkjet printer works by heating the ink every time a dot is required on the page. The print head contains a tiny ink reservoir and a heating element for each dot. The element vaporizes the ink, which consists mostly of water, by rapidly heating it.

As anyone who has opened a shaken bottle of fizzy juice can tell you, gas takes up more volume than liquid does, and as a result the expanding gas forces some of the ink out of the reservoir and onto the page. The gas bubble (which gives '*bubble jet printers*' their name) then cools and turns back to liquid, and more ink is sucked into the chamber to fill the empty space left by the ink that was ejected.

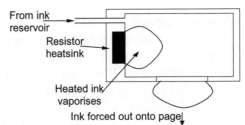

A nozzle in a thermal inkjet print head

This heating and cooling process can occur extremely quickly

– it can be repeated thousands of times a second! In addition, inkjet printer heads have rows of several dots, most commonly totalling 16 but which can number up to a hundred, all of which print simultaneously. As a result, thermal inkjet printers are much faster than continuous stream inkjets, some able to print thousands of characters per second. They also do not waste ink by spraying it continuously.

However, thermal inkjets are not without their drawbacks. There is a tiny resistor in the print head that carries out the heating of ink, thousands of times a second, every time a page is printed. Imagine if an electric cooker was turned on and off that much – it would not last as long as it would under normal use. As you might expect, then, thermal inkjet print heads need to be replaced comparatively often. So often, in fact, that thermal inkjet print heads are actually put inside the ink cartridge, which is thrown away when the ink runs out.

The quality of a modern thermal inkjet printer is comparable to mid-range laser printers, at about 600 dots per inch. Inkjet printers are also very quiet in operation – one model of printer was actually named the QuietJet.

Piezo-electric inkjets

The piezo-electric inkjet printing mechanism was actually invented before the bubble jet method, but until relatively recently has been more expensive. In modern systems the quality, speed and cost of piezo-electric inkjets are very similar to those of bubble jet printers. However, they work on a slightly different principle. A piezo crystal inside the print head reacts to electrical signals by changing shape. This change in shape moves a vibration plate between the crystal and the ink chamber. This in turn causes increased pressure in the chamber, which forces ink out of the chamber. Fortunately, surface tension will prevent excess ink from leaking out.

Since there is no heating element, the print head can be part of the printer instead of part of the ink cartridge, which is more ecologically sound.   Furthermore, the ink is not required either to be conductive, or to be able to cope with continual vaporising and condensing. Both of these factors mean that ink cartridges for a piezo-electric inkjet are very slightly cheaper.

Colour inkjet printers

Colour inkjet printers usually use four different ink reservoirs. Normally one cartridge is used for black ink, and another cartridge holds three ink reservoirs – cyan, magenta and yellow. Each colour has its own print head, and combinations of the four inks can theoretically produce any colour.

However, it should be noted that continuous stream inkjets are unable to use multiple print heads because their magnetic fields would interfere with one another.

Laser Printers

Laser printers, or page printers as they are sometimes referred to, are more expensive than dot matrix or inkjet printers, but provide considerably higher quality output. The speed of laser printers vary, with low-end models printing just 2 to 4 pages per minute (ppm) and many lasers printing 10 or even 12 ppm. However these figures usually assume that the same page is being printed repeatedly; printing out different pages of a document for example would reduce such figures noticeably.

The laser printer operates on the same principles as a photocopier, except that the page image comes from computer data rather than a scanned page. In fact, a photocopier is basically a scanner and laser printer in one, cutting out the computer in the middle! This is the reason why so many photocopier manufacturers also produce laser printers.

Printer memory

Laser printers always build up an image of a page before printing – the time taken to build up a page in the printer's memory is the reason why laser printers rarely achieve their top printing speed in ordinary home or office use. If the same page is printed many times, then the delay caused by collecting data from the PC and building up a page image in memory only happens once at the start of printing, after which time it can be ignored for the following pages. However, in many cases, each page printed will be a different page, and so the delay of building up an image affects every page and slows the printer down considerably.

If a binary page image is sent to a laser printer then building up a page image in printer memory is comparatively simple; however if ASCII text or a Postscript page description is sent to the printer then it has to be able to create a page from that data.

The page image has to be stored somewhere though, and so laser printers require substantial amounts of memory to store the page image until it is printed. The amount of printer memory affects the resolution (in dpi) of page that can be stored. For example, a laser printer with 1MB of memory could store an A4 page at a resolution of 300dpi, but at a resolution of 2400 x 600dpi the amount of memory required would be 16MB. For this reason many laser printers are capable of having their memory upgraded, so that higher resolution pages can be printed.

Once the page image is created in printer memory, it is then printed in exactly the same way a photocopier would print it. However, a laser printer is much more useful to a computer user than a simple photocopier, as the user can print out documents, spreadsheets, computer images etc.

Memory requirements for common laser printer resolutions

Note that these figures are for black and white printing only – colour printing requires additional memory by a factor of four.

Resolution	Dots per sq. in.	Dots per A4 page (8 x 11in)	Memory required
75dpi	75 x 75 = 5625 dots	5625 x 8 x 11 = 495,000 dots	64 KB
150dpi	150 x 150 = 22,500 dots	22,500 x 8 x 11 = 1,980,000 dots	256 KB
300dpi	300 x 300 = 90,000 dots	90,000 x 8 x 11 = 7,920,000 dots	1 MB
600dpi	600 x 600 = 360,000 dots	360,000 x 8 x 11 = 31,680,000 dots	4 MB
1200 x 600dpi	1200 x 600 = 720,000 dots	720,000 x 8 x 11 = 63,360,000 dots	8 MB
1200 x 1200dpi	1200 x 1200 = 1,440,000 dots	1,440,000 x 8 x 11 = 126,720,000 dots	16 MB
2400 x 600dpi	2400 x 600 = 1,440,000 dots	1,440,000 x 8 x 11 = 126,720,000 dots	16 MB

How Laser printers work

Unlike most other types of printer, the laser printer does not have one individual component that can be said to be the print head or the printer carriage. Instead, the laser, which gives 'laser printers' their name, remains stationary as the page moves through the printer. There is a rotating mirror inside the printer that repeatedly reflects the laser beam in a horizontal line.

Some very similar printers use a row of LED's instead of this laser and mirror arrangement. These are usually described as *'page printers'* rather than laser printers.

Both versions, however, result in a continuous horizontal line of light as the page passes through the printer.

However, the light is not fired directly at the page, as this would have no effect. Fortunately, the dry toner that is used in laser printers is easily attracted to electrostatic charge in the same way as dust is attracted to the static that builds up on your television screen. So, a laser printer must find a way to create this charge in a pattern that will draw the toner onto the page to form the desired printout.

The laser printer contains a drum that spins round as a page is printed. The drum is coated in a special *Organic PhotoConductive* (OPC) material, enabling it to be electrostatically charged with a high voltage wire, called a *"primary corona wire"*. The primary corona wire uses a grid between the wire and the drum to ensure a regulated charge over the whole drum surface.

The laser inside the printer then fires a beam of light across the drum as it turns round, usually by bouncing the laser beam off a rotating mirror. The varying light changes the electrostatic charge on parts of the drum. It is this pattern of electrostatically different areas that represent black and white areas on the final printed page.

As the drum rotates past the toner cartridge, the toner is attracted to those areas of the drum that have been struck by the laser beam. This pattern of toner has to be transferred onto the page, and this is achieved by using a stronger static charge than the drum, attracting the toner onto the page. In most laser printers a *'Transfer Corona'* wire charges the page as it feeds into the printer to achieve this effect.

Some laser printers work with a slightly different method, using positive and negative charges instead of strong and weak charges, but the principle is the same.

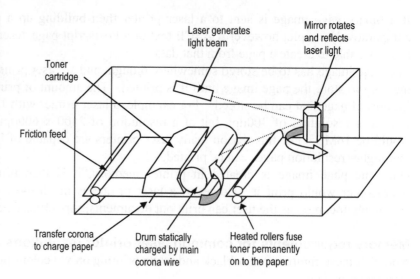

Toner cartridge

Friction feed

Laser generates light beam

Mirror rotates and reflects laser light

Before the page leaves the printer though, the toner has to be fused onto the page so that it will not drop back off. So, the page is passed between two heated rollers that melt the toner onto the page. Also, the drum has to be scraped clean in case any excess toner remains, before the next page is printed.

Transfer corona to charge paper

Drum statically charged by main corona wire

Heated rollers fuse toner permanently on to the paper

GDI Laser Printers

As mentioned above, laser printers require memory, with which to build up an image of the page before it is printed. However, it is possible for a printer to use the computer's memory to do this, thereby saving on production costs, as the printer does not have to be manufactured with expensive memory chips installed. Windows computers allow this via a system known as the GDI (Graphical Device Interface).

The Uninterruptible Power Supply

An uninterruptible power supply (UPS) runs the computer on its own batteries in the event of a power failure. They are available in a wide range of capacities. Some last for only a few minutes while more expensive models maintain the system for substantially longer periods. The smaller capacity models are adequate for many standalone PCs while the higher capacity models are common on network servers. The aim of UPS is not to maintain normal working for any prolonged period, as the cost of the batteries would be prohibitive. The UPS aims to allow the machine to close down naturally without loss or corruption of files. The battery pack is kept charged by a regulated mains supply. The diagram shows that the normal computer power supply is still used but is routed through the UPS card.

There are two major types of UPS, these being:

Off-Line Models

The Off-line UPS lets the computer power supply provide the power for the system under normal conditions. If the mains power fails completely or drops below a tolerable level (a 'brownout'), the UPS card senses the loss and takes control. The backup battery is then used to feed the

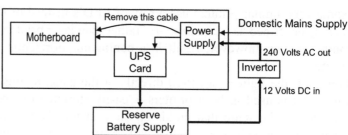

Remove this cable

Motherboard

Power Supply

Domestic Mains Supply

UPS Card

240 Volts AC out

Invertor

12 Volts DC in

Reserve Battery Supply

inverter and the inverter converts the battery's low voltage into the normal mains supply voltage. This provides enough mains power to alert the user and save files. This changeover period lasts a couple of milliseconds and most computers can handle this small loss. In the diagram, the bold lines indicate the activities that are activated upon mains power loss.

On-Line Models

The On-line UPS is similar to the above diagram. In this case, however, the domestic mains supply is not connected to the PC. The PC is permanently supplied by the inverter. The role of the domestic mains is to keep the batteries topped up.

This is a more costly option but it has these extra advantages:

- ○ Since the computer is not directly connected to the domestic mains, it cannot be affected by mains fluctuations, voltage spikes and other line noise.
- ○ There is no switchover delay, as the supply is constantly being fed. This means that there is no possibility of the machine going down during a changeover period. This is a more secure option for servers and machines where there should be no margin of error.

Selecting a UPS

Each UPS has a power rating which is measured in VA (Volt Amperes). This is equivalent to one Watt of power. To determine the VA rating for a particular station:

- Decide which devices require to be protected; this would include the computer and the monitor, but probably not the printer.
- Add together the power requirements of each of the protected devices.
- Since a UPS is usually around 80% efficient, multiply the total by 1.4 to provide the true working rating.

This gives the <u>minimum</u> rating required. For a longer protection time, increase the VA rating.

Typical UPS ratings are from 500VA to 2000VA.

Many modern UPS systems come with power monitoring software. This utility, as the name suggests, enables the user to view the performance of the UPS, and the mains supply. Most types of this software include additional facilities to automatically shut down applications and safely turn off the server in case of imminent power failure. This is vital to servers that are to be left unsupervised overnight.

System Selection

Choosing the correct computer system is a difficult decision to be made by home and professional users alike. This is due to the thousands of different products and their ever-changing specifications.   Any book, by the time it is published, is out of date in terms of hardware/software specifications and prices. However, the approaches to evaluating, choosing and purchasing hardware/software remain unchanged.

The first part of this chapter looks at the factors for business hardware purchases, while the last part looks at the hardware considerations for specifying a single computer.

Analysing IT requirements

In the present competitive climate, companies look to I.T. to improve their performance. To achieve the maximum effect for the minimum cost and effort, the new systems have to match a company's needs.

Capacity planning

Capacity planning is the prediction of future resource needs to meet future business requirements. It considers:

- Evaluating the current workload. This records and examines the number of transactions, the speed of transactions, usage of different parts of the system, response times, etc.
- Evaluating the future workload. This is forecasting company needs, the scope for tuning existing system, the need for extra resources, etc.

This process must take into account the projected size of organisation as growth in staff or number of computers users could require the installation or extension of a local area network or links between existing geographical branches.   Increased quantities also open the possibility of financial savings through bulk purchases or volume licences for software.

Other considerations

The planning must also consider the effects of expanding or renewing the IT structure.   The most important consideration is that of finance. All companies work on agreed budgets and this limits the available funds for any new project and often prevents the full implementation that may be considered necessary.

The system has to consider the business needs of the company. This means that it should contribute to improvements in areas such as workflow (how quickly and smoothly operations are conducted) and productivity (the amount of output for each hour of staff labour). The implementation of the new equipment should not disrupt the current business and the new equipment should easily assimilate with existing resources.

The new equipment may have other implications, depending on the nature of business and what new tasks the equipment will perform. For example, if the equipment stores customer and staff details, there are implications under the Data Protection Act. Similarly, if the company takes on new or specialised business, it may be forced to adopt more stringent security procedures.   In addition, if the extra equipment leads to the business offering new products or services, this involves the company in additional advertising and promotional costs.

The system has to also consider user needs (i.e. the people who will use the equipment or be affected by the equipment). This covers physical issues such the need for extra space (to abide by the laws on floor space per employee) and extra equipment (such as furniture, additional lighting and ventilation). It also covers personal issues, such as additional staff training, ergonomics (e.g. more frequent breaks or job rotation) and Health & Safety Laws.

The system that is purchased has to take into account the existing level of expertise of its employees. This may mean the specification of software that is specially written to exclude unnecessary features. Alternatively, it may mean an ongoing programme of training for existing staff and all new recruits.

As can be seen above, the considerations are not solely technical and a thorough selection process is required for large projects.

Locating systems

An appropriate location should be decided on before ordering a new computer system. This should take into account all the relevant Health & Safety concerns such as space, lighting, glare, and so on, as well as the immediate needs of a computer system such as electricity sockets, environmental conditions (e.g. not too humid or hot).

The selection process

The main stages of the selection process can be defined as:
- Definition of needs
- Evaluation of products
- Purchasing policy
- Post-delivery activity

Companies may well divide these into further sub-activities. For example, the evaluation process may involve both the technical staff (to evaluate the technical specification) and financial controllers (to evaluate purchasing, running and maintenance costs).

Definition of needs

The definition process can be treated as two separate, although linked, stages:
- Define the purpose of the purchase
- Define the equipment and software to meet that purpose

Defining equipment to meet a purpose is fairly simple. Reaching an agreement on what is required can be much more difficult. The best approach is to consult widely as there may be sectional and conflicting interests. This fact-finding exercise requires interviews and consultations with:

Management	to clarify business needs
Finance Dept	to clarify financial limits
MIS/DP Dept	to clarify required operational procedures
Users	to clarify day-to-day needs
Trade Unions	to clarify any problems on staffing, safety, demarcation, etc.
Support Dept	to clarify any technical objections to the new system

The results of these discussions should be clearly documented and the observation of the results usually produces two distinct problems:

Conflicting interests

Different pressures will be evident in the results. For example, expectations of the new system (from the management or the data processing department) may greatly exceed what it can deliver (as expressed by the users or support department). Similarly, the requirements (as expressed by users, trade unions or even management) may be countered by the finance department who want to save money or spend money in another area.

Needs and wants

There can be a very big difference between needs and wants. What people want is usually a wish-list, whereas needs express the minimum requirements necessary to get the job done. In the real-world, restraints often result in not even getting what is needed. The fact-finding exercise should result in specifying a system that best meets the main requirements of the business and the staff.

Creating a list

A list of equipment requirements should be provisionally agreed as the basis for the preparation of the detailed list of hardware and their specifications. In the light of the evaluation stage results, there may be some amendment to this list, due to financial or other constraints. Indeed, the hardware definition stage might also force a review of needs, due to technical or other considerations.

The exact number of machines and the exact software requirements has to be determined as the first priority. This may be a matter of negotiation, since users may well wish to have more software on their machines than they will normally use. Since most packages cost hundreds of pounds, over purchasing of software is extremely wasteful. If a number of machines are in the same room, then perhaps only one computer should be fitted with the software that users rarely use and users can share this machine when required.

If many users require access to the same packages, and especially if they require access to the same sets of data, consideration should be given to placing these machines on a local area network. This involves cabling the machines together so that they are all able to share the one version of each package and the one version of the communal data. The licence for multiple users on a network is generally appreciably cheaper than buying multiple copies to place on each individual machine.

Individual items

In some cases, the demand may be for a multi-purpose machine; the users may require to have word-processing, spreadsheet and database facilities on each machine in the office. In other cases, a single machine may be required to only run a single package, such as computer aided design software or video editing software. Some computers may be purchased to run as network servers, while others are bought as workstations or portable computers.

The important starting point is that

software needs determine the hardware requirements.

For example, a network server needs special server software such as Unix or Windows 2000 or XP. Each operating system has its own hardware requirements and this is the minimum specification for using the computer as a server. Similarly, the operating system chosen for workstations means that the computers must meet their minimum specification. This covers issues such as amount of memory and amount of hard disk space and is covered in the chapter on Windows Configuration.

When choosing equipment, there is no *'correct'* answer - there is only a correct choice for a particular set of circumstances. For example, a 21" monitor is entirely unnecessary for use with a computer used for normal text-based programs such as fleet control, many databases, network servers, etc. On the other hand, for some graphic-based programs - such as video editing, CAD (computer aided design), professional DTP, map drawing, etc. - a large-size monitor might be an essential purchase. The extensive screen activities involved in continually re-drawing the screen graphics will benefit from the purchase of an especially fast video cards. If a database is to be used regularly, then a fast hard disk will make the machine more productive. If a computer is used for graphics, CAD, audio or video editing, it will be working with huge files and will require a much larger hard disk than other computers.

There are also different requirements for add-ons. For example, database software only requires a simple dot-matrix printer, the typing pool requires a high-quality laser printer, the accountant requires a wide-carriage dot-matrix printer, while CAD software requires an expensive plotter.

This means that the final decisions must be based on knowing what equipment is available and on understanding what is suitable for each situation.

Finally, there is little point in buying a machine with every conceivable bell and whistle, if it is always breaking down and the technical support from the manufacturer is poor. Questions of warranty and after-sales service can be as important as the technical specifications.

Evaluation

For a large contract, or a likely repeat contract, a thorough evaluation process would be carried out. This is aimed at pinpointing problems in advance and thereby preventing future difficulties.
The evaluation process should include:
- EQUIPMENT TESTING (reliability, compatibility)
- EQUIPMENT COSTING (cost of purchase, installation, training, running, maintenance)

Equipment Testing

Testing of equipment should not be done in an ad hoc fashion, but should be carried out in accordance with a test plan. The test plan should be written up for any given item, to fulfil the requirements of a general test procedure applied to all computer hardware. The terms of the test procedure will very from one organisation to the next, but the following section should illustrate some of the more common requirements.

Reports should be made of each equipment test, to help in support of the equipment. (See the *'PC Support'* chapter)

Reliability

The single biggest factor in commercial computing equipment is reliability. This is even more important than the raw speed of a system. If a system breaks down, data may be lost or be temporarily inaccessible. This could have severe consequences for the organisation and must be taken into account during the purchasing of new equipment.

A reputable dealer will be willing to demonstrate equipment. Where a large order is involved, the dealer should be asked to loan equipment so that a thorough test can be carried out. As a minimum, the dealer should offer a 30-day money-back guarantee if the equipment is not suitable. This time should be used to check the machine performance under all possible conditions - running databases, number crunching, graphics, etc.

Specific quality checks include:

Checking for a CE mark.

All electrical goods sold must carry the CE mark. Products with this mark comply with all EEC directives regarding the manufacture and use of the equipment. It is an offence to supply equipment that does not comply with the regulations.

The purchaser need not accept the CE mark at face value and can request a certificate of conformity for the product or even a copy of test results that back up the certificate of conformity.

Further details can be found at
www.ce-marking.org/

Checking for ISO9000

The manufacturer/supplier of the goods should be checked for ISO9000 accreditation. ISO9000 is an important international standard that defines the quality systems, processes and procedures that should be used by industry. It is not a set of technical standards for hardware or software, but it does lay out the approved quality standards for procedures by which a company's design, manufacturing and servicing output can be judged.

Checking for MTBF

Many items of equipment are tested by manufacturers who produce figures on the likely running time before there are any problems. This is the MTBF (Mean Time Between Failures) and is measured in thousands of hours. Equipment with a high MTBF rate is likely to run with fewer faults than equipment with a lower rating. In most cases, it is appropriate to ask suppliers to provide MTBF figures so that can be compared to competing products.

Compatibility

Another important factor in a purchase is its compatibility with current and new hardware and software.

Typical questions are:

- Is it a UK version? Sometimes bargain hardware and software are non-UK versions being dumped. Hardware may be wired for 110 volts or software may not support UK currency or VAT rates.
- Does new software read old data? Ensure that working data import/export facilities exist.
- Does new software run on intended old machine? Consult the software's minimum requirements.
- Remember that SCSI hard drives use a SCSI bus, a PCI card needs a PCI bus, and so on.
- Is the machine's CPU Intel-compatible? A CPU chip should act exactly like an Intel chip, since most software assumes that a 100% Intel is in use.

PC or Mac

Although this book mainly concentrates on PC-based systems, the buyer should consider the compatibility of any new computer with other users, both inside and outside the organisation. While most business users have PC systems and PC software, many print houses, design houses, multimedia developers and similar trades, are committed users of Apple Macintosh computers. There are technical and creative arguments for both PC and Mac based systems. Where a company produces their own products in-house, either system can be used. Where a company has to trade files and techniques with other organisations, having the same system has obvious advantages and should be a major consideration when entering the selection process.

Equipment Costing

If cost is not a problem, then there are few other problems. The user can simply purchase the most powerful computer incorporating the latest technology, a large screen, high resolution monitor and a high definition colour laser printer. Suitable extras might be a flatbed scanner, high-quality video and sound card, modem, rewriteable DVD and CDR drive, digital camera, digital camcorder and multimedia editing suite. This setup covers a range of possible uses. For most individuals, and certainly most companies, there are severe financial constraints and expensive equipment is only purchased if it is absolutely essential. Therefore, the selection of computer systems becomes a vital process, as purchasing mistakes might prove costly.

Companies operate under financial planning that may be laid down for a number of years.
The two main financial expenditures are:

Capital Expenditure

This describes the large one-off purchases such as buildings, machinery, furniture and equipment (both office equipment and IT equipment). Outlay on these items may be spread over a number of years (in the case of purchasing expensive buildings), or may be bought in one financial year (in the case of buying furniture). In between, a company may have a rolling capital investment programme to modernise production equipment or renewing IT equipment.

Revenue Expenditure

This describes the ongoing expenses that come up week by week or month by month. This covers paying for ongoing training, maintenance and support, administration, consumables and energy consumption. So, everything from toilet rolls to printer paper come under this description.

There is a follow on effect on revenue expenditure from outlay on capital expenditure. For example, buying new office space (a capital outlay) results in extra heating, lighting, maintenance (revenue costs). Similarly, purchasing computer hardware and software is not a one-off expense. There is a range of added costs that result from the purchases. This is examined in detail next.

Total Cost of Ownership

The evaluation of costs for IT projects looks at the *'Total Cost of Ownership'* (TCO). This realises that the cost of computer hardware and software is not the price paid for their purchase; there are a great many extra factors to be considered.
The next few pages lay out the areas for examination when calculating the overall cost of implementing new hardware and software projects.

Purchase Cost

Many dealers reduce the advertised price of their products by omitting components from the package. Typical *'extras'* may be such essential components as monitors and hard disks. So, check the exact items included in any quoted price. Items to confirm include monitor, Windows, mouse and any bundled software. Ensure that there are no hidden extras.

Installation Costs

For a simple, single computer purchase, there may be no extra cost; the machine might be set up by the dealer as part of the delivery, or it may be installed by company support staff.
For larger or more complex purchases, there are other considerations:

- The time required for installing and testing multiple stations and their software.
- The time and material involved in installing a local area network of machines.
- The amount of software customisation required. This may be programs specially written by a software house or application packages customised to companies' needs. In both cases, time is required to fully test out the software.
- Duplication of effort when running the old manual system and the computerised system concurrently. This may be required until the robustness of the new system is proven.
- Environmental costs, such as improved seating or desks, air conditioning or alterations to the office lighting.
- Security costs, such as physical security, system security, power backup, data backup and standby facilities.

Running Costs

The organisation has to budget for the future replacement of faulty or obsolete equipment. This involves estimating the useful life span of the new purchases and the likely costs for replacements at the end of that period. In addition, an estimate has to be made of likely annual consumables such as disks and toner or ribbons for printers. An often overlooked cost for certain systems is the Data Protection Act 1998 and the workload it places on systems administrators. Another vital outlay is for insurance (against flooding, fires, theft, vandalism, power problems, etc.)

Maintenance Costs

The costs do not end when the systems are bought and installed. Provision has to be made to keep the systems running as smoothly as possible, with as little loss of processing time as possible from breakdowns. The main considerations are:

Warranties

Most warranties last a year, with a few dealers offering two or three year warranties. The first year usually covers all parts and labour and the type of cover thereafter has to be checked. Some, for example, only provide parts cover in the second and third years. Also, the conditions of the warranty vary and the most common arrangements are:

Back-to-Base

This is a cheap option for the supplier and the user. The repair is carried out at the supplier's premises reducing labour costs and delivering a cheaper maintenance contract. However, these policies have negative features:

- Loss of use of the machine for days.
- Risk of damage in transit.
- Costs in preparing the crate for transporting to the supplier.

This option is suitable for computers that are not in regular use or handle low priority work.

On-Site

An on-site policy is an expensive option since it includes the payment of the engineer's travelling time. It is a useful option for users as it involves little disruption and the symptoms and operations are more easily explained to the engineer. The guaranteed response time - i.e. the time delay before a visit - should be confirmed. Of course, a fast response time does not guarantee a fast repair and the item remains unusable during that period. This option is suitable for medium to high priority items.

Collect & Return

As the name suggests, the equipment is picked up by the suppliers (or their agent) and taken to a service centre for repair, before being returned. Confusingly, this title also sometimes describes a policy that is similar to a 'back-to-base' policy, except that the supplier pays for the shipping charges.

Parts Only

The warranty only covers the replacement of parts that become defective or worn-out during the warranty period. The costs of the technical work is charged to the company. This is a common practice during the later life of a warranty, where parts are more likely to fail. The company providing the warranty expects to recover some of the parts costs through the margins on the work charges.

Replacement Policies

For a price, a replacement, or 'swap out' policy can be obtained. The defective item is replaced with a working equivalent while the repair is being carried out (either on-site or at the supplier's premises). This allows the organisation to continue with the minimum disruption. Faster response times to effect the replacement are more expensive than slower responses. This is the best solution for essential items such as printers, peripherals, network servers, etc. In the case of defective computers, replacing the machine usually results in the data on the defective machine being temporarily unavailable - unless the data is transferable to the new machine, or the computer is a network node using centralised data.

Maintenance Contracts

When the normal guarantee period expires, some suppliers provide an extension to their cover and this cost should be confirmed. If there is no policy of extending maintenance cover, terms have to be sought from a separate maintenance company. In both cases, the terms of the service have to be considered.

In all warranty contracts, it pays to ask who carries out any maintenance work – the manufacturer or a third party. There is weight in the argument that a repair by the original manufacturer will be quicker or better, due to their more detailed knowledge of the equipment.

Other Support

Some manufacturers provide lifetime telephone support for their machines and the availability and quality of this should be checked (e.g. the times the service is available and whether software, peripherals and network problems are included). Others provide customer support for the first year and charge thereafter. This may be on an annual charge basis or on a per-call basis.

If many new computers are added to a business, the size of the support staff should be considered.

Finally, if a local area network is established, a network supervisor has to be trained and given time to administer the system.

Training Costs

A factor often overlooked in the costing process is the adequate training of the staff expected to use the new hardware and software. The cost of training soon repays itself in increased productivity. The degree of training required for personnel has to be determined (e.g. some staff to a basic level and others to an advanced level) and costed. For large organisations with extensive IT departments in-house training may be available, which is normally substantially cheaper than sending staff to external training companies. It is also more effective, as company trainers usually know the problems experienced by the staff.

Software Costs

The chapter on 'Software' looks at the range of available applications software. The selection process takes into account the limitations placed on software by hardware. More advanced applications require a more powerful computer system (usually processor, amount of memory and disk space). For example, a video editing software suite may require massive amounts of memory and disk storage. It would also benefit greatly from a computer with dual processors. If the budget does not allow for purchase of these computers, then the software will run more slowly or not run at all.

A company may decide that existing software packages do not cover the operations and activities that it requires. In this case, there are two alternatives:

- Have an existing package customised to match the company's requirements. Packages such as Access and Excel are often modified in this way, although the programming does require expertise (which can be expensive).

- A contract can be signed with a software house to write an application from scratch, especially to match the operations of the company. This is an expensive option but it minimises the amount (and cost) of staff training. If the data produced by the software has to be shared outside the company, the programme has to be written to create data that is compatible with the systems of the other organisations.

Cost benefit analysis

The above lists all the costs associated with new purchases. This has to be compared to the benefits that will accrue from using the new technology. This table shows examples of the benefits that can be expected from implementing new computer systems.

Better cash flow	(e.g. improved issuing of invoices and statements, automated acceptance of credit cards
Reduced cost levels	(e.g. automated re-ordering, reduced staff levels, shared resources, better space utilisation)
Increase sales	(e.g. improved customer lists, new markets such as web sites)
Increase profitability	(e.g. targeted mailshots, increased productivity)
Increasing capacity	(e.g. handling more traffic, ability to handle future growth)

Improved management information	(e.g. easier and quicker production of figures on sales, costs, margins, etc. in a more detailed way (i.e. sales by district or region) providing improved management forecasting)
Chance to reorganise	A computer system that mimics a currently inadequate manual system will simply produce inadequate results faster. The computer system should be used to evolve improved methods.
Company image	(e.g. faster response to customers, improved customer support)

The cost benefit analysis should quantify both the financial costs and financial benefits. It should also compare its chosen solution with other possible solutions (including the cost of doing nothing).

Purchasing Policy

Tendering or requesting quotes may result in finding the lowest price – but this does not necessarily mean that it is the best supplier. Issues of quality, reliability, support, warranties, etc. have to be considered.

The company should have a set of rules on general purchasing and most of them will apply to computing purchases. These rules may include:

- Dealing directly with the computer manufacturer. This cuts out the middle man and lowers prices - a system known as 'Direct Sales'.
- Choosing a company with a known track record.
- Checking how long a company has been trading.
- Checking a company's financial health. The Companies Act 1989 demands that all companies file annual returns and this information is open to public scrutiny. A search at one of the Companies House offices can be requested or their web site can be consulted at
  www.companies-house.gov.uk
  Checks will reveal whether the supplier's current assets exceed their current liabilities, any sudden changes from one year to the next, the level of turnover and profit, etc.
- Ensuring that the supplier is a member of the appropriate professional bodies.
- Asking for a reference from the supplier's existing customers.
- Getting copies of the supplier's warranties and terms and conditions for examination before placing an order.
- Placing orders that are conditional on specified delivery times, pricing, or an agreed returns or refunds policy.
- Keeping a copy of all material - adverts, order forms, invoices, receipts, correspondence and records of telephone conversations.

A company may have an overriding purchasing policy to always buy IBM products, buy British products, or buy from the cheapest quote. If a company insists on buying goods manufactured in Britain they can easily get the information from the supplier. A clause in the 1968 Trades Description Act prohibits a supplier from misleading customers on the 'history of the article', so they are obliged to provide details on the country of manufacture. If making a purchase from a non-UK supplier, any costs savings have to be weighed against difficulties with returned goods and problems of support . There are no additional import duties on goods purchased within the EC but extra duties will apply to other countries.

Pricing

Before placing an order, the final prices should be confirmed and this includes questions such as:

- Does the price include all parts and accessories.
- Is VAT included in the price.
- Are there printed manuals, can extra copies be bought, are all manuals on CD, are they printable (as good user documentation reduces support costs).
- Who pays for insurance against transit damage.

Tendering

Tendering is the process of creating a list of goods to be purchased, including quantities, specifications, conditions, etc. and requesting quotes from interested suppliers. This is only an option for very large contracts, as the cost of organising and controlling the process probably costs more than the money saved. For a very large project, such as networking an entire building, the bidders will make a free site survey. Most suppliers will visit the company in any case, to find out more facts and make suggestions. The tender document should place any conditions within the order. For example, an item might be purchased on condition that the seller's assurance that it is compatible with other equipment proves true. The process can be slow but should result in at least three quotes.

Payment methods

As explained earlier, purchasing goods means using cash from the company's capital account. For large orders, this can place a great strain on the company's cash flow and there are alternatives.
The three most popular payment methods are
Purchase
> Outright purchase is the most cost effective method in the longer term. Owning the equipment allows the company complete control over how it is used, updated, etc. Capital allowance are claimable against the company's tax liability. For companies that cannot afford the initial outlay, there remains the option of renting or leasing computing equipment, as explained below.

Rent
> Renting is the most expensive option. Short-term rental is particularly expensive but is useful for coping with sudden demands.

Lease
> Leasing is a common business option. The leasing company buys the equipment from the manufacturer and the customer has use of it during an agreed period in return for monthly payments. At the end of the lease period, the user returns the equipment to the supplier. This eases the strain on a company's cash flow and means that the problems of obsolescence of equipment remain with the leasing company (particularly if the contract allows a short notice of cancellation of the contract). Leasing also provides a cushion against inflation as a long-term leasing contract (particularly one that includes a clause on updating equipment) on a fixed rate ensures the company is unaffected by sudden large prices rises in new equipment.

The Purchase Contract

The purchase contract is a binding agreement between the company and the supplier and both sides will attempt to have their conditions inserted into the document. However, the buyer has the most leverage and the contract should cover the following issues:

Pricing	The quotes should specify the time period during which the prices are guaranteed to remain in force. Reject quotes that are *'subject to modification'*. Check the small print (e.g. 'E&OE' : errors and omissions excepted) for supplier get-out clauses. Insert a clause that makes all price alterations subject to agreement.
Timing	If timing is important, insert a delivery clause with daily penalties for non-delivery.
Delivery details	Specify days (e.g. weekdays) times (e.g. 9 to 5) and location (e.g. leave with porter) for delivery. This prevents possible delays in delivery and carrier surcharges for repeat visits.
Acceptance on delivery	Carriers are keen to dump the parcels, get a signature and get off. The document to be signed usually states that the goods have been received in good condition. It is therefore best to insert a clause that states that receiving goods unseen does not imply acceptance of goods.
Payment	The payment requirements are usually net 30 days, unless otherwise agreed.
Guarantee	Specify the terms of the warranty – type of coverage, duration of coverage, who pays for returns, etc.
Rejected goods	Insert a clause that states *"Goods not accepted for any reason remain the property of the supplier at all times"*. This clearly states that any rejected goods remain the property of the supplier and it is their responsibility to collect such goods.

A contract is the basis of a purchase – so it is important to ensure that the terms and conditions safeguard the company's interests.
If making a personal purchase, it is advisable to use a credit card, as buyers are covered by the credit card company's insurance scheme if the supplier ceases trading before the goods are dispatched. No goods should be charged for until they are despatched.

Post Delivery

When the system arrives, the contents of all the boxes should be checked and tested.

As most carriers will not wait until every box is opened and checked, the carrier's consignment sheet should have *"Goods not yet inspected"* written on it. Goods accepted *"sight unseen"* are easier to return. Even then, however, a very brief inspection of the packaging itself may be in order: spotting a broken seal or damaged packaging on a delivered item can indicate that the material inside is damaged.

Checking

The organisation should have a system for checking and documenting the receipt of all incoming goods. Failure to deliver in time is a breach of the supplier's contract and it may be that the lateness renders the equipment useless. In such a case, the box may be returned to the supplier. If the goods are in time, equipment testing can proceed. At its simplest this may be only a checklist to compare and sign if correct. The first check is to see that the goods have arrived within the required time. Each item is given an initial visual examination to check for obvious damage and to ensure that the item is of the type ordered - e.g. correct model, size, capacity, etc. If the item is present, correct and apparently undamaged, the checklist is ticked against that item.

Testing

Computer equipment should not be placed in a storage cupboard; it should be tested upon arrival. The extent of testing will depend upon the apparatus. The minimum check should be on basic functionality - i.e. does the printer actually print, do all the keys on the keyboard work, does the monitor display a satisfactory screen. Further checks can be conducted where required - e.g. do all the printer emulations work, does the monitor handle all the required resolutions, etc. All testing must be carried out within the manufacturer's instructions. Take care, before beginning tests, to remove all shipping protection. Printers and scanners are the devices that most often come with shipping protection, usually in the form of sticky tape, or foam or plastic covers.

If the system is in any way incomplete or non-functional, the supplier should be contacted immediately. Speed and accuracy in reporting any discrepancy or damage is important, both to the purchaser and the supplier. Suppliers must deliver the goods as advertised and purchasers are protected by consumer law. From the suppliers point of view, it is useful to know of potential problem areas so that they can reduce delivery problems and identify problems with their goods. In many cases, the initial contact with the supplier is carried out by the technician, so that the technical details can be clearly explained. The technician should also inform the administration of his/her own organisation since they will pursue any legal and financial consequences.

The company should only deal with the seller as sometimes the supplier will attempt to pass responsibility on to the manufacturer. Even if the goods are faulty, they were purchased from the seller, not the manufacturer. This means that it is the seller's responsibility to put things right.

Consumer Law

The main points of the Sale of Goods Act are:
- Goods must be accurately described
- Goods must be of merchantable quality
- Goods must be fit for the purpose for which they have been sold

The main consumer laws are the Consumer Protection Act 1987, the Fair Trading Act, the Sale and Supply of Goods Act 1994, the Trades Description Act, the Supply of Goods and Services Act 1982, the Distance Selling Regulations 2000, the EU E-Commerce Directive and the EU Directive on Sale of Goods and Associated Guarantees.

Information on these acts can be found on the following web sites:
> www.opsi.gov.uk/acts
> www.berr.gov.uk

Other useful websites are:
> www.asa.org.uk   (The Advertising Standards Agency)
> www.nacab.org.uk (The Citizens Advice Bureau)
> www.oft.gov.uk   (The Office of Fair Trading)

Hardware definition

The rest of this chapter discusses the relative merits of different computer components as an aid to decision making. For more details on a particular topic, the appropriate chapter can be read. To make an informed decision, the full range of facts must be available for comparison. These facts will include product specifications, independent reviews and reports from user groups. Hardware decisions are required on the items listed and guidance is given as to their respective merits for specific purposes.

Case types

A first consideration is the environment for using the system. The options are:

Tower This type of case (also called *'full tower'*) has a large, vertical case with plenty of space inside for the inclusion of extra equipment. The case should have extra drive bays, so that CD- ROMs, extra hard disks, etc. can be easily fitted. The main board used in these models should have plenty of unused expansion slots, so that extra equipment cards can be plugged in. This is the first choice for a system that carries out a lot of the office's extra activities. Examples of this would be using the machine as the server in a local area network or using the machine as the office's main resource for fax cards, modems, scanners, tape backup, etc. The unit normally sits on the floor and the monitor sits on the desktop. New tower units, like most other types of case, now come in ATX form rather than AT form.

Mini-Tower This type has a vertical construction as above but is not so tall. It can store less than a tower but is more expandable than the average desktop machine. It is a good compromise for size and expandability, and as such is now the most common form. It usually sits on the desktop with the monitor close by.

Mini-PC Also called 'small form factor', these systems are compact, almost cube-shaped, and for obvious reasons have limited scope for additional internal devices. They typically sport USB, sound, and other connectors on the front. On the inside, they make use of tubular connectors instead of ribbon cables, to reduce clutter. Although many of these use the FlexATX motherboard style, some use the MiniITX setup, which is smaller but incorporates some components (such as CPU and/or video chipset) into the board and are therefore not upgradeable.

Desktop This was once the most common of all case types and is a horizontal box of varying dimensions, on to which most users place the monitor.

Low-profile This is a smaller *'slim line'* version of the above. They are often of the *'small footprint'* variety, i.e. they have smaller breadth and depth dimensions than desktop machines and therefore take up less of the desk area. They are pleasing to the eye but have a major drawback with their expandability.

Since the case is of a low profile, there is not enough height in the machine to plug expansion cards straight into the board's expansion slots. A special *'plane'* board has to be fitted vertically into one of the expansion slots. The expansion cards then plug horizontally into one of the expansion slots on the plane board. This normally results in fewer slots being available in low-profile models. Unless future expansion of the machines is ruled out, this would not be the first choice for office machines. There are also 'slim-line' PC models available, which follow a similar philosophy but are designed to be placed vertically. As a result they often require plastic stands at the base to ensure they do not fall over.

Notebook These are about the size of an A4 book, hence the name. They use internal batteries, the car's 12 volt lighter socket or a mains adapter. They have a flat screen built in to the case lid. They are small enough to carry in a briefcase along with other material and are in regular use by those who require computing facilities away from the office.

Handheld This name covers two types of system: Palmtops (also called *'Personal Digital Assistants'* or PDAs), and WAP mobile phones. While a palmtop is a full-fledged computer in its own right (albeit one which is very limited in its capabilities), a WAP device is essentially a mobile phone with a few extra functions added. These include email and limited web browsing.

CPU Options

The type and speed of the computer's CPU have a great bearing on the system's ability to handle tasks. The difference between different chips and chip speeds becomes more noticeable with the increasing complexity of software. For example, programs designed to take full advantage of SSE3 code will only give this extra performance to those who own those machines.

Note: CPU types are covered in the chapter on Computer Architecture.

Other CPU factors:

Processor Upgrade Options: Some computers allow the CPU to be removed and replaced by a more up-to-date version. This may involve buying a computer whose motherboard supports such an upgrade option. Often, the upgrade is not as effective as a newly purchased system, since the other components in a new machine (i.e. disk speed, bus type, video cards) will have improved greatly since the older models was phased out. However, upgrading does provide a degree of *'future proofing'* - i.e. it allows the machine to partially keep up with new technology without the expense of being completely replaced. Recent changes in processor connections and the rapid pace of processor development have made processor upgrades less common.

Chipsets: The CPU is supported by a *'chipset'* on the motherboard (See the chapter on Computer Architecture). This set of supporting chips is designed to handle memory and peripheral interfacing. The older chipsets are cheaper but support less facilities – for example they may not contain onboard LAN and audio support, or may not support up-to-date RAM types such as DDR or RDRAM.

Portables: These are mainly battery powered and therefore require a low-power version of the CPU. The older portables only lasted around 3 hours on one charge of the internal batteries, while the newer chips are more low-powered to allow the machine to run for up to a full day on a single charge.

Motherboard options

Facilities   For those concerned with future-proofing their machine, consideration should be given to purchasing computers that support the latest bus speeds, memory types, and interfaces. For example the quad-pumped 800MHz bus, DDR3 memory modules, or the USB2 bus interface.

Expansion Slots   Each computer's main board has a number of extra slots into which additional hardware boards can be fitted. These are known as *'expansion slots'* and the more that are provided, the more expandable the machine becomes. Typical cards to plug into these slots are modems, video capture cards, sound cards and cards for the control of electronic apparatus. These slots are provided for different card types and a typical computer will offer a single AGP slot, and a number of PCI slots. If the machine is likely to have a range of add-ons fitted, the number of expansions slots provided on a motherboard is important.

External Ports Computers are supplied with at least one parallel port for the printer, one or more serial ports for add-ons such as a modem, and a dedicated, built-in mouse port in the form of a PS/2 socket. USB and FireWire sockets provide for various add-ons such as scanners and cameras.

BIOS   The BIOS chip is a key component in the system and well-known manufacturers like AMI, Award and Phoenix are safe choices. These manufacturers ensure that the code in the BIOS chip is compatible with new hardware developments. The main thing to look for in a BIOS is the range of hardware it supports – for example, booting from CD-ROM or external drive/memory stick.

Memory Options

Size   Machines are provided with a wide variety of memory amounts installed. The amount of memory required for a particular machine can be stated at the time of placing the order, or extra memory can be fitted at a later date as an upgrade (see the chapter on *'Hardware Installation'*). The memory requirements of a particular application will appear on its specification; this is printed in the application's manual and is usually printed on the box packaging. Assuming the computer uses Windows and Windows-based applications, the machine will need plenty of memory. Although the majority of Windows applications have relatively low memory requirements when measured against the capacity of an up to date system, if the user wishes to open several packages at one time this will require greater memory capacity. The version of Windows used will help determine the minimum realistic level of memory. For example, Windows XP systems should realistically be fitted with at least 256MB to ensure a reasonable speed, and Vista systems with upwards of 1GB.

The more memory that is fitted, the more efficiently Windows applications will run.

Speed   The type of memory impacts significantly on its speed. PC3-6400 memory, for example, is theoretically twice as fast as PC3200 memory. Various extra technologies can be applied to memory chips to improve performance. For example, if your motherboard supports DDR memory, then using DDR SDRAM chips will give better memory throughput.

Format   Modern motherboards use DIMMs, DDR DIMMs, or RIMMs as a means of holding memory chips, with SIMMs being found only in legacy systems.   Any system allows easy upgrading of memory, should the need arise. The user simply purchases extra memory modules and inserts them in unused slots, or replaces existing chips with higher-capacity chips.

Cache Memory   This is a small block of ultra-fast memory that acts as a buffer between the CPU proper and main memory. It greatly speeds up data transfers, particularly with databases. It is typically available in 32k, 64k, 128k, 256k and 512k cache sizes. In modern systems, cache is fully integrated onto the CPU, so the CPU selection, rather than the motherboard selection, will determine the level of cache.

Monitor Options

Size   The basic supplied size is 15" and this is acceptable for general purposes.   The supplying of 17" monitors is also common and provides an improved viewing area for the user.   For graphics applications such as CAD, artwork, multimedia and DTP, a larger size screen may be necessary.   These are normally 19" and 21" models or more.

Resolution   Machines are typically supplied with monitors capable of at least 1280 x 1024 resolution. Thanks to the modular driver system in Windows, virtually any application is able to take advantage of whatever resolution to which user sets their monitor.   There is currently a move to provide support for 1920x1080 resolution in order to allow processing of HD video.

Dot pitch   A dot pitch (or pixel pitch, for flat screens) of 0.28 is the basic quality for general uses. If affordable, a 0.25mm pitch or less is preferred for high-resolution work.

Refresh rate   The higher a monitor's screen refresh rate, the less is the flicker and the less is the risk of eyestrain for users spending prolonged periods at the machine.   A refresh rate of 70Hz or 72Hz is a satisfactory minimum.

Video cards   If a machine is to be used for Windows applications or extensive graphics work, a high performance video card or Windows accelerator card should be bought. Most cards supplied today have upwards of 128MB of video memory, which is more than sufficient for most day-to-day work. If high resolution or special 3D effects are required, a higher specification video card should be considered, perhaps with as much as 1GB of RAM. In some circumstances TV-Out, TV Tuner, or MPEG hardware might be wanted.

Other factors   If a machine is to be used for prolonged periods, or placed in an environment with bright light or shiny surfaces, an anti-glare screen should be fitted to the front of the monitor.   If a machine is in regular use, or is positioned next to other staff, a low-radiation model should be purchased. If a portable or notebook computer is in regular use, a separate monitor should be purchased, so that the user can connect the machine when appropriate (e.g. a salesperson may use the notebook with its small screen to collect orders during the day and then connect to the large external monitor for calculating and summarising information back at the hotel or head office).   An FST monitor (flatter, squarer tube) provides a screen that maintains its clarity for a longer period than the conventional tube.   It has no convergence problems and it is an ideal monitor for intricate design work. Trinitron monitors also provide better quality.

Screen Type   Certain systems require, or will benefit from, use of special display technologies such as LCD or plasma screens, projectors, and so on. These technologies, and their typical applications, are explained more fully in the chapter on *'Display Technology'*.

Hard Disk Options

Size   The purchase should be based on the fact that most computers use up more disk space than first predicted.   Calculation of the disk's size should not be a simple sum of all the expected software, since each application will generate its own sets of data. A machine used in a typing pool may only generate Word documents, and thus a small 80GB disk may be entirely adequate. A database server or multimedia capture machine might require 300GB, 500GB of storage or even more, while heavy-duty ISP servers will require RAID arrays with huge storage requirements. A single Windows application can require upwards of 250MB of hard disk space just to store its program files. Fortunately, few new systems have less than 100GB of hard disk space, even for budget entry-level PCs.   There is even an increasing trend toward the use of RAID systems in workstations rather than servers. This is due to the increased speed and security they can provide, but the increased cost means this applies mainly to high-end workstations such as multimedia stations.

Type   Hard drives on sale today are generally SATA or UltraDMA drives, with basic IDE and EIDE drives in use only on legacy systems. SCSI drives are normally only available as an optional extra, but may be desirable for multimedia and video editing activities. FireWire drives are also available, offering faster transfer rates and plug and play compatibility.
There are several sub-types of these systems. UltraDMA is also available in UDMA66, UDMA100, UDMA133. These require special low crosstalk cables and support from the BIOS, but in modern systems these are available by default. SCSI varieties include SCSI-2, Ultra-Wide (UW) and several others. See the '*Hard Disks*' chapter for details of the various hard disk types.

Speed   The speed of a disk is measured in average access time and can range from 4ms to 10ms.   If a disk is rated in excess of 10ms, it is probably old stock.   For applications that are '*disk-bound*', i.e. use a lot of disk access such as databases, a fast access time can have a significant effect on the machine's overall performance. Additionally, high-volume data applications such as video editing require fast access speeds.   Consideration should be given to a large internal cache, which also speeds up operations. Finally, the revolution speed of the drive, measured in rpm, affects the rate at which data is read from the disk. The higher the rpm, the better, but access time is usually the more important factor.

SMART   Self Monitoring And Reporting Technology is built into a great many modern drives. These monitor their own performance and warn the user if there is a danger of imminent failure.

Removable Media Options

Nowadays, many machines are supplied without a floppy disk. Larger capacity removable drives are now more commonplace. The name 'removable media' covers a variety of devices, including memory sticks, external drives, floptical drives, floppy disks and others. Since most of these are not part of the system unit they can be purchased later. The main choice is whether to include a floppy disk in the system unit, and this is generally not recommended unless compatibility is an issue or there is some other reason why floppies are particularly desirable.
When adding mass storage removable drives to a system, the most important aspects are usually storage capacity, cost, and portability. While memory sticks are the most portable of the common removable media options, they tend to provide less storage capacity for the same cost. For archiving purposes or for large scale data transfer, an external disk drive is a better choice.

Miscellaneous Options

Power Supply: A power supply has to be able to handle the current needs of the equipment fitted in the computer case - i.e. the motherboard, hard disk, floppy disks and any cards plugged into the expansion slots such as disk controllers and video cards.   The supply also has to cope with any future add-ons that are plugged into the expansion sockets such as modems, etc.   Additionally, the supply has a wiring loom that provides a few spare power connections.   These are left floating around in the case and can be used to power up add-ons that do not connect directly to the expansion bus, such as the CD-ROM or DVD drive.   A computer power supply of 250W would be needed if the machine is expected to host extra equipment.   For a tower machine used as a network server or power workstation, a 300W or 400W supply would be more appropriate. Another consideration with power supplies is their safety, since they handle mains voltages.   The supply should have a safety kitemark or other seal of approval. All power supplies in new machines are some form of the ATX type; unless you have a very old AT power connector motherboard this is the correct option. Pentium 4 systems use a variation on ATX known as ATX12V.

Keyboard: A cheap and nasty keyboard of an unknown brand can spoil an otherwise good machine. Where possible the machine should be purchased with a known brand name. Special keyboards are available for one-handed use, or with curved keypads for a more 'natural' feel.

Mouse: A poor mouse, with a sticky and jerky operation, hinders Windows operations and a quality mouse should be purchased with the machine. Consideration might also be given to *'wheel mice'* that give added functionality or to an optical mouse that needs less maintenance.

Printer: Quality of printout must be balanced against cost considerations. Dot matrix printers are the cheapest, but are only suitable for high-volume, low-quality printouts. Inkjets give decent quality at a reasonable price, but those who can afford it (such as medium to large size businesses) should consider laser printers, which are expensive but of the best quality. Laser quality is measured in dots per inch (dpi), and generally speaking higher dpi means higher price. 600dpi is a basic model but is sufficient for the great majority of needs.

CD-ROM: Every machine now comes with at least a CD-ROM, with most models offering either CD-R or DVD drives, but a DVD-RW drive offers the greatest flexibility. An expensive option that is only particularly useful for special requirements is a DVD-RAM drive, while a Blu-Ray might be considered for a media system or for some 'future proofing'.

Extras: These may include scanners, modems, sound cards, network cards, video capture cards, etc, as well as more unusual extras such as port replicators or noise reducing equipment, with the correct mix dependent upon the intended use for the machine. Most computers on sale include sound cards, network interfaces and modems as standard, as these are usually incorporated into the motherboard circuitry.

Technical Check List

Case	Type: Tower / Mini-Tower / Mini-PC / DeskTop / Low Profile Slim-Line / Portable / Notebook / Hand-held Power Supply : ATX or ATX12V (for Pentium 4 systems)
CPU	Type: Pentium III/ Celeron/ Athlon / Pentium 4 Speed: < 1GHz / 1 – 2GHz / 2GHz – 3GHz / > 3GHz
Motherboard	Chipset: 845 series / 865 series, 875 series/ 850 / SiS / Via / nVidia Memory Slot type: SDR DIMM / DDR DIMM / RIMM Number of free PCI slots: 1 / 2 / 3 / 4 Onboard devices: None / Graphics / Sound / Network / USB 2 / FireWire
Memory	Size: 64MB / 128MB / 256MB / 384MB / 512MB / 1GB Speed: 100MHz / 133MHz / 200MHz / 266MHz / 333MHz / 400MHz, / 533MHz / 800MHz / 1066MHz / 1200MHz Type: SDRAM / RDRAM / DDR
Hard Disk	Interface Type: UDMA / UDMA-66 / UDMA-100 / UDMA-133 / SCSI-2 / SCSI-Ultra / SCSI-UW / Serial ATA Access Time: 4ms / 5ms / 7ms / 9ms / 10ms / >10ms
Other Storage	Extra floppy drive / ZIP drive / JAZ drive / DAT tape / CD Writer / DVD-RAM / DVD-R / DVD+R / DVD+RW / DVD-RW / LS-120 / FireWire Hard disk / External SCSI drive / USB storage device
Monitor	Size: 15" / 17" / 18" / 20" / 21" / 22" / 24" Resolution: 800x600 / 1024x768 / 1280x1024 / 1600x1200 / Widescreen Dot Pitch: 0.28mm / 0.27mm / 0.26mm / 0.25mm Refresh Rate: 72Hz / 85Hz / Higher Radiation: Standard / Low radiation / Not applicable Type: CRT / FST / Trinitron / LCD / Plasma / Back projection Anti-glare: Yes / No Energy saving: Yes / No
Video Card	3D accelerator: Yes / No 3D systems supported: OpenGL / Glide / Direct3D Interface: PCI / AGP / AGP2x / AGP4x / AGP8x Memory: 16MB / 32MB / 64MB / 128MB / 256MB / 512MB Additional features: TV-Out / TV Tuner / MPEG hardware
CD-ROM	Interface : IDE / SCSI / USB / FireWire Speed : 32x / 36x / 40x / 44x / 48x / 52x / 56x
Ports	Serial: 1 / 2 Parallel: 1 / 2 Mouse: PS/2 / USB Keyboard : PS/2 / USB USB ports: 0 / 1 / 2 / 3+ Other ports : FireWire / IrDA / Games
Power Supply	Capacity: 200W / 230W / 250W / 300W / 350W Safety marked: Yes / No
Mouse	Type: PS/2 / Serial / USB Features: Mouse wheel / Cordless / Optical

Printer	Dot-Matrix: 24-pin / 48-pin InkJet: 600x600 / 1200x600 / 1440 x 720 2400 x 1200 / 2440 x 1220 Laser: 600 dpi / 1200dpi Colour printing: Yes / No Duplex (printing both sides simultaneously) Yes / No Handles A3 paper : Yes / No LAN compatible: Yes / No
Extras	DVD Player / Network Card / Sound system / Microphone / UPS / Modem / Webcam / Plotter / ISDN card / ADSL adapter
Warranty	1 year / 3 years / 5 years Back to base / On site / Collect and Deliver / Replacement
Operating System	Windows ME / 2000 / XP / Unix
Applications software	
Model / Price	Model: Price: £ Quantity Price: £

Hardware Installation

This chapter covers both computer system building and upgrading of an existing system.

The building of a computer system centres around the motherboard. All components connect to the motherboard – either by plugging in to the board (e.g. memory, CPU, video card, keyboard) or by being connected by cable to the board (e.g. hard disk, CD-ROM).

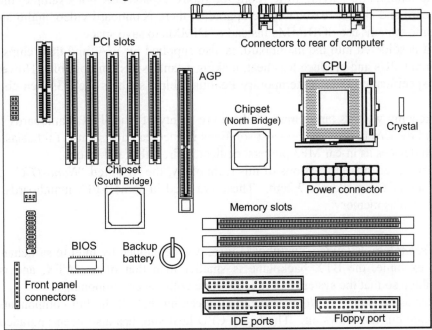

The diagram shows a typical layout of a motherboard. It is not intended to represent any particular model and the actual layout of components and sockets varies in different boards.

The main components of a computer system are explained next, including their functions and features.

Motherboard

There is a huge range of different motherboard types in circulation. As technology has developed, the board layout has altered to accommodate the new components, since the components are mostly incompatible with older versions. For example, a new CPU, or a new memory module will not fit in an older board as the sockets have different layouts and number of connecting pins. Similarly, the expansion slots have changed from ISA, through EISA, MCA, to PCI, USB, AGP and PCI-E. Therefore older cards, such as modems or sound cards will not fit into the newer expansion slots.

Even the size and shape of motherboards has changed. PC motherboards, from 1984 onwards, used a size and layout format *(called the 'form factor')* known as AT. A full-size AT board could be up to 12" by 13.8" and the smaller Baby-AT was rapidly introduced at 8.57" x 13". However, the sockets and slot connectors still matched those of the AT boards, allowing them to be fitted as a direct AT replacement.

In 1995, the current ATX form factor was introduced. This used a board the size of the Baby-AT, with an alternative 11.2" x 8.2" mini version. The motherboard components were re-sited so that the CPU did not block any of the space allocated for full-length expansion slots.

However, the ATX board is not a drop-in replacement for an AT board because:

- It has a different socket/slot layout so an ATX upgrade requires an ATX-type case. On an AT-based system, internal cables were often used to connect between sockets in the motherboard and the external connections provided on the computer's back panel. ATX motherboards mount many of the connectors (e.g. parallel port, serial port, etc.) directly on to the board. On many ATX boards, these connectors are stacked (see diagram later)
- It has a different supply voltage. The ATX case provides a 3.3v power supply (instead of the 5v supply used in AT boards). The AT case had a power supply with two separate power cables. These plugged into two power sockets on the motherboard. The ATX power supply plugs into a single power socket on the motherboard.
- ATX boards have different cooling arrangements.

Mini-ITX

The Mini-ITX form of mainboard, developed by VIA Technologies, measures 17cm squared. It is based on the earlier ITX form, which was never used because manufacturers preferred the alternative FlexATX form factor. The Mini-ITX itself was not intended for release but public response to two show models prompted them to reconsider. It is backward-compatible with the ATX power supply leads, but is intended for use with a 100-watt power supply.

The EPIA ("*Embedded Platform Innovation Architecture*") M-series mainboards which use the Mini-ITX form factor are intended to be an *"integrated solution"*, meaning that as much technology as possible is crammed onto the mainboard, leaving little room for future expansion. For example, the processor is soldered to the board and cannot reasonably be upgraded, there is onboard video, audio and networking capability, and some systems use SODIMMs instead of DIMMs to save space.

The CPU, since it is soldered into the mainboard, is also supplied by VIA, and their chips consume less power than Pentium CPUs and produce less heat, making a fanless system possible. However, they tend to be of a lower specification than contemporary Pentium chips, such as the C3/Eden chip at 533MHz upwards.

Furthermore, in keeping with its target market, there are plenty of Mini-ITX mainboards featuring low-end processors and devices to provide low-cost solutions for dedicated systems. Enthusiasts promote the Mini-ITX for such devices as in-car MP3 players, dedicated firewalls, and so on.

In addition, there are even smaller versions of this technology, the so-called *"Nano-ITX"*, at just 12cm x 12cm, and the '*Pico-ITX*', at 10cm x 7.2cm. These are used in some EPIA mainboards, using only a single SO-DIMM chip as memory.

BTX

The *"Balanced Technology Extended"* mainboard form was developed by Intel to suit changing needs in computing. For example, the BTX backplane is smaller than that of the ATX, and is designed to minimise heat buildup so that the system can reliably cope with faster components.

Heat is reduced by using '*inline cooling*', essentially meaning that all the hot components form a path down which a single big fan blows air. The lowly CPU heat sink has also been upgraded to a '*system cooling module*' that fits the entire underside of the mainboard.

The BTX form is fully backwards compatible with the ATX form in terms of the power supply, but in keeping with the BTX philosophy, there is a slimline power supply form available known as CFX12V. However, it is not backward compatible with ATX cases.

There are also smaller versions of BTX planned, in direct competition to MiniITX. These are named *"microBTX"* and *"picoBTX"*. The BTX has not attracted the commercial success that its creators had hoped, though, and development on the BTX line has ceased.

Cases and power supplies

Cases for both AT and ATX boards are available in desktop, mini-tower and tower sizes. They both have pre-drilled and tapped holes inside the case for mounting the motherboard. All cases are supplied with a power supply fitted and many have a case fan fitted, for keeping the case contents cool.

However, AT and ATX cases have three major differences:

- The case layout.
- How external connections are supplied.
- The power supply and powering arrangements.

The cases

Since the size of AT and ATX motherboards are different, the mounting holes on the boards have different spacing from each other. Although the component layout will vary from board to board, the mounting holes drilled in an AT or ATX motherboard should be in the same place for each type.

The connections

On older AT systems, many of the connections to the outside world were made by removing some of the blanking plates (also called 'slot covers') from the rear case chassis and slotting in replacement plates that had sockets. The sockets had cables that connected to sockets on the motherboard. So, for example, a serial port might be fitted in this way.

With ATX systems, many of the external connectors (see the illustration below) are directly mounted on the motherboard. The rear chassis of an ATX case is therefore manufactured with a cut-out window to allow the motherboard's on-board sockets to be accessed from outside the case.

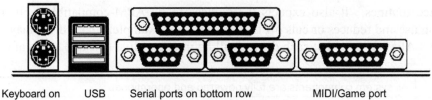

Keyboard on	USB	Serial ports on bottom row	MIDI/Game port
bottom row.	sockets	(COM1 and COM2). Parallel port	
Mouse on top row		on top row (LPT1)	

Where motherboards have built-in audio circuits (instead of using a sound card), a set of three sockets would be mounted under the MIDI port. These would provide the Microphone, Line In and Line Out sockets that are normally found on a sound card. Modern motherboards are also likely to also have modem, LAN, FireWire and possibly Serial ATA connectors.

The computer case also connects to the motherboard with cables that connect the devices on the front panel of the case. These connections include the power switch or button, a reset button, and LEDs to indicate that power is on or that the hard disk is active. In addition, a cable connects to the small internal loudspeaker built into the case. This is only used for sounding the *'beeps'* that are heard when the computer is first switched on and indicates the result of the system self-test.

The power supplies

The power supply converts the mains voltage of 230 volts AC down to a range of fixed DC voltages e.g. +5 volts or –12 volts. Negative voltages are not used by modern devices and are included for backward compatibility with older devices. The circuitry on the motherboard only uses the 5 volt positive supply.

There are three different types of power supply, with the ATX boards having two varieties:

AT	The cable from the power supply carried +5 volts, -5 volts, +12 volts and –12 volts and connected to the motherboard via two 6-pin sockets.
ATX	The cable from the power supply carries +3.3 volts, +5 volts, -5 volts, +12 volts and –12 volts and connects to the motherboard via a single 20-pin socket.
ATX12V	Designed for P4 motherboards, the supply has the normal 20-wire ATX power cable plus one (sometimes two) other cables. It provides a separate +12 volt cable that feeds only the CPU (to reduce system noise). This cable from the power supply plugs into a small square 4-pin socket on the motherboard. Some supplies also provide a 6-pin auxiliary power cable for use with heavily loaded systems such as servers and high-end workstations. This provides a +3.3 volt and a +5 volt supply.

When 3.3 volt CPUs were first introduced, power supplies did not provide a 3.3 volt supply and the motherboards used a voltage regulator to reduce the +5 volt input down to the required 3.3 volts.

Motherboards for AMD Athlon CPUs do not need or use the extra ATX12V power cables but do recommend the use of supplies of 250W or more.

A signal wire runs between the power supply and the motherboard (pin 1 on an AT cable and pin 8 on an ATX cable). This is called the *'Power_Good'* line and it is held at a high level as long as the power supply is able to feed the motherboard with the required voltages. If the power supply cannot maintain the required voltage levels for any reason (e.g. a drop in the mains voltage) the *Power_Good* line is brought low. The motherboard detects the change and stops processing.

A power supply has its own fan built into its case and this is additional to any fans used for cooling internal components (e.g. disk drives, motherboard components).

LVDS Monitor connectors

LVDS stands for Low Voltage Differential Signalling, and refers to a low-voltage method of transmitting data, rather than any specific connector type. In fact, LVDS is used in certain types of SCSI connector, and can even be transmitted via a plain old Cat 5 cable. Despite this, some PCs are listed as having an *'LVDS monitor connector'*. In most cases they are in fact referring to a white 20 or 40-pin square connector on the mainboard, rather than the actual connection between the base unit and the monitor, which in LVDS is typically a flat-panel LCD screen. The 20 or 40-pin connector attaches to a device that converts the TTL signals that drive a conventional CRT into the LVDS signals the flat panel display can understand. These signals are then transferred via the regular D-SUB or the newer DVI connector.

Power management

A motherboard that meets the APM (Advanced Power Management) specification can control the supply to individual devices in the computer, to save power. This is usually implemented in a BIOS chip and in software interface routines. It also expects the devices to be APM-compatible. It monitors which devices are not in use and reduces or cuts off their power. For example, a hard drive may be switched off when not in use. APM ensures that each device will be in one of five possible states at any one point in time.

Full On	All system components are fully powered and operational.
Standby	The CPU and some devices are powered down but the memory remains powered. This allows the system to be quickly switched into the fully on state.
Suspend	Most devices are powered down and the CPU is put into a low power state with its clock turned off, providing the greatest degree of power saving.
Hibernation	The state of all currently open programs and data is saved to disk and the computer is powered down. When the computer is next activated, all the saved data is loaded and the machine is returned to the position it was at prior to hibernation.
Off	The entire system is powered down and has to proceed through the whole bootup procedure when power is next applied.

The APM-compliant computer can be switched between states, either by user activity or by system events. For example, the user can press the 'Resume' button to switch the computer into a fully on state. Another *'wake-up'* activity may result from an incoming telephone call energising the modem into signalling the motherboard.

ACPI (Advanced Configuration and Power Management) is a development and extension of APM. The main activities are now co-ordinated by the operating system and include additional functions such as battery monitoring and thermal monitoring (e.g. closing down a system that is overheating). ACPI has a wider range of power saving options, with basic options of 'global, special sleep, microprocessor and device'. This means, for example, that the CPU or individual devices such as modems or hard drives have their own set of power saving states.

The full ACPI specification, all 507 pages, can be downloaded from www.acpi.info

AT supplies are *"hard switched"*; pressing the power supply button on the front of the case closes down the power supply. The mains supply is physically routed through the switch to the power supply. ATX systems with ACPI-enabled motherboards use *"soft-switching"*. The mains supply is wired directly to the power supply unit and is wired to the switch on the front of the case. Instead, the cable between the supply and the motherboard has a wire (on pin 14) that carries a signal from the board to the supply. This allows operating systems (such as Windows) to power down the supply via software. So, choosing the Windows *"Shut Down"* option saves all currently open data, closes down applications safely and then tells the supply to power down. In fact, a +5 volt supply is still fed to the motherboard on the *5v_Standby* line (pin 9) and an examination of a motherboard in this state usually reveals that an onboard indicator LED is lit. This line supplies sufficient power to the board to allow *wake-up* activities such as incoming calls to modems or network cards to be monitored and acted upon.

Even the power button on the front of the case supports this *'Soft Off'* system. Holding the button depressed for a few seconds soft switches the supply off.

CPU

The CPU is the heart of the computer and its functions and options are covered fully in the chapter on Computer Architecture. It plugs into a socket or slot on the motherboard and requires its own fan to keep the chip cool. The power cable from the fan plugs into a power socket on the motherboard.

Old motherboards used a square socket into which the CPU was fitted. The socket was unmistakable as it had hundreds of pins in the socket. For a while, CPUs were mounted on a separate card that plugged into a slot connector on the motherboard. This was known as a 'Single Edge Connector' ('*SEC*') arrangement, and examples included the Pentium II and early Pentium IIIs (slot 1 connector), and the Pentium II Xeon (slot 2 connector).

Manufacturers have returned to using multi-pin square sockets with a ZIF (zero insertion force) action. The layout ensures that CPUs can only be inserted the correct way.

Each motherboard has to have the correct socket for the CPU in use. For example, most Pentium IIIs used a Socket 370 (i.e. 370 pins), while current Intel Core 2 CPUs use a Socket 478 and Athlon CPUs use Socket A (462 pins). A table of types is shown later in this chapter (see *'Upgrading'*). It is common to buy a motherboard and CPU at the same time, to ensure compatibility.

The CPU is clocked at a rate determined by the basic system clock frequency as set by the crystal and the values set by the clock's jumper links.   The crystal is a motherboard component that is usually housed in a small tin case.

CPU caching was once implemented using memory chips mounted on IC sockets on the motherboard. Then some cache was supplied in plug-in form as COAST (cache on a stick) and COAST slots were provided on early motherboards. Now, modern CPUs have their cache memory built in to the CPU chip itself.

Chipsets

A motherboard uses a set of support chipsets to connect the CPU and memory through the buses to the devices such as disk drives, keyboard, I/O ports, etc.   A PCI chipset comprises two integrated circuits, called the North Bridge and South Bridge. Apart from the CPU, they are usually the two largest chips on the motherboard.

A range of competing chipsets are available. For example, the 845 chipset supports PC2100, while the 648 chipset supports PC2700 and AGP 8X.   Care is required in matching CPUs, motherboards and memory modules.   For example, the early 845 chipset for the P4 only supported SDRAM, while the newer version also supports DDR (as does the Athlon).

In addition to the PCI chipset, a motherboard has integrated peripheral chips. These circuits are used to interface to the standard I/O devices (e.g. serial and parallel ports, keyboard controller, etc.) and storage devices (e.g. IDE drives and floppy drive, etc.). Some motherboards provide additional onboard support chips to handle:

- Sound processing.
- Video capture (e.g. FireWire sockets).
- Ethernet interfaces.
- Raid controllers or SCSI drive controllers.
- Dual CPU sockets.

BIOS

The functions of the BIOS chip are covered elsewhere.

Early BIOS systems used ROM chips, where the code was permanently burnt into the chip. This meant that the system could only be updated by the replacing the BIOS chip with a new chip containing the new program routines. As a result ROM BIOS chips have been replaced by EEPROM, or *'Flash ROM'* which allow BIOS updates to be carried out in software. In fact, many systems, particularly portable systems, now have the BIOS permanently soldered onto the motherboard, and thus can only be updated by flash. There are numerous reasons why you may want to upgrade the BIOS, but they usually involve fixing bugs, improving compatibility, or overcoming limitations on hard disk size posed by the present BIOS.

Slots

The chapter on Computer Architecture examined the variety of expansion slots that are provided on motherboards.   Each type is generally identified by its size and colour:

Slot type	Colour of slot moulding	Approximate length
ISA	black	6"
PCI	white	3.5"
AGP	brown	3"
PCI-E x16	blue / yellow	3.5"

Slot type	Colour of slot moulding	Approximate length
PCI-E x8	blue / yellow	2.2"
PCI-E x4	white / yellow	1.5"
PCI-E x1	white / yellow	1"

The ISA slot is being phased out on many motherboards, although some boards continue to provide ISA slots for connecting older expansion cards (e.g. an ISA sound card or modem).

Motherboards are also available with differing memory module slots.

The common SDRAM DIMM module plugs into a motherboard slot that has 168 pins, while the DDR DIMM requires a slot with 184 pins.   RIMM modules also use a 184-pin slot. Although RIMMs and DDR DIMMs have same number of pins, they have locating notches in different places so that the wrong type cannot be fitted accidentally.

Connectors

There are a number of connector sockets or pin strips on the motherboard. Sockets are used to connect the leads from the power supply, the floppy drive and the IDE devices (such as hard drives or CD-ROMs). Blocks of pins are used to connect cables to the case's front panel LEDs (e.g. power indictor, disk activity indicator) to the panel's power/reset switches, to the CPU cooling fan and to the computer's internal speaker).

Miscellaneous

Each motherboard has an on-board battery that is kept charged when the computer is switched on. When the computer is switched off, the battery maintains power to the onboard clock and to the small area of memory used to store BIOS details.

The motherboard may also have a number of jumper blocks that are used to set the system's voltage settings, the CPU's clock speed and the processor multiplier value. The motherboard manual will supply the jumper setting details.

System Assembly

The next part of the chapter looks at putting a computer system together.

Before proceeding, consideration has to be given to component selection and compatibility.

Selection Issues

The last few pages explained that the CPU, motherboard and memory modules have to match. There are many motherboards in the marketplace, including models to older specifications, working with older memory types, older CPUs, etc. Even relatively new models use different chipsets that offer varying levels of support (e.g. a 400MHz or a 533MHz front side bus, USB 1 or USB 2, SDRAM only, DDR only or both) or facilities (e.g. on board SCSI or RAID controllers).

The technician also has to know the best component to fit for a particular situation. It is important to check that a card can be installed without any interrupt clashes, DMA clashes or I/O address clashes (see later). This would probably involve checking that the add-on card allowed for a range of different settings to be chosen, or is a plug-and-play type. Incorrect selection could lead to poor performance or the failure of the system to operate. These issues should be investigated and settled <u>before</u> the purchase of the items.

Compatibility Issues

The technician has to ensure that the components intended for assembly are fully compatible. This may involve physical, electronic and software considerations. A technical specification may indicate that a card is satisfactory for a particular purpose but other factors may come into play. For example, the new device may be a full-length card but the computer may only have a half-length expansion slot left unused.

- Check that the computer will work in the planned operating environment (e.g. is the temperature too high or too low, is the humidity too great, is the computer to be located close to sources of electrical interference such as machinery, does the site suffer from mains noise requiring the fitting of a mains filter, etc). Check the computer's specification for the temperature and humidity tolerances.
- Before installing any equipment, carry out a dry run to ensure that there is adequate space to house the equipment (e.g. a spare expansion slot if fitting a card or a spare bay if fitting a drive).
- The dry run should also check that all the necessary leads have sufficient connectors and will stretch to connect to the new equipment. This may include control/data cables from the disk controller, connector cable from a SCSI card, audio lead to a sound card, etc. It would certainly include making sure that there was a spare power lead on the power supply's cable loom and that the connection would reach to the new equipment. If there is no spare connection, a 'Y' connector can be bought. This involves removing a lead from an existing piece of equipment and inserting it into the Y connector. This connector has two outputs - one to go to the original piece of equipment and one for the new apparatus to be installed.

Assembling the components

The following pages are a step-by-step guide to assembling a computer system from a set of components. The detail may vary from system to system, depending upon the components involved.

Rushing into an assembly may produce a working system first time. It may also lead to damage or configuration problems. It is best to take time to read the instructions supplied with the components before carrying out any activity.

The final checklist before starting:
- Read the safe working and equipment handling notes in the chapter on PC Support.
- Check that all the required components, including cables, are present before starting.
- Check that all documentation (e.g. motherboard and hard drive manuals) is to hand.
- Check that all the necessary tools are available.

Preparing the case

- Remove the cover of the computer main unit. There are normally 4 or 5 screws along the rear, which secure the cover to the main chassis. In some models, the screws may be along the side of the casing. In a very few cases, it is simply a matter of pressing in two side buttons and hinging up the cover. Check the manual, as the some of the rear screws might be used for other purposes such as securing 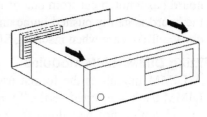 the fan casing or the power supply. In some tower cases, the front panel has to be removed first (read the manual).
- The screws should be placed in a safe place. If there is much disassembly work involved, the various screws should be placed in labelled envelopes.
- Where an add-on with an external interface is to be fitted (e.g. an internal modem or sound card) remove the blanking plate that blocks off the corresponding slot in the external casing. Do not remove more blanking plates than are required, as these are prevent dust from entering the case. This could lead to heat buildup and cause any of a wide range of ill effects, most of which will result in a crash of some kind.
- Make sure the power supply is set to 230v.

Installing the motherboard

- Fit an earthing strap to wrist and connect to an earthing point (e.g. the computer chassis). This minimises the risk of body static blowing any chips on the motherboard.
- Set any jumpers on the motherboard. Check the manual for details. Likely settings would be the processor voltage, clock speed, the CPU multiplication factor and disabling the on-board sound circuitry where an add-on sound card is to be fitted. Older motherboards used jumpers to set the clock speed but this is now mostly set in the BIOS.
- Hold the board over the case chassis and check that all the mounting holes on the motherboard line up with stand-offs on the chassis. In extreme cases, fresh holes may need to be drilled in the case to fit mounting posts. Never drill or file the motherboard as this may damage the tracks on the board.
- Slip the motherboard into the case, aligning the rear connectors with the open slot at the rear
- Match the holes on the motherboard up to the mounting holes in case chassis.
- Screw in the motherboard with brass bolts, using plastic stand-offs to keep the motherboard above the metal chassis surface.
- Connect the power cable(s) from power supply to the motherboard.
- Connect the cables from the motherboard to the case components (e.g. power switch, speaker, LEDs), as given in the motherboard and case documentation.

Installing the CPU

- Lift up the lever on the CPU ZIF socket (a large square white socket).
- Align pin 1 of the CPU to the motherboard socket pin 1 – the CPU should only fit one way. Different processor types have different numbers of pins; make sure the correct processor type is to be fitted to the correct socket type.
- Insert the CPU into the socket and close the ZIF lever.
- Spread some heat-sink compound on the top of the CPU.
- Fit the CPU heatsink using the clamp. Securing the clamp often requires a little bit of force and great care should be taken to ensure that the motherboard is not subject to undue pressure, to avoid cracking the board.
- Connect the power cable from the heatsink's fan to motherboard's fan power socket.

Fitting memory

Memory modules are available in the older SIMM and modern DIMM formats (see the chapter on memory). Before handling either, discharge your body static or preferably wear an earthing wristband.

Fitting SIMM Boards

These boards have holes to engage with pegs on the slots. Place the SIMM into the socket at an angle of about 30 degrees and engage the SIMM's pegs into the matching holes in the SIMM slot. The board has a notch cut from one of its sides, so that it cannot be inserted the wrong way round. When the board is gently pushed home and rotated vertically, it clicks into place in the bank's retaining side clips. Take care when inserting SIMMs since the pegs break quite easily.

Fitting DIMM/RIMM Modules

A DIMM module is the format used for DDR memory, the most common type currently in use.. A DIMM bank is inserted vertically into the DIMM socket. The socket has two keys and the DIMM has two matching notches along the bottom of the bank. This ensures that the DIMM is inserted the correct way round. When the DIMM is fully inserted, retaining clips at the side of the socket hold the DIMM in place.

A RIMM module is the format used for RDRAM (Rambus). It has identical dimensions to a DIMM module and is fitted in the same way. The two modules are not interchangeable and the notches on the DIMM modules are in different positions to those used in SIMM modules (see the chapter on memory) to prevent the accidental fitting of the wrong type of module.

In both cases, alter any DIP switch settings or jumper settings as necessary, after insertion of the memory bank. This configures the motherboard to recognise the new memory. This is only required by older motherboards, as newer boards automatically detect the amount of memory fitted.

Fitting IDE drives

There are three main steps involved in fitting a disk drive:

- Set any jumpers (on the drive or drive controller)
- Install the drive into the computer case and connect it to the rest of the system.
- Ensure that the system's software settings allow the PC to recognise the new drive.

The rear connectors

The diagram shows the connections that are present at the rear of a typical IDE disk drive. The disk drive is normally connected to the rest of the system by two cables.

The Molex power socket

This is shown at the right of the illustration. The power cables that feed out of the computer's power supply unit supply 12 volt and 5 volt to power the various peripherals such as hard disks, floppy disks, CD-ROMs and DVD players. One of the spare plugs is connected to the rear socket to power the disk drive. As can be seen, the socket on the drive is shaped with bevels on two

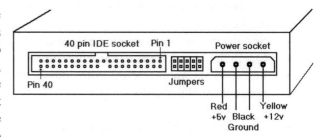

corners, such that the power cable can only be inserted one way. The diagram also shows the colours and voltages of the wires that connect to the power socket.

Control/Data socket

The cable that plugs into this socket has two purposes:

- To allow control signals from the main system to start and stop the drive motor, move the read/write head and other control functions.
- To allow data from the computer to be taken to the write head and to allow data read from the head to be taken back to the computer.

This cable is a grey ribbon, with a red strip along one edge. The red strip indicates that it is the wire for Pin 1 of the socket and this allows the user to fit the cable the correct way round. Pin 1 of the header socket is at the end near the power socket.   Some sockets and cables are designed so that they can only be fitted one way round, by engaging a bump on the edge of the plug into a notch in the socket.

In early systems, the control cable was a separate cable from the data cable and the system used three cables to attach the drive to the system.

Setting up an IDE drive

The chapter on disks explained the way that drives are set as 'masters' or 'slaves'.   This is achieved by adjusting settings on each drive, so that they are set as being unique.   These are found at the rear of the case on a *"jumper block"*.   The block has two rows of pins and various pins can be bridged with small metal connectors with plastic covers.

Single   The jumper settings on the drive alter the configuration and a common method of setting the jumpers is shown in the diagram.

Master   If the jumper block has no jumper links fitted, as shown in the first example, the drive is regarded as being a *'single'* drive.   This means that it is the only drive on the IDE cable and is automatically regarded as the master drive.

Slave

In the second example, a link has been inserted to bridge the middle set of pins (often marked as MASTER or MS), to configure the drive as a master.

The third example shows a link shorting the pins marked as SLAVE or SP (Slave Present), to configure the drive as a slave drive.

Although this is a common method of configuration, other methods are used and the disk's manual should advise.   If the manual is missing, the information can usually be found on the manufacturer's web site or from www.thetechpage.com, a website that has details on a huge number of drives.

Fitting

The steps for installing a hard disk are as follows:

- For very old legacy drives, ensure that the new disk's parameters are known; this is likely to be printed on a label on the disk.   If this is not provided, contact the supplier for the information on number of tracks, number of sectors per track, etc.   Do not proceed with the remaining steps until these facts are known, as the BIOS will have to be set up to these parameters.   This is not required with a modern BIOS, which has an *'IDE HDD Auto Detection'* facility that automatically detects and stores the parameters of each disk detected.

- Ensure that the new disk is configured as a *'master'* disk (see the notes above).

- Carefully remove the new disk drive from its anti-static bag.   Avoid touching any exposed electronic components and handle the drive by its casing.

- Fit the new drive into an unused bay and secure with screws. Where a 3.5" drive has to be fitted into a 5.25" drive bay, a mounting adaptor kit is required.   This uses fixing rails to bridge the gap.   The drive is screwed to the rails and the rails are screwed to the bay.

- Connect one of the spare power connectors on the power loom to the drive.   This has a unique shape and can only be connected one way round.

- Fit the data ribbon cable from the IDE connector on the motherboard to the disk drive. The motherboard has two IDE ports – the primary port and the secondary port. The cable should be attached to the primary IDE port.   The ports may be marked as '1' and '2'.   If not check the layout on the motherboard manual.

  Remember that the red end of the ribbon cable aligns to pin 1 - this is true for both ends.

Later, when the system is fully assembled and booted, the BIOS can be set to recognise the drive's parameters and the disk can be partitioned and formatted (see the chapter on Disks and Drives).

Fitting a second IDE hard disk

The following steps cover the addition of an extra IDE drive to a computer with an existing IDE drive.

- Ensure that the computer has:
  - A spare power connector (if not, purchase a 'Y' power adapter).
  - A power supply that is capable of handling the total system power requirements.
- IDE hard disks are supplied configured as masters so the system may need to be informed that a slave drive is connected (by setting a *'Slave Present'* jumper). In general, the newest drive should be used as the master, as its controller may have extra features that have been developed since the older drive was designed.
- Fit the drive into an unused bay and secure with the screws provided with the installation kit. Where a 3.5" drive has to be fitted into a 5.25" drive bay, a mounting adaptor kit is required. This uses fixing rails to bridge the gap. The drive is screwed to the rails and the rails are screwed to the bay.
- Fit the power cable and ribbon cable to the new disk drive. The drives can be connected to the ribbon cables in any order. There is no requirement for the master disk to be on the first connector.

Like the first drive, the BIOS can be set to recognise the drive's parameters and the disk can be partitioned and formatted (see the chapter on Disks and Drives). This will be carried out when the system is fully assembled and booted

Fitting a Serial ATA drive

A Serial ATA drive is physically secured into the case in the same way as any other drive. However it has some important differences from IDE drives:

- While an IDE drive is connected using a 40-wire cable, a Serial ATA drive uses only a 7-pin connection (the data is carried over two pairs of wires). This makes the cable much smaller and results in less blockage of airflow through the case.
- While an IDE cable can connect two drives, a separate cable is used for each Serial ATA drive that is attached to the motherboard. This means that the drives do not need to be set as 'master' or 'slave', making installation easier.
- While the computer has to be switched off to work with IDE drives, Serial ATA drives are *'hot swappable'*.

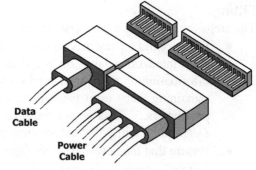

Data Cable

Power Cable

There are three ways that the drive can connect to the motherboard:

- Through an integrated controller on the motherboard' chipset. These *'native'* systems are designed to use the full capability of serial ATA.
- Through a *'bridge'* controller on the motherboard. This has to convert between the serial and parallel data formats and so some of the drive's performance is lost.
- Through an add-on controller card. These are available in both native and bridge formats. Add-on controller cards are particularly useful for servers, where RAID connections for 4, 8 or 12 channels are available.

A Serial ATA controller will recognise a Serial ATA drive automatically when the computer is booted up.

Once the computer is booted, the drive can be partitioned and formatted (see the chapter on Disks and Drives).

Serial ATA controllers are backwards compatible with IDE devices. This allows a Serial ATA controller to control a normal IDE drive, although an adapter has to be fitted between the cable and the drive.

Fitting removeable drives

This covers the fitting of a floppy disk drive and a CD-ROM. These are regarded as the basic requirements for a modern computer system. For example, Windows is supplied on a CD-ROM.

Other drives such as a DVD player, and a CD writer are covered later, since they are best fitted once a basic system is assembled and proved to be running. If all possible add-ons are fitted before switching the machine on, it is much harder to diagnose any problems that may manifest themselves.

Once the basic system is running, each add-on can be individually installed and tested. This makes the detection of clashes between incompatible components much easier to detect and overcome.

For each removeable device:
- Identify which plastic blanking plate on the front of the case covers the mouth of the drive bay being used for the new device.
- Remove the plate by popping it out from the case.
- In some instances, the case covers the mouth of each bay with a metal blanking plate. The plate is punched so that it is only held at a few points. The plate can be removed by gripping the plate and gently twisting it until the connecting points snap.
- Connect the appropriate cables, typically a power and a data cable, to the motherboard or controller.

Fitting a CD-ROM

CD-ROMs are available in either internal or external models. If the case has a spare front 5.25" drive bay then the user has the option of having an internal unit fitted. Otherwise, an external model can be fitted. With both models there is a further choice, as the CD-ROM can be connected to the motherboard in several ways. The steps for fitting depend on the type of CD-ROM drive.

Internal

- Choose the computer's drive bay and expansion slot that allow the connecting cables to reach both components without undue strain.
- Remove the front blanking plate; this is usually a plastic plate that can be popped out.
- Install the CD-ROM into the guides and firmly press into place.
- When the front of the ROM unit is flush with the front of the computer casing, secure the unit to the casing with the screws provided.
- Connect one of the spare power connectors on the power loom to the CD-ROM. This has a unique shape and can only be connected one way round.
- For an IDE drive connecting to the motherboard's first IDE slot, set the CD drive's jumper to make the unit a 'slave' device and connect the drive on an unused connector on the existing hard disk cable.
- For an IDE connecting to the motherboard's second IDE slot, set the CD drive's jumper to make the unit a 'master' device and connect an IDE interface cable between the drive and the second IDE slot on the motherboard.
- For a SCSI CD-ROM drive, set the drive's SCSI ID to an unused ID and connect the drive to an unused connector on the existing SCSI disk cable.

If the computer has an audio card fitted later, an audio cable can be fitted between the CD-ROM and the card's onboard audio input connector. This cable carries audio (i.e. from normal audio CDs) from the CD-ROM to the card and the cable is keyed to only connect one way round.

External

There are four current ways that an external CD-ROM can be connected to the system:

SCSI

This is useful where the computer already has an external SCSI connector. The cable from the CD-ROM is plugged into the computer's SCSI socket. On bootup, the SCSI's BIOS chip will recognise the new drive's presence.

USB

This is a simple way to connect an external CD-ROM to a computer. The cable from the CD-ROM is simply plugged into the computer's USB socket and the drive is immediately recognised.

FireWire

This is a simple way to connect an external CD-ROM to a computer with a FireWire connection. The cable from the CD-ROM is plugged into the computer's FireWire socket and the drive is immediately recognised.

PC Card

This is a popular way to connect an external CD-ROM to a laptop computer. The cable from the CD-ROM has a PC Card on the end and this card is plugged into one of the computer's PCMCIA slots. The drive is immediately recognised.

Fitting a graphics card

A few motherboards have the graphics circuitry mounted directly on to the board. This ties the user to a specific graphics performance and most users prefer to fit a separate graphics card. This usually provides an improved video performance and added features. The following steps are for fitting a graphics card to the motherboard.

- If the motherboard has on-board graphics, disabled it by setting a motherboard jumper or by changing the BIOS settings.
- Locate a free expansion slot. Remove the rear blanking plate currently blocking this slot. Insert the graphics card carefully into the expansion slot. The card's output socket should protrude from the empty slot.
- Secure the card using the same screw removed with the blanking plate.

When the computer is first booted up, the card will default to displaying in VGA mode. After Windows is installed, a software driver allows the resolution, colour depth, etc. to be user defined.

Attach external devices

Attach the keyboard, mouse, monitor, and power cable, as described in the chapter on Basics.

Configure the system

Switch on the computer and check that the BIOS reports the correct amount of installed memory and that it recognises the type and capacity of the disk drive. Also check that the floppy drive is capable of reading disks, as this is essential for installing the operating system. Other features, such as clock speed, power management, etc. should be set through the BIOS at this stage. See the chapter on *'Windows Configuration'* for details. The chapter on Disk & Drives covers partitioning and formatting hard disks.

Install the operating system

The installation activities depend upon the operating system that is being installed. In general, this will take the form of:

- On older systems, running a floppy disk program that installs a driver for the CD-ROM. This ensures that the CD-ROM drive is recognised by the system, allowing the operating system to be loaded from the installation CD.
- Inserting the Operating System installation CD and running the install program.

Full details for installing various versions of Microsoft Windows are provided in the chapter on Windows Configuration. Windows should detect the presence of the new hardware and automatically find and install its driver. These are specially written software programs, designed to drive the new graphics hardware to the best performance. If the card being fitted does not have a driver stored within the Window's system, the driver from the CD supplied with the video card should be installed.

Thereafter, run the Window's Settings/Control Panel/Display Settings to select the required screen resolution, colour depth and refresh rate.

Installing add-on cards

The previous pages should have resulted in a computer system with basic functions (i.e. floppy and CD-ROM operations) and a fully functioning operating system. At this stage, it would be appropriate to consider adding other hardware devices such as a sound card, modem, network card or video capture card.

Before considering adding specific cards to a computer, the following issues should be considered:

- That the cards are handled safely.
- That cards are added in a way that does not interfere with existing devices in the computer.

Handling procedures

There are a number of general safety, handling and organisational procedures that should be observed. These are designed to both protect the technician and safeguard the equipment. The general safety procedures were outlined in the chapter on PC Support. General rules on handling cards are:

- If any internal connectors are temporarily removed, record which socket they were removed from and note the orientation of the plug in that socket.
- When installing the card, ensure that the edge connector is properly lined up with the expansion socket.

- Avoid excessive force in installing the card; gently rocking the card from edge to edge with a firm pressure is sufficient.   If the card is hard to fit, check that there is no other problem such as an obstruction or a misalignment of the card with the slot.
- Avoid excessive force in plugging in connectors to the card.   If the plug is hard to fit, check that there is no other problem such as an obstruction or a reversal of the plug.
- Ensure that the card is securely screwed to the computer chassis.   The screw used to secure the blanking plate is used for this purpose.

Resource compatibility

Each device uses some of the system's resources and it is important that two devices do not clash over the use of these resources. A clash might result in a device not operating properly or the computer hanging.

The three resources are:

IRQ	The way that a device triggers a software activity (see chapter on Computer Architecture)
DMA	The way data transfer between the memory and certain devices is speeded up (see later).
Address space	The unique address for accessing a device (see later)

The general approach for fitting cards is:
- Check that each card's IRQs, DMA channels and I/O address locations do not clash with any existing card in the machine. If necessary, consult the manuals of the existing cards. If there is any clash, set the jumpers on the new card to avoid any collision. Plug and play cards, along with Window's PCI Bus IRQ Steering, should minimise this problem.
- Install the card.
- Install the driver.
- Check that the device works.
- Check that the device has not upset any other devices or operations. If so, examine the possibilities of using other IRQs, DMAs or I/O addresses.

In most cases, plug and play makes compatibility automatic and installation only involves fitting the card and installing the driver software.

Installing drivers

A device driver is a piece of software that interfaces a device to the rest of the system. A different driver is used for each device (e.g. a graphics card driver or a network card driver). The driver is usually provided on floppy or CD along with the card. As newer versions of the drivers are written, they can be downloaded from the web site of the card manufacturer. This corrects any bugs in the original driver or adds extra functionality. The add-on cards fitted to a Windows computer can be of two types:
- Plug and Play cards that are automatically detected.
- Cards that need to be set up manually.

Automatic Installation

If the computer's BIOS supports Plug and Play (all modern computers), then the addition of a new PnP card is detected during the bootup stage. If the device exists in the list held in the Window's 'INF' folder, then the driver is automatically installed. Otherwise, the *'Add New Hardware'* Wizard is called up and the user can choose to:
- Let Windows search for an appropriate driver for the card.
- Point to the folder that contains the driver.

The automatic search is through the driver database already installed on the computer. If the driver is found in the database, it is installed. If the driver is not already in the database, the user is prompted to browse through the computer's file system (including floppy disk, CD, etc) to point to the folder containing the driver (a .INF file).

The user is often asked to insert the original Windows installation CD, to access the driver stored there. Often, however, the version on the CD is older than the driver on the floppy disk or CD-ROM provided with the add-on card. If this is suspected, then the option for user control of the source folder should be chosen. Alternatively, the latest driver can often be downloaded from the web site of the card manufacturer. When the driver is installed, the system may prompt for the computer to be restarted. Sometimes, Windows will detect that a new card has been installed but will not be able to detect what the device is. If the "Unknown Device" message is displayed, then the manual method of device driver installation as outlined below has to be used.

Manual installation

The *'Control Panel'* has an *'Add New Hardware'* option that invokes an installation wizard to select and configure new hardware. The menu presents a choice of device type - e.g. display adapters, hard disk controllers and network adapters.

The example shows the menu displayed when *'Printers'* is chosen. The windows list all devices - by manufacturer- that are contained in its database. For newer models, the *'Have Disk'* option allows installation from CD or floppy.

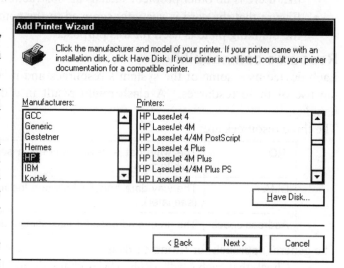

Windows 2000 has an *'Add/Remove Hardware'* option, which can Remove or Troubleshoot devices. However, it will only add devices that it detects.

Updating drivers

The *'Device Manager'* option (in Windows 2000 this is accessed through the '*System*' dialog in the *'Hardware'* tab) displays a list of all recognised devices on that computer.

Clicking on a device opens up a dialog box similar to that shown in the illustration.

Clicking the *'Driver'* tab displays the details of the driver that the computer uses to interface that device.

Clicking the '*Update Driver*' button provides an option for Windows to search for a driver or for the user to specify a location for a driver (e.g. on a floppy disk or CD-ROM).

Practical IRQ Considerations

Each IRQ number corresponds to a physical hardware line - e.g. an activity from a mouse connection or a modem connection. Each IRQ line is allocated to an interrupt number that links to the corresponding routine for handling that device. So, for example, a mouse might be attached to the COM1 port, which is IRQ1. Any mouse movement will trigger the IRQ1 interrupt and this will call the mouse handling routine. When the user installed the mouse driver, the routine was placed in memory and the address of the routine was placed in the interrupt vector table.

Sharing IRQs

It follows that only one routine can be linked to a single IRQ number at any one time. It is possible to have two or more add-on cards or devices set up with the same IRQ number, as long as they are not used simultaneously. If two devices have the same IRQ setting and both attempt to invoke a call at the same time unpredictable results can be expected, since only one device handler is in memory. Devices, such as a scanner and a modem are unlikely to ever be required at the same time. In this case, the two cards can both have IRQ settings at the same IRQ number.

From Windows 95 Release 2 onwards, Windows has the ability to handle multiple PCI devices with the same IRQ - and this is known as *"PCI Bus IRQ Steering"*.

If possible, every card should use a different IRQ setting. This is possible in a computer with few add-ons but conflicts become more likely as more and more adapter cards are added to a system.

Choosing an IRQ

When a new device is to be added to the system, its IRQ requirement must not clash with any existing IRQ requirements of cards already fitted to the system. Add-on cards allow some alteration of their IRQ settings, through the adjustment of jumpers or switches or through software setting. The documentation that accompanies the card will give details of the default IRQ setting and the other

```
IRQ  Address     Description       Detected     Handled By
---  ---------   ---------------   ----------   ---------------
 0   0566:00D2   Timer Click       Yes          MOUSE
 1   CF01:1923   Keyboard          Yes              Block Device
 2   F000:EA97   Second 8259A      Yes          BIOS
 3   F000:EA97   COM2: COM4:       COM2:        BIOS
 4   0566:02CD   COM1: COM3:       COM1:   Logitech Serial MOUSE
 5   F000:EA97   LPT2:             No           BIOS
 6   F000:EF57   Floppy Disk       Yes          BIOS
 7   0070:06F4   LPT1:             Yes          System Area
 8   F000:EA42   Real-Time Clock   Yes          BIOS
 9   F000:EECF   Redirected IRQ2   Yes          BIOS
10   F000:EA97   (Reserved)                     BIOS
11   C94C:091F   (Reserved)                     SCSIMGR$
12   F000:EA97   (Reserved)                     BIOS
13   F000:EED8   Math Coprocessor  Yes          BIOS
14   F000:E845   Fixed Disk        Yes          BIOS
15   F000:9272   (Reserved)                     BIOS
```

settings that it can adopt. Sometimes, there are only a few alternatives while other cards offer a range of 8 alternative IRQ settings to allow the greatest opportunity for fitting the card without interrupt clashes. The first stage is to check the usage of the IRQs within the existing system.

The *'Properties'* option within Windows Device Manager can be used for this purpose.

The table above shows the result of a diagnostic utility showing IRQs. These will vary with differing machine hardware configurations but most IRQ assignments will be similar.

Notes

- IRQ numbers 0, 1, 4, 5, 6, 7, 8, 9 and 14 are used in almost all machines.
- IRQ numbers 0, 1, 2, 8 and 13 are not wired to the expansions slots.
- **IRQ2**   When an IRQ between 8 and 15 is activated, it is using its own PIC, known as the slave PIC. This PIC does not have its own connection directly to the MI line of the CPU. It has to notify the CPU through the master PIC - the one that services IRQ0 to IRQ7. It does this through the master PIC's IRQ2 line and the Master PIC activates the CPU's MI pin. This process is known as *'cascading'* and is implemented in hardware - the actual interrupt 0A is not used. This often means that IRQ2 can be used for another device, being mapped to the IRQ9 line of the slave PIC; any card configured as IRQ2 is really using IRQ9.
- **IRQ3**   This is allocated for a second serial port, COM2. In the first example, a second port is installed on the machine so the IRQ is in use. Where a second port is not fitted, the line can be used by another device. If a second printer port is fitted but not in use, it may be possible to disable the second port's IRQ line, releasing IRQ3 for another device as shown below.
- **IRQ5**   This is allocated for a second parallel port, LPT2. Since a second port is rarely fitted,

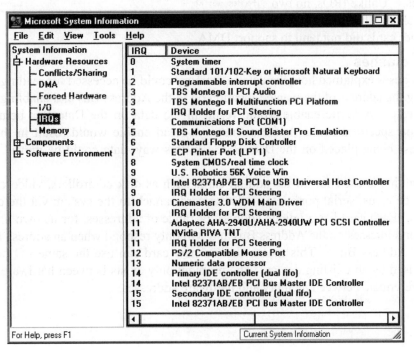

the IRQ can be used by another device.   If the second port is fitted but not in use, it may be possible to disable the second port's IRQ line, releasing IRQ5 for another device as in the example below.

- **IRQ7**   This is allocated for the first parallel port, LPT1. The printer port only needs an IRQ line if it is carrying out bi-directional data transfers.   Disabling the IRQ7 line of the printer port allows all the normal printing operations to be carried out, along with the usual out-of-paper and off-line detection.   In this way, IRQ7 can be released for another device.
- **IRQ10, 11, 12 and 15** are likely to be available for use, despite being displayed as *'Reserved'*. In the example, IRQ11 is being used for the SCSI controller card.

Windows 98 onwards provides information on IRQ usage, along with other useful information, via its *'System Information'* utility accessed from the *Start / Programs / Accessories / System Tool* buttons.

DMA

Some devices require data to be transferred between themselves and the memory at the fastest possible speed.   These are usually devices handling bulk data such as network cards, scanners, soundboards and hard disks.   Slower devices such as floppy drives and serial/parallel ports do not have as demanding a speed transfer requirement.   The slow devices use the CPU to organise the transfer of data between memory and the devices.   All the data has to pass through the CPU and this ties up a lot of processing time, slowing down the computer's throughput.

To handle the faster devices, the PC uses a special technique known as *'Direct Memory Access'*.   An extra chip handles the transfers to and from memory, leaving the CPU to get on with other tasks.   This results in a more efficient system and increased throughput.

The original XT had four DMA channels, three of which appeared on the expansion bus.   The AT onwards has eight DMA slots, with DMA4 being used to cascade to the CPU.   DMA Channels 0 through to 3 are used for 8-bit transfers, while Channels 5 to 7 are available for 16-bit transfers only.

Windows 98 onwards provides DMA information via its *'System Information'* utility accessed from the *'Start'* button's *'Programs / Accessories /System Tool'* options. The illustration shows typical DMA usage.

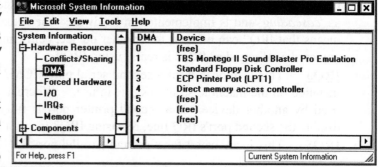

Some installation routines, such as that for sound cards, carry out their own check of DMA usage and report any possible clashes.   Unlike IRQs, no two devices can share the same DMA channel.   Older cards did not tend to support DMA.

I/O address clashes

The section on buses explained how the data in memory could be accessed for reading and writing.   This entailed placing the address of the wanted location on to the Address Bus and enabling the Read or Write lines as required.   A Write enable would result in the data on the Data Bus being written into the memory location specified in the Address Bus.   A Read enable would result in the data held in the specified address being placed on the Data Bus.   In this way, data could be moved round the internal system.

The same technique is used for all the add-on cards such as disk controllers, video cards, sound cards, network interface cards, serial ports, etc.   These cards attach to the system via the connections on the expansion slots.   Each card has a unique address, or range of addresses, for its own use.   The card will ignore any other addresses on the Address Bus and will only respond when an address from its own range appears on the Address Bus.   This means that no new card can use the same I/O port address as that already being used by an existing device. The problem only exists between hardware devices, since the system can differentiate between memory and hardware addresses.

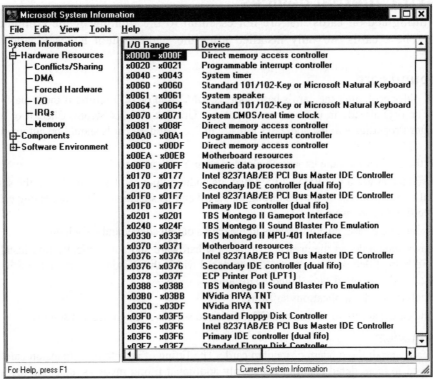

The illustration shows the lower range of I/O addresses and this will vary slightly dependent upon the machine configuration in use.

As can be seen, many of the addresses have their functions allocated, leaving a small range of addresses into which must be fitted additional cards.   The range 200h to 20Fh is often used for the fitting of a games port while the 300h to 31Fh range is the common area used for the addition of extra cards (e.g. a network card).   Again, Windows Device Manager can show some of the current I/O port address usage on the machine.

Altering existing values

Clicking the *'System'* icon in *'Control Panel'* displays a *'System Properties'* menu from which the *'Device Manager'* option displays a list of existing hardware. Clicking on an item displays the menu shown. The *'Resources'* option displays the current I/O and IRQ settings. Unchecking the *'Use automatic settings'* box allows the values to be altered. In the example shown, Windows reports that no conflict has been detected between this device and others. The *'Driver'* option displays the software drivers that handle the device. The *'General'* option displays information such as the detected manufacturer of the device.

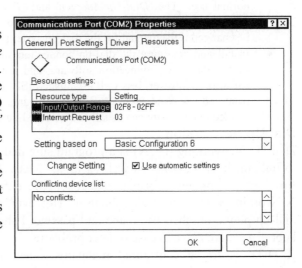

Fitting PC Cards

A laptop system does not have room for full size expansion slots. Instead it uses PC Cards, which are described in the 'Computer Architecture' chapter. The PC card is simply inserted into an empty slot of the correct Type, and held in place by closing the lever beside the slot. PC Cards are hot-swappable, which means they should be detected as soon as they are inserted. If the driver already exists on the system, it will use that driver automatically, so the driver installation process need only be performed once. However, when removing the card, the user should first stop the card driver using either the Control Panel, or the 'Remove Devices' icon in the system tray if it is available. Failure to properly stop the driver can sometimes result in a crash, or lost data.

Fitting extra internal devices

This covers fitting add-on cards that are not essential to the running of the computer but add greater functionality. These cards are only installed after the main system is tested and found to be fully functioning.

Fitting a sound card

- On an older card, alter the card's base address, DMA and/or IRQ setting if these clash with an address, DMA or IRQ already in use on the computer. Utilities such as Sleuth, Checkit or Windows Device Manager/Properties will list addresses already in use. Modern cards should be automatically configured through plug-and-play.
- Insert the card into a spare expansion slot and secure with a screw.
- If the computer has a CD-ROM drive fitted, its audio output can be connected to the sound card, so that normal music CDs can be played through the card and its speakers. The connecting cable can normally only be fitted in one way.
- Re-assemble the case, attach speakers to the card's output socket and switch on.
- Windows should detect the presence of the new hardware and automatically find install its driver. If the card being fitted does not have a driver stored within the Window's system, the driver from the CD supplied with the sound card should be installed.
- Install all the card's applications software.
- Test the card's ability to play music CDs, digitised sounds and synthesised sounds.

Installing a modem

- Physically install the modem or modem card. The fitting of an internal expansion card or PCMCIA card is explained in more detail elsewhere; the only additional fitting involves attaching the modem to the phone line. Most modems come with a telephone cord; the most likely problem is if the modem has a US-style modem jack, requiring an adapter to plug into a UK phone socket. Fitting an external modem involves ensuring the modem has power (this may not be necessary for USB modems), and connecting it to the PC serial or USB port as appropriate. A good external modem will still be automatically detected, however. If not, simply select Add New Hardware from the Control Panel and install manually.
- Install the modem driver. A Plug-and-Play modem should be detected automatically by Windows, as described earlier. Generally the modem will come with a driver disk that should be used when prompted by the Windows operating system to select a device driver. If not, the '*generic modem*' driver may suffice for normal use. The '*Dial-Up Adapter*' and '*TCP/IP*' Network components will be automatically installed. TCP/IP is by far the most common Internet protocol and is used by nearly all ISPs; the protocol should only be changed if the manual for the dial-up system specifically says to do so.
- Install and configure the dial-up connection software. Major ISPs such as Demon, AOL and FreeServe supply their own connection software, and the appropriate instructions should be followed to install the software. However, less well established ISPs may not have any connection software, or may simply use a front-end to Windows' connection software, Dial-Up Networking. Even those ISPs with proprietary connection software can usually be accessed through basic DUN if necessary.

Dial-Up Networking

Dial-Up Networking (DUN) is a program supplied with Windows 95 onwards. It can be used to dial in to bulletin boards (BBS) as well as ISPs. Many ISPs supply '*INS*' files, which contain information that will be entered into Dial-Up Networking without involving the user. However, details such as the dial-up phone number, username and password should be noted and kept in a secure place in case of later problems.

If DUN is to be configured manually, select it from the Start menu/Accessories/Communications or open Explorer and select My Computer/Dial-Up Networking. A wizard will pop up, prompting the user to enter details for the system he/she will be dialling into. This includes a name for the connection, and the telephone number to dial. Once a connection is set up, an icon will be added to the DUN screen. At this point the user can add new connections, or double-click on the icon to begin the dial-up process.

DUN will load up a connection window, as shown. Initially the Username will be taken from the current user's Windows login name, but this should be changed to reflect the username on the ISP. Similarly, the password will be blank at first, and the user should enter the correct password. If this is the first time using this connection, the '*Save Password*' checkbox can be ticked, allowing DUN to store the password so that the user need not enter it every time.

If there are problems connecting to the remote system, right clicking on a connection icon and selecting '*Properties*' gives access to a dialog from which many connection settings can be changed. These include the phone number, modem settings such as start and stop bits, as well as scripting that allows DUN to interact with the remote system on the user's behalf, entering the user name and password automatically. In most cases these properties should not be changed unless the manual states otherwise.

Installing ADSL

How ADSL works is explained in the chapter on Data Communications.

The steps for getting started with ADSL are:

- Check if ADSL is available in your exchange area. Large areas of the country are still to have their exchanges upgraded to provide this facility, although the level of availability is improving all the time.   Check out www.btopenworld.com/broadband/linecheck, enter your telephone number and a report on your exchange's suitability is displayed.
- Select an ISP. There is a fair difference in price between different suppliers, although the size and track record of the ISP might also be taken into consideration. The '*contention ratio*' – i.e. how many other users might share the bandwidth at any time – is also an important factor.   An ISP might offer a cheap rate because more users share the bandwidth, making for slow connections at peak times.
- Order an ADSL modem and filters (see below) if required.   Some ISPs provide these items as part of their bundled agreement.

If a user has a dedicated line just for ADSL use, the connection is very simple.

The ADSL modem has two leads.   One is plugged into the telephone socket on the wall and the other is connected to one of the computer's USB sockets.

Split installation

The most common method is to share the incoming telephone line between Internet use and normal telephone use.   The telephone operates over audio frequencies, while the ADSL data uses higher frequencies. This allows the telephone and the modem to be used at the same time.

However, a filter (sometimes called a microfilter) has to be fitted to prevent the telephone's components from downgrading the data signal.

For a simple installation, a splitter is used.   As the illustration shows, the unit connects to the telephone socket and provides two connections – one for the phone and one for the modem.   A filter is built in to the splitter.

The illustration shows a T-bar type of splitter.   Another common type is a small plastic case with a short lead that plugs into the telephone socket.

The diagrams show two possible wiring configurations.

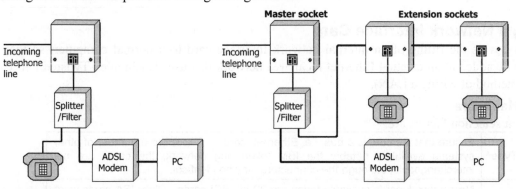

If the house telephone and the computer are in the same room, the configuration on the left can be used. The splitter will either be labelled "*telephone*" and "*ADSL*" or will have icons that indicate the purpose of each socket. The configuration on the right is for a house with multiple phone sockets. This uses only a single splitter/filter but requires that the wiring to the extensions be routed through the filter instead of being directly wired to the master socket.

Note: Although telephone symbols are used in the diagram, the sockets may be equally used for fax machines, answering machines, etc.

Splitterless installation

The diagram on the right above requires skill to rewire the telephone cable. A simpler alternative is to dispense with a splitter and only use filters.

This is a unit with a telephone plug at one end and a telephone socket at the other end. An example is shown in the illustration.

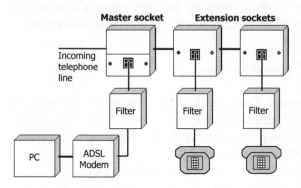

A filter is used for each telephone, fax machine or answering machine in use, as shown in the diagram.

Although a filter/splitter is shown connected to the master socket in the diagram, it can be fitted to any telephone socket in the house.

The modem does not really require a filter, as the modem does not affect normal telephone operation. However, a splitter/filter is often used, so that a telephone can be used from the same wall socket if required.

Setting up the modem

The steps for the installation of the modem are:

- Install the setup software supplied with the modem.
- Connect the modem to one of the computer's USB ports.
- The *'Found New Hardware'* wizard will report detection of the modem.
- If you are still waiting for the ISP to activate the service, the ADSL light on the modem will flash continuously. The modem may remain connected until the service is activated (see next).
- If the service has been activated, the USB and ADSL lights will both flash for some seconds before settling down to being permanently displaying green.

The modem is now ready to connect to the Internet.

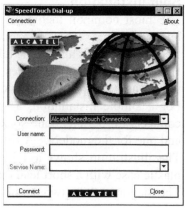

The illustration shows the dialog box used by the very popular Alcatel modem. Entering the user name (supplied by the ISP) and the password (the one that you supplied to the ISP along with the application) and clicking the *'Connect'* button connects the PC to the Internet via the ADSL connection.

All the usual services such as browsing, e-mail, downloading, chat, etc will work as normal, except for an increase in speed. These services are accessed using the software already installed on the computer. There is no need to install any ADSL-specific applications. There is not an ADSL version of Explorer, Outlook, etc.

Installing a Network Interface Card

This section covers the fitting of an internal network interface card to a normal computer, so that the machine can be added to an existing Ethernet local area network that uses Unshielded Twisted Pair cable (a common method of wiring a LAN).

Selecting Hardware

The important selection factors are:

Network Type	Ensure that the card is a bus, i.e. Ethernet, card. There are a number of other systems available, notably the IBM token ring network; the cards are not interchangeable, although the connectors may be identical.
Bus Width	Most network cards available today are 32-bit, PCI cards. Older ISA cards were be 16-bit (such as the NE2000 range) or even 8-bit (NE1000 range) and should be avoided. The larger bus sizes transfer more data at a time, and the cards are not physically interchangeable.
Card type	The cards are available in three types - DMA, shared memory and I/O mapped. A mixture of these cards is allowed on the same network. Card speeds include 10Mbps, 10/100 Mbps (i.e. it supports both 10Mbps and 100Mbps working), and 10/100/1000 Mbps (which also support 1Gbps working).

Fitting
- With older cards, check the card's IRQ and address space allocations to ensure that they do not conflict with the allocations for any existing card.   Alter the network card's jumpers if necessary.   With modern Plug and Play cards, including PC-Cards, the device should be detected by Windows.
- Insert the card into a spare PCI expansion slot and secure with a screw. (In the case of PC-Cards, simply push the card into the slot firmly)
- Refit the computer cover.
- Attach a UTP cable via the RJ-45 connector on the card.
- Attach the other end of the UTP cable either to the network hub, or in the case of a simple two-PC network, to the other PC.   In the latter case a slightly different cable, known as a cross-over cable, will be required,

Note: In a properly networked building, cable trunking will be used to connect various wall sockets to the hub(s). In this case the UTP '*drop*' cable will attach the PC to the wall socket, and the '*patch*' cable in the network room will attach the wall socket to the hub.

Testing Hardware
The Network Interface Card (NIC) will usually come with a floppy disk containing drivers. As well as the protocol and device drivers needed when installing software, there will often be a small diagnostic program, which can interrogate and configure the card, and be used to send simple packets between two machines fitted with the cards. By using this program, the NIC hardware and network media can be checked out before embarking on the installation of the software.

Installing Software
The computer only requires a few small pieces of software in order to function as a network node. These are the driver, protocol and client. See earlier in this chapter for driver installation and see the LANS chapter for a description of the protocol and client software and how to install them.
- Reboot the computer to install the network software.
- Enter the user login name and password when prompted.
  This should let the user into the network with the security provisions already set up on peer computers and/or network servers.

Setting up a small network
Building a peer-to-peer network is fairly simple. A number of manufacturers supply a network starter kit. This is designed for new or inexperienced user and it provides all the components, including the hub, two or more NICs, two or more connecting cables, and the appropriate software drivers. A hub is used as the central connecting point for all the computers and each computer needs its own network card and its own cable running from the card to the hub. The illustration shows a commonly-used 4-outlet hub but 8-and more outlets are also common.

If desired, each of the components can be purchased separately from PC stores or by mail order.

Hardware
The steps for assembling a network are:
- Fit a network card to each computer (see earlier).
- Find a location to place a hub. This should be situated so that all computers can be wired to it with the minimum of cable lengths. For a typical network the cable length should be no more than 100m.
- Plug the hub's mains adaptor into a power socket and connect the adaptor's low voltage lead to the hub.
- Wire each NIC to the central hub. Cat5 cables are available in a

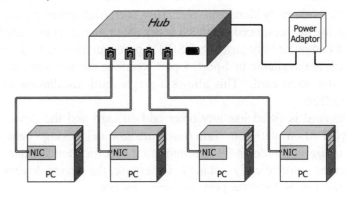

range of lengths. Each cable has a plug at each end, so there is no soldering or wiring required. Avoid running the cables near mains wiring, power wires, or high-voltage equipment such as faxes, to minimise any interference with the data signal.

- If a computer is switched on, then connecting the cable between the network card and the hub should light the LED above that connection socket in the hub. This light indicates that the wiring works and the computer is ready for data transmission and reception.

Software

The driver for each NIC should already have been installed in each computer, as explained earlier.

See the LANs chapter for details of installing and configuring the network client software.

Fitting a serial port

A motherboard provides two serial ports as standard and these are hard-wired on the board.

There are a variety of reasons for fitting an additional serial port card to a computer. These are:

- The on-board circuitry supports a slower speed than a new standard that is introduced. Therefore, fitting a serial card upgrades a slower system with a faster system (see the chapter on Data Communications).
- Overcoming a fault on the on-board serial circuits.
- Adding extra serial ports to the computer. This is useful where a user has three or more serial devices to attach to the computer.

Most I/O cards are provided with two serial outputs and one parallel output.

The card is easily installed by inserting the card into a spare expansion slot and securing it with a screw.

The most likely problems will arise from clashes between devices.

Since this is an additional card, the IRQ and I/O addresses already allocated to the existing serial ports should be checked to avoid conflicts. A computer may wish to work with a number of serial devices (e.g. mouse, modem, scanner, serial printer) and these should not share the same addresses. If the mouse, for example, is to be set to COM1 with IRQ4 then a modem or scanner card would have its jumpers set for other I/O and IRQ addresses from the table shown.

Port	I/O Address	IRQ Address
COM1	03F8	IRQ4
COM2	02F8	IRQ3
COM3	03E8	IRQ4
COM4	02E8	IRQ3
LPT1	0378	IRQ7
LPT2	0278	IRQ5

The problem with a serial card is that of avoiding address clashes with the other components being fitted to the motherboard.   The table above shows that while COM1 and COM3 have different I/O addresses, they have the same IRQ setting.   This may not be a problem where devices are never used simultaneously (i.e. a scanner on COM2 is never used at the same time as a modem on COM4).   Where devices are to be used simultaneously, (e.g. a mouse and a modem) they cannot share the same IRQ, as the computer would not know which device to service.   Since most computers do not require two parallel devices, one of the COM ports could use its IRQ address if it is not already in use.   So, for example, COM2 could be 02F8/IRQ3 while COM4 could be 02E8/IRQ5.

The Windows Device Manager/Properties dialog boxes will list addresses already in use.   If the address needs to be altered for any reason, the card should be set to the desired new addresses (usually by setting jumpers - consult the card's instructions).

Adding a USB 2.0 card

Although new motherboards support USB 2.0, there are many computers that only work to the old USB 1.1 standard.   The USB 1.1 standard is fine for attaching a mouse, a keyboard, a modem or other device with a relatively slow data rate.   However, high-speed devices, such as fast networks and MPEG-2 video capture devices, need the much faster data rate that is provided by a USB 2.0 port.

If a computer only provides USB 1.1 ports, an add-on card can be fitted to provide USB 2.0 ports. These cards are available in 2-port, 4-port, versions etc and some are also sold with FireWire and USB 2.0 ports on the same card. This allows a single card installation to upgrade an older computer to both faster interfaces.

The card is fitted like any other add-on card and the device should be detected when the computer is switched on, with the 'New Hardware Found' message being displayed. Depending upon the version of Windows (Windows 98 is a minimum specification for handling USB), the correct device drivers may then be automatically installed. Otherwise, the device drivers provided with the card have to be installed. When this is done, the ports are ready for use.

Adding a FireWire card

The FireWire interface is a popular high-speed connection for most digital video camcorders, along with some scanners and hard drives. Although USB 2.0 and FireWire are roughly equal in data transfer rates, digital camcorders do not have USB interfaces, so a FireWire card is essential for video capture.

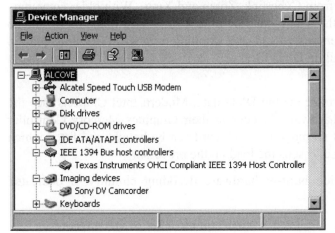

The card is fitted like any other add-on card and the device should be detected when the computer is switched on, with the *'New Hardware Found'* message being displayed. Depending upon the version of Windows, the correct device drivers may then be automatically installed. Otherwise, the device drivers provided with the card have to be installed. When this is done, the ports are ready for use.

The illustration shows Windows Device Manager reporting the installation of a FireWire host controller. In this example, a DV camcorder has been plugged into one of the FireWire ports and has also been detected by Windows.

Fitting a CD-writer

In terms of shape, data connectors, power connectors, and so on a CD-writer is identical to a CD-ROM drive, so fitting a writer is like fitting a CD-ROM (see earlier).

While a CD-ROM drive may only require a driver to be installed (only if Windows cannot automatically find and install that particular model's driver) a writer requires additional writing software. Basic CD writing facilities are built in to Windows XP. However, an additional package, such as *'Nero'* or *'WinOnCD'* is required for older operating systems, or for XP users who require more comprehensive CD writing facilities.

For best results (i.e. no corruption of the writing process and subsequent loss of disks) CD-Rs should be written to at a speed that the computer system can handle. Writing at a fast speed is only possible if the hard disk, the disk interface, and the overall computer system can supply data at a fast and consistent rate to the writer. Fortunately, some writing software packages provide a utility for testing the system for maximum performance (i.e. the fastest safe writing speed). Be aware, therefore, that having a fast speed CD-writer does not guarantee that CD-Rs can be reliably created at the writer's maximum speed.

Fitting A DVD drive

Like the CD-writer, a DVD drive is similar to a CD-ROM drive, so fitting a DVD drive is like fitting a CD-ROM. However there are more stringent hardware requirements that have to be met before a DVD drive can be used to display DVD films etc. As explained in the chapter on disks, the rate that the data is read off a DVD disk is much higher than for a CD running at the same rotational speed. This means that a PC equipped with a DVD needs a reasonable level of specification. Older legacy systems are likely to experience occasional disappointment at the DVD performance, as the data is not read, converted and fed to the monitor quickly enough to keep up a smooth video delivery.

DVD decoding

The data encoded on a DVD is subject to a form of encoding, in order to get large amounts of audio/video information onto the media and recover it intact. This encoding needs to be undone at the player end before the data can be displayed.

There are two ways of doing this:

Software decoding

This involves the use of specialist drivers supplied with the drive, or included with the player software. Modern versions of Microsoft Windows include media players that can cope with DVD decoding. When a movie is supplied on DVD, the DVD disk will often include a bespoke player to allow software decoding. Specialist software is also available from Cyberlink, Zoran and Xing. With older computers the disadvantage of using software to decode the data is that the processor is used much more, and so the overall system is more likely to become overstressed and start skipping frames or degrading quality. Modern PC's are however quite capable of handling DVD files.

Hardware decoding

The alternative is to use specialist hardware to decode the DVD data. Modern Intel Chipsets (see the architecture chapter) include the appropriate hardware decoder in their Graphics Memory Controller Hub or GMCH. For motherboards that are not so modern, a PCI card can be bought and fitted which does the same decoding work in hardware and so lessens the load on the processor.

Although modern graphics cards often provide built-in hardware decoding circuitry, a dedicated decoder card has additional benefits:

- It often provides composite and S-video outputs, for connection to a TV or video recorder.
- It provides a SPDIF (Sony/Philips Digital Interface) output, for connection to a surround sound system. This provides theatre-quality sound and is a major improvement compared to using the output from the normal audio out socket (which is usually still available).

In both cases, the drive is fitted using the same method as that for fitting a CD-ROM drive.

The steps for installing a DVD system are:

- Fit the DVD drive into a spare bay.
- If using a separate MPEG decoder card, fit it into a spare PCI slot.
- Connect the surround sound system to the decoder card's SPDIF socket.
- Replace the computer cover, re-insert the machine's power cable and switch the computer on.
- If the device is not automatically detected by Windows, install the driver supplied with the DVD player.
- If not using a separate decoder card, a third party DVD player should be installed after the system is rebooted (unless the computer already has this facility through Windows).

Fitting A UPS

An uninterruptible power supply (UPS) runs the computer on its own batteries in the event of a power failure. Its operation is described in the chapter on Computer Peripherals. It uses an internal card and an external unit that houses the storage batteries.

The installation steps are:

- Load the UPS software.
- Set the UPS card's I/O port address. With some cards this may happen at a later stage as some setup software auto-detects and informs the user what address to select. With others, the plug and play facility makes configuration automatic.
- Plug the card into a spare expansion socket and screw into place.
- Unplug the power cable coming from the power supply to connect to the motherboard.
- Connect this cable to the UPS card.
- Connect the additional supplied power cable from the UPS card to the motherboard.
- Connect the external UPS supply into the mains supply.
- Amend the machine's configuration files according to the manual, to load the monitoring routine. This program may be automatically carried out on running the setup program.

The battery pack is kept charged by a regulated mains supply. The normal computer power supply is still used but is routed through the UPS card.

Fitting extra external devices

This section covers devices that are added to a computer without having to open the computer case.

Fitting A Scanner

The operation, functions and features of scanner are covered in the chapter on computer peripherals. There are three different ways that your scanner can be connected to your computer:

Parallel

Where a scanner has the old parallel plug connector, the user can unplug the printer from the computer's parallel port and insert the scanner plug, or he/she can fit a parallel *'pass-through'* connector. This connector allows two parallel port devices to be connected at the same time and saves plugging and unplugging each time the scanner is to be used. This parallel interface scanner is easily carried round for use on another computer. The scanner software is installed on the new computer, the scanner is plugged in and the system can be used.

SCSI

This provides faster data transfers than the parallel port system and is useful where lots of photographs need to be scanned. A SCSI interface card is usually supplied with the scanner, although the scanner can also be fitted to a computer that has an existing SCSI card, by attaching a cable between the scanner and the SCSI card's external connection. With the introduction of fast USB scanner interfaces, SCSI scanners have become much less popular.

USB

This is now the most common way to connect a new scanner to a computer. It is easily connected - there is no special adapter card to fit, as with SCSI, or pass-through adapter, as with parallel. The cable from the scanner is simply plugged into the computer's USB socket, the scanner software is installed and the scanner is immediately recognised. The faster USB 2.0 version is now found in most models rather than the older USB 1.1 models.

FireWire

This is starting to appear as a fast transfer interface for scanners. The cable from the scanner is simply plugged into the computer's SCSI socket, the scanner software is installed and the scanner is immediately recognised.

While USB 2.0 and FireWire interfaces remove any data transfer bottlenecks, the final scanning speed is determined by the pace at which the scanner's mechanism operates.

Some scanners provide both SCSI and USB connections while others provide both a parallel and USB connection. However the scanner connects, the scanner's drivers and any software files, such as OCR, need to be installed.

Installing a printer

The installation of a printer can be broken down to the following steps:

1. Placing and physically connecting the printer.
2. Installing any relevant drivers and/or software.
3. Testing the printer.

Connecting the printer

A new printer may be supplied with some packaging attached. It is common for manufacturers to put cardboard or other packing inside hollow areas (such as paper trays) to prevent damage during transport, and some even put sticky tape over moving components so that they are not damaged. All of this should be removed - but consult the printer manual to ensure that you do not accidentally remove vital components!

Physically attaching the printer cable to the printer and the PC is the easy part. Simply plug the Centronics (or whatever other cable is used) cable into the printer, and the parallel (or other port) connector into the PC. Then attach the power cable. However, the manual should always be consulted, in case there are any other considerations. (e.g., the attachment of document trays, feeders, etc.).

Many printers are designed for use on a network and some may not even have a connector to a PC, having a network adapter instead. In this case, consult the network administrator as to how it should be connected, as it may affect the network as a whole.

Finding a place to put the printer sometimes causes more problems than actually connecting it up. Printers should not be too near users, especially if they are noisy dot matrix printers. There should be plenty of room to get into the printer to retrieve printouts, add blank paper or replace ink or toner cartridges. Health and safety considerations should be borne in mind when placing the printer in an office.

Installing printer software

All modern printers are capable of producing graphics, and almost all users wish to take advantage of that capability. In order to use this capability, a printer driver must be installed.

The vast majority of home and office PC's use a version of Microsoft Windows as the operating system, and it is Windows itself that handles printer drivers, not the individual software packages. This allows any software package that runs under Windows to access any printer driver Windows has installed.

When purchasing a new printer, it should be supplied with a floppy disk or CD-ROM containing driver software. There may be several ways to install this software.

The standard Windows method for installing driver software is through the Control Panel. For example in Windows 98, click on the Start bar, go to Settings, and select Control Panel. The Control Panel window will open up, and the option *'Printers'* is available. Double click on this. (Alternatively, in Windows 98, the Printers panel can be reached directly through Start/ Settings / Printers.)

The Printers window will contain all installed printer drivers, as well as an option to add new printer drivers, as shown. The default printer is indicated by a tick next to the icon.

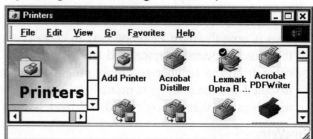

To install a new printer driver, double-click on the *"Add printer"* icon. An on-screen installation wizard will guide you through the process.

Here are the important steps:

The first question the wizard will ask is whether the printer is a network printer or a local printer. Unless you have purchased a network printer and have spoken with the network administrator regarding installation, you should not choose a network installation.

Next, the wizard will ask which type of printer to install a driver for. As shown below, it will offer a range of device drivers built in to the windows CD-ROM. If the printer is an exact match for any one of these printer models, then that printer driver can be used.

However, even if there is an exact match, it is always a good idea to check that there are no drivers available that are more up to date. These drivers may be more efficient, faster, or use more features of the printer, for example.

These printer drivers will likely be found either on the floppy disk or CD-ROM that was supplied with the printer, or on the printer company's Internet site.

In either case, if the up-to-date drivers can be located, then these should be used instead of the built-in Windows driver. In order to do this, the *"Have Disk"* button should be used instead of selecting one of the existing printer drivers.

Clicking on the *"Have Disk"* button will produce another window, allowing the user to locate the actual driver files, which should be found on the floppy disk or CD-ROM, possibly in a sub-folder.

Once the folder is located the user will be presented with a list of printer drivers located in that folder, via a window

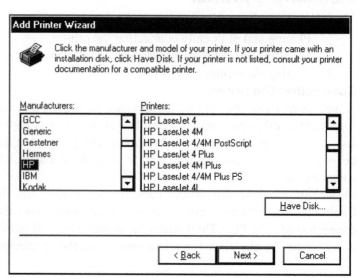

similar to the illustration.

Once a printer model has been selected, the wizard will ask which port the printer is connected to. (Assuming of course that it is not a network printer) In most cases this will be LPT1, although printers can be set up to print through COM (serial) ports, or to print to a file on disk.

A window is displayed on screen to allow the user to select a port.

The *"Configure Port"* button allows some settings to be changed that alter how the selected port operates. In most cases these settings should not be changed unless the printer manual recommends it.

The user is then asked to enter a display name for the printer driver. This is the name that will be displayed in the *"Printers"* window. So, for example, a user could install a printer driver for the HP LaserJet III printer, but give it a name that is more meaningful to the organisation, such as *"Finance Department Laser Printer"*.

The window also allows the user to set this new printer as the default printer. If there is currently no default printer or the new printer is to be used more often than any existing printer, then it should be set as the default printer. Since most non-networked systems only have access to one printer, they generally have just one printer driver and it is made the default printer.

Finally, the wizard will ask if the user wishes to print a test page, to check that the new printer driver is working correctly. If the printer is working correctly, then the test page will print out various details of the system, and a Windows icon.

Testing the printer

Every time a printer is installed, it should be tested. This applies whether it is a new installation or not – if you move a working printer from one PC to another, it should still be tested!

The Windows printer driver installation wizard ends with a test page being printed. If this test page prints out exactly as it should, then the printer can be used normally under Windows. This test page can also be repeated at a later date if problems occur.

Under some circumstances, it may be necessary to test the printer through a plain text application such as notepad or the Command Prompt - or it may even be necessary to test the printer without any PC attached at all. For example, if printing in Word is not working, then the user may wish to test printing through the Command Prompt to ensure that the printer cable and PC printer port are functional. If even Notepad will not print, then it may be necessary to attempt a printer self test to see if the printer is functioning at all.

These three common printer tests are described in more detail next.

Printer self test

The first test that should be carried out once a printer is physically installed, is the printer self test. This does not require that the printer be connected to a PC. Virtually all printers are capable of printing some form of self-test page.

In a laser printer, this is most commonly done through the control panel buttons. For example, the HP LaserJet series has a *'Menu'* button that cycles through various options, one of which enters a sub-menu containing various test and diagnostic printouts.

For a dot matrix or an inkjet printer, the self test is usually accessed by holding down a particular button. Sometimes it is necessary to do this while the printer is being powered up. Other printers, such as some Apple LaserWriters, print a test page automatically every time they are switched on.

The printer's manual should contain instructions on how to obtain a self test page – this should be consulted for every individual printer, to ensure the correct method is followed.

Self tests are also useful once the printer is installed fully. It can help in troubleshooting errors – a successful printer self test proves that there are no problems with the print head, printer carriage, printer power supply, or certain parts of the interface circuitry. In effect it implies that the fault is either with the PC, or with the communications equipment. (i.e. the ports, cables etc)

Command Prompt test print

One basic test for printers is to use some form of Command Prompt command that will result in a printout. For example, a plain text file (such as the WIN.INI that should be located in the Windows folder) can be printed in a typical PC setup by using a command such as the following:

```
TYPE C:\WINDOWS\WIN.INI > LPT1
```

This command will attempt to print the contents of the file 'WIN.INI'. Because this file is a text file, it is in plain ASCII format and will print on any printer, assuming that the printer is physically working and the communications equipment is correct and working.

The Command Prompt test print is usually not necessary at installation time. It is most useful to diagnose faults. Due to the fact that it is a plain ASCII file, it does not require any drivers, or printer languages. Therefore, if such a command fails to produce a printout, then it implies that the fault is either with the printer itself, or with the communications equipment.

On the other hand, if a Command Prompt test print is successful, then any fault that Windows programs experience with printing must lie with the drivers used by Windows, which are not necessary to print from the Command Prompt.

Windows test page

The Windows test page should be generated every time a printer driver is installed, to ensure that the printer is attached and functioning correctly. If problems develop after the installation however, it may be useful to be able to print this test page without having to reinstall the driver.

This can be done through the Printers section of the Control Panel. In the *'Printers'* window, right-click on the desired printer icon, and select the *'Properties'* option. A window appears, with various tabs describing the capabilities and settings of the printer.

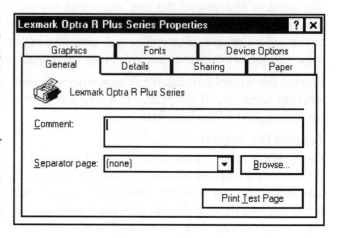

The default tab when the window opens up should be the *'General'* tab. This tab contains a button labelled *'Print Test Page'*. This button will generate the test page and send it to the printer.

The Windows Printer Test Page consists of a Windows logo (which will be printed in colour if it is a colour printer), a title, and some plain text. The text includes information on the printer driver, such as the printer name and model, driver files in use, and so on.

If the Windows Printer Test Page is created successfully, this shows that the driver is capable of printing to that device, but it does not guarantee that the driver is the most up-to-date version, or that every application will print perfectly. However, if the Windows Printer test page comes out properly, then any faults with printing to the device are probably caused by the software itself. For example, Microsoft Word may be unable to print due to insufficient memory, even though the printer and the Windows driver are quite functional.

Upgrading

Upgrading a computer consists of altering or adding to its component parts, so that the overall system is improved. The improvement may be speed or it may be added functionality. In some cases, the upgrade can be achieved by external add-ons, or it may result from additions or alterations inside the computer case itself. An example of an external improvement would be the fitting of an external modem or mouse, while an internal upgrade would be adding extra memory or a video capture card.

Note:

> If a major, or particularly tricky, upgrade is planned, the computer's data should be backed up before continuing.

Fitting a CPU upgrade

The CPU is the *'heart'* of the computer and fitting a faster CPU increases the performance of the computer. Although the process is simple, consideration should be given to the expected extra performance compared to the extra cost.

Consider the following points:

- Adding more RAM often has greater impact on performance than upgrading the CPU.

- Although the raw speed has been increased, many of the benefits of modern systems may still not available (e.g. improved chipsets, improved caching, USB ports, AGP slot, power management).
- Although the CPU is working at a faster pace after the upgrade, the rest of the system has not necessarily speeded up.   For example, the CPU might be clocked at a higher speed, while the main system stills runs at the same speed as prior to the upgrade. The motherboard will still be using slow memory chips.

Upgrading older CPUs

Overdrive chips are designed to fit in a motherboard that was designed for an earlier CPU type. This allows, for example, a 486 motherboard to use a Pentium CPU. However, since these chips are relatively expensive, a replacement CPU/motherboard/memory combination is usually a more cost-effective alternative to CPU upgrading.

Even where the CPU alone is being upgraded, it is not simply a matter of fitting a new CPU in place of the slower model.   The upgrade must be compatible with the existing motherboard and the main factors are:

Voltage

Older chips ran on 5 volts while modern CPUs run on 3.3 volts or less.   Fitting a 3.3 volt chip into a 5 volt socket, or a 2 volt chip into a 3.3 volt socket, would destroy the CPU and therefore some upgrade chips place an extra small board between the CPU and the motherboard.   This contains a voltage regulator, matching the newer chip with older motherboards.   On newer motherboards, the voltage can be established by setting jumpers or even through BIOS settings.

Socket type

The wide variation of CPU pin configurations and voltages prevents older motherboards from being upgraded through the simple replacement of the existing chip.

The upgrade can only be carried out with special *'Overdrive'* upgrades.   The Overdrive unit mounts the replacement CPU on a module that fits an older motherboard socket, thus allowing the connection of faster CPUs. The most well known supplier of Overdrive modules is Evergreen Technologies (www.evertech.com)

Typical overdrive upgrades		
From	To	Socket
Pentium 75MHz/100MHz	Pentium 400MHz	5 or 7
Pentium Pro 150MHz	Celeron 766MHz	8
Pentium III 350MHz	Celeron 1.2GHz	Slot 1
Pentium III	Celeron 1GHz	370
Pentium 4 1.3GHz	Pentium 4 2.4GHz	423
Pentium 4 1.4GHz	Pentium 4 2.4GHz	478

Overdrive upgrades for 486 motherboards are no longer produced but the table shows typical overdrive upgrades that are currently available.

Another approach, for motherboards with PCI slots, was the insertion of an Accelera PCI card.   This fitted any motherboard that had a PCI slot, and upgraded the system to a 1GHz Celeron CPU. However this concept never became as popular as the manufacturers had hoped.

Of course, if the existing motherboard already has a modern CPU ZIF socket, there is the likelihood that the CPU can be directly replaced with one that operates at a faster speed. So, for example, a 500MHz Pentium III module can be replaced by a 1GHz module or a Pentium 4 1.5GHz CPU can be replaced with a 2GHz version.   In some cases this might involve setting jumpers on the motherboard.

Overclocking

Most CPUs can run faster than the manufacturer's quoted speed. This has led to the practice of *'overclocking'* - adjusting the CPU clock speed by means of motherboard jumpers or BIOS configuration. This is implemented as a free alternative to buying a CPU upgrade. The principle is simple, as many systems contain user-accessible settings for adjusting the bus speed and the multiplier (see the chapter on *'Computer Architecture'*).

They set the CPU speed according to the formula
CPU speed = bus speed x CPU multiplier

For example, a bus speed of 100MHz and a 20x multiplier produces a CPU speed of approx. 2000MHz. Most motherboards can run at a variety of bus speeds and offer a selection of multiplier values. Therefore, if the multiplier were set to 22x, the CPU would be driven at 2200MHz. Alternatively, setting the bus speed to 110MHz and leaving a 20x multiplier also results in a 2200MHz speed.

The limitations on overclocking are:

- The CPU may not be able to run at the higher rate (this would be noticed at bootup).
- The CPU might run but crash more frequently.   Some enthusiasts increase the chip's supply voltage to overcome any instability but this greatly increases the risk of chip failure. Some motherboards allow the BIOS to adjust the CPU voltage in small increments. Experienced users may use this to tweak the CPU for optimum performance – but setting too high a voltage will lead to crashes, or the CPU being burnt out.
- The P4 CPU uses *'CPU throttling'*. The P4 has an internal diode that checks the CPU temperature and cuts off the chip's supply if it is running too hot.   This was intended to guard against cooling fan failure but also prevents some overclocking. This system is not present in AMD CPUs.
- The other parts of the system (e.g. memory) might not be able to cope with an increased bus speed. Rambus memory, in particular, does not perform well when clocked faster than its official speed rating.
- Faster CPU rates generate more heat from the CPU and the existing heat dissipation might not be sufficient. Some improvement in heat dissipation is possible with larger heat sinks and more powerful cooling fans.
- Slot 1 type processors, Pentium II, Pentium III, Xeons and some AMD Athlons, have speed and multipliers set by the positioning of a series of SMD resistors on the Printed Circuit Board that carries the processor and fits in the slot. Overclocking these is possible by moving these tiny components, but it is a very tricky operation and only for those with lots of experience of surface mount electronics.
- Many CPUs are now *'Clock-locked'* or *'Overclock Protected'*.   The chip is manufactured to run at a fixed multiplier rating and increasing the multiplier has no effect, or even decreases the CPU clock rate. In these cases, the bus speed may still be increased to a higher rate (e.g. a 100MHz motherboard may allow the setting of a non-standard rate of 110MHz or 120MHz). P4 CPUs with the Northwood core (chips with the suffix 'A' in their name) are more tolerant of changes in the bus speed than the older P4s with the older Williamette core.

Since overclocking pushes a CPU and associated components to their limits, the method should not be employed where the computer is used for vital operations.   Due to the risks involved with overclocking, the process is not always simple. Although the clock multiplier is sometimes set in the BIOS, it is often set physically using jumpers on the motherboard. The Front Side Bus speed can also be set in hardware or through the BIOS, depending on the motherboard.

The BIOS may also provide a reading of the CPU temperature and the effects of any alterations can be checked this way (the CPU temperature should not exceed 40°C)

Motherboard upgrade

The most dramatic upgrade performance comes from replacing the motherboard /CPU combination. This need not be over expensive, as all or most of the original components (case, disks, video card, etc) may be re-used on the new board.   Unfortunately, the memory modules of older boards (e.g. SIMMs) will not fit on modern boards, requiring a memory upgrade at the same time. Generally, an upgrade to last year's performance will cost far less than upgrading to the current top technology, while providing significant performance improvements.

Fitting the existing board

The steps for removing the old motherboard are:

- Carry out a backup of the disk's contents as a precaution.
- Dismantle the system as explained earlier.
- Note the way that the motherboard is mounted; where are the mounting holes?; are plastic stand-offs or mounting posts being used?
- Remove the add-on cards from the motherboard's expansion slots (e.g. video card and sound card).
- Unplug the cables from the motherboard, noting their function (e.g. cables to floppy drives, CD-ROMs, power supply, internal speaker, reset button, disk lights, keyboard lock).   Note

the orientation of cables that are temporarily removed from add-on cards (most cables have a red stripe on one side).

- Unscrew the motherboard and remove it.

The steps for fitting the replacement board and reconnecting the components are identical to those outlined earlier. If the board layout is different from the old board, the cards may not fit in their original order. If a cable is now found to be too short, the cards will need to be fitted on the board in the best order for all the connecting cables to reach.

Upgrading Memory

There are a number of very good reasons why a machine should have its memory size increased.

To handle modern applications

Early PCs were supplied with the basic 640k of RAM and most applications did not even use the full memory. With the development of ever-larger operating systems and user applications, 64MB has emerged as a realistic minimum requirement for modern software. If large files, multimedia, real time video capture and editing and so on are to be accommodated, main memory should be much greater as shown in the guide below (remember that these are minimum figures).

Category	Examples of Use	Min Recommended RAM
Light User	Word-processing, e-mail	256MB
Medium User	Database applications	512MB
Heavy User	Large databases, multi-tasking	1GB
Power User	Multimedia authoring, DTP, photo-editing, CAD	1GB
Design User	3D-CAD, CAM solid modelling, video editing	2GB

To achieve greater speed

Extra memory speeds up Windows applications. Windows uses a scheme called 'virtual memory' that utilises the hard disk's unused contiguous space as if it were an area of memory. Since the access time of a disk may be 10ms compared to memory speeds of 10ns (for some DIMMs) and as low as 1.2ns (for RIMMs), Windows will run much faster if it can directly use memory to store applications and parts of the operating system.

To handle more data

Most applications can use the extra memory to store and work with their documents. Databases, for example, may sort their records in memory rather than use slow disk operations.

To allow multi-tasking

Extended memory can be used to run several programs simultaneously.

To provide a disk cache

Smartdrv and VCACHE use a section of memory as a disk cache to speed up disk access times.

How to upgrade

The first step is to determine the kind of memory to be fitted. The most common formats are explained in the chapter on memory and the most likely types to be used in an upgrade are SIMMs, DIMMs or RIMMs as it is uneconomic to upgrade a computer that requires any older memory type.

The different sizes and possible combinations available should be carefully examined before the chips are purchased. For example, a Pentium using SIMM memory must upgrade SIMM memory boards at least two at a time, since chips are 32-bit and the Pentium has a 64-bit bus.

Older DIMM-based motherboards used PC-66 memory modules, which contain 66MHz SDRAM. Modern motherboards use PC-100, PC-133 or DDR modules. Fitting a faster memory module will not improve the computer's performance, as the module will only operate at the switching speed of the system (e.g. a PC-133 module will only switch at 66MHz on a 66MHz motherboard). On the other hand, fitting a slower module in a faster system will reduce the performance of the computer.

If you have an older 5v DIMM socket, ensure that only a 5v module is purchased, as newer 3.3v modules are incompatible. See the chapter on memory for more details.

Upgrading an IDE hard disk

There are many reasons why a new disk drive is fitted to a computer. It may be because the existing hard drive has failed. It may be because the existing disk is far too small to store all the user's applications and data. It may even be fitted as an extra disk to work along with the existing disk drive.

There are four main steps involved in replacing a disk drive:

- Removing the old drive.
- Setting any jumpers (on the drive or drive controller).
- Installing the drive into the computer case and connecting it to the rest of the system.
- Ensuring that the system's software settings allow the PC to recognize the new drive.

The detailed steps for replacing an old hard disk are:

- Ensure that the new disk's parameters are known; this is likely to be printed on a label on the disk. If this is not provided, contact the supplier (by telephone or website) for the information on number of tracks, number of sectors per track, etc. Do not proceed with the remaining steps until these facts are known, as the BIOS will have to be set up to these parameters. This is not required with a modern BIOS, which has an *'IDE HDD Auto Detection'* facility that automatically detects and stores the parameters of each disk detected.
- Ensure that the new disk is configured as a *'master'* disk (see the earlier notes).
- Make a complete backup of all the existing files on the old hard disk.
- Switch off the computer and remove the power cable and ribbon cable from the old drive.
- Unscrew and remove the old hard disk from its drive bay. Place the old drive to one side and retain the screws.
- Carefully remove the new disk drive from its anti-static bag. Avoid touching any exposed electronic components and handle the drive by its casing.
- Fit the new drive into the unused bay and secure with the same screws.
- Fit the power cable and ribbon cable to the new disk drive. Remember, the red end of the ribbon cable aligns to pin 1 - this is true for both ends.
- Refit the computer case and mains cable.
- Reboot the machine and run the BIOS setup program for that machine (see computer's manual).
- Alter the BIOS settings, so that the size and parameters of the new hard drive are saved to the machine's CMOS. This is through the *'IDE HDD Auto Detection'* facility in a modern BIOS. In an older system, the user will enter the settings from the keyboard.
- Partition and high-level format the disk, using FDISK and FORMAT utilities from a floppy boot disk (see chapter on hard drives). Format the active partition as a system disk (i.e. use FORMAT C:/S).
- Install the operating system and applications.
- Restore the data files from the backup files.

Upgrading to a UDMA hard disk

A general description of UDMA drives is given in the chapter on Disks and Drives. The instructions for handling and fitting IDE disks also apply to UDMA drives but there are some important differences.

Ultra-DMA disk drives will connect to existing IDE motherboards but will not provide the higher transfer rates unless the motherboard's chipsets directly support Ultra-DMA drives. For older motherboards, there is the option to replace the existing IDE controller card with an interface card. These cards have their own BIOS chips built in and these supplement the existing computer's BIOS. DMA/66 drives only provide top performance if connected to a DMA/66-compatible motherboard/BIOS with a special UDMA66 cable. The UDMA 66 drive may also need specialist BIOS support, possibly involving a flash upgrade. The same conditions apply to UDMA/100/133 drives.

If the UDMA drive is simply replacing an existing IDE drive, it is a straightforward one-for-one physical replacement, perhaps followed by the installation of the additional driver software. The power and data cables should be disconnected and the drive unscrewed and removed. The new drive should be screwed in place and all the cables connected to it.

The **blue** end of the connecting plugs into the controller card or motherboard. The **black** end connects to your master, or single, drive. The **grey** plug connects to a second slave drive.

The BIOS configuration, partitioning and high-level formatting are as before.

Using a new drive as the boot disk

Users may wish to use their new drive as the boot drive for two reasons:

- It is a faster drive than the original.
- They intend to remove the old drive.

The earlier section on replacing a drive involved the re-installation of Windows, all the applications and all the data. This could be avoided if the following steps were taken:

- Backup everything on the original drive.

- Ensure that a Windows emergency startup disk is to hand.   If not, create one.
- Fit the new drive as second drive.
- Format the new drive's active partition as a system disk (i.e. use FORMAT D:/S).
- Boot the machine back into Windows.
- Enter the Command Prompt from the Start Menu.
- Enter the command

c:\windows\command\xcopy c: d: /s/e/c/r/h/k

and press the *'Enter'* key.
This copies all the files from the old disk to the new disk, including hidden files, system files and the Windows registry.
Windows, all applications and data are now copied to the new drive.   Only the Windows temporary swap file is not copied.
- Close down Windows and switch off.
- Remove the old drive.
- Remove the new drive's *'Slave'* jumper.
- Insert the Windows emergency startup disk into the floppy drive and switch on.
- Use FDISK to make the new drive's partition active.
- Reboot the machine.   This will enter Windows and automatically create a new swap file.

Upgrading to a SCSI hard disk

The IDE interface only allows four devices to be attached.   If a computer has a ZIP drive, a DVD player and a CD-writer fitted, there is only support for a single hard disk drive.   Where more than four devices are required, a SCSI controller can be fitted.   A SCSI drive also has a better sustained data transfer rate than an IDE drive and is commonly used for video editing and other heavy-duty activities.

The basic SCSI system allows 7 devices to be added to the computer, while the higher-performance system allows 15 devices to be added.   One end of the cable connects to the controller card and the cable contains multiple plugs along its length to connect to the SCSI devices.

A general description of SCSI drives is given in the chapter on Disks and Drives. SCSI works well alongside existing hard disk systems inside the computer, as it does not use the computer's BIOS chip, relying instead upon additional software that talks to the additional SCSI controller card being fitted. The additional driver software comes with the new drive.   If, however, the drive is being used to replace an IDE system, then a SCSI interface card that has a BIOS ROM has to be fitted so that the disk will act as a bootup drive.

Fitting the SCSI system involves the following steps:

- Switch off the power to the computer.   Ensure that the mains plug is removed from the computers power socket.
- Fit an earthing strap to your wrist and connect it to the computer casing.
- Carefully remove the disk drive from its anti-static bag.   Avoid touching any exposed electronic components and handle the drive by its casing.
- Set the ID value of the SCSI drive.   Each SCSI device is given a unique device number (or ID).   With most SCSI controllers, the range of ID values is 0-7, with 7 being used by the controller itself.   Higher ID numbers are given greater priority when multiple SCSI devices are being accessed.   The ID is usually set using miniature rotary switches or jumpers on the drive case.
- If necessary, fit a terminator to the drive.   A terminating resistor is fitted to the last device on the cable in a SCSI system.   It is not required for IDE drives.   A terminator is a bank of resistors placed at the end of the SCSI chain.   Their job is to prevent signals that were sent up the cable from reflecting back down the cable, causing interference and losses.   A terminator may look like a plug or a solid resistor pack that is inserted into sockets on the drive's circuit board.   In some cases the termination is carried out by setting DIP switches and some modern SCSI devices *"auto-terminate"* which means that they work out the termination arrangements by themselves, without any human involvement.
- Fit the controller card in a spare expansion slot. In most cases, the SCSI controller is a card that plugs into a spare expansion slot, although some motherboards are now available with the controller circuitry already built into the motherboard.
- Fit the new drive into an unused bay and secure with the supplied screws.
- Connect the controller cable to the drive.
- Connect a power cable to the drive.
- Refit the computer case and mains cable.

- Install the software driver.
- Configure the SCSI software or the SCSI BIOS.
- Partition and high level format the disk.

Upgrading to a SATA disk

Although SATA supports '*hot swapping*' (adding, removing or replacing drives while the system is still running), this only works on systems which run a hot-swap capable operating system. This typically means server editions and is not usually done to Personal Computers.

The process for replacing an existing SATA disk is generally similar to replacing an IDE disk:

- Remove the old drive.
- Install the drive into the computer case and connect it to the rest of the system.
- Ensuring that the system's software settings allow the PC to recognize the new drive.

Since SATA is limited to one device per cable (unless '*port multipliers*' are installed) there are generally no jumpers or switches to set. However, it may still be necessary to enter the BIOS and run the hard disk auto-detect utility in order for the system to be properly configured to access the drive.

Upgrading a laptop system

With the limited space available in a laptop system, almost every piece of hardware is different in its installation. For example, PC Cards replace expansion cards. Other differences include:

Hard Disks

Although disks may technically use the IDE standard, they have a different style of connector, and are often 'clicked' into place rather than screwed in, as well as being considerably smaller than desktop hard disks. The manual will usually advise on how to remove the hard disk and replace it. Note however that some hard disks are available in Type III PC Card form, for those laptops that have the capability to use them.

Battery

It is unusual for batteries to be upgraded as such. However, it is a common practice to have a spare battery for a laptop. When battery power is low, the machine can be powered off and the battery replaced. If this is not a viable option, the machine can be attached to a wall socket via the AC adaptor while the battery is changed over. Changing the battery is in most cases as simple as changing the battery in a personal stereo – open the battery cover and slide the battery out.

Memory

Again, laptop memory modules are not the same as desktop modules. Ensure that you order the correct component; laptop memory normally has to be purchased from the same manufacturer that makes the laptop system, which can make them costly. The method of removing a chip and installing it is similar to that of a desktop system, but gaining access to the memory chips in the first place is usually very different. The process varies from machine to machine, so the manual should be consulted, but it often consists of unscrewing a plate at the bottom of the machine. In some older systems you may have to move important parts of the internals of a portable to gain proper access. Such installations should only be done by experienced technicians, and with great care, as it is all too easy to pull a connector out without realising, or even break a component.

Configuring Windows

What happens on switch-on

When a PC is powered up, a procedure known as *'bootstrapping'* occurs. This loads the operating system into the computer memory and sets up the system configuration. Programs cannot be run, or housekeeping tasks performed, until the operating system has been loaded. The normal usage of a PC consists of communication from interface to kernel to BIOS and finally to the machine hardware. The user will use the interface to choose which operation to perform. The interface passes this information to the kernel, which acts upon it. During those operations that require input or output to or from a hardware device, the kernel will communicate with the hardware, either via the BIOS or a device driver. The boot procedure follows the reverse order.

The main steps are:

1. The computer initiates a POST (Power On Self Test) procedure that is stored in the system ROM (i.e. the BIOS). The POST conducts a self-test of the main board, disks, printer, keyboard, memory, etc. If it finds any fault, it will display an error message and stop. Error messages can range from *"Hard disk failure"* to *"Time of day clock stopped"*. All checks are carried out with a *'hard reboot'* - i.e. switching the power on. A *'warm reboot'* results from pressing the computer's reset button. A warm reboot ignores some checks such as memory tests.

2. The presence of any *'ROM extensions'* is detected. Apart from the BIOS ROM that is present in all computers, some will have other ROM chips installed for extra control purposes. These are fitted on add-on cards such as video cards and disk controller cards. These extra ROMs contain code to control their own card's activities. If the BIOS finds an adapter card, it runs the code in the extra ROM so that the card's control code can be loaded into memory.

3. If the POST is successful, then control is passed to the bootstrap code resident in the BIOS ROM. This small piece of code sets up Plug and Play devices and then triggers the loading process. Although the code written into the BIOS of various manufacturers differ, all modern systems allow the user to configure which drives to attempt to boot from. For example, the BIOS may be configured to attempt to boot from the DVD drive before checking for hard disks. The BIOS therefore checks the MBR (*'Master Boot Record'*) of each drive that it may boot from, in order of the stored priority, until it finds a drive that contains boot information.

4. After finding an MBR that contains boot information, the BIOS will attempt to read that drive's boot sector, which is typically sector 1, track 0. If no boot sector is found on the disks, an error message is given and the system halts. Assuming however that the boot sector is found, the BIOS loads the code found there into memory, and hands the processing over to it. The boot sector code is used to load the kernel and remaining BIOS components. The kernel that is loaded by the bootstrap depends on the operating system installed on the hard disk, and therefore the remainder of the boot process is dependent on the OS that is installed.

Configuring a computer system

Configuring a computer system consists of:

- Setting the computer's BIOS as covered below. There are extensive options that set or optimise the computer's hardware. It is not recommended that inexperienced users make changes to the BIOS settings, as most settings affect fundamental hardware operation.
- In a Windows machine, the operating system must be configured. This entails setting options in the Control Panel, installing drivers as appropriate, and possibly setting INI files contents in some cases.

Setting a typical BIOS

The illustration shows a typical BIOS Main Menu screen, as displayed when the user hits a specific key (most commonly DEL or F2) during startup.   Exact BIOS contents vary widely between manufacturers and even between models and revisions of individual types of BIOS.

For specific details the manual should be consulted.

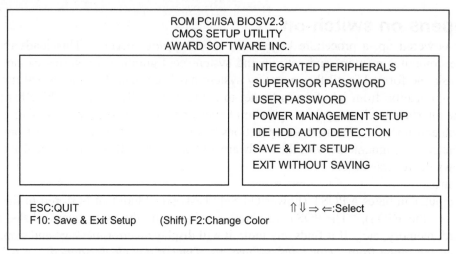

The top panel gives information about the BIOS publisher and the BIOS version.   The two panels in the centre of the screen contain options, where changes can be made. The lower panel contains summary instructions on how to use the system.

The options presented on the centre panels are:

Standard CMOS setup	This leads to another screen (see later), where the basic operating parameters of the BIOS, and so the PC is set.
BIOS features setup	This option leads to another screen (see later), where the less fundamental areas of BIOS operation can be modified or examined.
Chipset features setup	Under this option the user can alter aspects of the operation of the machine that are chipset specific. Typical items in this area include memory wait state and caching settings, temperature settings if they are available, etc. Modifications here are not advised, and are machine specific, so this area is not covered in any more depth.
Power Management setup	Modern ATX based PCs will typically have a series of sleep and wakeup modes. The machine is capable of going into low power modes if unattended or unused for periods of time, and of waking up from this sleep based on any of a number of stimuli. For example, LAN activity, Serial Modem activity, USB activity as well as mouse and keyboard activity can all cause the machine to burst into life. The exact detail of which modes it uses, and what delays are set, resides in the Power Management Setup page. Because this information is machine specific, no detail can be entered into beyond this basic outline.
PNP /PCI Configuration	Under this option the user can set whether or not the machine is Plug'N'Play or manually controlled. If the machine is set up not to be Plug'N'Play compatible, then the allocation of IRQs to expansion slots is carried out here.
Load BIOS defaults	This option does not take the user to a separate screen. Instead it loads all the BIOS settings with basic values, i.e. values that are guaranteed to get the machine running. That way, a scrambled CMOS can be quickly and conveniently recovered
Load Performance Defaults	This option is very similar to its immediate predecessor, but where the BIOS defaults turns off the processor's L2 cache and disables any ROM shadowing, this option tries to configure the machine to optimum performance levels.

Integrated Peripherals
Many motherboards have floppy and hard drives controllers, serial, parallel, USB, PS2 mouse and other peripherals integrated on the mainboard. The user might want to configure these, for example to decide which serial port is Com1, Com2, and so on. An Integrated Peripherals BIOS screen allows such adjustments to be made.

Supervisor Password
Selecting this option allows a supervisor password to be set. Such a password will be subsequently needed to access the BIOS. This is designed to stop casual 'passer by' abuse of the CMOS settings. It is not strong security, as most CMOSes can be readily reset.

User Password
This setting is used to add a password for the user. This appears at boot time and a password has to be entered before the machine will start. Like the supervisor password it is not a strong defence mechanism, but can discourage casual abuse of the system.

IDE HDD Auto detection
This option causes the BIOS to interrogate the hard disks in turn for their settings. Since most hard drives can operate in various modes (for example in LBA modes and cylinder translation modes), the auto detect will often return a number of options and ask the user to select which he/she wishes to set in the CMOS. A great many modern motherboards use an automatic option in the standard CMOS setup panel (see below) and so force the BIOS to detect the hard disk settings every time the machine is started.

Save & Exit setup
The current values are saved from RAM storage to CMOS, and the computer is rebooted, in order to force the CMOS to be re-read.

Exit Without Saving
The computer is rebooted, but the changes are not saved. This is useful if it is thought that a setting value might have been lost. By abandoning the session, the machine is in the same state as it was at the last boot.

```
                        ROM PCI/ISA BIOSV2.3
                        CMOS SETUP UTILITY
                        AWARD SOFTWARE INC.

  Date(mm:dd:yy) :Sat, Jun10 2000-03-29
  Time(hh:mm:ss)      : 14:05:58

  HARD DISKS        TYPE    SIZE   CYLS   HEAD  PRECOMP  LANDZ   SECTOR MODE
  Primary Master    :AUTO     0      0      0      0       0        0   AUTO
  Primary Slave     :AUTO     0      0      0      0       0        0   AUTO
  Secondary Master  :AUTO     0      0      0      0       0        0   AUTO
  Secondary Slave   :AUTO     0      0      0      0       0        0   AUTO

  Drive A: 1.44Mb 3.5 in.
  Drive B:  None                       ┌──────────────────────────────────┐
  Floppy Mode 3 Support :Disabled      │ Base Memory              640k     │
                                       │ Extended Base Memory   15360k     │
                                       │ Other Memory             384k     │
  Video ; EGA/VGA                      │ Total Memory           16384k     │
  HALT ON: No Errors                   └──────────────────────────────────┘

  ESC:QUIT                    ⇑ ⇓ ⇒ ⇐:Select            PU/PD/+/- :Modify
  F10: Save & Exit Setup      (Shift) F2:Change Color
```

Standard CMOS Settings

The standard CMOS settings are essentially the same on every machine. This is because in order to be fully IBM compatible the basic CMOS values must be compliant. Most machines have considerably more CMOS memory than the IBM standard minimum 42 bytes, and this is used to store the information that appears on other pages of the BIOS setup system.

The contents of the standard CMOS settings page are:
- Amounts of memory detected at POST.
- Date and Time stored in CMOS by Real Time Clock.
- Hard Disk type or parameters for type 47 drives or AUTO if the HDD is to be auto detected by the booting BIOS.
- Floppy Disk type. Mode 3 diskette support is sometimes offered.

- Primary Display Adapter type. This is usually simply EGA/VGA. It does not relate to the actual video adapter installed, but to a notional type stored in the CMOS's equipment byte, largely a legacy setting.

```
                            ROM PCI/ISA BIOSV2.3
                             CMOS SETUP UTILITY
                            AWARD SOFTWARE INC.

 Virus Warning              : Disabled    HDD S.M.A.R.T capability      : Disabled
 CPU Internal Cache         : Enabled     Report No FDD for Win95       : No
 External Cache             : Enabled     Video BIOS Shadow             : Enabled
 CPU L2 Cache ECC Checking  : Disabled
 Processor Number Feature   : Enabled
 Quick Power On Self Test   : Enabled
 CPU Update Data            : Enabled
 Boot from LAN First        : Enabled
 Boot Sequence              : A,C,SCSI
 Swap Floppy Drive          : Disabled
 VGA Boot from              : AGP
 Boot up Floppy Seek        : Enabled
 Boot up Numlock Status     : On
 Typematic Rate Setting     : Disabled    ┌──────────────────────────────────────────
 Typematic Rate(Chars /sec) : 6           │ ESC :  QUIT             ⇑ ⇓ ⇒ ⇐:Select
 Typematic Delay(mSec)      : 250         │ F1  :  Help             PU/PD  :Modify
 Security Option            : Setup       │ F5  :  Old Values       ShiftF2 :COLOR
 PCI/VGA Pallette Snoop     : Disabled    │ F6  :  Load BIOS Defaults
 Assign IRQ for VGA         : Enabled     │ F7  :  Load Performance Defaults
 OS Select for DRAM > 64MB  : Non OS2     │
```

Advanced BIOS Settings

The BIOS Features Setup page, or sometimes the Advanced BIOS options page, contains options that are not standard and differ from machine to machine.

A typical set is shown in the illustration and is detailed below:

Virus Warning	Enabling this makes the BIOS stop the machine and display an error message if any program tries to write to the first sector of the disk, where the Master Boot Record is stored. This can be useful, but is no substitute for a properly configured and updated virus checking program. It can on occasion interfere with operating system upgrades.
CPU Internal Cache	Disabling this option will cause the onboard cache memory on Pentium or better processors to be disabled. This will drastically slow the performance of the chip but can help to diagnose processor / memory speed problems. If enabling and disabling the onboard cache has no effect on performance then the chip's internal cache is suspect.
External Cache	This is very similar to the previous options, but it disables the L2 cache. Again this option can be used to diagnose processor /memory speed matching or to confirm the operation of the L2 cache circuits.
CPU L2 Cache ECC Checking	Enabling this option will force Cyclic Redundancy Checking to be carried out on the contents of the external cache memory. This will very slightly slow the machine, but can be used in mission critical situations to increase process integrity.
Processor Number Feature	This option enables a specific feature of Pentium III chips. It should be enabled for Intel PIII chips where desired, and disabled for anything else.
Quick Power On Self Test	Setting this to enabled will make the machine carry out only the most basic memory tests. This will cut the startup time to about 20% of the time taken with Full POST. The difference can be significant, especially on machines with lots of memory.
CPU Update Data	This option should be used once when a new CPU has been fitted to tell the bios to interrogate the mask type and stepping number so that the BIOS is always optimally matched to the processor.
Boot from LAN First	If enabled the machine will try to download a boot program from its network card. This is necessary when setting up diskless workstations such as terminal server /winframe machines.

Boot Sequence	This option decides where the machine looks for its system files on startup.
Swap Floppy Drive	On systems with two floppy disks the disk drive at the end of the cable (beyond the twist) is the A: drive. If it is necessary to use the other drive as A: then this option should be enabled.
VGA Boot from	Many modern machines have AGP slots for high speed graphics cards. The same machine will usually also have PCI slots, which can also hold a video card. The setting of this option decides which of the cards is the one that displays the information during bootup.
Boot up Floppy Seek	Used to decide whether the machine waits for its floppy drive to try and locate a system at boot time. If the machine usually boots from hard disk then this should be disabled to increase boot up speed.
Boot up Numlock Status	This option decides whether the keypad keys on the right of the keyboard start as number keys or cursor control keys. Most modern machines have dedicated cursor keys and so this option should be enabled.
Typematic Rate Setting // Typematic Rate // Typematic Delay	These options refer to the system built into the keyboard that makes it wait for a short time if a key is held down and then make the key repeat its signal. This typematic behaviour is controlled by these settings.
Security Option	A setting such as this allows the setup of security based options controlled by the BIOS. For instance, whether or not the Passwords setup elsewhere are asked for.
PCI/VGA Palette Snoop	It is possible to have Video Cards on both PCI and ISA busses at the same time. If this is the case then there is likely to be a conflict with regard to palette memory. By enabling this setting such conflicts can be eliminated.
Assign IRQ for VGA	This option will decide whether or not the VGA system uses one of the processors IRQ resources.
OS Select for DRAM > 64MB	IBM's OS2 operating system expects to find a *'hole'* in memory, that is to say an area of memory that cannot be addressed /read from /written to normally. This memory hole is located in a series of consecutive locations above 64MB. If the OS is IBM OS2 then the addressing hole should be installed, otherwise no memory hole setting should be selected.
HDD S.M.A.R.T capability	This option is set if the machine is fitted with Self Monitoring Analysis and Recording Technology. If the hard disk is suitably equipped then it can interrupt the processor to have the BIOS announce that it may need repaired or replaced.
Video BIOS Shadow	DRAM is considerably faster than PROM and so by copying the video BIOS program from its native ROM.

Multiple Booting

Multiple booting is different from multiple configurations, which is where the machine starts up the same Operating system with different configuration settings. With multiple booting, the machine can start up entirely different operating systems each time it is booted.

As explained elsewhere, any hard disk drive's partition table will allow a maximum of four partitions. Each partition can be any one of a variety of partition types, as noted in the table. Only one partition may be *active* at any time, and only the active partition is bootable.

In some cases, in order to use a partition of one type, another partition must also be used. For example, any creation of a Linux native partition will require the use of a Linux swap partition. This swap partition is one that Linux uses to swap out memory pages for faster access. Thus, a hard disk with a Linux native and a Linux swap partition could also support two further partitions before the four partition limit is reached.

It is also worth bearing in mind that a single partition, when allocated as an extended DOS partition (this nomenclature remains, even though DOS as an operating system is obsolete), can hold more than one logical drive. If all of the partitions are to be used with the same operating system then there is no issue, and partitioning can be used simply to keep the individual partitions below the 2GB maximum imposed by some file systems. On the other hand it is perfectly feasible to run different operating systems in different partitions on the same hard drive. Some operating systems can also access data from a partition used by another operating system. Linux, for example, can access a Windows FAT or FAT32 partition and read or write to files therein. In order to Boot with different operating systems, each time the machine is switched on a mechanism must be used for deciding which partition is active. This will in turn decide which OS boots up.

There are various ways of doing this as outlined below:

Boot Manager Partition

A popular and quite easy solution is to dedicate a small partition to a boot loader program. This technique came from other areas of computing and was adopted by DEC for its Alpha Processor systems and IBM for its OS2 operating system. Programs such as Partition Magic and System Commander use the OS2 loader intact, without modification. XOSL is a popular third-party boot manager. How such software works is by occupying a tiny active partition. The partition contains a small program, which on boot-up prompts for the user to choose an OS to load. It usually offers a time-out default choice as well. When an OS is chosen or the time runs out, the boot manager program passes control to the bootstrap loader on the partition selected, which then boots its operating system normally.

      Advantages: Simple, reliable.

      Disadvantages: Requires software to be purchased. Uses up one of the four partitions allowed.

Boot Loader

Some operating systems supply a boot loader program. For example Linux's boot loader is called LILO, and it does all of the same work as the boot manager outlined above, without needing a separate partition. In this way any partition can be loaded, as with a boot manager partition, but without the disadvantage of taking up one partition.

Windows XP has the capability of recognising previously installed Windows 2000 or Windows ME, and can be set up to multi-boot with a minimum of fuss so long as just these two operating systems are installed, and in that order.

      Advantages: Easy installation (usually installed automatically).

      Disadvantages: Not always available.

Program loader

This method of multi-booting uses a program inside one operating system to start another. Again, Linux is an example. A machine with both Windows and Linux installed can have a directory in the Windows partition, which contains an executable called **loadlin**, and a one-line batch file called linux.bat. The executable is a copy of the Linux kernel, which is the operating system's command line interpretation program. By running the batch file, the user can invoke Loadlin to load linux into memory and use the linux partition table entry for all further work. Thus, Linux is started up from within Windows.

Alternatively, there are numerous third-party applications available, such as VMWare or Connectix Virtual PC, which will create one or more 'virtual machines' out of a single physical system, enabling it to run one or more operating systems from within the main operating system.

      Advantages: Quick and simple to use.

      Disadvantages: Appropriate software and training in its use is required.

In addition there are other ways of running multiple Operating Systems that do not involve modifying Partition Tables. Among these are:

CD-ROM boot

Another option is to run the OS directly from a CD-ROM. For example BEOS, a recent OS, uses a tiny kernel and will happily run from a CD-ROM. It must be remembered that in order to use the CD as a boot device, the BIOS must support booting from CD-ROM or ATAPI devices. Many older machines don't allow booting from anything other than the first floppy disk and the first hard disk.

Installing an Operating System

Before installing Windows, or any other OS for that matter, it is important to make certain checks:

- Make sure the system meets the minimum requirements for the OS (e.g. minimum disk space required, minimum installed memory).
- Check for hardware and software compatibility with the new OS.
- Backup the system, if it is currently in use.
- Perform a virus check. If the system contains a boot sector virus, installing Windows will not solve the problem and all you will end up with is a fresh installation of Windows that has the virus. It may also be advisable to run a virus check on the installation media.
- Make a checklist of all components you will need. This generally means the installation disks, software and hardware manuals, user details (including passwords and other network data as needed), driver software, and any other media necessary. Don't forget to find the product key sticker that came with the disks or is attached to the computer. This sticker contains the activation code for the product and is a 25 digit sequence containing both numbers and letters.
- Go into the computer's BIOS and set it so that the first drive to be read at bootup is the DVD drive (unless using a brand new clean hard disk). This ensures that the Operating System CD is read first, otherwise the PC will just boot up using the existing operating system

Applications in modern Windows versions only load in software components when they are required. This requires less memory overheads and so more applications can effectively multitask. They also support multithreading, which allows different parts of the same application to run at the same time. A user, for example, can carry on using a word processor while it carries out a spell check or a file search.

Installing Windows XP

Like most versions of Windows, XP comes in two versions: one that is a full installation version, and one that is used to upgrade to XP from previous versions of Windows. However, Windows XP can only be installed if the currently installed operating system is Windows 98, Windows ME, Windows NT 4, or Windows 2000. Windows XP was marketed in two versions. The '*Home Edition*' is intended for personal home computers, while the '*Professional Edition*' is the same operating system with a few extra components such as Remote Desktop. If a machine has XP home edition installed, then the Pro edition can be installed over the top of it, to provide these extra functions.

Installing a new copy of Windows XP

The process for installing Windows XP on a new computer, or a computer that does not have a compatible operating system to install over, is as follows:

- Make sure that the system is capable of booting into the install procedure. In most cases this will mean booting straight from the CD-ROM.
- Boot up the machine from the appropriate drive to begin installation. The Windows install program will inspect the system's hardware, and load some rudimentary drivers as well as the Windows kernel. If booting from floppy, you may have to swap disks several times during the process. In addition, if you want to install XP onto a SCSI or RAID hard disk, you will have to press F6 at the appropriate time in order to install the correct driver.
- Select the setup type. Windows XP will ask the user whether to setup a new version of XP, repair an existing but damaged installation, or quit. Of course when beginning a new installation the first option should be chosen. The user will then have to agree to the Microsoft End User License Agreement before continuing.
- Set up partitions and file systems. Windows XP's installation routine includes the ability to partition and format drives, and select which partition to install onto. Windows XP can use FAT32 or NTFS file systems. NTFS provides better security and can be more reliable, but FAT32 might be needed for compatibility reasons, especially on a machine with multi-boot capability.
- Once the desired install partition is chosen, Windows XP will examine the disk, copy files onto it, load up INF files, and then reboot. When booting up again, the Windows GUI will be loaded, and the user will be asked to select regional options, including currency, language and so on.
- Enter the product key. Each copy of Windows XP, is supplied with its own key.

- Select a computer name, and an Administrator password. The computer name is used in LANs to identify each PC. The Administrator is a username that has full access to change any aspect of the system. In a home PC it may not be necessary to enforce strict security, but in a networked system it is usually advisable to give other users restricted access to change system settings, so that only the administrator has full access.
- Check the date, time, and time zone. Windows will display these settings, which should be verified by the user.
- Install networking software. Windows XP will display settings for TCP/IP and so on. These are only used in a computer network such as a LAN, so on a standalone system this can be ignored. In simple LANs the default settings may be acceptable, but you should consult the network administrator if you are not certain. Windows will then copy the appropriate files, install start menu items, register components, save settings, and reboot.
- Upon rebooting, the user will be asked to set up the Internet settings on the computer. If you already have an ISP, you can enter its details now. If not, you will have to come back later to set up your Internet settings. If the machine can attach to the Internet, Windows will ask you to register your copy of Windows XP online.
- Set up users. The system automatically comes with several usernames, including *'administrator'*, which is the user account used to manage the system; and *'guest'*, which is a logon for temporary users. All other users of the computer should have their own user account, as this will allow users to set up the system to suit themselves. Each user has their own *'My Documents'* folder, their own area of the registry to store program settings, their own Start Menu programs, and so on.

Installing an upgrade copy of Windows XP
The steps for installing Windows XP on a computer already has Windows 98 or another compatible operating system installed, are as follows:
- Insert the Windows XP installation disc. In most computers it should automatically run, bringing up the installation windows. If not, run SETUP.EXE from the CD-ROM drive. This can be done using Explorer, or by clicking *'Run'* on the Start Menu and typing *'D:\SETUP.EXE'*.
- You may wish to check your system is compatible first. Click on *'check system compatibility'*, and then *'check my system automatically'*. The install program will then look for any incompatible hardware and display a report as to whether the system is compatible with Windows XP.
- Click *'Install Windows XP'* to begin the installation procedure. The install program will then ask which type of installation to use – an upgrade or a full install. The full install option allows a system that is currently running a Windows operating system to perform a full installation of XP as described above. The upgrade option is the one used to install over an existing copy of Windows, preserving file associations, settings, and so on.
- Agree to the End User License Agreement, and enter the product key. Since we are installing over an existing version of Windows, many of the settings are already available. The install procedure will continue, rebooting occasionally.

Installing Vista
To install Vista for the first time,
- With the computer switched off, insert the Windows Vista DVD. In most computers it should automatically run, bringing up the installation windows.
- Switch on the computer.
- In response to *'Press any key to boot from CD'* press a key.
- Select the required user details (e.g. language, time and currency format, keyboard type) and press the *'Next'* button.
- When prompted, enter the product activation key (supplied with the Vista disks or on a label attached to the computer).
- Check the box to accept Microsoft's licence terms.
- Select the *'Custom'* option.
- If your main hard disk is partitioned, select the partition on which to install Vista.

- Enter a user name and password.
- Enter a name for the computer. This allows the computer to be individually identified when used on a network.

The computer will reboot itself several times during the installation. This is meant to happen and does not indicate a fault or any problem in the installation.

Microsoft describes this as a 'clean installation' as any existing data and settings on the computer are lost. In addition, any previously installed programs and applications will have to be re-installed.
This is not a problem if installing Vista on a brand new hard drive.

Upgrading XP to Vista
The steps for upgrading a computer with Windows XP to Vista are:
- If necessary, install XP's Service Pack 2.
- Insert the Windows Vista DVD. In most computers it should automatically run, bringing up the installation windows. If not, run SETUP.EXE from the DVD drive. This can be done using Explorer, or by clicking 'Run' on the Start Menu and typing 'D:\SETUP.EXE'.
- Click 'Install Now' in the opening screen.
- In response to "Get important updates for installation" click 'Go Online'.
- When prompted, enter the product activation key (supplied with the Vista disks or on a label attached to the computer).
- Check the box to accept Microsoft's licence terms.
- In response to being asked 'What type of installation do you want?' click 'Upgrade'. This option maintains the existing applications and settings.
- Microsoft may report on drivers or applications that are not compatible with Vista and these should be noted for further action.
- Choose various settings (automatic updates, time zone, password, etc).

The computer will reboot itself several times during the installation. This is meant to happen and does not indicate a fault or any problem in the installation.

Installing/Deleting Software
During an upgrade, existing applications from the previous operating system may have been added to the 'Programs' sub-menu of the 'Start' menu. Most application packages begin their installation procedures automatically upon inserting the installation CD in the CD drive.
Applications can also be added with these steps:
1. Open the 'Start' menu.
2. Choose the 'Settings' option.
3. Choose the 'Control Panel' option.
4. Choose 'Add or Remove Programs'.
5. Choose the 'Add New Programs' option. This displays the window shown.
6. Insert the CD that contains the new application.
7. Click the 'CD or Floppy' button.

The Install Wizard then carries out the required installation activities.

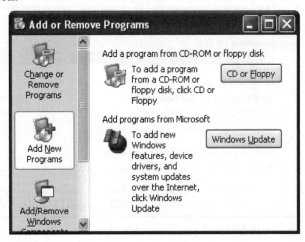

Most applications provide their own uninstall facilities.
They may also be removed using the 'Add or Remove Programs' option from the Control Panel.
This displays a window that list all the currently installed applications, including their size, etc.
The applications can be sorted and displayed by frequency of use, allowing the user to judge whether a program is heavily used and therefore should be kept.

The illustration shows the *'Family Tree Maker'* application being highlighted.

An application is removed by highlighting it from the pick list and clicking the *'Change/Remove'* button.

Adding/Deleting Windows Components

Since the *'Typical Setup'* only installs a selection of the available Windows components, extra components can be added later, using the *'Add/Remove Windows Components'* option within the *'Add or Remove Programs'* window. A list of linked components is displayed by category.

In the example shown, the *'Microsoft Fax'* box is unchecked indicating that it is not currently installed on the computer. The *'Internet Explorers'* box is checked indicating that all these components are installed.

The *'Internet Information Services'* box is checked but is also greyed. This indicates that only some of this category's components are installed.

Extra components can be installed by making its box active (i.e. a tick will appear in the box) and clicking the *'Next'* button. Similarly, components can be removed by making their boxes inactive (the tick is removed from the appropriate boxes) and clicking the *'Next'* button.

A text box explains the meaning of each category and each component as it is selected.

Highlighting a category and clicking the *'Details'* button displays the list of components within that category. This allows individual components to be selected or deselected.

Customising the Start Menu

When the computer boots into Windows, it displays a *'Start'* button on the bottom taskbar. Clicking this button displays a set of options, the contents of which vary slightly depending on the version of Windows. However, the illustration shows options on the right panel, which are commonly available.

If an option on the Start Menu has an arrowhead, then clicking on the entry or hovering the mouse over it will produce a sub-menu. In the example, the top three options have been added later by the user so that commonly used applications can be quickly accessed without hunting through sub-menus. Inside the *'Programs'* option is a structure of folders, and *'shortcuts'* which allow access to programs or data files.

These shortcuts are usually created by an installation program when an application is installed, but the user can create his or her own shortcuts by a variety of methods.

All Windows versions allow drag-and-drop shortcuts to be created. This is where the user locates a file using Explorer, and then drags and drops it somewhere else. If the file is a program, it will create a shortcut instead of copying the file.

The user can drag an application onto the Start Menu to create a shortcut there.

Alternatively, right-clicking on the Start Menu and selecting *'Explore'* from the menu will open up an Explorer window which starts inside the Start Menu folder. From here, the user can select 'File → New → Shortcut' and browse to select the program that the shortcut will point to.

Document Shortcuts

If a machine regularly uses a few data files (e.g. a database, an accounts main sheet, or a graphics template) these files can also be pointed to by shortcuts. The steps are identical to those above. This feature allows a regularly used data file to rest on the StartUp menu and be used by clicking on - without first having to run the application package and search for the file.

The Startup Group

Windows contains a *'StartUp'* folder. Any programs added to this folder are run automatically when Windows is started. This allows utilities such as virus checkers and printer monitoring software to run in the background. It also allows an application program to be run.

For instance, if a computer was used mainly for word processing, the machine could be configured to boot up straight into Microsoft Word. A shortcut that points to Word is placed in the StartUp folder and this will run Word. If the user wishes to run another package, exiting Word takes the machine into the normal Windows interface. Note, however, that not all programs loaded at startup are found in the Startup Group. Some are started via the Registry (explained later).

Altering the setup

The main configuration options as determined by the Windows Setup routine can be altered to suit personal choice or to accommodate changing hardware and software demands.

This can range from adding and deleting programs as already described, through to altering the configuration of hardware such as keyboard, monitor, modem, printers, mouse and sound cards. It includes the system settings such as date and time, fonts to be used, user passwords, etc.

These alterations are made via the *'Control Panel'*, which is accessed as an option from the *'Settings'* option on the *'Start'* menu. Some of the most common alterations are described next.

Display

Choosing the *'Display'* option in the *'Control Panel'* offers four or more choices, (depending on operating system, drivers and software) for altering display properties. The *'Settings'* menu, as shown in the illustration, alters the main display characteristics.

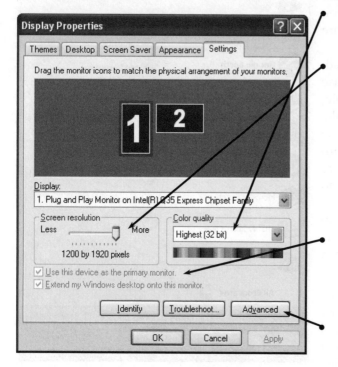

These are:

Selecting the number of colours to be used (this depends on the maximum number of colours offered by the video card).

Setting the screen resolution by clicking on the slider and moving it to the required setting (the maximum resolution depends on that supported by the screen and by the video card). Some systems also provide a second, similar option to select a 'desktop area'. These systems allow the user access to a desktop that is larger than the screen, by scrolling the portion of the desktop that is displayed on-screen at any one time.

Windows has the capability of supporting multiple monitors. These tickboxes are used to select how to use the monitors in a multi-screen system (e.g. whether to treat both monitor surfaces areas as a single large window).

The *'Advanced'* button provides further sub-options, depending on the hardware and software in use.

The five main components are General, Monitor, Adapter, Performance and Color Management. Other tabs are often available, but these depend on the hardware and software installed.

General — Select large or small fonts for use with text to be displayed on the desktop.

Monitor — Select the driver for the monitor in use (might require the disk that came with the monitor, if Windows does not have the correct one in its stored list).

Adapter — Select the driver for the graphics card in use (might require the floppy disk that came with the card, if Windows does not have the correct one in its stored list). Also allows user selection of the card's refresh rate.

Performance — Select the maximum rate at which the graphics card can handle data. This may be replaced by a tab placed there by a graphic card's installation to provide detailed control over the particular card's facilities.

Color Management — Select the colour profile that makes the monitor display colours exactly as they will be when they are used for colour prints.

Other display properties

This version of Windows is different again. It has tabs for:

- Themes. Allows desktop appearance settings to be saved and selected as 'themes'.
- Desktop. This tab allows the background image to be chosen, including using the 'browse' button to look for any GIF or JPG image to be used as a background.
- Screen Saver. This option lists a selection of possible screen savers and these can be previewed before one is selected. A *'Wait'* selection box sets the time delay before activating the screen saver. If *'My Pictures Slideshow'* is selected from the *'Screen saver'* drop-down list, This tab also provides monitor energy saving settings.
- Appearance. This option allows the screen display to be set to the user's preferences. This includes the colours for Window text, message boxes, etc. Alternatively, the user can choose from a number of default colours schemes.
- Settings. This tab has similar options to previous versions.

Mouse Customisation

From the *'Mouse'* option in *'Control Panel'*, the response of the mouse can be altered. The options available vary depending on the version of Windows installed, and indeed often on the Mouse driver being used. The tabs include:

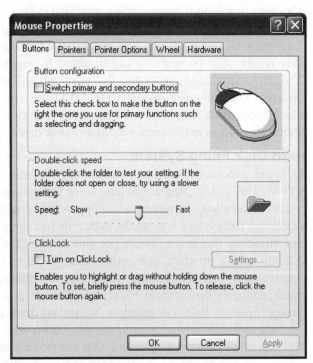

- Buttons. This allows the user to choose whether the mouse buttons are swapped for left-handed users; sets the double-click speed also allows access to the Clicklock accessibility function.

- Pointers. This tab allows the user to set which mouse pointer graphics to use for various operations such as *'Busy'* or *'Select'*, and save or select these settings in a mouse pointer 'scheme'.

- Pointer Options. This tab allows selection of the pointer speed, and whether to use mouse trails to aid visibility on an LCD monitor. Mit also has options for *'Snap To'* movement, pointer hiding while typing, and sonar-style circles to highlight the mouse position when the CTRL key is pressed.

- Wheel. This tab is only available for wheel mice, and sets how far to move the scroller when the wheel moves one notch.

- Hardware. This tab allows the user to change or view the properties of the Mouse driver in use.

Keyboard Customisation

If the *'Keyboard'* option is chosen from the *'Control Panel'*, the response of the keyboard can be altered. The *'Speed'* tab provides a slider control for setting the *'Repeat Delay'*. It determines how long a key has to be depressed before it begins to auto-repeat the character; dragging the slider to a faster or slower setting along a speed bar sets the value.

Setting the *'Repeat Rate'* determines the speed at which the key will auto-repeat the character. This setting is achieved by dragging the slider to a faster or slower setting along a bar. Below the speed bar there is a test box to test the settings, before exiting the window by clicking on the *'OK'* button.

Setting the *'Cursor Blink Rate'* determines the cursor's flash speed and is also set by dragging a slider.

Windows also allows access to keyboard drivers in two ways: either through the *'Hardware'* tab or through the Device Manager.

Note

Altering how programs display numbers and currencies are not set in this utility. Instead this is set by clicking *'Details'* in the *'Languages'* tab of the *'Regional and Language Options'* dialog from the Control Panel.

Setting the Date And Time

The computer's real-time clock can be set within Windows. The date and time settings within *'Regional Settings'* only control the way they are displayed; they do not alter the computer's internal clock. This facility is called up via the *'Date and Time'* option in *'Control Panel'*.

CD Autoplay

Windows is able to automatically play CDs/DVDs when they are inserted into the DVD drive. These can be normal audio CDs, Video CDs, or the growing number of applications (including the Windows installation CD) that have an *'autorun.inf'* file that commences the running of the application.

This facility can be enabled and disabled by right-clicking on the DVD drive in Explorer, selecting *'Properties'* and clicking on the *'Autoplay'* tab will allow the user to set autoplay options directly.

Different content types (music CDs, DVD movies, pictures, etc.) are listed and the user can decide which application should be used to access each type. Choosing *'Take no action'* means that the content is viewed and run in the same way as any disk drive.

Hard Disk Filing System

As noted previously, various versions of Windows may use different file systems: FAT16, FAT32, or NTFS. This is not often a problem, since the optimum file system should be chosen when the operating system is installed. However, when upgrading or when attaching a hard drive that is already formatted to a different file system, it is useful to be able to change the file system of a hard disk.

Unfortunately this is not always possible without the use of a third-party utility such as Partition Magic. Without such a program, converting from NTFS to FAT, or from FAT32 to FAT16, is only possible by repartitioning and reformatting the drive. Fortunately, Windows contains a program called *'convert'* which converts drives from FAT to NTFS. It is a command line program and therefore is accessed through *Start -> Run*. For example, to convert drive D: from FAT to NTFS, the user would type:

convert d: /fs:ntfs

The "/fs:ntfs" parameter specifies that the drive's new Filing System (FS) should be NTFS. This suggests that there are other options to convert to, but unfortunately this is not currently the case.

Notes:

- Examine the needs of the system carefully before changing the file system. If a legacy operating system needs access to the drive (e.g. in a multi-boot system), then the file system will have to remain of the type which the oldest OS can access.
- The file system conversion process is not reversible, unless third-party utilities are available to do so. Make certain the conversion is needed before proceeding.
- Do not interrupt the file system conversion process, as it could render the drive unusable.
- To find out the current filing system of a drive, right click it in Windows Explorer and look under the General tab. Alternatively, for more detailed information choose the *'Disk Management'* option in *'Administrative Tools'*, which is accessed through *'Control Panel'*.

Windows Fonts

Fonts are collections of alphabetic, numeric, punctuation and symbol characters as seen on the computer monitor or printed to paper. Fonts have three characteristics:

Type Face - the actual *shape* of the characters, such as Arial (a sans serif face i.e. plain outline with no feet or twirls), Times Roman (a serifed face used in many publications) and Gothic.

Type Size - the actual *height* of the characters as measured in points, there being 72 points to an inch. A 36-point headline, then, is half an inch high.

Type Style - such as bold, italics or underlined.

True Type fonts

True Type fonts do not store an exact bitmap picture of every typeface, size and style. Instead, it stores a description of a typeface. This description is stored as geometric mathematical formulae that outline the shape of the various parts of the character in normal, bold, italic and bold italic modes. When an application chooses to use a particular font, the font description is fetched and scaled to the required type size. Windows then generates a bitmap of the font for use with the screen or printer. This process is known as *'rasterising'*. A slight manipulation of the factors in the formulae allows the faces to be scaled to any size. This has two distinct advantages:

- The computer need only store the set of four descriptions for each typeface, compared to a set for every font size with bitmaps.
- The mathematical formulae of true type fonts maintain smooth curves even with large type sizes, whereas bitmaps tend to become very 'blocky' and ugly at larger sizes.

Fonts and printing

The fonts selected for use on a particular machine depends on the type of printer it is connected to. The common methods for printing text are:

- Using the font resident in the printer. Installing a printer's software may have resulted in fonts being added to the Windows system. If these fonts are used, Windows is compatible with the printer and, after a minimum of setup, the data is sent to the printer as a set of ASCII codes. This is a fast method, since there is no special translation required. However, the printer software may not have installed a matching set of screen fonts and Windows will have to use the closest match. Hence, the user will have lost WYSIWYG (What You See Is What You Get).

- Sending the bitmap straight to the printer. This may be from a bitmap font or may be the bitmap that was created by rasterising a True Type font. A normal A4 page would need around 1MB to store all the page's information. However, it is common for printers to only have an internal memory buffer of 512k or less. That is why a highly complex sheet is often ejected after only printing the top half of the page. The solution lies in adding more buffer memory to the printer or in using some method of compressing the data.

- Describing the fonts to be used to the printer. Once the printer has stored the definition of each font, the computer can send plain ASCII with the consequent saving in time. There are various methods dependent on the printer in use. These include PCL5 (Hewlett Packard's Printer Control Language 5) and Postscript. In each case the printer driver converts each font before sending it to the printer. Printers that support PDL (Microsoft's Page Description Language) have some True Type fonts already embedded in the printer. Since the fonts don't have to be downloaded, printing is greatly speeded up. They are also able to download True Type fonts at a faster rate than PCL5 or Postscript downloads.

Setting up fonts

Font management is through the *'Fonts'* option in the *'Control Panel'*. This displays a list of the fonts that are already installed in Windows. These are the fonts that are available within Windows applications such as Word, Excel, etc.

Any displayed font in the list can be deleted by highlighting the font from the pick list and choosing the *'Delete'* option from the *'File'* menu.

Additional fonts are installed via the *'Install New Font'* option on the *'File'* menu. This opens an *'Add Fonts'* window where the location of the new font can be given and the name of the font highlighted before clicking the *'OK'* button. A box can be checked to copy the font(s) from the original location into the Windows fonts directory.

Font Name	Filename	Size
Aardvark Bold	aardvrkb.ttf	27K
Adelaide	adelaidn.ttf	36K
Alefbet	alefbetn.ttf	20K
Algerian	Alger.ttf	68K
Algiers	algiersn.ttf	83K
Arabia	arabian.ttf	47K
Architecture	architen.ttf	33K
Arial	ARIAL.TTF	65K
Arial Black	Ariblk.ttf	47K
Arial Bold	ARIALBD.TTF	65K
Arial Bold Italic	ARIALBI.TTF	71K
Arial Italic	ARIALI.TTF	61K
Arial Narrow	Arialn.ttf	61K

336 font(s)

Maintaining fonts

Over a period of time, the number of fonts will grow as many applications add their own fonts into Windows. In many cases, the new fonts look very similar to existing fonts. As a result, no new facilities are added and yet the hard disk - and Windows' fonts menus - becomes rapidly expanded. The following fonts should always remain on the computer, as they are the standard Windows set and are used by many application packages and by Windows itself:

Font Name	Example
Arial	I am Arial
Courier New	I am Courier New
Symbol	ασδφγηφκλ
Times New Roman	I am Times New Roman
Wingdings	☺ ◆ ♎ ⚡ ♑ ♒ ♋ ♌

In addition, Microsoft uses fonts whose names start with MS - e.g. MS San Serif - for screen writing and these should also remain in Windows.

In a very congested system, there may be many fonts that are almost identical. This can be checked by choosing the 'List Fonts by Similarity' option in the 'View' menu of the 'Fonts' with 'Control Panel'. It will produce a screen similar to that shown.

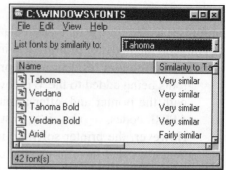

In the example it can be seen that the Verdana and Tahoma fonts are very similar, while the Arial font is only fairly similar to Tahoma. An inspection of these lists allows decisions to be made on which fonts are almost duplicates and can be removed from the system.

Printers

Printer options can be set up using the '*Printers and Faxes*' option from Control Panel or from the Start Menu. This produces a screen similar to that shown. The default printer is the one that is used when a job is printed without first specifically mentioning which printer should be used. It follows that the default printer should be the one that is mostly commonly used. If there is only one installed printer then it is automatically the default printer. The default printer choice is set using the '*Set as Default*' option when right-clicking on a printer that is not currently the default. Windows will indicate which is the default printer by putting a small black tick next to it.

Clicking the '*Add Printer*' icon runs the Add Printer Wizard, which steps the user through the installation options.

Double-clicking on a particular printer icon produces a status window for that printer, showing print jobs currently being processed. From this window, clicking the '*Printer*' menu and then the '*Properties*' option produces the printer

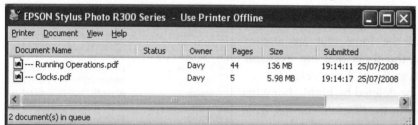

properties screen, which will be similar to that shown. As usual, the options vary depending on the version of Windows and the printer driver.

The '*General*' tab provides details about the printer's capabilities and allows a test page to be printed to check that the printer is functioning properly. Clicking the '*Printing Preferences*' button opens up a new window with many options for controlling the print quality, paper size, paper type, orientation, etc.

The '*Ports*' tab sets the printer port to be used for the printer connection. The pick list displays the possible ports to choose from (e.g. LPT1/2, COM1/2, USB or to PDF if a PDF driver is installed). This list can be altered by adding extra ports or deleting existing ports.

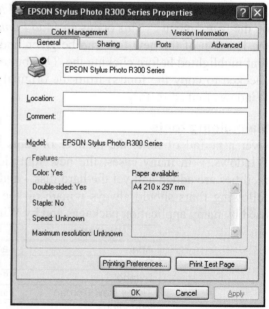

The '*Advanced*' tab sets the printer driver to be used with the printer. The pick list displays any drivers that are already installed and new drivers can be installed by clicking the '*New Driver*' button. This displays a pick list of all available Windows printer drivers. If the required driver is not in the list but is supplied with a printer, then it is installed by choosing the '*Have Disk*' option.

The '*Sharing*' tab, which is only available on networked computers, is used to enable the sharing of the printer over the network.

The '*Color Management*' tab uses profiles to match any colour content to be printed to the colour printing capabilities of the chosen printer.

Volume Control

Windows provides control over the audio volume from the desktop. The following steps install this facility to the desktop:

- From the *'Start'* button choose the *'Control Panel'* and *'Sound and Audio Devices'* options.
- Check the box marked *'Show volume icon in the taskbar'*.

A loudspeaker icon is added to the Windows taskbar. Clicking this icon opens the window shown.

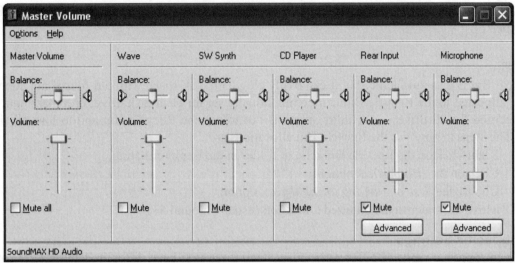

The *'Master Volume'* control settings affect the output of all audio devices. The mouse-controlled volume control slider that adjusts the audio volume. Checking the *'Mute'* box completely disables all audio output and all devices are silenced.

However, there are times when a more detailed control over the audio levels of individual audio sources is required. For example, it may be necessary to disable a microphone input when the sound card is recording from a tape deck, as the sound from the loudspeaker may be picked up by the microphone causing 'howling'. Alternatively, if both the microphone and tape deck sources are required, it may be necessary to mute the loudspeaker.

Each device can be individually muted or have its volume level set. This proves useful when creating multimedia productions and when working with audio recordings.

File Associations

Users can use applications to work with data in three ways:

1. Open the application (e.g. word processor, paint program, etc) and, once in the application, open the file to be worked on (e.g. letter, graphics file, etc).
2. Drag the file to be opened and drop it onto a program icon or link to a program.
3. Double-click on a file within Windows Explorer. This opens the application, followed by opening the file.

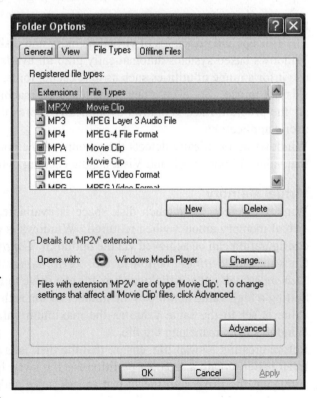

The last method makes use of *'file associations'*. A file's extension is linked to a corresponding application. As new applications are added to the computer, the file extensions used by the new application is added to the database of associations.

Although several applications may be able to process a file with a particular extension, only one can be the default association - i.e. the one activated when the file is double-clicked in Explorer. Of course, this does not prevent the other application processing the file using method 1.

The default associations can be viewed and altered within Windows Explorer. This is done by selecting '*Tools* → *Folder Options*' → '*File Types'* tab to show a dialog box similar to the one shown.

In the example, files with the *'MP2V'* extension are played using the Windows Media Player application. The *'Change'* option allows the default application to be altered.

A file does not have to be opened using the default file associations. Right-clicking on any file and selecting '*Open With*' will allow the user to open the file using any program. Furthermore, clicking the '*always use this program to open these files*' checkbox is another way to change the file association for that file type.

Recycle Bin

The Recycle Bin is a useful facility but it can easily clog hard disk space with old files if not controlled. The space allocated to the Recycle Bin can be individually set for each disk drive, or a maximum figure can be specified for all drives.   A third option is not to use the Recycle Bin and to lose all files on deletion. The steps to optimise the Recycle Bin allocations are:

- Right-click on the Recycle Bin icon or folder in the Explorer listing.
- Click on the *'Properties'* option.
- Choose the *'Use one setting for all drives'* option.
- Move the slider to the required allocation (usually around 5%).

Country Specific Settings

Windows can support a range of different languages and these may have different date/time formats (i.e. DD/MM/YY or MM/DD/YY), along with numeric and currency formats (i.e. £ symbols or $ symbols, using commas as numerical separators instead of full stops, etc.).

These options can be accessed via the *'Regional and Language Options'* in *'Control Panel'*.

The *'Regional Options'* tab offers drop-down menu of countries, and the desired country can be chosen from a pick list. This option controls the way applications will handle and present data, taking into account any special or accented characters in a language. It will display samples of the currency, time and date as displayed in that country. Also, the *'Customise'* button allows control over more specific details.

The '*Languages*' tab allows installation and removal of language options.

The '*Advanced*' tab is used to configure code pages where necessary.

Managing Memory

The concept and principles of virtual memory and disk caching are explained elsewhere in the book.

Windows based systems automatically grab all available physical memory in the computer, intending to use it for a range of utilities such as disk cache, fonts, etc.   This memory is held by Windows even when it is not in use. So, even a newly switched on machine will have all the available memory is allocated. As the program runs, Windows dynamically shares the memory between the system's resources and the user's applications.

Windows automatically detects the amount of memory available for disk caching and sizes the cache to that value. Windows XP and Vista handle caching dynamically without user intervention.

Virtual Memory

Windows detects how much disk space is available for virtual memory and automatically resizes the virtual memory amount when required. Windows is often left to organise its own management but user configuration can be achieved via the option in *'Control Panel'* → *'System'* → *'Advanced.*

Clicking the *'Settings'* button in the *'Performance'* followed by clicking the *'Change'* button in the *'Advanced'* tab opens a dialogue box to set a drive to be used along with minimum and maximum sizes.

Setting a high value minimises the number of times that the area will have to be resized. If the minimum value is set to the same value as the maximum value, the swap file size remains constant and saves Windows from managing the file.

Before creating a swap file, ensure that the disk is is is checked with ChkDisk and is defragmented. and Even better, create a separate partition for the swap file. Where there is more than one disk drive in the computer, the drive with the fastest access times and the highest data rate should be used for the swap file. This will improve overall performance.

Note:

There is a balance between disk cache size, swap file size and performance. If the disk cache minimum size is too large, there is not sufficient physical memory for processing and more is saved to slower virtual memory (increasing thrashing). If the maximum value is too small, handling of large files is slowed down. These problems mainly affect computers with small RAM sizes. The larger the amount of memory installed, the less the problems, and the smaller the size of the swap file needed.

Windows and DOS

New applications are designed for Windows but even now there are still some DOS programs in occasional use. It may be important that DOS utilities and applications can still be run under Windows. A DOS program can be run by using the *'Run'* option in the *'File'* menu of Program Manager, or by double clicking on an icon for a DOS package.

If fuller access to the DOS directory system is required, the user can shell out to DOS via the *'Command Prompt'* This is found under *'All Programs → Accessories'*. This opens a window in which the user can carry out all the normal DOS activities (e.g. DIR, COPY, etc.) or run a DOS package.

When first opened, the DOS window does not occupy the whole screen. For a larger viewing area, the window can be maximised by pressing the Alt and Enter keys. Pressing the same key combination a second time toggles the window down to the initial partial screen size.

Startup options

During the machine's bootup sequence, if the f8 key is hit before Windows begins loading, a menu is displayed, with several options, depending on the Windows version and setup.

These options may include the following:

- Normal. This boots into Windows normally as if this menu had been skipped.
- Safe Mode. The system will boot without loading any but the most basic drivers, (e.g. no CD-ROM, no sound card, basic VGA resolution) so that any problem software or drivers that are preventing a normal bootup can be changed or removed.
- Safe mode with Network Support. As above, but Network drivers will be loaded. This is useful for re-installing software over the network to save time when problems arise. This option will of course only appear if the system has network capabilities.
- Enable Boot Logging. The system boots normally but all bootup operations are recorded in the text file NTBTLOG.TXT for debugging purposes. This file is stored in the Windows folder and includes files and drivers loaded, and whether each loading was successful.
- Enable VGA Mode. Uses default monitor driver, ignoring the specific driver for the monitor. Diagnostic tool to see whether the normal video driver is
- Last Known Good Configuration. Uses the registry data that was saved at the last successful shutdown Used for troubleshooting.

Device Manager

The Device Manager is the most important tool for viewing and altering the configuration of the computer's hardware.

Device Manager is accessed via the *'System'* icon in the *'Control Panel.* S*electing the *'Hardware'* tab and clicking the *'Device Manager'* button displays the window shown in the illustration.

It offers different views of system devices:

- Listing all hardware in order of their type (e.g. all hard drives are grouped together regardless of the type of interface used to connect them).
- Listing all hardware in order of their type of connection (e.g. all SCSI devices such as disk drives and CD-ROMs are grouped together, while all the serial devices are listed together).

- Listing all devices in order of the computer resources they use (e.g. listing which IRQs are used by devices).

If an exclamation mark is displayed next to any device, it indicates that a conflict has been detected between the resources allocated to the device and resources required for its proper operation.

Double clicking on a device produces a screen that reports on the configuration and state of that device.

The example shows a report on an Ethernet Controller. The address space, IRQ and I/O channel used is clearly displayed. The bottom box also reports that the configuration of the device is not conflicting with the usage of other hardware devices in the computer.

Unchecking the *'Use automatic settings'* box allows the values to be altered. The setting to be altered can be double clicked and a new value can be entered.

The *'Driver'* option displays details of the current software driver being used to handle the device. Again, this can be altered if a newer driver is issued.

Similar reports are available for all devices on the system, including disk drives, the mouse, keyboard, monitor, modems, serial and parallel ports and network cards.

Hardware Profiles

Windows always stores at least one profile. Each profile contains details of the device drivers that are installed, disabled, or configured a certain way. Where is more than one profile, the user is asked at the bootup stage to select which profile to use. Windows then uses the selected profile to install a particular set of drivers during boot-up. This allows a user to boot up into any one profile, and load the set of drivers that are relevant to the situation. A common example is a laptop computer, which could have one profile for portable use, and another for use when attached to a docking station with extra facilities.

This facility is accessed via the *'System'* option in *'Control Panel'*. Clicking the *'Profiles'* button in the 'Hardware' tab displays a list of profiles that can be selected, deleted or renamed.

It is possible to create new profiles by selecting an existing profile, and clicking 'Copy'. This will create a new profile, and ask the user for a name to give the profile. Profiles can also be deleted or renamed from this window.

However, the main purpose of profiles is to select which drivers to install upon booting. This is not done in the Hardware Profiles dialog, but in the Device Manager dialog. Clicking the *'properties'* button while a device is selected will bring up the device properties dialog, as explained earlier. At the bottom of the *'General'* tab, depending on the type of driver selected, there may be one or more *'Device usage'* options, including *'Disable in this hardware profile'*; *'remove from this hardware profile'*; and *'exists in all hardware profiles'*.

The first option will not remove the driver, but will stop the driver from being loaded whenever booting into the current hardware profile. To set this up properly, first boot into the profile which is to have a driver disabled, click this box, and then reboot.

The second option simply specifies that the driver is totally removed from the current profile.

The third option specifies that the driver should appear in all hardware profiles. Obviously, this option is incompatible with the *'remove from this hardware profile'* option. The type and number of options available depends on the device driver. For example, peripherals such as SCSI cards or sound adapters can usually be freely disabled or removed, while more fundamental drivers such as the PCI bus or the hard disk drivers usually have no options available as they must be enabled for the system to work.

The Windows Registry

Early versions of Windows required a large collection of files supporting all the Windows components and applications. This was made up of the Windows INI files and usually separate INI files for each application. Added to this was the clutter of duplicated DLL files as different applications installed exactly the same DLL in various directories across the disk. Maintaining the system caused problems. Users found, for example, that deleting components for one application often removed a DLL that was shared with another application, thus preventing the second application from running.

With modern Windows versions, the collection of INI files and duplicate DLLs is replaced with a single database of all system and application information. This is the known as the Registry and it includes both hardware and software information.

Windows provides a program for editing the Registry, called *'REGEDIT'*. This application is accessed by choosing *'Run'* from the *'Start'* menu and entering 'REGEDIT' in the dialog box. This displays the Registry Editor as shown in the illustration.

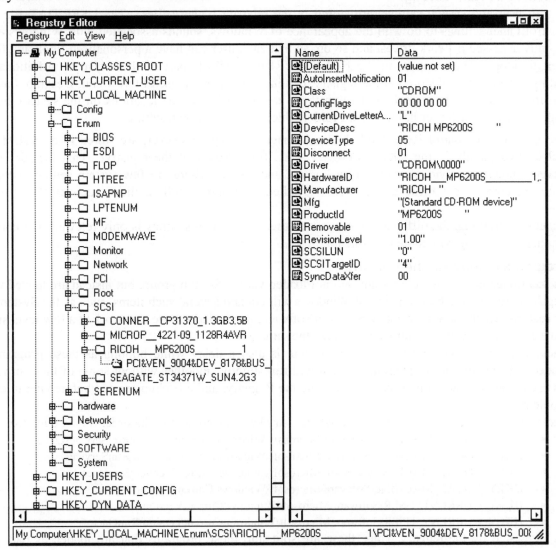

The left window of the Editor displays the Registry information under six sub-groups. The right window has two columns, displaying the name of each configuration detail and the data stored. The utility also has a *'Find'* facility, which can be used to locate a particular device in the Registry.

Warning   Altering the Registry should only be tackled by experienced users as incorrect changes can prevent Windows from booting up. Attempt the editing 'tips' in magazines at your peril.

Registry Backups

If the Registry is corrupted or damaged, some or all of the machine's configuration can be lost. There are many utilities that create backups of the Registry to provide a clean replacement copy in the event of problems. Examples of these utilities are Registry Mechanic, RegCure, Registry First Aid, Registry Easy, Registry Fix, Advanced Registry, WinRescue and Rescue Me.

Registry Security

The registry is a very intricate and important part of the Windows system, so ensuring that it runs efficiently will make for a smoother operation of Windows as a whole. Windows NT, 2000, and XP, are designed to be multi-user network systems, and security of such an important part of the system on a network is vital. Therefore, Windows NT based systems have *access rights* to various parts of the registry, which can be set by the administrator. As standard, the administrator has rights to view and change any part of the registry, while normal users as standard only have read/write access to their own HKEY_LOCAL_USER part of the registry. This will prevent tampering with system devices and so on.

User and System settings

Not all user and system settings are stored in the relevant registry files. The USER.DAT file stores Control Panel settings to do with the appearance of Windows, sounds associated with Windows events, recently accessed network drives, and so on, so that each user can have a personalised 'look and feel' to their desktop. These appear in the HKEY_CURRENT_USER part of the registry. Additional user settings, which are not stored in the registry, can include a personalised Start Menu, Desktop, Favorites folders, and so on. In a single-user setup these are stored in various locations on the system, but in a multi-user setup each user has their own folder which stores their own settings.

The majority of Control Panel (and Device Manager) settings, however, are stored in SYSTEM.DAT, and located mainly in the HKEY_LOCAL_MACHINE region of the registry. This includes device drivers, bindings, services which run at bootup, and so on. There are few system settings which are stored elsewhere, but these include fonts installed, and some shell facilities such as '*Send to*' and '*New...*'

Generally speaking, the differentiation between user and system settings is only relevant in a computer that has been set up with more than one logon.

Programs loaded via the Registry

As mentioned earlier, some programs are not loaded via the Startup group, but instead are loaded via the Registry. Even a basic installation of Windows will contain several such items, such as the System Tray or Task Manager. However, many pieces of software, particularly those that work at a low level such as virus scanners or display controls, are loaded the same way.

These take up memory when loaded, and there is also a delay while booting as these programs are loaded. If they are not needed, the system will run slightly smoother without some of these programs. As usual, caution should be used when editing the Registry, and a backup created beforehand in case of problems.

These programs are loaded in one of several Registry keys, listed here in the order they are loaded:

- HKEY_LOCAL_MACHINE\Software\Microsoft\Windows\CurrentVersion\RunServicesOnce
- HKEY_LOCAL_MACHINE\Software\Microsoft\Windows\CurrentVersion\RunServices
- HKEY_LOCAL_MACHINE\Software\Microsoft\Windows\CurrentVersion\RunOnce
- HKEY_LOCAL_MACHINE\Software\Microsoft\Windows\CurrentVersion\Run
- HKEY_CURRENT_USER\Software\Microsoft\Windows\CurrentVersion\Run
- HKEY_CURRENT_USER\Software\Microsoft\Windows\CurrentVersion\RunOnce

As suggested by the registry paths, these are split into those programs that are loaded as part of the machine settings and those which are loaded as part of an individual user's setup. The machine-specific Run settings are typically drivers, firewalls, virus scanners or other low-level items, so that they apply to all users. Many of these are classed as '*Services*', that is they provide functions to other programs rather than directly to the user.

The word '*Once*', as the name suggests, indicates that programs found within are run once and once only, and then removed from the registry. This facilitates the setup of certain programs.

Note: take care before removing items from the Run key, especially if they are Services. Make sure you realise their exact function before doing so, otherwise the system could suffer from potentially serious problems.

Accessibility Wizard

This allows the user with particular needs to set up his/her machine. The wizard interface guides the user step by step through a series of choices. Wizards are useful tools for administrators as they can be written, using Windows scripting, to do almost any task. They can however also represent a security hazard, and so "new" wizards should be checked for validity by a suitably experienced support person. Whilst the accessibility options are welcome additions to the operating system, they are no substitute for fully featured professional software for users with special needs. Microsoft recognises this and prompts the user to remind them of it.

Magnifier

This utility opens an extra screen window where the main screen contents are magnified around the area pointed to by the mouse cursor. This is primarily aimed at visually impaired but is also useful for viewing graphics or fine detail in a large spreadsheet, zooming in during presentations, etc.

This utility can be added by choosing the *'All Programs'*, *'Accessories'*, *'Accessibility'* and *'Magnifier'* options from the *'Start'* button.

The user can control the amount of screen space devoted to the magnified view and can set the degree of magnification.

Narrator

This utility is designed to help users with limited or no sight. Its control panel is shown in the illustration. Pressing the "VOICE" button brings up a new panel that allows the user to tweak the way the voice sounds, to suit their individual requirements.

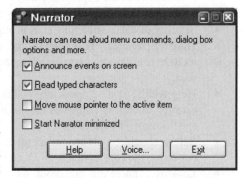

The initial settings are probably useful but the voice does rather drone on a bit, particularly when a "busy" window, with lots of toolbars, is opened. The voice will immediately read out the details of all of the toolbars. Whilst useful on smaller windows with only one or two controls, the narrators output can be utterly confusing when it is presented with a full functioned word processor or spreadsheet.

On-Screen Keyboard

The On Screen Keyboard allows users who cannot use a keyboard but who can use a mouse-like interface (or perhaps a puff switch) to use the PC, albeit slowly.

It also has uses for able-bodied users in situations where use of a keyboard is inappropriate, but use of a mouse, trackball, or touch screen is possible. Typical situations would include industrial settings where swarf, dirt or airborne contamination is a problem.

Multiple Monitors

Setting up a second monitor is an easy task. First, a second graphic card is installed and a monitor attached (see the chapter on *'Hardware Installation'*).

When the computer is switched back on, the *'Settings'*, *'Control Panel'*, *'Display'*, and *'Settings'* options are chosen from the *'Start'* button. This will open a window like the one shown earlier in the chapter (see 'Display'). Each icon will have a number, with monitor 1 being the one that will display the right side of the desktop and monitor 2 displaying the left side. The icons can be moved around with the mouse to alter the arrangement. Thus, monitor 2 can be switched to display the right side. If desired, the icons can even be positioned vertically if monitors are to be stacked. When the Monitor 2 icon is positioned, it should be clicked to highlight it, followed by clicking the *'Extend my Windows desktop onto this monitor'* box. Once set up, objects can be dragged from the main screen to the secondary screen.

For example, if Monitor 2 is the one on the right, dragging an object off the right hand side of Monitor 1 places the object into the secondary monitor.

Settings Transfer Wizard

This wizard is used, as the name suggests, to transfer settings and files from one computer to another. The program can be configured to act either as the original machine, or the new machine, depending on which direction the files are to be transferred.

The role of technical support

However technical support is provided, the computer technician's role in any organisation is to enable end users to reliably access computer and information facilities. Before technical support is provided, then, it is advisable to find out what the needs of the end users are.

End user requirements

As outlined in the '*Software and Data*' chapter, every organisation has a different purpose, and every organisation operates slightly differently. As a result, there is no single list of end user requirements that meets the needs of all businesses. The support technician's department must find out user requirements by discussion with the various computer using departments. Typical requirements include:

- Having access to the correct types of IT equipment to allow them to perform their role in the organisation, as well as that equipment being properly configured for their use.
- Reliably functioning hardware and software, including printers and related consumables.
- Availability of the appropriate data is of vital importance in nearly all cases. If the data is centralised via a network, this means ensuring that access is given to the correct users.
- Security of data. Often, this is as is important as the availability of the data.
- Disaster planning. If serious problems develop, the end user wants to minimise their impact. This can include fire, flood, computer virus, or something less dramatic such as accidental deletion of important data.
- Help with IT related operations. This can vary from having to train new users in the computer system, to creating document templates for use as invoices, or simply helping users who want to know a shortcut to specific software functions.
- Safety should be a concern of all workers, but working with computer equipment has specific safety concerns, the consideration of which is often the support department's concern.
- Legality. There are numerous legal concerns relating to data storage, 'hacking', licensing, and other computer matters. These must of course be followed, and users may need advice or aid from the IT department in doing so.

Sources of user support

A variety of user support mechanisms are used by organisations and these are:

Manufacturers

Where the goods are supplied directly by a manufacturer, they have the responsibility of ensuring that the product carries out its function correctly. This may take the form of repairing hardware or configuring software. The level of warranty support depends upon the terms of the contract, ranging from same-day, through to next-day, to two-working days and so on. The fastest response time is the most expensive but is necessary where products are used for essential operations (e.g. medical, financial, real-time, etc). Where a manufacturer is remote from an organisation, a local service company often provides a speedier response time. The service staff probably covers a wide range of products and will not necessarily be expert in the product to be serviced. This can be significant, as clear-up time is as important as the response time. After all, the user wants the visit to be effective as well as quick. In addition to direct maintenance, many hardware and software manufacturers run support lines, bulletin boards and Internet Web sites. These are dedicated to answering specific user problems, publishing FAQs (answer to frequently asked questions) and providing patches, upgrades and updated software drivers. Examples of this are Adaptec (manufacturers of hard disk controllers) and Microsoft (software producers).

Dealers

Where goods are supplied via a dealer, the dealer has the legal responsibility for the warranty, since the contract was with the dealer. Most dealers also offer extended warranties where, for an extra charge, the maintenance of the products is covered for a longer period. Dealers can also be contracted to provide improved response times since, in general, they are located closer to their customers. Many dealers will also provide user training as part of the sales package or for an additional charge.

Third-Party Support

Third party support is independent of the manufacturer and supplier of the products and the services cover a wide range of support levels. These range from supplying a diagnostics software package (where the user requires the knowledge and skills to use it) through to full-scale outsourcing (where all the organisation's problems are covered by an external company). In the first case, a one-off payment is made; with outsourcing, a negotiated annual fee covers the cost of the service. Although third-party charges can be expensive, they are often regarded as an efficient option compared to maintaining an in-house facility with permanent staff, accommodation, training costs, etc.

Other third-party services, which are covered later, are:

- Commercial held desks
- Support on CDs
- Training
- Consultancy

In-house Support

For smaller organisations with few computing resources, the cost of a permanent support staff is not justified. For larger organisations, in-house support groups provide the ability to call upon instant services. Additionally, the support staff has intimate knowledge of the organisation's needs and priorities and has local knowledge of the equipment and software in use. The scope of the services can also be much wider as staff can be trained in specialist areas.

Technical support functions

The type and amount of these facilities vary widely from place to place, as does the manner in which the support is provided. For example, a small business might have only one or two computer users, and only require access to a word processor and printer, while a university could have a large number of computers, connected via a complex network, with a wide range of peripherals and software. However, some of the most common duties of PC support staff include:

Hardware

- Advising on new purchases. Support technicians can provide invaluable information about the reliability of certain brand names and the quality of their after-service. Most technicians are also likely to have a very good appreciation of any shortfalls in the organisation's computing system and are among the staff most likely to be up to date on what equipment is necessary and available.
- Organising orders for replacement parts where necessary. Also ordering, managing, and installing consumables (including printer paper and ink) as needed. Printer paper and ink are the primary consumable items of most IT departments, but other items could include fax rolls, floppy disks, and perhaps even cleaning equipment in some cases.
- Installing and testing new computers; connecting computers to local area networks.
- Installing hardware upgrades, such as adding extra memory modules, modems, fax cards or network interface cards (with any corresponding driver software).
- Carrying out system preventative maintenance such as the periodic examination, cleaning and testing of equipment and running regular diagnostics checks.
- Carrying out first-line repairs such as replacing faulty boards or cables. The extent of the faultfinding and repair activities may vary widely with the organisation and with the capabilities and experience of their support technicians. Some sections may contain staff that are trained service technicians with the ability to repair equipment. Other staff need have no skills with a soldering iron; their role is to find the faulty component and have it replaced or sent for repair. Other organisations have maintenance contracts and PC support is confined to minor hardware and software problems.
- Where technicians are expected to send items off for repair, it is often their job to pack the items. This should be done with the same care you would hope to see put into an item being sent to your own company – careless packing can cause even more damage, either to the case or mechanical components, or to sensitive electronic parts inside. Goods damaged due to poor packing obviously cause delays in the item being repaired, and potentially higher costs.
- Technicians often undertake more general technical support on their organisation's computing equipment, for example portable appliance testing (PAT test) on IT equipment.

Software

- Installing new software. This involves installing and testing the software prior to its use by the organisation. It may also involve creating a training programme for the users.
- Installing and maintaining networked services. This can include email, gateways to the Internet, file servers, application servers, and print servers.
- Upgrading existing software - both system software and application software. This may involve upgrading Windows 98 to Windows XP/Vista, or replacing an application package with the latest version number, or upgrading available network protocols.
- Updating software. Many packages come with options for regular updates, and these should be installed as soon as they are received. For example, payroll software suppliers might be contracted to supply updates with any changes to Income Tax, National Insurance etc.
- Re-installing individual files that have been corrupted or inadvertently deleted.
- Re-configuring software as required, as users needs change.
- Removing viruses from computers and restoring working applications and data.

Operational

- Carrying out any necessary I.T. staff training, including the use of hardware, a new application package, or on carrying out new office procedures using existing equipment.
- Maintaining data security. This will probably include the regular backing up of important company data, either on individual standalone machines or on the network server. It may also involve the recovery of data and files from damaged disks.
- Advising and checking on Data Protection Act guidelines, and similar legislation.
- Advising and checking on Safety at Work regulations and local safety procedures as they relate to computers.
- Running a user help desk for users in the organisation.
- Maintaining records of machine configurations, the applications on each machine, the data held on each machine, the detailed fault histories of each piece of equipment, etc.
- Maintaining inventories of IT and computing equipment.
- Developing automated procedures to assist staff, such as document templates, macros for common tasks, and mail merge systems.

The authority of Technical Support

An important concern in most organisations is deciding what authority the technical support personnel have. Computers can store sensitive data, and expensive software. The hardware can also be expensive, and organisations do not implement Information Technology for its own sake, but to improve efficiency. As a result, each organisation must decide where the authority of the technical support staff ends.
Two main issues must be addressed:

- Purchasing of goods. Every department must purchase stationary and other goods. The IT department, however, deals with potentially very expensive computer equipment, and it must be decided just how much control over the purse strings should be given to the technical support personnel. It is normally the IT department's role to purchase consumables such as printer paper and ink. Most IT departments also have their own budget to buy replacements for faulty components such as video cards or mice. In most cases, though, purchasing new IT equipment, or upgrading existing equipment, is normally controlled by the Finance department, although the IT personnel should be consulted throughout.
- Access to data. As administrators of computer systems, IT personnel potentially have access to almost any data they wish. The IT department is often charged with overseeing the implementation of the rules of the Data Protection Act, and the security of the computer systems. This does not imply that the IT department has free run of the data, particularly if personal information is being stored. It is difficult to curtail the access rights of IT staff since they must work closely with the computer system, but clear guidelines should be laid out as to the limits of their authorisation. If the organisation has a separate Support department and MIS (Management Information Systems) department, then these functions can be separated, with Support staff dealing with maintenance of the system, and MIS dealing with the data issues, such as backups and security.

Assisting users to access support

There are times when the aim is to help the users to help themselves. This usually depends on the size of the organisation. If there is an internal support group, then the management will probably wish that all problems would be directed to the group. In a small company, where there is only a small training / PC support force, they may wish to show users how to get their own help.

The most common methods are:
Peer Support
This merely entails finding someone who already has the skills in a section, to provide the basic help that is mostly required. Of course, this may involve a process of training of key individuals in departments.
Using On-Line Support
There are now a number of bulletin boards that can provide answers to problems. Some, like the Microsoft On-Line board, are run by the software house concerned while others, like the Compuserve and CIX boards, are general service boards. All that is required is a modem connection from the PC to the telephone network. The user can then dial up, log in and either read existing help pages or leave a specific question on the board. Some areas of bulletin boards are free while others are chargeable; in all cases there are telephone call charges and possibly extra connect charges.
The recent growth of Internet subscribers means that many companies and individuals have access to this international network. Many Special Interest Groups exist on the Internet and these cover all kinds of hardware and software areas. Problems that are placed in this arena will receive replies from the best minds throughout the globe. There are very few queries that go unanswered on the Internet.
Another definition of on-line help is the mass of help information that is provided within many application packages. Some Windows applications even include very detailed built-in tutorials. This is not *'on-line'* in the sense of being connected to a telephone line; however, it does provide a high degree of assistance that is always available to the user. The time spent showing users how to access this information can save a great deal of support time in the longer run.
Using a Help Desk
Help desks, unlike bulletin boards, are able to provide immediate support for a problem. Dialling the help desk number and giving a customer number provides the verbal link between the user and, hopefully, the expert in the subject area. Help desks can either be internal (i.e. run by the company itself) or external (i.e. a commercial operation).
External Help Desks
These are normally run by software suppliers (e.g. IBM, WordPerfect), user groups or software maintenance firms. Some are free for the first year; most have annual charges; at least one provides a credit service, where advanced payment covers a specified number of calls to the hot line.
Internal Help Desk
This is run by the company's own PC support team and is dedicated to the company's particular hardware and software needs. In some cases, the support staff can take control of the user's computer in order to analyse and fix the problem; the support technician can see the users screen and can alter the flow and data on the user's machine from the remote help desk console. This is particularly useful where a company has sites that are scattered from the main office.
Fault Reports
In the case of both external and internal help desks, the user has to make some preparations prior to making the call. These are:
- To save any embarrassment, check the problem against manuals. With Windows, check out the hypertext Help menus.
- Make the call when the computer is switched on and the program is running, if possible.
- Complete a report form such as the example given later.

Running A Help Desk
Running an organisation's internal help desk tends to require a broader coverage than commercial help desks, which are mostly devoted to a particular product. The help from commercial desks concentrate on support of a particular item of hardware or software, although some general help lines are available.

Aims of a Help Desk

- Curing immediate problems, maintaining productivity and protecting data/equipment.
- To improve the long-term quality of IT in the organisation, through measures such as problem prevention, user training and informed future purchasing.

The task of a help desk is to solve user problems quickly and courteously.   The technicians on the desk cannot possibly know the solution to all problems. Their job is to know where to find the solutions to all problems.   Apart from the most obvious problems (e.g. printer out of paper), the degree of spontaneous help from a support technician will be in direct proportion to the knowledge and experience of that technician.   The remainder of the help must come from an organised system of initial remote diagnosis. The technician has to work from the information supplied by the user to identify solutions.

Scope of a Help Desk

Some organisations restrict the help desk's activities to that of clearing I.T. problems.   Other organisations expect a wider role from the desk, so that it becomes the clearing house for all company gadgets such as photocopiers, fax machines, telephones, lifts, coffee machines, shredders, etc.
These pages restrict themselves to the computer role of a help desk.

Fault reporting procedures

It is useful to have well-defined procedures for reporting faults. Ad-hoc fault reporting will inevitably lead to occasional misreporting of problems, or failure to deal with faults in a timely manner. This is especially true of larger organisations. A proper procedure for dealing with faults must be established, preferably by someone with experience in IT Support. Fault reports may be in one of several forms:

- Verbal – the support staff speaks to the user experiencing the problem, normally by telephone. Assuming records are being kept, the technician should be equipped with an on-screen or paper form that will prompt him or her to ask for the necessary information to record the fault properly. Even if the incident is dealt with in full over the phone it should still be recorded.
- Paper – Many organisations still implement a paper-based fault reporting procedure. The end user must fill out the appropriate details on the Support Request form before submitting it to the support department. Not only is this proof that the fault was reported properly, but paper forms are a material reminder to technicians of tasks still needing done.
- Online – A more modern method of fault reporting is to use the computers themselves to report faults. A web-based form can be used, or an email could be sent to the support department. This has the advantages of instant reporting, and reduced effort on the user's part. These can be disadvantages, though, if the users are inclined to report every trivial incident. Also, an on-line fault report form by its very nature requires that the user can access the network, which may not be possible if the fault is network-related. Modern online systems can also provide fault tracking (described elsewhere) direct to the user so that they may check on its progress.

Designing Support Forms

User Fault report forms, whether on-line, paper based, or notes of verbal reports, should be designed with an eye to ensuring that the salient details are recorded. At its simplest level, it may be sufficient to record the nature of the fault, the date of the report, and the staff member making the report. However, if any sort of fault tracking or quality assurance is to be practised, there will also need to be details of progress towards resolving the fault.

There may well be more than one type of form for use. For example, a small organisation might distribute Support Request forms to their users, who are expected to hand in these forms to the support department. Businesses that implement a Help Desk to provide phone support might accept Support Requests as well as producing a Fault Report form for every call dealt with.

Of course, the name and appearance given to the forms varies from place to place. In general, though, forms used to track the progress of Help Desk calls should include:

- A reference number. This can be selected by a call logging package, and in an automated system will allow quick viewing of faults reported, and their current status.
- Date and time the fault was reported. This should also identify the support staff member who received the fault report, if it was taken by phone.
- Contact details of the person reporting the fault. In-house support technicians could simply record the person's name, department, room number and extension number.   Third-party

support technicians may need full contact details: for example the contact's address is needed if technicians are to be called out to the site. However, this might be available from the company's customer records.

- Fault description. This should include a description of the system that has developed a fault, such as its location, machine number or serial number in case of users with access to multiple machines; as well as details of the fault's symptoms.
- Steps taken towards fault resolution. The form should record actions taken by technical support, identifying the members of staff who took these actions, and the date and time of such actions. This is important in insuring quality of service, especially when supplying third-party support, where technicians must adhere to SLAs. If the fault is resolved over the phone during the initial call, this should be recorded and the duration of the call logged.
- Third-party involvement. Often, faulty equipment can be returned to the supplier or manufacturer for replacement if it is under warranty. Also, some specialised repairs may need an item to be sent off to another third party. The fault report form should note these details: sending off faulty components for replacement does not resolve the problem, fitting the replacement when it arrives is the actual date of resolution.

Third-party user support departments should keep close track of the time taken to resolve the fault, how much downtime was incurred, costs of repair, and so on, to make sure of correct billing. On the other hand Service Level Agreements and contract details could be useful to ensure the customer is receiving the appropriate level of care.

The fault report form is more useful to the technician on site if it includes details of the computer hardware and system software, but not all users can be expected to be computer literate enough to provide full details. Maintaining of a database of client systems could be of use in this regard.

The following are sample Support Request and Fault Report forms.

User Support Request Form

		Date	
		Time	
Make		Model	
Location		On network?	
List of add-ons			
Software including version number			
Outline of Problem State as succinctly and clearly as possible; when does problem arise - what stage in program/process			
Any error messages			

Fault report form

Reference number		Date of report	
User name		Time of report	
Department		Date of resolution	
Extension number		Time of resolution	
Receiving technician			

Symptoms of fault	

System details

Machine number		Room number	
Base unit description		Operating System	
Additional Peripherals		Other relevant software	

Third parties

Time and date sent	Name of company	Reference number	Time and date received

Support activity

Time and date	Name of technician	Action taken	Outcome

Call management

Any large IT Help Desk that operates by phone should implement some form of call management. Smaller Help Desks might operate from a single office, meaning they could easily pass calls to the relevant person if they themselves do not know how to deal with an incident. In a Help Desk of any appreciable size, however, this is not an effective solution. There is a variety of call management software solutions available, however, some of them tailored for in-house Help Desks while others are intended for external Help Desks. A good call management application should keep track of any specialised skills the available personnel possess, so that calls may be routed to the appropriate person. Call management software often contains fault tracking and escalation functionality and reporting software as well as being able to direct incoming calls.

Help Desk technicians using Call Management should be able to access a database of clients, either external bodies or internal departments, and a list of details such as SLA agreements, service history, special requirements and so on. After briefly discussing the fault, the technician can then either deal with it, or use the software to find who is the appropriate person to pass the call on to.

Call logging packages

This software is created for use on help desks and provides the following facilities:

- Call logging; each call is recorded and saved.
- Call prioritising; the order of the queue of callers can be altered to match the estimated severity of the fault and the seniority of the person complaining.
- Call tracking; used where a fault is not cleared in the one call.

Support records

Keeping adequate records of Support Requests and Fault Reports is important, in order to ensure that individual requests and faults are dealt with in a timely manner. Well-kept records can facilitate additional services, though, such as *'fault tracking'*, and analysis of the support provided.

Installation records

It is usually useful to keep records on computer systems right from the start. Whenever a new system is installed, it is advisable to keep records of the installation settings, configuration of the equipment, and all tests performed on new equipment. This will often facilitate faultfinding since details of machine hardware and software will be to hand. Furthermore, these records may prove useful in auditing, and upgrading of systems.

Fault tracking

As the name suggests, this is a procedure whereby information on individual faults is kept. This is often used to report on the status of problems being investigated, but it also has additional uses. It can be used for information to measure the support department's efficiency against the Service Level Agreement, and control the fault escalation procedures explained previously.

A number of software-based fault tracking systems are available. Due to the wide-ranging nature of technical support, these come in a variety of forms. For example, some systems implement a web-based fault tracking system, while those organisations that have in-house support might prefer a more private, network-based fault tracking system.

It may well prove useful to keep track of the end-user's use of computer resources, for the purposes of determining user needs as well as aiding in diagnosing problems that arise. A simple questionnaire on important parts of the computer system can reveal basic trends in computer use, but proper logs are required for in-depth examination of resource usage or diagnosis of particularly troublesome faults.

Support logs such as the Support Requests and Fault Reports mentioned above are part of this logging process, but other logs can be of use, such as the Event Logs and audit information available in many modern operating systems, and any logs that may be generated by user software. In a network system, access logs (a record of those remote systems that have accessed the server) can also be of great use.

Prioritising requests

While it is possible to prioritise incoming calls, this is rarely encouraged. Instead, support requests that require additional attention should be prioritised. Again, an ad-hoc solution is workable only for the smallest of Help Desks, and even then is a flawed method.

Support requests may be prioritised on several levels, but the main priorities include:

- Person making the request. While this may at first sound unfair, it is sometimes the case that some staff members can get on with some aspects of their work without access to a computer, while others rely completely on information technology. It therefore makes sense to identify those users with greater needs and give them priority. In an external Help Desk, the client that requests technical support may still be prioritised, by means of determining which client has the more significant SLA agreement.
- Severity of fault. While some users require less access to computer equipment, it is nonetheless important to fix major faults in them. For example, a user whose machine develops a hard disk fault should be rectified as soon as possible in case further loss of data occurs, even if the user would normally be considered lower priority.
- Time the request was made. Regardless of other factors, the Help Desk should strive to fix requests as quickly as possible. If a user is kept waiting for their fault to be resolved, it reflects poorly on the Help Desk. A good prioritisation system will take into account how long a user has been waiting for support.

Service Level Agreements

Another factor in the provided support level is the Service Level Agreement or SLA agreed between the service organisation and the user. This model applies as much for an internal market within an organisation as it does for a 'real' user/vendor arrangement. It specifies the user responsibilities. It also specifies the service obligations in terms of response times, down times, schedules work, security, etc.

A typical SLA works in an increasing severity of a fault. Firstly, an *'incident'* is reported to the helpdesk, usually by telephone. If the helpdesk cannot get to the root of the 'incident' within a set time, say 30 minutes, then the '*incident'* is escalated to a *'fault'*. At this point a technician is despatched to hopefully cure the *'fault'*.

If the *'fault'* persists beyond the technicians visit then further escalation takes the *'fault'* to a *'problem'*, and so on. The SLA will typically guarantee the user against more than a certain number of faults per annum before service costs are levied, and different customers will negotiate different Service Level Agreements. Service Level Agreements, and how rarely customers incur additional service costs, are often quoted as major selling points by service organisations.

Support Level

The level of response and problem resolution for any user depends upon the importance of that user's work and the table shows typical examples:

User category	Type of work	Response Time
Occasional	Any non-essential or irregular user	Next-day or later
Regular	Typist, programmer, graphics designer	Same-day
Essential	Process control, medical, financial	Measured in hours or even minutes

This gives an indication for the needs of any given user. However, the support department must also take into account just how many computer users they will have to provide support for, and also how computer-literate those staff are. From such information, a new or developing support department can evaluate the amount of assistance it will have to provide, so that it can be determined how many of each type of support staff are needed.

Not all support staff are on-site technicians. The 'front desk' may be a call desk, email-based task system, or simply a collection point for support requests, but the skills needed for a front desk call manager are quite different from those needed of a 'second level' support technician.

Front desk support staff should be knowledgeable in dealing with people who may be frustrated and annoyed, as well as general support duties, while second-level technicians must be able to correct faults at the source, often requiring more in-depth knowledge of the hardware and/or software.

The analysis of user numbers, categories, and expected number of calls should allow the support department to gage the need for various levels of support staff, as well as identify areas in which training for support staff may be required.

Support provision analysis

Support records can be used to provide reports on the quality of service given. The provision of regular reports should be written in to any given SLA, so that the customer is informed of how well (or how poorly) the support department is meeting its SLA obligations.

Support inadequacies

Failures to meet the standards laid out in a SLA agreement are easily identified when proper records are kept. This can take many forms: support not being available at times specified in the SLA; failure to fully resolve support requests within an adequate timeframe; inability to resolve support requests relating to specific types of equipment; failure to provide the correct form of support (on-site, back-to-base, or swap-out); reduced levels of support when multiple requests are handled; greater downtime than allowed for in the SLA; and so on. Such reports are not only for the customer's benefit – either the support department should use the information to improve services to a level that they meet the agreement, or the SLA should be renegotiated.

Identifying support trends

Careful examination of support requests can reveal certain recurring themes. Individual users, or even entire departments, may have a tendency to report certain types of problems. Recurring problems with a specific computer system could be identified, or a widespread occurrence of a particular problem over various machines.

Detecting such trends in support can help technicians to recognise areas that may require improvement, and formulate recommendations to improve the quality of support provided, or reduce the need for support in the first place. For example, a user or department that often report a particular type of problem can indicate that appropriate training will reduce problems and therefore reduce the need for support. Recurring problems on a single machine could indicate that the machine requires complete reinstallation or even replacement, while widespread problems might be solved by installing updated versions of software on the network.

Identifying Problems

A large part of the PC support technician's life is spent handling *'non-routine conditions'* with hardware and software. This term describes any situation where the system does not perform as expected. This can vary from the keyboard *'hanging up'* to smoke belching from the system unit! From a user point of view, most problems are perceived as hardware faults whether the hardware or the software is at fault. For example, a user report that *'the printer won't work properly'* could be traced to a lost software printer driver or user inexperience with the application package.

The technician has to determine whether the complaint is of a hardware or software variety. This will often have to be diagnosed through effective questioning techniques, since the user will often blame the hardware for many software or user errors. There will usually be more hardware than software faults and always more operator errors than any other fault category. The questions asked allow the technician to determine the likely cause of the problem. Many problems are of a minor nature. Probably around a third of calls could be saved by training users in the basics of Windows and its applications. Possibly another third are *'printer out of paper'* or *'printer off line'* type of problems - i.e. problems that can be diagnosed and made good without a technician's visit to the actual machine. Of course, it is difficult to judge whether a user knows the answers to the questions being asked, since user understanding will vary enormously. If the organisation is sufficiently compact, it pays to get to know the users because this provides a basis on which to judge how much to trust their information. In large organisations, it may pay to have complaints routed through a section contact (the most computer-literate person in the section) so that the help desk becomes familiar with the contact and his/her capabilities.

But the support technician's task is not solely about fault diagnosis and elimination. The technician has to work to a company code, which probably includes the following principles:

- Providing a prompt response to user requests.
- Using a systematic method to diagnose faults.
- Evaluating down time of systems.
- Keeping records on hardware and software.
- Being economic with resources.
- Ensuring safe practices.
- Ensuring legal practices.

Providing a prompt response
The response to user complaints has to be as prompt as possible for the following reasons:

- To safeguard the health and safety of the workforce or the public.
- To reduce user frustration.
- To reduce machine downtime and maintain user productivity.
- To minimise the possibility of further damage to equipment or data.

The fault report form should include a section for the date and time of receiving the complaint. It should also contain an entry for the time of the first attendance and an entry for the time the fault was cleared. This is important to maintain a record of the efficiency of the support section. For office sites that are remote from the head office, an early response might be an initial phone call to identify the symptoms and suggest any simple remedies, with problem faults being attended to by as early a visit as is practical.

Evaluating down time
Once a fault is diagnosed, the user will require an evaluation of the likely downtime of the machine. All users will be eager to know how long the machine will be out of action and managers may wish to move employees to other jobs where a substantial delay is expected. In extreme cases, such as waiting for

replacement parts, another machine may have to be allocated and the backup disks from the faulty machine used to restore files to the replacement machine, in order to maintain office productivity.   An organisation's maintenance strategy will often contain response time and problem resolution time targets.

Factors in evaluating down time
- Does the company have a maintenance contract?
- If so, is it a 24-hour response contract?   Bear in mind that the response time is the time elapsing before a <u>visit</u> and not necessarily the time elapsing before a <u>repair</u>.   It is not uncommon for on-site technicians to take the machine back to their workshop for repair. The initial visit may be on site but the repair may still be carried out remotely.   This only happens when the fault is complex and therefore it may well involve waiting for parts, thus further delaying the machine's return to active service.   Press the visiting engineer for a realistic estimate of the time the machine will be gone.
- Is the problem affecting occasional, regular or essential users?
- If not maintained externally, is it a hardware or a software problem?
  IF HARDWARE:
  - Is the equipment under guarantee?
  - If guaranteed, is it a return to base guarantee?   The time taken to pack the faulty item and the delivery times adds to the delay in getting it back into service.
  - If guarantee is a site visit, what is the response time? Similar factors to those for maintenance contracts apply here (i.e. repair not be within time of first visit).
  - If not maintained externally, are there established sources of supply of replacement components; are the most commonly used replacement components (network cards, cables, etc.) kept in stock?

  Most hardware faults, apart from cables, mice, keyboards, etc., produce longer down times, caused by site visit delays or waiting for parts, etc.
  IF SOFTWARE:
  - Is it a machine configuration problem (e.g. incorrect settings, missing files, damaged Registry, etc.)?   For the experienced support technician, these difficulties are generally easily cured and the down time is therefore not significant.
  - Is it an application problem?   This could include simple user errors in using the package or tricky interrupt problems between different programs. The latter may take some time to resolve; the former may take even longer, since user training may be required.

Keeping an inventory
Every support group has a responsibility to maintain a current database of the organisation's hardware and software, down to individual machine level.   This should include case histories of all problems encountered on each machine. This is important to track recurring or developing problems and thus prevent future difficulties.   The data kept by a support group or help desk (see later) should be collected as part of a hardware and software 'audit'.
Items in an audit should include:

- The manufacturer, model, serial number of each computer in use.
- Details of hard disk types (i.e. IDE, UDMA 66, UDMA 100, SCSI or FireWire) and capacity.
- Details of floppy drive quantity, type and capacity (e.g. two 3.5" 1.4MB drives).
- Details of motherboard adaptor slots - number and type (e.g. ISA, PCI, AGP).
- The manufacturer, model, and serial number of each piece of ancillary equipment in use (e.g. printers, modems, plotters).
- The location of each item of equipment within the building.
- Any restrictions on access to the equipment (e.g. is computer in security room requiring special permission for access).
- Purchase date of equipment and details of guarantee and any maintenance agreements.

- Copies of the CMOS settings of each machine. Ideally these should be disk copies for easy restoration (using a CMOS saving/restoration utility). As a minimum, there should be manually recorded details, particularly of the hard disk drive parameters).
- Copies of each machine's configuration files. This includes the Windows Registry, INI files, and sometimes AUTOEXEC.BAT and CONFIG.SYS.
- Details of the cards fitted to each machine, including their purpose (e.g. scanner or fax card), manufacturer, model and serial numbers.
- Details of any hardware settings such as DIP switches or jumper settings on the motherboards and cards.
- Copies of all installation guides, hardware manuals and technical notes.
- Master copies of all the installation disks.
- Details of all the software used on the machine.
- Copies of all software master disks or CDs.
- Where practical, the original packing and anti-static storage bags, for the easier packing and return of faulty equipment.
- Details of the service history of each item of equipment.

It can be a time-consuming operation to collect data and document the entire existing system in an organisation. Because of this, the process may be best undertaken as part of a rolling programme. Each new purchase may automatically be documented at installation time, while each existing item may only be recorded at the time of a repair or as part of a major equipment service. Although tedious, this system pays dividends in the long run. The software audit ensures that future purchase requirements are more accurately identified. The hardware audit also aids future purchasing decisions and also prevents a whole range of potential difficulties - e.g. highlighting potential address clashes or IRQ clashes between existing and proposed new cards on a motherboard. The storing of copies of configuration information (CMOS settings, CONFIG.SYS, WIN.INI, Registry, etc.) can greatly speed up the restoration of a machine that has had its configuration inadvertently altered or deleted.

Personal Workbooks

It is good practice to keep a personal logbook, over and above any paperwork that is required by the manufacturer. Such a book will usually be hardbound and lined on one side only, with alternate pages left for sketches, diagrams, flowcharts and the like. As work is overtaken, detailed notes are made of equipment, configurations, observations, procedures and so on. There are various reasons for this.

- A lab-book can save the busy technician time by letting him/her quickly revisit an earlier chain of thought, without having to work through the case again.
- Good records let someone else take over a task if the original technician is on holiday, sick leave, or leaves the organisation for another job.
- Personal record books can also give valuable 'black box' information if a major incident occurs
- If personal records are well enough kept then the problematic equipment that keeps coming through the section can be identified and weeded.

The economics of PC Support work

Technically minded people have an affinity for the equipment that they are working with, and tend to want to repair equipment "no matter what". However, it is an unfortunate fact of life that all PC support work takes place within an organisation, which must perform economically, in order to survive. As a result, all PC support work must be financially viable. A competent support person must be aware of his/her own costs to his/her organisation, and be prepared to leave a solvable problem unsolved if it would cost his customer or his organisation too much to proceed. In establishing this *economic cut off point* for a repair, the costs of doing the repair must be weighed up against the cost of simply declaring the repair uneconomical and replacing the equipment.

Equipment, whose repair is deemed uneconomic, is said to be "written off". In general, this means that the equipment is removed from the organisation's inventories of assets, and usually its cost is declared to be lost. This accords with the terms of the practice of most organisations, whereby capital equipment like Information Technology is said to be amortised over a period of perhaps 5 years. This means that it is assumed for accounting purposes that the equipment loses 20% of its value each year over the first 5 years, after which it is considered to be worthless. Thus, a piece of equipment that has had light use and is still "as new" after 5 years might be technically entirely worthless. Because of the rapid pace of developments in PC technology, capital equipment on IT budgets is often amortised over 3 year periods or less. PC support personnel must be aware of the amortisation policy of the organisation that owns the equipment they are working on.

Replacing faulty components

As mentioned above, components or even whole systems may become uneconomic to repair. It is normally the technician's job to decide which systems are worth repair and which must be replaced. Replacement, of course, means the technician will have to install a new system, peripheral or upgrade, and in most cases this is identical to installing the item in the first place. For example, when replacing a faulty video card, the technician should follow all the same safety guidelines as if they were installing a new video card upgrade – see the chapter on *'Hardware Installation'* for details.

Financially, however, replacement must be justified. Every large company has a purchasing policy, and even an IT department that has its own budget has to take care not to overstretch its finances. Purchase of replacement IT components should be done in the same way as other capital items. For example, a replacement mouse, being of low cost, might be a routine matter, authorised by someone within the IT department. Purchasing a replacement for a faulty laser printer could be expensive, and may require the go-ahead from a separate Finance department.

Statistics of Equipment Failure

It is a fact of life that all equipment fails eventually. It is part of good practice to understand the ways in which equipment fails and to learn to recognise the so-called *'failure modes'*. Much has been written elsewhere on this subject and many resources are available. Among the failure modes to be aware of are:

*   Wear Failures. These are where equipment is subject to some force or action that causes its gradual erosion. Screen phosphors wear, paper path components and heads on printers wear, and fans and moving parts wear.
*   Cycling Failures. Some components will fail after going through a set cycle a large number of times. Switches, for example will happily work hundreds of thousands of cycles before becoming faulty. Note that cycling failures are very like wear failures except that wear is constant, whilst cycling is discrete.
*   Catastrophic Failures. Some components fail suddenly, often by design. Fuses are designed to operate in catastrophic failure modes, and some power supplies will fail catastrophically under stress to protect more expensive components elsewhere in the system.
*   Out of Spec Failures. Another common failure mode is when a component goes out of its stated specification range. A semiconductor device might be rated to perform for years at a set frequency. If the frequency is increased then the semiconductor overheats and shortens its own life expectancy. The practice of *'overclocking'* CPUs often leads to such failures.
*   Misuse Failures. Closely related to Out of Spec Failures are failures induced by abuse of the component. If a computer system box is used on a cushioned surface that blocks ventilation slots, then the temperature rises due to the restricted flow of air and eventually cause a failure. Misuse failures often need to be dealt with very tactfully. Helping a user to understand how they were involved in a fault may need a lot of diplomacy
*   Inservice failures. The final and most common failure mode is simple inservice failure. If an item of equipment is used for long enough it will suffer inservice failure, although the definition of 'long enough' may run to hundreds of years.

Studies have shown that most electronic equipment has a 'life' expectancy that can be characterised as follows: Suppose a large number of some device (think light bulbs) was subject to identical conditions. Some would fail almost immediately because they were not very well made.(1) This is referred to as *'infant mortality'* and can be eliminated by *'soak testing'* for a period before being put into service. There then follows a long time when practically no units fail.(2) This is called the working life of the product. Eventually there comes a time when the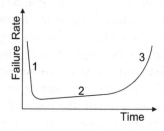
units will all start to wear out, and gradually the failure rate will increase.(3) This wear out phase ends when all of the units have failed. If the failure rate is plotted against time then the resulting curve looks like the graph illustrated. Such a graph is called a bathtub curve because of its characteristic shape.

Mean Time Between Failures

For any given component the average life is the time when 50% of a large sample of the components have failed. This is often called the Mean Time Between Failures or MTBF. Because of the shape of the bathtub curve, the mean time before failure is usually on the wearout phase, and so gives an indication of expected component lifetime

Mean Time To Service

Another quoted measure of system reliability is the Mean Time To Service or MTTS. This is weighted average of the MTBFs of all of the individual components in a system and represents the average time expected to elapse before some component or other fails.

Availability

Another oft-quoted statistic is the *'availability'* for a system. This is a measure of what percentage of the time the system is available. So, a server may be guaranteed to offer 99.9% availability, which means the manufacturer hopes it will be unavailable for less than 8 hours per year. 99.99% availability is the promise of less than 50mins per year downtime, or more realistically 8 hours per decade.

Aids to diagnosis

- Use an inventory of the organisation's computing system; know what software and hardware is on the reported machine - just by asking for the machine's identification code. Apart from diagnosis, this can be an aid to maintaining the office's normal operations. For example, if a machine has to be withdrawn to await spare parts, it can't be replaced by any other machine - account must be taken of any particular cards that may be inside the problem machine. Replacing the machine might otherwise lose the office its modem link or its fax connection.
- Use a remote access system to the user's computer. This is extremely useful in a largely dispersed organisation with computer sites remote from the help desk. Remote control software allows the help desk to link one of its computers to the computer at the remote site via modems. With this software, the help desk monitor will also display whatever the remote user is seeing. Even more important, the desk keyboard will act as if it were an additional keyboard on the remote computer. This way, the help desk technician can take full control of the remote system to examine many of its hardware aspects and all of its software aspects. Examples of this remote control software are Laplink Remote Assist, PCI Net Support Manager, Carbon Copy Solution and PCAnywhere.
- Consult the machine's previous case history. Use this information to detect a possible recurring fault or a developing problem. This also allows the desk to discover the most common faults, both within company and on any particular machine.

Help Desk Resources

As stated earlier, the help desk has to be the source of all knowledge and experience. The resources have to be built up to make this possible and the desk should not rely on the expertise stored in the head of an experienced technician. Fortunately, a number of different resources are available to build up the desk's reference abilities. These include:

- All hardware and software audit records as previously outlined.
- All software and hardware manuals and technical guides.
- Previous case histories of all equipment.
- Statistical records previously compiled from the above.
- Use of suppliers' and dealers' support lines.
- Use of consultants for major difficulties.
- Specially commissioned diagnostic packages as described later.
- Proprietary logging packages as described later.
- Technical information from various sources, as described below.

Technical data sources

In the rapidly changing computer world, computer and I.T. specialists require a constantly updated reference base. Such a reference base could consist of:

- Bought-in training material, such as training videos.
- Textbooks. These are widely available and often explore beyond the user manuals.

- Manuals. Despite being much maligned, often deservedly, manuals have an important role to play in providing the detail required on any one command or activity.
- Printouts from Internet news groups' on-line help sessions.   There are many news groups where queries can be placed and speedy answers received. Some of these are provided by software houses.   This can be a valuable source, since a problem experienced in one workplace has probably also been experienced and solved somewhere else.
- User Group newsletters, magazines and notes from group meetings. For the same reason as above, membership of user groups is advisable.   Most subject areas are covered and there are groups for Microsoft Application users, Windows users, Novell users, PhotoShop users, and many more. These are not hobbyists' clubs (although individual membership is accepted) and are usually composed of representatives from private companies, local authorities, health boards, etc.
- Notes taken during suppliers' on-line help sessions.   Many software and hardware suppliers run their own help desks and this issue is covered later.   However, the notes taken when on the telephone to these 'hot-lines' provide a useful insight into the workings of the particular package system and should be stored for future reference.   A standard form can be produced for this purpose.
- Notes taken from attendance at training courses.
- Computer magazines.   Subscriptions should be arranged for a range of magazines, after careful scrutiny of their general contents.   The best magazines provide cover of both hardware and software issues, although some specialise (in Unix, for example).   These are mostly monthly productions.   Typical contents include:
  - Product reviews, both of new hardware and new software. Hardware reviews generally provide performance benchmarks, so that different products can be compared. Software reviews provide a roundup of the packages' facilities in comparison to similar products from competitors.
  - Technological trends.   This can prove especially useful in aiding future planning of I.T. provision; planned spending on upgrades and extensions might be delayed awaiting the introduction of better systems.
  - 'How to' articles.   These cover issues as diverse as 'how to plan your network' and 'how to create macros in Word'.   These articles tend to present ideas in a popular way and can be either basic or advanced.
  - 'How things work' articles.   Similar to the above, usually with lots of helpful illustrations and diagrams.
  - Hints and tips. These sections may be categorised under database, spreadsheet, DTP, etc. headings, or there may be general sections.   Many useful small hints are available, some of which are not documented in the Windows manual, package manual or other source.

  Over a period of time, the shelves will begin to creak with the accumulated volumes of such magazines.   Finding a particular article requires a reference system to be built up. Maintaining this system is cumbersome and accessing data is slow. A more useful approach may be to simply cut out the articles and file them in cardboard wallets or boxes under appropriate headings.   For example, all articles on computer networking could be stored in a separate wallet, as with material on spreadsheet macros, Windows tips and so on.   In that way, all the material on a certain subject is easily accessed. The only overhead is the time spent breaking down the magazine into the wallets.
- Printouts of all help text files that are supplied with application packages and with hardware driver disks, etc.   These might be README.TXT or similarly named ASCII files and they provide up-to-date additions and modifications to the manuals.   They often cover known bugs and hardware clashes.   There are also a number of Windows files in .WRI format. And, of course, the many help pages in Windows applications are capable of being printed out; this means that the most frequently accessed help pages can be printed out and compiled into a separate booklet or included in wallets with similar information.
- Technical information on CD-ROM as supplied by some software houses.
- Trade papers.   These are weekly or monthly publications and are either general in nature or cover specialised areas such as local area networks or data communications.

Customised support packages

These are packages that are built to order and can cover specific software or hardware, or both. These packages are expensive but they address the specific needs of a support desk that may not be covered in general-release products. These are based on expert systems and lead the desk technician through the likely symptoms for different faults. If the organisation has staff with programming skills, then packages such as these can also be developed in-house.

Staff training

Staff need some knowledge to operate IT equipment properly. It is possible to ensure that any new employees have at least basic computing knowledge before being taken on, but every organisation upgrades to new software eventually, and existing employees will require training when this happens. The organisation can send employees to external training companies, but in many cases, it is the job of the in-house support department to provide training. This may be to reduce costs, or because the organisation uses proprietary software in which no external group can provide training.

Planning staff training

While being able to use the software is obviously important, an employee's time is valuable to the organisation he or she works for. A support department that provides training must aim to do so when it is convenient to the users, and not the other way around. The support staff should liase with managers and any other personnel concerned in order to work out a viable time scale for any large scale training programmes. If there are fewer staff, or if just a few new employees need to be trained, then there will probably be more room for timetabling the training.

Of course, if a company provides training to external organisations, such communication may not be possible. If the client has a large number of people to train with an external organisation, it is normally the client's responsibility to discuss with personnel the times that training should take place, and then negotiate with the training company. If there are fewer people to be trained, then the organisation may have no choice but to send them to attend an open seminar at a time set by the external training company.

Providing staff training

A detailed guide to the provision of training is beyond the scope of this book. However, the support personnel should take into account such factors as the current level of knowledge of the audience, as well as the level of training required. There is usually no need to train users in every detail of every function of the software they are using, but at the same time users will quickly grow tired of being taught how to use a mouse if they are already regular users of Windows software.

Simple demonstrations are usually the easiest and most effective way of training, and there are a variety of ways to do this. The simplest is just to ask the audience to watch the trainer perform an activity. However, a computer with an overhead projector would be more convenient, and better still there are a number of network training applications available that allow everyone in a class to see what the trainer is doing, on their own monitor.

Other effective aids to staff training include handouts, evaluation and feedback forms. The trainer should consider techniques such as demonstrations, presentations, practical exercises, individual tuition, and ongoing evaluation, as the application of training techniques will depend to a large extent on the personnel being trained.

Support staff training

An occasionally overlooked aspect of staff training in IT is that of training the support staff themselves. Information and Computer Technology is constantly evolving, and support staff should be well versed in the current state of the art. Planning the training of support staff is subject to the same timetabling concerns as planning for other members of staff. However, it can be more difficult to plan effectively, since support staff could be needed at any time if a fault develops. As such, in-house training can be more flexible, and the expensive option of bringing in external training groups can be avoided if the company is willing to accept the possibility of delays if faults do develop while technicians are not available. Of course, staggering the training will reduce the number of technicians away on training at any one time, but this may be small comfort if the number of support staff is small to begin with.

Ensuring Safe Practices

There are two separate issues involved:

- Safe practices as applied to users.
- Safe practices as applied to support staff.

Safe User Practices

The organisation should be raising user awareness on issues of safe working practice. Since support staff will spot many user deficiencies in this area, much of the direct input on good practice will come from technicians. The serious issues of staff's physical safety and well-being are covered later in this chapter. This leaves the instilling of good practice on equipment and data handling.

Good practice issues include:

- Cold Starts. Never use a computer that has been standing for a long time in a cold environment without first waiting until it has reached a normal room temperature. Writing to cold hard disks, which have been slightly reduced in dimension as a consequence, could result in data loss.
- Maintaining the machine's environment. No smoking, eating or drinking at the computer.
- Moisture. Similarly, a machine which been exposed to a moist atmosphere should be given time to normally dry out before being put into use. Placing voltages on damp circuitry is risking component breakdown as well as data loss.
- Viruses. All staff should appreciate the problems that can be caused by bringing in and using pirate software and be fully aware of any penalty that the company may impose on employees found bringing in or using virused software.
- Disk Handling. All staff should understand and implement rudimentary rules on handling floppy disks to prevent data loss (see section on disks and drives).
- Reporting any problems. The first person to detect any problem with a machine is the user. Users should be encouraged to report all problems, even those where there is uncertainty as to whether a fault actually exists. A quick call to the support room or the help desk will soon clear up whether the user is misusing the equipment or whether a problem is developing on the equipment.

Safe Technician Practices

The technician's good practice list is identical to those of the users with the addition of others particular to his/her job. These should include:

- Obtain training on manual handling procedures, to protect against back and other injuries when lifting and carrying heavy objects such as workstations, monitors and printers.
- Use proper tools. Using the same screwdriver for all jobs risks personal safety and can damage equipment. Use the proper tool for the job and always carry around a tool set composed of:
  - Box spanners. This is a preferred method of removing the screws that secure the computer's cover, power supply, expansion cards, etc. Using a screwdriver, particularly one of inadequate size, can chew up the head's slot, resulting in the whole screw having to be drilled out to remove it. Additionally, screwdrivers are prone to slip from the head's slot. This can have dire consequences such as scoring the computer's outer case, technicians stabbing themselves with the screwdriver or the screwdriver plunging though another component. With the box spanner, the screw head is held much more tightly and the chance of damaging the screw or other items is negligible.
  - Small and medium sized screwdrivers. If a DIP switch requires having its settings altered, a small screwdriver is ideal. For larger jobs, discard the small screwdriver and use the one up to the size of the task. Using too small a screwdriver can damage both the screw head being worked on as well as damaging the screwdriver itself.
  - Phillips head screwdriver. This is often used as an alternative to box spanners where the screw head is of the X-slot Phillips type. This is probably a slightly less safe method than a box spanner but has a lot more grip than a standard slot screwdriver. Where the screw has a rounded Phillips head, this screwdriver has to be used.
  - IC extraction/insertion tools. The pins of ICs (integrated circuit) chips are very fragile and are very easily bent or broken. Always attempt to use the specially designed tools for extracting and inserting chips. These are designed to remove chips in a straight upward motion to avoid pins being bent. Prising the chip's end with a screwdriver removes the chip by bending it in its connector and risks damage to the pins. If a pin becomes bent, an attempt to straighten it with a pair of fine pliers often results in the pins snapping off. An

IC insertion tool is designed to ensure that a chip's pins are all lined up correctly with the chip's holder. It also ensures that an even pressure is applied to the chip when it is being inserted into its holder.

- o A pair of fine pliers. These are useful in changing jumper settings and recovering screws that may fall into the computer case.
- o A multimeter. This can perform a range of tests such as checking the continuity of wires in a cable, checking fuses, checking that an earth point is actually at earth potential, checking that the voltage output of a power supply is within the tolerance range allows for a motherboard, etc.
- o A logic probe. The pins of the chips on the motherboard can be at earth potential, supply potential, high impedance or pulsing. While the multimeter displays high and low voltages, it cannot detect very fast pulses. The logic probe is placed on a chip pin or a motherboard track and detects a single-shot pulse or a regular pulse. The probe uses a set of LEDs to indicate the state of location being tested. See 'testing hardware' later in this chapter.

- Familiarise yourself with Safety laws, as covered later in the chapter.
- Read the equipment's safety notes, before starting a particular job.
- Never add or remove a card while a motherboard is powered up. In both cases there is a point when part of the card's edge connector is making contact with the socket on the motherboard, while other parts of the card's connector are unconnected. This could easily result in chips on the card being blown and having to be replaced.
- Never force cards into expansion slots or force connectors together. If there is a particular difficulty, check that the card is free to be slotted in - i.e. there is no debris in the expansion slot and its blanking plate and retaining screw have been removed. With cables, check that they are being aligned properly. Most cables terminate in plugs that have keys to ensure that they are only entered in the correct way round.

Electro-Static Discharge (ESD)

The electrostatic charge on the body can rise to several thousand volts and can wreak havoc on any chip that is touched, either directly or by touching part of the card or motherboard. For this reason, cards should always be left in their anti-static packing until required. When removed from the bag, they should be handled as little as possible and only be held by an edge that has little or no etched tracks.

Static build up can be prevented by the wearing of a static earthing band. This attaches to the technician's wrist and has a wire that earths the body to mains earth. The wire must contain a resistor of at least 1MegOhm to limit the current if live mains happens to be touched by the wearer. These can be purchased by mail order or from large computer stores such as PC World. Do not make up a simple wire connection between wrist and earth, as this can prove fatal if a live connection is accidentally touched.

Some also advocate leaving the computer's mains cable plugged in but switched off at the mains. Since the mains switch does not actually switch the earth connection, the earth is always connected through to the chassis of the computer. This allows the user to touch the chassis and dissipate any static charges prior to handling cards or components. Of course, this leaves open the possibility that the wall switch might accidentally be thrown. A kettle cable can be made for the job by having the live and neutral connections removed at the plug end. This special cable then earths the equipment safely with no danger of mains reaching the computer.

Technician benches are used regularly for repairing and upgrading computer systems. A more systematic approach to static dissipation can be organised in these situations. A conductive bench mat is available and this is attached to earth so that any equipment placed on the bench is kept static-free. Additional static protection is available by fitting a conductive floor mat and staff can be supplied with special smocks and shoes with conductive spikes.

Safe storage and disposal of components

When a card or other electronic component is installed, it is often a good idea to keep the anti-static bag, so that if it is ever removed and placed into storage, it can be kept safely. However, the component should always be placed *inside* the bag, and not on top of it, since static may still be able to build up on the outer surface of some bags (most anti-static bags only have the inside coated).

For longer term storage, components should ideally be kept in a temperature controlled environment. Excessive heat and moisture can be damaging, but excessive cold or dryness can cause static, which is equally damaging.

Items such as cases, keyboards, and printers are relatively simple to store since they have few or no exposed circuitry. Nonetheless, they must be stored safely: they cannot be simply piled on the floor, but should be kept in a dedicated storage area, with sufficient space. Batteries for laptops may have precise temperature ranges for storage, but no batteries should ever be stored long term in case of leakage.

Proper disposal of components can be trickier. In particular, there are certain items that pose a potential danger if not disposed of in the proper manner. Batteries, for example, contain hazardous chemicals, and cleaning fluids such as isopropyl alcohol are also potential hazards. The Environmental Protection Act of 1990 states that any organisation must have a *"Person Responsible"* for the safe disposal of waste. This person is to ensure that no hazardous waste escapes, and also to arrange transport to the appropriate waste disposal facility. It is an offence for an unlicensed organisation to transport potentially hazardous waste. The Person Responsible must provide an accurate description of the waste.

Employees and employers also have obligations according to COSHH (Control of Substances Hazardous to Health). Risk assessment must be carried out (explained later), to prevent or control risks from substances. The employer must maintain, test, and keep records about the testing of the appropriate safety equipment. Exposure to chemicals must be monitored, and health surveillance carried out as necessary. Information regarding hazardous substances in use must be supplied to employees.

The employee must use the appropriate protective equipment, and control measures, as well as presenting themselves for health surveillance. Employers must perform risk assessment (explained later), take action to prevent exposure to chemicals, keep appropriate protective equipment and control measures, keep records of all tests.

Chemicals should never be disposed of into the sink, and throwing batteries in the bin is environmentally unsound. They should be taken to the local Waste Disposal Centre to be dealt with properly. If in doubt, standard documents called Material Safety Data Sheets (MSDS) list a wide range of properties for any given chemical, and thus can give useful information on proper disposal of chemicals. MSDS are supplied as mandatory with chemicals. Batteries usually do not come with an MSDS but with an instruction manual, which should include details on safe disposal.

Toner cartridges for laser printers are also potentially dangerous, but they are also valuable to toner manufacturers for re-use. The obvious solution is to give the cartridge back to the manufacturer. In many cases they will pick up the toner, and a few even give a small fee for each cartridge collected.

The computer and most of its peripherals are extremely difficult to recycle, and the CRT monitor is particularly bad, thanks to extensive use of lead to prevent radiation leakage. The CRT also contains a vacuum tube, which can implode if subjected to shock. CRTs must be carried with care and taken to the local waste disposal to be dealt with properly.

Working with mains voltages

Although the computer motherboard operates on voltages between 2 volts and 12 volts, these are derived from a power supply in the computer case. The power supply connects to the alternating mains supply and converts this into various low level DC voltages. This means that a fault in the power supply can lead to some peripherals inside the case being at the full mains voltage.

- Ensure that plugs are wired correctly. This is not particular to computing equipment, of course. This is not simply a matter of making sure the correct wires attach to the correct pins. There must be no exposed wires – in fact, plugs should be wired so that there is some sheathed wire even inside the plug, in case a sharp tug on the cable should pull wires out of the plug.

- Never work on a live computer, particularly one that is faulty. A mains supply fault could result in lethal voltages present inside the computer case. With monitors, this is even more important, since around 25,000 volts is present inside the casing.

- Use a neon screwdriver. This is useful to confirm that there is no mains leakage to the computer casing or to the mains earth. The neon screwdriver is held in the hand and the tip of the screwdriver is placed on the area to be tested. The technician's thumb is placed over the cap at the end of the handle. If the neon bulb glows, then there is an unwanted mains voltage at the spot touched.

Mains protection

When a piece of equipment goes faulty such that the mains supply accesses areas of he apparatus that are not safe, a protection device should render the equipment harmless until it is repaired. Such devices are fuses, overload trips and RCDs.

Fuses

A fuse is simply a piece of wire that is placed in series with the live wire of the mains. This is usually inside the mains plug, but some equipment might have another fuse mounted on the equipment itself. The idea is that if the mains current exceeds a safe level, the fuse wire melts, thus shutting off the supply to the equipment. This prevents excessive current from overheating the equipment to the point of destruction and/or fire. Plug fuses are sold in a variety of ratings (2A, 3A, 5A, 7A, 10A and 13 amp) and the correct rating should be used with a particular piece of equipment. The rating is the highest current that the fuse can pass indefinitely without overheating. This rating is almost half of the fusing current which is the minimum current at which the fuse will blow instantaneously.

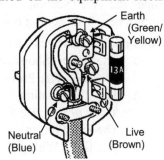

The rating for a fuse can be calculated thus

$$A = W/V$$

i.e. the rating in Amps is the equipment's power rating in Watts divided by the mains Voltage

So for example, a 1KWatt radiator needs a fuse rating of 1000/240 = 4 Amps, while a 200W monitor needs a rating of 200/240 = 1A.

These calculated values do not take into account that some appliances have a power surge when first switched on and therefore need a slightly higher fuse rating.

- Fitting a fuse close or below the calculated rating will result in the fuse blowing.
- Fitting a fuse well in excess of the calculated rating can result in the fuse failing to blow when a fault occurs. This allows excessive current to flow, overheating the equipment and risking damage and fire.
- Fuses should always be replaced with another of the correct rating. A 13A fuse should never be fitted in place of a 2A fuse for example – and a fuse should never be replaced with a nail or piece of wire!

While a blown fuse protects against fire or injury, it is often the result of some electrical problem. If a fuse blows regularly, the equipment is providing danger signs. The problem should never be overcome by fitting a higher rating fuse. Instead the equipment should be tested and/or replaced.

RCDs

The Residual Current Device, also known as ELCB (Earth Leakage Circuit Breaker), protects against a fault that allows current to flow to earth. It is designed for hand-held and portable equipment connecting between a portable appliance and the mains socket. In some cases, it is pre-fitted inside a mains socket.

It is commonly used with power tools, soldering irons and cord extension leads and is often used in wet operating conditions. The RCD acts as a circuit breaker that switches off the power if the amount of current leakage to earth exceeds a safe level.

Electric Shock

An electric shock is the result of an electric current flowing through a person's body. The degree of shock depends upon the voltage, the resistance of the person's body and the area of the body where the current flows. The effects of shock can be pain, flesh damage from burns, or even death. In addition, the shock may cause other injury through falling off ladders, being thrown across the room or dropping equipment. The contraction of the victim's muscles may result in the person being unable to let go of the faulty equipment.

- Switch off supply or source of shock. Do not try to pull the person free as this often results in two victims. If the supply cannot be easily reached, the victim can be prised from the danger using an insulating material such as a wooden brush handle.
- Apply immediate resuscitation techniques or quickly fetch a knowledgeable first-aider.

Health and Safety

There are many hazards to employees in the workplace; these are not confined to the 'dangerous' jobs such as mining, construction or heavy engineering.   Every day, employees suffer accidents at work or slowly impair their health by their work practices.

The Health and Safety at Work Act came into force in 1975 and acts as the basis for safety law in the UK.   It provides a legal framework outlining the responsibilities of both employers and employees, overseen by the Health and Safety Executive.   Any employer with more than five employees is obliged under the Act (Section 2(3)) to maintain a written policy on health and safety, open to view by all employees. The Act is a complex document and only the main points are covered in this section.

Other related measures, standards and recommendations are:

- The Office, Shops and Railway Premises Act of 1983.
- BS6266 - Fire Protection for Electronic Data Processing Installations.
- The Illuminating Engineering Society's (IES) recommendations on lighting standards, titled *'Code of Practice for Interior Lighting'*.
- The Fire Precautions Act 1971.
- The IEEE Wiring Regulations.
- The Health and Safety (First Aid) Regulations 1981.
- The Sex Discrimination Act 1986.
- The Race Relations Act.
- HSE pamphlet 23 - *"Hours of employment of women and young persons"*.
- HSE pamphlet 36 - *"Working with VDUs"*.
- BS7179 and ISO29241 standards on monitor image quality.
- The EEC Directive 90/270 on VDU radiation levels.

Before acting upon any information in this section, the appropriate material should be fully read over. As far as the computing environment is concerned, healthy surroundings are in the interests of all.   A smoky, dusty, damp or cold working environment is against the interests of the people who have to work there and is also damaging to the machines and their data.   In addition, the loss of skilled staff through ill health is not in the interests of anyone; employees lose out physically and the company loses out in loss of output. Implementing the legislation should not be viewed as a penalty but as an investment to retain and expand productivity with a more contented staff.

PC Support health and safety issues can be roughly divided into two:

- Those that are general to all offices - e.g. heating, lighting, working space, fire hazards, working ergonomics, etc.
- Those more peculiar to computer environments - keyboard injuries, damage from monitors, harmful ozone from laser printers, etc.

Note

It is not the job of the PC support technician to sort out the health and safety problems that he/she encounters.   The law ensures that proper machinery is in place with office safety representatives and probably safety committees.   However, it would be the responsibility of the technician, both legally and morally, to ensure that any situations that break the law - unintentionally or otherwise - are reported to management or safety representatives.

Some of the more common problems to be encountered are:

General

- Are work areas kept clean and tidy? Are waste bins emptied at least once a day?
- Are work areas overcrowded?   Is there the legal minimum of 11 cubic metres of space being provided per employee (with any roof area above 3m in height being excluded from the calculation)?   Are these area allocations compromised by excessive furniture, storage boxes, equipment, etc.?
- Is the working environment satisfactory? Is it properly lit to prevent eyestrain, headaches or accidents?
- Is the workplace properly ventilated to prevent headaches and sinus problems?   (see HSE Guidance Note on Ventilation of Buildings).
- Is there excessive temperature (not less than 60°F after the first hour and not exceeding 72°F)?

- Is the working environment excessively noisy? The 1972 Department of Employment *'Code of Practice for Reducing the Exposure of Employed Persons to Noise'* stipulates 90db(A) as the maximum steady exposure to noise for an eight-hour day or 40 hour week. For an office environment, a maximum figure of 60db(A) should be aimed for; conversations should be able to be conducted at a normal level.
- Is the furniture laid out to provide the best ergonomic conditions and reduce backache, neckache, etc.? Are all trailing cables kept safely inside a rubber cable cover to avoid trips?
- Is welfare accommodation satisfactory? Are there sufficient suitable sanitary conveniences, washing facilities (see Section 9 of the Office, Shops and Railway Premises Act) and places for keeping clothes (HSE booklet - "Cloakroom Accommodation and Working Facilities 1980)?
- Are there adequate canteen facilities? See the Department of Employment's Health and Safety at Work booklet 2.
- Are the floors, passageways and stairs safe? Are floor coverings well maintained? Are areas of movement free from obstruction and slippery substances?
- Are all electrical installations in safe condition? Are appliances checked regularly?
- Are the fire precautions adequate? Are all the fire exits in working order and free from obstructions? Are all flammable materials safely stored? Are fire alarms regularly tested? Does the building have a fire certificate? (required where a building houses more than 20 employees or where ten employees work above or below ground floor level)
- Are there adequate first-aid facilities? Are employees trained in first-aid techniques?
- Is there job design to minimise occupational stress? Has attention been paid to job rotation, job enrichment, staff training, removing job isolation, adjusting supervision levels, improving internal communication, providing adequate rest breaks and workplace creches, having clearly defined standards for employee/client communications?
- Computer equipment can be heavy. Has adequate information been supplied about safe lifting of heavy loads?
- Are all non-computer related safety procedures in place? For example: are fire alarm procedures posted where everyone can read them? are the legally required accident reporting procedures followed? is everyone aware of the nearest employee with first aid training?

Risk assessment

Other issues such as hazardous materials, operating plant and machinery, unsafe employer practices and unsafe employee practices threaten the safety of people and equipment. Organisations should have agreed health and safety procedures to examine all possible hazards and risks in the workplace.

A *'hazard'* is something that has the potential to cause harm, while a *'risk'* is an assessment of the likelihood of the hazard actually causing harm. All activities should be subjected to risk assessment, to see what hazards exist, what risk they may cause and what steps can be taken to eliminate or minimise them. For example, it is easy to identify some hazards, such as spilled chemicals, while other hazards (such as RSI or eyestrain) are not immediately noticeable. Similarly, some can be immediately eliminated (like the spilled chemicals) while others (such as lifting objects or typing at a keyboard) are necessary parts of the job. In these cases, the aim is to specify procedures (such as staff training on lifting or regular breaks for typists) that minimise the risk to staff or the public.

Portable Appliance Testing (PAT)

Electrical equipment deteriorates due to wear and tear, overloading, ageing, physical damage and environmental corrosion. The results can have safety or legal consequences and regular inspection and maintenance of apparatus has the following benefits:

- Minimises risk and injury to users of equipment and damage and loss of equipment.
- Complies with *'The Electricity at Work Regulations 1989'* and with all Health & Safety requirements. The Health and Safety Executive may demand proof of equipment tests when following up a report or an accident.
- Complies with insurance requirements and ISO 9000 & BS 5750 Quality Assurance procedures.

P.A.T. procedures ensure that portable appliances are safe to use, meet current regulations, are maintained and kept in good working order and are used in accordance with their planned function. Testing should also provide a means of recording and analysing results.

Types of appliance

A portable appliance is an item of equipment that connects to the power supply by means of a plug and socket and can be carried from one location to another. This covers computers, printers, photocopiers, well as lamps, vacuum cleaners, portable heaters and fans, etc. The regulations also cover hand-held equipment such as electric drills and soldering irons. Fixed installations (heating thermostat, air conditioning unit, etc.) and the building's own wiring, switches and fuses, while covered by The Electricity at Work Regulations 1989, are not included in PAT tests.

Types of test

Tests should comply with the guidelines and recommendations of *the 'Code of Practice for In-Service Inspection and Testing of Electrical Equipment'*, produced by the Institute of Electrical Engineers. This suggests test procedures and frequencies of testing depending on the type of equipment and the environment in which it is used.

Visual tests

The more often a piece of apparatus is used and/or moved, the more often it needs to be inspected and tested. Around 95% of faults or damage can be found on visual inspection. After disconnecting the apparatus, an examination should look for:

- Use of appliances in inappropriate conditions (e.g. excessively wet, dusty, etc.).
- Damage to the external casing of the appliance, or loose parts or screws.
- Internal damage due to vibration, shock, overheating, or ingress of liquid or dust.
- Damage to the cable or mains plug; incorrect or dangerous plug wiring or fuse rating.

If any faults are found, the appliance must not be used until repairs are carried out.

Electrical tests

After a visual inspection, the following electrical tests should be conducted, where appropriate.

Cord Test	This checks the polarity of the mains conductors, the wire insulation and the safety earth continuity where an earth conductor is used. This test ensures that the mains cable is safe to use.
Earth Continuity Test	This checks that there is earth continuity from the earth pin of the mains plug through to the areas most likely to become live in the event of an insulation fault. This verifies that the earth path will conduct currents in the event of an equipment fault.
Insulation Test	This checks the insulation of a cable by applying 500V DC between the live and neutral and earth, exposing any weaknesses not apparent to the naked eye. This test should not be done on computers or most electronic equipment. If in any doubt, the equipment manufacturer should be consulted.
Earth Leakage test	This checks that there are no voltage-induced, earth leakage paths (i.e. current flowing in the earth lead).

Testing hardware

There are numerous ways to test equipment at a more basic level than that which the POST works at. There are various forms of 'meter' that will measure electrical properties, for example. The ammeter measures current in amps; the voltmeter measures voltage; and the ohmmeter measures resistance in ohms. The multimeter is a device that is capable of performing all three functions.

When the multimeter is used to measure current, it must be inserted into the circuit, so that the current to be measured is flowing through the meter. When measuring the resistance of a component, that component should be removed from the circuit to eliminate the possibility that there is more than one path from one probe to the other. This makes measurement of current or resistance of any device on an integrated circuit infeasibly difficult in many cases.

However, reading the resistance between two points indicates whether current (or data) can flow from one of these points to the other. This is called a '*continuity test*' and can be used to ensure that there are no unexpected breaks in a cable, amongst other things. A continuity test should always be done on a system that is powered down, for safety reasons. Touch the two probes of the multimeter to the two locations to be tested between, and read the multimeter. If a reading of infinity is given, this means that current cannot flow between the two points. If it reads zero, the current can flow freely.

The measurement of voltage can be done in either AC (alternating current) or DC (Direct Current). A PC technician is unlikely to measure AC voltages, since all voltages at any point other than inside the actual power supply are DC. DC readings can check that the power's supply is reaching various points in the motherboard or component.

A multimeter may be digital or analog. An analog multimeter uses a needle on a scale to indicate the current, voltage, or resistance, and also has a mirror to aid in reading the measurements. If the viewer reads from the multimeter at a slight angle, the result will be incorrect, and this is known as a '*parallax error*'. The mirror will reflect the needle, and only when the reflection is hidden behind the needle itself is the measurement accurate. Digital multimeters do not suffer from parallax, and the only major downside to a digital multimeter is that it is difficult to notice a slowly changing current, which could be obvious when viewed as a slowly moving needle.

Other test equipment

Another testing device that could be of use to the PC technician is the digital thermometer, equipped with a temperature probe. However, this is only useful if the technician knows what temperature the device is expected to be at under normal operational circumstances. By comparing the expected result to the actual temperature measurement, the technician can see if the device is overheating.

The 'logic probe' is another test device, which is suited to very low level diagnostics. It shows the state of any 5 volt logic device, either 'high' (+5v), 'low' (+0v) or 'pulsing' (regularly changing between the two). For example, if a logic probe shows the reset line to be permanently low, this will be the cause of the PC never booting up. A logic pulser is the other side of the coin, supplying a constant pulse waveform. This can be useful, for example, in checking that the internal speaker is responding to input as it should.

An insulation tester can also be useful in some circumstances – attach one end to the device, and the other end to electrical ground to check the insulation on the device.

Documentation

Records of test results and maintenance should be kept throughout the active life of an appliance. This is part of the Health & Safety documentation and should include:

- An inventory of all electrical equipment (including extension cables), each appliance having a unique identification number.
- An inspection and test record form for each appliance.
- Labels for applying to apparatus, indicating a 'Pass' or 'Fail'. For items that pass the test, the label should indicate the due date for the next test.
- Failure reports for defective items.

Where an item is found to be dangerous, it should be disabled (usually by removing the plug or fuse).

Note: This is only an overview of PAT testing. Testing should only be conducted by trained, competent and qualified technicians who have the equipment and software necessary to carry out tests.

Fire procedures

Faulty electrical equipment or wiring is a common cause of fires, although there are other sources such as combustible fumes and liquids, and negligence (e.g. dropping lit cigarette ends, leaving open fires unattended). Only the very smallest of fires should be tackled and the alarm should be sounded even on these occasions, as small fires have a habit of quickly developing into major fires.

A range of fire extinguishers are available and the correct one has to be used for particular fires, to prevent making the situation worse or further endangering lives. Each type of extinguisher is colour coded for quick identification and the chart shows how each should be used.

Colour	Type	Purpose
Red	Water	Wood, textiles, paper, plastics, etc. Not for use on burning fat or oil Not for use on electrical appliances
Blue	Dry powder	Wood, textiles, paper, plastics, etc. Liquids such as grease, fats, oil, paint, petrol, etc. Safe on live electrical equipment.
Black	Carbon Dioxide CO_2	Grease, fats, oil, paint, petrol etc. Safe on live electrical equipment. (fumes from these extinguishers can be harmful if used in confined spaces)
Cream	Foam	Limited number of liquid fires.
Cream	AFFF (Aqueous film-forming foam)	Wood, textiles, paper, plastics, etc. Fires involving solids. Liquids such as grease, fats, oil, paint, petrol, etc

Each organisation should have its own evacuation procedures and notices should be posted throughout the building. Periodic fire drills should be conducted to ensure that the procedures are efficient.

Computer-related problems

All of the earlier questions on general office environments also apply to computer environments and can have a detrimental effect on staff and output.   In addition, there are other hazards that are encountered by computer users compared to other office staff.

VDU hazards   -   This issue is fully dealt with in the chapter on display technology.

RSI   -   The general points on ergonomics are also covered in the chapter on display technology. However, a serious problem affects workers who are employed on prolonged keyboard work, particularly fast data entry work.   This work can cause discomfort, pain or even crippling disability.   These symptoms are caused by the swelling and toughening of the muscles at the base of the wrist.   The muscles eventually become so thick that they press on the nerves that pass through the wrist.   The hand and wrist can become weakened to the point of irreversible damage.   This is known as *'repetitive strain injury'* and it is important that the symptoms are spotted at an early stage.   If diagnosed early enough, the damage can be arrested by means such as job rotation with non-repetitive tasks, reducing the work rate, introducing more work breaks or moving the employee to another job.   Surgery has also proved successful with RSI cases when detected before it has reached an irreversible stage.

Reporting problems

It is best if a working relationship is established in advance with the organisation's safety representatives and the company employee charged with responsibility for health and safety matters.   If the lines of communication are clearly understood in advance, it will reduce any tensions arising from any deficiencies that are reported.   Since the PC support staff are among the few employees who move around the entire building, they are the most likely to get soundings of employee complaints and problems.   Ideally, a report form should be devised and accepted as the standard method of notifying any potential or actual health and safety problem. This should be used to trigger a risk assessment.

Accident procedures

Despite all precautions, accidents and ill health at work may still occur and it is a legal requirement that these be recorded and reported to the Health & Safety Executive's Incident Contact Centre. This is a requirement of the Reporting of Injuries, Diseases and Dangerous Occurrences Regulations of 1995, known as RIDDOR. This provides the HSE with facts that allow them to advise on future improvements in prevention.   The areas that have to be reported are deaths, major injuries (including fractures, amputations, dislocations and loss of sight), accidents that result in an employee being off work for three days, work-related disease(including poisonings and skin diseases, lung diseases, infections) and dangerous occurrences (including fires, explosions, collapsing buildings, and the escape of flammable liquids).

Organisations must keep records of these occurrences, either in a log book, on report forms, or in a computer file.   The record should record the date, time, place, details of person(s) involved and a description of the event.   The HSE publish *"A Guide to the reporting of Injuries, Diseases, and Dangerous Occurrences Regulations 1995"* (ISBN 0-7176-1012-8)

Getting the full facts

For a more full account of safety regulations, contact the Health and Safety Executive, who can supply the *"Essentials of Health and Safety at Work"* and a range of other such material.   Many titles are free and they supply a twice-yearly list entitled *"Publications in Series"* which can be purchased at HSE centres or at bookshops that stock HMSO titles. Many of the free pamphlets can be obtained directly from the regional offices of the HSE (see the telephone book).

Their website address is www.hse.gov.uk

Ensuring legal practices

Apart from the Health and Safety regulations that technicians will wish to enforce, there are a number of other areas that could lead the organisation into legal difficulty. These are:

- The use of unauthorised software, (e.g. *'pirate'* copies of games or utilities).
- Licensing agreements (e.g. no more than 20 simultaneous users of a package on a network).
- Copyright.
- Data Protection Act.

These issues are covered elsewhere in detail.

System Maintenance

Preventative maintenance is preferable to waiting for equipment to fail and then repairing it. It is normally easier to carry out and is also cheaper in the long run. Repairs are often seen as money well spent, as it puts the organisation back into working order, while regular maintenance is often viewed as a tiresome and unproductive task. Any such attitudes - whether among management or support staff - need to be changed, as a defined maintenance programme will both reduce system failures and save money. There is a school of thought that advocates a policy of *'if it ain't broke don't fix it'* and it is certainly true that the over frequent pulling and prodding of equipment can cause problems. As often in life, a balanced approach to maintenance is the correct one. Elements of the computing system should get as much attention as they actually need in practice. This will mean there are different cycles of maintenance for different pieces of equipment. This chapter suggests that three levels of maintenance provide an adequate cover.

Regular Maintenance

The definition of *'regular'* depends on the organisation's structure and policy. For example, a widely dispersed organisation with far-distant local branches would pose problems for a weekly routine. Generally, a regular routine means a fortnightly or monthly cycle, depending on how harsh the computing environment.

The elements of regular maintenance are:

- Check all external cables for any mechanical damage (e.g. fraying, crushing, stretching, etc.). Also check that all cables are properly seated in their respective sockets and that none are only partly plugged in. These checks should be of video cables (between unit and monitor), printer cables (between the printer port on computer and the socket on the printer and the power cables (between the units and the mains supply) and any other cables such as mouse, modem or keyboard cables. Any partially connected cables will result in incorrect operation. In the case of power cables, poor connections might result in arcing (i.e. the mains supply jumping the gap between the plug and socket) at the connections and even result in fires in extreme cases.
- Clean the computer's outside case. This does not directly affect the performance of the machine. It simply keeps the computer looking smart and encourages best practice from its users. In a clean environment, this is a quick operation. If the cleaning removes a lot of dirt, then it indicates a dirtier environment and this may mean that these machines will require a more frequent internal clean (see later). After all, if the outside is getting dirty quickly, this must also apply to the inner machine.
  The rules for cleaning a computer case are:
  - Always use a proprietary case cleaning fluid; this is usually of the foam type. Never use normal domestic cleaning fluids, as these are often abrasive, either physically or chemically.
  - Always use a clean cloth of lint-free material, to avoid introducing lint fragments into the case via the ventilation slots.
  - Never spray or apply the cleaner directly to the case as this may penetrate the case via the ventilation slots. Always apply the cleaning fluid to the cloth, and then apply the cloth to the case.
- Clean the monitor. The monitor screen has a high voltage on its inside coating and this attracts dust very quickly, making the monitor the item most likely to need cleaned first in any system. Again, use a proprietary cleaning solution. The type purchased should be an anti-static cleaner; this type will avoid aggravating the always-present static problems inherent to monitors of the cathode ray tube type.
- Clean the laser printer. Running through special cleaning papers that are available in laser cleaning kits cleans the internal paper passages. The kits also include swab sticks for cleaning the corona wires. In some cases, the printer's ozone filter may also need to be replaced.
- Clean the keyboard. This is the hardware component that is subjected to most abuse. Greasy fingers pound it, its users drop biscuit crumbs and cigarette ash over it and even occasionally spill coffee or Coke over it. Not to mention dead skin cells and airborne dust. Like the monitor, it is almost certain to be in need of regular cleaning. If left untouched, it will eventually produce symptoms such as missing or repeated letters. Anything that obstructs the mechanical movement or alters the capacitance of the matrix will affect the keyboard's performance.

The steps to clean a keyboard depend upon the severity of the problem.

ROUTINE CLEANING
- Hold the keyboard upside down and gently shake it to dislodge loose crumbs, etc.
- Vacuum between the keys, ideally using a 'mini-vac' designed for the purpose. This produces a sucking action but cleaning is usually most effective with a blowing action which helps to dislodge particles. If available, use canned air that is available from electronic or office suppliers. A cheaper alternative is the use of a keyboard 'sweeper' brush or a photographic "puff-brush".
- Clean the keys with swabs dipped in cleaning solution.

PROBLEM KEYBOARD

In extreme cases, such as the spilling of sticky drinks over the keyboard, the keyboard may have to be dismantled for cleaning. In most cases, this will still only involve the removal of the keycaps and the cleaning of the external case beneath the caps. The steps are:
- Remove the keycaps. These can be gently prised off, always using an upward motion. Some keycaps have small springs under the caps and care must be taken to ensure that none of these are lost. Do not remove the space key cap unless necessary, as they can be very difficult to refit.
- Remove any sticky material from the keycaps and clean them in warm soapy water. Rinse the keys well to remove all traces of soap and ensure that they are properly dry before fitting again later.
- Use a low-pressure hose, hair dryer or canned air to blow an airstream down the key tubes, to loosen any internal particles. Do NOT put your mouth to the tube and blow your own air down the tube as this will introduce moisture into the matrix and possibly upset the capacitance between the plates.
- Carefully clean the board area under the keys, especially round the plunger mechanisms. Make sure that all debris and sticky substances are removed and that each key's plunger moves freely.

If the liquid has entered the internal matrix, the matrix will have to be dismantled for cleaning; this is a tricky task. The keyboard has to be carefully dismantled and even more carefully re-assembled after the cleaning operation. All the components have to correctly locate and the springs have to be correctly adjusted. It is a delicate and time-consuming operation. In the commercial environment, it is more cost-effective to completely replace a badly contaminated keyboard compared to the man-hours involved in a major strip-down.

- Clean the mouse. The normal opto-mechanical mouse uses a ball to rub against and rotate a couple of rollers that are housed inside the mouse casing. The mouse ball is designed to be pushed along a flat surface such as a desktop or a specially made mouse mat with the correct surface resistance. As the mouse moves, the ball picks up any dirt or dust on the mat and introduces it into the mouse casing. Eventually, the ball and the rollers both become coated and the result is that the mouse movement becomes jerky and erratic. The ball can be removed by rotating the ring that holds it in place; this is on the underside of the mouse casing. When the ball is removed, the rollers can be seen and these should be cleaned with a swab dipped in cleaning fluid. Make sure that all the perimeter of both rollers is cleaned. The mouse ball should be washed in warm soapy water and properly rinsed and dried before re-insertion into the mouse.

- Carry out backups of data. The '*Computer Security*' chapter details backup types, backup cycles, and how to determine the frequency of backups necessary. Windows is easily set up to automatically schedule regular backups. Alternatively, backup software is normally supplied along with the backup equipment, and any quality software will include scheduling capability. Additionally, the technician should ensure that the data being backed up is still the correct data. For example there is no point backing up spreadsheets from the server, if users are working on local copies of the data. This entails a certain amount of interaction with users, to make sure of proper identification of critical data.

- Update virus checking data, and scan the drives for viruses. Simply relying on a virus blocking program may not be enough, and regular scans in addition are recommended. See the '*Security*' chapter for details.

- Have a word with the users about the machines; this will pick up any training needs of the staff or may identify a problem not detected by the checks (e.g. intermittent problems).

Less Regular

Again, the definition of this time scale is loose but could be quarterly or six-monthly, dependent on the amount of use and the amount of changes that are predicted for the machines. The tests are aimed at picking up any deterioration of the disk surface or disk fragmentation due to prolonged file activities. The tests are also aimed at ensuring that the machine configuration is optimised for the current use of each machine. The elements of such a programme should include:

- Check the integrity of the surface of the machine's hard disk using ScanDisk or a similar utility.
- Defragmentation of the disk, where needed, with the Disk Defragmenter or a similar utility.
- Tidy the files and folders on the disk.
- Checking the machine's software and operating system configuration.
- Verify the integrity of backups. In a mission-critical environment, it may be necessary to verify every backup, sometimes even going so far as doing a full restore to an off-line computer. In most business environments, however, it is sufficient to perform occasional checks on files in and around critical areas of the system and data.
- Check that the computer's physical operating environment has not altered. Check for:
  - Exposure to excesses of temperature or of rapid temperature change.
  - Exposure to dampness, dust or vibration.
  - Exposure to strong magnetic fields such as lifts, machinery, office equipment.
  - Strong fields can corrupt disks, taint the monitor purity and produce unpredictable printing.
  - Exposure to strong radio signals such as a paging system or local taxi transmitter.

The utilities that are used for the above are explained later.

Annual Maintenance

These activities address the longer-term problems that arise with PCs and are as follows:

- Clean inside the computer unit's case. Over a period of time, dust settles on the components on the boards. This acts as a thermal insulator and reduces the ability of the component to dissipate its heat into the air. The result is overheating of components and an increase in their failure rate. Cleaning the board, therefore, increases the working life of the machine. The cover should be removed from the unit and the boards should be brushed down with a soft-bristled brush. Even better, use one of the small vacuums to ensure that the dust is completely removed and does not simply settle down on another part of the board. Since these are internal electronic components, it is important that an anti-static vacuum is used to avoid any chance of electrostatic buildup.

   Note: Before cleaning inside a computer, always make a backup of the hard disk contents as a precaution.

- Check the seating of internal cards and internal cables. Each time the computer is switched on it warms the components and they expand; when the computer is switched off again, the components contract. Different components expand and contract at different rates and this tends to make I.C. chips gradually lift out of their socket holders. Similarly, boards tend to lift out of their expansion slot sockets.
- Re-seat chips by applying a firm but even pressure over the whole surface of the chip; this ensures that none of the chip's pins are accidentally bent. You may have to support the underside of the board while applying the pressure, to prevent undue strain on the board. Don't forget to use a wrist earthing strap to prevent any damage to the chips from body static discharge. Similarly, when re-seating a card, ensure that the edge connector is properly lined up with the expansion socket. Avoid excessive force. The use of a rocking motion on the card - from edge to edge - will probably help the insertion process. Don't forget to tighten the card's securing screw once the card is inserted.
- Clean the edge connectors on expansion cards and cables. The accumulation of dirt on contacts increases their electrical resistance and can result in data transfer errors; the binary signal is reduced to a level where the next processing stage is unsure whether the signal represents a binary 1 or a binary 0. Edge connectors can be cleaned with a lint-free cloth or swab dipped in a liquid cleaning solution such as isopropyl alcohol. Do not use soap and water, as this can be abrasive to components. Take care, however, liquid cleaning compounds are one of the leading causes of chemical accidents. Cable connectors can be cleaned by unplugging and re-plugging the connector a number of times; this releases any trapped dirt and the abrasive effect cleans the joint between the connecting areas.

Don't forget to note the orientation of the cable, to ensure that the plug is re-inserted correctly in its socket. Some cables will have special markings and these should be noted before removing the connector. Ribbon cables, for example, usually identify pin 1 with a red stripe on the edge of the ribbon. Often the printed circuit board or the socket will also be marked with a '1' against pin 1 and this greatly reduces the possibility of errors. Other connectors only plug in one way round and this solves the problem. Of course, don't remove all the cables at the one time, in case you have trouble remembering what cable is attached to which connector.

- If the computer still uses floppy drive, clean the drive's read/write heads. Like an audio cassette player or VCR, the disk drive's performance degenerates if the head is coated in dirt or magnetic oxide. The coating increases the gap between the head and the magnetised surface and causes read and write errors to occur. The drive's head can be cleaned using a special cleaning disk that is readily available. Always use the *'wet'* cleaner type rather than an abrasive type; this uses a disk that is impregnated with cleaning fluid and has minimal abrasive effect. The disk is placed in the drive and spun like any normal floppy. The cleaning disk is removed and discarded, since it will probably now be holding the dirt particles. It is not a wise move to re-use the same disk; this may save money but introducing a disk with dirt particles is equivalent to using an abrasive type cleaner.   Hard disks are enclosed in airtight casings and are therefore not prone to the same degree of ingress of dirt.

- If still using a CRT monitor, de-gauss it if necessary.   If the screen displays a *'moiré'* pattern then the internal metal screen has become magnetised and requires to be de-magnetised with a de-gaussing coil (see the section on video).   This is usually only a problem with older monitors, since newer models have automatic de-gaussing circuitry.

Checking Hard Disk Integrity with XP/Vista

As explained in the *'Disks and Drives'* chapter, hard disks can develop a number of problems. These may be logical faults in the file system, such as lost clusters or allocation errors; or they may be physical faults, such as damaged sectors on the hard disk. If these faults are relatively minor, they may go unnoticed, so it is important to check the integrity, both physical and logical, of the hard disk at regular intervals.

Note: If a disk checking utility gives the user a message saying so, then the disk definitely has a fault. However, if no message is given, this does not necessarily mean that the disk is fault-free: it could simply mean that the fault is not one that the utility is capable of detecting.

There are various utilities that can detect and/or rectify hard disk faults. DOS used a tool called CHKDSK, which was useful but not very user-friendly. XP and Vista still provide the CHKDSK facility, presented to the user as 'error-checking'.

To test a disk for errors:

- Right-click the *'Start'* button and select *"Explore"*.
- Right-click the disk to be checked and select *"Properties"*
- In the properties dialog click the tab *"Tools"*. (the illustration shows the Vista window. The XP version is almost identical).
- Click on the *"Check now"* button.
- When the *"Check disk options"* dialog box appears, check both options and click *'Start'*. It has only two options: *'Automatically fix file system errors'*, and *'Scan for and attempt recovery of bad sectors'*. The first option will try to fix errors in system files as well as ordinary files, but may require the system to be rebooted first. The second option will perform a more thorough check of the disk, looking for bad sectors.

Windows will ask that the computer be shut down and restarted. When the computer restarts, it will first run the CHKDSK program.   If no errors are detected, it will load all the usual Windows files. If it detects errors, the utility reports on what was found and what was done.

Dealing with Hard Disk Integrity Problems

If any problems are detected, they should be repaired by a utility and the nature of the problems should be recorded. Norton provides for the creation of a text file report on the surface test and this can be printed out and filed away.   Where surface problems are detected, a more regular visit should be paid to the machine to ensure that the disk is not rapidly deteriorating. If a later visit shows even greater surface problems, it indicates disk deterioration and a replacement should be considered before any precious data is lost.   Of course, a problem with the disk surface may be a one off (e.g. jolting of the disk due to moving the machine from office to office or due to the effects of the office Xmas party) and will not repeat itself at a later test. In these cases, the sector corruption was not due to long-term deterioration of the surface but due to physical damage. If future checks show no further sector losses, the test routine can revert to the normal cycle.

Disk Defragmentation

Fragmentation is explained in the '*Disks and Drives*' chapter. A fragmented disk is extremely unlikely to cause any faults, but to optimise the speed of the machine it should be defragmented on a regular basis. Windows includes a Disk Defragmenter utility and is a total rewrite from earlier versions, to accommodate FAT, FAT 32, FAT32X, and NTFS filing systems. It is best to run the utility without any programs running in the background. To defragment a disk:

- Right-click the '*Start*' button and select *"Explore"*.
- Right-click the disk to be checked and select *"Properties"*
- In the properties dialog click the tab *"Tools"*.
- Click on the *"Defragment now"* button.

Defragmentation is a two-stage process. Firstly, the existing file system is analysed for fragmentation, then the fragmentation is removed by shuffling the contents of disk clusters to put fragments of the same file next to each other. Note that an analysis can be carried out without defragmentation and an analysis report can be produced, detailing how much fragmentation has been discovered.

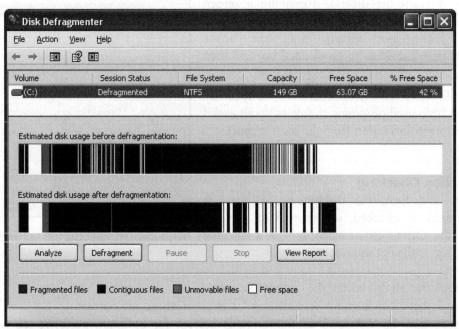

A window, as in the illustration, shows the progress of the defragmentation. Two *'spectrum'* style graphs are produced. One is from the analysis phase, which shows the state of the disk. The other is from the defrag-mentation phase, which initially looks just like the analysis display but which gradually changes with the defragmentation process, to show how much of the defragmentation process has been carried out.

The time taken to defragment a large drive can be quite long. Therefore, the user or support person may decide to schedule a defragmentation through the night when the machine is idle.

Tidying the disk contents

Over a period of time, the hard disk will accumulate unwanted files.   These might be files that were created and forgotten, data files left over from an abandoned project, or program files from an unused application. In addition, many programs including Windows create temporary files which are meant to be automatically deleted after their use; such files have extensions such as .A or .TMP. If the program should be unexpectedly halted, then the files are not deleted and still occupy disk space. Some of these temporary files can be quite large, and if they are allowed to accumulate they can take up a surprisingly large proportion of the disk.

It is almost impossible to identify every unnecessary file that can be safely deleted, however, so it may be useful to try more than one package. For example, the Windows utility can clean up the temporary folder, recycle bin and so on, but is powerless to detect duplicate files as some other utility programs can.

Other unwanted files should be identified, usually in consultation with the user, and then deleted.   In some cases, entire sub-directory structures may be deleted. This may result from unwanted applications or directories created for purposes that no longer exist. Note however that in the case of program files, the Uninstall Software option should be used rather than simply deleting the files, as the latter option may leave configuration information behind. Also take care when removing entire folders, and ensure that they do not contain any sub-folders that have data in them to be kept. The command does ask the user whether to continue but it is still too easy to delete huge chunks of the hard disk structure in a careless moment. Finally, any fonts which remain unused over long periods should be removed, since a large collection of fonts can slow down many office applications.

Using Disk Cleanup

The Windows disk cleanup utility is accessed by clicking *'Start'* then *'All Programs'* then *'Accessories'* then *'System Tools'* then *'Disk Cleanup'*.

When run, it scans the disk(s), displaying a screen showing all the files it has detected that can be removed.   The user simply ticks the boxes corresponding to the areas to be cleaned up, and then clicks *'OK'*.

The *'More Options'* tab offers to further save space by uninstalling little-used programs and deleting all saved System Restore points (apart from the most recent).

Configuration Checking

Every now and then, the machine's configuration settings should be checked, to ensure that are still correct for the current use of machine.   If a machine's main use has altered, the existing configuration may no longer be the optimum setting.

For example:

- Check that all drivers are the current version.
- Check that all updates for Windows and user applications are current.
- Check that the Windows configuration is correct for optimum performance with the current applications.   The Registry and INI files can be examined if you understand how they are composed; if not, check the configuration through Windows Control Panel, etc.
- Check that all Windows program are correctly set up, to reflect the applications currently in use. Programs may have been deleted or moved to other sub-directories and the given paths may no longer point to the programs' actual locations.

Task Scheduler

This utility sets up a computer to run a particular application or set of applications at a pre-set day and time.   In XP, it is accessed by clicking *'Start'* then *'All Programs'* then *'Accessories'* then *'System Tools'* then *'Scheduled Tasks'*.   In Vista, it is accessed by clicking *'Start'* then *'Control Panel'* then *'System and Maintenance'* then *'Administrative Tools'* then *'Task Scheduler'*.

The illustration shows the XP scheduler display.

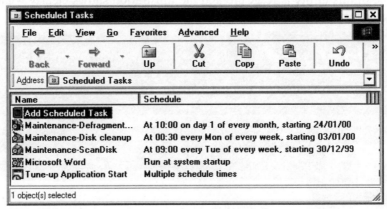

When the *'Add Scheduled Task'* bar is clicked, the utility lists all the applications on the computer and one can be selected.

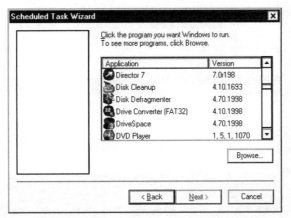

The user then has comprehensive choices on whether the application is run:

- On a periodic basis. This could be daily, weekly, or monthly. For weekly and monthly options, the user chooses which day of the week/month. All options include the setting the time when the application will run. An example use would be for interrupting the user's activities to run a backup.
- Each time the computer is booted up.   This would be useful where a particular computer is used mainly for a single purpose.   The computer could be set up to always boot up into a word processor, for example. Since more than one application appears in the list, the computer can be set up to run several applications when switched - e.g. word processor, spreadsheet, fax software, etc.

In the example, the computer has been set up for

- A monthly defragmentation.
- A monthly disk cleanup.
- A weekly scan of the disk surface.
- The automatic running of Microsoft Word when the computer is booted up.

The task Scheduler can also be used to schedule regular backups using the Backup utility supplied with Windows.   However, it is recommended that this be done via the Backup program rather than the Scheduler program, because Scheduler is unable to set specialised backup options.

Vista's Task Scheduler, while similar to XP, provides much more detailed control over the scheduling process.

Third Party Support Utilities

Registry Cleaner
It removes apparently unused registry entries. This can increase the efficiency of the system, by reducing the size of the registry that is loaded at bootup, and also reducing the entries that take up memory.

A typical example of this utility is RegCure and the illustration shows clearly what type of problems the scan will be looking for.

There are many other utility programs for registry cleanup. Some are bundled as part of a large suite of utilities and some are marketed as standalone products. Another product, Registry Mechanic, also provides a facility to compact the registry after it has been cleaned up.

Uninstallers
In the early days, installing a program involved placing all the files for the program in a single directory. Removing the program was achieved by deleting the directory and its contents. With Windows applications, the installation process may scatter the application's files over many directories. Several applications may also share the same program fragments such as DLLs. This means that uninstalling is a difficult process. Windows provides its own uninstall software, reached through *'Control Panel'* and *'Add/Remove Programs'*. However, add-on programs often do a more thorough uninstall.

Uninstaller software aids the removal of programs and can use two methods.

- When the uninstaller program is installed on the computer, it notes all the disk's current files. When an application is installed, the uninstaller software makes another record of the disk's files and detects the alterations. It knows what extra files were added and where they were stored, simplifying their later removal.
- The uninstaller software may also contain a database describing all the expected components that are associated with a particular application. It can then look for these components and delete them.

Duplicate Files

Over a period, copies of the same file will be stored in different directories of the computer's hard disk(s). This wastes disk space and confuses the user (e.g. which file is the most current). Utilities can detect and delete duplicate files or files that have not been accessed for a long time. Examples of this software are Clone Tools and Doublekiller.

Compression

File compression was explained in the chapter on Disks & Drives. Utilities for handling compressed files include PKZip, WinZip, TurboZip and ZipMagic.

Disk & File Protection

Backup Tools

The standard backup facilities provided within Windows are often sufficient for everyday needs. Other utilities offer added facilities such as saving files in compressed format, encrypting files as they are backed up, testing each file for viruses before backing up, etc. An example program is NovaBackup.

Computer Access

Sophisticated systems for preventing unauthorised access to computers, or allowing different users access to different parts of the disk directory are standard in machines running local area network operating systems. Products such as Bootlock and Winlock, enhance security on standalone computers.

Disk Image

While backup tools are essential for the safety of data files, a serious disk crash could result in Windows and all applications having to be reinstalled and customised again. Software utilities allow the entire image of the disk to be copied to removable media (e.g. CD, DVD, memory stick, external disk) or the network server, so that the original drive contents can be reinstalled to a disk in a single operation. Examples of this software are True Image, Norton Ghost and Quarterdecks' Diskclone.

Data Encryption/Decryption

Many data files store sensitive commercial information that should not be readily readable, particularly if the file is to be transmitted over a network. The solution lies in encrypting (scrambling) files before storing or transmitting them. The person reading that file has to apply a 'key' to decrypt (unscramble) them. PGP is the most common example of this type of utility.

Internet Tools

Internet browser add-ons provide a range of filters to prevent unwanted material being downloaded. These may be for reasons of:
- Censorship (e.g. preventing access to porn sites). Users of a computer can be prevented from accessing sites that appear on a database or are user entered. Examples are Net Nanny CYBERsitter, CyberPatrol, Norton Parental and McAfee Parental Controls.
- Financial saving (e.g. saving connect time downloading junk mail).
- Speed (e.g. saving waiting while adverts and banners are downloaded).

Additional features may include removing Internet 'cookies' and emptying the Internet cache.

Note

Many of the above non-Microsoft utilities are available as standalone products. Many are also available as *'suites'*, where a number of useful utilities are supplied as a single product. All the options are displayed in a common opening menu.

Printer Maintenance

Even ignoring printer faults, printers are probably the part of the system that requires the greatest amount of maintenance. Any printer that is in regular use will need paper and ink replaced fairly often. Heavy-duty printers in constant use may also need thorough cleaning and replacement drums every few months.

Printer paper

In most cases, printers will be loaded with A4 paper. The quality of paper purchased is the first concern. An inkjet printer with paper that is too absorbent will produce faded images and text. At the other extreme, paper that is not sufficiently absorbent will smudge. Thickness should also be considered – heavier paper is better quality, but if it is too thick some friction feed printers may not feed it properly. Of course, special requirements such as sticky labels, transparencies or fanfold paper for dot matrix printers might be another factor. Check the printer manual to ensure that the device handles the desired media. This especially applies to transparencies, which can melt if improperly used, jamming the printer.

Adding or replacing paper

Before adding paper or other media, it may be necessary to make sure the paper is the correct way up. This applies to headed paper, envelopes, and similar items, but not to plain paper. Additionally, plain A4 paper (but not fanfold) may benefit from being 'fanned' (rifling through the pages of the stack) before inserting into the printer, as it can help prevent the printer from picking up multiple sheets for each printed page.

The method for adding or replacing paper or other print media can vary depending on the printer. However, most tractor feed mechanisms follow a generally similar method, while most friction feed mechanisms follow another method.

Adding or replacing fanfold paper in a tractor feed mechanism normally involves lifting up flaps to allow access to the feed pins, and placing the paper over these so that the pins slot into the fanfold paper holes. The flaps are then closed and then the 'Line Feed' button is pressed until the paper reaches the print head. Note that some alteration of the position of the pins may be necessary to ensure the paper is held tight.

Adding or replacing copier paper in a friction feed mechanism normally consists simply of gaining access to the paper tray if necessary, and making sure the paper is stacked neatly and in the correct position. All friction feed printers have a maximum number of pages that can be safely fed into the tray or feeder mechanism. The paper tray can then be replaced if necessary.

Replacing ink

Although less regular than replacing paper, replacing the ink is usually no more difficult. The exact procedure depends on the type of printer and sometimes on the manufacturer - some replacement cartridges even have instructions printed on them. When in doubt, consult the manuals, especially with laser printers that often have high-energy capacitors, but in general the following is applicable to most cases.

Dot Matrix:

Replacing an ink ribbon usually means opening the front of the printer. The ribbon cartridge may be held in place by some mechanism or may lift straight out. This can simply be replaced with a new ribbon cartridge and the mechanism put back in place. However, it is usually advisable to make sure the ribbon itself is taut, and that it passes in between the rollers and the print head.

Inkjet:

The inkjet will have to be opened to gain access to the ink cartridge. Some may have to be switched on to replace the ink, and a button pressed to move the carriage into the correct position for replacement. Ink cartridges are held in place by a plastic clip that lifts up, usually exposing the cartridge for removal. Before replacing the ink, remove the tape covering the nozzles. The ink can then be replaced, and the clip pulled back down. Close the printer, and if necessary press any buttons required to make the printer initialise the new ink cartridge.

Laser:

Replacing toner in a laser is similar to doing so in a photocopier. Turn the printer off, and open it, normally. This is done by pressing in one or more holding flaps and lifting. Take care not to touch the print head (which will be very hot if it has been in use), the electronics (which could result in a nasty electric shock even if switched off), or the mirror if it is exposed. Most cartridge types simply pull out, but before replacing it with a new one there are some steps to be taken. Shake the toner cartridge firmly to dislodge any toner that has clumped together, and then remove the toner covering strip that prevents spillage during transit. Now the toner can be replaced, in the same manner as the previous cartridge was removed. Power the printer back on, and if it does not automatically run a self-test then perform one manually to ensure it is operating correctly.

A maintenance strategy

The tasks and their timings in the preceding pages are intended to be an indication of the likely elements of a company strategy on system maintenance. The final policy has to take into account any existing maintenance agreements with third parties, the conditions of any equipment guarantees, the current age and condition of the equipment, the severity of the working environment and the abilities of the staff in the support section. While the exact final policy is a matter for each organisation there is one matter that is clear - each organisation must have a clearly defined maintenance strategy. In this way the reporting and recording procedures, job descriptions, training needs, backup procedures, equipment stock levels, purchases and maintenance budgeting can all be easily understood and implemented.

Procedural support

Although installing, maintaining and troubleshooting equipment can take up a large proportion of an IT department's time, an often equally important task that may be part of the technicians' remit is that of Procedural Support. Small companies could benefit from automated procedures such as macros that facilitate data handling procedures. Even large organisations may not have bespoke software to handle every aspect of their computer usage – for example, a company could have specialised database software for customer details, but still use a generic word processing package to print out invoices or faxes. The main types of this area of User Support are as follows:

- Automated Procedures. Many computer related tasks can be repetitive, and repetitive tasks are the sort of thing that computers are good at. By using macro programming languages (such as Visual Basic for Applications), the IT department can create short programs called macros, that deal with the repetitive aspects of many operations. For example, a Microsoft Access database could have Visual Basic macros associated with it, so that certain keystroke combinations could be associated with macros that automatically enter sets of information. A wholesaler might sell mainly to just a few customers, and use 'Ctrl-A' to automatically enter the details of one particular customer into the appropriate data fields, saving the user from having to type this information. 'Ctrl-B' could be a macro for another customer, and so on. Many other packages can also have macros implemented, but of course this depends largely on the application itself.

- Standard documents. It is unprofessional for an organisation to write up documents in an ad hoc manner. A client could receive correspondence from several persons or departments within the organisation, and if they are all written in a makeshift manner it will give a shoddy impression. Documents such as faxes, receipts, orders, invoices, and so on can be standardised, using agreed-on fonts, formatting, and logos, so that all correspondence looks coherent and professional. Microsoft Word, the most widely used word processor on PCs, supports the concept of Document Templates for this purpose. Simply create a standard document and click 'File' → 'Save As' → 'Save As Type' → Document Template (*.DOT)', and the template will appear in the options when creating a new document. Additionally, Form Fields can be added to help ensure the document retains its standardisation, and Mail Merge facilities are also available in Microsoft Word.

Fault Finding

At some time in their useful lives, every computer will suffer from faults. In any reasonably sized organisation, diagnosing and repairing these faults is usually the realm of the IT support technician, but for home users the only options are to repair it yourself, or find someone knowledgeable to do it for you. For those working in a commercial or similar organisational environment, it is suggested that the chapter on PC Support is read. Furthermore, it is important anyone embarking on any troubleshooting must read at least the section on Health & Safety, to prevent both personal injury and damage to equipment.

Fault Finding Principles

Faultfinding should be carried out with certain principles always in mind. If these are adhered to, then faultfinding changes from being a daunting challenge to being an engaging and entertaining pursuit. These principles include.

- Start with an empty mind. It is very easy to set off down the wrong track altogether because of simple prejudices, i.e. making judgements before starting. Assuming that certain things are usually faulty, or that other things never give any trouble, can waste time energy and effort. Another factor that can cause confusion is the description of faults offered by the user. Although well meaning, system users are liable to assume that their understanding of the system is greater than it is. Start with the premise that anything and everything is possible.

- Concentrate on one fault only. Although you may be presented with a system that appears to have a series of faults, never attempt to fix more than one thing at a time. It may be that perceived multiple faults are all the result of a deeper underlying single problem. In the worst case, when there *are* multiple faults it simply means that by solving them in sequence the system gradually gets better.

- Observe carefully, using all of your senses:

See:	Screen contents, error messages, motion, lights (e.g. on the keyboard, printer, modem and disk drives), thermal footprints (even smoke!).
Hear:	Fans whirring, motors spinning, warning beeps, phone-lines tones, modem negotiations.
Feel:	Fans blowing, vibration from rotating parts, temperature of chips, electrostatic charge on screens.
Smell:	Components burning, dust, odour from spillages, ozone from office machines or from a high-voltage leak in the monitor, printer toner.
Time:	Start-up times, shutdown times, delays in running standard tasks, modem data transfer rates, Internet delays.
Sequences:	Noting the order of events (e.g. does the computer hang before or after a particular device is used).
Tests:	Noting the results of physical, electronic or software tests. Could include testing fuses, continuity of cables, results of POST card check, reports from diagnostic software, etc.
Differences:	Noting the performance comparisons between two identical computer's running the same application.
Memory:	Using your recollections and those of others.

  In practice, a number of these factors are used together in forming an opinion. For example, a disk drive may have an LED illuminated, indicating that power is reaching it. However, if no vibration can be felt by lightly touching the drive case, the motor is not spinning and therefore the drive is probably faulty.

- Concentrate on what you really observe, not on what you think that means. It is very easy to say that the whistling you observe could be a faulty hard disk bearing, particularly if there have been hard disk errors reported. However, it could equally well be the PSU fan, processor fan, CD drive, floppy disk or even the monitor's line output stage! Could some of these cause intermittent read faults?

Using a systematic method

The process of detecting the fault should not be intuitive, using inspiration or guesswork. Neither should it be a haphazard elimination process, trying out a series of random tests and equipment replacements until the problem is solved. For all but the simplest faults (i.e. broken cables or other visible effects), a systematic approach should be adopted. This may take the form of a flow chart, a checklist or even a computer expert system. In all these cases, the previous experience of technicians has shaped the best method of diagnosing problems. The experience embodied in the flow of questions and tests in the diagnostic system is then available to others.

If the system is followed, the technician should be provided with an answer that accurately diagnoses the problem.

Typical Systematic Methods

Breaking into logically discrete chunks

A good technician understands how the system he/she is working on works at a logical block level, and is able to point to the edges of the logical blocks. In that way, tests can be made at the inputs and outputs of each block - and decisions made based on the presence, absence or state of such signals.

These logical blocks do not need to be physically separate from each other. In the same way that a car contains an engine, clutch, gearbox, suspension etc and these units are often combined with each other, there are interlinked functional blocks within a PC's various subsystems. Many of these elements, for example, are on the motherboard.

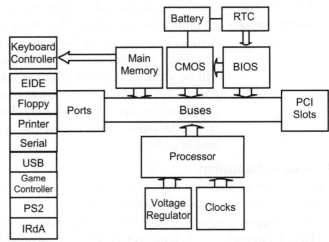

The illustration shows a simple block diagram of a PC system.

Hardware v Software faults

One of the major decisions to be made when assessing a reported fault is whether the fault is in the hardware or software. The usual way to find this out is to eliminate the software. This involves starting Windows and stepping through the startup (via f8), to eliminate drivers and handlers for everything except the device under investigation

Iteratively breaking the problem into sub-problems:

Once it has been decided that a fault lies in a certain area, that area can be subdivided into smaller sections that can be independently checked for faults. For example, a fault in a printer might be caused by a faulty interface, faulty paper handling, or faulty imaging, and each of these in turn can be broken down into further sub sections. Once the problem has been broken down into its logical component parts these should be tested methodically.

There are various ways to do this, among them:

Front to Back.

The first test is done on the input of the first logical block, then the output of that block, which is also the input to the next one, and so on. This methodology has the advantage that inputs are guaranteed to exist and be good on blocks that are working, and to not exist or be bad on blocks that are faulty. When a block can be found which has a good input but a bad output, the fault has been isolated.

Advantages: Good for tracing signals, intuitive.

Disadvantages: Signal paths can be tortuous, and can split/join at random.

Example: In a dialup TCP/IP stack, each software component depending on the previous one. The order is Application - transport layer – MAC layer – Winsock, and the links between each is easily tested.

Back to Front.

In this method, the output is checked. If it is not ok, then the input to the last stage is checked, and if necessary supplied to prove the last stage. Assuming all is well, the tester then moves to the previous stage and tests it, until a fault is found.

Advantages: Preferable for tracing power faults. The tester is not exposed to power until the fault is found, and is therefore safer.

Disadvantages: Always working *'beyond the fault'*. This usually means that there is very little output to test.

Example: Powered speakers don't work, try power at the speaker, then at the plugtop supply box, then at the four-way extension, and then at the mains, until good power is found. The last element that was bypassed is faulty.

Successive Binary Division

In this method, the first test is done in the middle, and depending on the outcome the next test is done either at the 25% or 75% mark. With each test, half of the remaining blocks are eliminated.

Advantages: Good for systems with a large chain of small blocks. Saves a lot of work.

Disadvantages: Of limited use on systems that are not linked in a chainlike manner.

Example: A room in a telesales office contains 60 PCs on a single 10Base2 Ethernet segment, terminated at either end. To find a cable fault, start at machine 30. The termination will be good on one half of the segment but not the other. Lets say the upper half is good. We now check the lower half by dividing into 1-15 and 16-30. If 1-15 is good, we then check 16-30 by dividing into 16-23 and 24-30. Eventually we find the fault in less than 6 tests (compared to an average of 30 tests doing it one machine at a time in order).

Trial by substitution:

One of the most common ways of testing equipment is to deploy an identical replacement and see if the fault *'goes away'* with the new component.

Advantages: Quick, simple and unambiguous results.

Disadvantages: A replacement has to be available. The fault that destroyed the original might also destroy the replacement.

Example: Workstation 13 has no picture on the monitor. Firstly, test the monitor by attaching it to the next workstation, and test the system by attaching it to the monitor at the next system.

Trial by symmetry

It is very easy to compare settings, responses and the like on two identical systems as a means to faultfinding. Indeed some systems have multiple identical channels that can be compared, audio comes in identical stereo pairs and video travels in groups of three (Red, Green, and Blue). Comparing and contrasting can be very enlightening.

Advantages: Simple informative, easily followed.

Disadvantages: Not always applicable

Example: System reports *"hard disk controller error"*. Inspection reveals twin IDE drives, master A and slave B. By swapping jumpers to make B master and A slave, we can compare the IDE controllers on the two drives. If the fault 'disappears' then A's Controller is faulty, if it does not then there is a slight chance that both controllers are faulty, but it is more likely that the IDE port on the motherboard is at fault.

Trial by Isolation

It is sometimes easiest to test components away from their parent system, particularly where the interactions between the component and its parent are complex. This might involve designing a test rig of some sort.

Advantages: Allows totally unambiguous tests.

Disadvantages: May involve some extra cost.

Example: NiMH battery for laptop computer appears to be faulty, but it is impossible to test while it is behind its little door powering the laptop. One possible solution is to charge the battery overnight in the computer and then test it outside the PC. Another is to build a dummy battery that makes the proper connections but allows wires to come out to the real battery now situated outside and accessible to test equipment.

Trial by integration

The opposite test strategy also applies. Some situations demand that the equipment under test is integrated in some host system before it can be tested.

Advantages : Usually go/no go solution.

Disadvantages: Needs an expensive host. Potential damage to host.

Example: PC Power supplies will generally not work without a load; therefore they are best tested by attaching them to a known mainboard or drive. Some workshops keep elderly or redundant equipment for this purpose.

Cascade Faults

Some faults cascade. That is to say a simple fault will cause a condition that causes another fault or faults. This is not a good thing. It is usually discovered when the support person fixes the perceived fault but it immediately recurs. The best advice is to isolate the most obvious suspects and then re-introduce them in a controlled order until the fault is found.

Advantages: The only positive thing that can be said about such a situation is that it is better than an intermittent fault!

Disadvantages: Expensive, difficult to fault-find.

Example: PC blows a fuse. Replacement fuse pops too. This suggests that we are not dealing with a tired fuse, but a condition that is causing the fuse to blow. Suspect the power supply and try a replacement. If all is well then the power supply was faulty, if not then something is drawing huge current to cause the supply to blow fuses as a safety measure. Isolate drives, motherboard, etc., and reconnect one at a time until the culprit is found.

Intermittent Faults

These are faults that do not always happen, or that happen only occasionally. They will never put in an appearance when you are waiting for them! They can only be found by detective work and intense observation. Sometimes observation by proxy! Get the user to note exactly what error messages occur, and when and what they were doing, and why. Then look for patterns; always first thing in the morning, always on hot days, always just after printing. Try to think laterally. Eventually a factor should emerge that explains the fault. If it does not then it may be necessary to embark on a program of trial replacements until the fault is isolated

Advantages: Because of their intermittent nature they won't be put at a high priority on the work list. However, they have a way of becoming a bit of an obsession with technicians.

Disadvantages: Can be frustrating and are a good way of getting the PC support group a bad name.

Example: Laser printer is intermittently blotchy; most days it gives perfect results, some days it is blotchy. Scanning the logs shows that this fault is hardly ever reported in months with an R in the name, but regularly reported May – August. It is also only ever reported in the afternoon. Investigations revealed that the corner where it sits is a suntrap and excess heat from the sun through the window causes the blotchiness. Such information may have been recovered from a well-documented logbook.

Causes of intermittent faults

There are occasions when there are no error messages displayed and the unit, keyboard, monitor, etc. all seem to be functioning satisfactorily. The problem seems to be an intermittent one, with the machine hanging up while lying idle, or crashing in the middle of a program. Either hardware or software can cause these problems.

If the fault develops when there is no software loaded, then the source is easier to determine; the fault must be a hardware one. While the source of the difficulty may be known, however, tracing the cause of the problem may be more difficult, since the fault cannot be reproduced to order.

Intermittent hardware problems may be:

- Overheating faults. As manufacturers race to bring ever faster performance machines on to the market, the CPU and other chips are forced to run at alarming clock rates and chip temperatures increase beyond the point of stability. So much so, that CPU chips have fans built on to their heat sinks, to dissipate the enormous amounts of heat that they generate.
- Design faults. Using memory chips that are not always able to keep up with the speed of the CPU. Try altering the clock speed or the memory timings (through the BIOS settings) and see if the intermittent fault disappears.
- Intermittent connections. These may be dry joints in soldered connections to the motherboard, power supply, disk drive, etc. These may be either component or wiring connections. The application of heat (by a hair dryer or similar) to an area of the board will expand any metal and hopefully expose the intermittent connection. Conversely, if the problem is already present, the application of a freeze spray (available from electronic component suppliers) to selected areas will cool the area and hopefully restore normal operations, thereby showing up the problem connection.
- Software problems are more difficult to detect, as the fault may only occur under specific circumstances. For example, it may require a particular clash of interrupts such as when using a particular function of an application over a local area network. There are so many possible permutations that this may take exhaustive tests to expose. A lot of time can be saved if users are encouraged to note down exactly what they were doing at the time of the fault.
- Lastly, the problem may be due to spikes or fluctuations in the mains supply affecting the data on the buses and causing the machine to crash. This may require the fitting of an uninterruptible power supply (UPS) to the computer. This is particularly important for local area network servers and other important machines in the company.

Breaking Loops

Very often a fault lies within a loop in a system, where the output is dependent on the input, which is dependent on the output. While this loop is intact it is very difficult to find faults. By breaking the loop, the problem is reduced to a straight line problem and the' front to back' or 'back to front' faultfinding techniques can be used.

Advantages: Simplifies a difficult problem.

Disadvantages: Finding a place to break the loop and a way of breaking it without upsetting the system can be tricky.

Example: Dot matrix printer suffering head jams. The ribbon is driven by the head motion and if the ribbon is removed, the controller notes the broken ribbon and stops the head to minimise damage. Remove the ribbon and run printer to see what is jamming head, but constantly twiddle the ribbon motion sensor with a screwdriver to simulate ribbon motion and allow system to function.

Environmentally based faults
Thermal

Heat can cause a great many faults. SIMMS were invented because on early PCs, the DIL packaged RAM chips moved a tiny fraction of a millimetre each time the machine heated up and cooled down. Eventually they would 'creep' out of their sockets. Technicians routinely solved memory faults by simply pressing all the RAM chips into place with their thumb. IBM proposed a solution whereby the chips were soldered but still replaceable and held against a spring to stop thermal effects and thus the SIMM was born. Extreme heat warps plastic, causes LCDs to lose their contrast, and causes mayhem with semiconductors. Even moderate heat causes component lifetimes to be shortened. Obstructing ventilation causes heat. Finally, heat sets laser printer toner. Clothes and hands that have become messed with toner should be washed in cold water (as hot water causes the toner to set).

Light

Light is more of an inconvenience than a hazard. Glare, both direct, from a bright window behind the screen, and reflected, say the reflection in the screen of a window across the room, are health and safety hazards. Flashing light at certain frequencies can lead to seizures and illnesses in certain people. Bright light can also erase EPROM bios chips if they are left for a long time with their window uncovered. Bright light will damage the photosensitive drum of a laser printer.

Dust

A coating of dust acts like a blanket and causes items to retain heat and so suffer thermal failure. Dust also wears moving parts that it comes in contact with, causes lightweight switches to stick and obstructs optical sensors and CD/DVD lenses. The contamination of a laser drum with dust can cause repeating patterns on every sheet printed. High voltages attract dust, and so screens and laser printers are particularly vulnerable. Ozone filters in laser printers also clog with dust.

Smoke

Smoke is a lot like dust, and does everything that dust does. In addition, smoke travels in directions other than down, and so tends to get more places. Cigarette smoke leaves a mucky brown tarry residue on the high voltage trays of monitors and can cause arcing. The effects of both smoke and dust can be partially alleviated by using an ioniser. This causes the particles to stick to surfaces close to the ioniser, thus keeping the air elsewhere cleaner.

Magnetic fields

Magnetic fields cause errors in magnetic storage devices, distortion on picture tubes, and induce a current in anything that contains a coil of wire. Sources of magnetic fields include loudspeakers, monitors, tools, fridge magnets, and electrical motors of all sorts. It is also produced by the mains transformers used to power loudspeakers, external modems, external zip drives and even halogen lamps. Audio leads, monitor screens, disks, etc. should all be kept a distance from such sources.

Electric / Electromagnetic fields

These fields are caused by the mains wiring, and all mains, radio frequency and oscillatory electrical circuits. They can act at a distance and can damage magnetic storage and induce unwanted voltages. Sources include microwave ovens, car ignition circuits, fluorescent lights, CB and amateur radio, mobile phones etc.

Judder /Jar/ Mechanical

Newton's laws of motion explain that there is no force on a moving body. However, starting and stopping causes forces, and the more sudden the jar the greater the force experienced. No system should be exposed to mechanical shocks.

Ingress of liquid

It goes almost without saying that ingress of liquid should be avoided. However should a keyboard have coffee or fizzy drinks spilled upon it then any damage tends to be a result of sugar or fruit acid, not the liquid. It may well be that washing the component in clean water and then carefully drying it out will restore it to full health.

Special cases

With both power supply systems, which are nearly all switch mode devices, and monitors, which tend also to be switch mode in their construction, there is a huge electronic complexity - and extreme danger from lethal voltages. The time taken to safely open, examine, fault find and repair such products far exceeds the economic cost of the device. Additionally, the risks involved are great, even for fully trained personnel. Both power supplies and monitors are now nearly commodity items and really do not warrant attempts at repair.

User Errors

The great bulk of faults reported to help desks are based on a simple misunderstanding or mistake on the part of the computer user. The user is part of the system, and a poorly trained user will almost certainly report more faults than a well-trained one.

Problems reported as faulty devices might in fact turn out to be devices that are unplugged, not switched on, or unconnected. Software 'bugs' can turn out to be misuse of software or misconceptions about what the software can do. Users with relatively little computer experience may well claim the computer is faulty when in fact they are simply using the wrong function or misunderstanding what their software is supposed to do.

And of course, users can be the source of most forms of real faults. Many users have spilled coffee or correction fluid over keyboards, some have jammed floppy drives with disks inserted incorrectly, and installation of unauthorised software such as games onto business PCs can result in reduced performance or even virus infection. It may be of use to identify those users who are less 'computer literate' and who may require a short training course in how to use their equipment properly.

Common equipment faults

Although there are a large number of faults that can occur in any given computer device, there are certain faults that manifest far more often than others. For example, the number of calls to technical support that turn out to be a simple case of a cable accidentally pulled out far outnumber those that involve malfunctioning hard disk electronics. The following pages describe the most common symptoms of system failure, and some typical causes and solutions to these problems. The possible causes are listed roughly in order of their probability.

However, this is far from an exhaustive list. Thankfully, serious computer faults are relatively rare, but they do happen, and a comprehensive guide to all possible failures in all components would not fit inside a single book. However, if the following guides to common faults are not of use, then systematic investigation in a manner as described previously in this chapter is the only definitive solution.

Power Problems

When the machine is first switched on, the main unit and the monitor should both be powered up. This should result in some form of screen output. This might be the result of the computer self-test or the normal Windows or other operating system screen.

If no video output is apparent, it would be wise to give the machine another hard boot, before carrying out the rest of the checks, since this could be caused by a minor, temporary glitch of some kind.

Symptom:	The computer does nothing; not even the fan inside the computer is turning.
Cause:	The power cable may not be properly attached. Make sure the power cable is properly attached, both to the base unit, and to the power outlet.
Cause:	The computer may not actually be switched on. Some computers have a power switch at the back of the case, as well as a power button at the front. If this is the case, make sure both are turned on.
Cause	The wall socket may not be supplying power in the first place. Check that the socket is supplying power, by attaching any other electrical device to the socket.
Cause :	The fuse may be blown. Replace the fuse in the PSU, if accessible, and/or the fuse in the power plug. Make sure that the replacement is of the same amperage!
Cause :	The power cable could be faulty. Try a known-good power cable.
Cause :	The PSU could be damaged. Do not attempt to fix any internal components unless fully trained in their repair, as they contain high-voltage capacitors that may still contain power even when switched off. Instead, replace the PSU or the entire base unit.

Symptom:	The computer does not beep and nothing appears on the screen, but the power supply's fan is turning.
Cause :	The motherboard may not be receiving power from the PSU. Make sure the PSU is attached to the motherboard. Replace the PSU with a known-good model if possible.
Cause :	The hard disk IDE cables may be attached incorrectly. In some systems, attaching an IDE cable upside down into a hard disk will actually stop the machine from responding at all. Fortunately, in modern systems, a key slot prevents incorrect insertion of cables. If it is an older PC, check that the IDE cables are attached correctly.
Cause :	The CPU may be unseated, or damaged. Make sure that a CPU is fitted and is held securely in place, with no bent pin (if it is of a socket type CPU fitting). Try the CPU in an otherwise working machine, if possible. Do not try a known-good CPU in this machine except as a last resort, as the fault could be severe enough to damage it!
Cause :	The BIOS or chipset could be malfunctioning. If the BIOS chip is replaceable, try putting the chip in an otherwise working machine. Again, do not place a known-good BIOS chip in this motherboard, as it could become damaged. The chipset is not generally replaceable, except by fitting a whole new motherboard.

Cause :   The motherboard may not be receiving a *'Power Good'* signal from the power supply. The Power Good line is a wire on the motherboard power connector that is used by the PSU to signal when it is safe for the PC to begin booting. If the Power Good signal is not received, it has the same effect as holding down the reset button permanently – the POST will not begin, and the hard drive will not initialise.

This could be caused by the PSU failing to stabilise the power supply for safe PC operation, or it could simply be a fault in the Power Good line, but either way the PSU should be replaced or sent to a competent electrical engineer.

Display faults

There are several components that must be functional in order for the display system as a whole to operate, and of course faults may develop in any of these. The most common symptoms and the faults that typically cause them, are as follows:

Symptom: Monitor power light does not come on.

Cause :   The monitor power cable may not be properly attached.
Make sure the power cable is properly attached, both to the monitor, and to the power outlet. Remember, in some cases, the monitor receives its mains supply from a cable attached to a rear socket on the computer, while other monitors have their own independent mains connections.

Cause :   The wall socket may not be supplying power in the first place.
Check that the socket is supplying power, by attaching any other electrical device to the socket. Of course, if the power is supplied via a socket on the PC, it will not supply power unless the PC is switched on.

Cause :   The monitor's fuse may be blown.
Replace the fuse in the monitor, if accessible, and/or the fuse in the monitor power plug if it attaches to a wall socket. Make sure that the replacement is of the same amperage!

Cause :   The power cable could be faulty.
Try a known-good power cable.

Cause :   The internal circuitry could be seriously damaged.
Do not attempt to fix any internal components unless fully trained in their repair, as they contain high-voltage capacitors that may still contain power even when switched off. Instead, replace the monitor.

Symptom: Monitor power light blinks, or is red instead of green.

Cause :   The monitor is receiving power, but is not receiving a data signal. Modern monitors are 'power saving' models, and therefore do not power up fully unless they have a picture to display. Make sure the computer is switched on and working. If the computer may be faulty, try the *'base unit faults'* section, later in this chapter.

Cause :   The video data cable (the VGA lead) may not be properly connected, or may contain bent pins. Make sure the computer is properly connected. Carefully unbend any bent pins using tweezers or fine nosed pliers.

Cause :   The computer may have suffered a serious crash. Try rebooting.

Cause :   The video adapter may have developed a fault. Disable or remove the current video adapter and replace it with a new video card.

Symptom: The power light is normal, but the screen is blank.

Cause :   If the monitor is <u>not</u> a power-saving model, it may be that the computer is not supplying an image to the monitor. Check under *'base unit faults'*, later in this chapter.

Cause :   The brightness may be turned right down. Change the brightness of the monitor, using either the OSD or the brightness knob.

Cause :   If the monitor is not a power saving model, this could be a symptom of any of the same faults that could cause the power light to blink in a power saving model. Try any of the solutions for the faults that would cause a power saving monitor to blink.

Symptom: The screen is flickering badly.

Cause : The display adapter may be set to a refresh rate that the monitor does not support. In the display adapter properties, set the screen refresh rate to one that the monitor supports.

Cause : In the case of older monitors, the current screen resolution may only be supported in an interlaced mode. Try reducing the resolution of the screen if this is an acceptable solution.

Cause : Occasionally, this symptom may be caused by slightly incorrect synchronisation. Randomly changing the vertical hold can sometimes jog it back into synch.

Symptom: The basic boot-up sequence appears normal, but upon entering Windows the display is unreadable.

Cause : The video adapter is probably set to a resolution that the monitor is not capable of supporting. Boot into Safe Mode by pressing f8 just before the Windows boot-up sequence begins, and selecting Safe Mode. When this loads, change to a lower resolution display and reboot.

Cause : The video adapter may be damaged. Replace it with a known-good model.

Cause : The monitor may be damaged. Replace it with a known-good model.

Symptom: The screen is corrupted, even during the boot-up sequence.

Cause : If the video adapter is a video card, it may not be firmly fitted. Try re-seating it in case it is simply a bad connection.

Cause : The cause may be faulty memory chips on the video adapter. Replace the video adapter.

Symptom: The screen has a distinct coloration to it, is distorted, or does not fit the screen properly.

Cause : The monitor settings may have been changed. Check the settings available on the monitor, such as horizontal and vertical position, Pincushion, Trapezoid, Rotation, and Colour Control.

Cause : The monitor might have become magnetised. Move the monitor away from any source of strong magnetic fields, such as speakers, fax machines etc. If this does not fix the problem, try 'degaussing', which is built in to all modern monitors.

Cause : In some cases the internal components may be slightly damaged. Replace the monitor.

Symptom: Windows boots into VGA mode, even though the adapter and monitor are capable of much better resolution.

Cause : The display settings may have been changed, deliberately or accidentally, to a lower resolution. Check the display properties, and change the resolution if possible.

Cause : The display driver may be corrupted, badly configured, or the wrong driver. Drivers are the pieces of software that are used to ensure the correct interface between the monitor, the video card and even particular application programs. For instance, Windows provides a set of drivers to match itself to most screen standards and most graphics cards. Check that the correct driver is in use; an nVidia driver will not drive an ATI video card, for example. Ensure that the correct driver is installed, and that it is set up properly. Most cards report their model during boot-up, check that this is the driver Windows has installed. Go to the manufacturer's website to see if there is an updated driver available. If so, install it.

Symptom: Graphics updates on the screen are slower than expected.
Cause : Badly configured settings. Many 3D cards come with additional configuration options in the Display Properties. Using this, disable any advanced 3D features in case any of these are incorrectly configured.
Cause : Incorrect or out-of-date graphics API. In addition to the actual device driver, there may be additional video software, such as Microsoft DirectX, or OpenGL drivers. This particularly applies to video cards optimised for 3D acceleration. Incorrectly configured or out-of-date drivers of these types rarely cause problems with the normal display, but could seriously affect the 3D performance of the card. Make sure the device driver and 3D system drivers are installed, up to date, and not corrupted.
Cause : Failing that, the software may not be fully compatible with that type of 3D interface or card – always check the software manual where 3D software is concerned. There may be a 'software render' mode that bypasses the card's 3D functions but is slower.

Symptom: Screen corruption occurs when dragging windows or icons, minimising, etc.
Cause : This is usually due to a driver problem. Check the display driver is current, configured correctly, and not corrupted. Re-install the driver if possible.
Cause : In rare cases it can be due to faulty video memory. Try a known-good video card to eliminate the possibility of hardware failure.

Hard disk faults

Hard disk problems tend to come in two forms: physical and logical faults. Physical faults include such problems as broken hard disks, faulty cables, or damaged interfaces. Logical faults imply that the hardware is working, but that the contents of the disk are somehow corrupted or set up incorrectly. In either case, the data on the hard disk is under threat. Taking adequate and regular backups is the only way to fully recover from a damaged hard disk system.

Symptom: "Hard disk 0 failure" or similar error message.
Cause : This typically happens on machines with very old BIOSes, or which are not set to autodetect hard disks. The figures for cylinders, heads, and sectors on the disk can be entered manually. Hopefully these figures will be printed on the side of the disk itself.
Cause : It is sometimes due to incorrect BIOS settings, i.e. the number of cylinders, heads and sectors. Run the autodetect procedure in the BIOS, or check the figures manually.
Cause : It can also indicate any of the faults that also cause a "No Boot Device" error. See the causes for that symptom.

Symptom: Failure to detect hard disk during bootup, "No Boot Device" or other error message.
Cause : The hard disk may not have a power cable attached. Connect a power cable from the PSU inside the PC to the hard disk.
Cause : The hard disk may not have a data cable properly attached. Check for bent pins before inserting the data cable, and make sure the cable is attached the correct way round. In some PCs it is possible to accidentally put the cable in upside down.
Cause : The hard disk could be attached to the wrong IDE port. In most cases the hard disk should be attached to the primary IDE connector. Usually the secondary IDE connector is only used if both primary connectors are already taken.
Cause : The 'master/slave' settings could be incorrect. If it is the main drive on the cable, for example if it is the boot disk, make sure the jumpers are set to 'master'. If it is the secondary drive on the cable, make sure it is set to 'slave'.
Cause : If the drive is a SCSI drive, it may have an incompatible ID. Check that the drive's SCSI ID is distinct from the ID of all other components attached to the SCSI card.
Cause : The cable, adapter, or hard disk could be physically damaged. Try replacing the cable, and then the adapter if possible, with known-good components. If neither of these work, replace the hard disk itself.

Symptom:	"Disk Boot Failure" message, or unspecified failure to boot from hard disk.
Cause :	This generally indicates corruption of the boot sector. The disk may still be accessible by booting from floppy (e.g. in order to backup files) but the hard disk itself will not boot. Depending on whether the boot sector is physically or logically corrupted, a reformat or even SYS command may fix this problem, or at worst the disk may be unsalvageable. In some cases, a disk repair package such as Norton Disk Doctor or SCANDISK may be able to repair damaged boot sectors. If a repair or reformat is performed, it will usually be necessary to backup important files before doing so, and restore the files once the disk is back in working order.
Cause :	In extreme cases, the master boot record (MBR) may be corrupt. If the MBR is corrupted, the only remedy may be to repartition the entire disk using FDISK.

Optical drive faults

Although CD-ROM and DVD-ROM differ greatly in capacity, they both operate using almost identical optical principles. Almost all faults apply equally to both types of device.

Symptom:	When accessed, the disc spins for a very long time and then an 'Error reading from disc' or similar error appears.
Cause :	The disc in the drive might be dirty. Again, CD cleaning kits are easily available, but it may be worth trying a known-good CD in the drive to make sure that this is the cause of the problem.
Cause :	The lens may be dirty. There are many CD-lens cleaning kits available and using one of these may alleviate the problem.
Cause :	The circuitry or mechanism in the drive could be faulty. Replace the drive.

Symptom:	"General Failure reading drive" error message.
Cause :	There may not be a readable CD in the drive. It may be empty, of an incompatible format, or badly scratched. It may even simply be dirty, in which case it can be cleaned and might begin working again.
Cause :	A dirty lens can also cause this problem. See the previous fault for details.
Cause :	The CD-ROM drive might not be connected properly to the IDE connector. This normally only applies to computers that have recently been worked on internally, however.

Floppy disk faults

Floppy disk drives are fairly simple devices in comparison to most computer equipment. Unlike most other computer devices, floppy disk faults are well understood, and relatively easy to diagnose and resolve.

Symptom:	The floppy drive does not spin, and the light does not come on.
Cause :	The power cable may not be connected properly. Connect a power cable from the PSU inside the PC to the hard disk.
Cause :	The data cable may not be connected properly. Ensure that the data cable properly connects the floppy drive to the floppy connector on the motherboard or adapter.
Cause :	The floppy drive, cable, or IDE adapter may be physically damaged. First try a known-good cable. If that does not work, try a known-good drive, and finally a known-good adapter if possible.

Symptom:	The floppy drive spins continually, and the light is on continually.
Cause :	The main cause of this fault is by plugging the data cable connector into the socket incorrectly, either at the floppy drive end or at the motherboard end. Ensure that the floppy connectors are inserted correctly.

Cause : The floppy drive, cable, or IDE adapter may be physically damaged. Try replacing these components with known-good components where possible.

Symptom: The drive lights but error messages appear when trying to access a floppy.
Cause : The disk may be unformatted or formatted incorrectly. If it is formatted incorrectly (e.g. A 2.8M disk in a 1.4M drive, or a Mac disk in a PC drive), then it is simply not accessible in the drive, and its contents must be accessed on another, compatible system. If it is unformatted, then simply formatting it should solve the problem. **Cause** : The disk may be damaged. check it thoroughly with a utility such as ScanDisk. **Cause** : The floppy drive may be dirty. Try cleaning it with a floppy drive head cleaner. **Cause** : The floppy drive, cable, or IDE adapter may be physically damaged. Try replacing these components with known-good components where possible.

Symptom: Unable to boot from floppy.
Cause : The disk may not in fact be a boot disk. Only disks that have been made bootable can be booted from. If this has not been done, then the disk will not boot. Use the '*create system disk*' option in Windows, or SYS command in DOS. **Cause** : The disk may be inaccessible. Any of the problems associated with being unable to access the disk may be the cause – see the symptom above.

SCSI Device faults

Both internal SCSI devices, such as hard disks and CD-ROM drives, and external SCSI devices, such as scanners, are subject to some of the same faults, since they all must connect to SCSI controllers. Some of these problems are listed below, but check the fault section for the relevant piece of equipment as well. For example, if a SCSI hard disk is faulty, check the hard disk fault section as well as this section.

Symptom: The SCSI device is not recognised during the adapter's initialisation at bootup.
Cause : The SCSI cable may not be properly terminated. Both the internal and the external chains must be terminated. Furthermore, if the chain is terminated before reaching a given device, the device will not be recognised. Make sure the last device on the chain is where the chain terminates. **Cause** : The SCSI ID numbers may be conflicting. Inspect the settings on each device (including the adapter) to make sure two devices do not share the same ID. **Cause** : Either the device or the SCSI adapter is faulty. Try the device in a known-good machine, and/or a known-good device in this machine, to determine the faulty component.

Symptom: The SCSI device is recognised during initialisation, but not in Windows.
Cause : If the device is a hard disk, it may not be partitioned and formatted. Or, it may be formatted to a standard that is not compatible. **Cause** : The operating system may not have the correct drivers for the device. Some devices may not be plug and play compatible, and most will require a driver disk.

Base unit faults

The motherboard is the 'backbone' of the computer, through which all data flows. Therefore, faults with the motherboard or any of the major components attached to it can easily prevent a system from functioning at all. Other components inside the base unit include the Power Supply Unit (PSU), which can cause some rather strange errors if it is not functioning properly. The base unit also includes the hard disk of course, and some IO devices, but these appear elsewhere.

Because the BIOS beep codes (see later in this chapter) vary, it is not possible to produce a definitive list of faults that cause a specific series of beeps. The common faults below, then, are based on general fault finding. If a system gives a beep code, it may save time if it is possible to consult a motherboard manual and find out what error the beep code refers to, rather than try all the options listed here.

Symptom:	The computer beeps more than once and nothing appears on the screen.
Cause :	The video adapter may not be functioning properly. If the video adapter is built in to the motherboard and is not functioning, look at the manual to see if it is possible to replace it with a video card. (this may involve setting jumpers on the motherboard as well as fitting a new card) If the system already uses a video card in an expansion slot, make sure it is seated firmly. Replace the card with a known good video card if possible.
Cause :	The memory may be malfunctioning, or attached incorrectly. Make sure the memory chips are seated properly; re-seat them in case there is a bad connection. Ensure that the chips are of the correct type. For example, DIMMs come in several voltages and some systems may require use of a certain type. Empty RIMM sockets must have continuity devices installed; SIMMs must be used in matched pairs in a Pentium system; and so on. Try the memory chips in an otherwise working system – do not try known-good chips in this system, except as a last resort, in case they become damaged.
Cause :	The Keyboard Controller (KBC) may be seriously damaged, or the keyboard may have a serious fault. Replace the KBC if this is possible, and try a known-good keyboard.

I/O faults

Input and Output devices also develop faults. For the purposes of faultfinding, the keyboard and mouse will be considered to be part of the computer in general, rather than as peripheral devices. It is assumed that most keyboards and mice are of the PS2 type connector. If a particular system uses a 6-pin DIN keyboard connector, a serial mouse, or USB keyboard or mouse, then some of these causes may not apply.

Symptom:	Keyboard failure on boot-up.
Cause :	The keyboard may be unplugged, or plugged in to the wrong port. Ensure that the keyboard is plugged in to the correct port on the computer base unit. With older, non-colour co-ordinated systems, it is easy to accidentally plug the keyboard into the mouse socket.
Cause :	The keyboard may have a key stuck down. Look for obviously jammed keys, and clean the keyboard.
Cause :	The keyboard (including the cable), the keyboard port, or the keyboard controller may be malfunctioning. Try replacing the keyboard with a known-good model. If this fails, try the inoperative keyboard in an otherwise functioning system. If this works, it indicates that the Keyboard Controller (KBC) on the motherboard of the first system may be damaged. In some systems the KBC can be replaced on its own but in many newer systems the entire motherboard may have to be replaced.
Symptom:	Keys on keyboard produce incorrect input when typing.
Cause :	The most likely cause is that the system is set up for the wrong country of keyboard. In Windows, the Regional Settings (or similar) in Control Panel determines the characters that correspond to each key on the keyboard. In DOS, it is the country code in the KEYB statement in CONFIG.SYS.
Cause :	In rare cases it may be due to a slightly faulty keyboard. Try cleaning the keyboard. If this does not work, replace the keyboard with a known-good model.

Symptom:	Keys on keyboard produce wildly inaccurate input, including beeps and control codes, when typing.
Cause :	This usually indicates a damaged cable. Replace the keyboard with a known-good model.
Cause :	It can also be indicative of a damaged KBC, or even keyboard port. If the good model still produces inaccurate input, open the case and ensure that the keyboard port has not become unseated from the motherboard. Replace the KBC if this is possible. Use a USB keyboard if possible. If not, the motherboard as a whole may need to be replaced.

Symptom: Mouse not detected when Windows boots up.
Cause : The mouse may not be attached, or may be attached to the wrong port. Ensure that the mouse is attached to the mouse port, and not to the keyboard port.
Cause : The mouse cable or the mouse itself may be damaged. Try replacing the mouse with a known-good model.
Cause : The mouse port may be damaged. a serial or USB mouse may have to be used, which in turn may necessitate the fitting of a new serial port.

Symptom: Mouse 'jumps' wildly around the screen.
Cause : This may indicate a damaged mouse cable. Try a known-good mouse.
Cause : The mouse may be of an incompatible type. Check that the correct mouse driver is installed. If the mouse is able to act in more than one mode, usually by a switch on the side of the mouse, try another mode.

Symptom: Mouse 'sticks' when moving around the screen.
Cause : The mouse ball or rollers may be dirty. The mouse ball may require cleaning fluid, but the rollers can often be cleaned with a pair of tweezers or a similar thin object. Don't use a sharp object, however, as they can easily damage the rollers.
Cause : Some mice use separate components for light emitters and detectors. You may be able to open the mouse, and move these optical elements closer together, as a temporary solution. However, this is indicative of a failing mouse and it will probably need replaced soon.
Cause : The mouse cable, or circuitry could be faulty. The only realistic solution is to replace the mouse.

Peripheral faults

Faults can also develop outside of the main computer system. Any external component can go wrong, and in fact the greatest number of technical support calls are due to one peripheral in particular – the printer.

Symptom: The printer does not seem to power up. The user will likely receive a *'Printer Not Responding'* error message.
Cause : The printer may not be attached to the power socket correctly. Check that the power cable is firmly attached both to the printer and to the power socket.
Cause : The power socket may not be supplying power. Try another electrical device in the socket to which the printer is attached, to check that it is powered.
Cause : The fuse may be blown. Not all printers have readily accessible fuses, but the power lead should have a fuse that can be replaced, or the entire power cable can often be replaced.
Cause : The printer may in fact be working fine, but has no 'on' light. Try using the printer.

Symptom: The printer is powered up, but will not print or do anything at all. The user may or may not receive a *'Printer Not Ready'* error message.
Cause : The printer cable may be unplugged, or damaged. Check that the data cable is firmly attached both to the printer, and to the PC's parallel or USB port.
Cause : The software may be trying to print to the wrong port. Check the printer properties, and ensure it is set to output to the same port as the printer is actually attached. For example, if the printer is on the first parallel port, it should be set to LPT1 in the printer properties.
Cause : The data port on the printer may not be functioning. Try a known-good printer.
Cause : The physical port on the PC could be damaged or disconnected. Try using the printer in another port if possible, but remember to change the output port in the printer properties. If using a parallel port, check that the port is attached to the motherboard.

Symptom: The printer prints, but the output is complete gibberish.

Cause : The wrong printer driver may be installed. Each printer uses its own set of codes to represent certain actions or data, and if the wrong driver is used, the output could essentially be random. Make sure the printer driver is for the correct model, and that it is up-to-date and uncorrupted. Re-install the driver if necessary.

Cause : There may be incorrect data in the print buffer, perhaps due to previous problems during printing. In Windows, double-click the printer icon in the system tray, and remove the current print job, then reset the printer.

Cause : The printer cable may be poorly connected, or damaged. Check the cable connections, and if necessary replace the cable with one that is known to work.

Cause : The printer may be set to emulate another printer. Ensure that the printer either has emulation disabled, or that it is emulating the printer whose driver is installed.

Symptom: The printouts are of poor quality.

Cause : If the printouts appear faded, the ink or toner may be running low. Replace the ink or toner cartridge.

Cause : If the printouts appear with vertical streaks of white, the print head may be clogged. If a printer cleaning kit is available, clean the print head. If it is an inkjet printer, replacing the ink cartridge may solve this problem.

Cause : The printer may be badly configured. Check the printer settings (e.g. a low dpi (dots per inch) setting, or being set to print in 'draft' mode, will affect the quality of the printouts.

Symptom: The printing has 'stalled'.

Cause : Printing might have deliberately been paused. Double-click on the printer in the Printers option of the Control Panel, and then select *'Printer'* → *'Resume Printing'*.

Cause : The printer may be out of paper, out of ink, or awaiting commands at the printer console. Less likely, though still a possibility, the printer cable may have become dislodged. Check the printer's status and make the necessary adjustments.

Cause : The print spooling software may have encountered problems. Rebooting may spur the spooler to try again; if not, you may have to delete the spooled print jobs to get the spooler to continue. The spooler in most Windows systems stores spooled print jobs in the 'C:\WINDOWS\SPOOL\PRINTERS\' folder.

Symptom: The software does not recognise the scanner.

Cause : The scanner may not be switched on.

Cause : With some systems, particular SCSI systems, the scanner must be switched on before the PC is powered up. Make sure the scanner is on before booting up.

Cause : The data cable could be damaged or not connected properly. Make sure there are no bent pins, and that the cable is firmly attached at both ends, to the correct ports. Replace the cable with a known working cable if one is available.

Cause : The driver may be incorrect. Scanners actually require two drivers – a scanner driver, and a TWAIN driver. The TWAIN driver provides an interface between any scanning device and any imaging software. Make sure that both the TWAIN system, and the scanner driver are up to date, correct, and uncorrupted. Re-install both if necessary.

Cause : If the scanner is attached via the parallel port, and is 'daisy-chained' through a printer, it may only work when the printer is also powered up.

Symptom: Scanned images are of poor quality.

Cause : The scanning interface may be badly configured. When scanning, a dialog box should appear, giving several options such as brightness, contrast, and resolution in dpi. Check that all of these options are at a suitable setting.

Cause : The scanning surface may be dirty. Clean the glass surface with a non-abrasive cleaner.

Cause : The scanning hardware may be damaged, necessitating replacing the scanner.

Symptom: The computer does not recognise the modem.

Cause : The modem may not be properly attached. If it is an external modem, make sure the cable is firmly attached to both the modem and the computer's port, and there are no bent pins. Replace it with a known-good cable if possible. If it is internal modem, re-seat the card firmly it in its socket to make sure there are not bad connections.

Cause : If it is an external modem, it may not be powered up. Make sure the modem is plugged in to a power socket, and is switched on.

Cause : The modem driver could be incorrect. Ensure that the driver is up-to-date and correct, and that the driver settings are correct. Re-install the driver if necessary.

Cause : The modem could be faulty. Try a known-good model.

Symptom: The modem will not dial out.

Cause : The modem may not be connected to the phone network. Ensure that the cable connecting the modem and the phone socket is firmly attached at both ends. Replace it with a known-good cable if possible.

Cause : The phone line may be having problems. If it is a shared line, check to make sure nobody or nothing else is using the line at the same time. Remember that a phone left off the hook will also stop the modem from dialling out.

Cause : The modem driver may be incorrect. Check that it is a current driver, with the correct settings.

Symptom: The modem will not connect properly to the remote system.

Cause : The number that the modem is dialling could be incorrect. Check the dial-up settings. In some cases this means using the Dial-Up Networking program to check the connection settings. Make sure it is dialling the correct number.

Cause : Other dial-up settings could also cause the problem. If the login username or password is incorrect, you will not be able to access the remote system. Other settings, such as whether to use SLIP or PPP, could also affect the system's ability to connect.

Cause : The remote system could be having problems. Contact whoever is at the other end of the system (for example your ISP) to see if there are any faults with their end.

Cause : The phone line could be at fault. If all other options have been exhausted, contact the phone service provider, to check on the quality of the line.

Symptom: The modem will not connect at full speed.

Cause : There may be degradation of the phone line's quality, due to having other devices on the line. For example, a home or office with several phones, a fax, and a modem attached, may find that the line quality is reduced because of all these devices being attached at the same time. Temporarily unplug some of these devices from the phone line and try again.

Cause : The phone socket or cable may be of poor quality. Try another phone socket, and then try a known-good modem cable.

Cause : The device properties may not be set up properly. In particular, the '*maximum speed*' setting in the '*Modem*' tab should be set at 115,200.

Cause : 56k modems frequently fail to achieve the full 56k speed. Due to the methods used, 56k modems can drop significantly in speed if the line quality is even slightly below par, or if the phone outlet is distant from the exchange. There is little that can be done about this, although a better quality modem might be able to squeeze some more speed out of the line.

Symptom: Windows does not recognise a peripheral device in the parallel, serial, USB or FireWire port.

Cause : The cable may be damaged. Try another cable if one is available.

Cause : The device could be faulty, or it may simply be switched off. Try using a known-good device where possible.

Cause : The correct driver may not be installed. Check that the driver exists in the Device Manager and that is has no problems. If it is missing or faulty, it can be re-installed or updated as necessary.

Cause : The port may be faulty. If a port (e.g. USB or FireWire) is located on an add-on card, the card can be replaced.   Where a port is on the motherboard (e.g. serial or USB), an add-on card can be fitted to provide a functioning port, can be replaced.

Common Networking faults

Networks can be extremely complex, and Network Support is very different from PC Support. However, PCs are increasingly being used with network access, so the more common faults should be considered by any PC Support technician.

Symptom: Unable to connect to the network.

Cause : There can be many reasons for this problem. The first thing to check is the physical side: make sure the cable is connected properly. In a typical office network this can be seen clearly by looking at the hub the system is connected to. If there is a lit LED next to that computer's cable, then the computer is connected properly.

Cause : The network settings may be incorrect on the local machine. For example, the driver for the network card might have a conflict in IRQs or I/O addresses; the system may be using the wrong protocols; or it may be set to log in to an incorrect or even non-existent domain or workgroup.

Cause : The server may not be set up to allow the machine to log on. It may not have your username and password, or it may be restricting access to certain physical machines on the network. This does not apply to Windows workgroups, where logins are ad hoc anyway.

Symptom: Unable to connect to a specific device on the network.

Cause : The system may not be attached properly to the network in the first place. See 'unable to connect to the network', above.

Cause : The remote device may not be set up correctly. If it is a remote PC, for example, it may not have File and Printer Sharing installed, and therefore is not broadcasting its existence on the domain or workgroup.

Cause : The remote device may have security restrictions in place.   Make sure you have legitimate access to the device.

Common OS faults

The computer hardware is not the only part of the system that can develop faults. All forms of software can cause problems. Faults in the Operating System, however, can be just as serious as hardware faults, in that they can often halt the system altogether.

Symptom: "Error in CONFIG.SYS line 1" or similar message.

Cause : There is a line in the CONFIG.SYS text file that is incorrect. In Windows ME and later, CONFIG.SYS should be empty, so this only occurs on older systems. The error message indicates which line, counted from the top, is causing the problem. The fault is often either a typing error, or a missing SYS file reference. Fix the typo, or check that the SYS file exists.

Symptom: "Bad or missing COMMAND.COM" message.

Cause : The file COMMAND.COM, which should be in the root directory of the boot drive, is either missing or corrupt. If COMMAND.COM is missing, boot from a system floppy disk, and type SYS C: (assuming of course the C: drive is the normal boot drive).

Symptom: "HIMEM.SYS not loaded" message.
Cause : Windows 95/98 requires the device driver HIMEM.SYS to be loaded during bootup. There should be a line in CONFIG.SYS similar to "DEVICE=C:\WINDOWS\HIMEM.SYS". If this is missing or has a typing error, it should be corrected.
Cause : If the file is referred to in CONFIG.SYS but the error still appears, it is because another command, which appears before HIMEM.SYS in the CONFIG.SYS, requires HIMEM.SYS to be loaded before it is executed. Move the HIMEM.SYS line to the top of the CONFIG.SYS file.

Symptom: "Missing or corrupt HIMEM.SYS" message.
Cause : The most likely cause of this error is that the line in CONFIG.SYS that loads HIMEM.SYS points to the wrong location. Make sure the path specified in CONFIG.SYS correctly refers to that file.
Cause : A less likely possibility is that the HIMEM.SYS file referred to in CONFIG.SYS is from a different version of Windows or DOS. Copy HIMEM.SYS from a boot floppy or another computer that is of the same version of Windows.
Cause : The possibility that HIMEM.SYS is in the correct place, but is actually damaged in some way, is extremely rare but cannot be discounted entirely. Try replacing it with a known-good copy from a working boot disk or machine with the same operating system.

Symptom: "Could not find NTLDR" message.
Cause : The file NTLDR, which is normally found in the root of the boot drive, is either missing or corrupt. This file is one of the few files used in the NT bootup process that are not system-specific, so it can be copied from an NT boot disk or another NT system.

Symptom: "Windows NT could not start because the following file is missing or corrupt" message.
Cause : This message will specify a file along with the error and, depending on the file, it can be caused by a huge range of software faults. Try booting into the Last Known Good Configuration and reversing any recent changes to the operating system. If that does not work, the only solution may be an Emergency Repair Disk or reinstallation of Windows.

Symptom: The GUI (Graphical User Interface) does not start.
Cause : The MSDOS.SYS might be configured such that the BootGUI setting is equal to 0, indicating the machine should boot to the CLI (Command Line Interface) instead of the GUI. Edit the MSDOS.SYS file to correct this.
Cause : It is highly unusual for the GUI to fail to load, without an appropriate error message being displayed. In such a case, it is probably indicative of a serious problem in the operating system, and restoration or reinstallation is likely to be the best option in such a case.

Symptom: The Operating System complains that it cannot find a file during GUI initialisation.
Cause : The Registry contains most of the settings for a Windows system, although for legacy reasons some settings can still be found in the WIN.INI or SYSTEM.INI files. Usually, this condition is the result of an application or driver being improperly installed or uninstalled. Try to find any software that has been added or removed recently, and then reinstall and/or uninstall the software fully. If there are problems in doing so, solve these before continuing.
Cause : If the problem persists, remove the reference to the files that are causing the error messages. In WIN.INI and SYSTEM.INI the reference can be 'commented out' so that it can be returned to its previous state if required. If the setting is in the Registry, you should make the proper system backup before editing.

Symptom: "The system is low on resources" message.
Cause : The most likely cause of such a message is running too many programs at once. Closing down programs will often solve the situation. However, some programs do not 'clean up' memory space after themselves properly, so after many programs are loaded and unloaded, a reboot may be necessary. To reduce the chance of the problem recurring, programs that are loaded on startup, such as Microsoft Office Find Fast, should be disabled where possible. **Cause** : There may be insufficient space on the hard disk for the swap file. Check the 'Virtual Memory' settings in the System Properties, and make sure there is enough room on the specified drive.

Common software faults

The increasingly huge range of application and utility software makes it impossible to cover the kind of faults that can occur in them. However, some of the more 'generic' faults are listed here. A simple reboot may allow the software to function fully. Although this is a temporary solution it may be the most expedient since software faults are notoriously difficult to diagnose fully. Also, defragmentation and disk scanning can help in some cases.

Symptom: "General Protection Fault" message.
Cause : This error message can have many causes, but by far the most common is that of a program trying to access an area of memory that has not been allocated to it. This can be the result of frequent loading and unloading of programs. When a GPF occurs it can often have a 'domino' effect on other programs, so it is recommended that the user reboot if possible. The reboot itself may temporarily solve the problem, since fewer programs will be running. Disabling other programs which are loaded on bootup, by removing them from the Startup Group or (with care) removing them from the 'Run' key in the Registry, may also help. **Cause** : If the problem is not solved, or if it occurs frequently, the application may require reinstallation, since one of its DLLs or other components may be corrupt or replaced by other applications. Use the most up-to-date version of the software available.

Symptom: "Invalid Page Fault" message.
Cause : The software has tried to access an area of memory that does not exist. The software may be corrupted. Try reinstalling the software. **Cause** : If reinstallation does not help, then the software may not be intended for use on that version of Windows. Make sure that the software is the most current version available for that operating system. **Cause** : As a last resort, try replacing the memory. Some of the more subtle memory failures may not be detected by POST but will produce faults during computer use.

Symptom: "Illegal Operation" message.
Cause: The software has tried to use an operation that does not exist, or use an operation in an incorrect way. This can be due to corruption of data in some way – try scanning the hard drive for faults, and checking the memory chips with a diagnostic utility. **Cause**: Other potential causes of this fault are badly written software, or incompatibilities between software, DLL libraries, or a combination of the two. These are extremely difficult to track down, and in most cases it is simpler to just install updated versions of the software used on the machine.

Symptom: "Windows Protection Error" message.

Cause: A virtual device driver (VxD file) has not loaded or unloaded properly. Often the driver is listed in the details of the error message. All of the usual driver problems can be the cause: incorrect settings, conflicts, or incorrect drivers. Make sure the driver is set correctly, and check the manufacturer's website to see if there are any known problems.

Cause: Sometimes there are 'hidden' settings for the driver, in the Registry. If these are incorrect they can cause this error, and in this case is extremely difficult to fix. Removing the driver software and reinstalling might fix the problem. If not, restoring the registry from an earlier state, or in Windows 9x, running "SETUP /I /p" may solve the problem. If not, the system may require complete reinstallation.

Symptom: "Invalid Working Directory" message.

Cause: This error can take different forms in different operating systems. It can also be seen as *"Cannot find the working folder for this program"*, or *"Invalid Startup Directory"*. Despite the differing descriptions, they all have the same cause. The folder specified in the PIF or the icon's properties is not valid. Check the properties for the icon and make sure all folders are valid.

Symptom: Unable to install the program.

Cause: Some typical causes of installation failure include insufficient hard disk space, incompatibilities between the application and the system it is to be installed on, and inability to access the necessary files. Where possible, close down all applications and utilities before beginning the installation, and ensure the system matches the minimum requirements of the application.

Cause: Older applications may not be written for the operating system you are using. Windows XP includes the Program Compatibility Wizard, which can help make an otherwise incompatible program install properly.

Symptom: Unable to execute the program.

Cause: The shortcut that is being used to execute the program may be corrupted. Use Explorer to locate the actual executable, rather than the shortcut, and run it that way. This is usually somewhere in the 'Program Files' folder, and normally has the .EXE extension. If this works, then the Shortcut should be recreated.

Cause: If it still does not run, the application or its files may be corrupt. Try reinstalling.

Symptom: The computer has 'frozen'; nothing appears to be happening; system has 'locked up'.

Cause: Computers often stall. There may be lengthy 'timeouts' in action, where nothing is being done deliberately, while awaiting a response from a device. Impatience can result in rebooting a system that was not in fact exhibiting any errors.

Cause: If the computer does nothing for a long period of time, then it is usually due to an error in an application. Occasionally, pressing Escape or Control-Break can spur a frozen application into action. More usually, however, it will have to be terminated, by pressing Control-Alt-Delete to bring up the Task Manager, and ending the task from there. If even this does not work, the system will have to be rebooted. If the application freezes frequently, its settings may have to be changed, or it may need to be reinstalled.

Cause: If the computer freezes frequently, while using a variety of applications, then it is more likely to be a problem either with the drivers, or with the operating system. Check that the drivers are all correct and up-to-date. Reinstalling the major drivers (such as video cards and modems) might solve any corruption. Otherwise, it may require the whole system to be reinstalled.

Hardware Diagnostics

Advanced hardware diagnostics are beyond the scope of this volume and beyond the means of most organisations whose business is not the manufacture or repair of computer equipment. However, there are basic hardware and software diagnostic tools available for small and medium organisations, and all PC support personnel should be familiar with them.

The following diagram represents a basic system to aid in diagnosis of a PC fault. It is simply an overview of the general type of steps to take in diagnosing a fault, and is not meant to be a comprehensive fault finding flowchart. It is intended to act as the basis of a systematic approach to locating hardware or device driver faults, and some of the methods involved are discussed in more detail in the following sections.

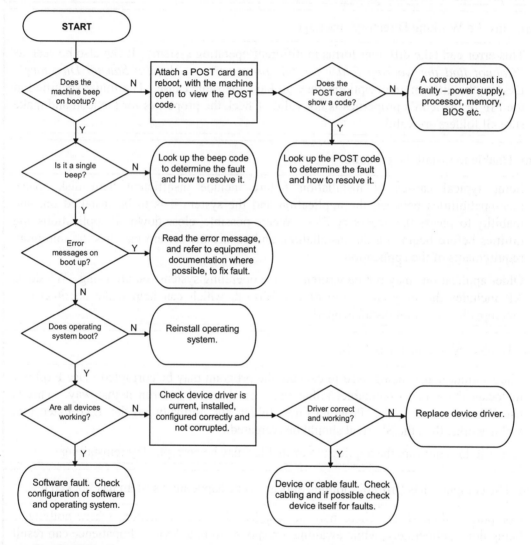

Power On Self Test

When the computer is first switched on, it automatically performs tests on the CPU, ROM, memory, motherboard, hard disk, etc. The machine will not carry on if it finds any fault and will in most cases warn the user by producing a series of warning beeps and/or displaying an error message on the screen.

If there is a single beep, (rarely two short beeps in the case of some very old machines) then the POST check has passed the computer system as operable. Note that the POST test is not nearly as thorough as the checks performed by quality diagnostic software. So, a POST failure definitely means a problem, while a POST pass does not necessarily mean that the machine is fully functional.

If there is more than one beep, or a continuous beep, then a fault has been found. The number and duration of the beeps represent a code that denotes a particular fault. Manufacturers of the various BIOS chips will assign each beep code to a different error. Therefore, the exact fault the code can be looked up on a list of beep codes for that specific BIOS make and model wherever possible. This may be supplied with the motherboard documentation, or can often be found on the BIOS manufacturer's website. For example, on some versions of AMI BIOS, two short beeps indicates a memory parity error, while on some versions of AST BIOS, the same code indicates a Keyboard controller failure. The following is a sample of some beep codes found on a typical system. (A Dell Dimension XPS)

Beep code	Error	Possible solution
1-2	Missing video card	Re-insert video card, or replace faulty card.
1-2-2-3	BIOS ROM checksum error	Replace battery on motherboard.
1-3-1-1	Memory refresh error	Re-insert memory, or replace faulty memory.
1-3-1-3	Keyboard error	Re-connect keyboard connector, or replace faulty keyboard.

POST Error Messages

If the POST is successful as far as being able to recognise and use a display adapter, then it can use that facility to output more easily recognisable error messages. Individual error messages for various faults can vary between BIOS manufacturer and version. Some older machines display a numeric code that should be looked up in a table of error codes like beep codes, while modern BIOS systems generally display a textual error.

Numeric error codes are organised into groups of related errors. For example, the error codes from 100 to 199 (called the 1xx series) may indicate system board errors, while the 6xx series may cover floppy disk errors. The errors range from older system problems (e.g. the 5xx series reports on CGA errors) to modern system errors (e.g. the 215xxxx series reports on SCSI CD-ROM errors).

If the computer fails to boot from the hard disk, it may display an error code from the 17xx series for ST506 systems, the 104xxx series for ESDI systems or the 210xxx series for SCSI systems. If so, the error code indicates the area that requires attention.

Even when a text error message is displayed, there is commonly additional documentation available to help diagnose the exact nature of the fault, and this may well be in the motherboard manual.

The most common messages include 'Keyboard Failure', 'Hard Disk Failure', or 'Memory Parity error', which clearly indicate the subsystem at fault. More detailed information is provided by some older systems, for example the 3xx series of errors indicated a variety of keyboard errors such as stuck keys, cable faults, and even keyboard locks. See the 'Common faults' section for information on potential causes of such faults.

P.O.S.T. Card

If a fault in a machine is so fundamental that it cannot even produce a beep sound or error message, or if for some other reason beep codes are not of use in locating a hardware fault, then there is a lower level diagnostic method available. This is to insert a POST card into one of the machine's expansion slots. The Power On Self Test card is a small expansion card that is used to help debug machines that appear to be "dead". During the earliest section of the POST process, the processor must ascertain that the major chips, like interrupt controllers, DMA controllers and the like are functioning. This part of the POST

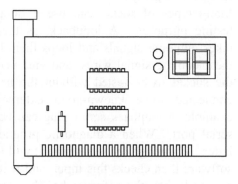

process is <u>before</u> the processor goes looking through address space for external adaptor cards, and so the video card cannot be used to output results. Therefore, another way is needed of letting the processor report on the testing process.

Fortunately, since the earliest days, the specification of the IBM PC and all its derivatives allowed for a single location in I/O space where the status of the POST process is put by the BIOS as it initialises.

The POST card simply monitors the value held at that address, and displays it on a couple of seven-segment LED displays. Most post cards also have LEDS that show the status of the various power lines. Unfortunately the actual POST result address used differs from machine to machine, so before we can use a POST card we have to know what type of machine we are dealing with, and perhaps set the post card to the correct address.

Once this is done, we can insert the card into the machine, switch it on and observe the LEDs on the card. As the machine performs each self-test, the number displayed on the card increments. If it stops, then the BIOS has become stuck at that test and cannot continue. Looking up the result tells us which test was being undertaken, and therefore where the trouble is likely to be. Like beep codes, BIOS error codes vary by manufacturer and version. The results corresponding to each code are published by the BIOS manufacturers on their website, and a booklet of them is often supplied with the POST card.

The table below gives a representative sample of the POST codes generated by AMIBIOS V2.2X.

00	Flag Test	3C	CPU speed calculation	78	Display Configuration Error messages
03	Register Test	3F	Read 8742 hardware switches	7B	Copy system BIOS to shadow memory
06	System Hardware Initialisation	42	Initialise interrupt vector area	7E	8254 Clock test
09	ROM BIOS Checksum	45	Verify CMOS configuration	81	MC146818 Real Time clock test
0C	Page Register Test	48	Test and initialise video system	84	Keyboard test
0F	8245 timer chip test	4B	Unexpected interrupt test	87	Determine keyboard test
12	Memory refresh initialise	4E	Start second protected mode test	8A	Stuck key test
15	8237 DMA controller test	51	Verify LDT instruction	8D	Initialise hardware interrupt vector
18	8237 DMA controller initialise	54	Verify TR instruction	90	Maths coprocessor test
1B	8259 Interrupt controller initialise	57	Verify LSL instruction	93	Determine com ports available
1E	8259 Interrupt controller test	5A	Verify LAR instruction	96	Determine LPT ports available
21	Memory refresh test	5D	Verify VERR instruction	99	Initialise BIOS data area
24	Base 64k address test	60	Address line A20 test	9C	Fixed /floppy controller test
27	Base 64k memory test	63	Unexpected exception test	9F	Floppy disk test
2A	8742 keyboard self test	66	Start third protected mode test	A2	Fixed disk test
2D	MC146818 CMOS test	69	Address line test	A5	External ROM scan
30	Start first protected mode test	6C	System memory test	A8	System keylock test
33	Memory sizing test	6F	Shadow memory test	AE	F1 error message test
36	First Protected mode test	72	Extended memory test	AF	System boot initialisation
39	First Protected mode test failed	75	Verify memory configuration	B1	Interrupt 19 boot loader

Once it has been used diagnostically, the POST card is removed until it is next needed, although it can also be used as a diagnostic tool for programs. Poking values or status bytes into the appropriate location can mean not having to interrupt the flow of a program to see what is going on.

The POST card is usually also the quickest way of diagnosing a PC with a suspect video channel. Inexpensive POST cards are becoming widely available which are preset to the most popular I/O address (080x), however they are arriving at a time where nearly all of the "glue logic" is becoming integrated onto the LSI chipset. Thus if an interrupt controller error or DMA refresh error is thrown up by the POST card, it serves only to tell that motherboard itself must be replaced.

Loopback plugs

Many types of socket can use a 'loopback' plug, for testing purposes. A loopback, as the name suggests, takes outgoing signals and loops them back around into the incoming signal wires, and vice versa. This allows the socket to be tested without the necessity of being connected to a known-good external device. For example, a loopback serial plug can be attached to the serial port. When a diagnostic program sends out the letter 'A' through the serial port, it will loop back and be received as input into the same serial port. The software then checks this input, and if it differs from the letter 'A' that was sent out, or if no input was received, then the software has detected a faulty port. The diagram shows the wiring inside a serial loopback plug. They can be created from a standard serial plug, with wires soldered between the pins as shown. However, loopback plugs are also readily available from electronics catalogues.

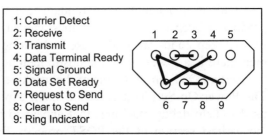

1: Carrier Detect
2: Receive
3: Transmit
4: Data Terminal Ready
5: Signal Ground
6: Data Set Ready
7: Request to Send
8: Clear to Send
9: Ring Indicator

Software Diagnostics

A huge range of utility programs exists to aid the user or technician in maintaining the system in peak performance. Hundreds of commercial products exist with varying strengths and weaknesses. Some, like QEMM and PCKWIK are concerned with maximising the machine's performance. Others, like WinSleuth and WinCheckit, are concerned with analysing and testing the system hardware. Some, like PC Tools and Norton Utilities, have elements of both testing and optimising. Of course, the programs have a large degree of overlap in terms of their functions. When the technician wishes to test out a system, one or more utility packages are probably available to him/her. Since the commercial products will vary from company to company, only the general utilities can usefully be covered in this section.

Some problems are easily diagnosed; a disconnected cable or a missing system file are quickly spotted and corrected.

Other problems are more difficult to diagnose. These include:
- Not having enough memory to run a program.
- Reduced or impaired component efficiency - e.g. the disk caching efficiency, the performance of the disk drive (date transfer rate, fragmentation, corruption of disk surface, etc).
- Experiencing conflicts between different programs.
- Experiencing conflicts between the addresses and IRQs (hardware interrupts) of different cards (e.g. a newly-installed sound card refuses to work).
- Problems with the size and location of video memory.
- Being unable to adequately test the printer ports, communications ports, mouse, keyboard, etc.

The list of such problems can become large and the use of diagnostic software can save many hours of experimentation. Microsoft supplies some utilities and these are therefore readily available on every machine. Additionally, the support engineer should carry disks with diagnostic software.

Windows XP/Vista Diagnostics

System Properties
The System Properties dialog box in XP and Vista provides a great deal of useful information.
Choosing the *'System'* icon within *'Control Panel'* brings up the *'System Properties'* dialog, with the
menu tab options shown in the illustration (the Vista window is very similar to that of the XP window shown).

The *'General'* tab provides basic machine information (e.g. CPU type, operating system in use, RAM size, etc.).

The *'Computer name'* tab allows the user to set information concerning the way the machine is connected to a network.

The *'Hardware'* tab contains several buttons which allow access to the Device Manager, Hardware Profiles, and Device Driver Signatures.

To get information on resources used in Windows XP, select the Device Manager menu option *'View'* → *'Resources by Type'*.

The *'Advanced'* tab gives access to Performance settings, User Profiles, and Startup/Shutdown settings.

The Performance settings dialog box allows changes to the visual effects used by XP, as well as the virtual memory assigned.

The *'System Restore'* tab allows the user to decide how much disk space on each drive to allocate to the System Restore utility. The more space is allocated, the more *'Restore points'* can be saved on the drive, providing greater flexibility in maintenance.

The *'Automatic Update'* tab sets how updates to the Windows system should be carried out. The options include manual updates, automatic download and installation, or downloading and installation after user confirmation.

The *'Remote'* tab is only available in Windows XP Professional, and provides access to the Remote Desktop, as described later in this chapter.

System Information

The System Information box also provides valuable information and is accessed by

  Programs → Accessories → System Tools → System Information

This utility offers a wide range of system hardware and software testing tools.   The opening window is as shown.

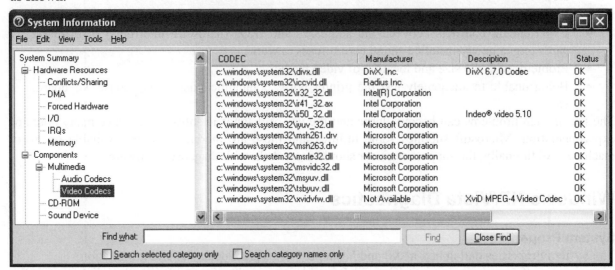

Choosing *'Hardware Resources'* offers reports on the machine's use of IRQs, DMA channels, I/O ports, etc.   It also reports on any hardware conflicts or any software sharing violations that it detects. These tools are useful for diagnostic purposes and they can also be used when installing new devices.

The example shows a report on the video CODECs that are installed on the computer.

The *'Tools'* drop-down menu provides some other utilities, including:

DirectX Diagnostic Tool

Checks out the PC's DirectX components to ensure that the video and audio modes all function correctly. It also checks mouse, keyboard and network functioning.

Dr Watson

Dr. Watson is an error logging program. When an error occurs and Dr. Watson is running, it will collect information regarding the crashed program, its status, and take a 'snapshot' of the system at the time. This snapshot shows what is running, what drivers are installed, and so on, in some detail, and is saved as a .WLG file.   This file is only useful to experienced technicians, and in many organisations inspecting the log for every crash would be a ridiculously time consuming operation.   But in important installations or circumstances it can be very helpful in determining the cause of problems. In many installations it is loaded at system startup to ensure that if a program error occurs, it records any useful information.

System Configuration

The System Configuration Utility provides user control over the configuration of the computer when it is booted up. This is very useful when the computer is experiencing setup problems, as it allows user control over which components from the setup script files are installed during bootup.

To load the System Configuration Utility, hold down the *'Windows'* key and press the *'R'* key.   In the dialog box that opens up, type in *'MSCONFIG'* and press Enter.

The utility provides several tabs, which vary depending on the operating system installed.   The XP version is shown in the illustration.   The Vista version drops the word 'Utility' from its heading and no longer has a SYSTEM.INI, WIN.INI tabs.

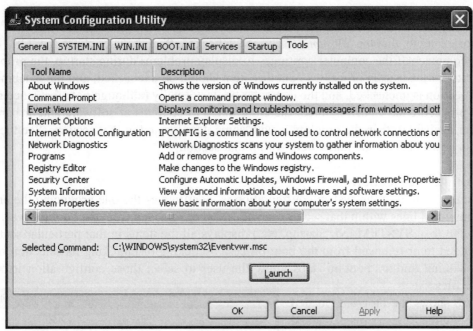

The following table shows the options available in various versions of Windows:

	General	Config.sys	Autoexec.bat	System.ini	Win.ini	Boot.ini	Static VxDs	Startup	Services	Environment	Tools	International
98	x	x	x	x	x			x				
ME	x			x	x		x	x		x		x
XP	x			x	x	x		x	x		x	
Vista	x					x		x	x		x	

The 'General' tab

There are two buttons on the *'General'* screen.

Launch System Restore

One option is to *"Create a restore point"*. This enables the user (or the support staff) to save the system's configuration when major changes are made or new software or drivers are installed. The *'report'* of the current system setup is saved to disk as a file. This is essentially a snapshot of the device drivers, settings, registry entries and so on that are in effect at that time. If subsequent changes are made to these settings which result in reduced performance or even PC failure, then the machine can be rolled back to a previous state by restoring the information in one of these reports. While this can take up a non-trivial amount of disk space, and requires some time to maintain, it can be invaluable in a support situation, as it can drastically reduce down time.

Each Restore Point takes up space on the hard disk, and there are settings in the File System Properties dialog of the System Properties to disable it or limit its hard disk space usage Note however, that you should not rely solely on this function, since in order to use System Restore your system must be able to boot at least into Safe Mode.

Expand File

This allows the user to select individual OS files and restore them to their original state from the copy in the Windows installation disk. This is useful if the file is suspected to have been corrupted.

The *'General'* tab also offers three bootup options:

Normal Startup

This is the normal setup, loading all the installed device drivers.

Diagnostic Startup

This offers a Safe Mode (loading only essential device drivers), as explained in the *'Startup options'* section of the *'Windows Configura*tion' chapter.

Selective Startup

This provides control over which files are loaded at startup and help trace the cause of problems. Consider, for example, that the *'System.ini'* box is unchecked, then the user clicks the 'OK' button and reboots the computer. If the computer continues to display problems during startup, the problem lies in another section of the startup process, so another item should be unchecked, and the machine rebooted again. If a section is unchecked, and the computer boots normally (although note that since many parts of the boot procedure have been ignored, there are likely to be items of software and/or hardware that are no longer available), then the problem is with some item located in that section. See the following for details on how to isolate the faulty item within that section.

Configuration Item Selection

When a particular section of the system configuration is identified as the one producing the error during startup, the individual lines within that section can be added or removed from the boot process.

Clicking on a tab (e.g. SYSTEM.INI, Startup, etc.) displays all the items in that particular section. Each item can be added to or removed from the boot process by ticking or unticking its selection box. The 'system.ini' 'win.ini' and/or 'boot.ini' tabs allow the user to select those configuration items that are found in those files.

The Startup tab shows the programs loaded during bootup via the Registry (as explained in the *'Windows Configuration'* chapter).

From any of these sections, the user can temporarily disable any setting or device found there, and then reboot to see if the system will run smoothly without that device or setting. The selection and boot process can continue until the problem device is identified. The example shows the *'Startup'* section contents of a system running Windows XP. The user can deselect any item that he or she believes may be causing the problem, one by one, until the problem item is located.

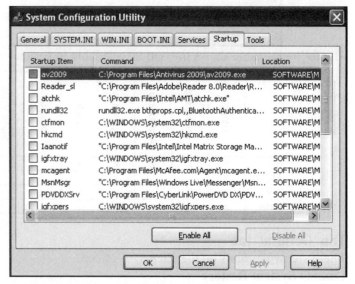

The 'Tools' tab

Clicking the Tools tab displays a long list of utilities as shown in the earlier illustration.

Many of these can be accessed by other ways but it is useful to group them conveniently into a single menu.

Most of the options are self-explanatory but a useful fault-finding tools is the Event Viewer.

This facility is based on event logging. The operating system keeps track of major events such as the boot up sequence, applications starting up and shutting down, errors, and so on. If a fault develops, careful inspection of these logs may provide clues as to what caused the problem.

The 'Services' tab

Services are system programs that provide system functions such as print spooling and automatic updates. The System Configuration Utility can be used to start and stop such services, but the *'Services'* utility from the *'Administrative Tools'* (reached via *'Control Panel'*) is more useful in that regard. It allows the administrator to start and stop services and decide which services to start automatically on boot up.

Microsoft's Help and Support Center

Windows provides a range of specialised help guides to aid users with common problems.

These are accessed through the *'Help and Support'* option accessed through the *'Start'* button.

These provide aids to understanding and troubleshooting problems.

Third Party Diagnostic and Repair Utilities

Each newer version of Windows provides more comprehensive diagnostic and repair tools. Although these are useful, a whole range of utility software is available, which greatly extends the tools supplied with Windows.

Many faults on computers can be either hardware problems or software configuration problems. The technician's most important tool is the set of utilities that check and report on the computer's hardware components. Finding faults without such utilities is possible but is much slower. These programs are used for a variety of purposes:

- Hardware testing (e.g. checking memory, printer and serial ports, etc)
- Hardware Performance (checking the working speed of the disk controller, video card, serial port, etc)
- Performance Tweaking (suggesting changes that would improve performance - e.g. swap file size, etc)

System restoration

Every Windows system can develop faults, and some are serious enough to make the operating system unusable. In such a situation it is convenient to restore the system to a previous state of operation, preventing the need to reinstall and set up all the software. Norton Ghost makes an exact copy of the user's entire hard disk, including Windows, applications, drivers, settings and user's data. In the event of a total hard disk disaster that destroys the disk contents, the Ghost image is written back to the disk after it has been cleaned up or replaced. The ghost images can be saved to CD, DVD or external drive via a USB or FireWire port. Similar products include Acronis True Image and PowerQuest Drive Image.

Virus Scanners

There are many software utilities that detect and eliminate viruses. These include AVG Anti-Virus (with an excellent free edition), Kapersky, Sophos, McAfee, Norton, F-Secure and Norton Anti-Virus.

Application Repairs

Over time, many pieces of software may be added and deleted from a hard disk. If software is badly written, badly installed or badly uninstalled, fragments may not be added/removed. This may cause programs to run erratically. Additionally, shortcuts to programs may not be installed or shortcuts may be left behind when applications are removed. Cleanup utilities remove abandoned fragments and ensure that all application links are working and relevant.

Note: Often, utility packages carry out many functions. It is common for these products to have virus checking, system checking, disk housekeeping, etc marketed under a single brand name. An examination of their specifications will allow the user to choose the package most appropriate to his/her needs.

Reinstalling Windows

Sometimes it is necessary to completely replace an existing installation of Windows. There may be corruption of essential files, or a fault in a DLL that is too difficult to trace. Or perhaps the system is simply becoming sluggish due to the number of files, registry entries and so on that have been added by software that is no longer in use. Th steps for re-installing are covered in the chapters on Windows configuration.

SMART monitoring software

SMART (Self Monitoring And Reporting Technology) is an interface that allows a hard disk to report status information to its host system. As the name suggests, a SMART capable disk incorporates monitoring electronics, and through the BIOS is able to report to the user when it senses that a disk failure may be imminent. SMART equipped drives measure such details as spin-up time, temperature, seek error rate, and so on. When analysed using the appropriate software (such as '*Drive Health*'), this can produce an estimation of when the disk will experience a '*Threshold Exceeded Condition*' (TEC) that essentially means an estimated date of failure. Note however that this only measures gradual deterioration, and is of no use with unpredictable events such as power spikes.

Computer Security

Computers are powerful tools, and can cope with huge amounts of data. But their usefulness in any organisation is also their vulnerability. Fires, floods and other disasters are a constant threat to computers and all the data that they contain. If an important file is accidentally or maliciously deleted, it can have serious repercussions. And the threat of hackers and viruses, although perhaps overestimated, is very real. The security of computer hardware, although important, is usually of less significance than the security of the data it holds. The IT department should try to provide '*Data Assurance*' – a strategy that intends to ensure that data is:

- Available. Obviously, the data assurance process should not obstruct the availability of data to those with proper authorisation.
- Confidential. On the other hand, a good data assurance strategy will ensure that only authorised users have access to the data.
- Accurate. The system should be able to ensure that the data held is up to date and error free, at least from a storage and communication point of view.
- Authentic. In many cases it is important to ensure that messages and data have not been tampered with, and also that it genuinely comes from the specified party.

The accuracy and authenticity of a document attest to its '*data integrity*' – the notion that the data is genuine and unchanged from its original form. In communications, a well-designed data assurance system will also provide proof that a message was sent and delivered in accordance with the above concerns. This should make it impossible to deny that a particular message was sent or received, a concept known as '*non-repudiation*'.

A Data Assurance strategy should consist of several aspects:

- Physical Security. The first step in providing security is ensuring that only authorised personnel are allowed access to computer equipment, especially servers and other network equipment.
- Software Security. In some organisations that are open to the public, such as colleges or libraries, it is not possible to guarantee physical security. Even in the most tightly controlled corporate building, it may be possible to access computer remotely, via the Internet or a modem. Whatever the reason, software exists to provide secure access to data only to authorised personnel.

Anti-Virus. Any system that accesses data from an external source is vulnerable to viruses. This includes accessing the Internet, or employees accessing floppy disks or CD-ROMs. Viruses are often destructive, and any virus will reduce the efficiency of a system, so the IT department should strive to prevent virus infection, and eliminate them if they do occur.

- Backups and Disaster Recovery. Even if all of the above security provisions are adequate, there is still the possibility of accidental deletion or corruption of data, due to user error, equipment failure, or catastrophe. The effects of such loss of data can be reduced or even removed by using a good backup strategy. This can range from nightly backups of non-essential systems, to off-site mirror images of entire servers in case of catastrophic failure.
- Document Management. In a large organisation it is easy for one hand not to know what the other is doing. It is often the network administrator's role to provide document management, also called '*Version Control*'. This is any system that is designed to ensure continuity among the user documents, whether they are complex database programs or word-processed mailshots.

Security Threats

Threats to an organisation's data take many forms. Environmental threats mainly consist of disastrous events such as fires, floods, earthquakes or lightning, and although thankfully rare their effects on computer equipment is obvious. Other physical threats include corruption or damage to media such as disk drives. However, the major threat to data is from individuals.

Threats unrelated to computers

Intruders can try to gain access to sensitive information in a number of ways, and computer 'hacking' is far from the only method of gaining unauthorised access. Intruders may go *'dumpster diving'*, looking for passwords or other confidential information that has been written down and then thrown in the trash. They may phone employees and gain such information under false pretences, sometimes referred to as *'social engineering'*. It may even be possible to simply catch a sneaky glimpse of a monitor screen while sensitive information is being displayed. Attempts to break system security are just one way for intruders to enter the system, and users should be made aware of this fact.

Operator error

A staggering 36,989,300 items of personal data lost in 2007.

Most of these were caused by:

Losses in the post	e.g. 25m child benefit details
Misposting	e.g. in May 2007, the tax credit and bank details of 42,00 were posted to the wrong people.
Theft	e.g. 41 laptops stolen from HRMC in a 12 month period. 658 laptops and 121 memory sticks lost from the Ministry of Defence between 2004 and 2008.
'Misplaced' drives/CDs	e.g. 15,000 Standard Life customers, 3m learner driver details

Other losses are caused by accidentally deleting or over-writing files.

In most cases, the majority of damage to or loss of data is attributable to user error, such as, rather than deliberate and malicious alteration or destruction of data. Even where the damage is deliberate, it is more likely to come from disgruntled or fraudulent employees rather than an outside "hacker".

Unauthorised access

Nonetheless, outside influences cannot be ignored, and such threats include fraud, commercial espionage and malicious damage. These are potentially extremely damaging and the problems are now addressed in Government legislation, known as the Computer Misuse Act of 1990.

Hacking into systems can be for reasons of industrial espionage, fraud or just to prove a point. It is the concern about keeping data secure that fuels the opposition to the government's proposals to introduce ID cards linked to a national database containing personal information on every citizen in the UK.

Systems connected to the Internet are very easily accessed by anyone, since that is its purpose. Systems that have a dial-up facility can be located by *'war dialling'* – calling a range of phone numbers in search of those that are attached to modems.

Even private communication systems with long-distance copper cables can be vulnerable to tapping – a well-financed intruder need only locate a wire and insert a tap to be able to read data being transferred. Fibre optic cable, using light instead of electricity, is far less vulnerable. Wireless networks present an easier target, however, since all an intruder needs is a laptop computer with the appropriate wireless setup to be able to communicate with the network. An intruder so equipped can easily drive around looking for a vulnerable wireless network, a process referred to as *'war driving'*.

Whatever means the network uses to communicate, there is always a potential way for intruders to gain access at some point. Unless the appropriate security measures are taken, including password authentication and data encryption, this remains a possible cause of loss or alteration of important data. Worryingly, however, the WEP (Wired Equivalency Protocol) that is used on many wireless networks is turned off by default, and even when turned on, estimates of the time taken to crack the encryption vary from several days down to just 15 minutes.

Password cracking

Attempts to break the security of a system can also be done several ways, depending on the system. Once the system is accessed, it can be attacked by trying to guess user passwords – many users simply use the word *'password'* or other non-secure words. This allows a malicious intruder to design a small program with a simple dictionary of words and names to repeatedly attempt login until it finds a correct password.

Many systems have 'stock' usernames, such as *"guest"* and *"administrator"*, and unless these are secured they present a problem. Guest logins can be given only cursory access rights, or preferably disabled altogether, but administrator logins must either be renamed and/or given a password that consists of random numbers and letters in order to make them secure.

Security holes

In some cases intruders need not be able to break through the password authentication system at all. For example, Denial of Service attacks often do not enter the system. However, it is possible in some cases to bypass the normal security restrictions. Normally this is done via a 'back door'. A back door is an undetected entrance to an otherwise secure system. Some administrators deliberately install backdoors, albeit secure ones, in case of malfunction or sabotage. But the kind of backdoors exploited by malicious intruders are normally introduced either by viruses or by badly written software.

For example, the most common security hole, making up 30 to 40% of all holes, is the '*buffer overflow*' error. This is a program error whereby an area of memory, called a buffer, is used to store incoming messages, but is not looked after properly. By flooding the buffer, it can become larger than the programmers intended, spilling over into main program memory. The intruder can thus overwrite legitimate program instructions with their own code, if the software is not patched appropriately.

Computer Misuse Act

It is generally accepted that breaches of data security are still mostly perpetrated by staff within a company, rather than the more publicised cases of 'hacking' from external sources. However, due to the increase in networking of PCs and the increase in remote access (i.e. accessing the company computers via a modem) the threat of data loss through hacking is increasing.

The Computer Misuse Act 1990 makes it an offence to:
- Make unauthorised access to computer material.
- Make unauthorised access with intent to commit or facilitate commission of other offences.
- Make unauthorised modification of computer material.

Case law in June 1992 established that the Act applies equally to hacking from a remote machine and on standalone PCs. In December 1993, case law established that the offender need not even touch the keyboard to commit the crime. One party enticed another party to copy confidential information. The court ruled that the party requesting the offence was the major offender. Using a program, erasing a file, altering a file, copying a file and even viewing a file are all offences, if the action is not authorised. The New Scotland Yard Computer Crime Unit (Tel 0207-230-1212) recommends that companies have a warning message displayed at the start-up of a computer, so that the user is left is no doubt about the possible consequences of his/her actions. Any subsequent activity is then being carried out in the full knowledge of the legal position. Penalties extend up to five years imprisonment or a fine, or both. Copies of the Act are available from HMSO suppliers.

Security Resources

With computer security a growing concern in the IT sector, there have evolved a number of groups and other resources that a concerned system manager can turn to for guidance. Naturally, the Internet is awash with web pages, newsgroups and other resources offering information on every aspect of security.

There are a number of groups designed to provide channels of communication between security experts in order to contain any potential threats, of which the most notable is the US government funded Computer Emergency Response Team (CERT). This group reports on a wide range of security topics, from potential security holes found in software applications, to new computer viruses. For example, CERT provided information that helped Symantec develop a tool to eliminate the '*Kournikova*' virus soon after it was discovered. Unfortunately, the growing number of applications and complexity of software means that CERT has its hands full trying to cope with the range of security problems in modern systems.

IT managers looking for guidance on security implementations also have resources other than the Internet. The US Department of Defence has created the '*Orange Book*' standard of security level classification, which defines four levels and several sub-levels of security. Class D is an unsecure system, while class C1 and C2 are password-authenticated, with C2 having auditing systems installed. Classes B1 to B3 and A1 require DOD clearance levels, and include improved security restrictions such as testing assurances and mathematical modelling.

Some data is more confidential - and more prone to misuse - than other data. The British Computer Society outlines a "*Scale For Sensitivity*" which ranks data on a scale of 0 to 10. Scale Value 0 covers items such as databanks of components, while Scale Value 5 covers bank and medical records. Scale Value 10 covers the most sensitive areas of diplomatic and defence secrets. Organisations can categorise their data and enforce security according to the degree of sensitivity of the data stored.

Company policy

The organisation should evolve a security policy. This should be a 'living document'; in other words the policy represents the company's strategy and is subject to change as new security threats or potential threats come to light. The policy should be well known and accepted by the staff. Staff should understand the need for some of the otherwise niggling procedures, as an educated workforce is the key to data security. However, managers of less sensitive systems should be wary not to implement over-zealous security procedures, which can prove counterproductive.

The evolution of the security strategy should identify all possible risks. It should cover networks, standalone PCs and remote access systems; it should involve the I.T. professionals and the day-to-day users. The commitment to security has to emanate from the top down and there is evidence of increasing understanding and action from top management.

The strategy should be enshrined in a company policy that details:

- Who is responsible for each level of security (who manages the network security, who carries out the backups, who controls document management, who carries out configuration management, etc.).
- Who will carry out the necessary staff education.
- Who will monitor the efficiency of the policy.
- What are the agreed penalties for breaches of security.
- What are the recovery systems in the event of data loss or corruption.

The policy should outline the main points of the Copyright, Designs and Patents Act, the Computer Misuse Act, the Trademarks Act and the Data Protection Act.

Achieving security

With a local area network, the access problem is partly solved by a series of passwords and accompanying rights to view, alter and delete data in various sub-directories. These are allocated by the network supervisor in a way that prohibits unauthorised access and use of files.

This is not sufficient in many cases, however. Passwords do not prevent theft of equipment, and many systems may store data locally even if they normally attach to a server. Nonetheless, it is obvious that network servers must be given greater physical security measures than ordinary workstations.

Physical security

The security of the IT equipment itself, rather than the data it contains, takes two main forms. The first is protecting the systems from being used by unauthorised persons. The other is locking down the equipment itself using hardware-based security.

Office security

A single computer or computer network that stores valuable programs or data can be physically protected by a security perimeter. This can take the simple form of situating the machine in a locked room or room with sign-in, swipe card or clearance badge access. More advanced security systems use *'biometrics'* – identifying legitimate personnel by physical characteristics such as fingerprints or retinal patterns. These are often more expensive than traditional methods, but if the data is important it is usually worth the expense.

No security system is unbreakable, of course. Keys for physical locks can be duplicated, and it has recently been revealed that so-called *'smartcards'* can be duplicated with the correct lab equipment. Even the latest biometrics, such as Iris Recognition and Lip Movement Recognition systems are no use if the intruder is able to break in through a window instead. A proper site security system will cover all points of entry adequately, while still providing for the necessary health and safety requirements.

Physical security may also mean purchasing a machine with a removable hard disk, so that the data can be stored in the safe at night. Another option is to install a key system to the computer so that it cannot be accessed without the physical presence of the key in the mechanism. Of course, the technician has to consider that a determined attempt at industrial sabotage will not be prevented by a password or keyed system; the machine may simply be stolen and entry gained at leisure. To prevent this, the machine can be bolted to the desk or can have steel cables connected to go round furniture and be locked. Equipment can also be fitted with an alarm system. The system might include provision to detect the proximity of a person's body or it may detect the physical movement of the computer. It may also be fitted with an anti-tamper device so that the computer alarm cannot be disabled (e.g. the PC Theft Alarm).

Each user in a network system is given a certain degree of access rights. In other words, each user or group of users is given the right to read and/or create certain documents. It is therefore important not only that the rights are given to the appropriate users, but also that users are not afforded a way to circumvent these access restrictions. This should include a staff policy that passwords should not be written down or shared; as well as securing their workstation when they are not using it, either by logging off or by using a password-protected screensaver.

Hardware-based security

Hardware-based devices are effective in preventing casual interference with the system. They are not capable of preventing the professional thief who will steal the machine, disable the security schemes and access the data. Examples of hardware security include:

- Many computers have key switches to disable the keyboard or even disable the power button.
- The use of floppy drive locks. These are blanking plates that can be fitted into the floppy drive and locked into place with a key. This prevents the unauthorised copying of files to floppy disk. If this is used in a network where all printing is to a central location, then the opportunity for removal of data is even further reduced.
- The use of *'dongles'* to prevent the illegal use of a piece of software. These were popular for many packages some time ago but most were withdrawn due to user hostility. These were devices that plugged into the serial or parallel port of the computer. The dongle was supplied with a particular application package and the circuitry inside ensured that the application could be run. If the dongle was removed, the application package would not run.
- The use of fingerprint scanners (e.g. the Datawise MT Digit and U.are.U fingerprint readers, or the reader built into the KeyTronic Secure Scanner Keyboard. The recognition software in the computer only allows access to those whose finger scans matched those previously stored in its database. Other biometric systems are being developed using face recognition, iris recognition and voice recognition.

Software Security

This comprises of two approaches – Intrusion Detection Software (IDS) and intrusion prevention software. Detection software does not prevent the breach of security but allows the culprit to be traced, while prevention software stops the security breach from happening. In addition, secure communications are becoming more important as networks grow and interconnect.

Intrusion Detection Software

- Audit/Logging systems, each computer creates a log of all files that were opened, with dates and times; it can also log the use of floppy disks or the serial port. These systems are regarded with some suspicion since they are also capable of monitoring the number of keystrokes entered by a user in a given period and can hence be used for employee performance monitoring.
- Monitoring systems (sometimes called '*black box*' monitors) that watch for signs that may indicate an attempt at unauthorised access. For example, the system could keep watch on TCP port connection requests, to find anyone attempting to break in by going methodically through TCP ports until it can find one that is not properly secured. Another method is to watch over important system files for signs of unauthorised alteration. These are forms of '*scanning software*'.
- Embedding of company information into application logos. When the package is installed for the first time, the user is prompted for the company name, address, etc. and this information is written into the application's .EXE file. Any subsequent installation does not prompt again and uses the previously saved data in the screen logo. This does not prevent illegal copying but makes it more conspicuous.
- '*Honeypot*' or '*deception*' systems are a special type of IDS software. The system administrator sets up a fake system, deliberately not implementing proper security measures. The idea is that malicious hackers will break into the honeypot server, usually so that the administrator can monitor the intruder's actions in the hope the intruder will inadvertently give the administrator information either on the intruder's techniques or on other targets that are being attacked.

Intrusion Prevention Software

- Password authentication systems. A set of users is defined by the appropriate IT personnel, and only those who have a username and the correct password will be granted access. This has some drawbacks, though, which are explained later. Passwords can be applied to networked systems, standalone systems, or even individual files in certain software packages. Secure Sockets Layer (SSL) is a protocol that is used for authentication between web servers and browsers, to enable secure online transactions. For local systems, a simple password logon system can provide security if implemented correctly.

- Methods that prevent unauthorised entry to company networks from modems. Authorised entry, via modems and remote access software such as Carbon Copy or PC Anywhere, requires the user to enter the correct password before allowing access to the main computer network. With patience, a hacker will eventually crack the password and be able to enter the network. An improved security system includes a *'callback'* or *'dialback'* facility. In this case, the user phones the main system and provides a valid user name and password as normal. The system software then consults a centrally held database to see what telephone number is associated with that password. It phones back the caller and allows the user's connection. In this way, a hacker will not gain access to the system even if he/she is able to work out the correct password since the call would not be coming from the authorised phone number. This callback facility is offered in Carbon Copy for Windows.

- Software that prevents unauthorised traffic between internal and external systems. These systems are commonly called *'firewalls'*, and are explained in detail later.

- The screen blanker, designed to turn off the screen after a pre-set time and requiring a password to restore normal viewing.

Secure Communications

- Using an encryption program to scramble files before they are stored on disk or sent over a communication line. The decryption software to unscramble the file can only be used by those who have the *'key'* code. A common example of this software is PGP (Pretty Good Privacy). This system, and the government's response to it, has caused some controversy

- A technique known as *'steganography'* can be used, in place of encryption. Steganography is the concealment of information within another, larger piece of data. At its simplest level, this could mean that the first letter of each word in a document would combine to create a new, hidden message. More advanced techniques based on similar principles can embed data within a graphic or audio file. Steganography can also be combined with encryption to improve its security even further.

- Sending *'Digital Signatures'* attached to each email or document. A public/private key system, similar to that used in PGP and such security systems, can be used to create a signature that is almost impossible to forge. The private key is used in conjunction with a *'message digest'* that is created by performing a hashing operation on the message itself, so the signature cannot be created without the key. This can be used in conjunction with *'digital certificates'* that hold public keys and information on the user of the public keys to prove the signature really is from the person it claims to be from.

Password systems built in to the BIOS

Many computers allow a user password to be allocated to a machine. This is stored in the CMOS memory and a user will not gain access to the computer unless the correct password is given. This prevents the machine from being accessed by unauthorised users but is only a crude system.

Password protection systems

A sophisticated system is often required so that users can share the same machine. Some users will be able to see budget data but be blocked from seeing personnel data. Other users will be able to see personnel data but will be blocked from viewing budget data. In other words, the machine provides selective viewing of sub-directories based on a user's password. This is available in both software implementations and hardware implementations (using add-on cards such as PC Access Control, Sysecure, StopLock, etc.). Beware of systems that encrypt the data on the hard disk. This is intended to thwart the person who gains unauthorised access to data. Check that there is no possibility that the authorised user ends up unable to decipher the data in the event of a hard disk fault or security card fault.

In a networked system, a username and password together make up a set of '*credentials*', and the system can allow access to only certain parts of the network based on these credentials. Thus, a server can allow the finance staff to see only financial data, and the personnel staff to see only personnel data.

Password systems have their problems, of course. Users can forget passwords if they are too difficult, locking them out of the system until the situation is rectified by the network administrator. Unfortunately, simple passwords are easily guessed by those wishing unauthorised access. The use of dictionaries to break into password systems mean that passwords should contain a mix of letters and numbers not based on any real word, if it is to be truly secure. Users must be discouraged from divulging passwords or writing them down to help remember them, as these are obvious security breaches.

Internet Security

Computers attached to the Internet should be subject to all the same security precautions as standalone PCs. However, the added potential for security problems presented by a link to external computers must be addressed. This mainly means ensuring that communications must be secure and safe.

Firewalls

The main current solution is to install a '*firewall*' – normally a hardware and software combination that stands between the organisation's internal network and the Internet. All communication between internal and external systems is vetted by the firewall. Its purpose is to prevent unauthorised external access to the network, with minimum effect on the normal legitimate operations of the organisation. The features of a typical firewall include:

- Monitoring of all incoming and outgoing traffic.
- Disallowing unauthorised access to internal systems from outside systems.
- Disallowing access to unauthorised external systems from internal systems. This could include non-business websites, IRC chat or file sharing networks.
- Suppressing outgoing traffic containing passwords or other confidential information.
- Suppressing incoming traffic containing viruses.
- Logging of all incoming and outgoing access. This can be simply for security reasons or can be used for auditing or billing.
- Traffic flow monitoring, to help prevent Denial Of Service attacks.

Most Firewall systems allow for a '*De-Militarised Zone*' (DMZ). This is an area internal to the organisation but outside of the firewall. This should include such systems as web servers or FTP sites. Access to systems in the DMZ must be well regulated.

Firewalls are not foolproof. For one thing, it only protects against Internet attacks, although some can be configured for dial-up protection as well. Firewalls can only protect against certain types of viruses, and have to be configured well in order to work well. Additionally, firewalls are rarely 'transparent' – that is, they rarely perform their function with no effect on the user whatsoever. However, they are still the single best method of Internet protection for networks.

An example of a firewall system is a '*TCP wrapper*'. As the name suggests, this is a group of data that 'wraps' round all transmissions. By inspecting the wrapper, the firewall server can decide which communications to allow through, and which to reject.

Setting up a firewall

There are two main types of firewall: software and hardware. A hardware firewall is a separate box from the PC, whose function is simply to examine incoming and outgoing IP packets and disallowing any packets considered unsafe or inappropriate. A software firewall, on the other hand, consists of software installed on a PC, but performs the same function.

A hardware firewall has some advantages: it is less likely to 'crash', is harder to 'hack', does not use up PC processor time, and is generally more efficient and reliable. However, there are also disadvantages, mainly cost and complexity.

In fact, there are popular software firewalls which are available in a freeware version. The most widely known example is ZoneLabs' ZoneAlarm software, which is available in a free version for non-business use only. ZoneAlarm works by dividing up traffic into 'zones'. The simplest example, where a PC is connected to the internet by a dial-up, ADSL or cable line, might only have one 'zone'. However, when that PC is then connected to another PC via a LAN, that LAN would become the second 'zone', and can be treated differently by the firewall. Zones can also be determined by IP address, DNS name, or subnet.

The screenshot above shows the "Zones" tab of the "Firewall" section in ZoneAlarm. This example shows two zones: the "WAN interface" being the internet connection, and the "Fast Ethernet Adapter" being the local area network connection. Each zone can be set to an "Internet" or "Trusted" zone. As the name suggests, the Internet zone can be set to have stronger security than the Trusted zone, meaning that IP packets sent on to the Internet will be inspected more thoroughly than packets sent on the LAN.

The "Main" tab of the "Firewall" section is where the security settings for these two zone types can be set. This version of ZoneAlarm has only three settings: Low, Medium or High. Zone Labs recommend that the Internet zone be set to High security, and the Trusted zone should be set to Medium.

This is just a basic security setting, protecting against the most common threats such as accidental sharing of resources over the Internet, or unwanted NetBIOS traffic that could be hacking attempts, most of which are threats from incoming packets.

However, it is also possible that the user may not wish to allow certain outgoing packets. To that end, ZoneAlarm, like most software firewalls, keeps track of individual programs and allows the user to decide which programs will be allowed to access communications.

The two Zone types have two different settings in this regard: one for where data is primarily incoming from the connection ("Access" to the connection) and one for where data is primarily outgoing over the connection (being a "Server"). Each of these four, then, can be set "Allow", "Block", or "Ask", as shown in the example screenshot. As might be expected, "Allow" will let the software use that Zone for that type of communication, and "Block" will not. Setting it to "Ask" means that ZoneAlarm will prompt the user when the software wishes to communicate through that Zone, to ask whether it should be allowed to do so.

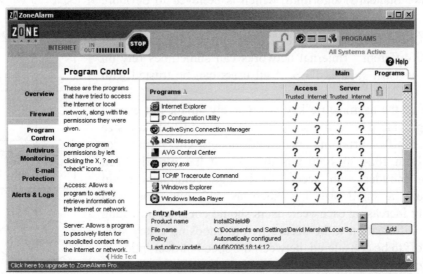

The example shows the "Programs" tab, of the "Program Control" section of ZoneAlarm. The screenshot shows several programs that have been set up in ZoneAlarm on a PC, with varying levels of access. A tick represents access allowed, a cross represents access blocked, while a question mark represents the 'Ask' setting. Note that it is not allowed for a program to have server access in a Zone without also having regular access, not is it allowed to have access to the Internet Zone without also having access to the Trusted Zone.

Proxy servers

Proxy servers are servers that connect multiple clients to the Internet, or public Intranet. They are often mentioned in the same breath as firewalls, but proxies do not necessarily have the same security features built in. One feature that all proxy servers share, however, is that of disguising IP addresses. A message sent from a system in the private network to the public network or Internet, will pass through the proxy server, and will be edited so that it appears to come from a different IP address. In such a way, nobody outside the network will know the true IP addresses of the client machines, reducing the possibility of security breach by malicious outsiders.

In addition, most proxy servers also act as a cache for Web pages, so that if several private clients request the same web page it will reduce the download time. Proxies are also often used to block access to certain resources – for example, to stop employees who should be at work from browsing illicit web sites. Some software, such as Microsoft's '*Proxy Server*' software, allows a server to act as both a proxy and a firewall.

Note that there are many other types of proxy, such as WINS proxies and management proxies – these have a quite different purpose and are not related to security issues.

Encryption

The information held in networks should be protected by the terms of the Data Protection Act and it is the organisation's responsibility to ensure that the Act's terms are met. One survey found that only around one half of companies, both public and private sector, used encryption to protect sensitive data.

Normal traffic on the Internet is carried in plain ASCII format. This is too insecure for organisations wishing to transmit confidential information over the Internet. One answer is to encrypt the message - apply a *'key'* (a mathematical algorithm) to scramble the contents before transmission. The receiving end can unscramble the message and recover the information, assuming that it also uses the same algorithm. Incoming traffic security is implemented using *'public'* and *'private'* keys. An organisation can hand out copies of the public key to all parties likely to send them data. The public key allows users to encrypt messages; they cannot be used to decrypt messages. The private key is held by the receiving organisation and this key can successfully decrypt all incoming messages. This is the basis of the popular encryption program called PGP (Pretty Good Privacy).

PGP should be distinguished from the algorithms it uses. PGP is a piece of software that provides public key encryption, but the actual encryption follows algorithms developed by other groups. PGP previously used an algorithm known as *'RSA'* (Rivest/Shamir/ Adleman, the creators of the algorithm), but now uses *'ElGamal'*, based on the DSS (Digital Signature Standard) algorithm, which is believed to be more secure.

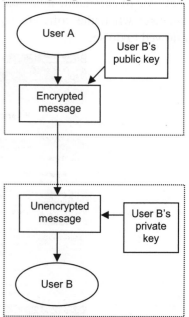

Both RSA and DSS use *'asymmetric keys'*, meaning that the public and private keys are different. (Internal networks can sometimes rely on symmetric key systems, such as DES, if all users can be trusted with the keys)

The actual size of the asymmetric key is relatively small, but even a small key can provide powerful encryption. Even a 512-bit key size could hold any of 10^{150} prime numbers, and modern encryption uses keys typically from 1024 to 4096 bits in size. It has already been proven that an intruder with access to enough computers could realistically break a small size key such as 512 bits, and with processing power increasing each year, users should consider how long they want their information to be secure before choosing a key size. There is a tradeoff to be considered, between the speed of decryption of messages by legitimate personnel, and the need for security.

The use of encryption is a controversial issue between governments and their citizens and organisations. Many governments have tried to enforce '*key escrow*' – a system whereby all private keys have to be given to a third party to allow government access to encrypted messages. This is usually met with wide opposition not only from human rights activists, but also from businessmen who need security for web commerce.

Denial Of Service

A relatively new problem for on-line businesses is Denial of Service (DoS). This is a process whereby malicious hackers deliberately reduce an Internet business system's functionality to the point where that service is effectively denied to all legitimate users. There are a number of ways this can be done, for example:

- Exploiting a flaw in the TCP/IP specification. For example the well-known *"Ping of Death"* method involves sending IP packets that exceed the maximum length given in the TCP/IP specification. This will cause some systems without appropriate patches to crash, hang or reboot.

- Exploiting a flaw in TCP/IP implementations. An example of this is the so-called *"Teardrop"* method, whereby fake fragments of IP packets are generated. These fragments appear to overlap each other, creating problems in reconstructing the IP packet at the receiving end. Again, this can cause a crash, a hung system or a reboot, unless an appropriate patch is installed.

- Flooding the system with unwanted data. For example, systems may be clogged by sending large numbers of ACK (Acknowledge) requests, preventing or slowing legitimate communications. Software to protect against this kind of attack is also usually available.

- Distributed Denial of Service (DDOS) attacks. This usually involves forcing large numbers of unwitting users into accessing a website at the same time, thus overloading it. This is most commonly accomplished by introducing viruses into user systems worldwide. Firewalls can help prevent this to some degree but are not foolproof.

More mundane DoS attacks could include using up system resources for purposes other than those for which they were designed, or sending many fake requests for goods. Many of these attacks are *'asymmetric'*, meaning that a small, old computer with relatively slow hardware can potentially crash a much more sophisticated system. The best way to counter such attacks is to make sure the operating system and software is up to date with the latest patches, and security software such as router filters are implemented.

Computer Viruses

Computer viruses of various types have gained a great deal of publicity and have diverted a great deal of resources to overcoming their effects. Nevertheless, viruses represent only a small part of an organisation's overall problems of security, integrity and reliability. While a definite area of concern, there are still much more important threats to an organisation. A company might fit virus protection software to all machines, to prevent the corruption of data. At the same time, little or no thought might be given to the physical security of the data; e.g. is it held in a machine in a secure room; is the computer password-protected, etc.

To date, apart from a number of well-publicised cases, virus problems are not yet general; many organisations carry out their daily work without any reported virus infection whatsoever. Nevertheless, computer viruses pose a mounting threat to data and have to be taken seriously. They can range from harmless messages to damage and/or loss of data. They are not the glamorous product of a *'hacker'*, as viewed by wide-eyed schoolboys. They are simply a nuisance that causes much extra work and anxiety to computer departments. As time progresses and systems become ever more complex and more interlinked (via local area networks and national networks), organisations come to rely more and more on the quality of their data as stored on computers. This, in turn, makes virus protection an indispensable part of an efficient computer system or network.

Virus Definitions

It is generally accepted that the first PC computer virus was *'Brain'* which appeared in January 1986 as a floppy disk virus. This changed the disk volume name and used up three extra disk sectors. This was fairly harmless but variations have been developed to infect hard disks, hide themselves from detection and destroy the disk's FAT. This is a good example of the evolution of viruses. Although there are now thousands of listed viruses, many are variants on others and far fewer viruses are commonly to be found. The general *'virus'* categories are:

- VIRUS - a program that attaches other runnable copies of itself to the machine code of other programs and may, or may not, carry out other activities (often described as the *'payload'*).
- WORM - similar to a virus but is aimed at attacking the resources of the computer system, rather than its files. It continually creates copies of itself without requiring user input, thereby clogging up a system. They are most dangerous to network systems.

- TROJAN HORSE - disguises itself as something else, such as a game, a utility or a graphics demonstration. When run, the program will carry out some irritating or harmful activity. A Trojan Horse (or simply '*Trojan*') generally does not replicate and so, when an infected file is deleted, it is gone from the system.
- TIME BOMB - a Trojan that is activated on a certain date or a certain time of day. While Time Bombs can be avoided by simply not using the machine on certain days, this is hardly an ideal solution.
- RETROVIRUS – A virus whose payload is concerned with disabling, corrupting, or otherwise preventing anti-virus software from being able to detect or remove viruses.
- MACRO VIRUS - a piece of code embedded inside Word document templates or Excel spreadsheets. Opening the document usually initiates the virus code.

In any discussion of viruses, the user should be aware that these terms are not mutually exclusive. A virus may be a worm, containing a trojan, which activates like a time bomb, contains retrovirus capability, and also includes the capability to spread via macros, for example.

Where the activity is initiated by a certain event, the program is also described as a '*Logic Bomb*'. Examples of triggering events are the number of times a program has been executed or the number of times the machine has been rebooted. Some may trigger in combination - i.e. when a certain file is run at a certain date or time. So, the elements of a logic bomb can be found in viruses and in Trojan horses.

Virus variants mean that there are an ever-increasing number of viruses to be detected.

Note: This section outlines virus problems and solutions. Since virus numbers increase at an alarming rate, every publication or anti-virus program is out of date as soon as it is produced. The examples, then, are not meant to represent the current state-of-the-art viruses; they are used to illustrate typical strains and their effects. The user is advised to maintain current lists of viruses and maintain the anti-virus software in as current an edition as possible.

The chapter does not dwell on the exact mechanisms that a virus uses. This is intentional; it is not the purpose of this material to point the way for potential virus writers.

The modification or loss of data through a virus is an offence under Section 3 of the Computer Misuse Act of 1990, which states:

3.(1) A person is guilty of an offence if -
   a) he does any act which causes an unauthorised modification of the contents of any computer: and
   b) at the time when he does the act he has the requisite intent and the requisite knowledge.

Since almost all viruses are imported from overseas, prosecutions under this Act will mostly apply to homegrown virus writers, or those who intentionally introduce an existing virus into a system.

Writing or owning a virus is not an offence but the infection of someone else's computer certainly constitutes an offence under the Act.

Virus Infection Methods

The vast majority of modern viruses are Windows based, due to the platform's popularity. In fact, there are '*virus toolkits*' available to allow those with little or no programming talent to create their own virus. There are two main methods of virus replication:

- File infection. At one time the most common method, this involves executable files being modified by the virus to contain a copy of the virus code. Infected files may come from magazine cover disks, web downloads, or friends' floppies.
- E-mail infection. The vast majority of viruses now spread via email. The user receives an email with an attachment containing the virus, which either runs automatically due to Windows Scripting or runs when the user tries to read the attachment.

File Infection

Viruses only infect executable code since they need to be able to gain access to computer processing time. Any machine code or script is therefore vulnerable to virus attack including:

- Directly executable files i.e. COM and EXE files.
- Overlay, driver or other transient files such as SYS, DLL, ICO, PIF, FON, CMD, SCR, OCX and VxD files.
- Disk boot sector or partition record.

- Data files that can contain macros, such as Excel, Word or Access files.
- Email systems that allow scripting, such as Outlook.

When an infected file is executed, the virus code becomes memory resident and is free to carry out its designed disruption. The virus has to ensure that its code is always run before any code of the file to which it is attached, since that is the only time that it can guarantee that it will capture processing time.

Files are infected by one of the following methods:

Appending: The most common method, it involves attaching the virus code to the end of the file. Every COM file has an initial jump instruction, which passes control to the program's main code.   The virus simply alters the jump address to the start of the virus code.   The virus code is run and control is finally directed to the actual program code.   Similarly, with EXE files, the code entry point is altered to the start of the virus code before passing control to the actual program. The virus code will contain a section to replicate itself, plus other

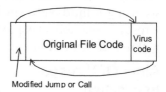

possible code sections for activities such as delivering any payload, any triggering routines and any stealth mechanisms. Since the program has extra code added to it, its overall size is increased - a good indication of a virused file.

Pre-Pending: Similar to the above, except that the virus code resides at the beginning of the affected program.   Only affects COM files and the overall file length is increased by the infection code.

Over-Writing: The virus code replaces the actual code at the beginning of the file, normally a COM file. In this way, the overall file size is unaffected.   When the program is run, the virus code is executed instead of the expected code.   Since the original code is lost, the program's intended function is lost and the file is irrecoverable.   Rarely used, since it is so easily spotted.   However, some programs will have an unused area at the end of its final sector and the virus code could position itself in this area without affecting the original program code, or altering the original file's size.   The *Chernobyl* virus uses this latter technique.

Companion: As previously explained, if two files have the same name, the one with the COM extension will take precedence over the one with the EXE extension.   This facility has been used by applications, with the COM file being used to set up any specialist configuration before loading the EXE file of the same name.   The virus writer takes advantage of this order to introduce a companion virus file.   The virus is created as a COM file with the same name as a normal program EXE file, with the COM file's attributes set to hide the file from normal view.   When the user attempts to run the EXE file, the COM file is run first and the virus activity is executed.

Cluster: Here, the file is left uninfected.   However, the Directory entry for the file is altered, so that the starting cluster points to the virus code instead of the wanted file.   The virus runs its own code then runs the file wanted by the user.   Many entries may be affected, each pointing to the same virus.

Email Infection

There are a number of methods used by virus writers to infect systems through email. It is not possible for the email message contents to be infectious; only attached elements may contain viruses. In general terms this means either a file attachment, or a Windows Script.

Virus Attachments

In this case, there is a file attached to the email, which contains a virus. The file itself must be of an executable type, most commonly an EXE or a macro such as VBS or DOC files. The text of the message is commonly designed by virus writers to tempt users into opening and running the infected attachment. These can be prevented either by having virus scanners built into the email reader or the mail server, or by never opening attachments.   Recently, viruses such as '*My Party*' have appeared, as .COM attachments. Since these files end in ".com", many users mistake them for web page addresses and click them without worrying about potential virus infection.

Script Attachments

Windows Scripting host is a small program that is available for all versions of Windows. It is capable of processing JScript and VBScript files, and with a few additions it can also handle Perl scripts. It can be used alongside web browsers, email clients, Microsoft Office applications, network administration programs and so on. It provides a number of functions in addition to those provided by these systems, as well as being able to make use of cookies, COM objects and more. As a result it is an extremely flexible tool for automating tasks, web pages and the like.

Unfortunately, this flexibility can be abused, as has been the case with several viruses that make use of the Windows Scripting Host. Script viruses mainly affect those with Microsoft Outlook as their email reader. Messages can contain scripts that automatically execute; virus writers take advantage of this to infect systems, sometimes without users even opening an email message. This can be prevented by setting up Microsoft Outlook not to use the Windows Scripting Host (WSH), although some users have gone so far as to delete the host executable, WSCRIPT.EXE, from their computer. If you are able to do so, using a third-party email reader such as Eudora or Opera instead of Outlook will stop many such viruses in one fell swoop, while changing File Associations for script files so that they load in Notepad will render them harmless.

Aims Of Viruses
Replication
The number one aim, sometimes the only aim, of a virus is to replicate itself on to other executable files. This is usually carried out unobtrusively, to avoid bringing itself to the attention of the user. There are only a few viruses that produce a message during the replication stage. Some viruses are restricted to this activity; they spend their lives on the machine with the aim to simply infect other programs. They can be termed *'passive viruses'* from the point of view that, while being a nuisance, they do not threaten the integrity of existing data. Of course, while many are passive types, some may be more lethal - it's just that the correct conditions have not been there for it to activate. Even those that do not aim to damage the host system can waste resources and time – email viruses such as '*Melissa*' have been known to cause so much network traffic that servers crash or become unusable. It makes sense, then, to treat all viruses seriously.

Survival
Once attached to a computer's files or resources, the virus may attempt to escape detection and elimination. This is covered more fully later.

Nuisance
These are sometimes termed *'irritant viruses'*. They display messages, change round keyboard responses, slow down the system, play a tune or affect the screen display in some way. They may also result in RAM being occupied while a genuine program is trying to run. '*Kakworm*' is an email nuisance virus that will cause a PC to shut down after 5pm on the 1st of any month. '*Cascade*' is an older nuisance virus that becomes memory-resident when an infected COM file is executed. The virus then infects other COM files and causes the letters of a piece of text to crumble to the bottom of the screen. '*Cascade*' began life as a Trojan horse that did not infect other files - another example of the evolution of viruses.

Security Breaches
Some viruses have more sophisticated, but no less damaging, intentions. They try to find a backdoor into systems, and thus have to be as inconspicuous as possible, causing no direct damage or nuisance. However, they are still a serious threat to those with infected PCs. For example, '*Nimda*' is a prepending virus that infects several Windows operating system files, and on Windows IIS internet servers it removes all guest login security restrictions. The '*Pretty Park*' email virus, once resident on a machine, will try to connect to IRC (Internet chat) lines and pass information on to the virus author, such as dial-up ISP user names and passwords, and ICQ numbers.

Denial Of Service
A few viruses are used for quasi-political aims. Some websites, for whatever reason, have been singled out for attack by virus writers, who use infected home or business PCs as '*zombies*' which are launched against that website in unison. The '*Anna Kournikova*' or '*SST-A*' time-bomb virus spreads via email, and lays dormant until the 26th of the month, at which point it tries to access a Netherlands computing component manufacturer's website. The aim here is to get enough infected zombies to access the site that it will not be able to cope with the demand, thus denying access to legitimate users of the site.

Damage
These are viruses that result in damage to files, disks or even hardware. Examples are deleting files, scrambling file contents, changing the disk logical structure, formatting the hard disk or changing

security settings. Even irritant viruses can result in problems. Consider the result of losing all screen display when in the middle of a complex set of data entry. Irritant screen messages can also result in a program crashing when the message is written during the execution of the application code.

- An example of drive damage is when virus code tells the read/write head of a floppy to move to an inner track that does not exist, causing the head to become jammed in the inner section of the floppy drive. Damage to hardware is, however, rare.   A sinister development in recent years has been the arrival of viruses, such as '*CIH'* or *'Magistr'*, which overwrite the PC's flash BIOS, resulting in the effective destruction of the PC. This moves virus protection away from being a matter of eliminating inconvenience and into the realm of truly protecting your PC investment. The AV scanners can all detect and repair infected files, and some motherboard manufacturers have started to address this in various ways, but it may be some time before a truly effective means of overcoming the threat from such programs is found.

Note:

If a file is <u>infected</u> by a virus it contains the virus code. If it is an executable file, the virus can be run from that file; if it is solely a data file, the virus is present but is never run.   If a data file contains macro code or code applets, these embedded mini-programs can be infected. Additionally, every file is capable of being <u>affected</u> by a virus - i.e. the file is corrupted or lengthened in some way.

Virus Activity

The activities of a virus can be viewed as different stages.   Not all stages need be coded in a virus, although some activities are common to all viruses. The main stages of activity are:

Activation - Caused when infected code is invoked

Trigger - Caused by the occurrence by a particular date, time or event.   This stage is only included as part of the code in a relatively few viruses.

Infection check - Tests to see if a targeted file is already infected. The virus can do this by examining the directory structure to find a suitable target, or it might lurk in memory waiting for an executable program to be run.

Infection - If not already infected, the targeted file has the virus code attached to it.   This stage would be omitted for simple Trojan Horse and Time Bomb viruses. More recent email viruses may infect by choosing names from the address book instead of file names, and the method of infection is indirect, but the principle is the same.

Activity - A particular action such as displaying a screen message, playing a tune, deleting a file, etc.

Evasion - Another stage, which may be present, is the virus evading detection.   This may involve deleting itself from the location where it carried out its particular activity, or some other method.

The simplest case is that shown for the Trojan Horse. It is activated when the infected file is invoked and it performs its particular task.

The second diagram shows the stages of a Time Bomb. As can be seen, it is similar to the Trojan Horse, with the addition of a triggering mechanism. It will not always run the virus tasks when the infected file is invoked; it will await the pre-determined circumstances.

The third diagram shows the infection stages of a typical virus. The virus makes an attempt at infecting its target file. The diagram shows that it will carry out a particular activity; this is not always the case, as certain viruses exist with the sole purpose of breeding.

Boot Sector Problems

As explained in the chapter on disks, the Boot Sector is the first sector of any floppy disk, or the first sector in a hard disk partition. The boot sector is a mere 512 bytes long and contains a small program that is loaded into memory by the BIOS when the POST check is completed. This program loads in the operating system components from the disk. This piece of code is the first code that can be modified after bootup, since any previously executed code was of the permanent type burnt into ROM.   The virus works by relocating the boot sector code into another sector and placing itself in the vacated position. When the boot sector code is to be executed, the DOS 13h interrupt (for disk read/write operations) is intercepted and the virus code is run before control is passed on to the genuine boot sector code. With a hard disk, this means that both the partition table and the DOS partition are affected.   The virus code is loaded into memory when the machine is booted up. In fact, the virus code is loaded before other system and program files. A large piece of virus code will fill the boot sector area and will place the remaining code into another disk sector. It then marks that sector as bad so that it will not be over-written. The most well known example of this type is *'Stoned'*. Although there have been no new boot sector viruses for quite some time, old examples of the type can still infect even the most up-to-date Windows PC. Its varieties include those that produce messages or affect the partition table.

Solutions

With an infected hard disk, a clean boot floppy should be used to boot and run the SYS command to create a new boot sector on the disk. For a bootable floppy disk, formatting the disk but choosing the *'copy system files only'* option will re-write the boot sector. With non-bootable floppy disks, the files should be copied from the disk (Note that only the files should be copied, never the entire disk), the disk should be formatted and the files should be copied back to the disk.

Partition Sector Problems

Some viruses, such as *'Michel-Angelo'* infect the Master Boot Record, or partition table. Again, no new viruses use this approach but modern systems can still be infected. This is the first sector on a hard disk and contains information about the disk (number of sectors in each partition, etc.) and a short piece of executable code to read the boot sector.   Every time the machine is booted up, the short program is executed.   The MBR virus infects the partition table code so that the virus code is run every time the machine is booted up.   When the partition sector is infected, the brute force recovery method is to back up all the disk's files, carry out a low-level format and re-partition the disk.

Solutions

In DOS, a quick solution is to boot the machine from a clean boot disk and give the command FDISK /MBR.   This eliminates the virus code from the master boot record on the hard disk but will not repair a damaged partition table. It is useful method to anticipate this problem and create backup copies of the partition table. This can be carried out with the DOS command MIRROR/PARTN. This creates a file called PARTNSAV.FIL on a floppy disk.   In the event of partition table corruption, the drive would not be recognised - but the machine can be booted from the floppy and the command UNFORMAT/PARTN can be given.   This will restore the partition table to the hard disk. Of course, this only cleans up the partition table.   A check will still have to be made of the actual executable files on the hard disk; otherwise an infected file might re-infect the partition table.

File Viruses

File viruses can have the following characteristics:

- **RESIDENT**   Many viruses operate as memory resident programs, either as part of macro space, Windows programs, or DOS TSRs.   When an infected file is executed, the virus code in the file is run first. This code places the virus in memory from where it executes.   The virus code is then free to infect other files, either immediately, as they are accessed, or at some trigger time.   Since the Windows system loads many files into memory at bootup, finding and eliminating a Windows virus can be a troublesome task.

- **NON-RESIDENT**   In these cases, the virus code is run once, before passing control on to the actual file's code. It does not install itself in memory. It only executes the virus code each time that the infected file is run.

- **STEALTH**   Stealth viruses are resident viruses that affect the system in such as way as to hide their existence from the user. Since most infected files have grown in size, reading the file size from the directory would reveal the infection. So, some stealth viruses detect the directory request, subtract the virus code length from the actual directory reading and present the user with the truncated file size. From the user's point of view, the file size has not been altered and it appears unlikely that the file has been infected.   The same technique is used to hide any alteration of the disk's boot record or partition table.   Such viruses will not be found by anti-virus checksumming systems which simply look for a file's size increasing. This is an old technique that appeared in *'Brain'*, the first recorded virus. However, using CHKDSK will result in the loss of these files! Additionally, viruses may ensure that when they infect a file, the normal file write update in the directory does not take place. This means that the date and time modified data is left unaltered, so that a change will not betray their presence. Fortunately, stealth viruses cannot hide their presence in memory and anti-virus software can detect memory-resident viruses.

On rare occasions, viruses infect both boot sectors and files. These are known as *'multipartite viruses'*.

Virus Detection/Prevention

Viruses can either be found by inspection of machines or by reported faults. Viruses often become noticeable when several machines exhibit the same characteristics. A problem on one machine could be a hardware or software fault but a number of machines showing the same effect could indicate a virus. Obvious virus problems are those where the effects are easily seen - e.g. unwanted screen messages, music, etc. Other problems may only be noticed after a while. Examples are file sizes being increased, data being corrupted or lost, cross-linked files, a file's date and time being altered, unusual error messages, a shrinking of the available main memory, programs taking longer to load than previously, the hard disk light coming on at unusual moments, etc. Virus protection software works in one of two ways, either through scanning existing files on a disk or memory, or by logging file characteristics and monitoring for any changes. The first method looks for the <u>existence</u> of viruses in a file or memory; the other method looks for the <u>effects</u> of a virus on a file. For added security, both methods should be used. Of course, a detection system is spotting a virus <u>after</u> it has affected the computer system; a prevention system is designed to spot a virus <u>before</u> it has a chance to affect the system.

Scanning Techniques

Anti-virus software detects the presence of a virus by looking for the characteristics that viruses portray. This can mean one of two things:

- A virus will have a distinctive piece of code within it (e.g. writing a message to the screen) that can be detected by the anti-virus software.
- Viruses have to open files, write to files, alter file sizes, write to the boot sector, write to the partition table, etc. Any unusual attempts to carry out these activities can be detected as a possible piece of virus code.

Broadly speaking, the presence of infected files can be detected by looking for the source of the infection or by spotting the telltale signs of effects of the infection. This can be achieved in two ways:

- the user loads and runs detection software as a specific activity.
- the detection software can be pre-loaded as a background program (or TSR in DOS) that tests every executable file for viruses before allowing them to be run. This slows program loading and uses up precious memory but is able to detect viruses before they can spread or cause damage.

These methods are complimentary to each other and both are encouraged.

Signature Scanning

This type of detector scans memory, the boot sector, the partition table and the executable files. It is searching for the occurrence of the string of instruction sequences that are mostly unique to particular viruses. This pattern is usually called its *'signature'* and is usually about 16 to 24 bytes in length. Although the virus code can be mostly randomly encrypted each time it infects a file, it still needs a section of unencrypted code to carry out the decryption of the other sections. This code section is its signature. This means that the software is virus-specific; if a new virus appears, a new version of the scanning software is required. The more up-to-date the version of scanning software, the more known signatures are searched for, thereby increasing the chances of detecting viruses. When a known signature is detected, the file or sector is reported to the user as being infected.

To prevent detection, some viruses randomly generate what appears as a completely new encrypted code each time it replicates itself. These are known as *'polymorphic'* viruses and the encryption code is often given the glamorous title of *'Mutation Engine'*. In these varieties, even the previously unencrypted code is altered. This is achieved in a number of ways - e.g. adding redundant instructions, changing the order of certain instructions, storing values in different registers or using alternative instructions that carry out the same end result as another set of instructions. This produces many possible permutations. When these viruses appear, a huge range of potential signatures would require to be searched for, making their detection almost impossible. An example is the *'Pogue'* virus, which plays music and corrupts hard disk data. In response, anti-virus software introduced the *'wildcard'* into their virus checking algorithms. This knows where some of the redundant instructions are situated and ignores their specific contents in the signature search. Unfortunately, the added complexity leads to slower operations.

Some systems use *'virus definitions'*. These are essentially just version numbers for virus signature files, but in terms of actually using the software, virus definitions and virus signatures are functionally the same.

Generic Scanning

A different type of scanning is to ignore signatures that can have many variations. Instead, the scanning software looks for machine code instructions that would result in executable files being written to. These are known as *'generic scanners'*, *'monitors'*, or *'heuristic scanners'*, since they look for points that are common to a range of viruses, rather than any specific virus. To that extent, they are more future-proofed. However, some applications require to re-write their EXE files to reflect a user's configuration and this might be reported as a virus. In development environments, such as software houses and colleges, EXE files are regularly created and modified and this could also lead to many spurious reports of file corruption. Even DOS commands such as FORMAT.COM and SYS.COM might be reported as viruses. This makes a generic scanner an imprecise weapon but it is useful nevertheless.

Some memory-resident versions of generic scanners overcome this by detecting the attempt to write to disk and providing the user with an option to continue with the operation or to abort. This can be used to prevent unauthorised disk formatting, programs going memory-resident, and writing to the disk boot sector. For example, if a memory-resident scanner intercepts a call to write to disk, its program tests whether the boot sector or FAT is being written to and prevents, or gives the user control over, that activity. This is successful unless the virus code writes directly to the hard disk controller via the BIOS, bypassing the DOS calls.   This is combated by detecting calls to INT 13, INT 26 and INT 40, which are direct BIOS disk calls.   Checks should include spotting attempts to change file attributes from read-only to read-write, renaming COM and EXE files, writing to executable files and writing to the boot sector.

File Fingerprinting (Checksumming)

The other detection method concerns itself with the original characteristics of a file and the effects of an infection. Every new .COM and .EXE file added to a disk can have a CRC check code (sometimes called a *'validation code'*) calculated and logged. Adding together the values of all the bytes in a file would produce a large number that could act as a simple checksum; using a mathematical formula to the bytes produces a figure that is more unique to that file. These checksums can be attached to the files concerned or they can be held in a separate database. The anti-virus software can then later check these codes for any sign that any file has been altered. This is a more efficient means of detecting virus attacks.   Of course, by definition, the viruses are only detected <u>after</u> they have infected the system; this method does not detect the infection process itself. The checking of the existing set of files on the disk can be an automatic process initiated through the Registry or Startup folder, or by a command in AUTOEXEC.BAT. Each file can have its checksum calculated and compared to its previous value. Any difference in values will result in an error report.   This can be a time-consuming business with large hard disks but is very effective. However, the calculation of checksums for new files has to be carried out regularly and added to the checksum list, if the system is to be maintained at an efficient level.

Viruses mostly work by changing the first 'jump' or 'call' instruction in a file; the pointer is altered to point to the added virus code rather than the normal program code. So, in many cases, testing the checksum of the first few dozen bytes will detect whether the file is infected. To counteract this, some viruses leave the first pointer untouched and alter the next pointer, which is embedded deeper in the file's code. This evades a simple checksum system and requires a checksum on the entire file to be carried out; this takes longer and occupies more storage space.

Anti-Virus Products

Ever-increasing ranges of anti-virus products are becoming available. Most are software products but a couple of hardware alternatives are around in the shape of cards that fit into the normal expansion bus. These are particularly useful in dealing with boot sector viruses, both on the hard disk and on floppies. Many anti-virus programs are normal commercial products and a few are shareware varieties. Considering the problems, then, a preferred anti-virus product should include the following facilities:

- The ability to run the utilities automatically, e.g. through the Registry, Startup folder or AUTOEXEC.BAT. If a utility has to be actively executed by a user, it will often be forgotten. The experience of creating backups has shown this.   The virus checking should be able to run without user-activation, if required.
- The ability to run its utilities as background programs or TSRs.   This should be able to scan all files that are executed, modified, copied or unarchived (i.e. restored from compressed form).
- The anti-virus software should be able to test itself for signs of viruses.

- The ability to check memory, disk partition tables, boot sectors, normal files and compressed files.
- The ability to choose between making all tests or making specified checks. A virus can infect an overlay file and although these are commonly given the extensions .OVR or .OVL, they can really be given any extension from a particular application. So, there is no way that a scanner can tell whether a file is a data file or an overlay file containing infected executable code. To be absolutely certain that a machine is virus-free, every file on the disk would have to be checked, not just the .COM and .EXE files. While this is slower, it is a more secure option.
- Few false detections. For example, the virus search strings embedded in one scanner's code should not be detected as a virus by another scanner. This can be avoided by a scanner that encrypts its search strings, which is common in modern anti-virus software. An uninfected machine should produce no false alarms.
- The ability to detect as large a range of viruses as possible.
- A range of protection systems, including specific and generic scanning and checksumming.
- The ability to handle 'stealth' viruses and macro viruses.
- The ability for users to add known signatures to their check list, including wildcards.
- The ability to prevent viruses writing to the boot sector or partition table.
- The ability to repair infected files.
- The ability to immunise files - fool the virus into believing that the files are already infected.
- Checking of incoming emails for viruses.
- A boot sector and partition table restoration facility.
- The ability to create a 'rescue' disk to store the partition table, boot sector, FAT and CMOS settings.
- A reasonable execution time, although this must in most cases remain subordinate to having the fullest tests carried out. The longer the list of possible signatures, the greater is the scanning time required; background virus monitors require processing time. These are facts of life that have to be lived with.
- A reference book, or dictionary, of all known viruses.
- The availability of regular updates.
- Help line and/or bulletin board service available.

Most up-to-date Anti-Virus software provides multiple functions. There are even on-line virus scanning services, ensuring that the signature file is at all times completely up to date.

The two main features of any virus checker are the protection software, which runs in the background in order to prevent infected programs from running; (known as 'on-access' scanning) and the scanner, which searches drives for infected files ('on-demand' and 'scheduled' scanning).

In theory, a combination of the two should prevent any known virus from entering the system, though it may not stop unknown viruses. The most popular anti-virus products perform both of these functions, and include Symantec's Norton Anti-Virus, McAfee VirusScan, Sophos Anti-Virus and F-Prot from Frisk software.

Testing your anti -virus product

The European Institute for Computer AntiVirus Research (EICAR) is an organisation that co-ordinates dissemination of information about viruses. As part of their efforts, they have created a non-virus that all virus scanning packages recognise. Thus, an anti-virus package can be confidence checked, without exposing the system to any danger.

The steps are:

- Create a text file using NotePad, Edit, or some other ASCII editor.
- Put the following text in the file
  X5O!P%@AP[4\PZX54(P^)7CC)7}$EICAR-STANDARD-ANTIVIRUS-TEST-FILE!$H+H*
  Note that the first 'O' is the upper-case letter (O) and not the number zero (0). Also, it is advisable to avoid entering any other text in the file, as some virus checkers will no longer recognise the string.
- Save the file as EICAR.TXT.
- Rename the file as EICAR.COM.
- Run your Anti –Virus package to check the directory that contains the file.

Using Anti-Virus Products

Many security applications bundle anti-virus facilities along with other utilities such as backups, system optimising, firewalls,   The anti-virus capabilities vary from package to package, but the basic steps for ensuring virus protection are similar.

These include:

Scheduling

Virus scans can be scheduled to run at any time, allowing time-consuming virus checks to be carried out when the user is not at the machine. Virus list updates and other programs can also be scheduled here.

Scanning options

This is the option that allows the user to run on-off checks, choosing which drives, folders or individual files to scan for potential viruses.   The user can also decide whether to check just the most vulnerable areas or carry out a check on every file.

Reports

This section is used to display reports on items in Quarantine, display the anti-virus log, or give information on the list of viruses and their individual threats

Once the package is told where to scan, it begins the scanning process. After checking memory for resident viruses to ensure a 'clean' uninterrupted scan, it will begin checking the chosen areas. During the scan, a screen will show how many files are scanned, and other details of the process.

If a virus is found, another window will pop up, allowing the user to decide what to do about it. Unless the user is experienced with PCs, the *'Automatic'* handling of viruses should be chosen.

Manual operation allows the user to choose whether to repair, delete, or quarantine the file, or exclude it from the virus check if the user is absolutely certain that it is a false alarm.

Finally, a window is displayed showing the results of the scan. This gives statistics including the total number of files and boot records scanned, the number of viruses found, and the number of files repaired, quarantined or deleted.

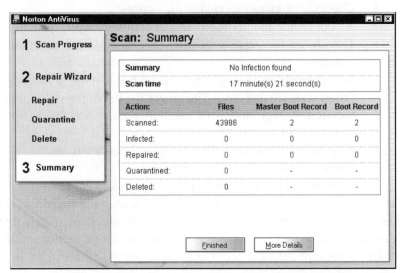

Virus Elimination

When a virus is detected, swift action should be taken, since delays will result in further potential data loss or corruption.   The action required should include:

- Immediately isolate the machine. Disconnect from any local area network or peer-to-peer system. No further activity should be carried out on the machine until the infection is cleared.
- Inform management and users.
- Collect any disks that were used in the machine.
- Test all machines that used disks taken from the infected machine or that may have been used to access its files in a peer-to-peer LAN.
- Check all machines in the organisation. If an infected game has passed round, employees will be reluctant to admit they used the disk. So, a check should be carried out nevertheless.
- Trace and eliminate the original source of the infection.   This is not always an easy task but overcoming the effects of a virus without eliminating the source of the infection only means that the whole process may start over again.
- If the virus is a new strain, report it to the various anti-virus software houses and the police Computer Crime Unit.

Microsoft Macro Viruses

Until recently, all viruses were contained inside the actual machine code of a program or routine. Data files were exempt from viruses, as they did not contain any executable code. The situation changed when Microsoft brought out Word 6, as it also introduced WordBasic to allow users to create their own *'macros'*. Similarly, Excel used Visual Basic for Applications to create spreadsheet macros. Office 97 uses Visual Basic 5 for both Word and Excel macros, while the popular Outlook email program may use Microsoft's scripting language. All known macro viruses can be detected using anti-viral toolkits.

Normal Macros

Macros are small, usually single-purpose, routines that are linked to a data document. Examples are macros to alter font characteristics in Word text or to carry out a sort on an Excel table. Macros can be invoked by clicking an icon or entering a particular keyboard combination. They can also be run each time that the Word or Excel document is opened. These legitimate macros are stored in a global template called *'normal.dot'*. The *'normal.dot'* template describes the document's characteristics such as customised toolbars, shortcut keys, macros, etc. These features, including the macros, are then usable by all documents that are based on the 'Normal' template. Legitimate macros can also be written to replace normal application activities. For example, macros such as *"FileSave"* and *"FileSaveAs"* will replace the normal file saving commands. The calls to the macros are embedded in the data document but the macro code resides in the *'normal.dot'* template.

Virus Macros

If a user opens a document that contains a macro virus, the virus code will run when its macro is activated. This may be through an *'AutoOpen'* macro (when the document is opened), an *'AutoNew'* macro (when a new document is created), etc. The virus spreads through copying the virus macros into the user's own 'Normal' template, so that all future documents can be similarly infected from there. All future documents that are created, amended, or sometimes simply opened, are in danger of having the virus macros calls copied into them. These documents are saved as new templates with the extension changed from 'DOT' to 'DOC' to appear like normal documents.

Web Viruses

With the rapid growth in the use of the Internet, there has been much concern expressed about its ability to spread viruses. The main areas of concern have been:

JAVA   Java Applets are small programs that are downloaded along with web pages. The Java specification describes a 'sandbox' that should keep viruses contained, but specific implementations in various browsers may contain security holes, and these can be exploited by viruses such as *'Strange Brew'*.

E-MAIL   As explained earlier, email viruses have overtaken traditional methods of virus infection.

CHAT   Some chat systems can transmit executable code, or even remotely run programs, and viruses have appeared that exploit these loopholes.

COOKIES   Cookies are small data files that some web sites store on the user's hard disk. Although there are privacy concerns, cookies contain no executable code and cannot be a source of viruses.

Virus Prevention

If an anti-virus strategy is adequately planned and implemented, the risk of virus infection is minimised. The adage *'Prevention is Better than Cure'* emphatically applies to viruses. A rigorous approach to virus prevention can save countless hours repairing the effects of a virus attack. The hours spent in implementing prevention measures will repay themselves many times over in preventing lost production caused by virus attacks. Nevertheless, viruses will still be a threat and it is far better to have a recovery strategy in place before any attack, than running round in a panic when the attack has already occurred.

There is a wide range of activities that can be carried out to provide as virus-free an environment as possible. Remember that a completely virus-free environment is still not a reality, since anti-virus software chases virus development. The degree of enforcement of the activities depends upon the importance of the system in use. Viruses finding themselves on to a home user's machine are less of a problem than viruses finding their way on to a network. Large organisations, with heavy reliance on their computing effort will want to make use of as many safeguards as possible. For these bodies, the data is far more precious than the hardware and the extra time and effort involved is worthwhile.

The organisation has to consider the amount of financial loss that would result from a loss of data. The losses could include:

- Repairing or replacing any damaged equipment.
- Lost output while the machines are down.
- Paying for incoming expert help (very expensive).
- Restoring available computer data (from backups).
- Re-entering available data held on paper.
- Re-collecting data not held on paper (e.g. telephone orders which were directly keyed into computers) and re-entering this data.

The strategy for virus prevention and elimination should be adopted as the organisation's policy at as high a management level as possible. This prevents friction at a later date, when machines are declared out of bounds and individual managers are losing precious processing time.

Virus prevention measures can tackle the problem both at the machine end and at the introduction of software into the system. Both activities are complimentary.

A virus-prevention strategy should therefore address both the existing machines and any new software that might be introduced to them. The anti-virus strategy should include:

- Naming staff responsible for maintaining current anti-virus software.
- Naming staff responsible for eliminating any virus outbreak.
- Securing outside consultants for anti-virus and data recovery work.
- Compiling detailed procedures for dealing with suspect files, disks, computers or networks.
- Staff training on virus issues.

Protecting the machine

The following practical measures are the responsibility of the whole organisation, although most will be carried out by the technical staff.

- Ensure that access to machines is restricted to only those who require it. This prevents unauthorised access and narrows down the source of any future virus problems. On a standalone machine, special password protection programs can be installed. On local area networks, the system passwords can be rigorously used. Machines should not then be left unattended and switched on, otherwise these passwords are ineffective.
- Where economically practicable, install anti-virus software on each machine. This is usually a cost-effective measure, as the alternative is to have the PC support technician running round all the machines with the single licensed copy. The extra cost of purchasing multiple copies is soon recovered. The purchase of a site licence can make their installation cheaper still.
- Create a 'rescue' disk. This is a boot disk that is tested as virus-free and contains a copy of the partition table, boot record and machine CMOS settings. This is normally provided as an option with anti-virus software.
- Ensure that the files and sub-directories of the disk are protected as far as possible. For a standalone machine, this involves setting most file attributes to read-only.
- On a local area network, sub-directory rights should be set to the minimum access rights possible. For example, if a server directory contains only program files, then access to the entire directory should be on a read-only basis. This is not always possible, as some applications need to write their configuration information. Individual files within read/write sub-directories should be set to read-only, where possible. Individual users on the network should be given no more rights than they actually require.
- Ensure that regular backups are carried out, so that the effects of a virus attack can be quickly overcome. Removing the virus may only be part of the recovery process. Deleted and corrupted files have to be replaced and carrying out a restore can be an effective method of replacing these files. Backup copies should not consist solely of a single backup. Copies of previous backups should also be kept, since a virus may not have been detected and the newest backup may itself be infected. From time to time, test that the restore procedures actually work. There is little point in rigorously backing up data if the restore mechanism is flawed (e.g. the tape player may not actually be recording the backup data).
- Enforce strict bans on users bringing in games, or even their own utilities. Although no longer the most common means of spreading viruses, the mobility of memory sticks and CD-ROMs

make this a potential risk area. Many organisations, where data integrity is crucial, have policies of dismissal where unofficial use of media is spotted. No disks or memory sticks should be brought into, or taken out of, the computer environment.   Where this is impossible, such as with users of portable computers, every disk taken from the laptop or notebook must be virus checked before being placed in a main machine. Note that this restriction should also be enforced with visiting computer service engineers; any diagnostic disks must be virus checked before being used on a machine.   Similarly, demonstration disks brought in by salespeople are a likely carrier of infection from company to company and should be rigorously checked before being run.

- Keep users informed about the risks of email viruses. Filter incoming mail through a mail server – this can reduce unwanted *'spam'* mail as well as potential virus infections. End-user machines can also install software to warn users before running any scripts received in emails.

- Ensure that only data is kept on portable storage. This minimises viruses spreading since there are no executable code for the virus to attach to.   If users are trained to write-protect the storage disks that only contain readable data, then virus spread via disk boot sectors is also minimised.

- Undertake a training campaign amongst staff, so that the problems from viruses are fully understood. This may well prove a more effective weapon than the big stick and training videos are available.

- Use several anti-virus products, as no single piece of software detects all the available viruses.

- Keep the most up-to-date possible versions of anti-virus software, to minimise the prospects of data loss or corruption.   The producers of anti-virus software supply monthly or quarterly updates. Most software is capable of updating via the Internet without user intervention if set up to do so, while other software must be updated by manually downloading and installing updates. These updates can be in two forms: virus signature updates (to spot new viruses) and engine updates (to fix bugs, add new code or otherwise change the virus checker itself).

- Buy books on computer security, virus protection and disaster recovery.   Evolve the best strategy for the organisation, taking into account the amount of data, its importance, cost, etc.

Installing/Using New Software
Included in the organisation's policy statement on virus prevention should be a section on the introduction of new software into the organisation.   This may involve the centralisation of software purchasing and installation so that the policy can be fully implemented.   The policy should include:

- Buy only from reputable dealers; avoid the bargains, which may be imitations.
- Don't be tempted to use pirate copies. It is illegal and it carries a high risk of infection.
- Do not use Internet or bulletin board software, postal shareware and public domain disks or 'free' disks supplied by magazines or dealers until they have been fully tested.
- Where copyright permits, make a copy of any downloaded applications or utilities and write protect the working set of files.
- Thoroughly test new software before introducing it to the working situation.   This should be carried out in a 'clean' environment. Ideally, this should be a standalone computer with no other hardware present except the operating system. Before testing the software, the hard disk contents can be completely erased and fresh system software and anti-virus software installed. Even the NVR (non-volatile RAM) area should be erased and re-written. This ensures that there are no unknown influences on the test. Equally, it ensures that any virused software is unable to affect any other working software.
- Test the software with as many anti-virus packages as possible. Each package tackles the checks in slightly different ways and has different strengths and weaknesses. The range of viruses found by each package is different. So, if several packages are used, the chances of detecting a virus are improved.
- If the tests do not expose any viruses, the software should be documented before being brought into use. This will involve noting, for each file, the file size, file checksum and creation date and time. This can be used to check if files are later affected and altered by viruses.
- Store the master set of disks in a secure place.

Backing up

The importance of regular backups cannot be stressed strongly enough. Countless users have kept a single copy of a file, or left their system without backups for long periods, thinking 'it will never happen to me', only to lose data irretrievably at a later date.

Users and systems administrators must realise that the only way an organisation can retrieve lost data is if it was backed up in the first place. Without a backup, there is little chance of an organisation being able to retrieve its data. When it can, it is often very costly and takes quite a long time. Data is the lifeblood of an organisation and if it is starved of its data, it is unlikely that it will be able to survive uninjured. If the data loss is complete then the organisation probably dies. Consider a credit card company who lost all of their customer's balances – they would probably never be able to get the money they are owed. If a bank had major problems and lost the balance of its customer's accounts, how would their customers react?

It should also be understood that most systems change on a frequent basis – especially the data element. As such, regular backups should be taken and the organisation should be prepared to lose any data that isn't backed up. Backups cannot be undertaken piecemeal, they are essential to the well being of the organisation. As such, it should be made someone's responsibility on their job description to take regular backups, and someone else's responsibility to ensure that they are taking place. If not, then backups may not happen, which could cause catastrophe to the organisation. Backups must be planned and a set of "idiots" instructions produced to ensure that everyone understands how to take a backup.

Backup Verification

It is no good simply backing up a computer and trusting the backup has worked – some drives do not generate an error message during backup but only during the restore procedure, by which time it is too late. The backup needs to be verified to ensure that the data has actually been copied. The test of the tape needs to be thorough – a backup is only as good as its test.

Sometimes, a tape listing will be made to check that data has been backed up. This is not always sufficient – the directory may be at the front of the tape, written correctly, while errors occur later in the tape. The only full and proper way to verify a backup is to restore all files.

Unless the organisation has a separate computer with the same version of the operating system installed, this is usually not possible and an alternative must be found. The files should never be restored onto the same computer – if the backup has failed then the original files will be corrupted.

If the organisation does not have a "spare" computer then it is best to write a script which places a copy of a master text file around the filing system in predetermined locations (usually around mission critical data – before and after). The backup should then be taken and these text files removed from the computer. An attempt should then be made to restore the text files from the backup and compare them to the master. If the copies verify OK then there is a high probability that the actual backup will be OK. If they do not, then another backup should immediately be made on another tape.

Frequency of backups

The frequency of backups is a matter for the individual organisation and is decided by asking *"how much extra effort would be required to reconstitute lost data if backups were carried out weekly instead of daily?"* or *"is there any data that can afford to be lost at all?"*. If data changes slowly on a particular machine, there is less need to carry out frequent backups. Where the data on a machine regularly changes, the degree of change should be reflected in the frequency of backing up. There are occasions, however, when frequent backups are important even for slowly changing data. Where the data being added contains vital information, a more frequent backup ensures that this information is not lost.

Types of Backup

Just as selecting the right backup device is important, there are 3 main backup techniques and the selection of the most appropriate technique is just as important.

Full Backup

Performing a full backup frequently, is usually the best way of protecting the system. This involves taking a copy of **all** the data, applications, and systems files (including the operating system) and storing it to tape. Literally, everything on the system is copied to tape.

Because of the volume of information being stored, this type of backup takes the longest to perform. Should the organisation need 24-hour access to its data then this kind of backup can be restrictive.

However, because all of the information is on one backup set, this type of backup is the quickest to restore the system. Often it is the time taken to rebuild the system that is critical, and as such, this type of backup may be the most appropriate.

Obviously if there is a lot of data and applications on the system, the backup device must be capable of holding all of this information. Sometimes full backups require a large number of tapes that need to be stored, but the expense of the tapes is usually small, especially compared to the potential losses if sufficient backups are not taken.

Because all information is stored on every backup set, it is possible to recover anything from any set. Thus if a change was made to the operating system which drastically affected users, the system could be quickly returned to a stable state on any of the days a full backup was taken. A good organisation could return to a month ago or even further.

Incremental backup

Incremental backups are a technique used to cut down on the time taken for a full backup. The first time a backup is made, it is a full backup. The second backup is an incremental backup, which means it will copy only the files modified (be they system or data) since the full backup. The next backup is also incremental, and will copy only the files modified (system or data) since the previous incremental backup, and so on.

This drastically cuts down on the time taken to backup but can lead to a complex chain of tapes, as each tape contains only files modified since the last backup. This means that it takes a lot longer to restore and that the backup is dependent upon more tapes, which increases the probability of failure. Should one tape fail in the batch, then they may be unable to continue with the restore or may have lost valuable data. In contrast to a full backup, where an older version of the file could be recovered from another tape.

When using this type of backup, the system administrator should try to keep to a minimum the number of days between a full backup. At most there should be 5 days in between full backups.

Differential Backup

Differential is really a compromise between the previous two backup techniques. With differential backup, a full backup is taken and then subsequent differential backups are taken. Each differential backup copies all files modified since the last full backup. This affords a higher level of protection than incremental backups but not as high as a full backup. It also takes longer to backup than an incremental backup but less time than a full backup. Finally, it takes longer to restore than a full backup and not as long as an incremental backup.

Choosing the Backup Technique

The choice of technique really depends upon the length of time available for the backup process. If the organisation can afford the time for a full backup then they should do this at least nightly. Using either of the other techniques is a compromise.

Backup Devices/Media

It is very important to purchase and use the correct hardware for the backup process and there are a number of factors that influence the choice of equipment. In this section some of the current backup devices are detailed with their strengths and weaknesses:

Tape Cartridge

Various forms of tape are used for backups, including Quarter Inch Cartridge (QIC), 8mm cassette, DAT cartridge, and Digital Linear Tape (DLT). Their cost and capability vary somewhat from one device to the next, but they are generally a cheap option for very large backups – typical modern tape drives can store around 80GB per tape. They are a common option in use with servers such as Unix, Novell, or Windows 2000 Servers.

CD-ROM

CD-ROMs are not really a backup device but are a good archiving device. Their relatively low capacity (generally 650MB) makes them unsuitable for industrial or commercial backup applications and there is little software to support writing to a multiple disk set. As they are WORM (Write Once Read Many times) technology, it would be a rather expensive way of backing up. The same applies to CDRWs. However, they do make an excellent archive medium and can easily be distributed. They are good for archiving as they support random access and are optically based (therefore last longer than magnetic sources).

DVD
The DVD is essentially an improved CD-ROM, and it shares much the same benefits and drawbacks of the CD. However, DVDs store considerably more (typically 4.7GB).

Removable devices
There are a wide variety of removable devices available nowadays, from memory sticks to portable hard disks. Memory sticks are useful for carrying around small amounts of data, while portable hard drives offer much greater capacity and are reliable and very fast.

Redundant Array of Inexpensive Disks (RAID)
These devices are not really backup devices, but are fault tolerant disk subsystems. See the LANs chapter for details of RAID. Whilst RAID systems afford high availability to data, they are not backup devices and **MUST** themselves be backed up at regular intervals.

Choosing the backup device
There are many factors that influence the choice of backup device. The most important factors are discussed below:

Budget
Often choice is made depending upon the amount of money available for the project. Unfortunately, with backup devices, cost (whilst important) should take a second place to other major factors. What is the point of buying a lower cost backup solution, which doesn't have sufficient capacity for the machine? It may also be found that a few hundred pounds has been saved on the device but that it requires attended operation (and therefore staff costs) to backup.

Capacity
The device must offer sufficient capacity (in unattended mode) to backup the system. A heavy contingency must be placed on this figure (of say 50% or more) to allow for future expansion of the system. Ideally purchase a backup device with a capacity, which far exceeds current needs.

Speed of the Device
Speed of the device is also of critical importance – especially the time taken to restore. The critical time for the speed of a backup device is the time it takes to restore. If a restore is required, then it is likely the organisation cannot function until it has taken place – time is then of utmost importance. The time taken to backup should also be as short as possible – especially if the organisation needs to cease trading whilst the backup takes place. In such cases, the backup intrudes upon business time and therefore the backup time becomes very important.

Type of device
The type of device also has a large impact upon choice. Standards such as DDS (Digital Data Storage) and DDS2 mean that there is more freedom with respect to devices. Should the old device fail, then it can be replaced with any drive from any manufacturer as long as it is compliant to the same standard. This can also afford a level of protection – should the device fail when it is needed most, then one can usually be sourced fairly easily. Of course, given the value of the data to the organisation, it may well choose to hold a spare device.

Tape handling
Backup devices and techniques to be used in backing up the data have so far been discussed. What must also happen is to ensure that the tapes are used in accordance with the manufacturer's guidelines (in terms of heat, humidity and acclimatisation) and to ensure that backup tapes are cycled.

Firstly the manufacturers issue instructions with tapes detailing constraints on their operating conditions. These include storage temperatures and humidity and usually they will detail a time taken for the tape to acclimatise to the environment of the tape drive. This can often take several hours and the tape should not be used until acclimatised - the use of non-acclimatised tapes can damage the drive and jeopardise the backup.

Selection and purchase of the tapes should be undertaken with caution. Firstly, only the best quality tapes should be purchased from a reputable manufacturer and supplier. The tapes purchased should be from multiple batches – in case of a batch problem.

Tapes have a finite life and will eventually wear out. The tapes will usually state an expected life or mean time between failure (MTBF) and a tape should never be used beyond these guidelines. Should a tape fail prematurely, then it may be prudent to discontinue use of all tapes from that batch.

In order to ensure reliability of the tapes, cycling is of utmost importance – each tape should be used frequently and to a similar extent. Tapes stretch as they are used, especially at first. If they are underused, then reliability may be impaired just as if they are overused. Systems Administrators should ensure that each tape is used a similar amount of times. This cannot be achieved by random selection, instead a specified cycling technique should be used. In addition, the organisation should:

- Replace tapes regularly (the purchase date should be written on the tape together with a tally for the number of times used).
- Upon receiving any errors, the tape should be replaced immediately.
- Clean the drive regularly following manufacturer's instructions.

Finally, backups should be stored '*offsite*' if possible. It is handy to have a backup nearby if a user accidentally deletes a file or some similar minor problem occurs. But if there is a serious problem, such as a fire, then the backup will have been destroyed along with the original. Therefore, if possible, always store tapes offsite in a fireproof safe to avoid this situation.

Backup Cycles

Using a single backup tape is not secure enough. The next time the system is backed up, the tape will have to be overwritten - the same tape containing the only copy of the data. Should there be a power loss whilst the computer is backing up, then the copy of the data on the hard drive may be lost, and the user will certainly lose the copy on tape as it will have only been partially written. Thus all of the data will have been lost.

In most cases however, there is a limited number of tapes available to back up onto – the administrator cannot simply keep backing up onto new tapes. The solution is a '*backup cycle*', where used tapes are re-used at a later date. This does even out the wear on tapes, but more importantly it provides archives dating back more than just the last backup. This can be useful if a file was lost or damaged several days ago and it has only just been noticed. The following are examples of backup cycles.

Grandfather/Father/Son

This is a simple but effective backup cycle. The first tape created becomes the son and is kept. The second tape created becomes the new son, the older one becoming the father. When the third tape is used, it becomes the son, the oldest tape becomes the grandfather and the previous son becomes the father. Thus there is a whole generation of backup tapes and it is possible to recover back to the third backup. In a daily cycle, this means that files lost up to three days ago can be recovered. As computer systems become larger with more users, often lost files are not noticed in three days. Consider a part time class at University – they may only be in once per week. If they discover a lost file at this point, it is too late to recover it using this method of cycling. Thus organisations have adopted more complex strategies for cycling.

4 Week Cycle

This cycle method aims to minimise tapes required while still providing good archiving capability. A backup (full or incremental) is taken each working day for four weeks. The last working day of each week, a full backup is taken, and stored elsewhere. This tape is then replaced with a fresh tape.

At the end of the four weeks, a new cycle starts. The same method is used, but the replacement tapes come from the four tapes from the previous cycle. Take care, however, not to use the last day's tapes only for that purpose – since they are being stored instead of used for most of the time, they might be underused which could cause problems.

Assuming a 5 day week, and that the entire backup fits on one tape, this method needs just 8 tapes to store adequate backups for most of a month. If further archives are required, then the last of the four weekly tapes could be stored as a monthly archive, using a similar tape replacement technique.

Using DOS Backup

DOS provides two commands to handle backups

- The BACKUP command creates the backup copies. This can be a copy of the contents of a single directory, with or without its lower subdirectories. This means that the user can start from the root directory and backup the entire disk, if required. As a refinement, the user can decide to only back up selected files, rather than all files in a directory.
- The RESTORE command recreates the copy on the original disk, if required.

Normally, the BACKUP command will be used regularly, say daily, while the RESTORE command will only be used in an emergency.

The basic syntax of the command is:

BACKUP C:\TEST.DIR*.*   A:

This makes a backup copy of all the files in the TEST.DIR directory of the hard disk on to the floppy drive.   It is important to note that this command deletes all the previous contents of the destination disk.

The BACKUP command does not work like the COPY or XCOPY commands, which copy the files in their original format.   With these commands, the individual files can still be individually accessed.

The BACKUP command copies the files over to the destination disk in a coded form and they cannot be accessed until they have been re-processed with the RESTORE command.   The main data files are compacted into a single file, along with a

```
Volume in drive A is BACKUP  001
Directory of A:\

BACKUP  001    166484 14/06/00  18:57
CONTROL 001       889 14/06/00  18:57
    2 file(s)   167373 bytes
              562176 bytes free
```

control file that is used to track the files in the backup file. An example of a backup disk is shown. If a backup requires several floppy disks to hold the data, the program will prompt for the disk to be changed. In that case, DOS numbers each disk label as BACKUP 001, BACKUP 002, etc. and the files on the disk are numbered as BACKUP.001 with CONTROL.001 onwards.

The BACKUP command allows the following parameters to provide added flexibility:

/s   Also backup the files in any sub-directories.

/a   Append the backup files to those already on the floppy disk. The destination disk is not deleted and the new backup data is merely added to the disk.

/m   Back up only those files that have changed since the last backup. This also turns off the 'archive' attribute on the original file, so that it will not be backed up in a future /m backup (unless it has been modified in the meantime, turning on the 'archive' attribute).

/l   Create a log file (BACKUP.LOG) of all the files backed up.   This text file lists all the files, along with date and time information, making it easier to trace backup activities.

/d:dd-mm-yy   Only back up files created or modified on, or after, the given date.

/t:hh:mm:ss   Only back up files created or modified on, or after, the given time.
If this parameter is used, the /d parameter must also be used.

These options can be entered in upper or lower case and can be used in any sequence or combination.

A typical BACKUP.LOG file might be as shown on the right. The date and time of the backup are stored, followed by details on the disk number, path, and filename of each file backed up.

```
14/08/2000  18:57:13
001  \WINDOWS\256COLOR.BMP
001  \WINDOWS\ARCADE.BMP
001  \WINDOWS\ARCHES.BMP
001  \WINDOWS\ARGYLE.BMP
```

Restoring Files

This command is used to restore backed up files to their original destination.   As with BACKUP, if the files are stored over several disks, the RESTORE program will prompt for the next disk to be inserted, as appropriate.   An example would be:

RESTORE A: C:\TEST.DIR

The destination directory must be specified as the same one from which the backup was made. If the files do not exist on the hard disk, then they are created. If they do exist, they will be over-written.

A range of parameters can be also be used with RESTORE.

/s   Also restores the files in any sub-directories.

/m   Only restores files that have been modified since the last backup. This saves time over-writing files that are unchanged since the backup.

/n   Only restores files that no longer exist on the original drive.

/p   Prompts for confirmation before restoring over newer or read-only files.

/b:dd-mm-yy   Only restores files modified on, or before, the given date.

/a:dd-mm-yy   Only restores files modified on, or after, the given date

/e:hh:mm:ss   Only restores files modified on, or before, the given time.
               If this parameter is used, the /d parameter must also be used.

Examples

RESTORE A: C:*.* /S

Restores all files, including any in any sub-directories from the A drive on to the hard disk root directory.

RESTORE A: C:\WINFILES*.DOC /m

Restores all the files with the .DOC extension that were modified since the last backup, in to the WINFILES directory.

Backup for Windows XP

The Windows XP backup utility is accessed through

'Start menu' → *'All Programs'* → *'Accessories'* → *'System Tools'* → *'Backup'*.

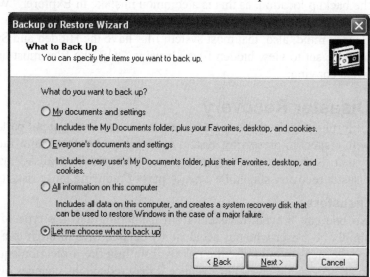

This displays a 'Backup or Restore Wizard' offering a choice to *'Back up files and settings'* or *'Restore files and settings'*.

The illustration shows the menu that displays when the backup option is chose.

Choosing any of the first three options and clicking *'Next'* opens a window that asks the user to choose a name for the backup and to select a folder where the backup will be saved.

Choosing the bottom option displays the drives and files menu shown in the illustration. The user can select entire drives, folders or individual files, in any combination that is required. When the *'Next'* button is clicked, the user is prompted to name the backup and choose a folder as the destination for the backup.

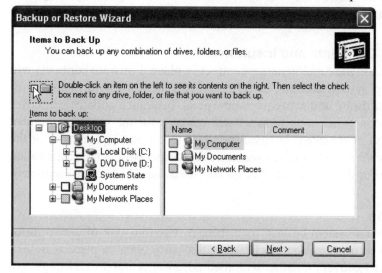

Scheduling backups

The Windows XP backup utility is accessed through

'Start menu' → *'All Programs'* → *'Accessories'* → *'System Tools'* → *'Scheduled Tasks*.

Click on *'Add Scheduled Task'* and choose *'Backup'* from the drop-down menu. The wizard then asks for the name of the backup to be scheduled how often the backup should occur (e.g. daily, monthly, on start-up) and the month day and hour of the backup. From then on, a scheduled task will run the backup job without user intervention.

Alternatively, in the backup wizard, after setting the files to be backed up, click the *'Advanced'* button. This allows access to settings such as the backup type (normal, differential etc), the name of the job, whether to use verification, and the backup time.

Restoring

If the files ever need to be restored, the *'Restore files and settings'* option should be chosen from the wizard.   tab of the *'Backup'* utility is selected. The set of files to be restored is chosen from those listed in the *'Items to restore'* box. This displays the folder and files structure of the backup set in the left panel.

Clicking any folder in the left panel results in its contents being displayed in the right panel. This way, individual files can be selected for backup, if desired.   The bottom left dialog box allows the choice of restoring files to their original folders, or selecting a new drive or folder for the restore.

Vista Backups

This operates in the same way as XP but with prettier screens and some refinements such as backing up files by type (e.g. the user can choose to backup all video files, selected audio files, etc.).

Manual Backups

It is not generally recommended to use Explorer copy system files, as this method is slow, and prone to user errors. Most modern backup software is quite capable of backing up system files such as USER.DAT and SYSTEM.DAT. For users of older software, however, it may be necessary to make backups of such files manually. The important thing to remember is to <u>copy</u> the file, and not <u>move</u> it, to the backup location, as this is a common mistake in Explorer. When copying files manually, the files are best copied to a separate drive, particularly a removeable device, for better security.

Bear in mind, also, that most system files have the Hidden and System attributes set. If using Explorer, it must be set to view hidden files. If using DOS, the files must have these attributes temporarily removed when copying.

Disaster Recovery

Unfortunately, backups and recovery only represent a small part of the tasks of the systems administrator with respect to preserving system availability. Another major factor in maintaining the availability of the system is disaster recovery planning. It should be realised that disasters must be faced, and as such, disaster recovery should be a major part of reducing those risks to an acceptable level.

Disasters

No one can prevent disasters from happening and the type of disaster cannot be controlled – it may simply be a user who has accidentally deleted files through to a fire in the computer room. It is possible to take steps to minimise the risk by installing fire protection equipment, etc. but this will rarely reduce it to an acceptable level. For instance it may reduce the chances of losing the data to fire but you could still lose the data to theft. Disaster Recovery is designed to plug the gap between the provision of such insurance and contracts and the needs of the organisation. However, disaster recovery is only as good as the last backup, and backups make up the majority of disaster planning.

Hardware & Software Maintenance Contracts and Insurance

Most organisations have a hardware and software maintenance contract in place. Software contracts will cover any new versions of the operating system and bug fixes to the present. Hardware maintenance contracts will cover any failures of the hardware and subsequent new parts. Insurance policies will cover loss or damage to the computer equipment. What none of these will cover is for the use of equipment whilst the organisation's is being repaired or replaced. In some instances repair and replacement of the computer equipment can take a considerable period of time (over a week) – especially in the case of total loss. In such circumstances it is possible for the organisation to go out of business before the equipment has been delivered.

Disaster Recovery Planning Options

Should access to information on a computer system be lost, then there is a serious risk of going out of business. Auditors now want proof that an organisation has Disaster Recovery plans in place. Below, the various schemes available for Disaster Recovery together with their advantages and disadvantages are discussed:

Self protection

Under this scheme the organisation provides for its own protection. It can be found that this is a very expensive solution - as another machine may need to be kept as a spare in case anything happens to the one currently in use. Each time the current machine is upgraded, the spare machine will also need to be upgraded. This will provide for the situation of a hardware failure. Should the organisation be burgled or be struck by fire or flood, then the probability is that both machines will be lost. It is best if the spare machine is resident on another site.

The organisation may also need another room in another building to which it can move should disaster strike. It will also need to ensure that it has the technical expertise and resources available to effect such a changeover.

This type of protection is becoming less and less common and is only really common with organisations large enough to protect themselves and with appropriate kit - e.g. a university could take computer equipment from academic use and use a room in another building.

Mutual protection with another organisation

This is probably the least recommended option. It relies upon two organisations being prepared to offer each other mutual protection in terms of accommodation and access to their computer systems. Such mutual protection should be agreed in contract before commencing but, if one of the organisations pulls out at the last minute, the legal wrangling process could see the demise of the other company.

The organisations that choose to team up in this way need to give some thought to their partners - as this could expose trade secrets and intellectual property rights. It is popular between schools, colleges and some universities but is becoming less popular. This type of protection demands high technical expertise as effectively two organisations have software and data resident on the same machine! The process of establishing such a complicated system could take so much time that the organisation would be out of business anyway!

Commercial plans

With the ever increasing usage of IT and the requirement of auditors that some sort of disaster recovery plan is in place, there has been an increase in the number of companies offering this sort of service. With a commercial plan, a company will provide access to a machine for an agreed annual fee.

Commercial plans with a reputable company that holds kit that can be utilised, represent one of the safest disaster recovery packages. Of course, the organisation will be expected to implement certain precautions themselves, such as taking regular backups and storing them in a fireproof safe.

There are many companies offering disaster recovery planning and the following is intended as a guide to selecting the appropriate service:

Equipment held and quantity.

If the equipment being held by the Disaster Recovery company is different to that of the organisation, then there will be a period of learning, which needs to take place with the users and systems staff. The time of the disaster is not usually the best time to acquire these skills. If the equipment is different, then it is possible that staff may be unproductive for a few days following the incident. In particular, the organisation should be wary of organisations that insist that they can make different hardware work effectively for them as a temporary measure. Who trains the system manager with the new commands? Who will teach the data entry clerks the new keystrokes & how long will it all take?

The number of machines held by the company should also be ascertained – they may hold 1 machine for every 10 clients – check the number of clients. If they have only 10 then there may be a reduced opportunity of getting a loan machine! Some companies operate this as insurance - with a no claims discount. Be sure the organisation trusts the company. A plan, which doesn't allow for testing should never be bought. Companies offer a number of different plans; the most appropriate one to the organisation should be selected. Measures should be taken to protect some stationary – perhaps some should be left in a bank safety deposit box!

The levels of recovery available

Time on someone else's machine

With this type of cover, a tape is sent to the Disaster Recovery provider and they load the data onto their machine. The organisation then uses their machine to access their data. This type of plan is only really suitable for small to medium sized businesses that have access to reasonably fast telecommunications (a fast modem or ISDN). It is usually the cheapest option available but can be expensive to operate (given the telephone costs). Sometimes this can be claimed under insurance. Printing can be a real issue with such plans.

Machine Delivered - organisation installs

This level of protection means that the disaster recovery contractor will deliver a machine within a given time span. The organisation then needs to install and commission the machine. This amounts to an agreement to "loan" the machine for an agreed period of time, after which it is usually possible to hire it for a longer period.

This is usually the next level in disaster recovery planning and is charged at a higher rate. The price will usually reflect how quickly the contractor will respond and the duration of the loan.

Whilst this is usually better than the first option, simply the loan of a machine may not be sufficient. If the organisation has the technical resources to install and commission the loan machine with their data, they need to ensure they are available (not ill or on holiday) when required. Usually, in the event of a real disaster, the organisation's technical people will be too busy to have time to install and commission the equipment.

Machine delivered and installed - organisation puts on data and applications

This is similar to the option above, except that the disaster recovery contractor will set up the machine (and possibly the network) which will save the organisation's technical people some time, However, the applications and data still need to be installed. Obviously the cost for this will be higher than just for delivery of the machine. However, in the event of a disaster it could be money well spent.

Machine delivered set up and tested

This represents an even more expensive option but is probably worth it because everything is down to the disaster recovery contractor. This means that at the time of a disaster the organisation's technical staff are more free to take a supervisory role and ensure the system is set up and working satisfactorily. With this type of plan, the contractors will turn up within a specified time period, there are fixed times for loan of the system (which can usually be extended on a hire basis).   With this kind of plan, the organisation should ensure that the contractor knows their requirements at the outset.

Full service - including "white room"

This service has nothing to do with the colour of the room, but is a term used by such contractors. Basically, it is a room or a building to which a company can move if their existing building becomes unusable. The room will usually be equipped with computer equipment, terminal and telephone points. This room is usually contracted for a fixed time period - but this could be an unknown length for the organisation and so hiring is again a possibility.

This is obviously much more expensive and only useful for organisations that don't have another site to which they could move. It does, however, allow them to continue business.

Data Recovery

When a hard disk, or other media fails, it is extremely difficult for ordinary users or even the typical IT service department to get any information from it at all. However, there are specialist data recovery companies that use special equipment to retrieve data from damaged media. Those areas which have become damaged are almost invariably lost, but other data may be retrievable. This is usually an extremely expensive option, but if extremely important data is not backed up properly and is lost, this may be the only option.

A compromise?

Most contractors will allow an organisation to take out an option and upgrade at the time of the disaster. Although slightly more expensive (in case of a disaster) it could be cheaper if the plan is never used.

Note that the organisation must be careful because the contractor may not have enough machines if everyone does this. In which case, it is likely that the clients who bought the higher level plan will be serviced first.   The organisation should always ensure that the machine will be configured to an appropriate specification.

Document Management

The IT department in an organisation is normally charged with organising the file structure on servers. Although this is an important part of maintaining the system's data, it is sometimes more important to look after the data files' contents, as well as their location. Although this is true of several types of data in many organisations, it is particularly important to those who develop software, because code can be changed very easily and interactions between code developed by different people or teams can become very complex if not managed properly.

'Version Control' systems are employed to keep track of documents that change regularly. A good version control system will organise files and resources, keep track of tasks assigned to personnel, and will protect any part of the system that may be undergoing change, as well as keeping a record of document updates and versions. There are a wide variety of document management solutions available, but for PC-based organisations the most widely used software is PVCS, from Merant.

Data Communications

The development of data communications

At first, the realm of data communications was rather specialised, involving terminals with little or no processing power communicating keypresses to a remote server that would carry out the processing. The growth of Personal Computers was a major factor in the advancement of data communications technology, both in terms of long-distance communications via telephone networks, and in terms of short-distance communication over a Local Area Network. PCs access data from the Internet, a bulletin board, or the office down the hall, and better communications means more efficient personal computing.

However, recent developments in wireless technology have indicated a possible change in direction again. Wireless communications provides the ability for '*mobile computing*'. Although the majority of networks are still wired, there is great promise in the idea of workers being able to carry their workstation with them, and yet still have access to all the centralised files and data they need to carry out their work. Wireless systems are already gaining in popularity in specialised fields, and they are almost certain to see use in traditional systems as they are gradually becoming more secure, faster, and more robust.

The use of data communications

Communications technologies can provide many benefits to an organisation. Conventional communications, such as telephone, fax, and voice mail, are essential to any organisation's ability to plan and carry out activities. When combined with computing, data communications can provide many additional capabilities:

File transfer; Centralised data; Videoconferencing; Email; Mailing lists; EPOS sales; EDI ordering and invoicing; Home banking and ATM bank machines; Distance learning; Distributed processing; Video on demand; Remote administration; Telemarketing/home shopping; Teleworking

Many of these capabilities allow effective operation from a remote location. For example, much of every bank's business now comes from EPOS or ATM machines, which link to centralised financial databases in the bank's main computer system. In this way, data communications can overcome many of the limitations imposed on a business by having remote installations.

Other problems that are eased by such technologies include technical support, which can be delivered from a remote location; or customer interaction, which can be standardised through the use of EDI or online sales. Communications networks can also bring other improvements:

- Speedier response to orders, invoices, requests and so on.
- Maintaining up-to-date records, available to all branches of the organisation.
- More effective decision making, due to the improved ease of discussion between managers.
- 'Roaming' users, able to work normally wherever they are physically located – perhaps even working from home.

A major benefit of communications networks is that of availability of information. As long as the network is configured properly, a user could have access to all the information they need to do their job, without even having to leave their desk. As well as making the employee's life easier, this is also an aid to productivity.

Well-designed communications networks are also scalable. That means that they are easily increased in size, if the organisation needs more connectivity between the locations it occupies. A distribution firm that dispatches orders through a computer network, for example, need only install a new node in one of its warehouses to provide full access to the necessary information.

At the end of the day, the aim of introducing a communication network into an organisation is to increase its efficiency and/or profitability, both by improving the organisation's speed and effectiveness and by introducing new markets and ways of reaching the customer.

The use of communications technologies will vary from one organisation to the next. Most high street outlets need ready access to financial data such as is available by EPOS, while wholesalers would be more concerned with implementing an EDI system to improve volume sales. Office-based businesses have different needs again, relying on the fast communication provided by email, and so on.

Development of communications applications

The first communications programs only connected terminals to servers. Even here, however, applications were developed to bring functions such as email, though the capabilities varied from one network to the next. Early email programs ran only on Local Area Networks, and were used mainly to pass short memos between separate departments or personnel within the same building. As communications technology progressed, however, so did the network applications.

Internal email within a single organisation is still possible, but most organisations have access to email on the Internet, which has evolved around a set of standard protocols. This enables all such organisations to communicate globally. Additionally, technologies such as MIME and UUEncode have arrived, allowing files to be attached to Internet emails, thus facilitating small-scale transfer of files and data along with email messages.

Other applications have also grown from simple LAN backgrounds. Applications for distributing and accessing information on a network stem from the basic principle of centralising data files on a local network. Although a number of programs appeared with the purpose of facilitating information access on a local network, the HTML standard, and the browser software that became associated with it, quickly became popular.

File transfer and remote access applications have also changed since the days of dumb terminals. FTP and Telnet are the standard now, thanks to the proliferation of the Internet.

Flexible Working

The integration of communications with networks allows for a much more flexible working environment:

TELEWORKING

> Packages allow modem access to the computer network over the normal telephone line. Work can now be carried out remotely from the work place - known as *'teleworking'*. This work might be able to be carried out at a time and a place that suits the user, since the network is available 24 hours a day. A salesperson can log in from his/her hotel in the evening and upload the day's orders. A programmer can write software from home and be paid by results. A director can control the business from the comfort of Monte Carlo. Students can download the week's work, write their essays and send them to their personal directories for marking. Lecturers can stay at home and still mark and tutor students.

DATA LOGGING

> Data logging (e.g. quantity measurement or salesmen's orders) on portable machines can be transferred via the telephone network to the office server for processing.

Limitations of communication technology

Every communication system has limitations, and computer data communications are no different. Speed is usually the prime limitation on the effectiveness of data transfer, but there may also be limitations of distance, particularly between wireless systems. Other factors may include software and protocol compatibility, maintenance overheads and of course, cost. Any system that communicates via a public network, such as the Internet, also has greater security concerns.

As with most computer technologies, the technical concerns can largely be overcome by using better quality, and therefore more expensive, connections and software. However, it is more important that the network is properly planned before implementation. A slow-speed network is quite sufficient if all that is needed is to transfer sales figures to head office at the end of each week; while a large commercial network would need much greater facilities. The type of services supplied over the network play a major role in determining the minimum quality of hardware and software needed.

Types of Data Communications

Almost all computer activities involve communication of some kind of data. Communications can take two forms: '*Analog*' or '*Digital*'.

Analogue	Data transmitted in analogue form has infinite potential variations. For example, colours on an ordinary television screen, or sounds recorded on a cassette tape. Dial-up phone connections, cable television (CATV) and cable internet are examples of analogue media.
Digital	Digital signals can be in one of only a set number of possible states for each item of data. For example computer data consists purely of ones and zeroes, with nothing in between. Printer cables, ISDN connections, and most types of local area network cables are all digital media.

It is possible to convert analogue data to digital and vice versa. For example a sound card must convert analogue sounds to digital data for storage, and back again to play the recorded sound. Similarly, a computer that uses an analogue transmission media such as a phone line must convert between analogue and digital, a process carried out by a modulator/demodulator, or '*modem*', as explained later in this chapter.

Furthermore, there are two ways in which data can be transmitted: '*Serial*' or '*Parallel*'.

Serial

This type of communication uses a single data line. This has the disadvantage that only one data bit can be transferred at a time, but has the advantage of lower cost.

Parallel

This type of system uses multiple data lines, to transfer multiple data bits in parallel with each other. All other things being equal, this would make parallel communications faster. However, the multiple connections make parallel links expensive, and the need to synchronise all the data lines makes them more complex. As a result parallel ports are in use only for very short distances indeed.

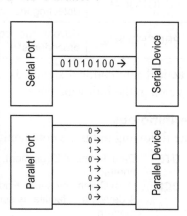

The various uses of data communications include:

- Internal and peripheral data communications. Within a computer, most data is moved round in parallel format on the various internal buses. Peripherals can communicate with the base unit in either serial or parallel format, depending on the type of connection. This type of communication is described in the '*Computer Architecture*' chapter.

- Local Area Networks. LANs, as they are known, are computer networks that span a short geographical distance, usually within a single building or even a single office. The '*LANs*' chapter describes this type of network.

- Metropolitan Area Networks. A MAN is a network that covers a larger area, perhaps several buildings, or even across town. They are most commonly composed of several LANs linked together through fibre optics, leased lines, or other longer-distance connections.

- Wide Area Networks. WANs are the longest distance networks, some of which span the entire globe. The Internet itself can be thought of as the largest single WAN on the planet. Most WANs, however, are less extravagant, consisting of local computers or LANs linked to main computer systems via phone lines, dedicated transmission lines, or through secure Internet connections.

Serial / Parallel Conversion

As can be seen, the computer deals with data internally in parallel format. However, with the exception of a few peripherals such as some models of scanners and printers, all communications are done in serial format. Therefore, the parallel data inside the computer has to be converted into a stream of bits to be sent out of the computer serially.

There are a number of chips that can perform this conversion:

- A chip called a '*UART* ' (Universal Asynchronous Receiver Transmitter) on the computer's motherboard is used to convert between parallel and serial data, for use with RS232 serial ports.

- The USB controller, whether on-board the motherboard or on a USB expansion card, converts parallel to serial data for the USB port. Similarly, the chipset for FireWire connectors, network cards, or internal modems, must perform the same function.

The conversions work in both directions, so that data can be transferred both in and out of the PC.

Interfaces

An interface is the point of connection between two pieces of electronic equipment. To communicate properly, the devices must both conform to the same specification.

The specification will include the following requirements, with the examples in brackets being for the RS232 interface:

MECHANICAL	Covers the physical elements such as the connection type (e.g. 9-pin or 25-pin layout) and cabling type (e.g. a 15m maximum between devices).
ELECTRICAL	Covers the signal voltage levels passing between devices (eg -5volts to -15volts representing logic 1) and the way that the data is passed (e.g. serially, synchronously, asynchronously).
FUNCTIONAL	Covers the purpose of each signal (e.g. carrying data, sending requests, and detecting the condition of connected devices).
PROCEDURAL	Covers the control and timing of signals between devices (e.g. handshaking procedures).

Practical international standards exist for both analogue and digital transmissions and these issues are covered in the following pages.

Terminology
The following terms are commonly used in describing communication equipment:

DTE   Data Terminal Equipment. A device that can send/receive data. Usually the microcomputer or printer.

DCE   Data Communications Equipment (mostly now called Data Circuit Terminating Equipment). A device that facilitates serial data communications. From a user point of view, this is usually a modem.

DSE   Data Switching Equipment.   The equipment used to route a call when there is no permanent link between two stations.

Serial Port
The serial ports are detected at power up and their addresses stored in memory. The normal base address for COM1 is 3F8h, COM2 is 2F8h, COM3 is 3E8h and COM4 is 2E8h. The port addresses in use on any particular computer can be found by using Windows Device Manager or the MSD utility.
The PC uses a standard known as RS232C and is implemented as COM1 and, if fitted, COM2.   An updated version known as RS-232D meets CCITT V.24, V2.28 and ISO IS2110 standards.

Physical Characteristics
The serial port is situated at the rear of most PCs. Serial ports are generally 9-pin D-type connectors, although the specification does allow for 25-pin D-type connectors. If the computer is 9-pin and the device is 25-pin - or vice versa - then a 9-pin to 25-pin adapter or a 9 to 25-way cable can be used to make the connection.   The connector at the rear of the PC is male (i.e. has pins) while the cable end is female (i.e. has sockets).

The RS232 standard was designed to minimise interference on the wires carrying the data signals.
To aid this, the voltages carried are higher than the normal range for digital signals carried inside the PC. The logic states inside the PC carry voltages typically no more than 5 volts. With RS232, binary 0 is represented by a voltage of +3 to +15 volts and binary 1 is represented by a voltage of -3 to -15 volts. Ideally, the signals would be +15v and -15v but by specifying a positive and a negative range, allowance is made for signal losses along the line.

Voltages between +3 volts and -3 volts cannot be converted to known values.   These indeterminate values may be caused by interference spikes or may be the result of losses of signal on the line. They are shown shaded in the diagram. The transition from a bit 0 to bit 1 is represented by a change of voltage on the appropriate output pin.

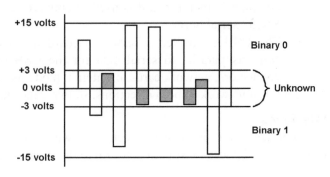

Serial Connectors

The connections for a 25-pin serial port are:

Pin	Purpose	Signal Direction	Signal Name
1	Frame Ground	-	FG
2	Transmit Data	Out	TXD
3	Receive Data	In	RXD
4	Request to Send	Out	RTS
5	Clear to Send	In	CTS
6	Data Set Ready	In	DSR
7	Signal Ground	-	SG
8	Data Carrier Detect	In	DCD
9	+ DC Test Voltage	In	+V
10	- DC Test Voltage	In	- V
11	Equaliser Mode	In	QM
12	Secondary DCD	In	DCD2
13	Secondary CTS	In	CTS2
14	Secondary TXD	Out	TXD2
15	Transmitter Clock	In	TC
16	Secondary RXD	In	RXD2
17	Receiver Clock	In	RC
18	Unused	-	NC
19	Secondary RTS	Out	RTS2
20	Data Terminal Ready	Out	DTR
21	Unused	In	NC
22	Ring Indicator	In	RI
23	Data Rate Selector	Out	DRS
24	Transmit Clock	Out	TC
25	Unused	-	NC

The connections for a 9-pin serial port are:

Pin	Purpose	Signal Direction	Signal Name
1	Carrier Detect	In	DCD
2	Receive Data	In	RXD
3	Transmit Data	Out	TXD
4	Data Terminal Ready	Out	DTR
5	Signal Ground	-	GND
6	Data Set Ready	In	DSR
7	Request to Send	Out	RTS
8	Clear to Send	In	CTS
9	Ring Indicator	In	RI

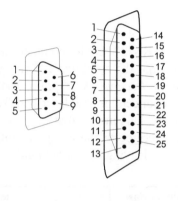

Note:

The tables show all the pins for the RS232 standard. In practice, most equipment uses a smaller number of connections, as explained later.

A summary of the signals is:

Voltage	Signal Name	Data Logic	Control Logic
+3 to +15	Space	0	True/High
-3 to -15	Mark	1	False/Low

Note that a positive voltage corresponds to a data bit logic of zero - but oddly also corresponds to a *'true'* logical statement. Hence, a positive value on *'Transmit Data'* or *'Receive Data'* lines indicates the presence of a zero bit, while a control line such as DTR indicates that it is ready by placing a *'true'* condition (i.e. a positive voltage) on its line. This is a source of confusion. Some books and manuals refer to the *'enabling'* of a control pin as going high (in the sense of the voltage on the pin) while others describe enabling as going low (in the sense of the logic value). Diagrams show a bar over a signal to indicate that it is enabled by going low (e.g. RD)

Modems

All data is held in binary format within the computer. Ideally, computers also wish to communicate in binary format. However, due to the characteristics of long analogue telephone cables, there is too much loss on digital signals for this method to be used. Telephone lines are designed to carry low frequency signals (from 300Hz to 3500Hz). To communicate, the binary data has to be converted into a signal in this audio range. The device that allows these conversions is known as a MODEM, which stands for MODulator/DEModulator.

The diagram shows two computers being connected via a telephone line. There is an external modem at each end between the computer and the line. The computer sending the data feeds the modem with a

stream of binary zeros and ones. The modem converts the 'zeros' into one audio tone and the binary 'ones' into a different audio tone. These audio tones can then be readily sent along a line. At low transmission rates this can easily be a standard telephone line. At the receiving end, the modem carries out the opposite function, converting one tone back to logic 0 and the other tone back to logic 1. In this way, the modem reconstitutes the original digital data sent from the first computer. This stream of digital information is then fed to the serial port of the receiving computer.

Essentially, the modem is a two-way device for connecting a computer to a telephone line.

The connection to the computer has to reflect the need to send data from the machine to the modem, and vice versa, including flow control of the data. Modems differ from printers in that they have a range of error-checking methods and, if an error is detected, a request can be made for the re-transmission of the affected data. Modems can be supplied as internal or external devices. The internal modem is a card that plugs into an empty expansion slot on the motherboard. Most current modems are Plug and Play compatible, and will configure themselves to COM3 or higher to avoid clashes with the existing COM ports that most computers already have. The link between the computer and the modem is via the normal address and data buses. The communication protocols to the external cable would be set within the communications program, using the Hayes AT command set.

The external modem is supplied as a freestanding unit that sits outside the computer casing. This saves using up an expansion slot on the motherboard, but requires to be fitted to the computer via a serial or USB port.

Modem Wiring

The diagram shows the basic RS232 cable connection between a computer and a modem. Note that the computer's *'Transmit Data'* pin does not connect to the modem's *'Receive Data'* pin as may have been expected. This is because all connections are described from the DTE (i.e. the computer) point of view. This means that the pins on the DCE (i.e. the modem) describe their <u>service</u> to the computer rather than the <u>direction</u> of the signals entering or leaving the modem unit. This could be expressed thus:

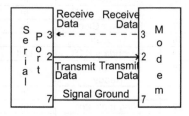

Simplified computer/modem link

Pin	Computer's point of view	Modem's point of view
Pin 2 (TXD)	Data that I wish to transmit	Data from the computer that I must transmit down the line
Pin 3 (RXD)	Data that I wish to receive	Data received from the line that I must pass on to the computer

Similarly, all other pins, such as RTS, CTS and DTR are wired directly to each other, i.e. pin 4 to pin 4, pin 5 to pin 5 and so on. The distinction between connecting DTE to other DTEs or to DCEs is important to avoid confusion and to prevent incorrect wiring of connections (see later).

Note

> This approach mainly applies to modems. With most other devices, the wiring follows expected practice with the computer's *'transmit'* pin being wired to a device's *'receive'* pin and the computer's *'receive'* pin being connected to the device's *'transmit'* pin.

Synchronisation of devices

If two devices are to communicate, the receiving device must run at the same speed as the sending device. To maintain the synchronisation of the two devices, each has a clock. The clock at the sending end tells the sending device when to transmit a bit of data on to the line. The clock at the receiving end tells the receiving device when it is time to check whether a 0 or a 1 has arrived. It is vital that the two clocks be kept at the same speed. If, for example, the transmitting clock sent 1200 data bits every second and the receiving device checked the line at the rate of 1300 times a second, the result would be the detection of 100 extra spurious bits of data which would completely disrupt the message.

Synchronous Mode

The easiest way to synchronise the two clocks involves the sending clock keeping the receiving clock in step. This would simplify matters, compared to alternative methods. The big drawback is that data has to be sent in a continuous synchronised stream, or in large blocks. This is not always possible or necessary, and it requires another wire between the devices. It is, however, less prone to distortion than other methods and is therefore usable at higher transmission speeds. It would not be found as a method for connecting computers to modems.

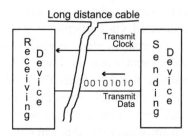

Simplified version of synchronous transmission

Asynchronous Mode

The most common method of connecting PCs is the asynchronous method. Here, there is no equal spacing between each character transmitted. A character being sent in real time via a keyboard, for example, could be sent at any unknown moment. For the system to be able to process a character, the hardware has to be told when a character is about to be received and when the transmission of the character has

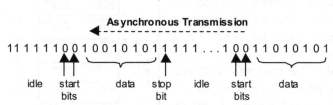

ceased. This involves enclosing the bits of the data with extra bits known as the START BITS and STOP BITS. As the names imply, the START BITS take the signal off the idle state, so giving a kick to the clock.   Incoming bits can now be sampled at the clock rate. The STOP BIT returns the system back to the idle state.   Conventionally, the least significant bit of the data (LSB) is transmitted first and the most significant bit (MSB) is transmitted last.   The idle state, also known as the *'mark'* condition, is a logic 1 while the logic 0 is known as a *'space'* condition.

Advantages

- Requires fewer connection wires.
- Works well with irregular data streams - e.g. keyboard entry transmissions.

Disadvantages

- Start bits can be missed. Data bits are then misread as start bits, producing errors.
- Interference pulses on the line can generate spurious start bits and non-existent bits are decoded.
- The system is slowed down, as a proportion of the data bits transmitted carry no useful information - they are for control purposes only.   For example, a system with 2 start bits and 1 stop bit requires 11 bits to transfer a single byte.

Parity Bit

For the transmission of ASCII files, a 7-bit code is sufficient to cover the ASCII range and the extra bit can be used by the receiving device for error checking.   The eighth bit is known as the parity bit and communication systems can use either even or odd parity - assuming that both devices know that they are checking by the same method. Depending on the system, parity may also be used on 8-bit data packets.

Even Parity

The sending device counts the number of 'one' bits in the character to be transmitted.   If the number of these data bits is even, as in the top diagram, the parity bit is set to zero. If the number of 'one' bits is odd, as in the lower diagram, the parity bit is set to one.   Thus the total number of 'ones' in the byte will always be even, no matter how many 'ones' are in the character being transmitted. If any of the data bits or parity bits is accidentally altered during

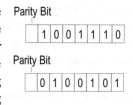

transmission, the receiving device can detect the problem by counting the number of bits. If the total is not an even number, there has been corruption of the data.   This provides an elementary check for data errors.

Odd Parity

Here, the sending device counts the number of 'one' bits in the byte to be transmitted.   If the number of these data bits is even, as in the top diagram, the parity bit is set to one. If the number of 'one' bits is already odd, as in the lower diagram, the parity bit is set to zero.   In this way, the total number of 'ones' in the group is always maintained at an odd value.

Note:

Parity checking is a useful facility but it is not foolproof. For example, two bits in a byte both being altered from zero to one would produce a correct parity check although the data in the byte had been corrupted. In practice, larger blocks of data are examined for corruption (see section later on Error Detection).

Flow Control

In a half-duplex link, only one of the computers can transmit at any one time. If a modem detects an incoming signal from the remote modem, it must prevent its own computer from transmitting data to ensure that it stays in 'receive' mode.   When the incoming signal stops, the modem can then allow the computer to send its data. Traffic on the link is regulated by having the modem control the flow of data out of the computer's serial port.   The process of control is known as *'handshaking'* and can be implemented in hardware or in software (XON/XOFF handshaking).

Hardware Handshaking

In the diagram, the numbers on the side of the computer serial port and the modem port represent the pin numbers to be found in the device connectors. When the computer and the modem are connected together and switched on, the computer's DTR (Data Terminal Ready) line on pin 4 on its serial port is enabled to inform the modem that it is operational and wishes to establish a connection.   The computer DTR pin is wired to the modem's DTR pin. The modem responds by enabling its DSR (Data Set Ready) line on pin 6 to inform the computer that it is switched on and ready for use.   In effect, DSR means *'Modem Ready'*.   At this stage, both devices know that the other is connected and active so data transfer is possible. This is done using the RTS and CTS lines to control the flow of information between the two devices.

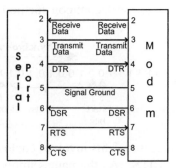

9-pin wiring of Modem Cable

A typical transmission sequence might be as below:
1. The computer wishes to send data to the modem.
2. The computer enables (i.e. high positive voltage) its RTS (Ready To Send) pin to inform the modem that it wishes to transmit. The modem receives this signal via its serial port's RTS line.
3. The modem has disabled its CTS (Clear To Send) pin (i.e. there must still be incoming data).
4. This condition is detected by the computer's CTS pin; no data is sent; the machine stays in receive mode.
5. The calling station stops transmitting and this is detected by the modem.
6. The modem enables its CTS line; this is detected by the computer's CTS pin and data is passed to the modem for transmission.
7. The computer sends a stream of text data out of its serial port TxD (Transmitted Data) pin.   This data stream is sent, via the modem cable, to the TxD pin of the modem.
8. The remote modem detects this incoming carrier and disables its CTS to ensure that the remote computer will read the data and not try to transit.

The CTS line is also used to prevent the computer sending data into the modem when the modem's memory buffer is full.   When the buffer is emptied, the CTS line is used to indicate that the modem is ready to receive more data.   Hardware handshaking is the preferred method for faster modems as there is no unnecessary data being passed around the system, occupying precious processing time. The hardware handshaking method is also used with a serial printer interface.

Xon/Xoff Handshaking

DTR handshaking uses extra wires to carry the control signals; the handshaking is implemented via hardware.   The other common method is to use a software handshake. This reduces the amount of connections to only three - one for data in each direction and one common line. While this simplifies the connections between the computer and the device, it leaves no obvious physical means for passing over handshake signals.   Yet, the computer still needs to know when transmission can and cannot take place. In this system, specific ASCII numbers, outside the printable range, are used as codes to represent *'stop transmission'* and *'start transmission'*. This is where the Xon/Xoff method derives its name.

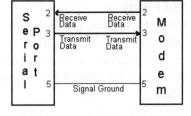

When the modem is switched on, it sends out an ASCII character known as DC1. This is the *'transmit enable'* code and is decimal 17 or 11 hex.   This code is received by the computer, which knows that it is able to commence transmitting data to the modem.   This is the Xon condition.   If there is incoming traffic, the modem sends out an ASCII DC3 character. This is the Xoff condition and is 19 in decimal (13 in hex). The computer receives this code and stops transmitting data.

Notes:
* This method is used with a serial printer. It sends out an Xoff code when its internal buffer is full. As it prints, it reduces the amount of characters in its buffer.   When the buffer has sufficient space, it sends out a DC1 code to the computer, which resumes the transmission of data to the printer.
* The ASCII codes DC1 and DC3 stand for Device Control 1 and Device Control 3.

- This method can transmit and receive text files, since the printable ASCII set ranges from 32 to 127. Binary files (i.e. containing machine code) contain a full range of possible numeric values. This would include the values for the DC1 and DC3 signals, which means that Xon/Xoff is not suitable for transmitting and receiving binary files.

RS232 Pins

A summary of the uses of the main pins on a computer's serial port is shown in the following table.

DTR (Data Terminal Ready)	The computer informs the modem that it is powered up and ready to be active, by switching this pin to an 'ON' state. Most modems require to receive this signal before they will operate.
DSR (Data Set Ready)	The modem informs the computer that it is powered up and ready to be active, by switching this pin to an 'ON' state. Most computer ports require this signal before they will operate.
CTS (Clear to Send)	The modem informs the computer that it able to accept data for transmission, by switching this pin to an 'ON' state. The computer will not send out data while this pin is 'OFF'.
RTS (Ready to Send)	The computer informs the modem that it wishes to give it data for transmission, by switching this pin to an 'ON' state. The modem responds by switching its CTS line 'ON' - unless its memory buffer is full, or it is receiving incoming data.
TXD (Transmit Data)	Carries the data from the computer to the modem's TXD pin, to transmit data. The data goes out the serial port's TXD pin and goes in the modem's TXD pin.
RXD (Receive Data)	Receives the data from the modem's RXD pin, to receive incoming data. The data comes out the modem's RXD pin and goes in the serial port's RXD pin.
DCD (Data Carrier Detect)	Used by the computer to determine whether the modem has an incoming carrier (i.e. whether the line is idle or not). Some communications packages must detect a DCD signal before they will carry on. This signal can be brought from the modem or can be provided locally by a 'wraparound'. This connects the computer's DTR pin to the computer's DCD pin to simulate an idle condition.
RI (Ring Indicator)	This pin could be used by an auto-answer modem. Its value is raised high when the phone rings. The modem informs the DTE via this change in the RI line and the DTE responds by setting its DTR line high. The modem then answers the call and data is passed from the telephone line to the DTE.
SG (Signal Ground)	This pin is used as the reference for all other signal voltages. So, if a pin swings +15 volts, it means that the pin is 15 volts higher than the voltage on SG. This pin should not be confused with electric earth or Frame Ground (FG).

Analogue signal modulation

A modem or radio broadcast network translates digital levels into differing tones on the telephone line or differing radio waves on the air.

This can be achieved by one of several different modulation methods:

- Amplitude Modulation (AM). The amplitude (strength) of the signal indicates the data to be transmitted. For example one amplitude could represent a 'one', and another a 'zero'.
- FSK (Frequency Shift Keying). Although FSK is sometimes called Frequency Modulation (FM), technically FSK is just one type of FM. This system operates by altering the <u>frequency</u> of the tone according to whether each bit in the incoming data stream is a binary zero or a binary one. For example the V21 system uses 1180Hz to represent a binary zero and 980Hz to represent a binary 1, while a V23 system uses 450Hz and 390Hz respectively.
- PSK (Phase Shift Keying), also called Phase Modulation (PM). Another method is to alter the <u>phase</u> of the tone dependent on the incoming data's binary state. Phase modulation would maintain the same frequency for a 1 and a 0 but would shift the waveform in time between the two states. This is used with V22 systems.
- QAM (Quadrature Amplitude Modulation). It is possible to combine both the alterations of the tone's phase and its amplitude so that a single baud can represent one of four bits. Therefore, a 2400 baud modem can transfer at 9600bps by using QAM technology. Trellis Coded Modulation (TCM) is an enhanced version that can transmit up to 10 bits per baud rate.

Digital line coding

Digital transmission media do not require modulation. However, a system must still be devised whereby data can be transmitted and recognised. There are a number of ways to do this, and the following is just a sample of the most widely used forms.

- Non-Return to Zero (NRZ) coding is the simplest method. A binary '1' is encoded as a certain electrical level, while a binary '0' is encoded as a different electrical level. This causes problems, however, in the receiving circuitry, which could lose track of the number of data digits received if they were all of the same electrical level.

- Return to Zero (RZ), by contrast, uses three levels of electrical signal. The positive level represents a binary '1', the negative level a binary '0', and the signal returns to zero halfway through to indicate the end of each binary digit. The requirement for three signal levels means it has to be a higher power signal, and another disadvantage is that half of the bandwidth is wasted on zero-level signals.

- Manchester coding is similar to RZ coding, but the transition is from one electrical level to the other, with no third level. This removes the need for higher power since only two discrete levels must be recognised. A version of Manchester coding is used in Ethernet networks.

- Alternate Mark Inversion (AMI) transmits a '0' as a zero level, with a '1' being sent as a positive signal the first time it appears, then a negative signal the next time, and so on. This system is still left with the problem of recognising long strings of zeroes.

- 8BZS (Eight Binary Zeroes Substitution) is based on AMI, but strings of eight zeros are replaced by a data sequence that introduces artificial changes in the signal for recognition purposes. These artificial changes include 'violation' codes that have a polarity opposite to that of a legitimate 1 signal, to distinguish it from normal data signals. 8BZS is used in the US for primary rate ISDN.

- 4 Binary 3 Ternary (4B3T) is a system that turns 4 binary digits into 3 ternary (base three) digits. This provides an extra 25% bandwidth, at the cost of again having to use three discrete levels of signal. 4B3T is used in Europe for primary rate ISDN lines.

- HDB3 (High Density Bipolar Order 3) is similar to 8BZS, but inserts violation codes in a run of 4 zeroes, instead of every 8 zeroes. HDB3 is used in Europe for basic rate ISDN lines.

- 2B1Q (2 Binary 1 Quaternary) is a coding scheme that requires quaternary transmission, in other words the cable must handle four distinct levels of signal. Four levels corresponds exactly to the number that can be stored in two bits. Thus, a 2B1Q signal requires twice as many discrete levels, but allows twice as much bandwidth. 2B1Q is used in the US for basic rate ISDN lines.

Data Compression

Smaller files are transmitted in a shorter time than larger files. This saves both user time and telephone connect time. This has led to the compression of files prior to their transmission. The compressed file is later decompressed at the receiving end. The most common ways to achieve data compression are V42bis and MNP levels, known as 'Classes'. It should be understood that modem compression systems have to achieve this compression at the point of transmission and this limits the degree of compression. It is much better to compress a file using a normal file compression package such as PKZip and then transfer this file over the network. Since packages such as PKZip do not have to analyse the entire file in real time, they can arrive at the highest possible compression ratio.

MNP stands for 'Microcom Networking Protocol' and covers both error detection and data compression. Each higher Class encompasses and expands on the features of the Class below. Class 1 through to Class 4 provides increasingly sophisticated techniques to reduce time delays caused by transmission errors. For example, MNP 3 acts like a synchronous modem, removing the need for start and stop bits and thereby increasing throughput. Microcom's options now extend to MNP 10, which is targeted at noisy systems such as radiophones. Its transmission speed slows down for noisy environments and returns to faster rates when the noise subsides, thus reducing losses. Of the MNP range, MNP 5 is the most commonly used and has become a de facto industry 'standard'. Like other compression systems, it uses a pattern recognition algorithm to replace long or regularly occurring strings of data with shorter tokens that represent those strings. At the receiving end, the communications software reverses the process and rebuilds the original data using the tokens. Although popular, it only compresses in about a 2:1 ratio. Consequently, the CCITT chose a different algorithm for its V42bis compression standard. It uses a more efficient system based a British Telecom version of the famous Lempel-Ziv algorithm, known as BTLV. With a V34 modem, this can produce an effective data transfer rate of 115,200bps.

Breakout Box

Every manufacturer uses the same serial port pins to represent the same functions and all manufacturers work with the same signal voltage levels. However, different devices will use different combinations of these pins. Some devices are wired as DTEs while others are wired as DCEs. While all devices will use the TXD, RXD and GND connections, there is a wide variation in the usage of the other pins. This means that some devices will require the use of a certain pin while other devices ignore that pin. In some cases, pins will require to be connected together before the device will operate. In other cases, that same wiring combination will prevent the device from operating. Wherever possible, the device manual should be consulted. The book *'RS-232 Made Easy'* by Martin Seyer shows the extent of the problem. It devotes 271 pages to charts and wiring diagrams of different computers, printers, modems, multiplexors, etc.

Often, technicians are working with equipment that has no documentation or with cables whose internal wiring is unknown.

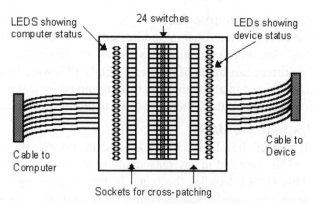

In these cases, a device known as a *'breakout box'* is invaluable. As the diagram shows, this is inserted in the cable between the computer and the device being connected. If the miniature switches are left in their *'on'* setting, every pin is connected straight through from computer to device. If all the switches are thrown to their *'off'* setting, the computer is completely disconnected from the device. In this disconnected mode, one row of the LEDs will display the signals that are coming from the computer while the other row of LEDs displays signals from the device. These LEDs are *'tri-state'* the three states being *'off'* along with positive (green) and negative (red) polarities. The breakout box is accompanied by a set of jumper leads that have a plug at each end. When the switches are in their *'off'* state, jumper leads can be inserted into the sockets to connect computer pins to device pins. For example, a lead may be plugged into socket 2 at the computer and socket 3 at the device end. This ability to criss-cross leads allows the technician to quickly test various combinations. When the correct working combination is determined, a cable can be wired up and soldered as a permanent replacement for the breakout box.

- Care must be taken when buying ready-made cables as some have pins strapped together (i.e. wired together) inside the plug. It is common to find pins 4 and 5 strapped, or even 4,5,6 and 8 strapped.
- Serial printer connections are mostly wired as DTEs.

Reading/Writing with RS232

As mentioned earlier, COM1's base address is 3F8h. This means that the memory location 3F8h is the start of a set of eight bytes that hold information and instructions to control the port's read and write operations. Each byte is known as a *'register'* and these are numbered from 0 through to 7.

The register table for COM1 is:

Register Number	Memory Address	Status	Purpose
0	3F8h	R/W	Data Buffer - stores the byte to be transmitted or the byte received
1	3F9h	R/W	Interrupt Enable - sets what activities will generate a processor interrupt
2	3FAh	Read	Interrupt ID - for 8250 - holds the cause of any particular interrupt. Also a FIFO Register for the 16550 UART
3	3FBh	Write	Line Control - sets the baud rate, stop bits, parity and word length
4	3FCh	R/W	Modem Control - e.g. sets the RTS and DTR lines
5	3FDh	Read	Line Status - stores whether there was a parity error, the user sent a BREAK signal, etc.
6	3FEh	Read	Modem Status - stores the status of the DCD, RI, DSR and CTS lines
7	3FFh	R/W	The 'Scratch-pad' - a general one-byte memory store

Register 6 holds the status of the DCD, RI, DSR and CTS lines as single bits in the 3FEh memory location, in the 8th, 7th, 6th and 5th bits respectively.

Transmission Speed

The speed of data transfer is measured in bits per second (bps). The highest rate for analogue modems is 56kbps. Modem rates used to be measured in '*baud*', and the baud rate and the bps rate were identical. This was only true when one signal on the line represented one single bit of information. Baud really measures the number of frequency changes on the line per second and ignores phase changes, amplitude changes and the fact that the data may be compressed (see later). All of these techniques mean that more data can be passed down a cable while running at a relatively low baud rate. So, when a modem claims a certain transfer rate, it need not be actually producing frequency changes at that rate down the cable. The value given may be the underline{effective} rate of transfer taking into account the effect of these techniques. These schemes were only introduced on newer modems and 'baud' and 'bps' are only really interchangeable terms for older models. All specifications are now usually given in bps.

Improving the interface

The notes on handshaking addressed the problem of the modem being slower than the serial interface. However, older computers have serial interfaces that are unable to transfer data at the rate required for the current fast breed of modems. Early PCs were fitted with an 8250 or 16450 type UART. The type of UART fitted in a machine can be determined by using third-party system information utilities.

For older computers, there are three upgrade approaches:

Upgrade the UART

If one of the older UARTs is used in the PC, the computer's serial interface can be upgraded. The 16550, supplied in any reasonably new machine, has an internal 16-byte FIFO (first in first out) buffer. This UART handles the bytes in the internal queue while more data is being fetched. This greatly speeds up transfer speeds compared to the earlier UARTs with their one-byte memory.

Fit an internal modem

If an internal modem is fitted to the computer, the data is passed to the modem via the expansion bus. This is a parallel connection system and does not need the services of a UART.

Fit a USB card

This add-on card also connects to the motherboard's expansion sockets and provides external ports for connecting a USB external modem. This provides the additional advantage of allowing future USB devices, such as a mouse or keyboard, to be attached to the computer.

Error Detection

Modem communication over the normal telephone network is always prone to losses due to poor line conditions. As transmission rates become faster, the losses are increased. If an interference pulse occurred on a line with a 28800bps system, the transmission would be affected 24 times more badly than a 1200bps system, since 24 times more data will have been transferred during that time. Serious attention has to be paid to detecting and correcting such errors. The parity bit system described earlier is only a rudimentary check and only applies to ASCII files. Since most files are not plain ASCII, they will require to use all eight bits of the byte and there is no parity bit.

CRC Checking

Data is transmitted in '*blocks*' or '*packets*' with a checksum created using the CRC (Cyclic Redundancy Check) method. When the data is compiled into a block prior to transmission, a mathematical formula (using polynomial codes) is applied to the data to produce a check number that is unique to the data stream in the block. These check digits are then transmitted along with the data. The receiver stores the incoming block of data in a buffer for examination. The same formula is applied to the data in the buffer and it should produce the same answer as that stored in the check bytes. If the computed CRC figure accords with the stored CRC figure, the data in the buffer is fit to be passed on and an 'ACK' signal is returned to the transmitting end to acknowledge the receipt of a block in good condition. If there has been any corruption of the data in the block, or even any corruption of the check bytes, then the formula will produce answers that do not match. In this case, the device will request that the block of data be re-transmitted. This is done by returning a 'NAK' signal to the transmitting end.

A number of different block transmission techniques and error detection methods are in common use. Error detection can occur at one or more stages in the transmission process – hardware error detection is covered by the modem V standards (see below). Software protocols, as described later in this chapter, also perform error checking.

Data Communications Standards

A variety of standards bodies exist, in order to help ensure compatibility between various systems. The main standards bodies in this field are the following organisations:

ANSI

The American National Standards Institute has created a number of standards, many of which are computer related. Some of these include terminal protocols and character sets for data transmission. A committee of ANSI developers created the FDDI protocol.

IEEE

The Institute of Electronic and Electrical Engineers have produced a number of standards. The most important data communications standards from the IEEE are the '802' series, dealing with local area networks (see the LANs chapter).

ISO

The International Standards Organisation has developed a number of datacomms standards, most important of which is the OSI model, explained in detail elsewhere in this chapter. They also developed the OSI standards to go with that reference model.

ITU-T

Formerly known as the CCITT, the International Telecommunications Union is organised by the United Nations and has developed a number of telecommunications standards, including the following:
- The V-series, dealing with telephone circuits
- The X-series, dealing with data networks. This includes the popular X.25 protocol.
- The G-series, dealing with digital networks (digital exchanges, multiplexing, PCM, etc.)
- The I-series, dealing with ISDN (see later)

V Standards

There is a wide range of definitions and the most common ones are shown in the table. The V standards get their name from the first letter of the word 'vitesse', the French for speed although not all V standards are concerned with transmission rate.   V24, for example, specifies the serial port standard and V42 and V42bis cover error correction.   The 'bis' added to a V number means that it is the second version of the standard.

V17	Fax 14,400 transmit/receive
V21	300bps transmit/receive. full duplex, dial-up
V22	1200bps transmit/receive. full duplex, dial-up
V22bis	2400bps transmit/receive. full duplex, dial-up
V23	1200bps transmit/75bps receive, asymmetric duplex, dial-up
V24	The RS232 standard
V27	4800bps transmit/receive. full duplex, leased line
V27ter	4800bps transmit/2400bps receive, half duplex, Group III Fax
V29	9600bps transmit/receive. full duplex, leased line Also 9600bps half duplex Group III Fax
V32	9600bps transmit/receive, full duplex, dial-up
V32bis	14,4000bps transmit/receive, full duplex, dial-up
V34	28,800bps
V34bis	31,200bps or 33,600bps
V42	Error correction using CRC
V42bis	Data compression using Lempel Ziv
V44	Improved compression standard, and storing of phone line performance information to reduce connection times.
V80	Videoconferencing
V90	56,000bps download, 33600bps upload
V92	56,000bps download, 48000bps upload, and also incorporates V.44 and other facilities.

56k Technology

56k modems use existing rented telephone lines and incur no extra standing charges beyond the normal telephone charges. ITU v.90 56k modems superseded the interim x2 and k56flex standards.

British telephone exchanges work digitally and communications between parts of the telephone network are digital.   Likewise, Internet Service Providers (ISPs) use digital links. Only the cable between the exchange and the subscriber's premises uses analogue techniques. The audio of a normal telephone conversation arrives at the exchange as an analogue signal and is converted into digital information for use in the main network. The audio is converted into 8-bit resolution at an 8KHz sampling rate. This provides a theoretical data rate of 64k but, according to Nyquist's theorem, the reliable bandwidth of a signal is half its sampling rate. So, the conversion supports around 32k, which explains the previous upper 33,600bps limit of analogue modems.

ISDN adaptors, being digital devices in the first place, do not require analogue to digital conversion and vice versa, and can operate at the full 64k per channel.

56k modems use similar techniques of avoiding analogue/digital conversion losses. Since the link from ISP to telecommunications network is digital, the only analog/digital conversion that is required is from the exchange to the

Communication stages	Existing technology	56k technology
Data stored at ISP	Digital	Digital
ISP to Network	Digital	Digital
Network to Network	Digital	Digital
Network to local exchange	Digital	Digital
Exchange to subscriber	Analogue (tones)	Analogue (data)
Subscriber conversion	Analogue tones to digital	Analogue data to digital

subscriber, instead of having an additional conversion to the ISP. Although theoretically speeds of 64k are attainable, practical concerns limit this to 56k. Such speeds are susceptible to line degradation, and some locations will find it difficult or impossible to achieve the full 56k rate.

Modem Commands

The computer connects to the modem by a single serial connection. The user normally interfaces with the communications package software and will decide on actions by pressing menu options or by clicking on icons or buttons.   Basic user choices could include engaging the telephone line, dialling a number, downloading a file and eventually terminating the connection with the remote station.   A whole range of other options might be required. For example, some telephone exchanges use the old rotary pulse dialling method while most exchanges use tone dialling.   The user might wish to have the modem's inbuilt loudspeaker turned off or a range of other refinements. Although the user makes these choices via the software, the computer has to then inform the modem of these decisions.   Since there is only a single serial connection between them, the computer has to send this information in the form of messages along the serial cable.   The modem, in turn, will send messages ('result codes') back to the computer to indicate that it cannot get any dial tone, the dialled number is busy, etc.

As long as the modem and the computer understand and use the same set of messages, there is no communications difficulty with the system. The most common way to use these strings is to save them with the communications software's setup information. When the user runs the communications package, the desired command string is automatically associated with the package's corresponding menu and button options. A default set of commands is offered by most packages and the user can alter them for local conditions (e.g. changing the string from a tone dial system to a pulse dial system).

Hayes AT Commands

A popular modem command set is the Hayes AT set developed by Hayes Microcomputer Products.   Like other command sets, the Hayes commands are independent of the speed or performance of the modem. An old slow modem and one of the latest models can both use the AT command set. Modems described as 'AT compatibles' refer to their acceptance of this set of commands, or a superset or a subset.

The Command Set

All Hayes commands consist of a string of characters, both alphabetic and numeric, that control modem functions.   Each individual command sent to the modem is preceded by the letters 'AT' which stands for ATtention. So, for example, sending the string ATM0 would silence the modem's speaker.

The illustration shows the display for the default setting offered in the 'Telix' communications package:

```
═┤ Modem and dialing parameter setup ┠══════════════════════════════════════

  A - Init string ...,...... ATZ^M~~~AT S7=45 S0=0 V1 X4^M~
  B - Dialing prefix 1 ::::: ATDT
  C - Dialing prefix 2 ::::: ATDT
  D - Dialing prefix 3 ::::: ATDT
  E - Dialing suffix ....... ^M
  F - Connect string ....... CONNECT
  G - No connect strings .. NO CARRIER                    BUSY
                            VOICE                         NO DIAL TONE
  H - Hang-up string ...... ~~~+++~~~ATH0^M
  I - Auto answer string .. ATS0=1^M
  J - Dial cancel string .. ^M

  K - Dial time ........... 30
  L - Redial pause ........ 1
  M - Auto baud detect ::::: Off
  N - Drop DTR to hangup .. On

  Change which setting?        (Return or Esc to exit)
```

The initialisation string is the one that is sent to the modem when the package is first run.
The '^M' string is the equivalent of pressing the Enter key if the string was entered at the keyboard and the '~' characters are pauses. A comma is also used as an alternative method of obtaining a pause.

The individual components of the initialisation string are explained in the following chart:

Command	Meaning
Z	Used to reset the modem to the factory default settings.
S7=45	Specifies that the modem will wait for 45 seconds after dialling. If there is no connection to the remote station within that time, the modem hangs up the line and sends a 'No Carrier' message to the computer. The range is 4 to 60 seconds.
S0=0	Used to set the number of rings before the modem auto-answers an incoming call. The permissible range is 0 to 255. A value of zero turns off the auto-answer.
V1	Specifies that result codes will be reported in text format. This is used when the communications session is under manual control. With automated systems, the results codes can be reported in numeric format, using 'V0', so that the numbers can be easier interpreted by the software.
X4	Used to enable the full range of result codes and supports both dial tone and engaged tone detection. Other permissible levels are X0, X1, X2 and X3 and are mainly available for backward compatibility with older models and some non-standard telephone systems.

Dialling Prefix

The dialling prefix in the example is 'ATDT'. The 'D' is an instruction to commence dialling and the 'T' instructs the modem to use tone dialling. If the string had been 'ATDP' it would instruct the modem to use pulse dialling. Pulse dialling is the default and only has to be given as instruction to the modem if the modem had previously been ordered to use tone dialling. The software would add the actual number to be dialled to the end of the string. So, typical strings might be:

ATD 0141-775-2889 or ATD01417752889 or ATD 9,0141775 2889

The first two strings are directly equivalent since any dashes or spaces between numbers are ignored. The third example is for use in offices where the user has to dial '9' for an outside line. The comma (or '~') is inserted to provide a time delay to allow the office exchange to engage an outside line.

Hang Up String

The hang up string is 'ATH0' which is the 'On Hook' condition, the equivalent of replacing a telephone on its rest. The row of three plus signs switches the modem into 'Local Mode' also known as 'Command Mode'. Generally, the modem wishes to ignore the computer when it is getting on with its communications session. If a long file transfer is underway it will not wish to be disturbed by the computer and will ignore most AT command strings. However, there still has to be a way that the user can interrupt a session and this is achieved with the '+++' string. To prevent accidental triggering (e.g. the data being sent happens to include three plus signs), this escape sequence is only recognised if it is prefaced and followed by a pause. The default pause is 1 second and this is achieved by the '~~~' string that surrounds the three plus signs.

Other common AT commands are:

F	Sets the speed at which the modem will operate. F1 is for V21, F2 is for V23, F3 is for V22, F4 is for V22bis while F5 is for V32/4800bps and F6 is for V32/9600 working. If the command is set at F0, the modem is instructed to make the connection at the fastest rate available.
I	Instructs the modem to return details of its description and version number.
W	Instructs the modem to wait for secondary dial tone before proceeding to dial out. Used for modems connected to office exchanges (PABXs). This is an alternative to use the use of delays as shown earlier.
&K	Instructs the modem to use a specific flow control. AT&K0 inhibits all flow control, AT&K1 enables hardware (RTS/CTS) control and AT&K2 enables software (Xon/Xoff) control.
\C	Determines the level of data compression. \C1 operates in MNP class 1 mode and the range extends up to \C5 for MNP class 5 mode.

The result codes returning from the modem to the computer include:

Number	Text equivalent	Meaning
0	OK	The last command executed without error.
1	CONNECT #	A connection is established at 300/300.
2	RING	An incoming call has been detected.
3	NO CARRIER	Carrier cannot be detected or carrier has been lost.
4	ERROR	An invalid command has been given.
5	CONNECT 1200	A connection is established at 1200/1200.
6	NO DIALTONE	No dial tone has been detected within the specified timeout period.
7	BUSY	An engaged tone or number unobtainable tone has been detected.

Modem Lights

Many external modems have lights to inform the user of their current state and to reassure the user of the success of the various activities. When a communication session is unsuccessful, the lights can be used to determine the likely

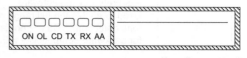

problem. The diagram shows the layout of a typical modem front panel although there is a wide variety both in the number of lights used and in the titles different manufacturers give to the same light function. A normal sequence for sending a piece of data by external modem would be:

1. The communications package fetches the data (from memory or from a disk file) to be sent.
2. The data is sent out the computer's RS232 or USB port.
3. The data is carried from the computer to the modem via a serial cable.
4. The data is converted to tones inside the modem.

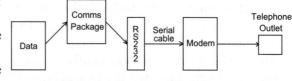

5. The tones are sent to the telephone line via a plug connected to a standard telephone socket.

The receiving process is a mirror image of the transmitting process with the data coming in the telephone socket, converted to digital signals and being received by the application via the serial cable and the RS232 or USB port. The modem's lights can indicate which parts of the process are working allowing the user to determine the source of the problem.

An explanation of the each modem light is:

Light	Meaning	Purpose
ON	Power On	The modem is correctly powered up from its power supply. Also known as 'MR' - Modem Ready or DSR - Data Set Ready.
OL	On Line	The modem is holding the telephone connection. This is the equivalent of a telephone being off its hook. Also known as 'OH' - Off Hook.
CD	Carrier Detect	The modem is in touch with a remote station and is receiving its carrier tones. This means that someone has answered an outgoing call, or the user's modem has answered an incoming call. When this light goes out, the link has been broken. Also known as 'DCD' - Data Carrier Detect.
TX	Transmit Data	This light flickers when data is being transmitted out of the modem. Also known as 'SD' - Send Data.
RX	Receive Data	This light will flicker when it is receiving data in from the telephone line. Also known as 'RD'.
AA	Auto Answer	This lights when the modem has been configured to automatically answer any incoming calls. This is used where a computer has to be left unattended.
HS	High Speed	This light indicates that the modem is working at its highest speed. In some modems, the light flickers for several of the higher speeds.
TR	Terminal Ready	This light indicates that the modem is both powered and in communication with the modem. The computer has sent a DTR signal through the serial port to the modem to inform it that is running a communications package. The modem lights is TR light in response.
RI	Ring Indicate	Indicates the presence of an incoming call. The equivalent of the telephone ringing.
TST	Test	This light indicates that the modem is performing a self-test.
LB	Low Battery	Used with portable modems to indicate that their battery supply is running low.
SQ	Signal Quality	A steady light indicates a good connection; a flickering light indicates a poor quality connection.

Soft Modems

Most computers are now supplied modems already fitted. In some cases these modems are based not on dedicated chips but on simple interface electronics driven by the processor. These don't work without the appropriate software and cause a drain on processor resources while they are in use. They generally are supplied with drivers for only one operating system and so are useless on any other operating system. They can be identified because very often they are on a simple riser card, which they share with USB ports or network connections that use the same trick. This is known as the AMR (Audio/Modem Riser) slot. Standalone boards are also offered for sale, which use this soft modem technology and are characterised by being noticeably inexpensive. Good retailers will confirm that a proposed purchase is a soft modem, and people with an electronics background can identify telltale signs of the necessary COM port and chipset on non soft modems.

Data Links

A range of possible connection methods between communication stations is possible. These include:

SIMPLEX	Data is sent in one direction only. No longer in common use and is mostly now found as a means of driving older printers where no information is fed back to the computer from the device.
HALF-DUPLEX	The link can carry data in both directions but not simultaneously. It is analogous to a CB radio user who has to be either in talk or in listen mode at any one time. A computer sends a packet of information and then switches into receive mode to wait for an acknowledgement from the other end. Once received, the computer can go back into transmit mode for the next packet. Used by Xmodem, Xmodem/CRC, Ymodem and Kermit protocols and common in domestic links to a host (e.g. CompuServe) and small businesses to a main link.
FULL-DUPLEX	The link can carry data in both directions simultaneously. It is analogous to a telephone user who can both talk and listen at the same time. Most modems work in this mode. It permits the use of sliding window protocols to speed up transmissions. Used by Zmodem, Sliding Windows Kermit, Sealink and the WXmodem file transfer protocols.

It should be noted that a simplex protocol can be used over a half-duplex channel and a half-duplex protocol can be used over a full-duplex channel. In a half-duplex modem, the entire bandwidth is available for use in the one direction. With a full-duplex system, the available bandwidth is divided into two sub-bands. The two sub-bands comprise the *'originate carrier'*, which carries data from the DTE to the DCE and the *'answer carrier'*, which carries data from the DCE to the DTE.

Bandwidth

Every communications line is only capable of carrying data over a certain band of frequencies. The range between the upper and lower limits is known as the *'bandwidth'*. With audio, radio and television applications, the bandwidth is usually measured in Hertz - with one Hertz being a single cycle per second. So, the bandwidth for transmitting voice may be less than 4KHz while music and colour TV signals may be 15KHz and 8MHz respectively. With data communications, users wish to know the maximum data rates that a channel can handle and this is measured in bps - bits per second.

Multiplexors

Many computers or terminals may wish connection to a single computer at a remote location. If each user were given a separate line to the remote computer, the cost would be unacceptable. So, one communication channel is shared between different users. This sharing can be achieved in terms of time or of frequency space. The device used at each end is known as a *'multiplexor'* or *'mux'*. Its job is to provide a *'transparent'* connection for the user. This means that neither the user nor the remote computer need know that a mux is in use; it requires no additional equipment or additional software. The local end *'multiplexes'* the channels while the remote end *'demultiplexes'* the channels.

Some data communications systems use a *'concentrator'*, which performs a similar but slightly different function. The concentrator divides one high-speed link evenly into several lower-speed channels. Thus, connections to a concentrator are at a set data rate, while a multiplexor must handle a variety of speeds and tries to maximise the usage of the high speed link. This type of concentrator should not be confused with a token ring concentrator, which is another name for a hub.

TDM

The *'Time Division Multiplexing'* technique is used to transmit multiple digital signals and it gives each terminal a share of the available line time.   The diagram shows four terminals sharing the same communication line.

The two multiplexors are synchronised so that both connect to point *'A'* at the same time, followed by both connecting to point *'B'* and so on. After *'D'*, connection *'A'* is returned to. During the connection to each point, a piece of data is transferred over the line.   Each terminal has a series of timeslots when it has exclusive use of the channel. In the example, each

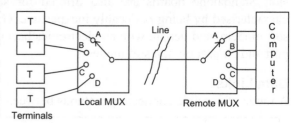

terminal only has one quarter of the line time.   With n terminals, each will have 1/n of the line time.   This needs a communications line with fast transfer rates, with its speed being the total of the combined speeds of the connected slow terminal connections. This is known as a *'synchronous multiplexor'*, and suffers from bandwidth wastage whenever one of the multiplexed channels is not transmitting data, since it still receives a slice of the multiplexor's time. Synchronous TDM is used with E1 and T1 type networks.

In contrast, an *'aysnchronous multiplexor'* only gives time to a terminal that is wishing to transmit data. It does this by tagging each packet of data with a number that indicates the multiplexing link that the packet belongs to. This allows the remote MUX to understand which link to pass the packet on to. As a result, each packet takes up more time on the MUX, but unless the system is fully utilised (which rarely happens) the freeing up of time slots will more than make up for this. Asynchronous TDM is used on ATM networks.

With a *'Statistical Multiplexor'*, a low speed channel is only given bandwidth on the high-speed channel if it has data to send.   The sum of the input speeds can now exceed that of the composite channel, since not all low speed channels are normally in use at any one time. To accommodate occasions of every channel wishing to transmit, buffering is used.   This makes most efficient use of the fast link but it cannot support synchronous data.

FDM

The other technique, known as *'Frequency Division Mulitplexing'*, also conveys a number of different users' data along a single line. In this case, all the users' data is transmitted simultaneously, with each terminal being transmitted at a different frequency band.   This *'broadband'* approach is further explained in the chapter on Local Area Networks.   The communication line used must have sufficient bandwidth to cope with the bandwidth of each channel, plus a margin between each channel, known as *'guard bands'*. This is the method used to transmit multiple analogue signals simultaneously. Cable TV (CATV) wiring uses FDM, with each frequency band being allocated to a particular television channel. Similarly, cable modem users must share the bandwidth of the cable with others along the same line.

Fibre optics use the same technique, but since physicists tend to refer to the *'wavelength'* rather than the *'frequency'* of light waves the method is called *'wavelength division multiplexing'*.

Transmission problems

No transmission technique is perfect, and every form of communication may be susceptible to signal loss or distortion. In a typical electrical signal over copper wire, these problems are due to several factors:

Attenuation – The reduction in power of an electrical signal as it travels.

Component Noise - caused by random or unwanted electron fluctuations within both inactive devices (such as resistors) and active devices (such as integrated circuits).

External Interference - caused by everything from natural sources (such as cosmic radiation and electric thunderstorms) to manmade sources (e.g. radiation from electrical appliances).

Crosstalk – interference between the various lines within the same communications medium.

Skew – This is not a signal loss as such, but if multiple lines carry part of one signal, it is possible that they may arrive at different times. This is one reason why most long-distance connections are serial.

Signal Bounce – an electrical signal on a wire that is not properly terminated by a resistor at the end of the cable, will not be absorbed. It will instead 'bounce' back from the end of the wire, possibly interfering with legitimate signals.

Attenuation

As an electrical signal moves along a communications wire line, its amplitude diminishes with every metre. These losses are caused by:

- Heat dissipation. A copper conductor has a finite resistance to the passage of electric current. Thicker wires reduce line resistance but are very expensive.
- Frequency dependent losses. The capacitive effect between the elements of a pair of communication wires leaks the signal across the wires, reducing the signal that arrives at the end of the cable. Higher data rates produce increased changes of signal on the line and increased capacitive losses.

Gain or loss is the ratio of the output voltage from a communications line or device (Vout), compared to the voltage fed into it (Vin). It is measured in units of *'decibels'* abbreviated to *'dB'*. This measurement is not linear - it follows a logarithmic scale. It is the ratio $20 \log_{10}$ (Vout/Vin).

Noise

Noise is unwanted electrical signals that exist on the communication channel along with the desired data. As long as the noise stays at a low level there is no serious problem - but when the noise increases to the point where it is treated as a legitimate logic level, it causes false triggering and corrupted messages.

External Interference

The effects of external noise can be reduced, or sometimes effectively eliminated, by using shielded cable. Shielded Twisted Pair (STP) is used in some LANs, and shielding is also available for longer distance links. However, shielded cable is significantly more expensive than unshielded cable, and in many situations it is most cost effective to use shielded cable only in areas where there is a risk of interference from nearby equipment.

Crosstalk

Crosstalk occurs in electrical communications media that use more than one cable. For example, one wire in a pair of coaxial cables laid alongside each other could be strong enough to exert an electromagnetic effect on the other wire. Crosstalk comes in two main forms: Near-End Crosstalk (NEXT) and Far-End Crosstalk (FEXT). Both types usually concern signal noise between the transmitting cable and the receiving cable. The effect is compounded by the fact that signals being received are by their nature weaker than those being transmitted.

As the name suggests, NEXT occurs at the end of the cable from which the signal is issued, while FEXT occurs at the end where the signal is received. Crosstalk can be reduced by twisting cable pairs round each other, to disperse their electromagnetic fields. UTP and STP both use this technique.

Crosstalk is also measured in decibels, but an equally important rating is the *'Attenuation to Crosstalk Ratio'* (ACR). This measures the difference, in decibels, between the signal after attenuation, to the amount of noise generated by crosstalk. If the attenuated signal is too close to the crosstalk rating, it becomes impossible to reliably detect the proper signal. For example, Category 5 UTP specifies a 3.1 dB ACR, which means that the signal should be approximately at least twice the crosstalk noise.

Practical links

The LANs chapter describes the main types of connections within a smaller area. There are three main options for long-distance connection to remote stations.

Leased Line

Here, BT or another telecommunications company provides a permanent, dedicated cable link between two stations. Since no other person can use the line, there is no waiting; the line is never engaged even at peak times. In addition, the lines are of high quality, providing fewer errors and are usually faster. Of course, they are less flexible as they only connect to a single remote site but are very popular with business to connect different branches. Examples of leased lines are the BT Kilostream, Megastream and Satstream systems. These do not use modems as the connection is digital.

Performances are:

Kilostream	2.4kbs up to 64kbps	Electronic mail, slow scan TV, fax, data, voice
Megastream	2Mbps up to 140Mbps	Often multiplexed (i.e. a group of connections share the bandwidth)
Satstream	2.4kbps up to 1.5Mbps	Satellite system used for short term links, remote site access and video conferencing

Dial-Up Line

Here, the user is sharing a network of cabling and switching apparatus. Lines are not exclusive but are cheaper due to the sharing of physical assets. Unlike a leased line, the user may often find a line is busy. Dial-up lines also suffer from poorer quality, producing a larger amount of errors. Increased errors require repeat transmissions and, since the user pays for the time used, error time costs money. Faster transmissions also usually result in more errors.

Virtual Private Networks

A Virtual Private Network (VPN) is, as its name suggests, the use of a public communications network to emulate a private communications network. The most common example of this is using the Internet (a public network) to transmit data, while restricting the users access to resources within an organisation. This is useful for teleworkers and remote sites.

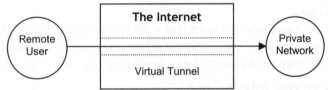

In order to access the VPN, the remote system uses '*tunnelling*'. Tunnelling is a system where data transmitted in one protocol is 'wrapped' inside a data packet in another protocol. For example, a VPN user might send a file to another user on the VPN. The file could be wrapped in an IP packet and a 'tunnel' made to send the data to the other user over the Internet, but it appears to both users that it was simply transmitted on a local network. VPNs typically make extensive use of encryption to ensure security of private data on a public network.

There are several competing VPN technologies:

- Point-to-Point Tunnelling Protocol (PPTP): The most widely known tunnelling system, created by Microsoft. It is a basic solution, including compression but very little security features. It also cannot transport non-IP packets.
- Layer 2 Forwarding Protocol (L2F): Developed by Cisco, L2F offers authentication (making sure the user is allowed to log on to the VPN) but not encryption. Like PPTP, it cannot be used on non-IP systems.
- Layer 2 Tunnelling Protocol (L2TP): A multi-vendor effort designed by the Internet Engineering Task Force, L2TP can be used with non-IP systems, and supersedes both PPTP and L2F.
- IP Security Protocol: Also designed by the IETF, the IP Security Protocol is designed specifically to provide authentication, secure encryption and data integrity functions. It operates at the OSI Network Layer. It is intended to complement the L2TP protocol.

Value Added Networks

A Value Added Network (VAN) is any type of network connection that is provided along with other services. For example, a basic ISP that only provides a point of presence on the Internet is not a VAN, but an ISP that provides access to a bulletin board or a specialised database to its users could be considered a VAN. However, in business terms, the name VAN is usually reserved for leased lines, which are provided along with a set of added extras. These usually include EDI (Electronic Data Interchange) services and secure communications. Other added extras might include guaranteed message delivery, additional error detection systems, and so on. VANs offering leased lines or access to specialised databases can be very expensive, and must be chosen carefully. The age and financial state of the business providing the VAN are issues to be considered, as well as the services provided and the cost. Other concerns can include security, availability, backups and disaster recovery plans implemented by the VAN vendor, and so on.

Communication Networks

A variety of services are available for data communications over a switched network system.

PSTN

The Public Switched Telephone Network is the normal network used for telephone connections. It is simple and cheap requiring modems to be plugged into the system instead of telephones. It is used by a wide range of both private and company users and is the main medium for information providers such as the Internet, and a range of bulletin boards.

The system is *'circuit switched'* - i.e. the telephone exchanges set up a link between the calling and called ends. The switching is physical with the older Strowger exchanges or is electronic with modern exchanges. In both cases, once the connection is established, the originating caller has sole use of the cable between both ends. If the caller is in Aberdeen and the called end is in Truro, there will be a connection spanning the entire country that is dedicated to the one call. When the call is terminated, the various channels that made up the connection can be used for other connections.

PSDN

The method of switching data traffic in the 1960's and 70's was *'Message Switching'* and this is still used with e-mail systems. It is a *'store and forward'* system, rather than today's real-time transmissions. Traffic is temporarily stored on disk and is sent on when a link is free. If there are three intermediate stations along the transmission route, the storing to disk and forwarding is repeated a further three times. It uses data links inefficiently and allows queues to build up, thus producing bottlenecks. Messages could take minutes or even hours to arrive.

The modern Public Switched Data Network is a parallel network to the telephone system but is dedicated to data communication. This is a *'packet switched'* system, which means that there is no permanent connection between the two stations during a session. The data to be transmitted is broken up into smaller chunks called *'packets'* and these are sent to the called end by the best route available at that time. The cabling between exchanges is used by all connections and the PSE (packet switched exchange)

ISDN

While the main Internet consists of a network of high-speed digital links, the connection between most users and their ISP is analogue. As the diagram shows, users link to the normal audio telephone network using modems. The analogue/digital conversion is explained earlier in this chapter.

The use of lines that were designed to carry low quality audio transmissions has led to innovative modem technology to squeeze the last drop of speed from them. There are, however, limits to the capacity of ordinary analogue systems. The ISDN (Integrated Services Digital Network) is a digital carrier network and it has been designed to also be used on the normal telephone line between a subscriber's house and the ISDN connection points at the telephone exchange. Once connected to the exchange's link, the rest of the link uses the high-speed ISDN data network that currently covers about 97% of the UK market.

Other countries using the ISDN system are Australia, Belgium, Denmark, Finland, France, Germany, Holland, Hong Kong, Italy, Japan, New Zealand, Norway, Singapore, Spain, Sweden, Switzerland and the USA.

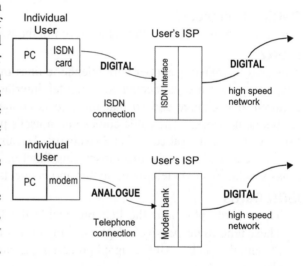

The UK currently has a solid commercial base of ISDN30 users but the take up of ISDN2 is slow compared to many other countries, probably due to the high connection and rental charges. The USA, in comparison, has a cheaper pricing policy and has over one million ISDN users. Overall, ISDN provides high-speed communic-ation over much of the developed world.

Key features of ISDN are:

- High bit-rate - a single ISDN channel has a throughput of 64kbps (i.e. kilobits per second). This compares favourably with the average modem used on an analogue telephone system where speeds of up to 56kbps are the norm.
- All-digital interfaces - no need for modems.
- Very fast call setup time (800mS compared to up to 30sec for a dial up connection).
- Reduced noise.
- Supports both circuit switched and packet switched services.
- Supports both digitised voice and digital data. The human voice is sampled at 8000Hz and quantised to 8 bits giving a 64kbps data rate and getting the maximum quality from the bandwidth of a single channel.

ISDN Services

There are two grades of service offered in the UK:

BTs Basic Rate Service - ISDN2

This service, also called BRI (Basic Rate Interface) is available from British Telecomms and it provides three digital channels into the user's premises. Two of these, known as the *'B* 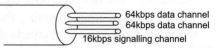 *Channels'*, (or Bearer channels) each provide a 64kbps digital data link. The third channel, the *'D Channel'*, (or Delta channel) provides a 16kbps digital link that is used for signalling purposes. When not in use for signalling, the D channel can also be used to carry digital data traffic.

Hence the maximum data capacity is 2 x 64k + 16k = 144Kbps.   This system is often called the 2B + D system.   The *'BT Home Highway'* service, in general terms, works out about twice the cost of a home telephone line.   Usage unit costs are the same as analogue telephone charges.   If both B channels are used at the same time, then each is charged as a separate call.   Most Internet providers support ISDN access and some charge extra for this service.   It is seen as useful for those in the UK that are unable to get broadband access.

Primary Rate Service - ISDN30

The Primary Rate Interface (PRI) is currently the other commonly used service. It provides thirty B Channels, allowing for a bandwidth of up to about 2Mbps, depending on the number of channels in use at any one time.  As each extra channel is brought into use, the bandwidth - and the usage unit costs - is increased.   ISDN30 is an essential service where the highest data transfer rates are required – until ADSL catches up.

Getting Connected

Connection to the ISDN system is achieved in the ways described below:

ISDN2

This uses the existing copper wire telephone lines into a user's premises. Instead of being connected to a telephone, they are connected to a digital interface as described below. Of course, alterations are required at exchange end so that the line is connected to the ISDN network instead of the switched telephone network.   The cable comes into a user's premises as a normal twisted pair and is taken into an ISDN wall socket - called an NTE (Network Terminating Equipment). Two connectors come out of the NTE (one pair of wires for the transmitting functions and one pair for the receiving functions). The NTE looks similar to a twin telephone socket and connects to a terminal adapter or ISDN card on a PC.

ISDN Cards

These cards plug into the PCI bus inside the PC and provide various levels of sophistication. These tend to be *'passive'* adaptors. This means that they act primarily as an interface between the PC and the NTE.   All the signal processing is carried out by the PC's own CPU.   This makes for a cheaper product.

Card prices vary dependent upon the facilities offered. Some cards can handle aggregation (see below), some only handle a single B channel, some provide data compression and so on.

Terminal Adaptors

Also known as an ISDN modem, it connects to the serial port of the PC.   It behaves in a similar way to a normal modem and has an extended set of Hayes AT commands. Some early models actually ran slower (at 19.2kbps or 28.4kbps) than the ISDN line.   Since the ISDN line is capable of handling 64kbps, the bandwidth was padded out with the insertion of null data.

External models are usually *'active'* adaptors.   In these models, all the signal processing and protocol handling is carried out by the electronics within the adaptor instead of the CPU.

Modern adaptors run at faster rates than the average serial port on a PC. To use them, the PC needs to have a fast 16550 UART inside, or have a high-speed add-on serial card fitted. Alternatively, terminal adaptors are now available for connection to a USB port.

An analogue telephone call can be made on one channel while the computer is using the other channel for Internet activity.

ISDN30

The ISDN2 is not powerful enough for many needs and the ISDN30 system provides for multi-channel use. All 30 channels allow for 1.92Mbps although, in practice, about eight channels are the maximum actually used.

Channel Aggregation

Channels can be grouped in various ways known as *'aggregation'* and *'bonding'* - to increase user bandwidth. Aggregation allows two or more channels to be used for a single call. This makes the effective data transfer rate double, triple, and so on. Bonding (Bandwidth On Demand Interoperability Group) is a dynamic equivalent of Aggregation. A bandwidth manager monitors the users needs at any one point and keeps the requisite number of ISDN channels open. These systems require that a channel aggregator be fitted at both ends of the link to maintain synchronisation.

ADSL

Asymmetric Digital Subscriber Line (ADSL) is the most common method of achieving broadband access to the Internet, with most of the UK able to have ADSL installed. *'Asymmetric'* refers to the fact that the data rate is different in different directions. In streaming media and Internet traffic this is quite acceptable, as the subscriber sends much less data back to the provider than he receives. The technique of using two line speeds on the same line is not new. V90, a common modem standard, can handle 56kbps downstream and 33kbps upstream. ADSL signalling rates are typically 6Mbps in one direction and 0.5Mbps in the other direction.

In the UK, however, ADSL bandwidth is usually shared, with contention ratios ranging from 10:1 to 50:1. During busy periods, this results in any one user's data transfer being slowed.

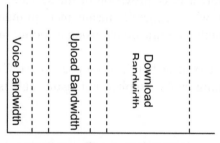

Frequency Range (0 to 1MHz)

ADSL technology connects the subscriber to the telephone exchange in the same way as a normal phone line, and it is still an analogue signal that is being transmitted. However, ADSL uses a much larger range of frequencies - up to 1MHz, compared to the 4KHz used for normal speech purposes. With a larger range, the ADSL connection still uses the same 0-4KHz bandwidth for voice signals, and the extra bandwidth is used for data. The signal is modulated using a form of QAM (as explained earlier), combined with a system known as Forward Error Correction (FEC) to reduce signal corruption.

At the subscriber's end, the incoming telephone line has a *'splitter'* attached. It sends the lower frequency audio signal to the telephone, and the higher frequency data signal to the ADSL modem. Typically this modem connects to a single PC but in some cases it shares the bandwidth between several PCs via a LAN or a router.

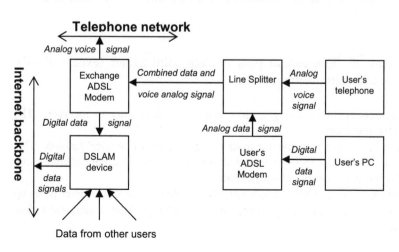

Data from other users

At the exchange end of the connection, an ADSL modem deals with the incoming signal, and passes it in a digital form to a multiplexing device known as a Digital Subscriber Line Access Multiplexer (DSLAM). The DSLAM combines the signals from many customers and transmits them over a high-speed connection, in many cases onto an Internet backbone line, from which the data is then passed on to the user's ISP.

Symmetric DSL was actually available before ADSL, and has variants known as HDSL (High-Rate DSL), SDSL (Single-line DSL) and VDSL (Very High-Rate DSL). HDSL runs over two or three paired wires and is designed to accommodate T1 and E1 signals, hence the data rates. (see below) Single-Line DSL and VDSL are single wire pair connections, both limited in range in order to achieve higher data rates.

Cable	Range	Speed upstream / downstream
HDSL (US)	Unlimited	1.544Mbps
HDSL (Europe)	Unlimited	2.048Mbps
SDSL	2.5km	1.5Mbps
VDSL	1km	13 to 523Mbps / 2.3Mbps
ADSL	4km	512kbps to 8Mbps / 256Kbps
RADSL	8km	Less than or equal to ADSL

ADSL also has its own variants. Rate Adaptive ADSL (RADSL) is able to adjust transmission speeds dynamically, and thus allows a greater distance between subscriber and exchange at the cost of potentially lower data rates (particularly upstream).

ADSL installation

Since ADSL uses existing phone lines, no additional cable installation to the site is required. However, being a digital technology, ADSL cannot use an ordinary modem. Instead, ADSL systems normally use an ADSL card or an external ADSL adapter that attaches via the USB port. The ADSL adapter is little more than an interface onto the cable, and is fitted via a new cable to the phone outlet.

Broadband Cable

A viable alternative to ADSL or ISDN is broadband cable. Although very different in operation from ADSL, it does share some characteristics. Bandwidth is shared with other cable users and in most cases cable Internet access is asymmetric, with download speeds being higher than upload speeds. Since cable does not rely on the telephone system, each cable provider has its own network. This means each cable network may be slightly different in terms of speed and contention ratios, although in most cases broadband cable is comparable to ADSL.

Unfortunately, since new cables need to be in place to provide cable access, provision of the service is limited to those areas that the cable companies decide to invest in, which generally means metropolitan areas. However, cable providers often supply cable television through the same outlet, using a splitter to send TV and data signals to the right appliances.

Physically, broadband cable delivers data to the subscriber via a coaxial or hybrid fibre coaxial (HFC) cable, typically reaching 750MHz in bandwidth. Costs vary depending on the supplier, but again cable is usually broadly similar to ADSL prices.

Cable installation

As implied by the name, broadband cable requires lines to be laid into the site. Typically, cable companies lay cable only in major cities, and only in areas that would bring the greatest return. This limits the availability of the service. However, if cable can be supplied to a site, the actual installation is relatively simple. The cable modem is normally an external box that connects via the USB port, and attaches to a coaxial cable wall outlet.

Wireless Communication

There is a growing trend to wireless connections. There are many applications for such devices: working 'on-the-go' from wherever you happen to be; instant communications from any location; and so on. There are many wireless technologies available and the following is an outline of the most common types.

Infrared

These systems rely on infrared (IR) light. IR light cannot pass through solid matter (except glass!), instead requiring a clear path between the transmitter and receiver.

This can be done one of three ways:

- Line of sight (LOS): These IR systems maintain a single, clear path from transmitter to receiver. The transmitter and receiver point directly at one another.
- Scatter: A wide angle of IR light can be emitted from the transmitter, in a 'diffuse' or 'scatter' fashion. This minimises the need to point the transmitter and receiver in exactly the right direction, but requires more power at the transmission end and is more susceptible to interference.
- Reflective: An IR light source is 'shone' onto a nearby object, usually a building, and the receiver picks up the light from that object. There still must be a clear line between the transmitter and the object, and a clear line between the object and the receiver.

Advantages	IR systems are cheap to implement, with relatively high bandwidth. The IrDA standards are international standards supported by most modern computer systems. No license is required to generate IrDA transmissions.
Disadvantages	Requires more power than radio links. Susceptible to interference from background light sources. Limited range and line of sight restrictions make it unsuitable for anything other than a local point-to-point connection, such as a connection between the LANs of two nearby buildings, or the connection between a wireless keyboard and the PC.

Infrared Standards

The most common infrared standard in computing was developed by a group of manufacturers known as the Infrared Data Association (IrDA). Uses for IrDA include:

- Wireless keyboards and mice.
- Wireless printers.
- Wireless LAN adapters.
- Wireless peer-to-peer computer networks.

The initial IrDA implementation, introduced in 1994, was seen as a direct replacement for the serial port and had a data rate of 115kbps. It uses RZI (Return-to-Zero Invert) modulation. This means that a light pulse is transmitted for each logic *'zero'* in the data stream; a logic *'one'* will not produce a light pulse. By 1995, a faster 4Mbps version had been introduced. It uses PPM (Pulse Position Modulation) where a constant stream of light pulses is transmitted. The time between each pulse is not evenly spaced and the exact position in time for the pulse indicates one of four binary values from 00 to 11. The transmission of these 4-bits has named the system 4PPM. 115kbps systems are common in applications such as wireless printer connection whereas the 4Mbps system is commonly implemented in portable computers.

Fibreless LASER

A LASER is a device that generates beams of 'coherent' light, sometimes but not always within the visible spectrum. Coherent light means that all the light waves are heading in one direction, rather than in a diffuse fashion like a lightbulb or torch. As a wireless technology, LASER is similar in many respects to Infrared.

Advantages	LASER beams are stronger than Infrared, making them much less susceptible to background interference.
Disadvantages	Due to the coherent light, a 'scatter' approach is not possible, and all connections must have precise line of sight.

Microwave

These systems transmit data on high-frequency microwaves. Microwaves can be used as a point-to-point link, providing a high-speed link between two locations on the ground. However, they can be used as an *'uplink'* to a satellite in Low Earth Orbit. When used in this way, the satellite will relay the data to another microwave receiver elsewhere on the planet, essentially giving this system unlimited range.

Early satellite systems had a reasonably high incoming (or *'downstream'*) data rate, but were forced to use modem or 64K ISDN links for outgoing (*'upstream'*) data. More recent satellite systems, however, contain a *'transceiver'* (transmitter/receiver) that enables communications in both directions via microwave signals. Such systems typically have a 1-2Mbps downstream connection, but still have a slower upstream connection, typically 128Kbps to 768Kbps.

Advantages	Terrestrial systems can have quite long range, and satellite systems have global reach. Bandwidth is also good. Portable systems allow 100% mobility anywhere on the surface of the Earth.
Disadvantages	Microwaves cannot penetrate any real amount of solid material, so they require line of sight just like IR and LASER systems, which can be a problem for long-range terrestrial links. Microwave frequencies also tend to be heavily regulated by the authorities. Prone to electromagnetic (EM) interference and atmospheric disturbances. The main disadvantage of microwave, however, is its prohibitive cost and complexity.

Narrow band radio

Information can be transmitted over radio waves in one of two ways. The simplest system, and the system with the most bandwidth, is 'Narrow Band'. This method utilises a small frequency band for data transmission. Obviously, this frequency band must be empty, or the transmissions will interfere with each other. As a result, most radio frequencies are regulated by the government. Even those frequencies which may be used, must be allocated wholly to the network – if two networks are to be installed, they must either use separate frequencies, or be sufficiently distant that they do not interfere with one another.

Advantages: High data rate. Radio signals can penetrate walls, so no line of sight is required.
                This makes it a viable technology for mobile computing.
Disadvantages   Susceptible to interference, as well as 'ghosts' where genuine signals bounce off
                objects and are received at slightly different times from one another. A whole
                frequency band must be allocated to the network. Radio signals can be picked up
                by unauthorised sources within range.

Spread-Spectrum radio

The counterpart to narrow band radio, spread-spectrum radio distributes the signal over a variety of bandwidths using an apparently random pattern. The receiving station knows this pattern, and can pick up the correct frequencies for the signals. DSSS (Direct Sequence Spread Spectrum) is a spread-spectrum standard defined by the IEEE, which uses the 2.4GHz frequency range that is available for use worldwide. FHSS (Frequency Hopping Spread Spectrum) uses the same range, but 'hops' in an apparently random (but in fact deterministic) fashion over frequencies, making it more secure.

Advantages: Like narrow band radio, spread-spectrum radio does not require line of sight. Due
                to the frequency hopping, this method is much more secure. Frequencies can be
                shared between networks, as long as patterns do not overlap.
Disadvantages   Lower bandwidth than narrow-band radio.
:

Cellular radio

This system uses radio 'cells' – geographic areas covered by a single radio transceiver. By planning the positioning of the cells, the system can potentially cover the entire area of a country. This is the system behind mobile phones, and it is increasingly being integrated into laptop and handheld computers. The de facto standard system for cellular radio in the UK and most of Europe is GSM – the Global Standard for Mobile communication. GSM is also used by some American mobile phone companies and other countries around the world, where it is often referred to as '*Personal Communications Services*' (PCS).

GSM uses TDMA (Time Division Multiple Access), which is similar to the TDM multiplexing technique explained earlier in this chapter, and operates at either 900 or 1800MHz frequency bands. It typically uses a circuit switching system at the exchange end (explained later).

Facilities available over GSM include SMS (Short Message Service), which is the exceptionally popular mobile phone message system. In addition, various systems can be used for data transfer on GSM, such as General Packet Radio Service (GPRS) at 115kbps; High Speed Circuit Switched Data (HSCSD) at 50Kbps; and EDGE (Enhanced Data Rates for GSM Evolution) at 384Kbps. These are often termed '2.5G' and are seen as an intermediate step between current '2G' technology and '3G' (see below).

Internet-enabled phones and cellular-based handheld computers use the Wireless Application Protocol (WAP) over GSM to connect to the Internet. Due to the smaller screen sizes and low data rates, HTML is not supported, instead a reduced-functionality equivalent known as Wireless Markup Language (WML) is used.

Advantages: Cellular radio provides the most mobile of all technologies, enabling access to the
                network anywhere so long as there is a transceiver within range.
Disadvantages   The main disadvantage of this technology is its speed. The widely touted third
                generation (3G) of mobile phones is supposed to improve this, but in the meantime
                speed is highly limited.

Third Generation Mobile Systems

The so-called third generation (3G) of mobile communications is widely touted as providing video conferencing, high-speed broadband data links, and various other benefits. Despite lengthy preparations and huge investments, 3G is still in development in most areas of the world. There is more than one contender to the 3G title, such as CDMA-2000, and TD-SCDMA, but the system that is most likely to gain the broadest coverage of the UK is the UMTS system.

UMTS

Universal Mobile Telecommunications System (UMTS) is an example of a third generation (3G) mobile phone technology. It is in fact composed of several mobile communications technologies, based on GSM, but using a packet-switched IP system, which could allow users to be charged by the amount of bandwidth used rather than the time spent online. It is available in Time Division or Wideband forms, and is expected to reach speeds of up to 2MBps. UMTS is planned for full implementation by 2008.

High-Speed Connections

While UTP may be the most common LAN networking choice, and technologies like Kilostream, Megastream and Satstream are suitable for Metropolitan Area Networks, Wide Area Networks (WANs) are very different. Technologies like ISDN, ADSL and Cable are all involved in getting data from the network (in this case the Internet) to the end user. But from the providers' point of view, it needs much higher speed and much longer distance links to provide sufficient bandwidth for all of this data. As can be imagined, the costs for such lines can be astronomical.

The majority of high-speed connections are fibre optical in nature, with the remainder being mainly copper T1, T3 or E1 wire lines.

The table shows some properties of various types of high-speed connections. The European E-rating and the US T-rating systems both use multiple 64Kbps signals, originally over twisted pair cable but now over a variety of media including optical fibre or satellite networks. The OCx system on the other hand, is used solely on optical fibre, and uses multiple 51Megabit signal streams.

Cable	Signals	Speed
E1 (Europe)	32 x 64Kbps	2.048Mbps
T1 (US)	24 x 64Kbps	1.544Mbps
T3 (US)	672 x 64Kbps	44.736 Mbps
OC-1	1 x 51.84Mbps	51.84Mbps
OC-3	3 x 51.84Mbps	155.52Mbps
OC-12	12 x 51.84Mbps	622.08Mbps
OC-48	48 x 51.84Mbps	2.43Gbps

Some of the technologies that utilise these high-speed connections are as below:

- One of the possible carriers for an ATM system is the OC-3 cable connection, which has the correct bandwidth. Of course, higher rated OCx cables can carry multiple ATM streams.
- The SONET (Synchronous Optical NETwork) system is based on OCx fibre cable carrying digital signals. It is a system that will guarantee a consistent media for data transfer, thereby providing the maximum bandwidth every step of the way. It is a hierarchical system similar in some ways to the existing digital copper cable of the phone network.
- The SMDS (Switched Multimegabit Data Service) system is a public network based on T1 and T3 lines transmitting datagrams which can encapsulate FDDI or LAN packets in order to bridge two LANs that are remote from each other. SMDS is intended for Metropolitan Area Networks, but has lost favour somewhat due to the upsurge of ATM based systems.
- "*Broadband ISDN*" is a name sometimes used to describe SMDS or ATM systems that provide both voice and data communications.

Circuit and Packet switching

The two main methods in which data is transferred from one specified location to another, are by 'circuit switched' and 'packet switched' systems.

- A Circuit Switched System involves creating a dedicated circuit between the transmitter and receiver for the duration of the message transfer, after which the circuit is freed up for use by other nodes on the network. The Frame Relay system or public PSTN phone network are examples of Circuit Switched systems. Such systems are known as '*connection-oriented*', and due to the need to maintain connections, Circuit Switching includes more overhead. As a result, Packet Switching is usually more popular in computing.
- In a Packet Switched network, only the very smallest message is sent as a complete block of data. All other messages are broken up into a collection of smaller units, known as '*packets*'. Each packet is transmitted to the destination where the collection of packets is re-assembled into a single block, with each packet being placed in its correct order like the original block. This allows the network to work at maximum efficiency, since each packet is routed along the currently fastest available link. X.25, and the IP protocol used by the Internet are examples of Packet Switched networks. Such systems are known as '*connectionless*'.

The Internet is the largest example of a packet-switched network, although the technique is used in most wide-area networks

Frame Relay

Based on the concept of circuit switching, Frame Relay transmissions consist of smaller packets, with less error detection data. The CCITT standard for Frame Relay defines a technology that has a top bandwidth of around 44Mbps, equal to a T3 link, though most connections are of equivalent speed to T1, which it can allocate dynamically to users of the service. Frame Relay is a public network, and a system connected to the network is said to be in the 'Frame Relay cloud'. As a public network, it is possible to implement a VPN through Frame Relay.

Network Routing

Most traffic travels long distances and passes through intermediate stations along the route. These intermediate nodes clean up the signal and pass it on to the next chosen station on the route. Since the data network is a collection of such stations, there are a number of alternative routes that a message could be sent.

For example, a message between Inverness and London may travel one of the following paths:

Inverness → Edinburgh → Newcastle → Leeds → London
Inverness → Glasgow → Liverpool → Birmingham → London
Inverness → Glasgow → Newcastle → Birmingham → Leeds → London

or any other permutation.   The performance of the network is determined by the way the links are used.

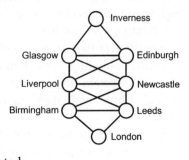

One routing strategy, called *'non-adaptive routing'* or *'static switching'*, provides each node on the network with a fixed table of routes. So, for example, all traffic between Inverness and London must pass through Edinburgh, Liverpool and Leeds.   The Edinburgh node's table would store the information that all messages for London from Inverness should be passed on to Liverpool, while Liverpool table would know to pass that message on to Leeds.   So for every possible source and destination in the system there is a routing table that has been calculated and permanently used by each station.   If a station is added, deleted or altered, all the routing tables that are affected have to be individually updated.

Availability

Non-adaptive routing is an efficient system where traffic demands are relatively light and unchanging. However, its weakness lies in its inability to automatically react to faults in the system. If the Leeds station broke down, then all traffic that was directed through it would be stopped until the fault was repaired. This would introduce unacceptable delays, particularly when the lines between other nodes were working perfectly. The *'availability'* of a station is simply the expected percentage of time that the station will work without problems. So, a station with an availability factor of 0.9 can be expected to work 90% of the time. However, the problem is magnified where a chain of stations is involved. If Inverness, Edinburgh, Liverpool, Leeds and London all had 0.9 availability factors, the overall availability of the Inverness to London route is 0.9 x 0.9 x 0.9 x0.9 x 0.9 = 0.59.   Where stations are connected in parallel (e.g. Edinburgh and Liverpool are parallel stations between Glasgow and Newcastle) the availability calculation shows a much more efficient system. If one node completely ceases (e.g. Edinburgh) the other node (e.g. Liverpool) remains 100% functional. This improvement cannot be utilised by non-adaptive methods, since the routing only directs traffic to a single node whether that node is functional or not.

Congestion Control

Each node is connected to a number of incoming/outgoing connections (the example shows Newcastle connecting to five other nodes while Inverness connects to two). Since each node only handles a defined amount of traffic at any one time, the system stops sending traffic to a busy node until the congestion eases. This routing is a wasteful, since one node may be congested while another is quiet.

Adaptive Routing

Adaptive routing responds to changes in the system (e.g. breakdowns, congestion) by automatically altering the traffic routes. The tables held by each node are no longer fixed; their path information is altered to reflect the current state of the network. There are two ways of implementing adaptive routing:

Centralised Routing

One node on the network constantly collects information on the status of every other network node. Each change in the system results in the centralised management system calculating the best new routes to maximise the efficient use of the system in its new state.   The new routing tables are then transmitted to each node for updating their routing activities.

Distributed Routing

With this method, there is no central control and each node carries out its own monitoring, calculation and distribution of routing information.   So, for example, if the Newcastle/Leeds link failed or became congested, Leeds would inform Liverpool and Birmingham. Each node responds to its own monitoring and to incoming status information by recalculating its own routing tables.

The calculation for routing tables, known as *'shortest path algorithms'*, would take into account the capacity of the alternate links (throughput in bps), the delays of each link, the cost of using each link and the error rate of each link. The calculation produces the most efficient new route to adopt.

P.C. links to large computers

Data communications allow a P.C. to access the resources of mainframe and other large computer systems. But mainframes were designed to connect to their own brand and design of *'terminals'*. A terminal's main function is to transfer the user's keystrokes to the mainframe and to display the mainframe's output on the user's monitor. The way this is achieved depends upon the design of the terminal and may range from simple ASCII screens to complex graphical screens. Terminals have no computational power other than that required to carry out their input and output functions - all the real program computation takes place inside the mainframe computer.

When a PC wishes to connect to the larger system, it has to communicate in exactly the same way as that expected by a terminal. This is achieved by the communications software, which allows the user to select a particular terminal *'emulation'*. The software ensures that communication between the PC and mainframe works identically to that with a terminal. The mainframe works normally, thinking its communicating with a standard terminal and the software in the PC does all the conversion work.

P.C. to P.C. links

Users may also wish to link their P.C. to another P.C. so that communication can take place or so that resources can be shared. This link can be either local or remote.

Local Connection

Used where the PCs are in the same room or office. This is commonly used for file transfers between a user's desktop computer in the workplace and the laptop computer that is carried around. Typical users include salespersons downloading current prices and uploading the previous day's orders and civil engineers bringing back information gathered on a site for analysis on the office machine.

In these cases, the PCs can be linked together using:
- A *'null modem'* serial cable connecting the two RS232 ports. The speed of file transfers depends on the maximum data transfer rate of the slowest serial port of the two computers and this speed can be set up using the communications software.
- A parallel cable connecting the two parallel ports. Data is transferred one byte at a time but the maximum transfer rate may be slowed by retransmissions due to transmissions errors.
- A USB or FireWire cable connecting to the USB or FireWire ports on both computers. Although this is another serial method, its transfer rate is far greater than with a serial cable. Special software is required to connect the PCs, however.
- Network cards fitted in each PC and linked together with LAN cabling. This is common with laptops that have PCMCIA card LAN adaptors. It is also reasonably popular as a means of games enthusiasts playing multi-player games. See the LANS chapter for information on how to set up a local Microsoft Network.

Of course, each computer has to run appropriate software to manage the connection.
Examples are:
- *'Direct Cable Connection'* provided with Windows.
- Laplink, which is a stand-alone product where either PC can access the other's files.
- Peer-to-Peer software such as Windows for Workgroups or Lantastic, which allows the sharing of each other's file and peripheral resources.

Laplink and similar programs are designed for use with either serial or USB connection between PCs, while network software expects the computers to have network interface cards and card driver software. Once connected, all the above systems allow file transfers from one machine's disks to the other's drives.

Null Modem Cable

A modem serial cable has no reversals in the cable wiring. Each pin on a plug is wired to the same plug pin number on the other end of the cable. This approach mainly applies to modems. The diagram shows a basic connection of two PCs

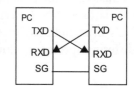

without hardware handshaking. The computer's *'transmit'* pin is wired to a device's *'receive'* pin and the computer's *'receive'* pin is connected to the device's *'transmit'* pin. In other words, one computer's TXD pin is wired to the other's RXD pin and vice versa.

With hardware handshaking, one computer's DTR pin would be wired to the other's DSR pin and vice versa and one computer's RTS line would connect to the other's CTS line. Some communication software refuses to work unless its DCD line is set on. In these case, the RTS and the CTS lines of the first PC should be wired together and taken to the DCD line of the second computer - and vice versa.

These are known as a *'null modem'* cables and they are widely used for transferring files across a serial port with packages such as Laplink.

Remote Connection

Where the PCs are at different sites, connection can be achieved over the public telephone network using modems at each end. Again, each computer requires remote connection software to be installed.

The software can provide two separate functions:

Remote Access

Here the incoming PC has access to the remote (known as the *'host'* or *'server'*) PC's resources such as files and peripherals. The user can download from the host system or can place data on the host system. Usually, either user can initiate the connection thereby making the called station the host. Laplink is an example of remote access software that can provide file transfers over a modem, even connecting into a remote Local Area Network. The data rates depend upon the speed of the serial ports, the modems and the quality of the transmission line.

Uses of remote access include:

- Teleworking - This covers a range of work activities such as an employee working from home, working from another branch, working from a customers premises and even group working with other individuals who are similarly located remotely.
- Distance learning - Enrolled students can access lessons, upload their course essays and e-mail enquiries to their tutor. This is an area of much development and the quality of material varies.

Remote Control

Here the incoming PC takes control of the remote PC's activities. The incoming machine's key and mouse activities control the remote machine and the incoming machine can see the same video output as that being displayed on the remote screen. This provides opportunities for remote diagnostics and debugging. The problems at a remote machine can be solved without visiting the remote site. Usually, one of the systems is permanently set up as the host while the other is used as the *'guest'* or *'client'*. Examples of this software are pcANYWHERE, Carbon Copy and Reachout. These products also allow remote control over a network so that any user on the LAN can be directly in communication with, and receive support from, a remote user.

OSI Standards

Where data has to be transmitted from one location and received at another location, there has to be a set of protocols which ensure that both the transmitting and receiving devices handle data in the same way. These should cover issues such as packet size, the organisation of packet contents, speed of transmission, types of synchronisation and error correction.

It must also cover the lowest level issue of how a single data bit is moved - e.g. voltage levels or current loop detection. As long as both sites use the same protocols, data movement is possible. Where sites are numbered in millions internationally, as in the Internet, there has to be an international set of standards. This prompted one description of OSI standards as *"the Esperanto of communications"*.

Application Layer		Application Layer
Presentation Layer		Presentation Layer
Session Layer		Session Layer
Transport Layer		Transport Layer
Network Layer		Network Layer
Data Link Layer		Data Link Layer
Physical Layer		Physical Layer

Networks, both LANs and WANs, were plagued by differing protocols for different proprietary products and this still inhibits the development of communications. The International Standards Organisation (*ISO*) addressed the problem and decided to introduce a model for the design of networks. This was known as the Open Systems Interconnection (*OSI*) model - mostly now known as the ISO/OSI model.

The model seeks to define the functions of the hardware and software involved in networks. It does this by creating seven levels of communication activity, known as *'layers'*. The seven layers, when interacting with each other, comprise the total system. The lowest layer performs the most basic hardware function. Each succeeding layer adds a greater level of sophistication to the process and the interface between each layer is clearly defined. The ISO/OSI model is not in itself a standard - it is more a set of measures to be used in comparing current and new products.

For a long time, few products emerged that used this model. This changed when the US and UK governments made OSI standards mandatory for most large government contracts. X.400 (Electronic messaging), X.500 and X.25 are some of the ISO/OSI standards.

The Seven Layers

The chart shows the differing levels of complexity handled by each layer. Layer 1 only works with single data bits while the upper layers handle entire messages. The highest layer is the layer seen by the user (e.g. e-mail or file transfer) while the rest should be hidden from the user.

The *'station'* referred to in the following descriptions could be any communications equipment. At its simplest, it comprises a PC and modem. The *'medium'* is any form of connection

Layer Number	Layer Name	Information Handled
7	Application	Message
6	Presentation	Message
5	Session	Message
4	Transport	Message
3	Network	Packet
2	Data Link	Frame
1	Physical	Bit

between the stations and covers from a telephone line to a vast switched network.

LAYER 1 - Physical Layer

The Physical Layer is concerned with moving data between the station and the medium that connects the stations. It sets up, maintains and disconnects the physical link between the stations. The layer defines the electrical (i.e. voltage levels) and mechanical (i.e. pin wiring) requirements for connecting the equipment to the medium. Examples of the Physical Layer are RS-232, X.21 and V35.

LAYER 2 - Data Link Layer

Layer 1 only accepts or sends a stream of data bits without paying any attention to the order or meaning of the bits. So Layer 2 ensures that any corruption of the data stream is detected. The data to be transmitted is fed into the Data Link Layer and it handles a block of data at a time, called a *'frame'*. A checksum is added to the frame and the frame is then passed on to Layer 1 for transmission. The receiving station's Layer 1 detects the incoming data stream and passes it on to Layer 2. If there is no corruption of the data it can be passed on for further processing. Layer 2 is also used for flow control and handles transmissions to and from the nearest DSE (data switching equipment). Examples of the Data Link Layer are Ethernet's CSMA/CD and HDLC (High-Level Data Link Control).

LAYER 3 - Network Layer

Most communication sessions between computers are not directly wired but are routed through a switched network or even a series of network devices. Layer 3 adds unique addressing information to packets so that they are routed to the correct receiving station. The enlarged packet is sent to the Data Link Layer where the error checksum is added and the packet is sent out on to the transmission media (via the Physical Layer). If the address of the receiving station does not match the packet address, the packet is ignored. If it has the matching address, the data is accepted and further processed.

Examples of this layer are X.25 used in wide area packet switched networks, Novell's IPX and the IP of Internet's TCP/IP.

LAYER 4 - Transport Layer

The Transport Layer acts as the interface between the user's activities and the requirements of the data communications network (i.e. the lower three layers). The message to be transmitted arrives at the Transport Layer and is often larger than the maximum size of data packet that can be handled by the lower system.   The Transport Layer splits the data into chunks that match the capacity of the network system in use (e.g. 4k blocks) and adds sequence numbers to each block before sending them to the Network Layer.   On a switched network, the various blocks may be sent via different routes. The Transport Layer on the receiving end does not care what route the blocks took.   It is only concerned with passing on the incoming blocks in the correct sequence.   If a block arrives out of sequence (e.g. block 2 is delayed in the network and arrives after block 3) the Transport Layer places the blocks back into sequence.   If a duplicate block arrives (e.g. block 2 arrives twice) the Transport Layer detects the duplicate block and ignores it.

The Transport Layer, therefore, provides a pipe between systems to exchange data, operating independently of both higher layer application protocols and lower layer network protocols - effectively the link between user applications and the network.

Examples of the Transport Layer are Novell's SPX and the TCP of Internet's TCP/IP.

LAYER 5 - Session Layer

The first four layers are *'communications oriented'*; they concentrate on the physical network and its rules.   Layers 5 to 7 are *'process oriented'* layers.   These are high level protocols to allow two OSI-based models to exchange data - regardless of the physical connecting medium.   The Session Layer establishes, controls and terminates the dialogue between the two user application processes.   It treats the session as a single activity, even although the Transport Layer may have used a number of different connections to complete the data transfer.   The layer also controls the flow of information to match the system currently in use (i.e. simplex, duplex, half-duplex).   The layer also inserts *'checkpoints'* into the data. This provides points from which to restart if the two ends get out of step (e.g. due to a connection failure).

Examples of this layer are Internet's TELNET and FTP, the HTTP protocol used in the World Wide Web, and Novell's NETBIOS emulator.

LAYER 6 - Presentation Layer

The two computers in the dialogue may use different methods of representing numbers and graphical characters.   The Presentation Layer has to ensure that machines with different data representations (e.g. ASCII 7-bit, BCD, etc) can still pass the same meaning from one user to another.   The data supplied to the Presentation Layer is converted from its existing format into a universal OSI format (known as ASN.1) before being passed to the Session Layer.   When the data arrives at the receiving end's Presentation Layer, it is converted from the universal format into the format used by that particular machine (which may or may not differ from that of the sending machine).   The data, in its acceptable format, is then passed up. The layer can also provide facilities such as compression/ decompression, encryption/decryption and terminal emulation.

LAYER 7 - Application Layer

The Application Layer is the link between the end user's application package and the communications system.   As such, it varies from program to program and from system to system.

Examples of this layer are X-Windows, the X400 standard for e-mail, Novell's DOS redirector and remote job entry functions.

OSI Summary

The chart shows the basic functions of each layer when sending a message - each layer processing data and passing it down one layer.   Receiving is the reverse process, with incoming data being processed and passed up one layer.

Layer Number	Layer Name	Purpose
7	Application	Routes data from application packages into the communication system
6	Presentation	Ensures that machines with different data representations can still understand each other
5	Session	Handles simplex/duplex operations over an entire communications session
4	Transport	Divides data into a series of sequenced blocks for transmission
3	Network	Handles the routing of data to the required station
2	Data Link	Carries out flow control and error checking
1	Physical	Handles the physical and electrical characteristics of the communications network

Protocols Overview

There are a variety of data communications protocols in use, from those used in the smallest local area network to the largest computer network of all, the Internet. A protocol is simply a common set of rules between two devices so that they may communicate.

In a basic point-to-point link, such as using a modem to dial a BBS, the protocol only needs to facilitate communication between the two machines.

On a network, including the Internet, the protocol must provide addressing information to indicate the recipient(s) of the data.

Other concerns the protocol should address include:

- Security: The transfer of data is a potential security risk if the protocol does not include satisfactory mechanisms to protect the information contained within. Some protocols, such as IPSec, are designed purely with security in mind. Other protocols are communications protocols that contain inherent security. But all too many protocols do not provide any real security. If a protocol is implemented that does not have acceptable security mechanisms then additional security protocols or procedures must be implemented on top of it, increasing the complexity of the system and therefore the potential for problems.

- Error detection and correction: Almost as important as the security of data is the need to ensure that the data is correct. Errors in transmission can be detected by the protocol in use. TCP, for example, implements considerably more error detection than UDP.

- Reliability: Finding and fixing errors in transmission is not the only component of a reliable protocol. The ability of the protocol to recover from network problems can provide vastly improved service. The Internet Protocol set, for example, is able to route messages in such a way that broken connections can be circumvented.

- Efficiency: Although the main determinant of communications speed is the physical media, the protocol in use can have a major effect. For example, the Ethernet protocol, by allowing transmission collisions to occur, has a low efficiency, reducing the effective speed of the network. The FDDI protocol, by contrast, is a robust and efficient system but requires a ring topology.

- Interoperability: The compatibility of the protocol with other networks can make administration easier, as well as improving the reach of the data communications system. If equipment from two sites or two organisations are not interoperable, then an intermediary is required, such as an EDI service provider.

- Cost. Although protocols themselves are not directly paid for, all of the above factors figure in to the cost of the network in some way, by making more efficient use of communications lines, making upgrades simpler, or increasing compatibility with external groups.

Routable vs non-routable protocols

Earlier in this chapter, the concept of routing was discussed. Protocols play their part in this process – some protocols are designed with routing in mind, while others are not. Routable protocols must allocate space within each transmitted packet, for routing information. This information will allow a device called a *'Router'* to pass such packets on from one segment of the network to another, in order to reach its destination. As a result, non-routable protocols are only useful for communication between nodes within a single network segment. Examples of routable protocols include TCP/IP and IPX/SPX, while NetBEUI is the most common non-routable protocol. IP uses either RIP (Routing Internet Protocol) or OSPF (Open Shortest Path First) protocol to achieve routing.

Addressing methods

Every DTE on a network has an address, to distinguish it from the other DTEs on the network. When data is transmitted, it is addressed to a particular DTE or group of DTEs.

There are three ways in which data can be logically addressed:

- Multicast: In this system, the DCE transmits data to multiple recipients. Routing multicast data only to the appropriate LAN segments requires intelligent routers, so most hubs simply transmit to all segments, using up bandwidth over the whole network. The most widely used multicast system is based on the IP protocol.

- Broadcast: This is like multicast transmission, but the data is received by all DTEs on the network. Obviously, this is not practical for the Internet, and is used mainly in small LANs. For example Ethernet is a broadcast protocol, used in many UTP networks. The node initiating communication must transmit to all other nodes on the network segment, because of the bus nature of the Ethernet system. Most wireless connections are also broadcast systems, which is one of the inherent security problems with wireless networks.

- Unicast: This is the most efficient method of addressing – the data is routed only to the network segment on which the receiving DTE is located, potentially freeing up bandwidth in other segments. The most widely known implementation of Unicast is the Internet, where almost all communications take place between one Internet client and another.
- Anycast: Multicast transmission can be used where only one reply is needed. For example, looking up a certain piece of data only requires one response from any of the systems in the Multicast list. This is known as 'anycast' addressing.

Protocol Binding

In a modern operating system such as Windows, each protocol suite, such as IP, must be *'bound'* to a particular data communications device. In this way, a single protocol can be installed, but it can have multiple bindings to multiple communications devices. For example, a server could have two network cards installed, to allow it to connect to more than one network segment. Both network cards can use the same protocol by using two bindings. Each binding communicates with its own driver, and can be configured differently, for example two network cards may have different IP addresses.

Common Protocols

TCP/IP Protocol Suite

The most common protocol in use today, TCP/IP is the de facto protocol of the Internet. Virtually, if not all dial-up ISPs (Internet Service Providers) use TCP/IP to connect a user to the Internet, and it is also very common in use in LANs. The TCP/IP protocol is explained more fully later in this chapter.

IPX/SPX Protocol

Rarely used for modem connections, IPX is mainly a LAN technology. Even when a LAN is connected to the Internet via a gateway, TCP/IP is usually installed as well as IPX, to handle Internet traffic.

X.25

This protocol, developed by CCITT and approved by ISO, is divided into three layers, and describes an interface between public and private packet switched networks. It is designed for data rates of up to 64Kbps, and although it is packet switched, it can run over circuit switched physical networks and provide more reliable 'virtual' connections. It is a communications suite that maps to the lower three layers of the OSI model. Public and private X.25 networks can be created.

NetBEUI and NetBIOS

The IBM-developed Network Basic Input/Output System (NetBIOS) is a non-routable protocol designed simply to allow communication between client and server processes. Microsoft's NetBIOS (NetBIOS Enhanced User Interface) works at a higher OSI layer but is still non-routable. As a result it is mainly used in older systems such as Windows for Workgroups. NetBIOS is an IBM protocol that was designed for the older LAN Manager system. It uses a 15-character name for each resource.

Appletalk

Apple's networking protocol is available in three main types: Localtalk (at 235Kbps), Ethertalk (10Mbps) or TokenTalk (16Mbps). It is used almost exclusively by Apple computer systems.

BBS Protocols

There are a variety of protocols that can be used when connecting a PC via modem to a Bulletin Board Service. They all provide error checking, but vary in speed and reliability. This includes XMODEM, YMODEM, ZMODEM, and Kermit protocols. For example, XMODEM uses a one-byte CRC for each 128-byte block, is limited to 9600bps, and can only transfer one file at a time. YMODEM has a two-byte CRC and is able to transfer multiple files at one time. Being older, most of these protocols do not follow OSI standards, and are designed only for one-to-one communication, providing no addressing or routing capabilities.

Other protocols

There are many other protocols in use. Wireless systems such as IrDA (Infrared) and WAP (for cellular radio) are becoming popular, while systems such as ATM are available for high-speed communications. These systems are explained in the LANs chapter.

TCP/IP

TCP/IP - *'Transmission Control Protocol over Internet Protocol'* - is the most commonly used set of communication protocols. It is used on the Internet, on Unix systems, on many local area networks, on wide area networks and as a means of connecting dissimilar systems (e.g. between minicomputers and mainframes). Novell provides IP as an alternative to its own IPX in Netware and it is supported by all versions of Windows. As long as a system has TCP/IP, it can communicate with any other TCP/IP-equipped system. This means that a PC can talk to a Macintosh or an Amiga can talk to a mainframe. Even better, the software is royalty-free - although many commercial products exist.

TCP/IP was introduced in the 1970's as a protocol suite to support ARPAnet, the American defence network that developed into the Internet.

The TCP/IP protocols embody four layers and these broadly compare with the OSI model as shown in the comparison chart.

TCP/IP Layer	Information handled	Corresponding OSI Layers
Application	Message	5,6,7
Transport	Segment	4
Internet	Datagram	3
Network Interface	Frame	1,2

The TCP component is concerned with maintaining the dialogue between two computers and keeping data packets in order, detecting any corrupted or missing packets and requesting retransmission. The TCP components are a set of communications routines that applications can call upon.

The IP component is concerned with the routing of packets to correct locations, from local organisations through to regions and then internationally.

TCP itself uses the routines that make up the IP component, but a few applications also directly use IP routines, bypassing the TCP layer.

Application Layer

The 'standard' set of TCP/IP applications include:

Telnet

The PC acts like a terminal to a remote Unix machine and the user can access resources in the same manner as a user that is locally connected to the system. With the growth of the World Wide Web, the use of Telnet has dwindled to use with universities, libraries and some bulletin boards.

FTP

The *'File Transfer Protocol'* allows files to be copied from one computer to another over the Internet. Users can directly use FTP (see the chapter on using the Internet). In Web sites, the FTP facility may be hidden from the user who clicks on a *'Download File'* icon without realising that this invokes the FTP.

E-Mail

This allows for the transfer of messages between computers even if one of the two machines is switched off.   Instead of sending the message directly to the remote computer, it is sent to a *'mail server'* which stores it for future reading by the remote station.   The remote station can, at any time and from any location, log in to the mail server and check for any messages that have been left.   The two common protocols for e-mail are SMTP and POP (Post Office Protocol).

NFS

The *'Network Filing System'* allows one computer to act as a file server to another remote computer. Since TCP/IP is machine-independent, a PC can use a remote Unix computer to save and recover files.

Remote Execution

A computer in one location initiates an activity on another remote computer.

These applications are under user control and consist of high-level activities (e.g. send this e-mail, fetch a copy of that file).   They pass information known as 'messages' down to the lower layers that work out how the tasks and operations will be achieved.

Transport Layer

There are two main protocol elements at this layer: TCP or UDP. The User Datagram Protocol (UDP) is a simple connectionless protocol that does little more than enable the use of ports (see later). TCP, however, allows much greater control, such as connections, acknowledgements of receipt, and so on.

Since packets can get lost in the system or can arrive out of sequence, the task of maintaining the correct data flow rests with the Transport Layer. This layer re-arranges out of order packets and ensures that lost packets are automatically re-sent.

In both TCP and UDP, messages from the Application Layer are broken into 'segments' and transmitted separately. Each segment has a 'header' added before the start of the data, containing information that enables the respective functions of the protocol. For example, the UDP header simply contains the port number and a checksum, while the TCP header contains sequence numbers, acknowledgements, options, and so on.

Internet Layer

With TCP/IP, information is sent in blocks known as 'datagrams'. For most TCP/IP use, a packet and a datagram are the same size of 500 octets. An octet is 8 bits - i.e. one byte; however, since some systems do not work on an 8-bit word, the octet is the preferred way to describe size. A packet and a datagram are not always the same size. For example, the X.25 interface creates data packets of 128 bytes and so several packets would be required to transport a single datagram. On the Internet, there is no distinction between packets and datagrams and they are often used interchangeably.

All data from TCP or UDP protocols is routed through the IP component of the system. This means that segments from the Transport Layer are sent down to the Internet Layer for processing and sending on to the Network Interface for transmission. The Internet Layer is concerned with getting the datagram to the correct location, as passed on to it from the Transport Layer along with the segments. The Internet Layer adds its own header to the datagram, containing data such as the protocol of the segment within, as well as the source and destination IP addresses and other information.

An IP Address is a four-byte number, normally expressed as four decimal numbers each separated by a dot. For example 128.96.0.255 is a valid number, but 128.96.0.256 is not (because 256 is more than can be stored by a single byte) and 128.96.0.254.3 is not (because it contains five numbers). On a proprietary network IP addresses can be allocated as the network manager sees fit. However, when using TCP/IP over the Internet, IP addresses must be allocated by the NIC – see the Internet chapter for details.

IP works out the best route to take for delivering the packet (i.e. directly or via a gateway) and passes it on to the Network Interface.

Network Interface

This layer transmits and receives datagrams over a particular physical network and is specific to the characteristics of that network - e.g. WANs, Ethernet LANs, Token Ring LANs, etc.

However, the data sections transmitted through the Network layer are referred to as 'frames', just as in the OSI model. The Network layer also adds its own header, depending on the system in use. For example, an Ethernet system would add a source and destination hardware Media Access Control (MAC) address, which identifies a unique node on the network, and may add a 'trailer' at the end of each frame to make sure the frame is of the correct size.

Packet construction

The diagram shows the layers of TCP/IP and how they contribute to the construction of packets sent across a network.

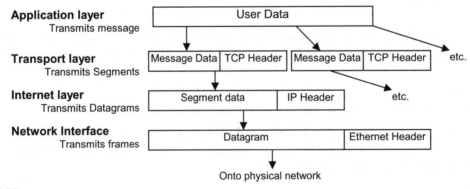

SLIP / PPP

IP is designed for routing in a large network. Many home and small business users only own a single modem and dial up into the Internet via a normal telephone line. The server that they dial requires all the sophistication of IP for its connection to the Internet but only requires a simpler system to interface to the dial-up line. The first protocol to allow telephone/modem connections to TCP/IP was SLIP (Serial Line Internet Protocol) and an improved version is PPP (Point to Point Protocol). This consists of a driver to the computer's serial port and out to a SLIP or PPP server.

Port Numbers

A server processes many different stations at any one time. Each process has to be identified with a particular station to ensure that datagrams do not get hopelessly mixed. Each process is identified by a 16-bit port number and this is generated by the application process initiating the contact. The more popular server applications are allocated their own port numbers e.g. FTP is port 21 while TELNET is port 23. A computer wishing to initiate a file transfer would specify its own port number as, say, 2345, while requesting a remote port 21.

Winsock

The combination of address and port number is referred to as a 'socket'. The TCP/IP software is known as the 'protocol stack' and is implemented as either a DOS TSR, a Windows 3.1 DLL or as a VxD in later versions of Windows. The Trumpet Winsock package and Windows (after v3.1) both provide both SLIP and PPP drivers. Winsock (Windows Socket Application Programming Interface) is the interface between a Windows version of a client application, such as FTP, and the TCP/IP protocol stack. The application calls routines from the Winsock DLL and it calls routines from the TCP/IP drivers. Each commercial implementation of a TCP/IP protocol stack will supply its own WINSOCK.DLL to work with its own proprietary brand of stack. In this way, writers of applications do not need to know what stack is in use, since it will always communicate with the Winsock DLL and let it carry out the operations to the stack. Applications that do not make use of Winsock have to write their own interface to the TCP/IP protocol stack.

Distinguishing IP applications

Simply having an individual IP address for each computer may not be sufficient. If a server, for example, allows Telnet access, HTTP (Web) access, and SMTP (email) access, then it must distinguish each of these applications from each other. Using a different IP address for each application is not a realistic option since it requires a separate network card and protocol binding for each application.

To overcome this problem, IP systems use 'ports' to distinguish the applications at the end point. A 16-bit number identifies each port, therefore this system allows approximately 65 thousand ports, which is normally much more than enough. Some services, such as FTP, HTTP and SMTP, use so-called 'well-known ports', which are defined in a standards document as being a particular number. This simplifies access to common services, in fact most users of these services are unaware that they are using ports.

For example, IP address 200.20.2.1 might be the address of a particular server, while 200.20.2.1:23 could be the address of that server, followed by the port number of their FTP facility.

The IP address together with the port number can be used to create a 'socket', which is essentially a construct that allows communications with an application. Thus, an application that knows the IP address and port number of a service can create a socket, and need not be concerned with the details of communication with that server.

IP Address allocation

The IP protocol requires that each system on an IP network must have its own unique address. The Internet chapter explains in detail the methods by which groups of IP addresses are allocated to organisations. However, the organisation must decide how to allocate its numbers amongst the machines attached to the Internet. IP can also be used in a LAN not attached to the Internet, and each machine must still be allocated an IP address. There are two ways of allocating IP addresses:

- Static. This is the simplest system, where each machine on the network has its IP address stored within the machine itself. This requires that allocation be carefully tracked to avoid allocating the same IP address to multiple systems. It also requires re-allocating addresses if machines are added to or taken off the network.
- Dynamic. In this type of system, IP addresses are stored in a central list on a server, and any machine that wishes to obtain an IP address for itself must contact the server. The server will allocate an IP address, and temporarily remove it from the list of available addresses. This ensure no duplication of address, and also potentially means that more machines can be attached to the network than there are IP numbers. The most common Dynamic allocation system is DHCP (Dynamic Host Configuration Protocol).

The type of address allocation can be chosen in the *'IP Address'* tab of the Properties of the TCP/IP protocol in Network Neighborhood, as shown.   *Select 'Obtain an IP address automatically'* to use DHCP, or *'Specify an IP Address'* to use static addressing, and then enter the IP address allocated.

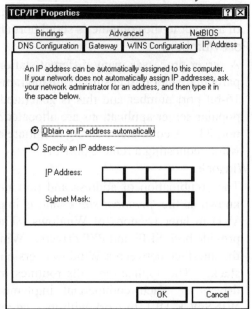

If Dynamic addressing is used, or if using a dial-up connection, a user's IP address may change every time the connection is used.   There are however tools that allow a user to find their machine's current IP address. IPCONFIG is a DOS mode program that will list IP details, while WINIPCFG is a Windows program that displays the same information as well as allowing the user to release or renew IP addresses.

Additionally, Windows 98 and later operating systems include a facility called Automatic Private IP Addressing (APIPA), which allows DHCP clients to use a private IP address (ie. one that begins with 169.254) when one is not available from the server.

There are other systems that allocate IP addresses.   For example, NAT (Network Address Translation) is a system that divides IP addresses on the local network into a 'public' side and a 'private' side, with the private NAT addresses only used internally. This allows private NAT addresses to be re-used in various locations, reducing the number of IP addresses needed overall. NAT can also form part of a firewall system, and in this capacity it will disguise the address of private NAT hosts.

Address Classes

As explained in the Internet chapter, IP addresses on the Internet come in three main classes: Class A, B and C. The class of network determines how many addresses (known as *'hosts'*) it can contain. It is possible to determine which type of network class an IP address belongs to, because each class is defined as follows:

Network Class	Range of addresses
Class A	1.0.0.1 to 126.255.255.254
Class B	128.0.0.1 to 191.255.255.254
Class C	224.0.0.1 to 255.255.255.254

Thus, the IP address of a machine on the Internet is composed of two parts – the first one, two or three bytes (for class A, B or C networks) are known as the *'network address'* and determine which network the machine is part of, while the remainder of the IP address is a unique identifier, which may be allocated in any manner the organisation sees fit.

For example, a company might own a Class B domain with IP addresses 128.0.0.1 up to 128.0.255.254, allowing it 65 thousand hosts. It could set aside all IP address beginning with 128.0.0 for the personnel department, and all IP addresses beginning with 128.0.1 for the finance department, and so on, thus allowing each department up to 254 hosts. These groups of smaller networks within the larger network are known as *'subnets'*.

Subnet masks

A *'subnet mask'*, or address mask, is a four-byte number, similar to an IP address, that is used to determine which subnet a machine belongs to. In the example above, every machine in the company would have a subnet mask of 255.255.255.0. A bitwise AND is applied between the subnet mask and the IP address of any individual machine, in order to find out the subnet it is located on. For example, IP address 128.0.1.55, with subnet mask 255.255.255.0, would turn out to have subnet address 128.0.1.0.

This information is used to aid in routing. For example, if a router can determine that the source and destination machines share the same subnet, they are local to that segment and the frame need not be passed on to another network segment. On the other hand, if they have different subnets, the frame will have to be routed to the remote machine's segment.

In most cases, the default subnet mask is 255.255.255.0, which means that the subnet takes up the first three of the four numbers in the IP address, thus allowing up to 254 addresses on the subnet. A custom mask would allow the network administrator to allocate larger ranges of IP addresses to a single subnet. For example a subnet mask of 255.255.0.0 specifies that all machines with the same first two of the four numbers in their IP address are considered to be within the same subnet.

Classless Inter-Domain Routing

This system, abbreviated to *'CIDR'*, is a modern IP address allocation system. It is no longer based on allocating domains to Class A, B, and C networks, but instead groups them by their subnet mask.

With the Class based IP system, a network must be either Class A, with 16 million IP addresses allocated to it; Class B, with 64 thousand, or Class C, with 254 useable IP addresses. There is no provision for any degrees in-between, so a company with 800 nodes in its network is forced to purchase 64 thousand addresses and will waste the vast majority of them. It would be much more efficient if such a network could be allocated around a thousand IP addresses.

In CIDR, this can be done. Groups of IP addresses are determined by their subnet mask, which is specified by using a shorthand convention of writing a slash prefix followed by the number of binary 'ones' in the subnet mask. For example:

Subnet mask	Binary equivalent	Slash prefix notation	Number of nodes
255.255.255.0	1111 1111 1111 1111 1111 1111 0000 0000	/24	254
255.255.0.0	1111 1111 1111 1111 0000 0000 0000 0000	/16	64516
255.0.0.0	1111 1111 0000 0000 0000 0000 0000 0000	/8	16387064
255.255.252.0	1111 1111 1111 1111 1111 1100 0000 0000	/22	1022
255.128.0.0	1111 1111 1111 1000 0000 0000 0000 0000	/13	32768

As can be seen, CIDR subnets can theoretically range from /1 to /31. However, in order to simplify top-level routing on the Internet, the vast majority of IP 'blocks' are allocated to major ISPs, who then allocate their addresses to their clients. Thus, most CIDR subnets range from /8 to /19.

For example, a network could have the address 192.40.0.0/13 – this indicates that the network's address for routing purposes is 192.40.0.0, and that it has been allocated 32 thousand IP addresses.

All modern Internet equipment recognises CIDR, but since there are still some legacy devices on the Internet they must also be able to understand the class-based system as well. When even this system starts to strain, which is not too far in the future, the IPv6 standard (explained in the *'Using the Internet'* chapter) is expected to take over, and provide for Internet routing in the future.

Hostnames and Domain names

IP addresses are useful, but they are difficult for humans to remember. For that reason, the Internet uses text-based *'domain names'* to represent IP addresses. This requires the use of a DNS (Domain Name Service) system to administrate the names. See the Internet chapter for details of the DNS system.

NetBIOS and IP

As explained earlier, NetBIOS was developed by IBM. However, many Microsoft networks use NetBEUI on top of NetBIOS, and quite often it is used alongside the IP protocol. NetBIOS names may use spaces and underscore characters not allowed in IP hostnames, and IP hostnames may be longer than the 15 characters allowed under NetBIOS. So, the NetBIOS name and the IP hostname of a machine may be different. In order to perform routing, the Microsoft server must perform *'name mapping'* between the NetBIOS name, and the IP address of the desired machine. This can be done using one of two methods – static or dynamic.

Static IP name mapping in NetBIOS involves the use of an ASCII text file called LMHOSTS, which simply lists NetBIOS names and the IP addresses they correspond to. In larger networks, however, this is both slow and time-consuming to maintain.

WINS (Windows Internet Naming Service) is a dynamic NetBIOS name mapping server application. Machines entering the network query the WINS server for an IP address, and the WINS server keeps track of their name and address until they leave the network again, in much the same way as DHCP dynamically allocates IP addresses.

Datacomms Applications

Worldwide data communications has opened a variety of new applications for industry, commerce and domestic users.   These can be broadly described as:

Remote Control	Remote monitoring, diagnostics, debugging, surveillance, process control.
File Transfer	The copying of files from a remote computer.
E-mail	The sending/receiving/storing/categorising of messages between users.
Information services	The availability of a mass of data, from test reports to train timetables.
Consumer applications	Multi-player games, home shopping, video-on-demand.

Access to these facilities can be provided in several ways.

Internal Organisation

Some of these services, such as remote control, file transfer and e-mail can be contained within an organisation. All activities are between the people and resources of that organisation.   The equipment used is exclusive to the organisation (e.g. internal networks, external leased private lines) and is not accessible by other users.

Home Bulletin Boards

Hundreds of bulletin board systems (BBS) are set up in a Sysop's (System Operator) home, with a telephone line attached to an auto-answer modem. These provide a wide range of files for downloading, e-mail, specialist groups and real-time chat. They are run on a hobby basis with no charge, or charges based on covering the cost of running the service. Bulletin boards have largely been overtaken by Internet provision.

Internet Providers

These services are run for profit and offer a greater range of facilities than the non-commercial bulletin boards. The company allows access to the resources on the payment of fees, which may include the following elements:

Standing charge	A monthly or quarterly charge, regardless of the amount of usage
Time charges	Charges based on each minute of connect time
Data charges	Charges for each Mb of data downloaded
Page charges	Charges for particular pages (e.g. financial information)

Free Internet access is provided by some companies, while the running costs may be recovered through advertising, support charges or commission from telephone companies.

Local Area Networks

Local Area Networks, usually shortened to *'LANs'*, is a constantly growing area of computing. In 1987, around a tenth of all PCs were connected to a network. Now, the large majority of all non-domestic PCs are attached to LANs.   This growth is due to their great contribution to office and industrial automation. The linking of PCs has developed from a *'good idea'* to a powerful aid to industrial and commercial efficiency. PC networks now carry out the tasks previously given to mainframe and mini systems.
The size of networks vary tremendously:
- Six linked computers in a typing pool.
- Hundreds of users in a medium company.
- Thousands of users at a university or large company.

There are many small networks in use, and quite a few very large systems. Around 75% of all commercial computers are networked.

What are LANS

In non-networked organisations, the sharing of information and inter-personal communication is via *people* - in a networked organisation this is achieved via *computers*.   There are a number of definitions of a LAN, some trying to state the likely maximum distance covered, or the maximum speed used.   In the ever-changing technology of computing, a more useful general definition might be:

"A local area network is a communication system used to interconnect all of an
organisation's computers, generally within a single building, or a single site".

In other words, a LAN would normally be owned and run within a single organisation, to link together the computers and peripherals found on a single location. This location could be a single office, or it could cover an entire commercial or production site.   In practice, the total distances covered range from a few yards (a typing pool) to over a mile (a shipyard or a university campus). Some networked systems allow much larger networks to operate as if they were all in the same building, though these are not truly LANs in the conventional sense.   Such networks are sometimes referred to as 'Virtual Area Networks' (or 'VANs', – but do not confuse this with Value Added Networks!). Though most computers on LANs are PCs, a LAN can encompass minicomputers, mainframes, super computers and even dumb terminals.

Why link users

Generally, 80% of an organisation's communications is from within that organisation.   Less than 5% of a company's entire written/verbal communications involves direct interaction with people outside the company.   So, most communication is within the organisation's own boundaries. Indeed, 90% of all information travels less than half a mile within the organisation - more than three-quarters travelling less than 600 ft.   So, much of an organisation's activities is based on the internal sharing of information.   In a normal paper-based company, one whose data is held on cards and stationary files, the files are held centrally.   Anyone wishing information can go to the appropriate cabinet and retrieve the desired data. However, in an office with many PCs, the information would be held on many different hard disks. Of course, the user of each PC could print out the machine's information and place it in the central filing area. The problems with this are:
- Wasted storage space and wasted effort.
- The information is never fully up-to-date.
- Only one person can look at the file at a time.

The filing cabinets can be dispensed with, if the information from PCs is transferred to floppy disks. This can solve some of the above problems but can cause new problems - those of data integrity.   For example, if a word-processed file is given to a colleague and both versions are modified, then neither is now complete. What is required is a central store of information, held in electronic form, which can be easily accessed from any PC in the system. Since most departments are using their own computers, it makes sense that communication between individuals or departments should ignore memos/telephone conversations/central filing cabinets and directly link the computers. The savings that can be made are potentially vast - it is estimated that around 1.4 trillion dollars is spent on staffing of offices in America alone. Even a relatively small saving from the increased productivity is a huge amount of money. The proportion of UK information-related jobs is over 40% and still increasing.

How

Each computer in the network has a special card installed, which allows the machines to be connected together with cables. Each machine has its own software to handle the network's activities. These computer stations are referred to as *'nodes'*.

In most cases there is a special computer called the *'server'* connected to the cable (large installations will use several servers), which has special software installed to allow it to act as the nerve centre of the system. The majority of servers are of the *'file server'* type. This kind of server has a set of large hard disks that hold all the application programs and data needed by the stations. The nodes send a message to the server, over the cable, requesting a copy of a particular program or item of data. The server responds by sending a copy of the program or data down the cable.

This is then held in the node's memory for use. In fact, the node sees the server disk as if it was the node's own local disk drive. All the usual file operations (such as copying etc) work as if the server hard disk was actually inside the node case. In this way, the activities of the network are invisible to the user.

Notes

- To ensure that all users have fair access to the network, the data travelling between machines on the media is split into small *'packets'*. These packets are interspersed on the cable with other users' packets.
- Very small LAN systems can use a similar method to the above, except that there is no special server for the system, as all the machines share each other's programs and data via the cable (this is known as a *'peer-to-peer'* system e.g. Microsoft Networks).
- For long distance communication within an organisation, or between organisations, wide area networks (WANs) are employed, either using the public network or private rented lines.
- LANs can be connected to WANs, if required. This allows users of a LAN in the Glasgow office to contact LAN users in the London office and exchange messages/data.
- LANs can also connect to other LANs; this is known as *'internetworking'*.

LANs and Multi-User Operating Systems

The acronym 'LAN' simply describes a method of connecting several devices within a relatively small area. This method can support a number of systems, such as the client/server system described above, the peer-to-peer system mentioned, or even a Multi-User Operating System, such as UNIX.

- A typical office LAN is a collection of stand-alone PCs that are all capable of independent processing. They share the same files and resources from the common server. However, each user will run a copy of an application in his/her own node's memory. A user can load an application from the server and spend all day creating data. Apart from the initial download of the application, there need be no further communication between the node and the server. At the end of the day, the data from the node memory may be sent down the cable to be stored in the server disk. At its busiest, every user is attempting to move files between the server and the nodes at the same time. At its quietest, the server is sitting unused, while all the individual nodes are carrying out activities in their own machines.
- An *'application server'*, in comparison, would connect to a number of terminals and carry out all the processing, for all the users, within the server. Each station would be given a small share of the server's CPU time on a *'time sharing'* basis, as explained in the Operating Systems chapter. However, since the user's waiting time between bursts of activity is also small, the station activity appears continuous. All the users' data is held and updated centrally; no data is held in the memory of individual stations. This system is ideal for situations where many users are doing essentially the same job (e.g. simultaneous sales producing simultaneous stock-control updates). Normally, the server is specially built for the job, with extra fast processing power. The normal PC operating system would not be up to handling the task and the more powerful (but less friendly) UNIX operating system is the most common operating system providing application services.

Advantages of a Local Area Network

The main advantages are listed below (although there is a degree of overlap between them):

Shared resources

Networks allow individual users to share the organisation's hardware and software resources.

Software

Any file on the server hard disk is available to every user.   Previously, this feature was often used by client systems to run applications directly from the file server's hard disk, saving disk space on client machines. Aside from database systems and application server networks, this practice has all but disappeared, due to the way Windows applications are installed. However, file servers are still an ideal way to store application installation routines, simplifying the installation of a new system and ensuring all newly installed applications are of the same software version.

Data

Similarly, any data in the organisation is available to every station in the entire building. This advantage has led to the development of LAN applications such as multi-user databases, where the input at any computer terminal updates the records for access by any other node on the system. Information is usually the most expensive item in an organisation, including its collection storage and maintenance. It varies regularly and to keep it up-to-date and available is both onerous and expensive. The distribution of the inputting and access to the database over the whole organisation provides the optimum use of the data.

Hardware

Peripherals are often a small part of cost of running a large computer system. However, specialised devices are often very expensive and are usually located in particular parts of the building. Such items include:

Plotters	Phototypesetters	Colour lasers
CD banks	High-speed data lines	Tape streamers

On a network, access to these devices would be available to all nodes, in any part of the building. This ensures the maximum use of these resources (e.g. most people only use a printer for less than 5% of the time they use a computer). It also allows connection of devices from different manufacturers. Finally, the hardware is easily expanded, with little disruption to the existing system.

Cost

There have been numerous attempts at '*thin client*' systems, and Network Computers in particular (explained in more detail later in this chapter). This concept is based on the idea that most of the expensive hardware can be at the server end, reducing the cost of the more numerous client systems. NCs can have smaller, or in some cases even non-existent hard disks, as well as slower processors and less memory, particularly if they are attached to an applications server. However, perhaps due to the constantly improving processing power of PCs for the same money, this concept is not as popular as it might be.

Efficiency

On a non-networked office, the failure of a machine meant that the programs and data in that machine could not be accessed until the machine was repaired.   This is not a problem on a computer network since, in the event of a node going down, a user can carry on his/her normal work from another node. Of course, if the server was to fail, that it is a very serious matter indeed, since it holds the entire programs/data for the whole company. This can be overcome by rigorous backup facilities and the use of backup ('*clustered*') servers that can take over in the event of a main server failure. This is an expensive solution - but cheap in comparison to potential losses from the lack of computer facilities. In general then, a network organisation is more efficient than a collection of individual PCs.

On top of the extra hardware efficiencies must be added all the benefits from file sharing and the flexible working possible on a network. There is now a growing trend of not only sharing resources but also sharing the actual processing power of the system. The collective computing power of the many individual PCs is awesome, if it can be properly tapped. If some of the processing tasks can be given to an idle CPU, then the overall processing is speeded up.

Speed

Ordinary telephone connections between computers, using modems, handle data at rates up to 56Kbps. ISDN can increase the rate to 64Kbps or 128Kbps, ADSL is typically 512Kbps to 8Mbps, and only the most expensive leased lines reach higher data rates.   In comparison, a LAN can work at

10Mbps, 100Mbps, 1Gbps, or even 10Gbps. Since a single character requires 8 bits to represent it, a 1Gbps service could theoretically transfer the equivalent of the entire contents of a CD-ROM in about a minute.

Communication

Most companies have resources that are not connected to the humble desktop PC. These include other networks, the company mainframe, and other branches over public or leased lines (e.g. Kilostream), etc. Connecting these resources to a network means that they are then all available to every station in the network.

Other communication benefits are:

- Outside resources - via modems, fax machines, ISDN lines, other leased lines and the public packet switched network. This gives access to vast on-line databases containing scientific, commercial, and industrial information.
- Electronic mail - The simplest version sends a message. The sender is informed if the destination station is not connected, otherwise a message appears on the destination screen. Mail servers will store a message if the destination is not connected and will deliver the message when the station does connect.
- FAX gateway - This is a dedicated PC with fax board(s). Cheaper than single-user boards. Most allow faxing via the existing e-mail system. These computer systems use the same standards as normal fax therefore they can communicate with any other fax machine in the world.

Security

With the exception of terminal based networks, the processing is carried out locally by the client. Despite this, control can easily be centralised in a LAN. The network supervisor has great control over who can enter the network, what directories are available to a particular user and what file activity is allowed.

Currency/Integrity

In non-networked companies, copies of the same data may reside in many different station hard disks. When an item of data is altered, the data on every machine has to be updated. This is time-consuming and error-prone. If one station is not updated, then the 'facts' depend on the machine interrogated. Networked data files avoid this problem entirely.

Disadvantages

Network systems, while providing distinct advantages, also create possible problems:

- An 'error' in one node may propagate through the network, as in the 1987 Stock Market crash.
- More costly to manage, in terms of time, management rules and technical skills.
- Always costs more to install and run than first thought.
- Less secure in at least one way - there are more access points to the same data.
- More complex software.
- Installation problems; a large LAN system takes at least 6 months to set up properly.
- Easy for viruses to propagate through.

LANs are now commonplace, from the home user who connects two PCs together to play networked computer games, through to the business that employs LANs in each of its office buildings, linked together via the Internet or a leased line.

Features of LANs

When viewing a LAN's characteristics, the following factors are a useful guide:

Simplicity

The system is relatively simple to configure and use. Working should be transparent to the novice user. Users can employ a large number of facilities with minimal training.

Expandability

New nodes can be added to the system with little hardware and software disruption.

Reliability

Reliability is of great importance in a network. For the server it is absolutely vital. LANs, once the initial settling down problems are overcome, are renowned for their reliability.

Integrity / Low Error Rate

WAN error rates can be up to 1 in 100,000. In comparison, LANs can be up to 1 in 100,000,000.

Connectivity

LAN systems have widely varied software and hardware, often even within the same organisation. Furthermore, any one LAN may need to be connected to another LAN, or to a WAN or the Internet. Many hardware and software incompatibilities exist. There are various standards that are intended to relieve this problem, from the OSI standard, to protocols such as TCP/IP and IPX, to cabling standards such as 10BaseT. Care must be taken in planning many aspects of a LAN, to provide for the capability to connect to other LANs if the need arises.

Speed

Important, as this is the potential system bottleneck. The measurement of data transfer speeds is difficult, since the actual speeds rarely correspond to the theoretical speeds. The basic measure of data transfer speed is *'bits per second'*, being the number of binary digits that can be transferred between one machine and another in a second. If it takes eight bits to represent each character and a 100Mbps system is in use, data should be transferred at the rate of 12.5 million characters per second. So, a 1MB file should theoretically be transferred between nodes in under a single second. However, the system has to transfer other information - such as the source address, the destination address, error-checking information etc., with each data packet. Also, the same medium has to be shared with other communicating nodes. Finally, in most LANs there is a huge loss in efficiency due to the way access to the transmission medium is regulated.

Networks are typically grouped together by their data transmission rates. Since these are constantly growing, such definitions are subject to change, and what is considered 'high speed' in one year or by one organisation may be considered 'medium speed' the following year or by another organisation. At the current time networks can generally be grouped as follows:

LOW SPEED-	Less than 4Mbps. Such systems are now a rarity, used only by legacy networks or in highly specialised cases such as high-interference areas.
MEDIUM SPEED-	Between 4Mbps and 16MBps. Typically used where the existing equipment will not support a high-speed network. These are also low-cost systems in relative terms.
HIGH SPEED-	Over 16Mbps, but typically 100Mbps. This is now the most common speed available for LANs, but is usually still considered 'high speed' because of the name given to the most common 100Mbps network – the so-called *'Fast Ethernet'*. The cable costs of high speed networks is higher, but over short distances such as a single building this is not usually prohibitive.
TOP SPEED-	1Gbps up to 10Gbps. Used for video, multimedia, or backbone links between LANs. Can be very expensive.

LAN Topologies

'Topology' refers to the way in which the nodes are connected to the media, to form the complete network system. In some cases there may be separate 'physical' and 'logical' topologies. The physical topology refers to how the cables physically connect the nodes together, while the logical topology refers to how data is transferred along the cables.

Today, the vast majority (well over 90%) of home and office LANs use a version of the Ethernet system, which uses a Bus topology. However, there are legacy systems and fiber optic networks that use a Ring topology; and many networks are physically wired as a Star topology even though they may logically be a Bus or Ring.

Bus

Invented by Xerox in the mid-70s, the Ethernet bus system is an international standard. The original configuration was a common data-carrying coaxial cable that wound its way through the different areas of the building and individual stations connected at any point on this cable. Current implement-ations use twisted pair cable instead of coaxial cable.

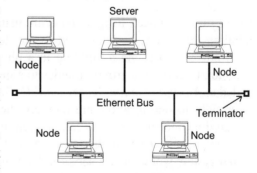

Each station has a *'tap'* on to the bus. Data from a node is transmitted in *'packets'* and each node on the network receives the transmission. Only a packet with the matching address is processed by the receiving node (i.e. station 17 only responds to packets with a destination address of 17). A failure in any one station affects only that station; the rest of the network functions normally.

Each end of an Ethernet coaxial cable had *'terminators'* fitted. These are special connectors that contain 50ohm resistors to absorb the signal thus preventing unwanted reflections of the transmission on the cable. If the signal were allowed to reach the end of a cable and reflect back down to the cable, it would interfere with the fresh signal and cause loss of data integrity. Ethernet can run on a wide variety of transmission media, both cabled and wireless systems. For example, early Ethernet ran on ThinNet or ThickNet coaxial cable at a speed of 10Mbps; modern Ethernet typically runs at 100Mbps on UTP or fibre optic cable.

Note that Ethernet is logically a bus; data placed on the bus is sent to all other nodes on the bus. However, a modern implementation of Ethernet is physically wired as a Star topology, with all of the nodes in a network segment attached to a central hub or switching hub. This is sometimes known as a *'star-wired bus'*.

Token-Ring

Ring topologies were slow to develop, until the *'token ring'* system was adopted by IBM. This system used to have around a third of the market but is now largely defunct as far as LANs are concerned, due largely to stagnation of IBM's Token Ring technology, and in particular its speed. It is aimed at the larger end of the market, since it covers great distances and allows large amounts of users, through linking of individual rings.

The ring is a closed loop, with nodes connected via repeating elements, known as *'ring interface units'*. These units boost the signal before passing it on, hence the greater distances covered. There is no central controller. All devices on the ring have equal status. The IBM Token Ring is a one-way system, with all data going clockwise, but the FDDI fibre optic system has dual rings, one going in either direction. Data circulates round the loop as a

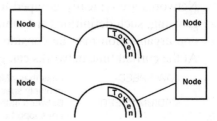

series of point-to-point links between adjacent nodes. The right to send data passes from one node to another in an ordered sequence determined by a token. The token grants permission to send data. A node with a message/data to send waits for an empty token to arrive. It then accepts the token, inserts the message/data into it and sends it on. This token passes the data in the form of a *'packet'*. The packet contains both the source and destination addresses, as well as the data itself. Each node checks the incoming packet, to see whether the destination code is its own. When the data arrives at the destination node, it is copied into a local buffer and the packet is marked to indicate its acceptance. The packet continues round the loop, returning to the sending node with the information that the data was received. Any node that is not the destination node passes the token on unaltered. Token Ring systems use coaxial, twisted pair or optic cable. Older versions operated at 4Mbps; newer versions run at 16Mbps; it can run at 100Mbps on fibre optic cable.

Advantages:

- Copes with heavy traffic better than bus systems (see later).
- Covers greater distances than bus systems, since the signal is re-generated at each node.

Disadvantages:

- If one repeater fails, the entire system goes down.

Like Ethernet, Token Ring systems are usually physically wired as a Star topology. Although the ring requires that nodes be connected in an electrical loop, the actual wiring need not be run round a building in a physical circle. In fact, it is very common to connect a group of nodes to a network via a *'concentrator'*, also called a *'Multiple Station Access Unit'* (MSAU). The wiring of these nodes is brought to one location and they are then connected together in a ring within the concentrator. As can be seen, the network topology is a ring but the cabling topology is that of a star. This system is therefore referred to by some as a *'star-wired ring'* topology. Of course, an actual system would have a server in the ring!

A variation on IBM's system is the *'Cambridge Ring'*, which circulates multiple tokens. This increases the throughput as nodes can use the first free circulating token.

Star

Star topology based networks constitute a tiny minority of the market, although most systems are physically wired as Star networks. The wiring to each node radiates from a single point - hence the *'star'* description. All traffic is switched and controlled by a central controller - the *'hub'*. A node wishing to transmit data to another node must make a request to the central controller, which will set up a dedicated path between the respective nodes. Once established, the nodes communicate as if they were on a dedicated point-to-point system.

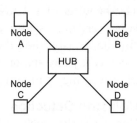

Advantages:
- Protocol may be simple - only the two stations involved in a link need to be involved.
- Because information transmission does not involve all parts of the network, the overall speed of the network may be higher than the maximum transmission rate allowed. For example, station A can transmit to station B, at the same time as station C transmits to station D.
- All data transmitted passes through the Central Hub, so the network can be easily monitored.
- Additional stations are easily and cheaply added, for the cost of the station plus the cabling.

Disadvantages:
- The initial cost of installing the network is high because the expensive Central Hub is required, even if the system only consists of a couple of nodes.
- Problems at the hub close the whole system down.

Note

Most networks using twisted pair cabling connect the computers to the network via hubs. These are different from the hubs mentioned in the star network. In a <u>star</u> network, the hub is the main server processor. Hubs in a <u>bus</u> system are only a means of station connection. The server is wired to the hub and stations connect to one of the hub's 8, 16 or more ports on the basis of one socket per UTP lead. Although wired like a star, it remains a bus system since all stations receive all transmissions. UTP hubs are mains operated, to supply the internal electronics used to balance the signals. A managed hub has more electronics to accept even more PCs and create sub-networks inside the hub. It programs connections between ports and can manage other hubs (e.g. for monitoring and diagnosis purposes).

Wireless

Wireless networks, since they have no cables, have no physical topology in a strict sense. Any system that is using the same wireless technology, the same frequency band, and the same low-level protocols is effectively a part of the network. As far as the 'topology' of a wireless network is concerned, any device in range of an Access Point (explained later) can gain access to a network. Therefore, the 'topology' basically consists of the Access Point (plus any LAN or WAN it is attached to) connected to all of the client nodes, and in that sense it is similar in some ways to a Star topology.

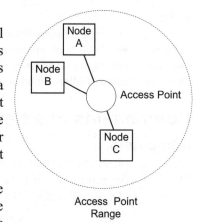

Access Point Range

Alternatively, wireless networks can utilise an 'ad-hoc' strategy. As the name suggests, ad-hoc networks connect whatever systems happen to be in range of one another at any time. Thus the topology varies depending on the location and number of nodes.

Wireless networks may be based on Ethernet using the 802.11 standard, although it is not really a bus topology. Other wireless networks may be based on Bluetooth, on proprietary protocols, or even irDA.

Advantages:
- No need to wire systems together, thus allowing mobility to users.

Disadvantages:
- Security systems must be implemented since the network is open to anyone with the appropriate equipment.
- Radio systems are more susceptible to interference, while infrared systems are limited to line of sight.

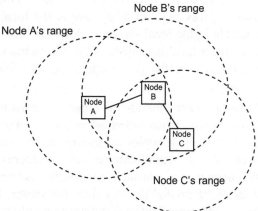

Example of a small ad-hoc network

LANs and collisions

The benefits of a LAN flow from the fact that many stations share the same transmission medium. However, this is also a potential source of problems. If two or more stations attempt to transmit simultaneously, then the signals interfere with each other. The result is that no useful intelligence is received by any station. This happening is known as a *'collision'*. All LANs, then, have to use a method of preventing or limiting this effect.

Collision Detection

Bus networks, such as Ethernet use this method. It is described as a Carrier Sense Multiple Access-Collision Detection system (CSMA-CD) and uses the principle of *'listen before speaking'*.   Here, a station that wishes to send a message will listen on the medium and only start to transmit when the medium is free. It is still possible, however, that two stations could sense the medium as free and begin to transmit simultaneously.   An Ethernet station, therefore, listens to its own broadcast, to see whether it is being interfered with. If a collision is detected, the stations immediately cease transmission. The stations then wait for a while before making another attempt at transmission. These are random delays, to prevent the same machines making their second attempt at the same time.

This improves overall throughput, since it greatly reduces wasted transmission time. However, where many stations are trying to use the medium (during peak spells) there will still be a great deal of wasted time, as the number of collisions will rise.   The rise in collisions and the subsequent decline in throughput develop at an alarming rate.

Collision Avoidance

Collision detection is an effective system and is the most common system. However, it has a serious flaw - the very act of detecting a collision means that the collision has already taken place!   The node can take measures to overcome the problem, but the damage (in terms of time wastage) has still occurred. An improved method would be to prevent the collision taking place in the first instance. By its design, a token-passing system can only have a single user packet on the system at any one time - therefore the possibility of a collision is nil.   This saves wasting time and increases throughput.

Note

As the traffic on a collision-detection system increases, the system performance deteriorates. Useful working is no more than 30-40% of the potential maximum of the system. The traffic on a token-passing system maintains a steady rate over a wide range of traffic demands. A 4Mbps token ring system can provide as much usable bandwidth as a 10Mbps Ethernet segment. A 16Mbps system can run at over 80% capacity without problems.

Components of a Network

Computers

At the simplest, the computers attached to a network can be normal run-of-the-mill PCs. The existing PCs in an organisation can have a network interface card fitted in one of the expansion sockets of the machine and a few files added to the hard disk; the result is a network node.

There is a growing market for LAN *'workstations'*. These can be specially built PCs with Ethernet hardware already built on to the board.   This opens up a new market for PCs.   Since most, or all, of the user's processing will take place at the local node, it would be efficient to have as fast a processor as possible in the local station.   However, since all, or most, of the user's data is held centrally, there is no need for a local hard disk. This allows manufacturers to offer high-performance machines for the LAN market, where the cost savings on the disk are spent on faster processors and/or higher resolution monitors.

Manufacturers provide a range of machines that are completely diskless - sometimes called a *'LANstation'*. This offers advantages as far as security is concerned. It greatly reduces the ability of users to purloin copies of data from the organisation, since it is impossible to download data from the network.   It also eliminates virus problems on the network, since users cannot bring in and use their favourite games.   In such systems, the station is fitted with a remote boot ROM system, which allows the node to be booted directly from the server; the node retrieves the files from the server that it needs to boot.   Also available are stations that only have a floppy drive fitted, to allow the transfer of data (where this is required), while retaining major cost benefits.

Network Computers

Network computers, NCs, are computer that have been designed as *'network centric computing'* systems. Earlier workstations were really cut-down PCs that were sold for connection to a network.   Network Computers have been specially designed as LAN stations. They are housed in cases about the size of this book and have no disks, no software and not even an operating system. A flash ROM in the NC contains a program that locates the server and downloads all its software from it. The server requires additional software to handle NCs.

Network Interface Cards

The network interface card (NIC) is a device to connect the computer on to the network cabling. In most cases, it is a card that fits into the expansion bus of the computer motherboard. In other cases, it is a separate unit that attaches to the computer's serial, parallel or PCMCIA port. External units are particularly useful for portable and notebook computers, where there is no space for internal expansion (these units are often referred to as *'lan adapters'*). Interface units come in a range of types, sizes and speeds. Performance of interface units is a key factor in network performance.

The interface card takes the data from the node computer and puts it into the appropriate format before sending it on the cable to another interface card. When the card receives data it puts it into a form that can be recognised by the computer. To achieve this, the card must perform many operations - e.g. buffers must be checked, requests must be acknowledged, sessions must be established, perhaps tokens are sent, collisions may be detected, etc.

The list of activities can be categorised thus:

- Host-card communications
- Packet formation
- Encoding/decoding
- Handshaking

- Buffering
- Parallel-serial conversion
- Cable access
- Transmission/reception

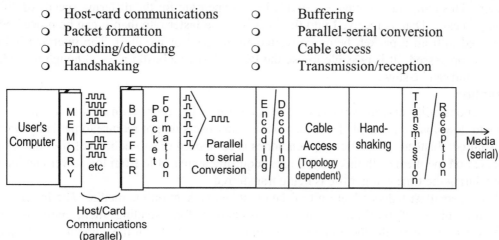

Host-Card Communications

The first need is to move data back and forward between the PC and the interface unit.
This can be achieved in three ways:

Direct Memory Access (DMA)

All Intel-based computers come with a DMA controller that handles the transfer of data from an input/output device to the PC's main memory, thereby relieving the PC's main processor. The controller informs the main CPU that it needs to perform DMA. The CPU then gives up control of the computer bus to the DMA controller. The DMA controller can then take data from the card and place it directly into memory. When all the data is in memory, the DMA controller passes control of the bus back to the computer CPU and informs it of the amount of data placed in memory. In a modern PCI system, the DMA is handled by a *'bus mastering'* system – see the Computer Architecture chapter for more details.

I/O Mapping

A common version is a *'memory-mapped'* system. The computer CPU allocates some of the 640k system memory to the interface unit (around 12k). Data is read from the card straight into this memory area. There are no extra instructions required to get data from the card, since it is already sitting in the computer memory. All that is required is the movement of data from one part of the memory to another, using standard memory movement instructions. The Western Digital token ring cards use the memory mapped method.

Shared Memory

This is similar to I/O mapping in that the CPU memory is shared with the card's processor. However, both the card and the CPU do their work on the data in the same area, eliminating any subsequent transfers.

Comparisons

- The shared Memory method is the fastest but is the least used for various cost and execution reasons.
- The DMA method allows the computer CPU to perform other tasks while it is transferring data (as long as these tasks don't involve memory access).
- I/O mapping takes up main memory and doesn't relieve the CPU from any work; although it is usually faster than the DMA method.

Bus Sizes

Interface cards were originally 8-bit but now have 16-bit or 32-bit connections to the computer data bus.   The wider the data bus, the more data can be transferred in a single operation - i.e. the wider bus cards have a faster performance.   The wider bus cards are, naturally, more expensive than more basic models.   The older 8-bit models are generally said to be *'NE1000 compatible'* with 16-bit cards being termed *'NE2000 compatible'* and 32-bit cards being *'NE3000 compatible'*.   A 16-bit MCA or ISA card handles around 3Mbps while a 32-bit PCI card handles 7Mbps.   This means that ISA cards can only handle up to 10Mbps systems, while PCI cards handle the faster 100Mbps/1Gbps systems.

Buffering

The interface units are mostly fitted with buffer chips to store data as it moves between the media and the computer.   This temporary storage is provided to compensate for the differing speeds of different parts of the process.   Data is received into the interface at a faster rate than it can be processed (e.g. being converted to/from a packet, being converted from serial or parallel). The interface holds the data while it is processed.   It is possible to use the PC's RAM as a buffer area, although this takes up main memory and can be slow.

Packet Formation

Part of the responsibility of a network is to give each user a fair proportion of media time.   So, if a user wishes to download a giant file from the server, other users do not require to patiently wait until this is transmitted.   Instead, all traffic between nodes is composed of subsections of files that can then be interspersed on the media.   In this way, a user requiring a small file from the server can have that need served during the time a larger file is being transferred.

A *'packet'* is the smallest independent unit of data that can be sent on the media.   The Interface Card has the responsibility of breaking a file into packets before sending them onto the media. Conversely, it will assemble the incoming packets into a coherent file for the computer.   The packet's size and layout are dependent on the network's access method.   Each packet has three sections:

- The header includes information on the packet's source and destination addresses.
- The data section contains the data being sent (e.g. word-processing or spreadsheet files, or program file).   The data section can be as large as 12k but is usually between 1k and 4k (e.g. Ethernet, has a data section size of 4kbytes).
- The trailer section contains information that is used for checking whether the data has arrived without any corruption.   The information is subjected to a mathematical calculation that aims to produce a unique number for each different packet (for the mathematically minded, a constant is derived from a polynomial expression).   This is called the *'cyclic redundancy check'* - CRC - and the resultant value is sent in the trailer section.   When a node receives the packet, the same calculation is applied to the information.   If it produces the same value as in the trailer, then no corruption has taken place - any corrupted data will result in a different calculated CRC value.

Parallel-Serial Conversion

The data that comes from the computer to the interface card is in parallel format. However, the media that carries the transmission is only capable of handling serial transmission.   The interface card has the task of converting the data from parallel to serial form.   Serial transmission is slower than parallel transmission, hence the need for buffering previously mentioned.

Encoding/Decoding

When data is made up into a packet and converted to serial format, it can be sent down the transmission medium, as a series of offs and ons.   At its simplest, the interface card could transmit a binary 1 as a positive voltage and a binary 0 as a negative voltage (i.e. NRZ as explained in the chapter on *'Data Communications'*).   At the other end, the card would translate the series of voltages into a stream of binary 0s and 1s.   However, most interface cards use a less error-prone method known as *'Manchester Coding'*.   This is a *'polar code'* - which means that it does not have positive and negative swings.   A logic high - i.e. a bit 1 - is represented by 0v and a logic low - i.e. bit 0 - is represented by -2.05v.   The serial data uses a *'50% duty cycle'* - which means that the time allocated to each bit of the data stream is divided into two periods. The first time period holds the actual bit representation. The second period provides a signal that is always the opposite of the first period. In this way, a constant change is guaranteed and this is used to ensure that the received signal is accurately synchronised, so that no false decoding occurs.

Media Access

The interface card also has the task of gaining access to the media (e.g. the cable).   This is no simple matter, since only one card can effectively communicate with the media at the one time.   Access is gained to the media in different ways, dependent on the network protocol in use (e.g. Ethernet, etc).

Handshaking

For successful transmission of a packet from one card to another, both cards have to be using the same parameters.   Typical parameters might be maximum packet size, buffer sizes, how many packets before an answer, acknowledge time-outs (how long to wait for an answer), etc.   Before the data packets are sent, the originating card transmits its parameters; the receiving card responds with its parameters.   The most sophisticated card then lowers its specification to match the other.

Transmission/Reception

The lowest level of card activity is to interface all this activity to the media itself.

The transmitting card translates the data stream into a signal of sufficient power to be successfully transmitted down the media.   At the other end, the receiving card has to take the varying signal and convert it back into the data stream for decoding, serial/parallel conversion and depacketing.

Modern network cards are 10Mbps, 100Mbps and 1000Mbps compatible.

Selecting a NIC

When connecting a system to the network, the computer must use a NIC.   However, selecting the appropriate NIC for a given system will depend on a number of factors, such as the following:

Internal card connection

Although all new cards are PCI based, older systems are still in use with ISA, EISA or other connectors.   As with every other type of card, the wider 32-bit bus of the PCI card can improve the speed of the network card, and older types of card should be replaced where practical.

Network media type

Every NIC allows access to at least one type of network, and some have multiple connectors to allow connection to more than one type of network, though only one at a time.   The various network media, such as Thin Ethernet and UTP, are discussed elsewhere, but they have a direct effect on NIC selection.   There is no point having a NIC with a Thin Ethernet connector, for example, if the network uses UTP.

Most NICs are internal cards.   However, some cards are available that have an AUI port (Auxiliary Unit Interface) – this does not connect directly to the network, but instead connects to an external *transceiver*. This transceiver (transmitter/receiver) deals with the physical connection to the media, thereby allowing the same network card to attach to any type of network, simply by replacing the transceiver.   There are transceivers available for almost every type of network, including fibre optic and wireless networks.   Transceivers are explained in more detail later in this chapter.

NIC Memory

Most NICs have a small area of onboard RAM used for buffering incoming and outgoing packets.   However, most of the data being transferred is held in system RAM, especially in an IO mapped or shared memory system. The amount of RAM only determines the number of incoming packets that can be buffered before overflow errors begin to occur. The NIC, like almost every type of other expansion card available, also has some ROM memory which is used for storing interface routines and so on.

A special type of ROM available in some NICs is a *'remote boot'* ROM. This chip contains routines which are called up by the computer system <u>before</u> trying to boot from the local hard disk. This allows the computer which has such a chip to communicate with a remote server, and use information stored there to boot up. This is useful in a Multi-User Operating System, or for remote administration purposes (see later).

Network Speed

Some network connections are capable of running at different speeds. For example, a UTP cable, depending on the wiring inside, may be capable of running at 10Mbps, 100Mbps, or 1Gbps. In order to utilise as much bandwidth as possible, the card should match the network speed. Some NICs are described as *'switching'* cards, able to run at either 10 or 100Mbps depending on the network it is attached to.

Configuring the NIC

Gone are the days when NICs were supplied with jumpers that had to be set physically to configure the card. Modern PC network cards are Plug-and-Play, needing little if any user configuration beyond installing the device driver. Of course, the system must still be configured with the correct protocols and client software – this is covered in the following pages.

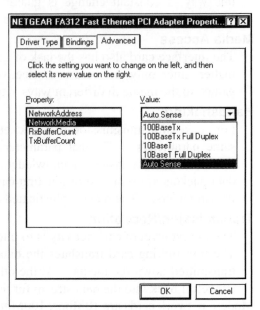

Every Network Operating System should include tools for configuring the network card. For example, in Windows systems, the user can click on the 'Properties' of the network card in the Network section of the Control Panel.

This will bring up a window similar to the one shown, where the user can configure various elements of the network card interface. This example shows setting the network media to use.

Node Software

To add a computer to a network, extra software is added to the computer, to allow it to interface with its new network card and to communicate with the network server.

The following software components have to be added:

Device drivers

This software controls input and output to and from the network card. The installation process varies. With Plug and Play cards, the device is automatically detected and the driver is chosen from Windows' own built-in list or from the NIC's installation disk. In this respect, installing the device driver is much the same as installing any other device driver, as explained in the 'Hardware Installation' chapter.

In Windows, these drivers are listed as Adapters, as can be seen by viewing the Network Neighbourhood Properties.

Sources of Device Drivers

As with any other hardware device, the NIC should come supplied with a driver disk, and may also have support built in to some versions of Windows. If not, the driver can be located in the same way as any other device driver, by searching on the Internet.

Network Protocols

The protocol is the method of communication between network clients and servers. It may be thought of as a language, in that only clients and servers who have the same protocol are able to understand each other. There are a variety of Protocols available, but by far the most common are TCP/IP that is widely used by Microsoft, and IPX/SPX which was created by Novell. Other protocols include Appletalk, SDLC or Token-ring.

There are a number of differences between protocols, but from a user's point of view the main difference is the software that uses those protocols. This software is called *'client software'* and is a separate component despite often being closely linked to the protocol. The exact procedure varies between Windows 95/98/ME and NT/2000/XP, but basically consists of a driver, similar in some respects to the device driver, being added.

In Windows 95/98/ME, installation of a network protocol is implemented through right-clicking on *'Network Neighborhood'*, then choosing the *'Properties'*, *'Add'* and *'Protocol'* options.   The appropriate protocol can then be chosen for installation.   When a protocol is installed in Windows, it is usually bound to all existing adapters, so some of these bindings may have to be removed if needed. The Network dialog can also be used to remove or configure any component, although in most cases the standard settings are acceptable.   The *'File and Print sharing'* allows the user to select to share either files, or printers, or both. If File and Printer Sharing is not installed then choosing to share files this way will install it automatically.

Each protocol has to be *'bound'* to a particular device driver. In other words the operating system has to be told which protocol(s) are to be used over which network device. In this way, it is possible to have more than one networking device. This is useful in Windows because Dial-Up Networking is considered a network device. For example, you could have an NE2000 network card, with IPX bound to it, in order to operate over a Novell network; and a modem, with Dial-Up Networking drivers, and TCP/IP bound to the DUN driver.

Installation of a network protocol, in DOS, is a matter of executing the appropriate TSR.   For example, an IPX network might require the running of the IPXODI.EXE file as well as the LSL.EXE file (although in most cases LSL is loaded before the device driver so that it can interrogate the device driver).

Open vs. proprietary protocols

TCP/IP was not developed by a single commercial organisation. As such, it is an 'open' protocol, allowing any software developer to build TCP/IP functionality into their software.   Proprietary protocols, on the other hand, are developed by a single organisation or group, and as such must be licensed before use. For example, the IPX/SPX protocols were developed by Novell, and remain their property.   As a result, the Windows operating system comes with IPX 'compatible' protocol drivers, rather than true IPX drivers. This can result in errors of compatibility between the various software components, increasing the installation and maintenance overheads of such a system. This is one of the reasons for the decline in IPX based and similar proprietary systems.

Client software

These are the programs, utilities and services that use the network protocols and the layers underneath.   Client software is not necessarily a driver file; anything that directly uses the network protocol is considered client software. For example, a Novell client (for logging in to NetWare networks) will use the IPX protocol, while the Microsoft client (for NT or other Microsoft server products) would use TCP/IP.   Internet packages, such as Telnet, FTP or Web Browsers, use TCP/IP. Other packages could use any one or more protocols.

In Windows, the client is considered a *'component'* just like the network adapter driver, and is part of Network Neighborhood properties.   It is installed in the same way as network protocols. Internet packages such as those listed above can directly utilise the network protocol without going through the Novell client (or similar client) but they are not considered as components.

However, note that after clicking *'Add'* from the *'Configuration'* tab, there is another option to install *'services'*.   A service in Windows is the inverse of client.   A client allows the PC access to a server's files or printers, while a service allows other PCs to access its files and printers. See peer-to-peer networks, later, for more details on file sharing.

LAN clients and the OSI Model

The various components required to connect to a LAN can be expressed in terms of the OSI model, as explained in the Data Communications chapter:

Layer 1 (Physical)	– Network cabling and connectors.
Layer 2 (Data Link)	– Network card and driver.
Layer 3 (Network)	– Network protocols such as SPX or IP.
Layer 4 (Transport)	– Network protocols such as IPX or TCP.
Layer 5 (Session)	– Client software such as the Novell client or Microsoft client.

There is usually considerable overlap in terms of OSI layers; for example some network protocols provide encryption or compression, which is technically part of OSI layer 6, the presentation layer.

Servers

Most networks are based on a *'client/server'* architecture, where one or more computers are at the operational heart of the system.   They handle all the other machines' disk storage requirements and may provide additional functions such as serving printer access, database access, web pages or so on. These central machines are called the *'servers'* or *'dedicated servers'*.   A *'non-dedicated server'* is a machine that carries out the functions of a file server, while also being able to be used as normal PC machine. This is often referred to as a *'peer to peer'* network. It is OK in small systems but would slow things down on a larger system, since the processor would have to share its time between network activities and the activities of the user at the server machine.

There are two types of server –

Utility servers -

These servers carry out the routine roles or the specialist roles in the network, where required (in a small organisation there may be no need of specialist utility servers).
Examples of this type are:

Standard :   file servers, print servers.
Specialist :   fax, mail, Internet and CD servers, modem pool servers,
                   micro-to-mainframe gateways.

Application servers -

These servers perform computational tasks for network users (see client/server software later)
Large systems will have a number of servers on the one network system.

Characteristics of servers

In the earliest days of networking, manufacturers marketed their LAN servers as specially made machines.   These were overpriced and users realised that a standard PC could be used as a server, if it was powerful and reliable enough.   Consequently, high-performance PCs now capture much of the server sales market.   Dedicated servers are still produced.   They are dedicated boxes of various shapes and sizes, often with no monitor or keyboard. Since most network activities can be organised from any node, the lack of add-ons is not a disadvantage. In fact, it is claimed as an advantage, as it provides an extra level of security.   Some of the advertised benefits of dedicated servers over PCs are hype. However, dedicated servers can have distinct advantages.

The following criteria may act as a yardstick for choosing a server:

Speed

The raw processing speed of the server CPU may not be vitally important as it may appear at first glance. Buying the fastest multiple processor server may not produce a very significant improvement over a machine with a slower, older chip.   This is because the speed of the processor is generally less a bottleneck than the speed of the server's disk drives and NICs.

Consider the following:

- A file server activity does not require much computing time, in comparison to the disk access time.
- If the transmission media (i.e. NICs, cable) is unable to transfer the data quickly, then there is no benefit in having the server process that data at a vastly faster rate.
- Consequently, faster computers do not necessarily produce faster server throughput.

The above is not true in all cases. The CPU speed is important in the following situations:
- Where the server acts as an application server, such as an SQL server.   In this case, the server has to perform considerable computational tasks in addition to a normal server role.
- Where the server Interface Card is not of the *'bus master'* type.   Here, the NIC circuitry does not relieve the server CPU of data transfer tasks - i.e. biggest part of server's work.
- Some PCs use a Digital Signal processing chip or a virtual peripheral, which means the CPU ends up doing many of the tasks mentioned earlier (like packet formation and parallel to serial conversion).
- If the machine is connected to two networks, (see below) it may be used to provide routing/bridging or packet filtering services between them using software.

Multi-Processing

Many servers are fitted with two processors and some include the option to fit further CPUs. This is particularly useful in client/server applications (see later).

The most common form of multi-processing is *Symmetric Multi-Processing* (SMP).   This involves multiple processors, all of which are running the same copy of the operating system and accessing the same memory and IO bus. Tasks are allocated to whatever processor may be free at the time, making the workload distribution reasonably symmetrical amongst the CPUs.   This system, however, is not 'scalable'. In other words, having 4 CPUs, for example, will fall short of having 4 times the processing speed.

In a *Massively Parallel Processing* (MPP) system, however, each CPU has its own copy of the operating system in memory. This has obvious memory overheads as well as maintenance requirements, but means that the system has much better scalability, providing almost the same speed increase with every processor added.

Bus Size

As explained in the section on NICs, the data bus size affects the throughput of any system, especially the server. As a result, servers were the first to use MCA and EISA systems, though now all servers use PCI. However, servers use the 64-bit version of PCI more often than it is found in a non-server system. The 'bus mastering' aspect of PCI is particularly useful in servers, which may have multiple NICs, or even multiple processors.

Memory

The memory of the server is used for a wide range of caching, buffering and other activities. The minimum RAM for reasonable performance is around 256MB. The system will run with less memory but the performance will degrade (e.g. a small disk cache allocation means more disk accesses, a small buffer allocation may result in lost packets).   The system may require more memory if it is carrying out heavy processing tasks such as handling databases.   Servers also generally use some of the fastest memory available, such as RAMBUS modules or high-speed DDR memory.

Storage

The server disk drive(s) store all application programs and data for the whole organisation.   The operating system alone might consume 2GB of disk space. This demands that the drives are the largest, fastest and most reliable that money can buy.

Disk Speed

While high-speed IDE drives are commonplace in PCs and low-end servers, in more sophisticated servers (and some high-spec workstations) SCSI (Small Computer Systems Interface) is preferred, and in high-end servers Fibre Channel is becoming popular. Current SCSI card data transfer rates are quoted by manufacturers as being 320MB/s.   However, even the fastest SCSI drives currently available cannot deliver a sustained data rate close to the interface's speed.   Huge data rates are delivered, but only for a few thousandths of a second, with the help of the drive's on board memory buffers. Where the high data rate of SCSI cards is more useful is in attaching a large number of drives, perhaps using RAID.

Disk Fault Tolerance

Due to the vital role of data in any organisation, it is not acceptable to have only a single copy on a single server drive.   Although organisations have rigorous and systematic backup procedures, this is insufficient for situations where data is rapidly changing. To ensure that data is always available, networks make use of multiple storage techniques such as disk shadowing and disk mirroring.   The objective is to keep two copies of the data on different drives, in case one copy is corrupted. Of course, there is still a problem if the two drives are in the same server - and that server breaks down!   In *'mission critical'* applications (those where it is essential that processing must continue), users employ a system of *'server mirroring'* or *'server clustering'*. Here, if a server goes down, a duplicate server kicks in immediately, with the same applications and data.   So, every update to the current server is also made to the shadow server.

Raid Technology

In large installations with multiple disk drives, access can be speeded up with a process known as *'striping'*.   The data is written/read in parallel fashion over different drives.   An extension of this principle is *'RAID'* technology.

This is a *'Redundant Array of Inexpensive (or Independent) Disks'* and uses the following features:
- A set of disks is configured to perform like a single large drive.
- Redundancy is built in; extra disks are used, not to store data, but to protect the data.
- Disks are *'hot swappable'*; they can be removed and replaced while the network remains operational; the network carries on without loss of data.

The table shows the levels of protection that are available.

RAID Level	Method	Advantages	Disadvantages
0	Basic disk striping	Improves performance	No protection. Any disk failing collapses the system.
1	Disks are mirrored	Improves performance. Easily implemented.	Expensive as it requires all data disks to be duplicated (mirrored).
0+1	Data striping on mirrored drives	Improves performance. High level of data protection.	Expense. Slower writes.
2	2 or 3 check disks for every 4 data disks.	Improves performance. High level of data protection.	Expensive. Rarely implemented.
3	One additional disk stores parity bits.	Common, low-cost choice, requiring only one additional disk.	Slows when many disk write requests are implemented.
4	One additional disk stores ECC data.	Improves performance. Can handle multiple read requests.	Only handles one write operation at a time.
5	ECC data spread over all array's disks	Can handle read and write requests simultaneously.	Slow to rebuild after a disk crash.
6	ECC data written to two separate disks.	Good data security, as two disks can fail and data can be rebuilt.	Slower performance than Level 5.

Reliability

Possibly the most important of all factors when purchasing a server is the issue of reliability. A reliable network of average speed is much more productive than a faster system that is always breaking down.

Influencing factors are:
- Whether servers have SETUP and diagnostics built in.   Some systems are configured to dial a service engineer as soon as a fault occurs.
- The use of an *'Uninterrupted Power Supply'* - (UPS).   This smoothes out mains spikes and fluctuations and - in the event of a complete power failure - provides a temporary supply to allow the data to be saved to disk.   Some servers have a built-in UPS.
- The use of a standby CPU, in case the main chip fails.   This is a bit extreme but might be regarded as important in mission-critical work.
- The replacement of NICs, graphics cards and disk controllers with built-in controllers and interfaces on the server main printed circuit board (PCB).   This provides an increased MTBF rate.   In other words, this area of the system does not break down so often!   It also frees up valuable expansion slots.

Quality of Service

The *'Quality of Service'* of any given server is a measure of the continuity of data transmission. Certain applications, such as streaming audio and video, require a guaranteed minimum bandwidth in order to avoid losing frames or stalling the streamed content. A server that has the required level of QoS can be specified to provide satisfactory bandwidth. However, this is largely a matter of the type of network connection used. For intranets within a single building, QoS can be guaranteed simply by using a high-speed network such as Gigabit Ethernet or Fibre optics. In a public network such as the Internet, however, transmission speeds are never guaranteed and QoS becomes difficult to measure.

Network Storage

One of the most common uses of a network server is as a file server – keeping data and/or program files on the server's hard disk for client nodes to access. However, this is no longer the only model of network storage available. Recently, the concept of a 'Storage Area Network' or '*SAN*' has been growing in popularity. Essentially a SAN consists of a high-speed network and server, typically using Fibre Channel, which serves files to clients. SANs often work alongside the normal, lower-speed network for high-bandwidth needs such as multimedia streaming or editing. There have been comments that the name SAN may become meaningless when ordinary network speeds grow to accommodate high-bandwidth needs.

Another approach to network storage is the NAS (Network Attached Storage) device. As the name suggests, a NAS device is simply a storage medium that is available through the local network. A NAS device bears many similarities to a file server, although it is in fact a client node, administered by the main server on the network, which just happens to be serving files to all other users. The benefit of NAS is the ability to attach or detach NAS serving nodes while the network is still fully operational. This would not be the case if the main server were also the file server.

Both SAN and NAS technology can prove expensive however, and are mainly in use in large corporate LANs, where they typically incorporate disk mirroring, archiving, RAID, and other services.

Network Operating Systems

The chapter on Operating Systems explained in depth the functions of an OS. A Network Operating System, or NOS, is a system that must provide functions relating to the operation of the network. Examples of NOS systems include Windows 2000 and XP, Novell, Unix and others. In most cases a NOS is an Operating System itself, but one which includes a set of programs dealing with network functionality.

As such, the Network Operating System provides additional network related functions such as the following:

- Resource sharing. The NOS must handle the sharing of files, devices, or applications to other computers.
- User management. A NOS must maintain a list of valid usernames and passwords, and keep track of which users are allowed to access which resources. In general, a NOS will not allow access to any resources unless the user is properly logged in.
- Network management. In all but the simplest networks, the NOS is used to manage network components, such as bridges and routers, as well as resolve any network addressing conflicts. Protocols such as SNMP (Simple Network Management Protocol) are used in this activity, which can also be an aid to troubleshooting. Network management may also include allocation of device addresses, such as in a system using DHCP.

Generally, the majority of NOS software runs on the server, but parts of it are handled by individual client machines as well.

Differences between stand-alone and Network Operating Systems

As noted above, the main difference between a stand-alone OS and a NOS is that the NOS must provide network related functions. In a typical server, the NOS still performs all the functions of a normal Operating System. It must control all the hardware in the server, and provide access to software and data on the server. However, it must allow access to these items only where authorisation is granted to do so. Windows Terminal Server or UNIX are examples of NOSes which are also Multi-User Operating Systems. In such a case, the NOS must provide access to the server's memory, and allow remote users to execute programs on the server's processor, again while making sure the user is authorised to do so. However, not all NOSes are Multi-User Operating Systems; Windows XP for example can share devices such as printers as well as file space, but does not normally execute programs for remote users.

NOS server software

The Operating System installed on a dedicated server quite often has NOS functions built in. Novell, Unix, Windows 2000 and XP Professional, for example, are all intended for use on servers, and come with network-related software functions. NOS server software will include functions for resource sharing, but focuses mainly on user and network management.

NOS requirements

The hardware requirements for server NOS software are usually quite high in comparison to standalone or network client systems. Windows 2000, for example, recommends at least 256MB of RAM, and Novell NetWare 6.5 recommends 512MB of RAM.

The server PC will normally be optimised for the NOS, using technology such as multiple processors, Uninterruptable Power Supplies, and heavy-duty cooling systems if necessary, as well as having a faster processor, more memory and more hard disk space than the typical client PC.

In addition to the files that are being shared, the NOS itself takes up some space on the hard disk. Quite often, a NOS will be installed on a separate partition from the shared files. This makes administration of the system easier and more logical. Windows 2000, for example, recommends a 2GB hard disk minimum, while NetWare 6.5 uses a 200MB Partition for the NOS and recommends at least 4GB of space for shared files.

Finally, the NOS may need peripherals for sharing over the network. In some cases printers and other shared devices are attached directly to a server (e.g. a print server). In other cases, the devices have their own connection to the network, but are still managed by the server's NOS.

With the current level of PC technology, almost any new PC can be used as a rudimentary server that is probably sufficient for most small businesses. Only when a large number of users is to be served does a specialised, high-specification server become an attractive option.

NOS client software

As explained, the NOS need not solely consist of the server OS. Non-dedicated servers can share resources, for example all current versions of Windows can share files and printers. And of course, every PC connected to the network must have a network address and be involved in transmitting and receiving data. In a sense, even Windows 95 can therefore be considered a very basic NOS.

Nonetheless, the major portion of the NOS resides on the server. Other than the potential for remote administration as explained later, network client NOS systems normally come with two specific pieces of software, named 'redirectors' and 'designators'. Both of these pieces of software are to do with accessing shared resources.

A Redirector is a piece of software that intercepts attempts to access a shared resource, and redirects the access information to the remote resource. For example, a Windows user can 'capture' a remote printer such as \\MIS\LASER, and assign it to a local printer port such as LPT2. The redirector must then intercept all calls to LPT2 and redirect them to the MIS Laser printer.

A Designator is a similar device, but dealing with shared folders. A Windows user can 'map' a drive letter, such as the F: drive, to a remote hard disk such as \\ACCOUNTS\SHARED, for example. The Designator then intercepts attempts to access the F: drive, and effectively substitutes the network address for the drive letter. For example, if the same user wished to create a file called 'Notes.doc' on this F: drive, the Designator would turn F:\Notes.doc into \\ACCOUNTS\SHARED\Notes.doc, and pass it on to the appropriate network drive.

Redirectors and Designators therefore work at the Presentation layer of the OSI model.

Using NOS client software

The first thing an NOS must do is connect to the network. This involves installing the NIC, drivers, protocols and so on; see the 'Installing Microsoft Networks' section for an example. In a client/server system, the client system will also have to be configured with server details.

One reason for this is that the user will be required to 'log in' (or 'log on') in order to use the system. Although Windows can supply a password system, it is not secure and not recommended for a business network. Instead, the main server (in Windows systems referred to as the 'primary domain controller') can maintain a secure password list, and client systems will ask the user for a username and password, verifying it from the server before allowing the user to even use the local system.

The client software should allow the user to browse the network. For example Windows Explorer allows access to Network Neighbourhood, which includes all the domains and workgroups visible to the user.

The client NOS should also allow access to shared resources, regardless of where those resources are located. In Windows systems, this is done by mapping network drives, or by capturing network printers. Windows Explorer can perform this function by clicking Tools / Map Network Drive, or by right-clicking on a network printer and choosing 'Capture Printer Port'.

NOS System compatibility

The intention of a network is to connect computers in order to share information and resources. This can only be achieved, however, if all the networking software is compatible. Whether using a peer-to-peer or client-server network, two systems can only communicate if they share the same protocols.

In a purely Windows-based system this is not a problem, as all systems will be equipped with the same network software. If, on the other hand, different systems are connected to the network (such as a Novell or UNIX server, and Macintosh clients) and are expected to work with each other, then the network manager must ensure that compatible software is used.

Using Windows clients with a Novell server, for example, will require installing the '*Novell Netware*' client and the '*IPX/SPX*' protocol component in Network Neighbourhood, while communicating with a UNIX box might require the TCP/IP protocol and Telnet software. Other systems may well require proprietary connection protocols and software.

Selecting a NOS

There are a wide variety of Network Operating Systems available, each of which have their own strengths and weaknesses. There is of course no single optimum solution for all networks, so network managers must select a NOS based on the size and type of systems already in use, any existing infrastructure, and what is needed from the network.

However, it is not as simple as simply selecting the server software. The network clients must have software to match, which may mean upgrading the clients' operating systems, or simply installing new software components. Additionally, network hardware must be specified.

The Development Life Cycle

Like many aspects of computing, selecting, planning, and installing a NOS should go through a well-documented process known as the development life cycle. This consists of four steps: User Requirements; Feasibility Study; Project Design; and Project Implementation.

User requirements

Just as with the selection of a single system, the process must begin with finding out what is needed of the network system. How much network traffic is expected? How critical are reliability, security, and speed concerns? What must the server provide? How many users are to be managed? What is the existing equipment and infrastructure? All of this information will be needed to make the correct choice.

Feasibility Study

At this stage, those involved with planning the network must weigh up their options. The NOS itself may only be part of the study; cabling, interfacing, and client upgrading might also be concerns, all of which must be weighed against the cost of the system, both in financial terms and in terms of implementation time. In fact, if the feasibility study finds that it is not worthwhile to implement a network, then it should not be installed at all – not every workplace will gain enough benefits from a network to outweigh the upheaval and cost of installing it.

Project Design

This stage involves the actual planning of the network. Now that the NOS has been decided upon, proposals can be made as to the implementation of the system. Structured cabling is discussed later in this chapter, if a well-laid out cable structure is required. The design stage must also address issues of network management, deciding where resources should be located (both physically and on the network) as well as user management and security.

Project Implementation

The final stage is the actual installation of the NOS. This might also involve installing network cabling, and existing client systems may need software upgrades to access the network fully.

Types of NOS available

The NOS consists both of software on the server and on client systems. The following are the most common examples of network systems:

Windows NT, 2000 or XP: These systems are relatively simple to administer, and are well supported as application servers (such as web servers, or database servers). The reliability of Windows has been compared unfavourably to some of the more well-established NOS systems, however.

Novell Netware: Netware comes with the NDS (Netware Directory Services) system that can be used to administer network resources centrally. This makes it ideal for a large to very large network including many shared resources. Earlier versions of Netware have been poor at application server work, however, and although this has changed they are still more commonly used as file servers and for network management.

Linux: Many versions of Unix are available, but Linux is the most common. It is probably the most reliable and secure network system available, which accounts for its longevity in the face of fierce competition from Novell and Microsoft. It is also very well supported as an application server, being an inherently multi-user system in all aspects.   Linux software is relatively inexpensive, with many components being freeware.

AppleTalk: This is the Apple Mac networking standard, but there is software available for PCs to interface with such a system. Like most Mac systems, Appletalk is very easy to learn and use.

Mainframe based networks: A number of network architectures have appeared, intended for connecting terminals to mainframe computers. With the decline in mainframe based systems, these have become marginalised, but are still in use in very large and/or very old networks. Examples include IBM's Systems Network Architecture (which has since been updated to include peer to peer networking), and Digital's DECNet. Such systems tend to be complex, but secure.

Installing the NOS

As already mentioned, modern server operating systems include NOS functions as standard. See the 'Configuring Windows' chapter for general details on installing Windows. However, installation on a server system has some important differences from installing a Windows system on a stand-alone system:

- File system. As previously mentioned, some server systems use a separate partition for the NOS and for the shared files, necessitating partitioning of the hard disk before or during installation. Also, if more than one file system is supported, the network manager must select the appropriate system. Specifically, Windows servers commonly support both NTFS and FAT filing systems – NTFS provides a degree of in-built security and is recommended for servers unless there are other overriding factors. All of this must be decided on before formatting the disk to prepare for installation.

- Licensing mode. Most NOS systems include software for keeping track of licenses. By tracking users logged in to the system, the NOS can ensure that licensing agreements are not exceeded. Application servers often take this further, keeping track of licenses for server applications in use. Of course, if this function is not provided, licenses must still be adhered to for legal reasons. See the Software & Data chapter for details of license agreements.

- Network structure. The Feasibility Study should have determined the structure of the network if there is no existing infrastructure. In Windows, there are two main groupings of network systems – workgroups and domains. A '*workgroup*' is a loose collection of peer systems, while a '*domain*' is a group of systems administered by the Primary Domain Controller (PDC). The grouping of users into domains must be planned, and the correct PDC server selected if more than one is available.

- Server Role. This must be selected while installing the server NOS. In a Windows system, a server may be a Primary Domain Controller, a Backup Domain Controller, or a stand-alone server.   Most commercial networks require security, and so domains should be used rather than workgroups, allowing the PDC to authenticate users before they are allowed to use a networked computer.

- Administrator privileges. At installation, there must be at least one account that has the ability to administrate the entire domain or server. In Windows systems this account defaults to the name '*administrator*' while in other systems it may be called by other names.

- Network services. Many servers are simply file servers, allowing remote users to access data. Other servers provide shared printers or other resources, while application servers run programs for users. This must be set up on the server appropriately.

Selecting a computer ID is important for a server system, especially the server that performs password authentication – if the server name changes, all the clients must be updated to reflect the changes! Similarly, the protocols installed on the server must match the clients, or they will not be able to communicate.

Remote administration

A true NOS will provide software to perform all of the network administration functions. However, in many cases, it is possible to access these functions without being present at the server itself. '*Remote Management*' software can be used to fulfil these roles from client machines. The network manager simply logs in using an account with the appropriate privileges, runs the remote management software, and controls the network from his current location. In fact, some NOS systems even provide a '*Remote Terminal*', where the network manager will be presented with a window showing the contents of the server's screen, and can interact with it as if he were typing at the keyboard of the actual server.

This means that a client system will run a program to perform management functions, and communicate management information with the server which will actually carry out the work. Often, the remote management software will reside in the server's shared file space, in a drive or folder to which only the network management personnel have authorised access. When the network manager runs the software, it is loaded from the server, and runs on the local system, but the changes are made to the server, since it actually administrates the system.

Remote installation

Some NOS systems provide even more advanced functions for system administration, allowing the server to control the installation of client operating systems remotely. A system that has a remote boot NIC (as explained in the earlier section on interface cards) can boot from the server, and install the system from there. This can be done one of two ways.

The first method is to install the client OS from a copy of the installation files located on the server.

The second method is to store a mirror image of a freshly installed system on a separate partition on the server, and copy this straight onto client machines that are to be installed. Windows 2000 and XP servers support both of these methods using a system called the Remote Installation Service (RIS).

Peer-to-peer LANs

Most medium and large systems use a dedicated server to control the network. There is a trend, in smaller organisation of say less than 10 users, to adopt a network system that has no main server. Instead, all the facilities of a node (i.e. local disk, local printer, etc.) are available to all others on the network. This is known as '*peer-to-peer*' working since there is no master PC. It is simple to implement but provides fewer facilities than a full network operating system. It is also slower, since all PCs also carry out some server activities. It is popular with hobbyists with several computers at home, for resource sharing or for playing multi-player games. Perhaps the most widely used peer-to-peer system is Microsoft Networking.

Installing Microsoft networks

The chapter on "*Operating Systems*" explains how to make use of Microsoft Networking once it is installed. The actual installation procedure is normally quite simple. It involves the following steps:

Cabling.

This is described in more detail elsewhere in this chapter. However, it is worth mentioning that for very simple 10BaseT networks involving just two peer computers, there is no need for a hub. A crossover cable can link the two cables directly – see later in this chapter for a description of a crossover cable.

Attaching.

Fitting the network card, and installing the device driver (covered in the hardware installation chapter).

Configuring.

This entails the installation and configuration of relevant software. This includes the network card driver, communication protocol, client software and network services. In the general case, these will be TCP/IP for the protocol, and Client for Microsoft Networks. At the user's discretion, the service '*File and Printer sharing for Microsoft Networks*' can be installed for additional functionality. When a network card driver is installed, or when Windows is installed on a system that already has a network card installed, TCP/IP and Client for Microsoft Networks will be installed by default. See the '*Network software*' section earlier in this chapter, if the protocol or client has to be changed, or if File and Printer sharing services are to be installed. Each individual component will come with some default configuration settings, and in some small networks these may be acceptable. However in most office networks some further configuration of each device will be required, and the Identification settings will also need to be configured.

TCP/IP configuration

The TCP/IP configuration dialog is explained in detail in the *'Data Communications'* chapter under *'IP address allocation'*. Which IP address is assigned is important, since a machine that tries to take up an IP address that is already in use will not be able to access the network.

If a LAN is attached to the Internet, it is also important to ensure that you only use the IP addresses that your organisation has been allocated. On a local network that is not attached to the Internet, any IP addresses can be used. However, there is a range of IP addresses that are free for use. These addresses can be used on a LAN, while having a separate IP address as far as the Internet is concerned. This allows the machines to treat the LAN and Internet totally separately, which can make many operations such as security configuration simpler. These *'reserved addresses'* come in the three main IP categories:

> Class A: 10.0.0.1 to 20.255.255.254
> Class B: 172.16.0.1 to 172.32.255.254
> Class C: 192.168.0.1 to 196.168.255.254

Any network node, be it a computer, router, printer or other device, may be allocated any of these IP addresses for internal use without causing any problems with Internet access. This may be particularly useful on a home network, where one machine may have an Internet connection that it wishes to share. Windows will often access a workgroup-based LAN without proper IP configuration but for such activities as Internet connection sharing the IP should be specified.

Other tabs on the TCP/IP configuration dialog, such as WINS, Gateway, DNS and NetBIOS, are generally only used when the LAN as a whole is designed to utilise these functions.

Client for Microsoft Networks configuration

The diagram opposite shows the configuration dialog box for the Client for Microsoft Windows. It is a simple dialog, which allows the user to connect to a Windows NT domain as a client in a client/server network, rather than being part of a workgroup in a peer-to-peer network as is the default.

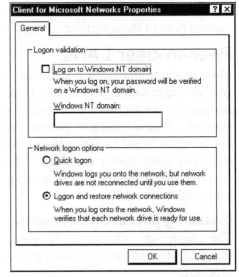

Windows also 'remembers' network drives that are mapped onto in Explorer, unless it is told not to during the mapping process. The *'Quick logon'* simply assumes that these mappings are available, while the full logon will carry out the full re-mapping process.

Identification configuration

Windows also has to be configured to attach to a Microsoft Network properly. In *Network Neighborhood / Properties*, the *'Identification'* tab allows the user to change the computer's details on the network. These details are normally entered as the machine is installed, but if installing a new network onto machines or changing the location or user of a machine, this tab allows the PC to be configured on the network.

Each Windows installation contains three pieces of network information: Computer name, Workgroup and Computer Description. The name and description are purely for identification purposes on the network, and Windows will give error messages if the Computer Name is the same as another machine's name in the same workgroup.

The Workgroup name tells Windows which Microsoft Workgroup the machine is part of. Machines within the same workgroup will be able to 'see' each other without having to navigate through layers of Network Neighborhood.

The '*Access Control*' tab allows the machine to be set up to share resources in one of two ways. The default is to use share-level access control, as described below. This can be changed to user-level access control, whereby a list of network users and groups is obtained, normally from a server, and access to shared resources can be controlled depending on specific usernames and groups.

File and printer sharing

While Microsoft Networking is a widely used method of connecting to NT servers, it is also useful in peer-to-peer networks in allowing file and printer sharing. File sharing through Microsoft Networking is not as flexible or as powerful as using a file server, but it is a relatively inexpensive method of networking.

Once Microsoft Networking and File and Printer Sharing drivers are both installed, the user may right-click on any drive, folder, or printer and select the '*Sharing*' option to set up sharing settings for that item. This will bring up a dialog similar to the one shown.

From here the user can control access to his local hard drive, folder or printer. The '*Share Name*' is the name displayed in Explorer on other machines when they view your machine's shared resources. '*Comment*' is just a description that is displayed when these resources are viewed with '*Details*' visible in Explorer.

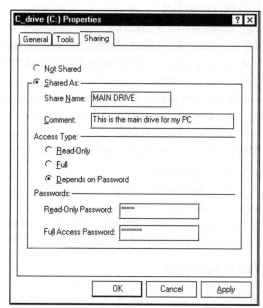

The '*Access Type*' determines how others may access the resource. Read-Only means that only read access is ever allowed, (optionally requiring a password) while '*Full*' means that only full access is ever allowed. (Again with an optional password)

The '*Depends on password*' option allows the user to set a password that will allow either type of access. Passwords may be up to 8 characters in length, and may be blank, but if the type of access depends on the password then the Full and Read-Only passwords must be different for obvious reasons.

The Sharing dialog for a printer is similar, but there are no access types, because printers are an output device only. A password may still be set for printer access.

Print servers

Many users are connected to a particular printer on the network. It is likely that several stations will send text files to the printer over the same period. A printer server will maintain a queue of such files. This appears to be similar to the PRINT command in MS-DOS in that 'spooling' is taking place. In fact, the print server handles the activity differently from MS-DOS. Each incoming print file is copied on to the disk of the print server. The file is then placed in the print queue to wait its turn. When the file is printed, it is deleted from the print server disk. It is also possible, in most networks, to place priorities on a file when it enters the queue, to change the order in which files are printed. A high priority file is allowed to 'jump the queue'.

This system is perfectly acceptable in small, compact systems. The fact that all the documents end up in the one laser printer tray in the one location is not necessarily a problem. However, if the organisation is

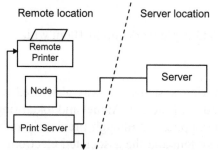

spread over a wide area, or many floors, then there could be a considerable inconvenience in collecting the printed material. In addition, there could be a problem of security, if sensitive documents are routed to a general pickup point (possibly breaching commercial or personal secrecy, not to mention the Data Protection Act).

One solution lies in re-directing the de-spooled files from the server to a node on the network. This workstation has a program in its memory that routes the print file to its local printer. However, ordinary users will use this local node. As such it is liable to be switched off or crashed by the users, making the print process vulnerable.

Note that the term *'remote printing'* means remote from the server, not necessarily remote from the user. Alternatively, a node on the network could be dedicated to handling an office's printing. The machine will not be used by staff, who will have their own workstations.

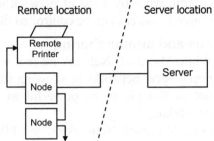

The file server directs the user requests for printing to this print server which then handles the entire associated file and print activities. This relieves the file server from much of its work and improves the overall efficiency of the system.

Another option for a print server is a printer with its own built-in network card.

LAN media

The topology of a network describes how one device connects to another. It does not take into account the data transfer speed achievable on the media between the devices. It is analogous to connecting two towns on a map.   The route may exist but the pathway could be anything from a country road to a motorway. In other words, the speed of a network is as fast as its slowest link.

There are two main performance factors when considering media:

- Transfer speed (easy to measure)
- Signal reliability

The three most common media types in networks are:

- Coaxial cable
- Twisted pair cable
- Fibre optic cable

Other transmission methods include wireless, infrared, and satellite and microwave techniques. Many systems use coaxial cable but most new installations are using twisted pair cabling.

Wire systems

By far the most common method of data transmission is to send a simple electrical pulse along a length of copper wire.   This is the basis of both the coaxial cable and twisted-pair systems.   Copper wire systems can be classified into two types: balanced and unbalanced. Unbalanced copper cable sends a single electrical signal, which is susceptible to interference and crosstalk. Balanced copper cables send a pair of equal but opposite electrical signals along a pair of connections, which helps to stabilise the signal and reduce interference and crosstalk Unbalanced cables include most forms of coaxial cable, cable TV wires, and IBM's STP cable, while UTP, STP, and IBM's Twinax cables are all balanced systems.

Advantages:

- LAN Cable and its connectors are relatively cheap.
- The cabling is relatively easily installed.
- The ends of the cables are easily connected.

Disadvantages:

- The electrical pulses on the cable are easily upset by electrical and magnetic disturbances.
- The pulses are also upset by temperature and humidity changes.
- The above necessitates careful routing of the network cables (e.g. if cable goes outside to connect to office blocks, it is best to use a pair of modems at either end, rather than use a simple cable link).
- Limited bandwidth compared to fibre optic systems.
- Segment length is short compared to fibre optic systems. Cat3 cable works up to 100m with cat4 and cat5 at 150m.

Twisted Pair

This type was initially used in IBM token-rings and Cambridge ring systems.   It was also used on StarLan networks (AT&T) and 3Com's Ethernet. The LAN standards of Ethernet, Arcnet and token-ring have been modified to allow them to run on twisted-pair and fibre-optic.   Although previously only common in small offices of 10-12 nodes, the faster speeds of the system and the associated electronics has led to a rapid expansion in twisted pair's use as the main medium for larger installations.

Twisted-pair cable is available in both shielded (STP) and unshielded (UTP) varieties.

Unshielded

The basic twisted pair system uses a cable, similar to telephone cable, made up of two insulated copper wires twisted together (usually a total of two pairs). They often use telephone-style jack sockets to connect PCs to the cabling system.

The wires are twisted to minimise crosstalk with other cables and to reduce the effects of external interference. It is the cheapest of the media types and, due to its construction, is the easiest to install. Unshielded twisted-pair cabling is used in 4Mbps token-ring systems. Although unshielded pair cable is used for Ethernet systems, additional apparatus such as bridges, equalisers and transceivers can result in the system being significantly more expensive than coaxial cable systems. Nevertheless, unshielded pair is the most common medium for low-cost, short-distance LANs. UTP cables follow the specifications in the chart.

Category	Bandwidth	Typical Data Rate
Cat 1	Up to 20KHz	20Kbps
Cat 2	Up to 4MHz	4Mbps
Cat 3	Up to 16MHz	10Mbps or 16Mbps
Cat 4	Up to 20MHz	16Mbps or 20Mbps
Cat 5	Up to 100MHz	100Mbps or 155Mbps
Cat 5e	Up to 100MHz	100Mbps up to 1Gbps
Cat 6	Up to 550MHz	Up to 1Gbps

Note however the differentiation between 'bandwidth' and 'data rate'. Generally speaking a cable can handle one data bit for each Hz. It is of course possible to use less than the maximum data throughput on any given cable. For example Cat3 cable was commonly used in 10Mbps systems despite its maximum bandwidth of 16MHz. On the other hand, it is also possible to exceed the data rate you would expect from such a system, by using data compression. For example ATM can run on Cat5 cable at 155Mbps despite the cable only having a bandwidth of 100MHz.

Shielded

To limit interference problems, the twisted pair can be covered in a metal braid that is grounded. This is known as 'shielded' cable and makes the cable vastly less prone to interference (around 1000 times better). The braid also provides great extra physical strength to the cable. It is this cable that is used for the IBM token-ring (16Mbps) and Cambridge ring system, which runs at 10Mbps. IBM offers both shielded and unshielded versions. The IBM shielded cable is rather more expensive. It consists of two pairs of twisted cable, each wrapped in plastic, then wrapped in aluminium file and copper braid; both pairs being enclosed in a final plastic sheath. The new Cat 7 cable will be shielded UTP.

Plug wiring

The diagram shows the wiring for the standard RJ-45 plug - the type used with twisted pair.

Token ring systems use pairs 1 and 3.
10Base-T uses pairs 2 and 3.
100Base-T4 uses all four pairs of wires.
100Base-VG uses all four pairs of wires.

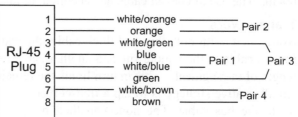

Pin	Function	Data Direction	Function	Pin
1	[TX+]	→	[RX+]	3
2	[TX-]	→	[RX-]	6
3	[RX+]	←	[TX+]	1
6	[RX-]	←	[TX-]	2

Where two nodes require to be connected to each other for PC to PC transfers or game playing, the transmit and receive pins in the cable have to be reversed to create a 'null modem' or 'UTP crossover' cable.

Coaxial cable

This cable is similar to the type used to connect TV aerials. This used to be the most popular choice of media, since it offered high speeds, greater bandwidth, fair distances and reasonable costs.

Coaxial cable is designed to minimise the 'skin effect' problem that affects all wire carriers. As the data transfer rate in a wire is increased, the current in that wire tends to flow along its outer skin. Since there is now less surface to carry the current, there is greater cable resistance, hence greater signal losses. Therefore, twisted pair is less efficient at higher speeds. To help overcome this skin effect, coaxial cable was introduced. Its outer conductor is in the shape of a tube. The copper in its construction is all effectively used. As a result, practically all network operating system software includes drivers for Ethernet cards.

There are two Ethernet standards - thin and thick coaxial cable. Both transmit at 10Mbps. These are called 10Base-2 and 10Base-5. The 10 indicates the maximum system speed in Mbps, the *'Base'* indicates the system runs in baseband mode (see later) and the final number indicates the maximum length allowed for a single cable segment (in hundreds of metres).

Ethernet Thin

Ethernet thin is also known as CheaperNet, ThinNet or 10BASE2. Coaxial cable has two conductors. The inner conductor is a solid copper core. The outer copper braid acts as the second conductor. The two conductors are held apart by plastic insulation. The cable is enclosed in a PVC casing. The bus cable has to visit every station that is used on the network, where it connects to the node with a BNC connector.

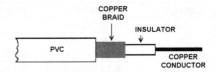
ETHERNET THIN CABLE

ThinNet environments are designed for 30 nodes per segment and a maximum segment length of 185m (extending to 925m with repeaters). It uses a 50 ohm cable (type RG58) which supports up to 10Mbps baseband working with an error rate of only 1 in 10^7. The coaxial cable has a minimum bending radius of some 15 cm (or six inches).

Ethernet Thick

Also known as Standard, ThickNet or 10BASE5. Its construction is similar to ThinNet, with an added layer of aluminised tape and an extra layer of copper braid. It is also a 50 ohm baseband cable and uses a coaxial n-type connector.

Due to its more complex construction, Standard Ethernet is somewhat more expensive than ThinNet. The size of ThickNet (10.3mm thick) also makes it expensive to install, as it is difficult to thread through existing cable runs.

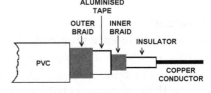
ETHERNET THICK CABLE

However, due its increased conductor size, it suffers fewer losses than ThinNet. Consequently, it covers greater distances (up to 500m, extending to 2500m with repeaters) and handles up to 100 users. Taps off the cable must be at least 2.5m apart. It is often used as a cabling *'spine'* - i.e. a main backbone from which ThinNet spurs can attach. Minimum bending radius with this type of cable can be 60cm. The use of coaxial cable has declined, in favour of twisted-pair.

Transceivers

Notice that, with both thin and thick cable, the station can be situated remotely from the bus cable. To route a cable to the remote site and another cable returning from the site would greatly add to the overall length of the segment. This in turn limits the remaining distance that can be covered by the cable.

An alternative strategy is to tap a transceiver on to the bus cable. The node can then be connected to the transceiver by a single cable. The bus cable is tapped into by connecting a transceiver. The special cable from the transceiver to the station can be up to 50m in length. These are expensive cables (costing more than ThickNet cable) and

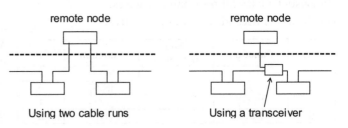
Using two cable runs   Using a transceiver

connect to the transceiver with an N series plug. The other end of the cable connects to the PC card with a 15-pin or 9-pin D connector. Transceivers have to be at least 2.5m apart and a maximum of 100 transceivers is allowed on a single bus.

Fibre Optic

All electrical conductors suffer from electrical resistance, poor insulation and electrical disturbance, due to unwanted electrical signals. These effects can be largely overcome by the use of optical fibre cables. This system uses light as a carrier instead of electrical pulses. The cable consists of a thin, flexible strand of glass, only slightly larger than a human hair. Plastic-clad silica or all-plastic versions are also available, but they are not as efficient or as easy to use. Most systems are made from very pure silica, covered with a glass clad.

A light source (either LED or laser) is fed into one end of the cable and the light travels along the cable core, reflecting off the cable's walls (the *'clad'*). There is total internal reflection within the cable, occurring at the core/cladding interface. Total internal reflection occurs because the core has a higher refractive index compared to the cladding.

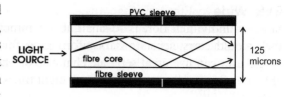

LED or laser light sources can be used. LED light sources are much lower powered and are used for shorter distances (a few kilometres) at speeds of around 200 Mbps. Laser sources are much more expensive but can handle longer distances and higher transmission speeds (around 1000 Mbps).

Disadvantages:
- Held back by lack of standards.
- Held back by lack of knowledge.
- Most expensive of the media types.
- Difficult to install.

Advantages:
- Handles much greater speeds (10-100 times faster than coax).
- Greater distances than coaxial cable (less attenuation).
- Performs faultlessly at 100Mbps, with a very lowest error rate of one faulty bit in every 10,000,000,000. Note however that fibre optic technology is capable of higher speeds.
- It is immune from electromagnetic interference. Ideal for 'noisy' environments e.g. lift shafts, shop floor production lines.
- Safe in most conditions. The cable carries only light, so there is no electrical energy to cause a spark in a hazardous or explosive environment (e.g. mines/oil plants/ gas plants).
- Greater security (very hard to tap into; no radiation therefore no unauthorised external monitoring).
- Electrical isolation, therefore no crosstalk.

Most networks do not support fibre optics as standard. It is available for token-ring and Ethernet systems and is expected to increase its share of use. Its main use is seen where there is a large volume of traffic or where very large files are used (e.g. video, multimedia, etc)

There are two kinds of optical cable - mono-mode (or single-mode) and multi-mode.

Mono Mode

Mono-mode fibre cable is only about 8 micro-metres in diameter and is used mostly in long-distance communications. Here, the diameter of the core is only a few times greater than the wavelength of the transmitted light and only a single ray is propagated, in almost a straight line. A large part of the power is propagated in the cladding near the core. The cable is difficult to connect to transmitters and receivers, since precise alignment is required. It supports a greater data rate than multi-mode, with a bandwidth of 1GHz over 1km being not uncommon.

Multi-Mode

Multi-mode fibre consists of a thicker core, with a surrounding fibre sleeve with different refractive qualities. Most of the power travels in the core. The core is many times greater than that used in single-mode. This allows WDM (Wavelength Division Multiplexing) since several different light signals at different frequencies can be transmitted simultaneously. Multi-mode cable is the most common system, since it requires a lower manufacturing tolerance, making it cheaper to produce. They are also easier to attach to hardware.

However, there is no agreement amongst manufacturers as to the dimension of multi-mode cable. All makes use an outer diameter of 125 micro-metres, with the exception of IBM who promote 140 micro-metres. Also, different manufacturers promote different inner core diameters (50 to 100 microns).

Light emitters

The problems of getting the light into the fibre are often the greatest cause of losses in the system. As the surface area of the light emitter and the end of the cable are so small, even a small misalignment can mean that the light does not even enter the cable. Alignment is very critical and needs expertise and the proper equipment. LEDs (Light Emitting Diode) deliver up to 100 microwatts into the cable. They are cheap, have long lives and work up to 100MHz. ILDs (Injection Laser Diodes) deliver a couple of milliwatts into the cable. They are expensive and require complex circuitry (not to mention coolers!) to maintain a stable output. They have bandwidths of over several hundred MegaHertz.

Byte-Wide

Since an individual fibre is so small, it is common to have more than a single fibre in a cable. Normally, they would carry separate data information for different users. In ultra-high performance systems, a single user can use eight separate channels on the cable, one for each bit of a byte. In effect, the user is able to make parallel transmissions at eight times the normal rate.

FDDI

In an attempt at standardisation, ANSI (the American National Standards Institute) has issued the FDDI (Fibre Distributed Data Interface) standard, covering data only. This promotes a 100 Mbps ring topology LAN with 125 micro-metre outer and a range of inner diameters (from 50 to 85 micro-metres) to suit different manufacturers. The system has two rings, the second being a backup (built-in resilience).
Its characteristics are:

- Supports 500 nodes
- Nodes can be up to 2km apart
- Maximum ring circumference of 100km
- Does not require amplifiers or signal conditioning apparatus

A successor, FDDI II, which includes digitised live voice and video, is being developed.
The main uses for FDDI are:

- Backbone connecting low-speed LAN systems together
- Use for high-performance workstations/image processing
- LANs to mainframes, minis and high-speed devices
- Future need to integrate voice/video on LAN (bandwidth)
- Increase of nodes on networks

Token-ring LANs are more easily supported by fibre-optic cabling than Ethernet.

Fibre Channel

The Fibre Channel specification is intended for fibre optic cables, but it can also run over twisted pair or even coaxial cable if necessary. It is both a network cabling technology and a hard disk connection method. It currently runs at 1Gbps or 2Gbps, although a 10Gbps version is in development. As a result, it is a competitor to SCSI, at least in the server market, where its high price tag may be justified.
Fibre Channel can have up to 125 devices attached, over a distance of up to 100 feet. As can be seen, this limits its potential for use in networking in general, but makes it ideal for use in a SAN, where its high speed can provide the bandwidth needed for high data rate activities.

Additionally, Fibre Channel is not a software protocol but a connection method. As a result, it can be used to carry a variety of signals, including SCSI signals or TCP/IP data. Unfortunately, the Fibre Channel specification leaves some aspects open to interpretation, which has created some difficulties in interconnection of FC devices.

Comparison of wire types

In planning any network, it is necessary to decide which type of cabling to use. Thin coaxial cable is now obsolete, and even Thick coaxial, previously delegated to linking network hubs, is largely replaced by Category 5 UTP or by fibre optic.
This is not due to price concerns: neither UTP nor Thin coaxial are particularly expensive for LAN use. In security terms, thick and thin coaxial can be tapped into using a so-called 'vampire jack', indeed this is how ThickNet is normally accessed! In contrast, UTP cannot easily be tapped, and realistically a potential intruder would have to access an unused wall socket. The main reason, though, is due to the fact that Ethernet over UTP cable is wired physically as a star, which makes it easier to organise and control than coaxial, which requires linking of one node to the next. For this reason, development has concentrated on UTP instead of thin coaxial, and UTP can now support 100 or even 1000 Megabits per second, while thin coaxial has remained stuck at 10 Megabits per second.
Shielded Twisted Pair is rated at 16Mbps by IBM, but in reality is capable of much higher speeds, reaching 100Mbps with the right equipment. It is necessarily expensive, due to the shielding, but its high resistance to interference makes it useful in areas using heavy machinery. Fibre optic cable, of course, is immune to electromagnetic interference, and can have a higher speed and similar (or even lower!) cost. It also provides better security, since it cannot be tapped into along the wire. The only problem is that

fibre optic is essentially a long thin strand of glass, making it difficult or impossible to bend round tight corners, and vulnerable to damage if exposed.

Cable troubleshooting tools

Wire systems have to rely on the physical medium of the cable, which is subject to several potential problems. Outright cable breaks are relatively easy to detect – in a 10BaseT network, the faulty cable will usually only prevent a single station from communicating, while in a 10Base2 network, Successive Binary Division can be used to detect the fault (see the chapter on *'Faultfinding'*).

However, as explained in the Data Communications chapter, electrical noise, crosstalk and other such factors can impede cable transmission reliability, with sometimes unpredictable and fluctuating effects. Cable testing equipment is available to detect such problems as Near-End CrossTalk (NEXT), attenuation and so on. The TIA standard 568-B specifies performance characteristics of UTP systems, so that the results of cable tests can be interpreted and the appropriate action taken.

Wake On LAN and others

Wake On Lan (WOL) is a standard that allows a network card to be attached directly to the mainboard. Assuming the PC is left on standby rather than switched off completely, it will still supply some power to a few devices, just enough to detect activity. One of these devices is the network card, which can then, on receiving the appropriate signal, begin the power-up or power-down procedure.

This is useful for various reasons. It is often used to 'wake' a gateway PC, to remotely access a work PC from home, or activate network nodes to run diagnostics.

In order for WOL to work, it must be supported by the mainboard, the BIOS, the network card, drivers, and the power supply, which must be at least ATX version 2.01. WOL-enabled software will also be required to do the waking from the remote location.

Wake-On-Ring is similar to WOL, but of course it depends on a modem ringing rather than a network card receiving data. They are used for similar purposes.

Keyboard-Power-on and Timer-Power-on are also similar in effect, but do not require any expansion cards or mainboard connectors. Keyboard-Power-on is simply the ability for a keyboard equipped with a power button to be used to start up the computer or send it into hibernation. Timer-Power-on is a less widely used method, which, as the name implies, activates or powers down a computer at a predetermined time.

Power over Ethernet

IEEE802.3af specification covers providing power over Ethernet cables, along with the data. This allows low-power devices, such as IP telephones, to connect to the network without requiring their own power supplies. It is particularly useful for devices that may be difficult to power otherwise, such as remote webcams, wireless LAN access points, etc.

Around 15W of power is available (48V at 0.4A) and this is provided either on the four unused wires on a CAT-5 cable's RJ-45 plug, or by superimposing the power on the data lines.

The system is most often described as Power Over Ethernet (PoE) or sometimes Power Over LAN (PoL)

Homeplug

For small home networks, a dedicated wired network system can involve a lot of work laying the cables and fitting networks cards inside the PCs. This option is 'wireless' in the sense that it does not a use dedicated cabling system to connect PCs. Instead, it uses the house mains wiring as the network cable, since it already exists in every room. Ethernet cables connect the PCs and any ADSL router, wireless LAN access point, etc. to Homeplug boxes which then plug into any wall outlet.

Earlier attempts at mains-borne networking were slow, but Homeplug units are available in a range of speeds depending upon their application:

	Max speed	Typical Uses
HomePlug 1.0	up to 14Mbps	Internet sharing, gaming and VOIP
HomePlug 1.0 Turbo	up to 85Mbps	TV over IP, on-line gaming
HomePlug AV	up to 200Mbps	Streaming HDTV

The house electricity meter acts as an effective filter, preventing data from entering the district mains supply. As an added precaution, the data on the wiring can be encrypted.

Wireless Systems

A network node does not have to be connected via wires. Although wireless LANs have taken their time to reach maturity, there has recently been an increase in the use of wireless LANs, and they are expected to become even more important in the foreseeable future, as so-called 'mobile computing' is an attractive prospect to employers and employees alike.

In a wireless LAN, transmissions are carried through the air on waves of various kinds, as shown:

Infrared	Data is transmitted by modulating a beam of light that has a wavelength below that of the visible spectrum.
Fibreless Laser	Data is transmitted by modulating a beam of light produced using a LASER, just like a fibre optic system, but the laser beam travels through air rather than along a fibre cable.
Microwave	Data is transmitted by modulation of a microwave emission.
Radio	Similar in concept to CB radio, data is transmitted via radio waves.
Satellite	Information is transmitted to and from satellites in orbit around the Earth, for almost total mobility.

The operation of these various forms of wireless are explained in the *'Data Communications'* chapter. Wireless transmission systems can have a variety of uses:

- To connect a number of computers together in a peer system, or *'wireless LAN'*.
- To connect a mobile user to a stationary wired network. Known as *'mobile computing'*.
- As a bridge between two LAN segments. This is known as a *'wireless extended LAN'*, and is a type of *'point to point'* network.
- As a backup connection between devices on an existing wire network.

Wireless peer-to-peer LANs

A number of peer systems can communicate with one another over wireless links, in similar fashion to a wired network. For example, several infrared laptop computers in a conference room could be connected to each other. However, lacking a central server, such systems are difficult to administer and troubleshoot, as well as being insecure. However, they are a simple solution for fast networking.

Wireless LANs are by their nature ad-hoc networks, at least in terms of their topology. Each node is only able to communicate with those other nodes that are within its wireless range, and therefore messages must be passed on via several 'hops' rather than directly along a bus. An exception to this is the infrared network, which has a very limited range (it is often quoted as a *'conference hall network'*) and often all nodes are able to communicate directly with each other.

The routing on a wireless network is achieved using either *'discovery'* techniques, or *'promiscuous mode'*. Using discovery techniques, each node periodically broadcasts, looking for new nodes within its range. Using *'promiscuous mode'*, a node listens to all network broadcasts, even ones which are not intended for that node, in order to gain knowledge of nodes nearby. Ad-hoc routing protocols are still largely in development, since the techniques are relatively new.

Point-to-point networks

These are wireless systems that simply connect two fixed points. This is most commonly implemented as a wireless bridge to form a Wireless Extended LAN, but may also be used as a backup to an existing cable connection. Most infrared and LASER systems are of this type, as the nature of the light wave being used makes mobile communication difficult with these technologies. However, spread-spectrum radio connections can also be used as wireless bridges. The bridge may span a small gap between two buildings, or could cover a distance of several miles.

Bluetooth

Bluetooth is an open interconnection standard that has been in preparation for a number of years but is only now beginning to make an impact. Bluetooth capable equipment offers short-range digital voice and data transmission by radio signals, for both point-to-point and multicast applications. Point-to-point transmission is useful for personal applications, where cables and infrared light links are currently used. Multicast will allow the use of networking, email, World Wide Web and no doubt other yet to be developed technologies. The use of radio links presents interesting problems. Higher frequencies only work between antennae that can see each other, so called "line of sight", whilst lower frequencies are subject to fading and interference. The Bluetooth standard overcomes these problems and incorporates encryption technology to ensure privacy where it is needed.

Bluetooth products are available, mostly hands-free phone adaptors and notebook PC Cards. Bluetooth peripherals for PCs do exist however, such as wireless Printing Modules.

Aloha

Although not a new networking protocol by any means, the Aloha system is becoming popular once again due to the emergence of wireless networking. It comes in several forms, including 'Pure Aloha', 'Slotted Aloha' and 'Spread Aloha'. All of these are designed for wireless systems.

Pure Aloha is the original form of the protocol, and bears a remarkable similarity to Ethernet, because that technology was based in part on techniques developed for Aloha. Pure Aloha uses Collision Detection, not Carrier Sensing, meaning that any station could begin transmitting and cause a collision at any time. This achieves a low throughput (quoted at just over 18% usage of bandwidth) but is easy to implement.

Slotted Aloha uses the same collision detection method, but uses Time Division Multiplexing (TDM) to split the media into fixed time slots. Each station can only begin transmitting at the commencement of each time slot, reducing collisions and increasing bandwidth usage to around 37%.

Spread Aloha is a more recent form of the protocol. It deals with spread-spectrum transmissions, in order to allow more than one frequency for transmission. This means a much higher throughput.

Mobile LAN access

Mobile computing is one of the most useful aspects of wireless technology. A portable laptop computer can be fitted with a wireless Network Interface Card, which will communicate with a nearby network, effectively connecting it to that network. This requires the network to have an 'access point' that will communicate data with the mobile computer. An Access Point is a specialised computer system that is attached to the network. It basically performs a function similar to a Gateway, in that it provides an interface between the local, wired network, and roaming, wireless systems. It must be equipped with both wireless and wired communications hardware, as well as software that will route messages between wireless clients and the wired network. Since the Access Point is open to potential interference, it should preferably include security of some kind as well.

Comparison of Mobile LAN speeds

Technology	Product	Data rate
Infrared	IrDA version 1	115.2Kbps
Infrared	IrDA version 2	115.2Kbps and 4Mbps
Narrow Band radio	10BaseRadio	10Mbps
Spread-Spectrum radio	802.11a or 802.11g	54Mbps
Spread-Spectrum radio	802.11b FHSS or DSSS	1Mbps, 2Mbps or 11Mbps
Spread-Spectrum radio	802.11 FHSS or DSSS	1Mbps or 2Mbps
Microwave	Mainly proprietary systems	Data rate increases with frequency, some systems offer 155Mbps
Cellular radio	GSM 3G	9600bps 384kbps

WiFi 802.11n

802.11n is a fast wireless network standard that is still in its early stages.

Current wi-fi systems, although fast, are not able to meet the demands of future business applications like high performance networking and consumer markets such as HDTV, streaming video and handheld platforms.

In early 2004, the IEEE set up a working group to develop this new standard. The standard would be called 802.11n and the working group was called 'Task Group n' (TGn). The new standard is required to have a minimum base throughput of 100 Mbps.

Different groups have produced specifications for the standard and these have been reduced to two main proposals from:

- The TGn Sync (Task Group n synchronisation) consortium, which includes Intel, Cisco, Sony, Phillips and Panasonic.
- The WwiSE (World-Wide Spectrum Efficiency) Alliance, which includes wi-fi manufacturers such as Motorola, Nokia, Broadcom, Texas Instruments and Conextant.

The technology

Both groups base their schemes on MIMO (Multiple In, Multiple Out) technology, sometimes called 'smart antenna systems'.

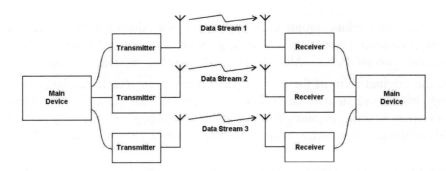

As the diagram shows, a MIMO device uses several aerials (antenna). The data stream from the sending device is split into three separate streams, with each stream being transmitted on its own frequency. The three streams are then combined into a single channel at the receiving end.

This system allows more data to be transferred than with a single radio channel.

The benefits of MIMO are:
- Faster transfers.
- Greater range (although there are concerns that in urban situations this could cause interference between systems).
- Fewer losses from multipath (i.e. reflected) signals interfering with the main signal. *'Antenna diversity'* and *'spatial multiplexing'* techniques are used.
- Since the aerials are spaced apart, the receivers can use the multiple signals to more effectively recover the original data from the signals.

This increased performance requires greater sophistication in the channel's electronics and multiple aerials means greater implementation costs.

Each device uses its same set of aerials for both transmission and reception.

Number of Channels

The 802.11n specification requires at least two aerials per device. The use of three or more aerials is an option within the specification, although four aerials is probably a maximum practical proposition (due to the increased complexity and costs involved).

Channel Width

The two main contenders currently differ on the width of each channel. Currently, 802.11a uses 20MHz channels and WwiSE supports maintaining 20MHz channels in 802.11n in the 2.5GHz spectrum. TGn, on the other hand, supports 40MHz channels in the 5GHz spectrum, as this would further increase the data rate (some say to 300Mbps while others are attempting 500Mbps).

The IEEE specifically requires that 802.11n devices must be backwards-compatible. So, even if a 40MHz bandwidth is finally settled on, the devices will still have to be able to support the existing 20MHz channels. Of course, a non-MIMO device joining a network may result in that network's speed and coverage being reduced.

The situation is less clear with the Pre-n devices that are currently available. As standalone MIMO devices, they are much better than existing standard devices. However, purchasers cannot be guaranteed that the devices will support all the features of the new standard – since the new standard does not yet exist! They may, for example, only communicate in 802.11g or 802.11a mode, or they may not support all the features that are eventually agreed.

WIMAX

The IEEE is completing the 802.16m standard, known as WIMAX, which will extend WiFi speeds to beyond 1Gbps.

An even faster WIMAX version is expected to provide long-range communication measured in kilometres, although there concerns regarding interference-free implementation of high-power long-range channels in closely-packed urban areas.

Transmission Methods

There are two main methods of transmitting over a cabled network:

Baseband

This is the most common method for LANs.   It is essentially a digital technique, with the node's signal being applied directly to the media, in a similar fashion to TTL or RS232 levels (i.e. +15v represents 0 and -15v represents 1).   There is no signal processing and the entire medium bandwidth is used for a single transmission at any one time.   Since only one transmission can be handled, high transmission rates are necessary.   It is also necessary to share the medium between nodes on a time-sharing basis known as TDM (time division multiplexing).

Digital signals are transmitted as a sequence of 0s and 1s. At its simplest, a negative voltage on the line represents a '0' condition, while a positive signal represents a '1' condition.   Changes of signal voltage cannot be used as a means of detecting '0' and '1' states, since a series of 0s or 1s could be sent - producing no voltage change.   It is necessary, therefore, to time each pulse to detect whether there are multiple occurrences of the same pulse.   This requires that the transmitting and receiving nodes be synchronised.   This is achieved by sending the data in a form known as *'Manchester coding'*, which uses the codes themselves to maintain the necessary synchronisation.

Broadband

Where an organisation has large/complex communication demands, a broadband system will normally be in operation. The advantages of the broadband system include:
- The ability to carry multiple channels
- The ability to carry analogue signals, e.g. voice and TV
- The ability to cover long distances. Analogue signals do not suffer from degradation to the same extent as digital signals and are easier to boost using analogue amplifiers.
- The ability to interface different baseband systems, using the broadband system as the network 'backbone'.

The disadvantages are:
- High initial cost - planning costs, equipment costs and setup costs.
- Each network adapter needs its own modem.
- Needs regular testing and adjustment (as with a radio, mistuning leads to loss of the information).
- Difficult to insert new stations

A better name for this system would be *'multi-band'* since the cable carries more than one data channel, using *'frequency division multiplexing'*.   The channels are separated by using each data source to modulate a different radio frequency, called the *'carrier'* frequency. These carriers are then placed on the media, where they occupy different parts of the radio spectrum. The channels are separated out at the receiving end into the required channels. This is the same technique as used by cable TV firms to place several TV channels on the one TV cable. Each data channel can then effectively be considered as a separate baseband channel, from an access and sharing point of view.

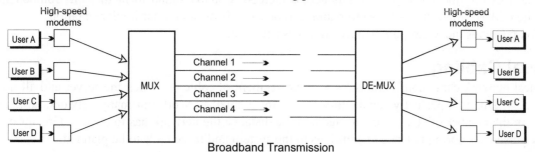

Broadband Transmission

Each channel operates independently of the others and can therefore run at different speeds using different access methods. For example, one channel could be dedicated to networking PCs while another connects IBM 3270 terminals to a mainframe computer. A node will usually be allocated to a particular channel (e.g. a node running AUTOCAD would be attached to the channel allocated to the transfer of the image files). A node could be allowed to choose which channel to connect to.

The width of a broadband channel depends on the data being carried. For data channels, the required bandwidth will increase with increasing data transfer rates. Ethernet, for example, will require 18MHz of bandwidth.   LocalNet, on the other hand, opts for 120 slow-speed channels (only 128Kbps) each channel requiring 300KHz of bandwidth.   Broadband systems are currently in use to carry multiple data channels and video for LAN applications, although it appears likely that it will be overtaken by fibre-optic systems.   The only PC network to use broadband is the IBM token ring system, which transmits on 50.75MHz and receives on 219MHz.

Notes:

The system uses cable TV equipment - i.e. one way only - and is therefore usually a twin cable system. An alternative is to split the bandwidth into transmit and receive bands.

The system uses expensive, high-speed, modems at each node. Modems can be a single pair of frequencies (1 for transmit, 1 for receive) or can be *'frequency agile'* - can access several channels.

Ethernet and IEEE standards

In the ideal world, all computer devices would easily connect together, using the same electronic methods and the same communication protocols.   However, due to the historical development of networks via competing manufacturers, many differences exist between the brand names - even where the products are supposed to conform to the same standard.

The chart shows the most common systems in use.

Ethernet Specification	IEEE Standard	Band	Usage
1Base5	802.3	Baseband	1Mbps using UTP, STP cable
10Base2	802.3	Baseband	10Mbps using thin coax cable
10Base5	802.3	Baseband	10Mbps using thick coax cable
10BaseF	802.3	Baseband	10Mbps using fibre optic cable
10BaseT	802.3	Baseband	10Mbps using UTP cable
10Broad36	802.3	Broadband	10Mbps using broadband cable
100BaseT	802.3u	Baseband	100Mbps using UTP, fibre optic cable
100VG-AnyLAN	802.12	Baseband	100Mbps using UTP cable
Gigabit Ethernet	802.3z and 802.3ab	Baseband	1000Mbps using fibre optic cable (802.3z) or copper cable (802.3ab)
10 Gigabit Ethernet	802.3ae	Baseband	10000Mbps using fibre optic cable

The IEEE Local Networks Standards Committee has developed the series of LAN standards listed below:

- IEEE 802.3 Covers the carrier sense multiple access and collision detection (CSMA/CD) access method and physical layer specification.   This is also known as *'Ethernet'* and was mainly developed by Xerox, Intel and DEC.   It was introduced in 1980.
- IEEE 802.5 Covers the token passing ring access method and physical layer specification mainly developed by IBM, introduced in 1985.
- 802.1 Covers the system overview, architecture, addressing, internetworking and network management.
- 802.4 Covers the token passing bus access method. Usually found in factory environments, where MAP (Manufacturing Automation Protocol) is its most popular implementation.
- 802.6 Covers the Metropolitan network access method.

Practical Cabling

The simplest network cable configuration is a single segment of cable on which the server and all nodes are located.   This is a perfectly satisfactory layout for a small network but many networks gradually grow both in the number of stations connected and the distance the network has to cover.   Greater usage and greater distances normally leads to additions to the system and these have to be planned.

Effect of segment length on collisions

Consider three nodes on a network, one attached at each extreme end and one in the middle of the segment length. The left-most node transmits a packet and needs to detect if it has collided with another packet on the cable, say one being sent by the right-most node. A user's packet, being in serial format, takes a finite time to place on the cable. It also takes a finite time to travel to the ends of the cable.   The distance between the two furthest nodes must be short enough for one node's packet to travel to all other nodes (the other end of the cable being the furthest cases) during the lifetime of the other's transmission. If this is the case, then the packets will corrupt each other and the collision will be detected. However, if the segment length is too great, the left node's packet will be completely sent before the right node's transmission arrives. A collision has still occurred but has not now been detected. Both packets still collide in the middle of the cable and both are corrupted.

This explains why a limit is placed on the length of a network segment.

Collision Domains

Another way to reduce collisions is to plan the network based on Collision Domains. A Collision Domain is the area of the network on which two computers may attempt to transmit at the same time, causing a collision. An Ethernet network that consists of a single segment, or of multiple segments connected by simple repeaters, is essentially a single Collision Domain.

However, using switched hubs lets nodes communicate over dedicated circuits, so that each segment attached to the switched hub is in its own Collision Domain. If every computer were attached directly to a switched hub then collisions can be eliminated. 10BaseT and 100BaseTX networks can use a combination of normal and switched hubs, but due to technical concerns the faster 1000BaseT network requires switched hubs anyway.

Extending a network

There are many reasons for wishing to extend the reach of a network. An organisation could have several small LANs, which it wishes to connect together. A new facility could be installed, requiring extension of the network to the new location, or perhaps there is simply a need for more users to access the network.

Generally, this is achieved by splitting the network into 'segments' (or 'partitions'). Indeed, virtually all WANs are made up of smaller LAN segments that are connected by long-distance links.

Segmentation has additional benefits:

- Local traffic. Users transferring data with other users in the same segment do not have to cross into other segments, meaning they have potentially better bandwidth.
- Reduced collisions. On an Ethernet system, having less users on each segment means less packet collisions, resulting in better efficiency. This only works, however, if the connection between segments is more 'intelligent' than a basic repeater; for example a switched hub or a router.

A range of hardware is available to allow a single segment to join with another segment, or several segments, to form a larger network.

Repeaters

Individual segments of a LAN bus can be connected with 'repeaters'. A repeater receives the transmission from one segment, amplifies and cleans up the signal and re-transmits it to the other segment. In this way, the maximum cable length and number of stations can be increased from the previous limits. Repeaters do not have any control over addressing or forwarding and therefore do not ease congestion and collision on the system. They operate at the OSI physical layer 1.

A multiport repeater has many outlet sockets and copies the transmission over multiple segments.

Bridges

A bridge connects two segments and passes traffic between them. It is used to extend the network size without breaking the limit on any segment size, attached device count, or number of repeaters per segment. It is very popular with small networks. A bridge can be a standalone piece of equipment but is often a PC with two NICs, one connecting to each segment.

A learning bridge builds up a picture of what addresses are on each side of the bridge and decides whether packets are allowed to cross the bridge. For this purpose, it operates at the Data Link Layer level 2 and uses the MAC (Media Access Control) sub-layer to check addresses. The only traffic allowed on a segment is traffic destined for a node on that segment. Since there is reduced traffic, there are also fewer collisions and less wasted traffic. However, when a bridge becomes busy, it places traffic in memory buffers and when these buffers become full, users' frames are discarded.

A bridge is also used as a connection between the building's main data backbone and separate segments for each floor. So, packets addressed to a node on the ground floor will not be sent on to the segments on the other floors; they will not pass through the first floor and second floor bridges.

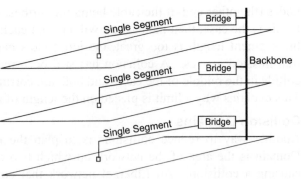

Routers

A router is like a bridge except that it works on OSI Network Layer level 3 protocols. Messages are transmitted to other segments dependent upon their protocol level address (e.g. TCP/IP address) rather than the MAC addresses. This means they can span differing lower-level protocols. For example an Ethernet and a token ring network could be connected via a router, as long as they both used TCP/IP at a higher level. Routers can also pass messages between different physical media, for example passing a message received on a UTP cable onto a ThinNet network. Routers are slower than bridges but are used for larger networks, since they are better at handling collisions and bandwidth utilisation. Routers can communicate with other routers on the network as to which route of the possible options is the most efficient.

A *'brouter'* is a device that operates as either a bridge or a router, depending on the packet being transferred.

Gateways

A gateway is used to connect two networks whose communications protocols are different. So, a gateway device might connect an Ethernet segment to a Unix system, a mainframe computer or an ISDN or X.25 communications line. Gateways handle a larger range of protocols than a router. The gateway device carries out the translation of information between the systems.

Design Restrictions

There is a *'5-4-3'* rule for connecting unbridged systems.
- The system must not have more than 5 repeated segments.
- The system must not have more 4 repeaters/hubs between any 2 stations.
- The system must have no more than 3 of the segments populated.

The layout of the network structure must follow these rules to ensure consistent network operation.
In addition, a maximum of 7 bridges is allowed in a system.

Structured Cabling

The above additions can, and often do, develop in a piecemeal way, as the organisation gradually expands.   They keep the network operating but a large collection of such segments and components may

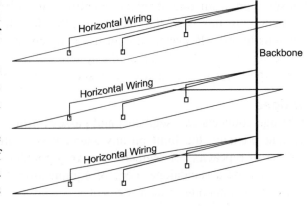

eventually not produce the efficient working that is required.   For systems that need reorganised, and particularly for new networks, the principle of structured cabling is important.

With structured cabling, the total system comprises simple wiring structures that are repeated in various locations, or various floors of the building and then combined.

The diagram shows a 3-floor building with the outline of a structured cabling layout. The type of cabling and type of hardware components offer a range of options to suit an organisation's operational needs as well as the building layout.
The main features should be:
- A fast cabling type for the building's data backbone. This vertical cabling carries the heavy data needs throughout the building. The backbone could be fibre optic, ThickNet or Cat 5 UTP depending upon the implementation decided upon.

- Floors are *'flood wired'*. Cables are not only routed to where computers currently sit; cables are taken to all places where a computer may be located in the future. This is usually a ratio of connections per square metre of floor space.
- Cabling provides enough spare capacity for future use (e.g. running two cables to each workspace).
- All cables on a particular floor are taken to a *'wiring closet'*. This is a small cupboard or room with a patch panel with connections for each cable.
- All further connections to equipment are carried out in the wiring closet, providing flexibility.
- Fast systems must provide slower speed ports for connecting to printers, routers and bridges that are not designed for fast speeds.
- Data hungry workstations, such as those used for CAD, Multimedia, video and DTP, can be linked to the main system using a fast network card.

Structured Cabling standards

There are several well-defined methods that can be followed in order to implement a structured cabling policy. The main standards are EIA 568A, EN/BS 50173, and ISO 11801. The first of these, EIA 568A, was developed by ANSI and is billed as a *"Commercial Building Telecommunications Cabling Standard"*. There are a number of related EIA standards alongside it to further clarify structured cabling practice, such as EIA-606, an administration standard.

Although this is an American standard it was the first structured cabling document, and the European EN/BS 50173 standard is very similar in concept. The ISO Standard 11801 is an international effort, and as such incorporates elements of both, and other structured cabling standards.

Cabling and safety concerns

Typical UTP or coaxial cabling is manufactured using PVC plastic. For small networks this may be entirely satisfactory. However, in flood-wired buildings this will result in a very large amount of plastic. There have been a few well-publicised cases of buildings containing large amounts of PVC cabling causing toxic fumes in the event of a fire.

Therefore, LSZH (Low-Smoke, Zero Halogen) cables are produced for such situations. These produce less smoke, and are more resistant to flames, but tend to be more expensive than ordinary cables. Such cabling is sometimes referred to as *'Plenum'* cable because it is intended for wiring in a Plenum space. Plenum spaces are hidden areas created by dropped ceilings, usually provided for air conditioning, heating and ventilation purposes, which are often used for running long network cables.

Fast Systems

A number of competing technologies exist for fast 100Mbps and above operation. FDDI has the best performance but is very expensive. The other options are:
- 100Base-T
- 100Base-VG
- Gigabit and 10-Gigabit Ethernet
- Ethernet switches
- ATM

100Base-T

Also known as Fast Ethernet, this remains a CSMA/CD Ethernet system.
It offers three options:
- 100Base-TX, which uses 2 pairs of the Cat 5 cable.
- 100Base-T4, which uses 4 pairs of Cat 3, Cat 4 or Cat 5 cable.
- 100Base-FX, which uses 2 strands of optical fibre.

100BaseTX and 100BaseT4 have a 100m maximum length between node and hub. The two furthest nodes cannot be greater than 200m apart (including 2 repeaters or hubs which cannot be more than 5m apart in between). Longer distances are achieved using switches or switching hubs.

Fast Ethernet requires new switched hubs and NICs.   Existing 10Mbps hubs and NICs can be retained for average users while power users have direct 100Mbps connections as shown in the diagram.

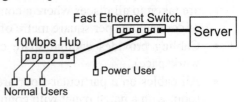

The server has a 100Mbps switched NIC and feeds 100Mbps to the Fast Ethernet switch.   Power users with heavy bandwidth needs are connected directly to this switch to maximise their bandwidth.   The switch also feeds 100Mbps to normal 10Mbps hubs which each feed connecting a number of normally loaded PCs.   The Fast switch could feed 100Mbps to another 100Mbps switch in a *'cascade'* of high-speed connections.   It is a simpler and cheaper system than 100VG but is less efficient at handling time-dependent data.

100VG-AnyLAN

100VG supports token ring frames but is mainly used with Ethernet.   It doesn't use the standard Ethernet CSMA/CD.   Instead, it uses *'Demand Priority Protocol'* which has a normal and high priority level. High priority transmissions are given precedence over lower priority activities to ensure adequate performance for time-critical applications such as process control, multimedia and live video.   It is a high performance system that uses up to 95% of its maximum theoretical capacity.

Like all modern wiring systems, it uses twisted pair connected to hubs and the hubs can be cascaded to three levels of depth as shown in the diagram.

100VG supports the following options

- 4 pairs of Cat 3, Cat 4 - with a 100m limit between node and hub and also between hubs.
- 2 or 4 pairs for Cat 5 - with a 150m limit between node and hub and also between hubs.

Since the system does not have to listen for collisions, the signalling pair used by 10Base-T is no longer used and all four pairs in the UTP can be used to carry data.   So, the multi-core cable designed to carry 10Mbps now carries 40Mbps. There is also much redundant data sent in a normal Manchester coded packet (see earlier explanation).   Two bits of data are transmitted for every bit of actual data.

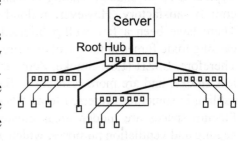

100Base-VG uses a method called 5B6B NRZ which uses 6 bits to represent every 5 bits instead of the 10 bits required by Manchester encoding.   The system uses round robin access (i.e. token ring access) inside the hub.   The hub checks each node in turn looking for traffic.   So, all ports get a fair share of the bandwidth, apart from any changed priorities imposed by the Demand Priority protocol.

With 100VG, packets are sent to the destination node only, not transmitted to all nodes as in a single bus segment.   It requires new hubs and NICs, since it is no longer based on the collision detection mechanism of layer 2.   The network can retain the existing cabling but a translation bridge is required between the 100VG and 10Base-T components.

Switched Ethernet

While 100Base-T retained CSMA/CD for its high-speed system, Switched Ethernet abandons shared access methods in favour of a point-to-point connection set up by switched components for the duration of the communication.   By eliminating collisions, the existing bandwidth is used much more effectively. As the diagram shows, the server, power users and normal hubs all connect to the switch.   The users then have *'bandwidth on demand'* - a guaranteed 10Mbps allocation.

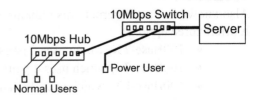

Switched Ethernet uses the existing servers, nodes, cabling and NICs but requires changes and additions to the cabling infrastructure (i.e. the addition of an Ethernet Switch and existing nodes reconfigured through extra hubs). It is a cheap option and is easily set up.   It is a great improvement over standard Ethernet but is not powerful enough for large throughput demands.

ATM

Asynchronous Transfer Mode is available in three options:
- 25Mbps for Cat 5, with a 150m limit between switch and node.
- 155Mbps for multi-mode fibre, with a 2km limit.
- 622Mbps for multi-mode fibre. Probably the upper limit that will be implemented in ATM.

It uses switching hubs and *'cells'* (packets of only 48 data bytes and 5 header bytes). Cells are transmitted over *'pipes'* (virtual channels) between a node, a switch and another node. The bandwidth for each channel can be set separately, allowing heavy users such as multimedia to run with a guaranteed bandwidth of 155Mbps right up to the node. At the moment, it is used largely for fast backbones.

Gigabit Ethernet

Used on both mono-mode and multi-mode fibres, it provides fast network backbones with a maximum of up to 3km cable length. It can be used on legacy category 5 UTP, but only if the cable is of good quality, meeting strict requirements for crosstalk and other electrical factors. Category 5e cable is certified to meet these requirements. It retains Ethernet's CSMA/CD method, making it easy to replace or extend an existing network. 10-Gigabit Ethernet, on the other hand, is full-duplex and fibre-optic only, and defines several new fibre optic media types, with cable lengths from 65 metres up to 40km.

Software on the network

Most modern software is capable of being run on a stand-alone PC or over a network. An application is loaded from the hard disk of the file server into the memory of the calling node. The program is then run in the machine memory. This means that the program can be downloaded to as many nodes as require it. This has encouraged the purchase of single copies of applications, rather than the multi-licence network versions. The lack of network facilities in the applications could sometimes be overcome by the network utilities of the operating system.

To prevent this, many single-user applications now test to see whether it is being used in a machine with a network operating system. If it detects such a system, it refuses to run. Some applications operate on a network as standard. Others require that network versions be purchased.

File Problems

The main difference between stand-alone and network use is in the ability to share files. The application program can be easily copied into the memory of several stations. The problems arise from stations trying to use the same data files.

Consider the case of two station users running Word, which is on the file server in single-user mode. Both users decide to load the same monthly report to make their own amendments/additions. The first user will successfully load the original file and begin working on it. While this is happening, the second user can also successfully load the original file and make other changes.

The problem arises when the users save their files, since only a single copy of a unique file-name can exist on the disk. Both users' amended versions are saved - but whoever saves second overwrites the file the first user saved. In other words, the amendments of the first user are lost - and the user will not even know it has happened. An even worse situation exists if both users try to save simultaneously. At best, a new file is created which has elements of both files. At worst, the disk file organisation may be affected, causing other files to be irretrievable.

There are other occasions when the user would wish an entire file to be used exclusively by a single user. For example, when packing a database (to remove records marked as deleted), no other user should have access to that file.

These problems are overcome by a system of *'file locking'*.

File Locking

This is enacted either by automatic or manual means.

Automatic Locking

The vendors of most Network Operating Systems use file-locking and record-locking techniques, to allow applications to control access to the files. Thus, spreadsheets, databases and word processors can run happily on the network.

The default locking mechanism overcomes the simultaneous update clashes by stopping file sharing completely. However, most application files are never updated and could therefore be shared by many simultaneous users. To provide this flexibility, the software will not lock a file that is set to be Read Only. It would seem to make sense, therefore, to set all shareable programs to be Read Only. Unfortunately some applications, usually for reasons of copy protection, write to their own program and overlay files and this makes them effectively unshareable.

In Novell and Windows NT, the supervisor of the network can ensure that certain files are only able to be read but cannot be amended (i.e. written to). This allows multiple users to download and run system files, review product information, etc. from databases and read text files.

When a file is allowed to be written to, it is marked accordingly (by changing a file attribute bit). When one of these files is opened by a user, the file is automatically 'locked' by the network operating system. When another user attempts to open the same file, either a 'file locked' message is presented, or the user may be allowed to open the file on a read-only basis (dependent on the application being used). If a non-LAN version of an application is in use, other miscellaneous error messages are liable to be generated.

Manual Locking

Automatic locking works well in those situations where the file is kept open (therefore kept locked) during the entire time that the file is being worked on by a user. However, a number of applications (such as spreadsheets and word processors) only open the file, read the contents into computer memory, then close the file again. The user works on the data within memory, the file being closed - and therefore free to be opened by other users. When the user is finished working on the data, the file is re-opened to write away the new details. This presents most of the original problems, since the file is only locked during the actual process of reading and writing the data. Apart from the short time needed for disk operations, the file is free to be opened by anyone.

Because of this, many network applications ensure that the file is kept open for the entire period between opening and closing the file. A more flexible approach is giving the user control over whether the file should be locked. After all, the user may only load in a spreadsheet to view it - with no intention of making any alterations. In that situation, this first user might be quite happy that a second user could load and alter the worksheet file.

Deadly Embrace

Also known as deadlock, this is an ever-present threat for application programmers.

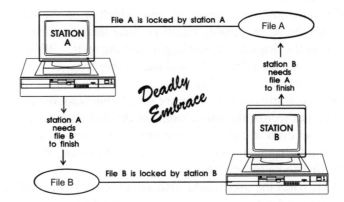

Consider the example shown in the diagram.

    Station A requires files A and B to be simultaneously open for its activities.
    Station B also requires files A and B to be simultaneously open for its activities.
    Station A wishes to use file A followed by file B, then end its program.
    Station B wishes to use file B followed by file A, then end its program.

Consider the following sequence:

- Station A accesses file A, locking the file to other users.
- Station B accesses file B, locking it to other users.
- Station A tries to open file B but is locked out.
- Station A cannot continue with its program, so file A is not closed.

- Station B tries to open file A but is similarly locked out.
- Station B cannot continue either, so file B is not closed.

Both stations now wait for the other to release the file they need to complete their program. This is an endless situation called *'deadlock'* or *'deadly embrace'*. The only solution is to terminate one of the programs, with any consequences that may produce.

The simplest way to prevent this problem is to write the software such that an application will acquire all its required resources <u>before</u> continuing with the program. This prevents deadlock but may result in valuable resources lying unused until the application is ready for it.

Record Locking

File locking is the most appropriate method for preventing possible concurrent updates but is unsuitable for databases, particularly large databases. A database is composed of a collection of individual records. A user is often only concerned with viewing/updating a single record in the file. It would be very inefficient if all other users had to wait for consecutive access to the file. A better method would be to lock at a record level, rather than file level. If a user wished access to a particular record, that record would be locked. This would allow the user to modify and save that record; all other users would only have read access to that record during that time. Of course, all the other records could be handled similarly, allowing many users concurrent access to the database - while only one user at a time could have write access to a particular record. In practice, it is usually more practical to lock a portion of the file, rather than individual records.

The above works well for modifying records but causes problems when a user wishes to add a new record to the file. Adding a record changes the file structure and many databases require that the entire file be locked during this alteration. Since the file can only be locked when there is only a single user and since the database is likely to be in continuous use by multiple users, additions to a file could be a time-consuming business.

The general solution is to design the database so that spare blank records are added to a database each time the system is used. This allows users to modify the blank records into new records - without the problems mentioned above.

Other Single-User Problems

Apart from the file-sharing problems already mentioned, there are other difficulties with using single-user software on networks:

Temporary Files

When running, a number of applications produce temporary files. During this period, a second user is effectively locked out. The solution is to direct the temporary output to different directories, using the applications configuration setups. Creating specific directories for different users overcomes the problem.

Configuration Files

Configuration files are used to determine the specific hardware, directories, etc. that an application will use. Since different nodes may have different hardware and directory requirements, the same copy of a program may not run on all stations. Dependent on the program, it is usually possible to overcome this by the use of individual batch files for each node.

Word Processing

Nowadays, word processors have an in-built spell-checker. There is no problem in simultaneous use of this dictionary, when users wish only to read the file. However, there is no control over users wishing to add new words to the dictionary. Since different nodes may well have different needs (e.g. to add financial, scientific or legal words to the dictionary) the file could soon become very large and contain many words never likely to be used by a particular node.

If the network application allows it, users could be granted personal extensions to the main dictionary - which would not be accessed by any other node's search. Of course, this option does not exist on single-user versions.

Copy Protection

Apart from the built-in check that certain applications make for their single-user version being used on a network, many programs have a general copy protection method built in. This prevents unauthorised copying of the program's master disks and often works by the timing of a disk operation or a direct read or write of the disk drive. Since this is impossible over a network, the program is treated as a pirate copy and will not function.

Purchasing Software

Most stand-alone applications are sold on a single-user basis.   This requires that the application be used by a single user on a single machine at a single site.

Borland (of Paradox, Turbo C, Turbo Pascal and Delphi fame) have no objection to the user and the site being varied, as long as only a single copy is being used at any one time. From a network point of view, a single copy can be downloaded to any one node at any one time. The responsibility of preventing concurrent use rests with the user.   Clearly, using single-user applications on a network can be difficult - not to mention illegal.   On the other hand, users don't wish to buy a complete package (disks, manuals, etc.) for every user on the network.

To meet this situation, an organisation can purchase a licence for a set number of concurrent users. For example, a 10-user licence would allow up to 10 users to run the application at the same time, from any of the stations on the network. When an 11th user attempts to use the application, access is denied until of the previous 10 users ceases running the application. Packages such as dBase and SuperCalc provide this method of licensing.

Languages

Networked application packages are very useful but do not meet everyone's needs. Consequently, there is a role for programming languages on a network. This means that the language has to have additional commands to make it operate a network - commands to implement the file locking facilities.

Client/Server Software

Up to recently, networks consisted simply of a collection of PCs which all processed independently. The linking of the stations was only used as a means of resource sharing and communications. As a consequence, many stations could be sitting idle while others were working flat out. The ideal world would have the idle stations carrying out some of the functions of the busy stations. Unfortunately, this is still some way off.   However, there are steps in this direction with the *'client/server'* systems.   In such a system, the user machine (the *'client'* or *'front end'*) concerns itself with the user interface/editing tasks, while the core data remains on the server end (or *'back-end'*).   The backend could, of course, be a mainframe, mini or high-end PC.   Not only does the data to be processed stay in the server, the actual processing of the data can now be done in the server end.

Advantages:

- Improves performance, due to reducing traffic on the network - since part of the processing coding remains on the server and the core data remains on the server. Since this is no longer required to be sent down the network, the normally heavy traffic can thereby be substantially reduced. With applications being ever more complex (thereby ever larger), the traffic reduction savings will become more and more significant.
- Makes savings on hardware upgrades.   With the increasing complexity of applications, came the demand for increased power from workstations. If the main tasks of the workstation are reduced to user interface activities then the node system can be relatively simple (therefore cheaper), while the high performance server `carries out the more demanding activities such as searching, sorting, producing statistics, etc. For example, why have a 600MHz Pentium III processor in each station. If calculations only account for 10% of the workload, then the station is being underused for 90% of the time.

Disadvantages:

- High initial software costs, due to having to buy both server software and client application software.
- The client database software (the software in each node) has to have SQL (Structured Query Language) capability and the database server software is more complex than normal server software.

The most common example of an application server is the SQL database server. Consider an earlier, non client-server type, network database package. A node would require to carry out all its processing in the node PC. So, to find out a count of all records matching search criteria (e.g. how many Glasgow-based customers in a file), the entire file would have to be copied along the network from the server to the node.   The processing of the records would then take place within the node PC.   This involves a substantial amount of network traffic.   If the network is a large user of databases, then the system would soon slow down to a snail's pace.

This is where SQL and client/server software comes in.   Structured Query Language provides a common database language, allowing the splitting of functions over different machines (of course, it can also be used on a single-user machine).   It is rapidly gaining acceptance as a standard and will provide some further compatibility between database applications.   Eventually, a single database server using SQL could be used to service requests from stations using different database packages.   The client (or 'Front End') is the node PC running the database package.   The client's job is to provide the user with the user interface - menus, output screens, query tools.   The database server (or 'Back End') carries out all the database functions such as storage allocation, indexing, record selection, file statistics, etc.   The user formulates a request in SQL, which is sent to the database server for implementation.   Thus, for a function such as narrowing a search to a subset of records, only the matching records are sent over the network. If the user requests a count of those records matching a set of criteria, then only the final figure is transmitted over the network.

This has the following benefits:

- Substantial reductions in network traffic, greatly enhancing overall network performance.
- More nodes can process the same file simultaneously; database servers are designed to be multi-tasking.

Implementations of the above techniques are now becoming available.   Open DataBase Connectivity (ODBC) makes connecting any Client based software, like Access, Excel or user-written programs in Pascal, C or Visual Basic practically trivial, and Back end drivers are readily available for major database packages such as Oracle, Sybase, DB2 and most mainframe systems.

Front-End and Back-End Processing

The previous sections have discussed Front End and Back End systems as being almost synonymous with

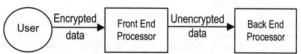

Client and Server systems.   However, in terms of data processing, both 'Front-End Processors' and 'Back-End Processors' are servers, and both perform data processing.

A typical example of Front-End and Back-End processing might be a sales system on the Internet.   The user wishing to purchase items online would communicate with the Front-End Processor, to select and order items. The Front-End Processor would provide security in the form of Encryption and Decryption, as well as other communications related functions such as error checking and data links.   However, the actual order information, once it has been decrypted and verified, would be passed on from the Front-End Processor to the Back-End Processor, which will take action on the order.

Using the Internet

Basics

The Internet is undoubtedly the largest computer resource on the planet. It enjoys a continual massive growth in the numbers using it and the facilities it offers. It is not a single entity; there is no Internet Ltd. At its simplest, it is a communications structure that links a huge number of independent PCs, networks and computer sites. The main features of Internet use are:

- Many computers systems throughout the world are permanently connected to each other (i.e. *'on-line'*), through an elaborate high-speed worldwide cabling system.
- Between them, these systems store a gigantic collection of information and opinion.
- The network allows the easy movement of information between the permanent sites on the Internet and the users who access the system.
- Individuals usually connect to the system using their own PCs, a modem and a line connection (e.g. telephone line, ADSL or cable). Many organisations (colleges, universities, etc) access the Internet through their own LAN.

Once connected, users have access to the material stored on the Internet. They can also send each other e-mail, download software and conduct commercial activity.

The facilities provided for Internet users include:

User Groups	Consumer reports	Press cuttings
Multi-user chat sessions	Software fixes, updates	Government statistics
Hardware/Software News	Research papers	Market information
On-line shopping	Search facilities	Travel information
On-line games	Newswire services	Downloading of programs
Distance learning	Latest drivers	Encyclopaedias
On-line magazines	Databases	Company information
Classified adverts	Webcams	Faxes

These facilities can be broadly categorised as:

Facility	What the user will do	What the user will see
Information Services	Access, read, copy and print material found on the Internet.	Text, graphics, sound, animations, video, forms.
E-Mail	Send/ receive/ store messages between users.	Plain ASCII messages or HTML text, sometimes with an added non-text *'attachment'*.
File Transfer	Copy files from a remote computer.	Files and directories.
Newsgroups/Chat	Exchange views in an open or closed forum of users with similar interests.	Questions, answers, opinions, blogs, displayed in plain ASCII text.

All of these facilities are covered later.

The background

The Internet began in the USA in the 70's as a Department of Defence sponsored interconnection of supercomputers for defence purposes and was called *'ARPAnet'* (Advanced Research Projects Agency). It was made up from a private web of leased lines between ARPA sites and defence contractors, with no public access. It is alleged that the system was designed to withstand a nuclear attack and therefore there was no central vulnerable 'master' computer. The system used a peer-to-peer method, where each computer could access another computer without the need for a centralised server. All the data was distributed throughout the system and there was no central store of data.

In 1971, there were only 23 computers connected to the network. During the 70's, remote connectivity, e-mail and file transfer was added and by 1977, there were over 100 computers connected to the network.

In the 80's, other academic networks joined ARPAnet to produce a large publicly funded university and research network. Universities use Unix servers, which have TCP/IP as their communication protocol. It became natural, therefore to adopt TCP/IP as the standard for the entire network, so that every computer could successfully communicate with each other. In 1982, ARPA adopted TCP/IP as the standard for the network.

In 1983, the military sections of the network spilt away to create their open network (MILNet), leaving behind a network largely used and run by academic institutions.

The Domain Name Server (DNS) system was introduced in 1984, allowing sites on the network to be identified by names rather than their IP addresses.

In 1987, there were over 10,000 computers connected to the network.

In 1989, the World Wide Web information service appeared, promoted by Tim Berners-Lee. Web pages, written in HTML could now contain graphics, audio and video instead of simple text. Hypertext allowed the pages to be linked, providing easy browsing. The user could jump from one resource to another, without having to know where it was actually stored. However, it was not until 1993 that the first graphic browser appeared ('Mosaic') that took best advantage of the WWW. This was followed in 1995 by the appearance of Netscape Navigator and in 1996 by Microsoft Explorer.

Note:

> The terms *"WWW"* and *"Internet"* are different. The Internet supplies many services such as e-mail, newsgroups, file transfer, etc. The World Wide Web uses the Internet to provide hyperlinked pages containing graphics, etc.

In 1989, there were over 100,000 computers connected to the network.

In 1990, the network backbone was taken over by a US Government agency, the National Science Foundation (NSFNET). In 1992, the huge growth in Internet use resulted in over one million computers being connected to the network.

In 1994, restrictions on commercial use of the network were removed and the network was turned over to the private sector. By 1995, most traffic on the Internet came from commercial communications and there were more .com domain names than there were .edu domain names. Of course, there is still a large presence on the Internet of education and research establishments.

The Structure

The original backbone has been extended throughout almost all major industrialised countries of the world, and is organised and run as a group effort by numerous telecommunications companies. It has been described as *"a network of networks"* and smaller localised clusters of networks are linked by high-speed telephone cables, microwave links, fibre optic cables, laser links and satellite links. Each stage of these links is paid for from the subscriptions of those using the local service.

In all, well over 10,000 separate networks are connected together. The British network connects main centres, known as POPs *('Points of Presence')*. These are the points where individual users connect to the overall system. The entire UK network is connected to the rest of the world through links from London to America, Stockholm and Paris.

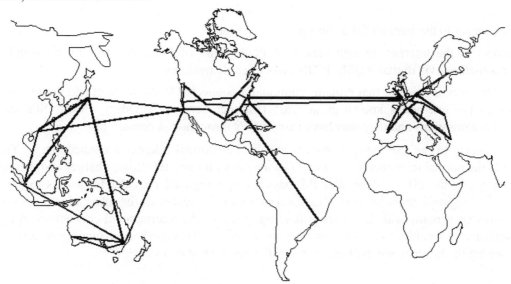

The diagram shows some of the major links used by the Internet.

The main links that carry the bulk of the traffic are called the *"Internet backbone"*. These link the USA, Europe, Japan, mainland Asia, etc. The main backbone sections use fibre optic paths running as fast as 2.48Gbps and copper lines running at 1.5Mbps (known as T1 lines) and 45Mbps (known as T3 lines). Other countries have slower links into the main backbone.

The USA began with four NSF-funded main routing centres (called Network Access Points or 'NAPs'), at San Francisco, Chicago, New York and Washington. There are now many more NAPs worldwide, and the network is always growing.

Routing messages

The chapter on *'Data Communications'* explained the principles of packet switching and how dynamic routing operated. In the Internet, a packet of data can also be routed along the section of the network that is the quickest at that point in time. So, for example, data from London to Tokyo may be directed along the London/Washington route or may be directed along the London/New York route. When the data gets to Los Angeles, it may be sent directly to Tokyo or may be directed via Australia. It all depends on which routes are congested and which are quiet at the time. These alternative routes provide a useful degree of *'redundancy'* – i.e. if one link breaks down, the alternative routes ensure that traffic continues to flow. Not surprisingly, the equipment that carries out these tasks is called a *"router"*. The network uses a mix of repeaters, hubs, bridges and gateways to provide the most efficient communication links.

A UK user may wish to talk to users in Germany or download a file from the USA, so the entire network has to be available to all the world's users. There is no centralised control of the traffic and since data packets can travel a variety of routes between the sending and receiving locations, all packets contain their own source and destination information as well as the data to be sent.

Connecting locally

Initially, the Internet was only for computers that were permanently connect to the network. Although individual users can now have their own permanent Internet connection (e.g. using ADSL), most private

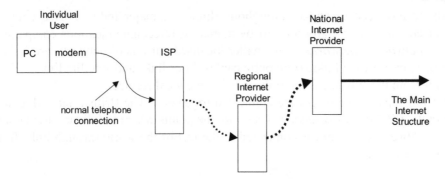

users only connect to the Internet for a short period at a time.

Users connect to the Internet through their own POP (Point of Presence), usually by simple dial-up modem or sometimes via digital ADSL/ ISDN links or cable modems.

A Point of Presence is a server that remains continually connected to the Internet and the provider of the connection to the Internet is known as an *'ISP'* (Internet Service Provider). Most ISPs are run by commercial organisations and they may have many POPs throughout a country or region.

The user connects to the ISP using a modem and his/her normal telephone connection. The ISP is accessed via the normal telephone network. The user pays for any telephone charges and usually pays a standing charge to the ISP. A smaller ISP pays a larger regional provider for access to the national network. The regional provider pays a national provider for access to the international network. The national provider, perhaps with government funding, pays for the international connection. A larger ISP may be sufficiently wealthy to provide its own main links. This method of funding results in no one actually owning the Internet and explains its title of *'a network of networks'*.

Internet Administration

Although there is little or no control of the Internet's data providers and users, several bodies administer the development of the general structure.

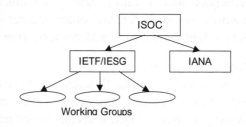

The Internet Society (ISOC) is the overall body that promotes Internet maintenance and evolution. It approves any new standards and protocols, ensuring that the whole structure remains compatible. The Society is a non-profit making body and is independent of any government control.

It has a President and a Board of 18 members and is located in Reston, USA.

A main component of the Internet Society is the Internet Engineering Task Force (IETF). IETF membership is open to any interested individual and the body consists of professionals from the networking industry (e.g. designers, manufacturers and operators). Its main function is to maintain standards regarding the physical network (i.e. the wiring structure internationally) to ensure the most efficient use and expansion of the communications links. Its technical work is carried out in specific topic areas such as Applications, Operations and Management, Routing, Security, etc. Each topic area is covered by a large number of working groups that look in detail at specific aspects. Each topic area is headed by an AD (Area Director) and each AD sits on the IESG (Internet Engineering Steering Group).

Another main body of the Internet Society is the Internet Architecture board (IAB). Its functions include reviewing the protocols and procedures used on the Internet and liasing with other national and international bodies that are concerned with communications standards. It also produces many papers to promote discussion and seek best experience and practice. These papers are known as RFCs (Request for Comment) and actively seek responses from interested parties.

ICANN (Internet Corporation for Assigned Names and Numbers) controls the allocation of domain names worldwide, with power for allocation in specific countires being devolved to approved national registrars (e.g. in the UK the domain name registrar is Nominet). Control remains with ICANN, which is non-profit, private sector corporation set up in 1998 by the US Department of Commerce. World control being wielded by a private corporation that is subject to US law (and a veto from the US Department of Commerce) has caused friction and complaints about its undemocratic nature.

The World Wide Web Consortium (W3C) controls the standards for HTML, the web page language.

User Addresses

Each Internet user is allocated a different identification code (their IP address) so that the station can be uniquely identified for routing, e-mail and other purposes. Each user is registered through one of the Network Information Centres (NICs). Each NIC allocates blocks of IP addresses, to ISPs. These ISPs then allocate them to individual users or groups of users.

All communication on the Internet uses the same protocol (methods of transmission and reception) to allow PCs to communicate with Unix systems, Macintoshes, etc. The Internet protocol is TCP/IP and is explained in the chapter on *'Data Communications'*.

The IP part of the protocol requires each station on the system to have a unique address. This IP address consists of four bytes, each storing a value between 0 and 255, and is written with a period separating them. Therefore, a valid IP address might be

175.73.44.11

The NIC issues blocks of addresses in three ways.

Class A addresses	Class A addresses are issued with the first byte fixed by the NIC. The provider receiving the Class A address can allocate over 16 million unique addresses.
Class B addresses	With Class B, the first two bytes are fixed, allowing the provider to allocate over 65,536 unique addressees.
Class C addresses	This has the first three bytes already allocated, allowing the provider a maximum of 254 unique addresses (the 0 and 255 address being used for other purposes).

Note: This 'class-based' system of IP allocation is largely outdated even though it is still in use by some networks, and is shown mainly for illustrative purposes. To alleviate the shortage of available IP numbers, most routers and other Internet equipment now understand and use the more versatile 'class-less' CIDR system of IP address allocation, as explained in the Data Communications chapter.

Domain Names

Using numbers for the IP address is very confusing and users prefer to be identified by an agreed text substitute. The text is easier to understand and consists of a hierarchy of allocated *'domain'* and *'sub-domain'* names. These text equivalents map on to the actual numeric addresses. When a user's account is set up, these details are stored in a DNS (domain name server) and all providers can access these servers to translate text names into the corresponding address for routing purposes.

The *'Top Level Domain'* (TLD) names are allocated by the NIC and the original set of TLDs is shown in the first table. These are specific categories on the Internet and show their organisational status. The list includes allocations for each country. For example, the letters *'uk'* indicate that it is a British TLD, with *'fr'* for France and so on. America is allocated *'us'* but it is rarely used; if no country is specified in an address, the domain is generally either US or multinational. The TLDs that

Top Level Domains	
com	commercial organisation
org	non-profit making organisation
gov	government
mil	military
edu	educational establishment
net	networking organisation
int	international organisation
uk, de, etc	country codes

are not specific to any country are called *'generic top level domains'* or *'gTLDs'*.

The *'uk'* top level domain is further allocated into sub-domains. These include sub-domains such as *'co'* (commercial) and *'ac'* (academic).

Where a site is stored on an ISP, the ISP name is included as a further sub-domain level name.

The example shows the domain name for the *'dumbreck'* site. The individual or organisation sponsoring the web site is known as the *'hostname'* or *'nodename'*. Hostnames can be from 3 to 22 characters in length. Since *'dumbreck'* is located on the Demon ISP, its full address is *'dumbreck.demon.co.uk'*

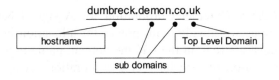

Larger organisations own their own web server and are not be a sub-domain of another ISP. Examples are *'tesco.co.uk'* and *'sony.com'*.

Every user has both a unique domain name (e.g. dumbreck) and a unique IP address.

The site address is written with the lowest level first, moving to the highest level. It is similar to writing an address on an envelope (i.e. name, address, city, and country).

Using DNS

It would be impossible for every Internet server in the world to keep a copy of every domain name of every user in the world and to maintain the constant daily changes. The DNS uses a distributed database approach, which means that the information on domain names is spread throughout many servers in the system. Each ISP keeps a database on its systems and users (e.g. Demon keeps its own database). Above these are the *'root servers'* and they store information on the lower domain levels.

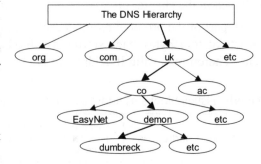

So, for instance, sending a message to
                sales@dumbreck.demon.co.uk
initiates a visit to a root server to find a server that handles .uk domains (i.e. a DNS server based in the UK).
A visit is then paid to that server, where information on .co domains is then requested. This is followed by a request to find the Demon server and a visit to the Demon server than results in the IP address being returned.

In this way, each intermediate server has much less updating to handle and all the major additions and deletions of individual domain names is handled by each ISP.

E-mail addresses

Internet subscribers with a single address have a potential e-mail problem. A domestic subscriber may wish e-mail to be sent to different family members. A company may have many employees who require individual or departmental e-mail addresses. Setting up separate Internet accounts for each person is far too costly. Fortunately, most ISPs are prepared to process multiple e-mail accounts for a single Internet account. Each user has an agreed e-mail name and this is used along with the @ symbol.

So, the following address would be easy to remember:

sales@dumbreck.demon.co.uk

This is the Dumbreck Publishing account and shows the account's host name is *'dumbreck'*; the domain name is called *'Demon'* which is one of the largest commercial Internet service providers based in the UK. Mail with that address is stored under the *'sales'* mail name.

If a number of computers were based at a site (as in universities), the full address might be:

eddie@science.lumchester.ac.uk

The computer's name is *'science'* and is one computer attached to the *'lumchester'* university in the UK. Eddie is a user of the *'science'* system.

Addressing shortages

The success of the Internet has caused difficulties in allocating names to all new subscribers.

The Problem

Each IP address contains four bytes. The first three bytes each store 256 usable combinations and the last byte stores 254 combinations. In theory, this provides for 256 x 256 x 256 x 254 = 4,264 million unique addresses. Since there are not 4 billion Internet users, the system would seem to have capacity for some time to come.

However, the way the addresses are allocated limits this. For example, each of the over 100 Class A addresses consumes well over ten million IP addresses, when very few organisations could hope to use even a tenth of that number. Even Class B addresses are over specified for the majority of users needs, wasting many more addresses.

To make matters worse, a range of IP addresses are reserved for use on internal networks. If these problems were not addressed, the Internet would already have run out of allocateable IP numbers, despite having many unused addresses.

Additionally, the requirement to associate a text name to each address (see *'Domain Names'* earlier) has resulted in a severe shortage. Users want meaningful text names for their address and there are not 4 billion combinations of useable names. If a set of four numbers was hard to remember, users would have little chance of recalling an address such as *'zzqq2bntr3xa.co.uk'*

This problem is worsened by the now common practice of *'cybersquatting'*. Cybersquatters are professional Domain Name hoarders, collecting those names that they feel are likely to be in demand in the near future. When another group or individual wants to register a domain name they could well find that it has already been taken up by an organisation whose only purpose there is to sell the name to them at an inflated price. Although occasionally court action can evict these groups from their domains, it is still a common practice, with some cybersquatters registering hundreds of names at a time.

The rapid rate of take-up of addresses means that there will soon be no meaningful names left to allocate.

The shortage is worsened in certain areas by:

- Americans being reluctant, until recently, to take up the *'.us'* TLD. As the originators of the Internet, they did not feel the need to use the 'us' TLD but, since 9/11, many have adopted the TLD as a demonstration of their 'Americanness'.
- Non-Americans wishing to appear multinational by adopting *'.com'* as a domain, instead of *'.co.uk'*

If some TLDs are fully occupied while others are underused, using up unused names cannot alter the balance. For example, an unused name in a *'.us'* domain cannot be used by a UK commercial company.

The Solution

The answer lies in the general expansion of the system through:

- Additional addresses
- Additional domain names

Additional Addresses

The original IP system, known as IPv4, has been supplemented by additional techniques such as CIDR (Classless Inter-Domain Routing), DHCP (Dynamic Host Configuration Protocol) and NAT (Network Address Translation) in order to reduce the strain on IP addresses. Even with these, IPv4 will run out of addresses eventually, and the replacement, IPv6, uses 16 bytes instead of 4. Even at conservative estimates this allows for over a thousand IP addresses for every square metre of land on Earth.

This vastly exceeds all foreseeable needs and is intended for future uses of the Internet. This would include connecting all domestic appliances to the Internet and communicating with each through their unique addresses. Office workers could switch on their central heating and microwave ovens before leaving the office. Similarly, commercial appliances could be remotely monitored and controlled. Automatic dispensing machines can be checked for low stock without leaving the depot and inhospitable sites can be remotely controlled (e.g. switching on defrosters at remote radio masts).

The new system is known as IPv6 and is being built in to modern software (e.g. the latest browsers) and hardware (e.g. network routers) in anticipation of its implementation.   Apart from more addresses, IPv6 also provides faster and more efficient operation, as well as additional features like streaming support.

Additional Domain Names

ICANN has introduced new TLDs, as shown in the table.

A rival company, New.net, has already set up its own group of 20 TLDs (including .ltd, .mp3, .shop and .video). However, these require new browser plug-ins, or co-operating ISPs, to allow access to sites with those TLDs. Co-operating ISPs amend their domain name servers to recognise these new TLD suffixes.

In 2002, the European Union agreed a new .eu TLD.

New Top Level Domains	
Info	Open to public
biz	Businesses
name	Individual's names
aero	Aviation groups
museum	Accredited museums
coop	Business cooperatives
pro	Professionals

Internet protocols

The chapter on *'Data Communications'* explained the operation of TCP/IP in some detail. The table shows the most important protocols used for Internet communication and outlines two different approaches for interfacing to the Internet.

http, ftp, smtp, pop3, telnet	Streaming media DNS lookups
TCP (connection based protocol)	UDP (connectionless protocol)
Internet Layer – IP addressing and routing	
Network Interface – modem, ADSL line, ISDN line, etc.	

TCP

TCP is a connection based protocol. This means that the communications required by the application do not start until after a success link has been established between both sides of an activity. It maintains a reliable connection, checks that all packets have been received and requests resending of any lost or corrupted packets. It is the more reliable of the two systems.

Several protocols run 'on top' of TCP, in the TCP/IP 'application layer', which is effectively equivalent to the OSI layers 5, 6 and 7 (Session, Presentation and Application layers).

They include:

HTTP : The *'Hypertext Transfer Protocol'* is the method used to read HTML files. Under HTTP, the browser sends the server requests in text format, and the server returns text files (HTML) that are interpreted and displayed on the screen.

SHTTP : *'Secure HTTP'* is basically HTTP with security built in. It provides message security, but not connection security, so other security specifications (such as SSL, 'Secure Sockets Layer') can be used alongside SHTTP. However, SSL has become more popular than SHTTP, and hypertext transfer using SSL security is generally called 'HTTPS'.

FTP : The *'File Transfer Protocol'* is the method where a user, employing *'FTP client'* software, can access a remote *'FTP server'* site, allowing files to be copied from the server to the user's computer (downloading) or from the user's computer to the server's disk system (uploading).

SMTP : The *'Simple Mail Transport Protocol'* is the original e-mail mechanism used by ARPAnet and can still be found in use today. Any message is sent in two parts – the header (which carries information on the sender and the recipient) and the body (which contains the actual e-mail message). SMTP is used to transmit e-mail messages from one mail server to another. It also allows a user to establish a link with his/her own mail server.

POP3 : While SMTP is used to both send and receive messages, the *'Post Office Protocol'* is only used to retrieve messages from a mail server. When a user is sent an e-mail, it is transmitted via SMTP and sits on the user's mail server until it is accessed. POP3 is the most popular method of accessing e-mail and messages can either be read or downloaded onto the user's PC (via his/her e-mail software). By default, messages are copied to the user's home computer and deleted from the mail server. All messages, including embedded attachments such as audio or video files are fully downloaded and can be viewed offline. This is known as the 'offline model'. POP3 has been adapted to also support the 'online model', where messages are download to the local PC but are not deleted from the mail server. POP3 is a retrieval mechanism only; if a user wants to send an e-mail, it is sent to the mail server using SMTP.

IMAP : The *'Internet Message Access Protocol'* is a newer e-mail protocol where the e-mail messages remain on the mail server. The user stays online while being presented with the e-mail message headers. Only the messages that interest the user need be read fully or downloaded. This saves a user a long wait while large numbers of junk mail messages and messages with unwanted graphics, etc. are downloaded in their entirety on to his/her local PC (as is the default with POP3). IMAP also allows the user to create storage folders in the mail server and is a preferred mode where multiple users share e-mail or where a user wishes to access e-mail from many different locations (e.g. travelling salesmen). The account can be set up so that the folders, address book, etc. will appear identical to the user, no matter what computer is used to check the e-mail. Users can log in from their home PC, another PC in the office, from an Internet café, etc.
Like POP3, IMAP is a retrieval mechanism only; if a user wants to send an e-mail, it is sent to the mail server using SMTP.

NNTP : Newsgroups use their own protocol, known as *'Network News Transfer Protocol'*, to post, distribute and retrieve news messages. A newsreader can be considered an NNTP client, which sends NNTP messages to the *'news server'*. It, in turn, distributes news items to other servers via the NNTP protocol.

In addition, there are various protocols that are based on the IP protocol. Some operate at the same level as the IP protocol, despite being based on it. These include:

SNMP : This is the *'Simple Network Management Protocol'*, and as its name suggests it is used to manage various aspects of network operation. An SNMP *'manager'* is a computer system that uses special software to send requests to various SNMP *'agents'* on the network. These requests are used to view or alter a wide range of settings, but the agent can also send a *'trap'* message without a request being sent, if it detects something unusual happening. Some typical SNMP agents include network printers, routers, and so on.

IGMP : The *'Internet Group Management Protocol'* is used by multicast systems (explained in the *'Data Communications'* chapter). A device with an IP address uses IGMP to register their membership in one or more multicast 'groups', and routers can use this information to send multicast messages to the correct targets on an IP system.

ICMP : This is the *'Internet Control Message Protocol'* and it is mainly used internally for diagnostic and control purposes. However, two applications that use ICMP include *'Ping'* and *'Traceroute'*. The 'Ping' program simply sends a test packet to a specified IP or DNS address and waits for an acknowledgement, thus proving that the address refers to a device that can be reached. Traceroute (called TRACERT on Windows systems) goes one step further, and shows the address and response speed of each network 'hop' between the local host and the specified IP or DNS address.

ARP : The *'Address Resolution Protocol'*'s purpose is to define a method by which any device on a broadcast network (such as an Ethernet network or the Internet in general) can query another device to find the hardware (or 'MAC') address that corresponds to a particular allocated IP address. The *'Reverse Address Resolution Protocol'* (RARP) was used to do the opposite, but has since been overtaken by such protocols as BOOTP and DHCP.

UDP

The User Datagram Protocol is connectionless. This means that it avoids all the complications of HTTP and is therefore much quicker. Reliability is sacrificed for speed. Datagrams (i.e. packets) are sent out one after the other, with no previous handshaking between systems and therefore no method of knowing whether all the packets were received successfully. While loss of packets would result in unusable data for many messages (e.g. sending executable programs, spreadsheets, etc.), other applications can accept the occasional loss of data in return for increased speed. A good example of this is streamed media, where an occasional loss of packet would only result in a tiny blip in an audio track, or a judder or unwanted line or artifact on a video stream. Unlike TCP, UDP does not place the incoming packets into their correct order and so streamed media needs an additional protocol, called RTP (Real-Time Transport Protocol) to reassemble incoming packets. UDP is also used for DNS lookups.

MIME and UUENCODE

The standard for sending text messages over the Internet is 7-bit ASCII text. This is fine for text-only messages but many users want to include non-text attachments to their e-mail messages. Examples are graphics, executables, spreadsheets - or any other form of binary file. The Internet Engineering Task Force produced a new MIME(Multipurpose Internet Mail Extensions) standard in 1993.

Where both the sending and receiving e-mail packages support MIME standards, non-ASCII files can be transmitted along with the messages. The e-mail message header contains details of each item included in the message, along with details of the file type.

For example, an entry in the header may describe attachments as

    Content-Type:image/jpeg
    Content-Type:video/mpeg

An older but still commonly used variant is UUencode (Unix-to-Unix encode), which converts 8-bit binary files into 7-bit versions for transmission. A UUdecoder at the receiving computer translates the file back into its original binary form.

Getting on the Internet

Connection to the Internet requires the following:

- A modem for telephone line access or a terminal adapter for an ISDN or ADSL link.
- A connection to a service provider. This is usually a dial-up or ADSL connection on a normal telephone line, or a permanent connection using an ISDN or Cable link.

- An account with an ISP
  (Internet Service Provider. All provide basic services such as WWW, e-mail and newsgroups, while some also provide free web site space, technical support, chat rooms, multiple email aliases and additional private services. Costs vary substantially between different suppliers. Some have fixed monthly charges, while other charge by the amount of data downloaded.
- Interface application software such as Explorer, Opera or Firefox.

The *'Hardware Installation'* chapter explains the major steps in installing a modem and the appropriate software.

ISPs

An Internet Service provider provides the user with a temporary dial-up connection to the Internet. The ISP has fast permanent links to the Internet and has a bank of modems for use by its subscribers. A subscriber accesses the ISP by dialling the POP telephone number, using the normal telephone line. The telephone exchange connects the subscriber to one of the ISP's modems and this temporary connection is maintained as long as the user wishes. The cost of the call is payable to the telephone company.

Once connected to the ISP, the caller has to provide a password to the ISP, to prove that he/she is a valid subscriber. This process is often embedded in the user's connecting software. The ISP's dialling code and the user's password are stored on the local computer, to automate the login. One click of an icon provides the telephone number for the modem and the ISP is provided with the password when requested. Once into the system, the user can access some of the bandwidth of the high-speed connection for Internet surfing, or can make use of the facilities that are stored locally on the ISP's own server. Some of these facilities are made available to all Internet users (e.g. subscriber's web sites or mirror sites). Other on-line providers such as AOL provide facilities that are restricted to their own subscribers. These subscribers can choose to view the ISP's internal material, or use the ISP as a link to the wider Internet.

World Wide Web

The World Wide Web, usually called the Web or WWW, produces the largest share of all Internet traffic. It combines all existing facilities within a modern graphical environment.   Its documents are read using a browser - a utility to assist the user through the Web.

The Web's features include:

- Hypertext browsing (*'point and click'* on links to other resources).
- Screens displaying graphics and animations.
- Playing video in AVI, MPEG or QuickTime format.
- Running downloaded sub-programs via Java.
- Audio on Demand and Video on Demand.
- 3-D VRML models.
- Real-time voice Telephony.

Typical uses of the WWW

Personal	Obtaining information on television programs, the weather, etc.
	Requesting product information (e.g. holiday brochures).
Professional	Searching for reference material (e.g. scientists, medical practitioners, journalists).
	Obtaining technical updates (e.g. for computer technicians, engineers).
Commercial	Conducting e-commerce (electronic commerce).
	Advertising goods and services.
	Taking orders for products; accepting VISA transactions.
	Obtaining the latest information (e.g. financial newspapers, the Stock Market).

The WWW uses special software to package these Internet contents. This is required at both the ISP end and at the user's end. This has led to the development of *'Web Servers'* and *'Web Browsers'*.

Web Servers

Web servers are computers permanently attached to the Internet.   A large company or organisation will have its own server to exclusively store its own web site.   Smaller web sites will rent out space on the drives of an ISP or web space may be supplied free as part of the rental agreement.   A single ISP may act as the host to tens of thousands of web sites for small companies, organisations and individuals.

A web site stored on a web server consists of a number of individual web *'pages'*.   Each page is written in HTML (the HyperText Markup Language).   HTML is the language designed to deliver text, graphics, audio, etc to users with the software able to interpret it.   The software that re-creates the web page at the user's end is called a *'Web Browser'*.

Web Browsers

Software that is used on the local computer is known as *'client'* software, while the ISP end uses *'server'* software.   The most used piece of client software is the Web client - known as the *'browser'*.   It translates the HTML files from the server into readable pages at the client end.   It uses the HTML script to build the page's text, graphics, etc in the order written in the script (see chapter on Web Site Creation).

It also makes extensive use of *'hypertext'*.   Hypertext replaced older, text menu-based access systems.

In the Web, the user is presented with an attractive graphical screen document. The document may contain graphical images and the screen text may have words or phrases that are highlighted. These highlighted areas point to information in another part of the document - or an entirely different document. The other documents may reside anywhere on the Internet. So, clicking on a hyperlink area (the highlighted text or icon) downloads the document pointed to by the hyperlink. This other document may consist of further text with further links, or it may even contain a video clip, an audio clip, a small Java program, etc. The hypertext features of the Web make it an ideal learning environment, where the user can explore paths that are of particular interest.

By far the most widely used Web browsing software is *'Microsoft Internet Explorer'*, with a small proportion of users having other browsers such as '*Netscape*', '*Opera*' or the open-source '*Mozilla*'. The browser developers strive to continually add new features (e.g. video, audio, animation, VRML, scripting) and some web sites insist that Internet Explorer be used for best results, since their sites are optimised to use the latest features of that browser.

Inconsistencies

The World Wide Web Consortium (W3C) issues regular updates to the standards for HTML, currently in main version 4. HTML is intended to be a language that is universally understood by all browsers.

However, the following problems exist:

- If the latest HTML innovation or add-ons for animations, audio, video, etc are used, then only browsers equipped with these facilities will be able to make use of all the site's features.
- Various brands of browser, and even different versions of the same brand, may produce different screen results while executing the same HTML command. In fact, even differently configured installations of the exact same software can produce varying results.
- Due to constant changes/additions, no browser software faithfully implements all available web content.

URLs

Every web site has its own unique domain name and every document on the site has its own reference (given by its file name and the name of any folder that it is stored in). The combination of the domain name, directory name (if any) and file name provide a unique description of that document. This description is known as the URL (Universal Resource Location). There is a separate URL for every single document on the entire Internet.

Internet browser software uses URLs to fetch documents, either through clicking on hyperlinks or by the user entering the URL from the keyboard.

The illustration shows part of the screen of the Internet Explorer browser.

The URL is a long single item of text without spaces and in the above example is

http://www.intel.com/index.htm

The part before the colon specifies the type of access. In the example *'http'* is used; this is the *'Hypertext Transfer Protocol'* and is the method required to read HTML files.

Other possible access options include FTP, Gopher or Archie. The remainder of the line specifies the server that is being accessed and may optionally include a path and file name at the end.

Since not every page is a hyperlinked document, the URL is valid for other access methods, as in this example:

ftp://ftp.cdrom.com/pub/cdrom/photo_cd/writeablecd.txt

The browser's '*bookmarks*' menu manages a user's database of URLs, allowing URLs to be added, deleted and given user-defined titles (e.g. *"stuff about disk specifications"*). Web sites can then be easily fetched from the pull-down pick list instead of having to be sought and manually entered.

Using Internet Explorer

Every web browser requires that the computer already have a valid IP address, either allocated statically on a network already linked to the Internet, or dynamically such as via a firewall or ISP.

Once an IP address is established, the first thing a user sees in Explorer is the default home page (see later). A typical Microsoft Explorer window is shown in the illustration.

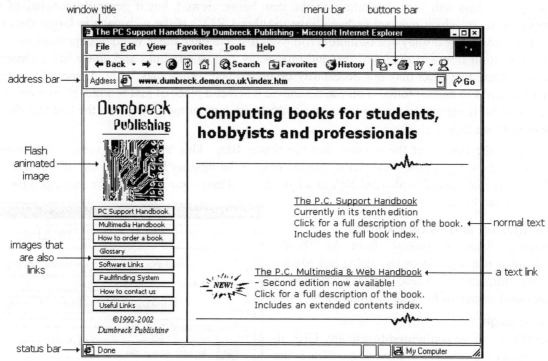

At the top of the window is the title, which all Windows applications normally show. Underneath is the menu bar, also common to most Windows applications. However, users rarely need to access these menus to navigate the web properly. In most cases, Explorer is set up to display the Buttons Bar below the menu bar. This toolbar contains a variety of buttons to aid navigation and usage of the web.

From left to right, those functions are:

- Back: As the web is navigated, Explorer stores a History of the locations that have been visited. The *'Back'* button returns the user from the page currently being viewed to the page last viewed. Of course, you can only go back as far as the first page that was displayed when Explorer started up.

- Forward: This is the opposite of the *'Back'* button, moving forwards through Explorer's History rather than back. Of course, if the *'Back'* button has not been pressed, the user is at the end of the History and therefore there are no pages forward of that point and the *'Forward'* button is greyed out.

- Stop: If a web page is taking a long time to load (perhaps because of a network fault or a page with a lot of graphics), the *'Stop'* button causes Explorer to stop downloading and display as much as it managed to download.

- Refresh: This button forces Explorer to reload the entire page and its contents. This is useful when the *'Stop'* button has halted downloading before a full page is loaded. It is also useful for web pages that update very frequently, such as pages of news or pages that record usage of your website.

- Home: The *'Home'* button is a short way to send the browser straight back to the page which has been set as the browser default home page.

- Search: The *'Search'* button opens up a special bar called the *'Explorer Bar'*. The Explorer bar appears in the left hand side of the main page view, with facilities that allow the user to enter criteria for sending to Microsoft's search engine on the web.

- Favorites: The *'Favorites'* button opens up the Explorer bar, displaying the contents of the user's *'Favorites'* folder. These contents are also accessible via the *'Favorites'* menu on the menu bar, and are also available to other programs.

- History: The *'History'* button opens up the Explorer bar, displaying the user's browser history. Explorer not only records the web pages visited in one session, but also the web pages accessed on previous dates.

Below the Button Bar lie the address bar and the links bar. The address bar contains a text box, which contains the URL of the current page being displayed. If the user wishes to go to a specific URL without having to follow links, he/she types the URL into this text box. As soon as the *'Enter'* key is pressed, Explorer tries to download the contents of the URL.

The main page view is normally located under all these toolbars and is where the web site contents are displayed.   This will vary depending on the item being viewed, but it generally consists of text and images, some of which may act as hyperlinks to other URLs. If the web page is larger than the main window size, it may display one or more scroll bars, just like most other Windows applications.

The illustration shows examples of text and images, as well as text links and image links. Depending on the web page, text links may not necessarily be underlined – they may be bold, specially coloured, or even displayed in normal fonts. You can determine whether a piece of text is a link by moving the mouse to point at it. If the mouse pointer turns into a hand with a pointing finger, then the text that the finger is pointing at is a link.

Finally, at the bottom of the window lies the Status Bar. This toolbar has various functions. Most notable of these is the download status, located next to the Internet Explorer icon.   It may, for example, tell the user that it has downloaded 50% of a 64k file, or it may simply display the message *"Done"* if the download has been completed.

Configuring and using Explorer

Selecting *'Internet Options'* from the *'Tools'* drop-down menu produces the dialog box shown in the illustration. These options provide a significant degree of browser configuration.

Home page

Explorer can be configured to use any URL to access any resource as a home page. This is the first option offered when the *'General'* tab is clicked.   The URL of the user's most-commonly used web site can be entered, or a blank screen (i.e. not linked to any web page) can be displayed.

Cache size

As a user browses through various web pages,

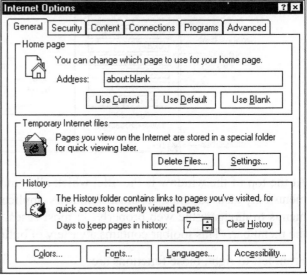

the page contents are displayed on the monitor screen. They are also stored on the user's hard disk, in a folder called *'Temporary Internet Files'*.   If the user returns to that site, the page contents are fetched from the hard disk instead of being downloaded over the Internet. This greatly speeds up the display of regularly visited pages.   Of course, this also means that hard disk space is required to store the pages.

The second option under the *'General'* tab allows the balance between speed of page access and loss of hard disk space to be set. Clicking the *'Settings'* button allows the amount of disk space to be set by dragging the slider or manually altering the value in the entry box.

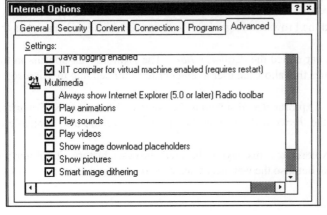

Turning off graphics

Downloading text is fast while downloading images is slow. If a user is more interested in the page text content than the pretty pictures, browsing can be greatly speeded up. The illustration shows the options available under the *'Advanced'* tab. Unchecking the *'Show Pictures'* box prevents graphics images from downloading. Bear in mind, however, that graphics images are often used as navigation buttons.

Security

Over the years, Internet security has become an ever bigger issue, due to the instances of hacking and virus attacks. Clicking the *'Security'* tab produces a menu that provides a variety of security options. The web sites that users visit can be categorised as *'Trusted Sites'* where security is low, *'Restricted Sites'* where security is high and an *'Internet Zone'* where security is medium. When the user enters a web site, its status is checked against the saved lists and the appropriate security action is taken for that site. So, for example, a Trusted Site may be allowed by the user to download files or run programs.
The security options for each zone can be set up using the *'Custom Level'* button. Examples of security measures are turning off ActiveX controls and JavaScript support (to prevent possible virus attacks) and turning off cookies (to prevent possible privacy intrusion).

Changing page text size

The point size used for web page text can be altered to allow easier viewing for users with visual impairment. The *'Text Size'* option of Explorer's *'View'* drop-down menu provides facilities to increase or decrease the screen text size.

Working full screen

Pressing the F11 key on the keyboard removes almost all of the toolbars from the Explorer window, and maximises the window, so that the web page displays on the entire screen. Full screen display is useful because some web pages are optimised for display on a full 800 x 600 screen, for example.

Saving a web page

An individual web page can be saved to the local hard disk, by selecting the *'Save As'* option from the *'File'* drop-down menu. This saves the complete page contents including text, graphics, etc.

Spyware

The name 'Spyware' is given to a piece of, usually unwanted, software that is installed along with another application. The user is usually not informed of the existence of the Spyware, although it is sometimes referred to in the licence agreement. When installed, the Spyware gathers information about the user's online browsing preferences and this is transmitted back to the producer of the utility – without the knowledge or explicit agreement of the user. The information is then used for targeted online advertising.

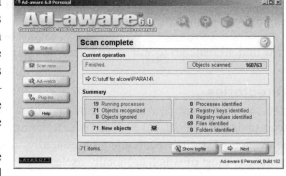

Ad-aware is a freeware utility that scans the computer's memory, Window's registry and hard drives. Any unwanted Spyware is detected and the user is given the option of deleting these elements.

Web Searches

The Web is a vast area to explore and help is required to locate resources.
There are two methods of searching the web:

- Using a *'Search Engine'* (typing in keywords to search for).
- Using a *'Directory'* (a hierarchy of menus).

Hundreds of web sites exist to point the user to their desired area of interest. They may provide little or no content of their own. They do not act primarily as information providers. They exist to organise the user's browsing and searching capability.

Search Engines

Search engines are software tools provided to aid users to locate the material that interests them. Google, with an index of over 3 billion web pages, is the most popular search engine. Teoma is another example of a standalone search engine. Many popular sites, such as Yahoo, Lycos and AltaVista, provide both searching and directory facilities. Yahoo now uses the Google search engine.
In a text search, the user enters the key word or words that describe the item and requests that a search is made of the Internet for items that match the given description. Searches can be made of the web sites or of the material stored in the user group directories.

There are a few golden rules of searching:

- Be as specific as possible. Searching on *'Computers'* will result in an enormous number of matches. Searching through all of these matches would take months. Searching for *"Compaq"*, for example, will narrow the search considerably and produce far fewer useless matches. Searching for a specific model of computer would narrow the search even further.
- If searching for a specific file, use the file extension in the search. A search for *'winzip'* will probably produce many matches that only contain comments such as *"winzip is great!"*. Searching for *"winzip.exe"* will reduce the number of wasted matches.
- Learn and use the differing search syntax available for the search engines used.

Searches allow for more than a single word to be entered and this produces a much more refined search. The common search syntax used by many search engines is shown in the following examples:

Search text	Result
car OR engine	Finds any matches on *'car'* (e.g. restaurant car) and also any other separate matches on *'engine'* (e.g. steam engine)
"car engine"	Finds matches on car and engine as a single entity; only references to car engines are displayed. Pages containing *'fire engine'*, *'sports car'* and/or *'engine car'* will not be found.
car engine car AND engine +car +engine	Finds matches only where both the words appear. *'engine'* on its own is not found. *'car'* on its own is not found. *'engine car'* and *'car engine'* will both be found.
car +engine	Finds all matches where *'engine'* appears but not necessarily containing *'car'*. *'racing car'* will not be found, while *'steam engine'* will be found.
car -engine	Finds matches on all car references, except those containing the word *'engine'*

Some search engines allow more complex searches to be built up, by combining various Boolean expressions using parenthesis.   For example

car and (engine or steering)

will find all matches to *'car engine'* and *'car steering'* but not *'car sales'* or *'steering rod'*.

Directories

Search engines are powerful but can have drawbacks.   Automated *'robots'* or *'spiders'* roam around the web updating the databases used by search engines. These do not attempt to evaluate the usefulness or relevance of a site's contents. Consequently, a simple search can result in hundreds or thousands of matches - most of which are totally useless.

Web directories (also known as *'portals'*), on the other hand, are compiled and updated by the directory site operators. They select sites and place them into categories that are accessed through user-selected menus. This makes them easy to use and they are ideal for the casual user.

The directory's menu hierarchy system is very popular and most packages use this method.

The illustration shows the main choices offered by Yahoo. The *'Computing'* option has a further list of sub-options. Some may have further sub-options in turn.   When there are no more menus, the user is offered a list of resources (such as reviews, shareware programs, academic papers, etc) that can be viewed or downloaded.

Business & Economy B2B, Finance, Shopping, Jobs...	**Recreation & Sports** Sports, Travel, Autos, Outdoors...
Computers & Internet Internet, WWW, Software, Games...	**Reference** Libraries, Dictionaries, Quotations...
Education College and University, K-12...	**Regional** Countries, Regions, US States...
Entertainment Picks, Movies, Humor, Music...	**Science** Animals, Astronomy, Engineering...
Government Elections, Military, Law, Taxes...	**Social Science** Archaeology, Economics, Languages...
Health Medicine, Diseases, Drugs, Fitness...	**Society & Culture** People, Environment, Religion...

Since directory operators make money from the advertising space they rent out, they tend to maintain their system to cover the most popular material on the web. When a user wants a specific specialised item, it is unlikely to be available via menus and therefore search engines provide the best route.

Browser Enhancements

A range of add-ons can be downloaded (many are free or are shareware) and installed on a computer to enhance its range of capabilities. These include:

Java

Java, which is essentially similar to the C++ programming language, can be used to create *'applets'*. These are small programs that can be downloaded along with HTML files and graphics files. They are then run within the calling PC. Applets range from simple animated icons and games through to database utilities. They require that the browser support Java.

Active-X

A set of rules developed by Microsoft, it provides around 1000 Windows controls. It is also designed to be downloaded and run within the local computer. Whereas Java is capable of running all platforms (i.e. - on any type of computer) that are Java-enabled, Active-X is solely designed for Windows. Its controls can be written in C, C++, Visual Basic and Java.

Real Time Telephony

Users with a sound card and a microphone, or compatible telephone, can talk in real time to other similarly equipped users throughout the world. Charges range from free to reduced call rates. Products such as *'Skype'* provide the software to call up one of a range of specially created servers. These list all users who are attached to the service and are currently on-line. Both parties in the conversation use the same software to ensure consistent results. Usually, calls between users of the same system are free, while calls to normal landline or mobile numbers is charged.

Flash Animation

Current browsers are supplied with Shockwave Flash plug-ins, while older browsers can be easily updated by downloading the appropriate plug-in. This allows the browser to display Flash animations, which can be anything from a small animated logo, up to multiple screens of web content. Flash can also be used to create menus, timing and many other effects. Furthermore, Flash files are quite compact, making Flash a versatile tool for web productions.

Streaming

When downloading files over the Internet, the user is only concerned that the total file is fetched successfully. Any delays in the network, due to congestion and re-routing of packets, only influence the downloading time and have no affect on the quality of the file being downloaded. This is not true of audio and video files that have to be presented to the user in <u>real time</u>. Any delays in transmission would result in the break up of the sound or video continuity. To overcome this, *'streaming'* is used. This reads a number of data packets and stores them in a LIFO (Last In First Out) buffer in the computer. The user will have a slight initial delay as the buffer is filled. These data packets are then fed out from the head of the buffer, while incoming packets are fed into the tail of the buffer. During periods of transmission delay, the user is fed information from the buffer, thus maintaining a constant audio or video stream. Users can listen, in real time, to radio programs from around the world. There are already hundreds of stations to choose from and the quality is equivalent to a normal AM radio.

Streaming requires the computer to use Windows Media Player, or to have *'RealOne'* or *'QuickTime'* installed; these are free add-ons to the user's browser.

Virtual Reality

VRML (Virtual Reality Modelling Language) is an ASCII description of a 3D scene such as a building, a human heart, a car engine, etc. When VRML viewers are embedded in browsers, clicking an icon takes the user on a screen walk around the objects.

Surround Video

Also known as *'panoramic video'*, it provides an environment that completely surrounds the user. Special cameras capture an entire location as a 360⁰ photograph and convert it to a graphics image. The left and right edges of the image are aligned and the whole scene can be thought of comprising a cylinder inside which the user is located. At any stage, the use can view about one-tenth of the image. Using the mouse or the keyboard moves the user round the image, giving the illusion that the user is situated in the middle of the scene. This is available as Apple's *'QuickTime VR'*, *'Surround Video'* and *'RealVR'*. Combining the panoramic background with the 3D objects available in Virtual Reality produce ever more realistic presentations.

Netiquette

Good browsing practice can benefit all Internet users.

- Switch off browser graphics when they are not essential.   This reduces download time, saves telephone costs and saves bandwidth for others.

- Access *'mirror'* sites where possible. These are replicas of other busy sites. Congestion is reduced at the main site and overall use of the bandwidth is improved.   Since many sites being mirrored are American, European mirror sites reduce the strain on the Trans-Atlantic links.

E-mail

This is one of the most used Internet services.   With multi-millions of users connected to the system, it is a cheap way for individuals and companies to exchange information, as there is no extra charge for this service.   Many believe that the Internet e-mail service will make the traditional fax services redundant. It is faster than postal services and, unlike fax, does not depend upon the receiving end being switched on and ready.   It is also an improvement on some telephone conversations, as the contents are recorded and exact details (such as numeric values, postcodes, spelling of names, etc) can be reviewed, preventing errors and misunderstandings.

E-mail facilities

E-mail can be used in a number of different modes.

- From a user to a provider.   The provider is permanently on-line and instantly receives the message.

- From a user to another user. The receiving user is not permanently attached to the Internet and the message is stored on his/her ISP's mail server.   The mail is available when he/she next logs in.

- From a user to a group of users.   A single e-mail is prepared and sent to multiple e-mail addresses. This is a useful tool for saving time.   It is also the method for issuing junk mail.

- Within groups of users. Subscribers can join *'Mailing Lists'* on a topic of their interest. New contributions on the topic are gathered centrally and a copy of each message is e-mailed to every subscriber on the mailing list.

- Including *'Attachments'*.   An e-mail can have one or more other files sent along with it.   The e-mail is sent as a single entity but the receiving user can extract the file(s) at the distant end.

Typical uses of e-mail

Personal Communicating with distant or overseas friends and relatives.
Requesting product information (e.g. holiday brochures).
Distance learning students maintaining contact with their lecturers, submitting examination scripts, etc

Professional Academic exchanges (e.g. between educationalists, scientists, medical practitioners).
Technical mailing lists (e.g. for computer technicians, engineers).

Commercial Press releases to promote a new product or service (sent to editors of newspapers, TV, radio, etc).
Mailshots to potential purchasers (sent to existing customers, bought-in mailing lists, etc).   Recipients may have requested regular mailshots, or may be victims of junk mail.
Answering customer queries.

Using e-mail software

The most widely used email client, ignoring web-based email providers such as Hotmail or Yahoo!, is Microsoft Outlook. Like many Microsoft products, Outlook contains many features that are unnecessary for the majority of users, but its basic features are similar to those provided by other email client software. Outlook can be configured to dial up your ISP automatically if it detects that the computer is not already online.   It can then check for new mail at regular intervals, such as every half hour. Alternatively, the user can select *Tools / Check For New Mail* to tell Outlook to retrieve mail. In some versions the '*Send and Retrieve*' button performs this function.

When mail is retrieved, it is stored in the *'Inbox'* folder, unless the user has set up rules to tell Outlook how to deal with mail. For example, if a user receives a lot of junk mail, he /she may set up a rule to automatically delete any mail with the words *'mortgage'* or *'credit'* in the subject line. Or a user who receives a lot of mail from a few clients can separate them into different folders using rules – each folder that contains unread messages will be shown in bold face. The messages are actually physically stored in a file on the hard disk, usually called *'outlook.pst'* in the Windows folder.

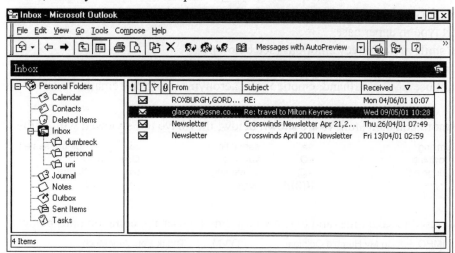

Clicking on any folder displays its contents in the right-hand panel, as shown in the illustration. The user can then double-click on any email to open it in a new window and read it. Messages can also be deleted, replied to, forwarded, printed or saved. Right-clicking on the *'From'* field while reading a message opens a pop-up box including options to add the email name to Outlook's Contact List.

To send an outgoing email, the user should click on *File / New / Mail Message* or click on the *'New'* button in the top left hand corner while browsing any mail folder. This will bring up a new window, which should be used to enter the message details.

The steps for composing a new e-mail message are:
1. Enter the e-mail address of the person(s) receiving the mail in the *'To:'* dialogue box. Clicking on the *'To'* button allows the user to select names from the contact list.
2. If the message is to be Cc'ed (Carbon Copied) to other addresses, enter them in the 'Cc' box. CC'ing an email recipient has the same effect as adding them to the *'To'* field, but is used to indicate that CC'ed recipients are included for information only.
3. Enter a summary of the e-mail in the *'Subject'* dialogue box. This is optional but it is good manners to inform the recipient of the reason for the e-mail.
4. Type the message into the main window. It is normally good netiquette to discuss only a single subject in each e-mail.
5. Use the *'Insert File'* option to attach any files to the e-mail. This is optional.
6. Click the *'Send'* button.

The message will then go to Outlook's *'Outbox'* folder. From there, it will be sent to your ISP's mail server when *'Send and Receive'* or *'Check for New Mail'* is selected. The ISP will pass the message on to the recipient's ISP within a matter of seconds, and the user will receive the message next time they check their mailbox. Messages can be composed off-line saving on telephone costs.

All recipients will know who received the message. Using *'bcc'* (blind carbon copy), all recipients will receive the e-mail and be unaware that it was also sent to others. E-mail software also allows messages to be read 'off-line' - i.e. when the computer is not connected to the ISP. Incoming messages are downloaded during a connected session and read later at the user's leisure. It also allows the user to write outgoing messages and mark them for posting. When the user next logs into the Internet, the messages are sent to the ISP. These both save telephone usage costs.

Messages can be saved or printed using the *'File'* menu and can be cut and pasted into other documents using the *'Edit'* menu. As can be seen from the illustration, Outlook provides many additional features as well as email, such as a Calendar, Journal, Notes, and Task List. Also, new subfolders can be created by the user to store email messages, notes, tasks and other Outlook objects.

E-mail Etiquette

As in verbal or written communication, there are certain rules when using the Internet and its services. These are often referred to *'netiquette'* and the specific advice for those sending e-mail messages is:

- Treat other users with respect. Avoid sexist, racist, culturally insensitive and judgmental language.
- Keep sentences short; the recipient is paying the phone time.
- Never forward a received e-mail to a third party without permission.
- Don't type in upper case.
- Use 'smileys' to convey emotions (see below).
- Learn and use e-mail acronyms (see below).
- Do not use SMS shorthand, emoticons or acronyms in official emails.

Smileys

Some of the more common smileys are shown below; they have to be viewed with a tilted head.

:-)	smiling	:->	sarcastic	:-x	my lips are sealed
:-(	frowning	I-O	yawning	O:-)	angelic
:-D	Laughing	:-@	screaming	:-I	indifferent
:'-(	Crying	{{{}}}	hugs	;-)	winking

Acronyms

Acronyms are used to save time (and to show how smart a user is), common ones being:

IMHO	In My Humble Opinion	TYVM	Thank You Very Much
IIRC	If I Recall Correctly	WRT	With Respect To
CMIIW	Correct Me If I'm Wrong	AFAIK	As Far As I Know
BTW	By The Way	IKWYM	I Know What You Mean
OTOH	On The Other Hand	TIA	Thanks In Advance

E-mail Viruses

E-mail is now the most common method for viruses to reproduce. Although the actual email message itself cannot contain a virus, they spread via email attachments. In most cases this means the attachment must be activated for the virus to spread, but there are a few exceptions. Viruses are explained in more detail elsewhere, but to reduce the risk of infection there are several things that can be done:

- Scan all incoming email before reading. Nearly all virus checkers and many software firewalls are capable of scanning incoming email for viruses, but they must be kept up to date, and even then are never 100% perfect – a brand new virus can often evade scanners until the anti-virus software developer updates their virus database.
- Never open any email attachment unless you are expecting it. Even email from your friends and colleagues cannot be assumed safe, since they themselves might have accidentally become infected somehow.
- Keep your email software up-to-date with any security patches available. Microsoft Outlook is the target for most viruses, so using different software altogether would provide good security if it is a realistic option. Webmail is also comparatively safe from viruses.

Spam

There has been a huge increase in the traffic of unwanted e-mails, offering everything from illegal get-rich-quick schemes to sexual services and aids. These unwanted e-mails, known as *'spam'*, waste a user's time, may cause offence, cost a user in download time and tie up much of the Internet's bandwidth.

Most email software has some elementary filtering facilities to reduce spam (Outlook calls the filters *'rules'*).

Unwanted bulk email is a constant nuisance to almost every email user. There are two main ways bulk emails are targeted: by collecting email addresses from web pages, newsgroups and other sources; or by trying random names at common DNS addresses. Therefore, simply keeping your email address to yourself may not be enough.

Having an unusual email address can stop spammers from guessing your address, while in order to stop email address harvesting, users should avoid posting their complete email address on any public forum such as the web, newsgroups, or so on. Some users replace the '@' or dots of their email with words for the same, or insert words, to stop their address ending up in the hands of spammers. For example, instead of 'davey@aol.com', a user might go by the address of 'daveyATaolDOTcom', or 'davey@NOSPAM.aol.com'.

However, once an email address ends up on one spammer's list, one way or another, it often finds its way onto many others, and this can result in a torrent of useless email filling the inbox. Then, all that can be done is to try to filter out unwanted mail. Some email providers have this function built in and filter out some spam before the user even sees it. However, no spam filter can ever be perfect, so the end user might need to consider installing their own filter, or setting up 'email rules' so that emails with certain contents are automatically detected as spam and dealt with. Note, however, that it is best to place suspected spam in a special spam folder rather than deleted right away, since the filter might accidentally mistake a normal email for spam.

The illustration shows Outlook being set to send all incoming e-mails with a subject line containing the word *'viagra'* into a specified folder. A set of such rules can be set up, barring e-mails from particular sources or filtering out e-mails destined for a particular user.

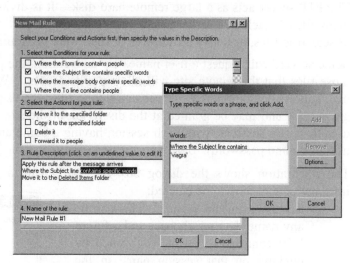

Other software, such as McAfee Spam Killer can filter out e-mails from particular countries known to be source of spam (often used by bulk emailers as a means of avoiding laws in their own countries).

The European Union's 'Privacy and Communications Directive' specifies that e-mail has to be on an opt-in basis (i.e. the user requests to placed on a mailing list) instead of the current opt-out basis (the user requests to be removed from a mailing list and hopes that the bulk mailer will respect the request). Since the Directive only applies to members of the EU, it does not affect spam from the rest of the world.

Scams
Fraudulent emails, or 'email scams; are generally a type of spam – they are very rarely targeted at specific individuals. The most well-known form of scam is that of a foreign official (classically a Nigerian royal family member) wishing to set up a foreign bank account with the recipient's help, for which they will be more than adequately compensated. Of course, the scammer is nothing of the sort: they simply want the recipient to send them money to help with the process, at which point the scammer will simply take the money and run.

Adequate filtering of spam email will mean that most scams are ignored automatically. However, all email users should be made aware of the existence of such scams, and every user should think carefully before entering into any email communication with a complete stranger.

Other scams, however, are less obvious. Popular banks have been a cover for some scammers trying to acquire bank details or credit card numbers to defraud their legitimate owners. At any mention of anything related to finance, the recipient of the email should check with the bank or any other relevant authority before taking any action whatsoever.

Encrypted mail
Where email is used to send private information, the users might consider using some form of security. It is rare, but possible at least in theory, for email to be intercepted between sender and recipient. It is also possible that the end user's email account could be compromised, or even that an email provider may be monitoring email contents. Encryption can provide a secure form of communication, as explained in the 'Computer Security' chapter.

File Transfer

The Internet supports FTP (*'File Transfer Protocol')* facilities that allow the user to:

DOWNLOAD: copy files from the remote server to his/her local drive.

UPLOAD: copy files from the local drive to the remote computer (where access is permitted).

Typical uses of FTP

Personal	Collecting clip art, shareware.
	Distance learning students downloading tests from a college's server.
Professional	Downloading case histories (e.g. lawyers).
	Uploading/Downloading scientific data (e.g. researchers).
Commercial	Uploading/downloading contracts, prices, specifications.
	Updating the contents of the company's web site.

A user, employing *'FTP client'* software, can access a remote *'FTP server'* site.

The FTP server acts as a large remote hard disk.   It is divided into many folders and each folder stores many files.   Each FTP server usually acts a host for a particular area of interest. It may store academic or scientific files, or it may be a source of shareware programs.

Some servers will request a user name. By convention, the password *'anonymous'* allows the user to see those files that the remote site will allow public access.   When prompted for a password, the user's e-mail address can be entered. To see non-public files, the user requires a security password.   This can be applied for and may be granted at the discretion of the site organisers.   FTP software often allows the user to set up sessions, with each session having a name and a set of parameters (e.g. ftp site address, user name and password). Selecting a session automates the logging process.

The illustration shows the dialog box for configuring a session.   There are three main pieces of information that have to be entered:

- The name of the session. This can be any name the user chooses and a future FTP connection can be established by clicking on that session name in the *'Profile Name'* list.
- The FTP site details (the address of the site and the operating system that it uses).
- The login details (see above).

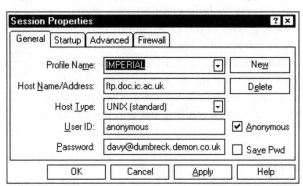

Clicking the 'OK' button establishes the connection between the user and the FTP site.

The client software, under the control of the user, sends commands to change directory or list files.   The server receives these commands and sends back the appropriate information.   This is the *'control'* connection.   Most FTP servers store their non-restricted material within the *'pub'* (i.e. public) directory.

Each directory contains a text file (e.g. 00-INDEX.TXT, README.TXT or INDEX.LST) that provides a brief description of each file in that folder. Highlighting that file, and clicking the *'View'* or *'Open'* button displays the text on the screen.

When the user clicks on a desired filename, a *'data'* connection is opened and the file can be transferred in either ASCII or binary mode (ASCII for text files, binary for programs, graphics, etc). When the file is transferred, the data connection is closed and the control connection remains active for further directory navigation and transfers. Closing the program breaks the control connection and returns the computer to its previous state.

The diagram shows a screen from WS_FTP, a popular Windows FTP client where the user is connected to an FTP site in Australia. The left panel shows the drives, directories and files of the computer initiating the transfer. The right panel shows the directories and files of the remote system. Highlighting a file in the right panel and clicking the leftwards arrow, copies the file to the directory that is active in the left panel. Sending files to a remote site (uploading) is looked at in the chapter on web site creation.

The menu buttons allow the user to create and delete directories, move around the directory structure, as well as viewing file contents, and renaming and deleting files. These options on the remote computer are subject to the restrictions imposed by the administrator of the remote system.

Many Web browsers offer automatic FTP facilities. If a file download hyperlink is clicked, the system switches into FTP mode and the only user involvement is in selecting the directory into which the file should be stored. This avoids the user having to learn how FTP operates, as the mechanisms are hidden by the browser's user interface.

Apart from the text files that store descriptions of the files in each directory, there is little more in the way of casual browsing. FTP users have to already know which FTP sites store particular information and this information can be obtained from publications or by asking within newsgroups.

To save on connect time, many files are stored in a compressed (usually ZIP) format. A ZIPped file will show as a single file in the FTP site and downloads as a single file. In practice, the ZIP file may contain a number of separate files that are bound together before compression. The unzipping process converts the single file back into its original parts and uncompresses each file. A range of utilities such PKZIP, WinZIP and TurboZip are designed for this purpose. Since some applications have many files, it is best to unzip files into their own directory/folder. This prevents the files being mixed into other files. ZIP utilities usually create folders when instructed.

Newsgroups

The Internet has scores of thousands of newsgroups (also known as user groups, special interest groups, conferences or forums) operating on a wide variety of subjects. A newsgroup is an electronic version of a notice board. Members contribute to discussions via e-mail and all contributions are stored for a period and are available for all wishing to read them. Any user can join these groups and read existing messages, contribute to existing discussions or send an e-mail to start a new discussion.

The topics are extremely varied. Some cover computer topics (programming, hardware, sales); some cover leisure (sports, music, hobbies); some are serious (politics, religion, support groups); some are frivolous (jokes, games); a small but highly publicised number of topics are unsavoury or illegal (pornography, hacking, pirate software).

Hierarchy	Content
comp	computing hardware and software
news	network news
rec	recreations, hobbies, art and sport
sci	science
biz	business
soc	social issues
talk	debate on controversial matters
alt	controversial or unusual contents
misc	subjects that don't fit any of the other hierarchies

There is no central control over newsgroups. Each newsgroup is organised and run by a volunteer. Newsgroups are all categorised within Usenet's hierarchy as shown in the table. If a newsgroup is *'moderated'* the incoming e-mail messages are read and approved before being placed in the newsgroup directory. This prevents illegal, abusive or irrelevant material from clogging up the newsgroup. Many groups are not moderated and this often leads to *'flame'* wars, where long, ongoing, abusive exchanges take place between contributors. Another approach is the *'digest'*, where the moderator produces regular summaries of the contributions received.

User groups are an extremely useful way to gain answers to technical or other queries since the correspondence for the most popular groups may be read by hundreds of thousands of users.

The overall service is called Usenet and newsgroup contents are viewed with a piece of software called a *'newsreader'*. This software is available in freeware, shareware and commercial packages.

Subscribing

When the user uses the newsreader for the first time, it does not have a built-in list of newsgroups. Since the list regularly alters, the current list has to be fetched from the news server. Once the list is downloaded, the user can browse through, highlight desired topics and click the *'subscribe'* option.

Off-line Reading

Once subscribed to a newsgroup, any fresh contributions to the group are downloaded each time the user logs on to the Internet. The user can read the messages at leisure after logging off the Internet, thus saving on telephone charges.

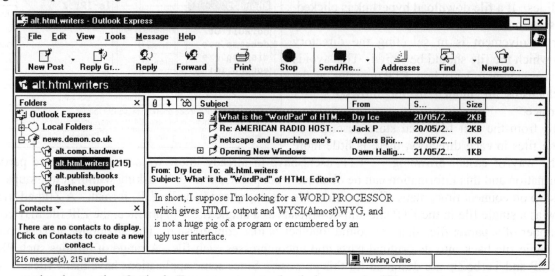

The example shows the Outlook Express newsreader being used offline to examine a newsgroup's content. The newsgroup shown is for web page authors, as indicated by the description [alt.html.writers] in the newsreader's title bar. The dots indicate sub-divisions of the hierarchy - i.e. the *'alt'* hierarchy has a sub-group called *'html'* and it has a further sub-group called *'writers'*.

Each subject is a *'thread'* that was begun by a user and added to by other participants. With controversial issues, it is common to have up to several hundred contributions to a thread.

The user is presented with a one-line summary of each thread, allowing the choice to read the messages in the thread. Message contents can be saved to disk or printed. Users can also opt to send a reply.

Messages are removed after a certain period and some are stored in archives. Common questions and experiences are regularly summarised and placed in the newsgroups as FAQs (Frequently Asked Questions).

The way that messages in newsgroups are handled can be altered by the user.

The illustration on the right shows the dialog box that appears when *'News'* is selected from the *'Message Rules'* choice of the *'Tools'* drop-down menu.

In the example, the application is being instructed to look for the word *'exams'* in the headers of all messages. If required, more than one condition can be checked. After selecting the word to be checked for, the user can decide on the treatment of the messages that match the condition. For example, the user can decide to highlight all such messages.

Another possible combination is to automatically delete all messages that over a certain size.

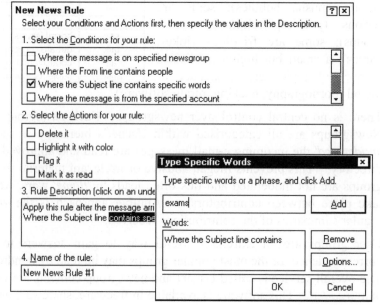

Remote Access

The chapter on Data Communications looks at the how remote control software allows a user to access and carry out operations on a computer that is distant from the user. At one time, this could only be carried out using the TELNET protocol, the part of the TCP/IP suite that acts as a terminal handler. Now, programs with graphical interfaces can be used to access resources on the web. However, not all important systems have a web site presence and TELNET remains the tool to access these computers. The output from TELNET sites is largely text-based, perhaps with some colours and simple lines and boxes.

Remote systems that offer public TELNET access include universities, libraries and some government departments.

The steps for using TELNET are as follows:
- Run the Telnet software.
- Enter the address of the remote site.
  Some example sites are fedworld.gov and atlas.gcal.ac.uk
- If a TELNET site specifies a particular port number, it should be entered into the *'Port'* box, otherwise the contents should be left to the default value.
- Enter the login name and password. This depends on the site. Many public sites expect *'guest'* to be used for the login name and password, while private sites require the user to provide the correct information (e.g. the login for gcal is *'library'*). The fedworld site allows public access after the user supplies registration details.
- Set up the local computer's emulation, so that it acts like the kind of terminal that the remote computer expects. Many sites use the VT100 emulation and the ANSI emulation can be used where a site provides coloured output.
- Use the site's on-screen menu system to look up the required resources. Many sites have a help system to explain how best to use the menus.

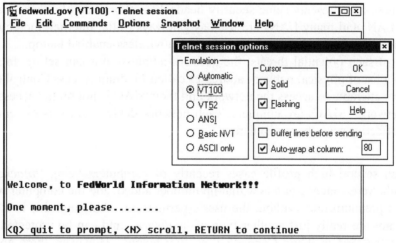

The illustration shows a user having logged in and waiting for the appearance of the opening menu. A pop-up dialog box has been called up to set the terminal emulation. Choosing the *'Log Entire Session'* from the *'Snapshot'* drop down menu allows the user to keep a record of all the browsing within the TELNET site.

While TELNET allows users access to a remote site to view its contents, it is not normally used to alter the remote site in any way. Although some systems allow varying levels of access to system resources the majority of current TELNET sites are for information only.

Another form of remote access is used to provide support to users in distant locations, allowing a technician to diagnose hardware and software faults, and even fix some software problems without travelling to the remote location. These systems are also used to copy files back and forth between computers, and use the remote system's printers, network, fax system, etc. Examples of this kind of software are PC Anywhere, Laplink and pcTelecommute.

Internet Safety

Valuable though the Internet may be as a tool for learning, commerce, and entertainment, it is not without its dangers. Every Internet application has slightly different vulnerabilities, and the major problems facing web servers are covered elsewhere in the book, so this section concentrates on the problems facing a typical home user.

Keeping your account safe

The most basic security issue is keeping your Internet access account safe. If an unauthorised person can get onto the Internet using an authorised person's account, then any trouble the unauthorised user causes might be blamed on the actual owner of the account.

Account security

Fortunately, this is rare. ISPs typically use a simple username and password system to make sure the user is who they are claiming to be. However, this system can easily be compromised. Windows systems allow the user to set the computer up so that it will remember the password for the user. While this is a handy time-saving device, it means that anyone who gains physical access to the computer also has access to the Internet account without needing to know the password. Account holders should carefully consider who would be able to use their computer, and if any of them are not trusted, take steps to secure the system.

The easiest way to secure such an account is to disable the option for Windows to remember the password. However, many home systems have separate logins for different family members. In this case, it is possible to set up the Internet connection for those who should be allowed access, and do not set it up for those who are not allowed. In this case, make sure all users log out of the computer when it is not in use.

Wireless LANs on the Internet

An increasingly common way to set up home networks is to use a Wireless LAN. Although a very convenient method, this presents some security headaches. For example, there may be shared files or printers on the LAN, and many LANs are used as gateways to the Internet, thereby effectively granting access to your account to anyone who walks past with a wireless-enabled laptop.

To protect against such potential threats, the network administrator can set up an Access Control List, which is simply a list of physical network addresses called Medium Access Control (MAC) addresses. If a wireless system attempts to access the network and their MAC is not on the access list, they are denied access to the network. MACs are unique to each network device, and it is extremely difficult to fake, making this an effective security mechanism.

Hijacking

There have been several high profile cases recently of computers being 'hijacked'. Their Internet connection details were changed or a new dial-up number added, and the computer was then made to dial the number, at a premium rate, without the user's permission. Although this is a connection problem, hijacking programs are really just another type of 'malware', and can be protected against in much the same way. See the 'Safety While Connected' section below. However, there are additional ways to protect against hijacking. The simplest is to just unplug the modem cable from the phone line when the Internet connection is not in use, or even switch to a non-phone based connection such as ADSL or cable.

Safety while connected

While connected to the Internet, every machine is at risk, even when you are not using a web browser or other Internet software. The threats here come from hacking attempts, viruses, and unwanted advertising.

- Hackers can try 'port scanning', checking various ports on any IP address on the Internet, until it finds a port which is not blocked, and for which there is a known security flaw. The hacker would then exploit this flaw to inspect or alter the machine's data or operation somehow.

- Viruses can spread automatically in a few extreme cases, such as the worms that can spread via port 445 on Windows computers. This port, if not secured, can allow hackers or viruses to access the system and even run programs remotely.

- Windows Messaging Service is a handy piece of software for sending messages from one computer user to another over a LAN. However, when an Internet-connected machine has this service enabled, it opens the door for unscrupulous advertisers to send the user unwanted advertisements.

There are various ways of protecting against such problems. The first, and most widely employed method, is to install a Firewall. All of the above problems are caused by incoming data on ports that are not secure, so a Firewall which blocks these ports by default can prevent all of the above problems.

However, no Firewall is perfect. There will always be new security holes to be discovered, and in order to operate at all there must be at least some ports which are open some of the time.

An NAT (see chapter on datacommunications) system will provide greater security. The NAT box will translate incoming ports on an IP address into local IP addresses on a LAN. Therefore, such vulnerable ports as 445 simply do not map to any service that can be exploited. In addition, the NAT box can also act as a Firewall in most cases. The downside is that some software may need additional modification to access the Internet through a NAT box.

In the end, the best way to be secure is to regularly check for security bulletins that would highlight any potential problem, allowing you to "plug the hole" before anyone has a chance to use it against your system.

IP spoofing

In an attempt to get around a Firewall, some hackers will try to spoof an IP address. This method involves tampering with the IP packets sent from the hacker's machine, so that they appear to be coming from a different computer entirely, usually one which the hacker hopes will be 'trusted' by your Firewall. Fortunately, most modern Firewalls will protect against IP Spoofing by checking up on all 'trusted' traffic, making sure that it did indeed come from the source from which it claims. The simplest example of this is using a hardware firewall that is also the gateway between the 'trusted' LAN and the 'untrusted' Internet. The incoming hacker's IP packets, which pretend to be from a trusted source, have been received by the Firewall from the Internet connection. The Firewall can thus be set up to discard IP packets which claim to come from a trusted source but are received on an untrusted connection.

Safe surfing

Once connected to the Internet, the most common activity is, of course, web surfing. However, this introduces additional security concerns, foremost of which are those of secure connections, client-side security, and storage of potentially sensitive information in cookies.

Secure connections

Some web pages ask for confidential information, for example personal or financial information. For most home users the most basic security measures are sufficient.

This involves two steps:

1) Make sure that you trust the web page owner with the information. You could use all the security technology in the world to make sure that the only person who receives your credit card details is the company whose web page you are looking at. However, if that "company" turns out to be a fly-by-night organisation who will not provide the goods you paid for, that security has been to no use.

2) Make sure that the connection to the web server is secure. Most browsers are able to use 'https', which is essentially http with SSL security protocols. Although 'shttp' (Secure HTTP) provides more in-built security-related mechanisms, the HTTPS system is considered secure enough for credit card transactions, as long as the encryption system used is 128-bit, and not the older 40-bit system. Simply hover the mouse over the padlock icon in the web browser to make sure that the web page is secure and uses 128-bit encryption.

Client-side security

Some viruses can spread from web pages. The HTML page itself cannot contain a virus: the virus is contained within some form of script or applet that is used by the web page.

There are several methods to help protect against such viruses, but most of these have also their down sides.

- Run a virus guard program at all times. A few virus checkers are able to check all incoming and outgoing data for viruses, though this of course significantly impacts on system performance.

- Completely disable web facilities such as ActiveX, Java, and plugins, which might provide a route for viruses to enter the system. This is a drastic measure, however, and results in reduced functionality of the web browser.

- Keep the web browser up to date with all security patches available. Again, since Internet Explorer is the most common browser, it is the target for many viruses, so using an alternative browser can provide some measure of security in this regard.

- Set up the browser so that any time an applet or other potential risk tries to run on the target machine, the user is given a dialog and allowed to choose whether to run the applet. This, however, puts the burden on the user, and quite often the user will choose to simply run the risk in order to be able to browse the web page.

Cookies

When cookies were introduced, there was a lot of discussion about potential security concerns. In truth, there are very few security concerns, although there are certain forms of cookie which track the user's web browsing habits in a manner similar to spyware.

However, some cookies are used to store information entered by the user, such as a login and password to the web server, to save the user from having to type these in for every page. While this sounds useful, it can be a security issue if the cookie is not encrypted – it means anyone who accesses that computer may be able to find out your password for that site.

Fortunately, unencrypted cookies containing passwords are now very rare. To provide added security, use a different password for each web resource, and if you are concerned that one of the sites might be storing unencrypted passwords in cookies, you can regularly clear out your cookies. This can usually be done using your browser; alternatively it can be done going into Windows Explorer, navigating to "C:\Windows\Temp\Cookies" and deleting all the cookies.

Safe chatting

Perhaps the area of the Internet that has been featured on the most television shows, are the 'chat rooms'. Although most chat programs now come with the option to send and receive files, thus making them just one more possible route for viruses to take, the main focus of the media has been on the effects which the Internet's anonymity can have on chat users.

This is really a social issue, however, which just happens to centre around computer use. Users on a chat system are more likely to be abusive than if they were talking face to face. Some people find it amusing to masquerade as someone they are not. And there is also a small minority who will use the anonymous nature of the Internet for deceptive and illegal purposes, such as the notorious '*child grooming*' which paedophiles are known to use in an attempt to convince children to meet up with them.

Aside from banning chatrooms, the only real way to tackle deceptive chat is to educate the users about the realities of the system. Most users on chat rooms use nicknames, and even those who do not use nicknames may not be using their real life name. And it is all too easy for chatters to lie about their age, their gender, their occupation, or any other aspect of their background. In essence, anything a chatter says to a user could be false, so making any decisions in your everyday life based solely on what an Internet chatter says is definitely a poor choice.

That is not to say that everyone on a chat room will lie at the drop of the hat – far from it. However, if anything is said in a chatroom which may influence a user to take a certain course of action, that user would be well advised to check up on the information through more reliable methods, such as checking official publications, speaking to appropriately qualified personnel, and so on.

Safe downloading

Whether downloading a file from a peer-to-peer network, an FTP site, a newgroup, a chatroom, or even a website, there is <u>always</u> a possibility of receiving a file that contains harmful data, sometimes grouped into the general heading of '*malware*'.

There are three main types of malware: Viruses, Spyware, and Adware.

- Viruses are explained in plenty of detail elsewhere. However, it cannot be stressed enough that <u>any</u> file from <u>any</u> source can potentially be infected, so every single file that is downloaded should be scanned for viruses.

- Spyware is any type of software that is intended to collect information about the user's computer, web surfing habits, or even about the user themselves, without the user consciously providing that information. This is an obvious problem if the user's privacy is valued. At the worst end of the scale, it may be possible to collect passwords or even credit card details by using Spyware, but the majority of Spyware is concerned simply with learning about users in order to bombard them with advertisements.

- Adware describes any type of software designed to provide the user with adverts. Often, these adverts are tailored to the user's web surfing habits so as to provide the advertiser with 'targeted marketing'. As a result, Spyware and Adware can often be inextricably linked.

Spyware and Adware have become so widely disliked that most of them have been forced to make deals with other software providers, where the malware is installed alongside the desired software, often without the user being informed.

To reduce the risk of becoming infected with viruses or malware, the user is advised to examine carefully the installation procedure and any documentation that comes with any software, but particularly with "free" software. It is most commonly freeware that comes bundled with malware, as no serious commercial vendor would risk alienating customers by bundling their software with undesirable addons.

However, it is all too easy to install a small, free utility or game to 'try it out', only to find that your system has now been loaded with spyware. If it is suspected that there is malware on a system, there are plenty of programs that can be used to remove them, such as "Ad-aware", "Hijack This!", or "Spybot Search & Destroy". However, none of these are 100% effective at finding and removing all forms of malware, so to be sure, it is best to use at least two different anti-spyware programs, and keep them up-to-date.

Aside from the problem of malware, downloading from the Internet can carry other risks. Depending on the source of the data, its legality may be dubious. Files traded on peer-to-peer systems have made news stories several times thanks to the booming illegal trade in copyrighted material. However, it is just as possible to find illegal files on web pages, FTP sites, or just about any other method of downloading. Anyone who participates in distributing or even just downloading of illegal files risks being cut off by their ISP, or even taken to court by the copyright holder, so the user should make every reasonable effort to ensure the legality of the file before downloading.

Factors affecting performance

There are two areas where the quality of the Internet service can be affected:

- General system problems that affect all services.
- Specific problems that affect each application.

General system problems

The movement of large files across the Internet places a strain on the system. In particular, the size of programs, sound files and video clips mean long download times.

The diagram shows that there are many hardware components involved in a single connection between a user and a web site. The link can only run as fast as its slowest component and a problem at any point slows or prevents the successful use of the link.

The example is of the most common connection method – using a modem/router on a telephone line.

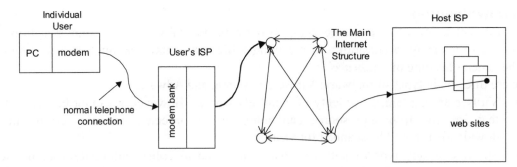

Modem/line speed

These are factors under the direct control of the user – the connection speed offered by the ISP, the speed of the modem and the computer's software settings. Where possible, users can upgrade to a faster performance ISDN or ADSL link.

Noisy telephone line

If the telephone line between the premises and the telephone exchange is noisy, messages are corrupted and have to be re-sent, lowering the effective transmission speed.

Users should insist that telephone operators check out and repair noisy lines. Better still, users should consider upgrading to an ADSL link, as it is both faster and cleaner.

Not enough lines to ISP

An ISP uses a set of modems (a modem bank) to provide entry points for subscribers. If an ISP has, say, 500 modems, then only 500 subscribers can access the ISP at any time. At peak times, all other users will receive a busy tone. ISPs have to balance the cost of providing extra lines and modems against the losses caused by customers switching to other providers.

Insufficient bandwidth between ISP and network

At a certain stage, an ISP may have increased the modem bank to an adequate size but not increased the capacity of the connection between the ISP and the main network. Although subscribers can all gain access to the ISP, the connections have to share the bandwidth and suffer low data transfer rates.

Network breakdowns

As the chapter on Data Communications explained, the network will have many connections between its nodes.   If one section of cable should break down or become congested, the traffic can be automatically re-routed around the problem area. This may result in traffic taking a longer path causing some time delays. Each link in the path is called a *'hop'* and 10 hops may be considered reasonable. The Internet only supports a maximum of 255 hops before abandoning the connection.

Congestion at remote server

This is a similar problem to the earlier discussion on the lack of modems at the user's ISP. If the remote ISP has too few modems then the user receives a *'host unavailable'* message. The user can still access resources on his/her own ISP with adequate speed, since there is no problem on that link.

Congestion at web site

Even if all other parts of the system are working perfectly, a busy web site can cause delays. This is particularly true where site space is rented from an ISP. The ISP only guarantees a specific bandwidth to a site and this slows the site down when it becomes more popular.

Peak congestion

Just like road or rail traffic, the Internet performance suffers from degradation caused by peaks in Internet usage. Heavy use of the available network bandwidth causes delays, no matter how fast an individual user's equipment might be (driving a sports car does not help when stuck in a traffic jam).

A UK user can look forward to better network performance if he/she logs on to UK sites at 2.00am, since most users are tucked up in bed. However, in other parts of the world, people are just newly logging on to the Internet. Accessing a US site during the US peak times produces delays, even if there are few other UK using the system.

Specific application problems

The above factors affect the overall performance of all Internet services. In addition, there are factors that affect the efficiency (reliability and speed) and the quality (how the user experiences the service) of individual Internet services.

E-mail	• Availability is a consideration for business users. A mail service with frequent interruptions or slow-downs to the service affects business efficiency.
	• Most mail readers download the full content of all messages (including all spam). Web-based services avoid this by only initially downloading message headers
	• POP3 automatically fetches messages, while SMTP requires the user to actively check for new mail.
	• Spam (i.e. unwanted junk mail) wastes users' time and wastes system resources.
WWW	• Lack of security (against fraud, hacking, viruses, etc.) can seriously affect web users.
	• Non-standard TLDs require an add-on to the browser.
	• Streaming of audio and video is seriously downgraded (i.e. glitches in the sound or loss of video frames) by insufficient system bandwidth.
	• Different browsers support non-standard features, so that the same material from a web site may display or operate differently for different users.
FTP	• A broken connection can mean the loss of a large file that is being downloaded, unless an intelligent download application like 'GetRight' is used (this resumes a download from the point that the connection was lost).
	• Command-based FTP programs are less intuitive than 'point-and-click' versions.
	• Some ISPs limit the amount of time that a user can stay online for a single session, limiting downloads of very large files.
Newsgroups	• The sheer amount of newsgroups and the quantity of messages in each group can result in users suffering from information overkill.
	• Only a percentage of all the newsgroups appear on an ISP's server. Although the most popular newsgroups appear on most servers, this can be a problem for a user with specialist interests.
	• Many newsgroups are not moderated, allowing endless arguments and inflammatory statements to fill the newsgroup.
Chat services	• Many chat rooms are filled with complete drivel and finding a useful discussion can be time consuming.
	• Although real-time, chat rooms can suffer from message lag (the time between typing an entry and it appearing on the chat room).
	• Each chat room has an owner who can disconnect users at his/her whim.
Remote Access	• Non-GUI applications, such as Telnet, require the user to learn how to use their menus.
	• There can be significant delays in controlling remote events (e.g. with pcAnywhere or similar, moving the mouse at the local end may produce slow and jerky pointer movements on the remote computer).
	• Since the user is manipulating the remote operating system, the speed and efficiency of that operating system determines the user's efficiency.

Economic Issues

Although the Internet began as a non-commercial communications link, the balance of net traffic is rapidly switching to commercial uses. Marketing, selling, on-line publishing and commercial databases form the basis of the emerging dominance of financial interests over academic and hobby interests. The arrival of Internet shopping allows subscribers to view goods, specifications and prices and place orders using electronic transactions (i.e. using VISA or other credit cards). Banking and financial dealing is available and the range of Internet pay services will expand.

Information has become one of the most prized commodities in the world. The creation, processing and marketing of financial, commercial and scientific information is a huge industry with enormous power.

The possession of information is a driving force in the success of institutions and entire nations. Those without knowledge and current information are destined to lag in the economic race.

This has led to the concept of the *'information rich'* and the *'information poor'*. The rich can afford to buy the information that makes them richer; the poor cannot afford access to the information and remain poor. Even within most developed countries, a large section of the population does not have Internet access. Within the system, premium services (financial newspapers, stock market information, company profiles, etc) are already only available by extra subscription. The Internet is used by the rich and powerful to maintain and extend their position. The *'digital divide'* is even greater between the developed and developing countries of the world. The industrialised countries that make up 15% of the world's population provide almost 90% of all Internet users. There are mores ISPs in the city of New York than in the whole of Africa. Many areas do not have the telephone structure that would support the Internet. In fact, 2 billion people on the planet are not even connected to an electricity supply. Internet access is very restricted in many countries due to financial hardship. This may be worsened if future improvements in the Internet infrastructure are financed by big business, as they may demand priority in use of the bandwidth (probably on a payment basis).

Social implications

Like the rest of life, Internet usage does not occur in a vacuum. The way that the Internet develops has a direct influence on many aspects of life – some for the better and some for the worse. The table looks at some of these issues, comparing the possible benefits and disadvantages.

	Potential benefits	Potential disadvantages
Home banking	Access any time of day or night.	Branch closures and redundancies.
Home working	Flexible and convenient, saves travelling time/costs.	Lack of personal contact with other staff/customers.
VOD	Watch movies at any time of day or night.	Video quality remains a problem.
E-mail	Much faster than posted mail.	Even more junk mail.
Distance learning	Opens up education to the disabled, single parents, residents of remote islands, shift workers, etc.	Lacks the face-face contact with teacher or lecturer.
E-commerce	Increases choice for those who do not live in large cities. Also benefits the elderly, the disabled, the sick, shift workers, etc.	Increases the risk of fraud.
Increased internationalisation	Encourages a greater awareness of the rest of the world (the global village).	Increased competition as overseas firms are opened to the home market.
No regulation	Provides a platform for minority views or specialist interests. Provides alternative viewpoints from national government norms (threatens autocratic regimes).	Potentially exposes browsers to illegal material (e.g. porn, plans on bomb-making).
Greater commercialisation	More consumer choice.	Dominance by monopolies, small traders pushed out. Increase of pay services.
Giant collections of information	Easy access to information on travel, health, entertainment, etc.	Increased threat to privacy.

Even from this small selection, it can be seen that there are many legal, economic, political and ethical problems facing Internet users. Some of these can be tackled and solved within organisations, while others are of much broader concern and require political will and intervention.

Legal Problems

A range of legal problems shows up the difficulties of obtaining a uniform enforceable framework for Internet use.

Privacy

The Data Protection Act (see the chapter on Software) is a UK law guaranteeing individuals rights to privacy regarding information stored about them on computers in the UK. Breaches of this Act within the UK are an offence but breaches committed from another country about a UK citizen would depend on whether that country had similar privacy protection.

Within the UK, as throughout much of the world, there has been great debate since 9/11 on the issue of personal privacy versus national security. On the one hand, the loss of some privacy might be regarded as a price worth paying for improved security. On the other hand, handing such power to a country's state apparatus (particularly to unelected and unaccountable bodies) might be regarded as a step too far and a threat to democracy in itself.

The European Union Council passed a *'Directive on Privacy and Electronic Communication'* in June 2002. This required EU member states to enforce its policies before October 2003. The policy mandates the retention of both the traffic data and location data of all communications over the Internet, including e-mails and chat rooms. The policy also covers use of mobile phones, landline phones, faxes, etc. This reverses the provision of previous data protection legislation requiring ISPs to destroy data after their billing operations.

In the UK, The Regulation of Investigatory Powers (RIP) Act was passed by parliament in the year 2000. This gave extensive new powers to government agencies to access e-mail and Internet traffic. Patricia Hewitt, as Minister for e-commerce, justified the move *"because crime has become global and digital and we have to combat this"*. However, the Bill appears to have political overtones as, for example, it specifically designates *"conduct by a large number of persons in pursuit of a common purpose"* as *"a serious crime"*.
In particular, the Bill stipulates that:

- All Internet Service Providers (ISPs) must provide *"interception capabilities"* that permit government monitoring of all Internet access through their systems. When served with an *"interception warrant"* ISPs will be required to intercept private email and convey the contents to the police or intelligence services.
- It is an offence to fail to comply with an interception warrant, with a maximum two-year prison sentence.
- It is an offence for an ISP to reveal that an individual is under surveillance or that his/her email is being read, punishable by a maximum five years prison sentence.
- It is an offence for an individual to reveal that the authorities are making attempts to read his/her mail, with a maximum five-year prison sentence.

While there may be valid arguments for government monitoring in some cases, many people feel that this approach is an infringement of civil liberties and breaks the European Convention on Human Rights.
The UK's *'Anti-Terrorism, Crime and Security Act 2001'* obliged ISPs to retain data beyond the time allowed for normal billing purposes *'if it is necessary to safeguard national security or to prevent, detect, or prosecute crimes related to national security'*. Like all such definitions, it begs the question of who decides what constitutes such a threat.

When an allegation was made that around one million requests for data were made each year, a Home Office spokesmen told the BBC News that the figure was estimated to be half that alleged. In other words, 500,000 requests are made each year to gather information on telephone calls, e-mails, credit card details, etc. A report by the Interception of Communications Commissioner stated that there were 350,000 information requests per year on average between 2005 and 2006 but this had risen to 519,260 in 2007. This figure would have been much higher if the Government's original proposals had been implemented.
The RIP Act allows dozens of bodies, including every local authority in the country and many quangos (non-government organisations), to have ease of access. A report by the Chief Surveillance Commissioner criticised councils for showing a *"serious misunderstanding of the concept of proportionality"*. An Act justified on the grounds of fighting serious global crime was being used to investigate fly tipping, etc!

The RIP Act also includes international collaboration between law enforcement bodies. It would allow the UK interception of *"communications of subjects on the territory of another country according to the law of that country"* at the request of *"the competent authority"* in that country. In other words, the governments of countries with questionable human rights records can request that the content of e-mails of refugees be sent to them - even when the e-mails are solely within the UK. In many of these countries, opposition to the government or just fighting for democratic rights is regarded as *"serious crime"*.

A committee of Euro-MPs reported on the operations of the multi-billion pound *"Echelon"* system. This system can scan over 2 million electronic communications each minute of the day! It reports on communications that contain key words that are entered by the operators. It is mainly run by the US National Security Agency, backed by the British spy centre at GCHQ Cheltenham, and supported by the Canadian, Australian and New Zealand governments. The information that is obtained is not shared with the UK's European partners and the US still denies that the system even exists! The European

Convention on human rights has no control over the situation, as the police, army and secret services are exempt from these laws.

Supporters of the system claim that such interception is necessary to combat terrorism, drug-dealing and the proliferation of weapons of mass destruction. Opponents of the system claim that there are serious issues of privacy and accountability. They point out that the European Parliament's investigation was instigated after complaints from several EU countries that American and British companies had won very profitable contracts through intercepting the details of rival bids. While interceptions in the UK are meant to require a Home Office Warrant, this would appear to be at odds with the 'blanket' approach adopted by the system. It is also extremely dubious whether the National Security Agency would apply for warrants.

Copyright

The international provisions on copyright apply to Internet material but is as difficult and expensive to pursue as other copyright wrangles.

Libel

The UK Defamation Act of 1996 holds that an ISP is not liable for libel if it acts solely as a transmitter of material that is libellous. It is held to be secondarily responsible as it is not the actual author or editor of the material.   This is in recognition of the instantaneous nature of e-mail and newsgroup postings that make vetting almost impossible.   The mechanics of processing a libel action for an individual from country A against an ISP based in country B that has posted a libellous piece from an individual from country C is complex.

Censorship

With the Internet connecting millions of web sites and tens of thousands of user groups, it is not at all surprising that some material causes offence to some users. This has provoked a fierce debate between those who seek to have greater control over Internet content and those who support uncensored Internet content.

The debate centres on whether an individual ISP is a 'broadcaster' or a' post office'.

If an ISP is regarded as a broadcaster, it is deemed to be consciously deciding on the content that it delivers, in the same way as a newspaper or a TV station chooses what material to deliver.   In this case, the ISP can be deemed responsible for the content on their servers. The fact that millions of pages may be added and altered each day, making content surveillance and control impossible, is considered irrelevant in this approach.

If an ISP is regarded as a post office, it is treated in the same way as the Royal Mail, British Telecom, Parcel Force, etc, is just a carrier - it distributes what it is given. The Internet does not cause crimes or outrages any more than crimes or outrages are caused by the existence of the telephone or the mail service. In this case, ISPs should not be held responsible for the content of individual websites.

The public debate has centred on defining offensive material and deciding on the course of action, if any, that should be taken.

Offensive Material

Like all moral debates, there are problems producing a satisfactory definition. Some moral questions, such as murder and rape, have international agreement. Other issues vary with the traditions of that country. Most Internet information is in English and most newsgroups promote English-speaking Christian culture and morality. What is regarded as satisfactory conduct in that arena may be disgusting and/or illegal in another part of the world. All kinds of moral laws and norms exist. For example, some countries practice capital and corporal punishment while other regard it as abhorrent. Some countries have strict laws on drugs while others are more relaxed. In some countries, the age of consent is as low as 13, while that is regarded as paedophilia in other countries. In one US state it is even illegal to have sex with the light on (see www.dumblaws.com).

Each country has its own laws on a range of issues (e.g. outlawing racial hatred, pornography, political views, etc) but the Internet is international by its nature.   If a user in country A is banned from viewing certain material in that country, the material is still available from country B by logging in to that web site.   The material can be sexual or political content. UK government reports that are 'classified' - i.e. banned from publication in the UK - are available freely in other countries that do not operate the same view of what is 'best' for British citizens.

Although Internet pornography generates much press and TV coverage, a survey found:

- 0.002% of newsgroups contained graphics with sexual content.
- Of these, most were of the 'soft' variety to be found in tabloid newspapers.
- The 'hard core' variety was mostly of sex between consenting adults.
- The remainder (i.e. a tiny proportion of the already minuscule 0.002%) displayed *'unlawful sexual practice'*, thereby falling under the UK Obscene Publications Act (see below).

Most of the sites that fell foul of the OPA are only accessible by credit card - not a commodity possessed by the children liable to be corrupted by this material. In fact, the use of credit cards has led to the world's largest clampdown on paedophiles, in *'Operation Ore'*. The organiser of an Internet porn ring in Texas was jailed for 1,335 years and the arrest uncovered the credit card details on 250,000 people throughout the world who had paid for the site content - 7,200 in the UK. Many have already been arrested and many more are under investigation.

Unfortunately, some material has found its way on to the Internet through peer-to-peer systems (Kazaa, etc.). Users searching for innocent content may be presented with offensive-sounding or illegal-sounding filenames. Downloading the files to see what they contain may result in committing an offence.

Actions

The Internet remains a great source of knowledge, assistance, commerce and entertainment for the vast majority of its users. It is one of the few areas that national governments have been unable to control. A large proportion of the Internet community, and the public at large, feel uneasy at some of the Internet's content but are totally against any censorship. A powerful lobby, representing some religious and political interests, demand sweeping control over the Internet. In the absence of a consensus, there remain the options of new legislation or accepting that the only laws to be enforced on Internet users and providers are the existing ones prevailing in each individual country.

The relevant UK laws are:

- The Obscene Publications Act of 1959, which makes the publication of an obscene article an offence. The definition of *'obscene'* is its tendency to deprave and corrupt.
- The Protection of Children Act of 1978, which states that the making of an indecent photograph of a child an offence (a child being someone under 16). The definition of *'making'* a photograph includes downloading an image since that results in another copy of the image.
- The Criminal Justice Act of 1988, which makes possession of an indecent photograph of a child an offence.
- The Telecommunications Act 1984 and the Criminal Justice and Police Order Act of 1994, which ensure that the OPA's provisions on pornography applied to the Internet in the UK.

Legal restrictions on the Internet have so far proven difficult to formulate and implement. In 1996, the American Communications Decency Act was overturned in their Supreme Court due to the Act's failure to adequately define offensive material.

There is now a trend for governments to pressurise Internet providers into acting as censors for all material that they provide to users. Since web sites and newsgroups are in permanent flux, the ability of ISPs to constantly monitor millions of pages every day is a totally impractical task. For the same reason, governments do not expect postal workers to open and read every letter before popping them in letterboxes. Easier targets are the semi-permanent newsgroups whose titles are suspect and UK providers have evolved their own voluntary code on these. Some newsgroups are already moderated by their organisers; any offensive or defamatory material received is not placed into the newsgroup. Another approach is self-regulation by the end-users. A variety of censoring software is available to prevent children, students or employees from gaining access to material that is deemed unsuitable by the person in control of the PC or local network. For example, Net Nanny allows a parent to maintain a dictionary of banned words - e.g. URLs and newsgroups, while WinWatch Home also allows children's on-line time to be restricted. Cyber Sentry and WebTrack are aimed at monitoring and controlling employees' access to the Internet. Already around two-thirds of libraries filter the Internet content that they allow on to their public access computers.

Useful websites discussing the issues are www.eff.org, www.iwf.org.uk and www.wiseuptothenet.co.uk

Web Site Creation

There is a spectacular expansion in the number of web sites on the Internet. Many are personal sites but there is also a huge number of commercial sites. Until a few years ago, only the largest companies tended to have web sites. Now, many small companies have their own site.

Web site uses

It is estimated that over 450 million people have internet access, including 34 million in the UK and over 170 million in the US. Reaching that amount of people by conventional means (e.g. TV adverts, newspapers, leaflets, circulars, catalogues, etc) is a very expensive business. The creation of private or commercial web sites opens up new and improved forms of communication across the globe. The variety of existing sites is immense but the most common categories are:

- E-commerce (promoting products or services, on-line stores).
- Public information (e.g. Inland Revenue, weather, etc).
- Social networking sites such as Bebo, Facebook and Friends Reunited.
- Private sites promoting ideas (e.g. politics, religion, music, art).
- Leisure (e.g. sports, hobbies, entertainment, radio stations).
- Reference (e.g. publications, dictionaries).
- Education (on-line learning).
- Support for products (e.g. on-line documentation, FAQs, software updates, drivers).

Web sites and multimedia

The production of multimedia presentations and the creation of web sites share many common areas. They both use text, graphics, audio and video in sets of screens that allow the absorption of information in a manner controlled by the viewer.   They both use similar equipment (still cameras, video cameras, video capture cards, scanners) and the raw material for integration often uses the same file formats (graphic, video and sound formats).   They differ in how they integrate and package these resources. More importantly, they differ greatly on how they <u>deliver</u> their final product.   Most multimedia, due to the large size of the files, is delivered on CD-ROM.   All the features of a multimedia CD-ROM are available as web site material but their widespread use is held back by the very slow rates of transferring data on the Internet.

Download problems

The single greatest problem with the Internet is the speed of access to web pages.   In part, this is due to the popularity of the medium. The congestion on the Internet results in times when transfer rates fall well below the capability of users' modems; sometimes data transfer rates fall to zero.   Even during a quiet(ish) period on the Net, the speed at which users can download pages is governed by the speed of their modems.   Telephone lines have a limited capacity and some users have older, slower modems.
This table shows the likely speeds for a range of internet connections.

Modem speed (in bits /sec)	Max theoretical transfer rate
56kbps	5.09KB per sec
ISDN	11.64KB per sec
Typical Cable	64KB per sec
Basic ADSL	512KB per sec
Typical ADSL	8Mb per sec

The values shown for cable modems and ADSL modems are typical values, as a range of speeds are available for both services.
These figures are optimistic, as few users achieve an average transfer rate that is close to the modem's maximum figure.   The times for downloading very large files are usually acceptable when using ftp, since users are storing the file contents and can carry on with another computer activity.   This is not the case with web browsing, as users expect to see page contents appear within a reasonable time.

If a web site is sited on a company's Intranet, the users have the benefit of the much faster communications channels (usually 10Mbps, 100Mbps or even 1Gbps). However this bandwidth has to be shared by scores, hundreds, or even thousands of users. While users can easily download small items such as e-mail, large files containing graphics, sound and video will only download in a reasonable time during periods when the intranet is little used by other users.

The consequence for web site designers is that they have to design for the lowest reasonable modem speed of 56kbps. Around 50% of Internet connections use ADSL. So, if a new, all-featured, site only performed adequately for users with ADSL lines, then the site would have a very limited appeal indeed to about half the potential market. This then is the starting point for web site design. Site builders do not have a free hand; they have to design with these severe restrictions in mind.

Site components

The main elements of a web site are:

Web Server

This is the computer connected to the Internet that stores the organisation's web pages. The server may be the property of a single organisation and only store the single web site. The majority of servers act as the host for many different users. The users may rent out space on the server or, in the case of many ISPs, a certain amount of web space may be provided to users as part of their normal rental agreement. Extra web space can usually be rented for an extra fee.

Web Site

Strictly speaking, the server location is termed the 'web site' but it is now customary to refer to each user's set of web pages as a web site. The diagram shows a web server that is the host for two separate web sites. A web site is the property of the person or organisation that owns and maintains the collection of files. Passwords are used to prevent unauthorised access and tampering with web site contents.

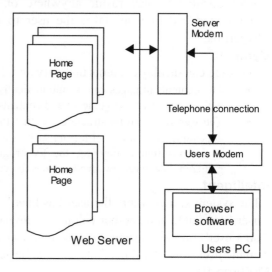

Web Page

This is a single page on the site. It may consist of a single text file, or may be made up of several files, each occupying parts of the screen, combined with other files storing graphics, sound or video. In either case, the user viewing the page sees it as a single screen display.

Home Page

Each site has a Home Page, which acts as a starting point, displaying the site's contents and providing links to other site pages. The Home Page may also display a welcome message and have an attractive format to entice viewers further into the site.

Intranets

Some companies have systems that use Internet facilities <u>within</u> their own network structure. These are called 'Intranets' and they may have no physical connection to the Internet. An Intranet is a self-contained system of company information, prices, projects, etc for employees to reference via browsers. It may or may not be connected to the Internet but provides similar services such as web pages, e-mail and FTP, although these are all internally organised. An Intranet is not designed to replace the network's file servers for standard file activities. It is likely to use its own internal IP addresses and these will probably not match external Internet assignments. Much freeware, shareware and commercial software is available for creating Web servers. Commercial products offer 'off-the-shelf' solutions that combine easy setup with added facilities such as monitoring, virus detection, encryption and security measures.

Extranets

An organisation with an Intranet often also provides a web site for the public. For security reasons, this web server will not be physically connected to the Intranet. There are certain resources, however, on the Intranet that it would be desirable to share with an authorised group of users such as customers, clients, partners and mobile employees.   These users would access the Extranet via the normal Internet.   Extranets require strict security using *'firewalls'* to prevent unauthorised access. The username and password of the individual logging in is used to determine which parts of the Extranet are available for viewing.

Technical characteristics

The main characteristics of web sites are:

Cross-platform

The script for every single HTML page on the entire Internet is stored in plain ASCII text and can therefore be read by every computer attached to the Internet.   This means that a script written using a PC can be read by the browser software sitting on a Macintosh, a UNIX system, etc.   This maximises the potential readership of sites and allows for easy interchange of documents between different hardware platforms.

Hyperlinking

The main benefit of web browsing is that users can navigate within sites and between sites by clicking on a piece of text or a graphic icon. These areas are the *'hyperlinks'* and they link information in one document with information in another part of the document - or an entirely different document.   The other documents may reside anywhere on the Internet.   So, clicking on a hyperlink area (the highlighted text or icon) takes the user to another retrieved document - the one pointed to by the hyperlink.

Dynamic

The page can display contents that vary and this can be implemented in two ways:

- The contents of pages can be automatically altered as an organisation's prices or specifications change, with each viewer seeing the altered contents.
- The web page can be structured so that the same URL will return different content to different users, depending on a variety of factors such as geographical location (e.g. displaying prices in pounds instead of dollars), time of day (e.g. the TV programme schedules) and reader profiles (e.g. using previously gathered data to review arcade games for younger users and car road tests for older users).

Intelligent

The system knows where the user has been!   It displays hypertext in two colours - one for links that a user has visited and another colour for unvisited links. *'Cookies'* can also be used to store information on a user's previous usage, to guide that user's future usage of the site.   Cookies are files that are stored on the user's own local machine and can be accessed by the remote site when the user logs into that site.

Multimedia

The original web page carried little more than text.   Now, the basic page can deliver a wide variety of file formats. Graphics, sound, animations and video are now commonplace. Files created in other packages (e.g. Paintshop graphics, Director movies, Premiere videos, Voyetra MIDI music, etc) are easily integrated into web sites. The introduction of the Java programming language into the Internet also provides platform-independent applets (little programs) that are downloaded from the server and run on the local computer. The one piece of code plays the same game or runs the same animation on PCs, UNIX boxes and Macintoshes.

Browser problems

In the ideal world, every browser would be capable of reading every web page and faithfully reproducing its contents. The page that was created by the original designer would be accurately displayed on every user's screen, regardless of what hardware or software they were using.

Unfortunately, the competition between different manufacturers and different software producers results in many incompatibilities. The different screen sizes and resolutions are covered later but the main headache for designers is the difference in operation and the variation in facilities offered by different browsers. There are constant updates to the 'standards' for web browsers but these are often ignored, varied or added to by browsers. Even if these are useful, they depart from the principle of an inclusive internet. They also cause problems for site designers.

Apart from differences between different products (e.g. Netscape and Explorer) there are differences between different versions of the same product, as new features are constantly added to newer versions.

This means that pages that run happily on a newer version of a browser may not work on an older version of the same browser.   Typical problems to be tackled include:
- Older browsers don't handle image maps.
- Older browsers don't handle Cascade Style Sheets.
- Not all CSS features are supported on all browsers, or are handled differently.
- Newer browsers have features that need to be installed as extra plug-ins in older versions.
- Netscape and Explorer use different techniques for handling DHTML.
- ActiveX and VBScript are only for use on Windows Explorer.
- XML is not fully supported on all browsers.

Design

Like software and multimedia projects, the impact of the final web site depends upon the amount of preparation that goes into the design. For all but the smallest of sites, a systematic approach to both content and design pays dividends. Other chapters ("*Multimedia*", '*Software & Data'*) cover storyboarding and project management, and these techniques would be used for creating any large web site.

Design characteristics
An effective web site is the result of effective design and this is characterised by two factors:
- Content   - what the site will contain and how it its pitched.
- Presentation   - how the contents will be displayed.

Content
Users don't log in to a site to marvel at the overall presentation. They only stay, and return, if the content is valuable to them. Soon, millions of students and hobbyists will have the ability to create reasonably advanced web pages. What will distinguish one site from another is the impact made by the page contents. In that respect, it is identical to writing for any publication. The site designer must <u>understand</u> the site content.   A thorough appreciation of the overall site flavour, down to the detail on each page is necessary to structure the contents to the best advantage. If the creator is not the site owner, the site contents must be fully discussed prior to design planning.

Presentation structures
A web site consists of many linked pages. The design of the page contents is accompanied by the design of the structure of the site.   The isssue of structures is discussed in the chapter on '*Multimedia'*.

Presentation

The contents are the main purpose for creating the site but the presentation of the site's pages has a great impact on drawing users into browsing its contents.   Most users decide their impression of a site within the first 10 seconds of viewing.

This highlights two factors:
- The site should be aesthetically pleasing.
- Pages should not take too long to download.

The following design characteristics should be studied before the final page contents and their presentation are decided.

Universality
The site has to be viewable by the maximum readership.   A decision must be reached on the balance between implementing the features of the newest HTML standards and latest browsers - and the effect of viewing numbers.   More functionality is offered by newer standards but, since not all viewers have browsers meeting these standards, this reduces the numbers capable of viewing the site.   As time goes by more viewers will update their software - but by that time, even newer features will have been added!

Regard should be paid to the needs of the over 5 million people in the UK who are registered as disabled. For example, visually-impaired surfers use special screen readers and these cannot cope with frames or buttons that use graphics instead of text links.

Page Size

Pages will be read on Macs with browsers whose screens are 465 pixels wide as well as PC's with 640x480 screens.   What looks good when designed on a 1024x768 screen may not look so good on these.   In addition, the screen size of the likely user must be considered.   Designing a highly-detailed page on a 21" monitor will not look the same when displayed on a 15" screen.

Scanability

Web site authors can learn from newspaper publishers. They know that readers don't read a page from top to bottom.   They scan the page, looking first at eye-catching components such as headlines, photographs and lists.   They only look at text after this initial scan.

For best results:

- Keep the most important points at the top of the page - like newspapers.
- Use headings and subheadings.
- Use bulleted lists.
- Use link menus as this improves scanability.

Simplicity

KISS - keep it simple, stupid!   Don't overdo the number of elements (lines, text, graphics, frames, and headings) on a page.   A fussy page is confusing and lacks clear navigation.

Style

Many sites revolve around the creator's flair or personality.   Some of the best sites are not the most polished, but are sometimes those showing the most vitality/originality.

Readability

The many tips for maximising readability include:

- Use *'white space'*.   These are not necessarily white, but are clear screen areas designed to rest the eye - and focus the eye on important objects.
- The text content of links should be explicit (e.g. not *'important'* or *'file57'*).
- If links are embedded within a sentence, they should be part of the text, not just stuck in

    eg do not use -   *"click here to read about my new video camera"*
    instead use -   *"My video camera provides the raw material for the ..."*

- It is OK to use links within the main body text but don't use whole sentences as links.
- Use lines to split the page into discrete areas by topic.
- Above all, spellcheck and grammar check text content.
- Use a consistent layout throughout the pages.   Use the same size of heading fonts, same method of navigation, same frame sizes, etc.
- Use margins, frames, tables and lists to break blocks of text into manageable chunks.

Finally, there are almost 9m disabled people in the UK. This includes many who are partially sighted and many blind surfers who use text readers to read page contents. Sites should also be designed for their ease of access. The Disabilities Rights Commission provides a code of conduct on site design and guidelines are also available from the Royal National Institute for the Blind (www.rnib.org.uk).

Consistency

A web site is easier to browse if the design uses consistent navigation methods. For example one page should not use text links to navigate while another page uses buttons.   Additionally, buttons should be in the same order and in the same place on each page.   It is also preferable to use consistent backgrounds for pages. Every page could use the same background or different backgrounds could be used for different sections of a site. Using different backgrounds for product information, ordering, special offers, etc., provide some sense of structure for the user.

Colours

Colour monitors' screens are covered in red, green and blue phosphor dots. Each dot can be lit to varying intensities to produce different colours. Common colour systems are:

24-bit

A 24-bit graphics card can vary the intensity of each dot to 256 different levels. This produces 256 x 256 x 256 = 16,777,216 different colours.   It uses 256 different values for each colour and needs three bytes (i.e. 24-bits) to store the colour of a single dot on the screen.   24-bit graphics are high quality but result in large file sizes, a potential problem on the Internet.

8-bit

The approach used by GIF and other low colour range images, is to use a pre-defined set of colour values, stored in a table. Each colour has a colour number or *'index'*. This table is called a *'CLUT'* (Colour Look-Up Table) and it stores a maximum of 256 values and these values are used to set the proportions of red, green and blue to be used in each colour.   256 values (i.e. 0 to 255) can be stored in a single byte, hence the name *'8-bit'*. Of course, an image may not use all of the colours in the table or it may use a different set of colour combinations.   The range of colours currently stored in the table is called the *'palette'*.   If an image contains colours not in the table, the extra colours are obtained on a 256-colour monitor by *'dithering'*. The browser produces a pattern consisting of some of the available colours. The result approximates to the wanted colour but often produces unwanted *'hatching'* or *'dotty'* effects.

8-bit monitor issues

Browsers use an 8-bit colour table that stores six levels for each colour, i.e. 6 red x 6 green x 6 blue = 216 different colours.   On an 8-bit colour system, all other colours not in this 216 colour table are dithered. Since the number of users viewing with 8-bit colour is very small, this is not a major problem. However, to ensure that images display at their best (i.e. without dithering) to the maximum number of users, the 'browser-safe' colours accepted by the major browsers should be used.

Hex	Decimal	Percentage
00	0	0%
33	51	20%
66	102	40%
99	153	60%
CC	204	80%
FF	255	100%

The six levels for each colour are shown in the table The percentage value shows the relative saturation while the decimal value expresses the RGB level.

HTML uses the hex values for each colour. So, for example, 000000 has all three colours turned off to produce black while FFFFFF has each colour at full saturation, producing white.

PCs and Macintosh computers can both use these 216 colours in their system palettes. However, of the standard Windows palette of 16 colours, only eight appear in the 216-colour palette.

Existing GIF files can be converted to this table's palette, using a graphics package such as Paintshop. This technique works best with clipart, graphs and other non-photographic images. Since photographs have a wide range of colours and many colours in the same range (e.g. lots of blues or lots of greens), converting to 216 colours will degrade the quality of the final display. The 216-colour palette may not already exist in a graphics package but all packages allow for the importing of new palettes. The palette can be downloaded from the Internet and stored in the graphics package.   Search the web for *'216 colours'* or use the graphic file offered in:

www.the-light.com/netcol.html

The site provides a graphics file that contains the palette.

24-bit colour issues

24-bit images are used most frequently in multimedia kiosks and on CDs, where size and display time is less of a problem. When full-colour images are used in web pages, they may occupy greater amounts of the site's storage capacity and take longer to download than their 8-bit equivalents. Of course, although this is not always the case and a 24-bit image can be reduced to 8-bit depth and the two files sizes compared before choosing a format. The big advantage of 24-bit colour is that it provides photographic quality and may be essential on some sites.

Graphics

Graphics play an important, even primary, role in making a site more attractive.   They can also be used to make navigation easier (i.e. by using navigation icons) and can impart information (e.g. displaying photographs, maps, graphs, etc).

Nevertheless, there are a few rules on the use of graphics.

- Do not place too many images on one page, as this is both distracting for the viewer, as well as lengthening download times.   There are exceptions where the user expects/wants to wait - e.g. to view goods or property, fanzine sites, etc.   In general, the purpose of every image should be questioned with unnecessary graphics being ruthlessly eliminated.

- Don't let the page background overpower the content. The background image must not obscure the foreground text or dominate the page.
- Use the <ALT> attribute on all <IMG> tags. This provides a text alternative for graphic images and is useful for browsers set to read pages in text-only mode. It also ensures the maximum readership of the site.
- Use thumbnail graphics (i.e. miniatures) on the page, with links to download the larger version. This speeds up the page download. Users can see the draft of the graphics and decide whether it is worth the extra time to download the larger version.
- Use graphics for bullets. This looks better than standard bullets. Keep the same graphic (e.g. a red ball) for all other page bullets. The graphic will be loaded into the local PC's browser cache and this reduces subsequent download times.
- Reuse other images in the same way. The download time overhead only happens once.
- Use image libraries. Graphic files are installed on many web servers. These can be used for the server's web sites, reducing the space used by each site. Since the server also provides more effective caching of its own graphics, this results in speedier access.
- Scanned images should be scanned at the average of 72dpi. Monitors range from about 70dpi to 100dpi. Scanning at greater resolutions increases file space and provides no extra resolution quality.

Graphic Types
The most common graphics formats are GIF and JPEG. They both use compression to minimise file size and download times.
- JPEG should be used for photographic images. These are in 24-bit colour but offer increased levels of compression with decreased picture quality.
- GIFs should be used for non-photographic images (e.g. clipart, logos, and banners). These files can be reduced to 8-colour or even Black & White (although B&W images save little space and are used mainly for aesthetic reasons). The big advantage of GIFs is that they can be organised in a variety of ways (transparent images, animated images and interlaced images - see later).

HTML implementation
When the design is complete and all the resources (text, graphics, etc) are gathered, the elements can be combined in the set of web pages to comprise the web site. These are implemented using HTML and are given the extension .HTM with the home page usually being called 'index.htm'.

The HyperText Markup Language is the language used for all web pages, although some other languages build round an HTML framework. An HTML script is written in plain ASCII, using any plain text editor (e.g. NotePad or EDIT) or word processor with the document saved a plain text file. Since ASCII characters are readable by all types of computer (UNIX, PC, Mac, etc) on the Internet, it forms the foundation of a platform-free language. One script is used for all machines, with each translating the script into its own machine-specific tasks.

A web page is simply a text file (known as a 'script') containing a list of commands. The script lines are used to display text and graphics, check whether the user has clicked on a particular object and jump to other parts of the script (or even other scripts). In these respects, an HTML page script is similar to a DOS batch file or the script for a program written in interpreted Basic.

However, the script may also contain information about what font style to use for text, which pieces of text are to be checked for user input and so on. This information is embedded in the HTML file as additional sets of ASCII characters. These are called 'tags' and are similar to the codes in Microsoft Word that turn italics or bold face off and on. With Word, these tags are normally hidden from the user; with HTML, the tags appear as part of the ASCII script. As long as all browsers know that the tag <I> turns on italics and </I> turns off italics, they can all make sense of the script file. How each machine displays and prints italics is nothing to do with the web page writer - the translation is up to the user's browser and operating system. Similarly, HTML may describe a piece of text as having a certain 'header' size, rather than as, say, 24-point Arial. Each machine will decide what font size and style it will use as a header. This makes the entire HTML language completely machine-independent and explains its popularity as a means of exchanging information between different computer systems.

Apart from all the text to be displayed on the screen, the HTML script file contains:
- tags which tell the browser how to display the various parts of the text (font size, underlining, etc).
- tags which instruct the browser to fetch an image and place it on a particular area of the screen.
- hyperlinks which take the user to another part of the document or to another HTML document.

There are many applications that are dedicated to simplifying the process. These vary from add-ons to Microsoft Word through to full-blown design packages. All packages still produce an HTML ASCII file as their final product (perhaps with the addition of some JavaScript).

Note: HTML pages using simple commands can be read by all browsers. If the latest HTML innovation or add-ons for animations, audio, video, etc are used, then only browsers equipped with these facilities will be able to make use of all the site's features. Various brands of browser, and even different versions of the same brand, may produce different screen results while executing the same HTML command. Due to constant changes and additions, no browser software faithfully implements every available command.

Basic structure

The illustration shows the minimum layout of an HTML script. Note that all the tags start with the '<' (i.e. the less than symbol) and end with the '>' (i.e. the greater than symbol). Repeating a tag reverses the earlier tag's effects, if the second tag is prefaced with a forward slash character. The effects of some tags need to be cancelled (e.g. turning on and off italics around a word or phrase). Other tags, such as drawing a line, need only appear once. Tags are not case sensitive; they can be entered in upper or lower case, although most writers use upper case for easier recognition.

```
<HTML>
<HEAD>
<TITLE>
    title text goes here
</TITLE>
</HEAD>
<BODY>
    main script goes here
    ...
    ...
</BODY>
</HTML>
```

The tags used in this basic script are:

- The 'HTML' tags are placed at the beginning and end of all HTML documents to tell browsers that the information enclosed is the valid section for translation.
- The 'HEAD' tag contains the web page '*header*', which can consist of the title and 'meta' tags, amongst others.
- The words placed between the 'TITLE' tags are those that are used when the page is added to a user's bookmark. It is also the text that is examined and displayed as the header in search engine results.
- The HEAD section can also contain 'META' tags that hold key words to help identify the site to search engines.
- Material placed between the two 'BODY' tags comprises the contents displayed in the user's browser window.

Order of tags

Tags may be '*nested*' - i.e. a new tag or set of tags may be placed within an existing set of tags. To ensure that the script produces the expected results in all browsers, cancellation tags should be placed in reverse order to the order of declaring them.

So, `<BLOCKQUOTE><I><B> blah blah blah </B></I></BLOCKQUOTE>` is correct while

`<BLOCKQUOTE><I><B> blah blah blah </BLOCKQUOTE></I></B>` is bad practice.

While some browsers may be more tolerant than others, failure to observe this rule may result in page formatting not looking the way that was anticipated.

Example script

This is a sample of a basic HTML script and its output, as seen by a browser.

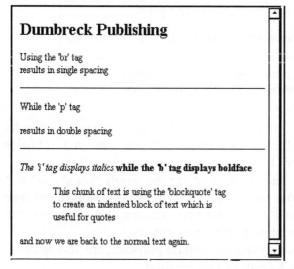

```
<HTML>
<HEAD>
<TITLE>A sample script</TITLE>
</HEAD>
<BODY BGCOLOR="#00FFFF" TEXT="BLUE">
<H1>Dumbreck Publishing</H1>
Using the 'br' tag<BR>
results in
single spacing
<HR>
While the 'p' tag<P>
results in double spacing
<HR>
<I>The 'i' tag displays italics</I>
<B>while the 'b' tag displays boldface</B>
<BLOCKQUOTE>This chunk of text is using the
'blockquote' tag to create an indented block of text which
is useful for quotes
</BLOCKQUOTE>
and now we are back to the normal text again.
</BODY>
</HTML>
```

Most tags also provide additional refinements. These are known as the tag's '*attributes*' and they may provide control over an object's size, colour and screen position. The inclusion of attributes is optional, although non-inclusion usually results in the adoption of the current or default values. For example, objects may be positioned on the left margin by default, while an attribute may be included in a tag to make a particular object right justified.

The various tags used in the above example are:

\<I\>   All text between this tag and a \</I\> tag is displayed in italics.

\<B\>   All text between this tag and a \</B\> tag is displayed in boldface.

BGCOLOR   This, along with 'TEXT' are optional attributes within the \<BODY\> tag.

    The BGCOLOR attribute sets the colour of the screen background and the TEXT attribute sets the colour of the all the text in the document (unless overruled).   Colour values can be specified in two ways:

    1. By naming the colour - eg   TEXT="BLUE" or BGCOLOR="YELLOW".   This is the simplest method when one of the sixteen colour names understood by browsers is required (see later for the full list).   The default text colour is black and the default background colour is white.

    2. When subtle colours, without any given name are required, values are set by giving the hex value of the amount of red, green and blue in the mix.   In the example above, the red value is 00, while the green and blue values are both FF.   This is entered as BGCOLOUR="#00FFFF" and results in a cyan background.   To obtain blue text, the text attribute could have been specified as "TEXT=#00FF00" - ie red fully off, blue fully on and green fully off.   The hash symbol '#' should be included to ensure that all browsers recognise the values as hexadecimal amounts.

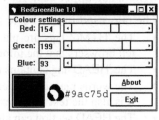

Software utilities such as RGB and RGB2WEB allow the writer to move sliders to mix the colours.   When the desired colour is viewed in the colour box, the decimal and hex values for that colour are displayed. The values can be noted and included in the page script or, in some utilities, the values can be copied straight from the utility and pasted directly into the page script.

\<BR\>   Provides the equivalent of a carriage return in word processing.   The remaining text is displayed on the next line.

\<P\>   The P tag is seen as the start of a new paragraph and an extra line of white space is inserted.

    It provides the equivalent of two carriage returns.

\<BLOCKQUOTE\>   Any text enclosed between this tag and the \</BLOCKQUOTE\> tag is treated as a quote and is indented from both sides of the page.   The \<BR\> tag can also be used between these tags.

\<HR\>   Draws a horizontal line, called the *'rule'*, across the page and is used to separate out or emphasise sections of text.   Without any attributes (i.e. used by itself as in the above example) it displays a line that is the width of the browser window.

    Optional attributes for the \<HR\> tag are:

ALIGN=	Use LEFT, RIGHT or CENTER to position the rule on the screen.
NOSHADE	Draws the rule as a solid block. The default is a 3-D shaded rule.
SIZE=	Sets the height of the rule in pixels.
WIDTH=	Sets the rule width in pixels or as a percentage of the window width eg WIDTH=50%

As many of the attributes as required can be used together as in this example:

        \<HR ALIGN=CENTER NOSHADE   SIZE=15   WIDTH=300\>

Text formatting

Note that there is no set width to a line of text.   Browsers word wrap the text into as many lines as its screen allows.   This, in turn, depends on the resolution of the monitor and font size used.   Lower resolution screens and larger fonts result in a paragraph of text spreading over more screen lines.

Also note that in the earlier example, separate script lines were used for the words *"results in"* and *"single spacing"* but the final output displayed it on the same line.   That is because normal carriage returns entered by an ASCII editor are ignored by browsers.   Browsers only respond to specific tag commands to move to a new line (apart from the word wrapping mentioned earlier).

Adding extra spaces between words or lines, for formatting and indentation purposes, are also ignored. All words are assembled into one giant paragraph unless formatting tags are used.

Font formats

Other font formats are <U> which turns on underlined text and <S> which turns on strikethrough text (eg ~~strikethrough~~).   Another tag called <TT> for *'teletype text'* is used to switch into a non-proportional font such as Courier. It is used to display numeric tables, as all columns can be guaranteed to align vertically. It can also be used to give a different appearance to programme listings of Pascal, C++, etc.

Other formatting tags are <SUP> which displays in superscript and <SUB> which displays in subscript.

The <SMALL> tag will display the content in a smaller than normal font until it is switched off with the </SMALL> tag.   Similarly, the <BIG> tag displays the content in a larger than normal font.   The actual size of the BIG and SMALL fonts will depend on the body font chosen by the user.

Heading tags

HTML provides a set of heading tags. These are <H1> through to <H6> and are used to provide headings and sub-headings to improve the document's formatting. All text enclosed by the <H1> and </H1> tags is displayed in the largest font size, with <H6> displaying the smallest font size.   As the example shows, cancelling a heading tag also results in a paragraph break.

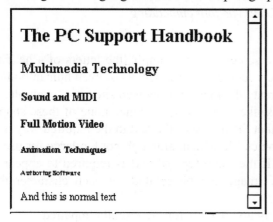

```
<HTML>
<HEAD>
<TITLE>Example heading sizes</TITLE>
</HEAD>
<BODY BGCOLOR="WHITE" TEXT="BLACK">
<H1>The PC Support Handbook</H1>
<H2>Multimedia Technology</H2>
<H3>Sound and MIDI</H3>
<H4>Full Motion Video</H4>
<H5>Animation Techniques</H5>
<H6>Authoring Software</H6>
<P>
And this is normal text
</BODY>
</HTML>
```

Headings should not be used to replace the <B> tag to emphasise parts of the text. Many search tools use the headings of a page to extract important information from a site.   The tools assume that if the writer found the text to be significant enough to be used as a heading, then it is important enough for search purposes.   While a subject heading is a good choice for extraction, an individual word or phrase - emphasised with a heading tag - devalues the site search if it not of any significance.   For example the phrase *"this should **NOT** be tried at home"* should use the <B> tag to embolden the word *'NOT'*.   If the word was emphasised using a heading tag, search engines would place an unwarranted significance to the word for search results.

Font faces

The viewer is able to set the typestyle that the browser uses to display web pages. This is set from the *'Fonts'* button on the *'Internet options'* choice in Internet Explorer's *'Tools'* menu.   Users can choose from Times New Roman, Arial, Verdana, Georgia, etc. The web site designer, however, may prefer that the viewer see the pages with a particular font. The pages, for example, may have been designed to look best with a sans serif font such as Arial or Verdana. There are a number of ways to influence what the user sees on his/screen and these are discussed below.

FACE

The FONT tag has a FACE attribute that specifies what font or style should be displayed. At it simplest, the lines

<FONT FACE="serif">   or   <FONT FACE="sans-serif">

can be included in the script.   This ensures that the viewer will see the main class of type, but does not specifies the actual font to be used.

The line

<FONT FACE="Verdana, Arial, Helvetica">

specifies that the Verdana font should be used as a first option. If the font is not present on the user's computer, the Arial font should be used, followed by Helvetica as the third option. If none of the fonts are installed on the user's machine, the default font will be used.

This is a very simple way of specifying fonts but it has two major drawbacks:
- Not every browser supports this attribute.
- Different computer systems use different names for their fonts (one system might have a Times font, while another has a Times Roman or a Times New Roman font).

Although the method is simple, it does not guarantee the required results for all those viewing the site. Since different fonts from the original may be used, the width of text characters may be different, causing lines of text to overflow.

Embedding Fonts

Bitstream have introduced a scheme to store their own TrueDoc fonts on their site. The designer creates links to their site at truedoc.com and these fonts can be displayed on a users web page. This requires a little JavaScript and the <FONT FACE= > tag using Cascading Style Sheets. The user does not require to download these fonts, as Navigator 4 onwards, and Explorer with a free Bitstream Active X control installed, can read the font elements from the TrueDoc site and display them. This allows designers to choose fonts in the knowledge that the user will see them the way the designer planned. Microsoft, of course, has developed a competing standard known as *'TrueType font embedding'*.

Graphic Text

There may be times when no existing font will do for a screen. For example, the letters of a heading may be required to be constructed from real world objects such as straws, pencils or even human bodies. Alternatively, a special font shape may be required to create the mood for the web site. For example, an oil company may wish the letters of the heading to look like drops of oil. Since none of these shapes will appear in any existing font, the only way to ensure that the user sees the text in the required way is to create the words as a graphic file. This results in a graphics file which, although not too large for use as a heading, could not be used as the entire body text. If the same type of text is required to appear in different headings throughout the web site, a graphic image can be created for each character that appears, so that these can be re-used throughout the pages.

Bear in mind, however, that graphic text cannot be read by text readers for the visually impaired.

Colours

Internet Explorer and Netscape recognise the following sixteen colour names:

- BLACK
- WHITE
- GRAY
- SILVER
- GREEN
- RED
- BLUE
- YELLOW
- MAROON
- OLIVE
- NAVY
- PURPLE
- LIME
- TEAL
- AQUA
- FUCHSIA

These colour values can be used to set the colour of the screen background, the main text, the borders and shading of objects and the various hyperlink states (e.g. unexplored or explored).

An alternative that is accepted by all browsers is using hex numbers for the RGB values.

To display white text on a black background use either:

```
<BODY BGCOLOR="BLACK" TEXT="WHITE">
```
or
```
<BODY BGCOLOR="#000000" TEXT="#FFFFFF">
```

The text of unexplored links is blue by default. This can be changed with LINK="colour"
```
<BODY BGCOLOR="BLACK" TEXT="WHITE"  LINK="YELLOW">
```

The text of explored links is purple/red by default. This can be changed with VLINK="colour"
```
<BODY BGCOLOR="BLACK" TEXT="WHITE" VLINK="LIME">
```

The <BODY TEXT=colour> tag changes the colour of the default text on a page. To change the colour of a particular paragraph, sentence, word or even a single 'letter', the <FONT> tag can be used with a COLOR attribute as in this example:
```
Do <FONT COLOR="RED"> NOT </FONT> try this at home
```

The word *'Do'* is displayed in the default text colour while the word 'NOT' is displayed in red. When the browser reads the </FONT> it again displays all text in the original default colour.

Again, the colour values can be entered as one of the given sixteen text values or can be entered as hex numbers.

Escape characters

There are times when the page has to display characters that are already used for formatting commands, such as & and > and <. Using them inside a normal text line may produce unexpected results in some browsers. In addition, some characters are not available in the standard ASCII set and can't be directly typed in from the keyboard.

HTML provides escape sequences to overcome these problems.

All escape characters begin with an ampersand character and are either followed by a text sequence or by a numeric sequence.

Text escape sequences include:

Sequence	Displayed character	Sequence	Displayed character
&gt	>	&amp	&
&lt	<	&quot	"

The numeric sequence places a hash symbol between the ampersand and the number and the range includes:

Sequence	Displayed character	Sequence	Displayed character
&#153	™	&#179	^{3}
&#169	©	&#188	¼
&#174	®	&#189	½
&#176	°	&#190	¾
&#178	^{2}	&#247	÷

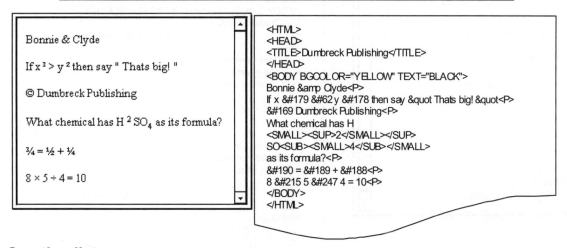

Bonnie & Clyde

If $x^3 > y^2$ then say " Thats big! "

© Dumbreck Publishing

What chemical has H_2SO_4 as its formula?

¾ = ½ + ¼

$8 \times 5 \div 4 = 10$

```
<HTML>
<HEAD>
<TITLE>Dumbreck Publishing</TITLE>
</HEAD>
<BODY BGCOLOR="YELLOW" TEXT="BLACK">
Bonnie &amp Clyde<P>
If x &#179 &#62 y &#178 then say &quot Thats big! &quot<P>
&#169 Dumbreck Publishing<P>
What chemical has H
<SMALL><SUP>2</SMALL></SUP>
SO<SUB><SMALL>4</SUB></SMALL>
as its formula?<P>
&#190 = &#189 + &#188<P>
8 &#215 5 &#247 4 = 10<P>
</BODY>
</HTML>
```

Creating lists

Most visitors to a web site dislike having to scroll through long paragraphs of text, trying to extract the main points.   Often, the information can be displayed more effectively as a list of main points.

HTML supports three types of lists and these are shown in the next example.

Unordered list

This is used when numbering the items has no relevance. The items appear as a bulleted list as shown in the example. The <UL> and </UL> tags indicate that the enclosed items are list items. Each individual list item has a <LI> tag.

The general layout is:
```
<UL>
<LI> first item to display
<LI> second item
<LI> third item
</UL>
```

The <UL> tag has a number of options, although the final effect may depend upon the browser used.

Use	Explanation	Example
TYPE="DISC"	The bullets are filled circles (this is the default)	●
TYPE="SQUARE"	The bullets are square	■
TYPE="CIRCLE"	The bullets are unfilled circles	O

So, for example   <UL TYPE="SQUARE">   displays an unordered list with square bullets.

Ordered list

This is used when numbering the items is significant, such a set of instructions.   The items appear as a bulleted list as shown in the example.

The general layout is:

```
<OL>
<LI> first item to display
<LI> second item
<LI> third item
</OL>
```

The <OL> tag has a number of attribute options:

Use	Explanation	Example
TYPE="1"	Standard Arabic numerals will number the list	1, 2, 3, 4, 5, 6, 7
TYPE="A"	Upper case letters will number the list	A, B, C, D, E, F
TYPE="a"	Lower case letters will number the list	a, b, c, d, e, f
TYPE="I"	Upper case Roman numerals will number the list	I, II, III, IV, V, VI, VII
TYPE="i"	Lower case Roman numerals will number the list	i, ii, iii, iv, v, vi, vii
START=	Alters the default starting point for numbering	See below

So,   <OL TYPE="A" START=G"> displays an ordered list with the items listed as G, H, I, J, etc.

While   <OL TYPE="1" START="10"> displays an ordered list numbered as 10, 11, 12, 13, 14, etc.

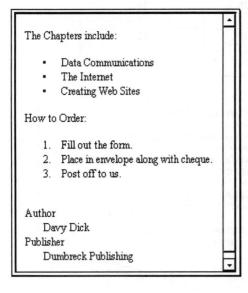

```
<HTML>
<HEAD>
<TITLE>Creating lists example</TITLE>
</HEAD>
<BODY BGCOLOR="WHITE" TEXT="BLACK">
The Chapters include:
<!--                              here is a bulleted list -->
<UL>
<LI>Data Communications
<LI>The Internet
<LI>Creating Web Sites
</UL>
How to Order:
<!--                              here is an ordered list -->
<OL>
<LI>Fill out the form.
<LI>Place in envelope along with cheque.
<LI>Post off to us.
</OL>
<!--                              here is a definition list -->
<DL>
<DT>Author
<DD>Davy Dick
<DT>Publisher
<DD>Dumbreck Publishing
</DL>
</BODY>
</HTML>
```

Definition list

Definition lists, sometimes called *'glossary lists'*, produce a list of terms and their descriptions.

The general layout is:

```
<DL>
<DT>  first term
<DD> first definition
<DT> second term
<DD> second definition
</DL>
```

The <DT> tag places the text in the left of the screen and the following <DD> tag indents the next line.

Comments

The script above inserted comments using the <!-- *comment* --> tag.   Comments make the script easier to understand but their content is ignored by browsers and is not displayed.

Nesting lists

Lists can be nested - one list is embedded within another list.   The example also shows the <BR> tag being used within a list to move to a new line without inserting another bullet.

The Chapters include:

    A. Data Communications
           ■ The RS232 port
           ■ OSI and TCP
    B. Creating Web Sites
          including HTML
    C. Multimedia
    D. and so on .....

```
<HTML>
<HEAD>
<TITLE>Nested lists example</TITLE>
</HEAD>
<BODY BGCOLOR="WHITE" TEXT="BLUE">
The Chapters include:
<OL TYPE = "A" >
<LI> Data Communications
<UL>
    <LI> The RS232 port
    <LI> OSI and TCP
</UL>
<LI> Creating Web Sites
<BR>
including HTML
<LI> Multimedia
<LI> and so on .....
</OL>
</BODY>
</HTML>
```

Aligning objects

By default, text and other objects such as graphics, tables etc, are aligned down the left of the screen.
An individual heading or paragraph can be positioned using the ALIGN attribute.
For example:

`<H2 ALIGN=CENTER> blah blah blah </H2>`	aligns text in the centre of the screen
`<H2 ALIGN=RIGHT> blah blah blah </H2>`	aligns text to the right edge of the screen
`<H2 ALIGN=LEFT> blah blah blah </H2>`	aligns text to the left edge of the screen

With this method, each item has its own individual ALIGN attribute.   Where a larger section of items share the same alignment, the entire section is enclosed by a set of <DIV> tags as in this example:

```
<DIV ALIGN=CENTER>
<H1> My Name </H1>
<H2> My address </H2>
</DIV>
```

The <DIV> tag has the advantage that it can enclose all kinds of objects such as paragraphs of text, headings, images, tables, etc.   When a <DIV> tag is used it alters that section's alignment, but the software remembers the previous alignment.   When the </DIV> tag is reached, the alignment reverts to this previous value.   To ensure that the script will work with all browser versions, always cancel a <DIV> tag before issuing another <DIV> tag.

Navigating the web site

So far, this chapter has considered:

- Web site contents.
- Design structures.
- Formatting of web page text.

The completed site consists of a collection of web pages held together by a set of 'hyperlinks'.   The links are another set of HTML tags and they are used to:

- Take the user to another part of the same web page
- Take the user to another web page in the same web site
- Take the user to another web site altogether.

The basis of all web navigation is the 'anchor tag' or 'link tag'.
The format of a link tag is:

```
<A HREF="where to jump"> Text for the hyperlink  </A>
```

The tag comprises several sections:

<A HREF="where to jump">	The 'A' indicates that it is an anchor tag - i.e. treat the tag as a link.
	The 'HREF' indicates that it is a hyperlink reference (other options can be placed here as can be seen later).
	The text part indicates what document or part of the document to jump to. This may point to another document using either:
	  • The URL (full hostname and filename) of a document on the WWW.
	  • The name of another document inside the same web site.
	It can also point to a 'label' within the currently displayed document.

Text for the hyperlink	The text that appears underlined on the screen waiting to be clicked.
</A>	The closing tag to indicate the end of the link definition.

Example link tags are:

        <A HREF="order.htm"> Ordering Information</A>
        <A HREF="http://www.dumbreck.demon.co.uk/index.html"> Dumbreck Publishing </A>
        <A HREF="#mboard"> Testing the motherboard </A>

Jumping within a web page

This is commonly used with large linear web pages such as FAQ pages and other technical pages.   The link tag points to a particular section of the document that is specially labelled. The label is embedded in the document and is known as the *'anchor'* with its own anchor tag. Labels can be spread throughout the document, allowing jumping both up and down through the document. This technique is similar to the GOTO command used in DOS batch files and some programming languages.   The link tag has a hash symbol before the name of the label to indicate that what follows is a label and not a URL.   So, "#Chapter1" points to an anchor within the document.   The format of the anchor tag is:

        <A NAME="anchor name"> The text to be displayed at the anchor point </A>

Note

In the next example, all the text is displayed on a single screen and clicking the hyperlinks has no apparent effect.   To test this page, the text sections have to be expanded so that the document requires several pages to display.

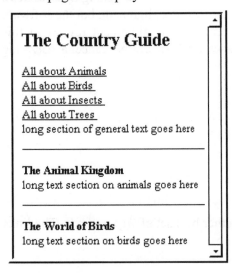

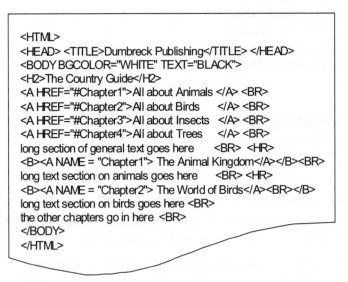

Jumping to another page

A web site usually consists of many pages and the user is encouraged to jump between the pages by clicking the hypertext links.

Consider the following hypertext link:

        <A HREF="order.htm"> Ordering Information</A>

The words *'Ordering Information'* will appear on the screen as the hypertext link.   Clicking on that text makes the browser load the web page called *'order.htm'*.   This assumes that the file called *'order.htm'* is in the same directory as the web page that is pointing to it.   This is the most common case for small to medium web sites.   It also simplifies the command since only the file name need be supplied.

Where the site's files are held in a number of directories, relative paths may can be specified as shown.

HREF="finance/order.htm"	The web page can be found in the directory called *'finance'* and the 'finance' directory is a sub-directory of the current directory.
HREF="book/finance/order.htm"	The web page can be found in the directory called *'finance'* which is a sub-directory of the *'book'* directory which, in turn, is a sub-directory of the current directory.
HREF="../order.htm"	The web page can be found in the directory above the current directory.
HREF="../../order.htm"	The web page can be found in the directory two levels above the current directory.
HREF="/d|/mysite/order.htm"	The web can be found in the *'mysite'* directory of the D: drive. Note that a vertical bar replaces the semi-colon normally found after a drive letter.

For simplicity, keep all the site's resources in the same directory - or use relative paths. This simplifies site maintenance, since the site can be moved to different disk directories without changing all the link references.

For larger web sites, it is common to organise the files into separate directories (one directory for sound files, one for video, clips, etc.). If the site is very large, these directories would be sub-divided into other directories (e.g. a directory for one set of audio files, with another directory for other audio files). Where thousands of html files are stored on a site, it is easy to leave old files in the system, forget to update certain files, and other errors associated with the sheer volume of files to maintain. In these circumstances, sets of html files would be stored in their own directories (e.g. one directory to store all product descriptions, one directory to store all FAQs, and so on).

Note:

While tags are not case sensitive, the directory and file functions of some operating systems (e.g. Unix) are case sensitive. So, for example, entering *'Order.htm'* or *'ORDER.HTM'* will result in the file not being found. Web space providers can supply details of any file naming restrictions that apply on their servers.

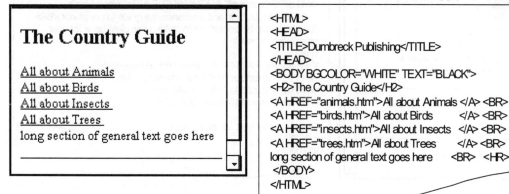

This is the earlier example altered from one large web document into a set of linked web pages. Clicking a hypertext link now loads the new web page instead of jumping to another part of the same document. The list of hypertext links at the top of the document is called a *'link menu'*.

Jumping to an anchor in another page

In the above example, a link loads a new web page and the user sees the top of that web page. It is possible to link not just to the top of the page but to any anchor within that new page. The opening tag has to contain both the name of the new page and the name of the anchor as in this example:

<A HREF="birds.htm#robins"> All about robins </A>

Jumping to another site

The link can take the user to any page on any site on the World Wide Web, just by placing the URL in the tag. This example takes the user to Dumbreck's home page:

<A HREF="http://www.dumbreck.demon.co.uk/index.html"> Dumbreck Publishing </A>

Graphic images

Graphics can make a huge impact on the effectiveness of a web page.

This section looks at *'Inline Graphics'* which are images that are loaded along with the web page (*'External Graphics'* are only loaded when the user asks for it, usually by clicking a link).

The image tag allows a GIF or JPEG image to be displayed on the web page.

The tag's basic format is:

```
<IMG SRC="filename">
```

A number of additional attributes provide for additional formatting of the image.   These are:

ALIGN=	Places the next line of text next to the TOP, MIDDLE or BOTTOM of the image. The first example below shows the result of using MIDDLE. Only one line of the text appears in the middle, with the remaining lines appearing under the graphic. The graphic, by default, is placed at the left margin of the page. If ALIGN=LEFT is used, as in the second example, the graphic is still on the left but the text flows down its right-hand side. Similarly, ALIGN=RIGHT places the graphic on the right margin.
BORDER=	Enlarges the border round the image, if required. The number entered is in pixels.
ALT=	Display a piece of text when the mouse hovers over the image. This is useful when users turn off the facility for viewing graphic images, as they can still get a description of the content.

An example image tag is:

```
<IMG SRC="world.gif" ALIGN=MIDDLE BORDER=10 ALT="World Map">
```

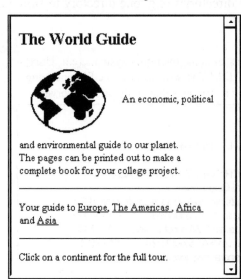

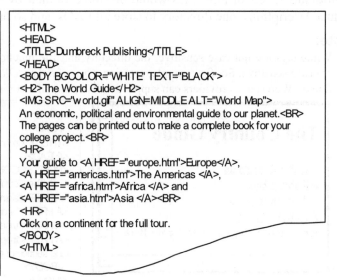

Changing the ALIGN setting to LEFT produces the result shown below.

CLEAR

In the example on the right, the first two sentences are both aligned down the side of the graphic image. Inserting a <P> or a <BR> after the first sentence will still leave the second sentence aligned down the graphic.

If the second sentence is required to appear below the graphic, the effects of the ALIGN=LEFT attribute can be cancelled by using the <BR CLEAR=LEFT> or <P CLEAR=LEFT> tag.   After this tag, the formatting of text resorts to normal.

Similarly, a <BR CLEAR=RIGHT> tag is used to cancel the effects of a previous ALIGN=RIGHT.

Using a graphic as a hyperlink

Many hyperlinks display underlined text that can be clicked to activate the link. It is also possible to use a graphic image as the hyperlink object, where they are often known as *'Hotspots'*. If an <IMG> tag is embedded inside a link tag, that graphic image becomes a clickable hotspot link.

In this example

```
<A HREF="worlddb.htm" > <IMG SRC="world.gif"> </A>
```

the graphic tag has simply replaced the hyperlink text.   When run, the globe graphic appears with a box outline round it to indicate that it is a clickable object.   The width of this outline is set, in pixels, with the BORDER attribute.

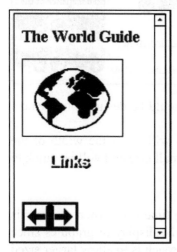

```
<HTML>
<HEAD>
<TITLE>Dumbreck Publishing</TITLE>
</HEAD>
<BODY BGCOLOR="WHITE' TEXT="BLACK">
<H2>The World Guide</H2>
<A HREF="worlddb.htm"> <IMG SRC="world.gif" BORDER= 1 ALT="World
Database"> </A>
<BR CLEAR=ALL><BR>
<A HREF="others.htm"> <IMG SRC="l_btn.gif" BORDER= 0 ALT="World Links">
</A>
<HR>
<A HREF="back.htm"> <IMG SRC="left.gif" ALT="Previous Page"> </A>
<A HREF="next.htm"> <IMG SRC="right.gif" ALT="Next Page">     </A>
</BODY>
</HTML>
```

When viewers look at a web page, it is common for many of them fail to appreciate that some of the graphics are hyperlink objects.   To avoid this, images can be created in the shape of a text button, as in the second part of the example. In this case, its use is more obvious and the box outline is removed by setting the BORDER value to zero.

The third part of the above example shows graphics images in the shape of direction arrows (i.e. navigation icons).   These, and UP and DOWN arrows, are very useful for linear structures.

Labels can be attached to each, to explain its function if this is required:

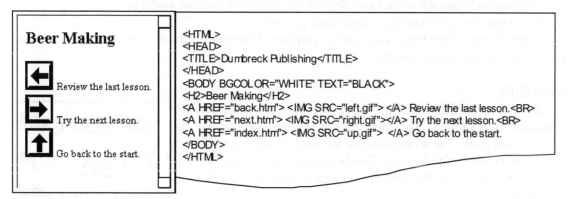

```
<HTML>
<HEAD>
<TITLE>Dumbreck Publishing</TITLE>
</HEAD>
<BODY BGCOLOR="WHITE" TEXT="BLACK">
<H2>Beer Making</H2>
<A HREF="back.htm"> <IMG SRC="left.gif"> </A> Review the last lesson.<BR>
<A HREF="next.htm"> <IMG SRC="right.gif"></A> Try the next lesson.<BR>
<A HREF="index.htm"> <IMG SRC="up.gif"> </A> Go back to the start.
</BODY>
</HTML>
```

Height/Width

The <IMG> tag has HEIGHT and WIDTH attributes and these have two uses.

- If the size of the image is known (most graphic editing packages such as Paint Shop Pro or Photoshop provide this information) its dimensions can be included in the <IMG> tag.
  This reduces display times in some browsers as they load each image and identify their dimensions before displaying the text.   If the files' dimensions are supplied to the browser, it can make space for them and allow the user to read the text while the graphics are loading.
- If the HEIGHT and WIDTH dimensions are different from the actual dimensions of the graphic, the browser will scale the graphic display proportionately.   The displayed image can be smaller or larger than the original. However, too much enlargement will make the image look too 'blocky' while shrinking an image is wasteful (create a smaller original version as it downloads faster).

Example use:

```
<IMG SRC="file.gif" HEIGHT=250 WIDTH=200>
```

Backgrounds

The background can be a solid colour using BGCOLOR="value" or can consist of a graphic file. A graphic background is introduced using the BACKGROUND attribute in the <BODY> tag.

<BODY BACKGROUND="virago.gif">

A single large graphic designed to cover the entire background is too large and takes too long to download. The browser overcomes this by taking a smaller file and *'tiling'* it. With tiling, the image is repeated vertically and horizontally to fill the screen. This saves the overheads of using large files.

The example shows the effect. In this case, the background image has only been tiled into the right hand frame as the BACKGROUND attribute has been inserted into the <TD> tag (explained later).

<TD WIDTH=200 BACKGROUND="virago.gif">

The graphic used has white space round the picture's edges and there is no visible 'join'. Where a pattern is used as a background, the design will require seamless joins on edges - i.e. the edges of the pattern should be designed to create a continuous pattern when tiles are butted together as a background.

A useful method is to create one short but wide strip of a pattern. This will cover the width of the screen and will be repeated down the screen. This graphic file will be of small size and will be quick to download.

External graphics

Inline graphics load as part of the web page. This consumes downloading time even when the user is only idly browsing. On the other hand, users are reluctant to switch off the display of graphics since many hyperlinks are made from graphic images. The most user-friendly approach is to allow larger sized graphics to be loaded only upon the specific request of the user. These are termed *'external graphics'* since they are not part of the normal web page. External graphics can be called up by clicking on a hyperlink. This can be a conventional hyperlink or, more helpfully, can be a thumbnail (i.e. a miniature version of the graphic). This allows users to click for more detail if they want. For example, a web site for an estate agent wishes to entice users to view as many pages as possible. Users can browse through many properties and only call up large graphic files for the properties that interest them.

<P>This <A HREF="kitchen.gif"> luxury kitchen </A> has to be seen to be believed<P>

This line of script uses a hyperlink to load and display the graphic if the user clicks it.

<A HREF="bigkitchen.gif"><IMG SRC="littlekitchen.gif"></A>

The line of script shows a thumbnail view of the graphic. Clicking on the thumbnail view loads and displays the file storing the larger version.

Transparent GIFs

When a graphic file is loaded, its display area occupies a rectangle on the screen. Consider this example. The white background area around the logo spoils the look of the page. The white area can be made transparent, allowing the screen content underneath to be seen. This is known as a *'transparent GIF'* and it stores all the colours of the image, with one colour nominated as the transparent colour.

Anywhere the transparent colour exists in the image, no pixels are displayed and the underlying screen content shows through.

To create a transparent GIF:

- Select the required transparent colour, ensuring that the colour does not already appear in the foreground part of the image. Use the colour selector to find out the palette index number.
- Ensure that the entire background is painted to that colour.
- In Paint Shop Pro, use the Colors/Set Color Transparency options to set the transparency value to the palette index number noted earlier. In PhotoShop, export the image as a GIF89a image, selecting the colours (more than one colour can be transparent) from the displayed color palette.

Animated GIFs

This graphic type is really a collection of graphic images embedded in a single file along with specific playback information (e.g. how long to wait between each frame, whether to show the sequence once only or continually repeat). Each frame's image is slightly different from the previous frame and playing the frames in succession provides the illusion of movement. Many web sites use animated GIFs (e.g. fluttering flags, waving hands, etc.) and huge amounts of these files are freely available on the Internet. They are embedded on a web page in the exact same way as an ordinary graphic file.

```
<IMG SRC="file.gif " HEIGHT=250 WIDTH=200>
```

A number of graphics applications such as Paint Shop Pro's *"Animation Shop"* and the *"GIF Construction Set"* can be used to create animated GIFs.

Multimedia

There are many facilities that are not yet built into browsers. Browsers are either configured to use the computer's existing facilities (sound card, video drivers, etc) or use browser add-ons such as Shockwave, Real Audio, etc. However, all browsers are capable of handling basic multimedia formats such as AU and WAV audio files and MPEG, AVI and MOV video files.

Sound

The <A> tag is capable of playing a sound file.

For example,

```
<A HREF="message.wav"> A word from our sponsors> </A>
```

displays a hypertext link that plays the message.wav file when clicked.

Internet Explorer inline sounds play automatically when the page is loaded, using the <BGSOUND> tag.

```
<BGSOUND SRC="message.wav">   or   <BGSOUND SRC="sun.mid">
```

BGSOUND has a LOOP attribute that sets the number of times the file is played. If the value is set to INFINITE, the file plays continuously until the page is exited.

This setting should be used carefully as continuous messages or music can be very annoying for users.

AU, MID and WAV files can be used with either of the two methods above.

The equivalent command for Netscape browsers is

```
<EMBED SRC="message.wav">
```

Video

The <A> tag is also capable of playing a video file. For example,

```
<A HREF="heaven.mov"> The winning goal> </A>
```

displays a hypertext link that plays the heaven.mov file when clicked. AVI, MPG and MOV files can be used with this method. Like inline sounds, inline AVI videos can play automatically when the page is loaded using the Internet Explorer DYNSRC attribute in the <IMG> tag.

```
<IMG DYNSRC="heaven.mov">
```

The LOOP attribute sets the number of times the file is played. If the value is set to INFINITE, the file plays continuously, although this value would not normally be used. The SRC="*file*" is used to display a static graphic for browsers that do not support DYNSRC.

The START attribute determines how the video file is activated. If it is given the value of FILEOPEN, it plays as soon as the page is loaded. If the value is MOUSEOVER, it does not play until the mouse passes over the blank playing screen. The CONTROLS attribute adds the stop/start button and position slider.

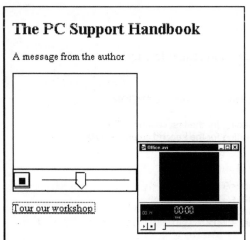

```
<HTML>
<HEAD><TITLE>Dumbreck Publishing</TITLE></HEAD>
<BODY BGCOLOR="#FFFFFF" FONT="BLACK">
<H2>The PC Support Handbook</H2>
<P>A message from the author<P>
<IMG DYNSRC="davy.avi" SRC="dave.gif"
          START=MOUSEOVER CONTROLS> <P>
<A HREF="office.avi" >Tour our workshop </A><P>
</BODY>
</HTML>
```

The script shows both methods, with the left-hand video screen being the result of using DYNSRC.

Flash

Flash is a major application for producing animation and interactive screens for web sites. Initially intended as a vector-based application to add small items of animated content to web pages (animated icons, rollover buttons, etc), Flash has become more powerful, using JavaScript-based scripting language, XML support, etc. Although primarily designed for vector images, it also handles sounds, images and video. It uses its scripting language to provide navigation, create menu structures, control animations, check user input, make calculations, etc. - all combined into an output suitable for a web site.

The steps in the process are as follows:

The web site stores two files- the HTML file that describes and calls up the Flash file, and the Flash (SWF) file itself. When a user downloads the HTML page, its code is read by the normal web browser software (e.g. Explorer or Netscape). This results in the SWF file being downloaded and displayed by the Flash plug-in. The screen outputs of both files are displayed on the user's screen. Sometimes, the HTML file only exists to call the SWF and has no screen output of its own. A web site designed purely in Flash stills needs a small HTML file to initially load it. In other cases, the main web page is made up of screen content displayed by HTML script lines, while the SWF file makes up a small animated part of the screen (e.g. an animated icon or a moving banner).

Many Flash animation files are available on the Internet and each has a .swf extension (e.g. *"project.swf"*) and requires a Flash plug-in for viewing them. Flash plug-ins are already included with most browsers. So the great majority of Internet users are automatically capable of viewing Flash files.

Like all animation formats, Flash deals with frames. Animation is handled by using '*keyframes*' which define important points in the animation along the '*timeline*'. At each keyframe, the contents of the layer can be modified. The real power of Flash animations is in using '*tweening*'. This involves defining the screen location of an object at keyframes, and letting Flash work out its location at the frames in between. While a raster image format such as GIF would need to store each frame individually, the vector format of Flash allows it to simply define the object and its location at each keyframe, making a great saving on space. Furthermore, Flash can be used to navigate the web, meaning that an entire website could be written in Flash. It can also produce moving buttons and similar effects without the developer having to worry about Java applets or JavaScript compatibility.

Another advantage of Flash, which stems from its vector base, is that of scalability. Flash objects can be scaled to fit any web page, without the pixellation that a scaled-up bitmap would suffer from.

Plug-in implications

Plug-ins are extra software that allows additional features not provided by the standard browser software. Initially, these are supplied by as an extra (usually a download) but the more popular ones are eventually integrated into the browsers. This means that older versions of browsers will need to download a plug-in before they can view the extra material. In addition, many plug-ins are not yet integrated into even the most modern browser. This means that careful thought has to be given to using page content that requires plug-ins. While they enhance the page viewing, they may be restricting the number of people who browse the site. Unless the content is compelling, users are mostly not willing to spend extra time downloading additional software – just to view a web page.

Creating tables

The <TABLE> tag allows sets of data to be laid out in a structured and readable way.

Its general format is:

```
<TABLE>                                         <TABLE>
<CAPTION> Caption for the table </CAPTION>      <CAPTION> Caption for the table </CAPTION>
    <TR>                                            <TR>
        <TH> Heading</TH>                               <TH> Heading for the first column </TH>
        <TD> Data for cell </TD>                        <TH> Heading for the second column </TH>
        <TD> Data for cell </TD>                        ....
    </TR>                                            </TR>
    <TR>                                            <TR>
        <TH> Heading</TH>                               <TD> Data </TD>
        <TD> Data  </TD>                                <TD> Data </TD>
        <TD> Data </TD>                                 <TD> Data </TD>
    </TR>                                               <TD> Data </TD>
    ....                                            </TR>
    ....                                            ....
</TABLE>                                         </TR>
                                                </TABLE>
```

Tables are defined row by row. The definition on the left is used when the headings are to appear down the first column of the table (as in the example below).   The other definition is used when the headings are to appear at the top of each column.   Headings are displayed in a bold typeface.

The other main components are:

- The optional <CAPTION> tag displays a centred heading for the table.
- The text between the optional <TH> and </TH> tags specifies the contents of the heading for the table.
- The <TR> and </TR> tags enclose the definition of a row and these sets would be repeated for each row required in the table.
- The <TD> and </TD> tags enclose the data that will appear in a cell in the row.   A set of these is required for each cell definition.

The contents of a cell can be text, a graphic image or a hyperlink.

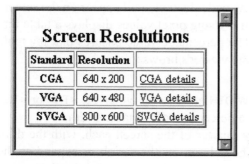

```
<HTML>
<HEAD><TITLE>Dumbreck Publishing</TITLE></HEAD>
<BODY BGCOLOR="#FFFFFF"  TEXT="#000000">
<TABLE BORDER=2>
<CAPTION><H2>Screen Resolutions</H2></CAPTION>
<TR ALIGN=CENTER>
  <TH> Standard</TH>
  <TD> <B>Resolution</B> </TD>
  <TD> <BR> </TD>
</TR>
<TR ALIGN=CENTER>
  <TH> CGA</TH>
  <TD> 640 x 200  </TD>
  <TD> <A HREF="cga.htm"> CGA details </TD>
</TR>
<TR ALIGN=CENTER>
  <TH> VGA</TH>
  <TD> 640 x 480 </TD>
  <TD> <A HREF="vga.htm"> VGA details </TD>
</TR>
<TR ALIGN= CENTER>
  <TH> SVGA</TH>
  <TD> 800 x 600 </TD>
  <TD> <A HREF="svga.htm"> SVGA details </TD>
</TR>
</TABLE>
</BODY>
</HTML>
```

In the example, the cell in the top right corner is empty and this is achieved by: <TD>
</TD>.

Formatting tables

The default positions for table components are:

	Vertical position	Horizontal position
ENTIRE TABLE	Defined by the script	At left of screen
HEADING CELLS	Centred	Centred
DATA CELLS	Centred	Left of cell

The table described so far leaves all table and cell formatting to the browser. A range of alterations can be made to the basic table definition to create more interest or to provide for irregular table shapes.

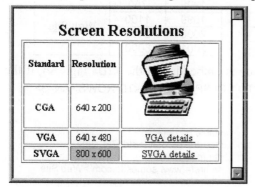

```
<HTML>
<HEAD><TITLE>Dumbreck Publishing</TITLE></HEAD>
<BODY BGCOLOR="#FFFFFF"  TEXT="#000000">
<TABLE BORDER=1 WIDTH=100% >
<CAPTION><H2>Screen Resolutions</H2></CAPTION>
<TR ALIGN=CENTER>
  <TH WIDTH=25%> Standard</TH>
  <TD WIDTH=25%> <B>Resolution</B> </TD>
  <TD ROWSPAN=2 WIDTH=50% > <IMG SRC="monitor.gif">
</TD>
</TR>
<TR ALIGN=CENTER>
  <TH> CGA </TH>
  <TD> 640 x 200  </TD>
</TR>
<TR ALIGN=CENTER>
  <TH> VGA</TH>
  <TD > 640 x 480 </TD>
  <TD COLSPAN=2>  <A HREF=vga.htm"> VGA details </TD>
</TR>
<TR ALIGN=CENTER>
  <TH> SVGA</TH>
  <TD BGCOLOR="#DDDDDD" > 800 x 600 </TD>
  <TD ALIGN=CENTER>   <A HREF=svga.htm"> SVGA  details
</TD>
</TR>
</TABLE></CENTER>
</BODY>
</HTML>
```

This example shows the result of using a number of these extra attributes and they are described next.

Border

The BORDER attribute determines the width of the border round each cell. A zero border value suppresses box drawing and is used to improve general screen formatting as described later.

The BORDERCOLOR attribute sets the colour around a particular cell as below:
        <TH BORDERCOLOR="RED"> VGA</TH>

The background colour of a cell can be set using the BGCOLOR attribute in the <TD> tag, e.g.
        <TD BGCOLOR="#DDDDDD" > cell data </TD>

Table alignment

By default, tables are displayed on the left of the screen, with text appearing above and below the table. As in the case of graph images discussed earlier, ALIGN=LEFT and ALIGN=RIGHT alters the default positioning.   To place the table in the centre of the screen, the tag <CENTER> is placed before the <TABLE> tag and </CENTER> is placed after the </TABLE> tag.

Cell alignment

The ALIGN attributes of LEFT, RIGHT and CENTER, along with VALIGN, are used to place the cell's contents in the required position within the cell. The CELLPADDING attribute is placed in the <TABLE> tag and determines the spacing between the cell walls and the text. The value is specified in pixels, e.g.

<TABLE CELLPADDING= 6>

The CELLSPACING attribute determines the width of the space between the cells, e.g.

<TABLE CELLSPACING=5>

The VALIGN attribute can be set to equal TOP, MIDDLE or BOTTOM, to position the cell contents in the vertical direction.

Table widths

The WIDTH attribute is added to the <TABLE> tag to specify how wide the table will appear on the screen. The value can be set in pixels or as a percentage of the screen.   Using pixel values displays a table that does not alter its width when the user's screen is resized.   The percentage value ensures that the table width grows or shrinks depending on the screen resolution of the viewer's browser.

Column widths

The width of each column can be individually set using the WIDTH attribute in either the <TH> or <TD> tag.   Again, it can be specified as a fixed amount of pixels or a percentage of the table width.

In the above example, the first two columns always occupy a quarter of the screen each, with the third column occupying the remainder of the screen width.   The column widths shrink or expand as the user's screen is resized but the columns always maintain the same ratio with respect to each other and to the overall screen width.

Merging cells

Many tables do not use a layout where there is a symmetrical matrix of cells (e.g. 5x5 or 8x7).

The examples show tables where cells have been merged - i.e. the data 'spans' more than a single cell. The first example shows a piece of data spanning the entire top row of cells.   The third example shows an entire column of cells being spanned by a single data item.   The middle example shows the first column being split into two separate vertical areas: the first data item spans the two upper rows of that column, while the second data item spans the two bottom rows.

Projected Sales		
	UK	USA
2002	8000	12000
2003	9000	18000

Male	Deaths	Injuries
	23	267
Female	Deaths	Injuries
	18	120

1998	750	
1999	1100	Web Site
2000	2100	
2001	5000	

To achieve the first effect, the COLSPAN or ROWSPAN attribute is embedded in the <TD> tag. So, if the data has to span the three cells, the value is set to three - e.g. <TD COLSPAN=3> or <TD ROWSPAN=3>

The scripts for these three layouts are:

```
<table border=1>
<tr>
<td colspan=3>Projected Sales</td>
</tr>
<td> </td><td>UK</td>
<td>USA</td></tr>
<tr><td>2002</td>
<td>8000</td>
<td>12000</td></tr>
<tr><td>2003</td>
<td>9000</td><td>18000</td></tr>
</table>
```

```
<table border=1>
<tr><td rowspan=2>Male</td>
<td>Deaths</td>
<td>Injuries</td></tr>
<tr><td>23</td>
<td>267</td></tr>
<tr><td rowspan=2>Female</td>
<td>Deaths</td>
<td>Injuries</td></tr>
<tr><td>18</td>
<td>120</td></tr>
</table>
```

```
<table border=1>
<tr><td>1998</td><td>750</td>
<td rowspan=4>
<a href="www.somesite.com">Web Site
</td></tr>
<tr><td>1999</td><td>1100</td>
</tr>
<tr><td>2000</td><td>2100</td>
</tr>
<tr><td>2001</td><td>5000</td>
</tr>
</table>
```

Screen layouts

Tables are also commonly used to lay out screen data.
The example layout shown is commonly used.

```
<HTML>
<HEAD><TITLE>Example frAME</TITLE></HEAD>
<BODY BGCOLOR="#FFFFFF">
<TABLE BORDER=1 WIDTH=300 CELLPADDING=16>
<TR>
 <TD WIDTH=150>
  <FONT COLOR="RED">
  <H2>Leeds <BR>Bikers Club</H2>
  </FONT>
  <IMG SRC="verago.gif"><P>
  <A HREF="ourbikes.avi">Watch our video</A><P>
  <A HREF="mailto:jake@leedsbikers.com">Ask for more
details</A>
 </TD>
<TD WIDTH=200 CELLPADDING=5>
 <FONT COLOR="OLIVE">
 Leeds Bikers Club is always looking for new members.<p>
 We meet every Thursday at 7.30pm,
 in the car park of the old mill.<p>
 Come along, bring your mates and try us out!
</TD>
</TR>
</TABLE>
</BODY>
</HTML>
```

The data is laid out in two columns. The left column displays a page headline, a graphic and a set of menu hyperlinks. The right column displays the main text. When the user clicks a hyperlink, the new page is in the same style, with the same content in the left column.

So, as the user navigates round the site, there is a constant unchanging menu on the left.

Column sizes are set with the WIDTH attribute.

CELLPADDING is used to create a space between the two columns. However, this also pushes the data down from the top of the column. An alternative is to insert a third column between the existing columns and adjust its width to the desired margin.

To insert a graphic image into a table cell, alter the TD (Table Data) tag to

```
<TD> <IMG SRC="filename.htm"></TD>
```

Frames

Frames are supported on all modern browsers. The *'Leeds Bikers Page'* example used a table to create two distinct window areas and the *'World Guide'* site could be re-written using tables to create the display shown. The aim was to display a menu of links on the left edge of the screen. Clicking a link alters the display on the right while the left column always displays the menu.

With tables, the whole screen is redrawn and the menu column is redrawn every time the right column displays new contents. The contents of each left column are identical for all pages yet have to be re-displayed after each hyperlink jump.

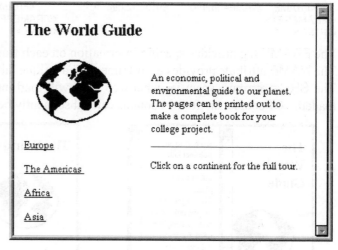

A more efficient way is to create distinct window areas called *'frames'*. Frames still produce the same visual display as before but the left frame's contents would not be refreshed when the right frame was redrawn. In the example, clicking a hyperlink only changes the contents of the right hand frame.

This technique can be extended so several different frames are present on the screen at the same time. For example, long documents may have a menu of links at the top of the document and a duplicate copy at the bottom of the document. For a user who is somewhere in the middle of a document, there is no menu or help in sight. With frames, a permanent menu can be placed at the bottom of the screen. The user can scroll the larger window's contents but the menu remains on screen at all times. Alternatively, a top frame can be used as a window to permanently display the web site banner and logo.

How frames work

The *'frame document'* is an HTML page that defines the size and position of each frame on the screen. The frame document does not contain any normal screen data such as text or graphics; it purely defines the screen layout.

The screen data is supplied from other HTML pages whose contents fill the screen frames.

Each frame is given a name and this name is used to link frames and files. In the example, there are three frames called *'Main'*, *'Menu'* and *'Banner'*. Hyperlinks are used to load different files into the *'Main'* or even *'Menu'* frames as the user navigates the site.

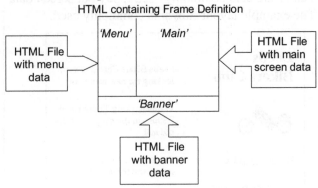

Defining frames

The basic format of a frame document is:

```
<HTML>
<HEAD><TITLE>Dumbreck Publishing</TITLE></HEAD>
<FRAMESET
        The frame definition .....
</FRAMESET>
</HTML>
```

The usual <BODY> tags are replaced by <FRAMESET> tags. These tags enclose the definition of the rows and columns that comprise the screen layout. A basic layout may simply consist of only two columns or it may simply consist of two rows. On the other hand, the layout may consist of a variety of frame combinations comprising both row and column shaped frames. Like tables, dimensions can be expressed either in pixel amounts or in percentages of the screen size.

Simple frame definitions are:

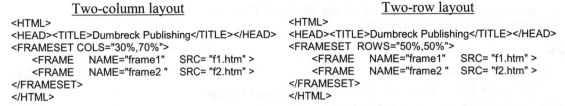

Two-column layout	Two-row layout
`<HTML>`	`<HTML>`
`<HEAD><TITLE>Dumbreck Publishing</TITLE></HEAD>`	`<HEAD><TITLE>Dumbreck Publishing</TITLE></HEAD>`
`<FRAMESET COLS="30%,70%">`	`<FRAMESET ROWS="50%,50%">`
`    <FRAME   NAME="frame1"   SRC= "f1.htm" >`	`    <FRAME   NAME="frame1"   SRC= "f1.htm" >`
`    <FRAME   NAME="frame2 "  SRC= "f2.htm" >`	`    <FRAME   NAME="frame2 "  SRC= "f2.htm" >`
`</FRAMESET>`	`</FRAMESET>`
`</HTML>`	`</HTML>`

The FRAME tag provides specific information on each frame that will be displayed.

The NAME attribute provides each frame with a unique label for linking purposes (see later).

The SRC= attribute specifies what web page will load into the frame when the frame document is first loaded. Of course, the frame contents can subsequently be changed as will be outlined shortly.

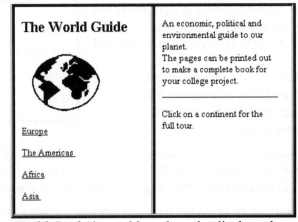

If a two-column definition was used for *'The World Guide'* it would produce the displays shown above. The right-hand screen is similar to the *'Leeds Bikers Page'* example using a table shown on a previous page. The left hand screen is the result of the user resizing the screen area and clearly shows that the display consists of two separate frame areas.

Complex definitions

More complex definitions are achieved by nesting a FRAMESET specification with another FRAMESET specification. Example scripts for splitting rows and columns are shown below, along with the screen displays that are achieved.

```
<HTML>
<HEAD><TITLE>Dumbreck Publishing</TITLE></HEAD>
<FRAMESET ROWS="90%,10%">
        <FRAMESET COLS="90%,90%">
                <FRAME SRC= "f1.htm" >
                <FRAME  SRC= "f2.htm" >
        </FRAMESET>
        <FRAME  SRC= "f3.htm" >
</FRAMESET>
</HTML>
```

```
<HTML>
<HEAD><TITLE>Dumbreck Publishing</TITLE></HEAD>
<FRAMESET COLS="40%,70%">
        <FRAME NAME="MENU" SRC= "f1.htm" >
        <FRAMESET ROWS="90%,90%">
                <FRAME  NAME="MAIN" SRC= "f2.htm" >
                <FRAME  NAME="BANNER" SRC= "f3.htm" >
        </FRAMESET>
</FRAMESET>
</HTML>
```

Notes

- The script lines are only indented for clarity. The browser ignores the spaces.
- Percentage values for **ROWS** and **COLS** don't necessarily add up to 100%. In the example, both column widths are set to 90%. Netscape and Internet Explorer add up the column percentages and distribute them proportionate to the screen. So, in the example, each column is allocated half of the users screen window width. Specifications of 40% and 120% would result in the first column occupying a quarter of the screen.
- **NAMEs** have been added to the **FRAME** definition in the second example.
- In these examples, the MAIN area's contents alter every time a new page is selected from the menu. The BANNER area would probably only be loaded once and remain on-screen at all times.
- The MENU area, like the BANNER area, might never be updated. Alternatively, it may be used to display sub-menus. The left display shows the opening menu frame. Clicking on the DISK hyperlink loads the page shown on the right into the MENU frame. Clicking any disk hyperlink option loads the matching data file into the MAIN frame. When the user clicks on the Main Menu hyperlink, the original page shown on the left is loaded into the MENU frame once again.

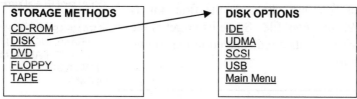

Attributes

The attributes available for FRAMESET definition are:

FRAMEBORDER   Setting the value to zero stops the display of the 3D border round frames. However, the space allocated for the border displays on the screen as a grey band.

FRAMESPACING   Setting the value to zero makes each frame butt on to the next frame, with no gaps. Example: <FRAMESET FRAMEBORDER="NO" FRAMESPACING=0>
Results in no borders being displayed around any frames and the screen appearing as a single display. Earlier versions of Explorer may need **FRAMEBORDER** to be set to zero instead of "NO".

The attributes available for FRAME definition are:

NORESIZE   The default, as with most Windows applications, allows the user to grab a window border and resize it.   The NORESIZE attribute prevents the user from altering frame sizes.

MARGINHEIGHT   Sets the margin, in pixels, above and below the document.

MARGINWIDTH   Sets the margin, in pixels, between the document and the sides of the frame.

SCROLLING   Controls the ability to scroll through a frame's document. It has three settings:

NO: The user cannot scroll through the document.   This should be used with caution. If the screen is small size and the user cannot resize the window, then some screen content will be prevented from displaying.

YES: Vertical and horizontal scrollbars are also displayed in the frame, even when the document is too small to need scrolling facilities.

AUTO: The scrollbars are only displayed if the document is too large for the size of the frame window.

Example:

```
<FRAME MARGINWIDTH=10 MARGINHEIGHT=15 NAME="MAIN" SRC="file5.htm>
```

results in a 15 pixel margin above and below the document and 10 pixels of space between the document and the frame's vertical sides.   By default, scrolling facilities are automatically triggered by large documents and the user is allowed to alter frame sizes by dragging them with the mouse.

Linking frames

The use of frames allows one frame's contents to loaded and displayed without altering the other frames on the screen.   Since each frame has been given a unique name, the data that is loaded can be directed ('targeted') towards that named frame. Since only a part of the screen is being updated, the transition is smoother. More importantly, less of the screen being updated means that less data has to be downloaded. This results in smaller files being fetched and navigation is therefore faster.

The first script shown creates a screen with two column frame areas.   The first column is called MENU and has the contents of file 'f1.htm' displayed in it.   The second column is called MAIN and initially displays the contents of the 'f2.htm' file.

The contents of the f1.htm file are shown. The HREF tags have a TARGET= attribute added to them.   This points to the name of the frame to be updated with the file being loaded.

The example file has four hyperlinks. If the first link is clicked, it loads the 'europe.htm' file. Since its target is the MAIN frame, the file's contents are displayed in that frame (i.e. the second column).

```
<HTML>
<HEAD><TITLE>Dumbreck Publishing</TITLE>
</HEAD>
<FRAMESET COLS ="*,*">
  <FRAME NAME="MENU" SRC="f1.htm">
  <FRAME NAME="MAIN" SRC="f2.htm">
</FRAMESET>
</HTML>
```

The left column's contents remain unaltered while a click on any of the hyperlinks in the menu results in the contents of the second frame being altered.

In the example, the one frame was the common target for all updating.   In this case the TARGET= attribute can

```
<HTML>
<HEAD>
<TITLE>Dumbreck Publishing</TITLE></HEAD>
<BODY BGCOLOR="#FFFFFF" FONT="BLACK">
<H2>The World Guide</H2>
<IMG SRC="world.gif" ALIGN = MIDDLE ALT="World Map"> <P>
<A HREF="europe.htm"   TARGET="MAIN" >Europe</A><P>
<A HREF="americas.htm" TARGET="MAIN" >The Americas </A><P>
<A HREF="africa.htm"     TARGET="MAIN" >Africa</A><P>
<A HREF="asia.htm"      TARGET="MAIN" >Asia </A><P>
</BODY>
<.HTML>
```

be removed from each HREF line and be replaced by the single line:

```
<BASE TARGET="MAIN">
```
This line is inserted between the <HEAD> tags.   Where different frames are being updated, this method cannot be used.

The technique of targeted frames can be used to refine the menu system shown earlier.   In the example on the right, the top-left corner box permanently displays a main menu.   Clicking on a menu option displays its corresponding sub-menu options in the lower-left corner box. Clicking on any sub-menu option then displays its contents in the main screen area.   This way, the main menu and sub-menu are visible at all times.

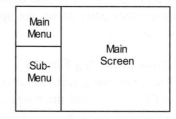

MAILTO

This is a very simple single line of script that allows a user to send an e-mail to the site owner while still inside the site.   The user does not have to leave the browser and enter his/her e-mail program to send the message.   The format is

```
<A HREF ="MAILTO: address"> hyperlink message</A>
```
A typical example is

```
<A HREF= MAILTO:sales@dumbreck.demon.co.uk>  Send us your comments </A>
```
When the hyperlink is clicked, the user is asked to provide a subject name for the e-mail and to provide the main text of the message.   When the user completes the details, the software sends the message and returns the user to the previously loaded web page.   An example of its use was seen in the *'Leeds Bikers Club'* site earlier.

Forms

Forms are the standard method of getting information from a browser to a server.   Forms are constructed from lines of HTML and are used to call a special script (called a *'CGI script'*) at the server end.   The CGI script then carries out the processing of the data passed to it.   Forms can sit anywhere on a web site, on any web page.   They can be placed on a separate web page or can be part of a web page.

A form can contain a single entry (e.g. What is your favourite girl band?), have relatively few entries (e.g. name and address for joining a newsletter mailing list) or can contain many entries (e.g. filling in questionnaires or for entering data for on-line credit card purchases).

The illustration shows the variety of options for entering data into a Form.   The script for this web page is described on the following pages.

Radio Buttons
The first question uses radio buttons to extract a user response. Only a single answer is expected (i.e. the book cannot be expensive and cheap at the same time).   A radio button method ensures that only one response can be entered.   If a second button is selected, the previous button becomes unselected.

Multiple selections
The second question allows more than one box to be checked, so the user can check none, some, or all of them.

Selection from a list
The third question provides a drop-down menu from which a user can select a single choice.

Text entry
There are a variety of ways that a user can enter text into a form. The simplest way is to provide a single box, allowing a single line of text to be entered.   The box may initially be empty or may contain an initial value. Providing an initial value

is useful when the response for a field is often the same for different users (e.g. a field requesting a delivery address for goods may supply an initial value of *'Same as Invoice Address'*).

A text entry box can also be designed, as in the illustration, to allow multiple lines to be entered. While most other entry boxes are specific, this box allows the user more freedom to enter data in their own words.

Implementing Forms

The script for a form is described in the following pages. The script is placed between <FORM> and </FORM> tags and the script can contain fields for entering information and normal text for headings, explanations and notes. All the rules on fonts and alignment apply within the form's script area in the same way as any other part of the HTML script.

The CGI script will be sent a number of items of information from a form and has to be able to distinguish between one item and the next. Therefore, every data entry field on the form has to be given its own name. The form is then submitted to the CGI script as a named item with the value given to it by the user.

For example, if fields were called *'name'* and *'age'*, the values would be sent to the script as

Name=Davy   and   age=21

These are referred to as *'name/value pairs'*.

Text entry options

The simplest entry method for a form is

What is your Post Code ? <INPUT NAME="postcode">

The first part is the text that will appear on the screen. The INPUT tag places a text entry box on the screen next to the text. The developer gives the field a name (*'postcode'* in our example).

What is your Post Code ?

When the user types information into the box, it is associated with the *'postcode'* field for sending to the CGI script. In the above example, the default entry box is far too long, since a Post Code only requires a maximum of eight characters, including the middle space.

The SIZE attribute can be added to specify the size of the text box, as in the following line of code:

What is your Post Code ? <INPUT NAME="postcode" SIZE=8>

This produces a smaller box but still allows the user to type in more than eight characters. To limit the characters accepted in a box, the attribute MAXLENGTH can be used, as below:

What is your Post Code ? <INPUT NAME="postcode" SIZE=8 MAXLENGTH=8>

An initial content can be placed into a text box, using the VALUE tag, as in this example:

Address for delivery <INPUT NAME="deladdress" VALUE="Same as the Invoice Address">

The screen display would look as in the illustration.

Address for delivery | Same as the Invoice Address

Where large sections of text input is expected from the user, the TEXTAREA tag is used. It has ROWS and COLS attributes that define the size of the text box. The results can be seen in the earlier *'Reader Survey'* illustration. The tag's format is:

```
Any suggestions:<br>
<TEXTAREA name="comments" rows=5 cols=40></TEXTAREA>
```

Multiple selections

The INPUT tag allows the user to enter text for sending to the CGI script. The use of the TYPE attribute allows the user to select from pre-written options. The form can be displayed with a set of check boxes. This allows the user to select multiple options from a displayed list.

The following code was used to create the checkboxes in the earlier *'Reader Survey'* illustration:

```
Which of the following chapters do you use most?<br>
<INPUT TYPE="checkbox" NAME="opsys"     VALUE="ON"> Operating Systems <br>
<INPUT TYPE="checkbox" NAME="support"    VALUE="ON"> PC Support  <br>
<INPUT TYPE="checkbox" NAME="websites"  VALUE="ON"> Web Sites<p>
```

The INPUT tag is using a TYPE attribute. If this attribute is not included in an INPUT tag it is assumed to be the same as entering 'TYPE="text"' (i.e. the input is assumed to be text).

The above code uses 'TYPE="checkbox"' and this and each field has a NAME and a VALUE that depends upon whether the box is checked.   In the example, VALUE="ON" is used, so checking the first box results in opsys=ON being sent to the CGI script.   In fact, the default value that is given to a checked field is 'ON', but other values could be substituted.

If required, some of the boxes could be displayed checked by default. This could be employed where users often choose these boxes from the list.

An example of use is:
```
Click any other facilities you require<br>
<INPUT TYPE="checkbox" NAME="catalogue"     CHECKED> Catalogue   <br>
<INPUT TYPE="checkbox" NAME="newsletter"    CHECKED> Newsletter  <br>
```

Radio Buttons
Radio buttons display a range of options to the user.   The user can only choose one option and so only one name/value pair is used. This means that all the radio buttons are given the same name.

The syntax for this code is:
```
How do you rate the book's contents?<br>
<INPUT TYPE="radio" NAME="content" VALUE="poor">       Poor
<INPUT TYPE="radio" NAME="content" VALUE="average">    Average
<INPUT TYPE="radio" NAME="content" VALUE="good">       Excellent
```

Again, the CHECKED attribute can be added, so that one option is initially selected.

Selecting from a list
Where a long set of options is to be chosen from, the screen may look cluttered with too many checkboxes or radio buttons. As an alternative, the SELECT tag allows a drop-down menu to be created, to save screen space.   The syntax is as shown in this example:
```
What course are you using the book for?<br>
<SELECT NAME="course" SIZE="1">
        <OPTION>   C&G
        <OPTION>   HNC/D
        <OPTION>   BSc/MSc
</SELECT>
```

The field has a single NAME and, when the user chooses from the menu, that particular entry after the OPTION attribute is associated with the NAME as the name/value pair for sending to the CGI script.

The SIZE attribute specifies how many lines of options are seen when the page is first displayed. The Up and Down arrow at the edge of the box allow the user to browse through the options.

Submitting the Form
When the user has completed the entries on the form, it can be submitted to the server by clicking on a *'submit'* button. The basic syntax to produce this button is:
```
<INPUT TYPE="submit ">
```
This produces an on-screen button with the words *'Submit Query'* on it.

The text in the button can be changed by specifying a new value for it, as in the following example script code:
```
<INPUT TYPE="submit" VALUE="Click to send">
```

If the user wishes to clear the entries and start over before submitting the form, the line:
```
<INPUT TYPE="reset">
```
clears all existing data from the forms' fields.   The default text in this button is 'Reset' and this can also be altered by using the VALUE attribute, as in the example below:
```
<INPUT TYPE="reset"  VALUE="Oops ! Clear the form">
```

The user sends the form to the server with the ACTION attribute of the FORM tag. This dictates what action will be taken when the submit button is pressed.   In the example below, the action is to send the form's data to the CGI script that is stored in the URL given in quotes.
```
<FORM ACTION="/cgi-bin/mailform"  METHOD="POST">
```
The example line is for a form running with Demon. Demon stores a cgi script called *'mailform'*.   This is Demon's own script and its purpose is to receive the input from the form's fields and send them as an e-mail to the web site owner.   The CGI script may well have another name with another ISP.

The 'ACTION' attribute points to the URL where the script is stored (in this case the cgi-bin folder of the server).

The URL address could equally have been entered in full as
      http://demon.co.uk/cgi-bin/mailform

The METHOD attribute determines the manner in which data is sent to the URL pointed to by the ACTION attribute. It can either have the value 'GET' or 'POST'.

If the GET attribute is used, the user entries are attached to the end of the CGI script's URL (a process known as *'URL encoding'*).

For the 'Reader Survey' example, the final URL might be:
      http://demon.co.uk/cgi-bin/mailform?value=good&content=fair&audio=ON&video=ON&....

A question mark separates the script URL from the data and each field's name/value pair is separated by an ampersand(&). This operates more quickly than the processing of POST data, but the reliable length of a URL is only 255 characters.

The POST method is the preferred method as the data is sent separately and has no limit to its size.

The complete script for producing the web page form shown in the earlier *'Reader Survey'* example is:

```
<HTML>
<HEAD><TITLE>Survey Form</TITLE></HEAD>
<BODY BGCOLOR="cyan"><FONT FACE="ARIAL,HELVETICA" SIZE="5">
<B>Reader Survey<br></font>

<FORM ACTION="/cgi-bin/mailform"  METHOD="POST">

<p><b>

How do you rate the book's contents?<br>
<INPUT TYPE="radio" NAME="content" VALUE="poor">        Poor
<INPUT TYPE="radio" NAME="content" VALUE="average">     Average
<INPUT TYPE="radio" NAME="content" VALUE="good">        Excellent
<p>

Which of the following chapters do you use most?<br>
<INPUT TYPE="checkbox" NAME="opsys"     VALUE="ON"> Operating Systems <br>
<INPUT TYPE="checkbox" NAME="support"    VALUE="ON"> PC Support  <br>
<INPUT TYPE="checkbox" NAME="websites"  VALUE="ON"> Web Sites<p>

What course are you using the book for?<br>
<SELECT NAME="course" SIZE="1">
   <OPTION>   C&G
   <OPTION>   HNC/D
   <OPTION>   BSc/MSc
</SELECT><p>

Any complaints, comments, suggestions?</b><br>
<TEXTAREA name="comments" rows=5 cols=40></TEXTAREA>
<p>

<INPUT TYPE="submit" VALUE="Send to us">
<INPUT TYPE="reset"  VALUE="Oops ! Clear the form"><P>

</FORM>
</BODY>
</HTML>
```

Web programming

As the last chapter showed, perfectly useful web sites can be created with just the use of HTML.

However, to produce the extra functionality and looks, developers look to new and emerging technologies. This might be in the form of animations or audio and video streaming. Or it might be through the use of programming languages, many designed especially for web use. Web programming is considered as having two realms of activity - those involved with the clients (i.e. those who browse the web site contents) and those involved with servers (those who provide the web site contents).

Client side programming

This concentrates mainly on <u>how</u> the browser presents information (i.e. layout, style, animation, etc). Client side programming means that all the program code is run at <u>browser</u> end. This has always been the case, for example, with HTML, but this has now been joined with a range of additional programs such as Java applets, JavaScript, Active X components, VBScript, APIs, DHTML, XML, and plug-ins. Because they run purely within the viewer's own computer, they have the following advantages:
- They do not require a special server setup.
- They perform quickly once they are downloaded.

On the other hand, they have the following disadvantages:
- The browser has to download the code in order to run it, resulting in slower page downloads.
- The code may contain commands that only work on certain browsers, or browser versions.
- There may be browser compatibility issues with some client-side software. Most notably, Active X and VBScript only work on the Windows platforms and only with Internet Explorer.

Server side programming

This concentrates mainly on <u>what</u> information is communicated between the server and browser. It can involve CGI scripts, Perl scripts, Server Side Includes, Active Server Pages, etc. In this case, the program code is run at <u>server</u> end and can be used to store, process and package information for display at the browser end. This supports, for example, databases and on-line purchasing.

Consider the operations required when a user is choosing holiday options at a travel agent's web site. The user completes a selection of criteria (e.g. dates, places, preferences, number travelling, etc). This information is sent to the server and is used to consult a database containing flight information, hotel vacancies, etc. The server then constructs a web page that displays the various holiday options that meet the users criteria, complete with costs. The server has carried out user requests, consulted databases, carried out calculations and prepared an individual web page just for that viewer. And all this has taken place within the server end.

Server side programming provides benefits such as:
- Processing takes place at server end, so program speed is not dependent on the age of the computer used for browsing.
- A huge range of facilities (search engines, database handling, maintaining site statistics, etc) are available.

The disadvantages are:
- It relies on what facilities are allowed by an ISP. Internet providers are reluctant to allow user programs that might introduce delays or system crashes and they often place limitations on what languages are allowed.
- Many facilities will only be available through an extra payment to the ISP.
- The program performance is dependent on how busy an ISP is at any time.

Scripting

Web programming is achieved by writing a script. This is a text file that contains a list of all the instructions that the server or browser has to carry out. The computer software (i.e. server software or browser software) reads each instruction in turn and carries out the instruction. The same script can be read by a PC, a Mac or a Linux system, as long as the software contains an interpreter that understands the script language. The script is therefore independent of any hardware platform.

Of course, there are many different languages, each using different instructions in their scripts. They have differences but they can all access the server's filing system, interface with databases and create dynamic pages. While JavaScript is so popular that it is built in to all browsers (e.g. Explorer, Opera, etc.), other languages have to be downloaded and installed as browser plug-ins. Similarly, language interpreters have to be installed on the server end and this has to be worked out with the ISP (unless the server is owned).

Active Server Pages

Another method of making dynamic web pages is Microsoft's ASP (Active Server Pages) extension for their servers based on their IIS (Internet Information Server) software, sitting on a Windows based Server such as NT or Windows 2000. Of course, this would mean that ASP facilities could only be used on IIS servers and these are a minority on the web (most servers use the free *'Apache'* web server software).   Third party providers supply extensions that attempt to make ASP compatible with other operating systems.

An ASP file is written in plain ASCII text and is saved with the extension .asp (e.g. *'testing.asp'*). The ASP file is essentially a normal HTML file with additional tags used to perform scripting. Those tags are placed around ASPScript code, which is very similar to VBScript (which is very similar to Visual Basic). HTML is parsed sequentially, and so is ASP script, so placement of script code within the HTML document can be very important. Although primarily designed for use with Visual Basic, ASP scripts can be written using JavaScript or Perl.

Javascript

JavaScript is a simple programming language that has many uses and has become popular on web sites. The JavaScript code is embedded within the HTML file and is interpreted by the client browser. The JavaScript interpreter that is built into Netscape, Explorer, etc, understands a range of pre-written functions. The only necessary tools for creating JavaScript code are a web browser (from Netscape 3+, IE 3+ onwards) and a plain text editor, although more advanced functions are available in packages that are specifically designed for JavaScript coding.

What it is used for

Using JavaScript, it is possible to:

- Customise HTML documents on the fly (e.g. adding current date and time).
- Write event handlers for elements on a page (e.g. rollover buttons).
- Validate data at the client side (e.g. checking that a form is only submitted when all fields have been entered).
- Perform other client-side computations (e.g. passwords, calculators).
- Detect what browser is being used and take the viewer to pages designed to work with that browser.

Event handlers

An event handler is a piece of script that remains inactive until triggered by some event.

The format of the statement is

event=activity

In other words

"when this event occurs, do this activity".

The event could be moving the mouse over a button, clicking a button, opening a web page, etc.

This is one the simplest examples of an event handler

```
<a href="test.htm" onMouseOver="alert('hi');" > test page </a>
```

The <a> tag places a hyperlink on the screen as usual but has onmouseover="alert('hi');" added to the line. onMouseOver is the event and "alert('hi');" is the activity.   When the mouse moves over the text of the hyperlink, an alert box pops up with a message.   Notice that this type of JavaScript does not require to be enclosed by <script> tags and is embedded amongst the rest of the HTML code.

A similar technique is widely used on menu pages, where buttons change colour/shape/size when a mouse is placed over them. This is referred to as *"button rollovers"*.

It uses the onMouseOver and onMouseOut functions that are built in to the browser's JavaScript interpreter. It needs two graphics files for each button. One image displays the button in its normal state, while the other image displays the altered button appearance when the mouse hovers over it.   The button usually changes colour or appears to have been depressed.

The screen will normally display the image called *'image1.gif'*. When the mouse hovers over the image, the onMouseOver function changes the graphic to display *'image2.gif'*.   When the mouse is moved away from the graphic, the onMouseOut function changes the graphic back to *'image1.gif'*.

Since these activities only display images after mouse movements, there is still a need to display the button when the page is first loaded. That is the purpose of the <img src="image1.gif" name="r"> line.

The image is given a name, in this case simply *"r"*, and this allows the event handlers to change the displayed image using the r.src= part of the statement.

```
<HTML >
<HEAD>
</HEAD>
<BODY>

<a href="nextpage.htm"
onMouseOver="r.src='image2.gif'"
onMouseOut= "r.src='image1.gif'">
<img src="image1.gif" name="r">
</a>

</BODY>
</HTML>
```

User-created functions

There is a long list of commands that are available in the JavaScript language and they can be used to create a script that is tailored to the site's needs. Also, the various pre-written functions can be combined to write a more complex program.

The JavaScript commands are placed within <SCRIPT> and </SCRIPT> tags as shown below:

```
<HTML>
<SCRIPT LANGUAGE="JavaScript">
JavaScript goes in here
</SCRIPT><HEAD>Usual header text in here</HEAD>
<BODY>
Usual HTML can go here
Usual HTML can go here
</BODY>
</HTML>
```

Browser detection

Since there are problems in producing JavaScript that runs on all versions of all browsers, you may wish to provide two versions of some web pages – one designed using Netscape-specific code and one using Explorer-specific code.

For this technique to work, a web page has to detect what browser is being used, so that the user is directed to the appropriate next page.

The example shows how the script can tell whether a user is browsing with Explorer or not. navigator.appName returns a text message that contains the name of the browser in use.   The if test then decides which web page the user will be taken to. Note that two equal signs are used when comparing values.

If more control is required, the version=navigator.appVersion line can be added.   This returns a long string that contains, amongst other details, the version number of the browser software.

indexOf searches through the text stored in **version** looking for the character *"5."* If it is present, it returns a number that indicates how far along the text it was found. If it was not found it returns the value of -1.

The line   if   (browser=="Microsoft   Internet   Explorer"   &&   versionposition>0) requires that two conditions be true.   The browser must be Explorer AND the version description must contain the phrase "5.".

The && symbols are used to indicate that BOTH conditions must be tested to be true before calling iepage.htm.

```
<script>
browser=navigator.appName;
if (browser=="Microsoft Internet Explorer")
  location.href="iepage.htm";
else
  location.href="nspage.htm"
</script>
```

Note: Some older browsers were written before the advent of JavaScript and will not understand what to do with the lines of script.   If the lines of script are enclosed with the usual comment tags, as shown below, they are ignored by older browsers while still working with JavaScript-aware browsers.

```
<SCRIPT LANGUAGE="JavaScript">
<!--
JavaScript goes in here
//-->
</SCRIPT>
```

```
<script>
browser=navigator.appName;
version=navigator.appVersion;
versionposition=(version.indexOf("5."));
if (browser=="Microsoft Internet Explorer" && versionposition>0)
  location.href="iepage.htm";
else
  location.href="nspage.htm"
</script>
```

Java applets

JavaScript is not the same as the more powerful Java language. JavaScript is used exclusively on the web, whereas Java is also used to create powerful software programs. When small Java applications are written for use in web wages, they are called *'applets'*.

Like Flash and JavaScript, there are many pre-written Java applets available for download over the Internet. These can handle passwords, navigation, scrolling, buttons, calculators, clocks, and so on.

The code for applet is not written as a text file (like HTML or JavaScript).   The applet is compiled into a file with the extension .class, as shown in the example. The additional lines of code required to call the applet are shown in bold.   The applet code can call other applets if required and can access graphic images and other resources.

```
<html>
<body>
<applet code="Clock.class" id="Clock">
</applet>
</body>
</html>
```

Cascading Style Sheets

While HTML is a powerful tool, its major drawback has always been its lack of control - it is impossible to set a standard style for the various types of content in all web pages within a site. Approaches involving lengthy, complicated scripts tend to work only under certain circumstances, and are difficult to maintain. Some HTML creation software has capabilities built in for version management, but this may involve extra expense, and is really a workaround rather than a solution.

An alternative is to use Cascading Style Sheets (CSS). This allows page styles (including fonts, background images, borders and so on) to be specified for various classes of objects on the web pages. These definitions cascade down through the various types – for example a font that falls into two categories as described in the Style Sheet will have the settings from both, with the type that is defined last in the Style Sheet having precedence wherever there may be a conflict in style. CSS is supported to varying degrees by Internet Explorer 3 and onwards, as well as Netscape Navigator 4 onwards. Browsers that do not support CSS will ignore the style part and continue to read the rest of the file, meaning that the HTML page will still display (albeit somewhat less attractively) on an old machine.

Inline Styles

The simplest way to use CSS is simply as an attribute of any text tag. For example the <H1> tag, the <P> tag, the <A> tag and so on can all use style definitions built in to the tag. This can give some greater control, and is useful to over-ride previously defined styles, but misses out on a lot of the power of CSS if it is the sole method used.

A simple inline style might look as follows:

```
<P STYLE="color: red">Red text</P>
```

Style Blocks

One way of using style sheets is to specify them inside the web page. In this method, the style sheet is placed inside the HEAD portion of the page source. The Style Sheet is specified within a <STYLE> tag.

Unfortunately, older browsers do not recognise the <STYLE> tag, and so will instead display the source text within that tag instead of using it as a style. Therefore, in order to preserve backwards compatibility, the contents of the <STYLE> tag should also be within an HTML comment block, so that older browsers are told to ignore it if they cannot handle CSS. The comment block begins with '<!--' and ends with '-->', and so the general structure of such an HTML file is as shown.

```
<HTML>
<HEAD>
<TITLE>Page title</TITLE>
<STYLE>
<!--
Style Sheet definitions
-->
</STYLE>
</HEAD>
<BODY>Page text</BODY>
</HTML>
```

Linked Style Sheets

However, style sheets can be even more useful when they are used outwith a web page's source. If a CSS sheet is stored separately, then each page on an entire site can use a single stylesheet. In this way, the style of all web pages will be the same, presenting a more consistent web site. Also, it means that changes of style require just one file to be updated rather than every single web page. Finally, having a linked style sheet can slightly reduce the size of individual HTML files.

An HTML file can link to a style sheet using the <LINK> tag, as shown. The HREF attribute is a URL to find the linked file, just like in an anchor, while the REL attribute indicates the relation of the link – in this case, a style sheet.

The TYPE attribute indicates the type of style sheet; there are a very few types of style sheets other than CSS, and they are not widely supported.

```
<HTML>
<HEAD>
<TITLE>Page title</TITLE>
<LINK HREF="style.css" REL=stylesheet
TYPE=text/css>
</HEAD>
<BODY>Page text</BODY>
</HTML>
```

In this case, the browser will expect to see a CSS style sheet called "style.css" in the same directory as the HTML page. This external style sheet is an ASCII text file containing style definitions exactly as they would appear within the <STYLE> tags if they were inside the web page itself (see below).

Alternatively, external style sheets can be imported into style blocks within a web page. This is done within the style block, using the @import statement, followed by the URL. To do this, though, the browser needs to know what kind of style sheet it is, so the <STYLE> tag itself should contain this information as an attribute.

The import statement could look as follows:

```
<STYLE TYPE="text/css">
@import URL("style.css");
</STYLE>
```

Note:

For both methods of using external style sheets, it is possible to use multiple links or imports, as well as style blocks, and even inline styles – this is the cascading aspect of CSS. If a type selector is defined multiple times, then the most recent values for any properties that are specified over-ride previous values. However, any properties that are left undefined in more recent style definitions retain their previous values.

For example, it is possible to have an external style sheet, an internal style block, and an inline style, all with properties applying to the <P> tag. The external sheet might make it indented and define a font face and font size, while the style block specifies an indent and a colour. The inline style might make the font bold and change the font face. In such a case, the resulting text will have the style block's indentation and colour, the inline style's bold weight and font face, and the style sheet's font size.

Fonts in Style Sheets

While <FONT> tags specify a single font that must be used if available, CSS allows the web page designer to suggest a group of fonts, and allow the browser to choose which of those fonts to use, or even override them entirely.

In addition, CSS stylesheets provide greater control over font types. This is achieved by having a number of *'selectors'* defined in the stylesheet, followed in braces by the style that should be applied to the selector when used within the web page. The most common kind of selector is a *'type selector'*, which simply applies a style to all text of a given type.

For example, to embolden all text that is specified as being of Header 1 (H1) type, the following style definition might be used:

```
<STYLE>
H1 {font-weight: bold}
</STYLE>
```

Any text within an <H1> tag will now be bold. The details within the braces (the '{' and '}' symbols) are the *'properties'* of the selector. If the selector is to have multiple properties defined then these should be separated by a semi-colon (;).

Furthermore, note that each definition is separated from its value by a colon (:). Some browsers will allow web pages to use an equal sign (=) instead of a colon, but this is contrary to the CSS standard and is not supported by all browsers. Consequently, it is recommended that designers use a colon.

Additionally, a property set can be applied to more than one type selector by separating the type selectors with a comma.

For example if you wish H1, H2 and H3 text to be both bold and italicised, the following style definition will do that:

```
<STYLE>
H1, H2, H3 {font-weight: bold; font-style: italic}
</STYLE>
```

Some properties are able to specify several sub-properties within them. For example, the 'font' property can be used to contain the font-style, font-size, and font-family properties, in that order. If the properties are accessed individually then they can be put in any order.

A font definition can thus be done in one of two ways:

```
<STYLE>
P {font-size: 50px; font-family: sans-serif; font-style: italic}
P {font: italic 50px sans-serif}
</STYLE>
```

For type selectors that apply to text, there are a number of possible properties.

The most common and widely-supported options are as follows:

Property	Usage
font-family	Defines the set of fonts that may be used. They should be separated by a comma, and the browser is allowed to use any font from the list that it has available. This includes Windows fonts, but there are also a number of generic fonts that indicate only a general type, most notably 'serif', 'sans-serif' and 'monospace'.
font-style	The style of font to use. eg: 'normal', 'italic' or 'oblique'.
font-size	The size of the font. As well as a size value, it can be specified as 'small', 'medium', 'large' and other such values.
font-weight	The weight (boldness) of the font. For example 'lighter', 'normal' or 'bold'.
color	The colour of the font. Like most HTML colour attributes, it can be defined as a string-value (eg 'red') or as RGB values from zero to 255, such as 'rgb(255,0,0)'
text-decoration	This property can specify 'underline', 'overline', or 'line-through' for text decoration.
text-indent	Indents are very hard to handle in basic HTML; this style sheet attribute makes it much easier.
text-align	Specifies the alignment of the text, using the keywords 'left', 'right', 'center' or 'justify'.
letter-spacing	The spacing between each letter in the text. Spacing can be set to zero or even negative values.

Where a size is specified (such as in font-size, or text-indent for example), the default measurement is in pixels but it can also be specified in points (eg. '20pt'), inches (eg. '1in'), millimetres (eg. '15mm') and other measurements.

Other options in Style Sheets

Style sheets are not all about fonts and text. Web site style includes background images, tables, borders and so on. The following properties can apply to almost any object in a CSS sheet.

Property	Usage
border	This property places a border round an object. The designer can specify the size of the border, and the border style and colour. For example {border: 3px double RGB(0,0,255)} would produce a 3 pixel blue double border. Other keywords include 'solid', 'dotted', and 'dashed'. Individual edges of the border can be specified using the properties 'border-top', 'border-left', 'border-bottom' and 'border-right'.
position	By choosing 'absolute' for the position, the exact position of the object within the window can be specified via the 'top' and 'left' properties. The 'relative' option for position specifies a location relative to the current location on the web page.
width, height	These are separate properties, and they can be used to specify how much space (in percentage or absolute terms) in the window they should occupy.
float	This property can accept the values 'none', 'left' or 'right', specifying whether an object is to be placed 'floating' on the left or right side of the window with text wrapping around.

Furthermore, there are some useful properties that can only be applied to certain HTML tags.

Property	Usage
background	This property applies to the BODY tag. It allows the designer to specify a colour, an image, whether the image is to repeat if it does not fill the window, whether it should scroll along with the page or stay fixed behind the page contents, and where the image should be positioned.
list-style	For the various types of lists, this property can set the style of bullet, images to be used as bullets, and the positioning of bullets.

The above lists are far from exhaustive, but the designer should be wary that CSS compatibility is sketchy at the best of times. While major properties such as font-styles and colour are relatively safe, the more in-depth CSS is used the more the web page will need to be tested on other browser platforms to ensure readability.

Both *'background'* and *'list-style'* properties are made up of other properties, in the same way as the *'font'* property discussed earlier.

A style sheet that makes use of these properties might contain the following definitions:

```
BODY {background: url(santa.jpg) no-repeat top right}
LI {list-style: url(bullet.gif) inside}
```

HTML editors/generators

The most basic editing tool is an ASCII editor such as Notepad. The author requires knowledge of the entire scripting language and layout, as there is no in-built assistance. However, it is best to use software packages that are dedicated to the production of web pages and entire web sites.

Text editors

An example of a text-based editor is shown in the illustration.

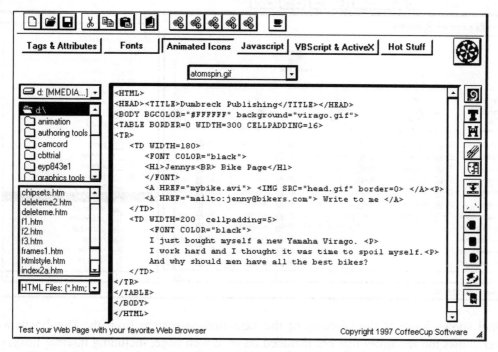

The main work area is a text screen and the script entries are placed in this text area. The cursor is placed where the item is to be added and the desired icon or menu option is selected. This method speeds up page development but the effect of the script is not seen until it is viewed from the computer's browser (called up via an on-screen icon).

This method involves an amount of trial-and-error - changing the script and viewing the result are separate operations.

These packages are continually increasing their features and the example package shown, *'Coffee Cup'*, also allows simple integration of graphics and Java applets into the script.

These editors are popular choices with writers with some previous HTML knowledge, who use them to get greater control over the site.

The drawback with these packages is that the writer is continually switching between the edit window and the viewing window. To overcome this, other packages, such as Hippie, display both windows on screen at the same time. Writers can edit their entries and view the script and the web page at the same time.

Graphics editors

These are the most popular packages, as the main work area is the web page rather than the HTML script. The writer can concentrate on the design and the package converts the screen layout into an HTML script. The script can still be edited directly for more complex work.

All the elements such as text, tables, images and buttons can be dragged from menus and dropped into the page editor (i.e. the design screen).   There are facilities for both beginners and experienced authors.

- For novices, the packages provide *'templates'*. These are pre-designed layouts for both personal and business pages.   Once loaded into the editor, a template is then edited to personalise the content. Templates offer comprehensive features such as *'Whats New'*, Table of Contents, Feedback forms and search forms. Beginners can also use *'Wizards'* which create a layout that results from answers to questions to the author.
- Advanced authors benefit from the simplification of tasks (e.g. resizing table widths or frame sizes by dragging with the mouse, or creating image maps simply by drawing an outline using the mouse).

The packages also integrate some of the graphic functions of other packages, such as providing a clipart library, a catalogue of image thumbnails, or image editing and animation facilities.

The illustration shows the Macromedia Dreamweaver package being used to display a site map.

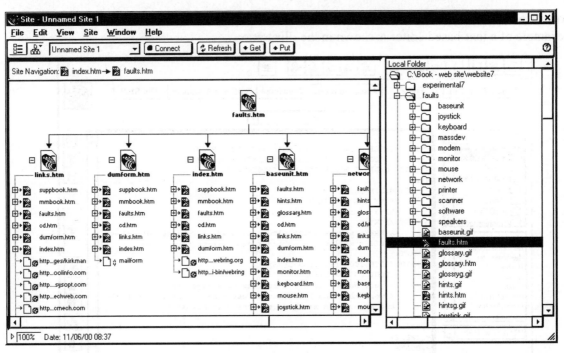

The left panel shows some of the contents of the fault-finding system from the Dumbreck web site. Dreamweaver shows the resources that are included on each web page, including internal links, external links and graphics files.

Site management

As a site expands, there are increasing problems of managing the project, resulting in unfinished pages going unnoticed or inadequate navigation (e.g. pages with no links, links pointing to non-existent pages, etc). The best editors provide not only page creation tools, but tools for managing the overall site.   This could include the graphical display of all pages and links, so that the author sees the overall structure. The package may also allow the author to create a *'To Do'* list.   The author creates the basic structure and the To Do list reminds him/her of the tasks still to be completed. Site management tools could also include improved uploading facilities and database tools.

Validation checkers

These facilities may be built in to editors and are also available as separate utilities.   They check the page documents prior to them being uploaded.   They report on any syntax errors (e.g. missing tags) and check for any browser versions that cannot handle all the commands in the page scripts. Examples are the freeware Xenu and Spyglass validators.

Site performance testers

This software reports on the time taken to load pages and the number of links that currently point to a page. These facilities can be obtained on-line from tester sites on the Internet.

Maximising promotion

Sites can be designed to maximise their search engine position, even before it is uploaded on to the server.

Search engines

Every day, large numbers of Internet users employ search facilities to find sites relating to their needs. Many software packages, called *'search engines'*, are available to aid these searches. The most famous are Alta Vista and Google, with others including HotBot, UK Plus, GOD and Excite. They use software utilities known as *'spiders'* or *'robots'* to search the Internet for new sites and alterations to existing sites. They note the content of web pages to compile indexes for user searches. The way that each package uses the information will vary with some giving greater emphasis to a particular feature than others.

Keywords

Keywords are the words that most distinguish the site's contents and the ones mostly likely to be used by someone searching the Internet for the site. Do not rely solely on keywords such as *'computer'*, *'car'* and *'employment'* as these are used by many existing sites and produce hundreds of thousands of matches for users of search engines. Use descriptive words such as *'fragmentation'*, *'Mercedes'* and *'welder'*. Even better, look at a competitor's web sites and examine the key words they use on their main pages.

There are companies that specialise in getting clients better ratings in search engines, although this has ultimate limits (not everyone can possibly be first in a search result).

<TITLE>

The text enclosed by the <TITLE> tags is not displayed on the screen but is the common starting point for text gathered by search engines. Therefore, the text should be as descriptive as possible, using keywords. This text is also used when a user decides to add the page as a bookmark in his/her browser. So, *"Great Bargains for All"* is useless ,while *"Printer Supplies"* is much more meaningful.

Page text

When analysing page content, search engines assume that writers place their most important information at the top of a page. Accordingly, search engines give greater weight to words at the top of the page. A web page, therefore should have a significant statement at the top of each page.

<META> tags

The <META> tag allows the site's description and associated keywords to be embedded in the web page, so that they can be automatically picked up by many of the search engine spiders. The script lines are located between the <HEAD> tags and have the following formats:

```
<META NAME="description" CONTENT="description of the site goes here">
<META NAME="keywords"   CONTENT="list of keywords goes here">
```

Repeatedly inserting a single word in the keywords list used to ensure a higher ranking in search results but modern search engines penalise this abuse by ignoring the entire keywords list. META keywords are particularly useful with sites whose main file uses frames. A page with frames contains a <FRAMESET> and little else, so a keywords list informs the spiders about the page's purpose.

ALT attributes

Some search engines use ALT attribute text in their calculations. So ALT text helps promote the site as

```
<HTML>
<HEAD>
<TITLE>The PC Support Handbook</TITLE>
<META name="description" content="Computer textbook for college and university students">
<META name="keywords" content="student textbook, technician handbook, computer basics,
software & data, operating systems & environments, computer architecture, computer video,
pc configuration, batch files, computer memory, windows configuration, disks & drives,
computer viruses, pc support, upgrading, system selection, data communications, the internet,
web site creation, local area networks, multimedia" >
</HEAD>
```

well as being helpful to users who have turned off their *'load images'* option.

<NOFRAMES> tags

Placing a site description between the <NOFRAMES> and </NOFRAMES> tags allows users with older browsers (i.e. ones not supporting frames) to view the page. The text is also included in search results.

Finding a server

Large organisations may decide that it is cost-effective to establish their own web server at their own site, incurring the expense of establishing, preparing and maintaining a permanent server connection to the Internet. Most organisations and individuals choose to use space on an existing web server. In most cases, an ISP (Internet Service Provider) provides a fixed amount of disk space as part of the standard user's rental. Additional web site space can be rented at an extra cost. The ISP will also offer more bandwidth for an extra charge. This is important for sites that expect many visitors or provides software for downloading.

If the server is rented from a host supplier, the range of facilities offered should be checked prior to signing an agreement. This should include:

- How much disk space is included in the agreement and how much does extra storage space cost.
- How much bandwidth is included in the price and how much does extra bandwidth cost.
- Does the server support facilities that might be used in the future, such as CGI scripting, Java, JavaScript, PHP, ASP, SSI, streaming, ODBC, Perl, MySQL, etc.
- Does the server have full physical security such as intruder alarms, water detection, fire alarms, backup power, access systems (e.g. swipe cards).
- Does the system provide measures to counter 'hacking' (see chapter on security).
- What reporting facilities does the host provide (e.g. weekly logs or monthly logs).
- How many e-mail addresses would be allocated.
- Does the host support discussion forums, mailing lists, etc.
- How long have they been trading, what is the current customer base, are they financially sound.
- What is their backup policy (e.g. frequency of backups, provision of virus protection).
- Is the supplier a backbone provider, or a reseller of bandwidth from an upstream provider.
- How much of the core capacity of the bandwidth is currently used (i.e. is the supplier working at the edge of its limit).
- If most customers come from the UK, what bandwidth is their line to London Telehouse (the main UK centre). If sales are in Europe, do they have a link to Amsterdam.
- Does provider have its own link to the USA (e.g. to the New York Telehouse). Suppliers with direct links can usually supply a better service but charge higher fees.

It is useful to request examples of existing customers and then check their access times at different times of day.

Capacity

The trader's target is that all viewers can navigate throughout the site with minimum delays between pages, to prevent them leaving the site too early. Therefore, the server has to have sufficient bandwidth to meet the expected amount of traffic. If a trader is using its own server, an eye has to be kept on the bandwidth usage, as it should never get above 80% of the system capacity. If the usage regularly exceeds this figure, the connection to the Internet should be upgraded. If the server is provided through an agreement with ISP, the trader should check whether the system bandwidth is dedicated to its server, or shared with other servers. Bursts above the agreed bandwidth are usually tolerated but abuse will lead to demands from the ISP for a new agreement on greater bandwidth provision. Very large increases may also require to be met with extra servers.

Web Server Software

The web server must run some kind of software that will service requests for HTML web pages. This is the Web Server software, and there are numerous products available to fill this role. The most widely used web server software, however, are the free '*Apache*' server and '*IIS*' from Microsoft.

While Apache is free, Microsoft IIS (Internet Information Services) is often considered to have a more user-friendly interface as well as providing better facilities. For example, IIS can act as an NNTP, SMTP and/or FTP server as well as serving HTTP requests. Some other capabilities available in IIS include:

- Indexing service: This is an automated search engine, built in to an IIS server. It creates an index of files, which is maintained any time a file is added, removed or changed. The user can then search the web site for keywords.
- Remote Administration: When combined with Microsoft Frontpage software, web pages on IIS servers can be managed from a remote location. This allows certain web pages to be kept by individual users on a local network, who may not have access to the server itself.

- Scripting: IIS supports Active Server Pages (ASP) which is a server-side programming language that allows for dynamic site content by giving users access to a dynamic local database. IIS also provides developer support for JavaScript, and VBScript client-side scripting languages.
- Secure Sockets Layer: SSL is a security mechanism that allows browsers and servers to agree on a level of security, including encryption and authentication.
- Windows Media Services: This is a specification that is used to provide streaming content, typically audio or video, on IIS web pages.

Getting a domain name

The web site name can be a problem for some companies. Finding an appropriate domain name may be difficult, as many obvious names are already allocated.

The domain name is usually in three parts, to describe the organisation, its type of activity and the country in which it is (nominally) based. So, ayrcoll.ac.uk describes Ayr College, which is an academic institution based in the UK. Some domains, like .gov, .ac, .org, .pro, .coop, .aero and .museum are only allocated on evidence that the applicant fits the particular category (e.g. only colleges, universities, etc. will be granted an .ac domain name).

Other domains include:

.org	Charities, professional bodies, trade unions, political parties
.gov, nhs	National government, local government bodies
.co, .com, .biz, .plc, .ltd	Business use
.info, .tv, .name	General use

While .co.uk and .com, are mostly used by commercial companies, there is no restrictions on applying for these domain names.

There are many companies involved in selling and managing domain names.   Nominet (www.nominet.org.uk) is the UK registrar of domain names and it provides a list of over 1,000 sellers and resellers. A search facility on the Nominet site can be used to check whether a domain name is already in use.   New.net have challenged the international registry (ICANN) by bringing out an 'unofficial' set of domains including .mp3, .sport, .travel, .club and .shop. At present, however, these require a special browser plug-in to access them.

There are charges for acquiring and maintaining a domain name. This comprises the registration fee (the one-off fee for setting up the arrangements), the management fee (a monthly fee for web forwarding, e-mail forwarding, etc.) and a NIC fee for the registrar.

Uploading

When the site contents are written and tested, they have to be copied from the local hard disk to the remote server's disk system.

The transfer is known as 'uploading' and the stages of the process are:
- Packaging the elements in a suitable uploading format.
- Testing the site before uploading.
- Transferring the files.
- Testing the final server version.

Format

Each server provider has different conditions and these should be checked before completing the site. Better still, check the conditions out before even starting the site design.

The issues to be considered are:
- The name of the server sub-directory allocated for the new site. This may be already created by the provider. In this case, providing the correct password at the ftp logon automatically directs uploading to the allocated directory.
- Avoid using absolute pathnames for graphic images, since the paths used to store them on the server disk will be different and the files will not be accessible (see earlier).
- The most common name for the main site file is expected to be index.htm, but some expect default.htm or another name.   The required main filename will be supplied by the ISP.
- Some providers support CGI scripting and offer image libraries and usage counters.
- The final site must fit within the maximum space allocated by the provider.

Pre-testing

Test all the links within the site to ensure that all the pages in structure function as expected.   Equally important, test the site with different browsers before uploading.   Some activities are peculiar to Netscape or Explorer and newer versions of the same browser support extra features not found in older versions.   To maximise the site's readership, a balance has to be struck between utilising the latest technological innovations and the ability of users to view the pages. If a site is being developed for a third party and there are major differences in the site when viewed by different browsers, the site should be reviewed along with the client. This may result in changing the design or withdrawing some features. The chapter on Multimedia covers testing methods, including user testing.

Transferring

The site is uploaded using an FTP session. The ISP hosts many separate sites on each of its servers, except for very large web sites that negotiated to pay for exclusive use of a server. This raises the ever-present threat to the security of a site. There have been many well-publicised illegal defacements of web sites, where hackers have gain entry to the site's files. As a minimum, each server allocates a directory to each customer and the customer is allowed to create sub-directories within that directory. The renter of that space is provided with a unique ID and a unique password, so that only authorised users have access to each structure.

When the FTP application is run, it produces a screen similar to that below. The details to be set up for an upload session are:

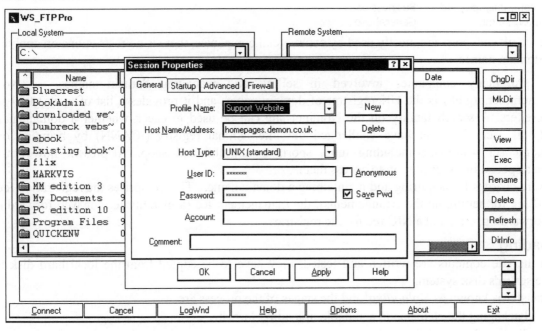

Profile Name:

A number of different profiles can be set up; one for uploading to the host server, others for downloading from particular sites, and so on.   The upload details can be saved as a profile and this can be called up each time the site needs to be updated.   The example entry is *'Support Web Site'* but this can be any name as it is purely for local use; it is not sent to the host server.

Host Details:

These are supplied by the server provider. The example uses a UNIX server and initially connects to the home pages area of the demon site.

User Details:

The user ID and the user password will have previously been agreed with the provider.

Initial Directories:

The Local Initial Directory is the directory on the hard drive that stores the web site files.

The Remote Initial Directory is the directory used for storing the files on the remote server.   This is usually left blank, as the correct password usually automatically directs uploading to the allocated directory.

Clicking *'OK'* and *'Connect'* produces the following results:

- The local computer connects to the remote site.
- The remote server returns a message to the local system. This appears at the bottom of the ftp screen.
- The left window displays all the files in the local disk's web site directory.
- The right window displays the receiving directory on the remote server. This directory will be empty. On subsequent visits to update the site's contents, the complete set of site files is displayed in this window.

Between the two window columns are two buttons. One displays an arrow going from the local window to the remote window (i.e. from the local site to the remote server). The other arrow points from the server to the local computer. These buttons are used to copy files between the two computers. Below the windows is a set of radio buttons. These allow the files to be transferred in ASCII or Binary mode. To upload the entire site:

- Set the transfer mode to ASCII.
- Highlight the HTML files in the local window.
- Click the right-pointing arrow to upload the text files.
- Set the transfer mode to Binary.
- Highlight the non-text files (e.g. graphics, audio, video, executables).
- Click the right-pointing arrow to upload these files.

As an alternate, some ftp packages allow a drag-and-drop method where files are highlighted by the mouse and *'dropped'* into the server window. In either case, the files will appear in the right window. This means that the entire population of Internet users can access them.

Final testing

After the site is uploaded, it should be tested. This involves logging on to the Internet as a normal user and entering the site address in the browser. The main page of the site should appear and each link should be tested, to see whether the expected pages appear and the text and graphics are displayed as expected. Test the site with the *'display graphics'* option disabled to ensure that <ALT> tags work.

Test the site with different browsers, to ensure that the site appearance is satisfactory on a range of browser packages.

Test the site with different versions of the same browser. For example, an older browser may not have the facility for displaying frames and this checks whether the <NOFRAMES> text works. If possible, the site should also be tested on different platforms. Many Internet users are not PC users and the site may not appear on other machines in quite the way that was planned.

Site Maintenance

When the site is uploaded and tested, it is ready for use by the browsing public. However, that is by no means the end of the story. Every site has its *'life cycle'* of use followed by modification, followed by a further period of use, followed by further modifications, and so on. The modifications could simply be corrections to errors in the initial site. More likely, they will be alterations and additions to improve the usefulness and relevance of the site.

Changes could include:

- Improving readability for the visually impaired.
- Linking to the company database, so that current price and stock information is always available.
- Adding e-commerce facilities.
- Providing updates and patches for software products.
- Providing FAQs
- Using Flash animations.
- Having monthly special offers.
- Providing company news.
- Publishing up-to-date product reviews.
- Providing a chat room for site visitors.
- Providing links to other web sites.

For a small company, regular maintenance is a fact of life. For a company that employs an outside agency to design a web site, there has to be provision in the contract covering regular site updates.

Promoting the site

The potential audience for a web site does not reflect all of society. Some countries have very low numbers on the Internet, while richer countries such as the USA have large numbers of Net users. There are more young people on the Net than there are older users. Within each country, Net usage is largely concentrated in the more affluent and professional sections of the population. The potential audience, therefore, is what actually exists and not what a site would wish to exist. The site's expectations have to reflect this reality. Sites for the unemployed, travelling people, pensioners, etc can expect fewer hits than sites for youth culture, consumer products, holidays, etc.

For most sites, especially commercial sites, the emphasis is on getting repeat visits. The more often a user returns to the site, the more likely he/she will subscribe to a product or idea. There are many strategies for increasing the *'stickiness'* of a site and these can be grouped under the following broad headings:

Access to software

All users like the idea of a *'freebie'* and sites attract support by offering various software such as:

- Free downloads (small free programs to entice users to buy larger and more powerful products).
- Evaluation software (fully-working programs that are time-limited or are being beta tested).
- Drivers and patches for existing software products.
- Screen savers.

Access to information

Another prime reason for users visiting web sites is to acquire information using:

- Product data pages.
- A site's internal search engine (i.e. to search the entire site for a keyword).
- Access to staff contacts (e.g. sales, despatch, technical support).
- Electronic Newsletters. These draw users into regular contact with the site, by inviting them to sign up to an e-mailing list for a regular newsletter. The list is used to send regular e-mails outlining site changes, special offers, events, etc. Before proceeding, there should be clear procedures that allow users to unsubscribe.

Site Events

These are designed to encourage users to pay regular visits to the site. Events will depend on the nature of the site but could be auctions, competitions, games, surveys, on-line interviews with celebrities or experts, pre-recorded audio broadcasts, FAQ series. These are all time-consuming as they require regular updating of the site contents but they make the site more attractive and encourage repeat visits. Where the site is updated regularly, displaying *"Last updated ......"* messages encourages return visits.

Advertising the site

The amount of time and money invested in publicising the site depends upon the nature of the site. Individuals and organisations will build a promotion strategy from the techniques listed below. Hobby sites may decide to generate extra hits using cost-free methods such as obtaining directory entries or hosting regular site events. Commercial sites may decide to embark on a range of advertising methods. Charities and special interest groups may decide upon publicity in the media. There is no 'correct' way to promote a site. Site owners will choose the mix of activities that produces the best results for their particular product/message. Before considering the items below, a company should begin by ensuring that all correspondence, adverts, etc. carries the URL for its web site.

Newspapers/Magazines/Radio

It is worth contacting newspapers (both national and local), relevant magazines and radio stations about the launch of a new site. This method only produces results if the site itself is newsworthy in some way (e.g. a charity site, a topical site, covering a niche market, etc). Coverage is free and widespread but may not be targeting the desired audience. This may work better for launching a helpline than launching a specialist site.

Press Releases

In addition to the printed press, sites can be publicised through on-line press releases. Several sites provide on-line daily or weekly information on new sites. Press releases should be short and sharp, using small paragraphs, if they are to be considered for inclusion.

Site Reviews

There are two types of reviews for web sites - *'Guides'* and *'Cool Sites'*.   A *'Guide'* provides a review of a selected number of sites and provides a site rating.   The *'Cool Site'* usually reviews and recommends a different site each day.   These both provide a high volume of extra traffic for a short time.

Magazine Adverts

The impact of paid advertising depends on the nature of the site and ensuring that the advertising matches the target group.   There will be fewer hits from groups who normally do not own/use a computer and advertising costs may determine whether to proceed.   On the other hand, adverts placed in magazines for computer users, electronic technicians, educationalists, government users and the IT industry can expect a better return.

Directories

These sites use categories to direct viewers, via menu options, to their chosen topics.   They are often described as the *'Yellow Pages'* of the Internet.   The menus have many categories and sub-categories. Inclusion on the directory, therefore, specifically targets those requiring the new site's information/ product.   Directory providers provide forms for site registration and these gather details on the URL, directory category (e.g. sport, travel, computers) and key details of the site contents.   In addition to directory services, most directory sites also provide search engine facilities.   Since most Internet purchases are made by users first initiating a search for their products, search engines play a huge part in influencing purchasing.   As a result, major search engines such as Google, Lycos and Alta Vista provide a *"paid for placement"* service, where a fee is charged for ensuring that a particular web site appears high up in a user's search rankings.   Companies offer assistance with search engine registration, providing experience in selecting keywords that improve the site's rankings – although, with a little thought and experience, the registration process can be undertaken by anyone.   Registrations should be renewed regularly (about every six months).

Newsgroups

There are over 30,000 newsgroups on the Internet and those with topics relevant to the site's contents can be selected for mailing.   This is a sensitive area, as some newsgroups do not allow advertising.   A posting to a newsgroup should not consist solely of the advert but should bring in the advert as part of a general contribution or answer to another's query.   So *"buy my product"* is counterproductive while *"...I hope that answers your question.   For more details see my web site ....."* is acceptable.

Links from other web sites

Other web sites may promote similar interests or products and have an interest in providing links between sites.   An academic or hobby site may be very happy to provide a one-way link to the new site.   Their link may point to the main page or directly to a page that contains their specific interest.   Other sites may swap links, with both sites providing links to the other site. The hits arising from web links is almost as high as that from search engines. There is no special procedure for attracting links: an e-mail request to the other sites soon produces their responses.

Banner campaigns

Here, advertising banners are placed on someone else's web site. The cost of advertising on popular directories and search engines is greater than on smaller non-commercial sites. The site owners can be e-mailed for more information. However, fewer than 1% of users seeing a banner actually click on it to jump to the new site (known as *'clickthrough'*).

Counters

One simple measure of a site's success is the extra sales/donations/members/enquiries that are generated. Then again, a site's purpose might be as an information provider.   Sites providing tax or weather information, music charts, train or TV timetables and so on are intended mainly to provide one-way traffic.   For these sites, the best measure of success is the *'hit rate'* - the number of times pages have been viewed.   These figures can be gathered using *'counters'*.   Counters can provide information on the origins of traffic, the total visits to the site and the number of hits on particular pages.   The ISP can be checked for these services.   The hit rate for sites is used in the same way as viewing figures for TV channels.   Increased viewers results in increased fees for advertising on these sites.

A large organisation will use its own resources to monitor web site usage. Smaller sites can use the counter facilities offered by many providers on the Internet. Some ISPs, such as Demon, provide a basic counter – informing the site administrator of the number of hits to a particular page. Other counter providers either charge for their service or are subsidised by advertising. These provide much more information, such as number of visits per day, the busiest time of day, the operating system used by the visitor, the visitor's screen resolution, and so on.

The simplest counting system requires a small text file to be stored on the web site, often called *'count.txt'*. This is a simple ASCII text file that can be read by any word processor. For example, it may contain the contents "2753" and this is made up of four text characters. A counter script sits on the ISP's site and is activated by a call to its URL. It reads the site's count file, converts it from text into an integer number, adds one to the number, converts it back into a text representation, and stores it back in the site. This piece of text can then be sent to the browser and the user can see a caption saying something like *"Total visitors since August 2002 : 2754"*. The number has to be stored as text so that it can be easily incorporated into the HTML page that is sent to the browser.

The web page that requests a hit counter update will include an HTML line something like:

```
<img src="/cgi-bin/count>
```

This is a demon counter script. A script from Tripod is very similar, with <img src=/bin/counter>

If the ISP makes no provision for counters, the developer can use counters provided by third parties. These are often 'free', in the sense that there is no charge for the service. These third parties often provide comprehensive information about site usage. The downside, of course, is that all the information that it has gathered on visitors to the site can also be used by the third party for targeted e-mail.

Copyright

There are two copyright issues to be considered when creating web site projects:

- The elements that are included in the project must be fairly and legally used.
- The finished work must be protected against abuse by another party.

Using other material

While professionals rarely react to their work being adopted for personal use, they will take action when their photographs, film clips, audio tracks, etc are re-used in a commercial product. Great care should be taken to protect against legal action. The Copyright Licensing Agency run a *'Copywatch'* scheme to detect illegal copying and advice can be sought from them (Tel 0207-631-5555). If in doubt, seek written permission from those who own the rights of the copyright. They may be prepared to give unconditional permission (after all, it is free publicity for their product), they may place conditions on its use or they may wish to charge some commission for its use. Where permission is granted, the finished product should acknowledge the source of the material.

An alternative is to stick to using copyright-free sound, pictures and clip-art collections. The original purchase price of the media should include a licence to reproduce it in any projects thereafter, without any further payments being required. There are many stock photographs that can be purchased in this way, although getting the appropriate image may not always be so easy.

Of course, home-created material is generally copyright-free, with the following conditions:

- Audio/video recordings and photographs must be made after obtaining any necessary permissions.
- General photographs, such as crowd scenes or country villages, present no problems.
- Rock concerts have strict bans on recordings the live performance of their artists.
- Photographs and recordings of individuals, without permission, raise questions of invasion of privacy, if not legal repercussions.
- The rich and famous have the financial/political muscle to deter unapproved recording.
- Altering someone else's work does not free it from copyright. For example, downloading an item of clip art and altering some colours or adding on an extra piece here or there does not get round copyright. The original work remains and is the copyright of the person who created it.
- Making an exact copy of another piece of work, starting from scratch, does not make the image free from copyright. The original work is the intellectual property of its creator.
- While media representations of objects are strictly controlled, there is less of a problem with creating images of the original objects. For example, there is not problem in taking a photograph of the Eiffel Tower, or creating an original drawing of a particular brand of car.

Protecting material

Once the project is completed, the entire work and individual elements (i.e. the written words, drawing, animations, photographs, video clips, etc) should be copyright protected.   The 1998 Copyright, Designs and Patents Act provides legal protection for computer material, as it is considered to be a *'literary'* work. The project does not have to be specially registered with any public body, filling in forms, etc. Copyright exists from the moment the work is produced.   This may require proof of *'originality'*.   In the event that there is a dispute over who first produced a particular image, photograph, video clip, or whatever, the judgement goes in favour of the individual who has the earliest proof of owning/using the material.

The UK is a member of four major international conventions on copyright and most countries of the world belong to at least one of them.   This provides some measure of international copyright protection, although the legal and financial implications of copyright action deter many people.

The CLA points out a distinction between those who create material in their own right and those who create material for their employer.   For example, if a lecturer writes student notes in college time, the material is commissioned, paid and owned by the college.   Similarly, if a multimedia designer creates material during the working day, it belongs to the company.   However, any work carried out in an employee's own time, using his/her own resources, is probably the property of the individual (unless the organisation's contract with the individual explicitly states otherwise).

Ensuring copyright

The work should contain the word *'copyright'*, followed by the name of the person or organisation and the date of origin.   The use of the copyright symbol © is not compulsory in UK, but is recommended as it is required in some other countries.

This, of course, does not prove that the date stated is genuine. The traditional method is to post a copy of the work to one's self, using registered post (to get a dated receipt).   The package remains sealed until it needs to be publicly opened to prove the date of originality.   For very expensive projects, the work should be deposited with a solicitor.

The copyright on an idea is a little more complex. For example, if someone wrote an article describing a great idea for a project, someone else is entirely free to adopt the idea and turn it into a commercial work. However, if he/she writes another article repeating the idea, it is an infringement of the idea's copyright.

Finally, designs are not copyright protected, although they may be registered at the Patent Office as a *'design right'*.

Moral/legal issues

The chapter on using the Internet looks at some of the trickier issues relating to content on web pages and how they may contravene laws on obscenity, privacy, libel or security.

Multimedia

The basics

There are many definitions of the term *'multimedia'*. At its simplest, it refers to using multiple forms of media. In practice, it is the convergence of graphics, audio, video, animation, and programming skills with imaginative and creative skills.

Multimedia uses the various types of visual and audio output to more effectively communicate with the user or viewer.

The kinds of facilities expected in a final multimedia package include:

- Still graphic images
- Digitised sound/music
- Plain text
- Animated graphics
- Synthesised sound/music
- Digitised photographs
- Moving video images

Multimedia is not just the repackaging of existing material. Early multimedia CD-ROMs used the large storage space of CD-ROM disks to store the entire text of books to CD, or place photographic albums on CD, and such.   While they undoubtedly help archive material, they were not true multimedia products. They missed out on the real value of multimedia authoring.

Multimedia is different from all communication mediums that have gone before.   At a visit to the cinema, the material is watched as a continuous sequence; the film has a start and a finish and the viewer watches the material in the order that the filmmakers decided. Watching television is similar. Although the viewer can flick channels, the content of any one channel is fixed and the order of the material is printed in television schedules in newspapers. Even interactive television provides only minor diversions from the main show. Similarly, books and videotapes are designed for sequential use. Audiocassettes, audio CDs and magazines are only slightly better, in that the user can jump between tracks or flick between pages, providing some control over the content.

Multimedia, on the other hand, contains audio, video, graphics, animations, video and text - but it is all under the control of the user! A distinguishing feature of multimedia is the ability of the user to interact with the media. This may be through choosing menu options or clicking the mouse on icons or areas of the screen.   The vast amounts of data are usually linked through hypertext systems or authoring packages. This is more correctly *'hypermedia'*, since it uses both multiple media elements and the ability to jump around the material. Of course, it is possible to create a multimedia production without any interactivity (e.g. a single TV advert probably contains video, audio, text and animation).   However, the general term multimedia has come to replace the more accurate term hypermedia in most areas.

This interaction is the key to the success of a multimedia product. The experts vary slightly, but generally agree that we recall 10% of what we read, 20% of what we see and 30% of what we both see and hear.   However, because we learn more from taking part in active learning, we recall a massive 70% of what we see, hear and do.   Multimedia packages allow the user to control the viewing process and decide what they want to see/do, how long they want to see/do it and what they want to see/do next.

Multimedia presentations

Having gathered the graphics, sound and music for the presentation, the author decides on the best way to present the information.

This will depend upon the purpose it is intended to achieve, although presentations are generally of two types:

Linear :

The user watches a sequence that has been already determined and has no influence over the presentation. This is best suited to exhibitions, point of sale and other information providing situations. Linear presentations can be created with simple software. Although they use multiple forms of media, they are not full multimedia products as there is no real interaction with the user.

Interactive :

The user can control the flow of the presentation, to explore particular areas, ignoring others and even returning to a particular area of the presentation. The package may have built-in intelligence to know where a user keeps going wrong and giving targeted advice. This is suited to the learning environment where the user controls the pace and the content of the presentation. Computer Based Training programmes use this method, as each run of the presentation can be different, changing with the needs of the student. CDs and DVDs for the domestic entertainment market use interactive techniques. Interactive presentations often use more sophisticated, and more expensive, software to create them.

Hypertext

Older applications tended to require the user to follow a fixed training pattern with clear end objectives. Options were allowed but they were temporary detours from the main path to be tread by the user. Although this has distinct advantages in certain situations, and is still implemented in some packages today, it does not follow the way humans think and approach issues. Few people learn a subject by systematically working through a linear path of material. Only fiction is read linearly. People learn by association; having grasped a concept it leads them to one or more linked concepts. For example, reading a car repair manual on fixing carburettors may inspire a reader to find out more about how the ignition systems works, what a catalytic converter is, or how to use a double-grommeted nut wrench. Hypertext builds a system that supports that way of thinking. Users can leave a particular subject area and explore something linked - or completely different; they can choose to return to the previous theme or can move onwards or sideways if they wish. Each person will use the system in a different way.

Users move from one subject to another by selecting menu options or by clicking the mouse on a highlighted word (a hypertext link) or on a particular area of the screen (a hotspot). Early systems were solely text based and graphical interfaces followed later.

The best definition of hypertext is that it:

"produces large, complex, richly connected and cross-referenced bodies of information"

Hypertext is widely implemented in Windows applications' help systems and this *'navigation'* process is a cornerstone of multimedia packages. The biggest example of hypertext is the World Wide Web.

Hypertext's benefits include good browsing abilities, rapid navigation, the ability to annotate results and the ability to save results and queries for later use. Reported problems with hypertext are disorientation (it is much easier to get lost than when page-hopping with a printed book) and *'cognitive overhead'* (the large variety of options stuns the brain's ability to easily consider alternatives).

Applications for multimedia

New uses are constantly being found for multimedia and these can be generally categorised as:

Training

Training is concerned with the acquisition of specific skills, of the mind or the hand. Examples are learning a foreign language or playing the guitar.

Education

Education is *'knowledge based'*; specific skills need not flow from the absorption of this knowledge. The theories of evolution, politics, religion, pure science, mathematics, etc. may be learned for their own sake rather than to be practised. The Educational Software & CD-ROM Yearbook is jam-packed with details of 1000 different educational CD-ROMs on subjects such as history, science, geography, art and architecture, economics, media studies, etc.

Distance learning

Distance learning assumes that the student is remote from the educational establishment. This could be for any of a variety of reasons, such as disability, family commitments, working overseas, shift working, etc. Those undertaking study communicate via downloading material, uploading exercises and carrying on e-mail dialogues with support lecturers. Students often use educational CDs or DVDs in a classroom where a teacher/lecturer is present to answer specific questions or to clear up any vagueness in the application's presentation. This immediate help is less available with distance learning students and the multimedia material has to reflect this. It must anticipate possible student problems, provide adequate help and guided support. The package should have facilities for student self-assessment, to reinforce students in their learning.

CBT/CAL

These systems embed the knowledge of a lecturer/teacher/trainer instructor into a training package that can be used anywhere at any time.

Computer Based Training (CBT) develops specific skills (e.g. typing tutors) while Computer Aided Learning (CAL) explores ideas (e.g. science and philosophy). Both applications provide user options and store user responses in variables. In this way, a user's progress is monitored and appropriate advice given. Users can be given assessments and told their scores. Users can be given a certain number of attempts at a multi-choice question. The support given for a wrong answer can depend on what incorrect choice is entered and previous experience of the user as judged by previous responses.

CBT/CAL provides an 'intelligent' system which users enjoy as they have more control over the learning experience. They can work at their own pace, reviewing a page, changing direction and stopping for a break.

Edutainment

Edutainment combines elements of education and entertainment in a manner that imparts knowledge to a user while wrapping the material up as an entertaining experience. Packages featuring the adventures of Peter Rabbit or Barney Bear provide children with animated stories. The text of the story is displayed on screen and each word is highlighted as the story is read out. Children can activate parts of the screen and can control the flow of the story by mouse clicks. Serious learning is taking place in conjunction with the attractive activities. Adult edutainment equivalents are CDs with conducted tours of 'The Louvre', investigating 'Great Artists' and exploring 'The Ultimate Human Body'.

Entertainment

These are solely aimed at providing fun with no attempt at any serious education, although in some packages a little general knowledge may be picked up along the way. Applications include multimedia databases on films and music, interactive music CDs and the guide to 'Wines, Spirits and Beers'. Other well-known applications of multimedia are the effects produced in films such as 'Toy Story', 'Monsters Inc' and the 'Jurassic Park' series of films, as well as the huge range of games that now exist on CD-ROM and DVD.

Simulation

Simulation provides a computer replica of a living or supposed situation and there are applications for use in both entertainment and industry. Leisure applications cover both the real world (e.g. flight simulators) and the imagined world (e.g. fighting the aliens on the planet Zog). Industry has many serious uses for simulations in situations where training staff can be hazardous both to the trainees and to real equipment. Typical applications are training French train drivers using simulations of railway routes and British firefighters learning to handle dangerous situations. Users can learn from their mistakes without any harm being done.

Marketing

Marketing covers the promotion of both opinions and products; it is aimed at altering the views and preferences of those who use the application. After viewing the application, users are hoped to desire certain products, holiday at a particular location, study at a particular university, etc. Example marketing applications are the 'virtual kitchens' demonstrated by Matsushita, unattended public information displays (known as kiosks) promoting clothes or holidays, and CD-ROM travel guides covering from the 'AA Days Out in Britain and Ireland' to 'Travel Mexico' and 'Voyage in Spain'.

Presentations

This is a specific form of marketing where the salesperson uses a multimedia presentation to enhance the effect of his/her delivery. The material is projected on to screens or video walls.

Home shopping

This also overlaps with marketing activities. While marketing promotes the demand for the product, home shopping provides the convenience to place the order. A growing number of product catalogues are provided on CD/DVD or many more are available on the World Wide Web. Users can log into a company's web site and use the search facilities to bring up details of desired products. The user can read the text descriptions and view the images. The product range is huge covering from computers to books and clothes. The user can instantly place an order and can pay with a credit card.

Reference

Reference material is readily available in book format but multimedia versions provide many extra facilities such as very quick subject searching and cross-referencing, the use of animations to aid explanations and sound and video clips of famous people and events. Examples of reference material are BOOKBANK (British books in print), specifications, dictionaries (e.g. the Oxford Compendium), the Guinness Book of Records and a range of impressive annually updated multimedia encyclopaedias (e.g. Compton's, Grolier, Hutchinson, Microsoft and Britannica). Archiving of reference material is another popular use, where the ability to quickly move around material and have easy search facilities provides added value. This allows for huge databases of material such as research results, specifications, legal documents, etc. These may include diagrams, personal signatures, scanned documents and even voiceprints. There is currently a huge growth in electronic publishing in the shape of news, books, technical manuals, public information, and promotional brochures.

Electronic Publishing

Electronic publishing is an area with anticipated rapid growth. Its contents can be electronic *'books'*, sales literature, or information banks. The contents of many daily papers are posted to the Internet and CDs/DVDs containing a year's contents can be purchased. CD versions involve a single payment, whereas on-line versions may involve paying for connect time compared to hard copy subscription charges. On-line versions provide constantly updated information while CD versions provide archive reference material. As in all publishing, copyright problems necessitate a legal framework to be adopted.

Virtual Reality

Virtual reality (VR) has received much publicity and is still in the development stage. Crude versions have appeared in amusement arcades and much work has been carried out in the areas of staff training and work simulation. VR produces an artificial world that is generated by computer.

It uses four elements:

- Database (to store the elements of the scenario - e.g. buildings, trees, roads, etc. These are not stored as graphics images; they are stored in descriptive format).
- Graphics engine (to convert object data in graphics shapes, implementing 3D shading and texture mapping).
- Input (to sense activities in the real world).
- Output (to stimulate human senses).

VR is produced in two ways:

Fully-immersive

The user wears a head-mounted display containing LCD screens for each eye, along with motion detectors. This is the most realistic method, as the user can only view the scene presented by the computer and there are no outside distractions. The helmet's sensors track head movements, such that turning the head to the left generates a picture that pans to the left. Similarly, sensors in data gloves detect movement and pressure and can provide feedback to simulate resistance (i.e. sensation of holding or moving an object).

Partially-immersive

The user views the artificial world through a window (i.e. the monitor) as in normal games use. It is less effective than fully-immersive systems, as the surrounding environment distracts from the effect of the simulation. The main outputs are to the user's sight and hearing. The main inputs are from helmet sensors, joystick, keyboard and foot levers.

Delivery methods

The finished multimedia products are supplied to the user in a number of different formats. Multimedia is often spoken of in the same breath as CD-ROM or DVD. However, CDs and DVDs are not always used for multimedia purposes, and multimedia does not necessarily require the use of a CD-ROM or DVD.

It is true that projects that are rich in video and photographic content requires lots of storage space and these are often best met by the capacity offered by a DVD. However, much effort has been put into making multimedia suitable for Internet distribution and the relative merits of these and other methods are discussed below.

The delivery of multimedia products can be either offline or online. The offline version is usually self-contained. All the project's elements are included on the CD-ROM or within the kiosk's hard disk.   The online version allows access to the material over local area networks, wide area networks or the Internet.

CD-ROM and DVD features

- Works on any multimedia PC, with predictable results. Most users have DVD drives.
- Available to PC users who have no Internet connection.
- Stores large amounts of information in a variety of formats (i.e. text, video, sound, animation).
- Allows fast user access.
- No ongoing costs to the user, after purchase, to access the information.
- Expensive for the producer to update regularly, due to production costs.
- The content is always available, undisturbed by telephone breakdown, busy periods, etc.

Internet features

- Can be potentially accessed by a huge audience.
- Provides two-way traffic (i.e. e-mail, form-filling, voting).
- The contents are dynamic - i.e. they are easily updated (daily, hourly, instantly as necessary).
- Slow for supplying large graphics and video to users, for those without broadband (although streaming techniques help to reduce the problem).
- Poses potential security problems. The site can be hacked into and the data can be altered.
- A huge web site is required to store the same amount of data as a DVD.
- Providers are charged by bandwidth usage.   The more popular the site, the more the Internet provider charges the web site owner, (unless they have their own equally expensive web server).
- Many users will incur telephone charges or download charges every time they access the material.
- Provides additional commercial opportunities (e.g. credit card transactions, auctions, gathering mailing lists, etc).

Some CD/DVDproducts now have web links, so that the viewer can get his/her modem to dial up a specific web site and fetch current data.   This allows, for example, educational institutions to produce CD-ROMs that can be updated less regularly, since the users can fetch any new material via the institution's web site.   Similarly, a manufacturer can create a CD-ROM catalogue of products and customers can click a hyperlink to fetch the current pricing and availability.

Intranet features

An intranet is a local area network serving a single organisation, with its own web server.   The only computers connected to the intranet are the ones used by the company's employees and the multimedia content stored on the web server is only available to this limited set of users.   There is no connection to the outside world and no one else can access the web server.   It is like the Internet in miniature. Companies can use intranets to store and distribute company training and it also becoming more popular in educational establishments.

Kiosk features

These are standalone applications designed for stores, museums, trade fairs, information points, etc.   The computer equipment is housed in a sealed unit and interacts with the public through its monitor and input device such as a touch sensitive screen (this screen has additional sensors that detect the presence of a finger or a stylus at a particular set of screen co-ordinates and use the information to determine menu options, etc.). The project is stored on hard disks and is potentially available 24-hours, 7 days a week.

Electronic presentations

The material is usually stored on a laptop computer and displayed via a projector on to a screen.   With large presentations, extra bright projectors, rear projectors or video walls may be used.

The multimedia machine

Most computers are capable of playing multimedia titles but the equipment for creating high-end multimedia products requires more power and more hardware.

The authoring computer

The requirements for computers that create multimedia products are more demanding than those used for simply playing multimedia. It is certainly possible to create basic multimedia projects with the simplest of computer systems, using little or no specialised hardware. A simple presentation involving text, graphics and limited animation, can be created on a basic computer without any extra hardware add-ons whatsoever. Of course, the more sophisticated presentations use sound clips, video sequences, complex animations, etc. and therefore require a high performance machine and special equipment to capture video, edit video, create multi-track sound, and so on.

The diagram shows some input devices (they bring data into the main computer) and some output devices (they receive data from the main computer systems). For example, the video capture card, CD drive, mouse, keyboard, tablet and touch screen are all input devices, while the CD writer and DVD writers are output devices (although they could be used as reading devices). Other devices, such as

memory, hard disks, modems and sound cards are both input and output devices. At one moment they may be sending information to the computer, while at other times they may be receiving information from the computer.

One range of add-ons is required for the production of multimedia applications, while other hardware is required for the delivery of such applications.

Hardware for creation

The list below is the minimum for a home-quality production facility.

The sound and video hardware would be upgraded for professional quality results.

Video Capture Card	Video Camera (preferably digital)
Sound Card (with hand microphone, tie-clip microphone or headset system)	Digital Still Camera
Graphics card (preferably with HD support)	Scanner
MIDI interface with Synthesiser/Keyboard	CD-ROM writer, DVD writer, Blu-Ray writer
VCR (if transferring old VHS tape footage)	Large, fast hard disks

Hardware for delivery

Completed multimedia products can either be distributed on CD-ROMs or via the Internet.

CD-ROM and DVD

CD-ROM or DVD player	Sound Card with speakers
Graphics card with MPEG, HD support	MIDI interface with Synthesiser/Keyboard

This has the advantage of using a known performance standard and quality is predictable. However, content can become outdated quickly and there is no contact between the manufacturer and the users. As it only offers single-user access and provides the most security, it is the obvious choice when the CD is itself the product designed for sale.

Internet

Graphics card with MPEG support	Sound Card with speakers
MIDI interface with Synthesiser/Keyboard	Modem, Cable, ADSL or ISDN link

This has the advantage that material can be easily updated and reaches a potentially larger market. Orders and queries can be dealt with on-line. However, the transfer of large graphics and video files is still a major obstacle on the Internet. Since data on the Internet can easily be accessed, it is the obvious choice for general promotional material for a product that can be ordered and supplied outwith the Internet.

Newer CD applications have Internet links to provide the best features of both methods. The core content (text descriptions, pictures, etc) resides on the CD-ROM while constantly changing information (e.g. prices) is downloaded as the application is viewed.

Multimedia Software

The range of software to support the creation of multimedia products includes:

	Purpose
Audio Editing, File Conversion	Audio files can be manipulated in many ways to create the final clip to be included in a production. These include cut and paste, mixing, merging, filtering out frequencies, adding echo effects, looping, muting, reversing, pitch altering, volume altering, panning, fading and waveform editing. Other utilities convert audio files into compressed MP3 versions.
Video Editing, conversions and effects	Most packages use 'Non-Linear Editing' where the video clips are digitised and individual sections of the clip (right down to a single frame) are easily accessed for editing and the usage of special effects. Typical facilities are cut and paste, adding filters, transitions between scenes such as fades and wipes, titling, warping and morphing (gradually transforming one object into another object). The clips are organised into the correct running order and saved as the finished video clip. Other utilities convert video files into compressed MPEG versions. Examples include Adobe Premiere, After Effects, DivX encoders, etc.
Graphic Creation	These packages are used to create drawings, charts, cartoons, etc from graphic elements such as lines, boxes, circles and polygons. The line widths, styles (e.g. dotted, arrowed) and colour are alterable and a variety of fill patterns are provided. Text of various sizes, types styles and colours can be added. Packages such as Paintbrush produce bitmap files while upmarket products produce vector images (although these can be converted to bitmaps).
Animation Graphic Effects	The most common effects are 3D objects using wireframes and rendered fills and animations. Many authoring packages include animation facilities but these are not as sophisticated as dedicated animation packages such as 3D Studio, etc..
Image Editing Photo Retouch	These packages (e.g. PhotoShop, etc.) are used to manipulate the contents of a photographic image. This includes altering the colours, altering contrast and brightness, and zooming, scaling and cropping of the image. It may also include special effects such as quantizing (producing an oil painting effect) and altering the data masks (producing a pop video effect). These packages are often used to alter the image's main contents (e.g. removing a blemish from someone's face, or removing the telegraph pole that seems to stick out of someone's head).
Authoring Packages	This is the key piece of software (e.g Director) that integrates all the sound, video, graphic and text components into a meaningful order to achieve a prescribed effect.
Web Authoring	These packages (e.g. HTML editors, Dreamweaver, JavaScript, Flash, etc.) are designed for creating web-based multimedia material. They may be the web equivalent of the authoring package (i.e. they integrate all the components into a set of interlinked web pages) or they provide animations and effects that are optimised for web use.
Music Software	These packages (e.g. Cubase, Sonar, etc.) provide facilities to compose, record, edit and mix music tracks. The audio tracks can be real world audio, recording via microphones or can be synthesised MIDI tracks.

Software for delivery

The software requirements for the delivery of multimedia are small.   Windows users already have the capability of playing WAV and AVI files.   Additional software drivers and CODECs are required to support a fuller range of playback modes.   For example, the playback of QuickTime and certain MPEG files may require their CODECs to be installed.   Sound cards require that their software be configured and if the user is downloading multimedia from the Internet, then communications, browser and specialist software (e.g. RealAudio or RealVideo) is required.

Creating a multimedia project

The main steps in designing projects for multimedia are similar to those for any software project, although there are extra considerations.

The main phases are:

Project brief	This states the main aims of the project and is supplied by the organisation commissioning the work.
Requirements analysis	This clarifies the brief and provides the specification of the project requirements.
Create/test prototype	This is a skeletal version of the project and is used to clear up any misunderstandings regarding their needs. The lessons from this stage are used to create the requirements specification.
Requirements specification	This states the project's technical requirements, detailed aims, navigation requirements, and screen layout specifications.
Design document	This provides a detailed overview, showing all navigational paths and sketches of screen content (showing media components, user interactions and screen layout). This should also include the creation of a storyboard and navigation maps.
Project plan	This states the financial and operational tasks in producing the project. It allocates individual responsibilities and creates the running order for events (e.g. shooting lists). Often a Gantt chart is used to plan the sequence of activities and milestones (dates for the completion of significant stages).
Test document	This includes the test specification, which in turn includes tests for usability and functionality, fitness for purpose and consistency. After testing, the test results are added, for comparison with the expected results.
Implementation	This is the main phase of the project, covering the capture/creation of material (i.e. record all the sound and video clips, photograph all the pictures, draw all the graphics) and their integration into a complete piece of work using an authoring package. The project is then mastered to its final distribution format (i.e. put on a web site, burned on to a CD-R, or saved as a kiosk master).
Project testing	This checks the project, to ensure that it passes all the tests specified in the test document.
Development report	This records the approach taken to the project, any assumptions made, any problems encountered, and any suggestions for future improvements.
Project assessment	This is a critical analysis of the project, noting its strengths and weaknesses and making comparisons between it and any other similar applications.

Requirements analysis

It is vital that a clear understanding of the project is achieved before any other work is undertaken.   This prevents many wasted hours and potential disputes with the client commissioning the project.

Client requirements

The client will provide a project brief, which is a short summary of the aims of the project. It identifies the client's main requirements (e.g. why they need it and what they expect it to achieve). The task of systems analysis is to convert the project brief into a project plan that can be implemented. A thorough set of discussions clarifies the detailed aims of the project. This would include issues such as the general content (e.g. education, training, entertainment).

It may also involve market research, to confirm that the project assumptions are correct (e.g. is there really a market for a Spice Girls CD game any more? Just how many small companies would be prepared to buy an interactive tutorial on completing VAT returns? and so on).

User requirements

The requirement analysis also identifies

- The target audience (the likely age, sex, previous knowledge/experience of those using the product, literacy level, social background). It should also identify any special needs, such as voice recognition, text readers, touch screens or special keyboard input, or Braille output.
- The mood (serious, light-hearted).

Context of use

The analysis stage also identifies the method of delivering the material (cd-rom, internet, kiosk, intranet) and these issues were covered earlier.

These discussions and investigations lead to the production of a project specification. This is essentially a requirements list covering educational requirements and technical requirements such as the proposed delivery system, screen resolution and colours, screen layout and project navigation).

The aim of the analysis phase is also to produce precise statements, which can act as a checklist in the later testing phase. Example statements might be that all menus should sit in a bottom panel, or that every screen should provide *'Help'* and *'Exit'* options.

Requirements Specification

This document covers the educational requirements and technical requirements and should be as factual as possible. It has to specify all the information components of the project.

The main elements in the requirements specification are:

Aim

This specifies the educational/entertainment requirements of the project and identifies the target audience. It also lists the assumptions of the target audience. For example, a tutorial on *'computers for beginners'* makes different assumptions from a tutorial on *'advanced networking techniques'*. In the first case, the users may not even know how to use mouse, while the other set of users will understand even advanced terminology used in the text. The project has to take into account the likely abilities and limitations of the users, understanding what they will want to do and what problems they may encounter using the package.

This section may also detail any educational requirements and tools. For example, a teaching application may begin by listing the expected learning outcomes from using the package and may include self-test questions at the end of each section. The package may supplement the learning of those doing badly in the self-assessments by supplying additional material and references for the subject areas in which the user scored less well. Educational packages may also include a glossary of terms or explanations of acronyms.

Technical requirements

This specifies all hardware requirements, including the specification of the computer and all peripherals. This is dependent upon the delivery method (CD, web, intranet, or kiosk). For example, projects designed for standalone kiosks have a specific set of requirements- such as the need for a touch screen or large screen monitor. Other possible factors are particular video/audio CODECs or add-ons (e.g. QuickTime), specialist drivers, sound card, and a particular amount of memory or hard disk space. The specification may also lay down performance requirements such as the speed of computer, the access time of a CD-drive or hard disk, the screen resolution, the colour depth and frame handling rates of graphics cards, or the lowest acceptable version of the operating system.

Navigation requirements

This specifies the general interface look (e.g. web-style, windows-style, image maps, etc.) It also details the specific navigational requirements of the project (see the later section on this topic).

Screen layout specification

This specifies the position of all the project's main elements and may include menus, buttons, active screen areas, video display areas, etc.

Some of these sections are inter-related. For example, if the technical requirements specify the use of a touch screen, then the screen layout specification will have to reflect this by stating that menu buttons have to be spaced slightly further apart. Similarly, designing a project to set and assess student performance in examinations or training exercises the project may mean that the project is specially designed for use on an intranet or extranet.

Design specification

The design phase lays out how the project will work in detail. A number of methods are used by different developers, but a top-down approach (where the main functions are outlined followed by subsidiary functions, continuing to the end of the outline) and flowcharts (showing the links between screen pages) are common development methods. The design phase produces all the content details. This will cover all internal resources (i.e. the company's own talent, hardware and raw material) and requirements for buying in skills (e.g. commissioning photographers, video camera teams, sound studios, graphics artists, animators, voice-over artists, etc).   Details of copyright would also be addressed at this stage.

Presentation structures

Thought has to be given on how screens are linked, which screens are linked and how the user is likely to view and use the project. Above all, navigation must be obvious and intuitive. For example if the project is an electronic book, screens could use a page metaphor. Individual screens would be displayed like book pages, with page turning arrows. The most likely structures to be implemented are:

Hierarchical structure tree

The project content is broken down into different sections and each section, in turn, sub-divides its information into more detailed options.   Generally, moving down provides more specific information while moving upwards provides more generalised information.   The diagram shows links moving <u>down</u> the structure.   When the user clicks the link (i.e. menu button, hyperlink, etc) the screen pointed to by the link is displayed. In practice, there will be links allowing the 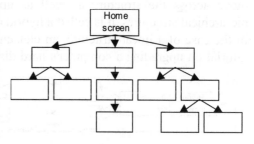 user to move back <u>up</u> to a previous screen and probably move directly to the home screen.

Linear structure

Some projects benefit from a linear structure where the user is prevented from jumping around the project. This known *as 'directed learning'*. These projects present ideas in a progressive fashion (i.e. 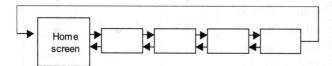 the user requires to acquire one piece of information before the next piece makes any sense).   Example projects are those where order is important (e.g. step-by step cookery or car maintenance instructions) or where ideas build on previous ideas (e.g. telling a story or developing certain training programmes). A linear structure only provides links that step the user forwards or backwards through the project to allow the user to review information. The project will also provide a link in the last screen to return the user to the home screen.

A web site variation on linear structures is a single large web page with links pointing to sections within that page. This is common on pages with large text content. The advantage for the site designer is that one large file is easier to update than a collection of files.   It also allows existing text documents to be quickly converted into hypertext pages.   From the user's point of view, a single large web page is easier to print out than a collection of smaller files.

There are also a number of disadvantages for users in this method.   The file is large and takes a long time to download.   The user spends time and telephone costs downloading whole chunks of the page that may be of no particular interest, just to get to the one required item.   Once the page is downloaded, it can be difficult to navigate.

In the example shown, the top of the page provides all the links to the sections of the document.   But once a user jumps halfway down a long document, there is no further navigation apart from links to return to the top of the page.   Adding links to point to other sections of the document is impractical in a document with lots of sections. Imagine if the example document had 50 sections instead of three.   While it may just be acceptable to have 50 links in the top menu, repeating the 50 links after every section makes the page extremely cumbersome.   However, this method is commonly used in reference works, where users are expected to be more patient and diligent.

Web structure

The web, or *'network'*, mesh matrix structure has an opening home screen with some initial links.   The user is encouraged to wander round the links without any particular order.   This is useful for projects where there is no evident strong link between one screen and another and there is no hierarchy of information.   An example of this type of project is one promoting a particular holiday resort.   The project may have many screens with information on travel, climate, currency, historical sites, restaurants, entertainment and so on.   Each screen can be read without having any special relevance to any other screen.

Hybrid structures

An entirely hierarchical structure is cumbersome to use, since the user has to go all the way back up the structure to navigate down another path.   It is more user-friendly to provide links that allow the user to move <u>across</u> the structure as well as up and down.   Since this combines elements of linear and hierarchical structures, it is called a hybrid or composite structure.

In the case of a linear structure, an element of choice can be built into the serial links. For example, a tutorial on upgrading a computer's hard disk has many logical steps. However, there are different steps

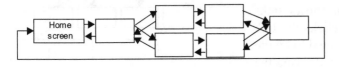

for fitting an IDE drive compared to fitting a SCSI drive. The user chooses which path to follow.   After the steps for that choice are navigated through, the user joins the main common linear path again.

A further variant is the *'menu structure'*. This is a simplification of the hierarchical structure, with linear elements. A number of routes are displayed in an opening menu.   Each route consists of a linear set of screens. When the set of screens is completed, the user is automatically returned to the opening menu.   This is different from the hierarchical structure, which allows further sub-routes at each lower level.   While the hierarchical structure is useful for further detailed information at each lower level, the menu structure is useful for taking a user through a collection of

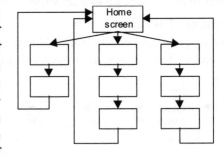

tasks. For example, a project on financial investments may have an opening menu's opening screen that offer options on different investment schemes (ISAs, TESSAs, Bonds, etc.). Choosing a particular menu option results in the user being taken through a linear presentation on that subject.

The two main guides that are produced from the design phase are:
- Navigation maps
- Storyboards

A project consists of many separate, but linked, screens. The navigation map describes how each screen is linked and the storyboard describes what happens inside each screen.

Navigation maps

This is required for all but the very simplest of projects. It details every connection between one part of the project and another. Users navigate (i.e. move round) the application by choosing menu options, clicking on icons, buttons or hypertext entries, or clicking on *'hotspots'* (active areas of the screen - e.g. a country on a map). The map shows where the user is taken on activating one of the navigation tools.

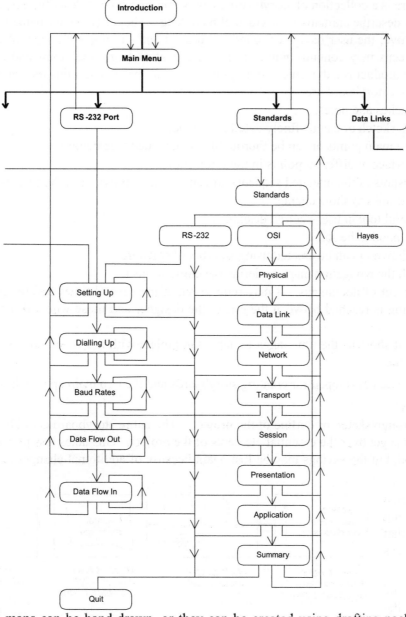

Navigation maps can be hand-drawn, or they can be created using drafting packages such as Visio, or even using Word's Flowchart AutoShapes.

Ideally, the method should allow quick and easy alterations and additions to the structure and this would favour a dedicated drafting package.

There is no preferred method or layout for creating navigation maps (unless an organisation has set its own internal standards). The over-riding requirement is that the map be legible and complete.

The diagram below illustrates part of a navigation map for a tutorial on data communications.

Notes:

Each screen has a direct link back to the main menu. Each screen has a direct link to quit. The *'Summary'* screen has a link back to the *'OSI'* sub-menu. Some screens show internal loops as shown on the extract on the right. These screens contain animations and the user can opt to re-run the animations as often as required, before moving on.

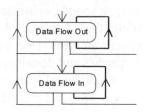

Storyboards

This is a set of sketches and notes that describe each scene, video clip, audio clip, text, navigation icon, and the mood to be set. A single storyboard might be enough to describe a small project whose screens are made up of static, or largely static material. Its purpose here is to document the layout and features of each screen (fonts, colours, navigation buttons, etc.).

Most often, though, there is a collection of storyboards, with some storyboards describing a particular set of screens, while others describe animations or video clip contents. They derive their name from the fact that a project is interactive; the user navigates round the project and - in doing so - is told a story. In addition, individual screens may contain their own dynamic content (e.g. video clips and animations). Since using the finished product is a dynamic activity, the storyboard has to chart this movement.

The essential features of a storyboard are:

- It is a set of sketches and notes.
- It can be a rough sketch or can be finely detailed (see below).
- It can convey the main points or can be thoroughly documented (see below).
- It shows the interface at different points in the interaction.
- It provides snapshots of the intended sequence to convey the impression of the final result.
- It provides key frames to show clients.
- It provides a useful tool in user-centred design.
- It describes the mood to be set.
- It can be hand-drawn or can be created using storyboard software.
- It combines with the navigation maps to define the entire project.
- It is not a static set of documents. It may require redrafting several times before agreement and understanding is reached between the client, the designer and those who will implement the project.
- Used correctly, it shortens the time taken to agree the project with the client, and also speeds up production time.

Many systems that have been developed for creating storyboards and the two main approaches are:

Schematic approach

This is basically just a rough sketch or outline of the project. The entire storyboard could be drawn and hand-written. The aim is get over the essential elements of the project. This takes less preparation time than the detailed method, but the savings may be lost again because of additional changes and additions at a later stage.

Consider the rough sketch in the illustration. Its aim is to illustrate the way that the opening screens unfold.

However, without the detailed notes under the

scrolling message on conditions of use	photo 2002/3 Range Credits	Chairman's message	Main Menu
18 point yellow Arial on a black background, music	photograph of latest model fades up	10 point black Arial on a light grey background	see Main Menu storyboard

boxes, there would be considerable possibilities for wasted time and wasted resources, as the output from the programmers is found not to match the expectations of the client. Storyboards that are more of a rough guide sometimes require more versions to be produced to even adequately define the overall parameters of the project.

Detailed approach

This approach provides full details of every screen, including descriptions of the text, fonts, graphics, images, sounds, animations, videos, button shapes and sizes, user responses, etc.

While this takes much longer to prepare, it eliminates most ambiguities at an early stage. It leaves less margin for error at the implementation stage and less scope for client misunderstanding.

It sketches and describes each scene, image, video clip, audio clip, text, and navigation icon. Each screen of the storyboard is accompanied by a full description, containing:

- Title and general description.
- Name and description, or description of function, of each object appearing on the screen.

Example

A college project displays course information to potential new students. After choosing a subject area (e.g. computing, media studies, applied science, etc), the viewer is presented with information on the courses on offer. The example below is the screen that describes a set of computing courses.

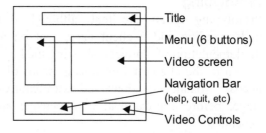

Title	Computing Courses Descriptions Screen
Description	The user chooses a course from the menu and is shown a short video showing the college's computing facilities and class activities.
Background	A light grey embossed image of the college main building.
Screen title	Displays the name of the computing department. Animates in from the left. Arial Bold Italic 36 point blue.
Menu button 1	Runs the video describing the HNC course in computing. Rollover button 100x30, chiselled 12 point text on dark marble face.
Menu button 2	Runs the video describing the HND course in information technology. Rollover button 100x30, chiselled 12 point text on dark marble face.
Menu button 3	Runs the video describing the HNC in multimedia. Rollover button 100x30, chiselled 12 point text on dark marble face.
Menu button 4	Runs the video describing the HND in networking. Rollover button 100x30, chiselled 12 point text on dark marble face.
Menu button 5	Runs the video describing the HNC in graphic design. Rollover button 100x30, chiselled 12 point text on dark marble face.
Menu button 6	Runs the video describing the HND in hardware support. Rollover button 100x30, chiselled 12 point text on dark marble face.
Video screen	Displays the video chosen from the menu bar. 320x 240 full-colour AVI.
Video controls	Provides user control over the play of the video clip. Stop/Pause/Replay.
Navigation bar	Provides user control over project navigation. Quit/Return to Main Screen/ Go to Enrolment Screen

Animation example

The above example works fine with screens that are static or have simple moving elements.

The storyboards for animations and video clips are more complex, in that they have to show the positions of objects at different points in time.

The next example shows the steps for an animation that shows one way that numbers can be sorted into ascending order. It shows movements and the resulting states for each stage of the animation.

A hand-drawn representation is perfectly satisfactory for this. There is no need to spend extra time producing perfect images. The aim is to show the order that events take place and the movements in the animation.

This animation would likely run in a window of the main screen. The main screen details (background, buttons, colours, etc.) would already have been described in a separate document. This sketch would therefore be accompanied with details of the animation's timing, along with the colour/content of the background and the size, font style and colour of the numeric elements.

It is helpful if a template is created containing the empty boxes that will contain the animation. The little time spent on preparing a master template is repaid later. The result is a cleaner presentation where the elements inside the boxes become the focus of attention.

Prototyping

Prototyping is an excellent, although time-consuming, way to develop an understanding and a client agreement on a project. A prototype is a partial implementation of a project, showing the key structural and layout details. This is shown to the client and used as a means of sharpening up the definition of their needs. Misunderstandings and extra features can be picked up and settled at this stage, before a great deal of expensive and possibly wasted effort has been expended.

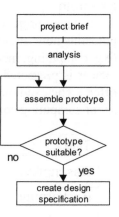

The last part of this chapter looks in detail at testing methods. Many of these can be applied to testing the prototype.

Prototype testing provides two valuable benefits:

- It identifies design or content problems at an early stage, before too much time has been wasted on a fuller implementation.

- It provides a fully working prototype to demonstrate to the client.

The Media Elements

The main media elements of a project will be recognised at an early stage, with the other elements being added later. The navigation maps describe how pages are linked and the screen content described in the storyboards need to be assembled.

Text

The display of multimedia text requires only a standard PC monitor and the main concern is how the text is accessed. The user requires to access specific subjects from a huge range of material. The text-handling software should be capable of detecting and displaying all stored material on the user's chosen subject. The user also requires the ability to explore cross-references in the material, to look at an item in further detail before returning to the main theme. These are the *'hypertext'* elements previously described. These may require the user to type in the data to be searched for or to select from a menu. Another method is to click the mouse on a key word or phrase within the displayed text. These elements can be seen in use in various Windows Help systems.

Text Creation

All multimedia applications employ text and the attributes used should reflect the nature of the application. The attributes to choose from are text face (what the basic face looks like), font (its size), style (normal, bold, italics, underlined), justification (left, right, centred) and colour. A psychedelic or bizarre collection of text faces and colours may fit the mood of some music applications but would be entirely inappropriate for a training package for funeral undertakers. Too much text on the screen repels viewers while text that is too small or too large makes the viewer uncomfortable. The number of words on any one line should be no more than 8 or 10 and each line should make a single point. Text should be presented with a mix of upper and lower case characters. Any one screen should not have text of many different colours. However, colours used to highlight titles or hypertext links are effective.

Similarly the choice of words used in the text is important; the grammar should suit the intended audience. Young children should not be bamboozled with complex words and older users should not be patronised. Jargon, abbreviations and acronyms should also be avoided.

The authoring packages that create multimedia projects all have the normal cut, paste and copy facilities to improve the screen layout.

Text Importation

Multimedia authoring packages do not generally have spell-checking or grammar-checking features and the author has to be very careful that misspelled words do not slip through and mar an otherwise professional project. All packages allow text to be imported into the project and this is the safest way to protect against typing or grammatical errors. Text can be entered into a word-processed file, which can be checked before being imported into the authoring package's project. The file types allowed by the authoring package should be checked and the text file should be saved in one of the acceptable formats. In some cases, this may mean converting a Word 2000 file, for instance, into an older Word format to be acceptable by an older authoring package.

Graphic Images

A graphic can be stored as a bitmap, or as a vector image. For multimedia purposes, the majority of uses are filled by bitmap images, with vectors used for animations.

Bitmaps

A bitmapped image is one in which every pixel on the screen or in the image is *mapped* to a *bit* of data. With a monochrome picture there is a direct correlation between the number of screen pixels and the number of bits to store the picture. Each bit only stores whether the pixel is white or black. With colour pictures, each pixel is represented by a group of bits that determine the pixel's colour.

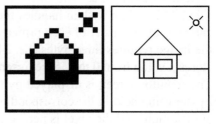

A simple bitmap   A vector image

Vectors

A vector image is one where the data represents not pixels, but *objects*. These objects could be text, circles, squares or such. The two example images display an extremely simplified image, shown in each type of format.   Note, however, that the bitmap has been rendered very crudely at small scale to show the basic idea; bitmaps are generally much more complex, and far more graphically impressive.

Depending on the image, either form could be more efficient. Bitmapping is far easier to use on complex coloured images such as digitised pictures, whereas a simple piece of computer-drawn clip-art would be much more efficiently stored as a vector oriented image. In the example above, the digitised picture would take up far less disk space. However, if a large bitmapped graphic could be easily converted to a vector image without loss of quality (which is not often the case) then the vector image would most likely be smaller in size.

As far as bitmapped images go, the only difference between one file format and another is the way the data is compressed, and how much extra information is needed, such as height and width of the picture, number of colours, etc. This information is normally stored in a portion of the file called a *'header'*.

Picture Scaling

The benefits of vector files lie in their *'scalability'*.   The user may wish to expand or shrink a picture so that it fits into a particular space in a document. This should be achieved with no loss of detail or picture distortion. The top diagram shows the result of scaling up a picture that contains a straight line to twice its height and width. Where there was a single pixel there is now a group of four pixels. Scaling the picture to four times its original size results in a group of 16 pixels for every original single pixel.   The result is a very *'blocky'* image, and this effect is known as *'pixellation'*.   The vector file on the other hand represents the line as *'draw a row of pixels between point A and point B'*.   Scaling the picture up still produces a single row of pixels, maintaining the fine detail.

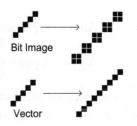

Bit Image

Vector

Image Properties

Although the content of bitmap images may vary widely, they all have basic properties that describe them. Every image has resolution and colour depth. Resolution describes the size of the image while colour depth describes how many colours appear in the image.

Resolution

As the chapter on display technology explained, the screen display surface can be depicted as a grid of separate picture elements (pixels). At any one moment, each element is individually controlled to display a particular colour and intensity. Modern monitor screens can easily handle a grid size of at least a thousand elements in each direction. The monitor's resolution describes its size when measured in pixels (i.e. how many pixels in the horizontal and vertical directions).

Similarly, the resolution of a graphic image is measured in terms of the number of pixels used for the image's width and height.

Colour Depth

The *'palette'* is the range of colours that the system is capable of displaying.   The table shows the most common colour depths used with graphic images.

Bit Depth	Number of Colours
8-bit colour	256 colours
16-bit	65,536 colours
24-bit	16.7 million colours

Typical working colour schemes

The 8-bit colour depth is commonly used for web graphics and clip art, while 16-bit and 24-bit depths are used for photo-realistic images. The 16-bit system is often described as *'high colour'* while the 24-bit system is described as *'true colour'*.

The 24-bit colour system handles the screen output in a straightforward manner. A 24-bit graphics card can vary the intensity of each primary colour (red, green and blue) to 256 different levels. Every pixel in the image requires three bytes (i.e. 24 bits), one for the intensity level of each primary colour. Each byte stores a value from 0 to 255, representing the 256 different intensity values.

The monitor screen is displayed by three guns and each gun's intensity is controlled at any one moment by the value held in the corresponding byte. Therefore, if all three values are 255, each gun's intensity is at maximum and the pixel is perceived as being white. If all values are at zero, the guns are switched off and the pixel is perceived as being black. The setting of different values for each gun produces the 16.7 million colours (i.e. 256 x 256 x 256). This is known as the *'RGB colour'* system and is used by JPEG files and other 24-bit file formats. This is also the method used by scanners, digital cameras, camcorders and monitors.

The 16-bit colour system only has 16 bits to store colour information on each pixel. Most commonly, it allocates 5 bits for red levels, 6 bits for green levels and 5 bits for blue levels. So the range of levels used to drive each monitor gun is less than with 24-bit systems and results in a set of 65,536 different colour combinations (i.e. 32 x 64 x 32).

File sizes

The final storage requirement for a bitmap image depends on its resolution and colour depth. The size of an uncompressed file is calculated thus:

$$\text{File Size} = \text{Bit Depth} \times \text{Screen Resolution} / 1024$$

Dividing by 1024 converts the answer into kilobytes. For very large files, the answer can be divided by a further 1024 to get the answer in megabytes.

Some example file sizes are:

An 8-bit image that fills a VGA screen would require

$$1 \times 640 \times 480 = 307{,}200 \text{ bytes}$$

An uncompressed true colour image at 800x600 requires

$$3 \times 800 \times 600 / 1024 / 1024 = 1.373\text{MB}$$

An uncompressed 1280 x 960 true colour image requires

$$3 \times 1280 \times 960 = 3{,}686{,}400 \text{ bytes or } 3.515\text{MB}.$$

The file sizes are often too big for practical use on web sites or in multimedia productions. The files can be reduced in size by various compression techniques. These attempt to store and convey the same image information using less bytes. In some cases, a little of the image quality is sacrificed to achieve this smaller file size. Files that degrade their quality are known as *'lossy'* systems.

File Formats

The most common graphic file formats on a PC are:

GIF: The acronym *'GIF'* is meant to be pronounced as *'jiff'*, but is usually pronounced *'giff'*. GIF was designed for fast transfer of graphics data over modems, and stands for Graphics Interchange Format. It compresses graphic images, making them smaller for faster transfer over the Internet. Now a very common file format, GIF files can be found on web sites and graphics packages everywhere. GIF files can have 2, 4, 8, 16, 32, 64, 128 or 256 colours. This doesn't mean that all those colours must be used, however.

PNG: The Portable Network Graphics standard was also produced for transferring bitmap graphics files over the Internet. It improves on GIFs by offering 24-bit colour and its own 'zlib' compression system.

PCX: These files use run-length encoding (RLE), which means that simple computer-generated pictures are stored fairly efficiently. It is comparatively inefficient at storing digitised or complicated pictures. Nonetheless, it has been around for some time and is now fairly common. PCX pictures may be found in monochrome (2 colours), 16 colours, 256 colours, 24-bit true colour, or even, rarely, in 4 colours.

BMP: BMP stands for Bit-Mapped Picture and is the Windows standard bitmap graphics file. BMP files are used for the background wallpaper in Windows. It is uncompressed, meaning that simple pictures will occupy much more file space than is strictly necessary. It also means that complicated, true colour pictures will not require a sophisticated decoder to display.

JPEG: When the Joint Photographic Experts Group was appointed by the CCITT to design a graphic compression and storage scheme, the JPEG file format was eventually created. It uses *'lossy'* compression, which means that slight detail is lost during compression. The level of detail loss is controllable, and a substantial space saving can be made even with very little detail loss. The JPEG compression standard is a complicated process involving several levels, and at first specialised hardware was needed to perform the process. There is a lossless version of JPEG, but this may require the extra hardware. JPEG files are stored in true 24-bit colour, and the JPEG scheme is much less efficient in storing images of any lower colour range.

WMF: The Windows Meta-File format is a comparatively simple vector oriented format born through the Windows interface. It is very effective for DTP. Like most vector formats, it is little used for multimedia.

Graphics Creation

Graphics creation software is available in *'painting'* format (for handling bitmapped images) and *'drawing'* format (for handling vector art).

The main considerations when creating graphics are:

FORMAT TYPE

Bitmaps can store photographic images while vector graphics consist of many drawn components. Bitmaps provide a range of manipulation options that are not available to vector images but lose much of their quality when scaled (see below). Vector images are scaleable with no loss of quality and would be the likely choice for creating symbols, line drawings and logos.

ELEMENTS

Unless the image is from a real-world source (i.e. scanned photograph, picture from a digital camera, or other bit image), it is constructed from a collection of squares, rectangles, circles, polygons, lines, arcs or bezier curves.

CONTENT

The elements have certain properties that can be altered for the maximum impact. These are element size (i.e. circle diameter, line width, rectangle dimensions) and appearance (e.g. box or circle colour, line type (plain, dotted).

LOCATION

Where the graphics appear on the screen and what proportion of the screen they occupy will depend on the nature of the final application. Large graphics are suitable where they have a crucial role in the presentation (e.g. a car repair program would use large and clear diagrams). Small graphics should be used where they should not distract the viewer from the main presentation. Similarly, graphics backgrounds should not overpower the foreground message.

PERSPECTIVE

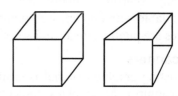

The monitor screen is two-dimensional; all screen content has only width and height. To provide the illusion of depth, images can be made to appear as if they recede into the background. The left box in the diagram has a front panel and rear panel of the same size. The rear panel in the right-hand box is smaller, which is perceived by the viewer as depth.

LAYER

Graphics layering allows one item to partially obscure another. In the boxes above, the front square is layered over the other lines and partially hides them from view.

Graphics Importation

Multimedia authoring packages do not generally provide more than elementary painting features that are sufficient for basic boxes and lines. For all other purposes, images are created in dedicated fully featured graphics packages and the finished item is imported into the authoring project.

Graphics Manipulation

The facilities offered by graphics packages vary and the most common manipulations are:

SCALING   The sides of the image can be pulled or squeezed so that it shrinks or expands to fill a given area. While this poses no problems for vector images, bitmaps will lose detail on shrinking and will become *'blocky'* when expanded.

CLIPPING/CROPPING Images often contain more detail than is required.   This distracts the viewer from the essential detail and occupies more disk space than is necessary. The image can be clipped or cropped.   This brings the picture in from the top or bottom, or left and right borders.   The example shows the continent of Africa being taken from a map of the globe.

Cropping

ROTATING   The text can be rotated from its normal horizontal axis to any degree and in any direction.   This can be used for visual effect or can be used to align the text along the outline of an object.

TRANSITIONS   As with text transitions, the graphic can be written to the screen in a pre-defined way such as being drawn from the left or filling in from the centre outwards.

FILLING   The diagram shows a number of squares that have been filled with either a plain solid colour, a fountain fill (e.g. linear, radial or conical gradations) or a pre-determined pattern (e.g. bricks, curtains, granite).

Plain   Linear Radial Conical Texture

REFLECTIONS   A mirror image of an object can be in either the vertical plane, as in the example, or in the horizontal plane. It is used for visual effect, or to save drawing time by drawing half of a symmetrical shape and creating an identical mirror image of the other half.

Reflections
Reflections

MORPHING   This takes two images and creates a set of intermediate images, showing the stages of transformation from one to the other. Morphing can be applied to objects (e.g. swords are turned into ploughshares) or photographs.

Gathering elements

Once the presentation's content is formulated, the designer has to decide on the source of any graphics and animations, special sound effects or musical accompaniment.   Some elements, such as photographs of products, have to be created in-house. Others, such as images of buttons and clip art, are available for use from a variety of clipart collections, many of them royalty free.

There are many varied ways to gather elements for a multimedia presentation.

Internet

The Internet is a very useful source. It provides access to the latest libraries of clip art, sound samples, pre-defined buttons, etc.   Some sites provide free clip art while others provide subscription services to royalty-free resources.

CD-ROM Sources

Many companies supply CDs, either singly or as collections, of royalty-free samples.   CD-ROMs are available with clip art, web graphics, digitised pictures, sound samples, and music clips.   Some of these files are public domain and some are copyrighted.

Scanners

Existing graphic material is easily incorporated into presentations using a scanner. It captures the graphics contents from any sheet of paper and converts it into a graphics file.   They can save the data in a variety of formats such as TIFF, BMP, PCX, GIF, or JPEG.   The scanner is able to handle line drawings, text and full photographs. Any material that is captured has to be within the laws of copyright. This means that pictures from newspapers and magazines cannot be used without

Flatbed Scanner

permission. Similarly, the law covers the illegal copying of company logos, company letterheads, bank notes, etc. Nevertheless, the device is very convenient for converting pen sketches, users' signatures and any authorised photographs.

The most common scanner is the flatbed model.   This is usually an A4 size device, where the sheet to be scanned is placed on a glass plate. In this respect, the scanner is similar to a photocopier. However, the data read is saved straight to a disk file rather than being used to directly produce a replica sheet. Modern flatbeds come with either USB or SCSI interfaces, though earlier models may use Parallel ports.

Flatbed scanner resolutions work up to around 9600dpi. 300dpi is generally considered as minimum standard for DTP work but screen-based multimedia does not require such high scanning resolutions. Dependent upon the monitor size and the screen mode only around 90 pixels are displayed for each screen inch. Any scanning at a higher dpi rate produces no improvement in quality, while consuming much more disk storage space. Modern scanners are 'Twain' compatible. This is the Windows interface agreed by major scanner manufacturers.

Screen Capture
Material for multimedia can be culled from almost anywhere, to do almost anything. For example, to create a CAL demonstration to teach people a certain technique in Microsoft Word, the *Alt+PrtScr* keystrokes can be used to capture the screen in the midst of using the technique. This can be pasted into a graphics package such as PhotoShop or Paint Shop Pro and saved as a normal graphics file (e.g. a GIF file or a JPEG file).

Still Capture
A still image can be taken from a video clip, using video editing software. Of course, a digitised picture can rarely be used *'as is'*. Generally, a digitised picture has to be manually re-touched, to remove such things as movement artefacts, (generated when a moving image is being digitised).

Digital Cameras
An alternative is to use a digital camera. These have all the features of normal cameras (e.g. zoom, focus, shutter speed, etc) but the image is digitised and saved to memory card or to mini-disc inside the camera. The number of pictures that can be stored depends upon the size of the flash memory or mini-disc, the picture resolution and the compression ratio. Older models took 320x240 or 640x480 pictures. Most budget models now take pictures at 1024x768 or greater, while semi-professional models handle around 3008x2000 (i.e.6 megapixels).

The quality from the higher resolution cameras rivals the resolution of a 35mm slide. There remains an argument that it is more effective to capture images using a 'real' camera, with the developed photographs being scanned with a high-resolution scanner. Most digital camcorders are now also able to capture still images. The images are either stored on the videotape or on memory modules such as the Sony Memory Stick. Digital cameras use a variety of methods to transfer the stored images to a PC, such as USB, serial and infrared links. Others use removable storage such as floppy disks or CD-R disks.

Copyright
While professionals rarely react to their work being adopted for personal use, they will take action when their photographs, film clips, audio tracks, etc are re-used in a commercial product. Great care should be taken to protect against legal action. The Copyright Licensing Agency run a *'Copywatch'* scheme to detect illegal copying and advice can be sought from them at 90 Tottenham Court Rd, London W1P 0LP (Tel 0171-436-5931). If in doubt, seek permission or stick to using copyright-free sound, pictures and clip-art collections. This is covered in more detail on the chapter on web site creation.

Animation
Animation is simply a collection of graphic images being displayed on the screen one after the other in quick succession. The eye possesses a persistence of vision such that, if the images are updated quickly enough, the viewer does not detect the sequence as a set of different pictures. In this way, animation creates the illusion of movement. This is the technique used to show movies in the film theatre or on television. There are two approaches to animation:

Bitmapped
Each frame is comprised of a separate bitmap image. The image can be computer-created or be a photographic image. Ideally, an animation should display at 25 or 30 frames per second. Anything below 10fps is regarded as too slow to maintain the illusion of continuous movement.

This type is mainly seen in *"animated GIFs"* which are widely used on web sites. Animation creation software ranges from simple programs such as GIF Animator, Animation Shop and Disney's Animation Studio to top-of-the-range professional products such as Autodesk Animator Pro.

The downside to this method is the file size required to store all the individual images.

Vector

Another approach, useful in cartoon work and web site animation, is to use vector drawn images to reduce the file size. It does mean, however, that the format does not handle photographic sequences. This type is used with packages such as *'Flash'* and *'Director'*.

Sound cards

Digitised sound is used in multimedia to accompany animations and graphics, giving a more convincing presentation. It can also be used to link sounds to events. Sound is fed into a sound card in analogue format, from a microphone or other audio source. However, the computer is only capable of storing data in digital format. So the card has to convert analogue sounds into a digital equivalent. This is achieved by a chip in the sound card called the *'ADC'* - the *'Analogue-to-Digital-Converter'*. The ADC converts a sample of sound into a series

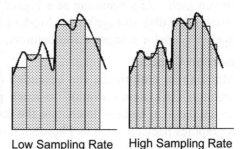

Low Sampling Rate   High Sampling Rate

of numbers that can be stored to disk for later replay. The numbers store the amplitude of the sound waveform at different points during the time of the sound sample.

Two factors determine the quality of digitised sound:

- The dynamic range (i.e. the accuracy in terms of absolute amplitudes).
- The sampling rate (i.e. the accuracy of the amplitude at any one instant).

Dynamic Range

The more complex the waveform to be stored, the greater total of different numbers required to store the sound. The span from the lowest amplitude to the greatest amplitude is known as the *'dynamic range'*. This is sometimes also described as *'resolution'* or *'bit-range'*.

In the left diagram, only a small number of bits are allocated to store the waveform so it is incapable of handling the small amplitude variations in the waveform and these details are averaged away. In that case, the card produces a series of numbers that approximate to the overall waveform but the harmonics that make a piano sound different from a guitar are lost as are the harmonics

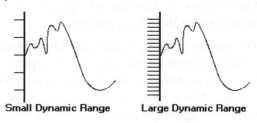

Small Dynamic Range   Large Dynamic Range

that differentiate between different human voices. The right-hand diagram shows a greater dynamic range allowing the same analogue signal to be converted into a greater number of digital levels. This allows for a greater clarity of reproduction, as the replayed sound is closer to the original sound. 16-bit sound cards handle a range of 65,536 different sound levels, giving a quality expected from a domestic audio CD system. This is usually sufficient for audio clips for web sites and multimedia projects.

Sampling Rate

The dynamic range determines the accuracy of the amplitude reading at any one point in time. Of equal importance is the frequency of taking these readings. If the readings are too infrequent, an amplitude change will pass undetected. If the readings are too frequent, the conversion will produce a giant series of amplitude readings. The timing of the conversions is known as the *'sampling rate'* and is measured in kilohertz (i.e. how many thousand amplitude conversions are carried out each second).

The left diagram shows the effects of a low sampling rate. The sound sample is converted into six samples with varying amplitude levels. When the sample is replayed, the sound card uses the six levels to reconstruct the sound wave. This sound wave is then amplified and sent to the loudspeakers.

As the diagram shows, the final output is an approximation of the original sound with a considerable loss of detail. The inertia in the loudspeaker cones acts to smooth the transitions between different output voltage levels from the card. The right-hand diagram shows the same sound sample with twice the sampling rate. The audio is now stored in twelve different samples and this is much more representative of the original sound source. In practice, the sampling rate must be at least double the frequency of the highest frequency to be sampled. Since the average human ear can only hear frequencies up to about 20KHz, a sampling rate of 44KHz is adequate for most uses. Indeed, the human voice itself does not produce sounds above much more than 3KHz.

Most sound cards operate up to 44.1KHz, the same rate as audio CD and sampling rates are adjustable down to as low as 4KHz.

Storage Overheads

Current sound cards have stereo channels, allowing each channel to process independent contents.   This improves the quality of the reproduced sound but requires double the disk space.   The table shows the amount of disk space required for even short digitised samples, with the top quality 44.1KHz sampling rate.   A four-minute song in stereo requires a staggering 42MB of disk space!

	bytes per sec	bytes per min
8-bit mono	44,100	2,646,000
8-bit stereo	88,200	5,292,000
16-bit mono	88,200	5,292,000
16-bit stereo	176,400	10,584,000

Minimising storage overheads

A number of techniques are employed to minimise the size of audio files and these include:

- Forcing the system down to a 22.05KHz sampling rate when recording in stereo.
- Using mono instead of stereo, where the stereophonic effect is not required (e.g. a voiceover).
- Compressing the file on recording and decompressing again on playback. This can use a CODEC chip (compression/decompression) to carry out these tasks in hardware to speed the process. Software CODECS such as ADPCM (see below) are available as alternatives to hardware implementations.   These systems offer a range of possible compression ratios, ranging from low-compression lossless samples to high-compression samples with loss of some detail.

Audio File Formats

All audio file formats are used to store the same audio content; only the manner of storage is different. The most important sound file formats are:

WAV: Introduced along with Windows, the WAV file format is a simple sound sample with a short file header.   The benefit of WAV files is that many Windows programs can use them with a single Windows sound driver.   Of course, the Windows sound driver is not limited to WAV files, but Windows programs themselves tend to prefer WAV files since they are the native format for Windows sound.

ADPCM: The *'Adaptive Delta Pulse Code Modulation'* system takes standard audio that has been encoded into its normal PCM values and compresses the data so that it requires less space than its .WAV equivalent.   By only storing the deltas (i.e. changes between samples) it requires about a quarter of the normal disk space.   This is also the technique employed by Sony for its Mini Disc recorder/players.

MP3: MP3 files use the compression standard laid down in MPEG-1 Audio Layer III.   Audio MPEG MP3 compression produces file sizes that are up to 12 times smaller than the standard digitised version, with no loss of quality.   This format is now widely supported on web sites and in multimedia applications. It is also a popular medium for storing music tracks. MP3 files are played through a computer that has the decompression software installed, or through a dedicated standalone device.

Audio or music tracks stored on audio CDs can also be converted to MP3 files, known as *'ripping'*. Programs such as AudioGrabber and RealJukebox read the digital information straight off a CD track and store it on the hard disk as an MP3 file (or WAV file).   This process also ignores the sound card and provides an identical digital copy. Ripping should only be carried out on copyright free music and sound CDs, as conversion of commercial audio CDs is a breach of copyright law.

Existing WAV files can be converted to MP3 files using applications such as the freeware BladeEnc. MP3 files can also be converted back to WAV files when required, using programs such as WinAmp.

Most applications are able to play MP3 files, including Windows 98 onwards.

WMA : Windows Media Audio is Microsoft's response to the MP3 format. The Windows Media Packager can convert MP3 and WAV files into a WMA format, producing a considerably smaller file size.

RA : Real Audio files can be downloaded from the Internet and played later.   However, their main advantage is their ability to be *'streamed'* - the audio is immediately sent to the soundcard for playing as it is received, without waiting until the whole file is downloaded.

Recording a sound

Although a wide range of digitised sound samples exists, there will be many occasions when a specific message is required. The audio input can come from a microphone or can be from the *'line in'* socket of a sound card to allow the sampling of music or voice from a variety of sources such as CD, cassette tape, video tape, etc. The provisions of copyright will apply to such samples. Sound cards provide their own software to create audio samples and Windows has its own simple utility called *'Sound Recorder'* as shown in the diagram. The right hand button has a microphone icon and clicking on this icon starts a recording process. The time of the sample is shown on screen as the recording is made. When the recording is finished, the user clicks on the button to the left of the microphone. The final sample length is displayed. Clicking the middle button will cause the sample to be replayed.

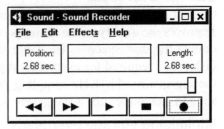

This system is adequate for day-to-day use but the more sophisticated software of the sound card utilities allows the selection of sampling rates. In Windows 98/ME/2000/XP/Vista, the Sound Recorder is found in the *'Entertainment'* option of *'Accessories'*.

Editing a sound

A user-created sound sample may not be immediately usable. It may contain unwanted pauses or require augmenting by special effects before it is used. The *'Sound Recorder'* utility has some basic tools. Clicking the arrow key icons moves the sample through different time stages of the waveform and the wave shape can be seen in a window while this is being adjusted. Facilities include deleting all silences or unwanted sounds before the chosen time point or after the chosen time point. This allows unwanted sections to be removed and results in a smaller sample file. Other facilities include introducing echo effects, reversing the sound sample and mixing in other sound samples. The finished file can be saved as a WAV file for later use. Audio editing software provides further facilities. These include the gradual fading up or down of sounds, the panning of sounds between stereo channels (i.e. the volume of the sound in the left channel is decreased while the volume in the right channel is increased), cut and paste operations and other waveform editing.

Video

Where a continuous sequence of movement is to be recorded, a video capture card is required.
The video card may accept a number of different video signals, such as the outputs from:
- An analogue camcorder connected to a card's VHS input socket.
- A video recorder connected to the card's VHS input socket.
- A digital camcorder connected to a card's FireWire socket.

In addition, a web cam can be connected directly to the computer's USB socket.

The recording device must also interface with the computer system through software. This may involve the installation of a device driver (to recognise the particular video source), CODECs (to handle the compression/decompression of files – see more details later) and software to handle the capture process.

Windows ME and XP supply their own video capture software (Microsoft Movie Maker) and most video capture cards supply their own device drivers and capture software).

Typical frame rates and their uses	
0fps	Still frame
10fps	Web video
15fps	Minimum acceptable for motion
24fps	Motion pictures
25fps	British television (PAL)
30fps	American television (NTSC)

Once the hardware and software is installed, these cards capture complete moving video sequences. The chart shows the number of frames displayed per second in various systems, to maintain the illusion of continual movement. The capturing of a sequence is carried out as a single operation.

File Formats

There are four main formats for storing video files:

AVI: The **A**udio **V**ideo **I**nterleave format is the Windows standard that stores the audio and video information as a single file. The video data and audio data is divided into blocks and interleaved in the file. Since both streams of data are stored next to each other in time, it aids the synchronisation process. Where video and audio files are held separately, the delays in reading both sets of data from disk and interpreting the separate streams leads to difficulty in keeping the sound synchronised to the picture. AVI files can be in compressed or uncompressed format depending whether one of the compression algorithms has been applied to them.

QuickTime: The *'Macintosh'* range of computers made by Apple has long led the field in innovation and is still the most popular system for use with art, design and DTP. Unfortunately, the Mac computer range is not compatible with PCs as they use a different processor range that uses different machine code instructions. Apple originally produced the QuickTime video format for their range of Macintosh machines. This format also interleaves audio and video information. QuickTime and AVI files can be played on a PC that has a QuickTime driver installed (see later).

MPEG : The Motion Picture Experts Group standard MPEG-1 compression forms the core of VideoCD as used in CD-I players, etc. and can store about 70 minutes of video on a single CD. The later version, MPEG-2, is used with DVD players. MPEG is explained more fully later.

Real Video & WMV : These are two *'streamed'* media formats for use on the Internet, from RealNetworks and Microsoft. They require special player software that downloads a video track as a set of separate blocks. This allows the video to be displayed immediately, without waiting until the whole file is downloaded. If the blocks arrive faster than they can be played, they are stored in a memory buffer. Of course, if the blocks arrive slower than required, the file cannot be played continuously.

Video Storage

Like animations, full-motion video can easily result in huge files.

Video has to store and play back between 15 and 30 individual screens per second. The storage capacity per second of video can be calculated thus:

File Size = Bit Depth x Screen Resolution x Frames/Sec

This is divided by 8 to get the answer in bytes and divided again by 1,048,576 to get the answer in MBs.

A 16Mcolour (i.e. 24 bits) MPEG-1 (i.e. 352x288) at a 25fps screen update would require

352 x 288 x 24 x 25 / 8 / 1048576 = 7.25MB/sec

Most common use	Screen Resolution	Frame Rate	Storage/Sec before compression
PAL MPEG-1	352 x 288	25	7.25MB
PAL MPEG-2	720 x 576	25	29.66MB
PAL MPEG-2 widescreen	1280 x 576	25	52.73MB
NTSC MPEG-1	352 x 240	30	7.25MB
NTSC MPEG-2	720 x 480	30	29.66MB
NTSC MPEG-2 widescreen	1013 x 480	30	41.73MB

The chart shows the amount of storage required for a range of popular displays.

The figures range from 7.25MBs per second for MPEG-1 to 52.73MBs per second for MPEG-2 widescreen. The saving and playing back of live video involves not only the storage but also the transfer of huge amounts of data. This requires a fast hard disk, a fast CPU and a fast video system.

These storage figures are not practical and a number of methods are introduced to reduce this size:

- Using only a portion of the screen to display the video. If the video occupies a quarter of the screen area, it only needs a quarter of the storage space. This is commonly used on CDs to accommodate the low performance of most disks/CPUs/video cards.
- Reducing the colour palette to 256 colours may mean a barely noticeable loss of colour gradation, but would result in a video clip that is a third of the size of a 16.78m colour clip.
- Lowering the frame rate at which the picture is displayed. This makes savings but the picture is jerkier.
- Compressing the files for storage and decompressing them when they are to be played. Unlike the other three methods, compression need not produce any deterioration in picture quality. The user has the option to make even bigger savings at the expense of some picture quality.

Codec Types

The CODEC (compressor/decompressor) is an engine that shrinks the files on saving and expands them again when they are to be used. CODECs can be implemented in either hardware or software. Hardware CODECs are more expensive but, because they use dedicated chips instead of the computer's CPU time, they are significantly more efficient.

The AVI (Audio Video Interleave) format is a popular Windows standard and is described earlier. Windows comes with many CODECs pre-installed.

These all result in files with 'AVI' extension and are:

Cinepak : Developed by Apple for their SuperMac computers and now licensed to Microsoft, it is currently the most popular of the Video for Windows CODECs. It is also supplied with Apple's QuickTime. It handles 8-bit colour (for animations and cartoons) and 24-bit (for everything else). This is a good general purpose CODEC for CD ROM distribution but has been replaced by more efficient CODECs for slow web data rates (below 30kbps).

Indeo : This system was initially developed by Intel as a CODEC for capture cards based on the Intel i750 video processor chip. Indeo 3.x had a slightly better compression ratio and compression time than Cinepak but introduced more artefacts. AVI files processed with the Indeo CODEC have had both interframe compression and run length encoding techniques applied (see earlier). Indeo 4.x, now renamed Video Interactive 4, took advantage of the new improvements in Pentium technology, such as MMX, to improve performance and quality. It also introduced transparency masks for their clips. This is the same technique as 'chroma key'. Version 5.0 is aimed at web video by including progressive download techniques.

RLE : Run Length Encoding takes a horizontal area of a colour and stores the length of the band rather than the individual pixels. This is very effective in animations where backgrounds are plain but produces poor results as a video CODEC.

M-JPEG

Motion-JPEG, called M-JPEG, is similar in basis to the JPEG graphic format. Each individual frame is compressed using JPEG techniques and each frame is stored individually and separately. By concentrating on individual frame compression, it produces less spectacular compression ratios (around 8:1) but provides 24-bit depth, higher quality and easier manipulation and editing. Its larger file size and subsequent increased data rate needs meant that it could not be supported by the slow speeds of early CD players and no mass-market M-JPEG players were produced. It is a popular storage and editing medium but is not used as for distribution. An M-JPEG clip would be converted into another format such as MPEG for distribution. It has the normal 'AVI' file extension, eg. 'wedding.avi'.

Other Codecs

Apart from the four CODECs supplied with Windows, there are some other very significant and popular CODECs that can be installed, such as MPEG, OpenDML M-JPEG and VDOWave.

QuickTime

Apple originally produced the QuickTime architecture for their range of Macintosh machines but it is now 'multi-platform' - versions are also produced for Windows and NT. Its files have the extension 'MOV', e.g. 'racing.mov', and are referred to as QuickTime movies. MOV files are 'cross platform' - if, for example, a MOV file is placed on a web site, it can be downloaded and played by any hardware system that has a QuickTime player.

MPEG

The Moving Pictures Experts Group format uses a complicated set of compression methods including spatial compression, Huffman coding and predictive compression - based on only saving the differences (or 'deltas') between successive frames. Depending on the quality and speed required, it may sometimes require expensive hardware, but can achieve surprising compression rates. These rates vary depending on the quality of the stored image, because MPEG compression is a type known as 'lossy' - i.e. the final image has lost small, less noticeable details in order to effect greater compression. Compression ratios up to 50:1 can be achieved before the picture quality deteriorates noticeably.

MPEG-1   Most systems are designed around MPEG-1 with data rates of around 1.4MBps and frame rates up to 30fps. It provides the lowest common formats as it can produce 340x240 at 30fps for American NTSC TV (or 352x288 at 25fps for European PAL TV) from a standard CD-ROM player; this is sometimes referred to as SIF - the Standard Interchange Format. It produces a result similar to television's VHS quality. Many video clips on CDs are designed for this format and don't therefore take advantage of the significant hardware improvements that modern PCs contain.   It is also a common multimedia format.

MPEG-2   MPEG-2 is a standard for higher quality with a resultant increase in data rates. It can deliver a screen resolution of 720x480 at a frame rate of 60fps.   This is the basis of DVD products. The increased demands of MPEG-2 have led to further improvements in component specifications.

MPEG-4   MPEG-4 Part 10 is the description given to a selection of video and audio encoding techniques. It is the standard to which individual codecs are designed and it defines a set of design levels (known as 'profiles').   Well-known codecs, such as DivX and XviD, come under this heading along with low-resolution/low bitrates for mobile phones and handheld video players.   At the other end of the range, it covers H.264 also referred to as AVC (Advanced Video Coding) for HDTV and Blu-Ray.   Different codecs encompass different levels of profiles but they are all designed to be backward compatible. Less well powered mobile devices such as mobile phones and video players are unable to meet the requirements of the upper profile levels.   HDTVs and other H.264 devices have the necessary CPU and graphics processing power to operate at the upper profiles – while still being able to handle video files that were created to a lower level of MPEG-4 profile.

Determining the CODEC used on an AVI File

Since an AVI file may have been encoded using one of a variety of CODECS, Windows provides a method to get a report on a file's configuration. If an AVI file is highlighted in *'Windows Explorer'* and the mouse right-hand button is clicked, the *'Properties'* option of the resulting menu produces the screen shown (with slight variations between different Windows versions).

The options include:

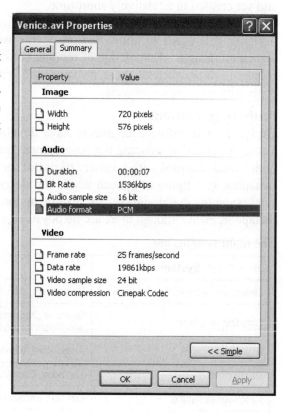

- The *'General'* option shows file dates, sizes, etc.
- The *'Details'* or *'Summary'* option shows that the file called *'Venice'* is designed to be run in a 720x576 screen at 25fps using a Cinepak CODEC.

Playback Systems

All video files have to be played back using some type of driver routine.   These routines can be implemented both in hardware or in software although hardware implementations are more efficient.

All AVI files compressed by a particular CODEC should be decompressed with that same CODEC.   So, an AVI file with Cinepak compression should be run using Cinepak decompression software.

Playing back MPEG

Clips that were created and saved using MPEG compression must be decompressed before the video information can be sent to the monitor. The machine showing these clips has to be fitted with an MPEG playback card or have MPEG decoding software routines.   The hardware implementation is potentially faster as the card contains chips that are dedicated to MPEG decoding.   This saves much of the computer's CPU time and is commonly implemented in graphics cards.

Software CODECs became more popular at one stage. The speed of CPUs and the general data transfer rates of computer systems have increased to a point where software MPEG decoding is possible, dispensing with the need for a dedicated decoder card.

Authoring Software

Having gathered the graphics, sound and music for the presentation, the developer's task is to integrate them and link them in the way laid down in his/her implementation plan. While it is possible to write simple applications directly at the keyboard, larger and more complex projects require a careful plan to be developed, as explained earlier.

All multimedia products can be written using conventional programming languages such as Pascal or C++, although they are time-consuming. Using GUI-oriented (graphical user interface) programming languages such as Delphi and Visual Basic provide pre-written routines for buttons, user input, etc., and so speed the development process. Best of all, multimedia authoring packages provide facilities to greatly speed up the development process. Although programming and authoring methods both require analysis and design skill, some authoring packages can produce very useful results with no coding skills whatsoever. Most packages are able to produce run-time versions - executable files that do not require the use of the original package to display them. Packages range from hobbyist products to those with full-blown commercial aspirations.

Approaches to authoring

An authoring system is an application that provides pre-programmed elements to speed the development of multimedia applications (e.g. ready-made buttons, etc). They create multimedia applications in a fraction of the time that would be required by script programming tools. Buttons, dialog boxes, etc. can be brought onto the screen, positioned and linked to functions - without writing any code. Interface design and screen editing are made much easier and quicker. Animations can be complex and detailed and yet created in a relatively short time.

Of course, there is still the same amount of time required to plan, design and create the content. The designer still needs to know how programs work and have an appreciation of heuristic thinking and algorithm design. Knowledge of module construction and basic screen construction skills are also still required. Nevertheless, these packages are learned much more quickly than programming languages, especially for simpler projects.

Authoring methods

Designers and software engineers have developed a number of approaches to multimedia authoring. These are aimed at reducing the development time through the provision of design systems that are easily understood, coupled with a variety of useful tools. Their methods are designed around 'metaphors'. A metaphor is a figure of speech where the description of one object is used to describe another object. For example, the designer can readily understand an authoring package that uses a 'page turning' metaphor, even although there are no physical pages that are turned.

The main systems are:

System	Typical products
Linear, frame-by-frame	PowerPoint, Illuminatus, Neobook, and many freeware/shareware products.
Scripting language	GLpro or programming languages such as Pascal or C++, with Visual Basic and Delphi supplying improved interface tools.
Iconic/flow control	Authorware, IconAuthor, Masterclass
Card/scripting	Toolbook, ClickWorks
Cast/score/scripting	Director, Emblaze, Flash
Hypermedia Linkage	Any HTML editor, with packages such as Dreamweaver supplying increased functionality and less scripting knowledge.

Linear, frame-by-frame metaphor

This is the simplest metaphor of all. The project is designed to run in a linear fashion. That means that it has a beginning and an end and the viewer is intended to watch the project's contents unfold a page at a time. There is little or no user control of the project, apart from perhaps pausing or exiting. This method is best suited to unattended presentations at exhibitions and in supermarkets and for some product promotions. Since the flow of material is determined for the viewer, there is only a single route to be followed and every piece of screen activity follows from the previous one in an orderly fashion.

Since the method is simple, the products are quickly assembled using basic authoring tools. There are a large number of freeware and shareware packages available for producing these kinds of projects and PowerPoint is the most common commercial product used for linear productions (although it can also offer some limited interactivity).

Programming

Programming requires scripts of code to be written by the developer. Early languages required complex scripts just to draw a box on the screen, while modern programming languages such as Delphi, Visual Basic and Visual C are blurring the boundaries between conventional programming and multimedia authoring. GUI-based development tools, such as Delphi and Visual Basic can bring in buttons, display graphics, and call up video and sound clips, etc. without resorting to heavy scripting.

Visual Basic, for example, uses a screen form (which can have a graphic image as a background), on which can be placed objects and controls. The developer then sets the properties that should apply to the controls. This is an *'event-driven'* system. Code is attached to a screen object and is only run when the object is activated. This allows some practical projects to be created without any coding. The package creates a compiled (i.e. self-running) product and provides comprehensive error checking and debugging facilities.

There are three types of scripting:

Scripting type	Example
Scripts to create the entire project.	GLPro is an authoring package that is entirely script-based, with no on-screen authoring.
Scripts that supplement authoring packages.	Director's Lingo script, Flash's ActionScript.
Internet advanced scripts.	JavaScript, Perl, etc.

Hypermedia linkage

This describes the linking of any number of separate resources to allow user access. The most common implementation is a web site, although CD's can use hyperlinks for navigation and for linking to wider resources through the Internet. This system produces the widest possible navigation facilities and the most likely methods for implementing these systems are HTML scripts, JavaScript, CGI scripts, etc.

Card/scripting

These are also sometimes called *'page-based'* systems. The project data is organised to simulate pages of a book, or a stack of cards. Each page has its own individual set of objects and its own layout. It can display graphics or play sounds, animations and video clips on any page.

It uses a book metaphor as its presentation format. Using navigation buttons, viewers can flick through the pages of the book in any order.

This presentation method is best used when a number of page sequences are used, although viewers can also jump between pages.

Examples of card-based authoring packages are Toolbook, Mediator and Illuminatus.

Iconic/flow control

This method makes the project's structure and links highly visible to the developer, as the main screens and user choices are represented on a flow chart.

These flow diagrams display the navigational links and flow of ideas. This aids the development of projects with complicated structures, as a top-down approach starts from the higher-level tasks and breaks them into lower levels tasks.

A flow chart plots the possible routes between activities; this is the *'navigation map'*. An activity is represented by an icon which could be a decision to be made, a user entry to be requested, a new screen of graphics to be shown, a video or sound clip to be run, and so on. At the design and implementation stages, groups of icons can be grouped together under a single icon - implementing a top-down design of sub-modules. Major points can be added to the flow line, and these can be returned to later to flesh out their sub-units and contents.

The example shows the second level of a package that displays a top menu with four choices (e.g. Memory Types, Organisation). Each choice produces a drop-down menu with other choices (e.g. Error Detection, Cache Memory).

Examples of such authoring packages are Authorware and IconAuthor.

Cast/score/scripting

These packages often use the terminology of the film producer or theatrical producer, with a *'stage'*, a *'cast'* and a *'score'*. Little wonder, then, that the most used package of this type is called *'Director'*.

The package uses a cast (i.e. the elements such as text, graphics, sound clips, video clips, user entry buttons or dialog boxes, screen effects, etc.) and a score (e.g. a chart of all events and when they will occur in time).

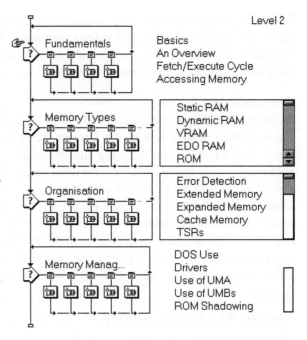

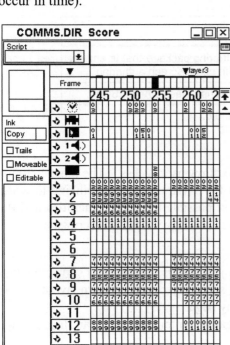

It is based on a *'timeline'* as in the example, where each vertical frame stores all the objects that are used during that particular timeslot.

Each object can therefore be controlled down to the precision of a single frame (for a 25fps production, this means control down to $1/25^{th}$ of a second). This allows animations to be set to precise durations, sound clips to be played at precise times that synchronise with other events, and so on.

All the project is laid out as a long chart of possible events (i.e. the timeline), navigation controls allow the user to jump to any point in the timeline. There is no concept of individual pages; just what will be displayed on the screen at any one time.

Other considerations

Apart from the design method, there are other considerations when choosing an authoring package:

- The range of drawing, animation, text manipulation facilities.
- The range of transitions and special effects.
- The range of packaging options (standalone executable, HTML file, Shockwave file, video clip, etc).
- Whether the package allows royalty-free distribution of the final project, or applies charges or conditions on the distribution. This may apply to a runtime module (a miniature version of the authoring package, with the development tools removed, leaving only the play functions).
- Whether the package can create cross-platform projects (e.g. can compile for PC or a Mac).

Scripting facilities

Some packages provide very simple navigation links but for greater control of navigation, and to support internal logic decisions, the author has to learn the programming language behind the package. The examples show typical simple scripts as used by the leading *'Director'* and *'Toolbook'* packages.

Director's Lingo
on mouseup   go to "quiz" end

Toolbook
TO HANDLE buttonClick   go to next page END buttonClick

Some authoring tools have no in-built scripting facilities (e.g. Illuminatus and Multimedia Fusion), some have very little (e.g. Mediator) and some have comprehensive facilities (e.g. Director and Toolbook).

Control facilities

In all multimedia presentations, the user approaches the application in an interactive way, expecting to be given control over the package. The three most important elements are:

Buttons

The user has to control the flow of information in a package. Normally this is achieved by the user clicking the mouse on on-screen *'buttons'* that represent a particular choice. The choice may be from a selection of menu options (i.e. where to go next) or might be from a selection of possible data entries (e.g. choosing a correct answer or saving or loading a set of data). Buttons can be the default grey variety provided in most authoring packages or can be user-defined such as pictures or shapes.

Alternatives to buttons are dialog boxes, where the user is asked to enter data (e.g. user name or age) and *'hot spots'* where areas of the screen act as equivalents of large buttons. Clicking a hot spot has the same effect as clicking a button but a hot spot can be an irregular shape. For example, this allows the user to click anywhere on the Isle of Wight in a screen map of the UK to see more information about that island.

Other on-screen system controls are:

- Radio buttons (i.e. only one option can be active at a time).
- Check boxes (i.e. more than option can be active at the same time).
- Scroll bars.
- File/directory selection.

Events

Normal conventional programs are written to be mainly sequential. The program starts at the beginning of the code and finishes at the end of the code. Multimedia products are explored in a different manner. With event-driven systems, code is attached to objects and remains inactive until it is called. Calls can be initiated by the user (e.g. clicking a mouse) or by the system (e.g. a timeout). The clicking of the button or hot spot is tied to a particular action. So clicking the *'Show Interview'* button always plays the same video clip. Clicking a *'More Details'* button may produce an entirely new screen with more information and a further set of buttons. Clicking the *'Quit'* button should exit the user from the package. These navigation activities are called *'simple branching'.* The earlier Director and Toolbook scripts showed examples of mouse events being detected and acted upon.

Control structures

For more control, *'conditional branching'* can be carried out. So, a user when presented with six buttons representing six levels of difficulty may only be allowed to pursue a higher level if the lower level has been successfully completed. The program has kept the user's previous performance in a set of variables and the branching allowed is a combination of what button the user pressed and what information is already stored. In a multi-choice question, the user may only be allowed three attempts.

Control can be passed to internal code using constructs such as:

     IF ...   e.g. if a user score is less than 50% ....
     REPEAT ...   e.g. repeat the question until the user chooses the correct answer.

Evaluation and testing

No projects work correctly first time. That is not a criticism of the team members or the team leaders. It is a result of the huge complexity arising from the size and scope of these projects. It is not an issue that only affects multimedia projects. All software suffers from the same problem (just how many bug fixes have Microsoft issued for their products?). The challenge is to recognise the inevitability of problems and to budget time and resources to tackle them.

Of course, prevention is better than cure and the organisation's culture should be one of minimising problems during the development process. A small design fault is easily fixed at the design stage. If it is missed and is allowed to shape the implementation of the project, it will be much more costly to put right at that later stage. The target of *'get it right first time'* minimises problems, reduces the hassle factor and saves a lot of money. Of course, extra money has to be spent on the testing but this is repaid many times over in the savings on bug fixing.

What can go wrong

To the question *'what can go wrong?'* there is only one answer - *'anything!'*

The problems are in three main categories:

Design flaws	These cover any mistakes made prior to commencing the implementation of the project. As such, they cover any shortcomings in the original specification. They could be learning issues (e.g. using the wrong criteria for self-assessment), navigation issues (e.g. poor module linkages) or omissions (e.g. forgetting to tell teams to use a particular font or colour).
Content errors	These cover any mistakes made on the actual screens of the project. Typical problems might include incorrect statements, misspellings, grammatical mistakes, poor quality images or video, or deviations from the design document criteria.
Programming errors	These cover any mistakes in the logic and operational flow of the project. Typical problems might include links that don't work, incorrect file handling, mistakes in calculations and running totals, and system crashes.

The testing stages are vital to ensure that the product meets the client's needs and to maintain the reputation of the company. Testing is the process of locating errors in the project, with the aim of eliminating them before the project is distributed. Some of the tests cover errors in content and screen design - although a tightly worded design document should limit these types of problems.

Much of the testing concerns the detection of flaws in the functions of the project, mainly navigation errors, errors when passing information between modules and other errors (such as search engines, database activities, file handling, etc). And, of course, there can be problems, even when the project meets the specification. Flaws in the specification may result in an unsatisfactory final product, or the client may wish to alter the specification.

Multimedia companies put in place procedures to minimise the disruption to a project's completion and these centre round two types of check:

Evaluation

Also known as *'validation'*, evaluation checks that the project performs according to the users' requirements. Validation tests ensure that the project has been built to the original specification and has not moved away from the client's original intention. These tests are on content, presentation and style, testing whether it addresses the agreed client group, and such issues.

Testing

Also known as *'verification'*, these tests ensure that the project functions perform correctly. This tests that all buttons work correctly, all navigation tools take the user to the intended destination, self-assessed tests provide correct marks, all video and audio clips play correctly, etc. Functionality testing covers internal screen functions and navigation between screens and this is covered later.

Design evaluation

This is designed to reach clarification and agreement with the client on the requirements specification and design document.   The intention is to have agreement on a detailed set of specifications that the client will sign off as acceptable as the basis for the project implementation.   Increasing the specific details in these specifications reduces the scope for future controversy, a problem known as *'feature creep'*.   If the client wishes to change the project at a later date, they can be clearly identified as alterations to the agreed specifications and will have to be paid for by the client.

Before meetings the clients, the organisation's own experts would carry out their own design evaluation, This aims to correct problems before meeting the clients and to sharpen the terms of the specification. This may take the form of a *'cognitive walkthrough'*, where the goals and sub-goals (and the actions necessary to meet these goals) of each task are compared against psychological criteria. This aims to identify the required cognitive processes and uncover any learning problems.   Another approach is *'heuristic evaluation'*, where tasks are compared to usability criteria such as checking whether the system is predictable, consistent, contains task-oriented dialogue, provides feedback, does not produce memory overload, etc.

Concurrent testing

This approach recognises the need for continuous assessment by those developing the project's modules. The policy of *'Test early, Test often'* aims to identify and rectify errors during the development of each module.   Bear in mind that a module may contain programming script (e.g. for file handling, database operations, mathematical calculations, etc.) that has an effect on other modules in the project. Correcting errors at this stage is more efficient and prevents a possible knock-on effect in other modules.

Usability tests

Sometimes called an implementation evaluation, this takes place after a runnable system has been produced and is a user-centred activity.   Its task is to identify user perceptions, user satisfaction and user problems. It focuses on the project's tasks rather than its features and requires participants that match as closely as possible the customers who will use the final project.

Usability testing seeks to determine how typical users of the project will understand, use, interact with, comprehend and recall the project. The tests may be extended to collect reactions from a broader range of users. Participants are invited to use the project and their responses are evaluated.

Simple activities such as surveys and questionnaires can gather broad opinions, while laboratory observations or observing users in their own viewing environment produces more detailed information. User observations are less focused on the opinions of the users and looks closely at the actual performance of users in navigating and using the project.   This take the form of a checklist that contains items on how quickly users can find a particular screen, if they can retrace their steps easily, if they can easily exit the system, etc.   It may also include tests on how well the material is comprehended. This may only be as simple as asking the user questions at certain times. For example, a user may be asked to explain what he/she thinks a screen is about, after only reading the first couple of lines of screen text.

The process may be filmed and the observer would have a checklist of what tasks were required, what the user did, how the system reacted and the observer's comments.   The observer should remain in the background so that the process is not influenced by his/her presence. Experience has shown that conducting iterative tests with only small samples (around 6 to 10 people) will find 90% of problems.

Test specification

The testing of individual modules and their interactions is not a random activity.   Every action that is included in the project has to be tested.   Every screen, every button, every multimedia element, every piece of programming script has to be tested.   This requires a systematic approach.   The testers already have the navigation map that can be used to test navigational links. They also have to build up a set of other tests.   Some are already available from the project specifications (layout, fonts, etc.). Other tests are developed as the implementation work proceeds.   When a task is undertaken, the necessary future tests are recorded.

Examples are:

- A project handles a database of 25 students for recording the results of student performance tests. Tests would include checking that the results were accurately stored and accurately recovered. It would also have to check what would result from a 26th student trying to join the group (e.g. error message, database corruption, system crash, etc.).

- A science project asks the user to enter a value between 5 and 15. Tests would ensure that the mathematical functions worked correctly (i.e. the value input by the user produces and displays the correct answer). It should also make *'boundary checks'*. This tests how the program responds to values that are at the boundaries of the acceptable/unacceptable range. It checks that the values of 5 or 15 accepted by the program, and checks what happens if the user enters 4 or 16.

- A web site uses a CGI script to check how often the site is visited. If the script is included on a splash page, the counter is incremented once for each visitor, as they only pass through the splash page once per visit. If the script is embedded in the home page, the counter can be incremented every time the user returns to the home page (depending on the user's web caching) - giving inaccurate results.

Testing stages

There are three main stages of project testing. The first two stages of testing are carried out in-house - within the organisation's own staff, while acceptance testing is carried out with the representative(s) of the client.

Unit testing

Often carried out by the programmer who created the screen or module (set of interlinked screens). This promotes *'quality at source'* - the programmer finds his/her own faults faster and clears them up quicker than an outside tester. The down side is that the programmer can often overlook the same fault, due to his/her familiarity with the work. It is almost universally true that everyone prefers programming to testing. This means that organisations have to create a climate that ensures that testing is carried out adequately.

Integration Testing

When the project is complete, all the screens and elements of the project are linked together. Integration testing checks that all the links work and that no errors have been introduced by the passing of information between modules. For example, ensuring that a shopping cart unit is not calculating goods in Euros while the payments unit is billing in pounds.

Acceptance testing

When the project is finished its internal debugging stages, it is ready to be presented to the client. The aim is to get the client's agreement for a final sign-off. This allows the project to be installed or distributed. As mentioned before, it is vital to get the client's sign-off for design stage at an earlier time, so that acceptance tests concentrates on the search for operational errors. If not, the client may start raising issues and requesting amendments to design issues (usually requiring substantial extra work). The larger the number of client representatives at the acceptance testing, the more chance there is of new demands emerging.

Top-down testing

Unit testing and integration testing are known collectively as *'bottom up'* testing. This method is useful for projects that have complicated units, such as shopping carts, forms, animations, etc. Each unit is tested and only added to the project when it is found to be operating satisfactorily.

An alternative approach is *'top-down'* testing. This fits in well with the *'prototyping'* method discussed earlier. The emphasis is on the overall structure, with the framework of the project being created at an early stage. All the project's units are created (most in a very elementary form) and all the units are linked. Tests then establish that a user can successfully navigate between all the units in the project. Any missing links, incorrect links (links pointing to the wrong unit) or logic problems (links that take a user to another unit depending on a set of conditions) are uncovered at this stage.

Once all links are proven to work, the individual unit's contents are fully developed.

Internal screen tests

These tests are designed to check that the screen layout and all internal functions (i.e. those that carry out activities within the screen but do not take the user to another screen) work correctly.

Typical tests are:

- Do all the typestyles, font sizes, colours and positions match those specified in the design document?

- Does the background, button design and hyperlink colours match those in the design document?
- Has all text been spell checked and grammar checked?
- Do button rollovers roll over?
- Do image map components change when the pointer hovers them?
- Does a long text window scroll?
- Are non-functioning controls greyed out or hidden? Do they still function despite being greyed?
- Do the user's media controls (e.g. volume control, video pause button) function as intended?
- If a web page, is the page size acceptable, or would it create problems with download times?

Navigation tests

These are designed to check that all controls that move the user around the project act in the way laid down in the navigation map.

The likely navigation elements in a project include:

Next screen	Previous screen
Next topic	Previous topic
Return to home screen	Exit
Return to top of this sub-menu	Move to new project area

The most efficient approach is to list all the areas of the project that function within their own boundaries. A typical example is a set of linear screens with a single access point to the first screen and one or more exit points that are all in the final screen.   These may be parts of main project content or may be subsidiary modules such as glossaries, search engines or help pages.   These modules can be tested on their own, as independent sub-programs.   The navigation through and back up the module's screens can be tested and the last screen should be tested to see that it does not include a *'next screen'* button (since there is no next screen in the module).

Alpha/Beta releases

In the commercial world, software developers produce two main testing stages. The *'alpha'* product is an early implementation of the product and is expected to contain lots of errors. It is intended for internal circulation only, so that these errors can be detected an eliminated. The testers are very thorough and very strict, so that the worst problems are eliminated before it goes out for more general testing. Once the alpha testing has eliminated the worst of the bugs, the *'beta'* version is provided to a selected audience outside the company, to people who have not been involved in its production. It is supplied on the basis that it will contain some errors and these new testers have not been party to any of the previous discussions and come to the product with a fresh eye. Since they do not have any preconceptions, they will detect problems that were overlooked by the company testers. The feedback from the beta stage is crucial in curing these problems, thus producing as reliable and useful a product as possible.

Final thoughts on testing

If projects are subject to such prolonged testing, why are they still distributed containing errors?

The project undergoes concurrent testing, unit testing, integration testing, usability testing and acceptance testing, yet errors still manage to pass through the testing procedures. A certain amount is inevitable, while other factors are predictable.   Developers are often pressurised to produce quantity and quality can suffer as a result. Early release dates leave little room for adequate testing. There may also be intense pressure to release a product before the competition complete theirs. The only way to ensure the best quality product is to factor sufficient testing resources into the project budget.

Index

P

T

Main index entries are in bold type.

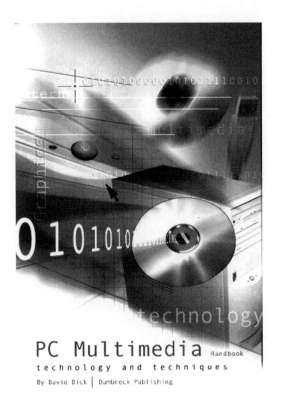

Check out our website

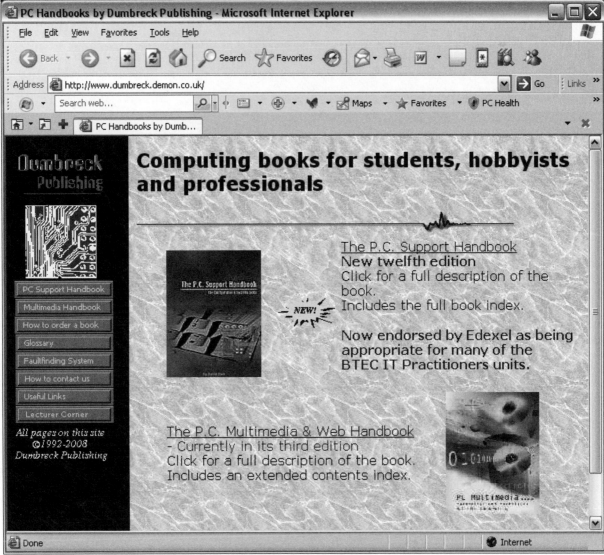

www.dumbreck.demon.co.uk

Website features:

- Details of the book's contents, including full indexes.
- How to place an order, receive bulk discount, etc.
- Quickly look up the meaning of acronymns (from AGP to ZIF).
- Reviews of the software packages that help you get the best out of our books. All programs are freeware or shareware.
- An expert system that guides you through the steps to identify your computer problem.
- Links to other websites with related content. These sites contain technical information, tutorials, etc.
- Sample mappings of the BTEC and SQA courses to the book's contents.

The online faultfinding section of the website covers the following areas: